French Warships
in the Age of Sail
1786-1861

French Warships
in the Age of Sail
1786-1861
Design, Construction,
Careers and Fates

RIF WINFIELD &
STEPHEN S ROBERTS

Seaforth
PUBLISHING

FRONTISPIECE: An oil painting by Jules Achille Noël celebrating the royal visit of Queen Victoria and Prince Albert to Cherbourg on 5 August 1858 at the invitation of Napoleon III. The French emperor welcomed his guests aboard the *Bretagne*, a three-decker screw ship of the line, the central focus of the painting. (© National Maritime Museum BHC0637)

Copyright © Rif Winfield & Stephen S Roberts 2015

This edition first published in Great Britain in 2015 by
Seaforth Publishing,
An imprint of Pen & Sword Books Ltd,
47 Church Street,
Barnsley
South Yorkshire S70 2AS

www.seaforthpublishing.com
Email: info@seaforthpublishing.com

British Library Cataloguing in Publication Data
A catalogue record for this book is available from the British Library

ISBN 978 1 84832 204 2

All rights reserved. No part of this publication may be reproduced or transmitted in any form or by any means, electronic or mechanical, including photocopying, recording, or any information storage and retrieval system, without prior permission in writing of both the copyright owner and the above publisher.

The right of Rif Winfield & Stephen S Roberts to be identified as the authors of this work has been asserted in accordance with the Copyright, Designs and Patents Act 1988.

Typeset and designed by Neil Sayer
Printed and bound by 1010 Printing International Ltd

Contents

Preface	7
Acknowledgments	8
Structure and Organisation of the Book	9
Historical Overview	11
Chronology	21
French Naval Operations	22
Dockyards and Infrastructure	29
French Navies and Naval Construction outside France, 1797-1814	32
Sources and Bibliography	35
Glossary and Abbreviations	39
List of the French Fleet as at 1 January 1786.	42

Chapter 1: The Three-deckers — 43
  (A) Vessels in service or on order at 1 January 1786 — 43
  (B) Vessels acquired from 1 January 1786 — 44
  (C) Vessels acquired from 25 March 1802 — 46
  (D) Vessels acquired from 26 June 1815 — 49
  (E) Screw three-deckers — 52

Chapter 2: Two-decker Ships of the Line, 80 to 100 guns — 55
  (A) Vessels in service or on order at 1 January 1786 — 55
  (B) Vessels acquired from 1 January 1786 — 56
  (C) Vessels acquired from 25 March 1802 — 57
  (D) Vessels acquired from 26 June 1815 — 62
  (E) Screw two-deckers, 2nd and 3rd Ranks — 66

Chapter 3: Two-decker Ships of the Line, 74 guns and below. — 76
Two-deckers with fewer than 60 guns — 76
  (A) Vessels in service or on order at 1 January 1786 — 76
  (B) Vessels acquired from 1 January 1786 — 77
  (C) Vessels acquired from 25 March 1802 — 77
64-gun two-deckers — 78
  (A) Vessels in service or on order at 1 January 1786 — 78
  (B) Vessels acquired from 1 January 1786 — 79
  (C) Vessels acquired from 25 March 1802 — 82
74-gun two-deckers — 83
  (A) Vessels in service or on order at 1 January 1786 — 83
  (B) Vessels acquired from 1 January 1786 — 88
  (C) Vessels acquired from 25 March 1802 — 94
  (D) Vessels acquired from 26 June 1815 — 102
  (E) Screw two-deckers, 4th (and 3rd) Rank — 102

Chapter 4: The Larger Frigates (24-, 30-, and 36-pounder Frigates) — 103
  (A) Larger frigates in service or on order at 1 January 1786 — 103
  (B) Larger frigates acquired from 1 January 1786 — 103
  (C) Larger frigates acquired from 25 March 1802 — 106
  (D) Larger frigates acquired from 26 June 1815 — 106
  (E) Screw frigates, 1st and 2nd Ranks — 115

Chapter 5: The Smaller Frigates (8-, 12-, and 18-pounder Frigates) — 121
8-pounder frigates — 121
  (A) Vessels in service or on order at 1 January 1785 — 121
12-pounder frigates — 122
  (A) Vessels in service or on order at 1 January 1785 — 122
  (B) Vessels acquired from 1 January 1786 — 128
  (C) Vessels acquired from 25 March 1802 — 134
18-pounder frigates — 135
  (A) Vessels in service or on order at 1 January 1785 — 135
  (B) Vessels acquired from 1 January 1786 — 137
  (C) Vessels acquired from 25 March 1802 — 144
  (D) Vessels acquired from 26 June 1815 — 157
  (E) Screw frigates, 3rd Rank — 160

Chapter 6: Corvettes — 163
  (A) Corvettes in service or on order at 1 January 1786 — 163
  (B) Corvettes acquired from 1 January 1786 — 166
  (C) Corvettes acquired from 25 March 1802 — 178
  (D) Sailing corvettes acquired from 26 June 1815 — 185
  (E) Screw corvettes — 194

Chapter 7: Brigs — 203
  (A) Brigs in service or on order at 1 January 1786 — 203
  (B) Brigs acquired from 1 January 1786 — 203
  (C) Brigs acquired from 25 March 1802 — 213
  (D) Brigs acquired from 26 June 1815 — 226

Chapter 8: Small Sailing Patrol Vessels — 238
  (A) Vessels in service or on order at 1 January 1786 — 238
  (B) Vessels acquired from 1 January 1786 — 240
  (C) Vessels acquired from 25 March 1802 — 251
  (D) Vessels acquired from 26 June 1815 — 259

Chapter 9: Sailing Gunboats and Coastal Vessels — 271
  (A) Vessels in service or on order at 1 January 1786 — 271
  (B) Vessels acquired from 1 January 1786 — 271
  (C) Vessels acquired from 25 March 1802 — 281
  (D) Vessels acquired from 26 June 1815 — 293

Chapter 10: Miscellaneous Sailing Vessels — 294
Lateen-rigged vessels — 294
  (A) Vessels in service or on order at 1 January 1786 — 294
  (B) Vessels acquired from 1 January 1786 — 295
  (C) Vessels acquired from 25 March 1802 — 302
  (D) Vessels acquired from 26 June 1815 — 307
Bomb (mortar) vessels — 309
  (A) Bomb vessels in service or on order at 1 January 1786 — 309
  (B) Bomb vessels acquired from 1 January 1786 — 309
  (C) Bomb vessels acquired from 25 March 1802 — 310
  (D) Bomb vessels acquired from 26 June 1815 — 311
Floating batteries — 312
  (A) Floating batteries in service or on order at 1 January 1786 — 312
  (B) Floating batteries acquired from 1 January 1786 — 312
  (C) Floating batteries acquired from 25 March 1802 — 312
Hydrographic vessels — 313
  (A) Hydrographic vessels acquired from 25 March 1802 — 313
  (B) Hydrographic vessels acquired from 26 June 1815 — 313
Yachts — 313
  (A) Yachts in service or on order at 1 January 1786 — 313
  (B) Yachts acquired from 1 January 1786 — 313

(C) Yachts acquired from 25 March 1802	313
(D) Yachts acquired from 26 June 1815	314

Chapter 11: Paddle Vessels 315
- (A) Early paddle vessels — 315
- (B) Paddle frigates and corvettes — 325
- (C) Larger paddle avisos — 338
- (D) Smaller paddle avisos (90nhp and less) — 345
- (E) Paddle yacht (later paddle corvette) — 351

Chapter 12: Screw Avisos and Screw Gunboats 353
- (A) Screw 1st and 2nd Class avisos — 353
- (B) Small screw avisos (90nhp and less) — 362
- (C) Screw gunboats — 363
- (D) Screw gun launches and sectional gun launches — 367
- (E) Screw sectional armoured floating batteries — 371

Chapter 13: The Larger Transports 373
Flûtes (corvettes de charge from 1821, transports from 1846) — 373
- (A) Flûtes in service or on order at 1 January 1786 — 373
- (B) Flûtes acquired from 1 January 1786 — 374
- (C) Flûtes acquired from 25 March 1802 — 378
- (D) Flûtes and corvettes de charge acquired from 26 June 1815 — 382

Gabarres (transports from 1846) — 383
- (A) Gabarres in service or on order at 1 January 1786 — 383
- (B) Gabarres acquired from 1 January 1786 — 385
- (C) Gabarres acquired from 25 March 1802 — 386
- (D) Gabarres acquired from 26 June 1815 — 391

Large transports — 394
- (A) Vessels acquired from 26 June 1815 — 394
- (B) Screw transports — 398

Chapter 14: The Smaller Transports 405
- (A) Smaller transports in service or on order at 1 January 1786 — 405
- (B) Smaller transports acquired from 1 January 1786 — 406
- (C) Smaller transports acquired from 25 March 1802 — 412
- (D) Smaller transports acquired from 26 June 1815 — 416

Postscript: Broadside Ironclads — 419
- Ironclad frigates — 419
- Ironclad floating batteries — 424

Appendix A. Standard Armaments of French Ships, 1786-1848 — 429
Appendix B. French Naval Artillery, 1786-1860 — 431
Appendix C. Resources Provided to the French Navy, 1816-1861 — 432
Appendix D. Strength of the French Navy 1818-1859 — 433
Appendix E. French Naval Programs, 1820-1857 — 435
Appendix F. French Ministers of Marine, 1780-1870 — 436
Appendix G: French Navy Shipbuilding Officials — 437
Appendix H. Selected French Naval Constructors, 1786-1861 — 438
Appendix I. French Naval Ship and Engine Builders, 1793-1861 — 442
Appendix J. Composition of the Crew for a French Ship of the Line, 1795 — 445

Index to Named Vessels — 447

Preface

This book provides a guide to every known named vessel which served in or was ordered for the French Navy between the start of 1786 and 1861. The earlier date reflects the effective beginning of the French reorganisation of naval construction brought in by Charles de la Croix, Marquis de Castries, Secretary of State for the Navy from 1780 to 1787, and Jean-Charles de Borda, France's Inspector of Naval Shipbuilding from 1784, mainly with the assistance of the naval architect Jacques-Noël Sané; vessels which were built before 1786 but which were still in existence are also included. The closing date is designed to identify the end of building French sailing warships; here there was clearly a substantial overlap between the sailing and steam eras, as steam-powered vessels (both paddle vessels and screw-propeller driven ships) were built in the previous decades; all such steam vessels built, ordered or acquired up to the end of 1861 are included herein.

This volume gives a summary of the main technical details of each class of vessel built for or otherwise acquired by the French Navy, including its dimensions and tonnage, its complement of men, and its armament. The designers and builders of each vessel are listed, along with its construction dates, highlights of its service in French hands, and its final disposal. It was initially hoped to give data on the service histories of each vessel (in the same way as was done in the earlier series on British Warships), but for reasons of space this has not been possible; just a few of the highlights of individual ship histories have been mentioned, notably in the listings of those French warships involved in the major battles and naval actions.

Essentially the authors of this volume split the 75-year period, with Rif taking responsibility for the eighteenth century vessels, Steve producing the material for 1815 onwards, and work on the 1800–1815 period being shared between the two authors, both of whom also assisted across this broad temporal division. Sometimes the dual authorship has resulted in different approaches, which we have tried to minimise in our final versions, but we apologise where the differences are obvious, although the changing nature of technology (notably the introduction of steam machinery and of rifled ordnance) has meant that this was sometimes unavoidable.

It is intended to produce another volume to cover the previous century-and-a-half of French naval construction, beginning with Cardinal Richelieu's self-appointment in October 1626 as *Grand maître, chef et surintendant général de la navigation et commerce de France* (effectively, absolute master of everything maritime) and his subsequent reorganisation of the feudal structure of French naval administration, and describing subsequent development up to 1786.

Acknowledgments

Many friends and colleagues assisted in the compilations of this volume, so we have numerous thanks to offer. Our colleague John ('Mike') Tredrea assisted in a considerable number of ways, including putting us in contact with others who readily supplied information. The Napoleonic period saw the acquisition of considerable numbers of vessels captured from other countries. Material on warships captured from the British Navy is primarily found from Rif's companion volume on *British Warships in the Age of Sail 1793-1817*. We are most grateful to Guido Ercole, author of *Vascelli e frigate della Serenissima*, for assistance with material on vessels acquired from the Venetian Navy both in 1797 and subsequently. Jim Bender supplied data and advice on captured Dutch vessels.

We are indebted to Grant Walker and his staff at the U.S. Naval Academy Museum at Annapolis for providing a number of illustrations from the Beverley R. Robinson collection, as well as for his courtesy and kindness to Steve Roberts on visits to that institution. Staff at the Caird Library in the National Maritime Museum at Greenwich have been an unfailing source of co-operation during many years of research, and our appreciation is also due to the personnel at the Brass Foundry, the NMM's out-station at Woolwich where their vast collection of ship's draughts are stored. The Royal Naval Museum at Portsmouth also contributed to our search for illustrations. Our thanks go also to former directors of the archives and library of the Service historique de la Marine in Paris, Messrs. Joël Audouy and Jean-Pierre Busson, who assisted Steve during his research in Paris.

Rif in particular needs to thank his wife Ann for her tolerance of the time he has given to this project, and for putting up with the piles of research documents around the house, while Steve wishes to remember his wife Sue Goetz Ross, who accompanied him on some of his research trips to France but who died long before he got the opportunity to publish his work in this book. Over a period of time, our information and much helpful advice and support has come from a number of individuals, both in France and around the world, including Leuewe Bouma, Deb Carlen, Fred Dittmar, Charles Haberlein, John Harland, David Hepper, John Houghton, Frank Lecalvé, Edel Moroney, Stuart Rankin, Christian de Saint Hubert, Eduard ('Ted') Sozaev, Adrian E. Tschoegl, Jane Winfield, Christopher C. Wright and Emir Yener. We offer our apologies to anyone we have inadvertently omitted from this page.

Information in a variety of published works in French has been invaluable in corroborating our information from French archives and in filling in gaps where we lacked details. The comprehensive listings compiled and published over a series of volumes by Cdt. Alain Demerliac have been an essential source of data, adding to our information on major ships and helping us to avoid overlooking some of the multitude of smaller craft. Indeed, in respect of most of the hundreds of vessels which were requisitioned by the Napoleonic Consulship and subsequently Empire for the putative invasion of Britain (for many of which we have no data other than names and often simply serial numbers) we would refer those interested to Cdt. Demerliac's 1800–1815 volume (see Bibliography). The published *répertoire* of Jean-Michel Roche has been a source of copious information, as have the earlier *répertoires* of Frank Lecalvé and of Jacques Vichot. The massive studies of a variety of warship types by Jean Boudriot, the doyen of French sailing warship design, are essential references for anyone working in this field. We have also benefited from the published studies by Henri le Masson, Philippe Masson, Gérard Piouffre and Henri Simoni as well as other volumes referenced in our Bibliography. We gratefully acknowledge our debt to all these authors and publications.

This publication would not have been possible without the enthusiastic co-operation and support of our publisher, Robert Gardiner. Robert has not only scoured every possible source for the 250-or-so illustrations which have graced this volume, and contributed most of their captions, but has also been a constant reference point for resolving queries and has settled issues from his own wide-ranging knowledge of the topic. To Rob, to his colleague Julian Mannering, and to the rest of the team at Seaforth, we wish to express our profound thanks.

Many of the ship drawings in this volume are attributed to the *Atlas du Génie Maritime*, for which we have two sources. One is a French collection of over 1,000 drawings that were compiled and printed between the early 1840s and the 1890s for the internal use of the *Génie Maritime*, the French naval construction corps, while the other is a collection of 383 original drawings associated with the printed French drawings that are now part of the DUILIOShip project at the Regia Scuola Superiore Navale di Genova. The French collection was at one time on the web site of the *Service Historique de la Défense* and parts of it remain on other web sites, while the Genoa collection is at http://www.duilioship.it/xmlui/handle/10621/21 under 'Atlas'. Most of the drawings reproduced here are associated with the first two volumes of the series, both printed at Toulon shortly before 1842 and entitled *Atlas du Génie Maritime rédigé par les officiers de ce corps et mis en ordre par A. Campaignac, Ingénieur de la Marine à Toulon*. The first volume contained 50 drawings relating to sailing vessels while the second volume contained 71 drawings of steam vessels and machinery. The internal arrangement plans are from a portion of the fifth volume that is entitled *Plans Réglementaires des Emménagements et des objets d'attache qui garnissent la Coque des Bâtimens de Guerre, approuvés à Paris le 20 Décembre 1838*; these drawings were originally lithographed at Brest by T. Souchou, *sous-ingénieur de la marine*.

The whole study of the history of French sailing vessels – both naval and commercial – exists primarily because of the life-long efforts of one champion, whose knowledge of the topic and commitment to pursuing it in print and in artistic representation have been the mainstay of research for many decades. Jean Pierre Paul Boudriot, born on 20 March 1921 at Dijon, died on 22 February 2015 at his Paris home as this book approached publication. His work as an architect and as a publisher equally known for his elegant productions on naval architecture and ancient weaponry made him one of the principal movers in the rebirth of interest in this subject matter. He was particularly celebrated for his authorship of the four-volume study of *Le vaisseau de 74 canons* and the numerous studies and monographs that followed it, of which many are mentioned in the Bibliography of this book. Graciously, he gave Steve much support and encouragement during his researches in France. To him, with thanks, we dedicate our own efforts in the hope that he would have approved of them.

Structure and Organisation of the Book

In most chapters, the vessels are listed chronologically, subdivided into five periods:
  (A) Vessels already in service or on order as at 1 January 1786, when the fleet reorganisation promulgated by Castries (the Secretary of State for the Navy) took effect (in Chapter 5 the starting point is actually the beginning of 1785 which better identifies the start of construction under the influence of Borda and Sané).
  (B) Vessels acquired from 1 January 1786 (up to 1802).
  (C) Vessels acquired from 25 March 1802 (up to 1815).
  (D) Vessels acquired from 26 June 1815 (excluding steam vessels).
  (E) Steam vessels (including conversions from sailing vessels).

Readers will observe that the start of period (C) marks the signing of the Treaty of Amiens, signifying the end of the French Revolutionary War; and that the start of period (D) marks the second abdication of Napoleon, and thus the effective end of the Napoleonic Wars. However, these dates have been varied slightly in individual chapters in order to better group together vessels of the same design or similar programs.

1. The dimensions given are those of the design of each class of vessels. These are given in French units of measurements in two formats for all vessels prior to 1815 – in French feet and inches (pieds and pouces), which were approximately 6.575% longer than the British/US feet and inches (324.8394 mm, compared with 304.8 mm for the British Imperial measurements) – followed by the metric equivalents in parenthesis. France officially adopted the metric system in 1799, following determination of the standard metre by the astronomers Jean-Baptiste-Joseph Delambre and Pierre-Francois-André Méchain for the French Academy of Sciences, but designers and shipwrights, being somewhat conservative in their approach, continued to use the pre-metric units in their designs for a number of years. By 1815 this had ceased, so for post-1815 vessels only the metric units are quoted.

Length: This dimension was commonly measured from the forward face of the stempost to the after face of the sternpost (*de l'extérieur de l'étrave à l'extérieur de l'etambot*) at the level of the gundeck (LD) port sills, or if the designer preferred at the height of the wing transom. This length is commonly called the length on deck (the gundeck) although it was also called the length between perpendiculars. Length however could also be taken as the distance at the same (gundeck) height between the rabbet of the stem and the rabbet of the stern (*de rablure en rablure*), the width of the rabbets being ignored; alternatively the length could be measured from rabbet to rabbet at the waterline. (The rabbet, or rabbit or rabbeting, was a wedge-shaped channel or groove cut into the face of the stempost, sternpost, keel, and wing transom to receive the planking.) Practices differed at different times and also between shipyards and even designers, which makes it difficult to interpret lengths recorded without further explanation as is the case with many written sources. The waterline length came into more common, but far from exclusive, use in the nineteenth century. The adoption of the screw propeller introduced another ambiguity as to whether the length was measured to the sternpost forward of the screw or the rudderpost aft of it.

Breadth: The moulded breadth was taken at the widest point of the vessel to the outside of the frame (*hors membrure*) but excluding the planking. The extreme breadth was taken in the same manner but included the hull planking (*hors bordage*); this measurement was used in earlier periods and reappeared in the nineteenth century.

Depth in hold (*creux*): The maximum depth inside the vessel below the deck beams of the lower deck (gundeck), measured at the point of the maximum breadth of the ship from the top of the keel to the lower horizontal of the midship beam (*maître-bau*). The British in contrast measured it from the upper side of the limber strakes to the upper side of the gundeck on the centreline amidships, producing dimensions that in some cases were significantly different from the French figures. The French measured the *creux* of ships without decks as the vertical distance from the top of the keel to the gunwale at the midships frame (*maître couple*).

2. Where known, two tonnages are quoted, separated by an oblique stroke (/). The first figure is the 'port' measurement, approximately equivalent to the British burthen tonnage and essentially an empirical measurement of the volume of the hold of the ship converted to tons by an arbitrary factor. The second figure is a displacement (or 'weight of water displaced' by the ship) at full load, i.e. when fully equipped and laden with men, stores and ordnance. The French also commonly recorded the draughts (fore and aft) corresponding to the recorded displacements.

3. The number of men is from multiple French sources, some of which recorded the established total of officers and ratings and some of which recorded men actually on board. The new organisational structure created from 1 January 1786 set established levels (separately for wartime and peacetime manning) for the ships of the line (*vaisseaux*) and frigates (*frégates*), but these altered according to operational needs in subsequent years. Clearly availability of personnel and losses while in service as well as the ability to pay crews led to large differences between established and actual manning.

4. The armament is that allocated to a class of vessel at the time of its entry into service (although sometimes the planned ordnance was altered even before the vessel or vessels entered service). Major subsequent alterations in armament are quoted where possible, but in wartime in particular additional guns were often added on the *gaillards* (a useful French term that encompassed both the quarterdecks and forecastles) too often for individual recording. The standard armaments for the various standard classes are shown in Appendix A and details of French naval artillery are provided in Appendix B.

5. Where known, the dockyard or port of construction of each individual vessel is given, along with its designer (*ingénieur-constructeur*) and the actual senior shipwright who oversaw the building (in many cases, this was the same person, but where this differed we have tried to give both names). As with shipwrights in Britain and elsewhere, skills were passed down the generations, and

thus surnames are inadequate to identify individuals; as a consequence, we have wherever possible included the first and middle names (*prénoms*) of the individuals. For steam vessels the builder of the machinery is named following the name of the shipbuilder, the two being separated by a forward slash (/).

6. The dates of construction given are usually three – 'K' signifies the keel laying date (*mise sur cale*), although some of the dates cited may be start of construction (*mise en chantier*) dates; 'L' signifies the date of launch (or of entry into the water in the case of vessels built in drydock); and 'C' signifies the completion date or date of entry into service. Where possible, and especially where it differs significantly from the *mise en chantier* or *mise sur cale* date, we have given the date on which the instruction to build was given by the Minister of Marine ('Ord') and/or the date upon which the vessel was formally allocated its name ('Named'). Beginning in 1800 actual commissioning dates or *dates de l'armement* ('Comm.') are also given where available. These are mostly from the *Répertoire* initially compiled by Baron de Lagatinerie (see Bibliography) and appear to represent the dates on which the ships began to go into commission and on which their crew muster lists were opened.

After the Revolution the French Navy inevitably suffered the effects of the ongoing ideological struggle within the country, the worst example being the surrender of the main Mediterranean fleet base at Toulon to Anglo-Spanish forces by the pro-Royalist authorities in 1793. It soon fell to the revolutionaries, but before the allies withdrew enormous damage was done to the port's facilities and many of the warships in harbour – as shown in this anonymous contemporary watercolour. Had the sabotage been better organised, the destruction could have been greater, but it was still a huge blow to French naval power in the Mediterranean. The revolutionary forces then took their revenge upon both the military and civilians who failed to be evacuated by the British Navy, with widespread mass executions following their return to control. (© National Maritime Museum PY3230)

Historical Overview

The French Navy in the 1780s

Louis XVI's *Marine Royale* finished the American War in far happier condition than when it emerged from the Seven Years War two decades earlier. Between 1780 and 1782 the older three-decked *Ville de Paris* and nine 74s had been lost, as well as lesser ships, but new construction had more than compensated, with the creation of four new three-deckers of 110 guns each, as well as three 80-gun and more than twenty 74-gun two-deckers added from 1778 onwards – the last of these were still joining the navy in the years immediately following the close of the war.

With Castries's support, Borda planned in the mid-1780s for a further major expansion of the battle fleet, and for lesser vessels. In 1786 he produced a comprehensive plan for new construction (identified throughout this book as his '1786 Programme'). Altogether the Programme provided for:
- 81 ships of the line (*vaisseaux*) – 9 three-deckers of 118 guns, 12 large two-deckers of 80 guns, and 60 of 74 guns.
- 70 frigates (*frégates*) – 20 with 18pdrs, 50 with 12pdrs.
- 60 corvettes – 20 carrying 24 x 8pdrs, 20 carrying 20 x 6pdrs, and 20 brig-rigged mounting 12 to 16 x 4pdrs or 6pdrs.
- 40 transports – 10 of 750 tons (i.e. flûtes), 10 gabarres of 500 tons, 10 gabarres of 400 tons, and 10 gabarres of 200 tons.
Total – 252 ships with 10,422 guns and 91,572 men.

The whole programme was approved by Castries (although somewhere along the way the number of 12pdr-armed frigates was reduced from 50 to 40). The design of ships of the line was to be standardised, and Borda turned for this to his colleague Jacques-Noël Sané, then acting as an *ingénieur sous-directeur* at Brest. A dozen 74-gun ships had already been ordered before the start of 1786 to the design of Sané's definitive *Téméraire* of 1782, and Borda ensured that this design, or derivations derived from it, was adopted for all future 74s. Moreover Sané followed this design with an equivalent scheme for an 80-gun variant of enlarged dimensions (an extra 10 feet in length, and 2½ feet broader), with an identical armament except that an additional pair of ports could be provided on each deck. At the same time he produced an equivalent design for a 118-gun three-decker, which likewise went into series production.

These three successful designs, with subtle improvements over the years, were to form the basis for all ships of the line constructed by France or its dependent navies over the next three decades. Each of these carried a principal lower-deck battery of 36pdr cannon – the standard principal weapon of the French battle fleet throughout the eighteenth and first half of the nineteenth centuries; as the French *livre* – at 489.5 grammes – was approximately 10% greater in weight than the British pound, in reality the French shot equated to 39lbs 11.5oz, compared with the standard British battle fleet weapon of 32lbs. While this significantly increased the firepower of an individual shot, the disadvantages of the French preference for 36pdrs were that the gun required a larger crew, took more time to reload which (when coupled with a relative lower standard of gun crew practice) resulted in a much lower rate of fire, and deformed the hull more quickly because of its heavier weight. This structural weakness was accentuated by the French practice of lighter construction – with more widely spaced scantlings, a practice derived from French strategic requirements which were for less frequent and less strenuous periods of deployment.

Borda matched the new battle fleet with similar major programmes for frigates, corvettes and lesser units, although here the designs of other constructors were developed as much as those of Sané. All new ships were to be fitted with copper sheathing. However from 1786 the growing financial difficulties resulted in a cutback of the planned construction. There were strikes by unpaid dockworkers at Brest and Toulon in 1789 (and pro-Jacobin radicals seized power at the latter dockyard in that year), and many new ships were poorly constructed or maintained. Although work on ships of the line and frigates did proceed, construction of lesser units virtually ceased until the outburst of war fever in 1792 led to a nationalist-inspired renewal of effort. The programme of 1786 for sixty corvettes (including twenty new brig-corvettes) was dropped (see Chapter 6 for details). On the other hand, the condition of existing vessels was improved, with every ship to be sheathed with copper as it underwent refit.

In addition to building new warships, a major effort was expended during the decade to develop the infrastructure that served the navy. The principal naval territorial divisions were organised around the three major dockyards at Brest and Rochefort on the Atlantic coast, and at Toulon on the Mediterranean, although there were lesser divisions based on Le Havre, Dunkirk and Bordeaux. While there were minor facilities on the Channel coast, there were no major bases to face France's traditional maritime enemy, Britain, whose bases at Portsmouth and Plymouth reinforced British command of the Channel. Brest, the most northerly of the major dockyards faced into the open Atlantic, and its prevailing westerly or south-westerly winds would always inhibit ships of the line sailing from there. Consequently work commenced in 1784 on the establishment of breakwaters at Cherbourg, chosen to provide a secure anchorage for their fleet in the Channel; ninety huge wooden cones with rocks inside them were planned to support piers within a north-facing harbour. Lesser schemes were put in hand at Dunkirk and elsewhere. The work at Cherbourg was inspected in 1786 by Louis XVI to underline its importance to strategic planning, but the difficulties of construction had been wildly under-estimated, and the looming financial crisis meant that the scheme was abandoned in late 1789.

Castries undertook a variety of other steps to improve the efficiency of the service. He tackled the bias in the recruitment of naval officers: formerly, the appointment of *enseignes* was from the *Gardes de la Marine* and the *Gardes de Pavillion*, institutions to which admission was limited to members of the nobility; Castries disbanded the *gardes* and substituted a system for recruiting *aspirants* who could now come from outside the nobility, opening training schools in Vannes and Alais. Also in 1786 he created a corps of seaman-gunners, signed up for eight years, and also introduced a new system of cadet entry, with a new rank of sub-lieutenant devised.

But from 1786 the worsening financial situation in France led to criticism that France should not afford the high cost of this new naval programme, and in the summer of 1787 Castries was forced to resign. After a brief interregnum, his post was filled by César-Henri, Comte de La Luzerne, who undertook to continue with the Borda-Sané plans. By 1788 France had seventy-one ships of the line, sixty-four frigates and some eighty smaller craft. There was a large corps of officers, mostly well trained, and a reorganised arrangement for the provision of crews.

The Revolution and its Aftermath: 1789 to 1799

The upheaval of 1789 brought these modernisation plans to a chaotic end, following the storming of the Bastille by the Paris mob in July, and the forced removal of Louis from Versailles to Paris in October. Discipline in the dockyards disintegrated, and many of the naval officers hastily departed the country. The newly established training schools for *aspirants* were closed on 15 May 1791 (when the Directorate was established, on 22 October 1795, new ones were opened at Brest, Toulon and Rochefort). In the heat of the Terror, Jean-Bon St Andre, the member of the Committee of Public Safety charged with the administration of the Navy, abolished the 5,400-strong corps of seamen-gunners, in the belief that gunners from the land artillery should be responsible for manning the guns of warships. Crews were poorly trained and ill-disciplined, with real power in many instances held by radical petty officers rather than those holding commissions.

While some experienced and competent officers remained, many of the newcomers were rapidly promoted from the ranks; this even applied to their senior commanders, with Villaret-Joyeuse (as an example) being raised from lieutenant to vice-admiral within the space of three years. For the main types of ships afloat the numbers of were kept up (see Appendix D to this book) but their readiness for service was neglected and only a reduced number was actually able to be put to sea when the occasion demanded. Stocks of supplies and fittings in the arsenals were allowed to deteriorate rapidly (a situation which was not fully corrected until after the Napoleonic period).

At the start of October 1792, the French Navy comprised some 246 warships according to William James (Vol. 1, Appendix 4), of which 86 were ships of the line. Of the latter, 27 were in commission and 13 were still under construction and nearing completion; 39 of these were at Brest, 10 at Lorient, 13 at Rochefort and 24 at Toulon. There were 78 frigates, 18 of them with a main battery of 18pdr guns, and the balance carrying 12pdr guns. In addition, there were 47 corvettes and avisos, 7 gunvessels and 28 flûtes and armed storeships. An official French tabulation dated around 1860 and reproduced in Appendix D shows that in 1792 there were 76 ships of the line afloat and 7 building, 71 frigates afloat and 6 building, and 81 other afloat and none building, for totals of 228 afloat and 13 building.

The consequence of this neglect, and misjudged policy by the republican regime, was that the French Navy fared disastrously during its first encounters with British and other naval forces when war broke out. The debacle of the occupation of Toulon in late 1793 resulted in the loss of a large proportion of the Mediterranean fleet, even though much was restored when the French republican forces took back control of that port in December. The battle fleet under Villaret-Joyeuse suffered a major defeat at the Battle of 13 Prairial in June 1794 (the 'Glorious First of June' in British terms), further reducing the ships available. France's land forces gained significant successes which resulted in the Netherlands (on 16 May 1795) and Spain (on 22 July 1795) leaving the First Coalition against France and effectively forced into becoming allies of the Republic; however this potential naval alliance was offset during 1797 when both countries suffered major losses to the British Navy – first Spain off Cape St Vincent on 14 February and then the Dutch (the newly organised Batavian Republic) at Camperdown on 11 October.

Equally seriously, the French entered the war with a severe shortage of smaller warships with which to operate a *guerre de course* against the merchant fleets of Britain and her coalition Allies, or to defend her own merchantmen against predatory warships. The Republic was forced, not only to initiate a series of orders to build more escort and coastal patrol vessels, but to acquire a number of privateers (both existing ones and others under construction) and even purchased merchantmen from commercial sources, to commission as naval cruisers. The chapters on corvette and brig acquisitions, and those on smaller vessels, demonstrate the scale of this programme. A variety of purpose-built designs were built in quantities, using a variety of designers, among which the contributions of Pierre-Alexandre-Laurent Forfait were prominent. Forfait was an *ingénieur-constructeur ordinaire* (the highest rank below the *ingénieurs sous-directeurs*) at Toulon in 1790 and held the same title at Brest in 1798. Some of these designers introduced some radical innovations, although there was a degree of over-gunning on some types, with vessels being fitted with guns of larger calibre than formerly – such as a range of large corvettes carrying 24pdr guns.

The error of disbanding the corps of seamen-gunners was belatedly recognised during the Directory, and in October 1795 a new naval gunnery corps (comprising seven *demi-brigades*) was established. In 1803 this was to be reconstituted as the *Artillerie de Marine*, comprising four regiments of three battalions each. Sadly, their specialist skills were never fully appreciated in Napoleon's land-centred strategy, and this force was to be increasingly deployed ashore, and was eventually expended wastefully in infantry roles during the disastrous 1813 campaigns.

However, during the early years of the Revolution, the enthusiastic French military machine carried all before it, overrunning most of their neighbours and defeating the principal Continental powers. At the beginning of 1798 France controlled northern Italy, much of the Low Counties and the Rhineland, their victories secured by the Treaty of Campo Formio. The Directory, which ran France from 1795, recognised that its sole remaining opponent, Britain, had to be conquered if the Revolutionary Wars were to end. It planned a series of invasions of the British Isles, and the rising star of its campaigns – General Napoleon Bonaparte – fresh from his victories over the Austrians in 1797, was appointed to lead the Armée d'Angleterre which had been assembled near Boulogne-sur-Mer; he was still only 28 years old.

Napoleon evaluated the situation and in early spring returned from Boulogne to Paris to advise the Directors that the firm control held by the British Navy over the Channel waters, coupled with a lack of suitable amphibious forces and equipment, meant that an invasion was totally unviable at that time. He had already devised an alternative strategy: in August 1797 he decided that to neutralise the massive economic benefits which Britain gained from its worldwide Empire – particularly the enormous trade with India - France first needed to seize Egypt. Thus Napoleon swiftly and secretly arranged for a force of thirteen ships of the line, under the command of Vice-Admiral Francois-Paul Brueys d'Aigalliers, to assemble at Toulon. Numerous smaller warships were added to this battle fleet (including the ships of the Venetian Navy, seized in 1797), which was to convoy 120 transports carrying 35,000 troops.

The whole fleet departed from Toulon on 19 May. The British were aware of the preparations but were completely ignorant of its destination, which was kept secret even from the invading force. Joined by 22 more transports at Ajaccio on 28 May, and bolstered by a convoy of a further 56 ships from Civitavecchia in early June, Napoleon arrived off Malta on 9 June, and by the 12th had secured the entire archipelago with its defences, Navy and Army, and the entire wealth of the Roman Catholic Church and the Knights Hospitaller in the islands. Moving on to Alexandria, where the fleet arrived on 1 July, Napoleon swiftly secured control of the land. However the arrival of Nelson's fleet at Alexandria on 1 August led to the annihilation of Bruey's battle fleet at the Battle of the Nile in Aboukir Bay on the same evening and during the following night.

Napoleon's Navy: 1799 to 1815

By 1799 the Directory Government in France was moving towards a crisis, with spiralling debts, a war unresolved and growing social unrest. The Coup of 18 Brumaire (9 November 1799) handed power to a Consulate comprising Napoleon Bonaparte, Abbé Emmanuel Sièyes and Pierre Roger Ducos, but in reality all power was held by the first-named, who by the end of the year was in firm control of France. Among the First Consul's early appointments was that of Pierre-Alexandre-Laurent Forfait, the

Outnumbered and outmatched in skill and experience, the French Navy did not enjoy much success in fleet engagements during the wars of 1793–1815, but one such occasion was the Battle of Algeciras in July 1801. An overconfident attack by a British squadron was beaten off, with the capture of the 74-gun *Hannibal*, which ran aground and surrendered. (Courtesy of Beverley R. Robinson Collection, US Naval Academy Museum)

veteran and skilled *ingénieur-constructeur*, to the post of Navy Minister, ensuring the development of Napoleon's planned invasion fleet. But Napoleon later disapproved of Forfait's poor administration and his financial interests in civilian shipbuilding. In 1801 the responsibility for the navy was given to Rear-Admiral Denis Decrès (Maritime Prefect at Lorient since returning from Egypt), who held office until the final fall of the Napoleonic regime. A tough-minded, financially honest and competent administrator, he proved a strong advocate of the *guerre de course* against enemy shipping, and as a former frigate commander he encouraged the construction of frigates following the defeat at Trafalgar.

The three principal dockyards were in a poor state. Brest was still suffering from the efforts of the previous decade; stocks of timber were very low, and the prospects of renewing them were poor because of the British blockade maintained rigorously between Ushant and Ireland. Consequently shipbuilding at the port suffered a major restraint from 1800 until 1812. Toulon had not recovered from the siege of 1793, at the close of which the British had destroyed not only ships on the stocks but much of the dockyard infrastructure. Only Rochefort was able to maintain its ability to produce major vessels while Lorient was also productive.

The renewal of war in May 1803 saw the French Navy having 23 ships of the line ready for service or in commission, with 25 frigates and 107 corvettes or smaller warships, plus some 167 small craft remaining from the invasion flotilla of the pre-1801 era. The largest component was in the Caribbean, where 12 ships of the line, 8 frigates and 28 smaller vessels were involved in the operations against San Domingo. There were only 5 ships of the line (at Brest and Toulon) and 10 frigates actually ready for sea in French or other European waters; the Brest and Toulon fleets were commanded by Truguet and Ganteaume respectively. However, Decrès advised Napoleon that this force could be increased within two months to 9 ships of the line and 13 frigates, and in six months to 21 ships of the line (including some to be deployed from the Caribbean) and 19 frigates. There were another 45 ships of the line under construction in French shipyards. More worryingly, the lack of seamen, timber and naval supplies mirrored the situation of 1793. The personnel resources had still not recovered from the chaos of the Revolution, and the loss of morale resulting from defeats such as at Aboukir. The forces of France's nominal allies were equally in poor condition, and in some cases were of unreliable loyalty. Against this the British Navy not only had more warships immediately available, but was also able to mobilise and commission its other warships out of 'Ordinary' (reserve) far more rapidly.

Napoleon's aim was to see French naval power resurrected. In 1803 he envisaged a ten-year scheme to build a battle fleet of 130 ships of the line, to be supported by 60 Spanish, 20 Batavian and 15 Genoese ships. More importantly in the short term, he demanded the re-establishment of an invasion force for the offensive against Britain to be composed of 310 armed vessels, to escort and support an invasion fleet capable of transporting 100,000 men. To this end he initiated not only a vast shipbuilding programme, but also the establishment of harbours and port facilities along the Pas-de-Calais coast, notably at Ambleteuse, Boulogne, Étaples and Wimereux. In July 1803 the projected number of armed vessels was raised from 310 to 1,410, and in August to 2,008, with an anticipated readiness date of November. He demanded of Decrès that by November there should be 20 ships of the line ready at Brest (the number actually reached there by that month was only 8), not to protect the invasion fleet in the Dover Straits but to initiate operations which would force the British to divert some of their forces to other areas; and he instructed that work should begin immediately on a large number of additional vessels.

By September 1803, Napoleon finally accepted that the flotilla would not be ready by November, and so postponed the planned action to January 1804. He instructed Ganteaume at Toulon to be ready to put to sea with ten ships of the line (although only seven were completed). A personal visit by the Emperor to Boulogne in November led him to conclude that the flotilla was unable to move at short notice and without the support of an adequate battle fleet. In the spring of 1804 he issued fresh instructions to Latouche-Tréville (who had succeeded Ganteaume at Toulon) to put to sea and, after a feint in the direction of Egypt (skilful misinformation had led to Nelson being convinced that a fresh occupation there was imminent), to round Spain, collect the ships blockaded at Rochefort, and to by-pass Brest (then blockaded by Cornwallis) to arrive finally at Cherbourg to support the invasion fleet. With the French Navy still crippled by lack of seamen and naval stores, even this was an impossible task until the close of 1804.

The seven demi-brigades of seamen-gunners, dating from 1795, were reorganised under the Empire in 1803 into a fresh body, the Imperial Corps of Naval Artillery (*Corps Impérial d'Artillerie de la Marine*). These formed the skilled members of gun crews aboard warships – the gun captains, the layers and trainers; ashore, their officers supervised the manufacture of naval ordnance and gun carriages, while the Corps also manned the batteries protecting the naval dockyards and other coastal installations. In 1803 they were composed of four regiments, two of which had four battalions, each of six companies, while the other two regiments had only two battalions. There were also separate battalions based on Martinique and Guadeloupe, formed in 1802.

Naval administration ashore was also reorganised into five naval districts (*arrondissements maritimes*) along the French coasts, each under a *préfet maritime*. These were centred on the five dockyards at Brest, Lorient, Rochefort, Toulon and Le Havre, although the administration of the last-named of these was moved to Cherbourg in 1809. Antwerp was subsequently incorporated as a sixth *arrondissement*, while Genoa was then added in 1805 (headquarters moved to La Spezia in 1807) and Amsterdam in 1809. Their maritime prefects controlled all shipping and harbour movements within their district (including private merchantmen), as well as supervising the dockyard construction and the supply of ordnance and other materials. Each maintained a register (*l'inscription maritime*) of all men within their district engaged in maritime activity, including merchant crews and fishermen. At Brest and at Toulon were created floating naval academies, specially equipped to train new officers on three-year intensive courses.

As far back as 1798, following French annexation of the Spanish Netherlands, Forfait had promoted the naval advantages of Antwerp. The rich hinterland had guaranteed the prospects of securing provisions, while the forests of the Ardennes and the Rhineland provided plentiful timber. In 1803 Napoleon decided to construct a dockyard there, with a dozen slipways planned for his intended shipbuilding programme. The maritime prefect whom he appointed here, Malouet, began immense construction works to meet the requirements of the Emperor and Decrès. The number of slipways – initially nine – was increased to the projected twelve in September 1809. Following the major British raid on Walcheren at the mouth of the Scheldt, Napoleon devoted considerable resources to improving the defences of Cadzand and Walcheren Islands, and to rebuilding the port of Flushing which had been burnt by the raiders.

The campaign of 1805 culminating with the destruction of most of the French and Spanish battle fleets off Cape Trafalgar is too well known to bear repetition here. Even before the two fleets had met in combat, Napoleon had already decided that command of the Channel, even for the few days required for an invasion fleet to be mobilised and to cross without being intercepted, was a chimera on which he should not build the future of the war. In August 1805 he had already begun to march the now retitled *Grand Armée* around Boulogne eastwards towards Ulm and the series of land campaigns that he would win in the next couple of years, commencing at Austerlitz on 2 December; in the summer of 1807 he reached a secret accord with Tsar Alexander at Tilsit, the naval consequences of that compact being that the French Emperor was empowered to annex the Danish, Swedish and Portuguese fleets to add to those of France and his other allies.

He was frustrated in his aim by the defection of his erstwhile Spanish allies, and by the seizure of the Danish fleet by Gambier at Copenhagen. His fertile mind turned to other means to secure his ambitions. The chapters of this book show the extensive plans he initiated in an attempt to make the French Navy the most powerful force. The massive constructions at Antwerp and at Cherbourg were accompanied by other projects along the northern coast of France, now extended eastwards to the Elbe, by similar schemes for the Atlantic bases at Brest, Lorient and Rochefort, and for enlarged facilities along the shores of the Mediterranean and Adriatic Seas, including Genoa, La Spezia, Venice, Trieste, Pola (Pula) and Cattaro (Kotor), all to become shipbuilding centres for the enlarged French Navy.

While Napoleon was determined to rebuild the battle fleet following the losses incurred at Trafalgar, Decrès believed that the maritime dominance of Britain could be defeated primarily by the war against commercial shipping – the *guerre de course* – and encouraged the depredations to British trade in which the French *corsairs* (privateers) excelled. British shipping suffered in the Baltic and in the West Indies, and also in the Indian Ocean where French frigates and privateers based on the Ile Bourbon (Réunion) and Ile de France (Mauritius) could fall 'like wolves' on the shipping lanes between India and the Cape. He sent out small squadrons, usually a pair of 18pdr frigates, sometimes with smaller units, to join in this economic warfare. Neutral ships were seized in European waters or in French ports for suspected trading with Britain, including at least 22 Portuguese merchantmen seized at Nantes in August and September 1807 and eight American schooners seized at Bayonne on 11 October 1810. The Continental System imposed by Napoleon on his allies was designed to cut off the supply of raw material to Britain and close the Continental market to British manufactured goods. It succeeded in imposing on the British population tremendous suffering and loss. When a failed harvest in 1812 brought near famine to Britain, the policy severely restricted Britain's importation of substitute grain, especially given French control of the Baltic trade from 1810, and came close to achieving its object. Nevertheless British trade overall continued to prosper, and on balance the Continental System must be deemed to have failed in its strategy.

The table below illustrated the relative lack of effectiveness of the *guerre de course*. The loss of some 500 ships per annum to privateers must be set against the gradual increase in the size of Britain's merchant marine – which reached 21,000 vessels by 1815. And while insurance rates rose to reflect these losses, leading to complaints by shipowners, at no time did these losses become unmanageable. Nor was Britain's ability to sustain the naval war seriously imperilled at any point.

Statistics of the Guerre de course, 1803 to 1814. Numbers of British merchantmen and French privateers taken:

Year	British ships	Privateers
1803	222	33
1804	387	53
1805	507	39
1806	519	33
1807	559	33
1808	469	49
1809	571	28
1810	619	67
1811	470	37
1812	475	34
1813	371	18
1814	145	16

Moreover, this form of warfare was very much reciprocated, and – except in the Mediterranean, where French coastal shipping was able to operate throughout the war – French merchant shipping was annihilated, and the French Channel ports in particular were devastated. Even in the Mediterranean, between about 1795 and 1815, the Barbary Coast states effectively changed over to monopolising the carrying trade between the Maghreb and southern Europe including trade with Italy and France. The Continental System was countered by a blockade of the European coast from Brest to the Elbe, proclaimed by the British government in May 1806. Over the period from 1802 to 1811, French exports increased slightly, while British exports declined. But France's unwilling allies suffered grievously – with no compensation from the French – and in the end it was this factor, reinforced by the military reverses in the Russian campaign of 1812, that triggered the internal revolts against the French Empire which arguably brought it to a collapse.

Napoleon's escape from Elba, and the Hundred Days which followed it until the ultimate débacle at Waterloo, had a limited naval effect. A fresh blockade of the French coast ensued, and finally it was to the British Navy – in the form of Captain Maitland of HMS *Bellerophon* – to whom the former Emperor eventually surrendered on 15 July 1815.

1816 to 1830: Rebuilding a Fleet

The French navy emerged from the Napoleonic Wars in a gravely weakened condition. It had lost almost a third of its ships of the line in the fall of Napoleon's empire. Its personnel were in disarray because of a shortage of seamen and the return from exile of many royalist officers. It had no money, because France was bankrupt from the war and had to pay an enormous indemnity to the victors before their troops would leave her soil. Most important, its naval policy had not worked: after 22 years of concerted French efforts to destroy the British navy and merchant marine, at 1 January 1815 Britain had 214 ships of the line built and building and a merchant marine that was larger and more prosperous than ever, while France was left with a navy and a merchant marine that had been all but driven from the seas.

The navy's main remaining assets were its ships and its administrative structure, but the ships disappeared rapidly. In mid-April 1814 the navy still had a large force of 104 ships of the line and 54 frigates afloat or under construction. By August this had fallen to 73 of the line and 42 frigates, due primarily to the surrender of ships located in European ports and building in shipyards outside France's new borders. By late 1819 the fleet had shrunk to 58 of the line and 34 frigates afloat or on the ways, most of the others having been found to be too rotten to be worth repairing. In 1817 the navy estimated that, at this rate of decay, the fleet would disappear completely in ten years.

In response Pierre Barthelémy, Baron Portal, Minister of Marine from 1818 to 1821, developed the Programme of 1820, the first of the comprehensive plans that shaped the evolution of the navy during the next forty years. This programme defined the composition of a realistically attainable fleet, set a target date for its completion, and determined the amount of money required per year to meet the target. In its final form, promulgated in 1824, the programme provided for a fleet of 40 ships of the line and 50 frigates afloat. Portal calculated that this force could be created in ten years with an annual budget of 65 million francs (of which 6 million were for the colonies). He secured a political consensus to work towards this fiscal goal, even though only 50 million francs could be provided in 1820. Portal's programme is listed along with subsequent French naval programmes in Appendix E.

Portal's programme took advantage of the few weaknesses that could be seen in Britain's naval position. It reversed the traditional relationship between battleships and cruising ships in the fleet – as recently as 1814, France had had twice as many ships of the line as frigates. The new programme emphasised frigates to exploit the enormous problems that Britain would face in trying to defend worldwide trade and colonies. It retained a battle fleet, not to stand up to Britain alone, but to serve as a nucleus for an anti-British coalition fleet. This battle fleet was also designed to ensure that France would face no other maritime challenges: if she could not be number one, she could at least be an undisputed number two.

Refinements were soon made to the programme. The navy realised that ships left on the building ways, if properly ventilated and covered by a protective shed, would last almost indefinitely without decaying and would also have a longer service life after launching because their timbers would be better seasoned. Equally important, maintaining ships in this way was highly economical. The navy eventually decided that a third of the planned 40 ships of the line and 50 frigates would not be launched but would be kept complete on the ways. An additional 13 battleships and 16 frigates would be on the ways at less advanced stages of construction. These decisions led to a large increase during the 1820s in the number of building ways in the dockyards and in the number of ships laid down on them. At the same time the navy's ordinary budget slowly increased, finally reaching the 65 million franc goal in 1830.

One reason the French navy survived the lean years after the Napoleonic Wars was the constant demand for its services. Within a few years naval stations were established in the Antilles, the Levant, and off the east coast of South America, and others were later created in the Pacific and in the Far East. Reoccupation and development of the few colonies left to France was given high priority. One of the navy's most famous shipwrecks occurred when the frigate *Méduse* was lost in 1816 while leading a force to reoccupy Senegal. A few small ships were assigned to each of the reoccupied colonies for local duties. Among these were the navy's first two steamers, *Voyageur* and *Africain*, built for Senegal in 1819. Scientific activities were also prominent. In 1820 (a relatively typical year), one corvette was in the process of circumnavigating the globe, two ships were surveying the Brazilian coast, three were producing definitive charts of the French coast, and one was charting the Mediterranean and Black Seas.

A series of crises gave the navy some new operational experience. In 1823 French troops invaded Spain to put down a revolution which had begun in 1820. Over 90 ships including four ships of the line supported this operation. In 1827, during the Greek war for independence, a French squadron joined British and Russian forces in annihilating the Turco-Egyptian fleet in the Battle of Navarino. In 1830, following several years of diplomatic disputes, the navy landed an army and took the city of Algiers. The invasion force included 11 ships of the line and 25 frigates.

Less sensational activities, including support for French occupation troops in Spain, Greece, and Algeria, large diplomatic missions to Haiti in 1825 and Brazil in 1828, and an expedition to Madagascar in 1829, created constant demands for additional ships and men. The active fleet of 76 ships planned in the 1820 budget exceeded the number of ships in commission in 1789, and unanticipated requirements increased the number of ships actually used during all or part of 1820 to 103. By 1828 this figure had exactly doubled to 206 ships, and it remained at this high level during the extensive operations in 1829 and 1830.

1830 to 1840: Retrenchment and Experimentation

In 1830 a liberal revolution brought to power King Louis-Philippe. The new king's backers believed that high government spending was one of the main causes of economic distress and political disorder, and they immediately imposed major budget cuts. The navy, which had just reached the expenditure level of 65 million francs per year called for by the Programme of 1820, was ordered to cut its budget request for 1831 to 60.5 million francs. The restrictions on spending continued in effect throughout the 1830s, and the ordinary navy budget did not again reach 65 million francs until 1838. Even more serious, extraordinary appropriations, which had funded the remarkable expansion of the navy's operations in the 1820s, were even more severely limited and did not reach the level of 1828-30 again until the crisis of 1840.

The impact of these cuts was particularly evident in the shipbuilding programme because the navy's other expenses, notably personnel and operations, were relatively inflexible. In late 1834 the navy increased the proportion of Portal's fleet to be kept on the ways from one-third to one-half to allow the dockyards to begin a few new ships with funds that otherwise would have been used to maintain some older ships. This change, along with other changes made to Portal's programme during the 1820s, was formalised in a new programme promulgated by royal ordinance on 1 February 1837. The programme also confirmed the navy's need for two ship classes, the 74-gun ship of the line and the 3rd Class frigate, which some politicians wanted to abolish.

Despite the new programme, the strength of the fleet declined in the late 1830s. The programme called for 53 ships of the line and 66 frigates afloat and on the ways, but between December 1834 and December 1839 the total number of battleships fell from 51 to 46 while frigates fell from 60 to 56. The deficit was in the number of ships under construction, a situation which was aggravated by the fact that operational requirements kept the number of frigates afloat substantially higher than in the new plan. The strength of the French fleet is summarised in Appendix D for the period 1789–1859.

The distribution of the fleet during the 1830s remained essentially as it had been at the end of the 1820s. The station cruisers remained busy,

In the post-1815 era the French Navy was employed on numerous overseas operations, supporting French colonial expansion or in the service of foreign policy objectives. In 1837-38, for example, France demanded reparations from Mexico for the sufferings of its expatriate citizens caught up in Mexico's political upheavals. Failing to obtain satisfaction, France sent a squadron of frigates and smaller vessels to bombard the fortress of San Juan de Ulúa (Saint Jean d'Ulloa) at Veracruz on 27 November 1838, which surrendered. It was an early outing for Paixhans' new shell guns, and combined with mortar fire from bomb vessels, their success against strong stone-built fortifications took naval observers by surprise. This print is after a painting by Théodore Gudin. (Courtesy of Beverley R. Robinson Collection, US Naval Academy Museum)

and were augmented by special forces sent in response to disputes with Colombia, Haiti, Mexico, and Argentina. An expeditionary force bombarded the fortifications of Veracruz in Mexico in 1838. The South Atlantic station began a blockade of Buenos Aires in the same year, and a special expedition finally secured a treaty from the Argentines in 1840. In Africa, the navy took possession of the mouth of the Gabon River in 1839 and subsequently established a few trading posts in the Gulf of Guinea. The navy was particularly active in scientific expeditions in the late 1830s, undertaking several circumnavigations of the globe.

The navy was also very active in Europe. In 1831 a squadron fought its way up the Tagus to Lisbon in a dispute with Portugal. Another squadron supported Belgian independence against the Dutch between 1831 and 1833, and another occupied Ancona following insurrections in Italy in 1832. Naval stations in Spain were re-established in 1834 in response to the Carlist revolution in Spain. In 1836 and 1837 a fleet was maintained off Tunis to prevent interference with the French occupation of the interior of Algeria. In 1838 this force was shifted to the Levant as relations between the Sultan of Turkey and his nominal vassal, Mohammed Ali of Egypt, approached breaking point.

1840 to 1852: Ferment

The Levant crisis gave the French navy its biggest test between 1815 and the Crimean War in 1854. War between Turkey and Egypt broke out in 1839, generating a crisis between France, which supported Mohammed Ali, and Britain, which supported Turkey. The French Levant squadron reached an average level of 16 ships, including 9 ships of the line, during the first half of 1840. It also reached a level of operational readiness that was admired even by British naval officers. In the meantime, the French decided to launch three ships of the line from its reserve of ships on the ways and take other measures to raise the number in commission to the twenty called for under the Programme of 1837.

Despite this demonstration of French naval strength, the British in July 1840 succeeded in forming a coalition with Austria, Prussia, and Russia to force Mohammed Ali to withdraw. An intense diplomatic crisis between Britain and France ensued, but France found it had no choice but to back down. The British squadron in the Levant was larger than the French (it contained about 14 ships of the line to the French 9) and it was backed by much greater resources at home in money and men. France tried to launch and commission 12 frigates then on the ways but suspended the effort when it realised it would not be able to find enough seamen to man them until the fishing fleet returned from the Grand Banks at the end of the year.

The crisis showed that the naval policy followed by France since 1815 had grave weaknesses that could no longer be ignored. It demonstrated that the fleet of the 1837 programme could not cope with the British battle fleet in cases such as 1840 in which France had no allies. It also showed that the policy of retaining ships on the ways for rapid launch during a crisis was an illusion. On the positive side, the crisis led to a relaxation of the fiscal constraints on the navy—it was clear that the navy's requirements had outgrown Portal's standard 65 million franc budget. The resources made available to the navy between 1786 and 1861, both money and men, are listed in Appendix C.

In the 1840s the navy focused its attention on steam as an alternative way to offset British sea power. The programme of 1837 had included 40 steamers of 150nhp and above, but since then much larger steamers had become practicable. In 1842 the French navy established a programme for a steam navy that would parallel the sail navy. It was to include 40 combat steamers: five 'steam frigates' of 540nhp, fifteen of 450nhp, and twenty 'steam corvettes' of 220nhp. The smaller ships already on hand (mostly the 160nhp *Sphinx* class) remained useful for messenger, transport, and colonial duties, and thirty were included in the programme.

At first, not much progress was made with the new programme because of lack of construction facilities and money, but studies of the role of steam in the fleet continued. The most famous was a pamphlet published in 1844 by François Ferdinand Philippe Louis Marie d'Orleans, Prince de Joinville, a son of the king who had chosen the navy as his career. Joinville claimed that steam would allow France to offset British supremacy in numbers by concentrating its forces at a point of its choosing, overwhelming local opposition, and either ravaging the coast or landing an army. His pamphlet triggered a major naval scare in Britain and the construction of many new fortifications along the British coast.

Joinville went on to direct a commission whose work led to a new steamer programme at the end of 1845. This programme increased the size of the planned steam fleet to 100 ships, including 10 frigates and 20 corvettes. Joinville wanted steam frigates to be true combatants, with an armament of 30 large guns and engines of 600nhp or more. His steam corvettes were also to be combatants, but were expected to serve primarily as avisos. They were to have around eight large guns and engines of 400nhp. The plans for the frigate *Isly* and the corvette *Roland* conformed to these guidelines. The remaining 70 ships were to carry out the now-traditional messenger and transport duties of steamers and were assigned two guns at most and engines ranging from 300 to 90nhp. This programme is listed along with other French naval programs in Appendix E.

The main strength of the navy remained in the sailing fleet, however. In the mid-1840s Parliament became concerned about its deterioration. The Minister of Marine, Vice-Adm. Ange-René-Armand, Baron de Mackau, took advantage of the opportunity and presented a new naval programme in 1846. In essence, it combined Portal's sail fleet and Joinville's steam fleet in a single programme which was to be achieved in seven years with the navy's regular budgets and special appropriations totalling 93 million francs.

The programme contained several innovative features, all involving steam. While drawing up the programme, the navy decided to reduce the number of ships of the line under construction over and above the programmemed 40 from 13 to 4, on the grounds that the progress of steam made it prudent not to build up too big a reserve of these expensive ships. (The corresponding reserve of 16 sail frigates was retained.) It also decided to adopt one of Joinville's recommendations and give part of the sailing fleet auxiliary steam propulsion. Parliamentary pressure caused the navy to increase the horsepower of these ships, and the final plan (not incorporated in the royal ordinance) called for four ships of the line with 500nhp engines, four frigates with 250nhp machinery, and four corvettes with 120nhp auxiliary machinery. This decision led, through many permutations, to the conversion of the ships of the line *Austerlitz* and *Jean Bart* and the construction of the corvettes *Biche* and *Sentinelle*. Parliamentary pressure also caused the navy to add to the programme two floating batteries of around 450nhp in response to the British blockships of the *Blenheim* type. These, however, were soon cancelled.

The execution of the Programme of 1846 was interrupted by the revolution of 1848, in which Louis-Philippe was overthrown and replaced by a second republic. The revolution ushered in a new period of fiscal retrenchment, which severely slowed down naval shipbuilding. The budgets of 1847 and 1848 had each included the planned annual instalments of 13.3 million francs, but the 1849 budget included only 2.7 million for the programme and later budgets included nothing. By the time naval activity revived in the early 1850s, further advances in steam technology had rendered the Programme of 1846 obsolete.

The navy's operations in the 1840s were concentrated first and foremost in the Mediterranean. The Levant crisis of 1840 was succeeded by a series of operations associated with the conquest of North Africa, including an expedition led by Joinville which bombarded the Moroccan port of

Mogador in 1844. A new crisis in Portugal caused the French to send another expedition to the Tagus in 1847. Elsewhere, Joinville in the frigate *Belle Poule* brought the ashes of Napoleon back to Paris from St. Helena in 1840. Expeditions were dispatched in 1842 and 1843 to occupy the Marquesas Islands in the Pacific, and French control was extended to the Society Islands in 1844. In 1843 the French occupied the islands of Nossi Bé and Mayotte off Madagascar, and a joint Anglo-French force bombarded Tamatave in 1845. In 1845 the French signed a treaty with Britain which required them to retain a force of 26 ships on the West African coast to help suppress the slave trade. Between 1845 and 1852 the navy was also involved in operations in Argentina, the dispute with that country having flared up again.

The 1848 revolution in France triggered revolutions throughout Europe, which kept the navy busy in European waters, especially in Sicily, at Rome, and in the Adriatic. Fiscal retrenchment, however, soon led to a substantial reduction in the number of ships in commission. Among the casualties was the West African station, which declined from 26 ships at the end of 1847 to its pre-treaty strength of around 8 ships at the end of 1849 and then to 3 ships at the end of 1851.

1852 to 1861: Towards a New Fleet

On 2 December 1851 Louis Napoleon carried out a coup d'état which gave him control of the government and made him, a year later, Emperor Napoleon III. The new regime quickly embarked on a revolutionary transformation of the battle fleet from sail to steam, which it finally codified in 1857 in a new naval programme just before another technological revolution took place.

In early 1852, the first French screw ship of the line to run trials, *Charlemagne*, demonstrated that the large screw-propelled warship was a practical reality. At this time, the navy estimated that Britain had afloat or under construction 10 such ships compared to 3 for France. Shortly thereafter, the new French government substantially increased the funds available to the navy for shipbuilding in 1852 and 1853, and in mid-1852 the navy decided to use the funds to convert seven more ships of the line along the lines of *Charlemagne*.

In justifying this programme, the Minister of Marine (then Théodore Ducos) told his senior advisory council in May 1852 that he felt France's strategy in a war with Britain should be to strike hard at British commerce while threatening a rapid, unexpected landing on the coasts of the United Kingdom. The need for speed and carefully coordinated operations ruled out the construction of additional sailing ships. Converted ships like *Charlemagne* could make a substantial contribution with their dependable speed of around 8 knots. (They were also a practical necessity, as they made use of existing materiel and could be completed more quickly than new ships.) Fast ships of the line like *Napoléon* would be even more appropriate, but the navy avoided committing itself to this type before the trials of the prototype. The sensational success of *Napoléon* in August 1852 caused the navy to start additional ships of the type as quickly as possible. Five new ships and one conversion (*Eylau*) were begun in 1853 alone.

In Britain, the return of a Bonaparte to absolute power in France aroused old fears and triggered a full-blown naval scare in 1852 and 1853. Between August and November 1852 the Admiralty responded to developments in France by ordering the conversion to steam of eleven additional ships of the line, and more soon followed.

Ironically, this period of rivalry soon gave way to a period of close

A eyewitness pencil drawing from the sketchbook of Captain George Pechell Mends, RN depicting the fifteen-strong French fleet rendezvousing with the British in Besika Bay on 14 June 1853, prior to the joint squadrons entering the Black Sea. As a naval officer Mends meticulously recorded the details of the French ships, which he listed (from the head of the line, right to left) as: *Ville de Paris* 130 Vice Flag, *Sané* [paddle frigate], *Jupiter* 90, *Bayard* 100, *Caton*, *Henri IV* 100, *Magellan*, *Valmy* 130 screw Rear Flag, *Napoléon* screw 90, *Mogador*, *Montebello* 120, *Charlemagne* screw 90. (© National Maritime Museum PZ0881-002)

cooperation as the two nations combined their efforts in the Crimean War against Russia. In September 1853 the fleets of the two powers entered the Dardanelles together, and they continued to coordinate their operations in the Black Sea and the Baltic until the end of the war in 1856. They also shared some of their latest technological developments, the British receiving the plans of the French armoured floating batteries and the French receiving plans of British gunboats.

In October 1853 *Napoléon* gave dramatic proof of the importance of steam by towing the three-decker sailing French flagship *Ville de Paris* up the Turkish straits against both wind and current while the British fleet had to wait for more favourable conditions. Subsequent operations reinforced the lesson that only screw steamers could be considered combatant warships. In October 1854, while preparing the list of construction work to be undertaken in 1855, the ministry of marine proposed converting to steam all 33 of its remaining sailing ships of the line in the next several years. One-third of the resultant fleet was to be fast battleships like *Napoléon* (including a few conversions like *Eylau*), and the remainder were to be conversions like *Charlemagne*. Conversions of existing ships of the line were carried out as quickly as the ships could be spared from war operations.

The Crimean War placed heavy operational demands on the navy. Fleets were required in both the Black Sea and the Baltic. The French used 12 ships of the line in the Baltic during 1854 and 3 in 1855; they used 16 in the Black Sea in 1854 and 31 during 1855 (including about 19 as transports). The principal naval engagements involving the French were all against fortifications: the capture of Bomarsund in the Baltic in August 1854, the bombardment of Sevastopol in the Black Sea in October 1854, the capture of Kinburn in the Black Sea in October 1855, and the bombardment of Sveaborg in the Baltic in November 1855. The bombardment of Sevastopol was carried out by ships of the line and was a failure – *Napoléon*, one of many ships damaged, was forced to withdraw after a shell produced a large leak in her side. In contrast, the bombardment of Kinburn exactly a year later made extensive use of technology developed during the war and was a success. The French armoured floating batteries proved practically impervious to the Russian shells, while groups of gunboats, mortar vessels, and armed paddle steamers also inflicted heavy damage on the defenders.

In May 1855 the Minister, Admiral of France Ferdinand-Alphonse Hamelin, circulated to the ports a list of questions raised by the October 1854 memo regarding the composition of the battle fleet. In August 1855 a navy commission, formed at the Emperor's direction to examine the responses, drafted a formal programme for the modernisation of the fleet. The key elements of its programme were a combat fleet of 40 fast battleships and 20 fast frigates and a fleet of transports large enough to transport an army of 40,000 men. While the combat fleet was being built, the navy was to rely on a transitional fleet of screw ships converted from sail, which was to be completed as quickly as possible. This plan called for the expenditure of 245 million francs in 13 years beginning in 1857. The commission was reconvened in December 1855 to consider the implications of the success of the armoured floating batteries at the bombardment of Kinburn in October. It completed the technical and fiscal details of the programme in November 1856, and the Emperor referred the plan to the Conseil d'Etat in January 1857 for study. Three changes were made during 1857. Two ship of the line conversions were deleted (*Friedland* and *Jemmapes*). The number of transports was reduced from 94 to 72, probably reflecting a decision to abandon all but five of the frigate conversions and instead convert some sailing frigates to steam frigates. The financial arrangements were also changed to provide for the expenditure of 235 million francs over 14 years beginning in 1858. The final programme was promulgated by imperial decree on 23 November 1857.

An Anglo-French squadron of steamers bombards Odessa in the Black Sea, 22 April 1854. Left to right, the attacking ships are: *Terrible* (RN), *Vauban*, *Mogador*, *Sampson* (RN), *Descartes*, *Retribution* (RN), *Tiger* (RN) and *Furious* (RN). (Courtesy of Beverley R. Robinson Collection, US Naval Academy Museum)

While refining the technical portion of the programme in late 1856, the navy's engineers under Stanislas-Charles-Henri-Laur Dupuy de Lôme, designer of *Napoléon*, had included a clause allowing the Minister of Marine to replace ship types in the programme with others equivalent in military strength and construction cost. Dupuy de Lôme knew better than most how quickly the programme would become obsolete, because he was already working on the plans for the world's first 'armoured frigates'. In March 1858 the Minister (Hamelin) ordered the first three of these, including *Gloire*, and simultaneously cancelled construction of two fast 70-gun ships of the line, *Desaix* and *Sébastopol*, which had not yet been laid down and a proposed class of fast 40-gun steam frigates. By October 1858 the navy had decided that the new armoured frigates were not just equivalent but superior to line of battle ships. At the same time, it replaced the fast frigates in the programme with smaller 'cruising frigates'. (Two similar 'station frigates', *Vénus* and *Minerve*, followed by a series of 'armoured corvettes', were eventually built in the 1860s.) The Programme of 1857 remained the legal basis for the modernisation of the French fleet to the end of the 1860s, but the ships built under it bore little resemblance to those in the initial 1855 proposal.

The navy saw considerable action in the 1850s besides the Crimean War. In 1851 a French force carried out a reprisal bombardment of the Moroccan port of Salé. In 1853 the navy occupied the Pacific island of New Caledonia. In 1855 the French in Senegal began to expand their control upriver into the interior of Africa. In 1856 Britain and France agreed upon joint operations for the revision of their treaties with China, and two joint naval and military campaigns were conducted before another treaty settlement was made in 1860. During this operation, the French occupied Saigon in 1859 and over the next few years took control of all of Cochinchina.

Elsewhere, the traditional Anglo-French rivalry was quick to revive. A French naval and military intervention in the Danube principalities after the Crimean War aroused British fears of a Franco-Russian alliance. The Franco-Austrian war of 1859, in which France helped Italy become independent, antagonised British conservatives as much as it delighted liberals. The French navy helped transport and supply the French armies in Italy and blockaded the northern Adriatic ports. Such activity focused British attention on the naval balance, and they found that France had reached near parity in fast steam ships of the line and had an advantage in the number of ironclad warships under construction. In February 1859 the Admiralty triggered the third major Anglo-French naval scare since 1844, which intensified in 1860-61 as France led the world into the ironclad era.

Impératrice Éugenie with the *Escadre de la Méditerranée* between May and December 1859. When this fleet anchored off Venice on 9 July 1859, without *Impératrice Éugenie* but with her sister *Impétueuse*, it included the fast three-decker *Bretagne*, the fast 90-gunners *Algésiras*, and *Arcole*, and the corvette *Monge*, all of which are probably visible here. *Impératrice Éugenie* sailed in May 1860 for the Far East where she remained until 1867. (Marius Bar)

Chronology

1774	(10 May)	Death of Louis XV ('le Bien-Aimé') and Accession of Louis XVI.
1789	(4 July)	Fall of the Bastille (effective start of the French Revolution)
1791	(1 Oct)	Inauguration of the Legislative Assembly following dissolution of the Estates-General.
1792	(20 April)	French declaration of war against Austria marking start of the War of the First Coalition.
	(June)	Declaration of War against Prussia.
	(21 Sept)	French National Convention meets.
	(22 Sept)	Proclamation of First French Republic under the rule of the Convention.
	(29 Sept)	Occupation of Nice and Villefranche-sur-Mer and seizure of Sardinian Navy's vessels.
1793	(21 Jan)	Execution of Louis XVI.
	(1 Feb)	Declarations of War against Britain and the Netherlands.
	(7 Mar)	Declaration of War against Spain.
	(6 Apr)	Formation of Committee of Public Safety, leading to start of the Reign of Terror.
	(27 Aug)	Occupation of Toulon by Anglo-Spanish forces.
	(17 Dec)	Evacuation of Toulon by Anglo-Spanish forces.
1794	(1 June)	Battle off Ushant ('13 Prairial'; 'Glorious First of June' in Britain).
1795	(13 Mar)	Action off Genoa ('Combat de Cap Noli' in France).
	(23 June)	Action off Groix / in Quiberon Bay between fleets under Vice-Adm. Villaret-Joyeuse and Vice-Adm. Lord Bridport.
	(13 July)	Battle off the Hyères.
	(26 Oct)	Establishment of the Directory (abolition of Committee of Public Safety).
1796	(May)	Napoleon's invasion of Italy.
1797	(14 Feb)	Battle of Cape St Vincent (an Anglo-Spanish battle not involving French vessels).
	(May)	Declaration of War against Venice and occupation of its territory (including Corfu).
	(11 Oct)	Battle of Camperdown (an Anglo-Dutch battle not involving French vessels).
1798	(1 Aug)	Battle of Aboukir Bay ('Battle of the Nile').
	(12 Oct)	Action off Tory Island
	(24 Dec)	Start of War of the Second Coalition against France (Britain, Russia, Austria, Portugal and the Ottoman Empire).
1799	(9 Nov)	Establishment of the Consulate, with Napoleon Bonaparte First Consul.
1801	(5 July)	Battle of Algeciras (Algésiras in French).
	(12 July)	Battle of Cadiz ('Battle of the Gut of Gibraltar' in Britain)
	(15 Aug)	British attack (led by Nelson) on Boulogne beaten off by French gunboats and small vessels under Vice-Adm. Latouche-Tréville.
1802	(25 Mar)	Treaty of Amiens signed (formal end of the French Revolutionary War).
1803	(18 May)	Resumption of War against Britain.
1804	(18 May)	Establishment of the First Empire, under Emperor Napoleon I.
1805	(22 July)	Calder's Action ('Bataille des Quinze-Vingt').
	(21 Oct)	Battle of Trafalgar.
	(4 Nov)	Action off Cape Ortegal.
1809	(12 Apr)	Assault on the French squadron in the Basque Roads.
1810	(2 Dec)	Surrender of Mauritius/Ile de France.
1811	(13 Mar)	Battle of Lissa.
1814	(6 Apr)	1st Abdication of Napoleon, and restoration of Bourbon Dynasty under Louis XVIII.
1815	(20 Mar)	Restoration of Napoleon; start of the 'Hundred Days'
	(22 June)	2nd Abdication of Napoleon; return of Louis XVIII.
1823		Siege and blockade of Cadiz.
1824	(16 Sept)	Death of Louis XVIII and Accession of Charles X.
1827	(20 Oct)	Battle of Navarino.
1830	(5 July)	Capture of Algiers by French Expeditionary Force.
	(2 Aug)	Abdication of Charles X; brief (7-day) reign of Henri V.
	(9 Aug)	Accession of Louis-Philippe.
1831	(11 July)	Forcing the Tagus (Tagus and Azores blockaded).
1836-1840		Rio de la Plata.
1838		Saint Jean d'Ulloa (Vera Cruz).
1840 (July-Nov)		Levant crisis.
1844	(6 Aug)	Bombardment of Tangiers and Mogador.
1845	(20 Nov)	Battle of Vuelta de Obligado (Rio de la Plata).
1848	(24 Feb)	Abdication of Louis-Philippe; establishment of 2nd French Republic.
	(10 Dec)	Prince Louis-Napoleon Bonaparte became President of the 2nd Republic.
1852	(2 Dec)	Louis-Napoleon Bonaparte became Emperor Napoleon III of 2nd Empire.
1854	(27 Mar)	Declaration of War against Russia ('Crimean War')
1857-1862		Actions in China.
From 1857		Actions in Indochina.
1859		Operations in the Adriatic.
1870	(4 Sept)	Deposition of Napoleon III and Proclamation of 3rd French Republic.

French Naval Operations

This section lists the forces of France and her allies involved in naval operations, together with vessels of its opponents in each major action. Single-ship combats are not included. For most operations after 1815 only French forces are shown.

OCCUPATION OF TOULON – 29 August 1793.
The French Mediterranean Fleet at Toulon – 31 ships of the line of which 4(#) were taken away by the British at the evacuation in December and 9(*) were destroyed.
2 x 120s – *Commerce de Marseille*# and *Dauphin Royal*.
4 x 80s – *Couronne, Languedoc, Tonnant* and *Triomphant**.
25 x 74s – *Alcide, Apollon, Barra, Censeur, Centaure*, Commerce de Bordeaux, Conquérant, Destin*, Duguay-Trouin*, Entrepranant, Généreux, Guerrier, Héros*, Heureux, Liberté*, Mercure, Orion, Patriote, Pompée#, Puissant#, Scipion*, Peuple Souverain, Suffisant*, Thémistocle** and *Tricolor**.
4 x 40s – *Arethuse#, Perle#*.
7 x 36s – *Alceste*# (given to Sardinians), *Aurore, Lutine, Prosélyte*, Topaze, Victorieuse**.
2 x 32s – *Iris** and *Montréal** (both ex-British 12pdr frigates).
3 x 28s – *Belette#, Poulette#*.
Also 12 corvettes including 24-gun *Auguste** and *Caroline**, 20-gun *Moselle*# and *Pluvier*, 18-gun *Mulet*#, *Petite Aurore*# (given to Spain) and *Sincère*#.
[Note that on 14 September four of the 'most unserviceable' 74s – the *Aquilon, Entreprenant, Orion* and *Patriote* – and the 20-gun brig-corvette *Pluvier* were allowed to sail (effectively disarmed) to other French dockyards with the 5,000 pro-Republican French seamen.]
Hood's fleet – 22 ships of the line.
2 x 100s – *Britannia* (flag of Vice-Adm. William Hotham) and *Victory* (flag of Vice-Adm. Samuel Hood and Rear-Adm. Sir Hyde Parker).
3 x 98s – *Princess Royal* (flag of Rear-Adm. Samuel Goodall), *St. George* (flag of Rear-Adm. John Gell) and *Windsor Castle* (flag of Vice-Adm. Phillips Cosby).
12 x 74s – *Alcide* (flag of Commodore Robert Linzee from September), *Bedford, Berwick, Captain, Colossus, Courageux, Egmont, Fortitude, Illustrious, Leviathan, Robust* and *Terrible*.
5 x 64s – *Agamemnon, Ardent, Diadem, Intrepid* (from end August) and *St. Albans*.
1 x 50 – *Romney*.
4 x 36s – *Aigle, Inconstant, Leda* and *Romulus*.
8 x 32s – *Aimable, Aquilon, Castor, Isis, Juno, Lowestoffe, Meleager* and *Mermaid*.
3 x 28s – *Dido, Nemesis* and *Tartar*.
1 x 24 – *Amphitrite*.
Also hospital ship *Dolphin* and store ship *Gorgon* (both ex 44s), store ship *Camel* (20), sloops *Eclair, Fury, Scout, Speedy, Tisiphone* and *Weazle*, and fireships *Conflagration* and *Vulcan*.

BATTLE OF 13 PRAIRIAL ('Glorious First of June') – 1 June 1794.
Villaret-Joyeuse's fleet – 26 ships of the line of which 6(#) were taken and 1(*) sunk.
1 x 120 – *Montagne* (flag of Rear-Adm. Louis Thomas Villaret-Joyeuse).
2 x 110s – *Républicain* (flag of Rear-Adm. Joseph-Marie Nielly) and *Terrible* (flag of Rear-Adm. François Joseph Bouvet).
4 x 80s – *Jacobin, Juste#, Sans Pareil#*, and *Scipion*.
19 x 74s – *Achille#, America#, Convention* (ex *Sceptre*), *Entreprenant, Éole, Gasparin, Impétueux#, Jemappes, Mucius* (ex-*Orion*), *Neptune, Northumberland#, Patriote, Pelletier, Téméraire, Tourville, Trajan, Trente-et-un Mai, Tyrannicide* and *Vengeur du Peuple**.
Also 18pdr frigate *Proserpine*, 12pdr frigates *Galatée, Gentille, Précieuse* and *Tamise* (ex HMS *Thames*), 12pdr corvette *Naïade* and brig *Papillon*.
Howe's fleet – 25 ships of the line.
3 x 100s – *Royal Charlotte* (flag of Adm. Earl Howe), *Royal George* (flag of Vice-Adm. Sir Alexander Hood) and *Royal Sovereign* (flag of Vice-Adm. Thomas Graves).
4 x 98s – *Barfleur* (flag of Rear-Adm. George Bowyer), *Glory, Impregnable* (flag of Rear-Adm. Benjamin Caldwell) and *Queen* (flag of Rear-Adm. Alan Gardner).
2 x 80s – *Caesar* and *Gibraltar*.
16 x 74s – *Alfred, Bellerophon* (flag of Rear-Adm. Thomas Pasley), *Brunswick, Culloden, Defence, Invincible, Leviathan, Majestic, Marlborough, Montagu, Orion, Ramillies, Russell, Thunderer, Tremendous* and *Valiant*.
2 x 38s – *Latona* and *Phaeton* (18pdr frigates)
4 x 32s – *Aquilon, Niger, Southampton* and *Venus* (12pdr frigates).
1 x 28-gun – *Pegasus* (9pdr frigate)
Also hospital ship *Charon* (ex 44), fireships *Comet* and *Incendiary*, sloop *Kingfisher*, and cutters *Ranger* and *Rattler*.

ACTION OFF CAPE NOLI – 13 March 1795.
Martin's fleet – 15 ships of the line, of which 2(#) were taken.
1 x 118 – *Sans Culotte* (flag of Rear-Adm. Pierre Martin).
3 x 80s – *Ca Ira#, Tonnant* and *Victoire*.
11 x 74s – *Alcide, Barra, Censeur#, Conquérant, Duquesne, Généreux, Guerrier, Heureux, Mercure, Peuple Souverain* and *Timoléon*.
1 x 40 – *Minerve*.
3 x 32s – *Alceste, Tamise* and *Vestale*.
1 x 20 – *Hazard*.
Also sloop *Scout*.
Hotham's fleet – 14 ships of the line (including the Neapolitan 74-gun *Tancredi*).
1 x 100 – *Britannia* (flag of Vice-Adm. William Hotham).
3 x 98s – *Princess Royal* (flag of Vice-Adm. Samuel Granston Goodall), *St George* (flag of Vice-Adm. Sir Hyde Parker) and *Windsor Castle* (flag of Rear-Adm. Robert Linzee).
8 x 74s – *Bedford, Captain, Courageux, Egmont, Fortitude, Illustrious, Terrible* and *Tancredi* (Neapolitan).
2 x 64s – *Agamemnon* and *Diadem*.
2 x 36s – *Inconstant* and *Romulus*.
4 x 32s – *Lowestoffe, Meleager, Minerva* (Neapolitan) and *Pilade* (Neapolitan).
1 x 26 – *Poulette*.
Also sloop *Moselle*, brig *Tarleton* and cutter *Fox*.

ACTION OFF ÎLE GROIX – 22 June 1795.
Villaret-Joyeuse's fleet – 12 ships of the line of which 3(#) were taken.
1 x 118 – *Peuple* (flag of Vice-Adm. Louis Thomas Villaret-Joyeuse).
11 x 74s – *Alexandre#, Droits de l'Homme, Formidable#, Fougueux, Jean Bart, Mucius, Nestor, Redoubtable, Tigre#, Wattigny* and *Zélé*.
Also 11 frigates and 7 smaller vessels.
Bridport's fleet – 14 ships of the line.

2 x 100s – *Queen Charlotte*, *Royal George* (flag of Adm. Sir Alexander Arthur Hood, Lord Bridport).
6 x 98s – *Barfleur*, *London* (flag of Vice-Adm. John Colpoys), *Prince*, *Prince George*, *Prince of Wales* (flag of Rear-Adm. Henry Harvey) and *Queen* (flag of Vice-Adm. Sir Alan Gardiner).
1 x 80 – *Sans Pareil* (flag of Rear-Adm. Lord Hugh Seymour).
5 x 74s – *Colossus*, *Irresistible*, *Orion*, *Russell* and *Valiant*.
1 x 44 – *Revolutionnaire*.
2 x 36s – *Nymphe* and *Thalia*.
2 x 32s – *Aquilon* and *Astraea*.
1 x 20 – *Babet*.
Also fireships *Incendiary* and *Megaera*, hospital ship *Charon* (ex 44) and luggers *Argus* and *Dolly*.

BATTLE OFF THE HYÈRES – 13 July 1795.
Martin's fleet – 17 ships of the line, of which one(*) was sunk.
1 x 118 – *Sans Culotte* (flag of Vice-Adm. Pierre Martin).
2 x 80s – *Formidable* and *Tonnant*.
14 x 74s – *Alcide**, *Barra*, *Conquérant*, *Duquesne*, *Généreux*, *Guerrier*, *Heureux*, *Jemappes*, *Jupiter*, *Mercure*, *Mont Blanc*, *Peuple Souverain*, *Révolution* and *Tyrannicide*.
Also 6 frigates and 2 brigs.
[Note the 80-gun *Formidable* had been renamed from *Figuieres* on 31 May, three weeks prior to the capture of the 74-gun *Formidable* which confusingly had been renamed from *Marat* on 25 May.]
Hotham's fleet – 23 ships of the line (including 2 Neapolitan 74s).
2 x 100s – *Britannia* (flag of Adm. William Hotham) and *Victory* (flag of Rear-Adm. Robert Mann).
4 x 98 – *Barfleur*, *Princess Royal* (flag of Vice-Adm. Samuel Goodall), *St. George* (flag of Vice-Adm. Sir Hyde Parker) and *Windsor Castle* (flag of Vice-Adm. Robert Linzee).
1 x 80 – *Gibraltar*.
14 x 74s – *Audacious*, *Bedford*, *Bombay Castle*, *Captain*, *Courageux*, *Culloden*, *Cumberland*, *Defence*, *Egmont*, *Fortitude*, *Guiscardo* (Neapolitan), *Samnito* (Neapolitan), *Saturn*, *Terrible*.
2 x 64s – *Agamemnon*, *Diadem*.
Also 2 frigates and five smaller.

EXPEDITION TO IRELAND – Dec 1796 to Jan 1797.
Morard de Galles's fleet – 17 ships of the line of which 2(*) were lost and 3(#) captured.
1 x 80 – *Indomptable* (flag of Vice-Adm. Justin-Bonaventure Morard de Galles).
16 x 74s – *Cassard*, *Constitution* (flag of Rear-Adm. Joseph Marie Nielly), *Droits de l'Homme* (flag of Rear-Adm. Francois Joseph Bouvet)*, *Éole*, *Fougueux*, *Mucius*, *Nestor*, *Patriote*, *Pégase*, *Pluton*, *Redoutable*, *Révolution*, *Séduisant* *, *Tourville*, *Trajan* and *Wattignies*.
1 x 44 (rasée) – *Scévola**.
3 x mortar frigates – *Impatiente**, *Immortalité*, and *Romaine*.
4 x 40s – *Tartu#*, *Bravoure*, *Cocarde*, and *Sirène*
5 x 32s – *Bellone*, *Fraternité*, *Résolue*, *Charente*, and *Surveillante*.
Also brigs *Affronteur*, *Atalante* #, *Mutine* #, *Renard*, *Vautour* and *Voltigeur*; powder vessel *Fidèle*; and 7 transports.

BATTLE OF ABOUKIR BAY ('Battle of the Nile') – 1 August 1798.
Bruey's fleet – 13 ships of the line of which 9(#) were taken and 2(*) sunk.
1 x 118 – *Orient** (flag of Vice-Adm. François Paul Brueys d'Aiguilliers).
3 x 80s – *Franklin#* (flag of Rear-Adm. Armand-Simon-Marie Blanquet du Chayla), *Guillaume Tell* (flag of Rear-Adm. Pierre Charles Comte de Villeneuve) and *Tonnant#*.
9 x 74s – *Aquilon#*, *Conquérant#*, *Généreux*, *Guerrier#*, *Heureux#*, *Mercure#*, *Peuple Souverain*, *Spartiate#* and *Timoléon**.
2 x 44s – *Diane* (flag of Rear-Adm. Denis Decrès) and *Justice* (18pdr frigates).
2 x 32s – *Artémise** and *Sérieuse** (12pdr frigates)
Also brigs *Alerte* and *Railleur*, and 3 bombs.
Nelson's fleet – 14 ships of the line (including a 50).
13 x 74s – *Alexander*, *Audacious*, *Bellerophon*, *Culloden*, *Defence*, *Goliath*, *Majestic*, *Minotaur*, *Orion*, *Swiftsure*, *Theseus*, *Vanguard* (flag of Rear-Adm. Horatio Nelson) and *Zealous*.
1 x 50 – *Leander*.
Also sloop *Mutine*.

BATTLE OF TORY ISLAND (off Donegal) – 12 October 1798.
Bompart's squadron – 1 ship of the line and 8 frigates
1 x 74 – *Hoche#* (flag of Commodore Jean Baptiste François Bompart)
3 x 40 (frigates) - *Romaine*, *Loire*, *Immortalité*.
5 x 36 (frigates) – *Coquille#*, *Bellone#*, *Résolue*, *Embuscade#*, *Sémillante*.
Note that this was the second (and more ill-prepared) attempt to land troops in Ireland. Besides the ships taken in the action itself (indicated by# above) the *Résolue*, *Loire* and *Immortalité* were captured a short time after, and only the *Romaine* and *Sémillante* returned to France.
Warren's squadron – 3 ships of the line and 5 frigates.
1 x 80 – *Foudroyant*.
2 x 74s – *Canada* (flag of Commodore Sir John Borlase Warren) and *Robust*.
3 x 44s – *Amelia*, *Anson* and *Magnanime*.
1 x 38 – *Ethalion*.
1 x 36 – *Melampus*.

BATTLE OF ALGECIRAS – 5 July 1801.
Linois's squadron – 3 ships of the line.
2 x 80s – *Formidable* (flag of Rear-Adm. Charles Comte de Linois) and *Indomptable*.
1 x 74 – *Desaix*.
1 x 40 – *Muiron* (18pdr frigate).
Saumarez's squadron – 6 ships of the line, of which 1(#) was taken by the French.
1 x 80 – *Caesar* (flag of Rear-Adm. Sir James Saumarez).
5 x 74s – *Audacious*, *Hannibal#*, *Pompée*, *Spencer* and *Venerable*.

BATTLE OF CADIZ ('Battle of the Gut of Gibraltar' in Britain) – 12 July 1801.
Linois's and Moreno's squadron – 9 ships of the line of which 1(#) French ship was taken and 2(*) Spanish were sunk by the British.
2 x 112s (Spanish) – *Real Carlos** and *San Hermenegildo**.
1 x 94 (Spanish) – *San Fernando*.
3 x 80s – *Argonauta* (Sp), *Formidable* (Fr) and *Indomptable* (Fr).
3 x 74s – *Desaix* (Fr), *St Antoine#* (Fr) and *San Augustin* (Sp).
1 x 44 (Spanish frigate) – *Sabina* (joint flag of Rear-Adm. Charles Comte de Linois and Vice-Adm. Don Juan Joaquin de Moreno).
2 x 40s (French) – *Libre* and *Muiron* (18pdr frigates).
Also lugger (Fr) *Vautour*.
Saumarez's squadron – 5 ships of the line.
1 x 80 – *Caesar* (flag of Rear-Adm. Sir James Saumarez).
4 x 74s – *Audacious*, *Spencer*, *Superb* and *Venerable*.
1 x 32 – *Thames* (12pdr frigate).
Also polacre *Calpe*, armed brig *Louisa* and the Portuguese frigate *Carlotta*.

ACTION OF 22 JULY 1805 ('Bataille des Quinze-Vingt' in France;

'Calder's Action' in Britain).
Franco-Spanish fleet – 20 ships of the line of which 2(#) Spanish ships were taken.
1 x 90 – *Argonauta* (flag of Adm. Don Frederico Gravina).
5 x 80s – *Bucentaure* (flag of Vice-Adm. Pierre Charles Jean-Baptiste Silvestre de Villeneuve), *Formidable* (flag of Rear-Adm. Pierre-Etienne René-Marie Dumanoir Le Pelley), *Indomptable*, *Neptune* (flag of Commodore Esprit-Tranquille Maistral) and *San Rafael*# (flag of Commodore Don Francisco de Montez).
12 x 74s – *Achille*, *Aigle*, *Algéciras*, *Atlas*, *Berwick*, *Firme*#, *Intrépide*, *Mont Blanc*, *Pluton* (flag of Commodore Baron Julien Marie Cosmao-Kerjulien), *Scipion*, *Swiftsure* and *Terrible*.
2 x 64s – *America* and *España*.
5 x 40s – *Cornélie*, *Didon*, *Hortense*, *Rhin* and *Thémis*.
1 x 36 – *Sirène*.
Also *Santa Magdalena*, 18-gun *Furet* and 16-gun *Naiade*.
Calder's fleet – 15 ships of the line.
4 x 98s – *Barfleur*, *Glory* (flag of Rear-Adm. Charles Stirling), *Prince of Wales* (flag of Vice-Adm. Sir Robert Calder) and *Windsor Castle*.
1 x 80 – *Malta*.
8 x 74s – *Ajax*, *Defiance*, *Dragon*, *Hero*, *Repulse*, *Thunderer*, *Triumph* and *Warrior*.
2 x 64s – *Agamemnon* and *Raisonnable*.
1 x 40 – *Egyptienne*.
1 x 36 – *Sirius*.
Also lugger *Nile* and cutter *Frisk*.

BATTLE OF TRAFALGAR – 20 October 1805.
Villeneuve's Franco-Spanish fleet – 33 ships of the line.
French component – 18 ships of the line of which 8(#) were taken, and 1(*) was sunk.
1 x 84 – *Neptune* (pennant of Commodore Esprit-Tranquille Maistral).
3 x 80s – *Bucentaure*# (flag of Vice-Adm. Pierre Charles Jean-Baptiste Silvestre de Villeneuve), *Formidable* (flag of Rear-Adm. Pierre-Etienne René-Marie Dumanoir Le Pelley) and *Indomptable*.
14 x 74s – *Achille**, *Aigle*#, *Algésiras*# (flag of Rear-Adm. Charles-René Magon de Médine), *Argonaute*, *Berwick*#, *Duguay-Trouin*, *Fougueux*#, *Héros*, *Intrépide*#, *Mont Blanc*, *Pluton* (pennant of Commodore Baron Julian Marie de Cosmao-Kerjulien), *Redoutable*#, *Scipion* and *Swiftsure*#.
5 x 40s – *Cornélie*, *Hermione*, *Hortense*, *Rhin* and *Thémis*.
Also 18-gun *Furet* and 16-gun *Argus*.
Spanish component – 15 ships of the line of which 11(#) were taken, although the *Santa Ana* was later retaken.
1 x 136 – *Santisima Trinidad*# (flag of Rear-Adm. Don Baltasar Hidalgo de Cisneros).
2 x 112s – *Principe de Asturias* (flag of Adm. Don Federico Gravina and Rear-Adm. Don Antonio Escaño) and *Santa Ana*# (flag of Vice-Adm, Don Ignacio Maria de Alava).
1 x 100 – *Rayo*#.
1 x 80 - *Neptuno*#.
9 x 74s - *Argonauta*#, *Bahama*#, *Monarca*#, *Montanez*, *San Augustin*#, *San Fernando de Asis*#, *San Ildefonso*# (pennant of Commodore Don Jose de Varga), *San Juan Nepomuceno*# and *San Justo*.
1 x 64s – *San Leandro*.
Nelson's fleet – 27 ships of the line.
3 x 100s – *Britannia* (flag of Rear-Adm. William Earl of Northesk), *Royal Sovereign* (flag of Vice-Adm. Cuthbert Collingwood) and *Victory* (flag of Vice-Adm. Lord Horatio Nelson).
4 x 98s – *Dreadnought*, *Neptune*, *Prince* and *Téméraire*.
1 x 80 – *Tonnant*.
16 x 74s – *Achille*, *Ajax*, *Belleisle*, *Bellerophon*, *Colossus*, *Conqueror*, *Defence*, *Defiance*, *Leviathan*, *Mars*, *Minotaur*, *Orion*, *Revenge*, *Spartiate*, *Swiftsure* and *Thunderer*.
3 x 64s – *Africa*, *Agamemnon* and *Polyphemus*.
1 x 38 – *Naiad*.
3 x 36s – *Euryalus*, *Phoebe* and *Sirius*.
Also 10-gun schooner *Pickle* and 8-gun *Entreprenante*.

ACTION OFF CAPE ORTEGAL ('Strachan's Action') – 3 November 1805.
Dumanoir's squadron – 4 ships of the line of which all were taken.
1 x 80 – *Formidable* (flag of Rear-Adm. Pierre-Etienne René-Marie Dumanoir Le Pelley).
3 x 74s – *Duguay-Trouin*, *Mont Blanc* and *Scipion*.
Strachan's squadron – 5 ships of the line.
1 x 80 – *Caesar* (pennant of Capt. Sir Richard John Strachan).
4 x 74s – *Bellona* (took no part), *Courageux*, *Hero* and *Namur*.
1 x 38 – *Revolutionnaire*.
2 x 36 – *Phoenix* and *Santa Margarita*.
1 x 32 – *Aeolus*.

SANTO DOMINGO – 6 February 1806.
Leissègues's squadron – 5 ships of the line, of which 2 (*) were destroyed and 3 (#) were taken.
1 x 118 (actually with 130 guns) – *Impérial** (flag of Vice-Adm. Corentin Urbain Leissègues)
1 x 80 – *Alexandre*#
3 x 74s – *Brave*#, *Diomède** and *Jupiter*#.
Also 40-gun *Comète* and *Félicité*, and corvette *Diligente*.
Duckworth's squadron – 7 ships of the line.
1 x 80 – *Canopus* (flag of Rear-Adm. Thomas Louis).
5 x 74s – *Atlas*, *Donegal*, *Northumberland* (flag of Rear-Ad. Alexander Cochrane), *Spencer* and *Superb* (flag of Vice-Adm. Sir John Thomas Duckworth).
1 x 64 – *Agamemnon*.
Also 40-gun *Acasta*, 36-gun *Magicienne*, 16-gun *Kingfisher* and 14-gun *Epervier*.

ASSAULT ON THE BASQUE ROADS ('Bataille de l'Ile d'Aix' in France) – 12 April 1809.
Allemand's fleet – 10 ships of the line, of which 3(*) were destroyed.
1 x 118 – *Océan* (flag of Vice-Adm. Zacharie Allemand).
2 x 80s – *Foudroyant* and *Ville de Varsovie**.
7 x 74s – *Aquilon**, *Cassard*, *Jemmapes*, *Patriote*, *Regulus*, *Tonnerre** and *Tourville*.
1 x 50 – *Calcutta* (flute)*.
4 x 40s – *Elbe*, *Hortense*, *Indienne** and *Pallas*.
Gambier's fleet – 11 ships of the line.
1 x 120 – *Caledonia* (flag of Adm. Lord James Gambier).
2 x 80s – *Caesar* (flag of Rear-Adm. Robert Stopford) and *Gibraltar*.
8 x 74s – *Bellona*, *Donegal*, *Hero*, *Illustrious*, *Resolution*, *Revenge*, *Theseus* and *Valiant*.
1 x 44 – *Indefatigable*.
2 x 38s – *Amelia* and *Impérieuse*.
2 x 36s – *Aigle* and *Emerald*.
3 x 32s – *Mediator* (flute), *Pallas* and *Unicorn*.
Also 3 x 18s – *Beagle*, *Doterel* and *Foxhound*, 10-gun *Lyra* and *Redpole*; *Aetna* (bomb), 7 gunbrigs, a schooner and 2 hired cutters; and transport *Cleveland*, 20 fireships, 3 explosion vessels, etc..

BATTLE OF GRAND PORT (Mauritius/Ile de France) – 22 August

1810.
Duperré's squadron – 2 frigates.
2 x 40s – *Bellone* (Commodore Baron Victor Guy Duperré) and *Minerve*.
2 ex-HEICo merchant prizes – *Ceylon* and *Windham*.
Also *Victor* 16.
Pym's squadron – 4 frigates, of which 2(*) were destroyed.
3 x 36s – *Iphigenia*, *Magicienne**, *Néréïde* and *Sirius**.
Also *Staunch* 14.

BATTLE OF LISSA – 13 March 1811.
Dubourdieu's Franco-Venetian squadron – 6 frigates, of which 3(#) were taken and 1(*) destroyed ; and 4 smaller vessels.
4 x 44s – *Corona*# (Ven), *Danae* (Fr), *Favorite** (Fr: flag of Commodore Bernard Dubourdieu) and *Flore*# (Fr).
2 x 32s – *Bellona*# (Ven) and *Carolina* (Ven).
Also 18-gun *Principessa Augusta*, 10-gun *Principessa di Bologna*, 6-gun *Eugenio* and 2-gun *Lodola* – all Venetian.
Hoste's squadron – 3 frigates and 1 post ship.
1 x 38 – *Active*.
2 x 32s – *Amphion* (pennant of Capt. William Hoste) and *Cerberus*.
1 x 22 – *Volage*.

ASSAULT ON CADIZ – 17 September to 1 October 1823. Ships marked (*) participated in the reduction of the fortress of Santi Petri on 20 September under Rear-Adm. des Rotours.
Rear-Adm. Duperrés' squadron
3 ships of the line – *Colosse* (74, flag of Rear-Adm. Victor-Guy, Baron Duperré), *Centaure* (80*, flag of Rear-Adm. Jean-Julien, Baron Angot des Rotours), *Trident* (74*).
11 frigates – *Guerrière* (58*), *Vénus* (50), *Hermione*, *Néréïde*, *Fleur-de-Lis*, *Antigone*, *Thémis*, *Eurydice*, *Galatée*, *Cybèle*, *Magicienne* (all 40).
4 corvettes – *Égérie* (20), *Sylphide* (20), *Isis* (18*), *Bayadère* (18).
5 brigs – *Dragon* (18), *Rusé*, *Zébre* (both 16), *Antilope* (schooner-brig, 16), *Lynx* (small brig, 12).
4 smaller – *Artésienne* (schooner, 6), *Dauphinoise* (schooner, 6), *Lilloise* (brig-aviso, 8), *Santo-Christo* (schooner, Spanish prize*).
10 bomb vessels – 7 French (of which bombarde *No.7* sunk) and 3 Spanish.
7 corvettes de charge and gabarres – *Moselle*, *Prudente*, *Zélée*, *Chameau*, *Bretonne*, *Marsouin*, *Lamproie*.

BATTLE OF NAVARINO – 20 October 1827.
de Rigny's French squadron
3 ships of the line – *Trident* (82), *Breslaw* (84), *Scipion* (82).
2 frigates – *Sirène* (58, flag of Rear-Adm. Henri-Marie-Daniel Gaultier de Rigny), *Armide* (44).
2 smaller – *Alcyone* (16), *Daphné* (6).
Codrington's British squadron
3 ships of the line – *Asia* (84, flag of Vice-Adm. Sir Edward Codrington), *Genoa* (76), *Albion* (74).
3 frigates – *Glasgow* (50), *Cambrian* (48), *Dartmouth* (42).
6 smaller – *Talbot* (28), *Rose* (18), *Philomel* (10), *Mosquito* (10), *Brisk* (10), *Hind* (6).
Count Geyden's Russian squadron
4 ships of the line – *Azov* (74, flag of Rear-Adm. Count Login Petrovich Geyden), *Gangut* (84), *Iezekil* (74), *Aleksandr Nevskiy* (74).
4 frigates – *Konstantin* (48), *Provornyy* (48), *Kastor* (36), *Elena* (36).
Ibrahim Pasha's Turco-Egyptian squadron (according to G. Douin, *Navarin*, 1927).
4 ships of the line – *Guhu-Reva* (or *Ghyu h Rèwan*, 74 or 80 or 84, Turkish flag of either Tahir Pasha, Kapudana Bey, or Padrona Bey), *Fatih Bahri* (74), *Burj Zafer* (74), plus 1 (74).
14 frigates – *Ihsania* (64, Egyptian), *Guerrière* (or *Murchid-i-Djihad*, 60, Egyptian, flag of Moharrem Bey), *Souriya* (56, Egyptian), *Leone* (60, Egyptian), *Belle Sultane* (54), plus 1 (64), 4 (56), 3 (54), 1 (50), 3 (Tunisian). Other names reported for Turkish frigates were *Fevz Nussret* (64), *Kaid Zafer* (64), *Keywan Bahri* (48), *Fryz Miraj* (48), and *Mejra Zafer* (48).
33 corvettes – 2 (44, Egyptian), 1 (32), 1 (28), 8 (24), 1 (22), 15 (20), 5 (16).
13 brigs and schooners – protecting 30 armed transports.
5 fire ships.

ALGERIAN EXPEDITION – 27 May to 5 July 1830.
Duperré's squadron
3 ships of the line – *Provence* (82, flag of Vice-Adm. Victor-Guy, Baron Duperré), *Trident*, *Breslaw* (all 82).
8 ships of the line armed as transports – *Duquesne*, *Algésiras* (both 86), *Ville de Marseille*, *Scipion*, *Nestor*, *Marengo*, *Superbe*, *Couronne* (all 82).
17 frigates – *Guerrière*, *Amphitrite*, *Pallas* (all 58), *Iphigénie*, *Didon*, *Surveillante*, *Belle Gabrielle*, *Herminie*, (all 60), *Sirène*, *Melpomène*, *Jeanne d'Arc*, *Vénus*, *Marie-Thérèse*, *Artémise* (all 58 or 52), *Circé*, *Duchesse de Berry*, *Bellone* (all 44).
7 frigates armed as transports – *Proserpine*, *Cybèle*, *Thémis*, *Thétis*, *Médée*, *Aréthuse*, *Magicienne* (all 44).
7 corvettes – *Créole*, *Victorieuse* (both 24), *Écho* (20), *Bayonnaise*, *Orythie*, *Cornélie*, *Perle* (all 18).
18 brigs – *Actéon*, *Adonis*, *Voltigeur*, *Hussard*, *Alerte*, *D'Assas*, *Ducouedic*, *Cygne*, *Griffon*, *Alacrity*, *Alcibiade* (all 20), *Cuirassier*, *Dragon*, *Endymion* (all 18), *Zèbre*, *Rusé*, *Euryale*, *Faune* (all 16), plus *Silène* (16) lost before the assault.
5 brig-avisos – *Comète*, *Cigogne*, *Badine*, *Capricieuse*, plus *Aventure* lost before the assault (all 16), *Lynx* (12).
1 gunbrig – *Alsacienne* (8).
2 schooners – *Daphné*, *Iris* (both 6).
8 bomb vessels – *Vésuve*, *Hécla*, *Volcan*, *Cyclope*, *Vulcain*, *Achéron Finistère*, *Dore*.
7 corvettes de charge – *Bonite*, *Tarn*, *Adour*, *Dordogne*, *Caravane*, *Lybio*, *Rhône*.
10 gabarres – *Vigogne*, *Robuste*, *Bayonnais*, *Chameau*, *Garonne*, *Lamproie*, *Lézard* (brig), *Truite*, *Marsouin*, *Astrolabe*.
1 transport – *Désirée*.
1 balancelle – *Africaine*.
7 steam vessels – *Sphinx*, *Ville du Havre*, *Pélican*, *Nageur*, *Souffleur*, *Coureur*, *Rapide*.

FORCING THE TAGUS – 11 July 1831.
Roussin's squadron
6 ships of the line – *Suffren* (90, flag of Rear-Adm. Albin-Reine, Baron Roussin), *Algésiras* (86), *Trident*, *Marengo*, *Ville de Marseille*, *Alger* (all 82).
4 frigates – *Pallas*, *Didon*, *Melpomène* (all 60), *Sirène* (52),
3 corvettes – *Églé*, *Perle*, *Diligente* (all 16),
4 brigs – *Hussard* (20), *Dragon*, *Endymion* (both 18), *Lynx* (12)

BLOCKADE OF THE SCHELDT AND SEIGE OF ANTWERP (BELGIAN INDEPENDENCE) – September to December 1832.
Ducrest de Villeneuve's squadron
1 ship of the line – *Suffren* (84, flag of Rear-Adm. Gabriel-Auguste-Ferdinand Ducrest de Villeneuve and from November 1832 Rear-Adm. Ange-René-Armand, Baron de Mackau).
8 frigates – *Melpomène* (58), *Calypso*, *Sirène*, *Atalante* (all 52), *Résolue*,

Médée, Flore (all 36), *Junon* (32).
5 corvettes – *Ariande, Héroïne* (both 32), *Créole, Naïade* (both 24), *Bayonnaise* (18).
3 brigs – *d'Assas* (20), *Endymion* (18), *Badine* (10).
2 smaller – *Vigilant* (6), *Constance* (4).

MEXICAN EXPEDITION – October to December 1838. Ships marked (*) participated in the reduction of San Juan de Ulúa at Veracruz on 27 November 1838.
Baudin's squadron
4 frigates – *Iphigénie* (60*), *Néréide* (52*, flag of Rear-Adm. Charles Baudin), *Gloire* (50*), *Médée* (46)
2 corvettes – *Créole**, *Naïade* (both 24).
5 brigs – *Alcibiade, Lapérouse, Voltigeur* (all 20), *Cuirassier* (18), *Zèbre* (16).
4 brig-avisos – *Eclipse, Dupetit-Thouars, Laurier, Dunois* (all 10).
4 bomb vessels – *Cyclope*, Vulcain*, Éclair, Volcan*
2 steam vessels – *Météore**, *Phaéton**,
3 corvettes de charge – *Fortune, Caravane, Sarcelle* (gabarre).

PLATA EXPEDITION – July to October 1840 (Treaty of 28 October 1840).
de Mackau's squadron
2 frigates – *Gloire* (50, flag of Vice-Adm. Ange-René-Armand, Baron de Mackau), *Atalante* (52).
6 corvettes – *Alcmène, Boussole* (both 30), *Triomphante* (28), *Bergère, Camille* (both 20), *Perle* (16).
10 brigs – *Alerte, Cassard, Cygne, d'Assas, Oreste* (all 20), *Cuirassier* (18), *Zèbre* (16), *Alcyone, Cerf, Lutin* (all 10).
7 gunbrigs – *Alouette, Bordelaise, Boulonnaise, Églantine, Tactique, Vedette, Vigie* (all 4).
2 steam vessels – *Styx, Tonnerre* (both 160nhp).
8 smaller (captured or purchased locally) – *Actif* (cutter), *Anna, Éclair, Firmessa, Forte, Martin-Garcia, San Martin, Vigilante* (all schooners).
7 corvettes de charge and gabarres – *Adour, Bonite, Fortune, Tarn, Expédition, Licorne, Bucéphale.*

LEVANT CRISIS – July to November 1840. The following ships comprised the French Mediterranean fleet in the Levant or en route as at 13 November 1840. In addition the newly-launched *Friedland* (120), *Jemmapes* (100), and *Inflexible* (90) were preparing to join.
Hugon's fleet
17 ships of the line – *Océan* (120, flag of Rear-Adm. Gaud-Aimable, Baron Hugon), *Montebello* (120, flag of Rear-Adm. Aaron-Louis-Frédéric Regnault, Baron de la Susse, second in command), *Souverain* (120), *Hercule* (100), *Iéna* (90), *Suffren* (90), *Diadème, Jupiter, Neptune* and *Santi-Petri* (all 86), *Alger, Généreux, Marengo, Sciption, Trident, Triton,* and *Ville de Marseille* (all 82).
1 frigate – *Médée* (46).
3 corvettes – *Embuscade* (30), *Brillante* (24), *Diligente* (16).
3 brigs – *Alcibiade* (20), *Bougainville* (10), *Flèche* (10).
1 schooner – *Mésange* (6).
1 steam vessel – *Phaeton,* (160nhp).

MOROCCAN EXPEDITION – August 1844. Ships marked (*) participated in the bombardments of Tangiers on 6 August 1844, Mogador on 15 August 1844, or both.

A major step in French colonial expansion came in 1830 with the occupation of Algeria, but this was neither quickly nor easily accomplished and opposition to French rule was encouraged by the neighbouring state of Morocco. This led France to take military action and on 6 August 1844 a French fleet bombarded Tangier – as shown in this print – followed rapidly by a land victory at Isly on 14 April and the bombardment of Mogador (modern Essaouira) on 15 April. All three actions provided names for later French warships. (Courtesy of Beverley R. Robinson Collection, US Naval Academy Museum)

Joinville's squadron
3 ships of the line – *Jemmapes* (103*), *Suffren* (92*, flag of Rear-Adm. François Ferdinand Philippe Louis Marie d'Orleans, Prince de Joinville), *Triton* (88*).
1 frigate – *Belle-Poule* (64*).
4 brigs – *Cassard* (21*), *Argus* (12*), *Volage* (11*), *Pandour* (11).
3 gunbrigs – *Tactique, Alouette, Vigie* (all 4).
11 steam vessels – *Asmodée*, *Groenland, Cuvier, Véloce*, *Gassendi*, *Pluton*, *Lavoisier, Phare*, *Grégeois, Var*, *Rubis*.

BATTLE OF VUELTA DE OBLIGADO (Rio de la Plata) – 20 November 1845.
Tréhouart's French squadron
4 sail – *Expéditive* (gabarre/corvette, 16), *Pandour* (brig-aviso, 10), *San Martin* (captured brig, 8, flag of Capitaine de Vaisseau François-Thomas Tréhourart), *Procida* (captured schooner-brig, 4).
1 steam vessel – *Fulton*.
Hotham's British squadron
4 sail – *Comus* (ship sloop, 18), *Philomel* (brig, 8), *Dolphin* (brig, 3), *Fanny* (collier brig, 1).
2 steam vessels – *Gorgon* (flag of Captain Charles Hotham), *Firebrand*.

FIRST BALTIC CAMPAIGN – April to September 1854
(Bombardment of Bomarsund 15 August 1854).
Parseval-Deschênes' fleet
9 ships of the line – *Inflexible* (90, flag of Vice-Adm. Alexandre-Ferdinand Parseval-Deschênes), *Austerlitz* (90, screw), *Tage* (90), *Hercule* (90), *Jemmapes* (90), *Duguesclin* (80), *Breslaw* (80), *Duperré* (70), *Trident* (70).
3 ships of the line armed as transports – *Donawerth, Saint-Louis, Tilsitt*.
6 frigates – *Sémillante* (56), *Andromaque* (56), *Vengeance* (56), *Poursuivante* (52), *Virginie* (52), *Zénobie* (52).
4 frigates armed as transports – *Algérie, Cléopatre, Persévérante, Sirène*.
2 paddle frigates – *Asmodée, Darien*.
3 screw corvettes – *Laplace, Phlégéton, Reine Hortense*.
2 paddle corvettes – *Souffleur, Laborieux*.
2 screw avisos – *Aigle, Lucifer*.
6 paddle avisos – *Goéland, Milan, Brandon, Cocyté, Fulton, Daim*.
2 transports – *Infatigable, Licorne*.

DEPARTURE FOR CRIMEA – 5 SEPTEMBER 1854.
First squadron, Vice-Adm. Hamelin (commander in chief)
7 ships of the line – *Ville de Paris* (112, flag of Vice-Adm. Ferdinand-Alphonse Hamelin), *Charlemagne* (screw, 80), *Jupiter* (82), *Suffren* (90), *Iéna* (90), *Marengo* (74), *Friedland* (116).
1 frigate-transport – *Néréide*.
Second squadron, Vice-Adm. Bruat
7 ships of the line – *Montebello* (118, screw, flag of Vice-Adm. Armand-Joseph Bruat), *Jean Bart* (78, screw), *Henri IV* (88), *Valmy* (118), *Ville de Marseille* (80), *Alger* (74), *Bayard* (84).
1 frigate-transport – *Calypso*.
Scouts
2 screw corvettes – *Primauguet, Caton*.
Convoy, Rear-Adm. Charner
1 ship of the line – *Napoléon* (94, screw, flag of Rear-Adm. Léonard-Victor-Joseph Charner).
8 paddle frigates and corvettes – *Vauban, Cacique, Mogador, Ulloa, Canada, Magellan, Caffarelli, Panama*.
2 paddle corvettes: *Lavoisier, Pluton*.
2 screw corvettes – *Roland, Mégère*.
2 steam frigates armed as transports – *Montezuma, Albatros*.
2 corvette-transports – *Euménide, Infernal, Coligny*.
1 frigate-transport – *Pandore*,
2 sail transports – *Allier, Girafe*.
Scouts and signal relay ships
1 screw frigate – *Pomone*,
2 paddle frigates – *Orénoque, Descartes*.
1 paddle corvette – *Berthollet*.
3 paddle avisos – *Dauphin, Ajaccio, Mouette*.

BOMBARDMENT OF SEBASTOPOL – 17 October 1854.
(only those vessels actually taking part in the bombardment are shown).
Bruat's French fleet
4 screw ships of the line – *Montebello* (118, flag of Vice-Adm. Armand-Joseph Bruat), *Napoléon* (92, flag of Rear-Adm. Léonard-Victor-Joseph Charner), *Charlemagne* (90), *Jean-Bart* (76).
10 sailing ships of the line – *Valmy* (120, flag of Rear-Adm. Jean Lugeol), *Friedland* (118), *Ville de Paris* (118, flag of Vice-Adm. Ferdinand Alphonse Hamelin), *Henri IV* (100), *Suffren* (90), *Jupiter* (90), *Bayard* (90), *Ville de Marseille* (80), *Alger* (74), *Marengo* (74).
Screw frigate – *Pomone* (40).
Deans Dundas's British fleet
3 screw ships of the line – *Agamemnon* (91, flag of Rear-Adm. Sir Edmund Lyons), *Vengeance* (84), *Sans Pareil* (70).
8 sailing ships of the line – *Britannia* (120, flag of Vice-Adm. James Whitley Deans Dundas and Rear-Adm. Montagu Stopford), *Trafalgar* (120), *Queen* (116), *Albion* (90), *London* (90), *Rodney* (90), *Vengeance* (80), *Bellerophon* (78).
1 sailing frigate – *Arethusa* (50).
3 other screw vessels – *Tribune* (31), *Lynx* (4).
5 paddle vessels – *Terrible* (21), *Sphinx* (6), *Sampson* (6), *Spitfire* (6), *Triton* (3).

SECOND BALTIC CAMPAIGN, May to August 1855 (Bombardment of Sveaborg 9-11 August 1855).
Pénaud's fleet
3 screw ships of the line – *Tourville* (90, flag of Rear-Adm. Charles-Eugène Pénaud), *Austerlitz* (100), *Duquesne* (90).
1 screw corvette – *D'Assas*.
2 screw avisos – *Aigle, Pélican*.
1 paddle aviso – *Tonnerre*.
4 First Class gunboats – *Aigrette, Avalanche, Dragonne, Fulminante*,
4 Second Class gunboats – *Tempête, Tourmente, Poudre, Redoute*.
5 sailing bomb vessels – *Tocsin, Fournaise, Trombe, Torche, Bombe*.
4 transports – *Marne* and *Saône* (screw), *Isis* (sailing frigate, hospital transport), *Galatée* (sailing corvette, transport).

BOMBARDMENT OF KINBURN – 17 October 1855.
Bruat's French fleet
5 screw ships of the line – *Montebello* (118, screw, flag of Adm. Armand-Joseph Bruat), *Fleurus, Ulm, Wagram, Jean-Bart*.
6 paddle frigates – *Vauban, Labrador, Asmodée* (flag of Rear-Adm. Marie Joseph Alphonse Pellion, known as Odet-Pellion), *Cacique, Descartes, Sané*.
3 screw corvettes – *Laplace, Primauguet et Roland*.
2 paddle corvettes – *Berthollet, Tisiphone*.
3 paddle avisos – *Milan, Brandon, Dauphin*.
1 screw aviso – *Lucifer*.
5 screw gunboats – *Alarme, Flamme, Flèche, Grenade, Mitraille*.
6 screw gun launches – *Tiralleuse, Stridente, Meurtrière, Mutine, Bourrasque, Rafale*.
3 screw floating batteries – *Lave, Tonnante, Dévastation*.

4 paddle mortar vessels (converted) – *Cassini, Ténare, Sésostris, Vautour.*
1 sailing mortar vessel (converted) – *Palinure.*
British fleet
6 screw ships of the line – *Royal Albert* (flag, Rear-Adm. Sir Edmund Lyons), *Algiers, Agamemnon, Princess Royal, St Jean d'Acre, Hannibal.*
3 screw frigates – *Curacoa, Tribune, Dauntless.*
8 paddle frigates – *Terrible, Odin, Valorous, Furious, Sidon, Leopard, Gladiator, Firebrand.*
3 paddle sloops – *Sphinx, Stromboli, Spiteful.*
1 paddle gunvessel – *Spitfire.*
6 sailing mortar vessels – *Raven, Magnet, Camel, Hardy, Flamer, Firm.*
6 screw gunvessels – *Lynx, Arrow, Viper, Snake, Wrangler, Beagle.*
5 screw gunboats – *Boxer, Clicker, Cracker, Fancy, Grinder.*

SEIZURE OF TOURANE, ANNAM – 1 September 1858.
Rigault de Genouilly's squadron
1 sailing frigate – *Némésis* (52, flag of Vice-Adm. Charles Rigault de Genouilly).
2 screw corvettes – *Phlégéton* (10), *Primauguet* (10).
5 screw gunboats – *Alarme, Avalanche, Dragonne, Fusée, Mitraille* (all 4).
4 screw transports – *Gironde, Saône, Dordogne, Meurthe.*
plus the Spanish aviso *El Cano.*

ADRIATIC CAMPAIGN – 9 July 1859.
Romain Desfossés' fleet
6 screw ships of the line – *Bretagne* (130, flag of Vice-Adm. Joseph-Romain Desfossés), *Algésiras, Arcole, Eylau, Redoutable, Alexandre* (all 90).
2 screw frigates – *Impétueuse* (56), *Isly* (40).
1 screw aviso – *Monge* (4).
1 paddle corvette – *Colbert* (5).
3 screw transports – *Isère, Ariège, Yonne,*
plus the Sardinian *Victor-Emmanuel* (frigate, 50), *Carlo-Alberto* (frigate, 40), *Malfatano* (paddle corvette, 4).
Bouët-Willaumez's siege fleet (all but the paddle steamers had some armour)

The French squadron sent to Cochinchina in action against the Kien-Chan coastal forts at Tourane (now Da Nang) on 18 November 1859. The sailing frigate *Némésis* is anchored to the left with the screw gunboats *Alarme* and *Avalanche* and the screw aviso *Prégent* inshore. The Spanish paddle corvette *Jorge Juan* is to the right. (Courtesy of Beverley R. Robinson Collection, US Naval Academy Museum)

4 paddle frigates – *Mogador* (flag of Rear-Adm. Louis-Édouard Bouët-Willaumez), *Vauban, Descartes* (all 20), *Gomer* (16).
3 armoured floating batteries – *Lave, Tonnante, Dévastation,*
7 First Class gunboats – *Éclair, Grenade, Fulminante, Étincelle, Flamme, Flèche, Aigrette* (all 4).
7 Second Class gunboats – *Sainte-Barbe, Tempête, Arquebuse, Redoute, Lance, Poudre, Salve* (all 2).
8 Third Class *chaloupes-canonnières* – *Tirailleuse, Alerte, Mutine* (all 3), *Nos. 1-4, No. 11* (all 1).

EXPEDITIONARY CORPS IN NORTHERN CHINA – 1860
(Capture of the Peiho forts, August 1860).
Charner's fleet
2 screw frigates – *Impératrice Eugénie* (56, flag of Vice-Adm. Léonard-Victor-Joseph Charner), *Renommée* (40).
5 sailing frigates – *Némésis* (52), *Persévérante* (56), *Vengeance* (56), plus *Andromaque* (56) and *Forte* (56) armed as transports.
2 screw corvettes – *Du Chayla* (16), *Phlégéton* (10).
2 screw avisos – *Forbin* (4), *Prégent* (2).
18 screw transports – *Calvados, Dordogne, Dryade, Durance, Entreprenante, Européen, Garonne, Gironde, Japon, Jura, Loire, Marne, Meurthe, Nièvre, Rhin, Rhône, Saône, Weser.*
5 screw gunboats – *Alarme, Avalanche, Dragonne, Fusée, Mitraille* (all 4).
9 *chaloupes-canonnières* Nos. *12, 13, 15, 16, 18, 22, 26, 27, 31* (all 1).
6 small paddle vessels – *Saïgon/Écho, Lily, Deroulède, Kien-Chan, Hong Kong, Ondine,*
3 small screw vessels – *Norzagaray, Alon-Prah, Peï-ho.*
5 small hired (?) vessels – *Tien-shan, Rose, Shang-haï, Contest, Feilon.*
1 hospital hulk at Saigon – *Duperré.*

Dockyards and Infrastructure

In 1776, when Louis XVI's new Secretary of State for the Navy, Antoine de Sartine, reorganised the navy's ports and dockyards (*arsénaux*), France had three major ports with dockyards (*grands ports*): Brest, Toulon, and Rochefort. In 1770 the navy acquired the former French East India Company's dockyard at L'Orient (Lorient) and, although the navy initially made little use of it, by 1795 Lorient had become the navy's fourth major port. In 1776 Cherbourg was selected for development into a major naval port in the Channel. Massive construction works began there in 1784, by 1795 Cherbourg was ranked as a secondary port, and by 1815 it had replaced Dunkirk and Le Havre as the main French Navy port and dockyard in the Channel. However at that time Cherbourg and Lorient were still inferior in stature and capabilities to the three traditional major ports.

The Brest dockyard was located on a minor river, the Penfeld, that flows into a magnificent sheltered bay – the *Rade de Brest* (Brest roadstead) – that, however, had a treacherous entrance (the *goulet*) and was susceptible to blockade by a determined enemy or by prevailing westerly winds. The town itself as well as the dockyard further upstream were well defended by fortifications built by Sébastien, Seigneur de Vauban, the greatest military engineer of his day, and the narrow gap of the *goulet*, defended by batteries on both sides, prevented a blockading fleet from entering the *Rade*. The disadvantages of the site were that land communications with the rest of France were poor, while local supplies were always inadequate.

The Rochefort dockyard was located on the Charente river 12 miles inland from its roadstead between the Île d'Aix and the Île d'Oléron. The original naval base in southwest France had been at Brouage (several miles to the southwest), but this became so silted up that Colbert decided in the 1660s to abandon it and replace it with Rochefort, where Vauban constructed fortifications and other facilities. It was easy to defend and nearly impossible to blockade, but access up the river was difficult and the roadstead proved vulnerable to raids.

Toulon had none of the geographic disadvantages of the other two original *grands ports*, but its very success (it became the principal French naval base after 1815) led to severe overcrowding within its original Vauban fortifications. It suffered greatly from the events of August 1793, when the citizens of the town showed their pro-Royalist sympathies by handing over their port and the majority of the French Mediterranean fleet to the Allied forces of Britain, Spain and Sardinia. When the Allies withdrew in December of that year, the Revolutionary forces punished the citizenry (apart from those who fled with the British ships) with widespread massacres, and destroyed much of the town. Rebuilding commenced early in 1794 and a major naval rebuilding program was begun, including new slipways and dockyard facilities. In the 1830s fifteen shipways were built to the east at Mourillon and, after the navy was allowed to breach the fortifications, a new dockyard was built in the 1850s to the west at Castigneau.

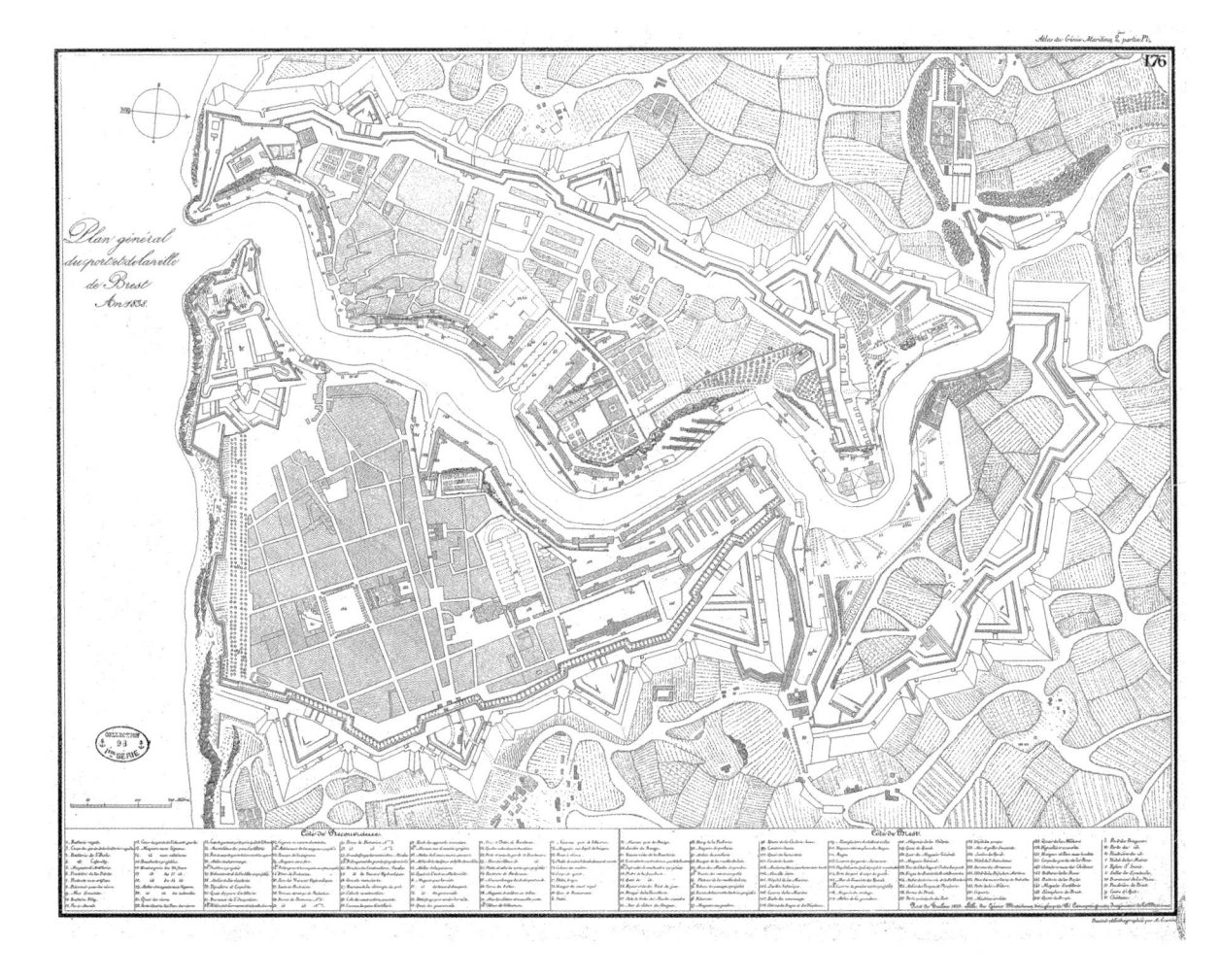

Plan of Brest dockyard in 1838. The dockyard extends along both sides of the Penfeld River. (Atlas du Génie Maritime, French collection, plate 176)

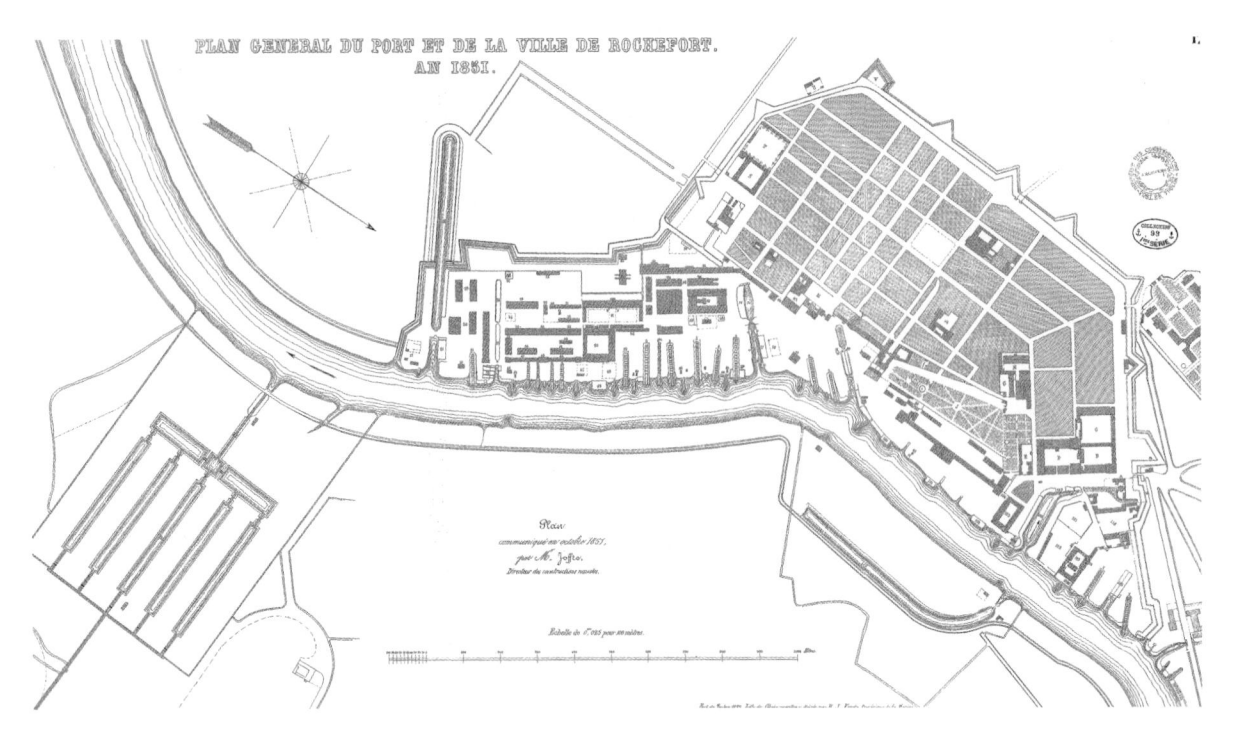

Plan of the town and dockyard of Rochefort in 1851. Across the Charente River are large basins for storing timber. (Atlas du Génie Maritime, French collection, plate 178)

Lorient, a southern Brittany river port with a protected anchorage but on a much smaller scale than Brest, was located on the west bank of the Scorff river near its mouth, with many of its shipbuilding ways on the east bank at Caudan, upriver from the main Lorient dockyard. This dockyard had been developed by the French East India Company (*Compagnie des Indes*) from 1719 onward as its principal base and shipbuilding centre, but in April 1770 its vessels and its dockyard installations had been seized by the state and handed to the French Navy. Between 1798 and 1803 the Crucy Brothers received contracts to build seven 74-gun ships of the line and two brigs at Caudan and in the main Lorient dockyard as well as three 74s in the Rochefort dockyard. At Cherbourg construction of the breakwaters and basins continued until 1858; ship construction began at the old dockyard in 1794 and at the new dockyard in 1810.

In addition to establishing three naval départements headed by the three major ports, the 1776 reorganisation also established three more with headquarters at Le Havre, Dunkirk, and Bordeaux. Le Havre had a small dockyard (the navy's first, with three shipways) while Bordeaux had the old *Chantier du Roi* (reduced by 1791 to a few shipways above the city on the Gironde riverbank), but much of the naval ship construction in these smaller ports between 1793 and 1814 was done by the many private shipbuilders located there. In 1776 the navy also maintained lesser administrative officials at Nantes, Saint-Malo, Marseille, Bayonne, and in Corsica. In 1795 these seven ports (less Corsica) were designated secondary ports.

After 1800 the navy built some shipways at Saint-Servan next to Saint-Malo by order of Lucien Bonaparte, whose wife was from Saint-Servan, the small dockyard being administered from Brest. Le Havre (at the mouth of the Seine) lacked the deep water necessary to harbour ships of the line, although it served as a major base for the gunboats and other flotilla craft gathered for the invasion of Britain during the Revolutionary War, and also provided a base for frigate squadrons despatched on raiding expeditions throughout the Napoleonic War; however in April/May 1804 Napoleon called for two or three 74s to be built there; one (never named) was laid down in June 1804, but work was subsequently suspended and never resumed. In 1815 the navy continued to maintain officials at Dunkirk, Le Havre, Nantes, Bordeaux, and Bayonne, although with the exception of Bayonne it no longer had active shipbuilding facilities in these locations. Bayonne launched its last navy ship in 1835 and new ship construction at Saint-Servan was terminated in 1838.

In 1777 Sartine established at Indret next to some shipways where frigates had been built in the 1760s a foundry to cast naval artillery using a technique just imported from Britain. Indret is located on the south bank of the Loire downstream from Nantes, Basse-Indre and Haute-Indre being on the opposite bank. In 1827 the navy contracted with Philippe Gengembre of Paris to convert the foundry into a plant for building steam engines. In addition to building the engines for many of the navy's early steamers, Indret built the hulls for some of them. Steam engine repair facilities were soon established at all five main dockyards and beginning in the mid-1840s these facilities built steam engines as well as maintaining them.

Traditionally the navy built all of its warships in its own dockyards. Sartine's ordinance of 1776 specified that, when the construction of ships was ordered in the secondary naval départements of Le Havre, Dunkirk, or Bordeaux, or in other ports, naval officers and *ingénieurs-constructeurs* would be sent to those locations to direct the work according to the rules that applied in the dockyards. However the increased wartime need for ships caused the government in January 1793 to open naval ship construction to private contractors. Contract activity was interrupted in August 1794 but resumed in September 1796 and remained a key part of French naval procurement until May 1814, when, with the return to peace, the navy stopped contracting for ships. The advent of steam engines soon caused the navy to resume construction by contract, first for steam machinery and between 1842 and 1848 for ship construction as well. The outbreak of the Crimean War prompted a general return to contract ship- and engine-building in 1854 that continued after that war.

During 1793-1814 contract shipbuilding was carried out on the Channel coast at Dieppe, Granville, Honfleur, Le Havre, and Saint-Malo; on the Loire river at Basse-Indre, Indret, Nantes, and Paimboeuf; on the southern Biscay coast at Bordeaux and Bayonne; and near Toulon at La Ciotat, La Seyne, and Marseille. After 1842 contract shipbuilding resumed in several of these locations plus in the suburbs of Paris, Dunkirk, and in 1860 at Ajaccio in Corsica. Steam engine construction took place initially

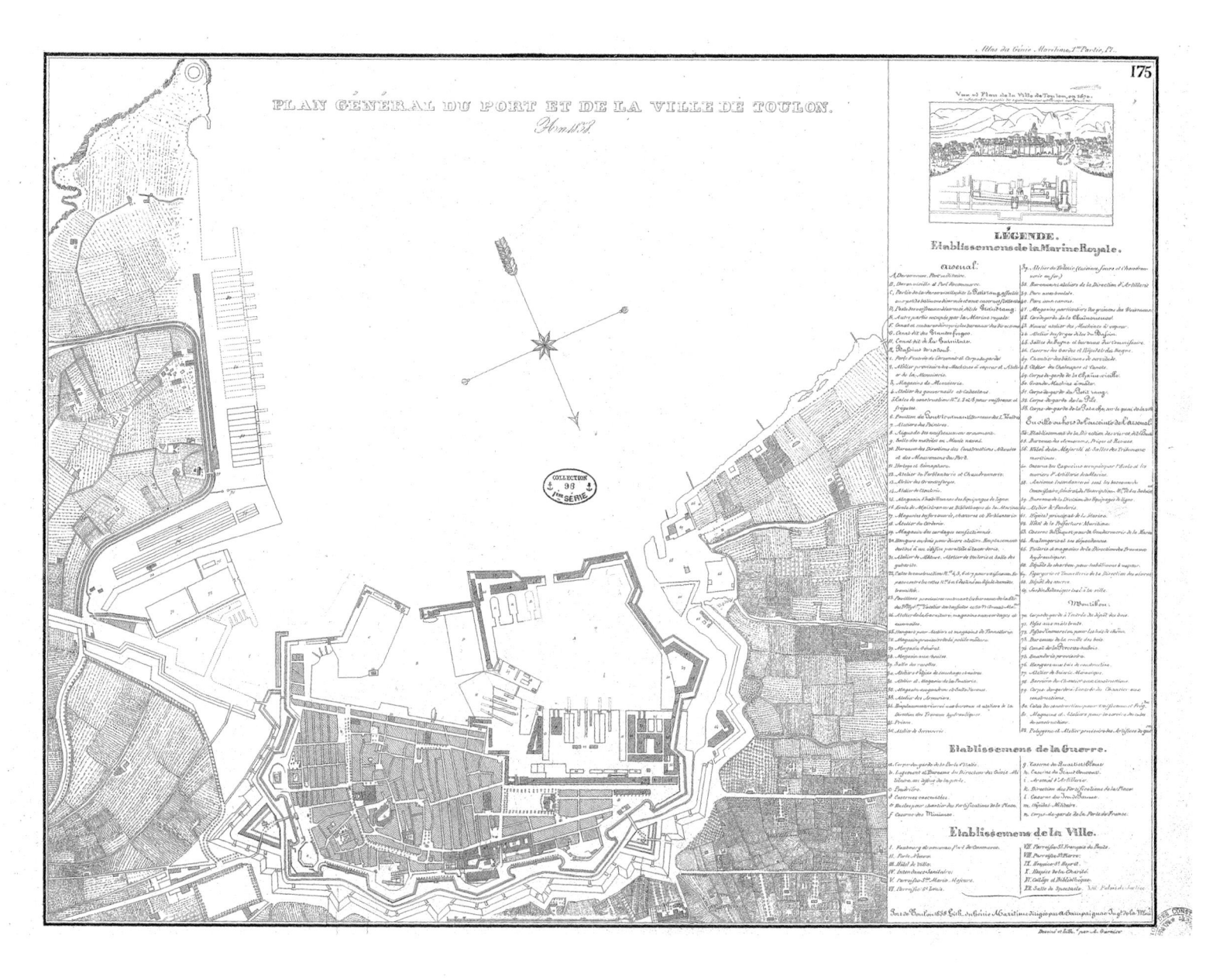

Plan of the town and dockyard of Toulon in 1838 showing the first major expansion outside the old fortifications, the row of shipways at Mourillon. (Atlas du Génie Maritime, French collection, plate 175)

in several suburbs of Paris and at Rouen, Landerneau (near Brest) and Fourchambault (in east-central France). In the 1830s and 1840s it spread from Paris to Arras (in northeast France), Le Creusot (in east-central France), Bitschwiller (in Alsace), La Ciotat, La Seyne and Marseille (all near Toulon), Nantes, and Le Havre. Appendix I contains a list of the individual private contractors and firms that carried out this ship- and engine-building activity for the French Navy between 1793 and 1861.

Between 1801 and 1805 the coastal port of Boulogne-sur-Mer became the centre of attention, as it was the focus of Napoleon's ambition to invade Britain, and thereby a port of crucial importance for both France and for Britain. Lying directly opposite Dover on the Kent coast, the ancient fishing port and peacetime packet centre for cross-Channel trade, situated at a gap in the cliffs around the mouth of the small river Liane, would have been the inevitable jumping-off point for the invasion fleet, and it was developed to hold the maximum number of specially-designed invasion barges and gunboats (see Chapter 9). Horatio Nelson was, on his return from Copenhagen, charged with the defence of the southeastern coast of England, and personally led two assaults on the well-protected invasion port during August 1801, without measurable success.

Not only Boulogne itself, but also the adjacent small ports of Wimereux and Ambleteuse immediately to its north, and Étaples a little to the south, were reconstructed to provide capacious harbours and basins to hold the thousands of invasion craft which were funnelled into the area. Their defences were augmented by the construction of new forts and gun emplacements, while a vast tented township was sited at Moulin-Herbert on the high land to the north of Boulogne to house Napoleon's 160,000-men *Armée de l'Angleterre*. On the other side of Cap Griz Nez, the Flanders ports of Calais, Dunkirk and Ostend were also developed to hold the reserve divisions of the Boulogne Flotilla. In the summer of 1805, when the main body of the Franco-Spanish fleet sought refuge in Cadiz, Napoleon was forced to confront the reality that he would not be able to provide the battle fleet coverage essential for the invasion crossing to be guaranteed, and on 26 August he postponed the operation indefinitely, and began to move his army out of its encampments.

French Navies and Naval Construction outside France, 1797-1814

As France expanded outside its traditional borders after 1793 it assumed control of or annexed some other naval powers and their fleets and dockyards. Some of these powers had long naval traditions and their own practices regarding ship design and construction.

Belgium

After occupying the former Austrian Netherlands twice, in November 1792 and June 1794 and after a failed annexation in February 1793, the French definitively annexed the Belgian territories in October 1795 and integrated them into France, eventually as eight new départements. The port of Antwerp, crippled by the Dutch closure of the Scheldt river between 1648 and 1792, began to revive in 1796. The French ordered a few frigates and brigs at Antwerp in April 1803 from the contractor Danet & Co, but this move was quickly overtaken by a decision in mid-1803 to build a new dockyard next to the citadel at Antwerp, with nine parallel shipways (a number increased to twelve in September 1809), capable of building ships of the line of up to 110 guns. Naval forces did not operate from Antwerp because of the difficulty of getting large ships up and down the Scheldt. Belgium became part of the Kingdom of the Netherlands in the post-war settlement and most of the French-built dockyard was razed.

Netherlands

The Stadhouder, the hereditary 'chief executive' of the Republic of the United Netherlands, held the title of Prince of Orange. Under the influence of the revolution in France and with armed assistance from the revolutionary French Republic Dutch revolutionaries proclaimed the Batavian Republic on 19 January 1795 with much popular support. Willem V, the incumbent Stadhouder, fled the country when the French invaded on 23 February 1795. In its brief existence the Batavian Republic replaced the confederal structure of the old Dutch Republic with a unitary state. This included disestablishing the five autonomous Dutch Admiralties (Amsterdam, Maas or Rotterdam, Zeeland, Friesland, and Noorderkwartier) and replacing them with a single 'Committee for Naval Affairs' on 27 February 1795. (In this book, the term 'Batavian' is used to signify the navy of both the Batavian Republic and the subsequent Kingdom of Holland until its annexation in 1810.) Much of the former Dutch Navy was taken by the British in Saldanha Bay in 1796, the Battle of Camperdown on 11 October 1797, and in the Texel in 1799.

On 5 June 1806 the Batavian Republic was converted into a monarchy, the Kingdom of Holland, to the throne of which Napoleon appointed his third surviving brother, Louis Bonaparte (who took the regnal name of Lodewijk I). In 1806 the French began construction of a 74-gun ship and two frigates at Flushing, but this attempt was disrupted in 1809 by the British Walcheren campaign. Louis proved too conscientious for the post, standing up to his brother in defence of Dutch interests. Napoleon invaded and forced Louis's abdication on 4 July 1810 in favour of Louis's elder surviving son, Napoleon-Louis (who briefly became Lodewijk II), but five days later Napoleon unilaterally annexed the kingdom and incorporated it into France as nine new départements. The French then integrated the remaining Dutch warships into the French fleet and began to build 74-gun ships of the line, frigates, and a single corvette to their own designs in the two main Dutch dockyards at Amsterdam and Rotterdam, where the work of the highly skilled Dutch naval constructors P. Glavimans Jr., R. Dorsman and P. Schuijt Jr., was overseen by French constructors. At the end of 1813 a Dutch uprising led to the restoration of independence (again as the United Provinces of the Netherlands) under the House of Orange. In the post-war settlement the state became the United Kingdom of the Netherlands on 16 March 1815 (including Belgium until 1830).

Venice

The Republic of Venice was neutral (and therefore 'at peace') when Napoleon delivered an ultimatum and then attacked the city in April 1797. Under the Treaty of Leoben Napoleon needed possession of Venice so he could give it and Venetian Istria and Dalmatia to Austria in exchange for the Austrian Netherlands and Lombardy. Following the Venetian capitulation French troops occupied the city on 16 May 1797 and ended the existence of the Venetian republic. They took control of the Venetian Navy ships then at Venice along with the reserve fleet on the slips and the supplies for them in the Venetian Arsenal, including their guns, On 28 June a French fleet under Rear-Adm. Comte de Brueys occupied the former Venetian territory of Corfu at the southern end of the Adriatic and took over more Venetian ships there. Since the city was to be handed over to Austria, the French in September and December 1797 sabotaged all of the ships in the Arsenal except for a few that were ready for immediate use and took the supplies, including more than 2,850 guns, to France.

To understand the types and numbers of ships that the French found in the Venetian Arsenal in May 1797 it is necessary to know the naval policy of the Venetian Government in the eighteenth century. Venice built ships on the Arsenal slips according to the yearly budgets of the State which permitted the maintenance of a navy of about 30 vessels. But these ships were launched only if necessary. If not necessary, they were maintained on the covered slips completed up to 22 'carati' ('ship's parts' or 24ths) and launched when they were needed, thus saving the fiscal reserves of the state. Venetian laws provided for a fleet of 12 ships – 4 First Rank and 8 Second/Third Rank or 'fregate grosse/leggere' (large/light frigates) when Venice was at peace and of 30/35 ships (20/25 First Rank and 10 frigates) in wartime. For this reason, in peacetime there was a 'fleet in being' of about 20 ships on the covered slips of the Arsenal. When a ship was on the slip, her rigging and guns were maintained in storage at the Arsenal.

The largest Venetian vessels had only two decks for two reasons. Their maximum width was limited to 39 Venetian feet (13.56 metres) because the *porta d'acqua* (the 'water gate') of the Venetian Arsenal has a width between the two little towers of only 40 Venetian feet (13.90m). And their draught could not exceed 20 Venetian feet (6.95m) which was the water depth at Venice in the eighteenth century. When the French started building 74-gun ships to French designs at Venice after 1806 the draught limit forced them to develop elaborate camels to float the new ships out of the city into deeper water. In 1780 the Venetian Arsenal adopted the 'double frame' method of constructing ships (*con struttura a doppia ordinata*) that was used in French and British vessels. Until 1779 Venice had used the 'single frame' method (*con struttura a ordinate singola*) that had originated in the Constantinople Arsenal during the Byzantine Empire in the Middle Ages to build first galleys and later galleons. It was also used by the Turkish Arsenal of Istanbul during the Morean Wars of the late 1600s and early 1700s. The 'single frame' method permitted the construction of hulls that were lighter and consequently speedier, but ships built with this method were more fragile. After the shipwrecks of *San Carlo Borromeo* in 1768 and *Tolleranza* and *Corriera Veneta* in 1771 the building method in Venice was changed. The prototype for the new method was the bomb vessel *Distruzion* (later the French brig *Destruction*, q.v.), built at the Arsenal in 1770-72 and launched in 1784.

The Cisalpine Republic and the Kingdom of Italy
The Cisalpine Republic was founded by Napoleon on 29 June 1797, comprising Lombardy, Emilia and the Marches. Napoleon became its President after France recovered the territory in June 1800. In January 1802 it was renamed the Italian Republic, still with Napoleon as its President. On 17 March 1805 the territory was renamed the Kingdom of Italy, with Napoleon becoming its King (Prince Eugene de Beauharnais was appointed his Viceroy in Italy on 7 June 1805). Venice became part of this kingdom under the Peace of Pressburg, signed on 26 December 1805, resulting in the second French occupation of the city. The French turned the Austrian naval forces at Venice into the navy of the Kingdom of Italy and made intensive use of the Venice Arsenal to build ships for both the French and Italian Navies, placing their first orders for 74-gun ships at the end of 1806. The Kingdom of Italy lasted until Napoleon's abdication on 11 April 1814 and the occupation by the Austrians of its territory including Venice later that month. A second small naval force, the Illyrian Navy, was established at Trieste after the French in 1809 formed the short-lived Illyrian Provinces from former Austrian territory north and east of the Adriatic. It took the place of a small force that the Austrians had maintained at Trieste after losing Venice in 1806.

Genoa
On 14 June 1797 Napoleon established the Ligurian Republic, most of which consisted of the old Republic of Genoa. Following a brief Austrian occupation, a new constitution of 1802, in accordance with Napoleon's desires, required the Republic to protect commerce and, to that end, establish a shipyard and maintain a navy of two 74-gun ships, two frigates, and two corvettes. The construction of the first frigate was ordered on 27 September 1802, and in the meantime the new brigs *Giano* and *Liguria* and the xebec *Serpente* were commissioned as privateers.

This program was of interest not only to the French but to Genoese shipbuilders and politicians. The only firm in the city capable of

A contemporary Dutch model of the 90-gun *Chattam*, launched at Rotterdam in 1800, one of the *Wreeker* class, the largest sailing warships so far built in the Netherlands. All eight ships of the class were incorporated into the French Imperial Navy in 1810. (Rijksmuseum, Amsterdam).

attempting to build ships of the line and frigates was the Compagnia Murio & Migone, located in the Lazzaretto district, and in April 1803 following the collapse of the Peace of Amiens Napoleon accepted an offer from this firm to build 'ready to operate' two 74-gun ships, two frigates, four brigs, and two 800-ton flûtes. A shipyard to perform the work would be established by the Ligurian Republic at French expense. War with Britain having again broken out, Napoleon on 23 May 1803 ordered Murat to occupy Liguria and strengthen its coast defences, and on 3 June 1803 he ordered Decrès to send a naval constructor and a naval commission to Genoa with plans for the construction of 74-gun ships and 44-gun frigates. In fact no ships of this size had ever been built at Genoa and no shipyards capable of building them existed. The French constructor Jean-Baptiste Lefebvre identified an area near the lazaretto at Foce as suitable for shipbuilding, and construction of the first shipway was begun in July 1803. On 8 August 1803 Napoleon ordered the immediate construction at Genoa of 2 ships of the line, 2 frigates, 4 brigs, and 4 large transports, and in August 1804 he approved the creation at Foce of a dockyard capable of building and maintaining in service a fleet of 10 ships of the line. In August 1805 the frigate *Pomone* and the brigs *Endymion* and *Cyclope* were ready for launching by Murio & Migone, with the 74-gun *Génois* scheduled for launching during the winter.

In June 1805 the territory of the Ligurian Republic was annexed by France and became three new French départements – Apennins, Gênes (Genoa) and Montenotte. At this time the small Ligurian Navy was incorporated into the French Navy. On 6 August 1805 an attempt was made to launch the *Génois*, but the ship hung up and hogged on the ways before new French engineers succeeded in launching her on 17 August. At this point the French took over direct control of shipbuilding at Genoa from the contractor and began steady but slow production of ships. After the fall of Napoleon the territory became part of the Kingdom of Sardinia, while several ships on the ways or in the harbour at Genoa were taken over by the British. Elsewhere in Italy, construction of a few brigs and schooners was undertaken in 1809 and 1811 at Leghorn (Livorno) and at Civitavecchia.

Naples

In January 1799 French troops entered Naples and declared the *République Parthénopéene* in the mainland portion of the Bourbon Kingdom of Naples. In the same month the French ordered three ships to be built for the French Navy at the Neapolitan dockyard at Castellammare di Stabia at the expense of the new Neapolitan republic, one 74 gun ship named *Marine Napolitaine* (*Armata Napoletana* in Italian) and two 18pdr frigates named *Partenope* and *Reconnaissance* (*Riconoscenza*). However the British and Russian fleets prevented the French from assisting the new republic and the French evacuated Naples on 7 May 1800, ending the plans to build the three ships.

On 23 January 1806 the Bourbon King of Naples, Ferdinand IV, fled Naples ahead of an advancing French army and was transported to Palermo in Sicily by his navy, most of which remained there with him. Following the overthrow of the Bourbon monarchy in Naples (as also in Spain, see below), Napoleon on 30 March 1806 appointed his elder brother Joseph Bonaparte to the Neapolitan throne (adopting the regnal name of Giuseppe). In 1807 Napoleon ordered the construction in Naples of two 80-gun ships of the line and 2 frigates for completion in 1808. On 4 July 1807 Napoleon asked Joseph about his progress in fulfilling this order, and on 7 July Joseph answered that the French engineer sent to Naples (Philippe Greslé) had never built a 74-gun ship and asked for a suitable officer. On 19 November 1807 Joseph confirmed the recent arrival of the engineer Jean-François Lafosse and reported that the timber for the ship had already been partially collected. In February 1808, however, he pointed out that the timber stocks at Castellammare were poorly guarded and that the thefts were frequent.

On 6 June 1808 Napoleon deposed his brother (whom he made King of Spain instead) and theoretically became the monarch himself for almost two months until on 1 August 1808 he appointed his brother-in-law Joachim Murat as King of Naples (who reigned as Gioaccino Napoleone). The first 74, *Capri,* was probably laid down before Murat's arrival in Naples in November 1808. She was followed on the ways by a second 74, *Gioacchino*, in 1810 and by the 80-gun *Vesuvio* in 1812. A frigate was begun at Naples in 1808, followed by a corvette in 1811. In December 1813 Murat abandoned Napoleon to keep his throne but, knowing that the Austrians planned to depose him, re-joined Napoleon in 1815 during the Hundred Days. He was deposed on 19 May 1815.and ended up before a firing squad. The Kingdom of the Two Sicilies (Sicily and Naples) was formed under a restored Bourbon monarchy in December 1815.

Portugal

On 14 August 1807 Napoleon presented an ultimatum to Portugal to close her ports to British shipping and to confiscate British goods. Portugal refused, and on 20 November a Franco-Spanish force under Jean-Andoche Junot invaded. The Portuguese royal family left Lisbon on 27 November to take refuge in Brazil and were accompanied or followed there by the serviceable ships of the Portuguese Navy, including 8 ships of the line, 4 frigates, 2 corvettes, 2 brigs, and 3 schooners. The French took over the ships left at Lisbon as unserviceable including 4 ships of the line and 6 frigates. Junot repaired many of them, but when the French evacuated Portugal under the terms of the Convention of Sintra on 30 August 1808 they reverted to Portuguese control.

Spain

The Spanish Kingdom, ruled by the House of Bourbon, was forcibly incorporated into the French Empire on 6 May 1808, when Carlos IV ceded the throne to Napoleon. Napoleon was theoretically the Spanish monarch for a month, before he appointed his elder brother Joseph Bonaparte to the throne on 6 June (adopting the regnal name of José). His nominal role continued until the restoration of the House of Bourbon on 13 December 1813. The Spanish Navy never came under direct French control and its ships are not listed in this volume.

Germany

Prussia, the leading power in northern Germany, had only a para-military maritime force of small craft designed for coastguard duties and enforcement of the Continental System, Frederick the Great having avoided developing a navy because it might divert resources from his army.

The Kingdom of Westphalia was created by Napoleon on 8 July 1807 from his conquests in Germany, and he appointed to its throne his youngest brother, Jérôme Bonaparte (who took the regnal name of Hieronymus Napoleon). The Duchy of Brunswick was annexed by France and in 1808 was ceded to Westphalia. With the French Empire collapsing in 1813, Jérôme fled on 26 October.

On 13 December 1810 Napoleon annexed the three Hanseatic cities of Bremen, Hamburg, and Lübeck (together with neighbouring parts of northern Hanover and the Duchy of Oldenburg), the cities becoming parts of two new French départements of Bouches du Weser and Bouches de l'Elbe. In late 1811 the French Navy ordered two corvettes to be built in each of these three cities; they were all begun but none were completed (see Chapter 6). In June 1813 orders were given to build three ships of the line and a frigate on four new slipways to be constructed at Altenbruck (near Cuxhaven on the west bank of the Elbe estuary), but this project was cancelled in October. Bremen was approached by Allied troops in late October 1813 and occupied by them in late November. Hamburg was besieged by the Allies in late October 1813 but the French held out there until May 1814 after the fall of the Empire.

Sources and Bibliography

ARCHIVAL SOURCES

1. Archives de la Défense, Marine, Fonds anciens (old records)
Series B: General Services
- B5-28 and B5-29: Naval programs and fleet lists, including a 'Liste générale des forces navales du Roi au 1 janvier 1789' and a corresponding list of ships under construction.

Series D: Materiel
- D1-4: 'État actuel de notre Marine,' memorandum ca. 1789.
- D1-63 to -69: Plans of ships.

2. Archives de la Défense, Marine, Fonds modernes (modern records)
Series BB: General Services
BB3: Correspondence
- BB3-309: Correspondence concerning the French Navy in the Adriatic (1800-1815).
- BB3-848: 'Réponse à une note de Son Excellence en date du 3 Mai,' memorandum dated 1 June 1818 with an undated fleet list attached.

BB4: Campaigns, expeditions, etc.
- BB4-115: List of ships of the line, frigates, and corvettes at sea belonging to the Republic of Venice in 1797 plus a list of such ships under construction, also lists of French forces in the Adriatic.

BB5: Movements of ships
1790-1801
- BB5-2: Register of light craft and cargo vessels begun 23 September 1795 for all the secondary vessels of the navy, covers the period to 1801.
- BB5-4: List of French vessels lost, taken, or destroyed from 1793 to 1796, plus a general statement (*état*) of ships taken, burned, or wrecked from 23 September 1799 to 1817.

1801-1807
- BB5-5: Register of corvettes, brigs, and light vessels from 1801 to 1803.
- BB5-6: Register of ships of the line and frigates from 1801 to 1807.
- BB5-7: Listing of monthly movements of warships from 1801 to 1807), also includes listings of ships under construction.
- BB5-8: Register of corvettes and brigs from 1804 to 1807.

1807-1828
- BB5-9: Register of corvettes and brigs from 1807 to 1826.
- BB5-10: Register of xebecs, feluccas, tartanes, galleys, and pinks from 1807 to 1814.
- BB5-11: Register of ships of the line from 1807 to 1828, with a detailed 'Situation matérielle de la Marine au 30 mai 1814' inside the front cover. The equivalent register for frigates did not survive.
- BB5-12: Register of mouches from 1807 to 1823 (29 ships).
- BB5-13: Register of schooners, luggers, and cutters from 1807 to 1825 (also contains the first steamers as well as canonnières and chasse-marées).
- BB5-14: Register of flûtes and gabarres from 1807 to 1823.
- BB5-15: Register of transports from 1807 to 1823.

Misc..
- BB5-57 to -62: Multiple fleet lists between 1791 and 1803, most for individual ports
- BB5-63: 'État de la flottille de Boulogne au 10 mars 1804'.
- BB5-64 to -86: Lists between 1804 and 1813, most for individual ports.
- BB5-87: 'Situation de la Marine au 1 avril 1814' and other lists, 1814 to 1816.

BB8: Papers of the Office of the Minister and various commissions
- BB8-824 to -900: Council of Admiralty (*Conseil d'Amirauté*).
- BB8-1106 to -1165: Council of Works (*Conseil des Travaux*).

Series DD: Materiel
DD1: Naval construction
Note: The six 0DD1 registers (matricules) cover the period from the mid-1840s to the mid-1850s.
- 0DD1-7: Register of sailing ships afloat (ships of the line, frigates, and corvettes).
- 0DD1-8: Same (brigs, light vessels, transports of 800 tons and less).
- 0DD1-9: Register of sailing ships under construction (all types).
- 0DD1-10: Register of steam vessels afloat (ships of the line, frigates, and corvettes).
- 0DD1-11: Register of steam vessels afloat (avisos and small).
- 0DD1-12: Register of steam vessels under construction.
- 1DD1: Outgoing correspondence of the Office of Naval Construction, including reports of the Director of Ports approved by the Minister of Marine.
- 4DD1: Contracts (including hulls and machinery).
- 7DD1: Dossiers relating to individual ships no longer in the navy, including *Devis d'armement et de campagne* and incoming correspondence and reports.
- 8DD1: Plans of ships.

Special collection (at Brest)
- 9S: Fonds Adam (materials collected by Adm. Marcel Adam that include notes taken in the archives at Brest, Lorient, and Rochefort by Pierre Le Conte and Cdt. Rouyer).

3. Archives Nationales, Paris
Records of national assemblies (Parliament),
- C-1010: Records of the Parliamentary investigation of the navy of 1849-51.

Section Outre-Mer, Senegal,
- Senegal XVI-43: Local naval station, 1817-1865.

PUBLISHED SOURCES

Acerra, Martine and Meyer, Jean, *La grande époque de la marine à voile*, Éditions Ouest-France, Rennes, 1987

__, *Marines et Révolution*, Éditions Ouest-France, Rennes, 1988

Aichelburg, Wladimir, Register der k.(u.)k. *Kriegsschiffe, von Abbondanza bis Zrinyi*, Neuer Wissenschaftlicher Verlag, Vienna, 2002

Babron, M, 'Les établissements impériaux de la Marine française: Indret,' *Revue maritime et coloniale*, vol. 23, no 89 (mai 1868), p. 123-148 and vol. 24, septembre 1868, p. 495-526, also published separately by Arthus Bertrand, Paris

Barrey, Philippe, 'Notice sur les constructeurs de navires Havrais,' *Recueil des publications de la Société Havraise d'études diverses*, 1907 pages 39-131

__, 'L'Arsenal du Havre pendant la révolution (1789-1801),' *Recueil des publications de la Société Havraise d'études diverses*, 1908 pages 277-308 and 331-396 and 1909 pages 17-62

Battesti, Michèle, *La Marine de Napoléon III*, 2 volumes, thesis for a doctorate in history, Service historique de la marine, Paris, 1997

Baxter, James Phinney III, *The Introduction of the Ironclad Warship*, Harvard University Press, Cambridge, 1933

Bazancourt, Baron César Lecat de, *L'Expédition de Crimée, La marine française dans la mer noire et la Baltique*, 2 volumes, Amyot, Paris, 1858

__, *Les expéditions de Chine et de Cochinchine*, 2 volumes, Amyot, Paris, 1861-62

Boudriot, Jean, *Le Vaisseau de 74 canons*, 4 volumes, Éditions des Quatre Seigneurs, Grenoble, 1973-77, also available in English

__ with Berti, Hubert, *Les Vaisseaux de 50 et 64 canons, Étude historique, 1650-1780*, Éditions A.N.C.R.E., Paris, 1985 & 1994

__ with Berti, Hubert, *Les vaisseaux de 74 à 120 canons, Étude historique, 1650-1850*, Éditions A.N.C.R.E., Paris, 1995

__ with Berti, Hubert, *La Frégate: Étude historique 1650-1850*, Éditions A.N.C.R.E., Paris, 1992, also available in English

__ and Berti, Hubert, *Frégate de 18 La Vénus de l'ingénieur Sané 1782, Monographie*, Éditions A.N.C.R.E., Paris, n.d.

__, *Monographie La Créole 1827: Historique de la corvette 1650-1850*, published by the author, Paris, 1990

__ and Berti, Hubert, *Brick de 24 Le Cygne de l'ingénieur Pestel (1806-1808), monographie*, Éditions A.N.C.R.E., Paris, 1987

__ and Berti, Hubert, *Cotre Le Cerf (1779-1780) du constructeur Denÿs, monographie*, Éditions A.N.C.R.E., Paris, n.d.

__ and Berti, Hubert, *Lougre Le Coureur (1776) du constructeur D. Denÿs, monographie*, Éditions A.N.C.R.E., Paris, n.d.

__, *Goélette La Jacinthe, 1825, de l'ingénieur-constructeur Delamorinière*, published by the author, Paris, 1989, also available in English

__ and Berti, Hubert, *Le Requin, 1750: Chébecs et bâtiments Méditerranéens*, Éditions A.N.C.R.E., Paris, 1987

__ with Berti, Hubert, *L'artillerie de mer: Marine française 1650-1850*, Éditions A.N.C.R.E., Paris, 1992

Brisou, Dominique, *Accueil, introduction et développement de l'énergie vapeur dans la marine militaire française au XIXe siècle*, 2 volumes, thesis for a doctorate in history, Service historique de la marine, Paris, 2001

Catalogus der Verzameling van Modellen van het Departement van Marine, Algemeene Lands-Drukkerij, 's Gravenhage, 1858.

Chasseriau, F, *Précis historique de la marine française, son organisation et ses lois*, 2 vols, Imprimerie royale, Paris, 1845

Chernyshev, A. A., *Rossiyskiy parusnyy flot, Spravochnik*, 2 volumes, Voyennoye Izdatel'stvo, Moscow, 1997-2002.

Chevalier, Édouard, *Histoire de la marine française de 1815 à 1870*, Hachette, Paris, 1900

__, *Histoire de la marine française sous la première République*, Hachette, Paris, 1886

__, *Histoire de la marine française sous le Consulat et l'Empire*, Hachette, Paris, 1886

Clowes, Sir William Laird, *The Royal Navy: A History from the Earliest Times to 1900* – volumes 3-6, Sampson Low, Marston and Company, London, 1898; republished by Chatham Publishing, London, 1996

Cormack, William S., *Revolution and Political Conflict in the French Navy 1789-1794*, Cambridge University Press, 1995.

Cossé, Yves. *Les frères Crucy, entrepreneurs de constructions navales (1793-1814)*, published by the author, Nantes, 1993. See also http://fr.wikipedia.org/wiki/Famille_Crucy

Crowdy, Terry, *French Warship Crews 1789-1805*, Osprey Publishing, Oxford, 2005

de Balincourt, Raoul, (Maurice Clément Marie Raoul Testu, marquis de Balincourt) and Le Conte, Pierre, 'La marine française d'hier: V: Navires à roues,' *Revue Maritime*, no. 154 (1932), pp. 472-512; no. 157 (1933), pp. 12-54

de Balincourt, Raoul and Le Conte, Pierre, 'La marine française d'hier: VI: Vaisseaux mixtes, *Revue Maritime*, no. 159 (1933), pp. 345-62; no. 160 (1933), pp. 483-509

Delacroix, Gérard, *Vaisseau de 118 canons Le Commerce de Marseille*, published by the author, L'Union, France, 2006

De la Roncière, Charles and Clerc-Rampal, G., *Histoire de la Marine Française*, Paris, Librairie Larousse, 1934.

Delattre, C.V. G, *Annales inédites de la flottille du fleuve Sénégal de 1819 à 1854, Première partie (de 1819 à 1835)*, Dakar, 1944, and Service historique de la marine, Paris, 1972

Demerliac, Cdt Alain, *La Marine de Louis XVI: Nomenclature des navires français de 1774 à 1792*, Éditions OMEGA, Nice, 1995

__, *La Marine de Louis XVI: Nomenclature des navires français de 1792 à 1799*, Éditions A.N.C.R.E., Nice, 1999

__, *La Marine du Consulat et du Premier Empire: Nomenclature des navires français de 1799 à 1815*, Éditions A.N.C.R.E., Nice, 2003

__, *La Marine de la Restauration et de Louis-Philippe 1er: Nomenclature des navires français de 1815 à 1848*, Éditions A.N.C.R.E., Nice, 2007

__, *La Marine de la Deuxième République et du Second Empire: Nomenclature des navires français de 1848 à 1871*, Éditions A.N.C.R.E., Nice, 2013.

Depeyre, Michel, *Tactiques at Stratégies Navales de la France et du Royaume-Uni de 1690 à 1805*, Economica, Paris, 1998.

Desbrière, Édouard, *The Naval Campaign of 1805*, Oxford University Press, 1933 (in translation by Constance Eastwick) – 2 volumes

D'Houry, Laurent-Charles, succeeded by Laurent-Étienne Testu et. al. and printed with government approval, *Almanach Royal*, later *Almanach National* and *Almanach Impérial*, Paris, annually from 1683 to 1919.

__, *État de la Marine*, Paris, 1785, 1789, 1803, 1816-17, and 1818. Publication taken over by the Navy before 1832

Dickinson, Henry Winram, *A Short History of the Steam Engine*, Macmillan Co., New York, 1939

Douin, Georges, *Navarin, 6 juillet-20 octobre 1827*, Institut français d'archeologie orientale pour la Société royale de géographie d'Égypte, 1927

Dupont, Adm. Maurice, *L'Amiral Decrès et Napoléon*, Economica, Paris, 1991

Dupuy de Lôme, Henri, *Mémoire sur la construction des bâtiments en fer*, A. Bertrand, Paris, 1844

Elting, John R., *Swords Around A Throne: Napoleons's Grande Armée* (esp. Chapter XV - *Matters Nautical: La Marine*), Weidenfeld & Nicolson (Phoenix Giant), London, 1988.

Ercole, Guido, *I Bucintoro della Serenissima, the ceremonial state barges of the Venetian Republic*, Gruppo Modellistico Trentino di studio e ricerca storica, Trento, 2015

__, *Galeazze, Un sogno veneziano*, Gruppo Modellistico Trentino di studio e ricerca storica, Trento, 2010

__, *Vascelli e fregate della Serenissima. Navi di linea della Marina veneziana, 1652-1797*, Gruppo Modellistico Trentino di studio e ricerca storica, Trento, 2011

Faivre, Jean-Paul, *Le contre-amiral Hamelin et la marine française, 1768-1839*, Nouvelles Éditions Latines, Paris, 1962

France, Assemblée Nationale Legislative, *Enquête parlementaire sur la situation et l'organisation des services de la marine militaire, ordonné par la loi du 31 octobre 1849*, 2 vols, Imprimerie nationale, Paris, 1851

France, Ministère de la Marine et des Colonies. *Rapport au Roi: Budget* (annual, 1820-1853). Each contains a list of ships of the navy as of the time that the budget was submitted

__. *Compte rendu par le Ministre de la Marine et des Colonies* (1821-1858, lists ships in commission)

___. *Annales Maritimes et Coloniales* (1809-1847). The editions from 1837 to 1847 contain 'États des bâtiments de la flotte' on a roughly annual basis. Replaced in 1848 by the *Nouvelles Annales de la Marine* (1849-1864) and, for official material, the *Bulletin officiel de la Marine*, below

___. *Bulletin officiel de la Marine* 1848-1964, particularly the entries after 1860 for 'Liste de la Flotte (Inscriptions — Radiations)'

Gardiner, Robert (ed.), *The Line of Battle: The Sailing Warship 1650-1840*, Conway Maritime Press, London, 1992

Gardiner, Robert, *Frigates of the Napoleonic Wars*, Chatham Publishing, London, 2000

___, *Steam, Steel and Shellfire: The Steam Warship 1815-1905*, Conway Maritime Press, London, 1992

___, *Warships of the Napoleonic Era*, Chatham Publishing, London, 1999

Gascoin, 'L'Ile d'Indret et l'établissement de la marine nationale,' *Cahiers des salorges*, nos. 7, 8 and 9 (1964), unpaged

Gervain, Baronne de, *Un ministre de la marine et son ministère sous la Restauration: Le baron Portal*, Plon, Paris, 1898

Gille, Eric, *Cent ans de cuirassés français*, Marines éditions, Nantes, 1999

Glete, Jan, *Navies and Nations: Warships, Navies and State Building in Europe and America, 1500-1860*, 2 volumes, Almqvist & Wiksell, Stockholm, 1993

Gogg, Karl, *Österreichs Kriegsmarine 1440-1848*, Verlag das Bergland-Buch, Salzburg, 1972

Goodwin, Peter, *The Ships of Trafalgar: The British, French and Spanish Fleets, 21 October 1805*, Conway Maritime Press, London, 2005

Gomart, Lieutenant de vaisseau, 'L'Escadre d'évolutions en Mediterranée de 1840 à 1848,' Thesis, Ecole de Guerre Navale, 1936-37

Granier, Contre-amiral Hubert, *Histoire des marins français, 1815-1870*, Marines éditions, Nantes, 2002

Gruss, Robert, *Dictionnaire Gruss de marine*, E.M.O.M., Paris, 1978

Guihéneuc, Olivier, 'Les origines du premier cuirassé de haut mer à vapeur: Le plan de Dupuy de Lôme en 1845,' *Revue Maritime*, no. 100 (**1928**), pp. 459-82

Hamelin, Ferdinand-Alphonse, *Rapport de Son Excellence M. le Ministre de la Marine à l'Empereur sur la transformation de la flotte*, Imprimerie impériale, Paris, 1857

Hampson, Norman, *La marine de l'an II, mobilisation de la flotte de l'Ocean 1793-1794*, Marcel Rivière, Paris, 1959

Harland, John, *Ships and Seamanship: The Maritime Prints of J J Baugean*, Chatham Publishing, London, 2000

Harland, John and Myers, Mark, *Seamanship in the Age of Sail*, Conway Maritime Press and Naval Institute Press, London and Annapolis, 1984.

Henry, Chris, *Napoleonic Naval Armaments 1792-1815*, Osprey Publishing, Oxford, 2004

Howard, Dr Frank, *Sailing Ships of War 1400-1860*, Conway Maritime Press, London, 1979

Ilari, Virgilio and Crociani, Piero, *La Marina italiana di Napoleone (1796-1814)*, Le Marine italiane del 1792-1815 N.1, https://archive.org/details/NapoleonsRoyalItalianNavy

___, *La Marina Napoletana di Murat (1806-1815)*, Le Marine italiane del 1792-1815 – 2, https://archive.org/details/MuratsRoyalNeapolitanNavy1806-1815

___, *La Marina Ligure di Napoleone (1797-1814)*, Le Marine italiane del 1792-1815 – 3, https://archive.org/details/NapoleonsLigurianNavy1797-1814

James, William, *The Naval History of Great Britain, from the Declaration of War by France in 1793 to the Accession of George IV* – 6 volumes, Richard Bentley & Son, London, 1886

Jenkins, Ernest H., *A History of the French Navy: From its Beginnings to the Present Day*, Macdonald and Jane's, London, 1973

[Joinville, François Ferdinand Philippe Louis Marie d'Orleans, Prince de,] 'Note sur l'état des forces navales de la France,' *Annales Maritimes*, no. 85 (1844), pp. 573-618

___, *Vieux Souvenirs, 1818-1848*, Calmann-Levy, Paris, 1894 and reprint edition, Mercure de France, Paris, 1970

Jurien de la Gravière, Jean-Pierre-Edmond, *Sketches of the Last Naval War (The French Navy)* – in 2 volumes, 1848

___, *Guerres maritimes sous la République et l'Empire*, Charpentier, Paris, 1853 and 1906

Knight, Roger, *Britain Against Napoleon: The Organisation of Victory 1793-1815*, Allen Lane, 2014 and Penguin Books, 2014

La Varende, Jean de, *Les Augustin-Normand: Sept générations de constructeurs de navires*, Imprimerie Floch, Mayenne, 1960

Lacour-Gayet, Georges, *La marine militaire de la France sous le règne de Louis XVI*, H. Champion, Paris, 1905

Langlois, H, 'La Dévastation. Épisodes et souvenirs de la guerre d'Orient. II Les batteries flottantes devant Kinburn et dans le Dniéper,' *Revue des Deux Mondes*, 1858, vol. 13, p. 739

Lecalvé, Frank, *Liste de la Flotte de Guerre Française*, published by the author, Toulon, 1993

Lecène, Paul, *Les Marins de la République et de l'Empire, 1793-1815*, Paris, Librairie Centrale, 1855.

Le Conte, Pierre, *Repertoire des navires de guerre français*, published by the author, Cherbourg, 1932

Lévêque, Pierre, *Histoire de la Marine du Consulat et de l'Empire* : in 2 volumes : Volume 1, *Du 18 brumaire à Trafalgar* ; Volume 2, *Après Trafalgar*, Éditions Historique Teissèdre, Paris, 2014.

Levi, Cesare Augusto, *Navi da guerra costruite nell Arsenale di Venezia dal 1664 al 1896*, Presso l'Autore, Venice, 1896

Loir, Maurice, *La marine royale en 1789*, Armand Colin, Paris, n.d. [1892].

Mackau, Ange-Réné-Armand, Baron de, Minister of Marine, 'Rapport au Roi: Compte rendu de l' établissement maritime en France depuis 1820. Sa situation présente. Vues du gouvernement pour l'avenir,' *Annales Maritimes*, no. 95 (1846), pp. **5-82**

Marestier, Jean-Baptiste, *Mémoire sur les bateaux à vapeur des Etats-Unis d'Amérique, avec un appendice sur diverses machines relatives à la marine*, Imprimerie royale, Paris, 1824

Masson, Philippe and Muracciole, José, *Napoléon et la marine*, J. Peyronnet & Cie., Paris, **1968**

Mazères, Adm. Louis, *Notice sur M. le baron Tupinier*, A. Leneveu, Paris, 1842

Musée national de la Marine; *Treasures of the Musée national de la Marine* (in English), Éditions de la Réunion des Musées Nationaux, Paris, 2006.

Norman, Capt. Charles Boswell, *The Corsairs of France*, Sampson Low, Marston, Searle & Rivington, London, 1887

Pacini, Eugène, *La Marine*, Paris, L.Curmer, 1844.

Paixhans, Henri-Joseph, *Expériences faites par la marine française sur une arme nouvelle*, Bachelier, Paris, **1825**

Penzo, Gilberto, *Navi Veneziane*, Lint, Trieste, 2000

Piouffre, Gérard and Simoni, Henri, *3 siècles de croiseurs français*, Marines éditions, Nantes, 2001

Pivka, Otto von, *Navies of the Napoleonic Era*, David & Charles, Newton Abbot (also Hippocrene Books, New York), 1980

Portal, Pierre-Barthélemy, Baron d'Albarédes, *Mémoires du baron Portal, contenant ses plans d'organisation de la puissance navale de la France*, Amyot, Paris, 1846

Quérat, Lieutenant de vaisseau, 'Le ministère Portal (29 décembre 1818-

12 décembre 1821),' Thesis, Ecole de Guerre Navale, 1936-37

Radogna, Lamberto, *Cronistoria delle unita' da guerra delle marine preunitarie*, Ufficio Storico della Marina Militare, Rome, 1981

__, *Storia della marina militare delle Due Sicilie*, Mursia, Milan, 1978

Répertoire alphabétique des bâtiments de tout rang armés et désarmés par l'État de 1800 à 1828 compris, et des Officiers qui, dans cet intervalle, en ont eu le commandement, by Baron De Lagatinerie, Paris, Imprimerie Royale, juillet 1830. Followed by supplements for 1-1-1829 to 31-12-1834 (1835), 1-1-1835 to 31-12-1844 (1852), 1-1-1845 to 31-12-1854 (1859), and 1-1-1855 to 31-12-1868 (1872)

Répertoire de l'École Impériale Polytechnique. Mallet-Gachelier, Paris, 1855

Roberts, David H., *Vocabulaire de Marine/A Marine Vocabulary*, A.N.C.R.E., Nice, 1994

Roberts, Stephen S., 'The French Transatlantic Steam Packet Programme of 1840', *The Mariner's Mirror*, Vol. 73 No. 3 (August 1987), pages 273-286.

__, 'The Introduction of Steam Technology in the French Navy, 1818-1852,' Ph.D. dissertation, University of Chicago, Chicago, Ill., June 1976

Roche, Lt. de vaisseau Jean-Michel, *Dictionnaire des Bâtiments de la Flotte de Guerre Française de Colbert à Nos Jours* – Tome I (1671-1870), Groupe Rezotel - Maury Millau, 2005

Rose, John Holland, *Lord Hood and the Defence of Toulon*, Cambridge University Press, Cambridge, 1922

Roux, Pierre-Henri, 'Le rôle de la marine française dans la crise franco-égyptienne de 1839-1840,' Thesis, Ecole de Guerre Navale, 1962

Schepen op de Admiraliteits-Werf Gebouwd, in Unger, J. H. W., *Rotterdamsch Jaarboekje*, zevende jaargang, P.M. Bazendijk, Rotterdam, 1900, pages 103-112

Smith, Digby, *The Greenhill Napoleonic Wars Data Book*, Greenhill Books, London, 1998

Taillemite, Étienne, *Dictionnaire des Marins Français*, E.M.O.M. 1992

__, *L'Histoire ignorée de la marine française*, Perrin, Paris, 1988

Teissèdre, Fabrice, *Souvenirs, Journal et Correspondance sur L'Expédition d'Égypte et l'Armée d'Orient*, Librairie Historique Teissèdre Fabrice, Paris, 1998.

__, *La marine et les colonies sous le premier Empire*, Librairie Historique Teissèdre Fabrice, Paris, 2000.

Thomazi, Auguste, *Napoléon et ses marins*, Berger-Levrault, Paris, 1950

Thompson, J. M. (ed), *Napoleon's Letters*, Prion, London, 1998

Tramond, Joannes and Reussner, André, *Éléments d'histoire maritime et coloniale contemporaine, 1815-1914*, Société d'éditions géographiques, maritimes et coloniales, Paris, 1924

Tredrea, John, and Sozaev, Eduard, *Russian Warships in the Age of Sail, 1696-1860*, Seaforth Publishing, Barnsley, 2010

Troude, Onésime-Joachim, *Batailles navales de la France*, Éditions Prosper Levot, Paris, 1867

Tupinier, Jean-Marguerite, 'Observations sur les dimensions des vaisseaux et des frégates dans la marine française,' *Annales Maritimes*, no. 17 (1822), pp. 1-87

__, 'Rapport sur le matériel de la marine, présenté en Mars 1838 à M. le vice-amiral de Rosamel, ministre,' *Annales Maritimes*, no. 67 (**1838**), pp. 133-318, **667-822**

__, *Mémoires du Baron Tupinier (1779-1850)*, Éd. Desjonquières, Mayenne, 1994

__, *Considerations sur la marine et son budget*, Imprimerie royale, Paris, 1841

Vandevelde, L., *Précis historique et critique de la campagne d'Italie en 1859*, Tanera, Paris, 1860

Vergé-Franceschi, Michel, *La Marine française au XVIIIe siècle*, Éditions SEDES, Paris, 1996

Vermeulen, A. J., *De schepen van de Koninklijke Marine en die der gouvernementsmarine, 1814-1962*, Bureau maritieme historie, Amsterdam, 1962

Vichot, Jacques (ed.), *L'Album de l'Amiral Willaumez*, A.A.A.M., Paris, n.d.

__, *L'Album de Marine du Duc d'Orleans*, A.A.A.M., Paris, n.d.

__, *Répertoire des Navires de Guerre Français*, Musée de la Marine, Paris, 1967

Villaret, 'Résumé des constructions exécutées au port de guerre de Rochefort depuis novembre 1802 jusqu'au 31 mars 1876,' *Bulletin de la Société de Géographie de Rochefort*, 1896, pages 105-130

Wheeler, Harold Felix Baker and Broadley, Alexander Meyrick, *Napoleon and the Invasion of England: The Story of the Great Terror*, London 1908, reprinted 2007 by Nonsuch Publishing, Stroud

Wilson, Herbert Wrigley, *Chapter II: The Armed Neutrality* (Sect. II) and *Chapter VIII: The Command of the Sea, 1803-15*, in The Cambridge Modern History, Vol IX – *Napoleon*, Cambridge University Press, 1906

Winfield, Rif, *British Warships in the Age of Sail 1793-1817: Design, Construction, Careers and Fates*, Chatham Publishing, 2005; 2nd edition by Seaforth Publishing, Barnsley, 2008

__, *British Warships in the Age of Sail 1817-1863: Design, Construction, Careers and Fates*, Seaforth Publishing, Barnsley, 2014

Zanco, Jean-Philippe, *Le ministère de la marine sous le Second Empire*, from a thesis for a doctorate in law, Service historique de la marine, Paris, 2003

Glossary and Abbreviations

This section serves not only to include the abbreviations used throughout the book, but to give translations for many of the terms likely to be encountered in material pertaining to the French Navy. For this reason, the French equivalents below are given in italics. In the available space here, only a fraction of the terms found can be given; the reader is encouraged to consult a bilingual maritime/naval directory like the recent one by David H. Roberts (see bibliography).

PERSONNEL AND NAVAL RANKS

The whole crew – officers, petty officers, seamen and boys – were termed the *équipage*; the commissioned officers comprised the *état-major*, including the officers of the Garrison (see below), the *commissaire* (Purser) and the vessels's chief medical officer. The formal composition of the *équipage* of a ship of the line of various rates, as at 25 October 1795 (3 Brumaire of Year IV) is tabulated in Appendix J.

Adm. The ranks of flag officer within the French Navy mirrored those in the British and other navies. There were three grades – in descending order these were Admiral (*Amiral* in French) – hereafter abbreviated to 'Adm.', Vice-Adm. (*Vice-Amiral*) and Rear-Adm. (*Contre-Amiral*). To make it easier for English-speaking readers, we have opted to retain the 'd' in references. Before 1831, there was only a single *Amiral*, the post being a dignitary, not held by a naval officer; from 1 March 1831 there were up to 3 Admirals allowed. The rank of *Vice-Amiral* was effectively the most senior naval rank. The rank of *Contre-Amiral* was so designated in 1791, and before that date the title was *Lieutenant-Général*.

Commodore An informal title intermediate between a *capitaine de vaisseau* and a flag officer. Captains of considerable seniority were often given this title when commanding three-decked ships of the line, or when serving as the senior captain of a small squadron. Before the Revolution, the ranks of *Chef d'escadre* and *Chef de division* were used, but these were subsequently merged into the senior grades of *capitaine de vaisseau*.

Capt. There were three designated ranks of Captain in the French Navy – *capitaine de vaisseau* (commanding ships of the line), *capitaine de frégate* (commanding frigates and some lesser units) and *capitaine de corvette* (from 1831 commanding corvettes and most lesser units). During the period of this book, the application of these terms varied. The second-in-command of a ship of the line was also a *capitaine de frégate* (although in the three-deckers, the term *Major de vaisseau* was also used prior to the Revolution).

A *capitaine de corvette* was essentially a senior lieutenant; the rank was created in 1831 for what had been the junior grade of *capitaine de frégate*, and in 1836 all other *capitaines de frégate* were also retitled *capitaines de corvette*, but in 1848 the rank of *capitaine de frégate* was restored and all *capitaines de corvette* were given that rank.

Lieut. As in the British Navy, the rank of commissioned officer below the captain was the *lieutenant de vaisseau*, of which there were several in ships of the line and frigates. Below these, the lowest rank of commissioned officer was the *enseigne de vaisseau* (before the Revolution, the term was *sous-lieutenants de vaisseau*) – roughly speaking equivalent to the senior midshipman in the British Navy or ensign in the US Navy. Most junior midshipmen would be termed *élèves* (from 1848 this designation became *aspirants*).

Petty Officers The senior non-commissioned officers (*officiers-mariniers*) were those who were the masters (*maîtres*) in various specialities, including those of manoeuvre (*premier maître*), of pilotage (*premier pilot*), of gunnery (*maître-canonnier*), of carpentry (*maître-charpentier*), of caulking (*maître-calfat*) and of sailmaking (*maître-voilier*), together with the boatswain (*maître d'équipage*). The *premier pilot* was the sailing master, and there were several grades of this rate of petty officer.

Seaman The basic grade was the *matelot*, but there were higher distinctions among the more skilled, including the *timonier* (quartermaster or helmsman) and *gabier* (topman, experienced in reefing or setting topsails); note that a *gabier de port* was a dockyard rigger.

Boy The underage members of the crew, such as the powder monkeys, were termed *mousses*; at age 16 the *mousse* would become a *novice* until the time he was able to qualify as a *matelot*.

Supernumeraries The *non-officier-mariners*, commonly known as in Britain as the 'idlers' (*fainéants*) as they did not have to stand as part of a watch, comprised the artisans working with weapons and metallic trades, the commissary personnel (stewards, cooks, etc) and the medical personnel.

Garrison As in British ships, there was on each ship a cadre of full-time professional soldiers or marines, separately organised in military regiments, and distinct from the seamen officers and crew, with their own officers who were directly responsible to the *capitaine de vaisseau* and *capitaine de frégate*. This was termed the garrison (*garnison*). They provided the artillery specialists, the infantry (when a landing party was required) and the ship's police force.

DECK LEVELS IN A WARSHIP (described in ascending order)

Cale	The hold, directly above the ship's keel (*quille*).
Marchepied	Platform; these were (in some vessels) non-continuous deck levels with the upper part of the hold.
Faux pont	Orlop deck; a (mainly) continuous deck level within the ship, usually at or below the waterline.
Premier pont	The lower deck of a two- or three-decked ship of the line (habitually called the gun deck in a British ship), carrying the largest-calibre – and heaviest – carriage-mounted guns.
Second pont	The middle deck in a three-decked ship of the line, or the upper deck in a two-decker.
Troisième pont	The upper deck in a three-decked ship of the line; this was the highest continuous deck of a ship, carrying the smaller carriage guns (although the guns on the *gaillards* – if any were mounted there - were smaller still).
Gaillards	This term describes the superstructure of a warship, above the continuous upper deck, encompassing both the quarterdeck (*gaillard d'arrière* in French) and the forecastle (*gaillard d'avant*) in English equivalent terminology. In the nineteenth century, warship evolution led to the area between these two decks – the waist – being gradually encroached upon, firstly by the introduction of gangways linking quarterdeck and forecastle along the side of the ship, and subsequently by filling it with beams to carry spare spars (hence the 'spardeck') and then eventually the reduction of the area between until they were covered by a series of slatted gratings to let light through to the upper deck below,

	but otherwise turning the *gaillards* into a continuous gun-bearing deck.
Dunette	On some ships of the line, there was a further level above the quarterdeck, traditionally described as the roundhouse (*dunette* in French), although this level rarely carried cannon by 1786.

PLEASE NOTE that in this volume we have retained the abbreviations 'LD' (for lower deck), 'MD' (for middle deck) and 'UD' (for upper deck) as more familiar to English-speaking readers; and have added the abbreviation 'SD' (for superstructure deck) to describe the gaillards (quarterdeck, spardeck and/or forecastle deck).

TOP HAMPER   The masts, spars, rigging and sails of a ship

Mât de misaine	The foremast (also *phare de l'avant* for a square-rigged ship)
Petit mât de hune	The fore topmast
Grand mât	The mainmast (also *phare du milieu* for a square-rigged ship)
Grand mât de hune	The main topmast
Mât d'artimon	The mizzen mast
Mât de perroquet de fougue	The mizzen topmast
Mâtreau	A spar, attached horizontal to the vertical mast
Vergue	A yard, a horizontal spar hoisted and fixed on a mast
Vergue de misaine	Fore yard
Vergue de petit hunier	Fore topsail yard
Vergue de petit perroquet	Fore topgallant yard
Grand-vergue	Main yard
Vergue de grand hunier	Main topsail yard
Vergue de grand perroquet	Main topgallant yard
Vergue d'artimon	Mizzen yard
Vergue de perroquet de fougue	Mizzen topsail yard
Vergue de perruche d'artimon	Mizzen topgallant yard
Vergue de vigie	Royal yard

Note the masts and spars as a whole were termed the *mâture*.

Basse voile	A lower sail (or course)
Voile au tiers	A lug sail
Voile aurique	Fore-and-aft sail
Voile carrée	Square sail
Voile de cacatois	Royal sail (i.e. a sail on a royal yard)
Voile de senault	A try-sail
Voile d'étai	Staysail
Agrès	Rigging
Cordage	Rope, ropework

OTHER PARTS AND FITTINGS OF A SHIP

Apotre	Knighthead
Étrave	Stem
Écoute	Sheet (as part of rigging)
Figure de proue	Figurehead
Galèrie de combat	Carpenter's walk
Poulaines	The 'heads'
Roue de gouvernail	Ship's (steering) wheel
Sabord	Gunport

SHIP DESIGN AND CONSTRUCTION

Écart	Scarph
Fonds	Underwater lines
Rentrée	Tumblehome
Tonture	Sheer (as of decks)

ARMAMENT / ORDNANCE

Affut	Gun carriage
Boulet	Shot (as in projectile); round shot was *boulet rond*
Bombe	Mortar shell
Canon	A carriage gun, in sizes from 36pdr down to 2pdr
Canon-obusier	Carriage gun firing explosive shells as developed by General Henri-Joseph Paixhans in 1822-23
Caronade	Carronade, a short-barrelled but large calibre gun effective only at short range; note French spelling difference. Usually mounted on a slide (*semelle*) rather than on a wheeled carriage
Gargousse	Cartridge for use with large-calibre guns
Obus	Explosive shell (as in projectile)
Obusier	Brass howitzer, superseded by the carronade in the early years of the nneteenth century
Pierrier	Swivel, a miniature muzzle-loading cannon mounted in a swivelling U-shaped fork at reinforced positions along a ship's side that fired grapeshot or small round shot, primarily against personnel. French *pierriers* (sometimes called *perriers*) made after 1786 fired roundshot of one (French) pound and had a bore of 53mm calibre. *Espingoles* were even smaller swivelling anti-personnel firearms that fired half-pound projectiles.

TYPES OF VESSEL The descriptions of certain vessels, notably those with traditional Mediterranean rigs, differed from British usage, and we have attempted here to identify the main types, including giving their equivalents in French. This list is necessarily limited to the types of vessel found in this book.

1. The following major types carried a ship rig (i.e. were square-rigged on three masts), although some corvettes (*brick-corvettes*) had a two-masted brig rig. The largest transports (flûtes and some gabarres) were also ship rigged.

Vaisseau	Literally 'vessel', but in naval use describing a ship of the line, with two or three batteries of carriage guns
Frégate	Frigate, a vessel with a single continuous battery of carriage guns (usually 13 or 14 pairs of guns).
Corvette	A vessel with a single continuous battery of carriage guns, but one smaller than the frigate (with 11 or fewer pairs of guns).

2. The following, designated by their rig, hull configuration, or function, illustrate the wide variety of smaller types in French service.

Aviso	An advice boat or despatch vessel, generally a converted craft, used with fleets or along a coast as a scout or to carry messages. The name is from the Spanish *barca de aviso*. From the 1840s the term came into widespread use for nearly all steam vessels (paddle or screw) smaller than steam corvettes
Balancelle	A small merchant or fishing vessel of Neapolitan origin with two pointed ends, a lateen mainsail, sometimes a second small sail right aft, and 8 to 10 banks of oars
Bateau-canonnier	An artillery boat (a small armed vessel that also transported artillery)
Bateau-plat	A flat-bottomed cargo vessel or lighter
Batterie flottante	A floating battery, often an old ship cut down and converted
Biscayenne (*chaloupe biscayenne*)	A Basque fishing or whaling craft of from 6 to 20 metres in length, without a deck, rigged with two lugsails, and capable of being rowed
Bombarde	A bomb or mortar vessel. By the end of the eighteenth century the term was also in use for square-rigged merchant vessels with similar characteristics including robust hulls and a ketch rig.

Brick	A brig (although the term *brig* was also used quite often in French), a two-masted vessel with a square-rigged foremast and a mainmast with both square and fore-and-aft sails		derived from galleys, as were those of the larger xebecs
		Flûte	A large square-rigged vessel derived from the Dutch *fluit*, frigate-built, designed to carry both cargo and personnel long distances. Analogous to the British storeship
Brick-goélette	A schooner-brig, in which the foremast was primarily square rigged and the mainmast was exclusively fore-and-aft rigged	*Gabarre*	A medium-sized square-rigged vessel optimised for carrying cargo, often on coastal routes
Brigantin	A brigantine, essentially a felucca modified for military use as a privateer. They resembled feluccas in typically having no deck, two masts with lateen sails (one amidships and one well forward), around 12 banks of oars, and an armament of two chase guns and some swivels. They had nothing in common with the eighteenth century Northern European two-masted brigantine, a brig without a square main course.	*Galère*	A galley, a warship propelled primarily by oars but also usually having two lateen-rigged masts (the *trinquet* forward and the *arbre de mestre* amidships).
		Galiote	A galiot. The Northern European galiot was a shallow-draught cargo-carrying two-masted vessel that was common in the coastal trade of Germany, Scandinavia, and the Netherlands. It had nothing in common with the Mediterranean *galiote à rames*, a military craft with lateen sails on two masts, around 16 banks of oars, and some swivels. This galiot, limited to North Africa after 1780, resembled the Mediterranean *brigantin* but had only minimal upperworks and was little more than a large *chaloupe* or launch. *Galiotes à bombes* were bombardes, q.v.
Brûlot	A fireship, generally converted from another type of vessel		
Caiche	A ketch, a two-masted vessel with a main mast stepped forwards and a mizzen mast fairly far aft		
Caïque	Originally a small oared launch carried by a Mediterranean galley, in the Boulogne Flotilla of 1803 a smaller (and unsuccessful) version of the troop-carrying *péniche*		
Canonnière or *chaloupe canonnière*	A gunboat	*Garde-côtes*.	A coast guard vessel; in the sailing navy generally a small converted craft
Chaloupe	A launch or a ship's longboat capable of carrying artillery. The British word 'sloop' derives from *chaloupe*, reflecting the origins of both the British sloop and the French corvette	*Goélette*	A schooner, a two-masted vessel with fore-and-aft rigged sails, in some cases with square topsails on one or both masts. Some later examples had three masts. The name is related to the Breton word for 'seagull'
Chasse-marée	A small two- or three-masted vessel with a rounded hull and a flush deck with a rig similar to that of a lugger, traditionally used for transporting material of all kinds, particularly in Brittany, but often lightly armed and used a coastal patrol craft in the Revolutionary and Napoleonic Wars	*Lougre*	A lugger, a vessel the size of a schooner or small brig with two or three masts rigged with *voiles au tiers* or *voiles à bourcet*, sails on yards suspended from the mast at a point on the yard about one third of the distance from one end. The result was a fast vessel in a cross-wind but one that required a large and well trained crew to come about. These military vessels were related to the cargo-carrying chasse-marées but had finer lines
Chatte	A type of double-ended sailing lighter or scow, of about 60 tons capacity with a single square-rigged mast amidships	*Mouche*	An advice boat or tender, used for scouting or carrying messages. The Napoleonic *mouches* were copied from a small Bermuda schooner
Chébec	A xebec or zebec, a fast Mediterranean armed vessel with a sharp beakhead or *éperon* and an overhanging stern or *cul-de-poule*. Typically they had lateen sails on three masts, though later many were rigged polacre fashion with square sails	*Péniche*	A pinnace, a lightly armed slender vessel without a deck whose primary purpose in the Boulogne Flotilla was carrying troops, who also manned the 20 pairs of oars. The word is used today for canal boats and landing craft
Cotre	A cutter, a vessel with a single mast carrying both square and fore-and-aft sails plus jibs rigged to a long bowsprit. Like luggers, the rig of these vessels became difficult to handle as they increased in size for naval use	*Pinque*	A pink, a Mediterranean merchant vessel with full hull lines for carrying cargo and up to three lateen-rigged masts, the mizzen sometimes having a square topsail. It had a beakhead like a xebec but had a square-cut stern. The Northern European pink was a cargo-carrier like the mercantile ketch but had three square-rigged masts
Demi-galère	A half-galley, or galley of less than maximum size. In contrast with a typical galley with 26 banks of oars, each oar with 5 oarsmen, a half-galley might have 20 banks of oars, each oar with 3 rowers. They typically had the usual two-masted galley rig (although a third small mast was later added right aft), one chase gun and two smaller guns forward, and some swivels	*Polacre*	A polacre or polacca, a Mediterranean merchant vessel based on the military *barque latine* with foremast raked forward for a lateen sail called a polacre and square sails on the main and mizzen. Its masts consisted of single poles and the square sails on them were rigged 'polacre fashion'. Vessels thus rigged could lower their sails quickly in a squall, even with a small crew
Demi-chebec	A half-xebec or smaller-sized xebec.		
Dogre	A dogger, a sturdy Northern European two-masted vessel, relatively short, wide-beamed and ketch-rigged. Initially employed as fishing vessels, these vessels with their round sterns were generally similar to the cargo-carrying Northern European galiots	*Ponton*	A hulk, often a former seagoing warship or other vessel struck from the active list and used as a stationary harbour vessel
		Prame	A pram, a flat-bottomed warship, usually heavily armed, designed for coastal waters and for grounding on a beach to put troops and horses ashore (an ancestor of the modern landing craft)
Felouque	A felucca, a small Mediterranean coastal merchant vessel that typically had no deck, one to three masts with lateen sails, and was also propelled by oars. Their hull form with its beakhead and *cul-de-poule* and its lateen rig were		
		Sloop	A sloop, in French usage generally a small cargo vessel

	with a single mast and a simplified cutter rig
Spéronare	A small Maltese merchant craft without a deck and with a single mast
Tartane	A tartan, a common Mediterranean coastal merchant vessel with a deck for cargo carrying, a beakhead forward and a small cabin in a pointed stern. They had one mast for a lateen sail and a jib, although some had a lateen-rigged foremast replacing the jib. When rigged polacre fashion with square sails they could resemble ketches
Trincadour	A small undecked vessel with two lugsails on horizontal rather than oblique yards, common in Biscayan coastal waters.

MISCELLANEOUS ABBREVIATIONS

BU	Broken up (or taken to pieces).
NMM	National Maritime Museum, Greenwich, UK.
PRO	Public Records Office, Kew, London; subsequently renamed the National Archives.
Comm.	Commissioned. Dates after 1800 tend to be early in the commissioning process.
Decomm., Recomm.	Decommissioned, Recommissioned.
Struck	Deleted from the fleet list. Represents the French *rayé* or in some cases *condamné*.

List of the French Fleet as at 1 January 1786

The start of 1786 marked a series of reforms of French naval administration put into effect by the Navy Minister (*Secrétaire d'État de la Marine*), the Marquis de Castries, with the promulgation on 1 January of a dozen ordnances and eleven regulations. Under these, the existing ships, frigates and corvettes of the navy were reorganised into nine Squadrons; five of these were based on Brest, two on Toulon, and two on Rochefort. In the list below, ships of the line ('vaisseaux de ligne') are followed by the number of guns with which each was established, while frigates and corvettes are followed by the calibre (in French pounds) of their principal batteries. The frigates included two small two-decked ships; the corvettes include brigs (#), cutters (*) and other avisos.

Brest
First Squadron
Ships of the Line: *Bretagne* (110), *Deux-Frères* (80), *America* (74), *Achille* (74), *Superbe* (74), *Patriote* (74), *Hercule* (74).
Frigates: *Résolution* (18pdr, 2-decker), *Nymphe* (18pdr), *Iphygénie* (12pdr), *Gentille* (12pdr), *Fine* (12pdr), *Prosélite* (12pdr), *Aigrette* (pdr).
Corvettes: *Badine* (8pdr), *Subtile* (6pdr), *Ballon* (4pdr*), *Courier* (4pdr*).

Second Squadron
Ships of the Line: *Terrible* (110), *Languedoc* (80), *Citoyen* (74), *Northumberland* (74), *Victoire* (74), *Fougueux* (74), *Brave* (74).
Frigates: *Expériment* (18pdr, 2-decker), *Vénus* (18pdr), *Engageante* (12pdr), *Résolue* (12pdr), *Bellone* (12pdr), *Cléopâtre* (12pdr), *Richemont* (12pdr).
Corvettes: *Belette* (8pdr), *Fanfaron* (4pdr#), *Pivert* (4pdr*), *Furet* (4pdr#).

Third Squadron
Ships of the Line: *Royal Louis* (110), *Auguste* (80), *Diadème* (74), *Magnanime* (74), *Illustre* (74), *Borée* (74), *Argonaute* (74).
Frigates: *Consolante* (18pdr), *Proserpine* (18pdr, bldg), *Atalante* (12pdr), *Gloire* (12pdr), *Félicité* (12pdr), *Danae* (12pdr), *Active* (8pdr).
Corvettes: *Blonde* (8dr), *Duc-de-Chartres* (6pdr), *Pilote-des-Indes* (6pdr), *Levrette* (4pdr#), *Tiercelet* (4pdr*).

Fourth Squadron
Ships of the Line: *Invincible* (110), *Saint-Esprit* (80), *Neptune* (74), *Pluton* (74), *Téméraire* (74), *Ferme* (74), *Zélé* (74).
Frigates: *Méduse* (18pdr), *Driade* (18pdr), *Amphitrite* (12pdr), *Amazone* (12pdr), *Galathée* (12pdr), *Émeraude* (12pdr), *Surveillante* (12pdr).
Corvettes: *Sincère* (6pdr), *Cérès* (6pdr), *Malin* (6pdr*), *Vaneau* (4pdr*).

Fifth Squadron
Ships of the Line: *Majestueux* (110), *Duc-de-Bourgogne* (80), *Sceptre* (74), *Audacieux* (74), *Léopard* (74), *Réfléchi* (64).
Frigates: *Didon* (18pdr, bldg), *Pénélope* (18pdr, bldg), *Calipso* (12pdr), *Capricieuse* (12pdr), *Précieuse* (12pdr), *Astrée* (12pdr), *Ariel* (8pdr).
Corvettes: *Vigilante* (6pdr), *Pandour* (6pdr#), *Hirondelle* (4pdr), *Papillon* (4pdr#).

Toulon
Sixth Squadron
Ships of the Line: *Triomphant* (80), *Héros* (74), *Suffisant* (74), *Dictateur* (74), *Heureux* (74), *Censeur* (74), *Souverain* (74).
Frigates: *Minerve* (18pdr), *Impérieuse* (18pdr, bldg), *Réunion* (12pdr), *Sérieuse* (12pdr), *Lutine* (12pdr), *Friponne* (12pdr), *Vestale* (12pdr), *Boudeuse* (12pdr), *Mignonne* (8pdr).
Corvettes: *Brune* (8pdr), *Sémillante* (8pdr), *Éclair* (6pdr), *Gerfaut* (4pdr*).

Seventh Squadron
Ships of the Line: *Couronne* (80), *Conquérant* (74), *Alcide* (74), *Mercure* (74), *Centaure* (74), *Puissant* (74), *Destin* (74), *Guerrier* (74).
Frigates: *Junon* (18pdr), *Modeste* (12pdr), *Iris* (12pdr), *Aurore* (12pdr), *Montréal* (12pdr), *Sensible* (12pdr), *Alceste* (12pdr), *Sultane* (12pdr), *Flore* (8pdr).
Corvettes: *Poulette* (8pdr), *Flèche* (6pdr), *Sardine* (6pdr), *Levrette* (4pdr#), *Tarleston* (4pdr#).

Rochefort
Eighth Squadron
Ships of the Line: *Séduisant* (74), *Généreux* (74), *Impétueux* (74), *Provence* (64), *Triton* (64), *Saint-Michel* (60), *Annibal* (50).
Frigates: *Pomone* (18pdr, bldg), *Andromaque* (12pdr), *Courageuse* (12pdr), *Médée* (12pdr), *Fée* (12pdr), *Gracieuse* (12pdr), *Guadeloupe* (8pdr).
Corvettes: *Alouette* (6pdr), *Fauvette* (6pdr), *Rossignol* (6pdr), *Chien-de-Chasse* (6pdr), *Hypocrite* (6pdr), *Sylphe* (4pdr).

Ninth Squadron
Ships of the Line: *Orion* (74), *Protecteur* (74), *Marseillais* (74), *Sphinx* (64), *Brillant* (64), *Amphion* (50), *Sagittaire* (50).
Frigates: *Fleur-de-Lys* (12pdr), *Railleuse* (12pdr), *Hermione* (12pdr), *Néréide* (12pdr), *Cérès* (12pdr), *Flore* (12pdr), *Pleïade* (8).
Corvettes: *Favorite* (6pdr), *Perdrix* (6pdr), *Tourtereau* (6pdr), *David* (6pdr), *Surprise* (4pdr*).

Source: Archives Nationales, fonds Marine, B5-28, *Répartition des forces navales du Roi, en 9 Escadres*.

1 The Three-deckers

(Vaisseaux à trois ponts)
(rated Vaisseaux de 1er Rang from 1824)

The first true three-decker built for the French Marine Royale was the *Saint Philippe*, which entered service in 1665. The first *large* French three-decker (*vaisseau de premier rang extraordinaire*) was the *Royal Louis*, completed 1668. In 1670 Colbert produced the first French system of rating, dividing the fleet into five Ranks (*Rangs*), the first of which comprised most of the three-deckers, while the second included some of the smaller three-deckers as well as the larger two-deckers. Forty-three of the First Rank and fourteen three-decked Second Rank were built for Louis XIV's Navy between 1661 and 1693, but changes in strategic thinking (and a general decline in the French Navy) meant that orders ceased abruptly in 1693 and no further three-decked vessels were built until 1757 (apart from the 110-gun *Foudroyant* in the 1720s and one attempted ship in the 1740s which was burnt before launching).

Two new ships – the 90-gun *Impétueux* (renamed *Ville de Paris* in 1762 while still building) and 124-gun *Royal Louis* – were built from 1757 onwards, but the former (enlarged to 104 guns in 1779) was lost to the British in 1782, and the latter had been deleted in 1773. A third three-decker – the 100-gun *Bretagne* – was approved in 1762 at the close of the Seven Years War to be built as one of seventeen new warships funded at the request of the Duc de Choiseul, and was still in service into the 1790s. No more were constructed until the outbreak of war against Britain in the late 1770s led to a batch of four new orders being placed for rapid construction.

Révolutionnaire (ex *Bretagne*) was the oldest French three-decker still in service at the beginning of the French Revolutionary Wars. She was badly damaged in the skirmishes leading up to the Battle of the Glorious First of June in 1794 – as shown in this drawing by Robert Cleveley of the French ship being raked by the 74-gun *Russell* on 28 May – and was towed into Rochefort but was never repaired. (© National Maritime Museum PX9715)

(A) Vessels in service or on order at 1 January 1786

Although the rank (*rang*) system had fallen into temporary disfavour by the 1780s, the three-deckers still constituted a distinct group within the French Navy, serving as the flagships of the battle fleet. As at 1783 five three-deckers remained in service, the older *Bretagne* (of 1766), and four newer vessels which had all been launched in 1780. Each carried 94 guns on their three complete gun-decks (*Invincible* had 2 fewer), including a principal battery of 30 guns (of 36 or 48 French pounds) on the lower deck, and all acquired a small number of lesser guns (8pdrs) on the gaillards, so that by 1786 each carried 110 guns in total, and was nominally 'established' with 950 men in wartime and 500 in peace. At the start of 1786 all five were at Brest, each with one of the five squadrons that the Brest fleet was to comprise.

In June 1803 Napoleon was to rule that any ship of the line needing a refit of 18/24ths or more should not be repaired but should instead be taken to pieces. This ruling was to affect all three of the pre-1786 three-deckers surviving into the Napoleonic War.

BRETAGNE. Ordered in 1764 to be built at Lorient to a design by Antoine Groignard, this ship was begun there in late 1764, but work ceased in January 1765 when the order was transferred to Brest. Her cost was funded as a gift to Louis XV by the États de Bretagne. She was completed at Brest with 100 guns (including just 6 x 8pdrs on the gaillards), but was re-armed in 1781, with 16 x 6pdrs added on the gaillards in lieu of the 8pdrs to bring her up to 110 guns; she was coppered at Brest in March 1781, and re-coppered at Brest in May to July 1786.

Dimensions & tons: 186ft 0in, 165 ft 0in x 50ft 0in x 24ft 6in (60.42, 53.60 x 16.24 x 7.96m). 2,600/4,666 tons. Draught 22½/24¾ft (7.31/8.04m). Men: 1,058.

Guns: LD 30 x 36pdrs; MD 32 x 24pdrs; UD 32 x 12pdrs; SD (from 1781) 16 x 6pdrs.

Bretagne Brest Dyd.
K: 10.6.1765. L: 24.5.1766. C: 9.1767.
Renamed *Révolutionnaire* in October 1793, she was severely damaged in action on 28 May 1794, and had to be towed into Rochefort, but was never restored to service. In early 1796 she was condemned and BU at Brest.

INVINCIBLE. 110-gun three-decker designed by François-Guillaume Clairin-Deslauriers. Originally built as a 92-gun ship, with no forecastle and without guns on her QD, the QD 8pdrs were added in 1781 and a forecastle added and armed in 1784.

Dimensions & tons: 184ft 0in, 167ft 0in x 50ft 0in x 24ft 6in (59.77, 54.25 x 16.24 x 7.96m). 2,400/4,670 tons. Draught 23½/25½ft (7.63/8.28m). Men: 1,058 (by 1795, 1,070 including 17 officers).

Guns: LD 30 x 48pdrs; MD 32 x 24pdrs; UD 30 x 12pdrs; SD 18 (Fc 6, QD 12) x 8pdrs; 4 x 36pdr obusiers were added in 1794.

Invincible Rochefort Dyd. (Constructeur, Jean-Denis Chevillard)
K: 2.1779. L: 20.3.1780. C: 5.1780.
Rebuilt and coppered at Brest in 1794. Re-armed there 1800-2, but disarmed on 11.3.1807 and condemned on 6.1.1808 in accordance with Napoleon's 1803 edict, before being BU to 12.1808.

ROYAL LOUIS. 110-gun three-decker designed by Léon-Michel Guignace. Unlike the other three-deckers of this era, she was completed as a 106-gun ship, including twelve 8pdrs on the gaillards; she was also completed with 48pdrs on the LD (the last French ship of the line to carry this calibre), but they were replaced by 36pdrs in December 1782.

Dimensions & tons: 186ft 0in, 164ft 0in x 50ft 0in x 24ft 6in (60.42, 53.27 x 16.24 x 7.96m). 2,400/4,835 tons. Draught 24/26½ft (7.80/8.61m). Men: 950 in 1786; 1,070 by 1794.

Guns: LD 30 x 36pdrs; MD 32 x 24pdrs; UD 32 x 12pdrs; SD 12 x 8pdrs (4 more 8pdrs were added in 1784, but they were replaced by 4 x 36pdr obusiers in 1794).

Royal Louis Brest Dyd. (Constructeur, Pierre-Alexandre Forfait)
K: 3.1779. L: 20.3.1780. C: 6.1780.
Renamed *Républicain* 29.9.1792; damaged at Battle of '13 Prairial' (Glorious First of June, 1794); wrecked off Brest 24.12.1794.

TERRIBLE Class. 110-gun three-deckers designed and built by Joseph-Marie-Blaise Coulomb. As with the *Invincible*, they were completed as 94-gun ships, with the forecastle added subsequently – and 8pdrs mounted here and on the QD. Both ships were condemned in accordance with Napoleon's 1803 edict.

Dimensions & tons: 186ft 8in, 169ft 0in x 50ft 0in x 25ft 0in (60.64, 54.90 x 16.24 x 8.12m). 2,500/4,700 tons. Draught 23/24½ft (7.47/7.96m). Men: 950 in 1786; 1,070 by 1794.

Guns: LD 30 x 36pdrs (initially 48pdrs in *Majestueux*); MD 32 x 24pdrs; UD 32 x 12pdrs; SD 16 x 8pdrs (4 x 36pdr obusiers replaced 4 x 8pdrs in 1793)

Terrible Toulon Dyd
Ord: 23.10.1778. K: 7.1779. L: 27.1.1780. C: 5.1780.
Damaged at Battle of '13 Prairial' (Glorious First of June, 1794). Condemned 5.1804 at Brest and BU.

Majestueux Toulon Dyd
Ord: 20.4.1780. K: 5.7.1780. L: 17.11.1780. C: 4.2.1781.
Renamed *Républicain* in 1797, repaired 1799-1800; BU 10.1808.

At least another three 110-gun ships (and two even larger vessels of 118 guns – see below) were projected in 1782, but were cancelled in 1783. One of these, to have been built by Joseph-Marie-Blaise Coulomb at Toulon, would presumably have been similar to the *Terrible* and *Majestueux*; funded by the Bordeaux Chamber of Commerce, this was provisionally named *Commerce de Bordeaux*. Another, to have been named *Généralités*, would have been built at Rochefort by François-Guillaume Clairin-Deslauriers, and may have been intended as similar to *Invincible*. The third, to have been funded by the Lyon Chamber of Commerce, would have borne the name *Commerce de Lyon*.

(B) Vessels acquired from 1 January 1786

The extension of the French three-decker to a ship of 118 guns (with 32 guns on the LD, an extra pair compared with the ships of the 1779-80 orders) had been envisaged in summer 1782, under the massive fleet expansion plans initiated by Castries and Borda. Two three-deckers of 118 guns were ordered to be built at Brest and Toulon on 7 July 1782, and a design for these was drawn up by Antoine Groignard and dated 30 August, providing for a ship of 194ft length. The Brest ship (to have been named *Ville de Paris*, or possibly *Commerce de la Ville de Paris*) would have been constructed by Jacques-Noël Sané, and doubtless Groignard's design formed the core of Sané's own 1786 concept for the *Commerce de Marseille* class. The Toulon ship would seemingly have been named *Commerce de Marseille* or *États de Bourgogne*, the names subsequently used for the ships ordered (or re-ordered) in 1786.

Under the standardised system laid down by Borda and Sané, the 118-gun ship became the approved three-decker design. Under the Program of construction planned by Borda, there were to be nine three-deckers built, one to head each of the nine squadrons into which the French Navy was to be divided. Five ships were begun between 1786 and 1794, all carrying 32 guns (of 36 French pounds) as their principal battery; another four ordered in 1793-94 were never begun. Besides the 118 carriage guns, each (except the *États de Bourgogne*) also carried 6 x 36pdr obusiers on the gaillards. After Trafalgar, a further group of these were begun from 1806 onwards to a modified design; these differed by carrying only 114 carriage guns, but additionally mounted a dozen 36pdr carronades on the gaillards; most of these were not completed by 1815, and all continued to serve for many years, with four being converted to steam screw vessels in 1852-54. A slightly shortened type of 110-gun three-decker was designed in 1804, with one fewer pair of gunports (and guns) to each deck, a reversion to the pre-1786 designs; two of these were built initially, although a further group to be of the same design were laid down at Antwerp in 1810-11 but were never completed.

COMMERCE DE MARSEILLE Class. A 1786 design by Jacques-Noël Sané, dated 23 October, to which five ships were laid down (two each at Toulon and Brest, and a fifth at Rochefort). The 1779 designs were stretched by about 10ft to make room for an additional pair of gunports on each deck, to raise the total ordnance to 118 guns. Apart from the *États de Bourgogne*, all also carried 6 x 36pdr obusiers on the gaillards. The total sail area was 3,250 sq.m.

Two ships were ordered on 30 September 1785 to be built at Brest and Toulon, apparently the re-orders of the ships cancelled in 1783. The Toulon ship was confirmed as *Commerce de Marseille* on 23 January 1786, while the Brest ship, the funding for which had been offered to the navy by the Estates of Burgundy, was named *États de Bourgogne* on 19 June. A third ship was projected at Toulon in 1786, possibly to have been named

THE THREE-DECKERS

The Admiralty draught of *Commerce de Marseille* as taken off at Plymouth in 1796. The largest British prize of the eighteenth century, her seventeen pairs of gunports of each deck and her excellent sailing qualities (outstanding for a three-decker) convinced the British to attempt to commission her, but she proved too weak structurally for prolonged service, and after a failed attempt to send her to the Caribbean as a storeship, she was relegated to a harbour prison hulk until broken up in 1802. (© National Maritime Museum J1853)

Six Corps, but was never ordered, and instead the third of the class was ordered at Toulon on 21 November 1789, and was named *Dauphin Royal* on 23 April 1790. Following Revolutionary practice, she was renamed *Sans Culotte* on 29 September 1792, but was renamed again (see below) after entering service. Four further ships were ordered in 1793, including one at Brest and one at Rochefort, although neither entered service until 1803-4; work on the Brest ship began on 17 October 1793, and she was briefly named *Peuple* in June 1794 but was renamed *Vengeur* on 9 July; the Rochefort ship was named *République Française* in September 1793, when work on her began.

The other two 1793 orders were for two ships to be built to the Sané design at Toulon, one to be named *Fleurus* and the other probably to be called *Quatorze Juillet*; neither was begun and they were cancelled in 1796. A final pair of orders were placed in 1794, again one at Brest and one at Rochefort – to be named *Liberté des Mers* and *Républicain*

A coloured lithograph of *Océan*, originally the *États de Bourgogne*, seen some time between the removal of the poop in 1847 and her final decommissioning in 1850. *Souverain*, a sister first commissioned in 1840, is in the background. (© National Maritime Museum PY0747)

respectively; again, neither was begun and the orders were rescinded in 1799.

> Dimensions & tons: 196ft 6in, 178ft 0in x 50ft 0in x 25ft 0in (63.83, 57.82 x 16.24 x 8.12m). 2,794 – 2,930/5,095 tons. Draught 23ft 5in/25ft 1in (7.61/8.15m). Men (1786): 1,117 in wartime/780 in peacetime. By October 1795 this was increased to 1,130, and by 1802 these totals had risen to those specified below for the *Austerlitz* class. The 1786 complement included 16 officers (17 by 1795) – comprising a *captaine de vaisseau*, a *major de vaisseau* (this rank for the captain's deputy was retitled *capitaine de frégate* after the Revolution), 6 lieutenants and 8 (later 9) *enseignes*.
> Guns: LD 32 x 36pdrs; MD 34 x 24pdrs; UD 34 x 12pdrs; SD 18 x 8pdrs + 6 x 36pdr obusiers.

États de Bourgogne Brest Dyd. (Constructeur, Jacques-Noël Sané)
> K: 12.8.1786. L: 8.11.1790. C: 12.1790.
> Renamed *Côte d'Or* 27.1.1793, *Montagne* 22.10.1793, *Peuple* 25.5.1795, and finally *Océan* 30.5.1795 (implemented upon her return to Lorient 26.6.1795). Poop deck (dunette) removed 1846-47. Decom. for the last time 1.8.1850. Rated floating battery 5.1851. Struck 31.12.1854 and then to be BU by a decision of 16.3.1855, also reported as condemned 14.5.1855, and BU at Brest.

Commerce de Marseille Toulon Dyd.
> K: 9.1786. L: 7.8.1788. C: 10.1790.
> Handed over to the British at Toulon 29.8.1793, and in 12.1793 taken to Britain, where she became HMS *Commerce de Marseille*, briefly used as a transport before being hulked at Plymouth, and finally sold to BU in 2.1802.

Dauphin Royal Toulon Dyd.
> K: 5.1790. L: 20.7.1791. C: 8.1793.
> Renamed *Orient* 21.5.1795. Blew up at Aboukir 2.8.1798 (with 940 of the 1,010 men aboard killed including Vice-Adm. Francois Paul Brueys d'Aiguilliers, and her Captain, Luc-Julien-Joseph Casabianca).

Vengeur Brest Dyd. (Constructeur, Pierre Ozanne)
> K: 17.10.1793. L: 1.10.1803. Comm: 11.1803. C: 2.1804.
> Renamed *Impérial* 4.2.1805 or 7.3.1805. Grounded 6.2.1806 in combat in the roadstead of Santo Domingo, where she was burned 9.2.1806 by the British.

République Française Rochefort Dyd. (Constructeur, Pierre Rolland, but completed after 1800 by Entreprise Destouches with their constructors Capon and Pelleteau)
> K: 21.3.1794, soon stopped, resumed 22.3.1800. L: 18.4.1802. Comm: 1.8.1803. C: 8.1803.
> Renamed *Majestueux* 5.2.1803. Struck 26.1.1839, hauled out at Toulon 11.4.1839 and BU.

(C) Vessels acquired from 25 March 1802

AUSTERLITZ Class. Following the losses which occurred at Trafalgar in October 1805 (although no French three-deckers were involved), a new 118-gun three-decker was ordered on 19 December 1805 as part of Napoleon's plans to reconstruct the battle fleet, and construction at Toulon began on 10 April 1806 (although the keel was not laid down until two months later). The frame for a second ship was ordered at Nantes from Crucy on 19 December 1805, initially named *Marengo* on 19 July 1806, but renamed *Ville de Vienne* a month later on 11 August 1806 (when a 74 at Lorient was named *Marengo*); construction of the ship was assigned to Rochefort in 1807 and the frame was placed on the ways there in May 1808. This ship was eventually launched in 1850 as *Ville de Paris* after further name changes (see below). A second frame ordered at Nantes on 19 December 1805 was not proceeded with because of a lack of timber there.

In 1807 a new règlement was applied to the armament of these ships, increasing the artillery on their gaillards from 18 x 8pdrs to 14 x 8pdrs and 12 x 36pdr carronades plus 6 x 36pdr bronze carronades on the dunette. In 1808 Sané found when measuring *Océan* for her major refit of that year that her beam had increased by 6 inches to 50ft 6in, and he worked this increase into the plans for the new ships. In 1851 a report of the Council of Works stated that the reason for the increase of beam was to allow 18pdrs to be carried on the UD and 12pdrs on the gaillards. The change to 18pdrs in the UD appears to have been implemented before the first of the new ships entered service in 1809. A decision of 17 December 1812 assigned the new ships an armament of LD 32 x 36pdrs, MD 34 x 24pdrs, UD 34 x 18pdrs, and SD 18 x 12pdrs, but this was not reflected in the artillery ordinance of 1817 which still showed 12pdrs on the UD.

The third ship was ordered at Toulon in 1809 as *Monarque*, but was renamed *Wagram* on 15 February 1810; the fourth was ordered at Toulon on 4 June 1810, and named as *Impérial* on 14 July; a fifth was also ordered in 1810 at Toulon, and named as *Montebello*.

A further ship was ordered to this design at Brest on 15 March 1811, and on 18 April was named as *Roi de Rome* after Napoleon's son born on 20 March 1811. She was renamed *Inflexible* on 21 May 1812 and *Sans Pareil* on 10 September 1812. There is much confusion over the successive names of this ship; the reconstruction presented here best fits the available data. This ship was never completed and she was broken up on the stocks in June 1816. March 1811 also saw a plan to built a three-decker of 118 guns at Trieste (the sole three-decker planned for construction outside France), but this never materialised. Also in 1811, a sister was ordered at Rochefort and named as *Tonnant*; construction was later suspended, and the ship was renamed *Louis XIV* in 1828 while still on the stocks.

Two further ships were ordered in 1812. The first, at Toulon, was named *Héros* on 21 May; the second, at Cherbourg, was named *Inflexible* on 10 September; the latter's name was altered to *Duc de Bordeaux* on 19 December 1820, but again changed to *Friedland* on 9 August 1830. Another two were ordered at Toulon during 1813; these were named *Souverain* and *Formidable*, but the latter name was altered to *Trocadero* in 1823; and a last vessel was begun at Cherbourg in October 1813 (using frames built at Le Havre) but was never named and was cancelled in March 1814.

In those ships of this and the preceding *Commerce de Marseille* class that were completed or received significant repairs after the early 1820s, the forecastle and quarterdeck were joined to form a complete spardeck upon which the guns assigned to this level were redistributed. The standard armament of the type was changed by the ordinance of 1828 to replace the long guns on the UD with 34 x 36pdr carronades and fit the SD with 16 x 36pdr carronades and 4 x 18pdr long guns, making the ships 120-gunners. The height above water of the LD was listed in the early 1830s as 1.62m at 7.88m mean draught. In the 1838 ordinance the old 120s were amalgamated with the new 120s, thus being assigned an armament of LD 32 x 30pdrs No.1; MD 30 x 30pdrs No.2 and 4 x 22cm No.1 shell; UD 34 x 16cm shell; and SD 16 x 30pdr carronades and 4 x 16cm shell. *Souverain* and *Friedland* were commissioned with this armament, except that *Souverain* had 20 x 30pdr carronades and no shell guns on the SD. New ordinances were issued in 1848 and later but by this time technology was moving so rapidly that the last two ships of this class to be completed (*Ville de Paris* and *Louis XIV*) received custom armaments as shown in their individual listings.

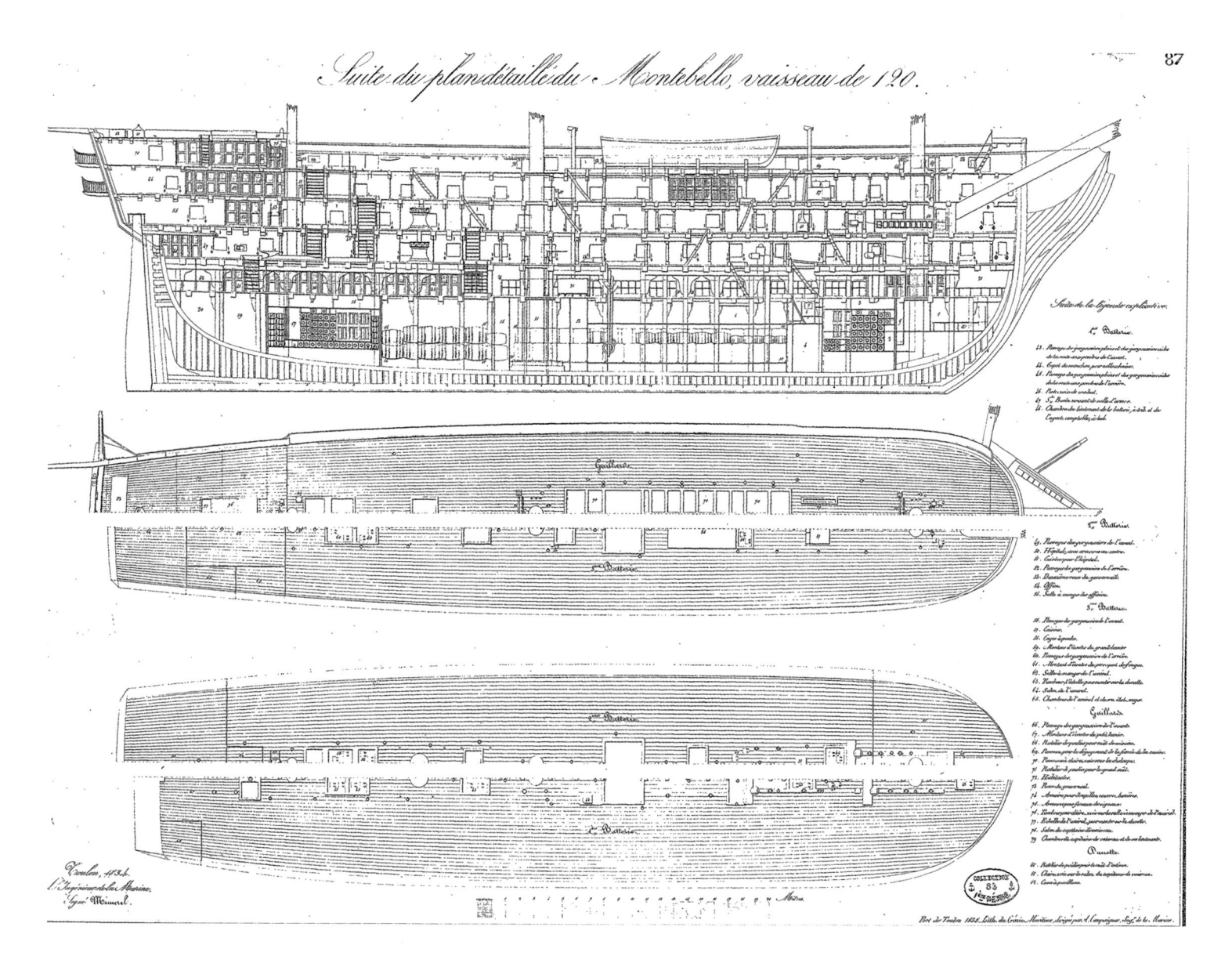

Official plan of the internal arrangements and deck layout of the *Montebello* as the ship was fitted in 1834. The post-war French Navy attempted to standardise the internal arrangements of each warship type, and produced drawings such as this one to act as a guide. (Atlas du Génie Maritime, French collection, plate 87)

Dimensions & tons: 196ft 6in, 178ft 0in x 50ft 6in x 25ft 0in (63.83, 57.82 x 16.40 x 8.12m). 2,794 – 2,930/5,095 tons. Draught 23ft 4in/25ft (7.60/8.14m). Men: 1,130 in wartime/825 in peacetime.

Guns: LD 32 x 36pdrs; MD 34 x 24pdrs; UD 34 x 18pdrs; SD 14 x 8pdrs + 12 x 36pdr carronades.

Austerlitz Toulon Dyd. (Constructeur, Jean-Baptiste Lefebvre)
   Ord: 19.12.1805 and named. K: 10.4.1806. On ways 6.1806. L: 15.8.1808. Comm: 16.8.1809. C: 8.1809.
   Never recommissioned after 18/24ths refit of 1821-22. Struck 8.3.1837, BU 1837.

Ville de Paris Rochefort Dyd. (Constructeurs, Rigault de Genouilly, Jean Chaumont, Antoine Bonnet-Lescure, Jean Clarke, Charles-Louis Duchalard, Henri De Lisleferme, Pierre Jean-Baptiste Rossin, and Louis Fabre d'Églantine)
   Ord: 19.7.1806 and named (as *Marengo*). On ways 5.1808. Comm: 1.4.1851. C: 9.1851.
   Guns as completed (1855): LD 24 x 30pdrs No.1, 4 x 22cm No.1 shell, 4 x 50pdrs; MD 28 x 30pdrs No.2, 6 x 22cm No.2 shell; UD 34 x 30pdrs No.3; SD 12 x 16cm shell.
   Renamed *Comte d'Artois* 8.7.1814, reverting to *Ville de Vienne* 22.3.1815 then *Comte d'Artois* again 15.7.1815; her final renaming on 9.8.1830 was as *Ville de Paris*. L: 5.10.1850. Decomm. 4.7.1855, steam 1858.

Wagram Toulon Dyd. (Constructeurs, François Poncet and others)
   Ord: 1809. K: 4.1809. L: 1.7.1810. Comm: 11.2.1811. C: 3.1811.
   Never recommissioned after 18/24ths refit of 1818-21. Struck 15.10.1836, BU 1837.

Impérial Toulon Dyd. (Constructeurs, Antoine Arnaud and Jean-Nicolas Guérin)
   Ord: 4.6.1810. K: 2.7.1810. Named 14.7.1810. L: 1.12.1811. C: 8.1812. Comm: 24.8.1812.
   Renamed *Royal Louis* 9.4.1814, *Impérial* 22.3.1815, and *Royal Louis* 15.7.1815. Decomm. 11.6.1816. Refit stopped, struck and ordered BU 31.3.1825.

A coloured lithograph by Louis Le Breton of *Friedland* tacking to enter the Bosphorus, with a British two-decker to starboard. A unit of the Anglo-French fleet sent to the Black Sea at the start of the Crimean War, *Friedland* took part in the first bombardment of Sebastopol on 17 October 1854. (© National Maritime Museum PW8088)

Montebello Toulon Dyd. (Constructeurs, Antoine Arnaud and Jean-Nicolas Guérin)
    Ord: 1810. K: 10.1810. L: 6.12.1812. Comm: 1.7.1813. C: 8.1813. Decomm. 12.8.1850, steam 1852.

Sans Pareil Brest Dyd. (Constructeurs, Pierre Degay and Charles Simon)
    Ord: 15.3.1811. Named: 18.4.1811 (*Roi de Rome*, after Napoleon's son born 20.3.1811). K: 4.1811. Suspended 4.1813 at 3.56/24ths (or about 350 tons), not launched. Dismantled on the open ways in 6.1816 to preserve her timbers, which were used in a major refit of *Wagram* in 1818-21.

Louis XIV Rochefort Dyd. (Constructeurs, Paul Filhon, Antoine Bonnet-Lescure, Jean-Baptiste Hubert, Louis Fabre d'Églantine, Antoine Auriol, Pierre Rossin, Bernard Chariot, and Jean Clarke)
    K: 4.1811. L: 28.2.1854. Comm: 24.3.1854. C: 9.1854.
    Guns as completed (1856): LD 28 x 30pdrs No.1, 4 x 22cm No.1 shell; MD 30 x 30pdrs No.2, 4 x 22cm No.2 shell; UD 34 x 30pdrs No.3; SD 12 x 30pdrs No.4.
    Decomm. 27.10.1855, steam 1857.

Héros Toulon Dyd. (Constructeurs, Antoine Arnaud and Jean-Nicolas Guérin)
    Ord: 20.2.1812. K: 4.1812. Named: 21.5.1812. L: 15.8.1813. C: 1.1814. Never commissioned.
    Named after the flagship of Suffren. Struck 10.3.1828 and hulked. Date BU unknown.

Friedland Cherbourg Dyd. (Constructeur, Jean-Michel Segondat)
    Ord: 20.2.1812. K: 1.5.1812. Named: 10.9.1812 (*Inflexible*). L: 4.4.1840. C: 8.1840. Comm: 5.10.1840.
    Frame begun at Le Havre 7.1811. Poop deck modified 3.1851. Decomm. 1.1.1856. Conversion to steam at Toulon or Cherbourg with a 600nhp engine to be built at Marseille proposed 1.1857, cancelled 1858. Struck 31.12.1864. Renamed *Colosse* 8.4.1865, hospital hulk, then relieved *Généreux* as barracks hulk for seamen at Toulon. Replaced by *Alexandre* and BU 1879.

Souverain Toulon Dyd. (Constructeurs, François Poncet and Antoine Arnaud or Jean-Nicolas Guérin, then Louis-Charles Barrallier)
    Ord: 20.3.1813. K: 4.1813. L: 25.8.1819. C: 7.1821. Comm: 16.4.1840.
    Decomm. 10.5.1852, converted to steam 1854.

Trocadéro Toulon Dyd. (Constructeur, Louis Barrallier)
    Ord: 20.3.1813. K: 9.1813. L: 14.4.1824. C: 10.1824. Never commissioned.
    Renamed in 10.1823 to commemorate a recent victory in Spain. Burned 24.3.1836 at Toulon when the temporary roof protecting her hull while in reserve and which had been left on board the ship caught fire during a refit in drydock.

COMMERCE DE PARIS Class. A smaller design by Jacques-Noël

Sané, to which two ships were ordered built at Rochefort and Toulon on 8 May and 14 May 1804 respectively as prototypes for three-deckers to be built at Antwerp, the design thus being analogous to the *petit modèle* 74. Sané shortened the plans of his 118-gun three-decker to produce a ship with one less gun on each side on each deck, thus in effect returning to the concept of the 1779 designs with a similar 110-gun armament and with virtually identical dimensions. The Toulon ship was funded by a gift donated by Parisian merchants on 27 May 1803, and her initial name of *Ville de Paris* (given on 7 November 1804) was accordingly changed to *Commerce de Paris* two weeks later on 22 November. The Rochefort ship was initially named *Victorieux* on 21 November 1804, but was renamed *Iéna* on 23 February 1807, then renamed again *Duc d'Angouleme* at her launch (although the name *Iéna* was briefly restored during the Hundred Days and then more permanently in 1830).

Four more to the same design were laid down at Antwerp in 1810-11, but none of the latter ships were completed; the first pair were named *Monarque* and *Hymen* on 23 July 1810 (the second in commemoration of Napoleon's marriage to Marie-Louise). The second pair were ordered on 15 March 1811, and named *Neptune* and *Terrible* on 26 August 1811. In October 1811 Napoleon asked for three 110-gun ships to be begun at Amsterdam, but only one was ordered; two more were ordered in 1812, one at Amsterdam and one at Rotterdam. The fabrication of the frame for the first Amsterdam ship was begun during the summer of 1813 but none of these ships was laid down.

Dimensions & tons: 186ft 0in, 183ft 6in wl, 167ft 6in x 50ft 0in x 25ft 0in (60.42, 59.61, 54.41 x 16.24 x 8.12m). 2,600/4,755 tons. Draught 23½/25ft (7.66/8.12m). Men: 1,070.

Guns: LD 30 x 36pdrs; MD 32 x 24pdrs; UD 32 x 12pdrs; SD 16 x 8pdrs; both later had 10 x 8pdrs + 10 x 36pdr carronades, then (*Commerce de Paris* only by 1824) 6 x 8pdrs, 12 x 36pdr carronades + 6 x 36pdr bronze carronades. As a rasée in 1833, *Iéna* (ex *Duc d'Angouleme*) had a unique armament derived from the *Suffren* class: LD 26 x 36pdrs, 4 x 22cm shell; UD 32 x 30pdrs; SD 26 x 36pdr carronades, 4 x 18pdrs.

Commerce de Paris Toulon Dyd. (Constructeur, Jean-Baptiste Lefebvre)
Ord: 14.5.1804. K: 10.1804. Named 7.11.1804 (*Ville de Paris*). L: 8.8.1806. C: 5.1807. Comm: 25.6.1807.

Renamed *Commerce* 11.8.1830 to avoid confusion with the newly renamed *Ville de Paris*. By 1839 *Commerce* needed a major refit, which if done would have included reducing her to a two-decker like *Iéna*, but instead she was struck 26.1.1839. On 5.10.1839 she was selected to replace *Orion* to house the Naval Academy at Brest, the previously proposed replacement, *Tourville* (74), not being large enough for the expanding school. The ship was raséed (her upper deck was removed) in 11-12.1839, she was renamed *Borda* 18.12.1839, and was recommissioned 1.12.1840 as the new school ship. She was replaced 18.8.1863 by the 120-gun ship *Valmy* which took the name *Borda*, on the same date the former *Commerce* took the name *Vulcain* and replaced the frigate *Uranie* as headquarters hulk for the reserves at Brest and as a mechanics training ship and floating workshop. Condemned 4.1884, sold at Brest 1885 and BU.

Duc d'Angoulême Rochefort Dyd. (Constructeur, Paul Filhon)
Ord: 8.5.1804. Named: 21.11.1804 (*Victorieux*). K:6.4.1805. L: 30.8.1814. Comm: 26.11.1814. C: 1.1815.

Renamed *Iéna* 22.3.1815 but restored to *Duc d'Angouleme* 15.7.1815. Raséed to a 90-gun two-decker at Brest between 1826 and 1833 (re-launched 9.7.1831) and proved very successful. Renamed *Iéna* again 9.8.1830. Used as transport in 1854, decomm. 17.7.1856. Recomm. 1.1.1862 as headquarters ship for the reserves at Toulon, struck 31.12.1864 and as a service craft continued to be used as a headquarters hulk and as a mechanics' training ship and floating workshop. BU 1886 (also reported as 1915).

Monarque Antwerp.
K: 4.1810. Named 23.7.1810. Was 18.5/24ths complete on 1.4.1814, not launched. Allocated to the French 8.1814 and sold for BU on the ways.

Hymen Antwerp.
K: 5.1810. Named 23.7.1810. Not launched. Was 18.5/24ths complete on 1.4.1814. Allocated to the Allies 8.1814 and sold by the Dutch for BU on the ways.

Neptune Antwerp.
Ord: 15.3.1811. K: 5.1811. Named 26.8.1811. Was 10.25/24ths complete on 1.4.1814, not launched. Allocated to the French 8.1814 and sold for BU on the ways.

Terrible Antwerp.
Ord: 15.3.1811. K: 6.1811. Named 26.8.1811. Was 5/24ths complete on 1.4.1814, not launched. Allocated to the Allies 8.1814 and sold by the Dutch for BU on the ways.

In May 1808 Napoleon attempted to purchase from Spain the 112-gun *Santa Ana* (built in 1782-84 at Ferrol), as well as the 94-gun *San Carlos* (built at Havana in 1764-65), but the opening of hostilities between France and Spain later that month terminated this project. He also ordered in June that two new three-deckers (either 118-gun or 110-gun, presumably to the Sané design) were to be built at Cartagena, but this was not pursued in the light of the breach.

(D) Vessels acquired from 26 June 1815

In 1817 the standard armament of the '118-gun' three-decker was 32 x 36pdrs on the LD, 34 x 24pdrs on the MD, and 34 x 18pdrs on the UD, with 12 x 36pdr carronades and 14 x 8pdrs on the gaillards for an actual total of 126 pieces of ordnance. This was retained for the Sané-designed ships, although on 18 September 1828 their UD guns were replaced by an equal number of 36pdr carronades, while the gaillards were re-armed with 16 more 36pdr carronades and 4 long 18pdrs.

Under the reforms proposed by Tupinier in May 1822 and adopted on 10 March 1824, these were eventually to be superseded by ten ships of the 1st Rank, each carrying 32 long 30pdrs on the LD, 34 short 30pdrs on the MD, and 34 30pdr carronades on the UD, with 16 30pdr carronades and 4 long 18pdrs on the gaillards. As no new 1st Rank ships were ordered until 1836, the distinction is only academic. However, this remained in theory the standard armament for 1st Rank ships until 14 April 1838, when 4 of their MD guns were replaced by an equal number of 22cm shell guns, while all 34 UD guns and the 4 18pdrs on the gaillards were replaced by equal numbers of 16cm shell guns.

On 20 July 1848 the number of shell guns was increased, with another 8 of the 22cm type were added to the LD and a further 4 on the MD, replacing 30pdr guns in equal numbers; on the gaillards 4 carronades were removed, bringing the rated total down to 116 guns. The standard armaments were changed again on 27 July 1849 to introduce a new 50pdr gun and two new 30pdrs, but by this time changes in ordnance technology were occurring rapidly and each new ship ended up receiving its own individual armament, some of which are shown in the descriptions of the individual ships.

VALMY – 120 guns. This ship was the sole new sailing three-decker to be completed by the French Navy following 1815. The budget for 1829

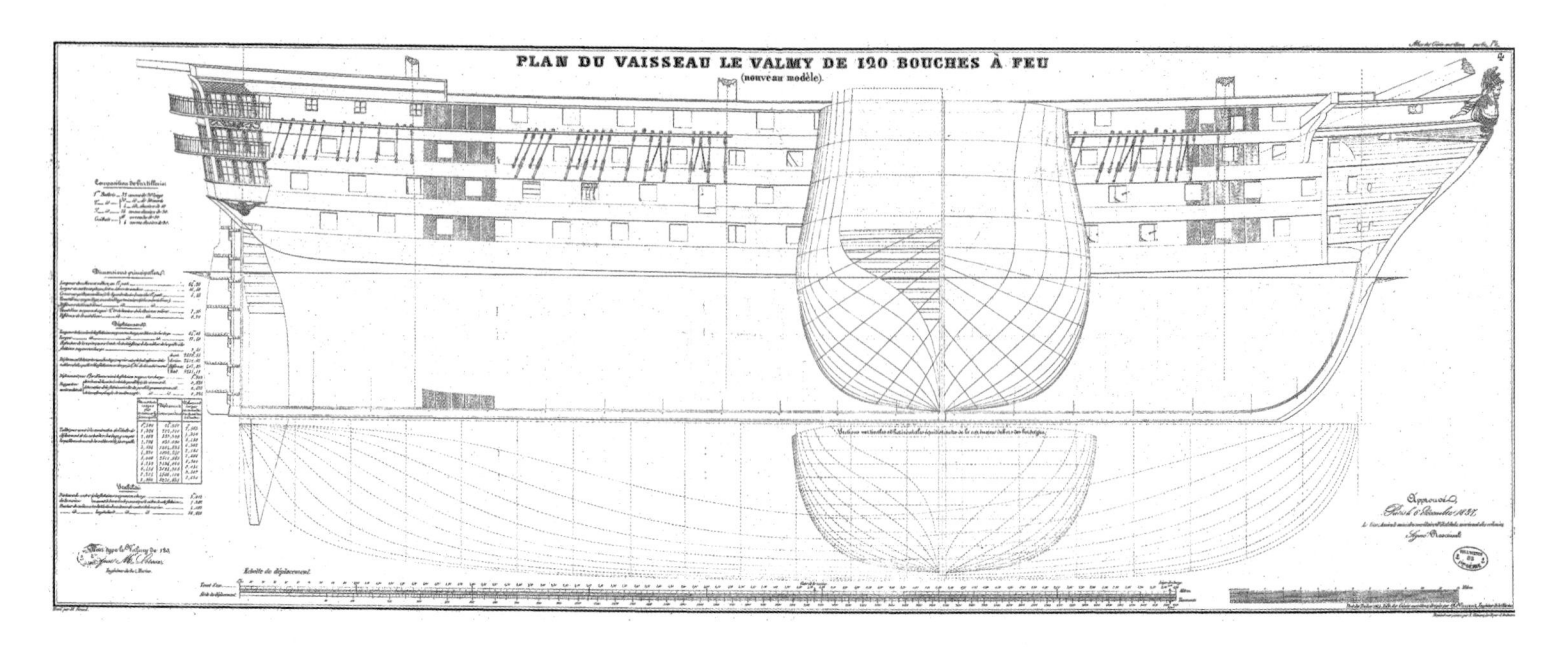

PLAN DU VAISSEAU LE VALMY DE 120 BOUCHES À FEU
(nouveau modèle)

The official sheer and body plan of *Valmy* as approved, 6 December 1837. A separate sail plan shows France's largest sailing warship with 3,351 sq.m. of canvas, not including royals. The sail area quoted on these draughts was primarily for stability calculation so only included the principal sails: in this case, courses, topsails and topgallants, plus a single headsail and the gaff spanker; some later draughts included royals, but these were added separately to the calculation. (Atlas du Génie Maritime, French collection, plate 4)

(presented in April 1828) included six ships of the line to be begun in 1829 at a new facility at Brest (the Anse St. Nicolas): the 1st Rank *Navarin* and *Formidable*, the 2nd Rank *Agamemnon* and *Hector*, and the 3rd Rank *Ajax* and *Diomède*. All but *Navarin* were cancelled in 1828 by a new Minister of Marine, Baron Guillaume Hyde de Neuville, who wanted to concentrate on frigate construction. *Navarin* was postponed on 16 November 1829 due to delays in completing the facility at Brest, reassigned to Toulon, and ordered built as a 100-gunner on 7 March 1832 after the navy could not decide whether it wanted 30pdr carronades or 16cm shell guns on the top decks of new three-deckers.

A three-decker named *Formidable* again appeared in the budget for 1837 (presented in January 1836) at Brest along with a 3rd Rank ship, *Argonaute*, at Toulon and a 2nd Rank frigate, *Clorinde*, at Brest. *Argonaute* and *Clorinde* were soon cancelled, but *Formidable* was renamed *Valmy* on 26 November 1836 and proceeded with. Her designer, Paul-Marie Leroux, generally followed the lines of Sané's *Montebello* (*Océan* type) but slightly increased the length and beam and reduced the tumblehome in the topsides. His plans were reviewed by the Council of Works on 22 May 1837 and approved by the Minister of Marine on 6 December 1837.

In this and the other large vessels of the post-Napoleonic navy the forecastle and quarterdeck were joined to form a complete spardeck, which although fully exposed could carry an unbroken tier of guns. Although the French had begun in the late 1820s to build some of their new warships with round sterns in an effort to strengthen them, *Valmy* was given a traditional square stern. *Valmy*'s designed draught was 7.95m mean and 8.30m aft with a displacement of 5231t and a height of the lower battery over the water of 2.00m. Initial trials showed that she was overweight and also raised questions regarding her stability, which was augmented by adding a 30cm thick, 3.00m high wood sheathing to the hull at the waterline. The modification also raised the actual height of her battery from 1.70m to 1.85m. Her designed armament was LD 32 x 30pdrs No.1; MD 34 x 30pdrs No.2; UD 34 x 30pdr carronades; SD 16 x 30pdr carronades, 4 x 18pdrs.

The French made several efforts to update their largest sailing warship. On 14 August 1855 the Council of Works reviewed plans by Henri-Jules Kerris at Toulon for removing the sheathing, lengthening her 13.44m amidships, and giving her 900nhp machinery. The result would have been a ship with the displacement and armament of the steam *Bretagne* but without that ship's fine lines. On 6 February 1856 it discussed plans by Jules Marielle for giving *Valmy* 500nhp machinery without lengthening her. When a set of 600nhp machinery was ordered from Napier on 20 February 1856 for *Louis XIV* the contract included an option for two more sets, the first of which was tentatively earmarked for *Valmy*, but this was cancelled in May 1856. The most ambitious plans were those submitted by Anselme De Roussel at Brest on 6 June 1859 for converting *Valmy* into an ironclad. Brest proposed removing two decks and fitting a battery armament of 20 x 50pdrs and 12 x 16cm rifles and a spardeck armament of 4 x 16cm rifles and 8 x 30pdr carronades (4 of which would be in a small armoured casemate with the conning station). On 5 July 1859 the Council of Works proposed modifying this project to retain part of the middle deck and form a much larger casemate with 18 x 16cm rifles, four of which could fire fore and aft over the lower ends. Armour in both proposals was 12cm, reduced to 10cm or 11cm at the edges and on the transverse bulkheads and the small casemates. None of these plans materialised and the ship remained in reserve after completing her Crimean War service in late 1855.

Dimensions & tons: 64.20m, 63.90m wl x 16.80m, 17.40m ext x 8.55m. 5,570 tons. Draught 8.00m/8.74m. After sheathing: Beam 18.11m ext and draught 8.21m mean / 8.59m aft. Men: 1089.

Guns: (1849) LD 24 x 30pdrs No.1, 8 x 22cm No.1 shell; MD 26 x 30pdrs No.2, 8 x 22cm No.2 shell; UD 34 x 16cm shell; SD 12 x 30pdr carronades, 4 x 16cm shell.

Valmy (ex *Formidable* 26.11.1836) Brest Dyd.
K: 1.3.1838. L: 25.9.1847. C: 1.1849. Comm: 12.2.1849.
Assumed the name *Borda* 18.8.1863 and replaced the former *Borda* (ex *Commerce de Paris*) as school hulk for the naval academy at Brest 1.10.1863. Struck 31.12.1864, continued training duty as a service craft. Replaced by *Intrépide* 1890, traded names with her replacement, and condemned and sold for BU 1891.

BRETAGNE Class – 120 guns. The budget for 1849 as presented in December 1847 included a new three-decker named *Terrible* to start construction at Brest in 1849, but she was cancelled during 1848 because of budget cuts. The budget for 1850, presented in August 1849, included two 1st Rank and one 4th Rank ships of the line to be begun in 1850. The 1st Rank ships, *Bretagne* at Brest and *Desaix* at Cherbourg, were finally ordered on 15 March 1851. (The 4th Rank ship, *La Tour d'Auvergne*, was not built.) The poor performance of *Valmy* in her trials caused the navy to return to Sané's classic three-decker design with minimal modifications for these ships. The modifications, carried out in mid-late 1851 by Joseph De Gasté for *Bretagne* and by Armand Forquenot for *Desaix*, were limited to a 20cm reduction in the tumblehome of each side and a slight increase in beam, which was justified on the grounds that the actual measurements of *Friedland*, *Montebello*, and *Souverain* exceeded their designed beam of 16.40m by 23cm, 24cm, and 12cm respectively. A proposal to give them 160nhp steam engines for 4.5kts was rejected to avoid compromising Sane's design. Machinery was to be added later if deemed useful.

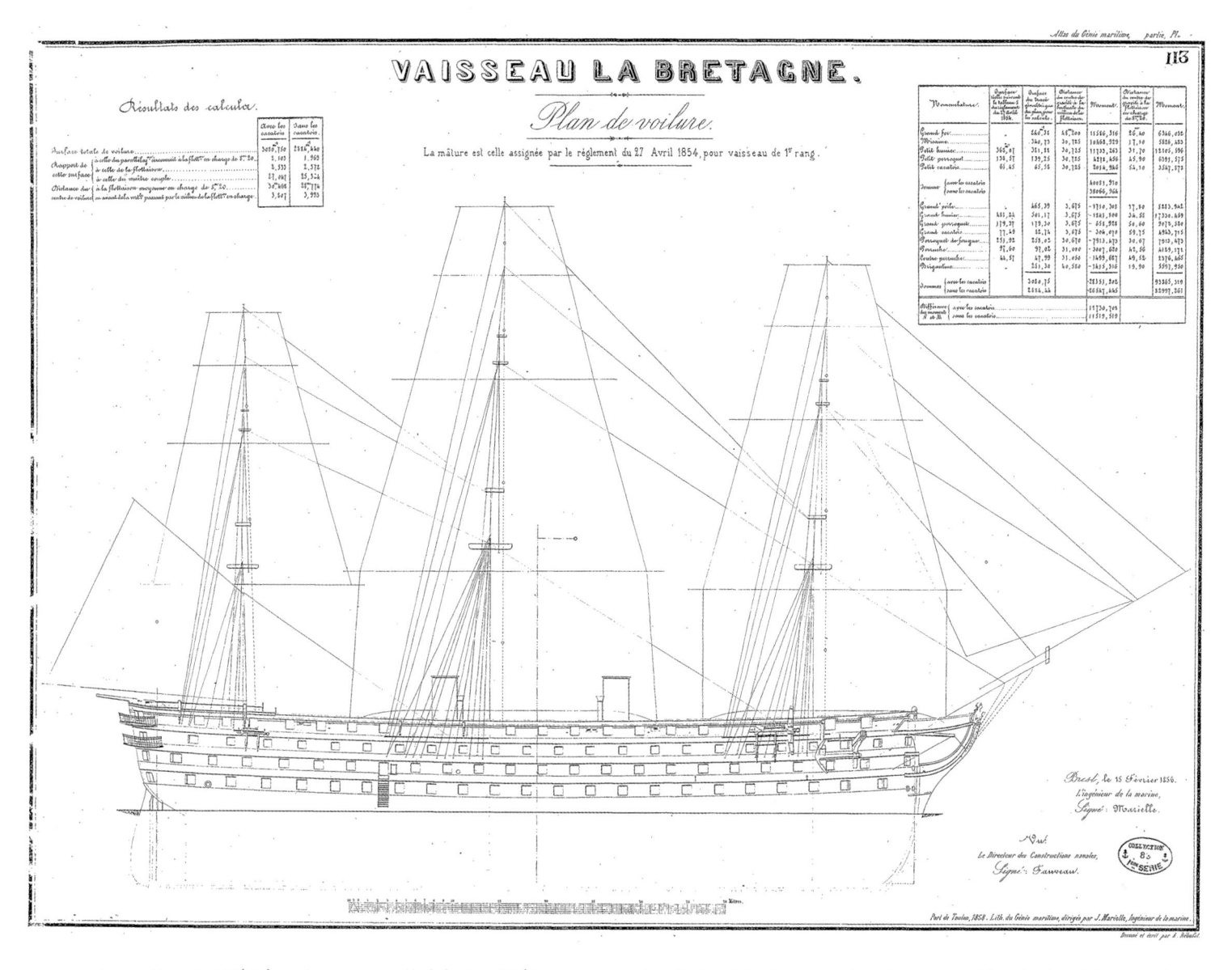

On 17 June 1852 the Minister of Marine suspended construction of these two ships and asked the ports to propose plans for lengthening them by 3.42m and giving them 540nhp engines. Brest submitted a plan on 4 September 1852, but in the meantime the *Napoléon* had achieved her brilliant trial results. The minister now wanted fast battleships and cancelled the two sailing ships on 10 September 1852.

The sail plan of the *Bretagne* as built with screw propulsion, dated 15 February 1856. The spar dimensions were as laid down by the regulation of 27 April 1854 for First Rates ('vaisseaux de 1er rang'), totalling 2,884 sq.m. (3,081 including royals). (Atlas du Génie Maritime, French collection, plate 113)

Under this decision *Bretagne,* which was 3/24ths complete, was to be transformed into a fast battleship, plans for which were to be prepared at Brest, while the construction of *Desaix* was abandoned. An order of 13 November 1852 stated that *Desaix*, which had barely been begun (a tenth of a 24th), had been replaced by a fast battleship of the *Napoléon* type (*Arcole*), which was to be 12/24ths built during 1853.

Dimensions & tons: As improved *Océan* class but with moulded beam increased to 16.64m. Tons unknown. Men: 1089.
Guns: (Designed) Probably similar to *Ville de Paris* as completed as a sailing ship c1851.

Bretagne Brest Dyd.
K: 4.8.1851. Not launched. Replaced 10.9.1852 by a fast battleship of the same name.

Desaix Cherbourg Dyd. (Constructeur, Amédée Mangin)
K: 27.10.1851. Not launched. Cancelled 10.9.1852.

(E) Screw three-deckers

Four of the three-deckers laid down in Napoleonic times were fitted with auxiliary screws from 1851 on. Two of the ships were fitted with 600hp engines built at Marseille and Toulon – *Souverain* in 1854 (originally launched in 1819) and *Ville de Paris* in 1858. In 1852 *Montebello* (first launched in 1812) was fitted with a 140hp engine built at Indret. And in 1854 *Louis XIV* (ex *Tonnant* renamed in 1828) was finally launched, fitted with a 600hp Napier engine. Plans to fit an engine to a fifth ship, *Friedland*, were abandoned and the engine was put instead into the two-decker *Turenne*. The navy also built one three-decker, *Bretagne*, with full steam power as in the smaller *Napoléon* class two-deckers, but the ship was not a success and was not repeated.

MONTEBELLO. On 9 June 1849 the Council of Works examined a proposal to give a 120-gun ship a steam engine considerably smaller than the one planned for *Charlemagne*. An engine of 120nhp would give the ship a maximum speed under steam of only 4 1/2 knots, but would not detract from its sailing qualities or military strength and would not require it to sacrifice any of its 6 months of provisions. On 13 December 1849 the Minister ordered the ports to prepare plans for fitting all four classes of ships of the line with such machinery, and on 12 February 1851 *Montebello* was chosen for the first conversion. Conversion plans by Stanislas-Charles-Henri Dupuy de Lôme were approved by the Council of Works on 28 May 1851. Her funnel was aft of the mainmast, the boiler having been placed in the old wine hold. The successful trials of ships with more powerful engines, first *Charlemagne* and then *Napoléon*, eclipsed this concept and *Montebello* remained the only French steam ship of the line of this low-powered type.

Dimensions & tons: 63.31m, 63.20m wl x 17.12m ext x 8.12m. 4,830t disp. Draught 7.19/7.99m. Men: 1063.
Machinery: 140nhp. Coal 199t.
Guns: (1852) LD 28 x 30pdrs No.1, 4 x 22cm No.1 shell; MD 28 x 30pdrs No.2, 4 x 22cm No.2 shell; UD 34 x 30pdrs No.3; SD 10 x 16cm shell.

Montebello Toulon Dyd/Indret.
Ord: 12.2.1851. Start: 1.4.1851. L: 23.8.1852. Comm: 25.8.1852. C: 8.1852.
Decomm. 13.9.1857. Relieved *Suffren* and served as gunnery training ship at Toulon 12.4.1860 to 28.11.1865. Struck 25.7.1867, barracks hulk at Toulon, Sold and BU 1889.

BRETAGNE. On 10 September 1852 Brest was ordered to prepare plans for the transformation of the sailing three-decker *Bretagne* (q.v.) to a fast battleship on the lines of *Napoléon*, using as many possible of the timbers cut for the sailing ship. Plans by Jules Marielle were approved on 13 December 1852 and a proposal to order the ship's machinery from Indret was approved two days later. The design by Charles-Henri Moll for this large propulsion plant was approved on 26 March 1853. As built (see below), *Bretagne* was heavier than intended: her designed displacement was 6,466 tons at 8.20m mean draught. When

Souverain after November 1876, when her engines were removed and she was fitted with 32 rifled guns to replace the 90-gun *Alexandre* as gunnery training ship at Toulon. This image shows most of her 1876 training armament of two 24cm, four 19cm, six 16cm, and two 10cm guns in the lower battery, sixteen 14cm and two 10cm in the middle battery, and none in the upper battery. Note the space for the screw forward of the rudder. (Marius Bar)

The internal arrangements of the *Ville de Paris* as lengthened and fitted for steam. The design received final ministerial approval on 16 January 1858. (Atlas du Génie Maritime, French collection, plate 638)

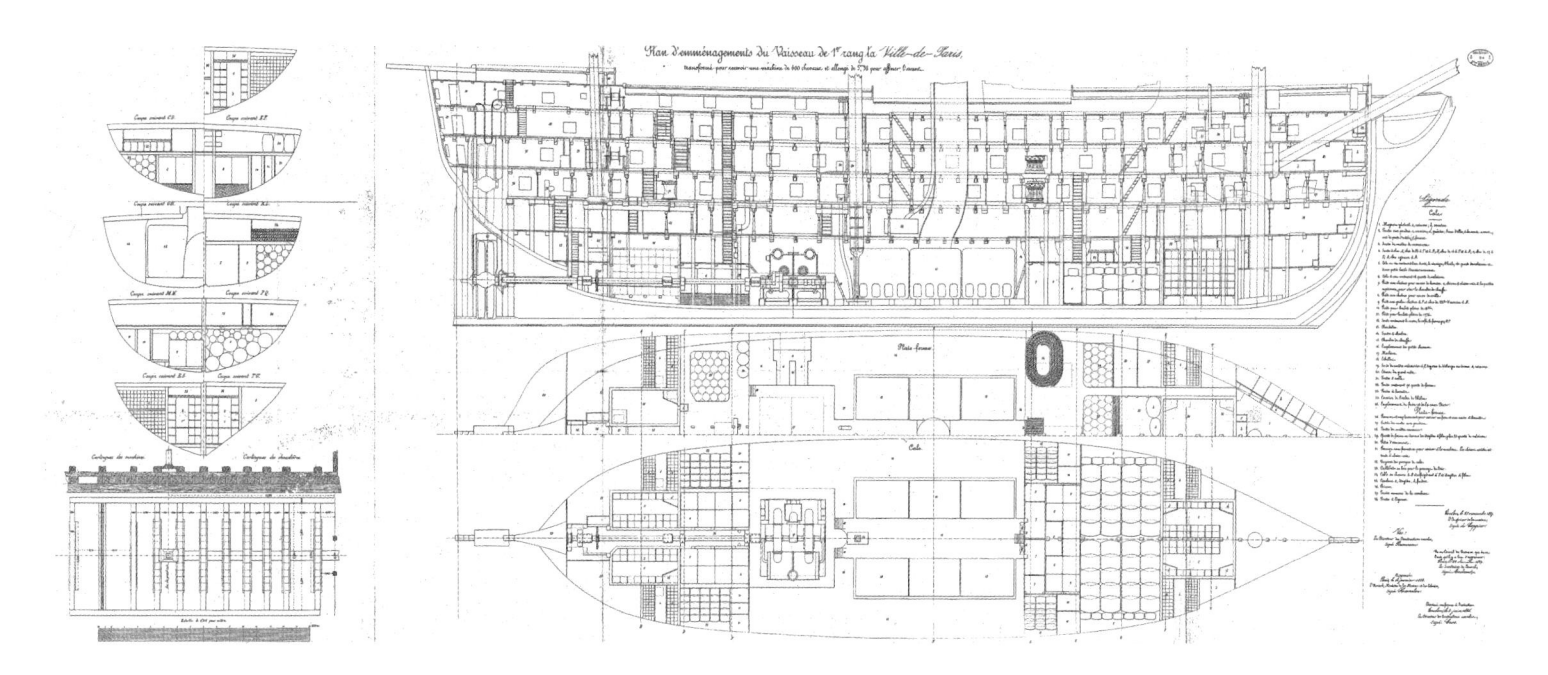

commissioned the height of her lower battery above the water was only 1.45m at 8.56m mean draught instead of the designed 1.76m. Her seagoing qualities were also disappointing, particularly when compared with the success of the *Napoléon* type. In January 1863 she left Toulon for Brest to replace her eight boilers, and she was decommissioned at Brest on 3 April 1863. However the navy evidently preferred to put new boilers in ironclads and in 1865 removed *Bretagne*'s machinery and fitted the ship as a barracks and school hulk.

Dimensions & tons: 81.00m, 81.00m wl, 78.50m x 18.08m ext, 17.40m x 8.35m. 6,874t disp. Draught 8.09/9.03m. Men: 1170.
Machinery: 1200nhp. 4 cylinders, 3327ihp, 12.8kts. Coal 590t.
Guns: (1855) LD 18 x 36pdrs, 18 x 22cm No.1 shell; MD 18 x 30pdrs No.2, 18 x 22cm No.2 shell; UD 38 x 30 No.3; SD 2 x 50pdrs, 18 x 30pdr carronades.

Bretagne Brest Dyd/Indret. (Constructeur, Marielle)
Ord: 13.12.1852. K: 1.1853. L: 17.2.1855. Comm: 1.6.1855. C: 6.1856.
Struck 26.7.1866, barracks hulk at Brest. Became gunnery school hulk in 1870 and school hulk for novices and apprentice seamen at Brest in 1873. Traded names with the ship that replaced her, *Ville de Bordeaux*, on 28.1.1880, condemned 1880, and BU 1881 at Brest.

SOUVERAIN. Toulon reported on 16 July 1853 that *Souverain* would probably need a refit and recommended fitting her with steam machinery larger than that in *Montebello*. Conversion plans by Louis-Auguste Silvestre du Perron were returned to him on 19 September 1853 for more work, but at the same time Toulon was directed to start work on the refit of the ship. On 5 April 1854 the Minister ordered Toulon to begin alterations of the stern based on new plans just completed by Silvestre du Perron. On 9 January 1854 the Forges et Chantiers de la Méditerranée (Philip Taylor) asked for an order for 650nhp engines for the ship but later renounced the project and Stanislas-Charles-Henri Dupuy de Lôme designed 600nhp machinery for construction at Toulon as a scaled down version of the 900nhp set he had designed for *Algésiras*. His plans were approved by the Minister on 21 December 1854. The ship was not lengthened, but fitting the stern with a hoisting screw and a second sternpost for the rudder increased her waterline length to 69.98m.

Dimensions & tons: 63.45m, 62.61m wl (to forward sternpost), 58.21m x 17.34m ext x 8.09m. 5,096t disp. Draught 7.48/8.38m. Men: 1079.
Machinery: 600nhp. 2 cylinders, return connecting rod, trials 1618ihp = 10.45kts. Coal 445t.
Guns: (1857) LD 16 x 36pdrs, 16 x 22cm No.1 shell; MD 24 x 30pdrs No.2, 8 x 22cm No.2 shell; UD 32 x 16cm shell; SD 2 x 16cm rifles, 12 x 30pdr carronades.

Souverain Toulon Dyd/Toulon.
Ord: 9.1853. Start: 11.1853. L: 11.1854. Comm: 16.3.1857. C: 6.1857.
Transported troops to Mexico 8-10.1862. Reclassified screw transport 1.1867, returned troops from Mexico 3-4.1867. Decomm. 21.2.1868. Her engines were removed 11.1876 and she replaced *Alexandre* as gunnery training ship at Toulon. Replaced as such by the ironclad *Couronne* 1885. Struck 8.12.1885, barracks hulk at Toulon for the Naval Infantry. Sold and BU 1905.

LOUIS XIV. This ship was among seven ships already afloat that were scheduled in late 1855 for conversion during 1856. Machinery for her was ordered from Napier in Britain by a contract approved on 20 February 1856 and an option under the contract was taken up on 19 March 1856 for a second 600nhp set for the proposed conversion of *Valmy* at Toulon. This second engine was cancelled in May 1856 and replaced with two of 500nhp for *Tage* and *Duguay Trouin*. *Louis XIV* was converted on plans by Bernard Chariot approved by the Council of Works on 2 September 1856.

Dimensions & tons: 63.90m, 63.28m wl x 17.40m ext x 8.13m. 5,170t disp. Draught 7.45/8.35m. Men: 1079.
Machinery: 600nhp. Coal 500t.
Guns: (1858) LD 28 x 30pdrs No.1, 4 x 22cm No.1 shell; MD 30 x 30pdrs No.2, 4 x 22cm No.2 shell; UD 34 x 30pdrs; SD 2 x 16cm rifles, 14 x 30pdr carronades.

Louis XIV Brest Dyd/Napier.
Ord: c10.1855. Start: 9.1856. L: 1857. Comm: 25.8.1857. C: 8.1857.

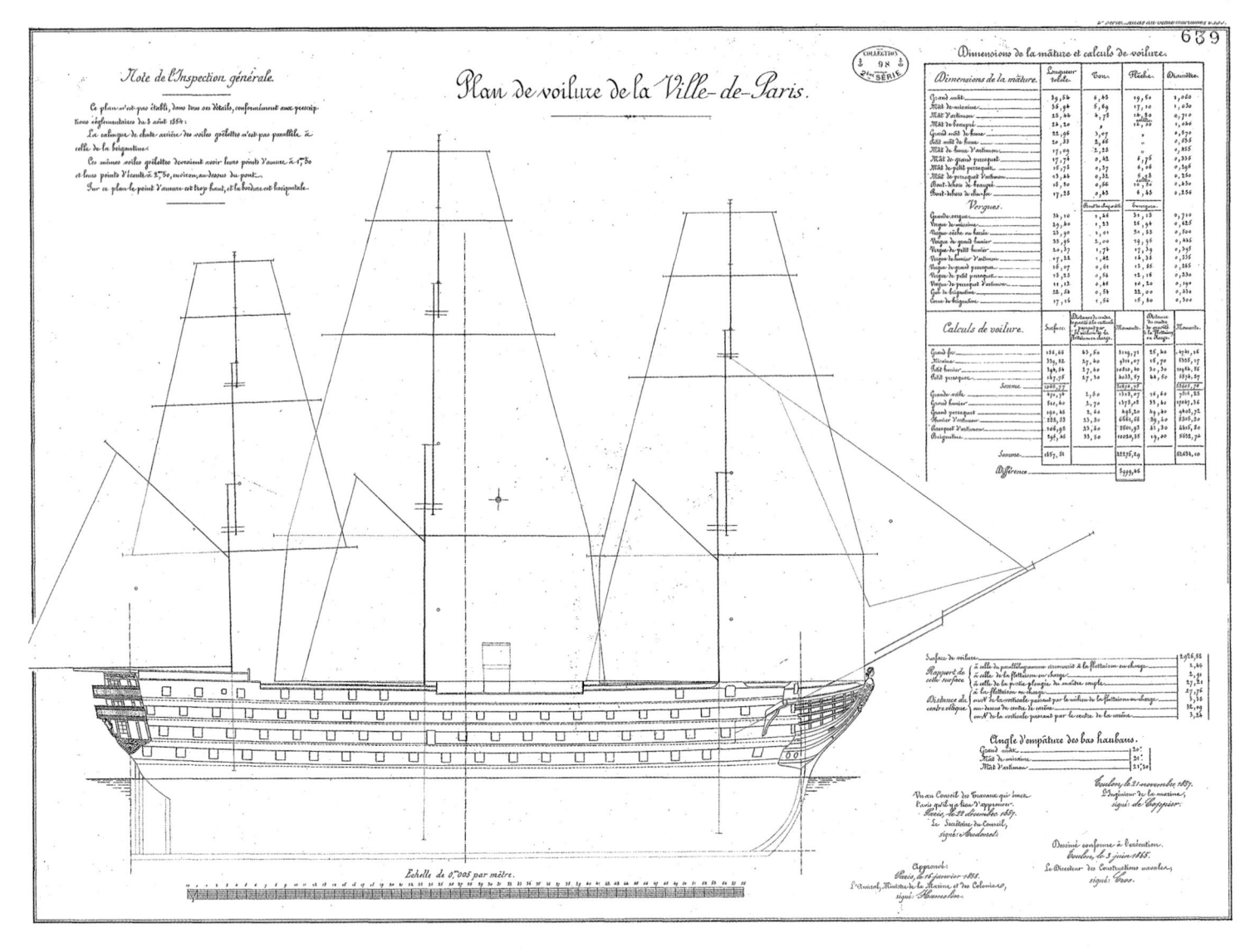

Official sail plan for the *Ville de Paris* agreeable to the regulations of 3 August 1854. Sail area for calculation totalled 1,858 sq.m. The plan is dated Toulon 21 November 1857 and was finally approved by the Minister of Marine on 16 January 1858. (Atlas du Génie Maritime, French collection, plate 639)

Became gunnery training ship at Brest 1861, moved to Toulon and relieved *Montebello* 1865, and continued to serve as training ship to 1872. Rated transport 3.1873. Struck 3.5.1880. Sold 1882 for BU, but alternatively reported as a school hulk at Hyères from 1885 to 1914 and then a barracks hulk at Toulon for a few more years.

VILLE DE PARIS. This ship and her sister *Friedland* were among seven ships already afloat that were scheduled in late 1855 for conversion during 1856. Their engines were ordered from the Forges et Chantiers de la Méditerranée by a contract approved on 11 June 1856. *Friedland*'s conversion, also planned for Toulon, was never ordered and her engines were used in *Turenne*. Hull plans for *Ville de Paris* by Hyacinthe De Coppier were approved on 1 September 1857 and provided for modifying the stern for the screw and lengthening the bow by 5.38m.

Dimensions & tons: 68.50m, 69.05m wl x 17.15m ext x 8.40m. 5,302t disp. Draught 7.34/8.34m. Men: 1079.

Machinery: 600nhp. Trials 1581ihp = 10.59kts. Coal 450t.

Guns: (1859) LD 16 x 36pdrs, 16 x 22cm No.1 shell; MD 24 x 30pdrs No.2, 8 x 22cm No.2 shell; UD 32 x 16cm shell; SD 2 x 16cm rifles, 8 x 16cm shell.

Ville de Paris Toulon Dyd/FCM.
  Ord: c10.1855. Start: 7.1857. L: 5.1858. Comm: 1.8.1858. C: 8.1858.
  Decomm. 20.9.1864. School for engineers at Brest 1864. Converted at Toulon to a steam transport 1867 to 1.1868 but remained in reserve. Struck 7.2.1882, barracks hulk at Toulon for the Naval Infantry. Sold 2.3.1898 at La Seyne, BU completed 7.1898.

2 Two-decker Ships of the Line, 80 to 100 guns

(Vaisseaux à deux ponts de 80 à 100)
(rated Vaisseaux de 2ème and 3ème Rang from 1824)

The French 80-gun ship resembled the contemporary three-deckers of around 1780 in that they similarly mounted thirty 36pdr guns on their lower decks, and they also carried a battery of thirty-two 24pdrs (18pdrs in early ships) on the deck above. The difference, of course, is that as two-deckers they lacked a third continuous gundeck. Most were of similar length to the three-deckers, but were several feet less in breadth.

The type had originated with the *Tonnant* of 1743 – the first two-decker in the French Navy to be pierced to carry thirty guns on the lower deck. Four more were built at the close of the War of 1744-48 (of which one – the *Duc de Bourgogne* – survived past 1786) and another in 1753, but four of the five were lost in 1758-59. Two replacements were ordered in 1762, and these – like all subsequent 80s, survived into the Revolutionary Era.

By about 1808 the progressive enclosure of the waist between the forecastle and quarterdeck to create a continuous structure had effectively turned this type into a three-decker with a flush spardeck. The addition of further ordnance on this spardeck had meant that the newer ships carried 90 guns, and this process continued after 1815. In 1824 improvements in construction meant that the designs could be stretched so that an extra pair of gunports and guns could be mounted on both the lower and upper decks, while three pairs were added to the spardeck to create 100-gun ships.

(A) Vessels in service or on order at 1 January 1786

In 1786 there were seven 80-gun ships extant. Each carried a battery of thirty 36pdrs on the lower deck, and – apart from the elderly *Duc de Bourgogne* - had 24pdrs on the upper deck; each was nominally established with a complement of 700 men in wartime and 490 in peace.

DUC DE BOURGOGNE. Designed by François-Guillaume Clairin-Deslauriers, and built by Antoine Groignard. This vessel was significantly shorter than the other six surviving 80s, and differed from them by carrying 18pdrs on its upper deck. Ordered as *Brave*, she was renamed at launch in honour of the birth of the new heir. Largely rebuilt between 1784 and 1794, she was renamed *Peuple* on 29 September 1792, then again as *Caton* in February 1794.
  Dimensions & tons: 173ft 0in x 44ft 0in x 21ft 0in (56.20 x 14.29 x 6.82m). 1,800/3,400 tons. Draught 21ft 10in (7.1m). Men: 860-910.
  Guns: LD 30 x 36pdrs; UD 32 x 18pdrs; SD 18 x 8pdrs.
Duc de Bourgogne Rochefort Dyd
  K: 1748. L: 20.10.1751. C: 1752.
  Condemned at Brest 10.1800 and BU in early 1801.

LANGUEDOC. Designed by Joseph-Marie-Blaise Coulomb, and ordered (and named) on 9 December 1761. By 1786 she mounted 86 guns (including 4 smaller weapons on the dunette). Her construction was funded by the États du Languedoc.
  Dimensions & tons: 188ft 0in, 168ft 0in x 48ft 4in x 23ft 2in (61.07, 54.57 x 15.70 x 7.52m). 2,100/3,850 tons. Draught 21ft 4in/22ft 7in. (6.93/7.33m). Men: 860-970.
  Guns: LD 30 x 36pdrs; UD 32 x 24pdrs; SD 18 x 8pdrs; in 1778 another 8 x 8pdrs were added (plus an extra pair of 24pdrs on the UD); in 1783, 18 x 8pdrs were removed (as was the extra pair of 24pdrs) and replaced by 12 x 12pdrs, while 4 x 4pdrs were mounted on the dunette roof.
Languedoc Toulon Dyd
  K: 5.1762. L: 14.5.1765. C: 11.1767.
  Renamed *Antifédéraliste* 21.4.1794, then *Victoire* 8.3.1795. Condemned 1798 and BU 1799.

SAINT ESPRIT. Designed by Joseph-Louis Ollivier, and ordered on 11 January 1762. Her construction was funded by the membership of the chivalric Order of the Holy Spirit (*Ordre du Saint-Esprit*).
  Dimensions & tons: 184ft 0in, 168ft 0in x 48ft 6in x 23ft 3in (59.77, 54.57 x 15.75 x 7.55m). 2,100/3,850 tons. Draught 21ft 4in/24ft (6.93/7.80m). Men: 860-970.
  Guns: LD 30 x 36pdrs; UD 32 x 24pdrs; SD 18 x 8pdrs.
Saint Esprit Brest Dyd
  K: 5.1762. L: 12.10.1765. C: 1766.
  Renamed *Scipion* 2.1794. Wrecked off Brest 26.1.1795.

AUGUSTE. Designed by Léon-Michel Guignace, and named on 20 February 1778. This was actually an 84-gun ship, carrying 4 extra 8pdrs on the gaillards (thus 84 guns in all); these were replaced in 1793-95 as shown below.
  Dimensions & tons: 186ft 0in, 171ft 0in x 46ft 0in x 23ft 0in (60.42, 55.55 x 14.94 x 7.47m). 2,100/3,850 tons. Draught 21/24ft (6.82/7.80m). Men: 850-860.
  Guns: LD 30 x 36pdrs; UD 32 x 24pdrs; SD 22 x 8pdrs; by 1795 carried 18 x 12pdrs and 6 x 36pdr obusiers.
Auguste Brest Dyd. (Constructeur, Pierre-Alexandre-Laurent Forfait)
  K: 12.1777. L: 18.9.1778. C: 1.1779.
  Renamed *Jacobin* 3.1793, then *Neuf Thermidor* in 12.1794. Wrecked 9.1.1795 off Brest.

TRIOMPHANT. Designed by Joseph-Marie Blaise Coulomb. Ordered 29 November 1777 and named on 20 February 1778.
  Dimensions & tons: 183ft 10in, 164ft 0in x 48ft 0in x 23ft 9in (59.72, 53.27 x 15.59 x 7.71m). 1,950/3,720 tons. Draught 22ft 4in/24ft (7.25/7.80m). Men: 860-910.
  Guns: LD 30 x 36pdrs; UD 32 x 24pdrs; SD 18 x 8pdrs.
Triomphant Toulon Dyd.
  K: 3.1778. L: 31.3.1779. C: 6.1779.
  Handed over to the Anglo-Spanish forces at Toulon in August 1793, and burnt by them at the evacuation on 18 December; recovered by the French and refloated in 1805, but not restored and BU in 1806.

COURONNE. Originally designed by Antoine Groignard, and built 1766-68 at Brest, but burnt accidentally in April 1781 and rebuilt over that year with 7½ft added to her length.

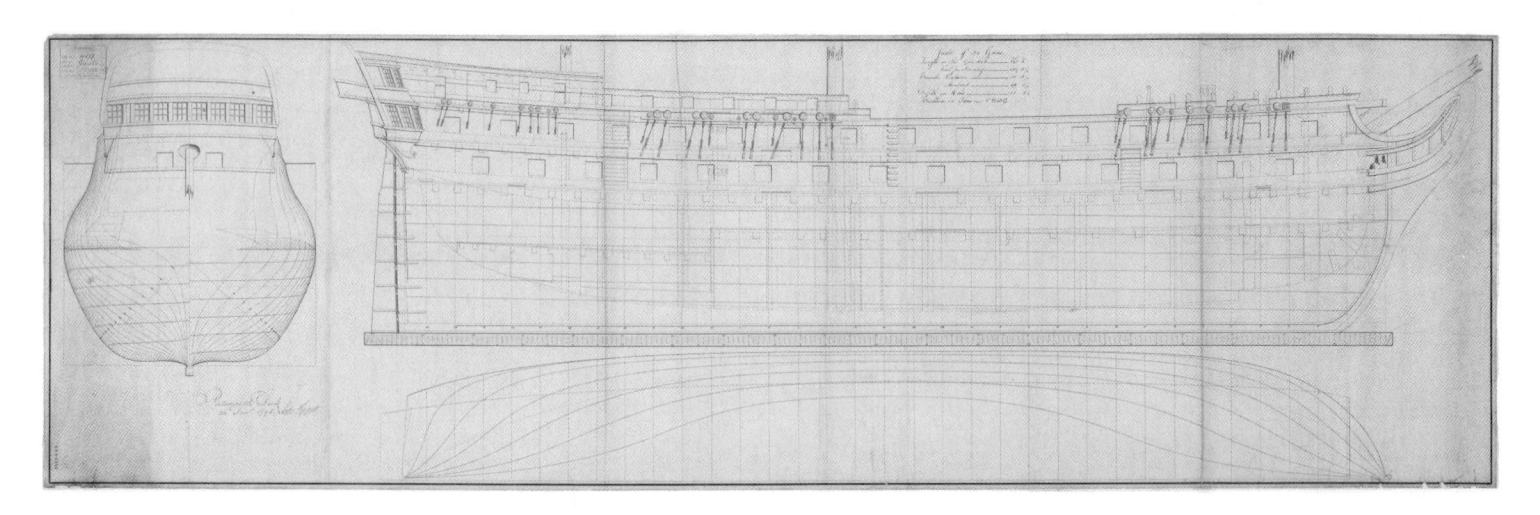

Admiralty sheer draught of *Juste* (ex *Deux Frères*) as taken off at Portsmouth, 24 January 1795. Despite having fifteen gunports on the lower deck, such was the length of these ships that there was no crowding in the battery and no need to bear the weight of guns right forward and right aft. (© National Maritime Museum J7772)

   Dimensions & tons: 190ft 6in, 168ft 6in x 46ft 0in x 23ft 0in
      (61.88, 54.74 x 14.94 x 7.47m). 2,100/3,850 tons. Draught
      22½/24ft (7.31/7.80m). Men: 860-970.
   Guns: LD 30 x 36pdrs; UD 32 x 24pdrs; SD 18 x 8pdrs.
Couronne Brest Dyd. (Constructeur, Pierre Degay)
   K: 5.1781. L: 18.9.1781. C: 10.1781.
   Renamed as *Ça Ira* on September 1792. Handed over to the Anglo-Spanish forces at Toulon in August 1793, but recovered by the French in December. Captured again by Hotham's squadron off Genoa on 14 March 1795, but burnt accidentally (again!) in April 1796.

DEUX FRÈRES. Designed by Antoine Groignard. The construction was funded by Louis XVI's two brothers (the Comte de Provence and the Comte d'Artois), and named for them on 20 July 1782.
   Dimensions & tons: 184ft 0in, 174ft 0in x 46ft 6in x 23ft 0in
      (59.77, 56.52 x 15.10 x 7.47m). 1,900/3,800 tons. Draught
      22/23ft (7.15/7.47m). Men: 850-860.
   Guns: LD 30 x 36pdrs; UD 32 x 24pdrs; SD 18 x 8pdrs; 4 x 36pdr obusiers were added by 1794.
Deux Frères Brest Dyd. (Constructeur, Pierre-Augustin Lamothe)
   K: 7.1782. L: 13 or 17.9.1784. C: 1785.
   Renamed as *Juste* on 29 September 1792. Captured by Howe's fleet off Ushant on 1 June 1794, and became HMS *Juste*. Condemned 1809 and BU 1811.

Another 80-gun ship, to have been named *Monarque*, was planned to be built in 1782 at Rochefort, probably to a design by François-Guillaume Clairin-Deslauriers along similar lines to his three-decker *Invincible*, but was cancelled in February 1783.

(B) Vessels acquired from 1 January 1786

The 1786 Program for new construction drafted by Borda (and approved by Castries) included the construction of twelve 80s, for which Sané's new draught for the *Tonnant* class was selected in 1787. The program also included nine new 118s and 60 new 74s. However, the arrival of a financial crisis soon after saw Castries attacked for attempting to maintain the construction program. Finally he felt compelled to resign, and was replaced as Navy Minister on 25 August 1787 by the Comte de Montmorin, who in turn on 26 December was superseded by the Comte de La Luzerne. Under the latter, who attempted to retain Castries's program, were ordered the first of a series of large and impressive two-deckers of 80 guns. These powerful ships were more than 10ft longer than the standard 74s, which gave them higher speed, but were just as weatherly as the smaller two-deckers, and they provided more effective flagships for flying squadrons than the high-sided three-deckers. Against this, their length and lighter French scantlings put a strain on the wooden technology of the day, tending towards structural weaknesses which made them prone to hogging and leakage. Although those captured by the British were highly prized, the resultant tendency of their captors to retain them in service for extended periods meant that they required greater than average time and expense to keep them fit for service.

TONNANT Class. The largest of the two-deckers designed by Jacques-Noël Sané, whose plans for the prototype were approved on 29 September 1787. With sixteen LD ports per side (although only fifteen were routinely provided with 36pdr guns) these were the most effective two-deckers of their era; their broadside of 1,102 *livres* (French pounds) equated to 1,190 English pounds, over 50% more than the standard British 74, and even greater than a British 100-gun three-decker. Five ships were ordered from 1787 to 1793, and all were completed during the 1790s; six more were ordered in January 1794 to be built (all at Toulon) but only three of these were named and commenced.

Two of these ships underwent name changes during construction; the *Formidable* was renamed *Figuières* on 4 December 1794, but her original name was restored on 31 May 1795, some 11 weeks after being launched; and *Foudroyant* was renamed *Dix-huit Fructidor* in December 1797 (in honour of the coup d'état carried out two months earlier – 4 September 1797 – when the three Jacobin members of the Directory arrested their royalist colleague François Barthélémy and caused the remaining moderate, Lazare-Nicolas Carnot, to flee the country, as well as removing many deputies from the Assembly) but the original name was restored in February 1800 after the Directory fell.
   Dimensions: 182ft 6in, 167ft 0in x 47ft 0in x 23ft 6in (59.28, 54.25
      x 15.27 x 7.64m). 2,034/3,868 tons. Draught 21ft 8in/24ft 0in
      (7.04/7.80m). Men (1786): 854 in wartime/594 in peacetime. By
      1802 these totals had risen to those specified in Section (C) below
      for the *Bucentaure* class. The 1786 complement included 12
      officers (14 by 1802).

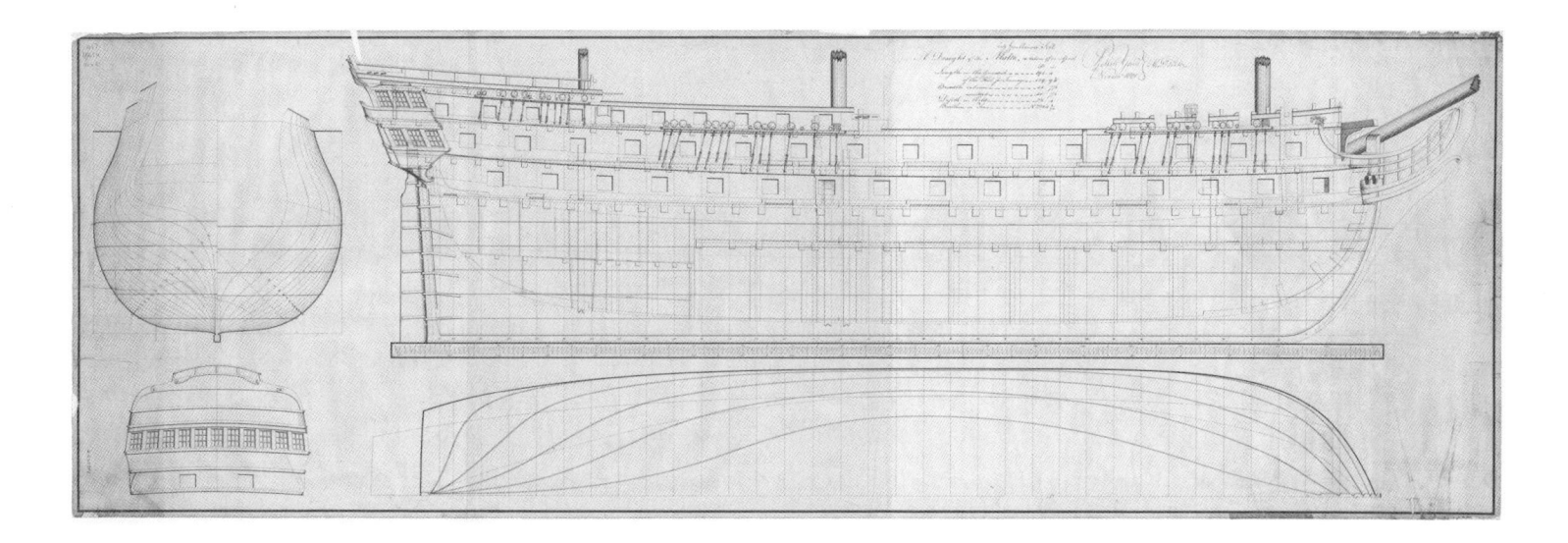

Admiralty sheer draught of *Malta* (ex *Guillaume Tell* of the *Tonnant* class) as taken off in April 1801. All but one of this class were captured or destroyed by the Royal Navy, and four were to enjoy long careers in their new service. The prizes were highly regarded by British officers, but they proved costly and time-consuming to maintain. (© National Maritime Museum J2377)

Guns: LD 30 x 36pdrs; UD 32 x 24pdrs; SD 18 x 12pdrs + 4 x 36pdr obusiers. By around 1807 the *Foudroyant* – last survivor among the eight – had on the gaillards 6 x 12pdrs and 12 x 36pdr carronades.

Tonnant Toulon Dyd.
  Ord: 19.10.1787. K: 11.1787. L: 24.10.1789. C: 9.1790.
  Handed over to Anglo-Spanish forces at Toulon in 8.1793, but restored to French Navy 12.1793. Captured by Nelson's fleet in Aboukir Bay 2.8.1798, becoming HMS *Tonnant* (broken up 1821).

Indomptable Brest Dyd.
  Ord: 19.10.1787 (named). K: 9.1788. L: 20.12.1790. C: 4.1793.
  Refitted at Toulon 1803-7.1804. Wrecked 22.10.1805 off Rota following the Battle of Trafalgar.

Sans Pareil Brest Dyd.
  Ord: 23.4.1790. K: 19.1790. L: 8.6.1793. C: 9.1793.
  Captured by Howe's fleet off Ushant in the in Glorious First of June Battle 1.6.1794, becoming HMS *Sans Pareil* (broken up 1842).

Indivisible Brest Dyd. (constructeurs, Léon-Michel Guignace and Jacques-Augustin Lamothe)
  Ord: by 31.8.1793 (named). K: 25.5.1793. L: 8.7.1799. C: 10.1799.
  Renamed *Alexandre* 5.2.1803. Captured by Duckworth's squadron in the roadstead of San Domingo 6.2.1806, becoming HMS *Alexandre* (hulk 1808, sold 5.1822).

Foudroyant Rochefort Dyd. (constructeur, Pierre Rolland; after 4.1798 by Entreprise Destouches)
  Ord: unknown. K: 11.1793. Construction interrupted 1795. L: 18.5.1799. C: 8.1800. Comm: 28.3.1801.
  Struck 26.10.1833, BU 1834.

Formidable Toulon Dyd. (constructeur, Jean-Jacques Le Roy and, from 1794, Jean-Jacques Abauzir)
  Named 5.10.1794. K: 8.1794. L: 17.3.1795. C: 27.10.1795.
  Captured by Strachan's squadron off Cape Ortegal 4.11.1805 after Trafalgar, becoming HMS *Brave* (hulk 1808, broken up 4.1816).

Guillaume Tell Toulon Dyd. (Constructeurs, Jean-Jacques Le Roy and, from 1794, Jean-Jacques Abauzir)
  Named 5.10.1794. K: 9.1794. L: 21.10.1795. C: 7.1796.
  Captured by HMS *Foudroyant*, *Lion* and *Penelope* off Malta 30.3.1800, becoming HMS *Malta* (hulk 1831, broken up 8.1840).

Franklin Toulon Dyd. (constructeur, Jean-Jacques Le Roy and, from 1794, Jean-Jacques Abauzir)
  Named 5.10.1794. K: 11.1794. L: 25.6.1797. C: 3.1798.
  Captured by Nelson's fleet in Aboukir Bay 2.8.1798, becoming HMS *Canopus* (broken up 1887).

(C) Vessels acquired from 25 March 1802

BUCENTAURE Class – 80 guns. A modified version of the *Tonnant* class, and officially recorded as being of the same class. *Neptune* (1803) was recorded as having been built to Sané's plans for *Alexandre* (ex *Indivisible*), while *Eylau* was built on the plans of *Bucentaure* which were sent from Toulon for the purpose. For ease of study, they are grouped below according to the dockyard in which they were built.

Recorded armaments on the gaillards in these ships varied over time. The two earliest ships, launched in 1803 (*Bucentaure* and *Neptune*), had 18 x 12pdrs and 6 x 36pdr obusiers (the 1786 ordinance), with *Neptune* allegedly also having 6 x 27pdr carronades. Two ships launched in 1806-8 (*Robuste* and *Donawerth*) had 10 x 12pdrs and 16 x 36pdr carronades, of which 6 were bronze guns. There followed two vessels launched in 1808-9 (*Ville de Varsovie* and *Eylau*) with 14 x 12pdrs and 10 x 36pdr carronades (a change called for in the new artillery Ordinance of 1807), *Eylau* also being credited with 4 obusiers. Finally came eight ships launched in 1810-12 (*Friedland*, *Sceptre*, *Tilsitt*, *Diadème*, *Conquérant*, *Auguste*, *Illustre*, and *Pacificateur*) with what evidently became the late wartime standard for the class, 14 x 12pdrs and 14 x 36pdr carronades (including 4 of bronze that may not have been carried), although the last three of these ships were, probably in error, listed with only 30 x 24pdrs on the UD.

  Dimensions: 182ft 6in, 167ft 0in x 47ft 0in x 23ft 6in (59.28, 54.25 x 15.27 x 7.64m). 2,034/3,868 tons. Draught 21ft 8in/24ft 0in (7.04/7.80m). Men: 866 in wartime/626 in peacetime.
  Guns: LD 30 x 36pdrs; UD 32 x 24pdrs; SD 18 x 12pdrs and 6 x 36pdr obusiers in the 1786 ordinance; in the 1806 règlement the SD armament was replaced by 14 x 12pdrs and 10 x 36pdr carronades.

PLAN DU VAISSEAU LE DUQUESNE, DE 86 BOUCHES A FEU.

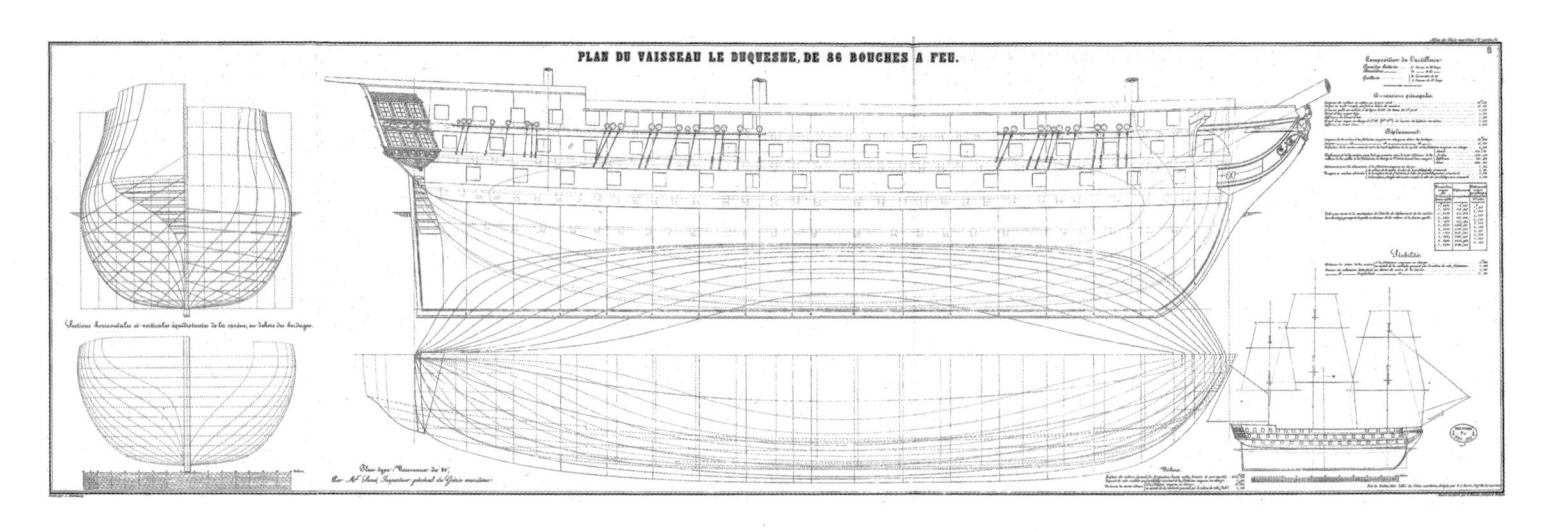

The Napoleonic naval administration introduced a remarkable degree of standardisation in warship building, and although designs were subject to minor variations between yards, the principal elements of the specification were centrally determined. The most widely adopted designs were the work of Jacques-Noël Sané, as with the 80-gun *Bucentaure* class, of which twenty-seven were laid down. This official sheer draught of *Duquesne* shows the post-war appearance of the class as 86-gun ships, with forecastle and quarterdeck barricades joined but no gunports in the waist; the bow was built up and enclosed resulting in a very heavy looking head, but this became the standard pattern in the French Navy. All plain sail (minus royals) totalled 2,852 sq.m. (Atlas du Génie Maritime, French collection, plate 8)

Toulon Group

Bucentaure Toulon Dyd
   Ord: 16.9.1802. Named 29.9.1802. K: 22.11.1802. L: 14.7.1803. Comm: 11.1.1804. C: 1.1804.
   French flagship at the Battle of Trafalgar, 21 October 1805, captured there by the British, retaken by her crew the next day while drifting in stormy weather but wrecked later that day off the entrance to Cadiz.

Neptune Toulon Dyd.
   Ord: 16.9.1802. Named 30.9.1802. K: 4.1.1803. L: 15.8.1803. Comm: 21.4.1804. C: 4.1804.
   Took refuge at Cadiz after Trafalgar, surrendered to Spanish insurgents there 14.6.1808, Spanish *Neptuno*. BU 1820.

Robuste Toulon Dyd. (Constructeur, Jean-Baptiste Lefebvre)
   Ord: 26.3.1805. K: 5.1805. L: 30.10.1806. Comm: 6.5.1807. C: 5.1807.
   Grounded near Sète 26.10.1809 with *Lion* (74) while being chased by the British and burnt to avoid capture.

Donawerth Toulon Dyd. (Constructeurs, François Poncet and others)
   Ord: 11.8.1806. K: 15.12. 1806. L: 4.7.1808. Comm: 1.10.1808. C: 10.1808.
   Beyond repair and struck 8.1823, BU completed 1.1824.

Sceptre Toulon Dyd. (Constructeurs, François Poncet and others)
   Ord: 26.12.1808. Named 27.3.1809. K: 3.1809. L: 15.8.1810. Comm: 17.3.1811. C: 3.1811.
   Struck 10.3.1828, became a barracks hulk at Toulon, and was destroyed by fire 16.1.1830.

Rochefort. A single vessel was built at Rochefort. Her frames were made at Bayonne from 30 April 1804 by Jean Baudry, and shipped to Rochefort. Initially to have taken the name *Tonnant*, she was renamed after the City of Warsaw on 14 May 1807. A second 80-gun ship was ordered at Rochefort in 1812 but was neither named nor built.

Ville de Varsovie Rochefort Dyd. (Constructeurs, Jean-François Chaumont, Paul Filhon, and A. Bonnet-Lescure)
   Ord: 30.4.1804 (frame). K: 22.3.1805. L: 10.5.1808. Comm: 18.6.1808. C: 7.1808.
   Grounded in the attack by fireships at Île d'Aix 12-13.4.1809, taken and burnt by the British.

Lorient Group. The first two ships of this type were ordered at Lorient on 27 April 1804 but the building ways they were to occupy were not large enough for them and they were re-ordered as 74-gun ships on 4 June 1804 before being named; they were completed as *Polonais* and *Golymin*. Instead, another ship was ordered to be built at Lorient on 4 June 1804, and named as *Saturne* on 26 February 1805; her frames were cut at Nantes by the Crucy Brothers, and she was ordered to be laid down at Lorient on 19 December 1805; her frames were 22/24ths cut by April 1806 and she was 4/24ths built by the end of that year; she was renamed *Eylau* on 2 July 1807 (to commemorate the battle fought on 7/8 February 1807). Two more were ordered on 29 October 1807 and named on 25 November; their fames were likewise cut at Nantes; the first was 6/24th built and the second 4/24th by 1 September 1810. Two later ships were built to this design at Lorient; the ship ordered in 1810 as *Brabançon* was renamed *Neptune* on 29 August 1814 following the restoration of the Bourbon monarchy, although the name *Brabançon* was restored from 22 March until 15 July 1815 (during the Hundred Days); the last ship was named *Algésiras* on 21 May 1812.

Eylau Lorient Dyd
   Ord: 11.11.1804 and 26.3.1805. K: 9.1805. L: 19.11.1808. Comm: 11.3.1809. C: 5.1809.
   Struck 1.6.1829, BU 1829 at Brest.

Diadème Lorient Dyd. (Constructeurs, François Etesse and others)
   Ord: 29.10.1807. K: 11.1807. L: 30.11.1811. Comm: 1.1.1812. C: 3.1812.
   Struck 21.1.1856, barracks hulk at Toulon, BU 1868.

Magnifique Lorient Dyd. (Constructeur, Aimé Jean-Louis Le Déan)
   Ord: 29.10.1807. '*Mise en chantier*' ordered at Lorient 26.12.1808. K: 12.1809. L: 29.10.1814. Comm: 1.11.1814. C: 11.1814.
   Decomm. 3.2.1815 and never recomm. Struck 23.9.1837, BU 12.1837.

Neptune Lorient Dyd. (Constructeur, Aimé Jean-Louis Le Déan)
   Ord: 23.7.1810 and named (*Brabançon*). K: 1.12.1810. L: 21.3.1818. C: 6.1818. Comm: 16.8.1839.
   Struck 11.1.1858, prison hulk at Toulon, BU 1868.

Algésiras Lorient Dyd
   Ord: 20.2.1812. K: 1.4.1812. L: 21.8.1823. C: 4.1824. Comm: 20.8.1828.
   Struck 1846, prison hulk at Toulon, mentioned for the last time 1847.

A coloured lithograph of the 86-gun *Algésiras* with topgallants struck riding out a storm. (© National Maritime Museum PY0826)

Antwerp 1st Group. During the summer of 1807, orders were placed at Antwerp for five ships to this design, intended for Napoleon's Scheldt Fleet; a sixth was ordered in 1809. All were constructed by Pierre Lair and others. Along with another pair ordered at Lorient in October, and a further Toulon order placed in 1808, these carried what evidently became the standard late wartime ordnance on the gaillards – 14 x 12pdrs and 14 x 36pdr carronades – thus making them 90-gun vessels.

Friedland Antwerp (Constructeurs, Pierre Lair and others)
  Ord: 2.6.1807 as a 74 named *Illustre*, ordered built as an 80 on 9.7.1807 and renamed *Friedland* 28.7.1807. K: 7.1807. L: 2.5.1810. Comm: 4.1.1811. C: 5.1811.
  Followed *Commerce de Lyon* (74) on the ways. Allocated to the Allies 1.8.1814 in the division of the Scheldt squadron and became the Dutch *Vlaming*. BU 1823.

Tilsitt Antwerp (Constructeurs, Pierre Lair and others)
  Ord: 6.1807. K: 6.1807. Named 28.7.1807. L: 15.8.1810. Comm: 4.1.1811 with a Flemish crew. C: 5.1811.
  Needed repairs 12.1813. Allocated to the Allies 1.8.1814 in the division of the Scheldt squadron and handed over to the Dutch 6.8.1814 as *Neptunus*. BU 1818 or 1823.

Pacificateur Antwerp (Constructeurs, Pierre Lair and others)
  Ord: 7.1807. Named 28.7.1807. K: 9.1807. L: 22.5.1811. Comm: 22.5.1811. C: 8.1811.
  Allocated to France 1.8.1814 in the division of the Scheldt squadron, arrived at Brest 20.9.1814. Struck 28.10.1823 and ordered BU but still on the list in 1.1824 and destroyed in 1824 in trials of Paixhans' new 22cm shell gun.

Illustre Antwerp (Constructeurs, Pierre Lair and others)
  Ord: 7.1807. Named 28.7.1807. K: 8.1807. L: 9.6.1811. Comm: 13.6.1811. C: 10.1811.
  Allocated to France 1.8.1814 in the division of the Scheldt squadron but delivered to the Allies in place of *Auguste* and renamed *Prins van Oranje*. Made cruises to the West Indies and the Mediterranean in 1815-17, sheer hulk at Flushing 1819, sold for BU 1825.

Auguste Antwerp (Constructeurs, Pierre Lair and others)
  Ord: 31.8.1807. K: 9.1807. Named 17.10.1807. L: 25.4.1811. Comm: 26.4.1811. C: 7.1811.
  Allocated to the Allies 1.8.1814 in the division of the Scheldt squadron but exchanged for *Illustre* which was not in condition to go to sea. Renamed *Illustre* 8.1814, arrived at Brest 7.10.1814. Was in bad condition 1822. Struck 3.1827.

Conquérant Antwerp (Constructeurs, Pierre Lair and others)
  Ord: 26.1.1809 (and named). K: 12.1808. L: 27.4.1812. Comm: 28.4.1812. C: 9.1812.
  Allocated to France 1.8.1814 in the division of the Scheldt squadron, arrived at Brest 6.10.1814. Struck 6.7.1831, barracks hulk at Toulon. BU 1841-42.

Cherbourg Group.

Zélandais Cherbourg Dyd. (Constructeurs, Jean-Michel Segondat and Charles Noël)
  K: 1.10.1810. L: 12.10.1813. Comm: 16.10.1813, C: 3.1814.
  Used a frame that was ordered at Le Havre 20.3.1804 and begun in

1-2.1805. Renamed *Duquesne* 29.4.1814, *Zélandais* 22.3.1815, and *Duquesne* 15.7.1815. Struck 19.11.1836, barracks hulk at Toulon. BU 1858.

Centaure Cherbourg Dyd. (Constructeur, Jean-Michel Segondat)
  Ord: 1811. K: 2.11.1811. Named 25.11.1811. L: 8.1.1818. C: 4.1818. Comm: 10.2.1823.
  Renamed *Santi Petri* 14.10.1823 after helping reduce a Spanish fort of that name on 20.9.1823. Struck 5.11.1849, prison hulk at Toulon, lost by fire 4.1.1862.

Jupiter Cherbourg Dyd. (Constructeurs, Jean-Michel Segondat, Joseph Daviel, and others)
  K: 5.11.1811. Named 25.11.1811. L: 22.10.1831. C: 9.1833. Comm: 20.11.1835.
  Struck 4.5.1863, barracks hulk at Rochefort, BU 1870.

Antwerp 2nd Group. Another five vessels were ordered to be built to this design at Antwerp, the first orders being placed on 15 March 1811; none of these was completed and all were BU on the stocks.

Alexandre Antwerp
  Ord: 15.3.1811. K: 6.1811. Was 14.5/24ths complete on 1.4.1814.
  Allocated to the Allies 1.8.1814 and sold by the Dutch for BU on the ways.

Mars Antwerp
  K: 4.1811. Was 6/24ths complete on 1.4.1814.
  Allocated to the Allies 1.8.1814 and sold by the Dutch for BU on the ways.

Tibre Antwerp
  Ord: 15.3.1811. K: 6.1811. Was 8/24ths complete on 1.4.1814.
  Allocated to the French 1.8.1814 and sold for BU on the ways.

Atlas Antwerp
  K: 7.1811. Was 8/24ths complete on 1.4.1814.
  Allocated to the French 1.8.1814 and sold for BU on the ways.

Fougueux Antwerp
  K: 6.1812. Was 6/24ths complete on 1.4.1814.
  Allocated to the French 1.8.1814 and sold for BU on the ways.

Italian-built Vessels. In or before February 1811 orders were issued to build an 80-gun ship at Venice and another for the French Navy at either Castellammare or at Naples. A month later an order was given to build a further ship at Trieste, and in 1813 a second ship was ordered at Venice, but no work was begun on either of these two, and no names were assigned.

Saturne Venice (Constructeurs, Jean-Marguerite Tupinier and Jean Dumonteil)
  K: 12.6.1812. On ways 20.6.1812. Was 10.7/24ths complete on 1.4.1814.
  Taken by the Austrians 20.4.1814 on the occupation of Venice and incorporated in the Austrian Navy on 16.5.1814 as *Saturno* after the Austrians took formal possession of the city. Renamed *Emo* 3.2.1816 after Angelo Emo, the last Grand Admiral of the Republic of Venice. Deteriorated on open slipway, inspected 3.4.1820 by a hull commission, dismantled 1823. Her probable intended armament was LD 30 x 36pdrs, UD 32x 24pdrs, SD 14x 12pdrs and 10x 36pdr carronades.

Vesuvio Castellammare di Stabia (for Murat's Neapolitan Navy)
  K: 8.1812. Named: 1814. L: 2.12.1824. C: by 7.1825.
  In 8.1808 Napoleon made one of his favourite marshals, Joachim Murat, King of Naples and Sicily. In around 1809 Murat ordered two 74-gun ships and two 44-gun frigates at Castellammare. In around 1812 an 80-gun ship was ordered to follow the second 74, *Gioacchino*, on the ways. In 12.1813 Murat abandoned Napoleon to keep his throne but, knowing that the Austrians planned to depose him, rejoined Napoleon in 1815 during the Hundred Days and ended up before a firing squad. The Kingdom of the Two Sicilies was formed under a restored Bourbon monarchy in 12.1815. The new 80, *Vesuvio*, entered service in its navy a decade later when on 13.7.1825 she carried the royal family from Leghorn to Naples. Her original armament was 58 x 24pdrs (LD & UD), 2 x 22cm and 2 x 16cm shell guns, and 16 x 24pdr carronades. She had a very active career until late 1844 when her keel was found to be badly warped. She was out of commission at Naples when Garibaldi entered the city on 7.9.1860 and was not inscribed on the list of the new Italian Navy on 17.3.1861. An attempt to sell her on 1.2.1862 failed and on 3.1.1865 she was towed to Castellammare for BU.

Besides the above, an order was issued in May 1808 for an 80-gun ship to be built at French-occupied Lisbon, but no work had been done on this by the time that the French evacuated the port in September of the same year. A plan of October 1811 to build three 110-gun and two 80-gun ships at Amsterdam resulted in an order for only one 110-gun ship.

PURCHASED RUSSIAN VESSELS (1809). When Russian forces abandoned the Mediterranean in September 1807 they left behind some ships that were unable to make the long voyage home. These moved to Trieste at the end of 1807 under Commodore I. O. Saltanov and remained there until October 1809 when, following orders from Moscow, the Russian flag was hauled down and the ships were sold to the French. An unusual feature of the armament of Russian ships was the edinorog. This was a weapon, unique to the Russians, that fired spherical hollow bombs and solid shot. A one-pood edinorog fired a 44-pound bomb shell or a 63-pound solid shot.

URIIL Class. This vessel, a sister *Tverdyy* (launched in 1805), and the slightly smaller *Rafail* (1802), were the Russian Baltic Fleet's first two-decker 80-gun ships. They were followed by a fourth and larger ship, *Smelyy* (1808) that was built by the the French emigré naval constructor Jacques Balthasar Le Brun de Sainte Catherine, probably as a copy of Sané's 80-gun ship. Le Brun had come to Russia from Turkey, where he had built *Sedd el Bahr* (see below). *Uriil* was named after the Archangel Uriel and her name was also rendered as *Arkhangel Uriil*.
  Dimensions & tons: 174ft 6in x 46ft 5in x 20ft 0in (56.69 x 15.09 x 6.50m). 1,500/3,000 tons. Draught 17ft 9in/19ft 8in (5.80m/6.40m). Men: 701.
  Guns: (Russian) LD 24 x 36pdrs, 4 x 60pdr edinorogs; UD 26 x 24pdrs, 4 x 24pdr edinorogs; SD 22 x 8pdrs.

Uriil (Russian *Arkhangel Uriil*) Admiralty Yard, St. Petersburg (constructed by M. Sarychev and Pospelov)
  K: 3.8.1800, L: 16.8.1802, C: by 1804.
  After serving in the Adriatic and Aegean since early 1806, *Uriil* left Corfu 19.9.1807 in the squadron of Vice Admiral Senyavin to return to St. Petersburg. On 23.9.1807 she was damaged during a violent storm, some of her beams being sprung. The admiral inspected the damage and sent the ship back to Corfu, where she arrived on 1.10.1807. On 12.12.1807 she departed Corfu in the squadron of Commodore I. O. Saltanov and arrived on 28.12.1807 at Trieste, where she remained until 10.1809. The guns were removed from one side of the ship and put on the pier on 13.5.1809 to defend against a threatened British attack. On 27.9.1809 the order was received to turn the ship over to the French, and the Russian flag was hauled down on 20.10.1809. The French found her to be beyond repair and she was BU 1810-11.

SED EL BAHR. Built by the French emigré naval constructor Jacques

Balthasar Le Brun de Sainte Catherine, reportedly as a copy of Sané's 80-gun ship. During the years when Le Brun was in effect the master shipwright of the Ottoman Empire (1793-99), he enacted a total transformation of Ottoman shipbuilding methods and technology. After leaving Turkey he served for thirty years more in Russia, where his influence was even greater (see the *Uriil* class, above). His former French assistant, Honoré Benoît, completed *Sedd el Bahr* after his departure. *Sedd el Bahr* means 'rampart of the sea'. A modern French reference lists her original armament as 32 x 42pdrs, 32 x 22pdrs, and 20 x 12pdrs and states that she suffered from corrosion of her iron nails and hull fastenings because of her copper sheathing.

Dimensions: Length (keel) 59 *zira* or (in French units) 138ft 5in.
Guns: 84; (Russian, 1807) 42 guns: LD 22pdrs, UD 12pdrs.

Sed el Bahr (ex Russian *Sedel-Bakhr*, ex Turkish *Sedd el Bahr* or *Seddülbahir*) Istanbul

Built (completed) 1799 or soon afterwards.
Turkish flagship captured by the Russians 1.7.1807 at the Battle of Mt. Athos by the Russian *Selafail* (74) and taken to Corfu for repairs. Placed in service using crew, rigging, etc., taken from other Russian ships. Departed Corfu 12.12.1807 in the squadron of Commodore I. O. Saltanov and arrived on 28.12.1807 at Trieste, where she remained until 10.1809. Helped defend against a threatened British attack there 17.5.1809. On 27.9.1809 the order was received to turn the ship over to the French, and the Russian flag was hauled down on 20.10.1809. In 7.1810 Napoleon ordered her repaired with the intent of sending her to Pola. This was not done, and she was BU 1811 at Trieste.

ANNEXED DUTCH VESSELS (1810). The Batavian Republic, successor to the Republic of the United Netherlands, was proclaimed on 19 January 1795, and on 27 February 1795 the five autonomous Dutch Admiralties (Amsterdam, Maas or Rotterdam, Zeeland, Friesland, and Noorderkwartier) were replaced with a single 'Committee for Naval Affairs'. In December 1795 the new Batavian naval organisation laid down the first Dutch 80-gun two-decker at Amsterdam.

WREEKER Class (80 and 90 guns). Although about four metres shorter than Sané's French 80-gun ships, *Wreeker* was the largest sailing warship built in the Netherlands up to that time. Her name was a variant of *Wreker* ('Avenger'). Seven sisters were subsequently laid down, including three at Rotterdam. The five Amsterdam ships had 30 ports each on the UD and LD and 20 guns on the gaillards. The three ships at Rotterdam were initially assigned ten more guns on the gaillards, where they had 10 behind ports and 20 in the open, causing them to be rated as 90-gun ships. The armament of *Wreeker* in 1801 was LD 28 x 36pdrs, UD 30 x 24pdrs, SD 22 x 12pdrs while *Chattam* in 1801 had LD 30 x 36pdrs, UD 30 x 24pdrs, SD 12 x 12pdrs on the quarterdeck plus 18 x 36pdr carronades in the waist and on the forecastle. The Amsterdam ships were built by the master shipwrights there, R. Dorsman followed by P. Schuijt Jnr, while the Rotterdam ships were built by that yard's master shipwright, Pieter Glavimans Jnr, who probably produced the overall design for the class.

Several renamings followed the establishment of the Kingdom of Holland. *Wreeker* was renamed *Koninklijke Hollander* on 10 June 1806 and *Kroonprins* on 15 February 1808. The first *De Ruyter* became *Admiraal Piet Hein* on 15 July 1806, *Rotterdam* two days later, and *Koninklijie Hollander* on 15 February 1808. *Leeuw* was changed to *Commercie van Amsterdam* on 27 December 1806 and *Amsterdamsche Handel* on 18 March 1808.

All eight ships were incorporated into the French Imperial Navy on 9 July 1810 when Napoleon annexed the Kingdom of Holland into the French Empire. All were given French versions of their Dutch names in July 1810 and most had those names shortened in April 1811. Napoleon decreed on 25 April 1811 that all would be ranked among the 80-gunners, and French records give the same 80-gun armament for all eight ships. *Evertsen* and *De Ruyter* were completed while under French control while *Amiral Piet Hein* was replaced on the ways by a *Piet Hein* built to a French 74-gun design.

Dimensions & tons: 169ft 11in, 159ft 6in x 44ft 5in x 19ft 2in (55.20, 51.80 x 14.44 x 6.23m). 1,500/2,900 tons. Draught 18ft 4in/19ft 2in (5.94/6.23m). Men: 673-819.
Guns: (French, c1811) LD 28 x 36pdrs, UD 30 x 30pdrs, SD 14 x 12pdrs, 2 x 60pdr carronades, 6 x 30pdr carronades.

Prince Royal (ex Dutch *Kroonprins* 7.1810) Amsterdam (constructed by R. Dorsman)
K: 1.12.1797. L: 28.7.1798. C: 1799.
Renamed *Prince* 4.1811. Was in the Texel squadron in 4.1814. Returned to the Dutch as *Prins* 22.4.1814. In bad condition at Nieuwediep in 1816 and converted to an accommodation ship for sailors and workers. BU 1819.

Amiral Zoutman (ex Dutch *Admiraal Zoutman* 7.1810) Amsterdam (constructed by R. Dorsman)
K: 10.10.1798. L: 15.9.1800. C: 1801.
Renamed *Zoutman* 4.1811. Was in the Texel squadron in 4.1814. Returned to the Dutch as *Admiraal Zoutman* 22.4.1814. Converted 1818 to an accommodation ship. Sold 10.1829 at Amsterdam and BU 1830.

Chatham (ex Dutch *Chattam* 7.1810) Rotterdam (constructed by P. Glavimans Jr.)
K: 5.1799. L: 24.5.1800. C: 1801.
Was out of commission at Vlissingen (Flushing) in 4.1814. Returned to the Dutch as *Chattam* 1.8.1814. BU 1823 at Vlissingen.

Royal Hollandais (ex Dutch *Koninklijie Hollander* 7.1810) Rotterdam (constructed by P. Glavimans Jr.)
K: 14.10.1804. L: 17.7.1806. C: 1807.
Renamed *Hollandais* 1811. Was in the Scheldt squadron as a floating battery in 4.1814. Returned to the Dutch as *Koninklijie Hollander* 1.8.1814. Guardship in Vlissingen 1815, BU there 1819.

Commerce d'Amsterdam (ex Dutch *Amsterdamsche Handel* 7.1810) Amsterdam (constructed by R. Dorsman)
K: 6.12.1804. L: 29.10.1806. C: 4.1811.
Renamed *Amsterdam* 4.1811. Was out of commission at Nieuwediep in 4.1814. Returned to the Dutch as *Amsterdam* 22.4.1814. Left the Texel for the East Indies in 1815 with a squadron under Rear Admiral A. A. Buyskes for colonial service. Began her return voyage 29.10.1817 but was blown ashore on 11.12.1817 by a storm in Algoa Bay, South Africa, and broke up there on 19-20.12.1817.

Amiral Evertsen (ex Dutch *Admiraal Evertsen* 7.1810) Amsterdam (constructed by R. Dorsman and P. Schuijt Jr.)
K: 2.2.1805. L: 19.11.1808. C: 9.1811.
Renamed *Evertsen* 4.1811. Sunk in shallow water at Medemblick 10.1811 by sabotage, refloated 11.1811. Was in the Texel squadron in 4.1814. Returned to the Dutch as *Admiral Evertsen* 22.4.1814. Departed the Texel 1815 and arrived at Batavia 26.4.1816. Started back to the Netherlands on 30.3.1819 but had to put in to Diego Garcia with a leak and was burned there. Her crew returned to Europe in the American merchantman *Pickering*.

Amiral de Ruyter (ex Dutch *Admiraal de Ruyter* 7.1810) Amsterdam (constructed by R. Dorsman and P. Schuijt Jr.)
K: 2.2.1806. L: 9.11.1808. C: 9.1811.
Renamed *De Ruyter* 4.1811. Sunk in shallow water at Medemblick

10.1811 by sabotage, refloated 11.1811. Was in the Texel squadron in 4.1814. Returned to the Dutch as *Admiraal de Ruyter* 22.4.1814. Sent to the East Indies, arrived in bad condition, turned over to the Colonial Navy in 11.1816, and BU 1818.

Amiral Piet Hein (ex Dutch *Admiraal Piet Hein* 7.1810) Rotterdam (constructed by P. Glavimans Jr.)

K: 20.2.1806. Was 6/24ths built as a Dutch 80-gun ship when on 14.2.1811 Napoleon ordered her disassembled and reworked as a 74 of the French *petit modèle*. Her timbers were reportedly already rotting on the slip. See *Piet Hein* (74) for the replacement ship.

(D) Vessels acquired from 26 June 1815

The artillery Ordinance of 1817 standardised the armament of the Sané '80-gun' two-decker at LD 30 x 36pdrs; UD 32 x 24pdrs; and gaillards 14 x 12pdrs and 14 x 36pdr carronades (including 4 of bronze on the dunette) for an actual total of 90 pieces of ordnance. This was probably the same armament that was fitted to eight ships in 1810-12. The *Centaure*, launched after the war, was credited with 2 x 12pdrs and 22 x 36pdr carronades on the gaillards along with two 16pdr carronades and one 12pdr carronade. The Ordinance of 1828 changed the armament on the gaillards to 20 x 36pdr carronades and 4 x 18pdrs (chase guns) for a total of 86 guns. The Ordinance of 1838 amalgamated this type into the new 90-gun type except for four fewer carronades on the gaillards, the resulting standard armament being LD 26 x 30pdrs No.1, 4 x 22cm No.1 shell; UD 32 x 30pdrs No.2; SD 20 x 30pdr carronades, 4 x 16cm shell. No ships were listed with this 30pdr armament, but two surviving ships, *Diadème* and *Neptune*, were listed, perhaps notionally, with the armament in the next standard ordinance (1848): LD 22 x 30pdrs No.1, 8 x 22cm No.1 shell; UD 24 x 30pdr No.2, 8 x 22cm No.2 shell; SD 20 x 30pdr carronades and 4 x 16cm shell.

In January 1820 the Minister of Marine, Baron Pierre Barthélémy Portal d'Albaredes, presented the navy's budget for 1820 to Parliament and stated, based on an analysis of the age and deterioration of the existing ships, that the navy would disappear if the current spending level of 45 million francs per year were continued but that with an annual expenditure of 65 millions a fleet of 38 ships of the line, 50 frigates, and a proportional number of lesser ships could be maintained. Portal made no reference to changing the types of ships composing the fleet, but this process had already begun with the laying down in 1819 of several 24pdr frigates under a policy set by Portal's predecessor, Comte Molé. In May 1822 Jean-Marguerite Tupinier, the Deputy Director of Ports and a *Directeur des Constructions de 2e classe* in the Génie Maritime, extended this restructuring to the battle line by proposing that the 80-gun ship be superseded by a 90-gun ship and that an even larger 100-gun two-decker be introduced between it and the three-deckers. The resulting Royal Ordinance of 10 March 1824 specified that the French battle fleet would consist of fifteen 90s and ten 100s, making them the core of the fleet, plus ten 120-gun three-deckers and five 82-gun two-deckers, the latter replacing the old 74s.

Under the 10 March 1824 ordinance the new 3nd Rank 90-gun ships carried 30 long 30pdrs on the LD, 32 short 30pdrs on the UD, and 24 x 30pdr carronades and 4 long 18pdr chase guns on the gaillards. The new 2nd Rank 100-gun ships had two more guns each of the same types on the LD and UD and six more carronades on the gaillards. On 14 April 1838 4 x 22cm (80pdr) shell guns replaced four of the 36pdrs on the LD and 4 x 16cm (30pdr) shell guns replaced the 18pdrs on the gaillards in each type. On 20 July 1848 the number of shell guns was increased, with another 4 of the 22cm type replacing an equivalent number of 30pdrs on the LD, 8 of the 22cm replacing 30pdr guns in equal numbers on the UD, and 4 carronades being removed on the gaillards, bringing the rated totals down to 96 and 86 guns. The standard armaments were changed again on 27 July 1849 to introduce a new 50pdr gun and two new 30pdrs, but by this time changes in ordnance technology were occurring rapidly and each new ship ended up receiving its own individual armament, some of which are shown in the descriptions of the individual ships.

Many of the numerous renamings of ships of the line after 1815, particularly those of the new 100-gun and 90-gun types, occurred on three occasions. The first bulk renaming was on 9 August 1830 when 'names no longer in harmony with the current order of things' were altered following the July 1830 revolution. At this time *Duc de Bordeaux* and *Comte d'Artois* (120), *Royal Charles*, *Dauphin Royal* and *Lys* (100), *Duc d'Angoulême* (an old 90), and *Duc de Berry* (82) became respectively *Friedland*, *Ville de Paris*, *Jemmapes*, *Fleurus*, *Ulm*, *Iéna*, and *Glorieux*. Eight frigates were similarly renamed. The second batch of name changes occurred on 23 November 1839 when six ships of the line were renamed after Napoleonic victories, the 100-gun ships *Ajax*, *Bucentaure*, and *Éole* becoming *Austerlitz*, *Wagram* and *Eylau* and the 90-gun *Achille*, *Alexandre*, and *Diomède* becoming *Breslaw*, *Donauwerth* and *Tilsitt*. Finally on 2 April 1850 the 90-gun *Hector*, *Sceptre* and *Achille* were given the

Official draught of *Hercule*, 100 guns, approved Paris 24 April 1824. With gunports filling the waist barricades, the ship was effectively a spardecked three-decker. The sail area, without royals, totalled 3,134 sq.m. (Atlas du Génie Maritime, French collection, plate 6)

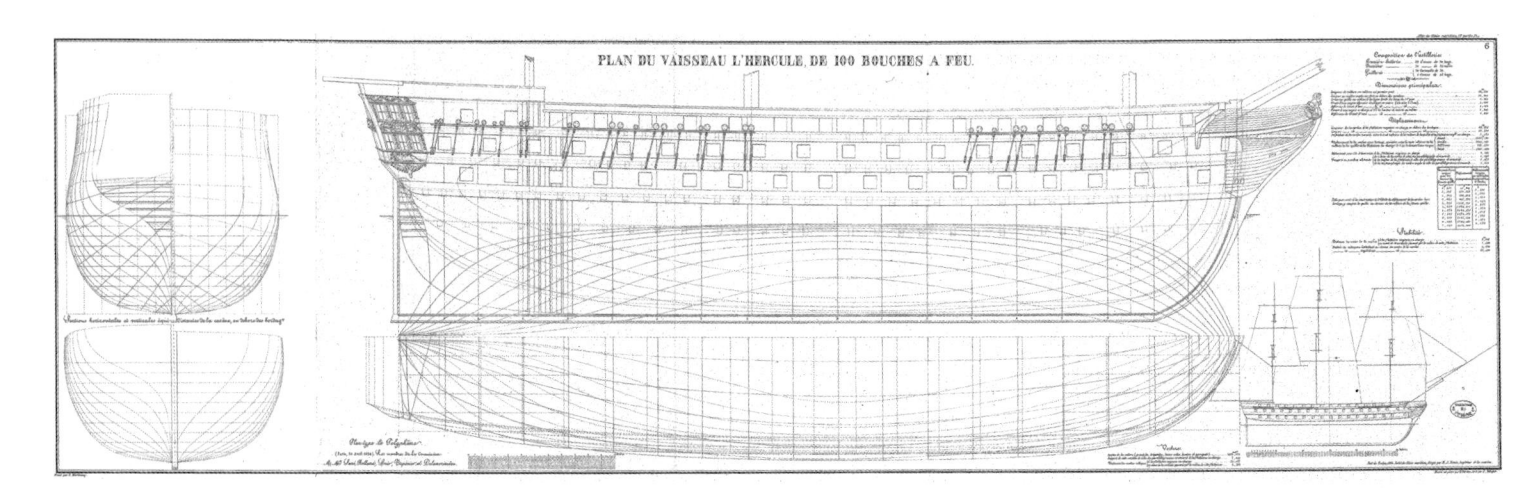

more French names of *Charlemagne*, *Masséna*, and *Saint Louis*. Details of these and other individual renamings are provided in the class tabulations.

HERCULE Class – 100 guns. This type was designed by a commission consisting of Jean-Marguerite Tupinier, Jacques-Noël Sané, Pierre Rolland, Pierre Lair, and Jean Delamorinière along lines suggested by Baron Tupinier. It was to fill the gap between the new standard French battleship, the 90-gun *Suffren* type, and the 120-gun three-deckers. Its lines were scaled up from those of Sané's now classic 80-gun ship, as were those of the *Suffren*s. The commission's plans, dated 24 April 1824 and signed by Sané, were approved by the Council of Works on 13 May 1824. In this and the other large vessels of the post-Napoleonic navy the forecastle and quarterdeck were joined to form a complete spardeck, which although fully exposed could carry an unbroken tier of guns. The designed height of the lower battery above the water was 2.00m at 7.64m mean draught, and the designed armament was LD 32 x 30pdrs No.1; UD 34 x 30pdrs No.2; SD 30 x 30pdr carronades, 4 x 18pdrs.

Nine ships were ordered to this design during the 1820s. *Jemmapes* (originally named *Indomptable* but renamed *Royal Charles* in 1824 in honour of the crown prince) was originally projected to be begun at Cherbourg in 1825 but was reassigned to Lorient before construction began in 1825. Two more ships, *Agamemnon* and *Hector*, were among five line of battle ships scheduled to be begun at Brest in 1829 but cancelled in late 1828 before orders were placed. They were replaced in the building program by frigates, which also were not built. Four more ships were ordered during the 1830s including *Navarin*, which was originally planned as a 120-gun ship to be begun in 1829 at a new facility at Brest

Morel-Fatio's depiction of the loss of *Henri IV*, along with the steam corvette *Pluton* on 14 November 1854. *Henri IV* was one of the first vessel in the French Navy ordered with a version of the round stern, as introduced into the Royal Navy by Sir Robert Seppings in the 1820s. (© National Maritime Museum PY0951)

(the Anse St. Nicolas) but was postponed on 16 November 1829 due to delays in completing the facility. *Navarin* was re-assigned to Toulon and on 7 March 1832 was ordered built as a 100-gun ship after the navy could not decide whether it wanted 30pdr carronades or 16cm shell guns on the uppermost decks of new three-deckers.

Early experience at sea with *Hercule* was favourable, but the next ship completed, *Jemmapes*, sailed badly, especially in bad weather, and was too crowded on the continuous spardeck. Both she and *Hercule* were modified at Toulon in 1847-49 in an effort to correct these problems, and the measures taken, including the removal of 8 x 30pdr carronades from the uppermost deck, were generally successful. By this time, however, the class was judged to be too close to the three-deckers in size and cost to be worth repeating in future programs. The last ships of this class completed as sailing ships (*Tage, Duguay Trouin,* and *Turenne*) were fitted with custom armaments as shown in their listings. *Henri IV* was one of the first French ships ordered to be fitted with a round stern, and others were subsequently fitted with them during construction or conversion to steam.

Dimensions & tons: 62.50m, 62.00m wl x 16.20m, 16.75m ext x 8.23m. 4,440 tons. Draught 7.31m/7.97m. Men: 916.
Guns: (*Hercule* and *Jemmapes* 1837-41) LD 28 x 30pdrs No.1, 4 x 22cm No.1 shell; UD 34 x 30pdrs No.2; SD 30 x 30pdr

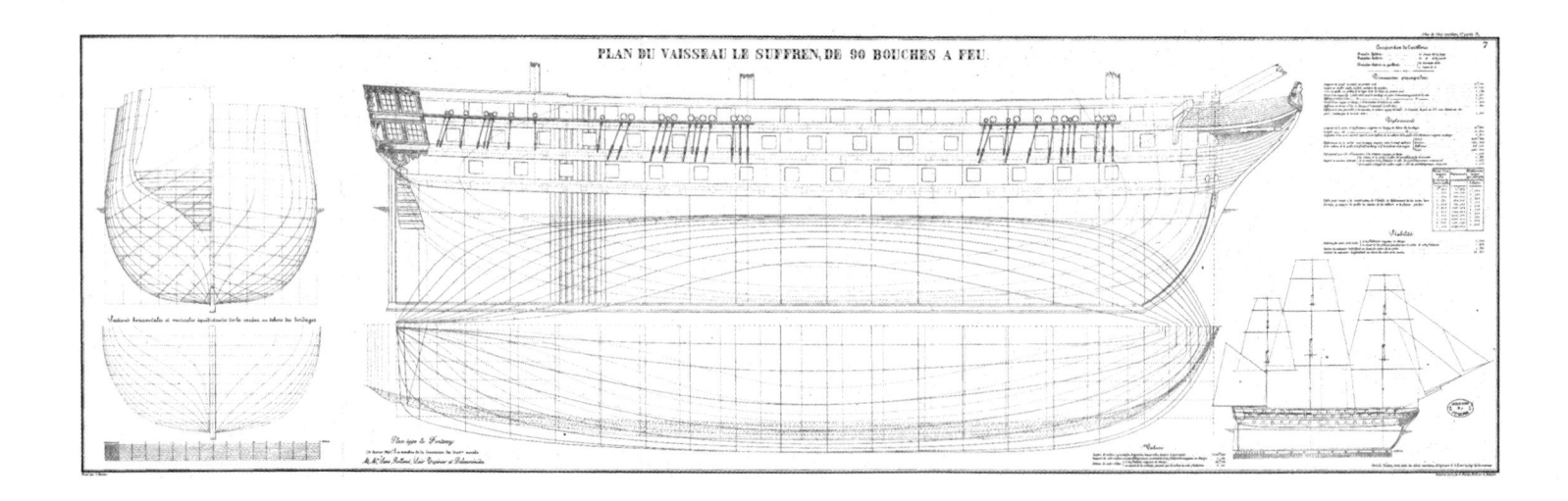

carronades, 4 x 16cm shell.

Hercule Toulon Dyd. (Constructeurs, Louis Barrallier and Firmin Joffre)
K: 6.1824. L: 29.7.1836. Comm: 1.5.1837. C: 8.1837.
Decomm. 3.10.1856. Converted to prison hulk at Brest 7.1859-1.1860, struck 23.3.1860. Prison hulk until 1873, ordered BU 25.9.1873, BU 1874-75.

Jemmapes (ex *Royal Charles* 9.8.1830, ex *Indomptable* 4.11.1824) Lorient Dyd. (Constructeurs, Aimé Le Déan and Jean-Baptiste Larchevesque-Thibaut)
Ord: 14.10.1824 and named (*Indomptable*). K: 26.4.1825. L: 2.4.1840. Comm: 16.10.1840. C: 5.1841.
Decomm. 25.9.1856. Struck 31.12.1864, barracks hulk at Cherbourg to 1889, BU 1890.

Tage (ex *Saint Louis* 1.12.1832, ex *Polyphème* 26.12.1828) Brest Dyd. (Constructeurs, Charles Desmarest, Jean Perroy, and Jean Le Jouteux)
K: 26.8.1824. L: 15.8.1847. C: 1.1854. Comm: 1.3.1854.
Guns as completed (1854) LD 28 x 30pdrs No.1, 4 x 22p No.1 shell; UD 30 x 30pdrs No.2, 4 x 22cm No.2 shell; SD 22 x 30pdr carronades, 4 x 16cm shell.
Decomm. c1856, steam 1857.

Fleurus (ex *Dauphin Royal* 9.8.1830, ex *Briarée* 10.1824) Toulon Dyd. (Constructeurs, Jean-Baptiste Bayle, Louis Sanial-Dufay, and Hyacinthe De Coppier)
K: 4.1825. Modified with round stern on plans by Jean Vincent in 1847. Not launched as sail. Steam 1853.

Ulm (ex *Lys* 9.8.1830) Rochefort Dyd. (Constructeurs, Jean-François Guillemard, Jean-Baptiste Hubert, Antoine Auriol, Louis Fabre d'Églantine, Gabriel Nosereau, Joseph Dreppe, Victorin-Gabriel Sabattier, and Jean Clarke)
K: 13.6.1825. Not launched as sail. Steam 1854.

Annibal Lorient Dyd-Caudan (Constructeurs, Charles Alexandre and Guillaume Masson)
K: 17.9.1827. Not launched as sail. Steam 1853, renamed *Prince Jérôme* 24.5.1854 during conversion.

Duguay Trouin Lorient Dyd-Caudan (Constructeurs, Charles Alexandre and others)
K: 17.9.1827. L: 29.3.1854. C: 4.1855. Comm: 16.7.1855.
Guns as completed (1855) as *Tage*.
Decomm. 6.9.1855, steam 1857.

Turenne Rochefort Dyd. (Constructeurs, Jean-François Guillemard, Amédée Lemoyne-Sérigny, Joseph Dreppe, Gabriel Nosereau, Antoine Auriol, Henri De Lisleferme, and Jean Clarke)
K: 13.6.1827. L: 15.4.1854. Comm: 24.5.1854. C: 6.1854.

The official draught of the new standard 90-gun ships of the *Suffren* class, dated 30 January 1824. Like the contemporary 100-gun design, these ships had a complete battery on the weather deck. The sail area was virtually identical to that of the 100-gun class at 3,130 sq.m. (Atlas du Génie Maritime, French collection, plate 7)

Guns as completed (1854) as *Tage* except SD 24 x 30pdrs No.3.
Modified with round stern to plans by Antoine Auriol approved 9.5.1846. Decomm. 7.2.1856, steam 1858.

Agamemnon Brest Dyd
Projected in 1828 to be begun in 1829 but cancelled in 1828.

Hector Brest Dyd
Projected in 1828 to be begun in 1829 but cancelled in 1828.

Henri IV Cherbourg Dyd. (Constructeurs, Paul Leroux, Jean-Baptiste Bayle, Alexandre Robiou de Lavrignais, and Louis Corrard)
Ord: 18.12.1828. K: 17.7.1829. L: 14.9.1848. C: 3.1850. Comm: 21.5.1850.
Blown ashore and lost 14.11.1854 in a storm at Eupatoria in the Crimea.

Austerlitz (ex *Ajax* 23.11.1839) Cherbourg Dyd. (Constructeurs, Jean-Baptiste Lefebvre, Louis-Alexandre Corrard and others)
Ord: 20.8.1831. K: 17.4.1832. Not launched as sail. Steam 1852.

Navarin Toulon Dyd. (Constructeurs, Jean Dumonteil, Jean-Baptiste Bayle, and Henri Kerris)
K: 5.1832. Not launched as sail. Steam 1854.

Wagram (ex *Bucentaure* 23.11.1839) Lorient Dyd-Caudan (Constructeurs, Charles Alexandre and others)
K: 23.2.1833. Not launched as sail. Steam 1854.

Eylau (ex *Éole* 23.11.1839) Toulon Dyd. (Constructeurs, Jacques Bonard and others)
K: 8.1833. Not launched as sail. Steam 1856.

SUFFREN Class – 90 guns. This type was designed by a commission consisting of Jean-Marguerite Tupinier, Jacques-Noël Sané, Pierre Rolland, Pierre Lair, and Jean Delamorinière along lines suggested by Baron Tupinier. It was intended to replace the 74 as the standard ship of the line in the French Navy (reinforced in battle fleets by a smaller number of 100-gun and 120-gun ships). The design superseded Sané's successful 80-gun type, following it as closely as possible but enlarged to carry a heavier armament at a greater height above the waterline (2.00m at 7.40m mean draught) instead of the 1.78m of the 80s. In this and the other large vessels of the post-Napoleonic navy the forecastle and quarterdeck were joined to form an additional complete deck, which although fully exposed could carry an unbroken tier of guns. Tumblehome was eliminated completely. The designed armament was LD 30 x 30pdrs No.1; UD 32 x 30pdrs No.2; SD 24 x 30pdr carronades, 4 x 18pdrs. The commission's plans were dated 30 January 1824.

Seven ships were begun in the 1820s to this design, but all except *Suffren* herself were not completed for many years; two more ships, *Ajax* and *Diomède*, were among five line of battle ships scheduled to be begun at Brest in 1829 but cancelled in late 1828 before orders were placed. They were replaced in the building program by frigates, which also were not built. Four more of this class were begun during the early 1830s but not completed for two decades; another, *Argonaute*, was scheduled to be begun at Toulon in 1837 but was deferred and cancelled in 1838. *Suffren* quickly earned the class a good reputation for sailing qualities.

Inflexible was completed with a round stern which served as a model for conversions of other ships. In 1847 Jean Vincent at Toulon developed an easy way of making this modification to ships on the ways, and on 2 March 1847 this was ordered applied to all ships under construction beginning with those at Toulon. Three more ships of this type ordered in 1848 are listed below as the Repeat *Suffren* class. The last ships of this class completed as sailing ships (*Bayard, Duguesclin, Breslaw,* and *Tilsitt*) were fitted with custom armaments as shown in their listings.

Dimensions & tons: 60.50m, 60.17m wl x 15.75m, 16.28m ext x 8.05m. 4,058t disp. Draught 7.10m/7.70m. Men: 811.
Guns: (*Suffren* and *Inflexible* 1839-40) LD 26 x 30pdrs No.1, 4 x 22cm No.1 shell; UD 32 x 30pdrs No.2; SD 24 x 30pdr carronades, 4 x 16cm shell.

Suffren Cherbourg Dyd. (Constructeur, Louis Bretocq)
Named: 27.8.1822. K: 21.8.1824. L: 27.8.1829. Comm: 10.3.1831. C: 3.1831.
Fitted as transport at Toulon 2-4.1854. Damaged aloft in combat 17.10.1854. Relieved the frigate *Uranie* and served as training ship for gunnery seamen at Toulon in 1855-60. Decomm 6.7.1860. Struck 4.4.1861, barracks and supply hulk at Toulon. Renamed *Ajax* 8.4.1865, replaced by *Jupiter* 1872, ordered BU 28.4.1874, BU 1874-76.

Bayard Lorient Dyd. (Constructeurs, Aimé Le Déan, Jean-Baptiste Larchevesque-Thibaut, and Pierre Thomeuf)
K: 1.7.1823. L: 28.8.1847. C: 8.1849. Comm: 1.5.1850.
Guns as completed (1851) LD 22 x 30pdrs No.1, 8 x 22cm No.1 shell; UD 24 x 30pdrs No.2, 8 x 22cm No.2 shell; SD 20 x 30pdr carronades, 4 x 16cm shell.
Decomm. 23.4.1856, steam 1858.

Duguesclin Rochefort Dyd. (Constructeurs, Jean-Baptiste Hubert, Jean Clarke, and Antoine Auriol)
K: 16.3.1823. L: 3.5.1848. C: 8.1848. Comm: 3.6.1850.
Guns as completed (c1850) as *Bayard*.
Decomm. 26.9.1856, steam 1858.

Inflexible Rochefort Dyd. (Constructeurs, Gustave Garnier and Amédée Lemoyne-Sérigny)
K: 18.8.1827. L: 21.11.1839. Comm: 24.8.1840. C: 8.1840.
Used as transport 1854. Decomm. 10.9.1856. Assigned 25.9.1860 to the school for boys at Brest and converted to training ship 10.1860-6.1861. Struck 31.12.1864. Continued in use as boys' training hulk until 1875, condemned and ordered BU 24.8.1875, BU 1876.

Breslaw (ex *Achille* 23.11.1839) Brest Dyd. (Constructeurs, Antoine Geoffroy, Jean-Michel Segondat, and Joseph Fauveau)
K: 26.5.1827. L: 31.7.1848. C: 1849. Comm: 1.3.1854.
Guns as completed (1854) LD 26 x 30pdrs No.1, 4 x 22cm No.1 shell; UD 28 x 30pdrs No.2, 4 x 22cm No.2 shell; SD 20 x 30pdr carronades, 4 x 16cm shell.
Sail transport 1854, decomm. 28.5.1855, steam 1856.

Donawerth (ex *Alexandre* 23.11.1839) Lorient Dyd-Caudan (Constructeurs, Charles Alexandre and Pierre Thomeuf)
K: 27.7.1827. L: 15.2.1854. Comm: 1.5.1854. C: 7.1854.
Decomm. 16.1.1856, steam 1857.

Fontenoy Toulon Dyd. (Constructeurs, Jacques Bonard, Jean-Baptiste Pironneau, Hyacinthe De Coppier, and Émile Dorian)
K: 6.1827. Not launched as sail. Steam 1858.

Ajax Brest Dyd
Projected in 1828 to be begun in 1829 but cancelled in 1828.

Diomède Brest Dyd
Projected in 1828 to be begun in 1829 but cancelled in 1828.

Tilsitt (ex *Diomède* 23.11.1839) Cherbourg Dyd. (Constructeurs, Jean-Baptiste Lefebvre and Louis Sollier)
Ord: 20.8.1831. K: 2.3.1832. L: 30.3.1854. Comm: 20.5.1854. C: 6.1854.
Guns as completed (1854) as *Breslaw* except SD 20 x 16cm shell. Modified with round stern in 1850 based on plans by Sollier.
Decomm. 13.11.1854, steam 1856.

Charlemagne (ex *Hector* 2.4.1850) Toulon Dyd. (Constructeurs, Jacques Bonard, Jean-Baptiste Pironneau, and Émile Dorian)
K: 4.1834. Not launched as sail. Steam 1851.

Masséna (ex *Sceptre* 2.4.1850) Toulon Dyd. (Constructeurs, Jacques Bonard, Jean-Antoine Vincent, Jean-Baptiste Pironneau, and others)
K: 9.1835. Not launched as sail. Steam 1860.

Castiglione Toulon Dyd. (Constructeurs, Jacques Bonard, Jean-Antoine Vincent, Jean-Baptiste Pironneau, and others)
K: 10.1835. Modified with round stern c1849. Not launched as sail. Steam 1860.

Argonaute Toulon Dyd
Projected in 1836 to be begun in 1837 but not laid down, cancelled c12.1838.

DUQUESNE Class – 90 guns. The budget for 1847, presented in December 1845, contained a new 3rd Rank ship of the line, *Duquesne,* to be begun at Brest in 1847, and the budget for 1848, presented in January 1847, added a second ship, *Tourville*, both to be begun at Brest in 1848. These ships were designed as raséed three-deckers. They were near copies of Sané's three-deck 110-gun *Iéna*, itself a slightly shortened version of the original *Océan* class. *Iéna* was raséed to a two-deck 90-gun ship in 1826-33 and proved highly successful. Paul Leroux's plans for the two new ships, which duplicated as closely as possible Sané's 110-gun design as raséed, were approved on 25 June 1847 with the stipulation that they be given round sterns, which had just been ordered used on all new ships of the line and frigates. Joseph De Gasté drafted the plans for the round sterns in 1852. Because of the origin of their design, these ships had a hull capacity substantially greater than other 3rd Rank ships and were re-rated as 2nd Rank ships when converted to steam.

Dimensions & tons: 60.42m, 59.61m wl x 16.24m, 16.69m ext x 8.12m. 3,750 tons. Draught 7.23m mean. Men: 811.
Guns: (Design) LD 26 x 30pdrs No.1, 4 x 22cm No.1 shell; UD 32 x 30pdrs No.2; SD 24 x 30pdr carronades, 4 x 16cm shell.

Duquesne Brest Dyd. (Constructeurs, Paul Leroux, Joseph Fauveau and others)
K: 4.8.1847. Not launched as sail. Steam 1853.

Tourville Brest Dyd. (Constructeurs, Alexandre Chedeville, Jean-Baptiste Pastoureau-Labesse, and Victor Gervaise)
K: 26.8.1847. Not launched as sail. Steam 1853.

REPEAT SUFFREN Class – 90 guns.
Two of these ships first appeared in the 1849 budget as already under

Napoléon, 90 guns, built to an innovative design by the young Dupuy de Lôme, was effectively the prototype of the fast steam line of battleship, in which screw propulsion took precedence over sail rather than being regarded as an auxiliary (this was symbolised by the non-hoisting screw, as the drag of the propeller when under sail was less of an issue in a ship optimised for steaming). The design was regarded as a great success and a large number of similar ships followed. (© National Maritime Museum PW8120)

construction, while the third, *Jean Bart*, was ordered on 16 October 1848 in the 1849 program of works for Lorient and was to be built on the plans of *Inflexible*, presumably with the latter's round stern. Technical specifications were as the original class, above, except that they were probably designed with the armament adopted as standard for this type on 14 April 1838: LD 26 x 30pdrs No.1, 4 x 22cm No.1 shell; UD 32 x 30pdrs No.2; SD 24 x 30pdr carronades, 4 x 16cm shell. Two of these repeat units were completed with steam propulsion and the third received it soon after completion.

Saint Louis (ex *Achille* 2.4.1850) Brest Dyd. (Constructeurs, Paul Leroux, Joseph Fauveau, and others)
    K: 13.7.1848. L: 25.4.1854. Comm: 20.5.1854. C: 6.1854. Decomm. 19.2.1856, steam 1857.

Alexandre Rochefort Dyd. (Constructeurs, Pierre Rossin, Henri De Lisleferme, Bernard Chariot, Victorin Sabattier, and Charles Brun)
    K: 30.5.1848. Not launched as sail. Steam 1857.

Jean Bart Lorient Dyd. (Constructeur, Pierre Thomeuf)
    Ord: 16.10.1848. K: 26.1.1849. Not launched as sail. Steam 1852.

(E) Screw two-deckers, 2nd and 3rd Ranks

NAPOLÉON – 3rd Rank. On 9 December 1846 the Minister of Marine ordered the ports to develop plans for installing screw machinery in several ships of the line and frigates then on the ways. The 30-year-old *sous-ingénieur de 1re classe* Stanislas-Charles-Henri Dupuy de Lôme felt that such conversions were a good way of using existing hulls, but also felt that a much more radical advance could be made if a new steam battleship were designed from scratch. While his colleagues prepared plans for sailing ships with auxiliary steam power (see below), he designed a true steamer which also had all the combat strength of 90-gun sailing ships of the line. The only thing he sacrificed was endurance – because the ship would have to replenish its coal supply fairly often, he reduced its supply of provisions and water to 2 months from the 4-6 months carried by sailing ships. The converted ships underwent a similar reduction, which effectively limited the new ships to operations in European waters. Dupuy de Lôme's plans were approved on 11 January 1848 and construction of one ship was ordered.

On 3 April 1848 the Director of Ports offered to the Minister of Marine a choice between three names for the then-unnamed ship, *Vengeur*, *Républicain*, and *Redoutable*, but the Minister, the astronomer François Arago, instead selected *24 Février*, the date of the declaration of

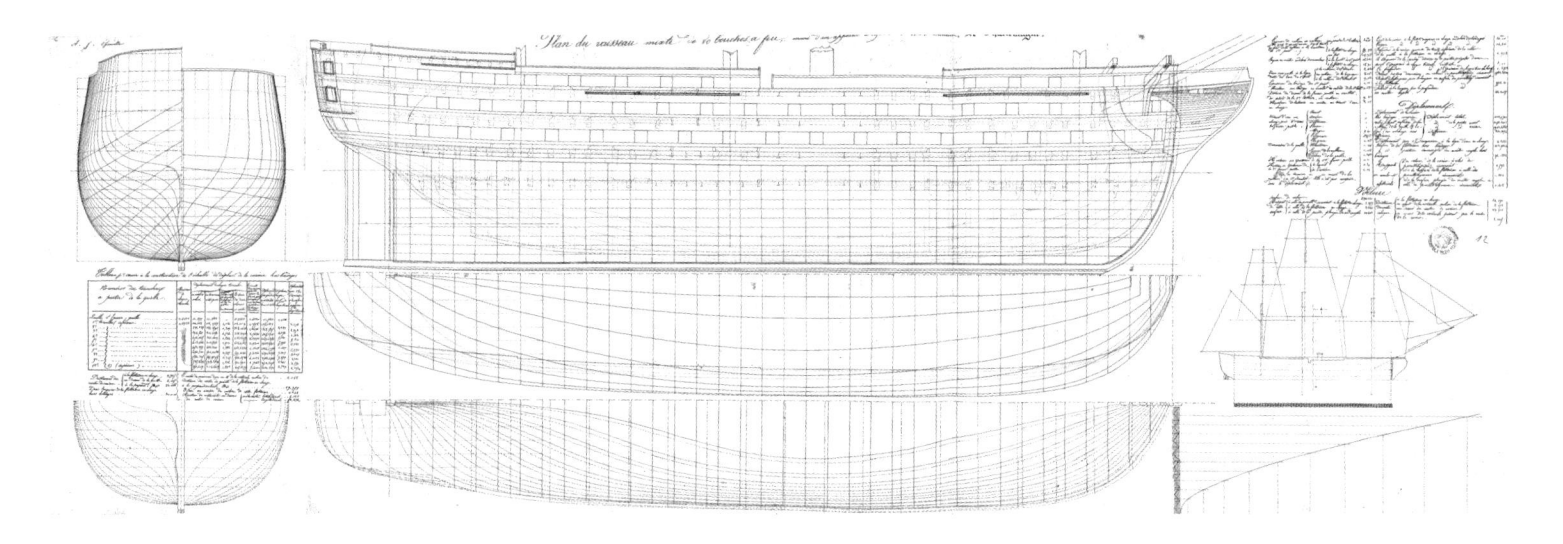

The lines of the 90-gun Charlemagne as converted to steam, with an elongated stern section to accommodate a hoisting screw. Despite a rig reduced to the scale of an 80-gun ship (2,802 sq.m.), in ideal conditions Charlemagne was still faster under sail than steam. (Atlas du Génie Maritime, Genoa collection, image 2-0012)

the French Second Republic, and Toulon was so informed on 8 April. The ship was launched under this name but on 27 May 1850 the new Minister, now the naval commodore Joseph Romain-Desfossés, notified Toulon that the President of the Republic (the future Napoleon III) had (on 17 May) accepted his proposal to rename her *Napoléon*. Her trials were regarded as a sensational success – on 30 August 1852 during a run from Toulon to Ajaccio she averaged 12.14 knots over a distance of 119 miles and reached 13 knots for short periods. Her armament was redistributed several times in the 1850s as the navy experimented with its new standard type of battleship. Her engines were highly successful on trials, but their gearing (as in most early geared screw machinery) created maintenance problems and new direct-drive engines were ultimately fitted. *Napoléon* and the comparable three-decker *Bretagne* had two funnels for their eight boilers, but the eight later ships of the *Napoléon* class (see the Later *Napoléon* class, below) had a single funnel. *Napoléon* and her later sisters were reclassified as 2nd Rank ships of the line in 1855 because of their length and speed.

   Dimensions & tons: 71.46m, 71.23m wl, 64.30m x 16.22m, 16.80m ext x 8.16m. 5,120 tons. Draught 7.46/8.26m. Men: 913.
   Machinery: 960nhp (designed by Moll). 2 cylinders, geared, 12.14kts sustained on trials. Coal 615 tons. Replaced 1861 by 900nhp engines (Mazeline), direct, 1798ihp, 12.94kts.
   Guns: (*Napoléon*, 1852) LD 32 x 30pdrs No.1, 4 x 22cm No.1 shell; UD 26 x 30pdrs No.2, 4 x 22cm No.2 shell; SD 14 x 16cm shell, 10 x 30pdr carronades.

Napoléon (ex *24 Février* 17.5.1850) Toulon Dyd/Indret.
   Ord: 11.1.1848. K: 7.2.1848. Named: 3.4.1848 (*24 Février*). L: 16.5.1850. Comm: 1.5.1852. C: 30.8.1852 (completion of trials with a 12.4-knot run from Toulon to Ajaccio).
   To reserve 13.2.1867. Prison ship for Communards at Brest 5.1871 to 4.1872. Decomm. 26.4.1872. Struck 6.11.1876, hulk at Brest. BU 1886.

CHARLEMAGNE – 3rd Rank. This conversion had its origins in a recommendation from Toulon on 11 November 1846 to fit screw machinery in the 74-gun *Nestor* during a planned refit. On 16 June 1848 the navy decided to ask Louis Benet at La Ciotat to have his British engineer (Barnes) design 450nhp engines for *Nestor*, and it ordered the engines from Benet by a contract signed on 19 May 1849. But on 16 April 1849 Paris received a report from Toulon that *Nestor* was too rotten to be worth refitting and a new hull, first *Castiglione* (ordered 21 May 1849) and then *Charlemagne*, was substituted. Jean-Baptiste Pironneau's plans for the conversion of the hull (including a round stern) were approved by the Council of Works on 26 January 1850, and on 17 September 1850 work was ordered begun. The conversion was limited to lengthening the stern 8ft 6in (2.60m) for a hoisting screw mechanism. Installation of her engines began in February 1851. *Charlemagne* and the other converted 90-gunners received the rig of sailing 80-gun ships (*Jupiter*, etc.). The ship did unexpectedly well on trials, developing 630nhp, maintaining a mean speed of 8.5kts, and reaching 9.45kts for short periods. She also did very well (11 knots) under sail.

   Dimensions & tons: 60.10m, 59.80m wl, 58.78m x 16.24m ext x 8.05m. 4,124 tons. Draught 6.90/7.90m. Men: 814.
   Machinery: 450nhp (designed by John Barnes). 4 cylinders, direct, 1206ihp, 9.5kts. Coal 260t.
   Guns: (1852) LD 24 x 30pdrs No.1, 6 x 22cm No.1 shell; UD 26 x 30pdrs No.2, 6 x 22cm No.2 shell; SD 18 x 16cm shell.

Charlemagne Toulon Dyd/Benet, La Ciotat.
   Ord: 17.9.1850. Start: 1850. L: 16.1.1851. Comm: 14.9.1851. C: 12.1851.
   Damaged by a shell exploding in the engine room 17.10.1854. Decomm. 16.9.1857. Converted to a steam transport at Lorient 1867-68 but, except for trials 1869-70, spent the rest of her career in reserve at Toulon. Struck 7.2.1882. BU 1884.

AUSTERLITZ - 2nd Rank. On 9 December 1846 the Minister of Marine ordered Rochefort and Indret to draft plans for putting 540nhp screw machinery in *Turenne*, under construction at Rochefort. Specifications for the conversion decided upon by the Council of Works on 30 June 1847 called for reducing provisions and spares from 6 to 2 months, water from 4 to 1 month, ballast from 320 to 70 tons, and rig from that of a 100-gun ship to that of a 90-gunner. The 930 tons thus made available were to accommodate the most powerful engine possible (650nhp) and 8 days of coal. On 30 November 1847 *Ulm* was substituted for *Turenne* and on 2 May 1849 *Austerlitz* was substituted for *Ulm*. Louis Alexandre Corrard, at Cherbourg, then began drafting the detailed plans and discovered that the specified changes made only 810 tons available. He recommended lengthening the ship, but on 24 December 1849 the ministry decided instead to reduce the size of the engines, already a tenth built, to 500nhp. Corrard was not notified of

this decision until 16 October 1850, and his final plans were approved by the Council of Works on 22 January 1851. Her engines were loaded at Indret by the transport *Cormoran* in December 1852 for transportation to Cherbourg and were installed between March and October 1853.
  Dimensions & tons: 70.62m, 70.32m wl x 16.80m ext x 8.23m. 4,467 tons. Draught 7.67m. Men: 883.
  Machinery: 500nhp. Direct, 10.2kts. Coal 378 tons.
  Guns: (1853) LD 30 x 30pdrs No.1, 2 x 22cm No.1 shell; UD 30 x 30pdrs No.2, 2 x 22cm No.2 shell; SD 4 x 30pdrs No.1, 16 x 16cm shell, 2 x 22cm No.1 shell.
Austerlitz Cherbourg Dyd/Indret.
  Ord: 5.11.1849. Start: 1850. L: 15.9.1852. Comm: 1.5.1853. C: 10.1853.
  To reserve 19.5.1862. Prison ship for Communards at Brest 5.1871 to 3.1872. Struck 22.7.1872. Became boys' training hulk at Brest 1874 (replacing *Inflexible*), relieved by *Fontenoy* and sold for BU 1895.

JEAN BART – 3rd Rank. On 9 December 1846 the Minister of Marine ordered Lorient to develop plans for installing screw machinery in the frigate *Vengeance* on the ways there. The frigate *Entreprenante* was substituted on 30 November 1847 and machinery of 400nhp was subsequently begun at Indret for her. On 23 October 1849 Indret reported that the same type of miscalculation had been made for this conversion as for *Austerlitz*. The frigate engines, however, were too far advanced to be reduced in size as were those of the battleship, and instead on 24 December they were ordered modified to 450nhp for a 3rd

A coloured lithograph depicting the newly converted screw line of battleship *Austerlitz* joining the Anglo-French fleet in the Baltic at the beginning of the Russian War. The ship has a new round stern with a projecting wrought-iron balcony for an admiral's walk. (© National Maritime Museum PU6155)

Rank ship of the line. *Jean Bart* was selected on 4 February 1850. The conversion, on plans by Pierre Thomeuf approved by the Council of Works on 6 April 1850, consisted of lengthening the stern 2.80m for a hoisting screw mechanism. The new stern was round. Between March 1861 and August 1862 the early Indret screw machinery in this ship was replaced at Brest with the Mazeline engines salvaged from *Duquesne*.
  Dimensions & tons: 63.60m, 60.70m wl, 57.50m x 16.26m ext x 8.05m. 4,070 tons. Draught 7.40m mean. Men: 814.
  Machinery: 450nhp (designed by Moll). 4 cylinders, direct, 1010ihp, 10kts. Coal 380 tons.
  Guns: (1853) LD 26 x 30pdrs No.1, 4 x 22cm No.1 shell; UD 26 x 30pdrs No.2, 4 x 22cm No.2 shell; SD 4 x 30pdrs No.1, 12 x 16cm shell.
Jean Bart Lorient Dyd/Indret.
  Ord: 4.2.1850. Start: 1850. L: 14.9.1852. Comm: 11.4.1853. C: 4.1853.
  Transported troops to Mexico 2-3.1863. Became seagoing training ship for *aspirants* (*École d'Application*) after refit at Brest 7-10.1864. Exchanged names with her replacement, *Donawerth*, 20.8.1868. Struck under name *Donawerth* 18.1.1869 and BU 1869.

ULM – 2nd Rank. Seven ships of the line then on the ways including *Ulm* were designated for conversion to screw propulsion in mid-1852. These seven conversions were prompted by the successful trials of *Charlemagne* and the burgeoning program of the British, who had reportedly already completed or ordered conversions of 10 ships of the line, 8 frigates, and 2 corvettes. The designs for the conversions packed 650nhp engines and their coal into the ships by various means, including reduction of the rig and a corresponding reduction in ballast. These and the other converted 100-gunners received the rig of sail 90-gun ships (*Suffren*, etc.). Unlike most other French screw conversions, these seven did not have a hoisting screw. Engines for all seven ships were ordered in August 1852, that of *Ulm* being assigned to Indret for comparison with the contract-built engines of the other six. Plans by Charles-Henri Moll (Indret) for *Ulm*'s engines were approved on 28 August 1852 and conversion plans by Victorin Sabattier were approved on 20 April 1853. Like most other conversions, she was fitted with a round stern copied from the sail *Inflexible*.

Dimensions & tons: 62.50m, 62.30m wl, 57.00m x 17.06m ext x 8.07m. 4,493 tons. Draught 7.10/8.20m. Men: 883.
Machinery: 650nhp. 10.38kts. Coal 500 tons.
Guns: (1855) LD 16 x 36pdrs, 16 x 22cm No.1 shell; UD 16 x 30pdrs No.2, 16 x 22cm No.2 shell; SD 2 x 50pdrs, 16 x 30pdrs No.4.

Ulm Rochefort Dyd/Indret.
Ord: 7.6.1852. Start: 1853. L: 13.5.1854. Comm: 6.11.1854. C: 11.1854.
Transported troops to Mexico 9-10.1862. Decomm. 12.6.1865. Struck 25.11.1867, coal hulk at Brest. BU 1890.

PRINCE JÉRÔME Class - 2nd Rank. These two ships were among seven ships on the ways that were designated for conversion in mid-1852. Their engines were ordered from Schneider by a contract approved on 18 August 1852. Plans by Guillaume Masson were approved by the Council of Works on 22 December 1852 with the provision that the stern above the waterline imitate that of *Inflexible*. Their beam included a sheathing about 20cm thick.

Dimensions & tons: 62.87m, 62.65m wl, 58.26m x 17.01m ext x 8.20m. 4,505 tons. Draught 7.20/8.04m. Men: 883.
Machinery: 650nhp. Coal 548 tons.
Guns: (*Wagram* 1855) LD 28 x 30pdrs No.1, 4 x 22cm No.1 shell; UD 28 x 30pdrs No.2, 4 x 22cm No.2 shell; SD 4 x 30pdrs No.1, 14 x 30pdrs No.4.

Prince Jérôme (ex *Annibal* 24.5.1854) Lorient Dyd/Schneider.
Ord: 13 & 27.11.1852. Start: 1853. L: 2.12.1853. Comm: 1.9.1854. C: 10.1854.
Trooping voyage to Mexico interrupted by a fire on board near Gibraltar 6.9.1862. Decomm. 1.1.1863. Renamed *Hoche* 19.9.1870. Struck 6.6.1872, engines removed, but hull in good condition and reinstated on the list 28.11.1872 as the sail transport *Loire* (1,372 tons burthen). Converted at Toulon 11.1872 to 3.1873 and made eight voyages transporting convicts to New Caledonia 1873-85. Struck 13.7.1886. Replaced the ironclad *Atalante* as headquarters hulk at Saigon 1887, replaced by the ironclad *Triomphante* 1895, BU 1897.

Wagram Lorient Dyd/Schneider.
Ord: 13 & 27.11.1852. Start: 1853. L: 12.6.1854. Comm: 16.1.1855. C: 1.1855.
Transported troops to Mexico 9-11.1862 and 2-3.1863. Decomm 10.8.1864. Became service craft at Brest at the beginning of 1867, cut down for use in trials with mines and torpedoes by the Commission on Underwater Defences, and sunk by a torpedo 29.4.1867. Struck 22.7.1867, experiments continued until she was cut in half and sunk 3.12.1867 in the river at Landerneau by the detonation of three torpedoes.

DUQUESNE Class - 2nd Rank. These two ships were among seven ships on the ways that were designated for conversion in mid-1852. Their engines were ordered from Mazeline by a contract approved on 18 August 1852. Unlike other new French 90-gun ships they were not of the *Suffren* class but were copies of a raséed 110-gunner, the *Iéna*. As a result, they had the hull capacity of a 2nd Rank battleship (and were rated as such after about 1855) but were shorter. Their conversion plans, by Victor Gervaise and Jean-Baptiste Pastoureau-Labesse, were approved on 4 April 1853. During conversion, they were lengthened 1.95m aft to provide finer lines for the screw. They had round sterns. They received the rig of a 90-gun sailing ship (*Suffren*, etc.). The original spardeck armament of *Tourville* was 4 x 30pdrs No.1, 12 x 30pdrs No.4 but it was changed during trials by a ministerial decree of 16 February 1855 to the one shown below, which was also fitted to *Duquesne*. The engines of *Tourville* were installed between April and December 1854.

Dimensions & tons: 62.84m, 61.40m wl, 56.75m x 16.88m ext x 8.12m. 4,566 tons. Draught 7.59/7.99m. Men: 814.
Machinery: 650nhp. 10kts (*Duquesne* 10.44kts). Coal 520 tons.
Guns: (*Tourville*, 1854) LD 26 x 30pdrs No.1, 4 x 22cm No.1 shell; UD 28 x 30pdrs No.2, 4 x 22cm No.2 shell; SD 2 x 50pdrs, 18 x 30pdr carronades.

Duquesne Brest Dyd/Mazeline.
Ord: 13 & 27.11.1852. Start: 1853. L: 2.12.1853. Comm: 12.10.1854. C: 10.1854.
Transported troops to Mexico 8-10.1862, to reserve 19.3.1863. Struck 6.9.1867. Became barracks and guard hulk at Brest, renamed *Veilleur* 1872, BU 1888.

Tourville Brest Dyd/Mazeline.
Ord: 13 & 27.11.1852. Start: early 1853. L: 31.10.1853. Comm: 28.8.1854. C: 12.1854.
Transported troops to Mexico 8-10.1862, to reserve 13.8.1864. Prison hulk for Communards at Brest 5.1871. Struck 12.8.1872, barracks hulk at Cherbourg, renamed *Nestor* 21.8.1873, BU 1877-78.

FLEURUS Class - 2nd Rank. These two ships were among seven ships on the ways that were designated in mid-1852 for conversion along the lines of *Charlemagne* and *Austerlitz*. Their engines were ordered from Schneider by a contract approved on 18 August 1852. They were converted on plans requested from Stanislas-Charles-Henri Dupuy de Lôme on 10 September 1852 and approved on 7 December 1852. Both retained their original square sterns as an economy measure. None of the converted 100-gun and 90-gun ships of the line retained the 2.00m lower battery height above water of their original sailing designs; *Navarin* was typical with her measurement of 1.85m at 7.72m mean draught in 1855.

Dimensions & tons: (*Fleurus*) 62.50m, 62.07m wl, 56.80m x 16.98m ext x 8.15m. 4,509 tons. Draught 7.80m mean. (*Navarin*) 62.00m wl x 16.88m ext x 8.15m. 4,562 tons. Draught 7.21/8.23m. Men: 883.
Machinery: 650nhp.
Guns: (*Fleurus* 1855) LD 24 x 30pdrs No.1, 8 x 22cm No.1 shell; UD 28 x 30pdrs No.2, 6 x 22cm No.2 shell; SD 22 x 30pdrs No.3, 2 x 16cm rifles.

Fleurus Toulon Dyd/Schneider.
Ord: 11.8.1852. Start: 1853. L: 2.12.1853. Comm: 1.7.1854. C: 10.1854.

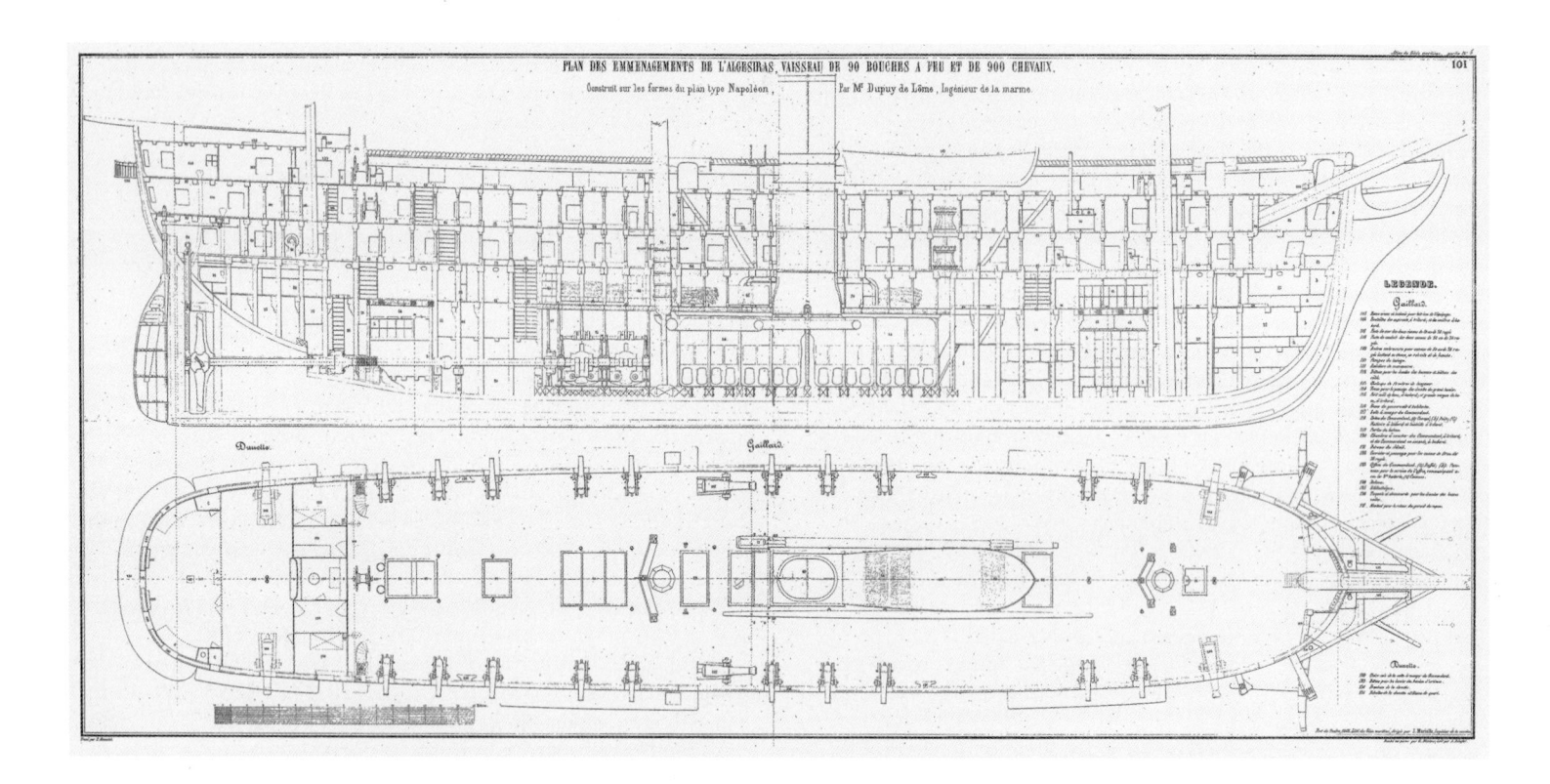

Trooping voyage to Mexico interrupted by collision near Gibraltar with transport *Charente* 6.9.1862. Decomm 28.4.1863. Engines condemned 21.5.67 and ship reclassified as a sailing ship. Refitted 8-9.1867 at Toulon as a headquarters ship for Saigon. In commission between 26.8.1867 and 25.5.1868 for the voyage to Indochina and then replaced *Duperré* as headquarters ship. Struck 17.8.1869 and listed among the service craft as a barracks hulk at Saigon. Condemned and sold at Saigon 1877.

Navarin Toulon Dyd/Schneider.
Ord: 11.8.1852. Start: 7.1853. L: 26.7.1854. Comm: 17.10.1854. C: 11.1854.

Transported troops to Mexico 8-10.1862. School ship for apprentice sailors at Toulon 1863. Returned troops from Mexico 3-4.1867. Engines removed and converted at Toulon to a sail transport 1873-74, made eight voyages carrying convicts to New Caledonia 1876-85. Struck 13.7.1886. Became barracks hulk for the torpedo school at Brest in 1886, floating workshop for the mobile defence force (*Défense mobile*) there in 1888, and headquarters hulk for the torpedo boats there in 1891. Sold 1908.

Later NAPOLÉON Class – 3rd Rank. In May 1852 two sisters to *Napoléon*, *Algésiras* and *Arcole*, replaced four 550nhp frigates in the building program. After *Napoléon*'s successful trials on 30 August 1852 they were ordered on 13 November 1852. For these ships Stanislas-Charles-Henri Dupuy de Lôme retained all the features of the original *Napoléon* except for the machinery arrangement, the engines being relocated from between two groups of boilers to aft of a single group. Six more sisters were ordered as rapidly as possible between February 1853 and April 1854. All but *Algésiras* (and *Napoléon*) had hoisting screws. The class received the rig of a 80-gun sailing ship (*Jupiter*, etc.). The height of the battery in *Algésiras* as completed was 1.94m. The ships were reclassified as 2nd Rank ships of the line in 1855 because of their length and speed.

Ville de Bordeaux was commissioned unusually early in the fitting-out

The internal arrangements of *Algésiras*, a sister of *Napoléon* but with different machinery. Like the later ships of the class, she had only one funnel, but retained the fixed propeller of the prototype whereas the later ships incorporated a lifting screw. (Atlas du Génie Maritime, French collection, plate 101)

process, and her machinery was not fully installed until September 1861. (Normally, French steamers began to go into commission no more than five months before their machinery installation was complete.) *Intrépide* was completed belatedly as a transport. Her original engines were ordered from Rochefort in 1853. Designed by Sabattier, they had 4 cylinders and were on Penn's system (presumably trunk engines). They were later split for use in two frigates (*Circé* and *Flore*) and replaced by a new set of 900nhp trunk engines from Indret.

Dimensions & tons: 71.46m, 71.23m wl, 64.30m x 16.22m, 16.80m ext x 8.16m. 5,121 tons. (*Ville de Nantes*: 72.55m, 71.76m wl. *Ville de Lyon*: 72.00m, 71.37m wl x 16.75m.) Draught 7.25/8.45m. Men: 913.

Machinery: *Algésiras*: 900nhp (designed by Dupuy de Lôme). 2 cylinders, direct, return connecting rod, 2,057ihp, 13.014kts sustained on trials. *Ville de Nantes*: 900nhp (designed by Dupuy de Lôme or Mangin). Direct. *Intrépide*: 900nhp. Trunk, trials 2,204ihp = 12.24kts. Others: 900nhp (designed by Moll). 4 cylinders, direct. Coal 570 tons.

Guns: (*Algésiras*, *Redoutable*, and *Impérial*) LD 18 x 36pdrs, 16 x 22cm No.1 shell; UD 34 x 30pdrs No.2; SD 20 x 16cm shell, 2 x 16cm rifles; (*Arcole*) as *Algésiras* except SD 20 x 30pdrs No.4, 2 x 16cm rifles. For the armaments of the three *Villes* as completed see their individual entries.

Algésiras Toulon Dyd/Toulon (Constructeur, Dupuy de Lôme)
Ord: 13.11.1852. K: 4.1853. L: 4.10.1855. Comm: 10.4.1856. C: 5.1856.
Decomm. 10.2.1865. Rebuilt as a transport in 1869-70 (when she

TWO-DECKER SHIPS OF THE LINE, 80 TO 100 GUNS

Impérial at Brest, probably photographed soon after completion in 1858. She appears to have her full original armament of 90 guns, which she retained into the early 1860s. (Marius Bar)

gained an additional deck and a poop), and still on transport duty in 1882. Refitted as torpedo school ship at Toulon 4.1889. Struck 20.11.1901. Became accommodation ship for torpedo apprentices at Toulon, burned accidentally 25.11.1906.

Arcole Cherbourg Dyd/Indret (Constructeurs, Prix-Charles Sochet and Louis Corrard)
   Ord: 13.11.1852. K: 4.3.1853. Named: 9.3.1853. L: 20.3.1855. Comm: 8.5.1856. C: 9.1856.
   To reserve 1.5.1864, struck 11.4.1870, hulk at Cherbourg. Prison hulk for Communards 5.1871, BU 72.

Redoutable Rochefort Dyd/Indret (Constructeurs, Victorin Sabattier and Henri Denis de Senneville)
   Ord: 17.2.1853. K: 11.4.1853. L: 25.10.1855. Comm: 24.11.1856. C: 11.1856.
   Decomm. 25.2.1865. Struck 15.11.1869, hulk at Brest. BU 1873-74 at Brest.

Impérial Brest Dyd/Indret (Constructeurs, Joseph Fauveau and others)
   Ord: 12.7.1853. K: 19.8.1853. L: 15.9.1856. Comm: 20.2.1858. C: 2.1858.
   Transported troops to Mexico 6-8.1862. To reserve 1.3.1865. Struck 15.11.1869, barracks hulk at Toulon, renamed *Jupiter* 19.9.1870, BU 1897.

Intrépide Rochefort Dyd/Rochefort (Constructeurs, Victorin Sabattier, Henri De Lisleferme, Henri Denis de Senneville and Auguste Boden)
   Ord: 23.8.1853. K: 2.9.1853. L: 17.9.1864. Comm: 8.5.1865. C: 9.1865. Conversion to a transport (4-30pdrs) begun 6.1863 before launching.

   Returned troops from Mexico 3-4.1867. Condemned 8.1887, engines removed and third deck added at Toulon 1887-89. Taken to Brest, then on 6.12.1889 struck, relieved the former *Valmy* as naval school hulk at Brest, and assumed the name *Borda*. Retired 1912, sank accidentally 5.1913 at Cherbourg, sold and BU in situ 1914-1922.

Ville de Nantes Cherbourg Dyd/Cherbourg (Constructeurs, Prix-Charles Sochet and others)
   Ord: 3.4.1854. K: 20.6.1854 (frame begun). On ways 7.1856. L: 7.8.1858. Comm: 25.10.1860. C: 10.1860.
   Guns (1863) LD 24-30pdrs No.1, 10-16cm rifles; UD 24-30pdrs No.2, 10-22cm No.2 shell; SD 4-16cm rifles, 6-16cm shell.
   In reserve from completion of trials in 1863 to 3.1867, decomm. 14.5.1867. Prison ship for Communards at Cherbourg 5.1871 to 4.1872. Struck 28.11.1872, hulk at Cherbourg. Sold for BU 1887.

Ville de Bordeaux Lorient Dyd/Indret (Constructeurs, Hippolyte Prétot and others)
   Ord: 3.4.1854. K: 26.6.1854. L: 21.5.1860. Comm: 5.11.1860. C: 11.1860.
   Guns (1862) as *Ville de Lyon* except SD 20 x 16cm shell, 2 x 16cm M1858 MLR.
   Transported troops to Mexico 8-10.1862, in reserve 1863 to 7.1866,

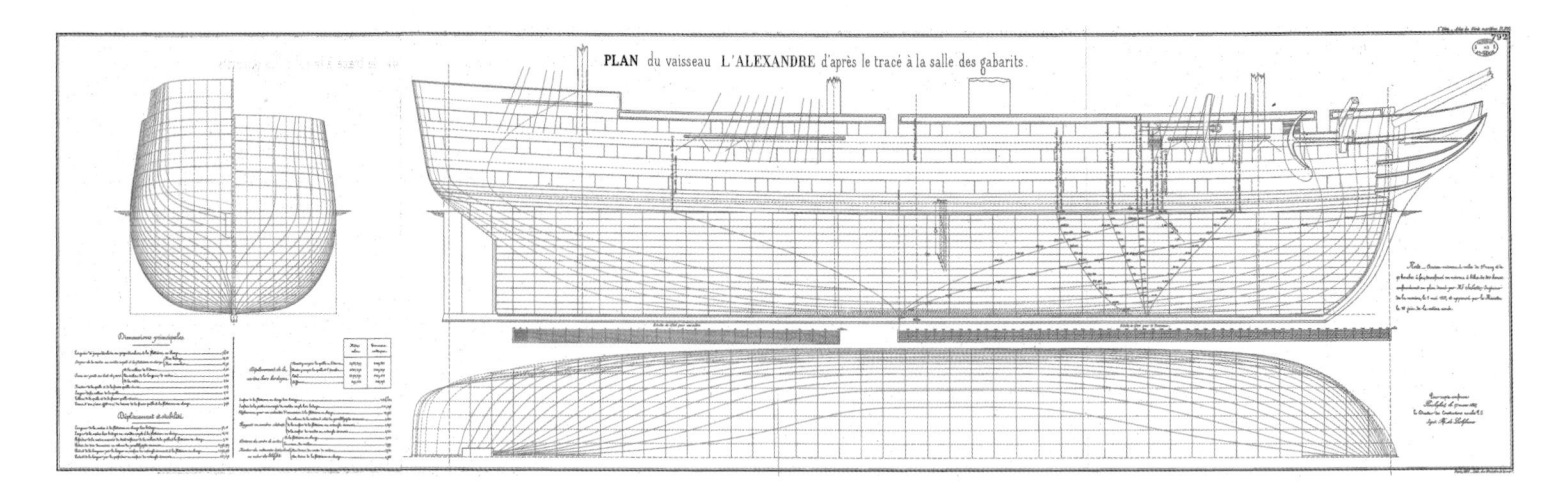

The official lines plan for the *Alexandre* as converted to screw propulsion, dated 5 May 1855 and formally approved on 18 June following; the plan was the work of Victorin-Gabriel Sabattier. The ship was cut in half and lengthened during the conversion process to accommodate high-powered machinery as in *Napoléon*, as indicated by the parallel section abaft the funnel. (Atlas du Génie Maritime, French collection, plate 792)

returned troops from Mexico 3-4.1867, and to reserve 12.6.1867. Prison ship for Communards at Brest 5.1871 to 5.1872. Struck 14.1.1879. Relieved *Bretagne* 1.1880 as school hulk for novices and apprentice seamen at Brest and assumed the name *Bretagne*. Replaced by *Fontenoy* and BU 1894.

Ville de Lyon Brest Dyd/Indret (Constructeurs, Joseph Fauveau and others)
Ord: 3.4.1854. K: 30.3.1855. L: 26.2.1861. Comm: 4.11.1861. C: 11.1861.
Guns as completed (1861) LD 34 x 16cm (30pdr) M1858 MLR; UD 34 x 30pdrs No.2; SD 12 x 30pdrs No.3, 2 x 16cm M1858 MLR.
Transported troops to Mexico 8-10.1862. School ship for novices and apprentice seamen at Brest 11.1863 to 1865. Returned troops from Mexico 3-4.1867, then to reserve 18.6.1867. Prison ship for Communards at Brest 5.1871 to 4.1872. Struck 28.6.1883, BU 1885 at Brest.

EYLAU - 2nd Rank. On 10 September 1852 the Minister of Marine ordered Stanislas-Charles-Henri Dupuy de Lôme to prepare plans for conversion of ships on the ways at Toulon to both fast battleships on the lines of *Napoléon* and mixed propulsion ships like *Austerlitz*. For the fast battleships Dupuy de Lôme proposed to cut ships on the ways in half at the midships section, slide the stern down the ways around 10 metres, and fill in the gap with new hull structure. This procedure would produce a hull with finer lines and capacity for a large steam engine and its coal. The conversion of *Eylau* to a fast battleship was ordered on 13 November 1852. Dupuy de Lôme's conversion plans dated 10 September 1852 were approved by the Council of Works on 12 January 1853. Her engines were ordered from François Cavé by a contract approved on 8 April 1853. *Eylau* retained her original square stern. The lengthening added two gunports per deck on each side.
Dimensions & tons: 69.22m, 68.72m wl, 64.12m x 16.80m ext x 8.07m. 5,023 tons. Draught 6.96/8.16m. Men: 913.
Machinery: 900nhp. 4 cylinders. Coal 765 tons.
Guns: (1857) LD 18 x 36pdrs, 16 x 22cm No.1 shell; UD 34 x 30pdrs No.2; SD 2 x 16cm rifles, 20 x 30pdrs No.4.
Eylau Toulon Dyd/Cavé.
Ord: 13.11.1852. Start: 5.7.1853. L: 15.5.1856. Comm: 8.3.1857. C: 3.1857.
Transported troops to Mexico 6-8.1862, returned 11.1862 with yellow fever on board. Third deck added and converted to transport at Toulon 1862 or early 1863. Decomm. 25.2.1865. Struck 22.2.1877, barracks hulk at Toulon. Replaced by a building ashore and sold 1905.

ALEXANDRE – 2nd Rank. On 19 October 1854 the Minister of Marine included *Alexandre* in a list of conversions to be begun in 1855. Three 3rd Rank ships still on the ways, *Alexandre*, *Masséna*, and *Castiglione* were to be given full steam power as in *Eylau* to provide a ratio in the fleet of one fast battleship for every two with auxiliary steam propulsion after the conversion program was completed. *Alexandre*'s conversion was given the go-ahead on 1 December 1854, and Victorin Sabattier's conversion plans were approved by the Council of Works on 29 May 1855. Machinery plans by Charles-Henri Moll (Indret) were approved on 12 April 1855. The ship was reclassified as a 2nd Rank ship of the line in 1855 because of her length and speed. She was cut in half amidships and, on 28 April 1856, lengthened by sliding the stern half 10.08m down the building ways. (The start of conversion dates shown for this ship and for *Eylau* and the *Masséna* class are the dates on which this lengthening took place; preparatory work began in June 1855 for *Alexandre*.) The lengthening added three gunports per deck on each side. Unlike the other three converted fast battleships she had a round stern.
Dimensions & tons: 73.38m, 72.03m wl, 67.75m x 16.25m ext x 8.05m. 5,292 tons. Draught 6.90m, 8.10m. Men: 913.
Machinery: 800nhp. Coal 600 tons.
Guns: (1858) LD 18 x 36pdrs, 16 x 22cm No.1 shell; UD 34 x 30pdrs No.2; SD 2 x 16cm rifles, 20 x 16cm shell.
Alexandre Rochefort Dyd/Indret.
Ord: 19.10.1854. Start: 28.4.1856. L: 27.3.1857. Comm: 1.9.1857. C: 14.4.1858 (began trials).
To reserve 20.7.1864. Engines condemned and ordered removed 20.11.1871, ship converted at Toulon to a transport for the deportation of convicts, but instead relieved *Louis XIV* 28.5.1872 as gunnery training ship at Toulon. Replaced by *Souverain*, struck 22.2.1877, replaced *Colosse* (ex *Friedland*) as barracks hulk for seamen at Toulon, sold for BU 1900.

MASSÉNA Class - 2nd Rank. The origin of the conversion of these two 3rd Rank ships was the same as for *Alexandre* except that they were carried out on plans by Stanislas-Charles-Henri Dupuy de Lôme with stern modifications by Henri Kerris approved by the Council of Works on 1 April 1856. Their conversion by lengthening and fitting with engines of 800nhp from Indret was approved on 19 October 1854. Machinery plans by Charles-Henri Moll (Indret) were approved on 12 April 1855. They were also reclassified as 2nd Rank ships of the line in 1855 because of their length and speed. They retained their original square sterns. The commissioning process for these two ships began early, and they did not have their machinery installations completed until May and December 1861 respectively.

Dimensions & tons: 73.97m, 72.99m wl, 67.70m x 16.28m ext x 8.04m. 5,137 tons. Draught 6.71/8.15m. Men: 913.
Machinery: 800nhp. Trials 2189ihp = 11.46kts (*Masséna*), 2259ihp = 11.77kts (*Castiglione*). Coal 550 tons.
Guns: (Both, 1863) LD 18 x 30pdrs No.1, 16 x 16cm M1858 MLR (16 x 22cm shell in *Castiglione*); UD 34 x 30pdrs No.2; SD 20 x 16cm shell, 2 x 16cm rifles.

Masséna Toulon Dyd./Indret.
Ord: 19.10.1854. Start: 12.3.1856. L: 15.3.1860. Comm: 21.4.1860. C: 11.1861.
Refitted as transport at Toulon 7.1866, returned troops from Mexico 2-4.1867, decomm. 10.6.1867. Struck 9.5.1879, barracks hulk at Toulon for the colonial infantry, renamed *Mars* 1892. Sank because of rotten timbers in the Missiessy Basin 18.6.1904, BU 1905-1906.

Castiglione Toulon Dyd/Indret.
Ord: 19.10.1854. Start: 2.1.1856. L: 4.7.1860. Comm: 15.7.1860. C: 1861.
Refitted as transport at Toulon 12.1866, returned troops from Mexico 3-4.1867, decomm. 1.6.1867. Struck 11.10.1881, barracks hulk for the Naval Infantry at Toulon, BU 1900.

BRESLAW Class – 3rd Rank. On 19 October 1854 the Minister of Marine included these two ships, which were already afloat, in a list of conversions to be undertaken in 1855, and on 6 November 1854 he ordered Brest to build engines for them. Victor Gervaize's plans for the machinery were approved on 11 January 1855 and his plans for the hull conversions were approved on 14 January 1856.

Dimensions & tons: 63.54m, 62.30m wl x 16.28m ext x 8.05m. 4,289 tons. Draught 7.12/8.44m. Men: 814.
Machinery: 500nhp. 2 cylinders, return connecting rod. Coal 430 tons.
Guns: (Both, 1859) LD 16 x 36pdrs, 14 x 22p No.1 shell; UD 30 x 30pdrs No.2; SD 2 x 16cm rifles, 12 x 30pdrs No.4, 6 x 30pdr carronades.

Breslaw Brest Dyd/Brest.
Ord: 19.10.1854. Start: c2.1856. L: 1856. Comm: 24.3.1858. C: 3.1858.
Transported troops to Mexico 9-10.1862. Decomm. 12.6.1865. Prison hulk for Communards at Brest 5.1871 to 1.1872. Struck 22.7.1872, guard hulk and after 1876 powder hulk at Brest. BU 1887.

Tilsitt Brest Dyd/Brest.
Ord: 19.10.1854. Start: 9.2.1856. L: 1856. C: 10.1859. Comm: 1.1.1860.
Transported troops to Mexico 8-10.1862 and 2-3.1863. Decomm. 11.2.1865. Prison ship for Communards at Brest 6.1871 to 4.1872. Struck 22.7.1872, hulk at Brest. Engines removed 1872. Left for Saigon 1.1877 to replace *Fleurus* as a barracks hulk. Sold there 1887.

DONAWERTH Class – 3rd Rank. On 19 October 1854 the Minister of Marine included these two ships, which were already afloat, in a list of conversions to be undertaken in 1855, but they were deferred when plans to build two battleship engines for them at Cherbourg were not carried out. Instead their engines were ordered from Mazeline by a contract approved on 11 July 1856. Conversion plans by Louis Corrard were approved by the Council of Works on 13 August 1856. The start dates below are the dates the ships were hauled out (*Saint Louis* followed *Donawerth* on the ways). The engines of *Donawerth* were installed between November 1857 and February 1858 and those of *Saint Louis* between February and August 1858.

Dimensions & tons: 60.50m, 60.28m wl, 57.00m x 15.75m, 16.28m ext x 8.05m. 4,231 tons. Draught 7.00/8.20m. Men: 814.
Machinery: 450nhp. 2 cylinders, return connecting rod, trials (*St. Louis*) 1411ihp = 9.86kts, (*Donawerth*) 1175ihp, 9kts. Coal 330t (*Donawerth* 380t).
Guns: (Both, 1859) LD 16 x 36pdrs, 14 x 22cm No.1 shell; UD 30 x 30pdrs No.2; SD 2 x 16cm rifles, 18 x 30pdr carronades.

Donawerth Cherbourg Dyd/Mazeline.
Ord: 19.10.1854. Start: 5.5.1856. L: 27.3.1857. C: 11.1857. Comm: 1.1.1858.
Decomm. 1.8.1864. Fitted as seagoing training ship for *aspirants* (*École d'Application*) 8-9.1868, renamed *Jean Bart* 20.9.1868, and served as such out of Brest until replaced by the frigate *Renommée* in 1873. Struck 13.4.1880. Became headquarters hulk for the reserves at Brest, renamed *Cyclope* 1886, BU 1897.

Saint Louis Cherbourg Dyd/Mazeline.
Ord: 19.10.1854. Start: 25.4.1857. L: 2.11.1857. Comm: 1.4.1858. C: 4.1858.
Transported troops to Mexico 8-10.1862 and 2-3.1863. Decomm. 1.7.1863. Raséed 1880 and became annex to the gunnery training ship at Toulon 1881 replacing the floating battery *Arrogante*. Renamed *Cacique* 1893. Struck 26.11.1894. BU 1895.

FONTENOY – 3rd Rank. On 19 October 1854 the Minister of Marine included this ship, which was still on the ways, in a list of conversions to be undertaken in 1855. At that time, it was intended to order 500nhp engines for her from Cavé. This was not done, and on 13 February 1856 Stanislas-Charles-Henri Dupuy de Lôme was asked to design engines for her similar to those in *Souverain* and *Algésiras*. Hyacinthe De Coppier's conversion plans were approved by the Council of Works on 4 March 1856.

Dimensions & tons: 62.46m, 62.27m wl, 59.96m x 16.28m ext x 7.91m. 4,051 tons. Draught 7.50m mean. Men: 814.
Machinery: 450nhp (designed by Dupuy de Lôme). 2 cylinders, return connecting rod, trials 1343ihp = 10.52kts. Coal 428 tons.
Guns: (c1859) LD 16 x 36pdrs, 14 x 22cm No.1 shell; UD 30 x 30pdrs No.2; SD 2 x 16cm rifles, 18 x 30pdr carronades.

Fontenoy Toulon Dyd/Toulon.
Ord: 19.10.1854. Start: 1857. L: 2.12.1858. C: 2.1859. Comm: 1.6.1859.
Transported troops to Mexico 9-10.1862 (collided with British steamer *Pactolus* on first attempt 1.1862) and brought them home 3-4.1867. Prison ship for Communards at Brest 5.1871 to 5.1872. Engines removed and converted to sail transport at Brest 1877-79. Made four voyages carrying convicts to New Caledonia 1882-86. Struck 10.2.1892. Designated 11.5.1894 to relieve *Austerlitz* as boys' training hulk at Brest, and at the same time replaced *Bretagne* (ex *Ville de Bordeaux*) and assumed the name *Bretagne*. Became *Fontenoy* again 1910 when she was replaced by the transport *Mytho*, BU 1911.

TAGE Class - 2nd Rank. These ships were among seven ships already afloat that were scheduled in late 1855 for conversion during 1856.

Conversion plans by Guillaume Cyr Masson for them were approved by the Council of Works on 12 December 1855 and modifications by Jean De Robert were approved on 24 May 1857. The ships differed in that *Tage* retained her original square stern while *Duguay Trouin* had hers converted from square to round. Their 500nhp engines were added to the contract of 20 February 1856 with Napier for the 600nhp machinery of *Louis XIV* by a supplement approved on 30 May 1856. The engines of both ships were brought from Glasgow by the navy transport *Nièvre*.

Dimensions & tons: (*Tage*) 64.07m, 63.72m wl, 61.20m x 16.75m ext x 8.23m. 4,707 tons. Draught 7.70/8.40m.

(*Duguay Trouin*) 64.90m, 62.25m wl x 16.80m ext x 8.23m. 4,636 tons. Draught 7.55/8.55m. Men: 883.

Machinery: 500nhp. Trials 8.97kts (*Tage*), 10.7kts (*Duguay Trouin*). Coal 500 tons.

Guns: (Both, 1858-60) LD 16 x 36pdrs, 16 x 22cm No.1 shell; UD 32 x 30pdrs No.2; SD 2 x 16cm rifles, 12 x 16cm shell, 6 x 30pdr carronades.

Tage Brest Dyd/Napier.
Ord: c10.1855. Start: 8.1857. L: 1857. Comm: 12.7.1858. C: 7.1858.
Decomm. 1.3.1861. Prison ship for Communards at Brest 5.1871. Assigned 30.11.1875 to carry deported convicts to New Caledonia, converted to sail transport 12.1875-10.1876 at Brest, and made five deportation voyages. Struck 6.5.1884, coal hulk at Brest, renamed *Vétéran* 1885, BU 1896.

Duguay Trouin Brest Dyd/Napier.
Ord: c10.1855. Start: 1857. L: 1857. Comm: 12.7.1858. C: 7.1858.
Decomm 9.4.1863. Used from 1.3.1867 to 9.5.1867 as a hospital ship at Brest for sick personnel returning from Mexico. Prison ship for Communards at Brest 5.1871 to 3.1872. Struck 22.7.1872, guard hulk at Brest, renamed *Vétéran* 1872, BU 1876-77.

Donawerth, photographed at Brest in September 1878 at the end of her long active career, having been renamed *Jean Bart* in 1868 for service as a seagoing training ship. She is seen with upper mast and yards struck, but there are still sails bent on the topsail and lower yards. The ship would see out another twenty years as a harbour hulk. (Marius Bar)

DUGUESCLIN Class – 3rd Rank. These ships were among seven ships already afloat that were scheduled in late 1855 for conversion during 1856. Their engines were ordered from Mazeline by a contract approved on 11 July 1856. Conversion plans by Pierre Armand Guieysse were approved on 28 October 1857. Both were to be converted at Cherbourg, but Brest had already begun work on *Duguesclin* and was allowed to complete it. *Bayard* was commissioned 24 August 1858, towed by the frigate *Souveraine* from Brest to Cherbourg for conversion between 19 and 22 September 1858, and decommissioned on 18 October 1858.

Dimensions & tons: 63.55m, 62.30m wl, 57.80m x 16.28m ext x 8.06m. 4,230 tons. Draught 6.93/8.23m. Men: 814.

Machinery: 450nhp. 2 cylinders, return connecting rod, 11.2 kts. Coal 280 tons.

Guns: (*Bayard* 1861) LD 30 x 16cm rifles; UD 30 x 30pdrs No.2; SD 4 x 16cm rifles, 12 x 16cm shell.

Duguesclin Brest Dyd/Mazeline.
Ord: c10.1855. Start: 1858. L: 1858. Comm: 1.8.1859. C: 8.1859.
Ran aground 14.12.1859 during speed trials on the point of Île Longue in the Brest roadstead. Determined to be a total loss 17.12.1859 and ordered scrapped in situ 3.1.1860. Refloated

Tage at Brest in the early 1880s as a sailing transport – note the large box-like sponson added amidships which housed the latrines needed for the ship's service transporting convicts. The rig includes double topsails, a later nineteenth century innovation designed to make sail-handling easier with smaller crews, but the ship also carries stunsail yards for fair-weather use. (USN NH-75902)

6.1860 and BU. Her engines were salvaged and installed in *Jean Bart*.

Bayard Cherbourg Dyd/Mazeline.
  Ord: c10.1855. Start: 10.1858. L: 1859. Comm: 1.5.1860 for trials (installation of engines completed at Cherbourg 10.1860, fully commissioned for trials 23.11.1860).
  Returned troops from Mexico 3-4.1867. Decomm. 1.7.1867. Converted to prison ship for Communards at Cherbourg 5.1871. Struck 20.6.1872, hulk at Cherbourg, renamed *Triton* 3.8.1876, BU 1879.

Modified *NAPOLÉON* Class – 2nd Rank. On 7 November 1856 Stanislas-Charles-Henri Dupuy de Lôme submitted a lengthy memorandum in which he outlined the characteristics required for the 2nd Rank steam line of battle ships in the new fleet program then being developed by the Ministry of Marine. He proposed a ship that had characteristics (below) very similar to the *Algesiras* and *Napoléon* classes, being about 5 metres longer and 400 tons heavier than *Napoléon* and having the same beam and depth of hull. The Council of Works concluded on 3 February 1857 that if the Minister wanted to build new vessels of this type the proposed design was excellent with two minor exceptions. Just over a year later the project was overtaken by the order to build the first French armoured frigates. The names *Prince Eugène* and *Prince Impérial* were mentioned in 1857 and 1858 for new ships of the line but no such ships were ordered and the names have not been authenticated.

  Dimensions & tons: 76.62m wl x 16.22m, 16.80m ext x 8.16m. 5,720 tons. Draught 7.13/8.23m. Men: 1,002.
  Machinery: 900nhp, 1 screw. Rig as *Napoléon*.
  Guns: LD 18 x 22cm No.1 shell, 18 x 36pdrs No.1 old model; UD 36 x 36pdrs No.1 lightened model; SD 2 x 17cm (30pdr) rifles, 22 x 36pdrs No.3 (96 guns).

TURENNE - 2nd Rank. On 4 November 1857 Jean De Robert submitted plans for installing in *Turenne*, which was already afloat, the engines ordered for the three-decker *Friedland*, whose conversion had not been proceeded with. He followed the plans of *Tage* very closely. On 11 November 1857 Toulon was directed to undertake the conversion when a drydock became available. The contract of 11 June 1856 with the Forges et Chantiers de la Méditerranée for the machinery of *Friedland* was modified by a supplement approved on 19 February 1858 to reflect its reassignment to *Turenne*.

  Dimensions & tons: 64.90m x 16.80m ext x 8.23m. 4,554 tons. Draught 7.35/8.35m. Men: 883.
  Machinery: 600nhp. Two cylinders, return connecting rod. Coal 500 tons.
  Guns: (1862) LD 16 x 36pdrs, 16 x 22cm No.1 shell; UD 32 x 30pdrs No.2; SD 18 x 30pdr carronades, 2 x 16cm rifles.

Turenne Brest Dyd/FCM.
  Ord: 11.11.1857. Start: 1858. L: 1858. C: 3.1859. Comm: 15.12.1859.
  Transported troops to Mexico 1-9.1862 and 2-3.1863. Rated screw transport 1.1863. To reserve 15.2.1865. Struck 25.11.1867, coal hulk at Brest, renamed *Éléphant* 1.2.75, BU 1886.

3 Two-decker Ships of the Line, 74 guns and below

(Vaisseaux à deux ponts de 74 à 56)
(rated Vaisseaux de 4ème rang from 1824)

The smaller two-deckers provided the mainstay of the battle fleet. By the early eighteenth century this had settled down to two principal types: the 60- to 64-gun ship with a principal battery of twenty-six 24pdrs on the lower deck; and the 74-gun ship with a principal battery of twenty-six 36pdrs on the lower deck. From 1734, with a few exceptions over the following decade, this became twenty-six 24pdrs for the smaller type; and from 1739 for new construction this became twenty-eight 36pdrs for the larger type.

By the 1770s the 64-gun ship was in decline, and by 1786 the few survivors had been relegated to hulks, with no more being built by France; however, a number of ships of this size were captured during the Revolutionary and Napoleonic Wars, and added to the French Navy. The 74-gun ship however quantitatively remained the principal unit of the battle fleet until after the Napoleonic era.

Two-deckers with fewer than 60 guns

The French Navy had dispensed with most of its remaining 50-gun ships and other small two-deckers well before 1786 except for two very elderly ships and three ships captured from the British in 1779-82, but acquired three more vessels during the French Revolutionary War.

(A) Vessels in service or on order at 1 January 1786

AMPHION. A one-off design of 50-gun ship by Jacques-Luc Coulomb, ordered on 19 January 1748 and named on 1 March.
  Dimensions & tons: 145ft 0in, 127ft 0in x 39ft 0in x 18ft 0in (47.10, 41.25 x 12.67 x 5.85m). 900/1,740 tons. Draught 16½ft/17ft 4in (5.36/5.63m). Men: 410-470.
  Guns: LD 24 x 24pdrs; UD 26 x 12pdrs; SD nil (6 x 6pdrs added later).
Amphion Brest Dyd.
  K: 3.1748. L: 28.7.1749. C: 1750.
  Condemned 1787 at Rochefort and BU.

SAGITTAIRE. A one-off design of 50-gun ship by Joseph Coulomb (while Coulomb supervised the building, the launch was overseen by Louis-Hilarion Chapelle). The first new 50-gun ship to be ordered since 1748, she was named on 18 October 1759.
  Dimensions & tons: 147ft 0in x 39ft 4in x 18ft 6in (47.75 x 12.78 x 6.0m). 1,000/1,800 tons. Draught 17ft/18ft 2in (5.52/5.90m). Men: 437-468.
  Guns: LD 24 x 24pdrs; UD 26 x 12pdrs; SD nil (6 x 6pdrs added later).
Sagittaire Toulon Dyd.
  K: 9.1759. L: 8.8.1761. C: 3.1762.
  Condemned 1786 at Lorient; hulked 4.1788 and sold for commerce 1790.

Ex BRITISH PRIZES (1779-1782). Three of the small British two-deckers captured during the American War remained in French service in 1786. These are listed below, with measurements in French units. One more (*Leander*) was taken in 1798.

EXPERIMENT Class. British 50-gun class (of two ships) designed by John Williams in 1772, and originally intended to mount a 24pdr main battery, but completed with 12pdrs instead. *Experiment* was captured on 24 September 1779 by the 50-gun *Sagittaire*. From January 1787, she was classed by the French as an 18pdr 'frigate', but apparently never changed from her 12pdr main armament and was reclassed as a 12pdr 'frigate' in June 1794.
  Dimensions & tons: 136ft 0in, 121ft 0in x 36ft 0in x 17ft 0in (44.18, 39.31 x 11.69 x 5.52m). 700/1,400 tons. Draught 16/17ft (5.20/5.52m). Men: 450.
  Guns: LD 20 x 12pdrs; UD 22 x 12pdrs; SD 8 (later 4) x 6pdrs.
Experiment Adams & Barnard, Deptford.
  K: 12.1772. L: 23.8.1774. C: 26.8.1775 at Deptford Dyd.
  Reclassed as a transport (with just 4 x 12pdrs and 8 x 6pdrs) 12.1797 and struck in 7.1800 at Rochefort.

ROEBUCK Class. British 44-gun class designed by Sir Thomas Slade in 1769, to which twenty ships were built. This type constituted the smallest two-deckers in service with the British, and this shallow-draught class was designed mainly for coastal warfare in the shallow seas off North America. The *Romulus* was taken by the 64-gun *Éveillé* (and the frigates *Gentille* and *Surveillante*) off the Chesapeake on 19 February 1781, and served the French Navy under her own name until April 1785. Her sister *Serapis*, captured by John Paul Jones in the American privateer *Bonhomme Richard* on 23 September 1779, had been transferred to the French Navy in December 1779 but was burnt by accident in July 1781.
  Dimensions & tons: 135ft 0in x 35ft 6in (43.85 x 11.53m). 700/1,350 tons. Draught 16ft (5.20m). Men: 400.
  Guns: LD 22 x 24pdrs; UD 24 x 12pdrs; SD 6 x 6pdrs.
Romulus Henry Adams, Buckler's Hard.
  K: 7.1776. L: 17.12.1777. C: 7.4.1778 at Portsmouth Dyd.
  Renamed (in French service) *Résolution* 6.11.1784, then possibly *Reine* 1.1787 but reverted to *Résolution* 3.1787. Struck and hulked at Mauritius 6.1789.

PORTLAND Class. British 50-gun class designed by John Williams in 1766, to which eleven ships were built. The *Hannibal* was captured by the 74-gun *Héros* and 64-gun *Artésien* off Sumatra on 21 October 1782, and put into French service as the *Annibal* (or perhaps *Petit Annibal*).
  Dimensions & tons (*Annibal*): 139ft 6in, 126ft 0in x 37ft 4in x 18ft 0in (45.32, 40.93 x 12.13 x 5.85m). 900/1,700 tons. Draught 17¼ft/19ft (5.60/6.17m). Men: 280 (*Annibal*); 350 (*Leander*).
  Guns: LD 22 x 24pdrs; UD 24 x 12pdrs; SD 6 x 6pdrs.
Annibal Henry Adams, Buckler's Hard.
  K: 7.1776. L: 26.12.1779. C: 22.2.1780 at Portsmouth Dyd.
  Struck 1787 at Rochefort.

After the Battle of the Nile, in the absence of any frigates, Nelson sent the 50-gun *Leander* home with his dispatches, but the ship was captured on 18 August 1798 by the 74-gun *Généreux*, herself one of the few French ships to escape from the battle. This lithograph was published much later, in 1837, so the detail of the ships is anachronistic, but it conveys the difference in size between the antagonists. The 50-gun ship was an obsolescent type that had long disappeared from the French Navy so the prize would not have been much value even if it had not been recaptured the following year. (Courtesy of Beverley R. Robinson Collection, US Naval Academy Museum)

(B) Vessels acquired from 1 January 1786

Ex BRITISH PRIZE (1798)

PORTLAND Class. The *Leander*, a second unit of this British 50-gun class described above, was taken off Crete by the 74-gun *Généreux* on 17 August 1798.
Leander Chatham Dyd.
  K: 1.3.1777. L: 1.7.1780. C: 21.8.1780.
  Taken by the Russians and Turks at Corfu 3.3.1799 and returned to British service.

Ex VENETIAN PRIZE (1797)

SAN MICHIEL ARCANGELO **Class, ships of the 2nd Rank (56 guns).** This class consisted of two ships completed in 1743-49 and two completed in 1773 (*Minerva* and *Concordia*). They were designed as 'large frigates usable as 2nd Rank ships of the line', carrying 40 guns as large frigates (LD 20 x 30lb; UD 20 x 14lb) or 56 guns as 2nd Rank ships of the line (LD 24 x 30lb; UD 24 x 14lb; SD 8 x 12lb). These guns were measured in Venetian *libbre-sottili*, the 30lb, 14lb, and 12lb guns being roughly equivalent to French 18pdr, 8pdr, and 6pdr guns. An additional function of these *fregate grosse* was to carry replacement masts and spars from Venice to its bases in the Levant. *Concordia* was hulked at Venice in 1793, leaving only *Minerva* active in 1797. She had been wrecked at Trapani on 5 November 1784 but returned to the fleet in 1787 and then served continuously at Corfu and at Venice.
  Dimensions (in Venetian measurements): 128.85ft max, 110ft keel x 35ft max x 27.5ft *puntale* (44.80m, 38.25m x 12.17m x 9.56m; in French units 137ft 11in, 117ft 9in x 37ft 6in x 29ft 5in). Draught 16.50ft (5.73m, 17ft 8in)
  Guns: LD 24 x 18pdrs; UD 26 x 8pdrs; SD 8 x 4pdrs.
Minerva Venice (laid down by Iseppo Coccon di Francesco)
  K: 1767. L: 24.12.1772. C: 19.7.1773.
  Was returning to Corfu from Venice when the Venetian Republic fell 12.5.1797. When the French took Corfu in 7.1797 they commissioned her for two weeks but found her in bad condition and hulked her in 8.1797. When the Russians arrived at Corfu on 3.3.1799 they found her hauled out and broke her up.

(C) Vessels acquired from 25 March 1802

Ex BRITISH PRIZE (1805)

CALCUTTA. This vessel was originally the East Indiaman *Warley*, launched on 16 October 1788 at Blackwall, and one of nine East Indiamen purchased as small two-deckers of 56 guns for convoy duties by the British Navy in March 1795; she was renamed *Calcutta* on 12 May 1795. She was captured on 26 September 1805 by *Magnanime* and

Armide of the squadron of Rear Admiral Allemand off the Scilly Isles (while her convoy escaped) and commissioned by the French Navy on the next day without change of name.

Dimensions & tons: 156ft 11in, 129ft 7¾in x 41ft 3½in x 17ft 2in (British measurements) (47.83, 39.52 x 12.59 x 5.23m). According to French records, 159ft 0in x 38ft 2in x 21ft 6in (51.65 x 12.39 x 6.98m). 1,100/2.200 tons. Draught (as re-measured by the French) 19ft 10in/20ft 8in (6.44/6.72m).

Guns: LD 28 x 18pdrs; UD 26 x 32pdr carronades (her original British guns); SD 2 x 18pdr carronades (by 1806, one 24pdr carronade) and 2 x 9pdr carronades.

Calcutta Perry & Co, Blackwall

Grounded, abandoned by her crew, and burned by the British 12-13.4.1809 following the British fireship attack at Île d'Aix; her commanding officer was executed by the French.

64-gun two-deckers

The origins of the 60/64-gun ship can be found in the early 1660s, and its main features remained constant for over a century. The type continued to carry a lower deck battery of twenty-four 24pdrs, and an upper deck almost always with twenty-six 12pdrs, until the 1730s when – commencing with the *Borée* of 1734 - space was provided for an additional pair of guns on both decks, and within a decade this became the new standard armament, with ten guns (6pdrs) remaining to the gaillards.

New construction of the type ceased in the 1770s, as the battle fleet concentrated on the more effective 74-gun type. Two new 64s were projected in 1782 – the *Oriflamme* and *Breton* (both to be laid down at Brest in 1783) – but were cancelled in February 1783. Subsequent acquisitions were only by capture of existing enemy vessels during the next few decades.

(A) Vessels in service or on order at 1 January 1786

SAINT MICHEL Class. One of a pair of 64-gun ships built at Brest to a design by Jean-Marie Helie; her sister *Vigilant* was captured off Louisbourg on 19 May 1745 by HMS *Superb*, *Eltham* and *Mermaid*, becoming HMS *Vigilant*. This was one of the last designs to have just 12 pairs of 24pdrs on the LD; other than the *Fier* of the same period, all future 64s would have 13 pairs of LD gunports (and consequently fewer SD guns), and the *Saint Michel* was reduced to a 60-gun ship in 1762 when two pairs of 6pdrs were removed.

Dimensions & tons: 143ft 6in, 130ft 6in x 38ft 6in x 18ft 9in (48.56, 41.01 x 13.16 x 6.23m). 1,242/2,150 tons. Draught 17ft/19½ft (5.90/6.82m). Men: 456-486.

Guns: LD 24 x 24pdrs; UD 26 x 12pdrs; SD 14 x 6pdrs (reduced to 10 x 6pdrs in 1762).

Saint Michel Brest Dyd.

K: 11.1739. L: 1.1741. C: 5.1741.

Struck in 1786. Transferred to the French East India Co. at Lorient for commerce in 5.1787, but never used by them.

TRITON. This old 64-gun ship remained in active service until 1783, following refits in the 1760s and thereafter, the last being in 1781 at Havana. She had been ordered on 9 November 1745 to a design by François Coulomb, and named on 11 March 1746. Disarmed at Toulon in April 1783, she was loaned for commerce (the Compagnie de Chine) from that September until August 1785.

Dimensions & tons: 149ft 6in, 126ft 3in x 40ft 6in x 19ft 2in (48.56, 41.01 x 13.16 x 6.23m). 1,242/2,150 tons. Draught 18ft 2in/21ft (5.90/6.82m). Men: 490-560.

Guns: LD 26 x 24pdrs; UD 28 x 12pdrs; SD 10 x 6pdrs.

Triton Toulon Dyd.

K: 1.1746. L: 4.8.1747. C: 12.1747.

Hulked as a guardship at Cherbourg in 1786. Removed from service in 1790 and sold for commerce in 1791, she was BU at Cherbourg in 1794.

HARDI Class. One of two ships built at Rochefort to a design by Pierre Morineau; her sister *Inflexible* was condemned in 1760 and taken to pieces by 1763.

Dimensions & tons: 149ft 0in x 40ft 6in x 20ft 9in (48.40 x 13.16 x 6.74m). 1,100/2,100 tons. Draught 19ft/20ft 2in (6.17/6.55m). Men: 530.

Guns: LD 26 x 24pdrs; UD 28 x 12pdrs; SD 10 x 6pdrs.

Hardi Rochefort Dyd.

K: 1748. L: 1750. C: 4.1751.

Reduced to a floating bath-house at Toulon in 1786, became a hulk there in 1788 and a floating prison hulk in 1791. Struck in 5.1798.

LION Class. Last of a class of four ships built at Toulon to a design by Pierre-Blaise Coulomb. The *Lion* and her sister *Sage* were ordered on 26 January 1749 and named on 17 June 1749. Of her sisters, the *Sage* was condemned at Brest in 1767 (and taken to pieces), the *Altier* at Toulon in 1770 (and sold) and the *Fantasque* at Lorient in 1784 (becoming a hulk at Martinique).

Dimensions & tons: 151ft 0in, 134ft 0in x 40ft 6in x 19ft 6in (49.05, 43.53 x 13.16 x 6.33m). 1,100/2,084 tons. Draught 17¾/21½ft (5.77/6.98m). Men: 492-572.

Guns: LD 26 x 24pdrs; UD 28 x 12pdrs; SD 10 x 6pdrs.

Lion Brest Dyd.

K: 7.1749. L: 22.5.1751. C: 1752.

Hulked at Toulon 12. 1783. Sold there 8.1785.

ARTESIEN Class. Survivors of a class of five ships built at Brest to a design by Joseph-Louis Ollivier. Of their sisters, the *Roland* was burnt by accident in 1779, *Protée* was captured by the British in 1780, and *Alexandre* was burnt at Mauritius in 1783 (condemned following an epidemic).

Dimensions & tons: 154ft 0in, 141ft 0in x 40ft 6in x 20ft 0in (50.03, 45.80 x 13.16 x 6.50m). 1,100/2,084 tons. Draught 18ft/19ft 10in (5.85/6.44m). Men: 570-580.

Guns: LD 26 x 24pdrs; UD 28 x 12pdrs; SD 10 x 6pdrs.

Artesien Brest Dyd.

K: 6.1764. L: 7.3.1765. C: 5.1765.

Condemned 1785-86 at Rochefort, and hulked.

Eveillé Brest Dyd.

K: 2.1771. L: 10.12.1772. C: 8.1773.

Condemned 1785-86 at Rochefort.

BRILLANT Group. Three very similar 64-gun ships were built at Brest and Rochefort to a series of designs by Antoine Groignard, of which the Brest-built *Solitaire* had been captured by the British in 1782.

Dimensions & tons: (*Brillant*) 157ft 0in, 142ft 0in x 40ft 6in x 20ft 0in (51.00, 46.13 x 13.16 x 6.50m). 1,200/2,300 tons. Draught 18¾/19¾ft (6.09/6.42m). Men: 489. (*Réfléchi*) 154ft 0in, 142ft

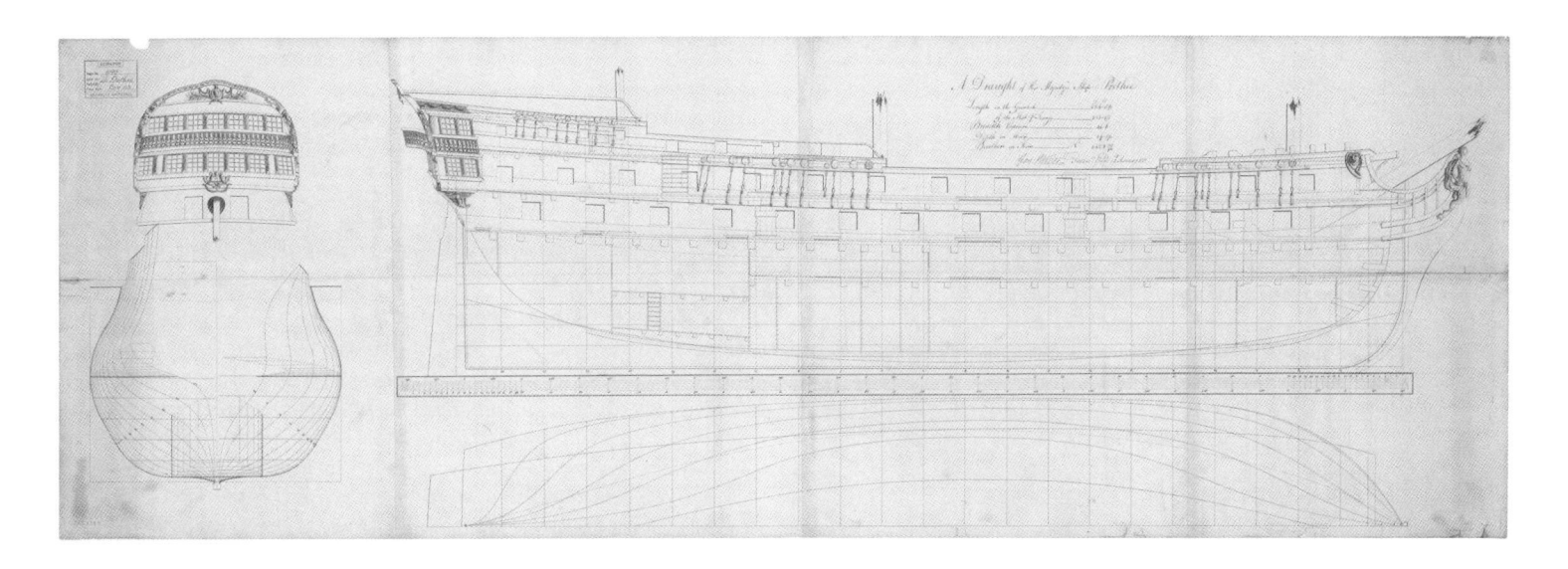

0in x 41ft 0in x 20ft 6in (50.03, 46.13 x 13.32 x 6.66m).
1,090/2,200 tons. Men: 491-560.
Guns: LD 26 x 24pdrs; UD 28 x 12pdrs; SD 10 x 6pdrs.
Brillant Brest Dyd.
K: 11.1772. L: 9.1774. C: 12.1774.
Hulked as guardship at Cherbourg 9.1787; condemned 9.1795 and BU there 1797.
Réfléchi Rochefort Dyd.
K: 5.1772. L: 25.11.1776. C: 2.1777.
Hulked at Brest 11.1788, raséed in 1793 and renamed *Turot*; not mentioned thereafter.

SPHINX. This vessel had been originally built in 1752-56 at Brest by Pierre Salinoc, but was 75% rebuilt there in 1775-76 to a design by Jacques-Noël Sané. She took part as a member of Suffren's squadron in the actions off India in 1781-82, and was refitted in 1784 on returning home.
Dimensions & tons: 151ft 0in, 135ft 0in x 41ft 0in x 20ft 6in (49.05, 43.85 x 13.32 x 6.66m). 1,200/2,200 tons. Draught 19ft 11in/21ft 5in (6.47/6.96m). Men: 491-560.
Guns: LD 26 x 24pdrs; UD 28 x 12pdrs; SD 10 x 6pdrs.
Sphinx Brest Dyd. (Constructeur, Joseph-Louis Ollivier).
K: 1.1775. L: 9.12.1776. C: 1777.
Hulked as floating battery at Rochefort 5.1793, disarmed 1.1802.

A two-ship class of 64s – the *Caton* and *Jason* – had been built at Toulon in the 1770s by Joseph-Marie-Blaise Coulomb, but both vessels were captured by the British in April 1782 in the Mona Passage off Puerto Rico and added to the British Navy as HMS *Caton* and *Argonaut*.

INDIEN Class. This group of vessels had been originally ordered by the French East India Company in the late 1760s and early 1770s to a design by Antoine Groignard and Gilles Cambry; all six vessels were built at Lorient-Caudan, a set of slipways on the opposite shore of the Scorff River immediately upstream from the main dockyard that had been in use since around 1750. The three earliest ships, *Actionnaire*, *Indien* and *Mars*, had been launched in 1767, 1768 and 1769 respectively (*Actionnaire*, the prototype, was about 2ft shorter than the others); all three had been acquired by the navy in April 1770, but *Mars* was burnt by accident in 1773, *Actionnaire* was captured by the British in 1782, and *Indien* was sold in 1784. The 1774-launched *Superbe* was retained by the Compagnie des Indes, but the final pair, *Sévère* of 1775 and *Maréchal*

The Admiralty draught of the *Protee*, 64 guns, as fitted out to British requirements in June 1781, but retaining the French decorative scheme. One of the *Artésien* class, the ship was typical of the type of small French two-deckers that survived in modest numbers into the French Revolutionary Wars, although none had been built since the 1770s. (© National Maritime Museum J3122)

de Broglie of 1774 (the latter renamed *Ajax* on 13 August 1779), were purchased by the navy in November 1778 and April 1779 respectively as part of the war preparations. They were the last 64-gun ships (other than prizes) to be added to the French Navy. *Sévère* was wrecked in January 1784, but *Ajax*, although struck from the list in 1786, was reinstated as a floating battery in June 1795.
Dimensions & tons: 157ft 6in, 148ft 0in x 40ft 6in x 17ft 6in (51.16, 48.08 x 13.16 x 5.68m). 1,300/2,250 tons. Draught 20/21ft (6.50/6.82m). Men: 600.
Guns: LD 26 x 24pdrs; UD 28 x 12pdrs; SD 10 x 6pdrs.
Ajax Lorient Dyd-Caudan.
K: 12.1772. L: 14.1.1774. C: 3.1774.
Floating battery at Verdon 6.1795. BU after 3.1801.

Although no further 64-gun ships were built after 1777, the 1786 Règlement provided for existing 64s to have a complement of 538 in wartime (377 in peacetime), including 12 officers.

(B) Vessels acquired from 1 January 1786

Ex VENETIAN PRIZES (1797). When the French occupied the city of Venice and its Arsenal in May 1797 they took over the Venetian Navy ships afloat there along with a reserve fleet of about 20 ships on the covered slips of the Arsenal. In June they also seized the Venetian fleet at Corfu. Since the city was to be handed over to Austria under the Treaty of Leoben, the French in September and December 1797 sabotaged all of the ships in the Arsenal except for a few that were ready for immediate use and took these and most of the supplies in the Arsenal to France.

LEON TRIONFANTE Class, ships of the 1st Rank (70, then 66 guns). This sixteen-ship class, which originated in a ship laid down in 1716, was built in four series of which the third (laid down in 1732) included *Vittoria* (launched in 1783), *La Guerriera* (launched in 1784 and burned while fitting out 1785), and *Medea* (launched in 1793), and the fourth (laid down in 1736-39) included *Eolo* (launched in 1784) and *San Giorgio* (launched in 1785). Another ship from the third series was on slip (*squero*) No.15 and one from the fourth series was on slip No.14 when the French took Venice in May 1797; the French sabotaged both on the ways on 27 September 1797. Both were salvaged as hulks by the Austrians, becoming *Pontone No.1* and *Pontone No.2* respectively in 1800. These ships were rated by the French as 64-gun ships.

> Dimensions (in Venetian measurements): 146.47ft max, 126ft keel x 37ft max x 28.50ft *puntale* (50.93m, 43.81m x 12.85m x 9.90m; in French units 156ft 10in, 134ft 10in x 39ft 7in x 30ft 6in). Draught 18.50ft (6.43m, 19ft 10in)
>
> Guns (Venetian: *Vittoria, San Giorgio, Eolo*): LD 28 x 40lb (*libbre-sottili*, equivalent to French 24pdrs); UD 28 x 30lb (18pdrs); SD: 14 x 14lb (8pdrs);
>
> Guns (Venetian:*Medea*): LD 26 x 40lb (24pdrs); UD 28 x 30lb (18pdrs); SD 12 x 14lb (8pdrs).

Vittoria Venice (laid down by Giacomo Moro in 1732, completed by Zuanne Zampin in 1746 and kept in reserve on the slip, launched by Andrea Chiribiri in 1783)

> K: 1732. L: 23.12.1783. C: 27.2.1784.
>
> Returned to Venice in 1796 but found not worth repairing, struck in early 1797 and sold. The buyer anchored her in the Giudecca canal where the French burned her when they entered the city in 5.1797.

Robert (ex French *Éole* 11.11.1797, ex Venetian *Eolo*) Venice (laid down by Zuan Battista de Zorzi in 1739 and kept in reserve on the slip, launched by Iseppo Livio in 1784)

> K: 1739. L: 23.12.1784. C: 23.2.1785.
>
> Dimensions & tons (in French measurements): 152ft deck, 137ft keel x 41ft mld x 19ft creux (49.37m, 44.50m x 13.32m x 6.17m). 1,100/2,000 tons. Draught: 15ft/17ft 6in (4.88m/5.68m). Men: 463-583.
>
> Guns (French, rearmed 1798): LD 26 x 18pdrs; UD 26 x 12pdrs; SD: 12 x 6pdrs.
>
> Taken by the French at Venice 20.5.1797. Renamed for General Jean Gilles Robert of the French Army, killed at Ferrara in a battle against the Austrian army on 10.10.1797. Refitted at Toulon 7-8.1798 with French guns. Condemned 10.1801 and became headquarters hulk at Toulon. Prison hulk 6.1807, sank at Toulon 1817, BU 1818.

Sandos (ex French *Saint Georges* 11.1797, ex Venetian *San Giorgio*) Venice (laid down by Zuanne Scabozzi in 1736 and kept in reserve on the slip, launched by Girolamo Manao in 1785)

> K: 1736. L: 23.4.1785. C: 30.6.1785.
>
> Dimensions & tons (in French measurements): as *Robert*.
>
> Comm. by the French 29.7.1797 at Corfu. Renamed for General Thomas Chegaray de Sandos of the French Army of Italy who died at Milan 11.1796 from injuries suffered during the Battle of Rivoli on 15.11.1796 against the Austrian army. She was in bad condition when taken and was used as a guardship until decomm. 31.10.1798. Hulk captured 3.1799 by the Russians, retaken by the French at Corfu 1807, and BU there 8.1807.

Frontin (ex French *Médée* 11.11.1797, ex Venetian *Medea*) Venice (laid down on slip No.12 by Francesco Novello in 1732, completed by Zuan Domenico Giacomazzo in 1746 and kept in reserve on the slip, launched by Andrea Spadon in 1793)

> K: 1732. L: 28.2.1793. C: 28.5.1793.
>
> Dimensions & tons (in French measurements): as *Robert*.
>
> Guns (French, rearmed 1798): LD 26 x 24pdrs; UD 26 x 18pdrs; SD: 12 x 6pdrs
>
> Seized by the French at Corfu 28.6.1797 and comm. 23.7.1797. Renamed for an adjutant-general of Napoleon who fell with General Beyrand at Castiglione delle Stiviere in a battle against the Austrian army on 6.8.1796. Refitted at Valletta 3.1798 and at Toulon 7-8.1798 with French guns. Fitted as 1,000-ton flûte in 11.1800 with 16 x 8pdrs, 6 x 6pdrs, 2 x 24pdr carronades, and 1 x 36pdr obusier. Condemned 1808, prison hulk at Toulon 1809. Ordered BU 31.3.1825 at Toulon.

***SAN CARLO BORROMEO* Class, ships of the 1st Rank (66 guns).** The name ship of this class, laid down in 1741, was originally to be the fourth vessel of the fourth series of the *Leon Trionfante* class, but was built to a revised design by Marco Nobile and was followed by five sisters. These five sisters had their sterns modified on the building ways after 1788 because of a steering defect discovered in *San Carlo Borromeo* in a storm in 1768, and they were thereafter referred to as the *San Carlo regolato* (regulated or modified) type. Only one of the sisters, *Vulcano*, was launched before the French took Venice in May 1797. Of the others, two on slips 16 and 18 were sabotaged by the French on 27 September 1797, one on slip No.2 was sabotaged on 28 December 1797, and one on slip No.23 followed on 30 December 1797.

> Dimensions (in Venetian measurements): 147.16ft max, 126ft keel x 38.00ft max x 28.25ft *puntale* (51.17m, 43.81m x 13.20m x 9.81m; in French units 157ft 6in, 134ft 10in x 40ft 8in x 30ft 3in). Draught 17.25ft (5.99m, 18ft 6in).
>
> Guns (Venetian): LD 26 x 40lb (24pdrs); UD 28 x 30lb (18pdrs); SD 12 x 14lb (8pdrs).

Causse (ex French *Vulcain* 11.11.1797, ex Venetian *Vulcano*) Venice (laid down on slip No.8 and completed by Marco Nobile in 1752, kept in reserve on the slip, adjusted by Andrea Chiribiri between 1789 and 1793 and then launched)

> K: 1752. L: 26.1.1793. C: 30.4.1793.
>
> Guns (French, rearmed 1798): LD 26 x 24pdrs; UD 26 x 18pdrs; SD: 12 x 6pdrs.
>
> Seized by the French at Corfu 28.6.1797 and comm. 23.7.1797. Renamed for General Jean Jacques Causse of the French Army of Italy, killed in Dego in a battle against the Austrian army on 16.4.1796. Converted to hospital ship with full armament of French guns at Toulon 4-5.1798 for the Egyptian expedition. Taken by the British 2.9.1801 at Alexandria and ceded to the Turks.

***FAMA* Class, large frigates (*fregate grosse*) 'usable as 2nd Rank ships' (64 guns).** Like the 1780 class of 1st Rank ships, this class of smaller two-deckers was built with the new 'double frame' method that was similar to that used in French and British vessels. (The earlier 'single frame' method had been inherited from the galleys of the middle ages.) The first four were laid down on 8 June 1782. The French took the first two at Corfu and launched the third and fourth at Venice during their first occupation of that city. All were given French guns, the first two at Toulon in 1798 and the second pair while fitting out at Venice in 1797. The French sabotaged one incomplete sister on slip No.17 on 27 September 1797 and one on slip No.3 on 28 December 1797. The ship on slip No.3 was salvaged by the Austrians during their first occupation and became the floating battery *Diamante*.

> Dimensions (in Venetian measurements): 138.00ft max. 122ft keel x 37.00ft max x 28.00ft *puntale* (48.00m, 42.42m x 12.86m x 9.73m; in French units 147ft 9in, 130ft 7in x 39ft 7in x 30ft 0in). Draught 17.50ft (6.08m, 18ft 9in).
>
> Guns (Venetian): LD 26 x 40lb (24pdrs); UD 26 x 30lb (18pdrs); SD 12 x 14lb (8pdrs).

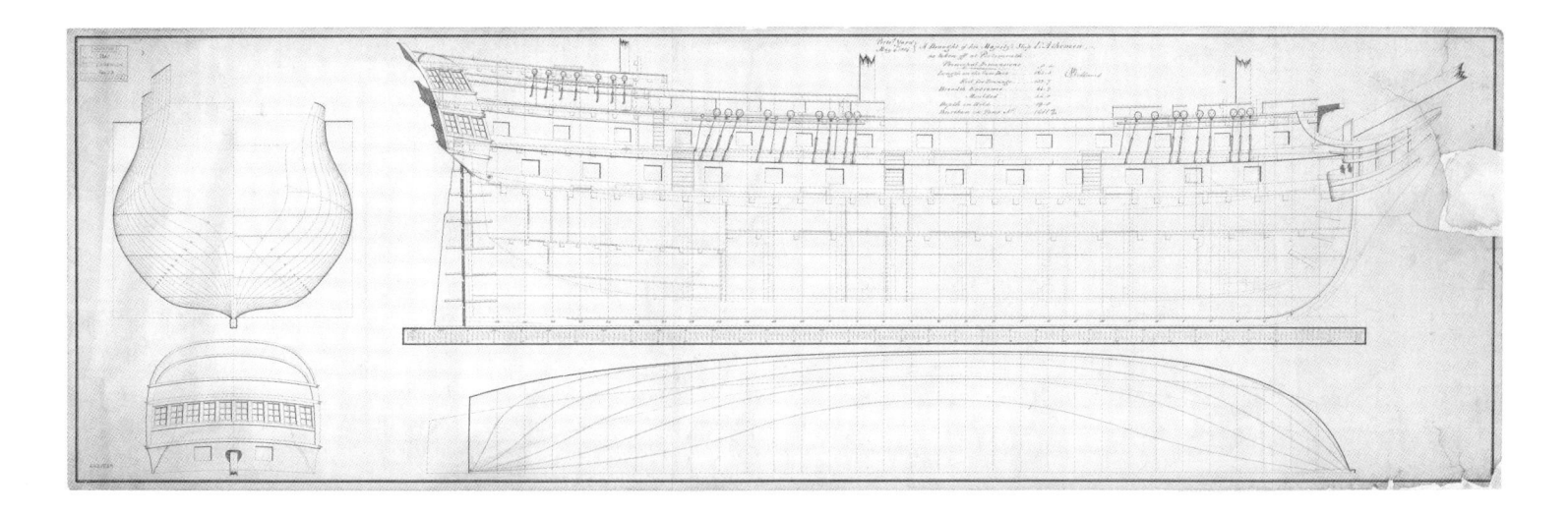

Dubois (ex French *Renommée* 11.11.1797, ex Venetian *Fama*) Venice (laid down and built by Domenico Giacomazzo, launched in 1784).
K: 8.6.1782. L: 31.3.1784. C: 19.5.1784.
Dimensions & tons (in French measurements): 150ft 0in deck, 139ft 0in keel x 40ft 0in mld x 18ft 6in creux (48.72m, 45.15m x 13.00m x 6.01m). 1,100/2,000 tons. Draught 16ft 0in/17ft 6in (5.20m/5.68m). (*Stengel*): 1,100/2,100 tons. Draught 16ft 0in/18ft 0in (5.20m/5.85m). Men: c500.
Guns (French, 1798): LD 26 x 24pdrs; UD 26 x 18pdrs; SD 12 x 6pdrs (in Venetian sources); or all guns as *Stengel* (in French records).
Seized by the French at Corfu 28.6.1797. Renamed for General Paul Alexis Dubois of the French Army, killed at Rovereto in a battle against Austrian Army on 4.9.1796. Fitted as flûte with full armament of French guns at Toulon 5.1798 for the Egyptian expedition. Damaged in collision 2.7.1798 with *Orient* (118) entering Alexandria and remained there as headquarters ship of General Jean Baptiste Kléber. Condemned 29.5.1800 at Alexandria, hulk scuttled 1801 in the entrance to the inner harbour at Alexandria to impede Anglo-Turkish landing operations.

Banel (ex French *Gloire* 11.11.1797, ex Venetian *Gloria Veneta*) Venice (laid down on slip No.22 in 1782 and completed by Andrea Chiribiri and Carlo Novello, kept in reserve on the slip, and launched in 1794)
K: 8.6.1782. L: 31.3.1794. C: 29.5.1794.
Guns (French, 1798): LD 26 x 18pdrs; UD 26 x 12pdrs; SD 12 x 6pdrs (in Venetian sources); or 26 x 18pdrs; 28 x 12pdrs; 10 x 6pdrs (in French records).
Seized by the French in the Venetian Arsenal in 5.1797. Renamed for General Pierre Banel of the French Army, killed during the attack on the Castle of Cosseria on 13.4.1796. She led the convoy carrying French troops to occupy the Venetian bases of Corfu on 28.6.1797. (The ships flew the Venetian flag, deceiving the defenders and allowing them to enter the harbour and occupy the fortress without firing a shot.) Immediately afterwards she sailed to Toulon and was refitted with French guns in 7-8.1798. Fitted as flûte at Toulon 11.1800. Departed Toulon 9.1.1802 with troops for Santo Domingo, wrecked 15.1.1802 on Cap Ténès (near Oran), Algeria.

Stengel Venice. (laid down on slip No.19 in 1782 by Giovanni Battista Gallina, completed by Iseppo Cason and kept in reserve on the slip, launched in 1797 during the first French occupation of Venice).
K: 8.6.1782. L: 2.10.1797. C: 17.11.1797.

When they occupied Malta in 1798 the French found one 64-gun ship under construction, which they completed as the *Athénien*, but the ship was captured when the island was taken by the British in 1800. This Admiralty draught, dated 6 May 1804, shows the ship in Royal Navy service as HMS *Athenian*. (© National Maritime Museum J3394)

Dimensions & tons (in French measurements): as *Dubois*.
Guns (French, 1797): as *Banel*.
Taken on the building ways by the French at Venice 20.5.1797. Named 1.6.1797 for Henri Christian de Stengel, a French cavalry general killed in the Battle of Mondovì on 21.4.1796. Launched and delivered during the first French occupation of Venice. Made a sortie from Ancona into the Adriatic under the French flag in 11-12.1798 together with *La Harpe* and *Beyrand*. Became a floating battery at Ancona 24.7.1799, captured by the Austrians there 14.11.1799. Returned to Venice 9.1800 and eventually sank there. Raised, fitted as floating battery (she was cut down to the second deck as with *Diamante*), and renamed *Megera* by the Austrians in 1805. Retaken by the French at Venice 27.12.1805, renamed *Stengel*, and transformed into a hulk. BU by the Austrians in 7.1814.

Beyrand Venice. (laid down on slip No.13 in 1782 by Iseppo Livio and launched by Livio in 1797 during the first French occupation of Venice)
K: 8.6.1782. L: 29.10.1797. C: 18.12.1797.
Dimensions & tons (in French measurements): as *Dubois*.
Guns (French, 1797): as *Banel*.
Taken on the building ways by the French at Venice 20.5.1797. Renamed for General Martial Beyrand of the French Army, killed with Adjutant-general Frontin at Castiglione delle Stiviere in a battle against the Austrian army on 6.8.1796. Made a sortie from Ancona into the Adriatic under the French flag in 11-12.1798 together with *La Harpe* and *Stengel*, became a floating battery at Ancona 7.1799, was sunk there 16.8.1799 by Austrian artillery and a Russo-Turkish naval squadron, and was captured in that condition 14.11.1799 by the Austrians. Refloated and taken to Venice in 1800, BU 3.1803.

Diamante Venice (slip No.3)
K: 1791. L: 1805? C: 1805.
Guns: 16 x 24pdrs.
Was 45.8% complete when sabotaged on slip No.3 by the French on 28.12.1797. Salvaged by the Austrians during their first occupation, cut down to the second deck and converted to the

floating battery *Diamante* (in French *Diamant*) with French 24pdrs in 1806/1807 during the second French occupation. Turned over to Napoleon's Italian Navy at Venice in 1811 as a prame. Left to the Austrians 4.1814 in the surrender of the French in Venice. BU 1825.

Ex MALTESE PRIZES (1798)
Athénien (ex French *Saint Jean*, ex Maltese *San Giovanni*, laid down at Valletta 1796)
   Dimensions & tons: 156ft 1in x 42ft 0in x 20ft 2in (50.7 x 13.64 x 6.55m). 1,200/2,300 tons. Draught 19ft 5in/20ft 6in (6.32m/6.66m).
   Guns: LD 26 x 20pdrs; UD 26 or 28 x 12pdrs? SD: 12 to 16 small.
   Taken on the ways 6.1798. L: 10.1798, C: 12.1799. Captured 9.1800 by the British at the surrender of Malta, became HMS *Athenian*.
Dego (ex Maltese *San Zaccharia*, laid down at Valletta around 1763 and completed 7.1765)
   Dimensions & tons: unknown.
   Guns: LD 26 x 20pdrs; UD 26 or 28 x 12pdrs? SD: 8 to 10 small.
   Taken at Valletta 6.1798 and recommissioned 7.1798 by the French. Captured 9.1800 by the British at the surrender of Malta and made into a prison hulk at Valletta. Sold by the British in 1802 or 1803.

(C) Vessels acquired from 25 March 1802

Ex PORTUGUESE PRIZES (1807)
Princesse de Beira (Portuguese *Princesa da Beira*. 3rd Class (64-68 guns). Constructed at Lisbon as *Nossa Senhora da Ajuda* by Manuel Vicente Nunes. Listed in 1769 as *São Pedro de Alcântara* and later as *Nossa Senhora da Ajuda e São Pedro de Alcântara*. Rebuilt 1793 and renamed *Princesa da Beira* 8.8.1793)
   K: 1757, L: 1759, C: 29.3.1759
   Dimensions & tons: Probably as *Saint Sébastien*. Men: 562
   Guns: (1793) LD 28 x 24pdrs; UD 28 x 12pdrs; SD 2 x 12pdrs, 10 x 6pdrs.
   Seized at Lisbon 30.11.1807 while in need of repairs and not repaired. Renamed *Portugaise* (*Portugesa*) 5.1808. Retaken in the evacuation of Lisbon early 9.1808 and returned to Portuguese service as *Princesse de Beira*. Became a prison hulk in 1808 and a sheer hulk in 1821, sold 14.7.1834.
Saint Sébastien (Portuguese *São Sebastião*, 3rd Class (64 guns), constructed at Rio de Janeiro by Antonio da Silva)
   K: 1764, L: 8.2.1767, C: 19.8.1767
   Dimensions & tons: 183ft 6in keel (sic) x 47ft 9in x 40ft 0in moulded depth (59.60m x 15.50m x 13.00m); recorded by the French as 182ft (Portuguese) x 44ft x 34ft 6in height. Draught 19ft 4in/21ft 4in (6.27/6.93m). Men: 576.
   Guns: LD 26 x 24pdrs; UD 26 x 12pdrs; SD 2 x 12pdrs, 10 x 6pdrs.
   Seized at Lisbon 30.11.1807 while in need of repairs and refitted 1807-8. Renamed *Brésil* (*Brasil*) 5.1808. Retaken in the evacuation of Lisbon early 9.1808 and returned to Portuguese service as *Sao Sebastiao*. Decomm. 13.1.1823, BU 1832.

New Construction Class. More than thirty years after the last French 64s had been launched, in May 1808 orders were issued to build by contract five 64s in France to a fresh design by Jacques-Noël Sané, which was dated 16 June. Two ships were to be built at Bordeaux, and one each at Dunkirk, at Paimboeuf (by Michel-Louis Crucy) and – probably – at St Nazaire. These ships were never begun or named. They would have carried the traditional 64-gun ordnance, except for the substitution of carronades for the quarterdeck guns.
   Dimensions & tons: 155ft 0in, 141ft 0in x 41ft 0in x 20ft 6in (50.34, 45.80 x 13.32 x 6.66m). 1,150/2,320 tons. Draught 19ft 3in/19ft 7in (6.26/6.36m).
   Guns: LD 26 x 24pdrs; UD 28 x 12pdrs; SD 2 x 6pdrs + 8 x 24pdr carronades.

PURCHASED RUSSIAN VESSEL (1809)

AZIYA **Class.** The design for this 66-gun class, of which construction began in 1772, was reportedly supplied by Admiral Grieg. The class ultimately included 28 ships, of which the *Aziya* that came into French hands in 1809 was the second ship of that name.
   Dimensions & tons: 150ft 1in x 139ft 2in x 41ft 7in x 17ft 10in (48.77, 45.20 x 13.51 x 5.79m). 1,100/2,000 tons. Draught 16ft 4in/17ft 6in (5.30/5.70m). Men: 571
   Guns: LD 24 x 24pdrs, 2 x 60pdr edinorogs; UD 24 x 12pdrs, 2 x 24pdr edinorogs, SD 14 x 6pdrs.
Asie (or *Asia*) (Russian *Aziya*) Solombala Works, Arkhangelsk (constructed by G. Ignatyev)
   K: 21.9.1794. L: 24.8.1796. C: by 3.7.1798.
   Arrived at Trieste from Corfu 28.12.1807 with the squadron of Captain 1st Rank Saltanov and participated in the defence against a threatened British attack there in 5.1809. Ordered transferred to France at Trieste 27.9.1809 and decomm. by the Russians 20.10.1809. BU by the French at Trieste 1810-11.

ANNEXED DUTCH VESSELS (1810). Around 26 Dutch 68-gun and nine 56-gun ships fell into the hands of the new Batavian Republic when it was proclaimed on 19 January 1795, but by the end of 1799 all of these older ships had been BU, hulked, or taken by the British Navy. The 68-gun ships measured about 167 Dutch feet in length and had originally been 64s or even 60s. In 1795 the Batavian Republic resumed construction of 68-gun ships, but with the 180-foot length of the older 74-gun type.

KORTENAAR **Class.** 68-gun ships designed for the Maas Admiralty, of which eight were built at Rotterdam (all by P. Glavimans, Jnr) and two elsewhere. The *Kortenaar* of this class, launched in 1795, was scuttled and burnt at Surabaya in 1807, and the *Oldenbarneveld* was removed in the same year. The *Schrikverwekker*, built at Amsterdam, was wrecked in the East Indies in 1806, the *Pluto*, built at Vlissingen, and the *Revolutie* were burnt in 1807 at Surabaya, and the *Neptunus,* renamed *Zeeland* in September 1806, was probably unserviceable by 1809. The armament of *Doggersbank* in 1801 was LD 26 x 36pdrs, UD 28 x 18pdrs, SD 16 x 8pdrs. Later ships had 30pdrs on the LD while *Kortenaar* had only 24pdrs.

The four surviving ships (the *Pieter Paulus* had been renamed *Utrecht* in 1807, and the *Hersteller* had been renamed *Commercie van Rotterdam* in February 1808 and then *Rotterdamsche Handel* a month later) were incorporated into the French Imperial Navy on 9 July 1810 when Napoleon annexed the Kingdom of Holland into the French Empire; the *Doggersbank* and *Utrecht* retained their names, while the *Johan de Witt* and *Rotterdamsche Handel* became the *Jean de Witt* and the *Commerce de Rotterdam* (shortened to *Rotterdam* a year later). The French ordered them rated as 64s on 25 April 1811. The *Utrecht* was unserviceable by 1813 and was condemned on 14 October 1813 (taken by the Dutch in the uprising of December 1813, and BU at Hellevoetsluis in 1815); the

remaining three were returned to the Dutch on 22 April 1814.
  Dimensions & tons: 156ft 10in, 148ft 7in x 41ft 10in x 18ft 9in (50.96, 48.27 x 13.59 x 6.09m). 1,200/2,300 tons. Draught 18ft 4in/19ft 2in (5.94m/6.23m). Men: 502-544.
  Guns: (French c1811) LD 26 x 30pdrs; UD 28 x 18pdrs; SD 14 x 8pdrs and 2 x 60pdr carronades (*Utrecht* had no carronades).
Doggersbank Rotterdam (constructed by P. Glavimans Jr.).
  K: 9.10.1797. L: 3.3.1798. C: end 1798.
  Became a barracks ship for sailors at Willemsoord in 1807. In the Texel squadron in 4.1814. Returned to the Dutch 22.4.1814 and renamed *Zeeland* 30.7.1814. Set out with a fleet for the Mediterranean 22.12.1814 but badly damaged by a storm and put in to Plymouth. Returned to Vlissingen 14.6.1815 and made a guardship on the Texel. Sold for BU 1839 at Nieuwediep.
Jean de Witt Rotterdam (constructed by P. Glavimans Jr.).
  K: 4.2.1798. L: 30.6.1798. C: 1799.
  Was out of commission at Nieuwediep in 4.1814. Returned to the Dutch as *Johan de Wit* 22.4.1814. BU 1817 at Vlissingen.
Commerce de Rotterdam Amsterdam (constructed by R. Dorsman)
  K: 4.1.1798. L: 8.9.1798. C: 1799.
  Renamed *Rotterdam* 1811. Was out of commission at Nieuwediep in 4.1814. Returned to the Dutch as *Rotterdam* 22.4.1814. Set out with a fleet for the Mediterranean 22.12.1814 but badly damaged by a storm and put in to Plymouth. Sold and BU 1815 in England.
Utrecht Rotterdam (constructed by P. Glavimans Jr.)
  K: 14.10.1798. L: 9.4.1800. C: 1801?
  Never commissioned by the Dutch. Unserviceable by 1813, condemned 14.10.1813. Taken by the Dutch in the uprising of 12.1813. BU at Hellevoetsluis 1815.

AMIRAL TROMP. A one-off reversion to the 68-gun design after intervening construction of the 80-gun type. She was constructed by Glavimans at Rotterdam from 1806 onwards as *Admiraal Tromp* (or *Maarten Harpertszoon Tromp*) with the same hull structure as the 180-foot *Utrecht* of 1798. She was taken into the French Navy in July 1810 and renamed *Amiral Tromp*; upon completion in 1811 her name was shortened to *Tromp*, but she was returned to the Dutch (name restored to

Guerrier, the oldest 74-gun ship in French service, was placed at the head of the line in Aboukir Bay, and was rapidly disabled by the fire of the *Goliath* and following ships, as shown in this eyewitness watercolour by Cooper Willyams of the opening stage of the Battle of the Nile. The French had pressed into service a number of old and relatively weak ships for the Egypt expedition, including the *Peuple Souverain* and *Conquérant*. (© National Maritime Museum D8132D)

Admiraal Tromp) on 1 August 1814.
  Dimensions & tons: 156ft 10in, 148ft 2in x 41ft 10in x 19ft 2in (50.96, 48.14 x 13.59 x 6.23m). 1,200/2,300 tons. Draught 18ft 4in/19ft 2in (5.94m/6.23m). Men: 502-544.
  Guns: (French) LD 26 x 24pdrs; UD 28 x 18pdrs; SD 4 x 8pdrs + 12 x 24pdr carronades (by a decision of 25.3.1813).
Admiral Tromp Rotterdam (constructed by P. Glavimans Jnr).
  K: 2.7.1806. L: 27.12.1808. C: 10.1811.
  Renamed *Tromp* 1811. In commission by the French between 20.2.1812 and 21.3.1814. In the Scheldt squadron as a floating battery in 4.1814. Returned to the Dutch as *Admiraal Tromp* 1.8.1814. Sailed from Vlissingen 16.3.1817 for the East Indies, handed over to the Colonial Navy 12.1820, BU 1823 in the East Indies.

74-gun two-deckers

(A) Vessels in service or on order at 1 January 1786

Although the French Navy had settled on the 74-gun two-decker as its standard two-decker battle fleet unit as early as 1719, the dozen ships of this rating which were built during the period up to 1737 were in effect broadened 70-gun ships, with four small 4pdr guns mounted on the dunette roof. With the design of Francois Coulomb's *Terrible* in 1737, room was found for an extra pair of gunports on the lower deck and similarly on the upper deck, and the ineffective 4pdrs were removed.

Henceforth all these 74s – without exception – carried the standard armament of 28 x 36pdrs on the LD, 30 x 18pdrs on the UD, and 16 x 8pdrs on the SD (gaillards). While Coulomb's first three 74s at Toulon were not significantly longer than the twelve 74s of 1719 to 1737, all the subsequent 74s were at least 160ft (equal to 170½ British feet, or 52 metres) in length, not matched by the British designs for this rating until the 1780s. Three of the six new 74s built during the War of 1744-48 had been lost by 1748, and Louis XV took advantage of the peace to order a number of new warships, with a dozen more 74s ordered in the next few years.

MAGNIFIQUE Class. Jacques-Luc Coulomb design, the last 74s to be designed before the peace agreement in 1748. Of the three ships built to this design, *Magnifique* was wrecked in 1782 and *Entreprenant* was burnt at Louisbourg in 1758. *Guerrier* was named on 18 September 1750 and served throughout the Seven Years War and (following reconstruction at Toulon in 1769-70) the American Revolutionary War, but was in reserve from April 1783 until September 1794.

Dimensions: 165ft 0in, ?157ft 0in x 43ft 0in x 20ft 4in (53.60, ?51.00 x 13.97 x 6.61m). 1,500/2,700 tons. Draught 19ft/20ft 5in (6.16/6.63m). Men: 670/750.

Guns: LD 28 x 36pdrs; UD 30 x 18pdrs; SD 16 x 8pdrs (i.e. 10 on QD, 6 on Fc).

Guerrier Toulon Dyd.
K: 3.11.1750. L: 9.9.1753. C: 1.1754.
Captured by Nelson's fleet at Aboukir 2.8.1798 and burnt as unrepairable.

DIADÈME Class. Design by Jean-Luc Coulomb. *Diadème* was named on 10 September 1755. *Zodiaque* of this design was sold in 1784.

Dimensions: 168ft 0in x 43ft 6in x 20ft 6in (54.57 x 14.13 x 6.66m). 1,500/2,800 tons. Draught 19½ft/21ft (6.33/6.82m). Men: 740/759 (as rasée 480).

Guns: LD 28 x 36pdrs; UD 30 x 18pdrs; SD 16 x 8pdrs. As rasée: UD 28 x 36pdrs; SD 14 x 18pdrs + 6 swivels.

Diadème Brest Dyd.
K: 9.1755. L: 26.6.1756. C: 11.1756.
Renamed *Brutus* 29.9.1792 and raséed 12.1793 – 5.1794. BU 1797 at Brest.

SOUVERAIN Class. Noël Pomet design. Named 25 October and 10 September 1755 respectively. *Souverain* was reconstructed to Antoine Groignard design at Toulon 26.9.1778 – 25.6.1779.

Dimensions: 164ft 0in x 43ft 6in x 21ft 6in (53.27 x 14.13 x 6.98m). 1,550/2,800 tons. Draught 19ft/22ft (6.17/7.15m). Men: 720.

Guns: LD 28 x 36pdrs; UD 30 x 18pdrs; SD 16 x 8pdrs.

Souverain Toulon Dyd.
K: 12.1755. L: 6.5.1757. C: 11.1757.
Renamed *Peuple Souverain* 9.1792. Captured by Nelson's fleet at Aboukir 2.8.1798 and became HMS *Guerrier*, as depot ship at Gibraltar; BU 1810.

Protecteur Toulon Dyd.
K: 29.5.1757. L: 22.5.1760. C: 4.1762.
Hulked as hospital ship at Rochefort 1.1789, and BU soon after.

ZÉLÉ Class. Joseph-Marie-Blaise Coulomb design, 1762; the longest 74 built to date, with length not to be repeated until the 1780s. She was funded by the *Receveurs Généraux des Finances*.

Dimensions: 168ft 0in, 151ft 6in x 43ft 6in x 20ft 9in (54.57, 49.21 x 14.13 x 6.74m). 1,500/2,900 tons. Draught 19½ft/20ft 8in (6.33/6.71m). Men: 720-727.

Guns: LD 28 x 36pdrs; UD 30 x 18pdrs; SD 16 x 8pdrs.

Zélé Toulon Dyd.
Named 9.12.1761. K: 2.1762. L: 1.7.1763. C: 1764.
Ordered BU at Brest 11.11.1804, ordered converted to hulk 7.1.1805 and renamed *Réserve*. BU 5.1806.

France lost twelve 74s to British action during the war years 1755-62: the *Espérance* in 1755, *en flûte*, the *Entreprenant*, *Prudent* and *Robuste* (*en flûte*) in 1758, the *Redoubtable*, *Téméraire*, *Centaure*, *Héros*, the brand new *Thesée*, and the older *Superbe* and *Juste* in 1759, and the *Courageux* in 1761, and with the *Florissant* having to be BU following battle damage, nine new 74s were laid down during the following decade.

MARSEILLAIS. One-off design by Joseph Chapelle, this ship was funded for the navy by the Chamber of Commerce of Marseille; ordered in 1761 or 1762 and named on 16 January 1762. Her figurehead was sculpted by Pierre Audibert. Construction was delayed by lack of timber. In 1793, 4 x 36pdr carronades were added to the gaillards armament.

Dimensions & tons: 168ft 0in, 146ft 6in x 43ft 6in x 21ft 0in (54.57, 47.59 x 14.13 x 6.82m). 1,550/2,900 tons. Draught 19ft 6in/20ft 8in (6.33/6.71m). Men: 720.

Guns: LD 28 x 36pdrs; UD 30 x 18pdrs; SD 16 x 8pdrs.

Marseillais Toulon Dyd.
K: 2.1763. L: 16.6.1766. C: 11.1767.
Renamed *Vengeur du Peuple* in 2.1794; burnt in Battle of Glorious First of June 1794.

CITOYEN Class. Design by Joseph-Louis Ollivier. The lead ship was funded by the Bankers & General Treasurers of the Army, and was ordered under the name *Cimeterre* in May 1757; renamed *Citoyen* 20 January 1762 on the stocks, she was intended to be launched on 10 August 1764, but stuck on the ways and did not reach the water until 17 days later. The *Conquérant*, originally built in 1745-47 at Brest (by Serpoulet to a François Coulomb design), was rebuilt to the lines of the *Citoyen* in a drydock at Brest from 17 March 1764. Two further ships were built to this design at Brest in 1766-68, but *Palmier* (also rebuilt from an earlier ship of 1750-52) was lost in 1782 and *Actif* was sold in 1784.

Dimensions & tons: 169ft 6in x 43ft 0in x 20ft 9in (55.06 x 13.97 x 6.74m). 1,500/3,000 tons. Draught 19ft 6in/21ft (6.33/6.82m) Men: 730.

Guns: LD 28 x 36pdrs; UD 30 x 18pdrs; SD 16 x 8pdrs. (*Conquérant* re-armed 2.1795: LD 28 x 18pdrs; UD 30 x 12pdrs; SD 16 x 6pdrs)

Citoyen Brest Dyd.
K: 7.1761. L: 27.8.1764. C: 12.1764.
Condemned 1790 and BU at Brest 1792-93.

Conquérant Brest Dyd.
K: 1.1765. L: 29.11.1765. C: 12.1765.
Condemned at Toulon 5.1796, but reprieved and returned to service in 1796. Captured by Nelson's fleet at the Battle of the Nile (Aboukir) 2.8.1798, becoming HMS *Conquerant*; never returned to service after arriving in Plymouth. BU 1.1803 at Plymouth.

BIEN-AIMÉ Class. Antoine Groignard design, 1768. The *Bien-Aimé* of this design was struck in 1784 at Brest and BU there in 1785 or 1786; the *Fendant*, a slightly shorter vessel developed from this design by Groignard and built by Chevillard at Rochefort in 1772-77, was lost in 9.1784.

Dimensions & tons: 170ft 0in, 160ft 0in x 43ft 6in x 21ft 5in (55.22, 51.97 x 14.13 x 6.96m). 1,500/2,884 tons. Draught 20ft/21ft 2in

(6.50/6.88m). Men: 656/727.
Guns: LD 28 x 36pdrs; UD 30 x 18pdrs; SD 16 x 8pdrs.
Victoire Lorient Dyd. (Constructeur, La Freté-Bernard).
K: 8.1768. L: 4.10.1770. C: 1.1773.
Disarmed at Brest 28.5.1782, condemned there 7.1792 and BU.

CÉSAR (or Modified ZÉLÉ) Class. Joseph-Marie-Blaise Coulomb design, 1762. *Destin*, ordered on 7 February 1770, was named on 20 March. The *César* of this design was captured 12 April 1782 by the British at the Battle of the Saintes, then destroyed by an explosion.
Dimensions & tons: 168ft 0in, 157ft 6in x 43ft 6in x 20ft 9in (54.57, 51.16 x 14.13 x 6.74m). 1,500/2,900 tons. Draught 19½ft/20ft 8in (6.33/6.71m). Men: 656/727.
Guns: LD 28 x 36pdrs; UD 30 x 18pdrs; SD 16 x 8pdrs.
Destin Toulon Dyd.
K: 4.1770. L: 21.10.1777. C: 28.5.1778.
Disarmed at Toulon 9.4.1783. Handed over to Anglo-Spanish forces at Toulon 28.8.1793, and burnt on the evacuation of Toulon 18.12.1793. Wreck raised and BU 1807.

NEPTUNE. A one-off design by Pierre-Augustin Lamothe in 1778, one of the first two new 74s to be ordered after a gap of some five years, and named on 20 February 1778.
Dimensions & tons: 168ft 6in, 146ft 6in x 44ft 0in x 22ft 0in (54.74, 47.59 x 14.29 x 7.15m). 1,500/2,856 tons. Draught 19½/20½ft (6.33/6.66m). Men: 662-750.
Guns: LD 28 x 36pdrs; UD 30 x 18pdrs; SD 16 x 8pdrs.
Neptune Brest Dyd.
K: 12.1777. L: 20.8.1778. C: 16.9.1778.
Wrecked in a storm off the north coast of Brittany 28.1.1795.

ANNIBAL Class. Jacques-Noël Sané's original design, dated 24 November 1777, was for a ship of 166ft length and 2,793 tons displacement. The *Annibal* was named on 20 February 1778, at the same time as the *Neptune*. Sané's amended plan for her was dated 10 January 1779. The plan for her near-sister *Northumberland*, which was a foot longer and 26 tons more in displacement than the *Annibal*'s dimensions quoted below, was dated 3 March 1780. Both ships were captured by Howe's fleet at the Battle of the Glorious First of June 1794 off Ushant, but were not commissioned into the RN.
Dimensions & tons: 168ft 0in, 151ft 6in x 44ft 0in x 21ft 6in (54.57, 49.21 x 14.29 x 6.98m). 1,478/2,939 tons. Draught 20ft 2in/22ft

Admiralty draught of *Northumberland* taken off in August 1795. The ship was never fitted for Royal Navy service and the draught records the ship as captured; note the French-style capstans and suction pumps as well as the original decorative scheme. The ship's name commemorates an earlier prize, a 64-gun ship taken from the British in 1744. (© National Maritime Museum J2685)

2in (6.55/7.20m). Men: 700-750.
Guns: LD 28 x 36pdrs; UD 30 x 18pdrs; SD 16 x 8pdrs.
Annibal Brest Dyd.
K: 12.1777. L: 5.10.1778. C: 1.1779.
Renamed *Achille* 21.1.1786. Captured on 1.6.1794, becoming HMS *Achille*; BU at Plymouth 2.1796.
Northumberland Brest Dyd.
K: 24.2.1779. L: 3.5.1780. C: 7.1780.
Captured on 1.6.1794, becoming HMS *Northumberland*; BU at Plymouth 11.1795.

SCIPION Class. François-Guillaume Clairin-Deslauriers design, 1778. The design of these ships was found to lack stability, and a further pair of orders placed at this port were considerably lengthened (see *Argonaute* class below). The *Pluton* was 'girdled' (sheathed) with 32cm of pine at Rochefort in 3-4.1799 to overcome her instability.
Dimensions & tons: 165ft 6in, ?155ft 0in x 43ft 6in x 21ft 6in (53.76, ?50.35 x 14.13 x 6.98m). 1,424/2,943 tons. Draught 20ft 2in/22ft 6in (6.55/7.31m). Men: 662/750.
Guns: LD 28 x 36pdrs; UD 30 x 18pdrs; SD 16 x 8pdrs.
Scipion Rochefort Dyd.
K: 10.4.1778. L: 19.9.1778. C: 2.1779.
Wrecked in Samana Bay (San Domingo) 19.10.1782.
Hercule Rochefort Dyd.
K: 1.4.1778. L: 5.10.1778. C: 2.1779.
Raséed 2.1794 – 6.1794, and renamed *Hydre* 5.1795.
Pluton Rochefort Dyd. (Constructeur, Henri Chevillard)
K: 10.4.1778. L: 5.11.1778. C: 2.1779.
Renamed *Dugommier* 17.12.1797. Condemned at Brest and ordered BU 7.1.1805.

HÉROS. A one-off design by Joseph-Marie-Blaise Coulomb, the *ingénieur-constructeur en chef* at Toulon from 1768; ordered on 29 November 1777 and named on 20 February 1778.
Dimensions & tons: 167ft 10in, 149ft 0in x 43ft 6in x 21ft 0in

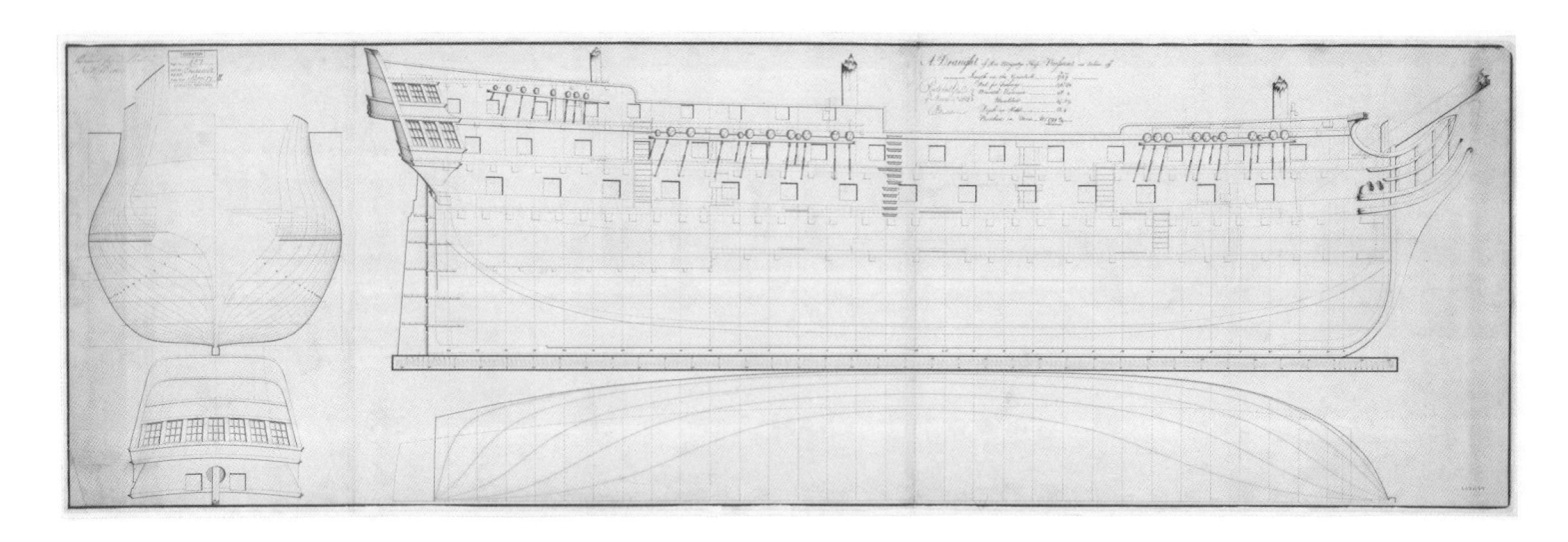

(54.52, 48.40 x 14.13 x 6.82m). 1,500/2,800 tons. Draught 19 6in/21ft (6.33/6.82m). Men: 707/750.

Guns: LD 28 x 36pdrs; UD 30 x 18pdrs; SD 16 x 8pdrs.

Héros Toulon Dyd.
K: 10.5.1778. L: 30.12.1778. C: 5.1779. Handed over to the Anglo-Spanish forces at Toulon 8.1793, and burnt 18.12.1793 by the Allies at the evacuation of that port; remains raised and BU 1806.

MAGNANIME Class. Jean-Denis Chevillard design, 1779.
Dimensions & tons: 171ft 3in, ?160ft 0in x 44ft 0in x 22ft 0in (55.63, ?51.97 x 14.29 x 7.15m). 1,500/2,950 tons. Draught 19/21ft (6.17/6.82m). Men: 660/750.

Guns: LD 28 x 36pdrs; UD 30 x 18pdrs; SD 16 x 8pdrs.

Magnanime Rochefort Dyd. (Constructeur, Jean-Denis Chevillard)
K: 10.1778. L: 27.8.1779. C: 12.1779.
Struck at Brest 1792 and BU there 1793.

Illustre Rochefort Dyd. (Constructeur, Jean-Denis Chevillard)
K: 8.1779. L: 23.2.1781. C: 3.1781.
Renamed *Mucius Scévola* 1.1791, shortened to *Scévola* 2.1794 and raséed 8.1793 – 2.1794. Wrecked in a storm 30.12.1796 during the attempted invasion of Ireland.

ARGONAUTE Class. François-Guillaume Clairin-Deslauriers extended design, approved in June 1779. The designer died at Rochefort on 10 October 1780, and his work was completed by Jean-Denis Chevillard, who was appointed his successor as *ingénieur-constructeur en chef* at that dockyard in July 1781. Both ships were raséed at Brest in 1793-94 to become heavy frigates (see Chapter 4 for revised ordnance).
Dimensions & tons: 170ft 0in, 159ft 0in x 44ft 0in x 22ft 0in (55.22, 51.65 x 14.29 x 7.15). Draught 21ft 0in/22ft 9in (6.82/7.39m). Men: 658/751.

Guns: LD 28 x 36pdrs; UD 30 x 18pdrs; SD 16 x 8pdrs.

Argonaute Rochefort Dyd. (Constructeur, Jean-Denis Chevillard)
K: 8.1779. L: 5.6.1781. C: 12.1781.
Raséed 12.1793-5.1794 and renamed *Flibustier* 6.1794. Disarmed 12.1795 and later BU.

Brave Rochefort Dyd. (Constructeur, Jean-Denis Chevillard)
K: 10.1779. L: 6.6.1781. C: 11.1781.
Hulked 1.1798 at Brest, and later BU.

SCEPTRE. A one-off design by Pierre-Augustin Lamothe in 1778.
Dimensions & tons: 166ft 6in, 151ft 0in x 44ft 3in x 21ft 6in. (54.09, 49.05 x 14.37 x 6.98m) 1,585/2,996 tons. Draught 20ft

Admiralty draught of *Puissant* taken off in November 1810. The ship spent the whole of her life after capture in harbour service, including a brief commission between 1812 and 1815 as the stationary flagship of the Commander-in-Chief, Portsmouth. (© National Maritime Museum J2662)

4in/22ft 4in (6.61/7.25m) Men: 700/750.

Guns: LD 28 x 36pdrs; UD 30 x 18pdrs; SD 16 x 8pdrs.

Sceptre Brest Dyd.
K: 25.5.1780. L: 21.9.1780. C: 10.1780 (built and commissioned in 105 days).
Renamed *Convention* 29.9.1792 and *Marengo* 8.1800. Condemned 8.4.1803; ordered BU 9.11.1803, provisionally used as prison and raséed 11.1803 as a prison hospital. BU begun 31.12.1811.

PÉGASE Class. Antoine Groignard design, 1781. All six were ordered in 1781 and named on 13 July 1781. The lead-ship *Pégase* (built at Brest in 1781) was captured by the British on 24 April 1782.
Dimensions & tons: 170ft 0in, 161ft 0in x 44ft 0in x 21ft 9in. (55.22, 52.30 x 14.29 x 7.07m) 1,515/3,000 tons. Draught 19ft 6in/21ft (6.33/6.82m). Men: 703/750.

Guns: LD 28 x 36pdrs; UD 30 x 18pdrs; SD 16 x 8pdrs.

Puissant Lorient Dyd. (Constructeur, Charles Segondat-Duvernet)
K: 8.1781. L: 13.3.1782. C: 6.1782.
Handed over to the Anglo-Spanish forces at Toulon 29.8.1793, and removed to Britain on evacuation of that port; sold 7.1816.

Dictateur Toulon Dyd.
K: 7.1782. L: 16.2.1782. C: 8.1782.
Handed over to the Anglo-Spanish forces at Toulon on 29.8.1793, then burnt there at the evacuation 18.12.1793; refloated 1805 then BU 1808.

Suffisant Toulon Dyd.
K: 7.1782. L: 6.3.1782. C: 8.1782.
Handed over to the Anglo-Spanish forces at Toulon on 29.8.1793, then burnt there at the evacuation 18.12.1793; refloated 1805 then BU 1806.

Alcide Rochefort Dyd.
K: 7.1781. L: 25.5.1782. C: 1.1783.
Caught fire and burnt off Fréjus 18.7.1795.

Censeur Rochefort Dyd.
K: 8.1781. L: 24.7.1782. C: 10.1783.
Captured by Hotham's squadron 14.3.1795; retaken 7.10.1795. Condemned at Cadiz and sold to Spain 6.1799 in exchange for the

Spanish *San Sebastián*, which became the French *Alliance*.

CENTAURE Class. Designed by Jean-Marie-Blaise Coulomb, original Jean-Denis Chevillard plan dated 28 March 1782. A development of Groignard's design for the *Victoire*, as amended by Coulomb.
Guns: LD 28 x 36pdrs; UD 30 x 18pdrs; SD 16 x 8pdrs.

(i) **First pair** – ordered 15.2.1782 and named 13.4.1782.
Dimensions & tons: 168ft 0in, 150ft 6in x 44ft 0in x 21ft 9in (54.57, 48.73 x 14.29 x 7.07m). 1,530/3,010 tons. Draught 20½ft/21ft 8in (6.66/7.04m). Men: 703-723.

Centaure Toulon Dyd.
K: 12.5.1782. L: 7.11.1782. C: 12.1782.
Handed over to the Anglo-Spanish forces at Toulon on 29.8.1793, then burnt there at the evacuation 18.12.1793; refloated 1805 then BU 1806.

Heureux Toulon Dyd.
K: 12.5.1782. L: 19.12.1782. C: 4.1783.
Captured at Aboukir 2.8.1798 by the British, then burnt 29.8.1798.

(ii) **Second pair** – ordered 1.6.1782 and named 21.8.1782.
Dimensions & tons: 173ft 3in, 156ft 0in x 43ft 7in x 22ft 0in (56.28, 50.67 x 14.16 x 7.34m). 1,550/3,100 tons. Draught 20ft 6in/22ft 8in (6.66/7.37m).

Séduisant Toulon Dyd.
K: 8.1782. L: 5.7.1783. C: 1783.
Renamed *Pelletier* 28.9.1793, but reverted to *Séduisant* 30.5.1795. Wrecked 16.12.1796 upon sailing from Brest.

Mercure Toulon Dyd.
K: 8.1782. L: 4.8.1783. C: 1783.
Captured at Aboukir 2.8.1798 by the British, then burnt 30.8.1798.

TÉMÉRAIRE Class. Jacques-Noël Sané design, 1782. From the middle of 1782 until the end of the Napoleonic era, all French 74s were built to this standard Sané design (including a few experimental variations to the basic design). Some 120 vessels to this design (including derivatives) would eventually be ordered between 1782 and 1813, of which the following twelve were ordered before 1786.
Dimensions & tons: 172ft 0in, 170ft 8in wl, 155ft 0in x 44ft 6in, 45ft 10in wl x 22ft 0in. (55.87, 50.35 x 14.46 x 7.15m) 1,537/3,069 tons. Draught 19ft 10in/22ft 0in (6.44/7.15m). Men (1786): 705 in wartime/495 in peacetime. The total included 12 officers, comprising a *capitaine de vaisseau* (to command), a *capitaine de frégate* (as second-in-command), 5 *lieutenants* and 5 *enseignes*.
Guns: (original) LD 28 x 36pdrs; UD 30 x 18pdrs; SD 16 x 8pdrs (plus 4 x 36pdr obusiers after 1787). (*Patriote*, 1810): LD 28 x 36pdrs; UD 30 x 18pdrs; SD 12 x 8pdrs, 10 x 36pdr carronades.

(i) **1782 Orders.** One ship was ordered on 15 February 1782 at Lorient and two at Rochefort, and all three were named on 13 April; two more were ordered at Brest and named on 1 June, while a second order was placed at Lorient on 1 June and named on 21 August. Four were begun in May (the name-ship of the class) and July; the other two were not begun until 1784. Another 74, to be named *Thésée* (probably to this design) was projected in 1782 at Rochefort, but was cancelled in February 1783.

Téméraire Brest Dyd.
K: 5.1782. L: 17.12.1782. C: 7.1783.
Condemned at Brest 9.11.1802, BU ordered 29.11.1802, BU 1803.

Superbe Brest Dyd.
K: 7.1782. L: 11.11.1784. C: 1785.
Lost off Brest 30.1.1795.

Audacieux Lorient Dyd. (Constructeur, Charles Segondat-Duvernet)
K: 8.7.1782. L: 28.10.1784. C: 1785.
Condemned at Brest 9.11.1802, BU ordered 29.11.1802. BU 2-3.1803.

Généreux Rochefort Dyd. (Constructeur, Henri Chevillard).
K: 24.7.1782. L: 21.6 or 7.1785. C: 10.1785.
Captured 18.2.1800 south of Sicily by the British, became HMS *Généreux*. Prison hulk 1805, BU 2.1816.

Orion Rochefort Dyd. (Constructeurs, Pierre Train and Joseph Niou)
K: 10.1784. L: 18.4.1787. C: 1788.
Renamed *Mucius Scévola* 11.1793, then *Mucius* 30.11.1793. Frame made at Bayonne, construction delayed by lack of carpenters. Condemned 13.10.1803, BU completed 8.4.1804.

Fougueux Lorient Dyd. (Constructeur, Charles Segondat-Duvernet)
K: 11.1784. L: 19.9.1785. C: 12.1785.
Had been begun 8.1782, stopped 1.11.1783, and parts put into storage until put back on the ways 11.1784. Captured by boarding at Trafalgar 21.10.1805, but abandoned by the British in the ensuing storm and went ashore 28.10.1805 on the Santi Petri reefs to the east of Cadiz.

(ii) **1784-85 Orders.** A second batch of six was ordered in 1784-85. The pair ordered at Toulon were known simply as *Vaisseau No.1* and *Vaisseau No.2* until named *Commerce de Bordeaux* and *Commerce de Marseille* respectively on 23 January and 27 January 1786; the second was amended to *Lys* on 17 July 1786. *Patriote* and *Léopard* at Brest were named on 28 January 1786.

Commerce de Bordeaux Toulon Dyd.
K: 9.1784. L: 15.9.1785. C: ?1786.
Renamed *Bonnet Rouge* 12.1793, then *Timoléon* 2.1794. Burnt by her crew at the Battle of the Nile (Aboukir) 2.8.1798 to avoid capture.

Lys Toulon Dyd.
K: 9.1784. L: 7.10.1785 C: 9.1787.
Renamed *Tricolore* 6.10.1792. Handed over to Anglo-Spanish forces at Toulon 8.1793, and burnt during the evacuation of that port 18.12.1793; raised and BU 1807.

Patriote Brest Dyd.
K: 10.1784. L: 3.10.1785. C: 4.1786.
Handed over to Anglo-Spanish forces at Toulon 8.1793, returned to the French 9.1793 to evacuate 1,400 counter-revolutionary sailors. Damaged by high winds 19.8.1806 and put in at Annapolis on 29.8.1806. Condemned 5.1820 at Rochefort, conversion to mooring hulk approved 16.1.1821, conversion completed 2.4.1821 and designated *Ponton No.4*. Grounded 1830, BU 1832-33.

Borée Lorient Dyd. (Constructeur, Charles Segondat-Duvernet)
K: 11.1784. L: 17.11.1785. C: 8.1787.
Renamed *Ça Ira* 4.1794, then *Agricola* 6.1794; raséed as a heavy frigate 4-7.1794.

Ferme Brest Dyd. (Constructeur, Lamothe).
K: 12.1784. L: 16.9.1785. C: 1786.
Renamed *Phocion* 10.1792. Handed over to the Spanish at Trinidad 11.1.1793 by her pro-Royalist crew; added to the Spanish Navy 1794; BU at La Guaira 1808.

Léopard Brest Dyd.
K: 15.11.1785. L: 22.6.1787. C: 7.1787.
Grounded off Cagliari 17 2.1793 and burnt two days later to avoid capture.

French losses of 74s during the war years 1780-82 amounted to eight ships – the *Intrepide*, *Orient*, *Palmier* and *Magnifique* by natural causes in 1781-82 and the *Glorieux*, *Hector*, *César*, and *Pégase* in combat in 1782.

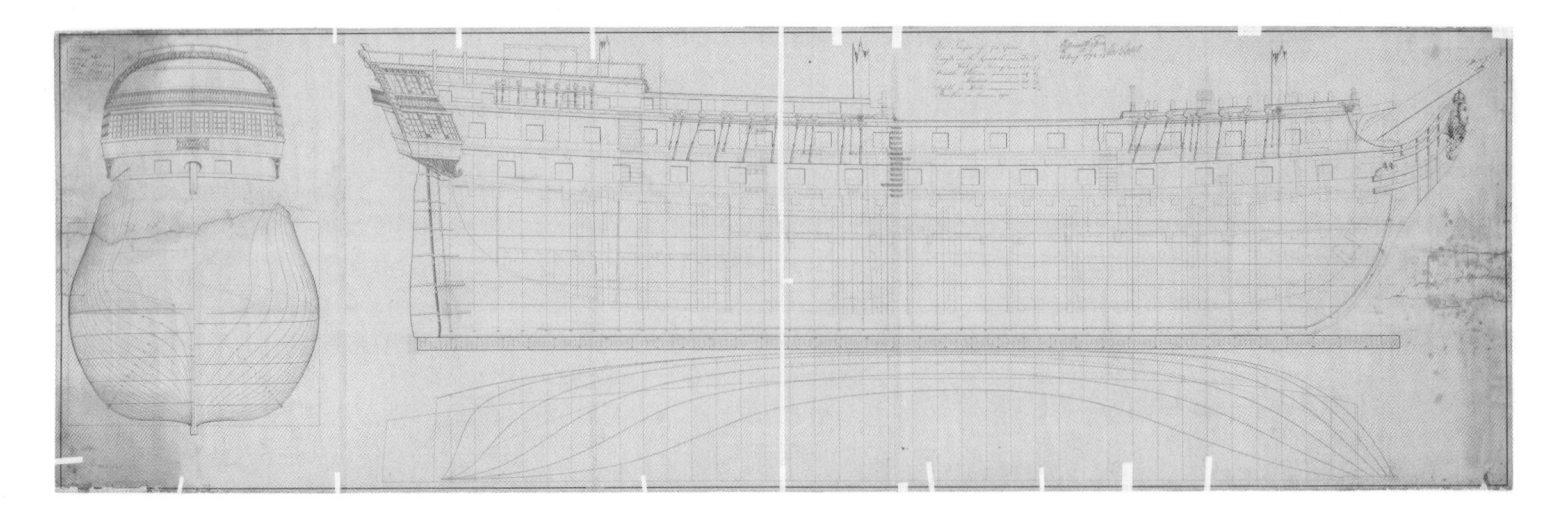

AMERICA. On 10 August 1782 the French 74 *Magnifique* (launched in 1749) struck a rock off Lovell's Island while entering Boston Harbour under the control of a Boston pilot. She was taking refuge there as part of Vaudreuil's squadron, after the Battle of the Saintes. On 3 September 1782 the American Congress presented the sole ship of the line built for the American Continental Navy during the war, *America*, to France as a replacement for *Magnifique*.

America was part of a building program authorised by the Continental Congress on 20 November 1776 that included three 74-gun ships of the line, five 36-gun frigates, an 18-gun brig, and a packet. Of the 74s, the construction of one at Philadelphia was prevented by the British occupation of that city, while work on one at Boston stopped before she was laid down. The third, built by Colonel James K. Hackett at Portsmouth, New Hampshire with his cousin William as master shipwright, was carried to completion, although work proceeded slowly despite the appointment by Congress in June 1779 of John Paul Jones as her commander and resident supervisor of construction. (He also changed the design of the ship's upperworks.) A draught and a half-model by Joshua Humphreys for an American 74-gun ship have been preserved, but they may have applied primarily to the Philadelphia ship. The American specifications given below for *America*, cited by the historian Robert W. Neeser from an unknown source, differ from those on the Humphrey draught, which were (American) 180ft, 166ft x 49ft x 19ft (54.86, 50.60 x 14.94 x 5.79m) with a draught of 21ft/24ft 6in (6.40/7.47m). The ship's reported American armament, also from an unknown source, was insignificant by European standards.

Magnifique's commander, Jean-Baptiste de Macarty-Macteigne, took charge of *America* immediately after her launch, placed the guns salvaged from *Magnifique* on board, and sailed *America* to France. The French described her as 'very long, very wide, with little depth of hull and a lot of tumblehome.' On 20 August 1786 Castries reported to the King that a careful inspection of *America* at Brest on 11 August had shown that the ship, although only four years old, was entirely rotten. All of her pieces were equally deteriorated although they had been fabricated with great care, indicating that North America was not a good source for ship timber. In addition a refit was inadvisable as 'the ship did not combine the qualities which a vessel of this class should have.' Consequently he recommended that the King order the demolition of the ship and the construction of another 74 under the same name, a recommendation that the King approved.

  Dimensions & tons: (American) 182ft 6in, 150ft 0in x 50ft 6in ext x 23ft (55.63, 45.72 x 16.59 x 7.56m). 1,982 tons.
  Dimensions & tons: (French) 172ft, 153ft x 47ft 4in x 21ft (55.87, 49.70 x 15.38 x 6.82m). 1,500/3,000 tons. Men (French): 13 to 17 officers and 690 men.
  Guns: (American) LD 30 x 18pdrs; UD 32 x 12pdrs; SD 14 x 9pdrs;
  Guns: (*Magnifique*) LD 28 x 36pdrs; UD 30 x 18pdrs; SD 16 x 8pdrs.
America James K. Hackett, Portsmouth, N.H.
  K: 5.1777. L: 5.11.1782. C: 6.1783.
  Given to France 3.9.1782. Struck 20.8.1786 and BU.

Admiralty draught of *Pompee* as captured, dated 26 August 1794. The ship was one of the very numerous *Téméraire* class, which was effectively the standard French 74 of this era. The draught shows the classic 'horse-shoe' shape stern favoured by Sané, and the standardised figurehead design approved in 1786 – still bearing the royal arms five years after the Revolution. (© National Maritime Museum J2666)

At the end of the period, the new 1786 Program for new construction drafted by Borda (and approved by Castries) included the construction of 60 new 74s, all to be to Sané's draught for the *Téméraire* class. The program also included nine new 118s and twelve new 80s, with sixty frigates (forty with 12pdr and twenty with 18pdr main batteries) and sixty corvettes and brigs.

(B) Vessels acquired from 1 January 1786

Later *TÉMÉRAIRE* Class (1786-1793 orders). In around 1787 (probably beginning with the *Tourville* below), the ordnance was increased by the addition of 4 x 36pdr obusiers, mounted on top of the dunette; in other vessels of this class, the gaillards armament was increased from 16 to 20 x 8pdrs. By 1807 the obusiers had been abolished and nearly all ships of this type had 14 or fewer 8pdrs, although they also had up to 14 x 36pdr carronades. To ease identification within this numerous group, the ships are grouped according to the dockyard in which they were built.
Lorient Group. The ship built as *Cassard* was renamed *Dix-Août* on 29 November 1793, but her original name was restored on 30 May 1795 after her launch.
Entreprenant Lorient Dyd. (Constructeur, Charles Segondat-Duvernet)
  K: 5.1786. L: 12.10.1787. C: 1788.
  Taken by Anglo-Spanish forces at Toulon 8.1793, returned to the French 9.1793 to evacuate 1,400 counter-revolutionary sailors and went to Brest. Condemned 9.11.1802 at Brest, BU ordered 29.11.1802, BU 1803.

Tourville Lorient Dyd. (Constructeur, Charles Segondat-Duvernet)
K: 1.6.1787. Named: 25.8.1787. L: 16.9.1788. C: 7.1790.
Decomm. at Brest 22.4.1818. Struck 26.10.1833 and hulked at Brest, BU 1841.

Éole Lorient Dyd. (Constructeur, Charles Segondat-Duvernet)
K: 2.6.1787. Named: 25.8.1787. L: 15.11.1789. C: 8.1790.
Sailed from Brest 13.12.1805 for the West Indies with a squadron under Rear Admiral Willaumez. Departed Martinique 1.7.1806, dismasted in a storm 19.8.1806, reached Annapolis 12.9.1806 assisted by 6 American ships. Ordered sold 3.10.1810, decomm. and condemned at Baltimore 1.1.1811. Sold there 1811.

Jean Bart Lorient Dyd. (Constructeur, Charles Segondat-Duvernet)
Ord: 19.10.1787 (and named). K: 1.6.1788. L: 7.11.1790. C: 2.1791.
Wrecked 26.2.1809 on the Palles rocks near Île d'Aix, wreck taken by the British and burned 4.1809.

Thémistocle Lorient Dyd. (Constructeur, Charles Segondat-Duvernet)
Ord: 19.10.1787. K: 1.9.1789. L: 12.9.1791. C: 9.1792.
Handed over to Anglo-Spanish forces at Toulon 8.1793, and burnt 18.12.1793 during evacuation of that port.

Trajan Lorient Dyd. (Constructeur, Charles Segondat-Duvernet)
Ord: 19.10.1787 (and named). K: 17.5.1790. L: 24.1.1792. C: 11.1792.
Renamed *Gaulois* 17.12.1797. Ordered BU at Brest 7.1.1805.

Tyrannicide Lorient Dyd. (Constructeur, Charles Segondat-Duvernet)
Ord: 25.3.1791. K: 1.11.1791. Named: 10.4.1793. L: 28.6.1793. Comm: 21.11.1793. C: 11.1793.
Renamed *Desaix* 19.7.1800. Wrecked 15.2.1802 on the reefs of Cape Français, Santo Domingo; sunken wreck destroyed by the British.

Droits de L'Homme Lorient Dyd.
Ord: 16.2.1793. K: 5.1793. Named 29.11.1793. L: 29.5.1794. C: 7.1794.
Wrecked off Audierne after combat against HMS *Indefatigable* and *Amazon* 13.1.1797, on returning from Ireland expedition.

Cassard Lorient Dyd.
Ord: 16.2.1793. K: 8.1793. L: 2.5.1795. C: 7.1795.
Renamed *Dix-Août* 24.2.1798 and *Brave* 5.2.1803. Captured at Santo Domingo 6.2.1806, sank 4.1806 off the Azores en route to England.

Wattignies (or *Watigny*) Lorient - Caudan (Constructeur, C.-V. Segondat-Duvernet)
Ord: 3.7.1793. K: 5.1793. Named: 29.11.1793. L: 8.10.1794. C: 12.1794.
Condemned at Brest and BU approved 5.9.1808, BU 1808-9.

Hercule Lorient - Caudan

Ord: 14.8.1793 (at Caudan, slip no.2). K: 6.1794. Named 10.7.1794. L: 5.10.1797. C: 2.1798.
Captured by the British Navy 20.4.1798, becoming HMS *Hercule*; deleted 12.1810.

Argonaute Lorient - Caudan (Constructeur, Pierre-Élisabeth Rolland)
Ord: 10.7.1794 (and named). K: 9.1794. L: 22.12.1798. C: 9.1799.
Projected 14.8.1793 at Caudan, slip no.3. Long construction period caused by a lack of timber. In bad condition at Cadiz following Trafalgar, ceded to Spain 18.12.1806 in exchange for Spanish *Vencador*. Became Spanish prison hulk *Argonauta*. On 25-26.3.1810 during the siege of Cadiz the 584 French prisoners on board seized the ship and cut her cables in hopes of drifting ashore behind French lines, but the ship grounded on an offshore mud bank and many of the prisoners were killed by gunfire from pursuing gunboats. The wreck was then burned.

Rochefort Group. The last three of the ships below were renamed before coming into service; the ship named *Pyrrhus* in 1789 was renamed *Mont Blanc* on 7 January 1793, the *Alexandre* (so named on 22 January 1792) was renamed *Jemmapes* on 7 January 1793, while the last ship, named *Lion* on 23 April 1790, was renamed *Marat* on 28 September 1793.

Impétueux Rochefort Dyd. (Constructeur, Henri Chevillard).
K: 1786. Named: 29.7.1786. L: 25.10.1787. C: 1788.
Captured by Howe's fleet at Battle of Glorious First of June 1.6.1794, becoming HMS *Impetueux*; burnt by accident at Portsmouth 24.8.1794.

Apollon Rochefort Dyd. (Constructeur, Joseph Niou).
K: 4.1787. Named: 29.7.1786. L: 21.5.1788? C: 1788.
Taken by Anglo-Spanish forces at Toulon in 8.1793, but restored to Revolutionary forces in 9.1793 at Rochefort (most officers and many seamen guillotined). Renamed *Gasparin* 2.1794, then *Apollon* 16.5.1795, and finally *Marceau* 17.12.1797; BU 6.1798.

Aquilon Rochefort Dyd. (Constructeur, Henri Chevillard)
K: 8.1787. Named: 29.7.1786. L: 8.6.1789. C: 6.1790.
Captured by Nelson's fleet at the Battle of the Nile (Aboukir) 2.8.1798, becoming HMS *Aboukir*; BU 3.1802 at Plymouth.

Thésée Rochefort Dyd. (Constructeur, Henri Chevillard)
Ord: 19.10.1787. K: 3.1788. L: 14.4.1790. C: 8.1790.
Renamed *Révolution* 7.1.1793 and *Finistèrre* 5.2.1803. Condemned 6.12.1804, ordered converted to a careening hulk (*ponton de carène*) at Brest 7.1.1805. BU 1816.

Pyrrhus Rochefort Dyd. (Constructeurs, Laglaine and Graciot)
Ord: 19.10.1787. K: 7.1789. L: 13.8.1791. C: 3.1793.
Frame cut at Bayonne. Renamed *Mont Blanc* 7.1.1793, *Trente et un Mai* 7.4.1794, *Républicain* 18.4.1795, and *Mont Blanc* 4.1.1796. Captured off Cape Ortegal 4.11.1805 after Trafalgar. HMS *Mont Blanc*, powder hulk 1811, sold for BU 3.1819.

Jemmapes Rochefort Dyd. (Constructeur, Jean-Denis Chevillard-cadet)
Ord: 19.10.1787. K: 8.1790. Named 22.1.1792 (*Alexandre*). L: 22.1.1794. C: 3.1794.
Condemned 5.1820 at Rochefort, conversion to hulk authorised 16.1.1821, conversion completed 2.4.1821. BU 1830 at Rochefort.

Marat Rochefort Dyd. (Constructeur, Jean-Denis Chevillard-cadet).
K: 8.1791. L: 29.4.1794. C: 6.1794.
Renamed *Formidable* 25.5.1795. Captured by HMS *Barfleur* in action off Ile Groix 22.6.1795, becoming HMS *Belleisle*; BU 1814.

Brest Group.

America Brest Dyd
K: 1787. L: 21.5.1788. C: 1789.
Captured by Howe's fleet at Battle of Glorious First of June 1.6.1794, becoming HMS *America*, but renamed HMS *Impetueux* 14.7.1795; BU 12.1813 at Chatham.

Duguay-Trouin Brest Dyd
K: 1787. Named: 25.8.1787. L: 30.10.1788. C: 7.1790.
Handed over to British at Toulon 8.1793, and burnt on the evacuation of Toulon 18.12.1793.

Jupiter Brest Dyd
Ord: 19.10.1787 (and named). K: 6.1788. L: 4.11.1789. C: 10.1790.
Renamed *Montagnard* 3.1794, *Démocrate* 18.5.1795, *Jupiter* 30.5.1795, and *Batave* 17.12.1797. Condemned 6.1.1807, BU at Brest completed 14.8.1807.

Vengeur Brest Dyd. (Constructeur, Pierre Ozanne)
Ord: 19.10.1787. K: 23.5.1788. L: 16.12.1789. C: 20.8.1790.
Grounded off Ajaccio 12.12.1792, abandoned and burnt 8.6.1793.

Suffren Brest Dyd
K: 15.1.1789. Named 24.3.1789. L: 31.5.1791. C: 12.1792.

Renamed *Redoutable* 20.5.1795. Captured at Trafalgar 21.10.1805, sank under tow 22.10.1805 in the ensuing storm.

Nestor Brest Dyd. (Constructeurs, Honoré Vial du Clairbois and Pierre-Élisabeth Rolland).

Named 23.4.1790. K: 10.1790. L: 22.7.1793. C: 10.1793.

Renamed *Cisalpin* 17.12.1797, then *Aquilon* 5.2.1803. Grounded on the Palles rocks after the British fireship attack at Ile d'Aix on 11.4.1809 and destroyed by the British 14.4.1809.

Tigre Brest Dyd. (Constructeurs, Honoré Vial du Clairbois).

Named 23.4.1790. K: 1.1791. L: 8.5.1793. C: 8.1793.

Captured by Bridport's fleet in the action of Ile Groix 22.6.1795; BU 1817.

Toulon Group.

Scipion Toulon Dyd

Ord: 19.10.1787. K: 1789. L: 30.7.1790. C: 11.1790

Captured by Anglo-Spanish forces at Toulon 29.8.1793 and (under French Royalist crew) burnt by accident at Livorno 20.11.1793.

Pompée Toulon Dyd

Ord: 19.10.1787. K: 1790. L: 28.5.1791. C: 2.1793.

Captured by Anglo-Spanish forces at Toulon 29.8.1793 and brought to Britain 12.1793, becoming HMS *Pompée*; hulked as prison ship at Plymouth 1810-11, BU at Woolwich 1.1817.

Duquesne Toulon Dyd

Named 25.8.1787. Ord: 19.1.1788. K: 1.1788. L: 2.9.1788. C: 1789.

Taken 25.7.1803 while leaving Santo Domingo with a crew of only 275 men. Became HMS *Duquesne*, BU 7.1805 after grounding in 1804.

Barra Toulon Dyd.

K: 11.1791. L: 23.3.1794. C: 2.1795.

Renamed *Pégase* 9.10.1795, then *Hoche* 17.12.1797. Captured by HMS *Robust* off Lough Swilly 12.10.1798, becoming HMS *Donegal*; BU at Portsmouth 1845.

VÉTÉRAN (Lengthened *Téméraire*) Class. In these two Brest-built ships, the *Téméraire* design was increased by 22in in length and 10in in breadth, to allow these vessels to carry an UD battery of 24pdrs instead of the 18pdrs mounted in all other 74s (with the complement raised to 735 to allow for the 11 men of a 24pdr gun crew *vice* the 9 men of an 18pdr gun crew). The LD armament was unchanged, except that a 15th gunport (chase port) was introduced at this level (without an extra gun being mounted there). The two were afforded a low priority for construction, and the experiment was not repeated. Each ship changed names twice during construction; the ship begun as *No.1* and then as *Lion* was renamed *Glorieux* on 24 February 1798, and renamed *Cassard* on 4 March 1798, while her sister, begun as *No. 2* and then as *Magnanime*, was renamed *Quatorze Juillet* on 7 May 1798 and then *Vétéran* on 6 December 1802. *Vétéran* did the whole cruise with Rear Admiral Willaumez in 1805-6 with 30 x 24pdrs on the upper deck satisfactorily, but after a few cruises the 24pdrs on both ships were replaced with 18pdrs.

Dimensions & tons: 173ft 10in, 157ft 0in x 45ft 4in x 22ft 3in. (56.47, 51.00 x 14.73 x 7.23m) 1,600/3,200 tons. Draught 20ft 10in/23ft (6.77/7.47m). Men: 735.

Guns (1803): LD 28 x 36pdrs; UD 30 x 24pdrs; SD 16 x 8pdrs, 4 x 36pdr obusiers. (After rearming c1806) 28 x 36pdrs, 30 x 18pdrs, 14 x 8pdrs, 14 x 36pdr carronades including 4 bronze.

Cassard Brest Dyd. (Constructeur, Pierre Ozanne)

K: 26.8.1793. Named summer 1794 (*Lion*). L: 24.9.1803. C: 12.1803. Comm: 16.2.1804.

Struck on 18.5.1818 and converted to a mooring hulk. BU 1831-32.

Vétéran Brest Dyd. (Constructeur, Pierre Ozanne)

Ord: 19.6.1794. Named 10.1794 (*Magnanime*). K: 10.11.1794. L: 18.7.1803. Comm: 24.9.1803. C: 12.1803.

Struck 26.10.1833, BU 1841-42.

Later *TÉMÉRAIRE* Class (1794-1801 orders). The majority of the 74-gun ship construction during this period was carried out at Lorient, including its annex at Caudan, which was made available by the navy to contractors, mainly the Crucy brothers, between 1798 and 1805. The Crucys also built ships on slips in the main dockyard there.

Brest. Three 74s were ordered to be built at Brest under the 1793 and 1794 Programs, but the first two were built to a lengthened variant of the design (see *Vétéran* class above); the other ship was initially labelled as *No.3* (of the 1794 Program) and then named *Quatorze Juillet* in 1795. The continuous disruptions at Brest (and wood shortages) meant that she was only 8/24ths complete by December 1806, and she was not launched until 1808, when she was again renamed. A further ship was commenced

Admiralty draught of *Spartiate* as fitted for Royal Navy service in 1802. Although the ship was laid up for three years after her capture at the Battle of the Nile, thereafter the *Spartiate* acquired a great reputation as a fast sailer, and was still in sea service as late as 1836. (© National Maritime Museum J2588)

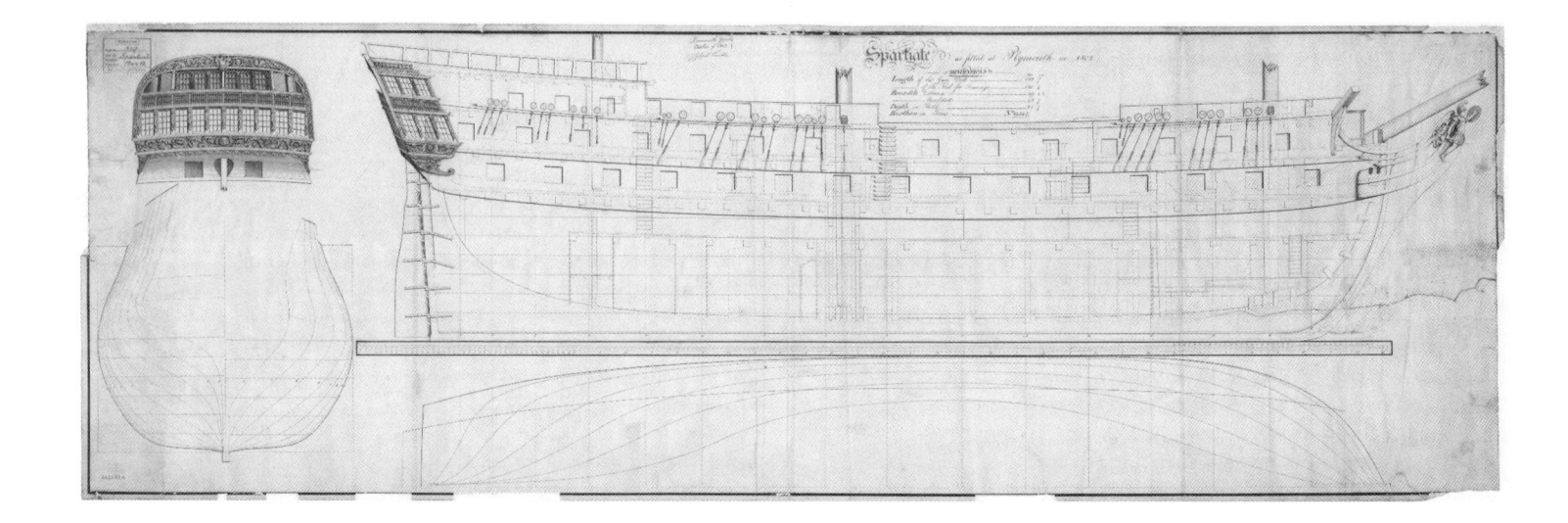

in 1801 at Brest, but was altered to a shorter design and its construction was cancelled in 1804 (see *Algésiras* class below). No further 74s were begun at Brest until 1808.

Tonnerre Brest Dyd. (Constructeurs, Pierre Ozanne, then Léon-Michel Guignace, then Pierre Degay)
> Ord: 16.4.1794. K: 22.9.1794. L: 9.6.1808. Comm: 21.7.1808. C: 9.1808.
>
> Grounded near Île Madame during British fireship attack at Île d'Aix 12.4.1809, burned by her crew and blew up.

Lorient Group. Several of these ships were renamed during construction; the first, initially named *Viala*, was renamed *Voltaire* on 9 October 1795 and subsequently *Constitution* on December 1795; the ship built as *Brutus* was renamed *Impétueux* on 5 February 1803; the last three, for which all the frames were cut at Nantes by Crucy Brothers under contract of 25 May 1801, with '*mise en chantier*' ordered at Lorient 2 November 1801, were all initially named on 7 January 1802, but the *Alcide* and *Courageux* exchanged names on 22 January 1802, and the last was again renamed *D'Hautpoul* on 14 May 1807 (named after the general killed in Murat's massive cavalry attack at Eylau in 1807).

Constitution Lorient - Caudan (Constructeur, C.-V. Segondat-Duvernet).
> K: 19.2.1794. Named 24.6.1794 (*Viala*). L: 28.9.1795. C: 5.1796.
>
> Renamed *Jupiter* 5.2.1803. Captured by the British Navy 6.2.1806 at Santo Domingo, becoming HMS *Maida*; sold 8.1814.

Quatorze Juillet Lorient – Caudan.
> Ord: 23.5.1794. K: 8.1794. Named 19.1.1795. L: 1.2.1798. C: 3.2.1798.
>
> Burnt by accident at Lorient 29.4.1798.

Union Lorient - Caudan (Constructeur, Rolland-aîné)
> Ord: 23.5.1794. K: 9.1794. Named 24.3.1795. L: 1.8.1799. C: 2.1800.
>
> Renamed *Diomède* 5.2.1803. Run aground at Saint Domingo 6.2.1806 to avoid capture, burnt by the British 9.2.1806.

Scipion Lorient - Caudan, by Louis, Antoine, & Mathurin Crucy (Constructeur, François Caro)
> K: 22.9.1798. Named 19.12.1798. L: 29.3.1801. C: 9.1801.
>
> Captured off Cape Ortegal 4.11.1805 after Trafalgar, HMS *Scipion*. BU 1819.

Impétueux Lorient - Caudan, by Louis, Antoine, & Mathurin Crucy (Constructeur, François Caro).
> Ord: 31.5.1798 (contract). K: 22.9.1798. Named: 19.12.1798 (*Brutus*). L: 24.1.1803. Comm: 26.3.1803. C: 3.1803.
>
> Dismasted in a violent storm 19.8.1806, drifted until 10.9.1806, chased by an British division at the mouth of the Chesapeake, ran ashore 14.9.1806 at Cape Henry and surrendered, burnt by the British.

Régulus Lorient - Caudan, by Louis, Antoine, & Mathurin Crucy.
> Ord: 5.4.1801. Named 7.1.1802. K: 7.1802. L: 12.4.1805. Comm: 15.4.1805. C: 7.1805.
>
> Burned 7.4.1814 in the Gironde with the brigs *Malais*, *Javan*, and *Sans-Souci* to avoid capture by the British.

Courageux Lorient Dyd, by Louis, Antoine, & Mathurin Crucy.
> Ord: 15.5.1801. Named 7.1.1802 (*Alcide*). K: 7.1802. L: 3.2.1806. Comm: 8.4.1806. C: 4.1806.
>
> Decomm. at Brest 2.1817. Struck 1827, receiving hulk for seamen (*cayenne flottante*) at Brest. Condemned 16.3.1831, BU 1831-32.

D'Hautpoul Lorient Dyd, by Louis, Antoine, & Mathurin Crucy.
> Ord: 15.5.1801. Named 7.1.1802 (*Courageux*). K: 6.1803. L: 2.9.1807. Comm: 3 or 23.12.1807. C: 2.1808.
>
> Captured 17.4.1809 off Puerto Rico, became HMS *Abercrombie*. Sold 4.1817.

Toulon Group. Eight 74s were intended to be built at Toulon under the 1794 Program, but only two were built and the other six were neither named nor commenced.

Jean-Jacques Rousseau Toulon Dyd. (Constructeurs, Jean-Jacques Le Roy and from 1794 Jean-Jacques Abauzir)
> K: 9.1794. Named 5.10.1794. L: 21.7.1795. C: 10.1796.
>
> Renamed *Marengo* 2.12.1802. Captured by the British Navy 13.3.1806 off the Cape Verde Islands while returning from the Indian Ocean with Linois, becoming HMS *Marengo*; prison hulk 9.1809; BU 11.1816.

Spartiate Toulon Dyd. (Constructeur, Jean-Jacques Abauzir)
> K: 11.1794. L: 24.11.1798. C: 3.1798.
>
> Captured by HMS *Theseus* and *Vanguard* at Aboukir 2.8.1798, becoming HMS *Spartiate*; hulked 8.1842 at Plymouth, BU 5.1857.

Rochefort Group. Three ships were built at Rochefort under the 1794 Program, initially labelled Nos.1, 2 and 3. The construction was interrupted in 1795, and in April 1798 the work was contracted out to Entreprise Destouches.

Duguay-Trouin Rochefort Dyd, after 4.1798 by Entreprise Destouches (Constructeurs, Pierre Rolland and after 1798 for the contractor by Jean-Marie Houssez)
> K: 15.11.1794. Named: 24.3.1795. L: 25.3.1800. C: 11.1800. Comm: 14.4.1801.
>
> Construction interrupted 1795. Captured off Cape Ortegal 4.11.1805 after Trafalgar, became HMS *Implacable*.

Aigle Rochefort Dyd, after 4.1798 by Entreprise Destouches (Constructeurs, Pierre Rolland, after 1798 for the contractor by Jean-Marie Houssez and Pelleteau)
> K: 26.12.1794. Named: 24.3.1795. L: 6.7.1800. C: 2.1801. Comm: 14.4.1801.
>
> Construction interrupted 1795. Captured 21.10.1805 at Trafalgar, wrecked 22.10.1805 off Puerto Santa Maria near Cadiz in the storm after the battle, could not be salvaged and wreck sold.

Héros Rochefort Dyd, after 4.1798 by Entreprise Destouches and/or S. Capon (Constructeurs, Pierre Rolland and after 1798 for the contractor by Jean-Marie Houssez and Capon).
> K: 15.1.1795. Named: 24.3.1795. L: 10.5.1801. Comm: 8.9.1801. C: 10.1801.
>
> Construction interrupted 1795. Surrendered 14.6.1808 to Spanish insurgents at Cadiz, Spanish *Heroe*, struck 1839 at Ferrol.

ALGÉSIRAS **(Shortened *Téméraire*) Class.** In 1801 two ships were begun at Lorient, which were shortened during construction to meet the design requirements of Pierre-Alexandre Forfait. In this variant the length was reduced by 65 cms (2.5in) from Sané's standard *Téméraire* model, resulting in dimensions of 170ft x 44ft 6in x 22ft (55.44 x 14.45 x 7.15m). A third ship to this modified design was begun at Brest but was never completed. After Forfait left the Ministry of Marine in October 1801, this type of shortened 74 was abandoned in favour of the 74 '*petit modèle*' whose prototype, *Borée*, was laid down in August 1803 (see Section (C) below).

Algésiras Lorient Dyd-Caudan, by Louis, Antoine, & Mathurin Crucy (Constructeur, François Caro).
> Ord: 26.8.1799. K: 20.7.1801. Named 14.11.1801. L: 8.7.1804. Comm: 27.8.1804. C: 9.1804.
>
> Captured 21.10.1805 by the British at Trafalgar, returned to her French crew during the ensuing storm and taken to Cadiz. Surrendered 14.6.1808 to Spanish insurgents at Cadiz, became Spanish *Algeciras*. Sank at Cadiz 1826 for lack of maintenance.

Suffren Lorient Dyd, by Louis, Antoine, & Mathurin Crucy (Constructeur, François Caro)

K: 8.1801. Named 14.11.1801. L: 23.9.1803. Comm: 10.12.1803. C: 12.1803.

Damaged in collision with *Trident* (74) in 1813 and was a careening ship (*vaisseau fosse*) at Toulon in 1814. Condemned 19.12.1815 and ordered to be fitted as a hulk or prison. Ordered 19.7.1816 to be fitted as *ponton de carène* and was converted to a prison hulk at Toulon in 7-9.1816. BU 1823.

Pacificateur Brest Dyd. (Constructeur, Antoine Geoffroy)
K: 5.1801. Cancelled 4.1804. Construction stopped 4.1804, Napoleon having ordered that nothing more should be built at Brest because of a criminal fire that ravaged the dockyard in 2.1804 and also because of difficulties in supplying the yard with timber.

Ex BRITISH PRIZES (1795-1801). One 74-gun ship was captured by the French off the Scillies in 1794 and another in the Mediterranean in 1795, and two more in the summer of 1801. All apparently retained their British guns, the French lacking a direct equivalent of the British 32pdrs. Listed below as re-measured by the French in French units of measurement.

ALFRED Class. Designed in 1772 by Sir John Williams, slightly enlarged from his *Royal Oak* design of 1765 but with greater breadth; four ships were built to this design (other projected sisters were cancelled or built to later designs), all in the Royal Dockyards, of which the *Alexander* was captured by the French in November 1794 and retaken 7½ months later.

Dimensions & tons: 164ft 0in, 145ft 0in x 44ft 0in x 20ft 3in (53.27, 47.10 x 14.29 x 6.58m). 1,400/2,700 tons. Draught 19½/20½ft (6.33/6.66m). Men: 666.

Guns: LD 28 x 32pdrs; UD 28 x 18pdrs; SD 18 x 9pdrs.

Alexandre Deptford Dyd.

The surrender of the *Alexander* after a two-hour fight against ships of Neilly's squadron on 6 November 1794. The capture of a British 74 was to be a rare event in these wars: only five were taken (including the recaptured *Censeur*), of which four were recaptured, the exception being the *Annibal* (ex *Hannibal*); notably all five British losses took place during the French Revolutionary War, and not a single one during the subsequent Napoleonic War, compared with the eighty-seven French ships of this rate which fell into British hands during the combined period. (Courtesy of Beverley R. Robinson Collection, US Naval Academy Museum)

K: 6.4.1774. L: 8.10.1778. C: 6.12.1778.

Captured by *Jean Bart* of Neilly's squadron off the Isles of Scilly 6.11.1794. Retaken off Lorient in Bridport's Action of 23.6.1795. Lazarette 1805; BU at Portsmouth 11.1819.

ELIZABETH Class. Designed in 1765 by Sir Thomas Slade, four ships were ordered in 1765-68, and a further four in 1779-82. Both ships were recaptured at Trafalgar in 1805, seemingly still armed with their original British guns.

Dimensions & tons: *Berwick* 162ft 0in, 148ft 0in x 44ft 0in x 20ft 4in (52.62, 48.08 x 14.29 x 6.61m). *Swiftsure* 160ft 6in, 146ft 6in x 43ft 2in x 20ft 4in (52.13, 47.58 x 14.02 x 6.61m). Each 1,400/2,700 tons. Draught *Berwick* 19½/20½ft (6.33/6.66m); *Swiftsure* 17ft 2in/21ft 10in (5.58/7.09m). Men: 666-690.

Guns: LD 28 x 32pdrs; UD 28 x 18pdrs; SD *Berwick* 18 x 9pdrs; *Swiftsure* 20 x 9pdrs plus 8 carronades (including 6 British).

Berwick Portsmouth Dyd.
K: 5.1769. L: 18.4.1775. C: 19.5.1778.

Captured 7.3.1795 by *Alceste* in the Gulf of Saint Florent, Corsica. Retaken by HMS *Achille* 21.10.1805 at Trafalgar, but wrecked off San Lucar a week later.

Swiftsure William & John Wells, Deptford.
K: 5.1784. L: 4.4.1787. C: 21.8.1787 at Woolwich Dyd.

Captured 24.6.1801 near Malta by *Dix-Août* and *Indivisible* of the Ganteaume division. Retaken by the British at Trafalgar 21.10.1805, renamed HMS *Irresistible*. prison ship 1808, BU 1816.

Modified *CULLODEN* Class. A later design by Sir Thomas Slade, to which seven ships were ordered in 1781-82. The *Hannibal* was taken by Linois's squadron at the Battle of Algeciras, and was retained by the French until BU in 1824.
  Dimensions & tons: 162ft 0in, 146ft 6in x 43ft 7½in x 20ft 6in (52.62, 47.59 x 14.17 x 6.66m). 1,400/2,700 tons. Men: 666-690.
  Guns: LD 28 x 32pdrs; UD 28 x 18pdrs; SD 18 x 9pdrs; later LD 28 x 32pdrs; UD 26 x 18pdrs; SD 8 x 9pdrs, 16 x 36pdr carronades including 6 bronze, all but the carronades presumably being her British guns retained in French service.

Annibal John Perry & Co, Blackwall.
  K: 4.1783. L: 15.4.1786. C: 8.1786 at Woolwich Dyd.
  Grounded then captured 6.7.1801 in the Battle of Algésiras by *Formidable, Indomptable,* and *Desaix* of the Linois division and immediately commissioned under the second senior officer of *Formidable*. Was a *ponton cayenne* (receiving hulk) at Toulon in 1.1821 and a floating prison there in 11.1822. Struck 27.12.1823, BU 1824.

Ex VENETIAN PRIZE (1797)

1780 CLASS, ships of the 1st Rank (70 guns). This class was built with the new 'double frame' method explained earlier. The lead ship was laid down in 1782 and launched in 1797 during the first French occupation of Venice. Three more were on the building ways when the French took Venice in May 1797; one on slip No.20 was sabotaged by them on 27 September 1797 and two on slips 5 and 7 were sabotaged on 28 December 1797. *Laharpe* was rated by the French as a 74-gun ship.
  Dimensions (in Venetian measurements): 162ft max, 139ft keel x 39.00ft max (56.33m, 48.33m x 13.56m; in French units 173ft 5in, 148ft 10in x 41ft 9in).

Laharpe (or *La Harpe*) Venice (laid down on slip 24 in 1782 by Andrea Paresi, continued by Andrea Chiribiri, completed by Andrea Spadon and kept in reserve on the slip, launched by Iseppo Fonda in 1797 during the first French occupation of Venice)
  K: 8.6.1782. L: 23.7.1797. C: 17.11.1797.
  Dimensions & tons (in French measurements): 160ft 6in deck, 148ft 0in keel x 42ft 2in mld x 20ft 6in creux (52.13m, 48.07 x 13.69m x 6.66m). 1,300/2,400 tons. Draught: 16ft 6in/18ft 6in (5.36m/6.01m).
  Guns (French): LD 28 x 24pdrs; UD 28 x 18pdrs; SD 14 x 8pdrs (in Venetian sources) or SD 18 x 8pdrs (in French records).
  Taken on the building ways at Venice 5.1797 and named 6.1797. Renamed for General Amédée Emmanuel Laharpe of the French Army, killed at Codogno in a battle against the Austrian army on 9.5.1796. Made a sortie from Ancona into the Adriatic under the French flag 11-12.1798 together with *Beyrand* and *Stengel*. Captured by the Austrians 14.11.1799 at the surrender of Ancona and taken back to Venice. Was refitting for further service when on 11.12.1802 the Austrian Archduke Charles ordered her converted to a prison hulk. Struck 1804, hulk retaken by the French at Venice 1.1806, BU 1809.

PURCHASED AND CEDED SPANISH VESSELS (1799-1800)

Saint Sébastien (Spanish *San Sebastián*, built at Pasajes 1783).
  Dimensions & tons: 164ft 1in, 145ft 11in x 44ft 6in x 21ft 0in (53.3, 47.4 x 14.45 x 6.82m). 1,500/2,800 tons. Draught: 20ft 0in/21ft 0in (6.50m/6.82m). Men: 706.
  Guns: (c1799) LD 28 x 24pdrs; UD 30 x 18pdrs; SD 16 x 8pdrs. SD changed 1804 to 8 x 8pdrs, 16 x 36pdr carronades.
  Purchased from Spain 5.1799 to receive the crew of *Censeur*, which had been condemned at Cadiz. Renamed *Alliance* 31.7.1799 a day after her arrival at Brest. Condemned and BU authorised 26.8.1807, BU 10.1807.

Atlante (or *Atalante*) (Spanish *Atlante*, constructed at Cartagena in 1755 by Edward Bryant to plans by Jorge Juan)
  Dimensions & tons: 164ft 5in, 145ft 7in x 44ft 7in x 22ft 3in (53.42, 47.3 x 14.48 x 7.24m). 1,450/2,900 tons. Men: 706.
  Guns: LD 28 x 24pdrs; UD 30 x 18pdrs; SD 16 x 8pdrs.
  Ceded to France under the Treaty of San Ildefonso of 1.10.1800 and comm. 23.9.1801 at Cadiz as *Atlante* or *Atalante*. Renamed *Atlas* 5.2.1803. Damaged in the Battle of Cape Finisterre (Calder's Action) 22.7.1805 and left at Vigo as a hospital ship 28.7.1805. Put in charge of Spanish caretakers there 15.6.1807, surrendered to Spanish insurgents 9.6.1808. Became Spanish *Atlas*, BU 1817.

Saint-Genard (Spanish *San-Genaro*, constructed by Edward Bryant to plans by Jorge Juan and built of cedar at Cartagena by contractors Juan and Agustin Monticelli. L: 23.12.1765)
  Dimensions & tons: 164ft 2in, 137ft 5in x 44ft 9in x 20ft 11in (53.34, 44.63 x 14.53 x 6.80m). 1,400/2,800 tons. Draught 19ft 8in/21ft 7in (6.40m/7.00m). Men: 706.
  Guns: (1797) LD 28 x 24pdrs; UD 30 x 18pdrs; SD 16 x 8pdrs. By around 1807 the SD had 12 x 8pdrs, 12 x 36pdr carronades. As school ship *Tourville* had 10 x 12pdrs, 8 x 6pdrs, and 3 x 36pdr carronades, all topside.
  Ceded to France under the Treaty of San Ildefonso of 1.10.1800 and comm. 22.7.1801 at Cadiz. Renamed *Ulysse* 5.2.1803. Selected 27.9.1810 as the ship for the *École Navale* created the same day at Brest. Renamed *Tourville* 14.1.1811 and began training duty 1.10.1811. She carried her students in the LD and instructors in the UD. The *École special de marine* at Brest was disbanded and *Tourville* was decomm. on 16.3.1815 upon the creation of the *École d'Angoulême*. Condemned 24.10.1815 and ordered converted to a sheer hulk and storage hulk at Brest. Hulked in 1816, BU 1822.

Saint Antoine (Spanish *San Antonio*, built at Cartagena 1785, design/construction probably as *Saint-Genard*).
  Dimensions & tons: 164ft 1in x 44ft 11in x 21ft 7in (53.29 x 14.58 x 7.0m). 1,450/2900 tons. Men: 530.
  Guns: (1785) LD 28 x 24pdrs; UD 30 x 18pdrs; SD 16 x 8pdrs.
  Ceded to France under the Treaty of San Ildefonso of 1.10.1800 and comm. 21.5.1801 at Toulon with a mixed Franco-Spanish crew. Captured 12.7.1801 by three British ships of the line off Gibraltar, became HMS *San Antonio*. Hulked 1807, sold 1827.

Intrépide (Spanish *Intrépido*, constructed at Ferrol by Tomas Bryant to plans of Romero Landa. L: 20.11.1790)
  Dimensions & tons: 162ft 11in, 146ft 3in x 44ft 7in x 21ft 5in (52.92, 47.50 x 14.48 x 6.96m). 1,450/2,784 tons. Draught 19ft 7in/20ft 10in (6.36m/6.78m). Men: 717.
  Guns: (1793) LD 28 x 24pdrs; UD 30 x 18pdrs; SD 16 x 8pdrs.
  Ceded to France 4.1801 at Cadiz under the Treaty of San Ildefonso of 1.10.1800 and comm. 30.6.1801 at Toulon. Captured at Trafalgar 21.10.1805 by the British who burned her.

Conquerant (Spanish *Conquistador*, constructed at Cartagena to plans by Romero Landa, as *Intrépide*, L: 9.12.1791)
  Dimensions & tons: as *Intrépide*.
  Guns: (1799) LD 28 x 24pdrs; UD 30 x 24pdrs; SD 18 x 12pdrs.
  Ceded to France under the Treaty of San Ildefonso of 1.10.1800 and

delivered at Brest 10.4.1802, on which date she was commissioned under her Spanish name. Condemned 6.1.1807, converted to hulk 26.2.1807, BU 9.1816.

Desaix (Spanish *Pelayo* or *Infante Don Pelayo*, constructed at Havana to plans by Romero Landa, probably as *Intrépide*. L: 22.12.1791)

Dimensions & tons: 163ft 1in, 146ft 11in x 45ft 3in x 27ft 3in (53.10, 47.72 x 14.70 x 8.85m). Draught 19ft 4in/19ft 5in (6.28m/6.30m).

Guns: (1802) LD 28 x 36pdrs; UD 30 x 24pdrs; SD 16 x 8pdrs. Originally had 24pdrs on the LD, rearmed with 36pdrs in 1799.

Ceded to France under the Treaty of San Ildefonso of 1.10.1800 and delivered by a Spanish crew at Brest 10.4.1802, on which date she was commissioned under her Spanish name. Renamed *Desaix* 20.7.1802. Found to be worm-eaten when docked 20.7.1803. Condemned at Brest 2.5.1804, BU ordered 4.5.1804 and completed 22.6.1804.

(C) Vessels acquired from 25 March 1802

Later *TÉMÉRAIRE* Class (1802-1806 orders). During this period, which extended from the signing of the Treaty of Amiens to the first year after the Battle of Trafalgar, orders for 74-gun ships continued to be placed in the three dockyards of Rochefort, Lorient, and Toulon.

Rochefort Group.

Magnanime Rochefort Dyd. (Constructeur, Pierre Rolland)

K: 6.5.1802 (keel laid 29.6.1802). L: 17.8.1803. Comm: 1.8.1803. C: 12.1803.

Began to go into commission before launch. Refit evaluated at 16/24ths on 9.12.1819, struck 4.1.1820 and proposal from Toulon approved to convert her to a floating prison to replace *St. Pierre* which could no longer remain afloat. Also reported as struck and converted to floating prison *Bagne No.1* in 1816. Last mentioned in 1820 and was probably BU then.

Lion Rochefort Dyd. (Constructeurs, Paul Filhon, later Antoine Bonjean)

K: 8.7.1802. L: 11.2.1804. Comm: 10.5.1804. C: 6.1804.

Grounded near Sète 26.10.1809 with *Robuste* (80) while being chased by the British and burnt to avoid capture.

Achille Rochefort Dyd, by Louis, Antoine, & Mathurin Crucy (Constructeurs, Jean-Charles Garrigues, Antoine Bonjean, and Charles Rigault de Genouilly)

K: 5.11.1802. L: 17.11.1804. Comm: 28.1.1805. C: 2.1805.

Caught fire and blew up at Trafalgar 21.10.1805.

Ajax Rochefort Dyd, by Louis, Antoine, & Mathurin Crucy (Constructeurs, Charles Rigault de Genouilly and Paul Filhon)

Ord: 6.4.1804 (frame). K: 23.11.1804. L: 17.6.1806. Comm: 26.8.1806. C: 9.1806.

Recomm. 1.4.1815 as floating battery for the defence of Toulon. Struck 10.3.1818 and converted to floating prison *No.1* to replace the ex-Venetian *Robert* at Toulon. Date BU unknown.

Triomphant Rochefort Dyd. (Constructeurs, Antoine Bonjean, Paul Filhon, and Jean-Baptiste Hubert)

Ord: 6.4.1804 (frame, begun 27.6.1804). K: 27.6.1806 (on the ways 8.1806). L: 31.3.1809. C: 5.1809. Comm: 1.7.1809.

Condemned 1.7.1822 at Brest. converted to storage hulk. BU 7-9.1825.

Lorient Group. The first two were ordered to be put in hand at Lorient on 4 June 1804, in place of two 80-gun ships (*Régulus* and *Algésiras*) ordered on 27 April 1804 that had been found to be too big for the available building ways. Frames for each were cut at Nantes by the Crucy Brothers under contracts of 25 February 1804 and 20 October 1804. Originally named *Glorieux* and *Inflexible* on 26 February 1805, the pair were renamed *Polonais* and *Golymin* respectively on 23 February 1807, the first to recognise 'the generous support given to a people long oppressed by the current enemies of France', and the second to commemorate the battle fought on Polish soil on 26 December 1806.

Polonais Lorient - Caudan (Constructeurs, François Etesse and others)

Ord: 11.11.1804 and 26.3.1805. Named 26.2.1805 (*Glorieux*). K: 2.1805. L: 27.5.1808. Comm: 25.6.1808.

Renamed *Lys* (*Lis*) 19.4.1814 following a visit by the Duc de Berry to Cherbourg. Renamed *Polonais* 22.3.1815 during the 100 days, reverted to *Lys* 15.7.1815. Condemned 1.7.1822 and converted to a storage hulk at Brest. BU 1825-26.

Golymin Lorient - Caudan (Constructeurs, François Etesse and others)

Ord: 11.11.1804 and 26.3.1805. Named 26.2.1805 (*Inflexible*). K: 6.1805. L: 8.12.1809. C: 10.1808.

Got underway 23.3.1814 to protect the entry into Brest of the frigates *Pallas* and *Circé*, struck a rock in the Goulet and sank there.

Marengo Lorient Dyd

Ord: 11.8.1806. Named 19.7.1806. K: 19.9.1806. L: 12.10.1810. Comm: 25.4.1811. C: 4.1811.

Followed *Courageux* on the ways. Struck 21.7.1858, converted 4.1860 to prison hulk at Toulon, renamed *Pluton* 8.4.1865, BU 1873.

Toulon Group.

Danube Toulon Dyd. (Constructeurs, François Poncet and others)

Ord: 11.8.1806. K: 1.6.1807. L: 21.12.1808. Comm: 27.8.1809. C: 8.1809.

School ship at Toulon 12.1822. Struck and ordered BU 18.12.1826.

Ulm Toulon Dyd. (Constructeurs, François Poncet and others)

Named: 31.7.1806. Ord: 11.8.1806. K: 2.3.1807. L: 25.5.1809. Comm: 28.8.1809. C: 8.1809.

Struck 1828 and hulked at Toulon. BU after 6.1830.

***PLUTON* Class** – *Petit modèle* ('Small model'). This variant of Sané's design was 166ft 2in long on the waterline (compared with the 170ft of the standard model) and its depth of hull was 9in less than the standard 74. Its mean draught was 1ft 1in less than the full-sized 74, and the height of its battery above the water was 5ft 3in instead of the 5ft 4in of the larger type. Two ships of the *petit modèle*, *Pluton* and *Borée*, were ordered at Toulon on 4 January 1803 as models for the 74s to be built at Antwerp. The design of *Borée* and the later ships was improved based on the trials of *Pluton*.

In March 1803, in response to Napoleon's decision to create a 'Squadron of the North', it was intended to build ten of a new type of 74, to Dutch design, drawing less than the *Téméraire* design of Sané. Five of these were to be built at Flushing and on the banks of the Scheldt, two at Nantes, and one each at Ostend, Bordeaux and Marseille. However, these were not ordered, and instead from June 1803 orders were placed for further units of the *Pluton* design. The first two of these orders, for a ship at Bordeaux and another at Marseille, were rescinded and all future building to this design took place outside the former French borders.

Nine to this design were ordered at Antwerp, one at Flushing, two at Genoa, ten at Venice and three at Amsterdam. The Flushing vessel was seized on the stocks by the British and completed for the British Navy, and the last five of the small 74s plus one 80 at Venice were not completed when Venice was occupied by the Austrians on 20 April 1814.

In 1803 three 74s were offered to the navy as gifts but were not built.

Ville de Rouen was offered in 6.1803 by a subscription at Rouen and was reportedly ordered at Saint-Malo. *Haute Garonne* was offered on 4.7.1803 in the form of a gift of 1,000,000 francs by the Conseil Général of that department but was not ordered. *Seine Inférieure* was offered by that department, to be built at Alet (Saint-Père), Solidor Point, Saint-Malo, and the Minister of Marine on 9.9.1803 ordered construction of the hull at Navy expense. The order was cancelled in 2.1805. These were most likely of the *petit modèle*, though firm evidence is lacking. In May 1808 there was an order issued to build three 74s at La Spezia (along with two frigates and two brigs); but as the shipyard there did not yet exist this order was transferred to Genoa soon after; it is unclear whether this order was for the *petit modèle* or the standard model of 74.

The ships ordered in 1803 and 1804 were to have had sixteen 8pdrs on the quarterdeck and forecastle plus four 36pdr obusiers on the roof of the dunette (giving them an actual total of 78 guns); the remainder were to have had only fourteen 8pdrs plus ten 36pdr carronades instead of the obusiers (giving them an actual total of 82 guns). In her short career from 1805 to 1808 *Pluton* carried 20 x 8pdrs and 6 x 36pdr carronades on her gaillards. Later gaillards armaments varied, though eight ships (*Anversois, César, Charlemagne, Commerce de Lyon, Dantzick, Duguesclin, Pultusk,* and *Ville de Berlin*) had what may have become a de facto standard for the class, 12 x 8pdrs and 14 x 36pdr carronades. Two Venice-built ships, *Mont Saint Bernard* and *Castiglione*, appear in contemporary French lists with only 10 x 8pdrs and 10 x 36pdr carronades topsides, but a modern Italian list shows them with 8 x 8pdrs and 16 x 36pdr carronades.

Dimensions & tons: 169ft, 166ft 2in wl x 44ft 0in x 21ft 3in (54.90, 53.97 x 14.29 x 6.90m). 1,381/2,781 tons. Draught: 18ft 10in/20ft 8in (6.12/6.72m).

Guns: (original) LD 28 x 36pdrs; UD 30 x 18pdrs; SD 16 x 8pdrs, 4 x 36pdr obusiers. (1806) LD 28 x 36pdrs; UD 30 x 18pdrs; SD 12 x 8pdrs; 10 x 36pdr carronades

Toulon Group.

Pluton Toulon Dyd. (Constructeur, Royer)
Ord: 4.1.1803. Named 7.2.1803. K: 19.8.1803. L: 17.1.1805. Comm: 16.3.1805. C: 3.1805.
Surrendered 14.6.1808 to Spanish insurgents at Cadiz, became Spanish *Pluton*. Hulked in 1816.

Borée Toulon Dyd. (Constructeur, Étienne Maillot)
Ord: 4.1.1803. Named 7.2.1803. K: 19.8.1803. L: 27.6.1805. Comm: 29.8.1805. C: 8.1805.
Condemned at Toulon 1828, prison hulk. Date BU unknown.

Genoa Group.

Génois Murio & Migone, Genoa (Constructeurs, Bianchi, Pierre-Alexandre Forfait, and possibly Jean-Baptiste Lefebvre)
K: 8.7.1803. Named: 24.4.1803. L: 17.8.1805. Comm: 2.11.1805. C: 11.1805.
First launch attempt failed on 6.8.1805. Condemned 14.8.1821 at Rochefort, BU 1821.

Breslaw (ex *Superbe* 14.5.1807) Murio & Migone (probably), Genoa (Constructeurs, Bianchi and François Pestel)
Ord: 24.10.1804 (contract, approved 19.1.1805). K: 3.1805. L: 3.5.1808. Comm: 9.8.1808. C: 12.1808.
Struck 19.11.1836 at Toulon. Date BU unknown, possibly 1837.

Antwerp Group.

Commerce de Lyon (ex *Ville de Lyon* 1804) Antwerp (Constructeurs, Pierre Dieudonné Jaunez and Mathurin Boucher)
Ord: 29.9.1803. K: 11.1803. On ways 7.2.1804. L: 9.4.1807. Comm: 10.4.1807. To Flushing 6.1807 for fitting out, C: 3.1808.
Allocated to France 1.8.1814 in the division of the Scheldt squadron, arrived at Brest 6.10.1814. Condemned there 23.2.1819, ordered BU 3.12.1819 but hulked instead, BU 1830-31.

Charlemagne Antwerp (Constructeur, Alexandre Notaire-Grandville)
Ord: 24.4.1804. K: 5.1804. L: 8.4.1807. Comm: 9.4.1807. C: 3.1808.
Allocated to the Allies 1.8.1814 in the division of the Scheldt squadron, she was ceded to Holland on 30.8.1814 and was renamed *Nassau*. She sailed for the East Indies 31.3.1816 with 300 passengers on board and was turned over to the Dutch Colonial Navy on 31.12.1818. She was raséed to a 32-gun ship in 1820 and participated in the blockade of Palembang. BU 1823.

Anversois Antwerp (Constructeur, Anne-Jean-Louis Leharivel-Durocher)
Ord: 24.4.1804. K: 6.1804. L: 7.6.1807. Comm: 8.6.1807. To Flushing 10.1807 for fitting out, C: 3.1808.
Renamed *Éole* 29.8.1814, but reverted to *Anversois* 22.3.1815 (during the Hundred Days) and then *Éole* again 15.7.1815. Allocated to France 1.8.1814 in the division of the Scheldt squadron, arrived at Brest 20.9.1814. At Brest 1818 in too poor condition to be sent to Lorient as a hulk (*Duguesclin* was sent instead). Condemned 23.2.1819, ordered BU 3.12.1819.

Duguesclin Antwerp (Constructeur, Pierre Dieudonné Jaunez)
Ord: 24.4.1804. K: 7.1804. L: 20.6.1807. Comm: 24.7.1807. To Flushing 9.1807 for fitting out, C: 3.1808.
Allocated to France 1.8.1814 in the division of the Scheldt squadron, arrived at Brest 6.10.1814. Condemned 6.1818, sent to Lorient and hulked there, BU approved 11.1.1820.

César Antwerp (Constructeur, Jean-Louis-Henri Barthélemy)
Ord: 24.4.1804. K: 9.1804. L: 21.6.1807. Comm: 23.6.1807. C: 3.1808.
Allocated to the Allies 1.8.1814 in the division of the Scheldt squadron and became the Dutch *Prins Frederik*. Sailed to the East Indies 31.8.1816, headed back to the Netherlands in 1819, but spent eight weeks in Simons Bay repairing a leak and ended up in Plymouth. She was sold in England in 1821 for BU.

Ville de Berlin (ex *Thésée* 1.6.1807) Antwerp (Constructeur, Philippe Moreau)
Ord: 24.4.1804. K: 3.1805. Named 1806 (*Thésée*). L: 6.9.1807. Comm: 21.9.1807. To Flushing 10.1807 for fitting out, C: 3.1808.
Allocated to France 1.8.1814 in the division of the Scheldt squadron, arrived at Brest 6.10.1814. Renamed *Atlas* 29.8.1814, *Ville de Berlin* 22.3.1815 (during the Hundred Days), and *Atlas* 15.7.1815. Condemned 23.2.1819 Ordered converted to storage hulk at Brest 3.12.1819 in replacement of *Tourville* (ex *Ulysse*). Date BU unknown.

Pultusk (ex *Audacieux* 23.2.1807, actually changed 14.5.1807) Antwerp (Constructeur, Mathurin Boucher)
Ord: 24.4.1804. Named 23.2.1805 (*Audacieux*). K: 4.1805. L: 20.9.1807. Comm: 21.9.1807. C: 3.1808.
Renamed for the 26 December 1806 battle in Poland. Manned by a Danish crew from 1808 to 5.1813. Allocated to the Allies 1.8.1814 in the division of the Scheldt squadron and became the Dutch *Waterloo*. She was BU in 1817 and a new 74-gun *Waterloo* was laid down in 1818.

Dantzick (*Dantzig*) (ex *Illustre* 4.6.1807) Antwerp (Constructeur, Jean-Louis-Henri Barthélemy)
Ord: 24.4.1804. K: 6.1805. L: 15.8.1807. Comm: 16.8.1807. To Flushing 9.1807 for fitting out, C: 3.1808.
Manned by a Danish crew from 1808 to 5.1813. Renamed *Achille* 29.8.1814, *Dantzick* 22.3.1815, and *Achille* 15.7.1815. Allocated

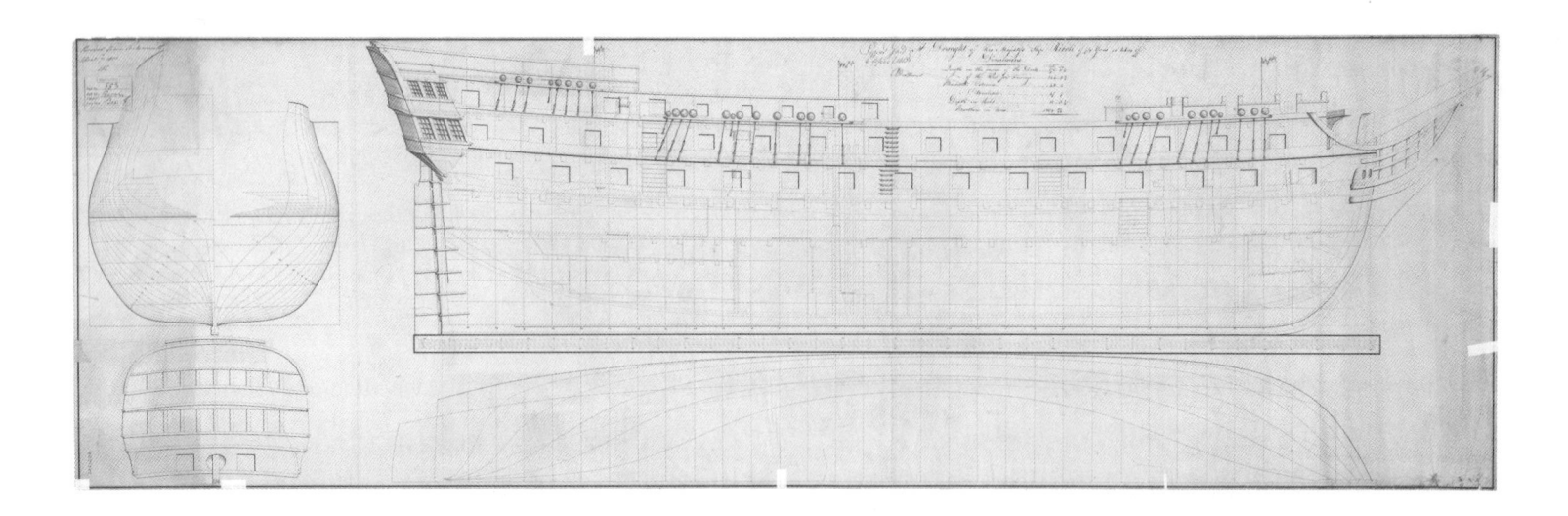

to France 1.8.1814 in the division of the Scheldt squadron, arrived at Brest 6.10.1814. Needed complete refit 10.6.1816, struck mid-1816.

Dalmate Antwerp

Ord: 11.8.1806. K: 22.8.1806. Named: 2.7.1807. L: 21.8.1808. Comm: 28.4.1809. C: 4.1809.

Manned by a Danish crew from 4.1809 to 5.1813. Renamed *Hector* 29.8.1814, *Dalmate* 22.3.1815, and *Hector* 15.7.1815. Allocated to France 1.8.1814 in the division of the Scheldt squadron, arrived at Brest 6.10.1814. Condemned and ordered BU at Rochefort 7.9.1819, BU reported completed 13.5.1820.

Albanais Antwerp

Ord: 11.8.1806 (following *ordre de mise en chantier* 31.7.1806 as *Vaisseau No.10*). K: 9.4.1807 (on the ways of *Charlemagne*). L: 2.10.1808. Comm: 1.10.1808. C: 4.1809.

Manned by a Danish crew from 4.1809 to 5.1813. Allocated to the Allies 1.8.1814 in the division of the Scheldt squadron and became the Dutch *Batavier*. Discarded and BU 1817.

Flushing order. A single vessel was ordered to be built at Vlissingen (Flushing). On 1 June 1808 Napoleon ordered that she should be launched before October, but she was delayed and was still on the stocks when the port was captured by the British during the Walcheren campaign a year later. The shipyard was burnt when the British withdrew.

Royal Hollandais (ex *Royal* 5.1808) Flushing

Ord: 14.8.1806. K: 8.1806.

Captured on the ways by the British 17.8.1809, dismantled 11-12.1809, timbers taken to Woolwich, and ship completed there on 25.4.1812 as HMS *Chatham* (74) with 24pdrs on the UD. Poor quality timber shortened her life and she was sold on 10.9.1817.

Venice Group.

Rigeneratore (ex *Severo* 1807) Venice (For Napoleon's Italian Navy, constructed by Andrea Salvini and Giuseppe Moro)

K: 26.12.1806. L: 7.7.1811. C: 30.1.1812.

Listed by the French as *Régénérateur*. Taken by the Austrians 20.4.1814 in the occupation of Venice and incorporated in the Austrian Navy on 16.5.1814 after the Austrians took formal possession of the city. Renamed *Severo* 5.1815. Raséed 1823 as 56-gun frigate *Bellona*, completed 9.8.1823. Decomm. 30.6.1830 after extensive cruising, BU completed 30.6.1831.

Reale Italiano Venice (for Napoleon's Italian Navy, constructed by Andrea Salvini)

K: 26.12.1806. L: 15.8.1812. C: 11.1813.

Admiralty draught of *Rivoli* as taken off in April 1813. The ship was of the 74-gun '*petit modèle*', a smaller type specifically designed to be built in many of the out-ports of the Napoleonic empire where the depth of water was a constraint. (© National Maritime Museum J3345)

Listed by the French as *Royal Italien*. Taken by the Austrians 20.4.1814 in the occupation of Venice and incorporated in the Austrian Navy on 16.5.1814 after the Austrians took formal possession of the city. Hauled out 7.1825, raséed, and completed 23.9.1829 as training frigate *Italiano*. Unserviceable 13.10.1835 and used from 19.11.1835 as target ship for experiments with French shell guns (including a 36pdr obusier) and rockets. Ship badly damaged, ordered BU 18.2.1836, completed 9.1836.

Rivoli Venice (Constructeur, Jean Tupinier)

K: 4.1.1807. Named 11.5.1807. L: 6.9.1810. Comm: 1.1.1811. C: 10.1811.

One of three 74s built at Venice for France in accordance with the convention of 16.4.1807. Lifted out of the Venetian lagoon 18.2.1812 by camels designed by Tupinier that reduced her draught by 2.35m. Immediately after departing Venice for Ancona four days later (22.2.1812) she was captured by HMS *Victorious* (74) assisted by HMS *Weazle* (18) and became HMS *Rivoli*. BU 1819.

Mont Saint Bernard (ex *Mont Blanc* end 1806) Venice (Constructeur, Jean Tupinier)

Ord: 4.1.1807. K: 14.3.1807. Named: 11.5.1807. L: 9.6.1811. Comm: 8.10.1811. C: 12.1811.

One of three 74s built at Venice for France in accordance with the convention of 16.4.1807. Initially served under the French flag as flagship of Admiral Duperré, then under the Italian flag as *Monte San Bernardo* or *San Bernardo*. Taken by the Austrians 20.4.1814 in the occupation of Venice and incorporated in the Austrian Navy on 16.5.1814 as after the Austrians took formal possession of the city. Burned by accident 14-15.9.1814 in the Darsena Nuova at Venice with *Castiglione*.

Castiglione Venice (Constructeur, Jean Tupinier)

Ord: 4.1.1807. K: 14.3.1807. Named: 11.5.1807. L: 2.8.1812. Comm: 19.9.1812. C: 10.1812.

One of three 74s built at Venice for France in accordance with the convention of 16.4.1807. Italy was to be paid for each of them. Taken by the Austrians 20.4.1814 in the occupation of Venice and incorporated in the Austrian Navy on 16.5.1814 after the Austrians took formal possession of the city. Burned by accident

14-15.9.1814 in the Darsena Nuova at Venice with *Monte San Bernardo*.

Duquesne (ex *Montebello* 12.1810) Venice (Constructeurs, Jean Tupinier, then Jean Dumonteil)
K: 12.1810. On ways: 21.3.1811. L: 7.11.1815. Was 22/24ths complete on 1.4.1814.
Taken on the ways by the Austrians 20.4.1814 in the occupation of Venice, incorporated in the Austrian Navy on 16.5.1814 after the Austrians took formal possession of the city, and launched as *Cesare*. Rotten timbers found in 1816 during careening, hull examined by a commission in 1820, ship still existed in 1824 but BU soon afterwards.

Montenotte Venice (Constructeurs, Jean Tupinier, then Jean Dumonteil)
K: 12.1810. On ways 12.1.1811. Not launched. Was 14/24ths complete on 1.4.1814.
Taken by the Austrians 20.4.1814 in the occupation of Venice, incorporated in the Austrian Navy on 16.5.1814 after the Austrians took formal possession of the city, and renamed *Kulm*. Deteriorated on open slipway and BU there 1818.

Lombardo Venice (for Napoleon's Italian Navy, constructed by Andrea Salvini and other Italian constructors)
K: 12.1810. On ways 27.7.1811. Not launched. Was 8.6/24ths complete on 1.4.1814.
Taken by the Austrians 20.4.1814 in the occupation of Venice and incorporated in the Austrian Navy on 16.5.1814 after the Austrians took formal possession of the city. Little progress made by 1824 but ship retained until ordered BU 9.1.1830. BU completed 4.1830.

Sigmaring Venice (for Napoleon's Italian Navy, constructed by Andrea Salvini and other Italian constructors)
K: 12.1810. On ways 27.7.1811. Not launched. Was 5.8/24ths complete on 1.4.1814.
Listed by the French as *Semmering*. Taken by the Austrians 20.4.1814 in the occupation of Venice, incorporated in the Austrian Navy on 16.5.1814 after the Austrians took formal possession of the city, and renamed *Hanau*. Ordered BU 26.8.1825, BU on slip 11.1825 to 2.1826.

Arcole Venice (Constructeurs, Jean Tupinier, then Jean Dumonteil)
K: 12.1810. Probably on ways 9.1811. Not launched. Was 2.5/24ths complete on 1.4.1814. Taken by the Austrians 20.4.1814 in the occupation of Venice, incorporated in the Austrian Navy on 16.5.1814 after the Austrians took formal possession of the city, and renamed *Tonante*. BU on slip 1821.

Rotterdam Group.
Piet Hein Rotterdam (Constructeurs, P. Glavimans Jr. and Alexandre Notaire-Grandville)
K: 1.6.1811. L: 1.5.1813.
In March 1806 the Dutch laid down at Rotterdam an 80-gun ship of the standard Dutch model named *Admiraal Piet Hein*. This ship was incorporated into the French Imperial Navy as *Amiral Piet Hein* on 9.7.1810 when Napoleon annexed the Kingdom of Holland into the French Empire. She was 6/24ths built when on 14.2.1811 Napoleon ordered her disassembled and reworked as a 74 of the French *petit modèle*. The new ship, renamed *Piet Hein* by the French in 4.1811, was laid down in 1811 and launched in 1813. Her length was 194 Dutch feet (54.90m), suggesting she may have differed slightly from the standard *Pluton* plans. While she was preparing for commissioning she was taken by the Dutch in their 12.1813 uprising. Renamed *Admiraal Piet Hein*, she had her bottom sheathed in copper in 1817 but was BU 1819 at Vlissingen.

Amsterdam Group.
Couronne Amsterdam (Constructeurs, P. Schuijt Jr. and Jean-François Guillemard)
Ord: 14.11.1811. K: 12.1811. L: 26.10.1813. C: 1816.
Was being commissioned when taken 12.1813 in the Dutch uprising and became the Dutch *Prins Willem de Eerste*. She made a Mediterranean cruise in 1816, was a barracks ship for sailors at Nieuwediep in 1823, and was sold for BU in 1829.

Audacieux Amsterdam (Constructeurs, P. Schuijt Jr. and Jean-François Guillemard)
K: 6.1812. L: 10.1816. C: 1817.
She was 10.5/24ths complete when taken 12.1813 in the Dutch uprising and became the Dutch *Coalitie*. Soon renamed *Wassenaer*, she made Mediterranean cruises between 1820 and 1824. While en route to the East Indies with troops for the Java War she stranded on the Dutch coast at Egmond on 16.1.1827 and her wreck broke up on 13.2.1827.

Polyphéme Amsterdam (Constructeurs, P. Schuijt Jr. and Jean-François Guillemard)
K: 6.1812. L: 7.1817. C: 1818.
Was 6/24ths complete when taken 12.1813 in the Dutch uprising and became the Dutch *Holland*. She made a Mediterranean cruise in 1824 and was sold in 1832 at Nieuwediep.

Trieste Order. In December 1811 an order was issued to build a *Pluton* class 74 at Trieste, to be named *Citoyen*, but this order was cancelled in 1812.

Napoleon took a personal interest in the problem of a limited-draught 74. On 12 October 1810 he wrote from Fontainebleau to his Minister of Marine, Denis Decrès: 'A vessel drawing 19½ft can get out of the Texel. I want you to propound the following problem to 10 of the best engineers, beginning with Sané: to produce designs for a vessel as powerfully armed as a 74-gunner, with a draught, when fully loaded, of 19½ft, and capable of as high a speed as possible. If there were any chance of getting a vessel as fast as our 74-gunners, all other considerations could go by the board.
It will be enough if this ship can only carry 3 months' provisions instead of the usual 6, and 3 months' supply of water in place of 4½.
If it is really necessary, the calibre of the guns can be changed to that of the English guns.
Again, if it is really necessary, these ships can carry bronze guns, which weigh much less.
You are to submit the engineers' report to me personally. N.'

Later *TÉMÉRAIRE* Class (1807-1813 orders). Of the dockyards building the small model 74s, Antwerp received its first order for a full-sized 74 in August 1807 and Genoa followed in April 1809. Venice and the Dutch yards continued to build the smaller model because of the depth limitations of their ports.

The recorded armaments on the gaillards (quarterdeck and forecastle) in the *Téméraire* class after around 1807 varied considerably. Typical examples were the 14 x 8pdrs and 10 x 36pdr carronades in *Éole, D'Hautpoul, Polonais,* and *Gaulois*, the 14 x 8pdrs and 14 x 36pdr carronades in *Courageux, Tonnerre, Golymin, Marengo, Trajan, Romulus,* and *Agamemnon*, the 12 x 8pdrs and 10 x 36pdr carronades in *Patriote* and *Triomphant*, and the 12 x 8pdrs and 12 x 36pdr carronades in *Tourville, Scipion,* and the *Jean Bart* of 1820. Two ships were listed with 20 x 36pdr carronades, with 8 x 8pdrs in *Régulus* and 6 x 8pdrs in *Magnanime*. Two others, *Ajax* and *Danube*, also had 6 x 8pdrs but with only 14 x 36pdr carronades. Two ships were listed with only 16 guns on the gaillards, *Lion* with 6 x 8pdrs and 10 x 36pdr carronades and *Ville de*

Marseille with 4 x 8pdrs and 12 x 36pdr carronades. Up to four of the 36pdr carronades in these ships were bronze guns.

Antwerp Group.

Trajan Antwerp (Constructeurs, Pierre Lair and others)
 Ord: 31.8.1807. K: 9.1807. Named 17.10.1807. L 15.8.1811. Comm: 21.11.1811. C: 4.1812.
 Allocated to France 1.8.1814 in the division of the Scheldt squadron, arrived at Brest 20.9.1814. Was in bad condition in 1822. Struck 9.3.1827, BU 1827-29.

Gaulois Antwerp (Constructeurs, Pierre Lair and others)
 Ord: 31.8.1807. K: 9.1807. Named 17.10.1807. L: 14.4.1812. C: 8.1812.
 Allocated to France 1.8.1814 in the division of the Scheldt squadron, arrived at Brest 20.9.1814. Needed a major refit 2.2.1822. Struck 9.3.1827, hulk at Brest. BU 1831.

Superbe Antwerp
 Either started 12.1808 and named 6.2.1809 or ordered and named 26.1.1809 and begun 23.8.1809. L: 5.7.1814. Comm: 16.7.1814. C: 9.1814.
 Allocated to France 1.8.1814 in the division of the Scheldt squadron. On 12.3.1822 was ordered raséed and converted to a 36pdr frigate and plans were drafted by Charles Desmarest on 2.4.1822, but this order was cancelled on 25.5.1822. Wrecked 15.12.1833 on the Greek island of Paros near its main town, Parikia.

Belliqueux Antwerp (Constructeurs, Pierre Lair and others)
 Ord: 15.3.1811. K: 7.1811 (slip No.9). Was 17.25/24ths complete on 1.4.1814. Allocated to the French 8.1814 and sold for BU on the ways.

Alcide Antwerp (Constructeurs, Pierre Lair and others)
 K: 8.1811. Was 6/24ths complete on 1.4.1814. Allocated to the French 8.1814 and sold for BU on the ways.

Aigle Antwerp (Constructeurs, Pierre Lair and others)
 K: 8.1811. Was 6/24ths complete on 1.4.1814. Allocated to the French 8.1814 and sold for BU on the ways.

Impétueux Antwerp (Constructeurs, Pierre Lair and others)
 K: 11.1811. Was 6/24ths complete on 1.4.1814. Allocated to the French 8.1814 and sold for BU on the ways.

Rochefort Group.

Triton (ex *Vénitien* 15.7.1815, ex *Triton* 22.3.1815, ex *Vénitien* 29.8.1814) Rochefort Dyd. (Constructeurs, Jean Chaumont and Antoine Bonnet-Lescure)
 Named: 31.7.1806 (*Vénitien*). K: c9.1814. L: 22.9.1823. C: 12.1826. Comm: 5.4.1834.
 Frame ordered at Bayonne 11.8.1806, cut there 10.1806 to 9.1811 by Jean Baudry. Frame still at Bayonne 1.2.1814. Construction suspended in 1814 at 4.24ths complete and resumed 11.1817. Used provisionally as a barracks at Rochefort from 7.1828 to 4.1831. Assigned to Cherbourg 22.9.1847 as a floating battery, later hulk, decomm. at Toulon 10.1847, and refitted at Brest 1.1848 en route to Cherbourg. Towed from Cherbourg to Rochefort 4.9.1849, condemned 5.11.1849, struck 16.5.1850, converted into sheer hulk at Rochefort 11.1850 to 9.1852, and BU 1870.

Duc de Berry (ex *Glorieux* 15.7.1815, ex *Duc de Berry* 22.3.1815, ex *Glorieux* 8.1814, ex *Couronne* 4.1812) Rochefort Dyd. (Constructeurs, Jean-Baptiste Hubert and Jean Chaumont)
 Ord: 21.8.1807. Named: 12.1807 (*Couronne*). K: 13.1.1812. L: 18.6.1818. C: 7.1818.

A mid-nineteenth century coloured lithograph of the Ville de Marseille *in heavy weather showing the post-war appearance of the later* Téméraire *class, with continuous barricades along the waist, a built-up bow, and quarter boats carried on davits. (© National Maritime Museum PY0949)*

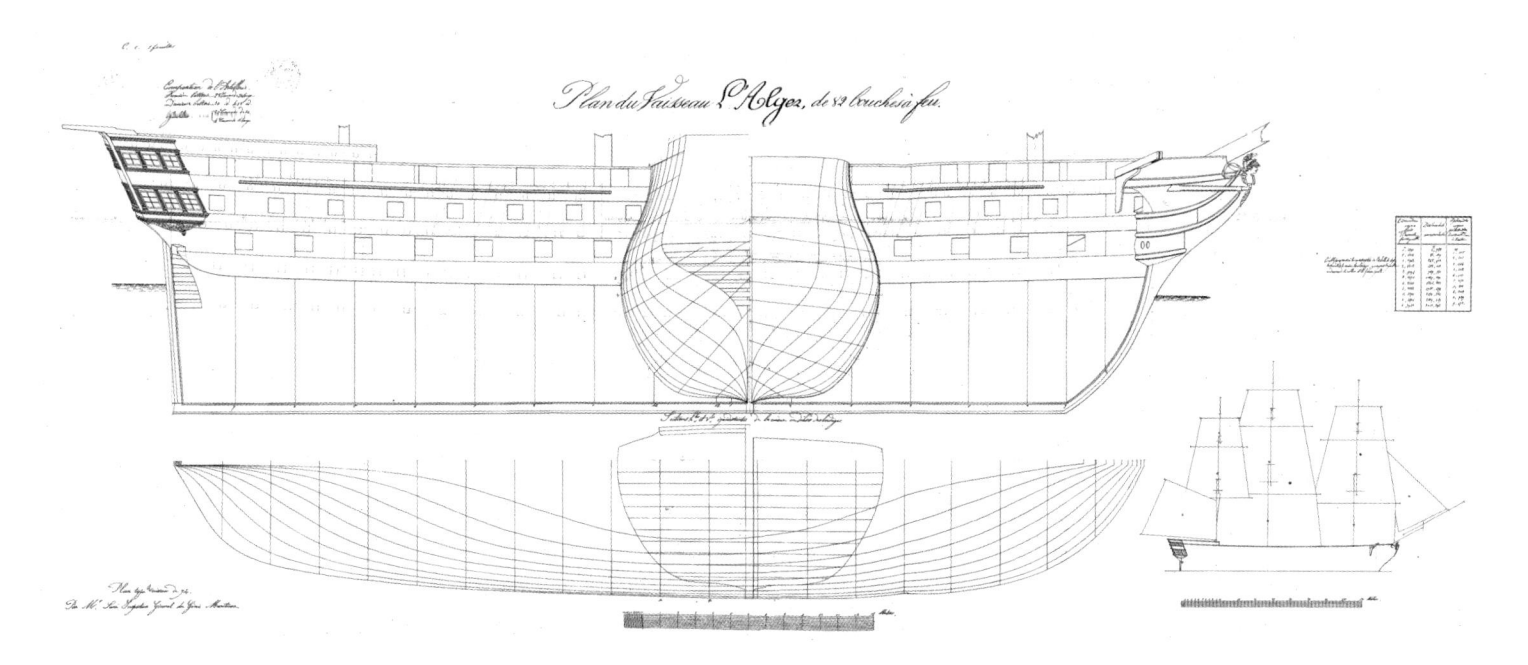

Frame cut at Bayonne beginning in 10.1807. Taken to Brest after launch but not commissioned as a 74. Reverted to *Glorieux* 9.8.1830 after the July Revolution. Renamed *Minerve* on 12.10.1831, hauled out and raséed 1833 to 10.1834, and classified as a 1st Rank frigate with 58 guns in 1834.

Italian Group.

Capri Castellammare di Stabia (for Murat's Neapolitan Navy, constructed by Jean-François Lafosse and Philippe Greslé)
   K: end 1808. L: 21.8.1810. Arrived at Naples 3.9.1810 for fitting out. C: 1.1812.
   After expelling the Bourbons from Naples in early 1806 Napoleon directed the construction there of two ships of the line and two frigates. The first 74, *Capri*, was laid down before Murat arrived in Naples in September 1808, while the second, *Gioacchino*, followed her on the ways in 1810. The 74s were built under the supervision of French engineers to the plans of *Duguay Trouin*, with all changes to the plans, even for improvements, strictly forbidden. After Murat defected to Napoleon during the Hundred Days *Capri* was handed over to the British on 28.4.1815 and taken by them to Malta. She was returned to the Neapolitans in 9.1816 and was sold for BU in 1847.

Gioacchino Castellammare di Stabia (for Murat's Neapolitan Navy, constructed by Jean-François Lafosse and Philippe Greslé)
   K: 9.1810. L: 1.8.1812. C: 5.1813. Comm: 5.6.1813.
   Built to the plans of *Duguay Trouin* with changes to the plans strictly forbidden. She followed *Capri* on the ways. After Murat defected to Napoleon during the Hundred Days, *Gioacchino* was handed over to the British on 28.4.1815 and taken by them to Malta. She was returned to the Neapolitans in 9.1816. Renamed *San Fernando*, she was badly damaged by fire on 10.5.1820 and was sold in 10.1820. A third 74 was reported as begun at Castellammare on 9.1812 but this ship was most likely *Vesuvio* (80, q.v.) following *Gioacchino* on the ways.

Brest Group.

Nestor Brest Dyd. (Constructeurs, Pierre Degay and others)
   K: 2.1809. L: 21.5.1810. Comm: 26.9.1810. C: 9.1810.
   Ordered raséed to frigate 12.3.1822, this order cancelled 22.5.1822. Plans were drawn up in 1846-49 for converting *Nestor* to steam (450nhp), and her conversion at Toulon was authorised on 24.4.1848, but she was found to be rotten. Struck on 29.8.1849 and converted to prison hulk. BU before 1865. The engine ordered for her was used in *Charlemagne* (90).

Orion Brest Dyd. (Constructeurs, Pierre Degay and others)
   K: 18.5.1810. L: 9.10.1813. Comm: 22.11.1813. C: 2.1814.
   Designated 7.5.1827 as school ship for the *élèves de 2e classe de Marine* (*École d'Angoulême*), commissioned for this purpose at Brest 1.10.1827. The *École d'Angoulême* was disbanded on 7.12.1830 but *Orion* on 1.11.1830 had become the first home of the *École Navale* (Naval Academy). Struck 26.9.1835, rerated as a service craft, and continued duty as a school hulk. Replaced 10.1840 by *Commerce* (110) under the name *Borda*, condemned and BU 1841.

Couronne Brest Dyd. (Constructeurs, Pierre Degay and Charles Simon or Mathieu Traon and Charles Desmarest)
   Ord: 20.2.1812. K: 15.10.1813. L: 26.8.1824. C: 1825. Comm: 23.2.1830.
   Was 4/24ths complete on 22.6.1814. Renamed *Barricade* 29.2.1848 and *Duperré* 12.1849. Fitted as transport at Cherbourg 10-12.1854 and as a hospital, retaining her rig, at Toulon 11.1859-1.1860. Towed out of Toulon 11.1.1860 by the screw corvette *Caton*, became barracks ship and headquarters ship at Saigon in 1861. Struck 17.8.1869 at Saigon, decomm. 1.1870. Some parts sold, the remainder burned.

Toulon Group.

Trident Toulon Dyd. (Constructeurs, Pierre Lair and others)
   Named: 27.3.1809. K: 15.11.1809. L: 9.6.1811. Comm: 1.1.1812. C: 9.1812.
   Fitted as a sail transport (1,638 tons, 34 guns, 510 men) 3.1854 at Toulon. Struck 11.1.1858, prison hulk at Toulon, BU 1874-75.

Romulus Toulon Dyd. (Constructeurs, Antoine Arnaud or Jean-Nicolas Guérin)
   Ord: 4.6.1810 (or begun 12.1809). Named: 23.7.1810. L: 31.5.1812. Comm: 21.9.1812. C: 9.1812.

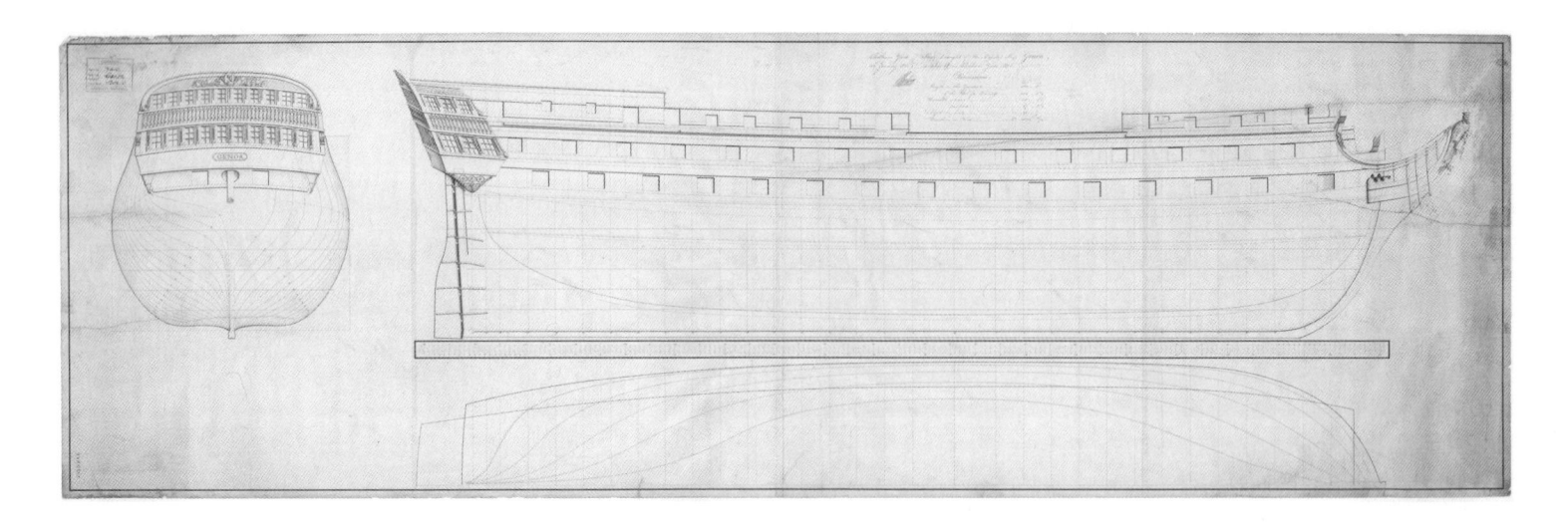

Hauled out and raséed 1820 to 6.3.1821 (re-launched), reclassified as a 1st Rank frigate 3.1821 and renamed *Guerrière* 19.6.1821.

Ville de Marseille Toulon Dyd. (Constructeur, Gustave Garnier)
Ord: 18.2.1811. K: 27.6.1811. L: 15.8.1812. Comm: 17.11.1812. C: 12.1812.
Floating barracks at Toulon from 2.1855. Struck 22.6.1858, barracks hulk at Toulon, BU 1877.

Colosse Toulon Dyd. (Constructeurs, Antoine Arnaud or Jean-Nicolas Guérin)
Ord: 20.2.1812. K: 7.1812. Named: 31.8.1812. L: 5.12.1813. C: 1.1814. Comm: 1.6.1819.
Renamed *Pallas* 24.10.1825. raséed 1825 to 10.1827, and reclassified as a 1st Rank frigate 10.1827.

Provence (ex *Hercule* 15.7.1815, ex *Kremlin* 20.4.1815, ex *Provence* 22.3.1815, ex *Kremlin* 19.4.1814) Toulon Dyd. (Constructeurs, François Poncet or Jean-Nicolas Guérin)
Ord: 2.1812. K: 9.1812. Named: 5.11.1812 (*Kremlin*). L: 26.5.1815. C: 8.1815. Comm: 1.4.1825.
Renamed *Alger* 15.7.1830 (commemorating her service as flagship of the force that captured Algiers). Was a floating hospital at Toulon in 1856. Struck 13.10.1858, barracks hulk at Toulon, BU 1882.

Genoa Group.

Agamemnon Genoa (Constructeur, Mathurin Boucher)
K: 4.1809. L: 23.2.1812. C: 8.1812.
Raséed 12.1822 to 12.1823, reclassified as a 1st Rank frigate 12.1823 and renamed *Amphitrite* 4.1824.

Scipion Genoa. (Constructeur, Mathurin Boucher)
Ord: 28.2.1812. K: 2.1812. L: 5.9.1813. Comm: 19.12.1813. C: 2.1814.
Struck 20.2.1846, probably became a hulk at Brest, date BU unknown.

Brillant Genoa (Constructeur, Mathurin Boucher)
K: 2.1812. L: 18.4.1815
Was 20/24ths complete on 1.4.1814. Taken 18.4.1814 by the British in the capitulation of Genoa. Launched there as HMS *Genoa* (74). BU 1838.

Brave Genoa
K: 9.1813. Was 4/24ths complete on 1.4.1814. Taken 18.4.1814 by the British in the capitulation of Genoa, dismantled, and timbers used to build HMS *Formidable* (80) at Chatham.

Cherbourg (ex Le Havre) orders. Following an instruction from Napoleon in early 1804 that two or three 74s should be built at Le Havre, frames for the first of these were ordered there on 20 March, and

Admiralty draught of *Genoa* (ex *Brillant*) as taken off in 1815. The ship was almost complete when captured, and was finished off with a British-style decorative scheme and the pattern of barricades then favoured in the Royal Navy, but needed a later refit to suit her internal arrangements for British requirements. (© National Maritime Museum J2786)

work began in June, and by 23 July the keel was assembled, but work ground to a halt; by 1 September 1810 the ship, now named *Duquesne*, was still only 6/24ths built, and the structure was then moved to Cherbourg, where work commenced on 6 May 1811, after she had been renamed *Duguay-Trouin* in February 1811. The other order or orders at Le Havre seem not to have been begun.

Duguay-Trouin Cherbourg Dyd. (Constructeurs, Jean-Michel Segondat and Noël-François Langlois)
K: 6 5.1811. L: 10.11.1813. Comm: 21.12.1813. C: 5.1814.
Condemned 12.1824 and on 10.2.1825 ordered converted to a storage hulk at Brest. Struck 1826 and BU.

Lorient Group.

Jean Bart Lorient Dyd. (Constructeurs, Aimé Le Déan and Pierre Le Grix)
Ord: 18.2.1811. Named: 18.4.1811. K: 21.6.1811. L: 25.8.1820. Comm: 1.10.1820. C: 12.1820.
Stayed at 6/24ths complete from 12.1812 to 1818. This ship had no poop. Floating storage at Brest from 1830. Struck 26.10.1833. BU 1833 at Brest.

Généreux Cherbourg Dyd. (Constructeurs, Louis Bretocq, Paul Leroux, and Anne-François Besuchet)
Named: 10.9.1812. K: 3.7.1813. L: 23.9.1831. C: 1832. Comm: 11.2.1839.
Frame cut at Le Havre between 2.1812 and 2.1813 by François Gréhan. Was 6/24ths complete on 1.4.1814. Ordered fitted as transport 1.1852 but instead used 1-7.1852 at Toulon to house political prisoners being deported to Algeria. Struck 21.11.1855, barracks hulk for seamen at Toulon until 1865, then BU.

PURCHASED SPANISH VESSEL (1806)

Vencedor (Spanish *Vencedor* constructed at Ferrol by Guillermo Turner and Ricardo Rooth to plans by Jorge Juan. L: 11.6.1755.)
Dimensions & tons: 164ft 1in, 137ft 10in x 44ft 8in x 21ft 7in (53.29, 44.77 x 14.52 x 7.01m). 1,450/2,900 tons. Draught 16ft 8in/18ft 6in (5.41/6.01m). Men: 706.
Guns: (French) LD 28 x 24pdrs; UD 28 x 18pdrs; SD 22 x 36pdr

carronades.

Purchased by France at Cadiz 18.12.1806 to replace *Argonaute*, which was in bad condition, and was probably renamed *Argonaute*. Surrendered 14.6.1808 to Spanish insurgents at Cadiz and reverted to *Vencedor*. The now-rotten ship was disabled in a storm while en route from Malaga to Mahon after participating in an unsuccessful assault with HMS *Rodney* (74) and was blown ashore and wrecked on Sardinia 31.10.1810.

Ex PORTUGUESE PRIZES (1807)

Maria Primeira (Portuguese *Maria 1*, ex *Coração de Jesus* 1793, 3rd Class (74 guns), constructed at Lisbon by Torcato José Clavina)
K: early 1788, L: 18.12.1789, C: 14.5.1790.
Dimensions & tons: 165ft 9in keel x 44ft 4in x 35ft 0in moulded depth (53.84 x 14.40 x 11.37m); recorded by the French as 166ft 7in, 149ft 11in x 44ft 7in x 35ft 2in height (54.10, 48.7 x 14.48 x 11.43m). 1,400/2,700 tons, Draught 20ft 6in (6.67m) or 19ft 8in/20ft 8in (6.40/6.71m). Men: 641.
Guns: (1793) LD 28 x 24pdrs; UD 28 x 18pdrs; SD 4 x 18pdrs, 12 or 14 x 9pdrs.
Seized at Lisbon 30.11.1807 while in need of repairs. Refit completed and renamed *Ville de Lisbonne* (*Cidade de Lisboa*) 5.1808. Retaken in the evacuation of Lisbon early 9.1808 and returned to Portuguese service, reverted to *D. Maria 1°* 9.1809. Grounded 4.3.1810 at Cadiz while supporting Spanish troops against the French, set on fire by French gunfire and sunk 8.3.1810.

Vasco da Gama (Portuguese *Vasco de Gama*, 2nd Class (80/94 guns), constructed at Lisbon by Torcato José Clavina)
K: 1788, L: 15.12.1792, C: 23.3.1793.
Dimensions & tons: Recorded by the French as 167ft 6in, 150ft 1in x 45ft 0in x 35ft 8in height (54.40, 48.77 x 14.63 x 11.58m). 1,500/3,000 tons. Draught 21ft 3in/22ft 6in (6.90m/7.30m). Men: 663.
Guns: (1793) LD 28 x 32pdrs; UD 28 x 24pdrs; SD 4 x 24pdrs, 20 x 8pdrs
Seized at Lisbon 30.11.1807. Retaken in the evacuation of Lisbon early 9.1808 and returned to Portuguese service. Sold to Brazil 1822, BU at Rio de Janeiro 1825.

Notre Dame des Martyrs (Portuguese *Nossa Senhora dos Martires*, built at Lisbon)
K: 3.1806. L: 24.8.1816. C: 1817.
Dimensions & tons: Recorded by the French as 184ft 8in x 51ft 10in x 43ft 2in height (60 x 16.85 x 14.03m). 1,600/3,206 tons.
Guns: 74 guns
Seized at Lisbon 30.11.1807 while on the building ways, construction continued. Renamed *Portugais* 5.1808. Retaken in the evacuation of Lisbon early 9.1808 and returned to Portuguese service. Probably renamed *Dom Joao Principe Regente* when returned and *Dom Joao VI* (*Sexto*) c3.1816. Launched 1816 and completed 1817. Harbour service 1833, struck 17.10.1846, BU at Lisbon 1852.

PURCHASED RUSSIAN VESSELS (1809)

YAROSLAV Class. A nineteen-ship 74-gun class designed by Katasanov for the Baltic Fleet in 1783. *Svyatoy Petr* was usually referred to as *Sankt Petr* to distinguish her from another *Svyatoy Petr* in the Black Sea.
Dimensions & tons: 159ft 6in, 144ft 8in x 43ft 10in x 18ft 9in (51.82, 47.00 x 14.22 x 6.10m). 1,400/2,600 tons. Draught 17ft 10in/19ft 8in (5.80m/6.40m). Men: 632
Guns: (Russian) LD 26 x 30pdrs, 2 x 60pdr edinorogs; UD 26 x 18pdrs, 2 x 24pdr edinorogs; SD 18 x 8pdrs. (The edinorog was a weapon unique to the Russians that fired spherical hollow bombs and solid shot.)

Moscou (Russian *Moskva*) Solombala Works, Arkhangelsk (constructed by G. Ignatyev)
K: 21.8.1798, L: 22.5.1799, C: by 8.9.1799.
Remained in the Mediterranean after the Treaty of Tilsitt of 7.1807. Arrived at Elba 10.1807 and at Toulon 3.5.1808. Sold to France with *Sviatoi Petr* on 27.9.1809 at Toulon in bad condition. Ordered converted at Toulon to school ship 27.9.1810, renamed *Duquesne* 5.2.1811, and commissioned 31.7.1811 at Toulon as the home of the *École des Élèves de la Marine* (similar to the school established at the same time at Brest). She carried her students in the LD and instructors in the UD. Decomm. 12.8.1815, the school having been disbanded. Condemned 2.1816 and became school hulk for the '*Compagnie des Élèves de Toulon*'. Cut down 12.1822 and made into a prison hulk. BU 1830-33.

Saint Pierre (Russian *Svyatoy Petr*) Solombala Works, Arkhangelsk (constructed by G. Ignatyev)
K: 20.11.1798, L: 22.7.1799, C: by 8.9.1799.
Remained in the Mediterranean after the Treaty of Tilsitt of 7.1807. Arrived at Elba 10.1807 and at Toulon 3.5.1808. Sold to France with *Moskva* 27.9.1809 at Toulon in bad condition. Became a depot ship at Toulon in 1810 and was in commission there as a station ship from 1.1.1812 to 31.12.1813. Fitted as prison hulk c10.1813 and used as such until around 1819.

SVYATOY PETR Class. A seven-ship 74-gun class designed by Katasanov for the Black Sea Fleet in 1794.
Dimensions & tons: 165ft 2in, 150ft 2in x 44ft 1in x 17ft 10in (53.64, 48.80 x 14.33 x 5.79m). 1,400/2,700 tons.
Guns: (Russian, 1798) LD 24 x 30pdrs and 4 x 60pdr edinorogs; UD 24 x 18pdrs and 4 x 24pdr edinorogs; SD 18 x 8pdrs.

Paraskeva (Russian *Svyataya Paraskeva*) Kherson (constructed by M. K. Surovtsov)
K: 4.11.1798, L: 6.11.1799, C: 1800.
Remained in the Mediterranean after the Treaty of Tilsitt of 7.1807. Arrived at Trieste from Corfu 28.12.1807 in bad condition and sold to France there 27.9.1809. BU at Trieste 1810-11 without being repaired or reactivated.

ANNEXED DUTCH VESSEL (1810). Seven Dutch 74-gun ships fell into the hands of the new Batavian Republic when it was proclaimed on 19 January 1795 with armed support from the French. Five of these had belonged to the Amsterdam Admiralty, but by the end of 1799 all had been BU or had been taken by the British Navy. The remaining pair had been built at Rotterdam for the Maas (Maze) Admiralty, and these served the Batavian Republic until 1806 when one was lost while the survivor was transferred to the successor Kingdom of Holland.

PRINS WILLEM DE EERSTE Class. The two ships to this design, nominally of 76 guns in Dutch service, were built at Rotterdam in 1785 and 1786. The *Prins Willem de Eerste* was renamed *Brutus* in 1795 and then *Braband* in 1806; she was incorporated into the French Imperial Navy on 9 July 1810 (renamed *Brabant*) when Napoleon annexed the Kingdom of Holland into the French Empire. Her sister-ship *Staaten-Generaal* was renamed *Bato* in 1798, but was burnt on 9 January 1806 at the Cape of Good Hope to avoid capture by the British Navy. *Brabant* was ordered rated as a 74 by the French on 25.4.1811. The armament of *Brutus* (later *Braband*) in 1801 was LD 28 x 36pdrs, UD 28 x 24pdrs, SD 16 x 12pdrs for a total of 72 guns; *Bato* had 76 guns with 30 x 18pdrs on the UD and 16 x 8pdrs on the gaillards.

Dimensions & tons: 161ft 3in, 156ft 10in wl, 149ft 11in x 42ft 4in x 19ft 2in (52.35, 50.96, 48.70 x 13.74 x 6.23m). 1,400/2,600 tons. Draught 18ft 5in/19ft 1in (6.00/6.20m). Men: 572-671.
Guns: (French) LD 28 x 36pdrs; UD 30 x 24pdrs; SD 16 x 12pdrs and 2 x 60pdr carronades.

Brabant Rotterdam (constructed by P. van Zwijndrecht).
K: 8.1782. L: 7.1785. C: 1786.
Dutch manned. Was out of commission at Nieuwediep in 4.1814. Returned to the Dutch 22.4.1814. Left the Texel in 1815 for the East Indies with troops but put into Portsmouth with damage and her crew continued the voyage the following year in *Prins Frederik* (ex *César*). BU 1820 at Vlissingen.

(D) Vessels acquired from 26 June 1815

The artillery Ordinance of 1817 standardised the armament of the Sané '74-gun' two-decker at LD 28 x 36pdrs; UD 30 x 18pdrs; and gaillards 14 x 8pdrs and 14 x 36pdr carronades (including 4 of bronze) for an actual total of 86 guns. In the ships that were completed or received significant repairs after the early 1820s the forecastle and quarterdeck were joined to form a complete spardeck upon which the guns assigned to this level were redistributed. The Ordinance of 1828 added another ten carronades on the gaillards in place of ten 8pdrs and replaced the remaining four 8pdrs with four long 18pdrs in the chase positions. This resulted in an armament of LD 28 x 36pdrs; UD 30 x 18pdrs; gaillards 20 x 36pdr carronades and 4 x 18pdrs for a total of 82 guns. In the Ordinance of 1838 shell guns replaced four of the 36pdrs on the LD and four of the 18pdrs on the UD, resulting in a standard armament of LD 24 x 36pdrs and 4 x 22cm No.1 shell; UD 26 x 18pdrs and 4 x 16cm shell; and gaillards 20 x 36pdr carronades and 4 x 18pdrs. The height of the lower battery of these former 74s was listed in the early 1830s as 1.78m at 6.73m mean draught.

The successor to the 74-gun ship, under the Tupinier revisions which were adopted on 10 March 1824, was the new 4th Rank of ships of the line. On these ships the 36pdrs and 18pdrs in the batteries were replaced by the equivalent number of long and short 30pdrs respectively, while the 8pdrs on the gaillards were superseded by twenty 30pdr carronades, again with four long 18pdrs in the chase positions. As with the surviving old 74s, on 14 April 1838 four of the 36pdrs on the LD were replaced by 22cm shell guns while on the gaillards 16cm shell guns replaced the four long 18pdrs (and two carronades were removed, reducing the total ordnance to 80 guns. On 20 July 1848 the number of 22cm shell guns was increased to eight on the LD and eight on the UD, each replacing a 30pdr, while another four carronades were subtracted, to bring the total to 76 guns of all types.

The new fleet structure adopted on 10 March 1824 contained only five 4th Rank ships in its total strength of 40 ships of the line. Only one new 4th Rank sailing ship of the line was ever ordered, and she was soon cancelled.

LA TOUR D'AUVERGNE – 74 guns. The budget for 1850, presented in August 1849, included one 4th Rank sailing ship of the line to be commenced in 1850 along with two three-deckers (*Bretagne* and *Desaix*). Although the 3rd Rank 90-gun ship was to be the mainstay of the fleet, the French Navy wanted to retain a few 4th Rank ships for use in shallow water or for coastal bombardment during combined expeditions. Because the old 74s were rapidly disappearing, the navy planned to build a maximum of four new ones to maintain the five in the fleet structure. On 27 February 1850 the Council of Works developed design specifications for the type, intended to make the ships significantly different from the 90-gun type in cost of construction and operation, crew size, and especially draught. To accomplish this it reduced the armament from 74 to 66 guns: LD 4 x 50pdrs (or 22cm No.1 shell) and 24 x 30pdrs No.1; UD 2 x 50pdrs, 28 x 30pdrs No.3; SD 2 x 30pdrs No.1, 6 x 30pdrs No.4. The hull lines of Sané's 80-gunner were to be followed as closely as possible, and all of the operational characteristics of the old 74s were to be retained except for a reduced supply of water. Space and weight were to be reserved for auxiliary steam machinery of 110-120nhp (later reduced to 80nhp, 110ihp) for 4.5 to 5 kts. The resulting hull specifications are shown below. The Council of Admiralty, discussing these technical decisions on 5 June 1850, felt that the reduction to 66 guns was too extreme, and specified the 74-gun armament shown below. The Council of Works tentatively approved a plan by Louis Lebouleur de Courlon on 25 June 1851, but in approving his modified plan on 21 January 1852 it recommended deferring the project until after the trials of *Charlemagne* and *Napoléon*. The success of these more powerfully engined ships later in 1852 put an end to the idea of a 4th Rank battleship with weak steam propulsion.

Dimensions & tons: 56.20m, 55.70m wl x 14.80m, 15.24m ext. 3,200t disp. Draught 6.84m mean. Men: 650-660.
Guns: (6.1850) LD 24 x 30pdrs No.1, 4 x 50pdrs; UD 26 x 30pdrs No.3, 4 x 22cm No.2 shell; SD 12 x 30pdr carronades, 4 x 30pdrs No.4.

La Tour d'Auvergne Brest Dyd.
Not laid down. Cancelled 1852.

(E) Screw two-deckers, 4th (later 3rd) Rank

SÉBASTOPOL Class – 70 guns. These two ships were ordered on 24 October 1855. They were successors to the old 4th Rank ships of the line but were rated as 3rd Rank ships under the new classification system of 1855. The creation of this type was probably motivated by the impending disappearance of ships of the line of modest dimensions and relatively shallow draught (the old 74s). The Crimean War showed that larger ships were often unable to carry out missions against the shore because of their excessive draught and revealed a need for 'scout battleships' able to approach the coast at will. Economy and a shortage of large timbers were also motivations. The data below are taken from specifications agreed on 4 September 1855 and plans by Amédée Mangin submitted by Cherbourg on 19 December 1855. The ship was about the same length as *Napoléon* but the beam and depth were less. It would have had the sail plan of a 74-gun ship. All seven plans drafted in accordance with these specifications were rejected on 10 June 1856 and a new set of specifications was adopted on 9 July 1856, including an increase of horsepower to 700, maximum draught to 7.15m, and crew to 740. Four sets of plans were examined on 13 January 1857. A decision was subsequently made not to create this type of ship because its draught as modified was only slightly less than that of a modified *Napoléon* then on the drawing boards and because it was becoming apparent that the advent of rifled artillery would require future capital ships to be armoured.

Dimensions & tons: 72.60m, 71.40m wl x 15.38m x 7.00m. 4,050t disp. Draught 6.40/7.00m. Men: 700.
Machinery: 650nhp. 12kts. Coal 520t.
Guns: LD 16 x 36pdrs, 16 x 22cm No.1 shell; UD 32 x 30pdrs No.2; SD 2 x 50pdrs, 4 x 30pdrs No.4.

Sébastopol Cherbourg Dyd.
Ord: 24.10.1855 and named. Not laid down. Cancelled 23.3.1858.
Desaix Rochefort Dyd.
Ord: 24.10.1855 and named. Not laid down. Cancelled 23.3.1858.

4 The Larger Frigates

(24-, 30-, and 36-pounder Frigates)
(1st and 2nd Rank from 1824)

This chapter covers those vessels of frigate construction (i.e. with their main battery at UD level, and with no ports on the LD) which were designed to carry a main battery of 24pdr or larger calibre guns – although in a number of the earlier cases the vessels actually mounted, or were later reduced to carry, guns of 18pdrs.

The problem with all of the smaller two-deckers (and a similar problem also affected small three-deckers) was that gunports or other openings on the LD brought the lower sills of those ports periously close to the waterline, so that in rough weather, or when the ship was heeling over, the LD gunports could not be opened in combat without risk of flooding the LD (and in extreme cases sinking the ship), thus making the main battery of the ship unusable. From the start of the 1740s, this problem was overcome by closing up all openings on the LD (other than ventilation scuttles) and moving the ship's primary armament to the UD.

Initial frigates were small, and their primary armament was 6pdr or 8pdr guns (upgraded to 12pdr guns in the late 1740s for two new French frigates, with more following in the 1750s in both France and Britain), but navies desired to obtain the same advantages for ships mounting heavier and more effective guns of 18pdr and 24pdr calibre, to replace the two-decked vessels of 44 guns or 50 guns.

(A) Larger frigates in service or on order at 1 January 1786

In early 1772 France experimentally ordered two large 'super-frigates' designed to carry an UD battery of 24pdr guns (at a date when even 18pdr-armed frigates had not been built); however the navy subsequently had second thoughts (allegedly at the instigation of Boux's rival constructeurs) about the structural stresses such ordnance would place on the hull, and the planned 24-pounder guns of this pair were replaced by 18-pounders, and they were subsequently employed as *flûtes*. Nevertheless, their great size places them in this chapter rather than the next. The navy did not order other 18pdr-armed frigates until 1781 (although one was built as a private venture, and another converted from a two-decker), and a new 24pdr-armed frigate was not attempted until 1782. By 1786 even this last frigate (*Pomone*) had been altered to carry the 18pdr guns.

POURVOYEUSE Class. A pair of very large 38-gun frigates designed by Jacques (or Louis?) Boux in early 1772 and named on 6 February 1772, and originally planned to carry 24pdr guns as their primary armament, although during construction it was decided to replace these by 18pdrs. They were both built by Pierre Train at Lorient. Intended for long-distance raiding operations, able to carry provisions for a crew of 350 men for up to a year, they were soon reclassified as *flutes* as there was no peacetime cruising role envisaged for these expensive-to-operate vessels.

Dimensions & tons: 154ft 0in, 139ft 0in x 38ft 0in x 16ft 5in (50.025, 45.15 x 12.34 x 5.33m.). 840/1,928 tons. Draught 19ft/19½ft (6.17/6.33m). Men: 300/327.

Guns (as completed): UD 26 x 18pdrs; QD 8 x 8pdrs; Fc 4 x 8pdrs.

Pourvoyeuse Lorient Dyd. (Constructeur, Pierre Train)
K: 3.1772. L: 10.11.1772. C: 1773.
In the Indies 1777 to 1783. Refitted about 1783 at Ile-de-France. Deleted 1786 at Brest.

Consolante Lorient Dyd. (Constructeur, Pierre Train)
K: 4.1772. L: 26.6.1775. C: 3.1776.
Refitted 11/12.1781 at Ile-de-France, and 7/10.1783 at Trincomalee. Deleted 1785 and became a hulk, BU 11.1804.

POMONE. 32 (later 40-44) guns. A one-off design by Baron Charles-Etienne Bombelle, with gunports designed to take 26 x 24pdrs and 6 x 8pdrs. She was listed in 1786 as carrying 18pdrs in her UD battery, so it is possible that she was completed with 18pdrs instead of the designed 24pdrs, but this long vessel, when taken by the British, was certainly carrying 24pdrs at that time, and so became the RN's prototype 24pdr-armed frigate (although she was later re-armed with 18pdrs in British service in 1799).

Dimensions & tons: 150ft 0in x 37ft 6in x 18ft 4in (48.73 x 12.18 x 5.96m). 700/1,400 tons. Draught 15ft 0in/15ft 10in (4.87/5.14m). Men: 325.

Guns: UD 26 x 24pdrs (see notes above); SD 6 x 8pdrs (SD re-armed 1794 with 12 x 8pdrs, 4 x 36pdr obusiers).

Pomone Rochefort Dyd. (Constructeurs, Hubert Pennevert & Henri Chevillard)
Ord: 13.4.1782 (named). K: 20.2.1783. L: 16.11.1785. C: 5.1787.
Taken by HMS *Flora* and *Arethusa* of Warren's squadron off Ile Bas 23.4.1794, becoming HMS *Pomone*; BU at Portsmouth 12.1802.

(B) Larger frigates acquired from 1 January 1786

At the outbreak of war against Britain and her allies, the French Navy began the conversion of several of the older 74-gun ships of questionable stability into large frigates. These retained the full battery of 36pdr guns on the main gundeck (which now became the upper deck), while their second battery was reduced by cutting away the waist and the existing superstructure. More frigates with (initially) 24pdr main batteries were constructed in the French Revolution, but the *Romaine* class, to which curious design (incorporating a heavy mortar into the design) numerous vessels were ordered, proved over-gunned, and no further 24-pounder armed frigates were begun until 1819. Meanwhile, France replaced all 24pdrs in the vessels below by 18pdrs so that by 1808 France once again had no frigate with the heavier guns.

RASÉED 74-GUN SHIPS. The conversion of five 74-gun ships to rasée frigates was begun at Brest between April 1793 and February 1794; all except the first ship (*Brave*) received new names when brought back into service. The lower deck battery was retained without change (except that this deck now became the 'upper deck'); The existing gaillards were removed, and the existing upper deck was partially cut away in the waist to create new gaillards. On the *Brave* a secondary

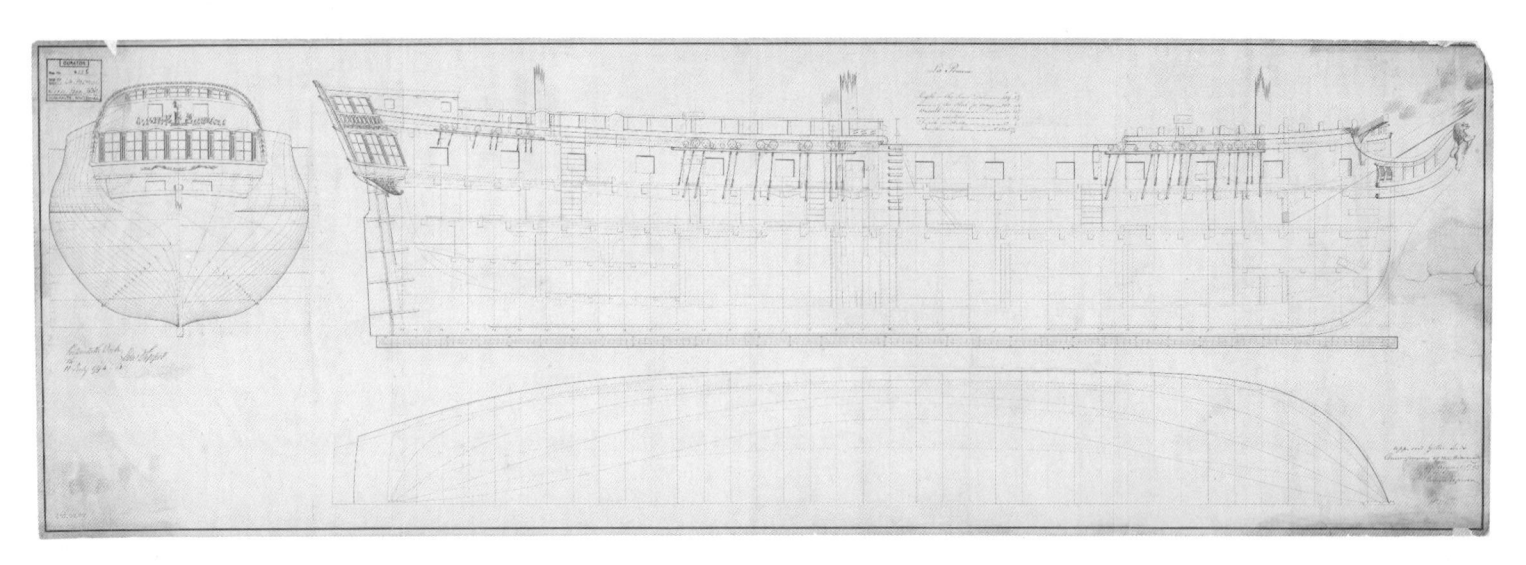

Admiralty draught of *Pomone* as captured, dated 11 July 1794. The origins of this one-off design are obscure, and French sources suggest the ship was designed for 18pdrs, but the length of the gundeck and the space between the ports suggests otherwise; the ship was definitely carrying 24pdrs when captured. *Pomone* was lightly built and did not survive long in British service, but HMS *Endymion*, which copied her hull form, was widely regarded as the fastest frigate in the Royal Navy and enjoyed a sea-going career that lasted over half a century. (© National Maritime Museum J5476)

battery of 12pdrs and 36pdr obusiers was mounted; on the other conversions this was enhanced to carry 18pdrs. A sixth ship (also renamed) was subsequently converted at Rochefort, with the same armament as the *Brave* but with one fewer pair of 12pdrs.

Guns: UD 28 x 36pdrs; SD (*Brave*) 20 x 12pdrs + 4/6 x 36pdr obusiers; *Scévola* had 2 x 12pdrs replaced by 2 x 18pdrs, while the other Brest conversions carried 14 x 18pdrs instead of 12pdrs, and no obusiers.

Brave Brest Dyd
Rasé began: 4.1793. C: 1.1794.
Struck 1.1798 at Brest.

Scévola (ex-*Illustre*) Brest Dyd
Rasé began: 8.1793. C: 2.1794.
Wrecked in an Atlantic storm 12.1796.

Flibustier (ex-*Argonaute*) Brest Dyd
Rasé began: 12.1793. C: 3.1794.
Removed from service 12.1795 at Rochefort.

Brutus (ex-*Diademe*) Brest Dyd
Rasé began: 12.1793. C: 5.1794.
Discarded 1797.

Hydre (ex-*Hercule*) Brest Dyd
Rasé began: 2.1794. C: 6.1794.
Discarded 1797.

Agricola (ex-*Borée*) Rochefort Dyd
Rasé began: 4.1794. C: 7.1794.
Hospital hulk 1796, BU 1803.

SEINE Class. 38-gun design by Pierre-Alexandre Forfait, with two ships being ordered in 1793 and two in 1794. While initially planned to carry a 24pdr battery, these ships were all completed with a main battery of 18pdrs, and thus appear in Chapter 5.

VENGEANCE Class. 48-gun design by Pierre Degay, ordered on 8 March 1793 and initially named *Bonne Foi* and *Fidelité* in November 1793, but were renamed before launch. Both built by the Crucy brothers Louis and Antoine at their Paimboeuf shipyard with their partner Jean Baudet acting as constructeur.

Dimensions & tons: 150ft 0in, 132ft 0in x 39ft 0in x 19ft 10in

This half-model of *Fisgard* (ex *Résistance*) highlights the curious underwater shape of this class, with its scow-like bow and long flat run aft. The ship also included technical innovations, like the screw-jacks that allowed the rake of the masts to be altered. Both the designer (Pierre Degay) and the private yard concerned specialised in privateers and this design shows how willing the French Navy was to consider unconventional ideas during the early years of the Revolution, a spirit of experimentation later replaced by Napoleonic standardisation. (© National Maritime Museum L0566-001)

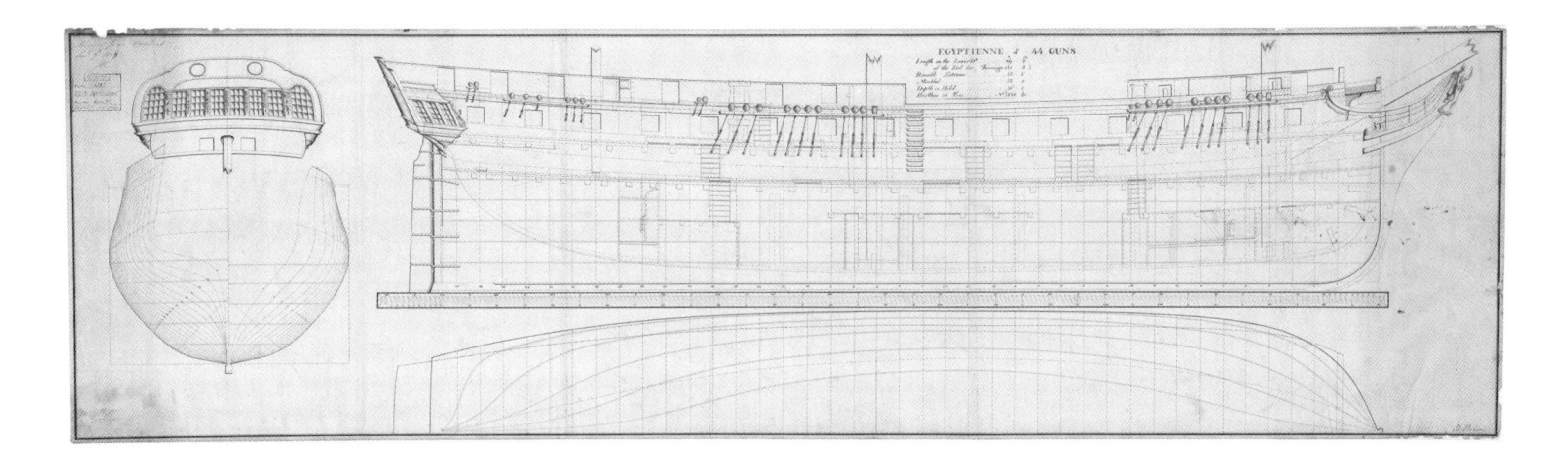

Admiralty draught of *Egyptienne* as fitted for Royal Navy service, dated January 1807, shortly before the ship was laid up. The largest French frigate design of the day, this *Forte* class was the work of François Caro, otherwise unknown as a warship designer, although he was associated with the Crucy brothers, who had considerable commercial shipbuilding interests. The design was influential, and although plans to build more came to nothing in the Napoleonic era, after the war it became the inspiration for the *Jeanne d'Arc* class. (© National Maritime Museum J3805)

(48.73, 42.88 x 12.67 x 6.44m). 806/1,556 tons. Draught (load) 16/18ft (5.20/5.85m). Men: 390.

Guns: UD 28 x 24pdrs; SD 20 x 12pdrs (6 Fc, 14 QD). However, these were replaced by 18pdrs on the UD, and 8pdrs on the SD.

Vengeance Louis & Antoine Crucy and Jean Baudet, Paimboeuf
K: 8.3.1793. L: 9.1794. C: 4.1795.
Taken 21.8.1800 in the Mona Channel off Puerto Rico by HMS *Seine*, becoming HMS *Vengeance*; BU 1801.

Résistance Louis & Antoine Crucy and Jean Baudet, Paimboeuf
K: 4.1794. L: 28.9.1795. C: 5.1796.
Taken 9.3.1797 in the Iroise estuary by HMS *San Fiorenzo* & *Nymphe*, becoming HMS *Fisgard*; sold 8.1814.

FORTE Class. 50-gun design by François Caro, the prototype being ordered on 5 July 1794 at Lorient and named 5 days later. The second ship was ordered at Toulon on 15 June 1798 and named in September. On 23 February 1805, Napoleon instructed Decrès to begin work on five more 24-pounder frigates of this class, three at Le Havre and one each at Saint-Servan and at Nantes, but these were never actually ordered.

Dimensions & tons: 160ft 0in, 148ft 0in x 40ft 0in x 17ft 5in (51.97, 48.08 x 12.99 x 5.66m). 1,012/2,042 tons. Draught (load) 16/18ft (5.20/5.85m). Men: 330.

Guns: UD 30 x 24pdrs; SD 20 x 8pdrs (6 Fc, 14 QD), also 4 x 36pdr obusiers (2 Fc, 2 QD).

Forte Lorient Dyd
K: 30.5.1794. L: 26.9.1794. C: 5.1795.
Taken 1.3.1799 by HMS *Sibylle* in the Bay of Bengal, becoming HMS *Forte*; wrecked 1.1801 in the Red Sea.

Égyptienne Toulon Dyd
K: 26.9.1798. L: 17.7.1799. C: 11.1799.
Captured by British Navy at Alexandria 2.9.1801, becoming HMS *Egyptienne*; sold 4.1817 to BU.

ROMAINE Class. 30-gun design by Pierre-Alexandre Forfait, to have carried a 12in mortar on a turntable platform just forward of the mizzen mast, and a main battery of 24pdrs, and designated *frégates-bombardes*. The ships also featured a shot furnace, but these proved impractical, dangerous to the ships themselves, and were later discarded. Experience quickly led to the mortars being removed (in most ships they were never fitted).

Twenty-four frigates to this design were originally envisaged, and twenty of these were ordered between October 1793 and April 1794, but only nine were completed to this design. Three further vessels begun in 1795-98 were intended to be of this class – the *Pallas* at Saint-Malo, and the *Furieuse* and *Guerrière* at Cherbourg – but all were completed as 18-pounder frigates (see Chapter 5). Another two ships – the *Fatalité* (ordered in 1793 at St Malo, ex *Frégate No.2*) and *Nouvelle* (ordered in 1794 at Lorient) were never completed; the remainder of the original program appears never to have been begun.

The hull dimensions of these ships were actually smaller than those of contemporary French 18-pounder frigates and they proved to be over-gunned. On 29 September 1800 the 24 x 24pdrs in *Incorruptible* were ordered replaced with 18pdrs because the weight of the 24pdrs reduced her speed and fatigued her hull. Most or all of the surviving units were similarly re-armed between 1802 and 1808.

Dimensions & tons: 139ft 8in, 124ft 0in x 36ft 4in x 17ft 9in (45.37, 40.28 x 11.80 x 5.76m). 700/1,700 tons. Draught 15½/15½ft (5.04m). Men: 340.

Guns: UD 20 to 24 x 24pdrs; SD 10 x 8pdrs. (later 24 x 18pdrs, 12 x 8pdrs & 4 x 36pdr obusiers)

Romaine Louis Deros, Le Havre
Ord: ?10.1793. K: 4.1794. L: 1.10.1794. C: 12.1794.
Condemned at Brest 2.1804; BU 1816.

Immortalité Lorient Dyd. (Constructeur: Pierre-Joseph Pénétreau)
Ord: 23.11.1793. K: 5.1794. L: 7.1.1795. C: 2.1795.
Captured by HMS *Fisgard* 20.10.1798, becoming HMS *Immortalité*.

Impatiente Lorient Dyd. (Constructeur: Charles-Jean-François Segondat-Duvernet)
Ord: 23.11.1793. K: 5.1794. L: 12.3.1795. C: 5.1795.
Wrecked off Cape Clear 29.12.1796.

Incorruptible Michel Colin-Olivier, Dieppe
Ord: 12.12.1793. K: 3.1794. L: 20.5.1795. C: 12.1795.
Decomm. at Toulon 27.2.1814. As of mid-1818 was to be converted to a hulk or BU. Struck in 1818 or 1819, prison hulk at Toulon, BU after 2.1830.

Revanche Michel Colin-Olivier, Dieppe
K: 3.1794. L: 31.8.1795. C: 12.1795.
Hauled out at Saint-Malo and converted to a flûte (500 tons, 24 guns) 1807-8, reconverted to a frigate 1811. Decomm. at Brest 11.3.1818. Struck early 1819, BU 10-11.1824 at Brest.

Libre Le Havre
K: 9.1794. L: 10.2.1796. C: 1.1798.

This detailed portrait by Antoine Roux makes the *Incorruptible* look like a conventional frigate, but the class she belonged to constituted a radically new concept described as *frégates-bombardes*. They were designed for maximum firepower on a small displacement, with a 24pdr main battery, a 12in mortar and a furnace for red-hot shot. Much was expected of them, with a large number planned, but in practice they proved over-ambitious, and they were either completed as conventional 18pdr frigates or converted as such after minimal service. Their principal identifying feature was only twelve upper deck gunports, compared with fourteen for most 18pdr frigates. (© National Maritime Museum A0652)

Captured off Rochefort by HMS *Loire* and *Egyptienne* 24.12.1805, but not added to British Navy.

Comète Le Havre
K: 10.1794. L: 11.3.1796. C: 1.1798.
Hulked 6.1808 at Bayonne and BU 1810.

Désirée Dunkirk
Ord: 19.3.1794. K: 10.2.1794. L: 23.4.1796. C: 12.1798.
Captured off Dunkirk by HMS *Dart* 8.7.1800, becoming HMS *Desirée*; hulked 1823 and sold 8.1832.

Poursuivante Dunkirk
Ord: 19.3.1794. K: 20.2.1794. L: 23.5.1796. C: 5.1798.
Condemned 8.1805 at Rochefort, hulked 1.1807 and BU.

(C) Larger frigates acquired from 25 March 1802

Between 1798 and 1813 France ordered no new frigates armed with 24-pounder guns and raséed no more 74-gun line of battle ships, preferring to focus exclusively on frigates armed with 18-pounders (see Chapter 5), notwithstanding Napoleon's instructions to Decrès in 1805. In addition, the French replaced the 24-pounders on those surviving frigates which carried the heavier guns by 18-pounders between 1802 and 1808 (as the *Vengeance* and *Forte* class ships had all fallen into British hands between 1797 and 1801, this meant solely the surviving *Romaine* class ships), and by the end of 1808 no French frigate carried guns heavier than 18-pounders.

However, Napoleon remained enthusiastic about the advantages of 24pdr-armed large frigates, and upon reading reports that the British were building ships to match the new American 44-gun frigates, he issued fresh instructions to Decrès; in August 1813 three new 24-pounder frigates, each with 50 guns, were ordered to be built at Cherbourg, Rochefort and Toulon; no names or designs were ever confirmed, and the construction due to begin in November was postponed, while the orders were finally cancelled in April 1814.

(D) Larger sailing frigates acquired from 26 June 1815

On 19 May 1817 the naval constructors in the ports were invited to submit plans in a competition to produce a new type of 50-gun frigate armed with 24pdr guns. The specifications for the new class, including the dimensions, were based on the experimental frigate *Forte* designed by François Caro in 1794 with 30 x 24pdrs and 20 x 8pdrs. In October 1817 a new Minister of Marine, Count Louis Mathieu Molé, presented to the Council of Ministers a draft decree that provided for a fleet of 38 ships of the line and 60 frigates and specified that the next eight frigates to be built would have 24pdr guns. Six of these were to be laid down in 1819. On 13 July 1819 the number of 36pdr carronades was increased from 18 to 26, making the ships 58-gunners. The carronades were a response to the 32pdr carronades on British and American frigates. In this and the other large vessels of the post-Napoleonic navy the forecastle and quarterdeck were joined to form a complete spardeck, which although fully exposed could carry an unbroken tier of guns. The ships' captains complained repeatedly about the excessive artillery which, among other things, reduced the height of the battery above the water from 1.95m in the 50-gun design to 1.73m as built. After 1823 various reductions were made in the armaments of individual ships as shown in the listings below.

JEANNE D'ARC Class – 24pdr frigates (2nd Rank from 1824), 58 guns. The first ship of the new 24pdr type to be completed, *Jeanne*

d'Arc, and one sister were designed by Charles-Michel Simon.
> Dimensions & tons: 51.98m wl x 13.16m x 6.98m. 2,275 tons disp. Draught 6.51m. Men: 441.
> Guns: (as built) UD 30 x 24pdrs; SD 26 x 36pdr carronades, 2 x 18pdrs (2 x 24pdrs in *Amazone* c1824).

Jeanne d'Arc Brest Dyd.
> K: 17.2.1819. L: 5.8.1820. Comm: 9.1.1821. C: 1.1821.
> Struck 26.10.1833. Still existed in 1850 as a training ship for seamen at Brest. Disappeared before hulks were added to the navy List in 1865.

Amazone Brest Dyd.
> K: 4.1820. L: 1.5.1821. Comm: 1.7.1821. C: 7.1821.
> Guns as reduced (c1827) UD 30 x 24pdrs; SD 18 x 24pdr carronades, 2 x 18pdrs, changed in 1828 to UD 28-24pdrs; SD 22-24pdr carronades, 2-18pdrs.
> Served as gunnery training ship at Toulon in 1840, relieving the corvettes *Alcmène* and *Sabine* which the school had used since its creation in 1837. Struck 13.3.1841. Towed from Cherbourg to Brest in 1841 for use as a hulk but reported BU at Brest in 1842.

CLORINDE – 24pdr frigate (2nd Rank from 1824), 58 guns. *Clorinde* was similar to *Jeanne d'Arc* and was designed by Louis Bretocq.
> Dimensions & tons: 50.60m wl x 13.16m. 2,220 tons disp. Men: 441.
> Guns: (1823) UD 30 x 24pdrs; SD 26 x 36pdr carronades, 2 x 24pdrs.

Clorinde Cherbourg Dyd.
> K: 2.1.1819. L: 5.2.1821. Comm: 15.1.1821 (sic). C: 7.1821.
> Guns as reduced (1828) UD 28 x 24pdrs; SD 22 x 24pdr carronades, 2 x 18pdrs.
> Struck 26.10.1833. BU at Brest 8.1834 to 9.1835.

VESTALE Class – 24pdr frigates (2nd Rank from 1824), 58 guns. These ships were similar to *Jeanne d'Arc* and were designed by Paul Filhon.
> Dimensions & tons: 51.97m wl (*Vénus* 52.60m) x 13.16m x. 7.05m. c2,300 tons disp. Draught 6.35m mean Men: 441.
> Guns: (*Vénus* 1824) UD 30 x 24pdrs; SD 26 x 24pdr carronades, 2 x 18pdrs.

Vestale Rochefort Dyd.
> K: 6.1820. L: 6.5.1822. Comm: 16.9.1822. C: 9.1822.
> Guns as reduced (1827) UD 28 x 24pdrs; SD 22 x 24pdr carronades, 2 x 18pdrs.
> Struck 26.5.1834.

Vénus Lorient Dyd. (Constructeurs: Jean-Charles Garrigues (?) and others)
> K: 2.1820. L: 12.3.1823. Comm: 1.4.1823. C: 6.1823.
> Guns as reduced (1827) UD 26 x 24pdrs; SD 22 x 24pdr carronades, 2 x 18pdrs.
> Relieved *Amazone* and served as gunnery training ship at Toulon in 1840-44. Condemned and renamed *Utile* 9.1846 as coal hulk at Gorée. BU after 1852.

Atalante Lorient Dyd. (Constructeurs: Jean Segondat and Joseph Fauveau)
> Ord: 16.1.1821. Named: 27.3.1821. K: 12.6.1821. L: 2.4.1825. Comm: 17.6.1828. C: 6.1828.
> Guns (probably as completed) UD 28 x 24pdrs; SD 2 x 18pdrs, 22 x 24pdr carronades.
> Fitted 1848 as powder storage vessel at Lorient. Struck 28.12.1850 and cut down to storage hulk at Lorient, initially *Ponton No.2*, renamed *Bache* 7.1865. Out of service 1877, BU 1885.

MARIE THÉRÈSE Class – 24pdr frigates (2nd Rank from 1824), 58 guns. These ships were similar to *Jeanne d'Arc* and were designed by Honoré Garnier Saint-Maurice.
> Dimensions & tons: 51.96m wl x 13.15m x 7.04m. 2,130 tons disp. Draught 5.71m/6.43m. Men: 441.
> Guns: (*M.T.* 1823) UD 30 x 24pdrs; SD 24 (later 26) x 24pdr carronades, 2 x 18pdrs.

Marie Thérèse (ex *Cérès*, renamed at launch) Toulon Dyd. (Constructeurs: Garnier Saint-Maurice and François-Timothée Pestel)
> K: 6.1820. L: 17.5.1823. Comm: 1.7.1823. C: 7.1823.
> Guns as reduced (1840) UD 30 x 24pdrs; SD 20 x 24pdr carronades, 2 x 18pdrs.
> Renamed *Calypso* 9.8.1830. Converted to hulk at Rochefort 12.1855 to 3.1856, struck 23.4.1856. Mooring hulk at Rochefort until 1882. BU 1885.

Sirène (*Syrène*) Toulon Dyd. (Constructeurs: Garnier Saint-Maurice and Pestel)
> K: 7.1820. L: 25.7.1823. Comm: 3.12.1824. C: 12.1824.
> Guns as reduced (1834) UD 28 x 24pdrs; SD 22 x 24pdr carronades, 2 x 18pdrs.
> Probably used as transport (2 guns) during Crimean War. Struck 20.7.1861, coal hulk at Brest. BU 1871.

RASÉED 74-GUN SHIPS – 36pdr frigates (1st Rank from 1824), 58 guns. Formerly the 74-gun ships *Romulus* (1812), *Agamemnon* (1812), *Colosse* (1813), and *Glorieux* (1818) respectively, these ships were raséed (cut down a deck) and converted to large frigates. The former upper deck became an open spardeck with a second unbroken tier of guns. The conversions reduced the draught by 37cm and increased the height of the battery by the same amount to 2.10m. The successful trials of *Guerrière* caused Jean-Marguerite Tupinier, the Deputy Director of Ports and a *Directeur des Constructions de 2ᵉ classe* in the Génie Maritime, to recommend in May 1822 that France develop a new type of frigate with 60 guns along her lines. The 60-gun *Surveillante* class and its successors were the result.
> Dimensions & tons: 55.87m, 54.82m wl (*Guerrière*) x 14.45m, 14.87m ext x 7.15m. 2,537 tons disp. Draught 6.08m/6.74m. Men: 513.
> Guns: (*Guerrière* and *Pallas*, c1828) UD 28 x 36pdrs; SD 28 x 36pdr carronades, 2 x 18pdrs; (*Guerrière* and *Pallas* c1830) UD 26 x 36pdrs, 2 x 22cm shell; SD28 x 36pdr carronades, 2 x 18pdrs; (*Minerve* as completed 1837) UD 26 x 36pdrs, 2 x 22cm shell; SD 28 x 36pdr carronades, 2 x 18pdrs.

Guerrière Toulon Dyd. Ex 74-gun ship *Romulus*.
> Rasé began: 1820. L: 6.3.1821. Comm: 2.4.1821.
> Hauled out and raséed by Louis Barrallier 1820-6.3.1821 (re-launched), reclassified as a 1st Rank frigate 3.1821 and renamed *Guerrière* 19.6.1821.Struck 29.11.1840 at Brest and BU.

Amphitrite Brest Dyd. Ex 74-gun ship *Agamemnon*.
> Rasé began: 12.1822. L: 27.12.1823. Comm: 17.4.1824.
> Raséed 12.1822-12.1823, reclassified as a 1st Rank frigate 12.1823 and renamed *Amphitrite* 4.1824. Struck 20.1.1836, hulk at Toulon, date BU unknown.

Pallas Brest Dyd. Ex 74-gun ship *Colosse*.
> Rasé began: 1825. L: 10.1827. Comm: 26.6.1828.
> Renamed *Pallas* 24.10.1825. Raséed 1825-10.1827, and reclassified as a 1st Rank frigate 10.1827. Struck 25.9.1840, hulk at Toulon. BU 1854.

Minerve Brest Dyd. Ex 74-gun ship *Glorieux*.
> Rasé began: 28.10.1831. L: 14.9.1833. Comm: 16.10.1836.

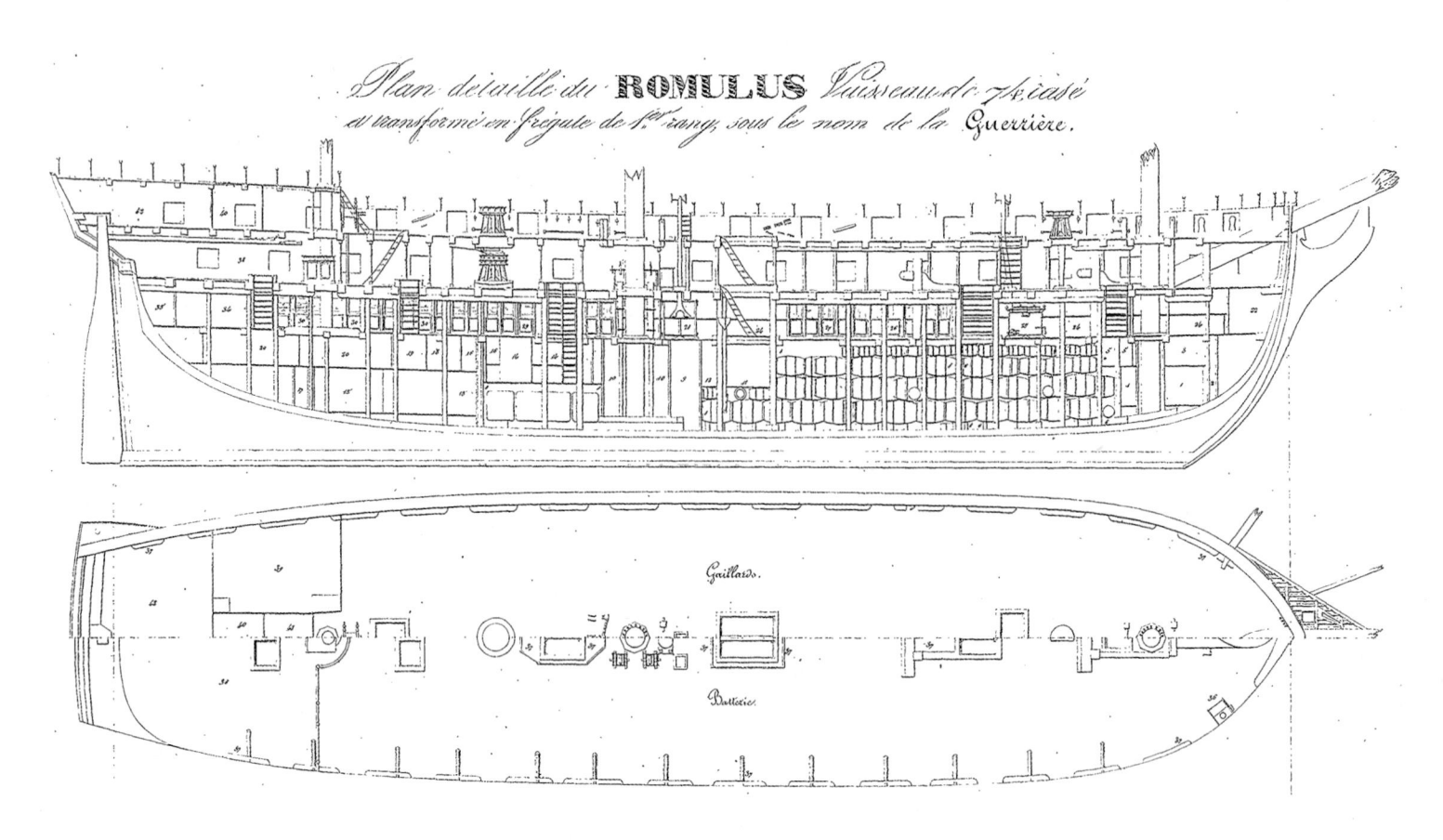

Plan detaillé du **ROMULUS** *Vaisseau de 74 rasé et transformé en frégate de 1er rang, sous le nom de la Guerrière.*

Detail from the official internal arrangements drawing of the 74-gun *Romulus* as cut down (raséed) to a 1st Rank frigate and renamed *Guerrière*; profile draught dated 1 April 1821 and signed by Barrallier. The conversion involved removing the quarterdeck, gangways and forecastle, although a section of the quarterdeck aft was retained to provide a roof over the captain's accommodation. (Atlas du Génie Maritime, French collection, plate 88)

Renamed *Minerve* on 12.10.1831, hauled out and raséed 1833-10.1834, and classified as a 1st Rank frigate with 58 guns in 1834. Relieved *Iphigénie* as gunnery training ship at Toulon. School ship for seamen-gunners at Toulon 6.8.1848 to 15.11.1849 and 1.1.1850 to 11.1850, the break being for a refit at Toulon. Sailed from Lisbon to Brest 6.1850 with 546 seamen-gunners, left Cherbourg 9.1850 for Brest and Toulon, damaged by a storm 6.12.1850 and turned back to Brest for repairs. Struck 12.12.1853, school hulk at Brest, renamed *Aberwrac'h* 7.1865, BU 1872-74.

Eight more 24-pounder frigates were planned during 1822-23. As of April 1822 the navy planned to begin five new 24-pounder frigates during 1822: *Melpomène* at Cherbourg, *Terpsichore* at Brest, *Dryade* at Rochefort, and *Didon* and *Iphigénie* at Toulon. These five ships were probably ordered on 4 December 1821. In December 1822 the proposed 1824 budget showed that a sixth, *Surveillante* at Lorient, was to be begun in 1823 and projected two more for commencement during 1824, *Belle Gabrielle* at Cherbourg and *Herminie* at Lorient. However the proposed budget for 1825 showed that by 1 January 1824 all of these had been reprogrammed as 30-pounder frigates and that four of them, *Surveillante, Terpsichore, Dryade,* and *Iphigénie* had been begun as such during 1823.

SURVEILLANTE Class – 30pdr frigates (1st Rank from 1824), 60 guns. In 1822 the ministry held a competition among the naval constructors in the ports to produce plans for a new type of 60-gun frigate. In February 1823 Mathurin Boucher completed the plans for *Surveillante*, in which he introduced some new techniques for stiffening the frames of long frigate hulls. *Herminie* was built on the same plans modified in November 1825 with a different stern. In this and the other large vessels of the post-Napoleonic navy the forecastle and quarterdeck were joined to form a complete spardeck, which although fully exposed could carry an unbroken tier of guns. The designed height of battery of this class was 2.00m at 6.41m mean draught. One more ship of this type added to the building program in 1847 is listed below as the Repeat *Surveillante* class.

Dimensions & tons: 54.40m, 54.00m wl x 14.10m, 14.50m ext x 7.00m. 2,558 tons disp. Draught 6.09m/6.59m. Men: 513.

Guns: (*Surveillante* and *Melpomène*, c1830) UD 30 x 30pdrs No.1; SD 28 x 30pdr carronades, 2 x 12pdrs (*Surveillante*) or 18pdrs. (*Belle Gabrielle*, c1830) UD 30 x 30pdrs No.1, SD 26 x 30pdr carronades, 4 x 18pdrs. Some later armaments are shown in the individual listings below.

Surveillante Lorient Dyd.
K: 12.9.1823. L: 29.7.1825. Comm: 25.8.1825. C: 9.1825.
Struck 22.8.1844. BU at Brest 3-7.1845.

Belle Gabrielle Cherbourg Dyd. (Constructeurs: Louis Bretocq and Joseph Daviel)
K: 13.4.1824. L: 28.6.1828. Comm: 1.8.1828. C: 8.1828.
Renamed *Indépendante* 9.8.1830. Struck 24.10.1860, careening hulk (*ponton-fosse*) until 1890. Renamed *Écurie* 1866. BU 1894.

Melpomène Cherbourg Dyd. (Constructeurs: Louis Bretocq and others)
Named: 16.4.1822. Ord: 4.12.1822 and 30.12.1824. K: 17.5.1825. L: 28.7.1828. C: 2.1830. Comm: 1.3.1830.
Struck 20.3.1845. Renamed *Travailleuse* c1865, sheer hulk at Toulon 1866-74, BU 1878.

Herminie Lorient Dyd.

K: 1825. L: 25.8.1828. Comm: 1.10.1828. C: 10.1828.
Wrecked at Bermuda 3.12.1838 on return voyage from Mexico.
Belle Poule Cherbourg Dyd. (Constructeur: Joseph Daviel)
   Ord: 29.11.1827. K: 1.4.1828. L: 26.3.1834. C: 1834. Comm: 6.6.1839.
   Guns (c1842) UD 26 x 30pdrs No.1, 4 x 22cm No.1 shell; SD 24 x 30pdr carronades, 6 x 16cm shell.
   Brought the ashes of Napoleon home from St. Helena 1840. Transport (9 guns) 1.1852, frigate 1.1856. Used as a powder storage vessel at Genoa c6.1859. Struck 19.3.1861, powder hulk at Toulon. Renamed *Poudrière* c1865. Barracks and storage hulk at Toulon 1868. Sold and BU 1888.
Sémillante Lorient Dyd. (Constructeurs: Charles-Robert Alexandre and Pierre Thomeuf)
   Ord: 11.12.1826 and named. K: 19.3.1827. L: 6.2.1841. C: 3.1845. Comm: 22.3.1854.
   Was in reduced commission (*commission de port* or *commission de rade*) from 1.3.1845 but was not placed in full commission until 1854. Used as transport (6 guns) during Crimean War. Wrecked in a storm in the Strait of Bonifacio 16.2.1855, with no survivors from the 710 souls on board.
Andromaque Lorient Dyd. (Constructeurs: Charles-Robert Alexandre and Pierre Thomeuf)
   K: 29.5.1827. L: 8.3.1841. C: 1.1854. Comm: 1.4.1854.
   Guns as completed (1854) as *Forte*.
   Used as transport (6 guns) during Crimean War and for the China expedition of 1859-62. Still transport (12 guns) in 1866. Struck 17.8.1869. Used as floating storage at Port Said until 10.1872, then hulk at Toulon. Sheer hulk 1874, replaced ex-*Melpomène*. BU 1905.

A lithograph of the *Belle Poule* and her consort *Favorite* becalmed after leaving Bahia, Brazil during the voyage to bring home Napoleon's remains from St Helena in 1840. The other ships may be Brazilian. The print is not very detailed but the two complete gun batteries in this class of frigate are evident. (© National Maritime Museum PY0858)

Forte Cherbourg Dyd. (Constructeur: Anne-François Besuchet)
   Ord: 18.12.1828. K: 5.6.1829. L: 16.9.1841. C: 12.1841. Comm: 20.2.1852.
   Guns as completed (1852) UD 26 x 30pdrs No.1, 4 x 22cm No.1 shell; SD 26 x 30pdr carronades, 4 x 16cm shell.
   Was in reduced commission (*commission de port*) from 1.12.1844 to 1.7.1850, commissioned in 1852 to carry deportees to Cayenne. Fitted as transport 1859-62 for expedition to China (26 guns), refitted as frigate 1864. Struck 6.1.1868, coal hulk at Cherbourg, moved to Rochefort as a mooring hulk 7.1876, condemned 6.1893, sold and BU 1894.

IPHIGÉNIE – 30pdr frigate (1st Rank from 1824), 60 guns. On 30 August 1823 the Maritime Prefect at Toulon recommended building frigates on the lines of a successful 74-gun ship designed by Colomb in 1768, *César*, which he argued would be far superior to the 58-gun frigates of the *Marie Thérèse* type then under construction. One such ship was built on plans by Jean-François Delamorinière dated 13 July 1824.
   Dimensions & tons: 54.22m, 53.92m wl x 14.13m, 14.52m ext x 7.09m. 2,676 tons disp. Draught 6.26m mean. Men: 513.
   Guns: (1827) UD 30 x 30pdrs No.1; SD 28 x 30pdr carronades, 2 x 18pdrs.
Iphigénie Toulon Dyd. (Constructeur: Pierre Rolland)

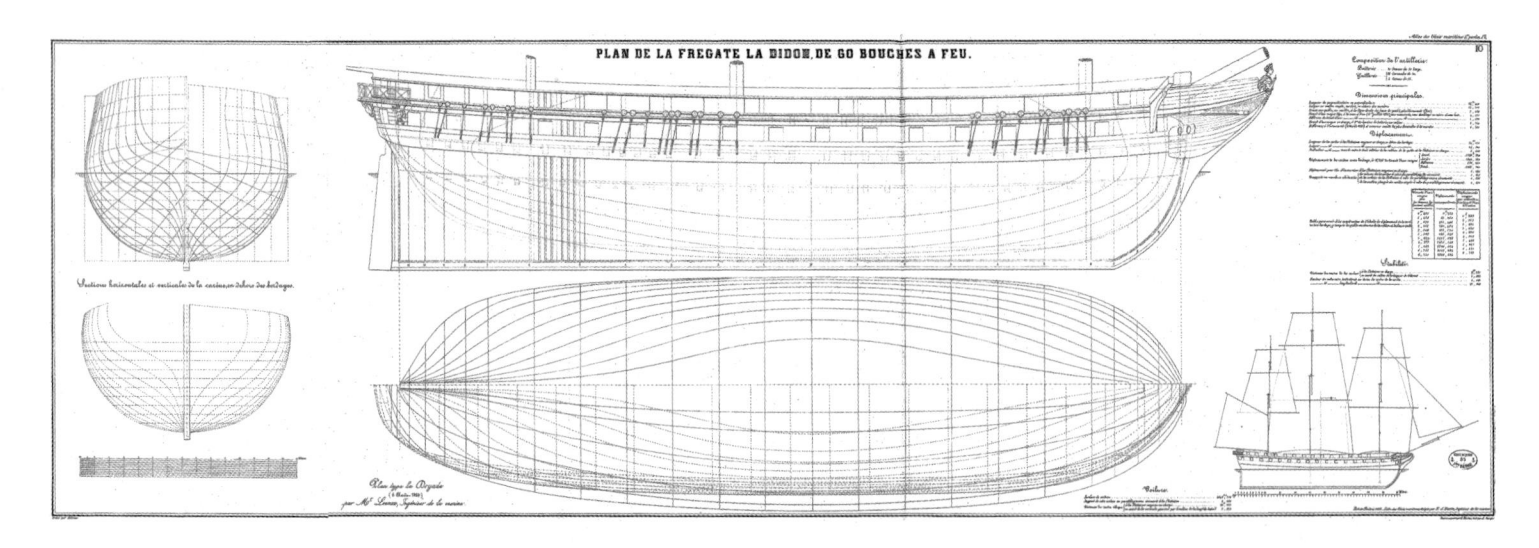

K: 8.1824. L: 3.5.1827. Comm: 28.9.1827. C: 9.1827.
Served as gunnery training ship at Toulon in 1844-50 with 50 guns and with masts and spars removed from her predecessor, the 2nd Rank frigate *Vénus*. Fitted as transport (4 guns) 1863. Barracks for Prussian prisoners at Rochefort 12.1870 to 2.1871, then prison hulk there 6-11.1871. Struck 1.7.1872. Mooring hulk at Rochefort 11.1873. Mooring and powder hulk there 1.1877, renamed *Druide* 1877. BU 1888.

TERPSICHORE – 30pdr frigate (1st Rank from 1824), 60 guns. Plans for this standard 60-gun frigate were completed by Philippe-Jacques Moreau in August 1823 and approved by the Council of Works on 13 May 1824.
Dimensions & tons: 54.00m wl x 14.05m. 2,707 tons disp. Men: 513.
Guns: (1828) UD 30 x 30pdrs No.1; SD 28 x 30pdr carronades, 2 x 18pdrs.
Terpsichore Brest Dyd.
K: 26.7.1824. L: 12.5.1827. Comm: 20.3.1828. C: 4.1828.
Struck 6.2.1839. BU at Brest 2-6.1839.

DIDON Class – 30pdr frigates (1st Rank from 1824), 60 guns. Plans for this class of standard 60-gun frigates were completed by Paul-Marie Leroux in August 1824. One more ship of this type added to the building program in 1847 is listed below as the Repeat *Didon* class.
Dimensions & tons: 54.40m, 54.00m wl x 14.10m, 14.50m ext x 7.05m. 2,497 tons disp. Draught 5.96m/6.72m. Men: 513.
Guns: (*Dryade* and *Didon*, c1828) UD 30 x 30pdrs No.1; SD 26 x 30pdr carronades, 4 x 18pdrs.
Dryade Rochefort Dyd.
K: 18.10.1824. L: 12.7.1828. Comm: 16.8.1828. C: 10.1828.
Renamed *Caroline* 12.7.1828 in honour of the Duchess of Berry, who attended her launch; reverted to *Dryade* 9.8.1830. Struck 9.3.1838.
Didon Toulon Dyd. (Constructeurs: François Pestel and Louis Lefébure de Cerisy, later Jean Vincent)
K: 3.1825. L: 15.7.1828. Comm: 1.8.1828. C: 8.1828.
Used as transport (6 guns) during Crimean War, later carried 20 guns as transport or 56 guns as frigate. Fitted as a guard station (*corps de garde*) at the mouth of the Donai River (probably at Bien Hoa) in Indochina in 1863, decomm. 1.4.1865, struck 28.3.1867 and BU 1867.
Renommée Rochefort Dyd. (Constructeurs: Alphonse Levesque, Charles

Official lines plan of the 60-gun *Didon* (described as 'plan-type la *Dryade*'), dated 6 August 1824 and signed Leroux. The ship has a round stern with a projecting walkway, supposedly inspired by British practice, but in 1831 the French Navy instituted a design competition for an improved stern intended to be fitted to both frigates and ships of the line. The sail plan shows a total area of 2,640 sq.m. (Atlas du Génie Maritime, French collection, plate 10)

Robert, Antoine Auriol, Gabriel Nosereau, and Pierre Jean-Baptiste Rossin)
K: 8.7.1826. L: 28.7.1847. C: 1.1849. Not commissioned as sail. Steam 1858.
Sémiramis Rochefort Dyd. (Constructeurs: Amédée Laimant, Jean Clarke, Henri Denis de Senneville, and Alfred Lebelin de Dionne)
K: 6.7.1829. Not launched as sail. Steam 1861.

URANIE – 1st Rank frigate, 60 guns. Plans for this standard 60-gun frigate were completed by Louis-Charles Barrallier in April 1826.
Dimensions & tons: 54.52m, 54.00m wl x 14.10m, 14.52m ext x 7.10m. 2,560 tons disp. Draught 6.11m/6.37m. Men: 513.
Guns: (1840) UD 28 x 30pdrs No.1, 2 x 22cm shell; SD 26 x 30pdr carronades, 4 x 16cm shell.
Uranie Toulon Dyd. (Constructeurs: Louis Barrallier and Jean Vincent)
K: 9.1826. L: 28.7.1832. C: 1833. Comm: 20.10.1840.
Relieved *Minerve* and served as gunnery training ship at Toulon 1851-55. Converted to a headquarters hulk and repair ship for the reserve at Brest between 1862 and 31.12.1864, on which date she was struck. BU 1883.

ARTÉMISE Class – 2nd Rank frigates, 52 guns. In response to the problems with the *Jeanne d'Arc* type, the ministry issued specifications for a second-class frigate with a slightly increased beam and a more realistic armament of 52 guns, mostly 24pdrs. Jean-Baptiste Hubert completed the plans for the first ships of this type in 1826. The designed height of battery of this class was 2.00m at 6.31m mean draught. The standard artillery of this type was changed in 1838 to a 50-gun armament of 30pdrs after successful trials in at least one ship, *Artémise*. *Cléopâtre* and *Danaé* were commissioned briefly in 1838 to move from Saint-Servan to Brest and were commissioned later for active service as indicated below. Four more ships of this type added to the building program in 1847 are listed below as the Repeat *Artémise* class.
Dimensions & tons: 52.80m, 52.00m wl x 13.40m, 13.78m ext x 7.05m. Beam of Lorient ships 13.72m/13.36m. 2,300 tons disp.

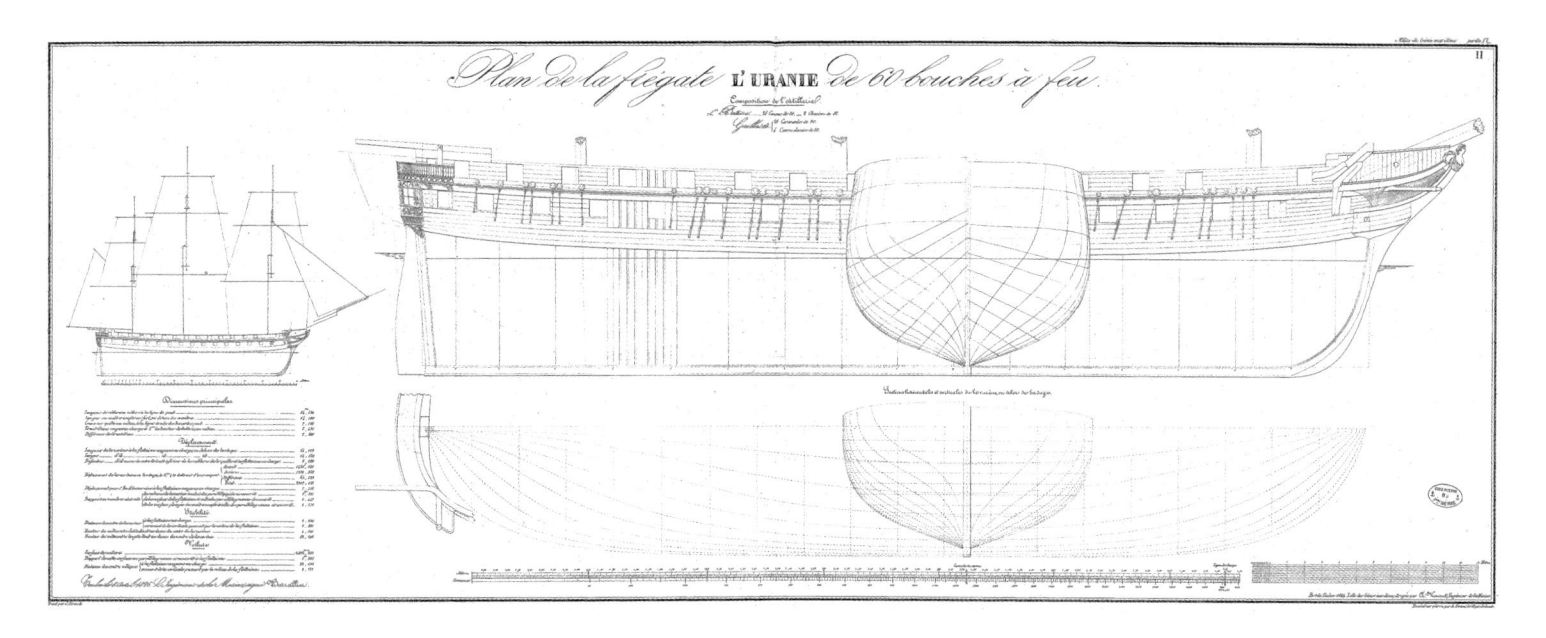

Official lines plan of the *Uranie*, dated 8 April 1826, a version by Barrallier of the standard 60-gun specification. The stern is round but more elaborately decorated than *Didon*'s. Total sail area, without royals, was 2,594 sq.m. (Atlas du Génie Maritime, French collection, plate 11)

Draught 5.90m/6.70m. Men: 441.

Guns: (*Artémise* c1830 and *Andromède* c1836) UD 28 x 24pdrs; SD 22 x 24pdr carronades, 2 x 18pdrs. Some later armaments are shown in the individual listings below.

Artémise Lorient Dyd. (Constructeurs: Jean Segondat and Jean-Baptiste Lebas)

K: 5.9.1826. L: 22.11.1828. Comm: 22.1.1829. C: 1.1829.

Struck 3.10.1840. Cut down to hulk at Lorient 1841-42. Renamed *Arc en Ciel* c1844. BU 1887.

Andromède Lorient Dyd. (Constructeurs: Jean Segondat, Jean-Baptiste Bayle, and Louis D'Ingler)

K: 2.4.1827. L: 5.4.1833. Comm: 12.9.1836. C: 10.1836.

Struck 24.10.1860, mooring hulk at Rochefort until 1886. Renamed *Athlète* 1883. BU 1887.

Néréide Lorient Dyd. (Constructeurs: Jean Chaumont and Pierre Thomeuf)

K: 1.8.1828. L: 17.2.1836. C: 4.1837. Comm: 16.9.1837.

Guns as completed (1837) UD 28 x 30pdrs No.2; SD 18 x 30pdr carronades, 4 x 16cm shell.

Fitted as transport 8-12.1863 at Brest, reclassified *frégate de transport* 1.1873. Struck 30.12.1887, guard hulk at Brest. BU 1896.

Although the first post-war 24pdr frigate specification was based on the highly regarded *Forte* design, the armament was increased and the resulting 58-gun *Jeanne d'Arc* class was considered over-gunned. A revised, less ambitious requirement for a 2nd Rank frigate of 52 guns produced a number of different designs, including this *Artémise* class of seven ships by Jean-Baptiste Hubert. These designs varied most visibly in their sterns, Hubert's being most unusual in having two levels of quarter galleries and a traditional square plan. This is the official lines plan of 1826, but as engraved in 1849, when the class had been re-rated as 50 guns. It gives the sail area as 2,175 sq.m. (Atlas du Génie Maritime, French collection, plate 15)

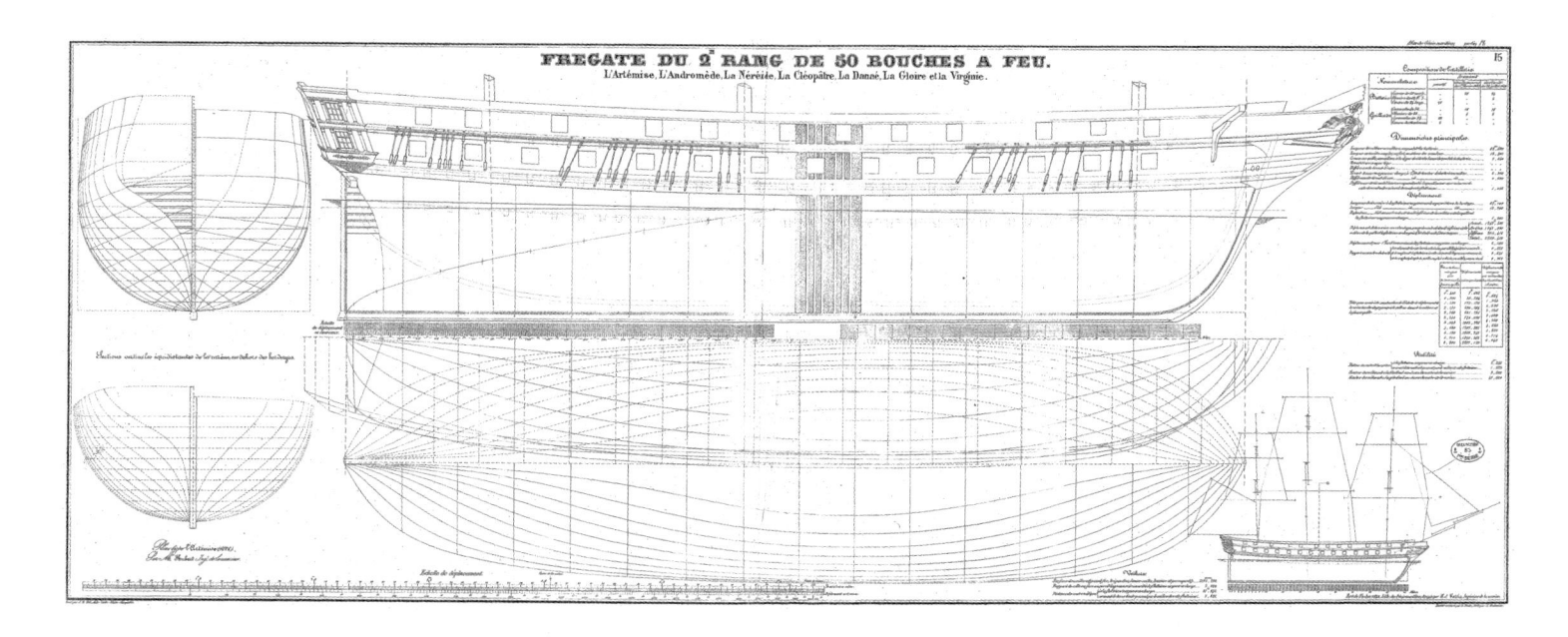

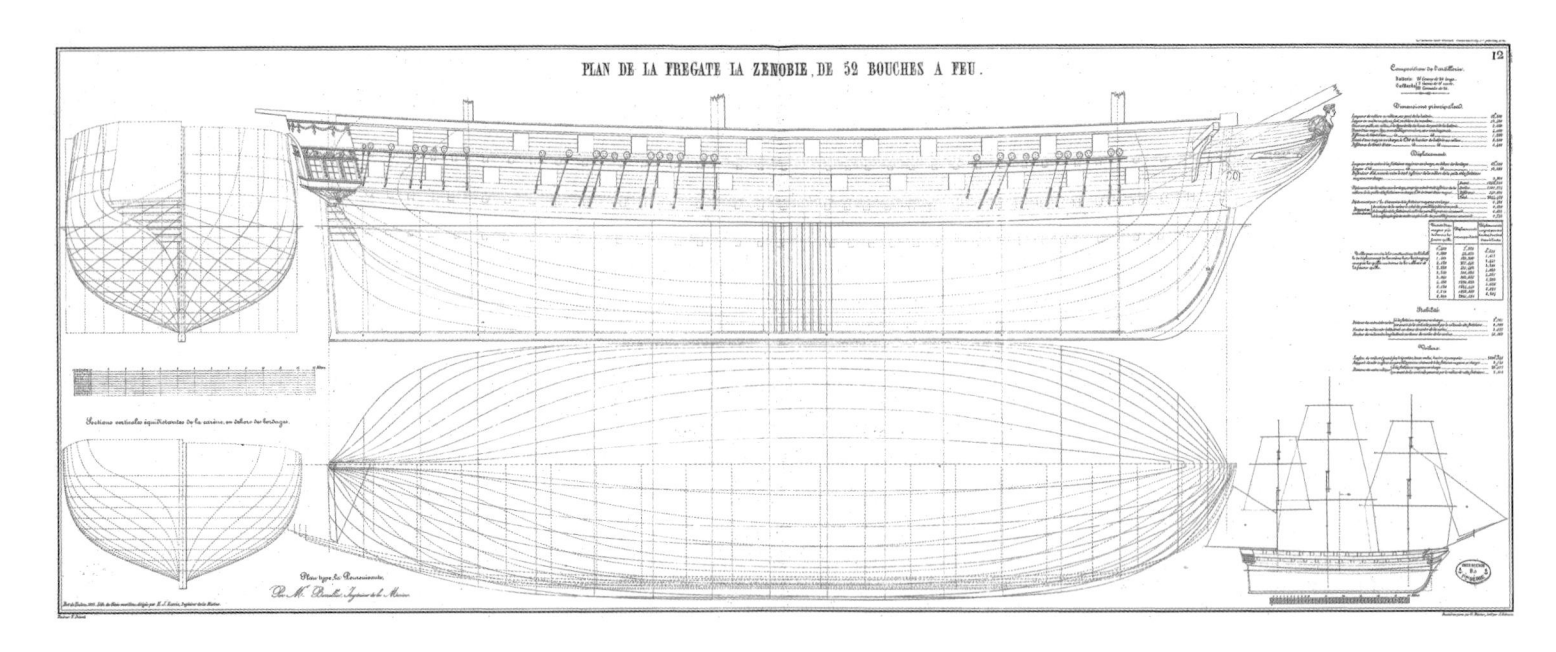

Gloire Rochefort Dyd.
K: 2.4.1827. L: 12.12.1837. Comm: 1.1.1838. C: 4.1838.
Guns (1839?) UD 24 x 30pdrs No.2, 4 x 16cm shell; SD 18 x 30pdr carronades, 4 x 16cm shell.
Grounded and lost 10.8.1847 off the southwest coast of Korea near Gunsan with the corvette *Victorieuse*.

Cléopâtre Saint-Servan (Constructeurs: Charles Alexandre and from 1835 Joseph Daviel and Georges Allix)
K: 1.9.1827. L: 23.4.1838. C: 6.1838. Comm: 21.7.1842.
Guns as completed (c1842) as *Néréide*.
In commission 24.4.1838 to 21.7.1838 to be towed by the steamer *Tonnerre* from Saint-Servan to Brest. Used as transport (2 guns) during Crimean War. Struck 31.12.1864, storage hulk at Cherbourg, BU 1869.

Danaé Saint-Servan (Constructeurs: Charles Alexandre and from 1835 Joseph Daviel and Georges Allix)
K: 27.9.1827. L: 23.5.1838. C: 8.1838. Comm: 12.10.1840.
Guns as completed (c1840) as *Néréide*.
Towed 6.1838 by the steamer *Tonnerre* from Saint-Servan to Brest. Converted to steam 1858.

Virginie (ex *Niobé* 23.11.1839) Rochefort Dyd. (Constructeurs: Jean-Baptiste Bayle, Gabriel Nosereau, Jean Le Jouteux, and Gustave Garnier)
K: 26.6.1827. L: 25.4.1842. Comm: 11.4.1844. C: 5.1844.
Guns as completed (c1844) UD 26 x 30pdrs No.2, 2 x 22cm No.2 shell; SD 18 x 30pdr carronades, 4 x 16cm shell.
Fitted as transport 1867, reclassified as such 5.1872. Struck 13.5.1881, storage hulk (*magasin à salaisons*) at Brest. BU 1888.

POURSUIVANTE Class – 2nd Rank frigates, 52 guns. Plans for these standard 52-gun frigates were completed by Louis-Charles Barrallier in February 1827.
Dimensions & tons: 52.50m, 52.00m wl x 13.40m, 13.78m ext x 7.05m. 2,303 tons disp. Draught 6.10m/6.50m. Men: 441.
Guns: (*Poursuivante* and *Zénobie*, 1847-48) UD 28 x 30pdrs No.2; SD 18 x 30pdr carronades, 4 x 16cm shell. In 1848-50 4 x 30pdrs No.2 on the UD were replaced by 4 x 22cm No.2 shell. (*Sibylle* 1851) UD 24 x 30pdrs No.2, 4 x 22cm No.2 shell; SD 18 x 30pdr carronades, 4 x 16cm shell.

Poursuivante Toulon Dyd. (Constructeurs: Barrallier and (in 1841-42) Stanislas-Charles-Henri Dupuy de Lôme)

Barrallier's version of the 52-gun design was the *Poursuivante* class of three ships, including the *Zénobie* shown in this official draught. The ship had a conventional single-level stern, although the upper finishing above the quarter gallery looks very awkward. The ship spent nearly twenty years on the stocks, so her appearance as completed is not certain, although this version of the draught was not engraved until 1855. Sail area was 2,260 sq.m. (Atlas du Génie Maritime, French collection, plate 12)

K: 5.5.1827. L: 16.11.1844. C: 3.1846. Comm: 27.1.1847.
Rearmed as *Zénobie* by 1854. Fitted as floating workshop at Cherbourg in 1862-63. Struck 31.12.1864, headquarters hulk for the reserve fleet at Cherbourg until 1889. Sold for BU 2.1891.

Zénobie Toulon Dyd. (Constructeurs: Barrallier, Jules Aurous, and Jean-Baptiste Bayle)
K: 3.1828. L: 29.7.1847. C: 8.1848. Comm: 1.1.1849.
Converted to steam 1858.

Sibylle (sometimes *Sybille* in error) Toulon Dyd. (Constructeur: Barrallier)
K: 9.1829. L: 7.11.1847. C: 1.1849. Comm: 8.4.1851.
Fitted as transport 1860, reclassified as such 5.1872. Struck 13.5.1881, workshop hulk at Toulon. BU 1883.

NÉMÉSIS Class – 2nd Rank frigates, 52 guns. Plans for this standard 52-gun frigate class were completed by Jean-Baptiste Perroy in April 1828. Plans were never assigned to the cancelled 2nd Rank frigate *Clorinde* of the 1837 program (see below), but as she was to have been built at Brest she is listed here.
Dimensions & tons: 52.45m, 52.00m wl x 13.40m, 13.78m ext x 7.05m. 2,303 tons disp. Draught 6.30m mean. Men: 441.
Guns: (*Pandore* 1848) UD 24 x 30pdrs No.2, 4 x 22cm No.2 shell; SD 18 or 20 x 30pdr carronades, 4 x 16cm shell; (*Némésis* 1857) UD 20 x 30pdrs No.2, 8 x 22cm No.2 shell; SD 16 x 30pdr carronades, 2 x 30pdrs No.1.

Pandore Brest Dyd. (Constructeur: Perroy)
Ord: 22.12.1828. K: 7.9.1829. L: 26.3.1846. C: 7.1847. Comm: 3.11.1849.
Used as transport during Crimean War. Converted to steam 1858.

Némésis Brest Dyd. (Constructeur: Perroy)
K: 14.9.1828. L: 14.4.1847. C: 1848. Comm: 26.3.1855.
Commissioned in 1855 as a transport for Crimean War, then refitted

The *Reine Blanche* of the *Alceste* class, a 52-gun frigate designed by Paul Leroux, approved 27 March 1829. The ship sported a round stern with projecting walkway, as seen in some of the contemporary 1st Rank 60-gun frigates. Although intended to carry 24pdrs, by the time this ship completed the gun establishment had been altered to short 30pdrs, 30pdr carronades and four 30pdr shell guns. Sail area totalled 2,245 sq.m. (Atlas du Génie Maritime, French collection, plate 13)

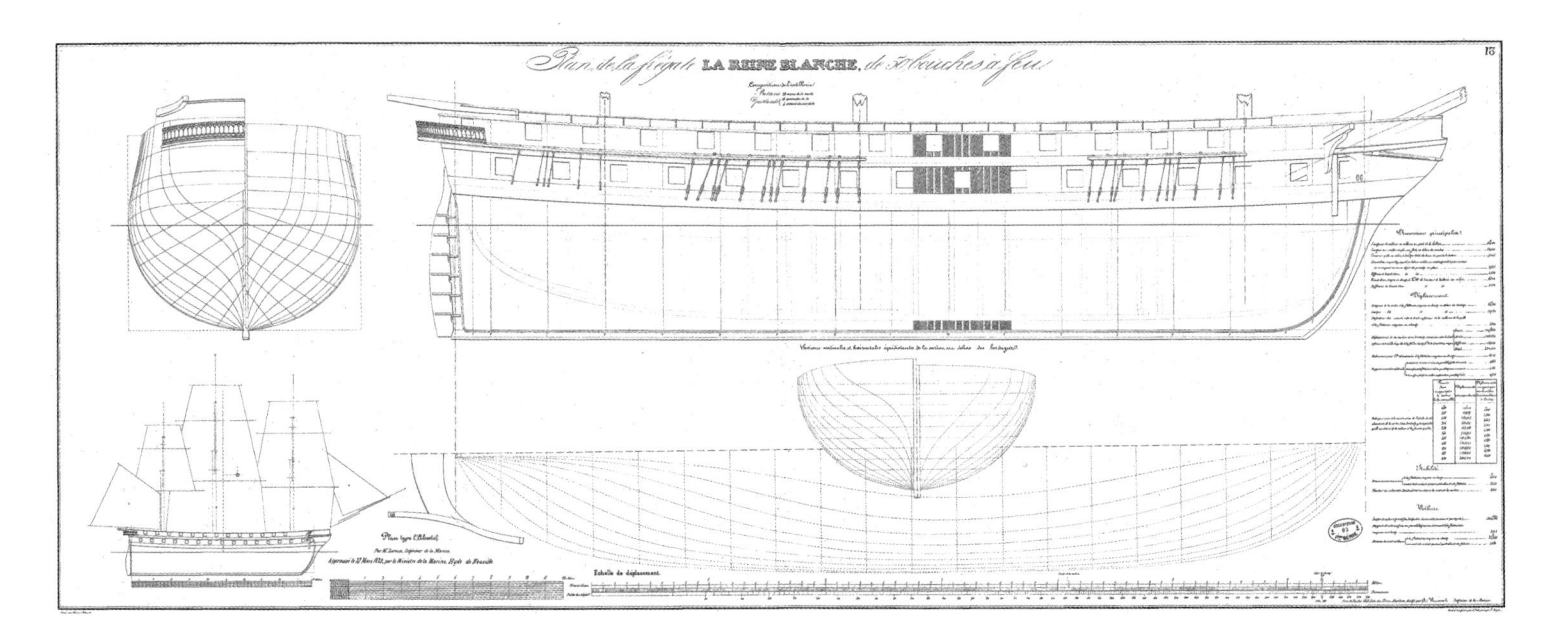

as a frigate. School ship at Lorient 1864. Struck 19.4.1866, barracks hulk at Lorient, also seamen's training ship from 1875. BU 1888.

Clorinde Brest Dyd

Projected in 1836 to be begun in 1837 but not laid down, cancelled c12.1838.

ALCESTE Class – 2nd Rank frigates, 52 guns. Paul Leroux completed plans for these standard 52-gun frigates in August 1828. *Reine Blanche* had a round stern.

Dimensions & tons: 52.46m, 52.00m wl x 13.40m, 13.78m ext x 7.05m. 2,360 tons disp. Draught 6.10m/6.50m. Men: 441.

Guns: (*Reine Blanche* 1841) UD 28 x 30pdrs No.2; SD 18 x 30pdr carronades, 4 x 16cm shell; (*Alceste* 1853?) UD 24 x 30pdrs No.2, 4 x 22cm No.2 shell; SD 18 or 20 x 30pdr carronades, 4 x 16cm shell.

Reine Blanche Cherbourg Dyd. (Constructeurs: Jean-Baptiste Lefebvre and others)

Ord: 16.11.1829 and named. K: 27.6.1830. L: 15.9.1837. C: 9.1840. Comm: 1.11.1840.

Used as transport (2 guns) during Crimean War. Struck 23.6.1859 at Brest, became a mooring hulk at Rochefort. Renamed *Vigoreux* 8.4.1865. BU 1885.

Alceste Cherbourg Dyd. (Constructeurs: Paul Leroux, Jean-Baptiste Lamaëstre, Paul Picot de Moras, and Charles Moll)

Ord: 18.12.1828. K: 26.5.1829. L: 28.3.1846. C: 1.1849. Comm: 9.4.1853.

Converted into a convict transport for New Caledonia at Rochefort 1867-68, reclassified as sail transport 1.1873. Struck 31.5.1886, hospital hulk at Gabon. BU 1891.

PERSÉVÉRANTE Class – 1st Rank frigates, 60 guns. This standard 60-gun frigate was designed at Brest by Charles-Michel Simon, whose plans were dated 19 June 1829. Plans were never assigned to the two cancelled 1st Rank frigates of the 1830 program (see below), but as they were to have been built at Brest they are listed here.

Dimensions & tons: 54.00m wl x 14.00m, 14.48m ext x 7.25m. 2,628 tons disp. Draught 6.54m mean. Men: 513.

Guns: (1854) UD 26 x 30pdrs No.1, 2 x 50pdrs, 2 x 22cm No.1 shell; SD 22 x 16cm shell, 2 x 30pdrs No.1.

Persévérante Brest Dyd. (Constructeur: Charles-Michel Simon)

Ord: 22.12.1828. K: 1.10.1829. L: 28.6.1847. C: 1848. Comm: 13.7.1854.

Commissioned in 1854 as a transport with 205 men, was manned as frigate by 1.1856. Decomm. 30.9.1864. Struck 28.3.1867. BU 1867-68.

Valentine Brest Dyd

Projected in 1829 to be begun in 1830, postponed to 1831 and then cancelled in 1831.

Jeanne d'Albret Brest Dyd

Projected in 1829 to be begun in 1830, postponed to 1831 and then cancelled in 1831.

VENGEANCE Class – 1st Rank frigates, 60 guns. Mathurin Boucher completed plans for this class in September 1829 with slightly smaller dimensions than his earlier *Surveillante* class. *Entreprenante* was originally projected to be begun at Brest in 1829 but was reassigned to Lorient before construction began in 1829. Similarly, *Duchesse d'Orleans* was originally projected to be begun at Toulon in 1830 but was reassigned to Lorient before construction began in 1830.

Dimensions & tons: 53.64m wl x 14.00m x 7.25m. 2,500 tons disp. Draught 6.25m/6.75m. Men: 513.

Guns: (planned) UD 28 x 30pdrs, 2 x 22cm shell, SD 26 x 30pdr carronades, 4 x 16cm shell.

Vengeance Lorient Dyd. (Constructeurs: Charles Alexandre and others including Charles Nettre)

K: 5.10.1829. L: 1.7.1848. C: 1.1850. Comm: 1.4.1854.

Used as transport with 6 guns during Crimean War, refitted as frigate with 56 guns 1.1857. Floating hospital at Lorient 1863, floating barracks there 1864. Struck 19.4.1866, barracks hulk at Lorient. Also school for apprentice seamen from 3.1872 to 1894. BU 1898.

Entreprenante Lorient Dyd-Caudan (Constructeurs: Louis D'Ingler, Charles-Louis Duchalard, and Louis Édouard Lecointre)

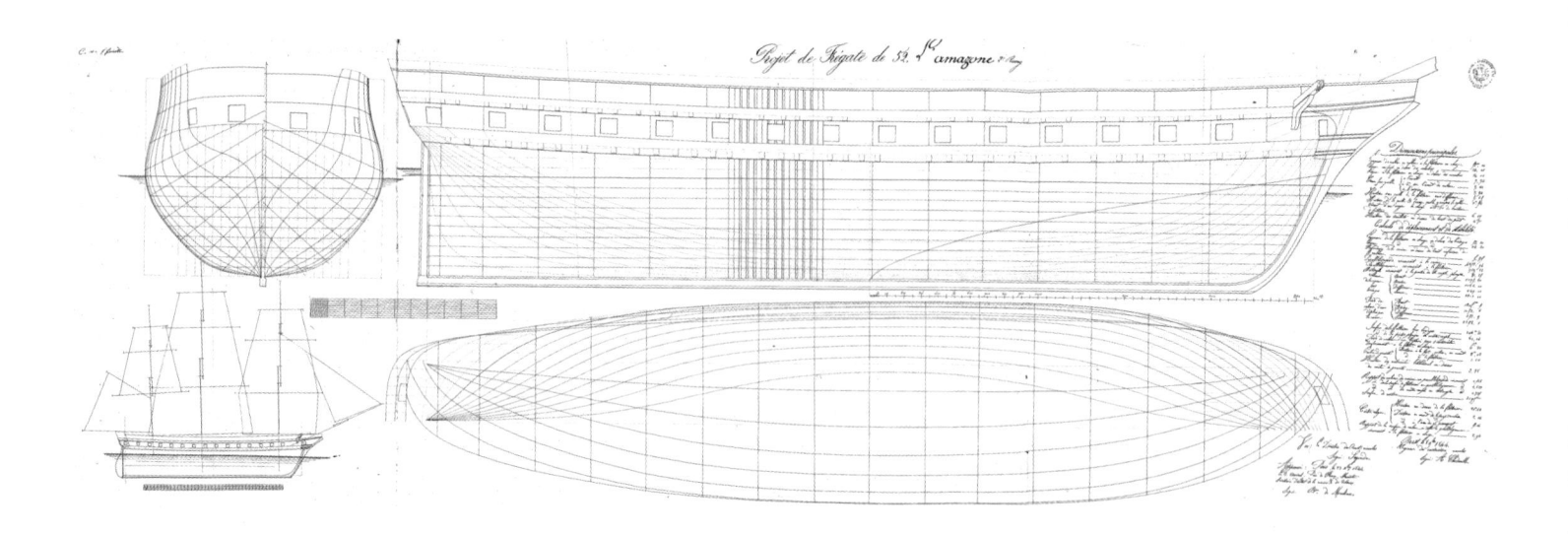

K: 5.10.1829. Not launched as sail. Steam transport 1858.
Victoire (ex *Duchesse d'Orléans* 29.2.1848) Lorient Dyd. (Constructeurs: Charles Alexandre and others)
   Ord: 16.11.1829 and named (*Duchesse d'Orléans*). K: 29.6.1830. Not launched as sail. Steam 1861.

The building program for 1830 (planned in early 1829) included ten frigates to be begun in 1830. Five were of the 1st Rank: *Reine Blanche* at Cherbourg, *Duchesse d'Orléans* at Toulon, and *Valentine, Jeanne d'Albret*, and *Douze Avril* at a new facility to be built at Brest. The other five were of the 2nd Rank: *Oriflamme* at Saint-Servan, *Pénélope* at Lorient, *Héliopolis* at Rochefort, and *Bouvines* and *Dame de Beaujeu* at the new facility at Brest. However the planned Brest facility did not materialize, and the five ships to have been built there were postponed on 16 November 1829. All five 2nd Rank ships plus *Douze Avril* (renamed *Charte*) were reprogrammed in 1829-30 as 3rd Rank frigates, *Dame de Beaujeu* being renamed *Psyché* and *Oriflamme* later being renamed *Érigone*. *Valentine* and *Jeanne d'Albret* were re-listed in 1830 to be begun in 1831, still as 1st Rank frigates at Brest, but they were cancelled in 1831. The only ship in the 1830 program to be built as a 2nd Rank frigate was *Reine Blanche*, which had been changed from the 1st Rank before being laid down at Cherbourg in June 1830. This in turn left *Duchesse d'Orléans*, laid down in June 1830 at Lorient after reassignment from Toulon, as the only ship of this group to be built as a 1st Rank frigate.

In 1837 one new 2nd Rank frigate, *Clorinde*, was scheduled to be begun at Brest, but she was deferred and cancelled in 1838. This was one of seven ships programmed, then cancelled in the mid-1830s, the others being the 90-gun *Argonaute* and five 3rd Rank frigates. With her cancellation, no new 1st or 2nd Rank frigates were laid down between 1830 and 1845. All of these ships are listed above in their respective classes.

AMAZONE Class – 2nd Rank frigates, 50 guns. The navy decided on 30 September 1844 to start four frigates in 1845 (*Bellone, Amazone, Astrée*, and *Magicienne*) using funds for some transports which had just been cancelled, and on 4 October 1844 the Minister of Marine ordered the ports to prepare drawings. Plans by Alexandre Chedeville for *Amazone* were approved on 23 December 1844 and after plans sent by Cherbourg for *Bellone* were rejected on 25 June 1845 Chedeville's plans were used for both ships.
   Dimensions & tons: 52.00m wl x 14.07m x 7.19m. 2,260 tons disp.
      Draught 6.30m mean. Men: 441.

A new generation of frigates – the last to be designed as pure sailing vessels – was planned in 1844. There were to be three new designs for 50-guns ships, one of which was the *Amazone* class shown here in the original draught dated 8 November 1844 and signed A Chedeville. Although this design was officially approved on 23 December 1844, none of this programme would be completed as a sailing ship, all being converted to steam before entering service. (Atlas du Génie Maritime, Genoa collection, image 1-0018)

   Guns: (Designed) UD 28 x 30pdrs No.2; SD 18 x 30pdr carronades, 4 x 16cm shell.
Bellone Cherbourg Dyd. (Constructeurs: Louis Nicolas Sollier, Amédée Cazavan, and Chedeville)
   K: 26.8.1845. L: 26.3.1853. Not commissioned as sail. Steam 1858.
Amazone Brest Dyd. (Constructeurs: Paul Leroux and others)
   K: 2.1.1845. Not launched as sail. Steam transport 1858.

ASTREE Class – 2nd Rank frigates, 50 guns. These ships were designed by Pierre Le Grix using the same specifications as for *Amazone*. The plans were approved on 12 June 1845. *Dryade* was added to the building program with the repeat *Artémise* class (below) by a decision of 16 March 1847.
   Dimensions & tons: 52.00m wl x 14.06m x 7.04m. 2,258 tons disp.
      Draught 6.19m mean. Men: 441.
   Guns: (Designed) As *Amazone*.
Astrée Lorient Dyd-Caudan (Constructeurs: Paul Masson and Louis Sollier)
   K: 26.7.1845. Not launched as sail. Steam 1859.
Dryade Lorient Dyd. (Constructeurs: Le Grix and Louis-Édouard Lecointre)
   K: 26.3.1847. Not launched as sail. Steam transport 1856.

MAGICIENNE Class – 2nd Rank frigates, 50 guns. These ships were designed by Prix-Charles Sochet using the same specifications as for *Amazone*. The plans were approved on 24 January 1845. *Thémis* was added to the building program with the repeat *Artémise* class (below) by a decision of 16 March 1847.
   Dimensions & tons: 52.00m wl x 14.00m x 7.09m. 2,183 tons disp.
      Draught 6.20m mean. Men: 441.
   Guns: (Designed) As *Amazone*.
Magicienne Toulon Dyd. (Constructeur: Hyacinthe De Coppier)
   K: 26.6.1845. Not launched as sail. Steam 1861.
Thémis Toulon Dyd. (Constructeur: Hyacinthe De Coppier)

K: 4.1847. Not launched as sail. Steam 1862.

REPEAT *SURVEILLANTE* Class – 1st Rank frigate, 60 guns. This ship was added to the building program by a decision of 16 March 1847 that followed the promulgation of a new naval program on 22 November 1846. Technical specifications were as the original class as designed by Mathurin Boucher in 1823 (above) except that she was probably designed with the armament adopted as a standard for this type on 14 April 1838: UD 28 x 30pdrs No.1, 2 x 22cm shell; SD 26 x 30pdr carronades, 4 x 16cm shell. Her plans were based on those of *Belle Poule*.
Pallas Lorient Dyd-Caudan.
   K: 3.6.1848. Not launched as sail. Steam 1860.

REPEAT *DIDON* Class – 1st Rank frigate, 60 guns. This ship was added to the building program by a decision of 16 March 1847. Technical specifications were as the original class as designed by Paul-Marie Leroux in 1824 (above) except that she was probably designed with the armament adopted as a standard for this type on 14 April 1838 that is shown for *Pallas*, above. Her plans were based on those of *Didon*.
Guerrière Brest Dyd. (Constructeurs: Paul Leroux, Émile Courbebaisse, and others)
   K: 8.6.1848. Not launched as sail. Steam 1860.

REPEAT *ARTÉMISE* Class – 2nd Rank frigates, 50 guns. These ships were added to the building program by a decision of 16 March 1847 that followed the promulgation of a new naval program on 22 November 1846. Technical specifications were as the original class as designed by Jean-Baptiste Hubert in 1826 (above) except that they were probably designed with the armament adopted as a standard for this type on 14 April 1838 that is shown above for *Amazone*.
Circé Rochefort Dyd. (Constructeurs: Henri De Lisleferme, Auguste Boden, Albin Vidal, Jean-Félix De Robert, and Henri Denis de Senneville.)
   K: 24.4.1847. Not launched as sail. Steam 1860.
Hermione Brest Dyd. (Constructeurs: Paul Leroux and others)
   K: 10.5.1847. Not launched as sail. Steam 1860.
Junon Brest Dyd. (Constructeurs: Paul Leroux, later Joseph Fauveau and others)
   K: 27.4.1847. Not launched as sail. Steam 1861.
Flore Rochefort Dyd. (Constructeurs: Henri Denis de Senneville, Auguste Boden, Jean Baron, and Eugène De Lacalle)
   K: 26.7.1847. Not launched as sail. Steam 1869.

***AMPHITRITE* Group (1847-1849)** – 1st Rank frigates. In addition to *Guerrière* and *Pallas*, above, four first-class frigates were projected to be begun in 1847-49: *Amphitrite* at Toulon in 1847, *Melpomène* at Cherbourg and *Impérieuse* at Rochefort in 1848, and *Vénus* at Brest in 1849. On 16 March 1847 the ministry requested new plans for the three ships originally scheduled for 1847, *Guerrière*, *Pallas*, and *Amphitrite*, but eventually decided to use the plans of *Didon* and *Belle Poule* for the first two. Plans were probably never chosen for the other four, and they were cancelled in 1848 because of budget reductions following the revolution of that year. One designer proposed fitting in *Amphitrite* a steam engine of 200nhp which could develop 5kts in calm seas.
Amphitrite Toulon Dyd
   Projected in 1847 to be begun in 1847, cancelled in 1848.
Melpomène Cherbourg Dyd
   Projected in 1847 to be begun in 1848, cancelled in 1848.
Impérieuse Rochefort Dyd
   Projected in 1847 to be begun in 1848, cancelled in 1848.
Vénus Brest Dyd
   Projected in 1848 to be begun in 1849, cancelled in 1848.

(E) Screw frigates, 1st and 2nd Ranks

On 9 December 1846 the Minister of Marine ordered Lorient to develop plans for installing auxiliary screw machinery in the frigate *Vengeance* on the ways there. The frigate *Entreprenante* was substituted on 30 November 1847 and machinery of 400nhp was subsequently begun at Indret for her. Because of a design miscalculation these engines had to be reassigned to the ship of the line *Jean Bart*. By February 1847 it was also intended to fit the frigate *Persévérante* with a screw propeller, but Brest appears to have put a quick end to this idea by arguing in April 1847 that making this alteration to a ship that was practically ready for launching would be very costly.

On 9 September 1851 the Minister of Marine initiated work on plans for a new construction steam frigate that had been included in the 1852 budget. The ship was to have the operational characteristics of a 3rd Rank frigate plus full steam power capable of producing a speed of 11 knots. On 19 November 1851 the Council of Works specified that the ships would have 34 guns, engines of 500nhp, and a length not over 65 metres. On 19 March 1852 it was proposed to order six of these ships in 1852, but in March or April the Minister of Marine deleted four of these in favour of two sisters to *Napoléon* and scheduled the other two to be begun in 1853. On 27 August 1852 the two ships were named *Impétueuse* and *Foudre* and were ordered built respectively at Lorient on plans by Pierre Guieysse and at Toulon on plans by Stanislas-Charles-Henri Dupuy de Lôme. Indret was to provide the engines for both. But on 10 September 1852 a new Minister, motivated by the success of *Napoléon*'s trials, asked instead for plans for fast first-class frigates carrying 60 guns at 12 knots. After a lengthy design process the hulls of six ships were ordered on 10 October 1853.

***IMPERATRICE EUGÉNIE* Class** – 1st Rank screw frigates. Stanislas-Charles-Henri Dupuy de Lôme's plans were approved on 16 December 1853 for four new steam frigates ordered on 10 October 1853 at Toulon and Brest. The machinery of all but *Audacieuse* was ordered from Schneider by a contract approved on 24 August 1854. The ships made over 12 knots on trials, but their seakeeping qualities were poor and their rapid construction caused their service to be short.
   Dimensions & tons: 74.76m, 73.98m wl, 68.28m x 14.36m, 14.78m ext x 6.80m. 3,797 tons disp. Draught 5.78/6.88m. Men: 530.
   Machinery: 800nhp. 4 cylinders, return connecting rod, 1,950ihp, 12.5kts. Coal 640t.
   Guns: (*Imperatrice Eugénie* and *Ardente*, 1856) UD 30 x 30pdrs No.1, 6 x 22cm No.1 shell; SD 18 x 30pdrs No.3, 2 x 16cm rifles; (*Audacieuse* 1856) same but SD 18 x 30pdrs No.3, 2 x 30pdr carronades; (*Foudre* 1859) same but SD 16 x 30pdrs No.3, 4 x 30pdr carronades.
Imperatrice Eugénie Toulon Dyd/Schneider (Constructeurs: Jean-Baptiste Pironneau and others)
   Ord: 10.10.1853. K: 4.1854. L: 21.8.1856. Comm: 21.3.1857. C: 3.1857.
   Decomm. 6.12.1867. Renamed *Touraine* 19.9.1870. Engines removed 1872. Struck 8.2.1878, storage hulk. BU 1887.
Foudre Toulon Dyd/Schneider.
   Ord: 10.10.1853. K: 5.8.1854. L: 2.12.1856. Comm: 15.5.1857. C: 5.1857.
   Decomm. 1.3.1868. Prison ship for Communards at Rochefort 7.1871 to 1.1872. Struck 1.7.1872, mooring hulk at Rochefort.

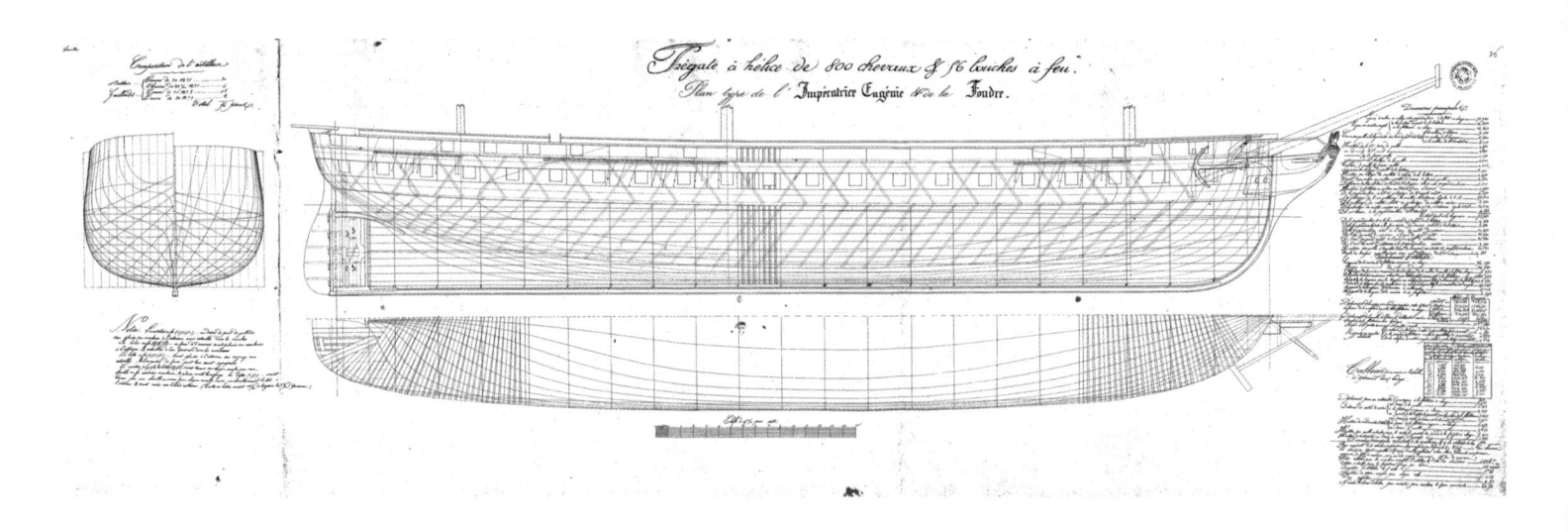

Original but undated draught of *Impératrice Eugénie* and *Foudre*, showing diagonal bracing that strengthened the long, low hull. The impression of great length is enhanced by twenty-one gunports in the lower battery, although only eighteen were armed. These 1st Rank ships were intended as the frigate equivalent of the fast battleships, and, like them, the earliest examples did not have a hoisting screw. (Atlas du Génie Maritime, Genoa collection, image 2-0025)

Renamed *Ulloa* 1891, sold 1895 for BU.
Audacieuse Brest Dyd/Mazeline (Constructeur: Gustave Alexandre Zédé)
    Ord: 10.10.1853. K: 6.6.1854. L: 22.1.1856. Comm: 3.6.1856. C: 6.1856.
    Decomm. 3.12.1864. Struck 11.4.1870. BU 1872 at Cherbourg.
Ardente Brest Dyd/Schneider (Constructeurs: Joseph Fauveau and others)
    Ord: 10.10.1853. K: 6.6.1854. L: 25.5.1857. Comm: 1.6.1858. C: 6.1858.
    Decomm. 14.10.1862 after major machinery failure. Struck 15.11.1869. BU 1871 at Brest.

IMPÉTUEUSE Class – 1st Rank screw frigates. A plan by Georges-Baptiste-François Allix was approved on 21 November 1853 for the two remaining fast steam frigates ordered on 10 October 1853. They were very similar to those designed by Dupuy de Lôme, but their lines were slightly fuller and they had hoisting screws. The machinery for these two ships and for *Audacieuse* was ordered from Mazeline by a contract approved on 8 June 1854.
    Dimensions & tons: 72.21m, 72.00m wl, 69.00m x 14.30m, 14.72m ext x 7.11m. 3,773 tons disp. Draught 6.63m mean. Men: 530.
    Machinery: 800nhp. 4 cylinders, return connecting rod, 2,228ihp, 12.04kts. Coal 520 tons.
    Guns: (*Impétueuse*, 1856) UD 30 x 30pdrs No.1, 6 x 22cm No.1 shell; SD 2 x 16cm rifles, 18 x 30pdrs No.3. SD altered by 1857 to 4 x 16cm rifles, 16 x 30pdrs No.3; (*Souveraine* 1856) UD 26 x 30pdrs No.1, 8 x 22cm No.1 shell; SD 2 x 16cm rifles, 20 x 30pdr carronades.
Impétueuse Cherbourg Dyd/Mazeline (Constructeurs: Prix-Charles Sochet and others)
    Ord: 10.10.1853. K: 20.1.1854. L: 15.8.1856. Comm: 15.11.1856. C: 12.1856.
    Decomm. 20.4.1865. Struck 3.11.1869. Hospital hulk at Cherbourg for Communard prisoners 5.1871 to 3.1872. BU 1874.
Souveraine Lorient Dyd/Mazeline (Constructeurs: Hippolyte Louis Prétot and others)
    Ord: 10.10.1853. K: 15.5.1854. L: 3.6.1856. Comm: 10.1.1857. C: 1.1857.
    Decomm. 9.2.1865. Hospital ship for prisoners at Brest 6-11.1871. Struck 24.5.1872, school hulk for seamen at Brest until 1891, also headquarters hulk from 1878. BU 1892.

The navy reverted to a smaller design for its next class of new construction steam frigates. On 20 November 1855 the Council of Works proposed specifications for second-class ships of the *Isly* type with 650nhp, a length not over 75m, and 40 guns. The proposed armament was UD 12 x 36pdrs, 12 x 22cm No.1 shell; SD 2 x 36pdrs, 2 x 22cm No.1 shell, 12 x 36pdr carronades. Plans by Achille-Antoine Guesnet were approved by the Council of Works on 23 December 1856, but construction of the still-unnamed ships was abandoned along with the *Sébastopol* class 70-gun ships of the line on 23 March 1858.

In the meantime, the navy in January 1853 examined the question of converting five 1st Rank frigates still on the ways to steam frigates without lengthening them. On 12 July 1853 the Council of Works instead selected an option that lengthened the ships amidships by five intervals between ports to provide space for powerful steam engines. Two plans were approved by the Council on 19 November 1853 but these conversions were then set aside, probably because of an emphasis on battleship conversions and the outbreak of the Crimean War.

On 12 December 1855 the Council of Works proposed specifications for converting frigates of all three ranks to either steam frigates or steam transports without lengthening the hulls. These specifications were approved by the Minister of Marine on 24 December. Second Rank frigates were to receive engines of 200nhp and crews of 440 men. Their height of battery above the water would be reduced to 1.80 metres, and their boilers would not rise above the waterline. The sailing rig would be that normally assigned to 2nd Rank frigates and the ships would carry four months of provisions. Plans for two conversions to transports were discussed by the Council of Works on 8 January 1856 and ultimately five of these conversions (four 2nd Rank and one 1st Rank) were carried out, all as auxiliary-propulsion frigates rather than transports.

RENOMMÉE – 1st Rank screw frigate. This ship was among five frigates already afloat that were selected in 1856 to receive engines of 200nhp without being lengthened. Her engines were ordered from Schneider by a contract approved on 6 June 1856. She was converted on plans by Henri De Lisleferme. The plans for the modification of her stern

THE LARGER FRIGATES

The nineteenth-century French Navy liked to have more than one design for each specification for comparative purposes, and the alternative to Dupuy de Lôme's Impératrice Eugénie *class was the* Impétueuse *design by Georges-Baptiste-François Allix, although the differences were relatively small scale.* Impétueuse, *seen here, was based at Cherbourg, and was in commission from 1856 to 1860 and again from 1862 to 1865. During these periods she spent most of her time in the Mediterranean. (Marius Bar)*

were approved by the Council of Works on 8 January 1856, plans for conversion to a transport were approved in principle on 22 July 1856, and the final frigate plans probably followed soon afterwards. Her machinery was installed between February and September 1858.
 Dimensions & tons: 57.80m, 55.60m wl, 52.32m x 14.50m ext x 7.05m. 2,650 tons disp. Draught 6.05/7.05m. Men: 498.
 Machinery: 200nhp. Trials 787ihp = 9.21kts. Coal 200t.
 Guns: (5.1859) UD 26 x 30pdrs No.1, 4 x 22cm shell; SD 2 x 50pdrs, 24 x 30pdr carronades. Soon (8-9.1859) modified to UD 24 x 30pdrs No.1; SD 2 x 16cm rifles, 24 x 30pdr carronades.
Renommée Rochefort Dyd/Schneider (converted by De Lisleferme)
 Conversion began: 1.1856. L: ?. Comm: 1.2.1858.
 Converted to a steam transport with an additional battery deck in 1.1869. Hospital ship for prisoners at Rochefort 6.1871 to 5.1872. Seagoing training ship at Brest 8.1873 to 9.1876 in place of *Jean Bart* (ex *Donauwerth*). Struck 15.11.1878, guard hulk at Brest. Replaced *Somme* as headquarters hulk at Brest 1882-97. BU 1898.

DANAÉ – 2nd Rank screw frigate. This ship was among five frigates already afloat that were selected in 1856 to receive engines of 200nhp without being lengthened. Her engines were ordered from Schneider by a contract approved on 6 June 1856. She was converted on plans by Émile Courbebaisse that were first discussed by the Council of Works on 8 January 1856 and that received final approval on 9 July 1856. She was scheduled to be drydocked in late June 1856 for hull modifications that would take about three months.
 Dimensions & tons: 60.00m, 57.36m wl, 52.15m x 13.88m ext x 7.08m. 2,438 tons disp. Draught 6.12/7.12m. Men: 388.
 Machinery: 200nhp. Coal 188 tons.
 Guns: (1858) UD 24 x 30pdrs No.2, 4 x 22cm No.2 shell; SD 2 x 16cm rifles, 8 x 16cm shell.
Danaé Brest Dyd/Schneider.
 Conversion began: 6.1856 (docked). L: 1856. Comm: 1.9.1858.
 Converted to a steam transport in 1868. Struck 18.1.1878. BU 1879 at Brest.

ZÉNOBIE – 2nd Rank screw frigate. This ship was among five frigates already afloat that were selected in 1856 to receive engines of 200nhp without being lengthened. Her engines were ordered from Schneider by a contract approved on 6 June 1856. She was converted on plans by Henri De Lisleferme that received final approval by the Council of Works on 30 December 1856. Her engines were reused in the refit of the transport *Ariège* in 1871-73.
 Dimensions & tons: 57.14m, 54.50m wl, 52.00m x 13.78m ext x 7.05m. 2,485 tons disp. Draught 6.03/6.69m. Men: 388.
 Machinery: 200nhp. 8.92kts. Coal 180t.
 Guns: (1859) UD 24 x 30pdrs No.2, 4 x 22cm No.2 shell; SD 2 x 16cm rifles, 8 x 16cm shell.
Zénobie Rochefort Dyd/Schneider.
 Conversion began: 16.10.1856. L: ?. Comm: 11.9.1859.
 Struck 7.8.1868 at Toulon, not hulked and probably BU 1868.

BELLONE – 2nd Rank screw frigate. This ship was among five frigates already afloat that were selected in 1856 to receive engines of 200nhp without being lengthened. Her engines were ordered from Schneider by a contract approved on 6 June 1856. She was converted without lengthening except for adjustments aft for the screw on plans by Marie-Pierre Carlet that were first reviewed by the Council of Works on 8 November 1856 and that received final approval on 7 April 1857.
 Dimensions & tons: 56.50m, 53.55m wl, 51.46m x 14.40m ext x 7.11m. 2,328 tons disp. Draught 5.74/6.74m. Men: 388.
 Machinery: 200nhp. trials 939ihp = 9.78kts.
 Guns: (1862) UD 24 x 30pdrs No.2, 4 x 22cm No.2 shell; SD 2 x 16cm rifles, 8 x 16cm shell.
Bellone Cherbourg Dyd/Schneider.
 Conversion began (hauled out): 26.5.1857. L: 11.8.1858. Comm: 1.8.1859.
 Struck 22.2.1877, mooring hulk at Lorient and storage for harbour defence forces. BU 1895.

PANDORE – 2nd Rank screw frigate. This ship was among five frigates already afloat that were selected in 1856 to receive engines of 200nhp without being lengthened. Machinery was ordered from Schneider for the frigate *Résolue* by a contract approved on 6 June 1856 and soon reassigned to this ship. She was converted on plans for her stern by Henri De Lisleferme that were similar to those for *Zénobie* and that were approved by the Council of Works on 1 July 1856.

    Dimensions & tons: 56.80m, 54.40m wl, 50.85m x 13.76m ext x 7.05m. 2,341 tons disp. Draught 5.94/6.94m. Men: 388.

    Machinery: 200nhp. 9.68kts.. Coal 180t.

    Guns: (1860) UD 22 x 30pdrs No.2, 4 x 22cm No.2 shell; SD 2 x 30pdrs No.1, 8 x 16cm shell.

Pandore Rochefort Dyd/Schneider.

    Conversion began: 9.11.1856. L: ?. Comm: 11.5.1859.

    Converted to a steam transport in 1868. Used as prison ship at Rochefort 5.1871 to 4.1872. Struck 2.11.1877, coal hulk. Mooring hulk at Rochefort 1889. BU 1893.

In 1856 the navy also converted four frigates that were still on the ways into screw transports. These ships, *Entreprenante* (1st Rank), *Dryade* and *Amazone* (2nd Rank), and *Cérès* (3rd Rank) were lengthened between 20 and 23 metres to accommodate engines of 250nhp (200nhp in the smaller *Cérès*) and their sides were raised to allow them to be fitted with a second enclosed battery deck. Full listings for these ships may be found in Chapter 13. They continued to be carried on the fleet lists as frigates until 7 January 1859, when the Minister of Marine decided that because of their increased size and weak engines they were unsuitable for use as frigates and would henceforth be listed with the large transports. Between December 1855 and March 1856 plans were also reviewed by the Council of Works for the conversion to transports of four other frigate hulls then on the ways, *Guerrière* (1st Rank) and *Junon*, *Hermione*, *Thémis* and *Magicienne* (2nd Rank), but these projects did not advance further.

On 15 April 1856 the Council of Works reviewed plans by Albin Vidal for the conversion of a 2nd Rank frigate on the ways, *Circé*, to a 'high speed' screw frigate, and plans by Anselme De Roussel for conversion of two more, *Thémis* and *Magicienne*, followed on 13 May 1856. Work on these plans continued through the end of 1856, but it was only in 1858 that the navy began nine such conversions of 1st and 2nd Rank frigate hulls. The ships were given full steam power and were lengthened substantially (by 20 to 25 metres) to accommodate large steam engines. The resulting ships slightly exceeded the length of the *Imperatrice Eugénie* type but had 600 instead of 800 nominal horsepower machinery. The engines for eight of the conversions were ordered in June 1858, in most cases well before the plans for the modified hulls received final approval, and the engines for the ninth (*Sémiramis*) were ordered in October 1858.

PALLAS – 1st Rank screw frigate. This ship was among nine frigates still on the ways that were selected in 1858 to be lengthened to receive large engines of 600nhp. Her engines were ordered from Schneider by a contract approved on 4 June 1858. She was lengthened by 22.05m on the ways and converted on plans completed by Guillaume Masson in late 1858. In 1878 she was assigned 4 Hotchkiss machine guns, 2 towing torpedoes, and 2 torpedo launches.

    Dimensions & tons: 77.80m, 76.95m wl, 73.46m x 14.56m ext x 6.91m. 3,618 tons disp. Draught 5.74/6.86m. Men: 466.

    Machinery: 600nhp. 2 cylinders, return connecting rod, trials 1427ihp = 11.74kts. Coal 420t.

    Guns: (1862) UD 30 x 16cm M1858 MLR; SD 4 x 16cm M1858 MLR.

Pallas Lorient Dyd-Caudan/Schneider.

    Conversion began: 1859. L: 15.8.1860. C: 8.1861. Comm: 1.12.1861.

    Struck 23.10.1883, mooring hulk at Rochefort. Sold or BU 1910.

VICTOIRE – 1st Rank screw frigate. This ship was among nine frigates still on the ways that were selected in 1858 to be lengthened to receive large engines of 600nhp. Her engines were ordered from Schneider by a contract approved on 4 June 1858. She was lengthened by about 22m on the ways and converted on plans completed by Guillaume Masson in late 1858. In 1878 she was assigned 2 Hotchkiss machine guns, 2 towing torpedoes, and 2 torpedo launches.

    Dimensions & tons: 77.16m, 76.31m wl, 72.82m x 14.44m ext x 7.13m. 3,582 tons disp. Draught 6.56m mean. Men: 466.

    Machinery: 600nhp. 2 cylinders, return connecting rod, trials 1349ihp = 10.93kts. Coal 362 tons.

    Guns: (1863) UD 8 x 30pdrs No.1, 22 x 16cm rifles; SD 4 x 16cm rifles.

Victoire Lorient Dyd-Caudan/Schneider.

    Conversion began: 6.1859. L: 21.8.1861. Comm: 1.8.1862. C: 12.1863.

    Struck 13.2.1880 at Brest. BU 1882.

GUERRIÈRE – 1st Rank screw frigate. This ship was among nine frigates still on the ways that were selected in 1858 to be lengthened to receive large engines of 600nhp. Her engines were ordered from Schneider by a contract approved on 4 June 1858. She was lengthened by about 22.5m on the ways and converted on plans by Émile Courbebaisse that were approved by the Council of Works on 4 May 1858 with modifications by Jean-Félix De Robert approved on 21 December 1858.

    Dimensions & tons: 78.10m, 77.00m wl, 72.80m x 14.56m ext x 6.96m. 3,597 tons disp. Draught 5.98/7.08m. Men: 466.

    Machinery: 600nhp. 2 cylinders, return connecting rod, 12.3kts. Coal 478t.

    Guns: (1861) UD 30 x 16cm M1858 MLR; SD 4 x 16cm M1858 MLR.

Guerrière Brest Dyd/Schneider (converted by Courbebaisse and others)

    Conversion began: 4.2.1859. L: 3.5.1860. Comm: 18.9.1860. C: 9.1860.

    Converted to a 1,300-ton steam transport at Lorient 1868-69 with an additional battery deck. Struck 28.5.1888, barracks hulk at Toulon. BU 1912.

SÉMIRAMIS – 1st Rank screw frigate. On 19 May 1857 the Council of Works considered plans by Henri De Lisleferme for the conversion of this sail frigate on the ways at Rochefort to a transport, probably with 250nhp engines to be built at Rochefort, but this project was not pursued. On 27 January 1858 the Minister informed Rochefort that *Sémiramis* was to be converted by lengthening into a fast frigate of 600nhp, and after a decision in March not to build her engines at Rochefort her engines were added by a supplement approved on 11 October 1858 to a contract with Schneider of 4 June 1858 for five other 600nhp frigate engines. She was lengthened by 20.94m on the ways and converted on plans by Henri De Lisleferme and Alfred Lebelin de Dionne that were completed in late 1858.

    Dimensions & tons: 77.33m, 75.05m wl, 71.35m x 14.50m ext x 6.92m. 3,830 tons disp. Draught 6.08/6.98m. Men: 466.

    Machinery: 600nhp. 2 cylinders, return connecting rod, trials 1664ihp = 12.1kts. Coal 500t.

    Guns: (1864) UD 30 x 16cm rifles; SD 4 x 16cm rifles.

Sémiramis Rochefort Dyd/Schneider (converted by De Lisleferme and Lebelin de Dionne)

    Conversion began: 1859. L: 8.8.1861. Comm: 16.12.1861. C:

Thémis was a 2nd Rank frigate lengthened and converted to steam during construction. The ship was based at Toulon for nearly her entire active career, which ended in 1882. After 1875 she was armed with twelve 16cm rifles in the battery and six more on the gaillards. (USN NH-74985, from an ONI album of French warships)

6.1862.

Struck 3.5.1877, headquarters hulk at Landévennec near Brest, BU 1895. Replaced successively by the frigate *Magicienne*, the cruiser *Aréthuse*, and the station battleship *Victorieuse*, all of which assumed her name.

MAGICIENNE Class – 2nd Rank screw frigates. These ships were among nine frigates still on the ways that were selected in 1858 to be lengthened to receive large engines of 600nhp. Their engines were ordered from the Forges et Chantiers de la Méditerranée by a contract approved on 4 June 1858. They were lengthened by about 22m on the ways and converted on plans by Anselme De Roussel. The Council of Works approved these plans on 26 January 1858 but with the recommendation that, because of the vulnerability of their machinery, the ships should be used in wartime as transports and in peacetime as station cruisers with a reduced armament. Installation of their machinery was completed in September 1862 and May 1863 respectively.

Dimensions & tons: 75.69m, 74.36m wl, 69.76m x 14.40m ext x 7.06m. 3,408 tons disp. Draught 6.38m mean. Men: 415.
Machinery: 600nhp. 2 cylinders, trials (*Thémis*) 1611ihp = 11.0kts. Coal 450 tons.
Guns: (*Magicienne*, 1862) UD 24 x 16cm M1858 MLR; SD 4 x 16cm M1858 MLR; (*Thémis* 1865) UD 24 x 16cm rifles; SD 4 x 16cm rifles.

Magicienne Toulon Dyd/FCM (converted by Hyacinthe De Coppier)
Conversion began: 10.1859. L: 26.12.1861. Comm: 8.1.1862. C: 9.1862.
Struck 19.4.1886. Replaced *Pomone* as a barracks hulk and reserve headquarters ship at Brest. In 1895 replaced *Sémiramis* as headquarters hulk at Landevennec and assumed that ship's name. Replaced by *Aréthuse* 1899 and reverted to *Magicienne*, sold for BU 1900.

Thémis Toulon Dyd/FCM. (converted by Hyacinthe De Coppier)
Conversion began: 1858. L: 29.4.1862. Comm: 21.11.1862. C: 12.1862.
Struck 7.11.1882, mooring and storage hulk at Lorient. Sold 1930, burned in Lorient harbour 1.7.1931.

HERMIONE Class – 2nd Rank screw frigates. These ships were among nine frigates still on the ways that were selected in 1858 to be lengthened to receive large engines of 600nhp. Their engines were ordered from Schneider by a contract approved on 4 June 1858. They were lengthened by about 25m on the ways and converted on plans by Émile Courbebaisse that were approved by the Council of Works on 4 May 1858 with modifications by Gustave Zédé approved on 12 December 1858. Zédé's plans reproduced the forward and amidships arrangements of Courbebaisse but added two metres aft. The armament given them in 1861 was found to be too heavy and was subsequently reduced.

Dimensions & tons: 78.75m, 78.30m wl, 73.66m x 13.88m ext x 7.05m. 3,550 tons disp. Draught 6.12/7.28m. Men: 415.
Machinery: 600nhp. 2 cylinders, return connecting rod, trials 12.3kts (*Hermione*), 11.60kts (*Junon*). Coal 500t.
Guns: (Both 1861) UD 24 x 16cm M1858 MLR; SD 4 x 16cm M1858 MLR.

Hermione Brest Dyd/Schneider.
Conversion began: 16.4.1859. L: 15.8.1860. Comm: 1.12.1860. C: 12.1860.
Converted to a steam transport with two battery decks 1868. Struck 11.5.1877, school hulk for mechanics at Toulon. BU 1892.

Junon Brest Dyd/Schneider.
Conversion began: 1859. L: 28.1.1861. Comm: 16.4.1861. C:

Flore at Algiers, probably near the end of her service between 1876 and 1884 as the seagoing training ship for the *École d'Application* based at Brest. In 1883 she had eighteen 14cm rifles in the battery amidships (barely visible on this image) and four more on the gaillards including a prominent chase gun forward. (USN NH-74800, from an ONI album of French warships)

4.1861.

Struck 24.3.1872, barracks hulk at Saigon to 1874. BU 1876.

ASTRÉE – 2nd Rank screw frigate. This ship was among nine frigates still on the ways that were selected in 1858 to be lengthened to receive large engines of 600nhp. Her engines were ordered from the Forges et Chantiers de la Méditerranée by a contract approved on 4 June 1858. She was lengthened by about 24m on the ways and converted on plans by Louis Sollier. Installation of her machinery was completed in December 1860.

Dimensions & tons: 77.58m, 76.58m wl, 73.73m x 14.04m, 14.40m ext x 7.03m. 3,564 tons disp. Draught 6.36m mean. Men: 415.
Machinery: 600nhp. 2 cylinders, trials 1411ihp = 11.21kts. Coal 464t.
Guns: (1865) UD 24 x 16cm rifles; SD 4 x 16cm rifles.

Astrée Lorient Dyd-Caudan/FCM (converted by Sollier)
Conversion began: 1859. L: 24.12.1859. Comm: 9.3.1860. C: 12.1860.
Struck 3.5.1877, barracks and storage hulk at Lorient. Renamed *Ponton No.2* in 1913 to free name for a new submarine. Sold or BU 1922.

CIRCÉ Class – 2nd Rank screw frigates. In March 1858 these two sailing frigates on the ways at Rochefort were each allocated half of a 4-cylinder 900nhp engine built there for the ship of the line *Intrépide*. Plans by Charles-Marie Brun for dividing the engine (originally designed by Victorin Sabattier) were approved by the Council of Works on 30 March 1858, and plans by Albin Vidal for converting the ships, initially reviewed in April 1858, were approved on 28 September 1858. They were lengthened by about 22m on the ways.

Dimensions & tons: 75.75m (*Flore* 76.05m) deck, 74.60m wl, 70.00m x 13.40m, 13.84m ext x 6.97m. 3,136 tons disp. Draught 6.20m mean. Men: 415.
Machinery: 480nhp. 2-cylinder trunk, trials (*Flore*) 1465ihp = 12.49kts. Coal 377t.
Guns: (*Circé*, 1866) UD 12 x 30pdrs No.1, 14 x 16cm rifles; SD 4 x 30pdrs No.1; (*Flore* 1870) UD 12 x 16cm M1864-6 BLR; SD 4 x 16cm M1864-6 BLR.

Circé Rochefort Dyd/Rochefort (converted by Vidal and others)
Conversion began: 1858?. L: 15.10.1860. Comm: 12.11.1862. C: 11.1862.
Struck 22.7.1872, hulk at Brest. BU 1875.

Flore Rochefort Dyd/Rochefort (converted by Vidal, Jean Baron, and others)
Conversion began: 1860. L: 27.2.1869. Comm: 12.1869.
Designated in June 1876 to replace *Renommée* as seagoing training ship at Brest and so served from 9.1876 to 1884. Struck 18.10.1886, headquarters hulk of the Maritime Prefect at Brest 1888, also a school for seamanship 1892. Sold for BU 1901.

On 1 June 1860 the *Moniteur de la Flotte* reported in its unofficial section that a 1st Rank steam frigate to be called *Ville de Nice* was to be laid down at Brest. No mention of this ship has been found in official French Navy records.

5 The Smaller Frigates

(8-, 12-, and 18-pounder Frigates)
(3rd Rank from 1824)

This chapter covers those frigates with a principal battery of 12pdr guns and (separately) those with a principal battery of 18pdr guns; these are preceded by the small group of surviving frigates with batteries of 8pdr guns. The majority of frigates built for France before 1786 had been armed with a main battery of 8-pounder or 12-pounder guns, but construction was increasingly concentrated on the heavier 18-pounder armed frigates, although the 12-pounder types continued to be built until well into the Revolutionary War.

This distinction by caibre is more significant than the actual number of carriage guns, although the 8pdr and 12pdr types with few exceptions mounted an UD battery of 26 guns (with a standard secondary armament on the gaillards of 6 guns of 4pdr and 6pdr calibre respectively), while most 18pdr types mounted an UD battery of 28 guns (with a secondary armament on the gaillards of 12 guns raising the total to 40 guns). However there were exceptions, notable after the introduction of 36pdr obusiers (and later of carronades).

French frigates were not as heavily built as their British equivalents, with lighter scantlings and more space between deck beams and frame timbers, as well as a weaker system of fastening. Largely this reflected a different strategic analysis in the two navies. French cruising vessels were not intended to spend so much time at sea, and they had relatively fewer cabins, platforms in the hold, storerooms and magazines. They could carry fewer provisions and the messing (eating) facilities were comparatively poorer. A consequence of this type of construction was that new French frigates were significantly faster, but the more lightly they were built, the more rapidly their hulls would distort through sea service (by hogging, sagging or racking) with resultant reduction in their seagoing advantages.

At the start of 1785 there were 74 frigates on the official List (excluding hulked vessels), but this included the ex-British prizes *Guadeloupe* and *Barboude* (see following pages) and fifteen others actually rated as 20-gun vessels (corvettes). Of the remaining 57, eight frigates were 18pdr-armed, 42 frigates mounted 12pdrs, three carried British 9pdr guns (all prizes taken from the British – *Active*, *Ariel* and *Crescent*) and four carried 8pdrs.

8-pounder frigates

(A) Vessels in service or on order at 1 January 1785

The heyday of the 8pdr frigate had been between the 1740s and the 1760s, with only one pair being built subsequently as production centred on 12pdr vessels. No further 8pdr types had been built at all after the *Alcmène* and *Aimable* of 1773-76, both of which had been captured by the British during the American War, and thereafter their role was taken over by the 8pdr-armed corvettes (see next chapter); by 1786 the only remaining 8pdr frigates were a motley collection of older vessels, mostly reduced to harbour service. As no further frigates of this rating were acquired, this part of the chapter therefore is not divided into sections but only gives brief details of the vessels remaining in 1786 and of construction plans from the mid-1760s. Of those on the List at the start of 1786, the *Aigrette* was based at Brest and the *Flore*, *Mignonne* and *Pleiade* were based at Toulon.

PLEIADE. 32 guns. A single ship built to a one-off design by Joseph Coulomb, ordered in 1752 and named on 7 January 1753; this was the oldest frigate in the French Navy in 1786 (although she was refitted several times during her 30 years of service), and was sold later that year.
    Dimensions & tons: 120ft 0in, 105ft 0in x 29ft 10in x 15ft 10in (38.98, 34.11 x 9.69 x 5.14m). 478/860 tons. Draught 13ft 4in/14ft 8in (4.33/4.76m). Men: 187-234.
    Guns: UD 26 x 8pdrs; SD 6 x 4pdrs (later).
Pleiade Toulon Dyd.
    K: 4.1754. L: 17.11.1755. C: 4.1756.
    Condemned and struck at Toulon in 7.1786, and sold to BU.

BLONDE Class. 32 guns. The *Aigrette* was the sole survivor of this class of frigates, all five built at Le Havre just before the Seven Years War to a design by Jean-Joseph Ginoux. Of her sisters, the *Brune*, *Vestale* and *Felicité* had been lost in 1761 (although *Vestale* later re-entered the French Navy in 1785 as the 12pdr-armed *Flore Américaine* – see later in this chapter) and the *Blonde* in 1782. The survivor had been refitted at Rochefort in 1767. The performance of these vessels proved mediocre, leading to post-war orders being transferred to Brest.
    Dimensions & tons: 127ft 0in, 113ft 0in x 32ft 0in x 16ft 0in (41.25, 36.71 x 10.39 x 5.20m). 480/880 tons. Draught 13ft 2in/13ft 8in (4.28/4.44m). Men: 154-253.
    Guns: UD 26 x 8pdrs; SD 6 x 4pdrs.
Aigrette Le Havre
    K: 9.1755. L: 3.1756. C: 7.1756.
    Condemned and struck at Brest 10.1789.

To recover from losses incurred during the Seven Years War, a substantial program of frigate replacement was ordered in 1765-66. An order for the first unit was placed at Toulon in August 1765 (see *Mignonne* below), and a second (*Étoile*) in January 1766; two larger frigates were ordered at the same shipyard in February 1766 (*Coquette* and *Fine*), to be laid down in 1769, but were cancelled unstarted during 1769. Two more 8pdr frigates to a Deslauriers design (*Oiseau* and *Nymphe*) were ordered in 1766 at Bayonne, but the orders were moved to Rochefort in 1767; *Oiseau* was taken by the British at the end of January 1779, while *Nymphe* was never built. Another pair (*Amour* and *Psyché*) were ordered in the same year from Jean-Hyacinthe Raffeau at Nantes, but the orders were transferred to Brest in February 1767, and then cancelled in 1769. Two more were originally ordered from Ginoux at Le Havre in October 1766 (*Flore* and *Zephyr*), but the orders were shifted to Brest in December (see below).

MIGNONNE. 30 (later 32) guns. A single ship built to a one-off design by Jean-Baptiste Doumet-Revest. Ordered on 5 August 1765 and originally named as *Précieuse* on 31 March 1766, her name was changed to *Mignonne* on 16 February 1767. A second ship was ordered in January 1766 (named *Étoile*), with a slightly altered plan approved on 31 May, but was cancelled in 1767.

Dimensions & tons: 120ft 0in, 108ft 0in x 32ft 0in x 15ft 9in (38.98, 35.08 x 10.39 x 5.12m). 500/880 tons. Draught 13ft/14ft (4.22/4.55m). Men: 157-200.

Guns: UD 26 x 8pdrs; SD 4 x 4pdrs (6 x 4pdrs from 1789).

Mignonne Toulon Dyd. (Constructeur, Claude Saussillon)
K: 10.1765. L: 26.4.1767. C: 7.1768.
Raséed to a corvette at Toulon in 1793, but captured (in poor condition) by Adm. Hood's squadron at the surrender of Calvi on 10.8.1794, becoming HMS *Mignonne*; burnt 7.1797 at Port-Ferrajo.

FLORE. 32 guns. This frigate, along with the *Zephyr*, was originally ordered to a Ginoux design at Le Havre in October 1766, but the orders were moved to Brest in December, where *Flore* was built to a one-off design by Antoine Groignard, and named on 9 November (the *Zephyr* was built to a similar design by Joseph-Louis Ollivier, but was burnt by accident in 1779). She undertook an extended scientific research voyage in 1771-72 to Africa, the Caribbean and Northern Europe (Jean-Charles de Borda, the later co-architect with Sané of the 1786 naval modernisation program, was aboard to evaluate the latest advances in chronometers). A modified version of this Groignard design was finally used for the last pair of 8pdr frigates – the *Alcmène* and *Aimable* built by Jean-Baptiste Doumet-Revest at Toulon – but both had been captured in 1779 and 1782 respectively.

Dimensions & tons: 126ft 0in, 117ft 0in x 32ft 6in x 16ft 4in (40.93, 38.01 x 10.56 x 5.31m). 540/950 tons. Draught 13ft 5in/14ft 0in (4.36/4.55m). Men: 174-230.

Guns: UD 26 x 8pdrs; SD 6 x 4pdrs (later).

Flore Brest Dyd.
K: 2.1768. L: 11.11.1768. C: 1769.
Condemned at Toulon in 1785, struck and sold in 1787.

Ex BRITISH PRIZES (1778-1783). While no further 8pdr frigates were built for the French Navy after 1776, nine British Sixth Rates (with 9pdr British guns) were captured during the American War. All retained their original names in French service, except that the *Unicorn* was renamed *Licorne*. Of these the *Fox* was wrecked and the *Sphinx* was retaken by the British in 1779, while the *Unicorn* and *Lively* were retaken in 1781, but the other five – three re-armed with French 8pdrs – remained in the French Navy until 1786, although *Guadeloupe* was reduced to 20 guns (usually rated a corvette). These are listed below, with measurements in French units.

ENTERPRIZE Class. 28 guns, designed by John Williams in 1770. Twenty-seven 28-gun frigates to this design were built of which the *Fox* had been captured in 1778 and *Crescent* was taken by *Friponne* on 19.6.1781. The *Fox* had been lost in March 1779, and *Crescent* would be wrecked in 1786.

Dimensions & tons: 116ft 0in, 104ft 0in x 31ft 6in x 17ft 0in (37.68, 33.78 x 10.23 x 5.52m). 450/850 tons. Draught 14ft/15ft (4.55/4.87m). Men: 210 (war) 130 (peace).

Guns: UD 24 x 9pdrs; SD 4 x 3pdrs. By 1784 *Crescent*'s SD guns had been replaced by 2 x 2 French 6pdrs.

Crescent James Martin Hillhouse, Bristol.
K: 19.8.1777. L: 3.1779. C: 30.6.1779 at Plymouth Dyd.
Wrecked at Petite-Goave (San Domingo) 1.1786.

COVENTRY Class. 28 guns, designed by Thomas Slade in 1756. Eighteen 28-gun frigates to this design were built (including five built of fir instead of oak) of which three – all oak-built – were captured by the French in 1778, 1781 and 1783.

Dimensions & tons: 116ft 0in, 100ft 0in x 31ft 8in x 15ft 0in (37.68, 32.48 x 10.29 x 4.87m). 450/850 tons. Draught 13ft 6in/15ft 4in (4.39/4.98m). Men: 210 (war) 130 (peace).

Guns (from 1780): UD 24 x 9pdrs; SD 4 x 6pdrs + 6 x 18pdr carronades (British); from 1783 *Guadeloupe* had UD 20 x 8pdrs, SD 6 x 4pdrs; from 1793 *Active* had UD 24 x 8pdrs, SD 4 x 4pdrs.

Active Thomas Stanton, Rotherhithe
K: 13.6.1757. L: 11.1.1758. C: 2.3.1758 (at Deptford Dyd).
Captured by *Charmante* and *Dédaigneuse* off San Domingo 1.9.1778. Condemned 11.1794 at Brest and BU 1795.

Guadeloupe Plymouth Dyd
K: 8.5.1759. L: 5.12.1763. C: 11.7.1764 (at Plymouth Dyd).
Scuttled in the York River, Virginia 10.10.1781, but salved by the French and entered their service 4.1783 after repairs; struck at Rochefort 1786.

Coventry Henry Adams, Buckler's Hard
K: 31.5.1756. L: 30.5.1757. C: 31.7.1757 (at Portsmouth Dyd).
Captured by Suffren's squadron off Ganjam in the Bay of Bengal 12.1.1783. Disarmed at Brest 1.1785 and BU 1786.

SPHINX Class. 20 guns, designed by John Williams in 1773. Ten 20-gun post ships were built to this design, of which three were captured by the French in 1779-80, but the *Sphinx* had been retaken in December 1779 and the *Unicorn* in April 1781.

Dimensions & tons: 105ft 0in, 93ft 0in x 28ft 2in x 11ft 0in (34.11, 30.21 x 9.15 x 3.57m). 350/650 tons. Draught 13ft 0in/14ft 6in (4.22/4.71m). Men: 210 (war) 130 (peace).

Guns: UD 20 x 9pdrs (British); in French service 2 x 4pdrs and 4 x 3pdrs were mounted on the gaillards.

Ariel John Perry, Blackwall
K: 7.1776. L: 7.7.1777. C: 12.8.1777 (at Woolwich Dyd).
Captured by *Amazone* off Georgia 10.9.1779. Lent to the US and served John Paul Jones as USS *Ariel* between Oct 1780 and June 1781, when the US returned her to French control. Burnt on the Schelt in 3.1793.

There was additionally an even smaller 'frigate' armed with 6pdr guns, the former British sloop *Barbuda* (a prize – originally the *Charming Sally*, taken from the Americans in 1780) which was captured by the French on 23 January 1782 and became the French *Barboude*; of just 320 tons and carrying 16 x 6pdrs (UD) and 6 x 4pdrs, she was struck at Brest in 1786 and sold, becoming the privateer *Inabordable*; however she was re-acquired by the navy at Le Havre in May 1793 and was renamed *Légère* in June 1793, but was wrecked at Cherbourg in December.

12-pounder frigates

(A) Vessels in service or on order at 1 January 1785

Only four 12pdr-armed frigates had been built for the navy in France before or during the Seven Years War (two in 1748-50 – Pierre Morineau's 26-gun *Hermione* at Rochefort and Joseph Chapelle's 24-gun *Gracieuse* at Toulon – and two larger in 1756-58 – Ginoux's *Danaë* and *Hébé* at Le Havre), while one building at Toulon as a privateer was acquired on the stocks in 1757 – *Chimère*. All five had been lost or discarded before 1786. However nineteen had been built in the five years following the armistice in 1762, of which the six below were still in existence in 1786. Of the others, the *Terpsichore* of 1763 and the larger

Renommée of 1767 (the only Brest-built 12pdr frigate of this decade) were BU in 1783, although both these Groignard-designed vessels nominally remained on the List at the start of 1785 (rated as 30-gun frigates), while the two modified *Boudeuse* class built at Indret (see below), all six of the *Infidèle* class built at Le Havre and three of the four *Dédaigneuse* class at Bordeaux were gone before 1786.

Of those on the 1785 List, all were formally rated at 26 guns with 220 or 240 men in wartime and 150 in peace, but under the new regulations from 1 January 1786 they were raised to 270 men in wartime and 188 in peacetime, while 6 x 6pdr on the gaillards became a standard addition, although in practice this minimum ordnance was increased by several extra 6pdrs and by 36pdr obusiers.

SULTANE. 32 (originally 26) guns, designed by Jean-Baptiste Doumet-Revest. Refitted at Toulon 1783-84, but relegated to a floating hospital 9.1792 and possibly renamed *Victoire* or *Victorieuse* c7.1793.
    Dimensions & tons: 130ft 0in x 34ft 0in x 17ft 4in (42.23 x 11.04 x 5.63m). 650/1,100 tons. Draught 14/15ft (4.55/4.87m). Men: 220 (war) 150 (peace); as 32-gun ships 250 (later 287).
    Guns: UD 26 x 12pdrs; SD 6 x 6pdrs.
Sultane Toulon Dyd. (Constructeur, Coulomb)
    K: 3.1764. Named 16.4.1764. L: 28.6.1765. C: 3.1766.
    Handed over to the British at Toulon on 29.8.1793 and burnt on evacuation of that port on 18.12.1793.

BOUDEUSE. 32 (originally 26) guns, designed by Jean-Hyacinthe Raffeau. Under Louis-Antoine de Bougainville, this frigate completed France's first circumnavigation of the world between 15 November 1766 and 16 March 1769 (accompanied by the flûte *Étoile*). Refitted at Brest 1775-76.

Rafeau had subsequently also built two further frigates at Indret in 1766-67 as lengthened (130ft) versions of the *Boudeuse* design, with a 14th pair of 12pdrs, but both ships were converted to flûtes at Brest in April 1780; the *Sensible* was hulked in 1783 and the *Indiscrète* condemned in 1784.
    Dimensions & tons: 125ft 0in, 118ft 0in x 32ft 8in x 16ft 6in (40.60, 38.33 x 10.61 x 5.36m). 580/1,030 tons. Draught 13ft 5in/13ft 10in (4.36/4.49m). Men: 240 (war, later 250) 150 (peace).
    Guns: UD 26 x 12pdrs; SD 6 x 6pdrs (2 x 36pdr obusiers added in 1794).
Boudeuse Indret
    K: 5.1765. Named 6.6.1765. L: 25.3.1766. C: 10.1766.
    Arrived at Valetta with supplies for the beleaguered and famished French garrison 4.2.1799 (dodging the British blockade). Condemned at Valletta 7.1800 and BU to provide firewood for Maltese bakeries.

DÉDAIGNEUSE Class. 32 (originally 26) guns, designed by Léon-Michel Guignace. Of the original four ships, all built at the Chantier du Roi at Bordeaux, the *Belle Poule* was taken by the British in 1780, the *Dédaigneuse* was sold in 1784, and the *Tourterelle* was also struck in 1784. The survivor, *Amphitrite*, was originally named as *Impérieuse* on 21 March 1766 but was renamed while building in February 1767.
    Dimensions & tons: 132ft 6in, 119ft 0in x 34ft 6in x 17ft 6in (43.04, 38.66 x 11.21 x 5.68m). 620/1,150 tons. Draught 14/15ft (4.55/4.87m). Men: 192-220 (later 260).
    Guns: UD 26 x 12pdrs; SD 6 x 6pdrs.
Amphitrite Bordeaux
    K: 11.1766. L: 26.10.1768. C: 9.1769.
    Wrecked either on 21.1.1791 or 30.4.1791 off the coast of Brittany.

ENGAGEANTE. 32 (originally 26) guns, designed by Jean-François Etienne, ordered on 18 August 1765 and named on 28 March 1766. Refitted at Rochefort 1779-80. An intended sister was ordered at Toulon in February 1766 (likewise to have been built by Joseph Chapelle), and was named as *Coquette* on 31 March, but was cancelled in 1769.
    Dimensions & tons: 134ft 0in, 120ft 0in x 35ft 5in x 17ft 10in (43.53, 38.98 x 11.50 x 5.79m). 600/1,010 tons. Draught 13½/14½ft (4.39/4.71m). Men: 190 (later 250).
    Guns: UD 26 x 12pdrs; SD 6 x 6pdrs (4 x 36pdr obusiers added in 1794).
Engageante Toulon Dyd. (Constructeur, Joseph Chapelle)
    K: 10.1765. L: 14.11.1766. C: 4.1768.
    Captured by HMS *Concord* in the Channel on 23.4.1794, becoming HMS *Engageante*; hospital ship 7.1794; BU at Plymouth 5.1811.

AURORE. 32 (originally 26) guns, designed by Jean-Denis Chevillard. Ordered in early 1766 and named *Envieuse* on 31 March, but renamed *Aurore* in February 1767. Refitted at Toulon 1777-78 and 1784-85.
    Dimensions & tons: 128ft 0in x 33ft 4in x 17ft 0in (41.58 x 10.83 x 5.52m). 600/1,100 tons. Draught 14ft 5in/15ft 4in (4.68/4.98m). Men: 190 (later 250).
    Guns: UD 26 x 12pdrs; SD 6 x 6pdrs.
Aurore Rochefort Dyd.
    K: 9.1766. L: 23.11.1768. C: 1769.
    Handed over to the British at Toulon on 29.8.1793 and removed by them on evacuation of that port on 18.12.1793, becoming HMS *Aurora*; hulked as prison ship at Gibraltar 1799, and BU there in 1803.

ATALANTE. 32 guns, designed by Jacques-Luc Coulomb as a modified (broadened) version of his *Chimère* of 1758.
    Dimensions & tons: 137ft 0in, 122ft 0in x 35ft 7in x 17ft 11in (44.50, 39.63 x 11.56 x 5.82m). 611/1,140 tons. Draught 13½/14½ft (4.39/4.71m). Men: 225 (later 260).
    Guns: UD 26 x 12pdrs; SD 6 x 6pdrs.
Atalante Toulon Dyd.
    K: 4.1767. L: 1.5.1768. C: 3.1769.
    Captured by HMS *Swiftsure* off Cork on 6.5.1794, becoming HMS *Espion*; floating battery 1798, then troop transport 1799; wrecked on the Goodwins 16.11.1799.

After 1768, no further frigates were built for the French Navy until after the death of Louis XV in 1774 (except the two 'super-frigates' of the *Pourvoyeuse* class, designed for 24pdrs but completed with 18pdrs, and the final pair of 8pdr frigates, which had gone before 1786). A new series of 12pdr frigates, built to designs from several contributors, began in early 1777. As most of the later ships survived until 1786, it is convenient from this point to list all construction.

CHARMANTE Class. 32 guns, Jean-Denis Chevillard design. Two ships were built in 1777 at Rochefort, although both *Charmante* and *Junon* had been wrecked in 1780. The design was revived in 1785 when three more were built at Rochefort (see below).

NYMPHE Class. 32 guns, Pierre-Augustin Lamothe design. All three built at Brest (*Astrée* was first intended to be built at St. Malo). The lead ship to this design – *Nymphe* (built 1777) – had been captured by the British in 1780.
    Dimensions & tons: 135ft 0in, 119ft 0in x 34ft 6in x 17ft 6in (43.85, 38.65 x 11.21 x 5.68m). 600/1,100 tons. Draught 15¾/16½ft (5.12/5.36m). Men: 290.

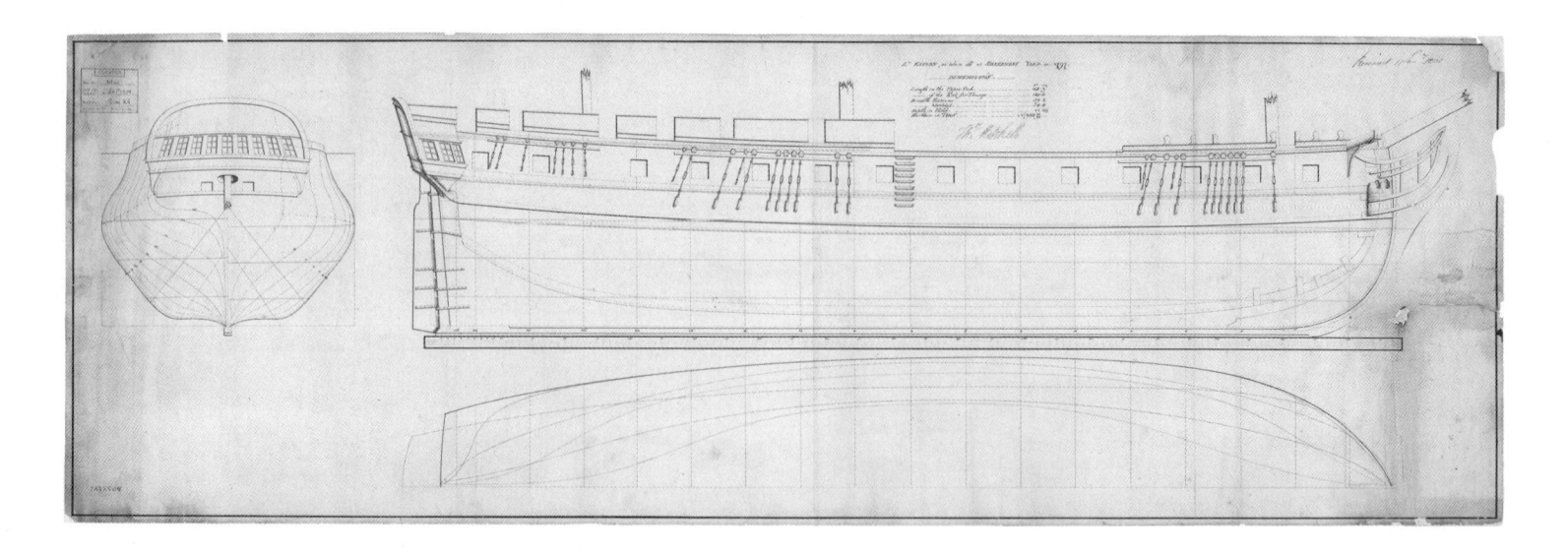

Admiralty draught of *Espion* (ex *Atalante*) as taken off at Sheerness in 1797, with quarterdeck barricades modified for carronades (the larger ports between the shrouds). The midship section is typical of French frigate design in the mid-eighteenth century, with hollow garboards and exaggerated 'two-turn' bilge, combined with extreme tumblehome above the waterline. The basic concept persisted in many frigate designs into the Napoleonic era but the midship section tended to become less extreme, the lines filling out and becoming more rounded. (© National Maritime Museum J5316)

Guns: UD 26 x 12pdrs; SD 6 x 6pdrs.
Andromaque Brest Dyd.
  Named 29.9.1777. K: 8.1777. L: 24.12.1777. C: 4.1778.
  Run ashore to avoid capture by Warren's squadron 22.8.1796 and burnt.
Astrée Brest Dyd.
  Named 4.12.1778. K: 8.1779. L: 16.5.1780. C: 7.1780.
  Lost 5.1795 in the Atlantic, cause unknown.

SIBYLLE Class. 32 guns, Jacques-Noël Sané design. The lead ship to this design – *Sibylle* (built in Brest 1777) – had been captured by the British in 1783; a second ship – *Diane* (built in St. Malo 1779) – had been wrecked in 1780.
  Dimensions & tons: 135ft 2in, 120ft 6in x 34ft 6in x 17ft 6in (43.91, 39.14 x 11.21 x 5.68m). 600/1,080 tons. Draught 14½/16½ft (4.71/5.36m). Men: 270.
  Guns: UD 26 x 12pdrs; SD 6 x 6pdrs.
Néréïde Saint-Malo (Constructeur, Geoffroy)
  K: 10.1778. L: 31.5.1779. C: 8.1779.
  Taken by HMS *Phoebe* off the Isles of Scilly 20.12.1797, becoming HMS *Nereide*. Recaptured 28.8.1810 by Duperré's squadron at the Battle of Grand Port, Île de France, but retaken by the British 4.12.1810 in the capitulation of Île de France and sold there for BU 1.3.1816.
Fine Nantes (Constructeur, Jean-Jacques Maistral)
  K: 10.1778. L: 11.8.1779. C: 10.1779.
  Wrecked 3.1794 in Chesapeake Bay.
Émeraude Nantes (Constructeur, Jean-Jacques Maistral)
  K: 12.1778. L: 25.10.1779. C: 12.1779.
  Condemned 1797 at Brest and BU.

CONCORDE Class. 32 guns, Henri Chevillard design, with three ships all built at Rochefort. The lead ship to this design – *Concorde* (built in 1777) – had been captured by the British in 1783.

  Dimensions & tons: 136ft 0in, 111ft 6in x 34ft 6in x 17ft 8in (44.18, 36.22 x 11.21 x 5.74m). 550/1,100 tons. Draught 13½/14¾ft (4.38/4.79m). Men: 280-300.
  Guns: UD 26 x 12pdrs; SD 6 x 6pdrs.
Courageuse Rochefort Dyd.
  K: 9.1777. L: 28.2.1778. C: 4.1778.
  Taken by HMS *Centaur* off Toulon 18.6.1799, becoming HMS *Courageux* (note change in gender!), used as prison or receiving ship at Malta; BU 1802.
Hermione Rochefort Dyd.
  K: 3.1778. L: 28.4.1779. C: 6.1779.
  Sailed 21.3.1780 from Rochefort (with General Gilbert du Motier, Marquis de Lafayette, aboard) to Boston, arriving 28.4.1780; a replica of this ship departed Île d'Aix for America on 18.4.2015, 235 years later. Wrecked 20.9.1793 near the Pointe du Croisic by a coastal pilot while escorting a convoy from the Loire to Brest.

FORTUNÉE Class. 32 guns, a one-off design by Pierre-Alexandre Forfait. The sole ship to this design – *Fortunée* (built at Brest 1777) – had been captured by the British in 1779.

IPHIGÉNIE Class. 32 guns, Léon-Michel Guignace design. Two ships built at Lorient and seven (by contract) at St. Malo. One ship to this design – *Prudente* (built at St. Malo 1778) – had been captured by the British at San Domingo on 22 June 1779.
  Dimensions & tons: 134ft 0in, ?120ft 0in x 34ft 6in x 17ft 6in (43.53, 38.98 x 11.21 x 5.68m). 620/1,150 tons. Draught 14/15ft (4.55/4.87m). Men: 270-290.
  Guns: UD 26 x 12pdrs; SD 6 x 6pdrs.
Iphigénie Lorient Dyd.
  K: 2.1777. L: 16.10.1777. C: 3.1778.
  Captured by the British at Toulon 29.8.1793, burnt at evacuation of Toulon 12.1793 but recovered by France and repaired. Captured by Spanish squadron 10.2.1795.
Surveillante Lorient Dyd.
  K: 8.1777. L: 26.3.1778. C: 5.1778.
  Lost in Bantry Bay during expedition to Ireland 1.1797.
Résolue Lemarchand, Saint-Malo
  K: 4.1777. L: 16.3.1778. C: 4.1778.
  Seized off Tellicherry by HMS *Phoenix* and *Perseverance* 11.1791, but restored to France. Captured by HMS *Melampus* in the Irish Sea 14.10.1798, becoming HMS *Resolue* but never commissioned (used

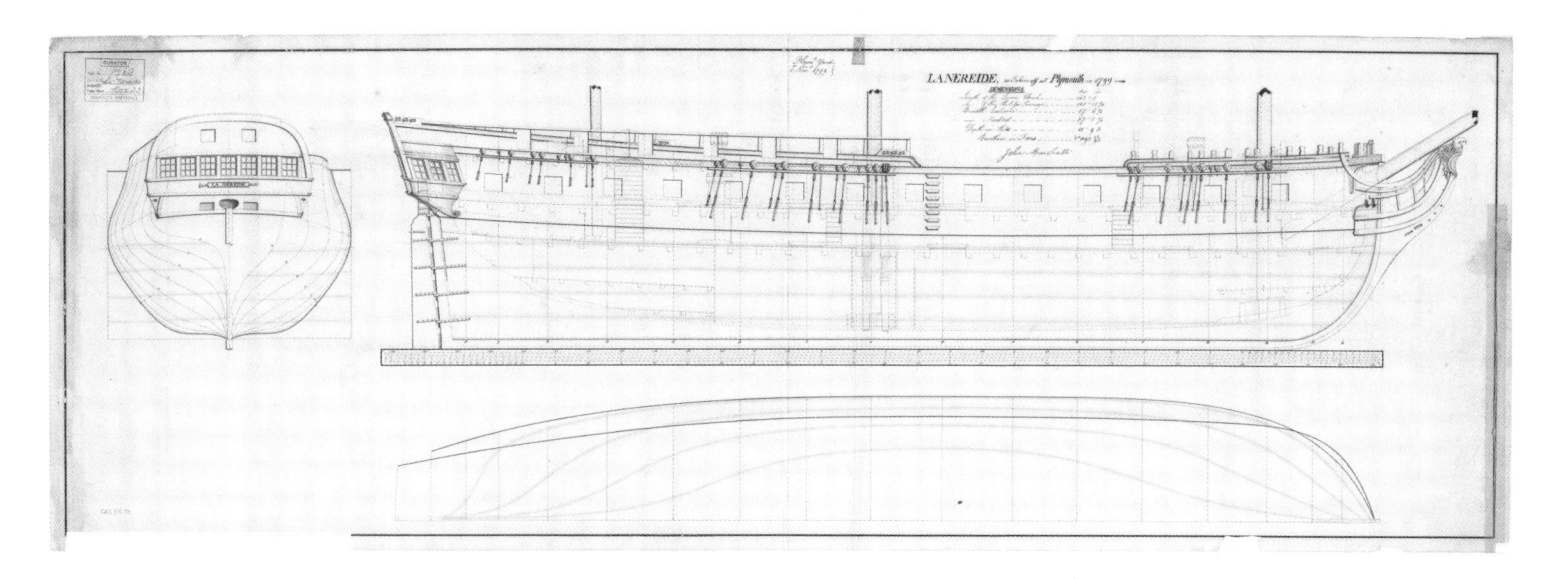

Admiralty draught of *Nereide* as taken off at Plymouth, dated 8 November 1799. Although the quarterdeck rails have been altered to Royal Navy practice, the ship still has French capstans, pumps and a republican figurehead with its Cap of Liberty. The design of this *Sibylle* class ship was an early example of the work of Jacques-Noël Sané, who was to dominate French naval architecture for a generation, although for this class he followed the prevailing style of hull form. (© National Maritime Museum J5485)

as receiving ship); BU at Portsmouth 8.1811

Gentille Saint-Malo
  K: 7.1777. L: 18.6.1778. C: 8.1778.
  Captured by HMS *Hannibal* in the Channel 11.4.1795, becoming HMS *Gentille*. Sold 9.1802 at Portsmouth.

Amazone Saint-Malo
  K: 8.1777. L: 11.5.1778. C: 7.1778.
  Captured by HMS *Santa Margarita* 28.7.1782, but retaken next day; wrecked 1.1797 on the Penmarchs.

Gloire Saint-Malo
  K: 1.1778. L: 9.7.1778. C: 1.10.1778.
  Captured by HMS *Astraea* in the Channel 10.4.1795, becoming HMS *Gloire*. Sold 24.3.1802 at Deptford.

Bellone Saint-Malo
  K: 1.1778. L: 22.8.1778. C: 2.1779.
  Captured by HMS *Melampus* and *Ethalion* in the Irish Sea 12.10.1798, becoming HMS *Proserpine*; sold 27.8.1806.

Médée Saint-Malo
  K: 1.1778. L: 20.9.1778. C: 2.1779.
  Captured by HEICo *Exeter* and *Bombay Castle* off Rio de Janeiro 4.7.1800, becoming HMS *Medee* but never commissioned (used as prison ship); sold 1805.

MAGICIENNE Class. 32 guns, Joseph-Marie-Blaise Coulomb design. Seven ships were built to this design at Toulon, the first two being ordered on 7 February 1777; of this pair the *Magicienne* (built 1778) was captured by HMS *Chatham* off Boston on 2 July 1781. A further five ships were built at Toulon from 1785 on (see Section B).
  Dimensions & tons: 136ft 0in, 119ft 0in x 34ft 6in x 17ft 10in (44.18, 38.66 x 11.21 x 5.79m). 600/1,100 tons. Draught 15/16ft (4.87/5.20m). Men: 265-285.
  Guns: UD 26 x 12pdrs; SD 6 x 6pdrs.

Précieuse Toulon Dyd.
  Ord: 7.2.1777, named 9.5.1777. K: 6.8.1777. L: 22.8.1778. C: 11.1778.
  Condemned 10.1814 and BU 1816 at Brest.

Sérieuse Toulon Dyd.
  Ord: 28.8.1778, named 4.12.1778. K: 3.1779. L: 28.8.1779. C: 10.1779.
  Sunk by Nelson's fleet at Aboukir Bay 1.8.1798.

Lutine Toulon Dyd.
  Ord: 23.10.1778, named 4.12.1778. K: 3.1779. L: 11.9.1779. C: 11.1779.
  Handed over to the British at Toulon 29.8.1793, becoming HMS *Lutine*; wrecked in the Frisian Islands 9.10.1799.

Vestale Toulon Dyd.
  Ord: 20.4.1780, named 16.6.1780. K: 5.1780. L: 14.10.1780. C: 2.1781.
  Captured by HMS *Terpsichore* off Cadiz 12.12.1796, but retaken same day by her own crew; taken again by HMS *Clyde* off Bordeaux 19.8.1799 but not added to British Navy.

Alceste Toulon Dyd.
  Ord: 20.4.1780, named 16.6.1780. K: 5.1780. L: 28.10.1780. C: 2.1781.
  Captured by the British at Toulon 29.8.1793, and transferred to the Sardinian Navy, but retaken by *Boudeuse* 10.6.1794; taken again by HMS *Bellona* off Toulon 18.6.1799, becoming HMS *Alceste*; sold at Sheerness 20.5.1802.

Iris Toulon Dyd.
  K: 5.1781. L: 29.10.1781. C: 2.1782.
  Captured by the British at Toulon 29.8.1793, burnt at evacuation of Toulon 12.1793.

CÉRÈS Class. 32 guns, designed by Charles-Étienne Bombelle. Similar to Chevillard's *Concorde* class of 1777.
  Dimensions & tons: 136ft 0in, 123ft 0in x 34ft 6in x 17ft 6in (44.18, 39.96 x 11.21 x 5.72m). 564/1,100 tons. Draught 13ft 9in/15ft 4in (4.47/4.98m). Men: 270.
  Guns: UD 26 x 12pdrs; SD 6 x 6pdrs.

Cérès Rochefort Dyd.
  K: 5.1779. L: 24.11.1779. C: 1.1780.
  Struck at Rochefort 7.1787 and BU there.

Fée Rochefort Dyd.
  K: 5.1779. L: 19.4.1780. C: 7.1780.
  Struck at Rochefort 5.1789 and BU there 1790.

GALATÉE Class. 32 guns, designed by Raymond-Antoine Haran. The

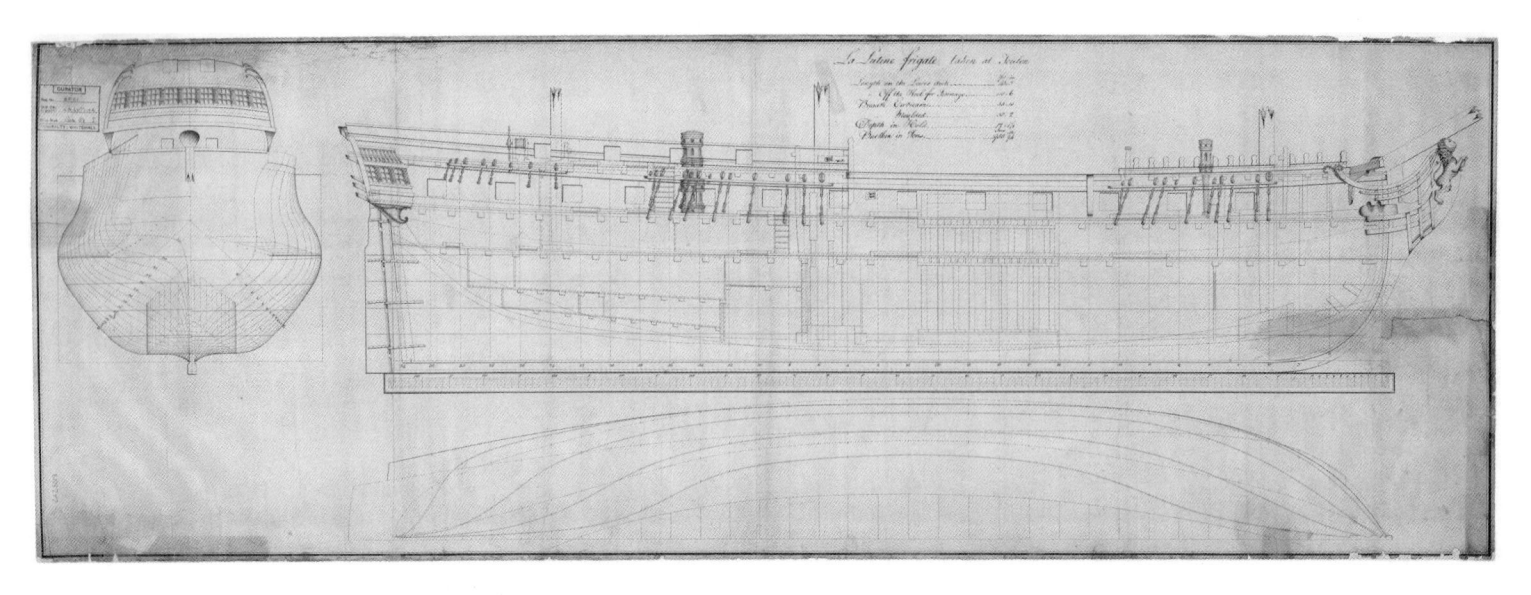

Admiralty draught of *Lutine* as captured at Toulon. Although undated, the draught shows the original French fittings and decorations, including the support structure for a bomb bed in the hold for one or two mortars that were added in September 1792. When the ship was wrecked in 1799, her bell was recovered and now hangs in the Lloyd's building, where it is still rung to announce important news. (© National Maritime Museum J5937)

third unit was ordered in early 1782 and named on 13 April 1782. Three more were built during the Revolutionary era (see below).

Dimensions & tons: 137ft 0in, 124ft 0in x 34ft 6in x 17ft 6in (44.50, 40.28 x 11.21 x 5.72m). 600/1,150 tons. Draught 14ft 8in/16ft (4.76/5.20m). Men: 220 (war) 150 (peace); later 280, then 322.
Guns: UD 26 x 12pdrs; SD 6 x 6pdrs.

Railleuse Bordeaux
K: 11.1777. L: 11.8.1779. C: 2.1780.
Refitted 1783 at Rochefort. Struck 1797 at Rochefort, and sold 17.1.1798 becoming privateer *Égyptienne*; as such, she was badly mauled on 23.3.1804 in action against HMS *Osprey* off Barbadoes, and four days later was captured by HMS *Hippomenes*; she became the prison ship HMS *Antigua* at that island, BU 1816.

Galatée Rochefort Dyd.
K: 3.1778. L: 28.6.1779. C: 9.1779.
Wrecked 23.4.1795 on the Penmarchs.

Fleur de Lys Rochefort Dyd.
K: 1.1783. L: 2.12.1785. C: 1786.
Renamed *Pique* 6.1792. Captured by HMS *Blanche* off Guadeloupe 6.1.1795, becoming HMS *Pique*; lost in action off the Penmarchs 30.6.1798.

CAPRICIEUSE Class. 32 guns, designed by Charles Segondat-Duvernet. These ships had 14 pairs of UD gunports, but usually carried only 26 x 12pdrs, although *Friponne* carried 28 x 12pdrs from 1788. Two ships were ordered in 1778; a third (*Danaë*) was modified while building to carry 18pdrs instead of 12pdrs, and appears in that section, but in early 1794 was re-armed at Brest with 12pdrs. The lead ship to this design – original *Capricieuse* (built in Lorient 1779) – had been captured by the British in 1780, and a second ship to this name and to the same design was launched in 1786: see Section (B) for details. While built at Lorient, the *Friponne* was based at Toulon.

Dimensions & tons: 136ft 0in x 34ft 6in x 17ft 6in (44.18 x 11.21 x 5.68m). 600/1,100 tons. Draught unknown. Men: 220 (war) 150 (peace); later 270.
Guns: UD 26 x 12pdrs; SD 6 x 6pdrs, 2 x 36pdr obusiers. *Friponne* had 16 x 6pdrs from 1788 to 1794.

Admiralty draught of *Pique* as taken off at Portsmouth, dated 23 February 1797. The ship has received a substantial refit for British service, although the French capstans have been retained. (© National Maritime Museum J5451)

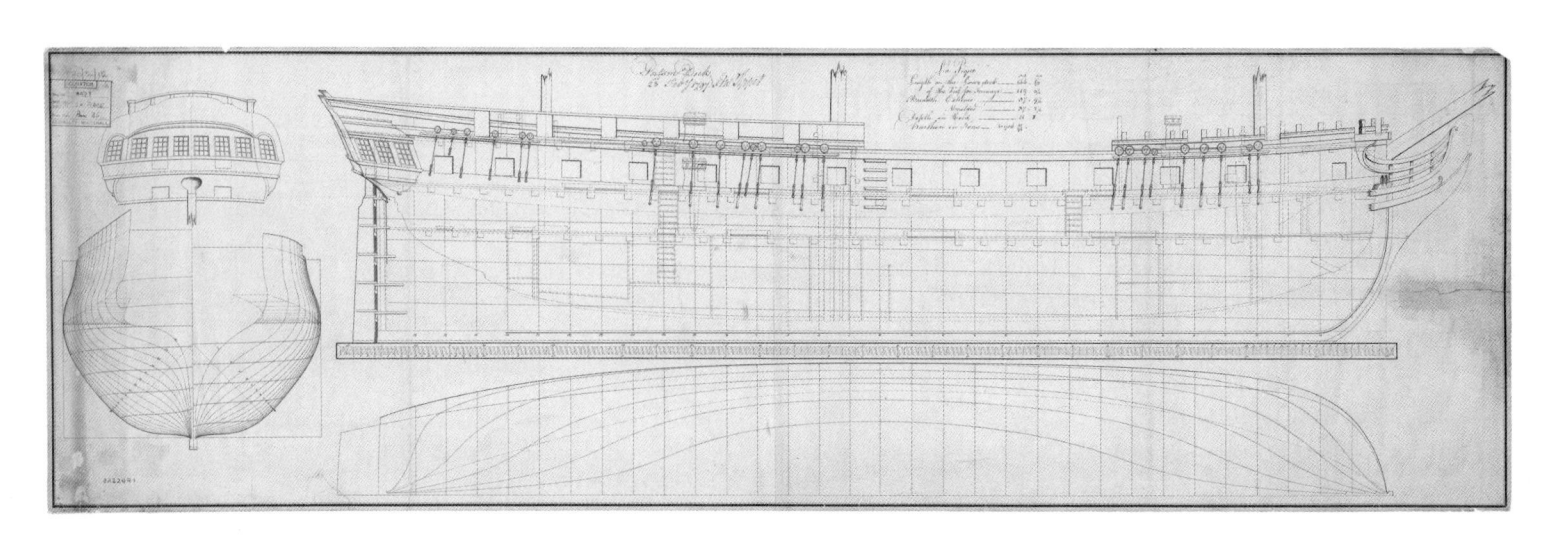

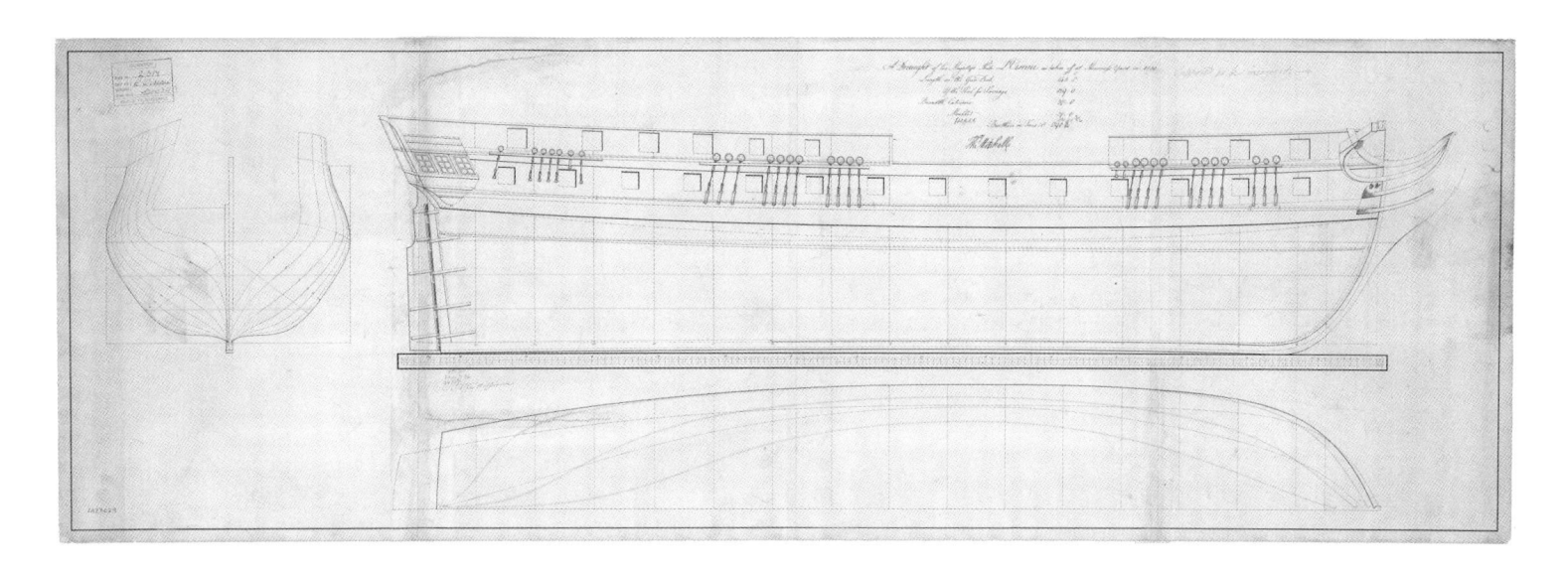

Friponne Lorient Dyd.
K: 12.1778. Named 4.12.1778. L: 20.3.1780. C: 6.1780.
Handed over to the Anglo-Spanish forces at Toulon in 8.1793, but restored to France in 12.1793. Struck at Brest 12.1796.

VÉNUS Class. 32 guns, designed by Jacques-Noël Sané. While only carrying 13 pairs of 12pdrs, these ships had 14 pairs of UD gunports. The lead ship to this design – *Vénus* (built at St. Malo in 1777-79) – had been wrecked in 1781. From May 1783 to 1793, the *Cléopâtre* carried 18pdrs (loaded at Trincomalee) *vice* 12pdrs.
  Dimensions & tons: 137ft 11in, 124ft 0in x 34ft 7in x 17ft 9in (44.80, 40.28 x 11.23 x 5.77m). 600/1,082 tons. Draught 15/16ft (4.87/5.20m). Men: 220 (war) 150 (peace); later 270.
  Guns: UD 26 x 12pdrs; SD 6 x 6pdrs (10 x 6pdrs in 1793).
Cléopâtre Benjamin Dubois, Saint-Malo (Constructeur, Geoffroy)
  K: 1780. L: 19.8.1781. C: 12.1781.
  Captured off Guernsey by HMS *Nymphe* 19.6.1793, becoming HMS *Oiseau*; prison hulk 1810, then sold 18.9.1816 to BU.

At least two more 12pdr frigates were ordered in 1782. The *Favorite* was begun at Rochefort in March 1783, and was 1/8 built when cancelled in June 1783. Another frigate, possibly to have been named *Cybèle*, was ordered built by contract by Deslandes at Granville in January 1782, but was cancelled in February 1783.

Ex BRITISH PRIZES (1778-1781). Four British Fifth Rates (with 12pdr British guns) were captured during the American War. The original names of three were slightly changed in French hands, with *Minerva* being altered to *Minerve*, *Montreal* to *Montréal*, and *Richmond* (probably) to *Richemont*. Of these the *Minerve* was retaken by the British in 1781, while the fourth frigate – the *Iris*, originally the American *Hancock* – was sold in 1784. The other two frigates –re-armed with French 12pdrs, and listed as 26-gun frigates (the French normally excluded SD guns from the official count) – remained in the French Navy until 1793, and are listed below, with measurements in French units.

NIGER Class. 32 guns, designed by Thomas Slade in 1757. Ten 32-gun frigates to this design were built, including the *Montreal* captured by the French in 1779.
  Dimensions & tons: 121ft 0in, 106ft 0in x 33ft 0in x 15ft 9in (39.31, 34.43 x 10.72 x 5.12m). 550/1,000 tons. Draught 14/16½ft (4.55/5.36m). Men: 220 (war) 150 (peace).
  Guns: UD 26 x 12pdrs; SD 6 x 6pdrs.
Montréal Sheerness Dyd
  K: 26.4.1760. L: 15.9.1761. C: 10.10.1761.
  Captured by *Bourgogne* and *Victoire* off Gibraltar 1.5.1779; powder hulk at Toulon 8.1793, handed over to Anglo-Spanish forces and burnt 18.12.1793 on the evacuation of Toulon.

RICHMOND Class. 32 guns, designed by William Bately in 1756. Six 32-gun frigates to this design were built, including the prototype captured by the French in 1781 (and the *Thames* captured in 1793 – see Section B).
  Dimensions & tons: 123ft 6in, 105ft 9in x 32ft 2in x 17ft 0in (40.12, 34.35 x 10.45 x 5.52m). 550/1,000 tons. Draught 14/15ft (4.55/4.87m). Men: 220 (war) 150 (peace).
  Guns: UD 26 x 12pdrs; SD 6 x 6pdrs.
Richemont John Buxton, Deptford
  K: 4.1756. L: 12.11.1757. C: 7.12.1757.
  Captured by *Bourgogne* and *Aigrette* in the Chesapeake 11.9.1781; burnt at Sardinia 19.5.1793 to avoid capture by the Spanish Navy.

FLORE AMÉRICAINE. 32 guns. This purchased vessel was originally the French 8pdr-armed frigate *Vestale* of 1756 (see beginning of this chapter) which had been captured in early 1761 by the British and re-armed with a 12pdr main battery. She was scuttled and partly burnt at the evacuation of Rhode Island on 5 August 1778 to prevent her capture by the French, but was refloated by the Americans in early 1783, repaired and brought to Bordeaux, where the French Navy repurchased her in September 1784.
  Dimensions & tons: 126ft 6in, 113ft 0in x 32ft 2in x 16ft 4in (41.09, 36.71 x 10.45 x 5.31m). 411/900 tons. Draught 14/15ft (4.55/4.87m). Men: 181-184 (254 in 1793-95).
  Guns (1784): UD 26 x 12pdrs; SD 6 x 6pdrs. The 12pdrs were replaced by 26 x 8pdrs in 1788. When re-acquired in 1793, she

Admiralty draught of *Oiseau* (ex *Cléopâtre*) as taken off at Sheerness in 1800. The dimensions on this minimally detailed sheer plan vary somewhat from those recorded in official Navy Lists and the draught may have been made carelessly or in a hurry. It shows the ship after a major refit; the original appearance would have been very similar to *Nereide* reproduced earlier, as this Sané design was virtually a repeat of his *Sibylle* class. (© National Maritime Museum J5938)

was re-armed with 26 x 8pdrs and 8 x 6pdrs.

Flore Americaine Le Havre
K: 9.1755. L: 3.1756. C: 7.1756.

Captured by HMS *Unicorn* off the Penmarchs on 8.1.1761 and renamed *Flora*. Repurchased 9.1784 from the Americans as *Flore Américaine* (there already being an 8pdr-armed *Flore* in French service – see earlier page). Refitted 1-5.1786. Renamed *Flore* 1787, re-rated as a corvette 1788 and re-armed with 8pdr guns again. Struck and hulked at Rochefort 2.1789, being disarmed in 1791. Sold 4.7.1792, renamed *Citoyenne Française* 4.1793 and commissioned as a Bordeaux privateer in 5.1793. Requisitioned by the French Navy in 8.1793 but returned to former owners in 12.1795 and resumed her career as a privateer. Captured as *Flore* by HMS *Anson* and *Phaeton* in the Channel 6.9.1798 but not added to the RN.

(B) Vessels acquired from 1 January 1785

While for most types of warships construction under the influence of Borda and Sané commenced in 1786, Castries took earlier action to renovate the vital frigate fleet, and orders for new frigates were placed from early 1785, albeit some of these as repeats of earlier designs. The 1786 Program for new construction envisaged the building of sixty new frigates, of which forty would carry 12pdrs in their battery and twenty would carry 18pdrs. The complements were raised to 270 men in wartime and 188 in peacetime, while 6 x 6pdrs on the gaillards became a standard addition, although in practice this minimum ordnance was increased by several extra 6pdrs and by 36pdr obusiers.

FÉLICITÉ Class. 32 guns. Design by Pierre-Alexandre Forfait, as approved by Léon-Michel Guignace. This was the first post-war design to be built, but was probably very similar to Forfait's earlier *Fortunée* of 1777, which had been lost to the British in 1779. They carried 19,209 sq.ft of sail. Although only 6 x 6pdr guns were carried on the gaillards, there were ports for 14 guns there.

Dimensions & tons: 136ft 0in, 119ft 0in x 34ft 8in x 17ft 9in (44.18, 38.66 x 11.26 x 5.77m) 600/1,140 tons. Draught 16ft 2in / 17ft 4in (5.25/5.63m). Men: 270 in wartime/188 in peacetime; included 6 officers.

Guns: UD 26 x 12pdrs; SD 6 x 6pdrs.

Félicité Brest Dyd.
K: 1.1.1785. L: 4.8.1785. C: 28.8.1785.

Captured by HMS *Latona* and *Cherub* in the Caribbean 18.6.1809; sold to Haitian King Christophe 7.1809, becoming Haitian *Amethyste*; taken by Haitian rebels 1811 and renamed *Heureuse Revolution*; captured again by HMS *Southampton* 3.2.1812, resuming original name, then returned to Christophe's government as *Amethyste*; sold 1818.

Calypso Brest Dyd.
K: 4.7.1785. L: 2.12.1785. C: 1.1786.

Her Royalist crew 'emigrated' (i.e. defected) in her to Trinidad and handed her over to the Spaniards there in 1.1793.

Fidèle Le Havre.
K: 10.1788. L: 22.8.1789. C: 9.1789.

Condemned 10.1802 at Brest, hulked 5.1804, powder hulk 5.1805, last mentioned 6.1813.

Fortunée Le Havre.
K: 5.12.1789. L: 28.9.1791. C: 5.1792.

Burned 2.1794 to avoid capture by the British in the loss of Saint-Florent (San Fiorenzo), Corsica.

PROSÉLYTE. 32 guns. A one-off design by the Marquis Charles-Louis du Crest.

Dimensions & tons: 138ft 0in x 36ft 0in x 15ft 9in (44.83 x 11.69 x 5.12m) 672/1,100 tons. Draught 13ft 4in / 15ft 2in (4.33/4.93m). Men: 270 in wartime/188 in peacetime; included 6 officers.

Guns: UD 26 x 12pdrs; SD 6 x 6pdrs.

Prosélyte Le Havre.
K: 2.1785. L: 2.1786. C: 6.1786.

Captured by the British Navy at the surrender of Toulon 29.8.1793 and commissioned there 12.1793, becoming HMS *Proselyte* (as a floating battery); destroyed in attack on Bastia 11.4.1794.

MAGICIENNE Class. 32 guns. Five further ships to this Joseph-Marie-Blaise Coulomb design of 1777 were built at Toulon from 1785

Admiralty draught of *Modeste* as taken off at Deptford, dated 2 April 1800. Following her capture in 1793, the ship had been laid up as soon as she reached a British port, so despite the passage of time this draught shows her original appearance as taken – she was about to be converted to a troopship so presumably the Navy Board wanted a record of the design. (© National Maritime Museum J5684)

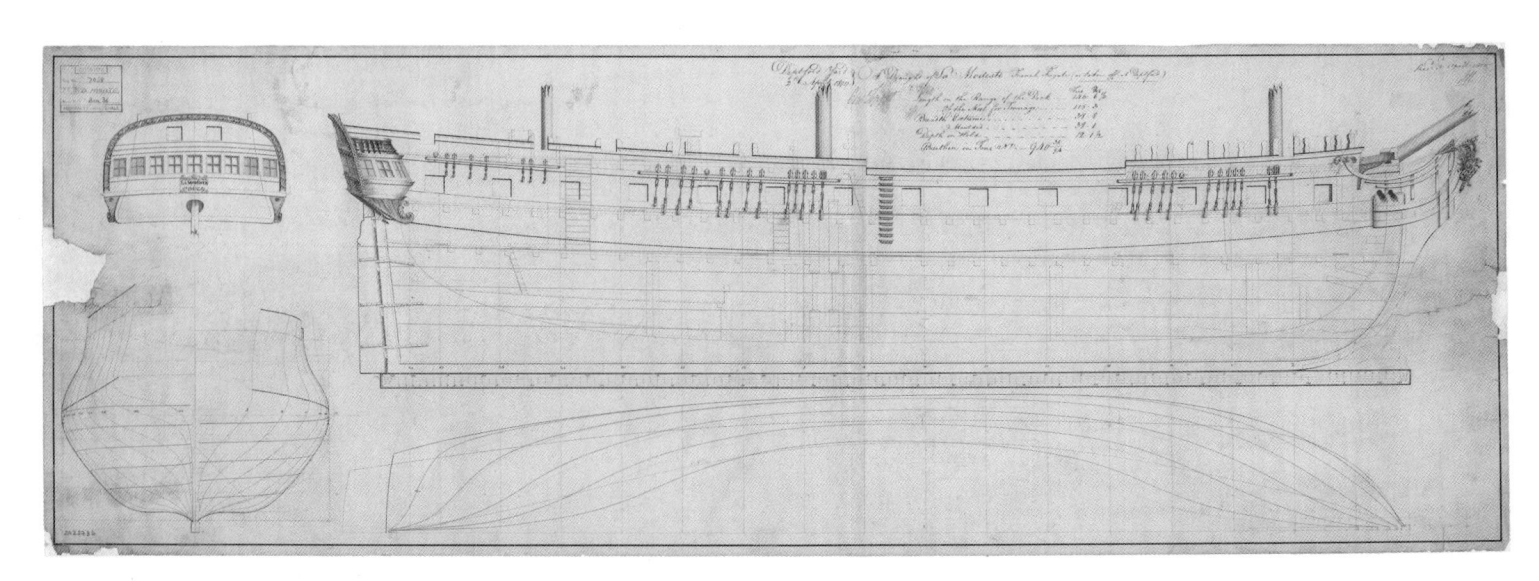

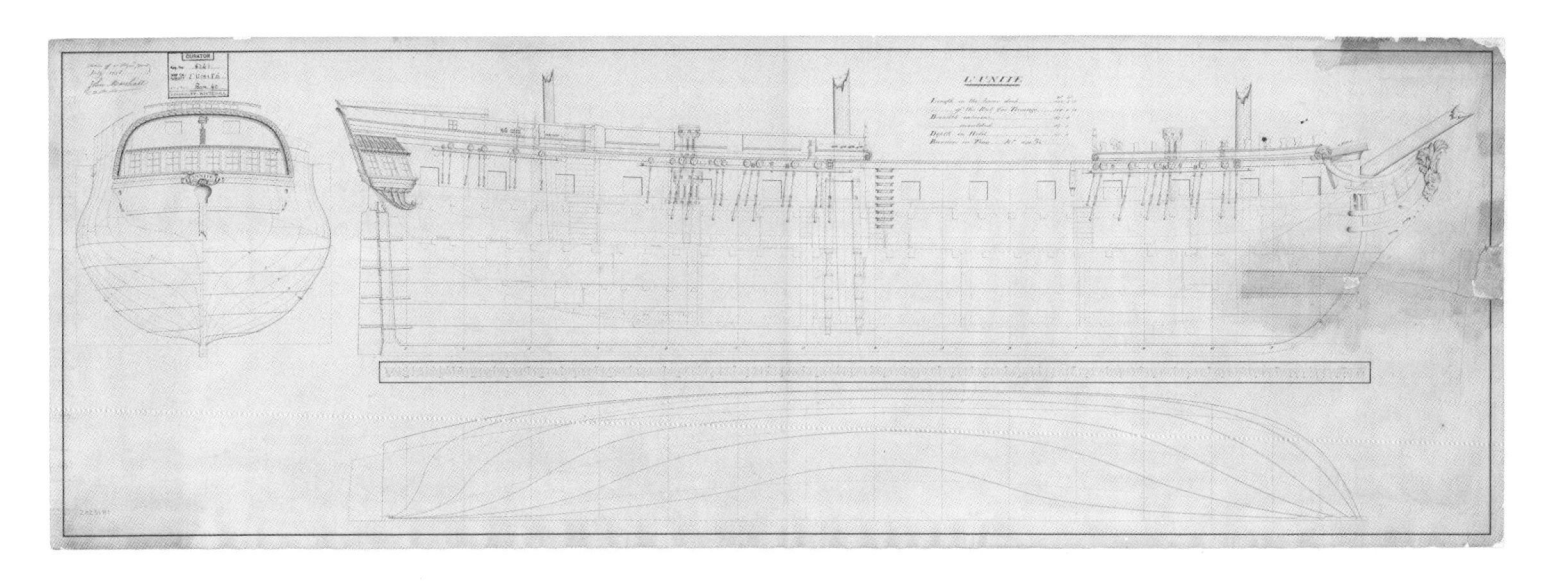

on – see Section (A) for details.
Réunion Toulon Dyd.
K: 2.1785. L: 23.2.1786. C: 1.1787.
Captured by HMS *Crescent* off Barfleur 20.10.1793, becoming HMS *Reunion*; wrecked in the Swin 7.12.1796.
Modeste Toulon Dyd.
K: 2.1785. L: 18.3.1786. C: 1.1787.
Captured by HMS *Bedford* and *Captain* at Genoa 7.10.1793, becoming HMS *Modeste*. Re-armed in British service with 26 x 18pdrs *vice* 12pdrs. To Trinity House 1803-5. BU 6.1814 at Deptford.
Sensible Toulon Dyd.
Named 23.1.1786. K: 2.1786. L: 9.8.1787. C: 3.1788.
Captured by HMS *Seahorse* off Sicily 27.6.1798, becoming HMS *Sensible* (troopship); grounded off Mullaitivu north of Trincomalee 3.3.1802.
Topaze Toulon Dyd.
Named 14.3.1789. K: 2.1789. L: 26.9.1790. C: 2.1781.
Handed over to the British at Toulon 29.8.1793, becoming HMS *Topaze*; sold 1.9.1814 at Portsmouth.
Artémise Toulon Dyd.
K: 12.1791. L: 25.9.1794. C: 11.1794.
Captured on the stocks by the British at Toulon 29.8.1793, but recovered at the evacuation in 12.1793. Named *Aurore* 24.7.1794, then *Artémise* at launch. Sunk to avoid capture by Nelson's fleet at Aboukir Bay 2.8.1798.

CAPRICIEUSE Class. 32 guns. Further ships to this Segondat-Duvernet design of 1778; see Section (A) for details; the original *Capricieuse* had been lost in 1780, and a replacement of the same name was ordered in 1785; another was ordered on 31 January 1789 at Lorient, and named on 14 March.
Capricieuse Lorient Dyd.
K: 9.1785. Named 28.1.1786. L: 20.11.1786. C: 9.1787.
Wrecked 10.1788 but salved and repaired. Renamed *Charente* 28.9.1793. Wrecked 1.1800 off Lorient.
Prudente Lorient Dyd.
K: 5.1789. L: 21.9.1790. C: 10.1790.
Wrecked late 1799 (date uncertain).

CHARMANTE Class. 32 guns. Design by Jean-Denis Chevillard. The lead ships to this design, *Charmante* and *Junon* (both built at Rochefort in

Admiralty draught of *Unite* (ex *Gracieuse*) taken off at Plymouth Yard, July 1796, which preserves the detail of the ship as captured, right down to the republican imagery on the taffrail – the *fasces*, a Roman symbol of authority (later adopted by Fascist parties of the 1930s) and a *bonnet rouge*, the so-called Cap of Liberty widely worn during the French Revolution. Notice the small poop cabin, or dunette, carried by some French frigates; this was usually removed before any prize frigate entered British service. (© National Maritime Museum J6091)

1777-78) had both been wrecked in 1780.
Dimensions & tons: 136ft 0in, 121ft 9in x 34ft 6in x 17ft 6in (44.18, 39.55 x 11.21 x 5.68m) 535/1,089 tons. Draught 15ft 3in / 16ft 7in (4.95/5.39m). Men: 270 in wartime/188 in peacetime; included 6 officers.
Guns: UD 26 x 12pdrs; SD 6 x 6pdrs.
Gracieuse Rochefort Dyd. (Constructeur, Joseph Niou).
K: 11.1785. L: 18.5.1787. C: 5.1788.
Renamed *Unité* 28.9.1793, then would have become *Variante* 4.1796, but was captured by HMS *Revolutionnaire* off Île d'Yeu 11.4.1796, becoming HMS *Unite*; sold 5.1802.
Inconstante Rochefort Dyd. (Constructeur, Hubert Pennevert).
Ord: 31.1.1789. K: 11.1789. L: 9.9.1790. C: 2.1791.
Captured by HMS *Penelope* and *Iphigenia* off San Domingo 25.11.1793, becoming HMS *Convert*; wrecked 8.2.1794 off Grand Cayman.
Hélène Rochefort Dyd. (Constructeur, Pierre Duhamel).
K: early 1789. L: 18.5.1791. C: 6.1792.
Captured by the Spanish at San Pietro (Sardinia) 19.2.1793, becoming Spanish Navy's *Sirena*.

AGLAË. 32 guns. A one-off design by Pierre Duhamel.
Dimensions & tons: 136ft 0in x 34ft 6in x 17ft 6in (44.18 x 11.21 x 5.68m) 700/1,200 tons. Draught 15ft 1in / 16ft 5in (4.90/5.33m). Men: 270 in wartime/188 in peacetime; included 6 officers.
Guns: UD 26 x 12pdrs; SD 6 x 6pdrs (from 1793, 10 x 6pdrs, 2 x 36pdr obusiers).
Aglaë Rochefort Dyd.
Ord: 4.11.1786. K: 1787. L: 6.5.1788. C: 1788.
Major refit at Rochefort 2 – 8.1793, then renamed *Fraternité* 28.9.1793. Lost (cause unknown) in the Atlantic after sailing from San Domingo for France 5.8.1802.

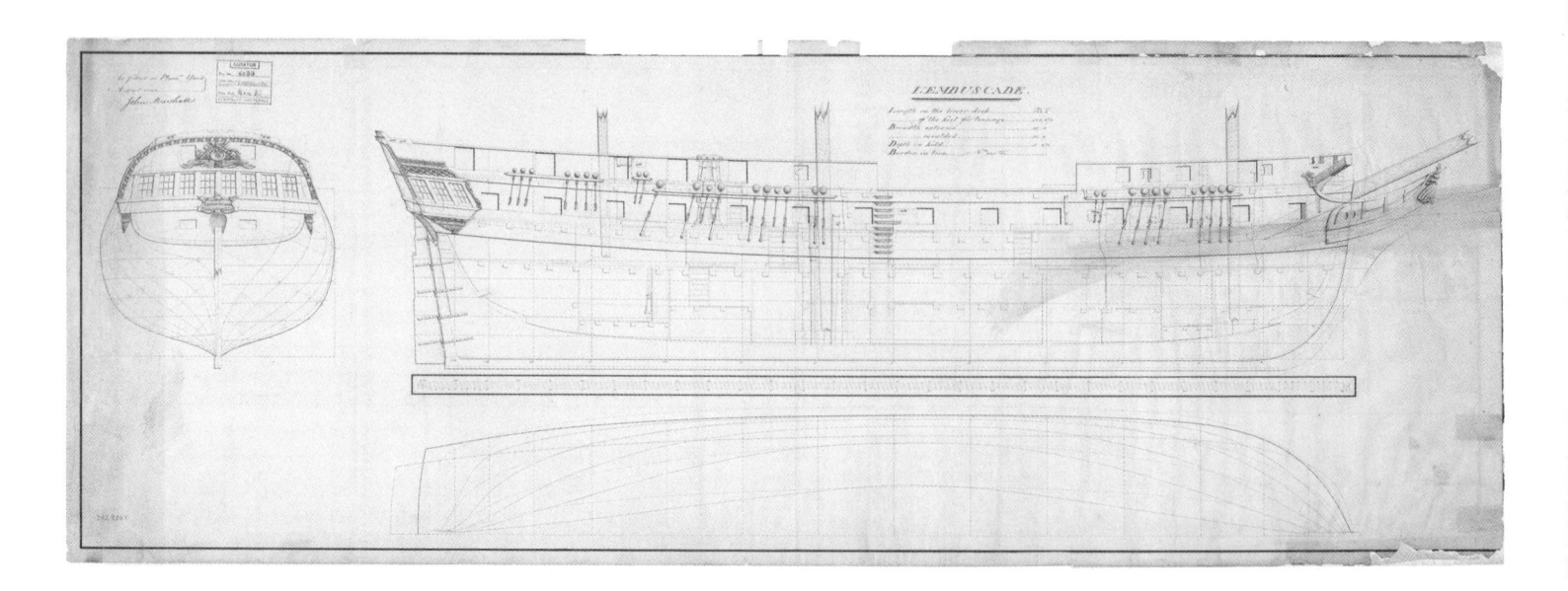

Admiralty draught of *Ambuscade* (ex *Embuscade*) as fitted at Plymouth in 1800. This one-off design exhibits an unusual midship section for a ship of this period, anticipating the shape that was to become common a few decades later. The designer, Vial du Clairbois, was a noted writer on naval architecture but he also translated into French the works of the great Swedish naval architect F H af Chapman; this hull form appears to be heavily influenced by Chapman's ideas. (© National Maritime Museum J5387)

EMBUSCADE. 34 guns. A one-off design by Honoré-Sébastien Vial du Clairbois.
    Dimensions & tons: 135ft 6in x 34ft 7in x 17ft 8in (44.02 x 11.23 x 5.74m) 563/1,200 tons. Draught 16ft 0in (5.20m). Men: 270 in wartime/188 in peacetime; included 6 officers.
    Guns: UD 26 x 12pdrs; SD 6 x 6pdrs, 2 x 36pdr obusiers (from 1794, 10 x 6pdrs).
Embuscade Rochefort Dyd.
    Ord: 19.10.1787. K: 1788. L: 21.9.1789. C: 6.1790.
    Captured by Warren's squadron in Lough Swilly (NW Ireland) 12.10.1798, becoming HMS *Ambuscade*; renamed HMS *Seine* 1.1804; BU 8.1813.

SÉMILLANTE Class. 32 guns. Designed and probably built by Pierre-Joseph Pénétreau.
    Dimensions & tons: 140ft 0in, 124ft 0in x 35ft 6in x 17ft 5in (45.47, 40.28 x 11.53 x 5.66m) 600 tons. Draught 14ft 10in / 16ft 4in (5.3m). Men: 270 in wartime/188 in peacetime; included 6 officers.
    Guns: UD 26 x 12pdrs; SD 6 x 6pdrs.
Sémillante Lorient Dyd.
    Named 23.4.1790. K: 12.1790. L: 25.11.1791. C: 5.1792.
    Given to Surcouf at Mauritius 9.1808 (in exchange for *Revenant*), and renamed *Charles* as a privateer. Captured by the British 12.1809 but not added to their Navy.
Insurgente Lorient Dyd.
    Ord: 3.9.1790. K: 5.11.1791. L: 27.4.1793. C: 6.1793.
    Captured by USS *Constellation* 8.2.1799 off Nevis, becoming USS *Insurgent*; wrecked 9.1800 in a hurricane.

Later GALATÉE Class. 36-40 guns. Design by Raymond-Antoine Haran. Further units to Haran's 32-gun design of 1778 (see Section A), but with additional guns on the gaillards. The first was ordered in 1792, was initially called *Frégate No.1*, and was named *Charente Inférieure* in May 1793. The final pair were ordered at Bordeaux on 17 June 1793, the first initially to be named *Panthère* but the names *République Française* and *Macreuse* respectively were assigned in January 1794; the second was renamed in October 1794 as shown below, but the two were again renamed in 1795 after entering service.
    Dimensions & tons: 137ft 0in, 124ft 0in x 34ft 6in x 17ft 6in (44.50, 40.28 x 11.21 x 5.68m) 590/1,150 tons. Draught 14ft 10in / 16ft 4in (4.82/5.31m). Men: 282 in wartime/209 in peacetime; included 7 officers.
    Guns: UD 26 x 12pdrs; SD 12 x 6pdrs (2 or 4 x 6pdrs replaced by 36pdr obusiers in some ships).
Charente Inférieure Rochefort Dyd.
    K: 2 (or 9).1792. L: 25 or 30.6.1793. C: 12.1793.
    Renamed *Tribune* 10.1794. Captured by HMS *Unicorn* in the Channel 8.6.1796, becoming HMS *Tribune*; wrecked off Halifax 7.11.1797.
Républicaine Française Bordeaux.
    Ord: 17.6.1793. K: 7.1793. L: 3.1.1794. C: 3.1794.
    Renamed *Renommée* 30.5.1795. Captured by HMS *Alfred* off San Domingo 12.7.1796, becoming HMS *Renommee*; BU at Deptford 9.1810.
Décade Française Pierre Guibert, Bordeaux.
    K: 3.1794. L: 10.10.1794. C: 1.1795.
    Renamed *Décade* 30.5.1795. Captured by HMS *Magnanime* and *Naiad* off Finisterre 24.8.1798, becoming HMS *Decade*; sold at Deptford 21.2.1811.

COCARDE NATIONALE Class. 40 guns. Built by Pierre Duhamel, but allegedly designed by Frédéric Roux. The first pair were ordered on 16 May 1793; the third about the same date. Two further ships were ordered at Saint-Malo in 1794 to a (possibly modified) design by Duhamel; these two ships, to have been named *Admirable* and *Imprenable*, were never begun; called *No.2* and *No.3* until May 1795, they were to have carried 28 x 12pdrs, 10 x 6pdrs, and 4 x 36pdr obusiers.
    Dimensions & tons: 136ft 6in x 34ft 8in x 17ft 4in (44.34 x 11.26 x 5.63m). 590/1,190 tons. Draught 14ft 6in / 16ft 3in (4.71/5.28m). Men: 282 in wartime/209 in peacetime; included 7 officers.
    Guns: UD 28 x 12pdrs; SD 12 x 6pdrs (8pdrs in *Cocarde*); 4 x 36pdr obusiers added later.
Cocarde Nationale Saint-Malo.
    K: 8.1793. L: 29.4.1794. C: 7.1794.

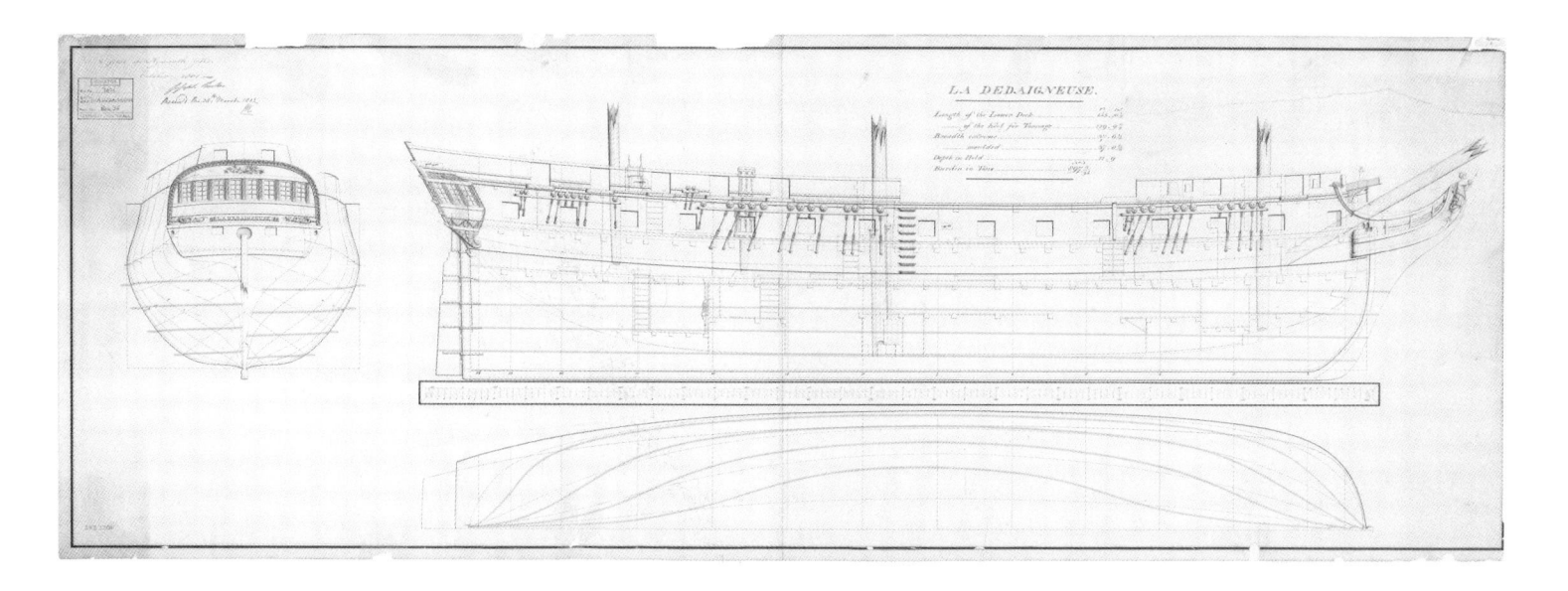

Renamed *Cocarde* 6.1796. Out of service 29.12.1802 and struck 14.6.1803.

Régénérée Saint-Malo.
K: 9.1793. L: 1.11.1794. C: 4.1795.
Captured by the British Navy at the surrender of Alexandria 27.9.1801, becoming HMS *Alexandria*; BU 4.1804.

Bravoure Saint-Servan.
K: 10.1793. L: 11.1795. C: 11.1796.
Wrecked 2.9.1801 about 4 miles south of Leghorn (while under chase by HMS *Minerve*).

COQUILLE Class. 40 guns. Design by Raymond-Antoine Haran, all five being built at Bayonne. The first pair were begun by Haran as *Patriote* and *Fidèle*, but were renamed as shown below on 30 May 1795.
Dimensions & tons: 137ft 6in x 34ft 9in x 17ft 7in (44.67 x 11.29 x 5.71m). 590/1,180 tons. Draught 14ft 10in / 16ft 4in (4.82/5.31m).
Men: 282 in wartime/209 in peacetime; included 7 officers.
Guns: UD 28 x 12pdrs (*Dédaigneuse* only 26 x 12pdrs); SD 12 x 6pdrs (2 or 4 of the 6pdrs substituted by 36pdr obusiers in some ships).

Coquille Bayonne
K: 5.1793. L: 10.1794. C: 4.1795.
Captured by Warren's squadron in Lough Swilly (NW Ireland) 12.10.1798, with 18 dead and 31 wounded, becoming HMS *Coquille*, but was burnt 14.12.1798 by accident at Plymouth while preparing for service.

Sirène Bayonne
K: 6.1794. L: 1795. C: 1795.
Hulked 4.1808 at Lorient; ordered to be BU 10.10.1825.

Dédaigneuse Bayonne (Constructeur, Jean Baudry)
K: 6.1794. L: 12.1797. C: 27.4.1799.
Captured by HMS *Sirius*, *Amethyst* and *Oiseau* off Ferrol 28.1.1801, becoming HMS *Dédaigneuse*; hulked 8.1812 as receiving ship at Deptford; sold 21.5.1823.

Franchise Bayonne (Constructeur, Jean Baudry)
K: 8.1794. L: 7.10.1797. C: 5.1798.
Captured by HMS *Minotaur*, *Thunderer* and *Albion* in the Channel 28.5.1803. becoming HMS *Franchise*; BU 11.1815.

Thémis Bayonne (Constructeur, Jean Baudry)
K: 9.1796. L: 13.8.1799. Comm: 10.2.1801.
Captured by the British Navy 6.1814 at the surrender of Corfu, but not added to their Navy.

Admiralty draught of *Dedaigneuse* as fitted at Plymouth, dated October 1801. Although the French decorative scheme has been retained, the draught shows a thorough refit to suit the ship for Royal Navy service. This includes a major overhaul of the internal arrangements, with the addition of platforms, magazines and storerooms below decks, the replacement of suction pumps with the more efficient chain pumps and, more visibly, the erection of barricades along the quarterdeck and forecastle. (© National Maritime Museum J5640)

Eight 12pdr frigates were included in the large construction programme proposed for Toulon in January 1794, but these were never begun or named.

HEUREUSE Class. 38 guns. Design by Pierre Degay. With the Bayonne quintet listed above, these were the last 12pdr-armed frigates to be built for the French Navy.
Dimensions & tons: 136ft 0in x 34ft 5in x 17ft 4in (44.18 x 11.18 x 5.63m) 600/1,100 tons. Men: 282 in wartime/209 in peacetime; included 7 officers.
Guns: UD 26 x 12pdrs; SD 12 x 12pdrs.

Heureuse Louis & Antoine Crucy, Basse-Indre.
K: 1.1795. L: 31.1.1798. C: 9.1798.
Wrecked 27.12.1798 off St Nazaire, being finally abandoned 9.1.1799.

Chiffonne Louis & Antoine Crucy, Basse-Indre.
K: 10.11.1794. L: 31.8.1799. C: 12.1800. Comm: 31.1.1801.
Captured by HMS *Sybille* off the Seychelles 20.8.1801, becoming HMS *Chiffonne*; sold 9.1814.

Ex VENETIAN PRIZES (1797). On 16 May 1797 French troops entered and seized the city-state of Venice and ended the existence of that republic; among other ships the French acquired one 12pdr frigate (*Bellona*) as well as two 18pdr frigates building on the stocks. On 28 June a French fleet under Rear-Adm. Comte de Brueys occupied the former Venetian territory of Corfu at the southern end of the Adriatic, and took over six Venetian frigates there (as well as six 64-gun ships of the line – see Chapter 3).

Venetian modified COSTANZA (2nd Class), light frigate (*fregata leggera*) with 11 ports. The first two ships of this class were laid down in 1757 and the third and last, *Brillante*, followed in 1774. *Brillante* was

A line and wash portrait of *Chiffonne* by John Shertcliffe, 1804. It is captioned 'The ship which Charles Adams took from the French at the Seychelles Islands', and appears to be done from life. (© National Maritime Museum A1580)

an enlarged version of previous light frigates with two feet added to the keel and 11 instead of 10 battery ports per side. Like the earlier ships she was of 'old construction' – *con struttura a ordinate singola* (built using the old method of the 'single frame', inherited from the galleys of the middle ages). She was rearmed with roughly equivalent French guns at Toulon in early 1798 for reasons of standardisation.

Dimensions (in Venetian measurements): 108.93ft max, 93ft keel x 28.50ft max x 23.75ft *puntale* (37.87m, 32.33m x 9.91m x 8.26m; in French units 116ft 7in, 99ft 7in x 30ft 6in x 25ft 5in). Draught 14.25ft (4.95m, 15ft 3in).

Guns (Venetian): UD 22 x 20lb (12pdrs); SD 16 x 12lb (6pdrs)
Guns (French, 1798): UD 22 x 12pdrs; SD 16 x 6pdrs.

Montenotte (ex French *Brillante* 11.11.1797, ex Venetian *Brillante*) Venice (laid down by Giacomo Giacomazzo in 1774, completed in 1778).

K: 15.1.1774. L: 1778. C: 26.5.1778.

Seized 6.1797 at Corfu by the French Bourdé division and comm. at Corfu 23.7.1797. Helped transport Napoleon's army to Egypt in 1798. Used as a fully-armed flûte from 4.1798. Condemned 5.1801 at Alexandria. Scuttled 21.8.1801 in the entrance to the inner harbour at Alexandria to impede Anglo-Turkish landing operations, BU in situ.

Venetian PALLADE Class, light transport-frigate (*fregata leggera da trasporto*) with 12 ports (3rd Rank). This ship was of 'new construction' – *con struttura a ordinate doppia* (built using the new method of the 'double frame', similar to that used in French and British vessels). It had a full armament in the battery but omitted the armament on the gaillards and had increased beam for use as a transport. *Pallade*'s only sister, *Venere*, was lost in a storm in 1787.

Dimensions (in Venetian measurements): 122.00ft max, 105.00ft keel x 32ft max x 23.75m *puntale* (42.42m, 36.51m x 11.13m x 8.26m; in French units 130ft 7in, 112ft 5in x 34ft 3in x 25ft 5in). Draught 14.25ft (4.95m, 15ft 3in)

Guns (Venetian): UD 24 x 20lb (12pdrs); SD none.

Pallade Venice (laid down by Piero Beltrame in 1784 and launched in 1786).

K: 1784 L: 3.5.1786. C: 19.8.1786.

Was on the list of Venetian ships to be taken over by the French, but when her commander heard of the fall of the Venetian Republic and the occupation of Corfu he took her to Cagliari, Sardinia, instead of back to Corfu, released her crew, and scuttled her to avoid delivering her to the French. She thus became the last ship to fly the flag of San Marco at sea. The hulk was raised in late 1800 and sold for BU, and her 24 guns were brought back by the brigantine *Marc'Aurelio* to Venice in 8.1802 during the first Austrian occupation.

Venetian CERERE Class, light frigates (*fregate leggere*) with 12 ports (3rd Rank). This class was built with the new 'double frame' method. It was derived from the *Pallade* class but lacked that ship's transport features and had a full armament. Only one ship, *Cerere*, was completed before the French took Venice in May 1797. She was the last ship launched at the Venice Arsenal during the Republic. Of the two sisters on the building ways, the French sabotaged one on slip No.10 on 27 September 1797 and one on slip No.31 on 29 December 1797. The

Austrians salvaged the vessel on slip No.10 and completed her as the 32-gun corvette *Aquila*, but after the treaty of Pressburg she was given back to the French in 1806. The ship on slip No.31 was 89.6% complete when destroyed and was BU in June 1804.

Dimensions (in Venetian measurements): 122.00ft max. 105.00ft keel x 32.00ft max x 23.75ft *puntale* (42.42m, 36.51m x 11.13m x 8.26m; in French units 130ft 7in, 112ft 5in x 34ft 3in x 25ft 5in). Draught 14.25ft (4.95m, 15ft 3in).

Dimensions & tons (in French measurements): 132ft deck, 124ft keel x 35ft mld x 15ft creux (42.87, 40.28 x 11.37 x 4.87m). 550/1,050 tons. Draught 12/13ft (3.90/4.22m). Men: 286.

Dimensions & tons (*Aquila* in French measurements): 121.48ft, 100.05ft keel x 36.76ft x 15.79ft (39.46m, 32.5m x 11.94m x 5.13m). 500/950 tons. Draught 12.31/13.36ft (4.00/4.34m). Men: 261.

Guns (Venetian): UD 24 x 20lb (12pdrs); SD 8 x 12lb (6pdrs).
Guns (*Aquila*): 22 x 12pdrs, 4 x 6pdrs, 6 x 12pdr carronades (1805).

Mantoue (ex French *Cérès* 11.11.1797, ex Venetian *Cerere*) Venice (laid down on slip No.26 by Giovanni Battista Gallina in 1788, completed by Iseppo Cason, and launched in 1794)
K: 23.5.1788. L: 18.6.1794. C: 30.6.1794.
Seized by the French Bourdé division 6.1797 at Corfu and incorporated in the French Navy 7.1797. Helped transport Napoleon's army to Egypt in 1798. Was serving as a transport in 4.1798. Taken by the British 2.9.1801 at Alexandria and then probably ceded to the Turks.

Aquila (Austrian *Aquila*) Venice (laid down on slip No.10 by Gerolamo Manao in 1791, completed after 1800 by Francesco Coccon)
K: 1791. L: 29.9.1802. C: 4.1804 or 10.1805.
Was 62.5% completed when sabotaged on slip No.10 by the French on 27.9.1797. Taken by the Austrians there on 18.1.1798. Named *Aquila* by the Austrians 9.1800 and launched and completed by them. Protected Austrian merchant ships in the Adriatic 11.1805. Turned over to Napoleon's Italian Navy in 1806 after Austria's defeat at Austerlitz and the subsequent Treaty of Pressburg. Used as a floating battery at Ancona from 10.1810 to 2.1814. Taken by the Austrians following the French evacuation of that city and BU.

Venetian *PALMA* Class, light frigates (*fregate leggere*) with 13 ports (3rd Rank). This class was built with the new 'double frame' method. Three ships of this type were completed before the French took Venice in May 1797; the French took two of these at Corfu and one while under repair at Venice. Three more were on the building ways, of which the French sabotaged two on slips 1 and 6 on 28 December 1797 and one on slip No.25 on 30 December 1797. The Austrians salvaged the two on slips 1 and 6 and in 1801 or 1802 decided to complete them as the 34-gun *Adria* class. However in January 1806 they had to cede the still-inactive ships to the French, who gave them to the subordinate Italian Navy which never used them.

Dimensions (in Venetian measurements): 122.00ft max, 105.00ft keel x 33.45ft max x 23.20ft *puntale* (42.42m, 36.51m x 11.63m x 8.06m; in French units 130ft 7in, 112ft 5in x 35ft 10in x 24ft 10in). Draught 16.20ft (5.63m, 17ft 4in).

Dimensions & tons (in French measurements): 133ft deck, 125ft keel x 35ft mld x 19ft creux (43.20, 40.60 x 11.37 x 6.17m). 600/1,100 tons. Draught 12/14ft (3.90/4.55m). Men: 286.

Dimensions & tons (*Adria* class in French measurements): 142.38ft x 37.19ft x 20.35ft (46.25 x 12.08 x 6.61m). 600/1,200 tons. Draught 15.48/16.84ft (5.03/5.47m). Men: 280.

Guns (Venetian): UD 26 x 20lb (12pdrs); SD 12 x 12lb (6pdrs).
Guns (*Adria* class): UD 24 x 12pdrs; SD 10 x 6pdrs.

Lonato (ex French *Palme* 11.11.1797, ex Venetian *Palma*) Venice (laid down at beginning of 1782 by Giacomo Giacomazzo and launched in 1784)
K: 1782. L: 25.3.1784. C: 19.5.1784.
Seized by the French at Corfu 7.1797. In bad condition and rearmed only with French 8pdrs. Condemned at Corfu 7.1798. Taken 3.1799 by the Russians at Corfu while semi-submerged and BU.

Bellone (Venetian *Bellona*) Venice (built by Andrea Chiribiri)
K: 7.8.1785. L: 27.3.1788. C: 29.4.1788.
Taken by the French at Venice 5.1797. Not commissioned by the French, scuttled 28-30.12.1797 in the Arsenal. Hauled out under an Austrian order of 6.1798 and repairs completed 1.1800 by Andrea Spadon and Andrea Chiribiri. Armed with a dozen 30lb (18pdr) guns found in a warehouse. Found in bad condition 23.10.1801, ordered BU by the French 3.1807.

Léoben (ex French *Méduse* 11.11.1797, ex Venetian *Medusa*) Venice (laid down on slip No.25 in 1788 by Gerolamo Manao and completed in 1791)
K: 21.4.1788. L: 3.9.1791. C: 9.9.1791.
Seized by the French at Corfu and comm. 30.7.1797. Helped transport Napoleon's army to Egypt in 1798. Was serving as a transport with 30 guns in 4.1798. Decomm. 11.9.1801, taken by the British 2.9.1801 at Alexandria, used as a hospital ship under her French name (corrupted to *La Bion*), and then ceded to the Turks.

Adria (Austrian *Adria*) Venice (laid down on slip No.1 in 1788, she was entrusted to Pietro Beltrame and was ready to be launched in 5.1797; completed after 1803 by Romualdo Battistella)
K: 21.4.1788. L: 6.6.1803. C: 11.1805.
Was ready for launch when sabotaged on slip No.1 by the French on 28.12.1797. Taken by the Austrians on the building ways 18.1.1798 in overturned and damaged condition. Named *Adria* 6.1803 and completion ordered. Completion authorised 11.1805 for use against French privateers. To Italian (French) control 15-19.1.1806. Never commissioned, BU beginning 6.1809.

Austerlitz (Austrian *Austria*) Venice (laid down on slip No.6 in 1789, she was entrusted to Carlo Novello and was ready to be launched in 5.1797).
K: 2.6.1789. L: 21.9.1803. C: 12.1805.
Was ready for launch when sabotaged on slip No.6 by the French on 28.12.1797. Taken by the Austrians on the building ways 18.1.1798 in overturned and damaged condition. Named *Austria* 9.1803. Commissioning delayed until 1805 due to lack of suitable guns. Ordered commissioned 1.10.1805. To Italian (French) control 15-19.1.1806 and renamed *Austerlitz* by the French. Never commissioned, ordered BU 12.10.1809.

Ex MALTESE PRIZES (1798). Malta was captured by the French on 12 June 1798, and the warships operated by the Knights of Malta were seized and added to the French Navy. Besides two 64-gun ships (see Chapter 3), the frigates *Santa Elisabetta* and *Santa Maria* (both launched at Valletta in 1782) were incorporated and renamed *Carthaginoise* and *Bérouse* respectively. However the latter was in such poor condition that she was not brought into service and was quickly BU.

Carthaginoise (Maltese *Santa Elisabetta*, launched at Valletta in 1782). Name also reported as *Carthagénaise*.
Dimensions & tons: unknown
Guns: 32 guns, including UD 26? x 12pdrs.
Recomm. by the French 7.1798. Captured 9.1800 by the British in the capitulation of Malta, but found to have been pillaged for firewood, and was BU.

Ex BRITISH PRIZES (1793-1801). Four British Fifth Rates (with 12pdr British guns) were captured during the French Revolutionary War (all were subsequently retaken), and are listed below, with measurements in French units. Their original names were slightly altered for three of them in French hands, with *Thames* being altered to *Tamise*, *Ambuscade* to *Embuscade*, and *Success* to *Succès*.

RICHMOND Class. 32 guns (36 in French service), designed by William Bately in 1756. The *Thames* was a sister to the *Richmond* captured by the French in 1781 (see Section A above).
 Dimensions & tons: 123ft 0in, 105ft 0in x 32ft 3in x 12ft 8in (39.96, 34.11 x 10.48 x 4.12m). 550/1,000 tons. Draught 14ft 3in/15ft 1in (4.63/4.90m). Men: 296.
 Guns: UD 26 x 12pdrs; SD 8 x 6pdrs + 2 x 36pdr obusiers.
Tamise Henry Adams, Buckler's Hard
 K: 2.1757. L: 10.4.1758. C: 29.5.1758 at Portsmouth Dyd.
 Captured by *Carmagnole* and two other frigates off Ushant 24.10.1793; retaken by HMS *Santa Margarita* off Waterford 8.6.1796, becoming HMS *Thames* again. BU at Woolwich 9.1803.

AMAZON Class. 32 guns (36/40/38 in French service), designed by Sir John Williams in 1770, to which three ships were built in 1771-73 and a further fifteen from 1778 onwards, of which the *Castor* was captured (for just 20 days) in 1794, *Ambuscade* in 1798 and *Success* in 1801 (a fourth sister - *Cleopatra* – was later captured in 1805 – see next section).
 Dimensions & tons: 122ft 4in, 109ft x 33ft x 18ft 8in (39.74, 35.40 x 10.72 x 6.07m). 550/1,000 tons. Draught 15ft/16ft (4.87/5.20m). Men: 270-286.
 Guns: UD 26 x 12pdrs; SD 6 x 6pdrs, 4 (*Castor*) or 6 (*Ambuscade* and *Success*) x 24pdr carronades. *Ambuscade*'s SD was re-armed in French service with 8 x 8pdrs and 6 x 36pdr obusiers.
Castor Joseph Graham, Harwich
 K: 1.1783. L: 26.5.1785. C: 11.7.1786 (at Chatham Dyd).
 Captured 9.5.1794 by Nielly's squadron off Cape Clear 9.5.1794. Retaken by HMS *Carysfort* off Land's End 29.5.1794.
Embuscade Adams & Barnard, Deptford
 K: 4.1771. L: 17.9.1773. C: 1.10.1773 (at Deptford Dyd).
 Taken by boarding by *Bayonnaise* 14.12.1798 west of Île d'Aix. Retaken 29.5.1803 by HMS *Victory* off Cape Ortegal, returned to service as HMS *Ambuscade*.
Succès John Sutton, Liverpool
 K: 8.5.1779. L: 10.4.1781. C: 7.1781 (at builder).
 Captured 13.2.1801 by Gantaume's squadron in the Mediterranean and taken into Toulon 13.2.1801. Grounded at Vado 1.9.1801 while being pursued by HMS *Pomone*, *Phoenix*, and *Minerve* and retaken by them 2.9.1801.

There were also two requisitioned vessels with 12pdr batteries acquired

The *Psyche* was built as a privateer and purchased for the French Navy before being captured by the British. The ship was designed and built by the same team responsible for the *Résistance* (later HMS *Fisgard* – see Chapter 4), and as demonstrated by this half model employed a scaled-down version of the same unusual hull form. (© National Maritime Museum L0775)

in 1794 and 1795 respectively. The first was the former British East Indiaman *Princess Royal*, built in 1786 on the Thames and captured in September 1793 by three French privateers; initially fitted for service as a privateer, she was requisitioned at Île de France (Mauritius) by the French Navy in January 1794 under the name *Duguay-Trouin*, carrying 26 x 12pdrs, 2 x 9pdrs and 6 x 6pdrs (British guns) with 403 men, but was retaken by HMS *Orpheus* (HMS *Centurion* and *Resistance* were also in the vicinity) in the Indian Ocean on 5 May 1794. The second acquisition was the *Droits du Peuple*, probably also a requisitioned privateer put into service with the French Navy in 1795 with 36 (or 40) guns; she was wrecked off Trondheim in November 1795.

(C) Vessels acquired from 25 March 1802

PSYCHÉ. 36 guns, purchased June 1804. This frigate was built at Basse-Indre in 1798-99 as a privateer to a Pierre Degay design, but was purchased for the French Navy in 1804 at Île-de-France (Reunion) by General Decaen.
 Dimensions & tons: 129ft 0in, 114ft 0in x 34ft 0in x 15ft 6in (41.90, 37.03 x 11.04 x 5.03m) 600/801 tons. Draught 16ft/16ft 2in (5.20/5.26m). Men: 240.
 Guns: UD 26 x 12pdrs; SD 6 x 6pdrs, 4 x 36pdr obusiers. Later 24 x 12pdrs; 12 x 12pdr carronades.
Psyché Louis & Antoine Crucy, Basse-Indre.
 K: 2.1798. L: late 1798. C: 1799.
 Captured 14.2.1805 by HMS *San Fiorenzo* (42) off SW India, becoming HMS *Psyche*; sold 1812.

Ex BRITISH PRIZE (1805)

AMAZON Class. Eighteen ships were built to this 1771 design by Sir John Williams, of which the *Cleopatra* was captured by the *Ville de Milan* off Bermuda on 17 February 1805, but was retaken (along with her captor) six days later.
 Dimensions & tons: 121ft 7in, 108ft 8in x 33ft 0in x 15ft 5in (39.50, 35.30 x 10.72 x 5.00m). 600/1,000 tons. Draught 14¾ft/15¾ft (4.80/5.10m). Men: 270.

Guns: UD 26 x 12pdrs; SD 10 x 24pdr carronades, 2 x 6pdrs.
Cléopâtre James Martin Hilhouse, Bristol.
  K: 6.7.1778. L: 26.11.1779. C: 9.7.1780 at builder's yard.
  Retaken (along with the damaged *Ville de Milan*) 23.2.1805 off Bermuda by HMS *Leander* (52) and returned to service as HMS *Cleopatra*. BU 9.1814 at Deptford.

Ex PORTUGUESE PRIZES (1807)

Triton (Portuguese *Tritão*, ex *Nossa Senhora das Necessidades* c1794, 5th Class (44 guns), launched 30.6.1783 at Lisbon)
  Dimensions & tons: 150ft 6in x 33ft 9in x 24ft 11in (48.89 x 10.97 x 8.10m). 500/900 tons. Draught 12ft 2in (3.96m) mean. Men: 329
  Guns: (1783) 30 x 18pdrs, 14 x 9pdrs; (1795) 30 x 18pdrs, 10 x 9pdrs; (by 1807?) 30 x 12pdrs, 12 x 6pdrs.
  Seized at Lisbon 30.11.1807. Retaken in the evacuation of Lisbon early 9.1808 and returned to Portuguese service. BU 1819.
Vénus (Portuguese *Vénus*, 5th class (36 guns), launched 22.2.1792 at Bahia, Brazil)
  Dimensions & tons: dimensions unknown. 500/900 tons. Men: 300.
  Guns: (1792) 26 x 18pdrs, 10 x 9pdrs
  Seized at Lisbon 30.11.1807. Retaken in the evacuation of Lisbon early 9.1808 and returned to Portuguese service. BU 1827.

CAROLINA Class. Two small 32- or 34-gun vessels – *Carolina* and *Bellona* - sometimes called frigates and quite similar in size and ordnance to the last Venetian 12pdr frigates, were launched at Venice in 1808 for Napoleon's Italian Navy. These were normally considered as corvettes by the time they entered service, and details appear in Chapter 6.

PURCHASED RUSSIAN VESSEL (1809)

AVTROIL. Originally the Swedish 24-gun rowing frigate *Af Trolle*, this 12-pounder frigate was captured on 13 August 1789 by the Russians.
  Dimensions & tons: 108ft 4in x 28ft 11in x 7ft 0in (35.20 x 9.40 x 2.29m). Tons unknown. Men: 210.
  Guns: UD 24 x 12pdrs; SD 8 x 4pdrs
Avtroil (ex Swedish *Af Trolle*) Djurgard, Stockholm (constructed by H. Sohlberg)
  Built 1767.
  To the Mediterranean 1804 with Commodore Greig's squadron carrying marines. Arrived at Trieste from Corfu 28.12.1807 with the squadron of Commodore Saltanov and was in the detachment of smaller ships that arrived at Venice 20.1.1808. Ordered sold to France 9.1809, decomm. 11.1809 at Venice, Russian crew left for home 24.3.1810. Found unserviceable by the French in 1810 and BU at Venice.

18-pounder frigates

(A) Vessels in service or on order at 1 January 1785

While the standard primary armament of the frigate before 1779 was the 12-pounder gun, in late 1778 Britain developed designs for 'heavy' frigates with a main battery of (either 26 or 28) 18-pounder guns, plus a number of lesser guns on the gaillards). In France, which followed suit in 1781, the early designs with 26 guns in their main battery soon gave way to those with 28 guns.

It is worthwhile recording that the idea of building 18pdr-armed frigates underwent a long gestation. In June 1757 a Capt. Shirley submitted a scheme to the British Navy for a 'super-frigate' measuring 146 x 37 (British) feet, carrying 28 x 18pdrs on the UD and 12 x 9pdrs or 6pdrs on the superstructures; however, his proposal was brusquely rejected by their Lordships. Across the Channel, towards the close of the Seven Years War, the Brest Assistant Constructeur Pierre Lamothe took a similar plan to Louis XV on 22 November 1762, with a design for a frigate of 145 x 37 (French) feet, to carry 30 x 18pdrs and 20 x 8pdrs, outclassing not only all existing frigates but also the two-decker 50-gun ship type. His timing was inauspicious, but in January 1769 the undeterred Lamothe took a modified version to his superiors. Again he was turned down, but in November Joseph-Marie-Blaise Coulomb revived the idea, suggesting such a vessel be built for trade predation, to carry 26 x 18pdrs and 10 x 8pdrs in wartime, but only fitted with 12pdrs in peacetime so as to not unnecessarily strain the hull structure. Nevertheless, no action followed.

Meanwhile, the two *Pourvoyeuse* class frigates designed for 24-pounder guns in the early 1770s (see Chapter 4) had been completed with an 18pdr main battery, and two further 18pdr-armed frigates were brought into French service in 1780 and 1782, although the latter quickly fell into British hands. The former two-decked 56-gun *Bordelais* (built at Bordeaux 1762-63) was hulked at Lorient in May 1779, but was rebuilt there by Arnous as a frigate with funds provided by the Comte d'Artois (Louis's brother) at his own expense, and renamed *Artois*; carrying 28 x 18pdrs (and 12 x 8pdrs), she was captured (less than two months after recommissioning) by HMS *Romney* on 1 July 1780, becoming HMS *Artois* (and was sold in 1786). The privateer *Aigle*, built at St. Malo by Dujardin to an early Jacques-Noël Sané design, with 26 x 18pdrs and 10 (later 14) x 8pdrs, was purchased in April 1782 by the French Navy; she was captured in the Delaware on 14 September 1782, becoming HMS *Aigle* until she was wrecked on 19 July 1798 off Cape Farina (Morocco).

DANAË. 36 guns. Originally begun to the lines of the 12pdr-armed *Capricieuse* class, this ship was completed to an amended design by Charles Segondat-Duvernet, as the first 18pdr frigate launched for the French Navy in 1781 (more than two years after the British ordered their first 18pdr frigates). However, her main battery was reduced to 12pdrs (and her SD guns reduced) following a refit at Brest in early 1784.
  Dimensions & tons: 140ft (45.5m); other dimensions unknown. 700 tons burthen. Men: 271 (as 12pdr ship).
  Guns: UD 26 x 18pdrs; SD 10 x 8pdrs or 6pdrs; (1785) UD 28 x 12pdrs, SD 6 x 8pdrs.
Danaë Lorient Dyd
  K: 9.1781. L: 27.5.1782. C: 10.1782.
  Struck in 1795. Last mentioned 1.1796 at Brest, fate unknown.

MINERVE Class. 36-40 guns. Joseph-Marie-Blaise Coulomb design. Two ships were ordered on 30 October 1781 and named on 28 November. Four more would be ordered to the same design from 1785 on. These ships were not as well regarded by the French as were Sané's contemporary ships, but their fuller hull form proved popular with the British Navy, who copied the lines.
  Dimensions & tons: 142ft 0in, 128ft 0in x 36ft 0in x 18ft 9in (46.13, 41.58 x 11.69 x 6.09m). 700/1,330 tons. Draught 16ft 3in/16ft 10in (5.28/5.47m). Men: 324 (later 335).
  Guns: UD 26 x 18pdrs; SD 10 (later 14) x 8pdrs.
Minerve Toulon Dyd.
  Ord: 30.10.1781. K: 1.1782. L: 31.7.1782. C: 10.1782.
  Captured 18.2.1794 at seizure of San Fiorenzo (Saint-Florent, Corsica) by the British, becoming HMS *San Fiorenzo*, troopship 1810, then

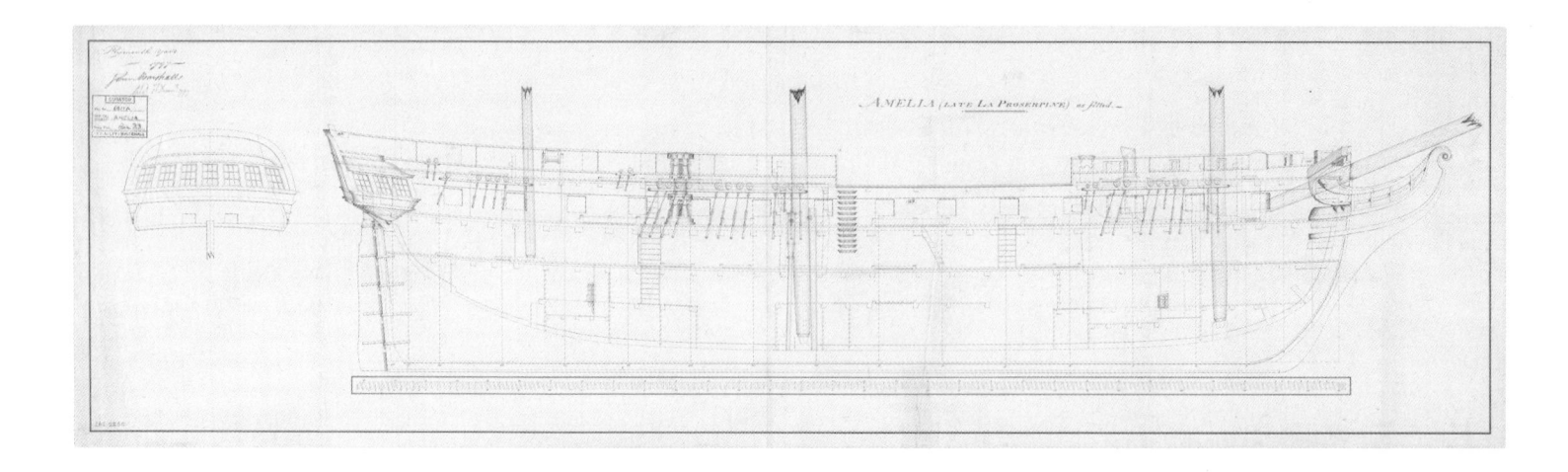

receiving ship 1812, BU at Deptford 9.1837.
Junon Toulon Dyd.
  Ord: 30.10.1781. K: 2.1782. L: 14.8.1782. C: 2.1783.
  Captured 18.6.1799 by HMS *Bellona* off Toulon, becoming HMS *Princess Charlotte*; renamed *Andromache* 1.1812; BU at Deptford 1828.

NYMPHE. 34 guns. One-off design by Pierre-Augustin Lamothe, Jnr, and built as a replacement for his father's 12pdr frigate of the same name which had been captured in August 1780. The design was revived for three more frigates from 1785 onwards.
  Dimensions & tons: 144ft 5in x 36ft 8in x 19ft 3in (46.91 x 11.91 x 6.25m). 744/1,423 tons. Draught 15ft/17ft (4.87/5.52m). Men: 324.
  Guns: UD 26 x 18pdrs; SD 8 x 8pdrs; (1792) UD 26 x 12pdrs; SD 10 x 6pdrs.
Nymphe Brest Dyd.
  Ord: 5.12.1781 (named). K: 12.1781. L: 30.5.1782. C: 8.1782.
  Wrecked at Nourmoutier 30.12.1793 while fighting the Chouans.

HÉBÉ Class. 38 guns. Four frigates were built to this 1782 design by Jacques-Noël Sané in 1781-85. The name-ship was captured by the British a month after completion, and her lines copied, but she is included below for the completion of the class list. From this both France and Britain developed the design further, so that it became the basis of numerous vessels in both navies. The original design was revived by France for two more ships in 1790 and 1792.
  Dimensions & tons: 142ft 6in, 129ft 0in x 36ft 8in x 19ft 0in (46.29, 41.90 x 11.91 x 6.17m). 700/1,350 tons. Draught 16/17ft (5.20/5.52m). Men: 324 (later 350).
  Guns: UD 26 x 18pdrs; SD 8-12 x 8pdrs (*Hébé* 12 x 8pdrs; *Vénus* 8 x 8pdrs; others 10 x 8pdrs). The *Dryade* additionally carried 4 x 16pdr carronades, but in 1794 these were removed, and she and *Proserpine* each received 4 x 36pdr obusiers; they also each received a 14th pair of 18pdrs around that time.
Hébé Saint-Malo
  K: 12.1781. L: 25.6.1782. C: 8.1782.
  Captured by HMS *Rainbow* in the Channel 4.9.1782, becoming HMS *Hebe*; transport 1798; renamed *Blonde* 24.12.1804 and refitted as frigate, BU at Deptford 6.1811.
Vénus Brest Dyd
  K: 11.1781. L: 14.7.1782. C: 10.1782.
  Wrecked in a typhoon in the Indian Ocean 31.12.1788.
Dryade Saint-Malo

Admiralty draught, received by the Navy Board on 1 December 1797, of the *Amelia* (ex *Proserpine*) as fitted at Plymouth for Royal Navy service. The most noticeable British fittings are the drumhead capstans, chain pumps (recognisable by their square backcases) and lightrooms to the fore and aft magazines. Ex French frigates often had additional barricades fitted around the forecastle and, if absent, along the quarterdeck. The ship has a billet head in lieu of a figurehead, a short-lived austerity measure of the time that was very unpopular with officers and crews alike. (© National Maritime Museum J5593)

  K: 1782. L: 3.2.1783. C: 4.1783.
  Struck and hulked 1796, BU 1801.
Proserpine Brest Dyd.
  K: 12.1784. L: 25.6.1785. C: 8.1785.
  Captured off Cape Clear by HMS *Dryad* 13.6.1796, becoming HMS *Amelia*; BU at Deptford 12.1816.

MÉDUSE Class. 36 (later 40-44 guns). A design by Charles Segondat-Duvernet for a ship that was ordered on 15 February 1782 and named on 13 April. A second ship was ordered in late 1784. The design was re-used for another single ship ordered in 1787 (*Uranie*, to a somewhat lengthened design), as well as another probably derivative (*Vertu*) in 1793, and was revived for four more ships in 1803-5.
  Dimensions & tons: 143ft 6in, 131ft 0in x 37ft 0in x 19ft 0in (46.61 x 12.02 x 6.17m). 700/1,370 tons. Draught 15ft 10in/16ft 6in (5.14/5.36m). Men: 324 (later 340).
  Guns: UD 26 x 18pdrs; SD 10 x 8pdrs. In 1788, 4 x 16pdr 'carronades' added to *Méduse*, which was re-armed 1794 with UD 28 x 18pdrs; SD 12 x 8pdrs, 4 x 36pdr obusiers.
Méduse Lorient Dyd.
  K: 6.1782. L: 18.11.1782. C: 3.1783.
  Burnt by accident in the Atlantic 3.12.1796.
Didon Lorient Dyd.
  K: 1.1785. L: 20.8.1785. C: 3.1787.
  Grounded by accident and burnt 9.1792 in the West Indies, although other sources suggest that she was renamed *Royaliste* in 10.1792 and handed over by her pro-monarchist crew to the Spanish at Trinidad (later fate unknown).

Thus in 1785 (prior to the launch of *Proserpine*) there were eight 18pdr-armed frigates – including the *Consolante* and *Pourvoyeuse* detailed in Chapter 4, but excluding the (re-armed with 12pdrs) *Danaë*. The Coulomb-designed *Minerve* and *Junon* were attached to the Toulon fleet, while the other six were under the Brest naval department.

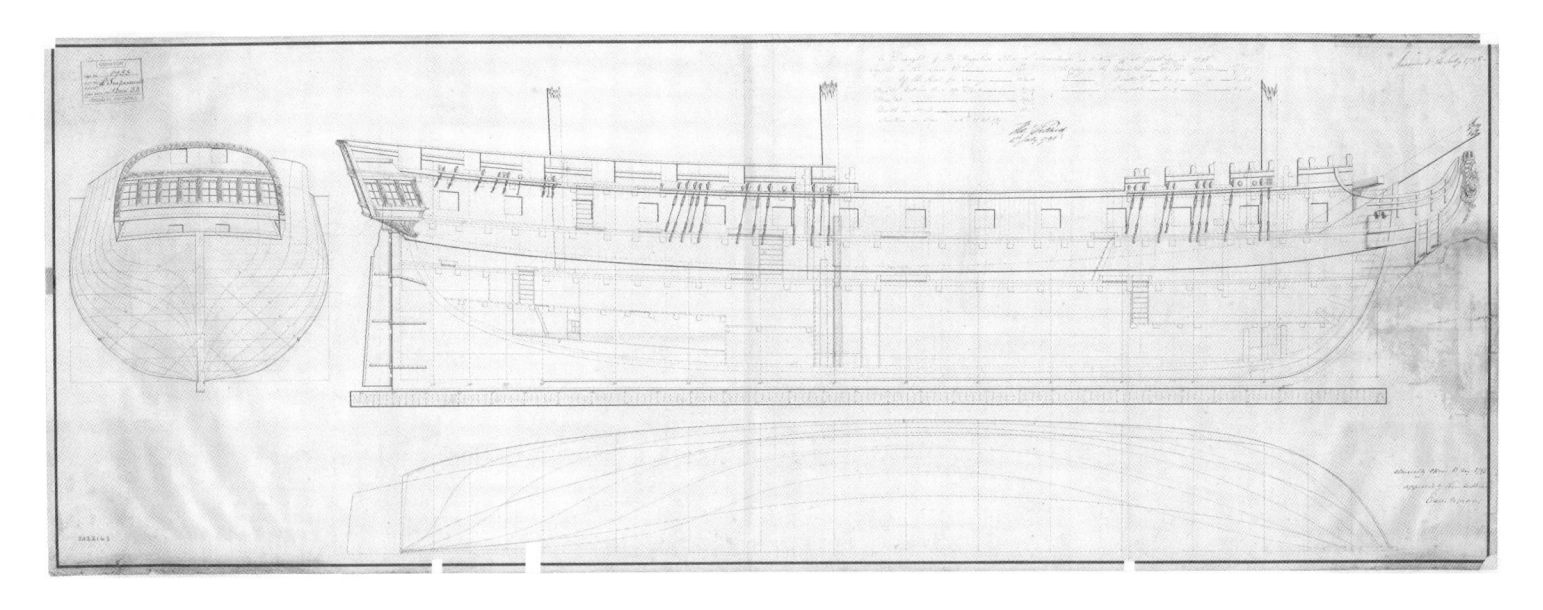

Admiralty draught of *Imperieuse* as taken off at Chatham, dated 14 July 1795. The lines of this ship were ordered to be used as the basis for HMS *Boadicea* while the same Admiralty Order instructed that the *San Fiorenzo* (ex *Minerve*) be used as a model for HMS *Sirius*. *Imperieuse* had been built to Coulomb's original design for the *Minerve* class while the second *Minerve* had been built to an altered version of that design, and these were evidently regarded as different designs by the British. (© National Maritime Museum J3767)

(B) Vessels acquired from 1 January 1785

The 1786 Program provided for twenty 18pdr-armed frigates to be built. Unlike the ships of the line, for which the Sané designs were used exclusively from 1786 until 1815, frigate designs of several ingénieurs-constructeurs were employed so that differing characteristics could be evaluated, and the conflicting views were not finally resolved during the Napoleonic era, although after 1805 the Sané-derived designs were adopted for all new construction. There were two differing approaches in these designs, reflecting two concepts of frigate operations.

The mainstream or 'standard' design of Sané, originating with his *Hébé* draught, evolved through various modifications, culminating in his *Pallas* class of 1805. These ships were built with fuller lines than the alternative stream. Other designers who favoured the same approach included Pierre Rolland, to whose *Armide* draught construction continued (at Rochefort, Bordeaux, Cherbourg and Bayonne) throughout the First Empire. A different concept was taken by Forfait and those who followed him, like Tellier, Francois Pestel and Jean-Francois Gauthier, Compared with Sane's classical lines, Forfait gave a significant amount of deadrise to the floors amidships, producing amidships sections with shapes closer to a 'V' than a 'U' and moving more of the hull volumes to the bow and stern.

MINERVE Class. 36-40 guns. Four further frigates were ordered to this 1782 design by Joseph-Marie-Blaise Coulomb, to which two vessels had been constructed prior to 1785 (see above), but the plans for the final two were altered to lengthened designs to allow them to carry a 14th pair of 18pdrs (see below). All were constructed at Toulon.

Dimensions & tons: 142ft, 128ft x 36ft x 18ft 9in (46.13, 41.58 x 11.69 x 6.09m). 700/1,330 tons. Draught 16ft 3in/16ft 10in (5.28/5.47m). Men: 324 in wartime/230 in peacetime; included 7 officers (a *capitaine de frégate* in command, 3 *lieutenents* and 3 *enseignes*).

Guns: UD 26 or 28 x 18pdrs; SD 10-14 x 8pdrs.

Impérieuse Toulon Dyd
Ord: 11.1785. K: 2.1786. L: 11.7.1787. C: 5.1788.
Chased by British ships of the line into La Spezia 12.10.1793 and taken there by HMS *Captain*, becoming HMS *Imperieuse*. Renamed HMS *Unite* 3.9.1803. Hospital hulk 1836, BU 1858.

Melpomène Toulon Dyd.
Ord: 1787. K: 2.1788. L: 6.8.1789. C: 4.1792.
Taken by the British at the surrender of Calvi 10.8.1794, and became HMS *Melpomene*; sold 14.12.1815 at Sheerness.

NYMPHE Class. 34-44 guns. Three further frigates were built to this 1782 design by Pierre-Augustin Lamothe, to which the prototype had been launched in 1782 (see above).

Dimensions & tons: 144ft 5in x 36ft 8in x 19ft 3in (46.91 x 11.91 x 6.25m). 744/1,423 tons. Draught 15ft/17ft (4.87/5.52m). Men: *Thétis*: 324.

Guns: *Thétis*: 26 x 18pdrs; 8 x 8pdrs; *Cybèle & Concorde*: 28 x 18pdrs; 12 x 8pdrs; 4 x 36pdr obusiers,

Thétis Brest Dyd.
Ord: 4.11.1786. K: 9.1787. L: 16.6.1788. C: 10.1788.
Taken by HMS *Amethyst* off Lorient 10.11.1808, and became HMS *Brune*; BU 1838.

Cybèle Brest Dyd.
Ord: 1787. K: 6.1788. L: 7.7.1789. C: 5.1790.
Wrecked 24.2.1809 in action off Sables d'Olonne.

Concorde Brest Dyd.
Ord: 1790? K: 4.1790. L: 25.10.1791. C: 2.1793.
Taken by HMS *Belliqueux* off Rio de Janeiro 4.8.1800, but not added to British Navy.

PÉNÉLOPE. 36 guns. A one-off design probably by Pierre-Augustin Lamothe (or possibly Jacques-Noël Sané).

Dimensions & tons: dimensions unknown. 700 tons. Men: 324.
Guns: UD 26 x 18pdrs: SD 10 x 8pdrs.

Pénélope Brest Dyd. (Constructeur, Pierre Rolland)
Ord: 30.9.1785. K: 28.11.1785. Named 28.1.1786. L: 12.7.1787. C: 7.1787.
Wrecked in False Bay (South Africa) 10.1788.

Admiralty draught of *Revolutionnaire* as taken off at Portsmouth, dated 12 February 1795. The ship is shown substantially as captured, and many later proposed modifications are pencilled onto the draught. A very long hull with a sharp V-shaped mid-section, the underwater shape was radically different from the usual French section with its 'two-turn' bilge, and became a hallmark of Forfait's designs, and those of his followers. The ship had a reputation as an outstanding sailer, once running 129 miles in 9½ hours, an average speed of 13½ knots. (© National Maritime Museum J5332)

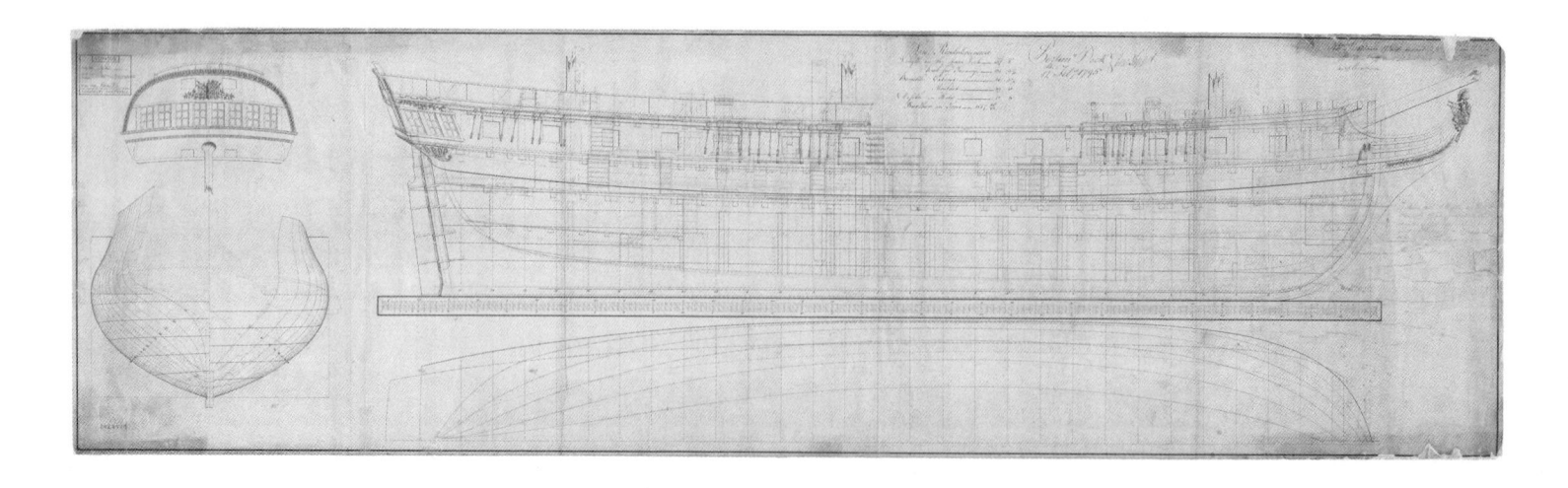

Lengthened *MÉDUSE* Class. 44 guns. A further ship to this 1782 design by Charles Segondat-Duvernet, with the design extended by another 4ft in length and 6in in breadth.

Dimensions & tons: 147ft 6in, 135ft 0in x 37ft 6in x 19ft 3in (47.91, 43.85 x 12.18 x 6.25m). 700/1,400 tons. Draught 15ft 10in/16ft 6in (5.14/5.36m). Men: 324.

Guns: UD 28 x 18pdrs; SD 12 x 8pdrs; 4 x 36pdr obusiers.

Uranie Lorient Dyd.

Ord: 10.9.1787. K: 31.12.1787. L: 31.10.1788. C: 5.1791.

Renamed *Tartu* 31.12.1793. Taken by HMS *Polyphemus* in the Irish Sea 31.12.1796, and became HMS *Uranie*; sold at Plymouth 10.1807.

Modified *MINERVE* Class. 36-40 guns. The fifth 18pdr frigate ordered to this 1782 design by Joseph-Marie-Blaise Coulomb, was slightly lengthened by Jacques Brun Sainte Catherine to allow a 14th pair of UD gunports.

Dimensions & tons: 142ft 5in, 126ft 6in x 36ft x 18ft 9in (46.26, 41.09 x 11.69 x 6.09m). 700/1,362 tons. Draught 14ft 11in/16ft 4in (4.85/5.31m). Men: 324.

Guns: UD 26 x 18pdrs (although pierced for 28 ports); SD 10-14 x 8pdrs.

Perle Toulon Dyd.

Ord: 1789. K: 6.1789. L: 27.8.1790. C: 9.1792.

Taken over by the British at the surrender of Toulon 29.8.1793, and became HMS *Amethyst* (carrying 28 UD 18pdrs); wrecked off Alderney 30.12.1795.

ARÉTHUSE Class. 36-40 guns. A new one-off design by Pierre Ozanne.

Dimensions & tons: 142ft 2in, 126ft x 36ft 6in x 19ft 0in (46.18, 40.93 x 11.86 x 6.17m). 793/1,314 tons. Draught 15ft/17ft (4.87/5.52). Men: 324.

Guns: UD 26 x 18pdrs; SD 10-14 x 8pdrs.

Aréthuse Brest Dyd.

Ord: 31.7.1789. K: 12.1789. L: 3.3.1791. C: 9.1792.

Taken over by the British at the surrender of Toulon 29.8.1793, and became HMS *Undaunted*; wrecked off the Morant Keys (in the Caribbean) 31.8.1796.

By 1790, the French had built 17 frigates of 18pdr design (of which 14 remained), and 3 more were with the builders to be completed in 1790-91 to complete the original program of 20.

HÉBÉ Class. 38-40 guns. Two further frigates were built to this 1782 design by Jacques-Noël Sané, to which four vessels had been constructed prior to 1785 (see above). The ships had 28 ports in the battery, and the final vessel (*Carmagnole*) carried a 14th pair of 18pdrs and therefore a larger complement.

Dimensions & tons: 142ft 6in, 129ft 0in x 36ft 8in x 19ft 0in (46.29, 41.90 x 11.91 x 6.17m). 700/1,350 tons. Draught 16/17ft (5.20/5.52m). Men: 325/361 in *Sibylle*; 335/360 in *Carmagnole*.

Guns: *Sibylle*: 26 x 18pdrs; 14 x 8pdrs; 2 x 36pdr obusiers; *Carmagnole*: 28 x 18pdrs; 10 x 8pdrs; 4 x 36pdr obusiers.

Sibylle Toulon Dyd.

K: 4.1790. L: 30.7.1791. C: 5.1792.

Taken by HMS *Rodney* off Mykonos 17.6.1794, and became HMS *Sybille*; sold 7.8.1833.

Carmagnole Brest Dyd. (Constructeur, Lamothe).

K: 3.1792. L: 21.5.1793. C: 7.1793.

Name changed to *Rassurante* 30.5.1795, but restored to *Carmagnole* 24.2.1798. Wrecked off Flushing 9.11.1800 during a storm and BU in situ.

Lengthened *MINERVE* Class. 42 guns. The sixth and final 18pdr frigate ordered to a J-M-B Coulomb design was re-designed by Jacques Brun Sainte Catherine, and while building was given the name of the first of this class following that ship's loss.

Dimensions & tons: 148ft 0in, 147ft 0in wl, 132ft 0in x 37ft 0in x 19ft 3in (48.07, 47.75, 42.87 x 12.02 x 6.25m). 700/1,450 tons. Draught 16ft 5in/17ft 3in (5.32/5.60m). Men: 340 in wartime/260 in peacetime.

Guns: UD 28 x 18pdrs; SD 12 x 8pdrs, 2 x 36pdr obusiers; (1804 after being retaken) UD 28 x 18pdrs; SD 6 x 8pdrs, 14 x 36pdr obusiers.

Minerve Toulon Dyd

K: late 1791. L: 4.9.1794. C: 10.1794.

Captured 23.6.1795 by HMS *Dido* (28) off Minorca, becoming HMS *Minerva*. Retaken by the gunboats *Terrible* and *Chiffonne* 3.7.1803 after grounding on the breakwater at Cherbourg. Renamed *Canonnière* 8.1803 as a new *Minerve* was under construction. Sold at

THE SMALLER FRIGATES

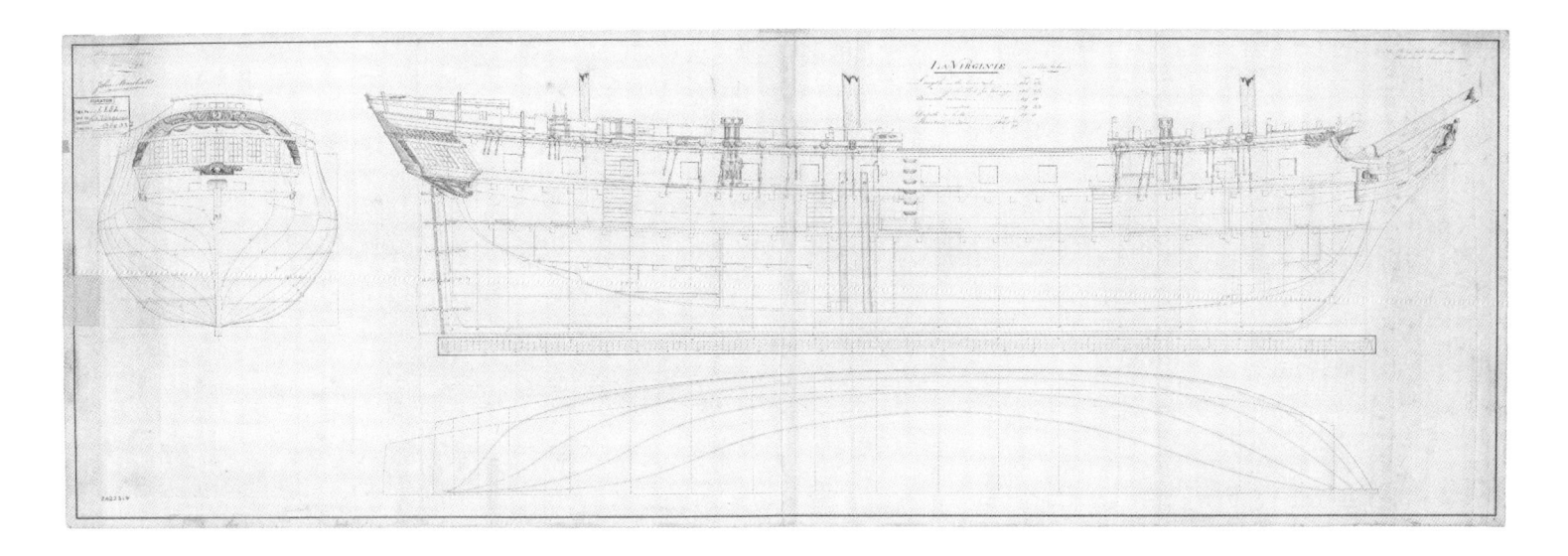

Île de France 6.1809 and renamed *Confiance*. Recaptured 3.2.1810 by HMS *Valiant* (74) off Belleisle with £150,000 cargo, but not re-added to British Navy.

SEINE Class. 42-48 guns. Designed by Pierre-Alexandre-Laurent Forfait. It was originally intended to build the first four of these large ships with a battery of 24pdrs, but this was altered to 18pdrs fairly early on. Two more ships (*Furieuse* and *Guerrière*) were originally ordered as bomb-frigates of the *Romaine* class (see previous Chapter), but were later ordered built to the *Seine* design, and two more ships (*Valeureuse* and *Infatigable*) were begun to the *Seine* design in 1797. The constructeurs of *Guerrière* (Jean-François Lafosse) and of the two 1797 ships (Charles-Henri Tellier), modified Forfait's design, Lafosse substantially and Tellier slightly, and these three ships are listed in their own classes below. The Admiralty draught of *Furieuse* shows a more rounded hull form than Forfait's favourite 'V' section, possibly because the ship utilised frames already cut for the original *Romaine* design.

    Dimensions & tons: 146ft 4in, 130ft 0in x 37ft 2in x 18ft 0in (47.53, 42.22 x 12.07 x 5.85m). 700/1,311 tons. Draught 15ft 6in/17ft (5.03/5.52m). Men: 340 in wartime/260 in peacetime.

    Guns: UD 28 x 18pdrs; SD 10 x 8pdrs, 4 x 36pdr obusiers. From 2nd ship (*Révolutionnaire*) another 2 x 8pdrs added; *Furieuse* had 16 x 6pdrs and 4 x 36pdr obusiers on the SD.

Seine Le Havre.
    K: 5.1793. L: 19.12.1793. C: 3.1794.
    Captured 30.6.1798 in the Channel by 44-gun *Pique* and 48-gun *Jason*, becoming HMS *Seine*. Grounded off the Elbe 21.7.1803 and burnt to avoid recapture the next day.

Révolutionnaire Le Havre.
    Ord: 3.7.1793. K: 10.1793. L: 28.5.1794. C: 7.1794 (armed at Havre 8.1794).
    Captured 21.10.1794 off Ushant by 44-gun *Artois* and 3 other frigates, becoming HMS *Revolutionnaire*. BU at Portsmouth 4.10.1822.

Spartiate Le Havre (Constructeur, Forfait)
    K: 5.1794. Named 5.10.1794. L: end 11.1794. C: 12.1794.
    Renamed *Pensée* 5.1795. Condemned 12.11.1804 at Brest and ordered converted to headquarters hulk, Replaced 5.9.1832 as hulk by *Nymphe* and BU 1833.

Indienne Jean Fouache, Le Havre
    K: 12.1794. L: 2.9.1796. C: 10.1796.
    Grounded and burnt 16.4.1809 near Île d'Aix to avoid capture by the RN.

Admiralty draught of *Virginie*, annotated 'as when taken' and dated Plymouth May 1796. Designed by Jacques-Noël Sané, who was to employ only minor modifications to this hull form for most of his frigates, this class displayed a handsome profile, with long head, exaggerated rake to the stern and low barricades, only spoiled by the addition of a dunette aft. (© National Maritime Museum J5490)

Furieuse Cherbourg (commercial port). (Constructeur, Aubert)
    Ord: 2.1794. K: 25.3.1795. L: 22.9.1797. C: 5.1798.
    Reduced to 18-gun flûte (185 men: 2 x 8pdrs, 4 x 4pdrs, 12 x 36pdr obusiers) 10.1808. Taken 6.7.1809 while *en flûte* by HMS *Bonne Citoyenne* (20) off the Azores, becoming HMS *Furious*. BU 1816 at Deptford.

MONTAGNE. 44 guns. One-off design by Joseph-Marie-Blaise Coulomb; built and completed in less than a year, but this brand new frigate was lost within a few weeks of entering service. She was initially called *Frégate No.2*.

    Dimensions & tons: not recorded. Men: 340 in wartime/260 in peacetime.

    Guns: UD 28 x 18pdrs; SD 12 x 8pdrs, 4 x 36pdr obusiers.

Montagne Rochefort Dyd. (Constructeur, Jean-Denis Chevillard)
    K: 8.1793. L: 26.6.1794. C: 8.1794.
    Renamed *Volontaire* 10.7.1794. Wrecked on the Penmarchs 23.8.1794.

VERTU. 44 guns. One-off design by Charles Segondat-Duvernet, possibly a variant of his *Méduse* design of 1782 to which he had previously built three ships at Lorient. Her 18pdrs were replaced with 12pdrs in 1802.

    Dimensions & tons: 144ft 0in x 36ft 6in x 19ft (46.77 x 11.95 x 6.17m). 646/1,350 tons. Draught 16ft/17ft 6in (5.20/5.68m). Men: 340 in wartime/260 in peacetime.

    Guns: UD 28 x 18pdrs; SD 12 x 8pdrs, 4 x 36pdr obusiers.

Vertu Lorient Dyd. (Constructeur, Segondat)
    Ord: 16.2.1793. K: 10.1793. Named 29.11.1793. L: 28.6.1794. C: 8.1794.
    Seized 30.11.1803 by RN at the capture of San Domingo, and added to RN as HMS *Virtu*. BU 1810.

VIRGINIE (*JUSTICE*) Class. 44 guns. A class of nine ships to a design by Jacques-Noël Sané. The Brest quartet were simply called *Nos.1-4*

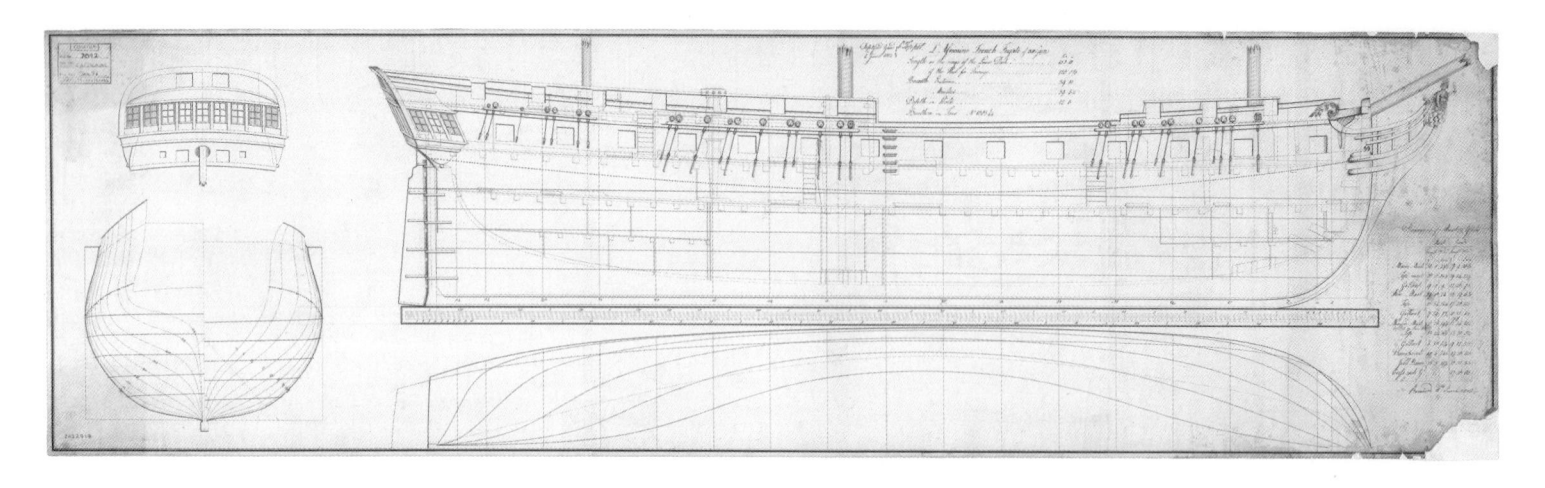

until July 1794. For three similar ships constructed at Saint-Malo by François Pestel see the *Consolante* class, below. *Rhin* was paid for by the four newly-conquered *départements* on the Rhine.
  Dimensions & tons: 146ft, 144ft wl, 130ft 6in x 36ft 8in x 19ft 0in (47.42, 46.77, 42.38 x 11.91 x 6.17m). 720/1,390 tons. Draught 16ft/17ft (5.20/5.52m). Men: 340 in wartime/260 in peacetime.
  Guns: UD 28 x 18pdrs; SD 12 x 8pdrs, 4 x 36pdr obusiers (6 in *Rhin*).
Virginie Brest Dyd. (Constructeur, Jacques-Noël Sané).
  Ord: 17.10.1793. K: 11.1793. Named 10.7.1794. L: 26.7.1794. C: 12.1794.
  Captured 22.4.1796 off the Lizard by HMS *Indefatigable* (46) and *Concorde* (36), becoming HMS *Virginie*; receiving ship 1810; sold 11.7.1827 to BU.
Justice (ex *Courageuse*) Brest Dyd. (Constructeur, Jacques-Noël Sané).
  Ord: 17.10.1793. K: 12.1793. L: 8.1794. C: 12.1794.
  Named *Courageuse* in error 5.10.1794 as this name was already in use, renamed *Justice* 20.4.1795. Taken 27.9.1801 by the British with *Égyptienne* and *Régénérée* at the surrender of Alexandria, given to the Turks and subsequent fate unknown.
Cornélie Brest Dyd. (Constructeur, Pierre Ozanne).
  Ord: 17.10.1793. K: 22.3.1794. L: 19.9.1797. C: 4.1798.
  Captured 14.6.1808 at Cadiz by the Spanish, becoming the Spanish Navy's *Cornelia*. Sold 21.10.1815 at Havana and BU.
Zéphyr Brest Dyd. (Constructeur, Pierre Ozanne).
  Ord: 17.10.1793. K: 26.3.1794. Named 11.7.1794. Not launched.
  Suspended 8.1795 for lack of timber and funding, resumed when a commanding officer was assigned 17.6.1802. Construction abandoned 4.1804 along with the 74-gun *Pacificateur* when 8/24ths built and BU. Napoleon decreed on 24.8.1804 that nothing more would be built at Brest because of difficulties supplying timber and because of a criminal fire that ravaged the dockyard in 2.1804.
Harmonie Bordeaux (Constructeur, François Etesse?).
  K: 5.1794. L: 12.1795. C: 5.1796.
  Run ashore 4.1797 at Santo Domingo after being attacked by two British ships of the line and burned by her crew.
Volontaire Bordeaux (Constructeur, probably François Etesse)
  K: 29.9.1794. L: 7.6.1796. C: 1797?
  Captured 4.3.1806 in Table Bay by a British division, becoming HMS *Volontaire*. BU 2.1816.
Rhin Toulon Dyd. (Constructeur, Poncet).
  Ord: 6.4.1801 (named). K: 6.1801. L: 15.4.1802. Comm: 9.10.1802. C: 10.1802.
  Captured 28.7.1806 off Île d'Aix by HMS *Mars* (74), becoming HMS

Admiralty draught of *Africaine* dated Deptford 6 June 1802. One recurring Royal Navy criticism of French frigates was their inability to stow the 6 months' provisions required of British cruising ships, but this was not a problem with the fuller hull form of this ship, one of a few designed by Raymond-Antoine Haran. Despite her rounder midship section, the ship still performed very well under sail. (© National Maritime Museum J5714)

  Rhin. Hulk 1838, sold 24.5.1884.
Surveillante Louis, Antoine, & Mathurin Crucy, Basse-Indre.
  Ord: 6.7.1800 (contract). Named 16.5.1801. K: 6.1801. L: 30.5.1802. Comm: 11.12.1802. C: 12.1802.
  Captured 29.11.1803 by the British in the surrender of Cap François, Santo Domingo, becoming HMS *Surveillante*. BU 8.1814.
Belle Poule Louis, Antoine, & Mathurin Crucy, Basse-Indre.
  Ord: 6.7.1800 (contract). Named 16.5.1801. K: 6.1801. L: 18.4.1802. Comm: 23.9.1802. C: 9.1802.
  Captured 13.3.1806 while returning from the Indian Ocean with *Marengo* (74) by HMS *Amazon* (46) and *Foudroyant* (80) off La Palma in the Canary Islands, becoming HMS *Belle Poule*. Sold 4.1816.

PRENEUSE Class. 44 guns. Designed by Raymond-Antoine Haran. *Preneuse* was initially called *Frégate No.3* (*No.1* at Rochefort being *Charente Inférieure* and *No.2* being *Montagne*).
  Dimensions & tons: 147ft, 140ft 6in x 36ft 6in x 19ft (47.75, 45.63 x 11.85 x 6.17m). 722/1,400 tons. Draught 16ft 5in/17ft 10in. (5.33/5.79m). Men: 340 in wartime/260 in peacetime.
  Guns: UD 28 x 18pdrs; SD 12 x 8pdrs, 4 x 36pdr obusiers.
Preneuse Rochefort Dyd
  Ord: 24.4.1794. K: 4.1794. L: 16.2.1795. C: 7.1795.
  Pursued 11.12.1799 by HMS *Tremendous* (74), *Adamant* (50), and *Jupiter* (50), ran aground on Île de France and scuttled, then burned by the British.
Africaine Rochefort Dyd
  K: 3.1795. Named: 23.3.1795. L: 3.1.1798. C: 5.1798.
  Captured 19.2.1801 by HMS *Phoebe* (44) east of Gibraltar while carrying 300 troops to Egypt, becoming HMS *Africaine*. Retaken 13.9.1810 by *Iphigénie* and *Astrée* but immediately retaken by HMS *Boadicea* (38). BU 9.1816.

LOIRE. 44 guns. A one-off design by Pierre Degay. Offered to the Republic by the Département of Loire-Inférieur (nowadays called Loire-Atlantique) via a public subscription opened on 12 April 1794 that yielded part of her cost. She originally bore the name of that département, but was renamed simply *Loire* in 1796. She was taken downriver to

Paimbeuf after launching and completed there by the Crucy brothers under a contract of September 1797.

Dimensions & tons: 142ft 6in x 37ft x 19ft 2in (46.29 x 12.02 x 6.22m). 700/1,350 tons. Men: 340 in wartime/260 in peacetime.
Guns: UD 26 x 18pdrs; SD 12 x 8pdrs, 6 x 36pdr obusiers (the obusiers being added in 1798).

Loire Frères Bourmaud, Nantes
K: 4.1794. L: 23.3.1796. C: 12.1797.
Captured 18.10.1798 off Ireland by HMS *Anson* and *Kangaroo*, becoming HMS *Loire*. BU 4.1818.

DIANE. 44 guns. Designed by Pierre-Joseph Pénétreau. Six 18pdr frigates were projected to be built at Toulon in January 1794, as part of a major construction programme at that port that included four additional slipways; eighteen frigates and corvettes in all were to be built in Mediterranean ports, but *Diane* was the only one to be named and laid down.

Dimensions & tons: 146ft 6in, 135ft x 37ft x 19ft (47.58, 43.85 x 12.02 x 6.17m). 750/1,466 tons. Draught 16ft 1in/17ft 5in (5.23/5.65m). Men: 340 in wartime/260 in peacetime.
Guns: UD 28 x 18pdrs; SD 12 x 8pdrs, 4 x 36pdr obusiers.

Diane Toulon Dyd.
Named: 24.7.1794. K: 9.1794. L: 10.2.1796. C: 3.1796.
With Rear-Adm. Denis Decrès (Napoleon's future Minister of Marine) aboard in command of the frigate squadron, *Diane* took part in the Battle of the Nile on 2 August 1798, but escaped undamaged. She was captured 27.8.1800 with only 114 men on board by HMS *Success* (32), *Northumberland* (74), and *Genereux* (74) when leaving Malta, becoming HMS *Niobe*. BU 11.1816.

CRÉOLE. 40 guns. Designed by Jacques-Augustin Lamothe
Dimensions & tons: 144ft 6in x 36ft 8in x 19ft 3in (46.93 x 11.91 x 6.25m). 700/1,350 tons. Men: 340 in wartime/260 in peacetime.
Guns: UD 28 x 18pdrs; SD 12 x 8pdrs.

Créole Louis & Antoine Crucy, Basse-Indre
K: 5.1.1794. L: 27.6.1797. C: 3.1798.
Loaned 19.10.1797 to a privateer at Nantes. Captured 29.6.1803 by HMS *Cumberland* (74) and *Vanguard* (74) off Santo Domingo, becoming HMS *Creole*. While being taken to Britain from Jamaica sprang a leak 26.12.1803 and foundered in the Atlantic 3.1.1804.

CONSOLANTE Class. 44 guns. *Consolante* was built by François Pestel to plans of Sané (probably those of *Virginie* or *Justice*, above) that he modified, and the latter two were probably also built to Pestel's modified plans although they are sometimes attributed to Sané. Differences from Sané's designs visible on British draughts of *Didon* dated 1811 include an extra (15th) pair of (chase) ports forward and a steeper rise of floor in the underwater hull. *Consolante* and *Didon* were called *No.1* and *No.2* until 4.1795 and 6.1795 respectively; the second was then named as *Fâcheuse*, but was renamed *Didon* in 1799; the only other use of the name *Fâcheux* ('Regrettable' or 'Unfortunate') had been for three fire ships in the 1600s. A *No.3* was also ordered to plans by Sané at Saint-Malo in 1794 and named *Farouche* in early 1795; if built she would probably also have been to Pestel's version of the Sané design, but the order was cancelled around 1796 as the ship had not been begun. However, a further ship to the same design was then ordered at St Malo in 1799.

Dimensions & tons: 147ft 0in, 146ft wl, 131ft 0in x 37ft 6in x 19ft 0in (47.75, 47.42, 42.55 x 12.18 x 6.17m). 750/1,400 tons. Draught 15ft/18ft (4.87/5.85m). Men: 340 in wartime/260 in peacetime.
Guns: (*Consolante* and *Didon*) UD 28 x 18pdrs; SD 12 x 8pdrs, 4 x 36pdr obusiers; (*Atalante*, all British): UD 28 x 16pdrs (British 18pdrs); SD 14 x 32pdr carronades, 2 x 9pdrs.

Consolante Entreprise Ethéart, Saint-Malo (Constructeurs, François Pestel and Pierre Ozanne)
K: 4.1795. L: 22.7.1800. Comm: 23.9.1800. C: 9.1800.
Wrecked on Isla Margarita 27.1.1803 while en route from Guadeloupe to Spanish South America, wreck abandoned 11.2.1803.

Didon Entreprise Ethéart, Saint-Malo (Constructeur, François Pestel)
K: 22.9.1796. L: 1.8.1799. Comm: 23.9.1800. C: 9.1800.
Captured 10.8.1805 by HMS *Phoenix* (42) west of Finisterre, becoming HMS *Didon*. BU 8.1811.

Atalante Entreprise Ethéart, Saint-Malo (Constructeur, François Pestel)
K: 9.1799. L: 29.6.1802. Comm: 1.7.1802. C: 7.1802.
Wrecked 3.11.1805 in Table Bay, Cape of Good Hope, in a storm; refloated by 7.11.1805 and repaired, but driven ashore in Table Bay by Home Popham's squadron 10.1.1806 and burnt to avoid capture.

Admiralty draught of *Didon* dated Plymouth 9 July 1811. It had been planned to give the ship a major reconstruction, but this was cancelled – presumably because the ship was beyond economic repair – and she was broken up in August 1811. Only the lines of the body plan was drawn, which suggests that the draught was produced as a record of the shape of the ship before she was taken to pieces. The resemblance of this Pestel ship to Sané designs is apparent. (© National Maritime Museum J5729)

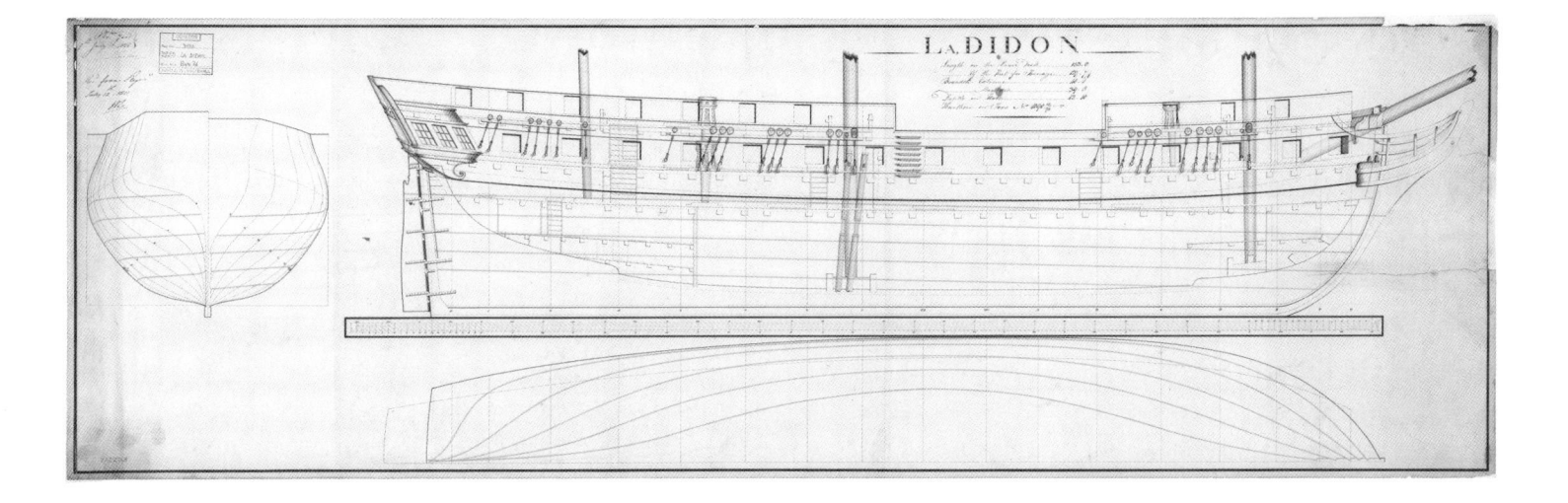

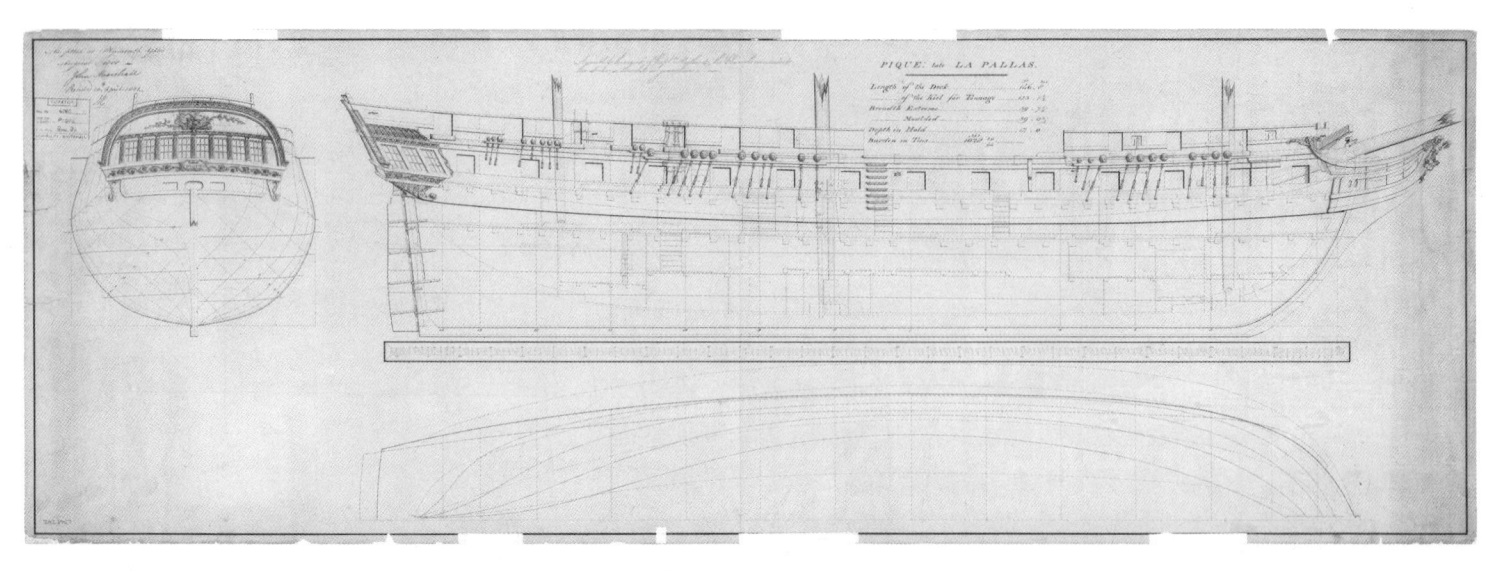

Admiralty draught of *Pique* (ex *Pallas*) as fitted at Plymouth August 1800. Although a modification of the *Romaine* class, this design employed a very similar hull form, the main visual difference being an extra pair of gunports on the upper deck. The shape may have been determined by timber cut for the frames before the ship was reordered to a new design – the *Furieuse*, nominally reordered to the larger *Seine* design also has a similar shape of midship section. (© National Maritime Museum J5385)

GUERRIÈRE. 44 guns. Design of Pierre-Alexandre Forfait modified by Jean-François Lafosse. This was the second of two ships that had been originally ordered at Cherbourg as bomb-frigates of the *Romaine* class (see previous Chapter) and were later ordered built to Forfait's *Seine* design. Unlike the first of these, *Furieuse* (listed with the *Seine* class), *Guerrière* was considerably modified by her constructeur and emerged with different specifications. She was the first frigate built at the old arsenal at Cherbourg, *Furieuse* having been built in the commercial port. *Guerrière* earned a place in United States naval history by being destroyed in 1812 while in British service by the large 24-pounder frigate USS *Constitution*.

Dimensions & tons: 145ft x 36ft 10in x 19ft (47.10 x 11.96 x 6.17m). 700/1,446 tons. Draught 15ft (4.87m) mean. Men: 340 in wartime/260 in peacetime.

Guns: UD 28 x 18pdrs; SD 16 x 8pdrs, 4 x 36pdr obusiers; (1806) UD 28 x 18pdrs; SD 8 x 8pdrs, 8 x 36pdr carronades, 4 x 36pdr obusiers (30 ports).

Guerrière Cherbourg Dyd. (Constructeur, Jean-François Lafosse).
Ord: 2.1794. K: 22.9.1796. L: 15.9.1799. C: 5.1800. Comm: 7.11.1800.
Captured 19.7.1806 by HMS *Blanche* (36) off the Faroes, becoming HMS *Guerriere*; taken by USS *Constitution* 19.8.1812 and burnt.

PALLAS. 40-42 guns. Design of Pierre-Alexandre Forfait modified by François Pestel. Ordered in 1794 as a bomb-frigate of the *Romaine* class (see previous Chapter) with 20 x 24pdrs, 12 x 8pdrs, and 1 x 12in mortar but later ordered built as a regular frigate with 26 x 18pdrs. François Pestel, constructeur at Saint-Malo, modified the original plans of Forfait to produce this ship. She was called *No.1* and then *Première* until being named in 1798.

Dimensions & tons: 140ft, 124ft x 36ft x 17ft 9in (45.47. 40.28 x 11.69 x 5.76m).700/1,071-1,200 tons. Draught 15ft 6in/15ft 6in (5.03/5.03m). Men: 340 in wartime/260 in peacetime.

Guns: UD 26 x 18pdrs; SD 14 x 8pdrs and possibly 2 x 36pdr obusiers

Pallas Saint-Malo
K: 11.1795. L: 12.1798. C: 9.1799.
After leaving Cancale for Brest on her first sortie she was captured 6.2.1800 off Bréhat by HMS *Loire*, *Danae* and others, becoming HMS *Aeolus*, renamed HMS *Pique* 1801. Sold 22.7.1819 for BU.

***VALEUREUSE* Class**. 44 guns. Design of Pierre-Alexandre Forfait modified by Charles-Henri Tellier. These, originally the last two ships of the *Seine* class, were built in 1797-1800 by Tellier, a student of Forfait who lightly modified his master's design including lengthening it by eight inches after Forfait went to Venice in 1797.

Dimensions & tons: 147ft, 130ft 0in x 37ft 2in x 18ft 0in (47.75, 42.22 x 12.07 x 5.85m). 712-759/1,341 tons. Draught 15ft 9in/16ft 11in (5.11/5.49m). Men: 340 in wartime/260 in peacetime.

Guns: UD 28 x 18pdrs; SD 12 x 8pdrs, 4 x 36pdr obusiers.

Valeureuse Le Havre (Constructeur, Charles-Henri Tellier)
K: 19.7.1797. L: 13.8.1798. C: 3.1800. Comm: 23.9.1801.
Separated from the Willaumez squadron in a violent storm 19.8.1806, arrived in Delaware Bay 31.8.1806 in deplorable condition, sold at Marcus Hook, Pennsylvania.

Infatigable Le Havre (Constructeur, Charles-Henri Tellier)
K: 19.7.1797. L: 6.4.1799. C: 3.1800. Comm: 25.6.1801.
Captured 25.9.1806 with *Armide*, *Gloire*, and *Minerve* after leaving Rochefort by HMS *Mars* (74) and the British blockading squadron, becoming HMS *Immortalité* (not commissioned); BU at Plymouth 1.1811.

***URANIE* Class**. 40-44 guns. Design by Jean-François Gauthier. The construction of these two was undertaken by the Crucy brothers supervised by the navy constructeur Pierre Degay. The Crucys regained possession of the yard at Basse-Indre in September 1796 from the French Navy, which had taken it over in August 1794 and then leased it back. On 29 May 1797 the Minister of Marine ordered that the frigates *Clorinde* and *Uranie* be armed with 18-pounder guns, and they may have been contracted for at about the same time. The report that *Clorinde* was named *Havraise* until 1800 would appear to be in error.

Dimensions & tons: 145ft 6in, 138ft 6in x 37ft 6in x 18ft 0in (47.26, 45.00 x 12.18 x 5.85m). 700/1,350 tons. Men: 340 in wartime/260 in peacetime.

Guns: UD 28 x 18pdrs; SD 12 x 8pdrs (*Uranie* also had 4 x 36pdr obusiers).

Uranie Louis, Antoine, & Mathurin Crucy, Basse-Indre (Constructeur, Pierre Degay)

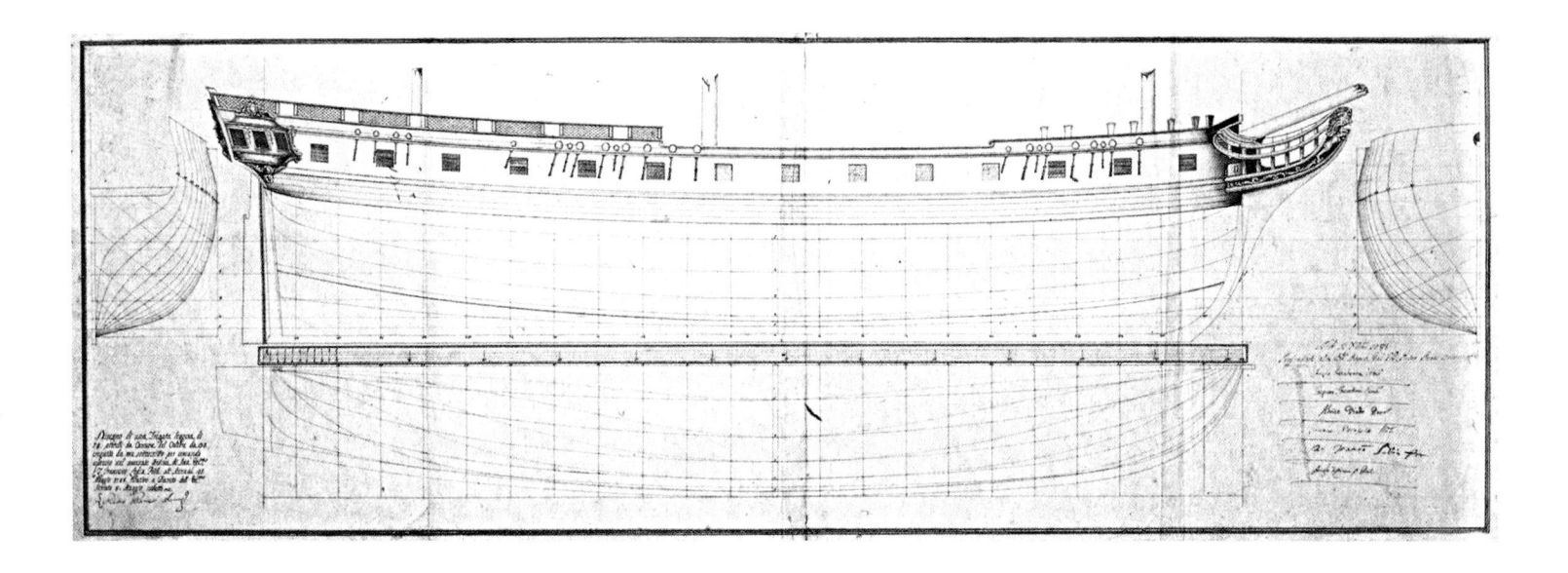

K: 24.9.1797. L: 31.10.1800. Comm: 27.4.1801. C: 6.1801.
Scuttled and burnt 3.2.1814 at Brindisi to avoid capture by the British Navy after Murat turned against Napoleon.

Clorinde Louis, Antoine, & Mathurin Crucy, Basse-Indre (Constructeur, Pierre Degay)
K: 24.9.1797. L: 1.11.1800. Comm: 27.6.1801. C: 6.1801.
Captured 30.11.1803 by the British during the capitulation of Santo Domingo, becoming HMS *Clorinde*; sold 6.3.1817.

A new 18pdr frigate order was placed at Brest in 1799, the first there for several years, as a first sign that the problems which had beset that dockyard were being overcome. However the optimism must have been premature, as the frigate was neither named nor laid down. If built, she would probably have been to Sané's *Virginie* design.

Ex VENETIAN PRIZES (1797)
Venetian 44-Gun Class, light frigates (*fregate leggere*) with 14 battery ports per side (3rd Rank). This class was built with the new 'double frame' method. Both ships were taken by the French on the building ways at Venice 20 May 1797, named by the French for deceased French military heroes of 1796-97, and completed for French service. As of May 1797 no other ships of this class were under construction or planned.

Dimensions (in Venetian measurements): 132.00ft max, 112.68ft keel x 33.45ft max x 23.20ft *puntale* (45.90m, 39.18m x 11.63m x 8.06m; in French units 141ft 4in, 120ft 7½in x 35ft 10in x 24ft 10in). Draught 16.50ft (5.73m, 17ft 8in).
Dimensions & tons (in French measurements): 147ft deck, 136ft keel x 36.33ft mld x 19.15ft creux (47.75, 44.17 x 11.80 x 6.22m). 680/1,300 tons. Draught 14.5/15.75ft (4.71/5.11m). Men: 340.
Guns (French): UD 28 x 18pdrs, SD 16 x 6pdrs or 12 x 6pdrs; (*Muiron* c1802) UD 28 x 12pdrs, SD 12 x 6pdrs.

Muiron Venice (laid down by Andrea Chiribiri on slip No.11 in 1789, completed by Andrea Calvin and launched in 1797 during the first French occupation of Venice).
K: 13.5.1789. L: 6.8.1797. C: 2.11.1797.
Brought Napoleon back from Egypt in 1799. Napoleon later ordered that she be preserved and a commemorative inscription was carved in gold on her stern ('*La Muiron, prise en 1797 dans l'Arsenal de Venise, par le Conquérant de l'Italie. Elle ramena d'Egypte en 1799 le Sauveur de la France*' or 'The *Muiron*, taken in 1797 in the Arsenal

Design draught for the Venetian 44-gun frigates that became the French *Muiron* and *Carrère*. (Biblioteca Civica, Trieste)

of Venice, by the Conqueror of Italy. She brought back from Egypt in 1799 the Saviour of France.'). Used as a transport to and from Santo Domingo in 1802. Damaged in collision with *Pomone* 30.1.1807 near Toulon, repaired. Became a headquarters hulk at Toulon 6.1807. Replaced by the frigate *Médée* of 1811 (which was renamed *Muiron*) and sold and BU in 1850.

Carrère Venice (laid down by Andrea Spadon on slip No.21 in 1789, completed by Francesco Coccon and launched in 1797 during the first French occupation of Venice).
K: 2.6.1789. L: 20.8.1797. C: 2.11.1797.
Named 1.6.1797. Accompanied *Muiron* back from Egypt in 1799, taking on board the French Generals Lennes, Murat, and Marmont. Captured 3.8.1801 off Elba by HMS *Phoenix* (36), *Pomone* (46), and *Pearl* (32), becoming HMS *Carrere*. When captured the 'very fine frigate' *Carrère*, according to the *London Gazette*, was armed with twenty-six 18pdrs with two spare ports in the battery, twelve brass 8pdrs, and two brass 36pdr carronades on her quarterdeck and forecastle (sic). The British commissioned her in the Mediterranean in 1801 with 28 x 18 pdrs, 12 x 32 pdr carronades and 4 x 9 pdrs, and Capt. Frederick Lewis Maitland brought her to Portsmouth on 24.9.1802. Not recommissioned, she was sold on 1.9.1814.

LOANED NEAPOLITAN VESSELS (1801).
The Bourbon Kingdom of Naples, previously allied against Bonaparte, was forced to conclude a treaty with France on 28 March 1801 (the Peace of Florence) under which British vessels were excluded from Neapolitan ports; as a consequence, on 14 July 1801 three Neapolitan 36-gun frigates stationed at Ancona were 'loaned' to France. Measurements and other particulars of these are uncertain, as is whether they were built to similar designs. Following the Peace of Amiens signed on 27 March 1802, France evacuated Neapolitan and Roman territory, two of these frigates were restored to the Kingdom of Naples at Toulon on 26 November and the third at Naples on 5 May 1803, all reverting to their original names.

Cérès (Neapolitan frigate *Cerere* launched at Naples 3.3.1783.)

Dimensions & tons: unknown.

Guns: (French) UD 28 x 18pdrs, SD 12 x 8pdrs.

Borrowed 14.7.1801 at Ancona from the Neapolitan Navy. Returned 26.11.1802 at Toulon and reverted to *Cerere*. Captured 14.2.1806 at Naples by the French after escorting the deposed Bourbon king and queen of Naples to Palermo and then returning to Naples for the queen's luggage. *Cerere* and the corvette *Fama* became the nucleus of the Neapolitan Navy of Joseph Bonaparte and later of Murat. Hauled out 1811 for reconstruction, re-launched 4.8.1812 and completed 12.1812 under the direction of Jean-François Lafosse. Reverted to Bourbon control 30.5.1815, sold 5.1820 and BU.

Minerve (Neapolitan frigate *Minerva* launched at Naples 19.10.1783).
Dimensions & tons: unknown.

Guns: (1801?) 28 x 18pdrs, 12 x 8pdrs; (1813) 26 x 18pdrs, 14 x 24pdr carronades, 2 x 12pdrs, 2 x 6pdrs.

Borrowed 14.7.1801 at Ancona from the Neapolitan Navy. Renamed *Sibylle* 24.12.1801. Returned 5.5.1803 at Naples and reverted to *Minerva*. Remained loyal to the Bourbons 1806-15. Wrecked 9.4.1821 in a storm while at anchor near Naples, wreck sold for BU.

Aréthuse (Neapolitan frigate *Aretusa* launched at Castellammare di Stabia 10.8.1789).
Dimensions & tons: unknown.

Guns: (French) 28 x 18pdrs, 12 x 8pdrs; (Neapolitan) 26 x 18pdrs; 14 x 18pdr carronades

Borrowed 14.7.1801 at Ancona from the Neapolitan Navy. Returned 26.11.1802 at Toulon and reverted to *Aretusa*. Taken 2.1806 by the French at the Naples dockyard while not in seagoing condition, said to have later rejoined the forces loyal to the Bourbons at Palermo but was not active for either side. Decomm. 6.1815 at Messina and sold for BU.

(C) Vessels acquired from 25 March 1802

On 7 April 1803 a program of fifteen 18-pounder frigates was directed, the ships to be completed by September 1804. These included two at Dunkirk (*Milanaise* and *Vistule*), two at Le Havre (not ordered), one at Cherbourg (*Manche*), one at Brest (not ordered, to follow *Zéphir*), one at Lorient (not ordered, to follow *Hermione*), two at Nantes (*Calypso* and *Topaze*, to follow *Président* and *Gloire*), one at Rochefort (*Ville de Milan*, to follow *Armide*), one at Bordeaux (*Pénélope*), one at Toulon (*Hermione*, to follow *Hortense*), one each at Villefranche and Marseille (ordered in June 1803 but never begun), and one at Antwerp (by contract with Danet, soon increased to two: *Néréide* and *Vénus*). No ships were planned at Saint-Malo to follow *Bellone*, *Piémontaise*, and *Sultane*. In June 1803, the Départements of Deux-Nèthes (Antwerp/Brabant) and Maine-et-Loire each offered to fund the construction of a frigate, to be named after their département and with *Deux-Nèthes* to be built at Antwerp, but these projects were never ordered. Before the end of the year the two Antwerp ships had been cancelled, *Calypso* had been moved from Nantes to Lorient, *Ville de Milan* had been cancelled at Rochefort and her name transferred to *Hermione* at Lorient, and *Pomone* had been ordered at a new yard at Genoa.

HORTENSE Class. 44-gun design by Jacques-Noël Sané. A slight modification of his previous design. *Hortense* was ordered on 6 April 1801 with *Rhin* but her designed keel length was extended c1802, and for convenience she is included here rather than in Section (B). The second ship at Toulon was originally named as *République Italienne* on 2 September 1803 and was to be paid for as a gift by the Italian Republic, but she was renamed *Hermione* on 26 December 1803 as part of a name swap that also involved *Ville de Milan* at Lorient. The Cherbourg vessel was initially named *Département de la Manche*, but the name was shortened to *Manche* after April 1806. The two frigates (*Néréide* and *Vénus*) ordered on 18 April 1803 from Danet at Antwerp would presumably have been of this design, but this order was cancelled in June 1803 with two brigs and like them may have been replaced with an order for prames. *Caroline* may have been built in place of the frigate *Deux-Nèthes* that was offered in June 1803 by a public subscription in the Département of that name to be built at Antwerp but not proceeded with. *Hortense* was named for Hortense de Beauharnais, Napoleon's stepdaughter, while *Caroline* and *Pauline* were named for two of his sisters.

Dimensions & tons: 144ft 0in, 130ft 5½in x 36ft 8in x 19ft 0in (46.77, 42.41 x 11.91 x 6.17m). 720/1,390 tons. Draught 16ft 5in/18ft 3in (5.33/5.93m). Men: 340 in wartime/260 in peacetime; included 8 officers.

Guns: (*Hortense*) UD 28 x 18pdrs; SD 12 x 8pdrs, 4 x 36pdr obusier. Later SD armaments: (*Hortense*, *Pomone*, *Pauline*, 1805-7) 8 x 8pdrs, 8 x 36pdr carronades; (*Manche* and *Caroline*, 1806) 8 x 8pdrs, 10 x 36pdr carronades; (*Hortense* and *Pauline*, 1810) 8 x 8pdrs, 8 x 24pdr carronades. (*Hermione*) UD 28 x 18pdrs; SD 4 x 8pdrs, 8 x 36pdr carronades, 4 x 29pdr carronades (probably British 32pdrs)

Hortense Toulon Dyd.
Ord: 6.4.1801. Named 30.9.1802. K: 14.12.1802. L: 3.7.1803. C: 1.1804.
Renamed *Flore* 14.3.1814, *Hortense* 22.3.1815, and *Flore* 15.7.1815. Struck 25.11.1840 at Brest and BU.

Néréide Danet, Antwerp
Ord: 18.4.1803. Order cancelled 6.1803.

Vénus Danet, Antwerp
Ord: 18.4.1803. Order cancelled 6.1803.

Pomone Murio & Migone, Genoa (Constructeurs, Bianchi and Jean-Baptiste Lefebvre).
K: 8.1803. Named 6.2.1804. L: 10.2.1805. C: 5.1805. Comm: 19.9.1805.
Captured 29.11.1811 by HMS *Active*, *Alceste*, and *Unite* (all 38) off Pelagosa while escorting the flûte *Persane* (also captured) from Corfu to Trieste in company with *Pauline*, becoming HMS *Ambuscade* (not commissioned); BU 11.1812 at Woolwich.

Hermione (ex *République Italienne* 26.12.1803) Toulon Dyd.
Ord: 2.9.1803 and named. K: 10.1803. L: 2.12.1804. Comm: 13.2.1805. C: 3.1805.
Wrecked 18.8.1808 near Trépied in the entrance to Brest, wreck burned by the British.

Département de la Manche Cherbourg Dyd. (Constructeur, Jacques Bonard)
Ord: 6.10.1803 and 30.1.1804. K: 22.6.1804. L: 5.4.1806. C: 9.1806.
Named commonly shortened to *Manche* after c4.1806. Taken by the British 4.12.1810 in the capitulation of Île de France (Mauritius) and sold there for BU.

Caroline Antwerp (Constructeur, Anne-Jean-Louis Leharivel-Durocher)
Ord: 24.4.1804. K: 5.1804. L: 15.8.1806. C: 12.1806.
Captured 21.9.1809 by HMS *Sirius* (36) and *Raisonnable* (64) during Rowley's raid on Saint Paul de La Réunion, becoming HMS *Bourbonnaise*; paid off 2.1810 and BU at Plymouth 4.1817.

Pauline Toulon Dyd.
Ord: 21.3.1806 and named. K: 5.1806. L: 18.4.1807. Comm:

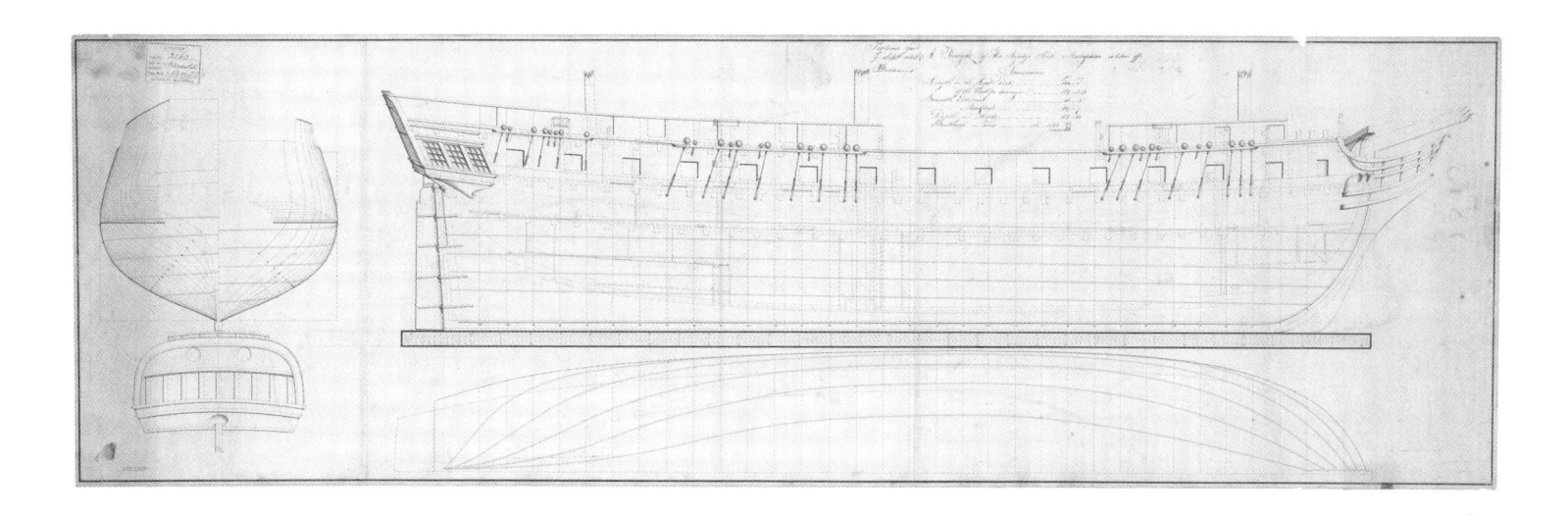

15.5.1807. C: 7.1807. Renamed *Bellone* 11.4.1814, *Pauline* 22.3.1815, and *Bellone* 15.7.1815. Reclassified 1840 as a corvette de charge of about 700 tons but not converted, struck at Toulon 11.12.1841.

Admiralty draught of *Madagascar* (ex *Néréïde*) as taken off at Portsmouth, dated 9 September 1813. It is interesting that Pestel's inspiration for this hull form seems to be the work of Forfait rather than the Sané models he followed earlier. (© National Maritime Museum J5811)

PIÉMONTAISE Class. 44 guns. This design was closer to those of Forfait than those of Pestel's original model, Sané, judging by a draught of *Néréïde* taken off by the British in 1813, although some of Pestel's ships continued to be attributed to Sané. *Piémontaise* was officially begun (*mise en chantier*) in December 1802, but work commenced on 22 March 1803. *Italienne* was begun (*mise en chantier*) in March 1803 but not laid down (*mise sur cale*) until 5.1805. The name *Italienne* was initially assigned to *Topaze* by an order of 10 May 1805 but this order was not carried out because that ship had already sailed and the name was instead given to *Sultane*. Some or all of the ships listed officially as built at Saint-Malo may have been built on the new slipways at neighbouring Saint-Servan.

  Dimensions & tons: 147ft 0in, 131ft 0in x 37ft 6in x 19ft 0in (47.75, 42.55 x 12.18 x 6.17m). 750/1,400 tons. Draught 16ft 3in/17ft 4in (5.28/5.62m). Men: 340 in wartime/260 in peacetime.
  Guns: (*Piémontaise*) UD 28 x 18pdrs; SD 14 x 36pdr obusiers, 4 x 8pdrs. Later SD armaments: (*Bellone*, 1808, and probably *Italienne*, 1806) 8 x 8pdrs, 8 x 36pdr carronades; (*Danaë*, probably) 14 x 24pdr carronades, 2 x 8pdrs.

Piémontaise Entreprise Ethéart, Saint-Malo.
  K: 12.1802. L: 15.11.1804. Comm: 6.12.1804. C: 4.1805.
  Captured 8.3.1808 by HMS *San Fiorenzo* (42) off Cape Comorin, India, becoming HMS *Piemontaise*. BU 1.1813.

Italienne (ex *Sultane* 5.1805) Entreprise Ethéart, Saint-Malo (Constructeur, Jean Denaix)
  Ord: 14.2.1803 (contract). K: 3.1803. L: 15.8.1806. Comm: 11.9.1806. C: 12.1806.
  Severely damaged 24.2.1809 with frigates *Calypso* and *Cybèle* in action at Sables d'Olonne with three British ships of the line, a frigate and a brig. Took refuge in the port after the battle but not repaired. Struck 11.1813, hulk sold c1816.

Bellone Entreprise Ethéart, Saint-Malo (Constructeur, Jean Denaix)
  Ord: 14.2.1803 (contract). K: 9.1803. L: 2.1808. C: 7.1808.
  Captured 4.12.1810 in the capitulation of Île de France (Mauritius), becoming HMS *Junon*. BU 2.1817.

Danaë Murio & Migone, Genoa (Constructeur, Jean-Baptiste Lefebvre)
  Named: 6.2.1804. Ord: 1.1805. K: 10.1805. L: 18.8.1807. C: 2.1808. Comm: 1.6.1808.
  Blew up (cause unknown) 4.9.1812 in the roadstead of Trieste with only one survivor.

Néréïde Saint-Malo
  Ord: 28.12.1805. K: 3.1806. L: 18.4.1809. Comm: 8.5.1809. C: 5.1809.
  With *Renommée* and *Clorinde* engaged HMS *Phoebe*, *Galatea*, *Astraea* (all 36), and *Racehorse* (18) 19.5.1811 off Tamatave, taken 25.5.1811 at the fall of Tamatave becoming HMS *Madagascar*. BU 1819.

GLOIRE Class. 44 guns. Designed by Pierre-Alexandre Forfait, a slightly modified version of his *Seine* class. Four were built by the Crucy brothers at Basse-Indre and Lorient and three were constructed at Le Havre to Forfait's plans (of the *Pensée*) by François-Toussaint Gréhan. The first pair were initially ordered at Lorient on 25 January 1801 and on 6 July 1801 a contract was awarded to the Crucy Brothers to build them there, but the order was transferred to Basse-Indre on 3 August 1802. *Calypso* was ordered from the Crucy brothers at Basse-Indre on 22 August 1803 but was transferred to their facility at Lorient on 14 October 1803 and may not have been laid down until September 1805.

  Dimensions & tons: 147ft 0in, 131ft 0in x 37ft 4in x 18ft 6in (47.75, 42.55 x 12.13 x 6.01m). 700/1,400 tons. Draught: 15ft 8in/16ft 10in (5.09/5.47m). Men: 340 in wartime/260 in peacetime.
  Guns: (*Gloire*, *Président*, 1803-4) UD 28 x 18pdrs; SD 12 x 8pdrs, 4 x 36pdr obusiers. Later SD armaments: (*Junon*, *Gloire*, and perhaps *Vénus*, 1806) 8 x 8pdrs, 8 x 36pdr carronades (10 in *Gloire*); (*Calypso* and *Amazone*, 1807-9) 14 x 36pdr carronades, 2 x 8pdrs. (*Topaze*) UD 28 x 18pdrs; SD 16 x 24pdr carronades, 6 x 8pdrs, for a total of 50 guns.

Gloire Louis, Antoine, & Mathurin Crucy, Basse-Indre.
  Ord: 25.1.1801 (Lorient). Named: 16.5.1801. K: 9.1802. L: 20.7.1803. Comm: 24.10.1803. C: 10.1803.
  Captured 25.9.1806 in the Atlantic by HMS *Mars* (74) and *Centaur* (74), becoming HMS *Gloire*. Frigates *Armide*, *Minerve*, and *Infatigable* were taken in the same action. BU 9.1812.

Président (ex *Minerve* 26.12.1803) Louis, Antoine, & Mathurin Crucy,

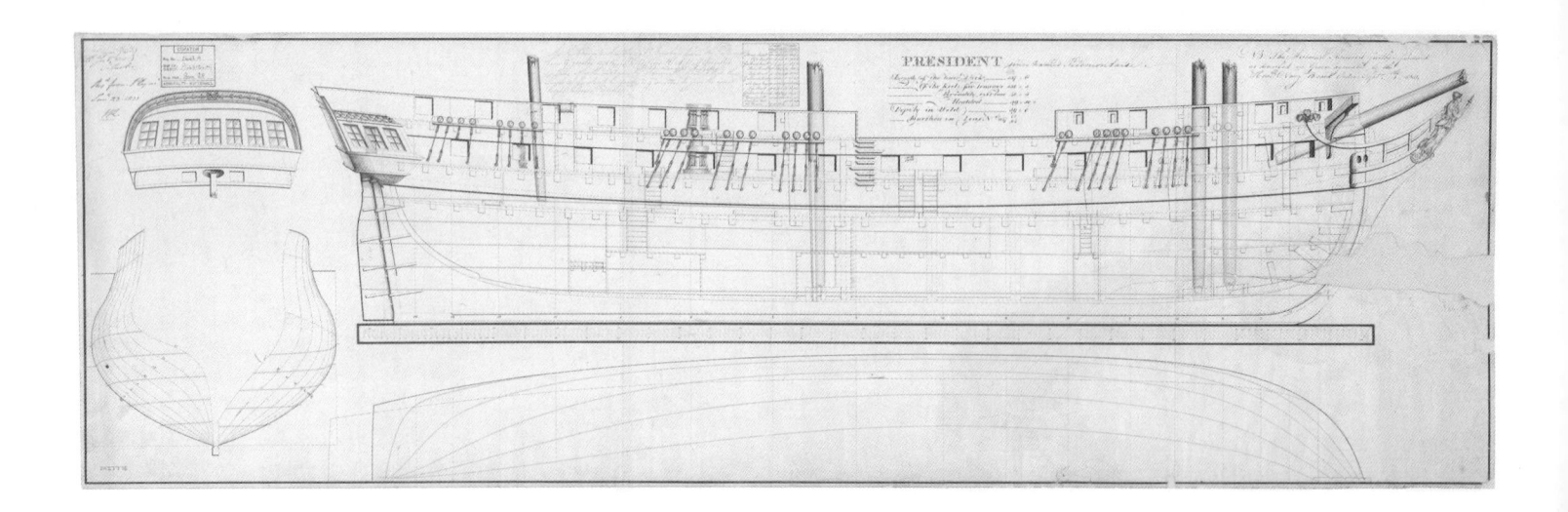

Basse-Indre.
>Ord: 25.1.1801 (Lorient). K: 9.1802. L: 4.6.1804. Comm: 20.7.1804. C: 8.1804.
>Captured 28.9.1806 off Morbihan near Belle-Île by HMS *Canopus* (80) and *Despatch* (18), becoming HMS *President* and in 1815 HMS *Piedmontaise*. BU 12.1815.

Calypso Lorient Dyd, by Louis, Antoine, & Mathurin Crucy
>Ord: 22.8.1803 (Basse-Indre). Named: 16.9.1803. K: 9.1803. L: 8.1.1807. Comm: 23.4.1807. C: 4.1807.
>Grounded during combat at Sables d'Olonne 27.2.1809, refloated and taken into Sables d'Olonne but found unusable. Struck 1.1813 and sold 1814.

Topaze Louis, Antoine, & Mathurin Crucy, Basse-Indre.
>Ord: 1.9.1803. K: 12.1803. L: 1.3.1805. Comm: 22.3.1805. C: 4.1805.
>Captured 22.1.1809 off Guadeloupe by HMS *Cleopatra* (32), *Jason* (32) and *Hazard* (16), becoming HMS *Jewel* and on 25.5.1809 HMS *Alcmene*. BU 2.1816.

Junon Le Havre (Constructeur, François-Toussaint Gréhan).
>Ord: 26.3.1805. K: 4.1805. L: 16.8.1806. Comm: 23.11.1806. C: 11.1806.
>Captured 10.2.1809 by HMS *Horatio* (48), *Latona* (38) and others off Iles des Saintes, becoming HMS *Junon*; retaken 13.12.1809 by *Renommée* and *Clorinde* in mid-Atlantic, in bad condition and burnt the same day.

Vénus Le Havre (Constructeur, François-Toussaint Gréhan).
>Ord: 26.3.1805. K: 4.1805. L: 5.4.1806. C: 7.1806. Comm: 22.11.1806.
>Captured 18.9.1810 in the Indian Ocean by HMS *Boadicea* (46) assisted by *Otter* (16), and *Staunch* (12), becoming HMS *Nereide*. BU 5.1816.

Amazone Le Havre (Constructeur, François-Toussaint Gréhan).
>Ord: 26.3.1805. K: 5.1806. L: 17.9.1807. Comm: 2.1.1809. C: 2.1809.
>Took refuge 23.3.1811 with bottom damage at Gatteville near Barfleur, then attacked by HMS *Berwick* (74), *Amelia* (38), and two brigs and scuttled there 24.3.1811.

ARMIDE Class. 44 guns. A series of fifteen ordered to a design by Pierre-Jacques-Nicolas Rolland, although three of these were later cancelled, and another three were not launched until after 1815. A younger son of Pierre-Nicolas Rolland (constructeur at Brest in the

Admiralty draught of *President* (renamed *Piedmontaise* in 1815) dated Plymouth 21 January 1811. This Forfait hull form was adopted for the post-war British *Seringapatam* class – to which pencil annotations on the draught refer – but the design was never entirely satisfactory in Royal Navy service and later ships were subject to considerable modification. The British ships never matched the sailing qualities of their French prototype, the official conclusion being that they were much more heavily built. (© National Maritime Museum J3962)

1780s), Pierre-Jacques-Nicolas was chief constructeur at Rochefort from 19 April 1804 until 1811. Rolland's designs were generally similar to those of Sané, of whom he had been a pupil, and as Inspector-General of the Génie Maritime he was allowed to continue using his own plans at Rochefort and Bordeaux after Sané's plans became standard elsewhere in 1810. The Courau's shipyard at Bordeaux was located next to the navy's Chantier du Roi, and they may have used its slipways.
>Dimensions & tons: 144ft 8in, 133ft 6in x 37ft 0in x 19ft 0in (46.99, 43.40 x 12.02 x 6.17m). 759/1,430 tons. Draught 15ft 8in/17ft 4in (5.09/5.63m). Men: 340 in wartime/260 in peacetime.
>Guns (*Armide*): UD 28 x 18pdrs; SD 8 x 12pdrs, 4 x 36pdr obusiers. Later SD armaments: (*Minerve*, 1805) 12 x 8pdrs; (*Pénélope, Flore, Amphitrite,* and *Niémen*, 1807-9) 8 x 8pdrs, 8 x 36pdr carronades; (*Saale*, 1811, and some of the previous group modified) 8 x 8pdrs, 8 x 24pdr carronades; (*Alcmene, Circé,* and *Antigone*, 1812-16) 14 x 24pdr carronades, 2 x 8pdrs; (*Magicienne*, 1825) UD 28 x 18pdrs; SD 16 x 24pdr carronades, 2 x 8pdrs. (*Antigone*) UD 28 x 18pdrs; SD 14 x 24pdr carronades, 2 x 8pdrs.

Armide Rochefort Dyd.
>K: 16.11.1802. L: 24.4.1804. C: 5.1804. Comm: 1.6.1804.
>Captured 25.9.1806 by HMS *Monarch* (74) and *Centaur* (74) while breaking out of Rochefort, becoming HMS *Armide*. The frigates *Infatigable, Gloire,* and *Minerve* were taken in the same action. BU 11.1815.

Pénélope Bordeaux (Constructeurs, Paul Filhon, Jean-Baptiste Hérel from 9.1804, Jean Chaumont from 7.1806).
>Frame begun 1802. Ord: 22.8.1803. K: 12.2.1804. L: 28.10.1806. Comm: 6.11.1806. C: 1.1807.
>Condemned 1826 at Toulon, hulked, BU after 11.1829.

Ville de Milan Rochefort Dyd
>Ord: 2.9.1803 as a gift from the Italian Republic. Name transferred to *Hermione* at Lorient 26.12.1803 and this vessel cancelled 2.1804.

Minerve Rochefort Dyd. (Constructeurs, Jean-Baptiste Hérel, from

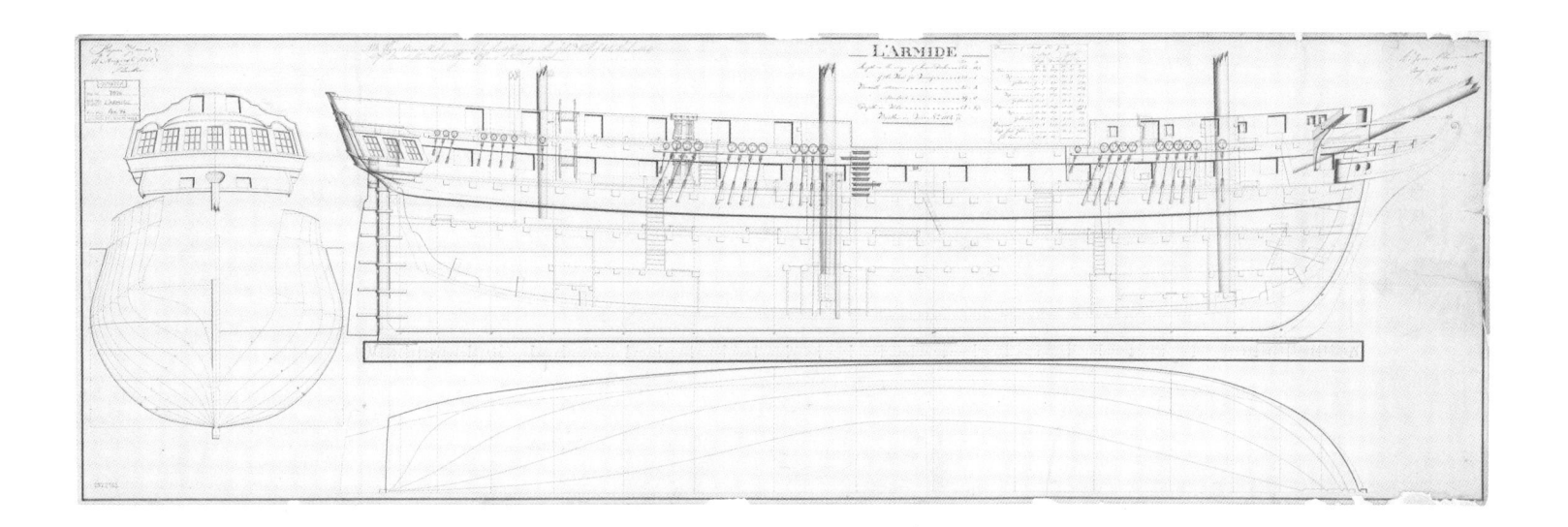

9.1804 Jean-Charles Rigault de Genouilly).
   K: 11.5.1804. L: 9.9.1805. Comm: 25.11.1805. C: 11.1805.
   Captured 25.9.1806 while in the Soleil division with *Gloire, Infatigable, Armide, Thétis* and the brigs *Sylphe* and *Lynx*. These ships had left Île d'Aix on 24.9.1806 and were intercepted and pursued the next day by 7 ships of the line including *Revenge* (74) and *Monarch* (74). Became HMS *Alceste*, wrecked 18.2.1817 in the China Sea.

Flore Rochefort Dyd. (Constructeurs, Jean-Baptiste Hérel, then Jean-Baptiste Hubert)
   Ord: 3.8.1804. K: 1.7.1804. L: 11.11.1806. Comm: 1.1.1807. C: 3.1807.
   Wrecked 30.11.1811 in a squall off Chioggia, near Venice.

Amphitrite Cherbourg Dyd. (Constructeurs, Jacques Bonard, from 12.1806 Jean-Michel Segondat)
   Ord: 6.1.1806. K: 8.1806. L: 11.4.1808. Comm: 1.7.1808. C: 7.1808.
   Burned 3.2.1809 by her crew at Fort Royal, Martinique, to avoid capture during the British assault on the island.

Niémen François, Jean-Baptiste, & Laurent Courau, Bordeaux (Constructeurs, Jean Chaumont, from 8.1808 Antoine Bonnet-Lescure)
   K: 5.1807. L: 8.11.1808. Comm: 22.11.1808. C: 1.1809.
   Captured 6.4.1809 in the Gironde off Cordouan by HMS *Amethust* (46) and *Arethusa* (48) two days after leaving Bordeaux for Martinique, becoming HMS *Niemen*. BU 9.1815.

Saale (ex-*Andromède* 22.4.1807) Rochefort Dyd. (Constructeurs, Jean-Charles Rigault de Genouilly, then Antoine Bonnet-Lescure)
   Ord: 24.11.1806 and named. K: 10.12.1806. L: 28.10.1810. C: 2.1811. Comm: 6.11.1811.
   Renamed *Amphitrite* 24.9.1814, *Saale* 22.3.1815, and *Amphitrite* 15.7.1815. Struck 1821 at Rochefort, BU there 4-6.1821.

Alcmène Cherbourg Dyd. (Constructeur, Jean-Michel Segondat)
   K: 4.7.1810. L: 3.10.1811. Comm: 1.1.1812. C: 3.1812.
   Boarded and captured 16.1.1814 near La Palma in the Canary Islands by HMS *Venerable* (74), becoming HMS *Dunira* and, in 1814, HMS *Immortalite*. Sold 1.1837.

Circé Rochefort Dyd. (Constructeur, Pierre Rolland)
   K: 2.1810. L: 15.12.1811. C: 3.1812. Comm: 22.4.1812.
   Converted to a 28-gun corvette (q.v.) 1831-33. Struck 26.4.1844 at Brest and BU the same year.

Andromède Bayonne (Constructeur, Jean Baudry)
   Ord: 16.5.1808. K: 22.6.1808. Cancelled 4.1814 when about 6/24ths complete. Dismantled on the ways 2-3.1815 and timbers sent to Rochefort.

Émeraude Bayonne (Constructeur, Jean Baudry)
   Ord: 16.5.1808. K: 22.6.1808. Cancelled 4.1814 when about 6/24ths complete. Disposition as *Andromède*.

Cornélie François, Jean-Baptiste, & Laurent Courau, Bordeaux (Constructeurs, Jean-Baptiste Hubert and Antoine Bonnet-Lescure)
   K: 1.1812. Was 22/24ths complete when capsized on the ways 10.3.1814 by Royalist insurgents from Bordeaux vandalizing the Couraus' property because they supported Napoleon. Damaged hulk sold 10.1814 to its builders, who probably used some of her timbers to complete *Antigone*, below.

Antigone François, Jean-Baptiste, & Laurent Courau, Bordeaux (Constructeurs, Jean-Baptiste Hubert and Antoine Bonnet-Lescure)
   K: 1.1812. L: 13.3.1816. Comm: 9.5.1816. C: 5.1816.
   Struck 3.8.1829 at Lorient, then cut down to a careening hulk (*ponton de carène*) at Brest.

Cléopâtre Cherbourg Dyd. (Constructeurs, Jean-Michel Segondat and Paul Leroux)
   K: 10.3.1812. Named: 20.4.1812. L: 1.4.1817. Comm: 1.4.1817. C: 6.1817.
   Drydocked at Brest for inspection 4.8.1823, struck 30.9.1823, BU in dock 1823-24. Her short life was attributed to the fact that she had been built on open building ways and had been continuously in service since then.

Magicienne Rochefort Dyd. (Constructeurs, Jean-Baptiste Hubert, then Pierre Rolland)
   K: 1.1813. L: 11.4.1823. Comm: 22.5.1823. C: 5.1823.
   Lost on the Palawan Reef in the Philippines 29.11.1840.

HERMIONE (VILLE DE MILAN). 46 guns. A one-off ship built at Lorient to plans by Antoine Geoffroy that were inspired by Forfait and

Admiralty draught of *Armide* as refitted for British service, dated 11 August 1810. The rounded midship section in this Rolland design retains only a hint of the classic 'two-turn' bilge, which by this date was largely the preserve of Sané. The large ports in the barricades indicate that, apart from two long 9pdr chase guns, the forecastle and quarterdeck armament of British frigates by this date was entirely comprised of 32pdr carronades. The draught also lists the mast and spar dimensions, but these are mostly the standard sizes for a British 38-gun frigate, except for the spanker gaff and boom, which may be a consequence of the mizzen mast being shifted aft in 1813. (© National Maritime Museum J5733)

probably rectified by Sané. She may originally have been included in a contract of 6 July 1800 with the Crucy brothers to build the 74-gun *Suffren* and *Algesiras* at Lorient but if so she was reassigned in 1802. A frigate named *Ville de Milan* had been ordered at Rochefort on 2 September 1803 as a gift from the Italian Republic (see the *Armide* class below), but in December this name was transferred to *Hermione* at Lorient and the name *Hermione* was transferred to *République Italienne* at Toulon.

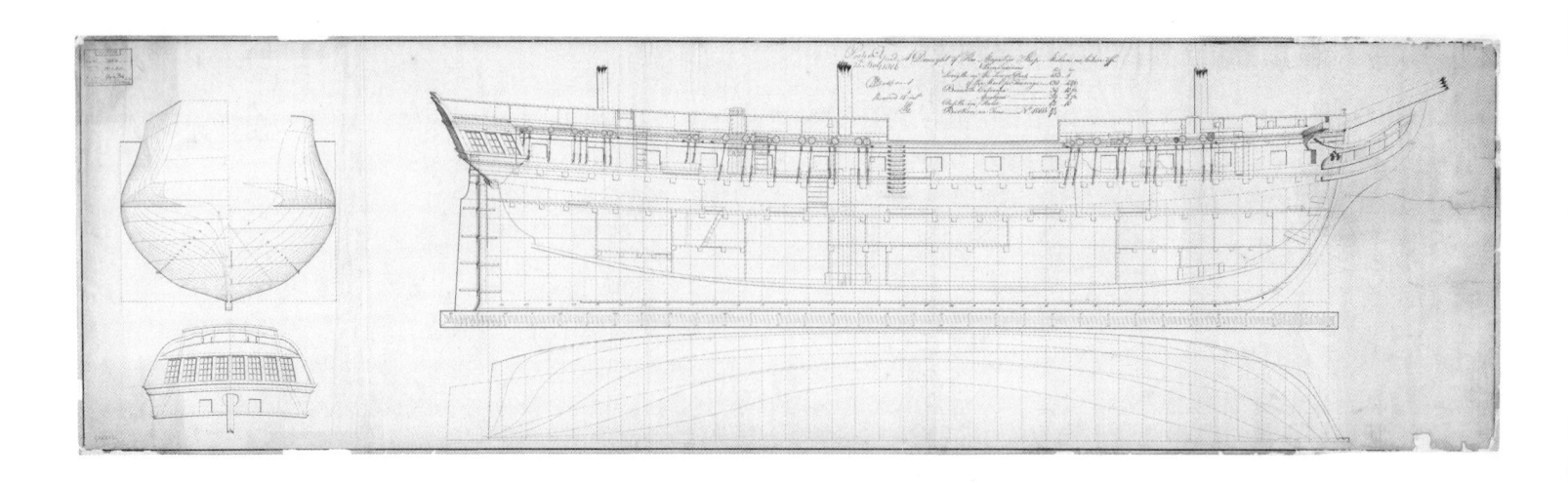

> Dimensions & tons: 144ft 8in x 37ft 7in x 18ft 6in (47.0 x 12.2 x 6.0m). 700/1,350 tons. Draught 16ft 8in/17ft 4in (5.41/5.62m). Men: 340 in wartime/260 in peacetime.
>
> Guns: UD 28 x 18pdrs; SD 14 x 36pdr obusiers, 4 x 8pdrs. Battery reduced to 26 x 18pdrs in 1805.

Hermione Lorient Dyd. (Constructeur, Antoine Geoffroy)
> Ord: 30.9.1802 and named. K: 1.1803. L: 15.11.1803. Comm: 24.2.1804. C: 2.1804.
>
> Renamed *Ville de Milan* 26.12.1803. Coming from Martinique boarded and captured HMS *Cleopatra* 18.2.1805 but both badly damaged ships then captured 23.2.1805 off Bermuda by HMS *Leander* (52) and Cambridge (80). Became HMS *Milan*, BU 12.1815.

Later MÉDUSE Class. 44 guns. This design by Charles Segondat-Duvernet was used for a quartet of frigates built at Dunkirk closely following the designer's earlier plan for the *Méduse* of 1782 (to which four ships had been built at Lorient between 1782 and 1793 – see Section A).

> Dimensions & tons: 143ft 6in, 134ft 10in x 37ft 0in x 19ft 0in (46.61, 43.80 x 12.02 x 6.17m). 760/1,350 tons. Draught 16ft 9in/18ft 10in (5.44/6.12m). Men: 340 in wartime/260 in peacetime.
>
> Guns: UD 28 x 18pdrs; SD 8 x 8pdrs, 8 x 24pdr carronades. (*Milanaise* was originally fitted with 8 x 36pdr obusiers until 36pdr and then 24pdr carronades were supplied).

Milanaise (ex *Amphitrite* 10.5.1805) Dunkirk (Constructeur, Louis Bretocq)
> Ord: 22.3.1803. K: 31.5.1803. L: 23.9.1805. Comm: 23.9.1805. C: 3.1806.
>
> Renamed *Sirène* 30.8.1814, *Milanaise* 22.3.1815, and *Sirène* 15.7.1815. At Brest 1818 in need of 20/24ths repairs, struck 1818-19 and hulked (possibly at Cherbourg). BU 1837.

Vistule (ex *Nymphe* 22.4.1807) Dunkirk (Constructeur, Louis Bretocq)
> Ord: 22.3.1803. K: 4.2.1805. L: 22.8.1808. Comm: 27.2.1812. C: 2.1812.

Admiralty draught of *Milan* as taken off at Portsmouth, dated 24 May 1806. The hull form of this one-off design by Geoffroy was an interesting combination of a Forfait-style 'V' section, with a hint of the 'two-turn' bilge shape. (© National Maritime Museum J5688)

> Renamed *Danaë* 30.8.1814, *Vistule* 22.3.1815, and *Danaë* 15.7.1815. Struck 1818, BU at Brest 7-8.1818.

Oder (ex *Iphigénie* 22.4.1807) Dunkirk (Constructeur, Louis Bretocq)
> Ord: 14.10.1805 and named. K: 11.1805 (on the ways: 6.11.1806). L: 14.7.1813. Comm: 9.11.1813. C: 11.1813.
>
> Renamed *Thémis* 30.8.1814, *Oder* 22.3.1815, and *Thémis* 15.7.1815. Struck 6.7.1831, prison hulk at Toulon. Last mentioned 1832.

Perle Dunkirk (Constructeur, Louis Bretocq)
> K: 5.1808. L: 13.8.1813. Comm: 9.11.1813. C: 11.1813.
>
> Used in 1814 to return French prisoners from Lisbon and Stettin, then put in reserve. Drydocked at Brest for inspection 4.8.1823, struck 30.9.1823, then BU in dock. See *Cléopâtre* for a similarly short career.

PALLAS Class. 44 guns. A class of 62 ships built to plans by Jacques-Noël Sané that were essentially identical to those of *Hortense*. From 1805 the standard design of Sané became predominant and – while other classes of frigate were contributed by other designers – Sané's design was used for the vast majority of 18-pounder frigates built thereafter for the First Empire up to 1814. Many of the frigates of this class were ordered at yards outside France, and all 62 ships that were named and begun are detailed below according to place of construction in the order of the start of construction of the first ship. Besides these 62 frigates, other 18-pounder frigates were ordered or projected during the First Empire, but were not completed (and in most cases not laid down on the stocks). The only one of these that received a name was *Vestale*, ordered in October 1810 to be laid down in March 1811 at Leghorn (Livorno) but not begun.

> Dimensions & tons: 144ft 6in, 130ft 6in x 36ft 8in x 19ft 0in (46.93, 42.41 x 11.91 x 6.20m). 760/1,390 tons. Draught 15ft 5in/17ft 4in (5.01/5.63m). Men: 340 in wartime/260 in peacetime.
>
> Guns: UD 28 x 18pdrs; SD 8 x 8pdrs, 8 x 36pdr carronades (8 ships, 1807-9, with *Clorinde* receiving only 2 x 8pdrs). The 36pdrs in three or four of these ships were replaced with 24pdrs in 1810, and beginning in 1810 all the later units except those noted individually received the new standard spardeck armament of 16 x 24pdr carronades and 2 x 18pdrs.

Basse-Indre Group. The seven frigates at Basse-Indre were fabricated under contract by the two brothers Mathurin and Antoine Crucy, who received this yard in the breakup in 1806 of the firm operated by the three Crucy brothers. Mathurin left the firm in 1809 and Antoine delegated the work at the yard to his senior shipwright, Bonissant until he retired in 1812. By then the silting of the estuary had made further frigate construction at Basse-Indre impracticable.

Pallas Mathurin & Antoine Crucy, Basse-Indre.
   Ord: 26.3.1805. Named: 2.4.1805. K: 10.1805. L: 9.4.1808. C: 6.1808.
   Unserviceable 11.1821 at Brest and struck, BU 5-7.1824.

Elbe (ex-*Aréthuse* 14.5.1807) Mathurin & Antoine Crucy, Basse-Indre.
   Ord: 26.3.1805. K: 10.1805. L: 23.5.1808. C: 11.7.1808. C: 7.1808.
   Renamed *Calypso* 30.8.1814, *Elbe* 22.3.1815, and *Calypso* 15.7.1815. Struck 8.11.1824 at Brest and hulked. BU 1841.

Renommée Mathurin & Antoine Crucy, Basse-Indre.
   Ord: 26.3.1805 and named. K: 10.1805. L: 20.8.1808. C: 3.1809. Comm: 1.7.1809.
   Sent from Brest 3.2.1811 with *Clorinde* and *Néréide* to reinforce Île de France, which had already fallen. Pursued by the English from Île de France and captured 20.5.1811 off Foulpointe, Madagascar by HMS *Astraea* (36), becoming HMS *Java*. Taken by USS *Constitution* 29.12.1812 and burnt 1.1.1813.

Nymphe Mathurin & Antoine Crucy, Basse-Indre
   Ord: 25.4.1807 (contract). K: 7.1807. Named 10.10.1807. L: 1.5.1810. C: 8.1810. Comm: 1.1.1811.
   Struck 5.9.1832 at Brest and ordered converted to headquarters hulk to replace *Pensée*. Was a guard hulk and disembarkation platform at Brest c1855. Unserviceable 6.1872, BU 1872-73.

Ariane Mathurin & Antoine Crucy, Basse-Indre
   Ord: 25.4.1807 (contract). K: 7.1807. L: 7.4.1811. Comm: 20.6.1811. C: 6.1811.
   Intercepted with *Andromaque* and the brig *Mameluck* by HMS *Northumberland* (74) and *Growler* (12) while returning from an Atlantic cruise, the two frigates grounded on 22.5.1812 while trying to take refuge at Lorient and were burnt to avoid capture, subsequently exploding.

Andromaque Antoine Crucy, Basse-Indre
   Ord: 10.11.1808 and 26.12.1808. K: 4.1809. L: 21.5.1811. Comm: 1.8.1811. C: 8.1811.
   Lost 22.5.1812 with *Ariane*, above.

Rubis Antoine Crucy, Basse-Indre
   Ord: 21.10.1809 (contract 5.5.1810). K: 6.1810. Named 26.10.1810. L: 25.5.1812. Comm: 7.8.1812. C: 8.1812.
   Wrecked in a storm 5.2.1813 on Tamara Island, Guinea, and burned by her crew, who returned home in the captured Portuguese ship *Serra*.

Flushing Group. One of the two frigates ordered to be built to this design at Flushing (Vlissingen) for the French Navy was launched and nearly complete when the port was seized by the British during the Walcheren campaign in August 1809. The second (never named) was due to be begun that same month on the slipway vacated by her sister but was never started.

Fidèle Flushing
   Ord: 14.8.1806. K: 8.1806 and 4.1807. L: 6.1809. C: 9.1809.
   Captured 16.8.1809 by the British at the seizure of Flushing. Sailed to Woolwich, arriving 26.12.1809. Commissioned 2.1811 as HMS *Laurel*. Wrecked 31.1.1812 on the Govinas rock in the Teigneuse Passage near Quiberon Point.

Le Havre Group. The three frigates ordered at Le Havre were constructed by François-Toussaint Gréhan. *Élisa* was named after one of Napoleon's sisters.

Élisa Le Havre
   Ord: 20.5.1806. K: 8.1806. L: 22.9.1808. Comm: 1.11.1809. C: 11.1809.
   Wrecked 22.12.1810 near Réville after departing La Hogue at night to escape British blockaders.

Gloire Le Havre
   Ord: 26.12.1808. K: 2.1809. L: 3.11.1811. Comm: 15.11.1811. C: 2.1812.
   Unserviceable 11.1822, struck 1822 at Brest and hulked. BU 10.1828 to 1.1829.

Cybèle Le Havre
   K: 4.1810. L: 11.4.1815. Comm: 1.2.1816. C: 2.1816.
   Converted to a 28-gun corvette (q.v.) 1833-36, struck 4.3.1850 at Toulon, hulk *Remise* 1850, BU 1894.

Paimboeuf Group. The seven frigates built by contract at Paimboeuf were fabricated by Louis Crucy and his son, Michel-Louis Crucy, who received this yard in the breakup in 1806 of the firm operated by the three Crucy brothers. The new enterprise was in the name of the son only, but the father took an active role. The firm encountered financial difficulties and was dissolved on 15 October 1813. It was proposed that another shipbuilder, Auguste Guibert, would take over the yard (and he did finish two brigs there), but in May 1814 the Minister of Marine decided on account of the return of peace to revert to construction of warships only in the navy's dockyards. The final pair of frigates (*Astrée* and *Armide*) were then still on the stocks at Paimboeuf about one quarter complete, and their construction was halted on 25 May 1814. Their timbers were moved to Lorient, where they were re-started on the stocks in September 1814.

Clorinde Louis & Michel-Louis Crucy, Paimboeuf
   Ord: 19.7.1806 and named. K: 7.1806. L: 6.8.1808. C: 3.1809. Comm: 1.5.1809.
   Captured off Ushant 26.2.1814 by HMS *Dryad* (36) and *Achates* (16), becoming HMS *Aurora*; coal hulk 3.1832, BU at Plymouth 5.1851.

Méduse Louis & Michel-Louis Crucy, Paimboeuf
   Ord: 11.3.1807 (contract). K: 8.1807. L: 1.7.1810. Comm: 26.9.1810. C: 9.1810.
   Stranded 2.7.1816 on the Bank of Arguin while en route to retake possession of Senegal under the command of a recently returned émigré, abandoned 5.7.1816 with most of the approximately 250 persons in the ship's boats surviving and most of the roughly 150 on a hastily improvised raft perishing.

Aréthuse Louis & Michel-Louis Crucy, Paimboeuf
   Ord: 26.12.1808. K: 3.1809. L: 11.5.1812. Comm: 27.6.1812. C: 7.1812.
   Converted to a 28-gun corvette (q.v.) 1833-34. Struck 11.6.1851, coal hulk at Brest. Unserviceable 1865 and BU.

Sultane Louis & Michel-Louis Crucy, Paimboeuf
   Ord: 21.10.1809 (contract 16.11.1809). K: 1.1810. L: 30.5.1813. Comm: 1.9.1813. C: 9.1813.
   Captured 26.3.1814 by HMS *Hannibal* (74) off Île de Batz, Brittany, becoming HMS *Sultane* but never commissioned; BU 3.8.1819.

Étoile (ex *Hymenée* 7.1810) Louis & Michel-Louis Crucy, Paimboeuf
   Ord: 21.10.1809 (contract 16.11.1809). K: 8.1810. L: 28.7.1813. Comm: 1.9.1813. C: 10.1813.
   Captured off La Hougue 27.3.1814 by HMS *Hebrus* (42) and *Sparrow* (18), becoming HMS *Topaze*; hulked 2.1823, BU 12.1851.

Astrée Louis & Michel-Louis Crucy, Paimboeuf, later Lorient (Constructeur at Lorient, Pierre Le Grix)
   Ord: 25.3.1812 (contract). K: 5.1812 (at Paimboeuf), 9.1814 (at

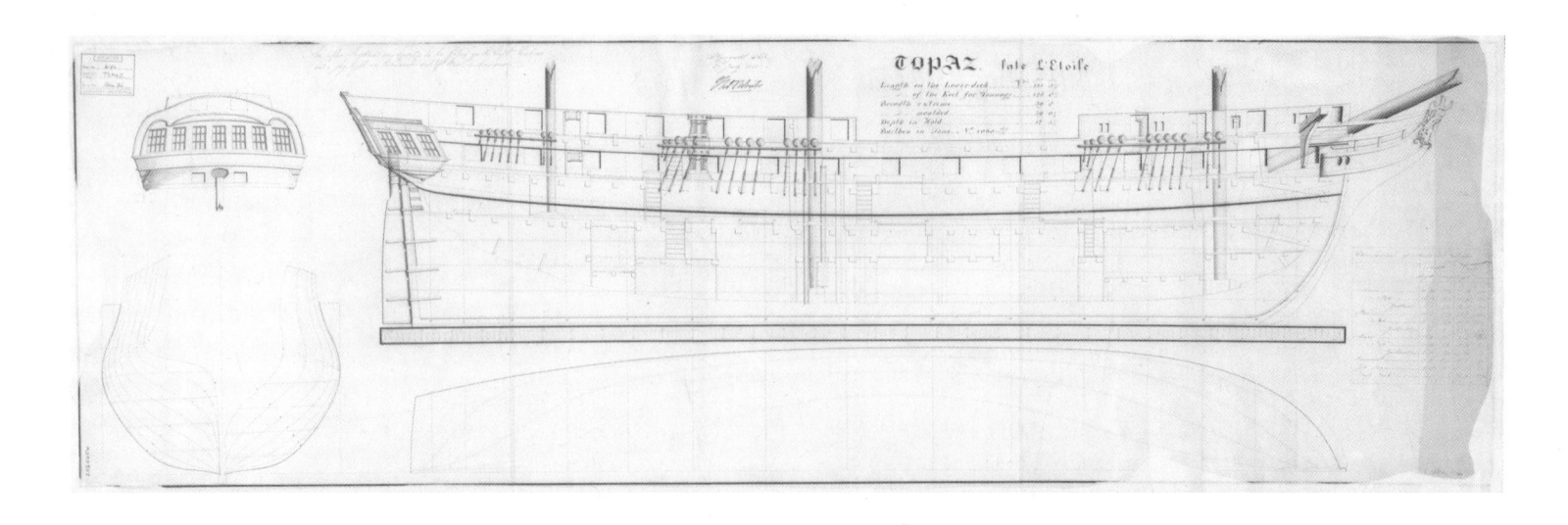

Admiralty draught of *Topaze* as refitted, dated 27 July 1815. Note the secondary (emergency) steering wheel ahead of the main cabin bulkhead. This was a British innovation introduced in 1808, but rarely depicted on draughts – except those of prizes as refitted for Royal Navy service. (© National Maritime Museum J5454)

Lorient). L: 28.4.1820. Comm: 3.10.1821. C: 10.1821.

Struck 29.10.1842, cut down to hulk at Rochefort between 7.1844 and 2.1845.

Armide Louis & Michel-Louis Crucy, Paimboeuf, later Lorient (Constructeur at Lorient from c1819, Joseph Fauveau)

Ord: 25.3.1812 (contract). K: 5.1812 (at Paimboeuf), 9.1814 (at Lorient). L: 1.5.1821. Comm: 5.3.1823.

Guns as completed: UD 28 x 18pdrs; SD 16 x 24pdr carronades, 2 x short 18pdrs.

Fitted as hospital ship at Lorient between 1843 and 11.1844, and as such was redesignated as an 800-ton transport by a decision of 14.5.1851. Training ship 6.1859. Struck 22.12.1864, training hulk, storage hulk for provisions 1866 at Lorient, renamed *Entrepôt* 1866, ordered BU 26.3.1888.

Venice Group (i) These two frigates were begun in December 1806 as part of the first large naval construction program initiated by the French at Venice that also included five 74-gun ships of the line. The two frigates were built for Napoleon's Italian Navy with the 74-gun *Reale Italiano* and *Rigeneratore*, the brigs *Friedland* (November) and *Nettuno*, and the schooners *Psiche, Ortensia,* and *Gloria*. The other three 74s of this program were for the Imperial French Navy. Two more brigs, two corvettes (the *Carolina* class) and the small *corvetta-brig Carlotta* for the Italians followed in early 1807. The Italians rated these two frigates at 36 guns and called them *frigate leggere* in contrast to the later *Princesse de Bologne* group which they rated at 44 guns and called *frigate pesanti*, but all were probably built to the standard French 18-pounder design just as the 74s were built to the standard French 74-gun design. The armaments in French records are listed below. The Italian naval constructor supervising work on these frigates was Battistella, whom Andrea Salvini had put in charge of frigate construction at Venice. The British regarded *Corona* as very weakly built even by (weak) French standards and initially intended to arm their prize with 32pdr carronades in the battery, but ended up giving her lightweight 24pdr Gover short-barrel guns instead.

Corona Venice (constructed by Battistella)

K: 26.12.1806. L: 27.12.1807. C: 12.1808.

Guns: UD 28 x 18pdrs; SD 10 x 8pdrs, 2 x 36pdr carronades. At Venice in 1809 and at Ancona in 1810. On 22.10.1810 she went into the port of Lissa (now Vis in Croatia), where she captured several enemy vessels. Captured 13.3.1811 at the Battle of Lissa by HMS *Active* (38) and Hoste's squadron, becoming HMS *Daedalus*; wrecked off Ceylon 2.7.1813.

Favorita Venice (constructed by Battistella)

K: 28.12.1806. L: 4.10.1808. C: 1809.

Guns: UD 28 x 18pdrs; SD 8 x 8pdrs, 8 x 36pdr carronades. Became French *Favorite* when traded for 3 brigs (*Cyclope, Écureuil,* and *Mercure*) in 4.1810. Received her guns in 6.1810. . At Ancona on 1.10.1810 together with the Italian frigates *Corona* and *Bellona* and the brig *Mercurio*. On 22.10.1810 went into the port of Lissa (now Vis in Croatia) flying the British flag and captured several enemy vessels. Was the French flagship at the Battle of Lissa 13.3.1811, beached and burned on Lissa after receiving heavy damage and losing most of her officers.

Toulon Group. The following five frigates were built at Toulon Dockyard to this design, the first three being constructed by François-Frédéric Poncet and others. On 11 April 1814 the *Amélie* and *Adrienne* (both named after sisters of Bonaparte who had died as children) were renamed *Junon* and *Aurore*; as in other such renamings their Napoleonic names were restored on 22 March 1815, and their Bourbon names were reinstated on 15 July.

Amélie Toulon Dyd

Ord: 10.10.1807 and named. K: 11.1807. L: 21.7.1808. C: 1.1809. Comm: 1.2.1809.

Renamed *Junon* 11.4.1814, *Amélie* 22.3.1815, and *Junon* 15.7.1815. Struck 17.8.1842 at Toulon.

Adrienne Toulon Dyd

Ord: 10.10.1807. K: 8.1808. L: 15.8.1809. Comm: 13.11.1809. C: 11.1809.

Renamed *Aurore* 11.4.1814, *Adrienne* 22.3.1815, and *Aurore* 15.7.1815. Renamed *Dauphine* 5.9.1829, reverted to *Aurore* 9.8.1830. Reclassified as an 800-ton corvette de charge in 1840, converted at Toulon in 1841-46, reclassified as a transport 1.1846 with the other corvettes de charge. Struck 5.7.1847 at Toulon, probably BU 1849.

Melpomène Toulon Dyd

Ord: 18.1.1810. Named 23.7.1810. K: 12.1810. L: 17.5.1812. Comm: 1.6.1812. C: 6.1812.

Left Toulon 24.4.1815 to pick up Napoleon's mother at Naples, captured 30.4.1815 by HMS *Rivoli* (74) between the islands of Ischia and Procida off Naples; sold 6.1821 at Portsmouth. (*Dryade* succeeded in a similar mission 3-5.1815.)

Rancune Toulon Dyd. (Constructeurs, Auguste-François Arnaud and from 1813 Jean-Nicolas Guérin)

Ord: 20.2.1812. K: 7.1812. Named 31.8.1812. L: 30.9.1813. Comm: 1.11.1813. C: 11.1813.

Renamed *Néréide* 30.8.1814, *Rancune* 22.3.1815, and *Néréide* 15.7.1815. Struck 1825, converted to school hulk and in 11.1829 to prison hulk at Toulon. BU after 6.1830.

Thétis Toulon Dyd. (Constructeurs, Louis Barrallier, Jean-François Lafosse, and others)

K: 9.1813. L: 3.5.1819. C: 3.1822. Comm: 8.3.1822.

Guns as completed: UD 28 x 18pdrs; SD 16 x 24pdr carronades, 2 x short 18pdrs.

Redesignated as an 800-ton transport 14.5.1851 and became a boys' training ship at Brest 9.1851. Condemned 12.12.1853, struck 1.1854, remained in use as a boys' training hulk at Brest until 8.1861. Coal hulk 15.1.1865, renamed *Lanninon* 4.1865. BU 1866.

Saint-Malo Group. The two frigates ordered at Saint-Malo in 1807-8 were constructed by Jean Denaix, although the second was completed by Antoine Bonjean. They were possibly intended at first to be built to Pestel's *Piémontaise* design, and *Illyrienne* (though not *Prégel*) has been recorded as a Pestel ship, but it seems likely that Denaix used the Sané design instead. Although listed officially as built at Saint-Malo they may have been built on the new slipways at neighbouring Saint-Servan.

Prégel Saint-Malo

K: 7.1807. L: 30.10.1810. Comm: 1.1.1811. C: 2.1812.

Renamed *Eurydice* 30.8.1814, *Prégel* 22.3.1815, and *Eurydice* 15.7.1815. Struck 20.6.1825. BU at Brest 7-11.1825.

Illyrienne Saint-Malo

Ord: 26.12.1808. K: 11.1809. L: 13.11.1811. Comm: 13.1.1812. C: 3.1812.

Renamed *Hermione* 30.8.1814, *Illyrienne* 22.3.1815, and *Hermione* 15.7.1815. Condemned at Rochefort 12.1840, struck 14.4.1841, converted to hulk at Rochefort 5-8.1841.

Cherbourg Group. The two frigates ordered at Cherbourg were constructed by Jean-Michel Segondat; their frames were ordered at the same time at Le Havre.

Astrée Cherbourg Dyd.

K: 20.4.1808. L: 1.5.1809. Comm: 22.7.1809. C: 7.1809.

Captured in the capitulation of Île de France (Mauritius) 4.12.1810, becoming HMS *Pomone*; BU at Deptford 6.1816.

Iphigénie Cherbourg Dyd

K: 5.1809. L: 20.5.1810. C: 11.1810.

Captured by HMS *Venerable* (74) and *Cyane* (22) off the Canaries 20.1.1814, becoming HMS *Palma* and on 8.11.1814 HMS *Gloire*; sold to BU 10.9.1817.

Naples Group. One ship, built for Murat's Neapolitan Navy. In 1807 Napoleon directed the construction at Naples of two ships of the line and two frigates. Plans for the first frigate were dated 6 March 1808. On September 17 1808, just 11 days after his arrival at Naples, Murat announced that a frigate would be laid down there that week and that the 74-gun ship begun earlier at Castellammare (*Capri*) would be ready within ten months. The second frigate, (*Principessa*) *Letizia*, was built as a corvette.

Carolina Naples (Constructeurs, Jean-François Lafosse and Philippe Greslé)

K: 1808. L: 16.6.1811. Comm: 5.6.1813.

When on 30 May 1815 Murat called for Italian support for Napoleon, *Carolina* and the corvette *Letizia* were being blockaded in port at Brindisi by the British. The British convoyed the ships to Naples where on 1 June 1815 they declared loyalty to the Bourbon monarchy and were renamed *Amalia* and *Cristina* respectively. Hauled out for major repairs 1841-42. Joined the Sardinian squadron in late 1860 and renamed *Caracciolo*, inscribed on the Italian Navy list 17.3.1861 as a 2nd Class sailing frigate. Downgraded to a 2nd Class sailing corvette 14.6.1863, decomm. 12.10.1864, struck 18.6.1865.

Genoa Group. The three frigates ordered at Genoa in 1808-11 were constructed by Mathurin Boucher after he succeeded François Pestel there in mid-1808, although Pestel's plans were reportedly used for the first two.

Médée Genoa

K: 7.1808. L: 5.5.1811. Comm: 26.8.1811. C: 8.1811.

Struck 6.2.1849, headquarters hulk at Toulon, renamed *Muiron* 1850 and replaced the old frigate hulk of that name. Struck by lightning and sunk 1882 at Toulon.

Galatée (*Galathée*) Genoa

K: 11.1808. L: 3.5.1812. Comm: 1.9.1812. C: 9.1812.

Struck at Toulon 6.5.1837 after being damaged in collision with *Trident* (74), BU 3-5.1838.

Dryade Genoa

K: 7.1811. L: 4.10.1812. C: 1.1813. Comm: 1.1.1814.

Renamed *Fleur de Lis* 11.1814 to honour a visit by the Comte d'Artois, the future King Charles X but reverted to *Dryade* 22.3.1815. Sent to Naples 3.1815 to pick up Napoleon's mother (Laetitia), blockaded for a while at Gaeta in May, then embarked Jérôme and Laetitia Bonaparte and brought them to Toulon. (*Melpomène* was lost 4.1815 on a similar mission.) Renamed *Fleur de Lis* 15.7.1815 after the fall of Napoleon and *Résolue* 9.8.1830 after the fall of Charles X. Wrecked 23.6.1833 in a storm at Cape Lévi near Cherbourg, BU in situ.

Lorient Group. The first of these two frigates, *Eurydice*, was ordered on the plans of *Cornélie*, showing how little Sané's frigate designs had changed since the 1790s. Her frame was ordered at Nantes on 15 October 1808 and she was built in the Caudan annex to the Lorient dockyard. *Eurydice* was renamed *Atalante* in September 1811 because a former Batavian frigate annexed in 1810 already had the name *Eurydice*. In July 1814 she was named for the only surviving child of Louis XVI and Marie Antoinette. *Didon* was ordered (*commandée*) on 18 January 1810, and the order to begin construction (*ordre de mise en chantier*) was given on 13 August 1810. She was named on 28 February 1811. On 13 August 1816 it was decided that *Didon* would take the name *Duchesse de Berry* on the day of her launch, the Duchess having married into the French royal family in April.

Atalante (ex *Eurydice* 9.9.1811) Lorient Dyd-Caudan (Constructeurs, Antoine Bonjean and Joseph Fauveau.)

Ord: 1.7.1809. Named: 31.7.1809. K: 4.1810. L: 24.6.1812. Comm: 18.12.1812. C: 12.1812.

Renamed *Duchesse d'Angoulême* 7.1814, *Atalante* 22.3.1815, and *Duchesse d'Angoulême* 15.7.1815. Struck 2.6.1825 at Brest, BU there 6-7.1825.

Duchesse de Berry (ex *Didon* 25.8.1816) Lorient Dyd-Caudan (Constructeur, François Etesse, later Aimé Le Déan and others)

K: 9.1810. L: 25.8.1816. Comm: 25.3.1817. C: 3.1817.

Renamed *Victoire* 9.8.1830. Reclassified 1840 as a corvette de charge but not converted, struck 11.12.1841.

Antwerp Group. The five frigates at Antwerp were all constructed by Pierre Lair and others. The two completed units received an extra pair of 24pdr carronades for a total of 16 x 24pdr carronades and 2 x 8pdrs on the spardeck.

Terpsichore Antwerp

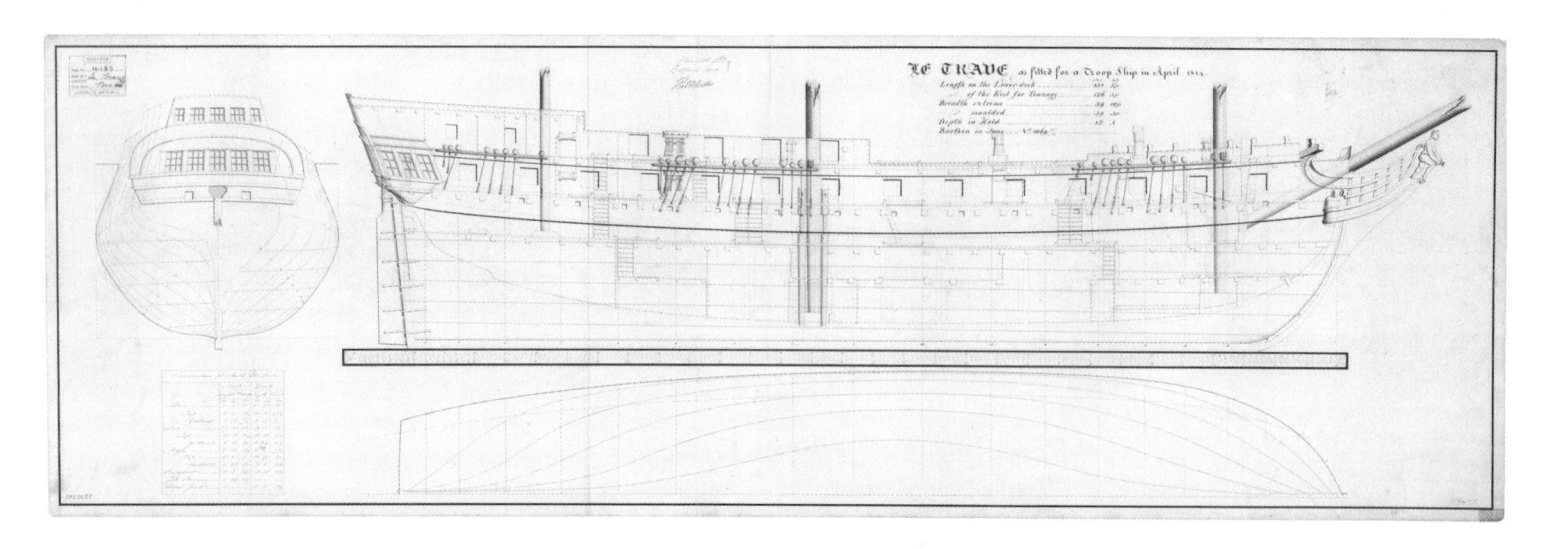

Admiralty draught of *Trave* 'as fitted for a Troop Ship in April 1814', dated Plymouth 27 April 1815. The most visible alteration for her new role is the addition of a poop cabin to house the army officers commanding the troops, but there is also a row of small scuttles on the lower deck to ventilate the troop spaces. (© National Maritime Museum J5610)

K: 5.1810. L: 26.2.1812. C: 5.1812.
Captured 3.2.1814 by HMS *Majestic* (58) off the Azores, becoming HMS *Modeste* (not commissioned); BU at Portsmouth 8.1816.

Érigone Antwerp
K: 5.1810. L: 25.3.1812. Comm: 26.3.1812. C: 6.1812.
Struck 8.11.1824 at Brest, BU there 11.1824 to 5.1825.

Précieuse Antwerp
K: 5.1812. Was 6/24ths complete on 1.4.1814.
Allocated to the Allies 8.1814 and sold by the Dutch for BU on the ways.

Ruppel Antwerp
K: 5.1812. Was 5/24ths complete on 1.4.1814.
Allocated to the French 8.1814 and sold for BU on the ways.

Inconstante Antwerp
K: 5.1812. Was 8.5/24ths complete on 1.4.1814.
Allocated to the French 8.1814 and sold for BU on the ways.

Amsterdam Group. Two frigates ordered at Amsterdam as sisters to the 50-gun *Van der Werff* were built instead under French direction as standard Sané 44-gun frigates. Ultimately six Sané-designed frigates were built for the French at Amsterdam, where P. Schuijt Jr. was the senior Dutch naval constructor. The French constructeur Jean-François Guillemard, assigned to Antwerp, oversaw the Dutch work at Amsterdam. The first four Amsterdam ships were armed with UD 28 x 18pdrs; SD 8 x 8pdrs, 8 x 36pdr carronades while the later ones were to have received the 16 x 18pdr carronades given to *Van der Werff* and the Sané ships at Rotterdam.

Yssel Amsterdam
Ord: 9.1810. K: 10.1810. L: 5.1811. C: 2.1812.
Was in the Texel squadron in 4.1814. Returned to the Dutch as *Ijssel* 22.4.1814 at Nieuwdiep in accordance with the capitulation of Vice Admiral Verhuell after the fall of the Empire. Left with a squadron for the Mediterranean 22.12.1814 but was dismasted in a storm and took refuge at Plymouth. Left Plymouth 16.6.1815 with a squadron for the Mediterranean and again damaged in a storm 3.11.1815. Not worth full repairs, was patched up at Gibraltar and sent home. Struck 1826 and sold at Hellevoetsluis, but capsized while being taken out of port.

Meuse Amsterdam
Ord: 9.1810 replacing *Alcide*. K: 10.1810. L: 17.12.1811. C: 6.1812.
Was in the Texel squadron in 4.1814. Returned to the Dutch as *Maas* 22.4.1814. BU 1816 at Nieuwdiep, replaced by a new *Maas* laid down in 1818 and launched in 1822.

Trave Amsterdam
Ord: 9.1810. K: 3.1811. L: 12.5.1812. C: 8.1812.
Captured 23.10.1813 in the Channel by HMS *Andromache* (36) and *Achates* (14), becoming HMS *Trave*. Sold 6.1821.

Weser Amsterdam
Ord: 9.1810. K: 3.1811. L: 12.5.1812. C: 8.1812.
Captured 21.10.1813 in the Channel by HMS *Scylla* (18) and *Royalist* (18), becoming HMS *Weser*. Sold 9.1817.

Ambitieuse Amsterdam
K: 1.1813. L: 11.1814. C: c1817.
Was 4.5/24ths complete when seized on the stocks 14.11.1813 in the Dutch uprising with the other ships under construction at Amsterdam. Taken into the Dutch Navy in 12.1813 as *Koningin*, then completed as *Wilhelmina*. Sent to the East Indies 1817, found unfit in 1820 for the return voyage and turned over 1821 to the Colonial Navy. Later BU.

Immortelle Amsterdam
K: 1. 1813. L: 11.1814. C: c1816.
Was 7.5/24ths complete when seized on the stocks 14.11.1813 in the Dutch uprising with the other ships under construction at Amsterdam. Taken into the Dutch navy in 12.1813 and completed as *Frederica Sophia Wilhelmina*. Participated in bombardment of Algiers 1816. BU 1819 at Hellevoetsluis.

Rotterdam Group. After completing *Van der Werff* to a Dutch 50-gun design with six guns removed from the spardeck by the French, Rotterdam built five frigates to Sané's French design with the same reduced Dutch-style spardeck armament of 16 x 18pdr carronades. The senior Dutch constructor at Rotterdam was P. Glavimans Jr., who was also the principal Dutch ship designer. The French constructeur Alexandre Notaire-Grandville, assigned to Antwerp, oversaw the Dutch work at Rotterdam. The two Rotterdam frigates retained by the French, *Jahde* and *Ems*, received the normal French spardeck armament of 14 x 24pdr carronades and 2 x 8pdrs in 1815.

Jahde Rotterdam
K: 6.1811. L: 9.5.1812. Comm: 11.5.1812. C: 9.1812.
Renamed *Africaine* 6.8.1814 for a mission to India but was in too bad condition and on 9.8.1814 *Ems* was selected for the mission and

renamed *Africaine* and *Jahde* was renamed *Psyché*. Reverted to *Jahde* 22.3.1815 and *Psyché* 15.7.1815. Struck 1821 at Brest, BU there 8-10.1823.

Ems Rotterdam
K: 6.1811. L: 26.5.1812. Comm: 27.5.1812. C: 10.1812.
Renamed *Africaine* 9.8.1814 (see *Jahde* above), *Ems* 22.3.1815, and *Africaine* 15.7.1815. Wrecked 16.5.1822 in fog on Sable Island, Nova Scotia.

Amstel Rotterdam
K: 1.1812. L: 13.9.1814. C: c1815.
Was 14/24ths complete when taken 12.1813 in the Dutch uprising. Launched and completed by the Dutch Navy. Participated in bombardment of Algiers 1816 and in overseas cruises 1825-27. Guardship at Hellevoetsluis 1841, sold for BU 1841.

Vestale Rotterdam
K: 3.1813. L: 10.1816. C: 1.2.1819.
Was 6/24ths complete when taken 12.1813 in the Dutch uprising. Launched and completed by the Dutch Navy as *Rhijn* or *Rijn*. Cruised to the Mediterranean in 1821. Lengthened 6.3 metres in 1828 at Vlissingen to be fitted as a steamer but then rebuilt in 1830 at Amsterdam as a 54-gun frigate. Extensive overseas cruising 1838-51, out of service 1.4.1851. Guardship at Hellevoetsluis1852, struck 1874.

Fidèle Rotterdam
K: 3.1813. L: 22.11.1817. C: c1818.
Was 4/24ths complete when taken 12.1813 in the Dutch uprising. Launched and completed by the Dutch Navy as *Schelde*. Cruised in the Mediterranean and was reputed to be fast under sail. Guardship at Hellevoetsluis 1.9.1842, BU 1853.

Venice Group (ii). At the end of 1810 the French initiated a second large naval construction program at Venice that included five more 74-gun ships of the line and eight 18pdr-armed frigates. The first five of these eight frigates were laid down at the same time as the five 74s, and the sixth was laid down soon after the 80-gun *Saturne*; the other pair were barely begun when the war ended. The Italians called these 44-gun vessels heavy frigates (*fregate pesanti*). The Italian naval constructor supervising the first two frigates was Romualdo Battistella, whom Andrea Salvini had put in charge of frigate construction at Venice, although he would have worked under the overall direction of Jean Tupinier and his successor from August 1813, Jean Dumonteil. These first two frigates were first named *Atalanta* and *Costituzione*, but were renamed *Principessa di Bologna* and *Piave* in March 1811; they were completed for Napoleon's Italian Navy. The Italian constructor for the later units, all of which were still building when the Austrian's occupied Venice on 20 April 1814, may have been Giacomo or Francesco Coccon. The first three units received or were to receive an armament of UD 28 x 18pdrs; SD 8 x 8pdrs, 8 x 36pdr carronades; the later units would probably have received an identical armament.

Principessa di Bologna Venice
K: 11.1810. L: 3.9.1811 (3.5.1811?). C: 12.1811.
Name in French *Princesse de Bologne*. Taken by the Austrians 20.4.1814 at the occupation of Venice and incorporated in the Austrian Navy on 16.5.1814 after the Austrians took formal possession of the city. Renamed *Lipsia* 13.5.1815. Ordered BU 1.5.1826, BU completed 30.9.1826.

Piave Venice
K: 1.1811. L: 15.8.1812. C: 7.1813.
Taken by the Austrians 20.4.1814 in the occupation of Venice and incorporated in the Austrian Navy 16.5.1814. Renamed *Austria* 3.1815. Ordered BU 1.5.1826, BU completed 1.1827.

Anfitrite Venice
K: 9.1811. L: 7.11.1815. C: 1815.
Name in French *Amphitrite*. Taken by the Austrians 20.4.1814 in the occupation of Venice. Was then on the ways 5 months from completion (23/24ths built). Renamed *Augusta* 1815. Launched (perhaps as *Principessa Augusta*) in the presence of the Austrian emperor. Harbour guardship at Venice 12.7.1821. Ordered BU 26.11.1825, BU completed 4.1826.

Ebe Venice
K: 26.9.1811. L: 14.7.1821. C: 8.1821.
Name in French *Hébé*. Taken by the Austrians 20.4.1814 in the occupation of Venice. Was then on the ways 9 months from completion (75% complete). Station ship at Venice 1835. Ordered BU 28.7.1845 but hulk still existed 1.1.1847.

Guerriera Venice
K: 26.9.1811. L: 12.9.1829. C: 1.1830.
Name in French *Guerrière*. Taken by the Austrians 20.4.1814 in the occupation of Venice. Was then on the ways 18 months from completion (30% complete). Renamed *Juno* 18.11.1849. Guardship at Trieste 1850, barracks hulk at Pola 1851. Sold 15.5.1858 or 28.12.1858.

Corona Venice
K: 8.1812. L: not launched.
Taken by the Austrians 20.4.1814 in the occupation of Venice. Was then 33% complete. Materials probably used in 1818 rebuild of corvette *Carolina* (q.v.), although it is also reported that *Corona*, not *Carolina*, was renamed *Adria* in 1815 and was completed with materials from the broken up *Carolina*.

Moscava Venice
K: 5.1813. L: 7.8.1827. C: 1828.
Name in French *Moskowa*. Taken by the Austrians 20.4.1814 in the occupation of Venice. Was then on the ways 19 months from completion (30% complete). Renamed *Medea* 1814. Ordered BU 5.9.1841, hauled out 20.7.1842, BU 1843-44.

Venere Venice
K: 20.7.1813. L: 12.6.1832. C: 11.1832.
Name in French *Vénus*. Taken by the Austrians 20.4.1814 in the occupation of Venice. Was then on the ways 22 months from completion. Nearly destroyed 11-12.8.1849 by explosive boat while at anchor near Chioggia during the blockade of Venice. Renamed *Venus* 19.10.1849. School ship at Trieste 1860, later at Venice and Pola, struck from the active fleet list 13.2.1868 and from the fleet list 5.1.1872, handed over 25.1.1872 in part payment for the new corvette *Aurora*.

Brest Group. The two ships ordered at Brest were constructed by Pierre Degay and others.

Cérès Brest Dyd
K: 5.1810. L: 12.8.1812. Comm: 8.9.1812. C: 1.1813.
Captured 6.1.1814 between Brazil and Cape Verde Islands by HMS *Niger* (46) and *Tagus* (40), becoming HMS *Seine* (not commissioned); BU at Deptford 5.1823.

Constance Brest Dyd
Ord: 20.2.1812. K: 8.1812. Named: 31.8.1812. L: 2.9.1818. C: 1819. Comm: 1.3.1823.
Struck 19.11.1836 at Brest and hulked, BU 1843 at Brest.

Trieste Group. In 1810 Napoleon ordered that a ship of the line and a frigate be built at Trieste, where previously only gunboats had been built. The ship of the line was probably the 74-gun *Citoyen* of the *Pluton* class, which was ordered in December 1811 but cancelled in 1812. The frigate was constructed by Jean-Baptiste Lefebvre and probably the Italian constructor at Trieste, Vincenzo Panfilli. A subsequent plan of March 1811 to build at Trieste one 120-gun ship, one 80-gun ship, and two more frigates was not pursued.

Istrienne Trieste

Ord: 9.8.1811 and 26.10.1812. K: 4.1813. Suspended c7.1813 when 6/24ths built. Abandoned 10.1813 in the fall of Trieste.

Other Groups (never begun). In April 1807 the names *Corbineau* and *Dahlmann* were selected for two new frigates but were never assigned; in October of that year, Napoleon ordered a frigate (and two brigs) built at Corfu, but this was never done. In May 1808 two frigates (with three 74s and two brigs) were ordered built at La Spezia, which Napoleon had just declared a military port and where the navy had sent François Pestel to establish a shipyard, but as that yard did not yet exist the orders were quickly moved to Genoa where they probably became *Médée* and *Galatée*.

During the last few years of the French Empire, a number of other orders were placed or proposed for additional frigates, many of which were never named or begun as the tide of war ebbed back towards France. In many cases their intended designs went unrecorded (and perhaps were never decided), but it may be surmised that these would have been standard Sané-type units similar to the *Pallas*. In February 1811 it was intended to build a frigate at Castellammare or at Naples for the French Navy (together with an 80-gun ship of the line), but no work was begun. A frigate was projected at Medemblick (North Holland) in October 1811, and in 1812 six further frigates were ordered that were never built or even named; these were one each at Dordrecht and at Helvoetsluys in Holland, at Marseille and at Saint-Malo, and two at La Ciotat. In June 1813 it was intended to build a frigate (as well as three ships of the line) at a shipyard to be established at Altenbruck on the River Elbe, but this was abandoned in October 1813. Also in June three new frigates were ordered from Marseille and Villefranche, but the orders were suspended in November, and cancelled in April 1814.

ANNEXED DUTCH VESSELS (1810). About 20 Dutch ships of between 32 and 44 guns fell into the hands of the new Batavian Republic when it was proclaimed on 19 January 1795 with armed support from the French. These included eight 40- or 44-gun two-deckers and twelve 36-gun frigates. By the end of 1799 all of these older ships had been BU, hulked, or taken by the British Navy. In 1795 the new Batavian Republic experimented with large frigates by cutting down a 68-gun two-decker dating from 1784 (*Zevenwolden*) to produce the 168-foot (Dutch measurement) 24pdr frigate *Mars* and by building the 160-foot 24pdr frigate *Amphitrite* at Amsterdam and the 160-foot *Eendragt* at Rotterdam. The British captured *Mars* and *Amphitrite* in 1799 while *Eendragt* was sold in Batavia as unserviceable in 1804. Her armament in 1801 was 28 x 24pdrs and 16 x 30pdr carronades. After these experiments the Dutch concentrated on building a new 32-gun class of smaller frigates until 1806 when they adopted a 160-foot 18pdr design. The six surviving 32-gun frigates that were still afloat in Dutch hands in 1810 were annexed to the French Navy with the incorporation into France of the Kingdom of Holland.

JUNO **Class.** Between 1797 and 1805 the Dutch launched twelve 145-foot (Dutch measurement) 32-gun frigates. The Dutch listed the first of these, *Juno*, with 26 x 18pdrs and 8 x 8pdrs, while a later unit was listed in 1801 with 26 x 18pdrs, 8 x 24pdr carronades, and 2 x 8pdr chase guns. *Juno* was wrecked on Amboin Island in March 1803. *Proserpina*, *Pallas*, *Maria Reijgersbergen*, *Phenix*, the first *Kenau Hasselaar*, and *Gelderland* (ex *Orpheus*) were taken by the British between 1804 and 1808, and *Irene* was wrecked in the Orkneys. The British considered them 12pdr frigates and rearmed the captured *Gelderland* with 26 x 12pdrs; 12 x 32pdr carronades, and 2 x 6pdrs for a total of 40 guns. The French in January 1811 listed *Frise* and *Kenau Hasselaar* as 40-gun frigates armed with 12pdrs and *Eurydice* and *Minerve* as 40-gun frigates armed with 18pdrs. In January 1812 all four were listed with 18pdrs.

   Dimensions & tons: 126ft 4in, 117ft 11in x 34ft 10in x 13ft 1in (41.05, 38.33 x 11.32 x 4.25m). 600/1,100 tons. Draught 14ft 4in/15ft 8in (4.66/5.10m). Men: 230.

   Guns: 32 guns (26 ports, Dutch rating). (*Frise*, French, 1810) 40 guns, 12pdrs and 24pdr carronades.

Eurydice (ex Dutch *Euridice*) Rotterdam (constructed by P. Glavimans Jr.).

   K: 12.1801. L: 4.1802. C: 1803.

   Was out of commission at Vlissingen (Flushing) in 4.1814. Allocated to the Allies 8.1814 under the Treaty of Paris and returned to the Dutch. Overseas cruises 1815-25, at Antwerp 1830. Barracks ship at Vlissingen 1842, sold for BU 1847.

Kenau Hasselaar Rotterdam (constructed by P. Glavimans Jr.).

   K: 6.1804. L: 12.1805. C: 1807.

   Ex Dutch *Diana* 1807. Was out of commission at Vlissingen (Flushing) in 4.1814. Allocated to the Allies 8.1814 under the Treaty of Paris and returned to the Dutch. Found unfit for further service 1828, guardship at Nieuwdiep, BU there 1841.

Frise (ex Dutch *Vriesland* 25.3.1811) Flushing (constructed by P. Schuijt Jr.)

   K: 6.1802. L: 10.1803. C: 1806.

   Ex Dutch *Aurora* 1806. Severely damaged in 1810 by an explosion. Was out of commission at Vlissingen (Flushing) in 4.1814. Allocated to the Allies 8.1814 under the Treaty of Paris and returned to the Dutch. BU 1817.

Minerve (ex Dutch *Minerva*) Flushing.

   K: 10.1804. L: 7.1.1806. C: 1806.

   Was out of commission in the Scheldt squadron in 4.1814. Allocated to the Allies 8.1814 under the Treaty of Paris and returned to the Dutch. Guardship at Vlissingen 1823, sold there 1835 for BU.

DAGERAAD **Class.** In 1807 the Dutch began two frigates at Amsterdam that at 150 Dutch feet in length were enlarged versions of the previous group. They were also rated at 32 guns. The French listed both in 1811 as 40-gun frigates armed with 18pdrs.

   Dimensions & tons: 130ft 9in, 122ft 0in x 35ft 11in x 13ft 7in (42.46, 39.63 x 11.68 x 4.43m). 600/1,150 tons. Draught 15ft 0in/16fr 1in (4.87/5.25m). Men: 243-323.

   Guns: 32 guns (Dutch rating). (French) UD 28 x 18pdrs; SD 8 x 24pdr carronades.

Aurore (ex Dutch *Aurora*) Amsterdam (constructed by P. Schuijt Jr.).

   K: 5.1807. L: 6.1808. C: 1809.

   Ex Dutch *Dageraad* 1809. Was in the Texel squadron in 4.1814. Returned to the Dutch 22.4.1814 and reverted to *Dageraad*. Left with a squadron for the Mediterranean 22.12.1814 but lost a mast in a storm and took refuge at Plymouth. Left Plymouth 16.6.1815 with a squadron for the Mediterranean, participated in the bombardment of Algiers and brought some Dutch captives home in 1816. Made a round trip to Batavia in 1821-22. Sent back there 1824 but found unfit, transferred to the Colonial Navy, renamed *Aurora*, and BU soon after.

Maria (ex Dutch *Maria Reigersbergen*) Amsterdam (constructed by P. Schuijt Jr.).

   K: 5.1807. L: 6.1808. C: 1809.

   Was in the Texel squadron in 4.1814. Returned to the Dutch 22.4.1814. Overseas cruises 1815-26, later hospital ship at Nieuwediep. Sold 1842 for BU.

KONINGIN. In 1806 the Dutch laid down their first frigate that was roughly equivalent to the 44-gun 18pdr frigates then being built in

A contemporary Dutch model of the Euridice. *Assuming the detail is correct, the ship had only thirteen main battery gunports a side. Dutch frigates were marked by more height between decks than was usual in other navies, which allowed them to fit small ports for light and air on the lower deck, a feature accurately portrayed on this model. (Rijksmuseum, Amsterdam)*

France. She had a heavy spardeck armament and was rated at 50 guns.
  Dimensions & tons: 139ft 5in, 129ft 10in x 38ft 4in x 14ft 8in (45.30, 42.18 x 12.46 x 4.79m). 700/1,350 tons. Draught 15ft 0in/16ft 8in (4.90/5.44m).
  Guns (Dutch): UD 28 x 18pdrs; SD 22 x 18pdr carronades.
Reine (ex Dutch *Koningin*) Rotterdam (constructed by P. Glavimans Jr.).
  K: 1806. L: 11.1810. C: 3.1811.
  Ex Dutch *Jason* 1808, ex *Phoenix* 1807. Annexed by the French 7.1810 while on the stocks. Wrecked and capsized 10.5.1811 near Willemstad, declared lost 7.1811.

VAN DER WERFF Class. For three more frigates ordered in 1808-9 the Dutch constructor P. Glavimans Jnr. produced a design for 50-gun frigates somewhat larger than *Koningen*. Like *Koningen* they had a heavy spardeck armament. The two ships of this class at Amsterdam were cancelled and replaced with ships built to Sané's standard French design, but the Rotterdam ship was completed by the French to the Dutch design reduced to 44 guns.
  Dimensions & tons: 142ft 9in x 37ft 11in x 19ft 2in (46.40 x 12.33 x 6.23m).
  Guns: (Dutch) UD 28 x 18pdrs; SD 22 x 18pdr carronades; (French) UD 28 x 18pdrs; SD 16 x 18pdr carronades
Van der Werff Rotterdam.
  K: 12.1809. L: 1.1.1812. Comm: 1.8.1812. C: 8.1812.
  Was out of commission in the Scheldt squadron as a floating battery in 4.1814. Ceded 1.8.1814 to the Allies with two brigs and a cutter in accordance with the treaty of 30.5.1814 as compensation for the Allied share in four frigates and two brigs that had been sent from Flushing to Brest. Returned to the Dutch, made a West Indies cruise 1815-16, and put into Falmouth 20.4.1816 on the way home with a leak. Sent to the East Indies in 1820 and participated in the blockade of Palembang that year. Declared unfit for the trip home 31.10.1821 and transferred to the Colonial Navy, later BU.
Ridder van Unie Amsterdam.
  K: c1809. Cancelled 9.1810, dismantled on stocks and materials used for *Ijssel*.
Alcide Amsterdam.
  K: c1809. Cancelled 9.1810 and replaced by *Meuse*, timbers used for *Willem I*.

Ex BRITISH PRIZES (1809-1810). Three British Fifth Rates were captured by the French in 1809 and 1810, one of which had been purchased by the RN from the East India Co. in 1805. The French altered the name of HMS *Iphigenia* to *Iphigénie*. The French continued to use *Proserpine* until 1865 while the British recaptured the other two, *Iphigenia* and *Ceylon* (ex *Bombay*) within four months of their capture.

AMPHION Class.
  Dimensions & tons: 130ft 7in, 130ft 3in wl, 124ft 4in x 35ft 7in x

20ft 2in (42.41, 42.30 wl, 40.40 x 11.56 x 6.54m). 1,434t disp. Draught 15ft 8in/16ft 9in (5.08/5.44m). Men: 319.

Guns: UD 26 x 18pdrs; SD 4 x 9pdrs, 10 x 24pdr carronades. (1828) UD 26 x 18pdrs; SD 16 x 24pdr carronades, 2 x 18pdrs.

Proserpine Thomas Steemson, Paull (near Hull)

K: 9.1805. L:6.8.1807. C: 27.11.1807.

Captured by *Pauline* and *Pénélope* off Toulon 28.2.1809 and commissioned at Toulon 1.5.1809. Reclassified as a 800-ton corvette de charge in 1840 and as an 800-ton transport 1.1846. Fitted as a hospital ship 10.1852 at Brest. Sent to Cayenne, French Guiana 1856 and converted to a prison hulk there 1.1857. Struck 20.7.1865, BU 1865-66 in French Guiana.

PERSEVERANCE Class.

Dimensions & tons: 130ft 3in, 118ft 3in x 37ft 0in x 19ft 1in (42.3, 38.4 x 12.03 x 6.20m). 700/1,300 tons. Draught 16ft 7in/17ft 10in (5.40/5.80m). Men: 258.

Guns: UD 26 x 18pdrs; SD 14 x 32pdr carronades, 2 x 9pdrs.

Iphigénie Chatham Dyd

K: 2.1806. L: 26.4.1808. C: 24.6.1808.

Captured 28.8.1810 at the end of the Battle of Grand Port, Île de France. Retaken by the British 4.12.1810 in the capitulation of Île de France and restored to service as HMS *Iphigenia*. Training ship 1833, BU 5.1851 at Deptford.

CEYLON (ex *Bombay*, purchased by Admiral Pellew from the HEICo 1805 and renamed 1.7.1808.)

Dimensions & tons: 122 ft 0in x 32ft 7in x 10ft 11in (39.62 x 10.58 x 3.56m). 672 tons. Men: 215.

Guns: UD 24 x 18pdrs; SD 14 x 24pdr carronades, 2 x 9pdrs.

Ceylon Bombay Dyd, built 1793.

Captured 18.9.1810 by *Vénus* and the corvette *Victor* (ex *Iéna*) off Reunion. Had on board General Abercrombie, commander of the British expedition against Île de France with his staff and his army's money. However *Vénus* was then taken by HMS *Boadicea* (38), *Otter* (16), and *Staunch* (12) which also retook *Ceylon* after *Victor* failed to tow her into port. Returned to service as HMS *Ceylon*. Hulk at Malta 1832, sold 4.7.1857. The French also captured an Indiaman named *Ceylon* on 3.7.1810 (see transports) and used her under the name *Ceylan* until the capitulation of Île de France in 12.1810.

Ex PORTUGUESE PRIZES (1807-1809)

Amazone (Portuguese *Amazona*, 5th Class (50-54 guns), launched 1798 at Pará, Brazil)

Dimensions & tons: 148ft 5in x 37ft 1in (48.2 x 12.04m). 1,500 tons disp. Men: 349

Guns: (1798) 22 x 24pdrs, 22 x 12pdrs, 2 x 12pdrs, 4 x 6pdrs; (by 1807?) UD 28 x 18pdrs; SD 10 x 18pdrs, 8 x 12pdrs, 8 x 18pdr obusiers.

Seized at Lisbon 30.11.1807. Retaken in the evacuation of Lisbon early 9.1808 and returned to Portuguese service. Retaken 11.7.1831 on the Tagus by the French, taken to Brest 9.1834, docked in 1835, sold a few years later.

Pérola (*Perle*) (Portuguese *Pérola*, 5th Class (44 guns), launched 1797 at Pará, Brazil)

Dimensions & tons: unknown.

Guns: (1797) 32 x 18pdrs, 12 x 9pdrs

Seized at Lisbon 30.11.1807. Retaken in the evacuation of Lisbon early 9.1808 and returned to Portuguese service. Retaken 7.1831 on the Tagus by the French, taken to Brest 9.1834, docked in 1835, sold a few years later.

Phénix (Portuguese *Fenix*, ex *Nossa Senhora da Graça* 1793, 5th Class (44 guns), launched 13.8.1787 at Bahia, Brazil)

Dimensions & tons: 151ft 1in x 39ft 5in (49.07 x 12.80m). 1,500 tons. Men: 379

Guns: (1787) 30 x 18pdrs, 14 x 9pdrs

Seized at Lisbon 30.11.1807. Retaken in the evacuation of Lisbon early 9.1808 and returned to Portuguese service. Burned 1819.

Carlotta (Portuguese *Princesa Carlota*, 5th Class (44 guns), launched 6.10.1791 at Bahia, Brazil)

Dimensions & tons: 152ft 0in x 39ft 5in (49.38 x 12.80m). 1,500 tons. Men: 379

Guns: (1791) 32 x 18pdrs, 14 x 9pdrs; (1797) 44 x 18pdrs, 10 x 9pdrs; (by 1807?) UD 28 x 18pdrs, SD 20 x 9pdrs.

Seized at Lisbon 30.11.1807. Retaken in the evacuation of Lisbon early 9.1808 and returned to Portuguese service. BU 1812.

Minerve (Portuguese *Minerva*, ex *Nossa Senhora da Vitória* c1792, 5th Class (48-50 guns), launched 19.7.1788 at Lisbon)

Dimensions & tons: 147ft 1in x 35ft 8in (47.78 x 11.58m). 1,400 tons. Men: 349.

Guns: (1788) 22 x 18pdrs, 22 x 9pdrs, 4 x 6pdrs.

Captured 22.11.1809 in the Indian Ocean by *Bellone*. Taken by the British 4.12.1810 in the capitulation of Île de France (Mauritius) and sold there for BU.

PURCHASED RUSSIAN VESSELS (1809)

GRIGORIY VELIKIYA ARMENII. 50-gun Black Sea Fleet frigate (designed for 62 guns) that was said to be the most powerful Russian frigate of the eighteenth century. As built she had 28 ports in her battery plus bridle ports and had a substantial armament on her quarterdeck and forecastle but lacked a continuous upper gun deck.

Dimensions & tons: 148ft 3in x 41ft 9in x 17ft 4in (48.16m x 13.56m x 5.64m). Tons unknown. Men: 428.

Guns: (original, probably no longer carried) UD 28 x 30pdrs; SD 22 x 18pdrs (all brass).

Grigoriy Velikiya Armenii Nikolayev (constructed by A. P. Sokolov)

K: 30.9.1790. L: 12.6.1791. C: 1791.

Served in the Mediterranean from 1798 to 1803, transported troops from the Black Sea to Corfu in 1804 and remained as a stationary hospital ship. Sold 1809 at Corfu, Russian crew transported to Italy and then home to Russia. Found unserviceable by the French in 1810 and BU at Corfu.

MIKHAIL. 50-gun Black Sea frigate. Named after the youngest son of Tsar Paul I; sometimes incorrectly called *Svyatoy Mikhail*.

Dimensions & tons: 149ft 2in x 39ft 5in x 14ft 9in (48.46 x 12.80 x 4.80m). Tons unknown.

Guns: (original, probably no longer carried) UD 24 x 24pdrs, 2 edinorogs; SD 18 x 12pdrs, 4 edinorogs.

Mikhail Kherson (constructed by A. S. Katasanov)

K: 6.11.1795. L: 31.10.1796. C: 1797.

Served in the Mediterranean from 1798 to 1803, carried troops from the Black Sea to Corfu in 1804, arrived at Venice 9.1807 in poor condition, moved to Trieste 12.1807 as part of Commodore Saltanov's squadron, and resisted a British attack there in 5.1809. Ordered sold to France 27.9.1809, decommissioned 20.10.1809 at Trieste, Russian crew left for Russia 24.3.1810. Found unserviceable by the French in 1810 and BU at Trieste.

CORCYRE. The Russian 38-gun medium frigate *Legkiy* of the Baltic

Fleet, built of pine, was initially armed with UD 26 x short 24pdrs and SD 10 x 6pdrs; she was sent to the Mediterranean 1806 with Ignatyev's squadron, arrived at Trieste from Corfu 28.12.1807 with the squadron of Commodore Saltanov, and resisted a threatened British attack there in May 1809. She was ordered to be sold to France 27 September 1809, was decommissioned 20 October 1809 at Trieste, and her Russian crew left for Russia on 24 October. Renamed and re-armed by the French but only fitted *en flûte* January-March 1811 at Trieste.

Dimensions & tons: 136ft 1in x 37ft 6in x 12ft 8in (44.20 x 12.19 x 4.11m). Men: 280 (at capture had 170 seamen and 130 soldiers aboard).

Guns: (1810) UD 26 x 18pdrs; SD 12 x 6pdrs (at time of her capture as a flûte mounted just 2 x 6pdrs here).

Corcyre Solombala Works, Arkhangelsk (constructed by G. Ignatyev)
K: 18.10.1800. L: 7.5.1803. C: 7.1803.
Captured 27.11.1811 off Brindisi by HMS *Eagle* (74).

(D) Vessels acquired from 26 June 1815

No further frigates with a battery of less than 18pdr calibre guns were ordered after 1814, although there were thirty 18pdr frigates of wartime construction (plus the *Proserpine*, captured in 1809 from the British) in service at the end of 1814, and another nine were under construction (including *Cybèle*, launched during the Hundred Days).

Under the ordnance establishments of 1817, the remaining 18pdr frigates retained their primary battery of 18pdrs, but were re-armed on the gaillards with 14 x 24pdr carronades and just 2 x 8pdrs in the chase positions. In 1828, one pair of carronades were subtracted, and the long (chase) 8pdrs were replaced by a pair of short (lightweight) 18pdrs; by now, the survivors were re-rated as 3rd Rank frigates (compared with the 30pdr-armed 1st Rank and 24pdr-armed 2nd Rank). In 1838, for the dwindling number of pre-1815 18pdr frigates, four of the UD battery guns were replaced by an equal number of 16cm shell guns.

The navy was slow to introduce new designs of 3rd Rank frigates after the Napoleonic Wars because a substantial number of ships of this type had survived the war and because some people (including some members of Parliament) felt France should concentrate on larger frigates. This began to change after March 1828 when Baron Guillaume Hyde de Neuville became Minister of Marine, cancelled five out of six line of battle ships proposed to be begun in 1829 but not yet ordered (*Formidable, Agamemnon, Hector, Ajax,* and *Diomède*), and focused on frigate construction instead. The building program for 1829 (planned in early 1828) included 8 frigates and the 1830 program (planned in early 1829) included 10 more. These frigates were all of the 1st and 2nd Ranks but beginning in late 1829 the 1830 program was reshaped and six of the ten 1830 ships emerged as 3rd Rank frigates. Of these, the former 2nd Rank *Pénélope* and *Héliopolis* were begun in 1830 while the former 1st Rank *Charte* (ex *Douze Avril*) and former 2nd Rank *Érigone* (ex *Oriflamme*), *Bouvines*, and *Psyché* (ex *Dame de Beaujeu*) were reprogrammed to begin in 1831. *Charte* and *Érigone* were built after additional delays but *Bouvines* and *Psyché* (both at Brest) were cancelled in 1831.

PÉNÉLOPE Class – 46 guns. On 31 December 1829 the engineers in the navy's ports were asked for plans for new 3rd Rank frigates, and among those accepted was this design by Jean-François Guillemard that was used for *Pénélope* and a sister ordered later (*Jeanne d'Arc*). The designed armament was 28 x 18pdrs in the battery and 16 x 30pdr carronades and 2 x 18pdrs on the gaillards. As in the other large vessels of the post-Napoleonic navy the forecastle and quarterdeck (gaillards) were joined to form a complete spardeck, which although fully exposed could carry a row of guns distributed throughout its length. By the late 1830s the designed armament had been altered to 24 x 18pdrs and 4 x 16cm shell guns in the battery and 16 x 30pdr carronades and 2 x 18pdrs on the gaillards.

The 14 April 1838 artillery ordinance, which adopted 30pdr guns as the main armament of all new ships, directed a change to short 30pdrs (No.2) instead of 18pdrs in new 3rd Rank frigates (specifically 22 x 30pdrs No.2 and 4 x 16cm shell guns in the battery and 14 x 30pdr

This official lines plan of *Armide*, engraved in 1834, illustrates the post-war appearance of surviving 18pdr frigates (this ship, of the standard Sané-designed *Pallas* class, was not completed until 1823). The waist barricades are now complete, although no guns were mounted there, and the small dunette has become an elaborate second set of galleries. Now rated as a 46, the new establishment for the gaillards was sixteen 24pdr carronades and two short 18pdr chase guns. The sail plan, as shown, totals 1,947 sq.m. of canvas. (Atlas du Génie Maritime, French collection, plate 16)

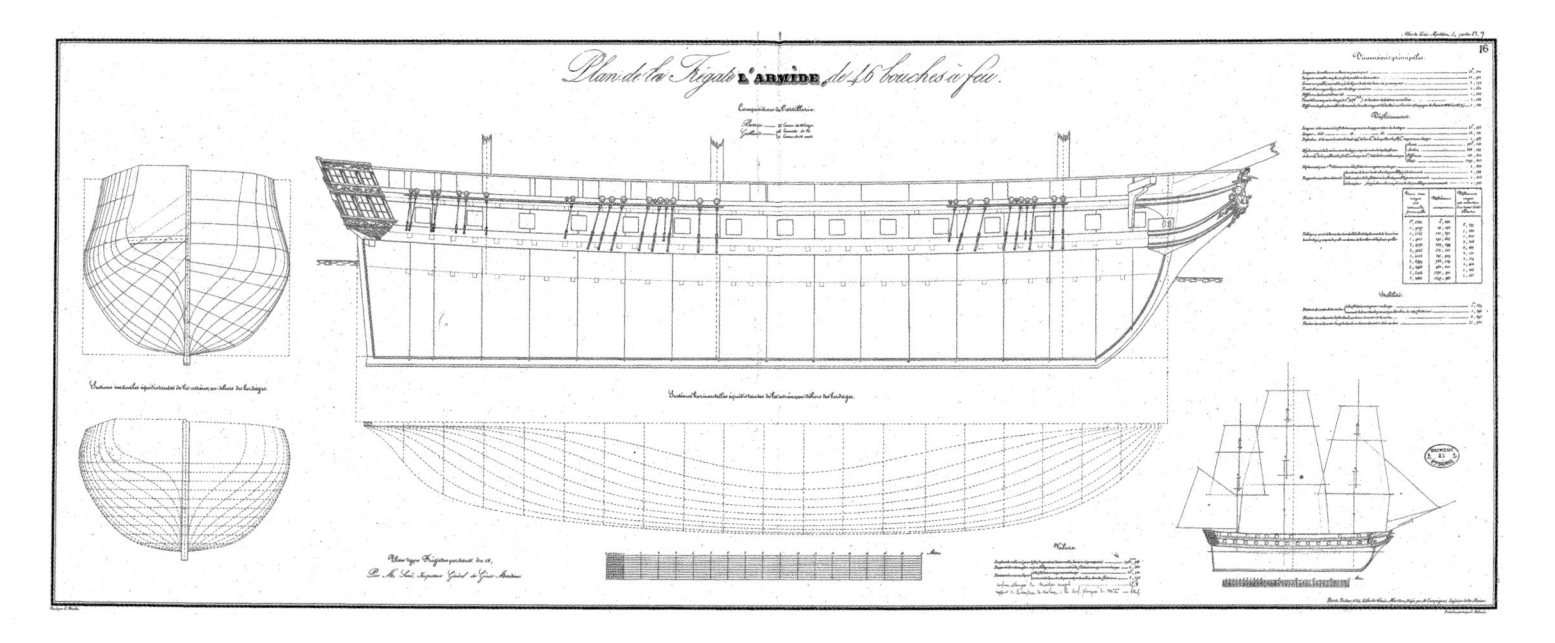

carronades on the gaillards). However this modification was difficult to implement for the new ships already under construction as it required rearranging the ships' gunports. On 13 July 1839 the navy decided it could easily make the change in *Jeanne d'Arc* and *Héliopolis* (of the *Érigone* class) which were then only 8/24ths complete, but not in the others, of which *Érigone* had been afloat since 1836 and *Charte, Africaine* and *Pénélope* were 21 or 22/24ths complete. *Jeanne d'Arc* and *Héliopolis* were to be modified with 28 ports including 2 chase ports while the other four were to be completed with 18pdrs. By 1846, however, the 18pdr was no longer considered satisfactory as a frigate armament, and when commissioned in 1848 *Pénélope* received 16cm shell guns in her battery instead.

> Dimensions & tons: 48.33m, 48.00m wl x 12.40m x 6.56m. 1,695 tons disp. Draught 5.67m mean. Men: 327.
>
> Guns: (*Pénélope* 1848) UD 24 x 16cm shell, 4 x 30pdrs No.2; SD 10 x 30pdr carronades, 2 x 16cm shell; (*Jeanne d'Arc* 1852) UD 22 x 30pdrs No.3, 2 x 30pdrs No.1, 2 x 22cm No.2 shell; SD 14 x 30pdr carronades, 2 x 30pdrs No.3.

Pénélope Lorient Dyd-Caudan (Constructeurs: Guillemard and Jean-Baptiste Larchevesque-Thibaut)
> Ord: 16.11.1829 and named. K: 26.9.1830. L: 25.11.1840. C: 1841. Comm: 20.9.1848.
>
> Used as school ship at Lorient 6-12.1861 and as floating barracks from 1862. Struck 22.12.1864, barracks hulk at Lorient. BU 1889.

Jeanne d'Arc Lorient Dyd-Caudan (Constructeurs: Charles Alexandre and Pierre Thomeuf)
> K: 16.7.1835. L: 8.11.1847. C: 5.1851. Comm: 21.1.1852.
>
> Ordered converted to a floating hospital at St. Nazaire 1862 and loaned to the Sanitary Service until 1869. Struck 22.12.1864, renamed *Prudence* 4.1865. Was at St. Nazaire in 1869 and Pauillac in 1872. By 1880 was attached to the training station for naval fusiliers (*dépôt des apprentis-fusiliers*) at Lorient. Mooring hulk at Lorient 1888. On 10.2.1898 the Minister authorised Lorient to condemn her and deliver her to the Domaines for sale. BU 1898.

ÉRIGONE Class – 46 guns. Three of the 3rd Rank frigates that emerged from the programmatic turmoil of the early 1830s and one more ordered later (*Africaine*) were built on plans by Jean-Baptiste Hubert. A 3rd Rank frigate named *Oriflamme* was scheduled to be begun in 1830 at Saint-Servan following the launch of the corvette *Sapho* but was suspended on 1 July 1830 when the navy decided to keep *Sapho* on the ways because she was not then needed. *Oriflamme* was reprogrammed in September 1830 to be begun there in 1831 but the corvette *Sabine* was laid down instead and *Oriflamme* was again rescheduled on 3 August 1831 under the name *Érigone* to be commenced in 1832 on the ways of the corvette *Blonde*. *Charte* was listed as a 3rd Rank frigate to be begun at Brest in 1831, was then reordered on 20 August 1831 for construction in 1832, and was then delayed to 1833. *Héliopolis* was begun as intended in 1830, but her construction was carried on so slowly that she became the last of the group to be completed. Plans were never assigned to the two cancelled 3rd Rank frigates that emerged from the 1830 program, *Bouvines* and *Psyché*, but as they would have been built at Brest with *Charte* they are listed here. *Charte* was commissioned in 1843 with a battery of 16pdr shell guns, and plans for alterations to *Héliopolis* to carry an armament of 30pdrs instead of 18pdrs were approved in 1844. *Érigone* and *Africaine*, which had been in service since 1840, thus became the French Navy's last frigates completed with 18-pounder guns.

> Dimensions & tons: 48.80m, 48.00m wl x 12.40m x 6.50m. 1,701 tons disp. Draught 5.33m/5.97m. Men: 327.
>
> Guns: (*Érigone* and *Africaine* 1840) UD 24 x 18pdrs, 4 x 16cm shell; SD 16 x 30pdr carronades, 2 x 18pdrs; (*Charte* 1843) UD 24 x 16cm shell, 4 x 30pdrs No.2; SD 16 x 30pdr carronades, 2 x 16cm shell; (*Héliopolis* 1854) UD 24 x 30pdrs No.2, 2 x 22cm No.2 shell; SD 8 x 16cm shell, 2 x 30pdrs No.1.

Érigone (ex *Oriflamme* 3.8.1831) Saint-Servan (Constructeurs: Charles Alexandre and, from 1835, Joseph Daviel)
> Ord: 16.11.1829 and named (*Oriflamme*). K: 26.9.1832. L: 27.9.1836. C: 1837. Comm: 1.6.1840.
>
> Used as convict transport (4 guns) in 1852-53 and as transport 1854-57. Struck 31.12.1864, storage and guard hulk at Brest. BU 1879.

Africaine Saint-Servan (Constructeur: Georges Allix)
> K: 1.2.1835. L: 9.8.1839. Comm: 26.11.1840. C: 11.1840.
>
> Used as transport (2 guns) in 1855-56 and as convict transport 1856-57. In service as service craft 1.5.1861 to 15.6.1863, then in commission 1.7.1863 to 18.1.1864. Struck 7.3.1867, storage hulk at Martinique. BU 1871.

Charte (ex *Douze Avril* 9.8.1830) Brest Dyd. (Constructeurs: Jean-Michel Segondat and others)
> Named 16.11.1829 (*Douze Avril*). K: 26.7.1833. L: 6.8.1842. Comm: 23.5.1843. C: 5.1843.
>
> Her original name was the date of the return of Louis XVIII to Paris in 1814. Renamed *Constitution* 29.2.1848. Used as transport (4 guns) during Crimean War. Fitted as a transport (4 guns) 1868 and reclassified as a frigate-transport 1.1873. Struck 31.12.1879 at Toulon. BU 1881-82.

Héliopolis Rochefort Dyd. (Constructeurs: Henri De Lisleferme, Antoine Auriol, Charles Moll, Henri de Senneville, and Armand Forquenot)
> Ord: 16.11.1829 and named. K: 8.1830. L: 25.8.1847. C: 7.1849. Comm: 20.2.1854.
>
> Out of commission at Toulon from 1856 to 1880 (listed as 4-gun sail transport 1869 and reclassified as a frigate-transport 1.1873). Struck 27.2.1880, powder hulk at Toulon to 1885. Sold for BU 1887.

Bouvines Brest Dyd
> Projected in 1830 to be begun in 1831 but not laid down, cancelled in 1831.

Psyché (1) Brest Dyd
> Projected in 1830 to be begun in 1831 but not laid down, cancelled in 1831.

POMONE Group (1835-1837) In addition to *Jeanne d'Arc* and *Africaine*, above, one new 3rd Rank frigate was scheduled to be begun in 1835, *Pomone* at Brest, and four more were scheduled for 1836, *Antigone* at Cherbourg, and *Nymphe*, *Thémis*, and *Psyché* at Toulon. Plans first drafted by Paul Leroux in 1831 in accordance with specifications dated 31 December 1829 were approved for the first of these, *Pomone*, on 20 June 1835, with the comment that compared with the old 3rd Rank frigates theses plans offered the advantage of having a more spacious hold that was more compatible with the navy's current procedures for fitting out ships. However these plans were never formally assigned to the other four ships, and all five ships were deferred around 31 October 1835 because of doubts in Parliament and elsewhere over the usefulness of 3rd Rank frigates. Three ships were cancelled in 1836 and the other two in 1837.

Pomone Brest Dyd
> Projected in 1834 to be begun in 1835 but not laid down, cancelled in 1836.

Nymphe Toulon Dyd
> Projected in 1835 to be begun in 1836 but not laid down, cancelled

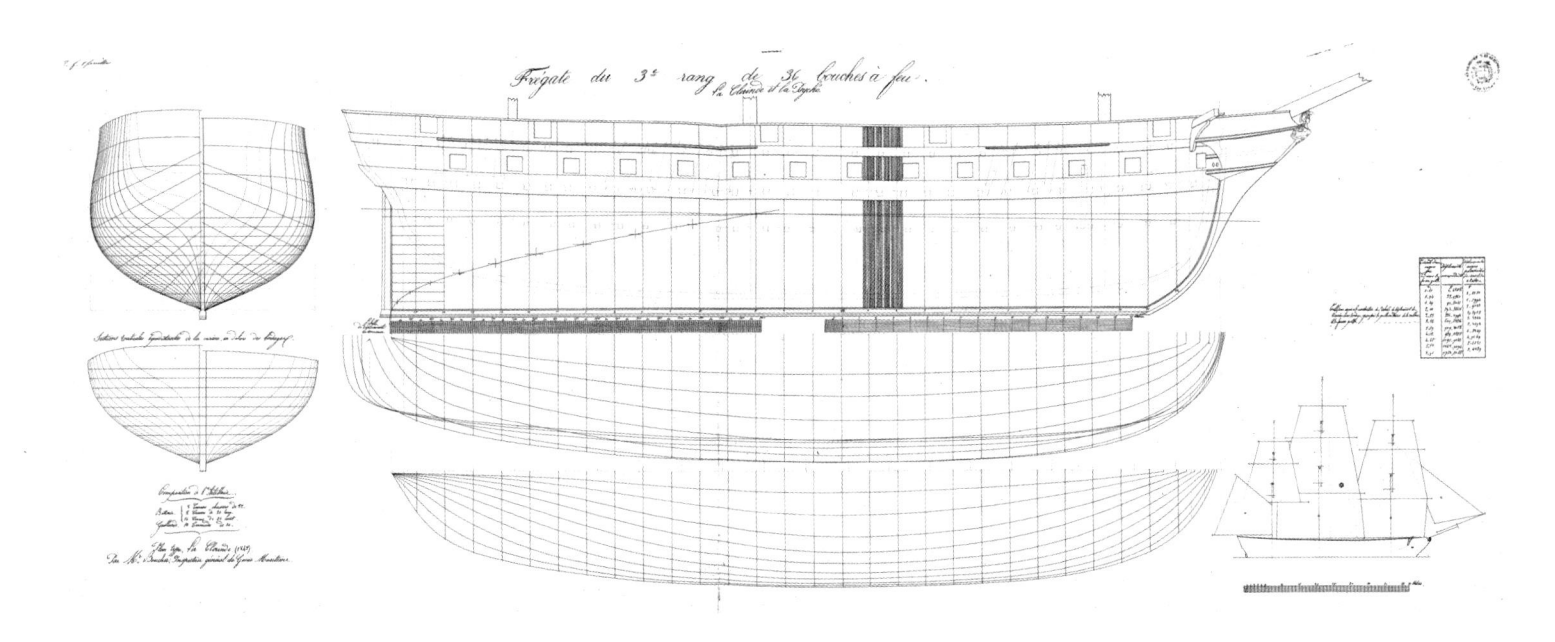

The original lines plan for *Clorinde* and *Psyché*, dated 1843, a new type of 3rd Rank frigate intended to carry a main armament of 30pdr guns. At this point the planned armament was sixteen short 30pdrs, two long 30pdrs and eight 22cm shell guns in the battery, and ten 30pdr carronades on the gaillards, but the armament varied later. This early form of the draught does not include a calculation of sail area, although a later engraved version quotes 1,838 sq.m. (Atlas du Génie Maritime, Genoa collection, image 1-0022)

in 1836.
Thémis Toulon Dyd
   Projected in 1835 to be begun in 1836 but not laid down, cancelled in 1836.
Psyché (2) Toulon Dyd
   Projected in 1835 to be begun in 1836 but not laid down, cancelled in 1837.
Antigone Cherbourg Dyd
   Projected in 1835 to be begun in 1836 but not laid down, cancelled in 1837.

PSYCHÉ (3) Class – 40 guns. In 1841 Mathurin Boucher began to work on plans for three new 3rd Rank frigates, *Clorinde*, *Psyché*, and *Pomone*, that were to be begun in 1842. In these the beam was increased by 60cm compared with the *Héliopolis* type to allow them to carry short 30pdrs in the battery instead of 18pdrs as specified for 3rd Rank frigates in the artillery ordinance of 14 April 1838, although this armament was already beginning to look insufficient to compete with the heavy shell guns in the latest steamers. The design also increased the height of battery from 2.00 to 2.11m but retained the displacement of 1,700 tons. The program was experimental, as both Boucher and the Council of Admiralty wanted to try out both large shell guns (22cm 80pdrs) and auxiliary steam propulsion in 3rd Rank frigates. As a result *Clorinde* and *Pomone* were given a mix of 30pdrs and 22cm shell guns in the battery, *Pomone* (see Section E) was also given auxiliary steam propulsion, and *Psyché* was given a battery almost exclusively of 22cm shell guns. The first two ships, with 26 guns in the battery, were pierced with 28 ports including 2 chase ports instead of the 30 in *Héliopolis* and the 32 in *Pénélope*, while *Psyché*, with only 22 guns in the battery, got a special arrangement.

Three more 3rd Rank frigates (*Résolue, Isis* and *Cérès*) were added in the 1846 building program, of which *Isis* was to be built to Boucher's design. For these the Minister on 23 May 1846 specified a conservative armament with 26 guns in the battery including 2 or 4 x 22cm shell guns instead of the 8 in *Clorinde* and the 18 in *Psyché*. On 27 July 1846 the Minister told Brest to use the plan of *Psyché* for *Iris*, but the engineer in charge of her mistakenly distributed her frames as in the *Héliopolis* type, which had 28 smaller guns in the battery. Boucher pointed out that, while she could not carry the newly specified armament, she could be pierced to carry *Psyché*'s armament. In the event, however, *Isis* was first commissioned as a transport during the Crimean War and never embarked a frigate armament. *Armorique* was added in the 1850 building program to be built to Boucher's design; another 3rd Rank frigate was planned in the 1851 program but was neither named nor ordered. *Armorique* was the last sail frigate ordered by the French.

   Dimensions & tons: 48.29m, 48.00m wl x 13.30m ext, 13.00m x 6.60m. 1,708 tons disp. Draught 5.27m/6.15m. Men: 327.
   Guns: (*Clorinde*, as designed 1844) UD 14 x 30pdrs No.2, 8 x 22cm No.2 shell, 4 x 30pdrs No.1; SD 4 x 16cm shell, 4 x 30pdrs No.2; (*Psyché*, as completed 1846) UD 18 x 22cm No.2 shell, 4 x 30pdrs No.2; SD 4 x 16cm shell, 4 x 30pdrs No.2.

Psyché (3) Brest Dyd. (Constructeurs: Jean-Michel Segondat and Philippe Binet)
   K: 14.6.1842. L: 28.9.1844. C: 1.1845. Comm: 6.7.1846.
   Used as transport (4 guns) during Crimean War. In service as a service craft (*frégate bâtiment de servitude*) at Landévennec (Brest) 16.6.1863. Struck 15.7.1867, headquarters hulk for the reserves at Landévennec until 9.1877. BU 1879.
Clorinde Cherbourg Dyd. (Constructeur: Charles Moll)
   Named: 1.7.1841. Ord: 21.7.1841. K: 5.6.1843. L: 19.8.1845. C: 12.1848 (built to 23/24ths, completion deferred). Not commissioned as sail. Steam 1857.
Isis Brest Dyd. (Constructeur: Alexandre Chedeville)
   K: 3.8.1846. L: 29.7.1851. C: 1851. Comm: 26.3.1855
   Commissioned 1855 as transport. Reclassified as a frigate-transport 1.1873. Replaced *Cornélie* as seagoing seamen's training ship 29.9.1875, relieved by *Résolue* 10.1878. Struck 12.11.1886, annex to headquarters hulk for the mobile defence force (*Défense mobile*) at Cherbourg until 1894, then became the headquarters hulk. BU 1900.
Armorique Lorient Dyd-Caudan (Constructeurs: Guillaume Masson, Nicolas Le Moine, and Charles Layre)

The original lines plan of the Pomone, as reconstructed with a round stern in 1847. The steam machinery of modest power was regarded as auxiliary to the sail, and indeed the ship was faster under canvas than steam. (Atlas du Génie Maritime, Genoa collection, image 2-0018)

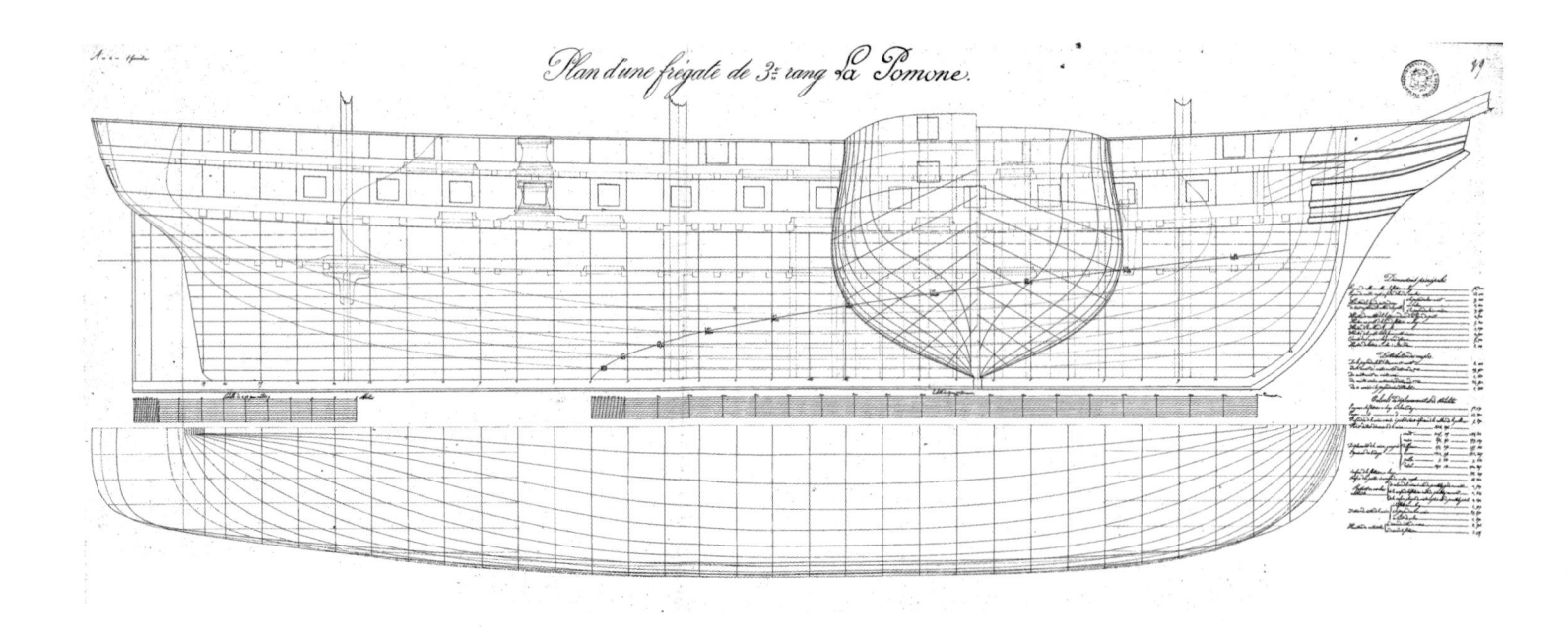

K: 19.4.1850. Not launched as sail, but converted on the stocks to a steam frigate 1858-62 (see Section E).

ALGERIE – 40 guns. In 1843 Rochefort asked to build this ship to use up some wood that was available there. Plans for her by Jean-Baptiste Hubert, approved on 5 September 1844, essentially duplicated those of *Héliopolis* with the beam increased by 40cm to accommodate an armament of 30pdrs instead of 18pdrs. She had a round stern.
 Dimensions & tons: 49.50m, 48.25m wl x 13.00m x 6.60m. 1,725 tons disp. Draught 5.62m mean. Men: 327.
 Guns: (1849) UD 24 x 30pdrs No.2, 2 x 22cm No.2 shell; SD 8 x 30pdr carronades, 4 x 16cm shell, 2 x 30pdrs No.2.
Algérie Rochefort Dyd. (Constructeurs: Antoine Auriol, later Bernard Chariot)
 K: 26.10.1844. L: 4.3.1848. Comm: 23.3.1849. C: 3.1849. Struck 15.7.1867. BU 1867.

CÉRÈS – 40 guns. On 23 May 1846 the Minister specified a new armament for 3rd Rank frigates with 24 or 22 x 30pdrs No.2 and 2 or 4 x 22cm shell guns in the battery. This decision led to the construction of *Cérès*, *Résolue*, and *Isis*, with *Armorique* following later. Plans by Pierre Le Grix for *Cérès* were approved on 16 November 1846, although he was directed to substitute a round stern for the square one in the plans.
 Dimensions & tons: 48.00m wl x 13.00m x 6.67m. 1,757 tons disp. Draught 5.70m mean. Men: 327.
 Guns: (Designed, 1846) UD 24 or 22 x 30pdrs No.2, 2 or 4 x 22cm shell guns; SD 10 x 16cm shell
Cérès Lorient Dyd-Caudan (Constructeurs: Le Grix and Louis-Édouard Lecointre)
 K: 2.1.1847. Not launched as sail. Steam transport 1857.

RÉSOLUE – 40 guns. This ship was designed by Charles Moll using the same specifications as for *Cérès*. The plans were approved on 3 August 1846. *Résolue* was launched in 1863 as a sailing ship but completed in 1872 as a steam frigate.
 Dimensions & tons: 48.00m wl x 13.00m (est.). 1,725 tons disp. (est.). Men: 327.
 Guns: (Designed, 1846) As *Cérès*.
Résolue Cherbourg Dyd. (Constructeurs: Alexandre De Lavrignais, Adrien Joyeux, and Louis Sollier)
 Ord: 14.10.1845. K: 22.10.1846. L: 18.6.1863. Not commissioned as sail. Completed as steam frigate 1869-72

(E) Screw frigates, 3rd Rank

France's first experimental screw frigate, ordered in 1842, was a modified 3rd Rank sailing frigate with auxiliary screw propulsion, and the second was a comparable vessel lengthened to accommodate full steam power. When the French began converting sailing frigates to steam later in the 1840s and in the 1850s, however, the larger 1st and 2nd Rank frigates were found to be more suitable because of their greater capacity, and of the three 3rd Rank frigate conversions undertaken only one proceeded uneventfully.

POMONE. Construction of this ship was proposed by the Director of Materiel, Mathurin Boucher, on 30 December 1841 as part of a program of experimental frigates which also included the sail *Clorinde* and *Psyché*. He argued that the advent of the screw made possible a new concept, the mixed propulsion warship. Such a ship would be basically a sailing ship, retaining all the characteristics of its sailing equivalents, notably performance under canvas, armament, and endurance. It would, however, also have modest steam power for use in calms, in entering and leaving port, and to assist in carrying out difficult manoeuvres. He designed *Pomone* as a standard 3rd Rank sail frigate with an extra 3.32m section amidships for 160nhp machinery (soon increased to 220nhp).

The building of the ship was ordered on 20 April 1842 and her engines were ordered from Rosen and Mazeline by a contract approved on 14 September 1843. The design for the screw installation was provided by Count Rosen, a representative of John Ericsson, and featured

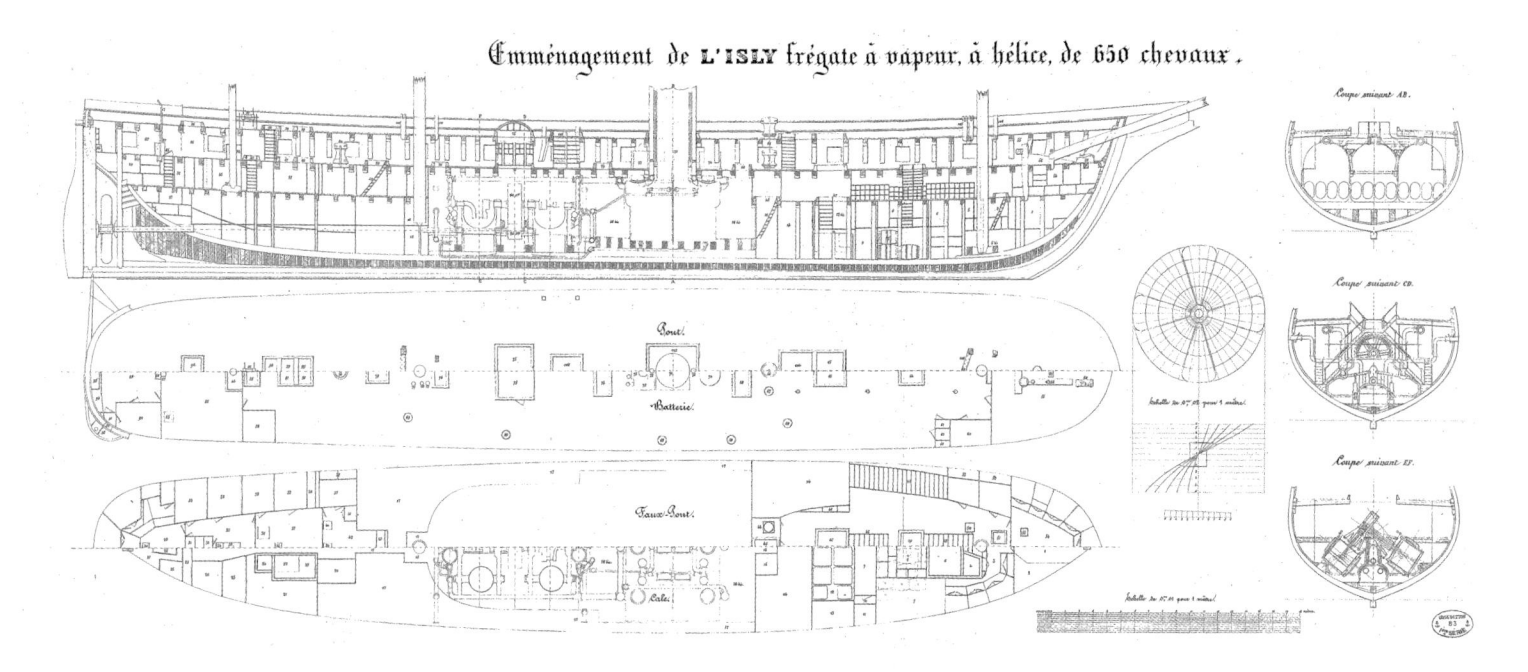

Emménagement de L'ISLY frégate à vapeur, à hélice, de 650 chevaux.

The internal arrangements of *Isly*, the French Navy's first high-powered screw frigate in which steam was intended to take precedence over sail. The original four-cylinder oscillating machinery shown here was plagued with troubles and in 1853 it was replaced by engines from the same manufacturer but to a fixed-cylinder design. (Atlas du Génie Maritime, French collection, plate 104)

two rudders, one on each side of the stern, ahead of a multi-bladed 4.20m diameter Ericsson propeller. When the ship ran her first steam trials in August 1846 she was unable to steer, and her stern was rebuilt in 1847 with a hoisting two-bladed propeller forward of a single rudder. (The stern was also changed from square to round.) She ran successful trials in October 1847 and was ready for service in February 1848. She recorded speeds of 7½ knots under steam in calm seas, 10½ knots under steam and sail, and 12 knots under sail.

Dimensions & tons: 54.77m, 52.00m wl x 13.00m, 13.30m ext x 6.70m. 2,010 tons disp. Draught 5.53/6.17m. Men: 388.
Machinery: 220nhp. 2 cylinders, direct, return connecting rod, 574ihp, 7kts. Coal 150-400 tons.
Guns: (1848) UD 4 x 30pdrs No.1, 14 x 30pdrs No.2, 8 x 22cm No.2 shell; SD 2 x 30pdrs No.2, 8 x 16cm shell.

Pomone Lorient Dyd/Mazeline (Constructeur: Jean-Baptiste Larchevesque-Thibaut)
K: 26.10.1842. L: 20.6.1845. C: 5.1846. Comm: 10.7.1846.
Struck at Lorient 15.11.1862, reinscribed on the list 12.5.1863 as a 500-ton screw transport. Struck 3.5.1877, barracks hulk at Brest. BU 1887.

ISLY. In contrast to *Pomone*, this ship was designed with full steam power and secondary sail power. She was the screw counterpart of the paddle frigate *Mogador*, in which new technology such as tubular boilers was exploited to increase the horsepower of large steam frigates from 450nhp to 650nhp. She was briefly listed as *Monge* when first proposed on 4 October 1845 but had become *Isly* by December 1845. Specifications in 1845 called for an armament 16 x 22cm No.1 and 8 'larger guns' on the gun deck and 4 x 50pdrs topsides. Plans for her hull by Jean-Baptiste Lebas were approved in July 1846, the hull was ordered on 7 August 1846, and her first set of machinery was ordered from François Cavé by a contract approved on 21 June 1847. Because of her full steam power, she was to have received a light rig with square sails on the foremast only, but in 1851 the rig was increased.

Her machinery proved to be structurally weak and was rejected after lengthy trials in 1851. The ship was decommissioned at Toulon in May 1852, and in a supplement approved on 6 April 1853 Cavé agreed to supply new engines for the ship under the original contract. In 1855 she received a new armament of UD 12 x 36pdrs, 12 x 22cm No.1 shell; SD 8 x 36pdrs, 2 x 22cm No.1 shell. When *Isly* ran trials with her second set of machinery in May 1856 her displacement was 2,915 tons and her mean draught 6.25m (6.92m aft). She pitched excessively with her new armament and her captain recommended removing eight guns – by 1861 she carried 12 x 30pdrs No.1 and 16 x 16cm rifles. She had the proportions of a 3rd Rank frigate but became a 2nd Rank frigate under the new classification scheme of 1855. Due to her machinery problems she entered service a full decade after being laid down and lost most of her significance as France's pioneer high-powered screw frigate.

Dimensions & tons: 73.40m, 70.00m wl, 64.2m x 13.00m, 13.24m ext x 6.73m. 2,675 tons disp. Draught 5.90m mean. Men: 415.
Machinery: 650nhp. First set: 4 oscillating cylinders, geared. Second set: 4 fixed cylinders, direct, 1530ihp, trials 12.4kts (reached over 13kts).
Guns: (1850) UD 8 x 30pdrs No.1, 8 x 22cm No.1 shell; SD 4 x 30pdrs No.1.

Isly Brest Dyd/Cavé (Constructeurs: Paul Leroux and others)
Ord: 7.8.1846. K: 26.8.1846. L: 19.7.1849. Comm: 5.10.1850. C: 12.1850.
Struck 22.7.1872, hulk at Brest. BU 1875.

CLORINDE. The hull of this sailing frigate, already afloat, was converted on plans by Adrien Joyeux approved in October 1856. The ship was designed to receive 400nhp engines with Belleville boilers which were to have been built at Cherbourg. This machinery never materialised, and smaller engines were finally ordered from Schneider by a contract signed on 3 February 1860. These were installed between September and December 1861. She was lengthened by about 2.70m.

Dimensions & tons: 51.95m, 51.00m wl, 47.15m x 13.28m ext x 6.60m. 1,720 tons disp. Draught 5.70m mean. Men: 388.
Machinery: 180nhp. Trials 563ihp = 8.79kts. Coal 142t.
Guns: (10.1861) 20 x 16cm rifles; (1867) UD 14 x 16cm rifles; SD 4

Résolue, France's last 40-gun frigate, carried a small steam engine between 1871 and 1877 but is shown here while serving as a sail training ship for seamen between 1878 and 1890. (Marius Bar)

x 16cm rifles.

Clorinde Cherbourg Dyd/Schneider.
   Start: 16.9.1856 (hauled out). L: 23.5.1857. Comm: 11.9.1861.
   Struck 26.1.1888, barracks hulk at Lorient, renamed *Tibre* 26.5.1911, BU 1922.

ARMORIQUE. This frigate was lengthened by about 28m on the ways and converted to a steam frigate on plans by Nicolas Le Moine approved in June 1858 for engines ordered from Indret in March 1858. She was rated as a spardecked corvette (*corvette à batterie*) between January 1862 and January 1872.

   Dimensions & tons: 76.95m, 76.00m wl, 71.80m x 13.50m ext x 6.56m. 2,890 tons disp. Draught 5.15/6.25m. Men: 345.
   Machinery: 400nhp. Trunk, trials 1175ihp = 10.37kts.
   Guns: (1863) UD 14 x 30pdrs No.1, 4 x 16cm rifles; SD 4 x 16cm rifles.

Armorique Lorient Dyd-Caudan/Indret (converted by Nicolas Le Moine and probably Charles Layre)
   Conversion began: ?. L: 1.3.1862. Comm: 7.4.1863. C: 4.1863.
   Struck 8.11.1884, school hulk for boys at Rochefort. Mooring hulk by 1900. Sold 1911 and BU.

RÉSOLUE. Engines of 200nhp were ordered for this ship, then on the ways, from Schneider by a contract approved on 6 June 1856 but were quickly reassigned to *Pandore*. Trunk engines of 400nhp were then ordered for her from Indret in March 1858, and drawings for lengthening her hull from 48.25m to 72.55m (wl) on the ways were drafted by Adrien Joyeux in April 1859. This conversion, however, was not carried out and the ship was re-listed as a sailing ship in January 1862 and launched as such in 1863 without being lengthened. She remained idle until being listed again as a screw frigate in January 1870 and receiving much smaller machinery by Claparède in 1869-71. Claparède had taken over the location at Saint-Denis vacated by Cavé around 1850.

   Dimensions & tons: 49.77m, 48.55m wl, 44.91m x 13.41m ext x 6.60m. 1,871 tons disp. Draught 5.15/6.71m. Men: 299.
   Machinery: 150nhp. Trials 697ihp = 9.55kts. Coal 145t.
   Guns: (1872) UD 12 x 16cm M1858-60 MLR; SD 4 x 14cm No.2 M1867 MLR.

Résolue Cherbourg Dyd/Claparède, Saint-Denis.
   Conversion began: c1869. Comm: 2.10.1872.
   Engines ordered removed at Cherbourg 16.10.1877. Listed as a sail transport 1.1878, replaced the sail frigate *Isis* 9.1878 as seagoing seamen's training ship (*École de matelotage et timonerie*) at Cherbourg, and listed as a sail frigate 1.1879. Decomm. 26.8.1882. Training ship for apprentice seamen (*École des apprentis gabiers et timoniers*) at Brest 17.9.1883, relieved by a new *Melpomène* 15.9.1890 and decomm. 20.9.1890. Struck 31.12.1890. Coal hulk at Rochefort 1891, mooring hulk there 1893. Sold 1913 and BU.

6 Corvettes

The early French corvettes were small two-masted vessels, developed from the *barques longues* of the seventeenth century. In fact, for many years the two terms were virtually synonymous, until the classification *barque longue* was dropped in 1746. By the 1740s the corvettes were miniature frigates, sometimes with a ship rig (three-masted), also with a set of long oars (sweeps) for rowing. They measured 50 to 80ft in length on the upper deck, well under the 86 to 100ft of contemporary light frigates (*frégates légères*). These vessels were used as raiders of enemy shipping, to escort French merchant vessels, and to support a fleet by scouting and carrying despatches. From the mid-eighteenth century they underwent a significant growth in size, with the new type of corvette carrying a battery of 16 or 18 guns on their UD. In 1758 the mathematician and archivist Alexandre Savérien was defining the corvette as any warship with fewer than 20 guns.

Most of the existing French corvettes were lost during the Seven Years War. Following this, a royal decision in October 1763 introduced the calibre of 6pdr guns to the ranks of the corvette; previously this had been borne by the larger *frégates légères*, whose role the corvette would largely take. In practice, some corvettes had already been built with 6pdrs by this date, but no further 4pdr-armed corvettes were built thereafter (although some were acquired by capture or purchase), so new construction consisted of 6pdr-armed types, carrying batteries of 12, 16 or 18 guns on hulls roughly similar in size and displacement to their pre-war (4pdr-armed) predecessors. The regulations of October 1765 split corvettes into two Orders, the first carrying 20 x 6pdrs and the second generally with 12 x 4pdrs.

A further enlargement, to corvettes with a battery of 8pdr guns, was made in 1779 with the *Coquette* class, but both 8pdr and 6pdr types continued through the Napoleonic era. During the Revolutionary period even heavier armaments of 12pdr and even 18pdr batteries were tried, and in the early years of the new century a smaller series of corvette-gunboats were built with 24pdr guns. As with the British Navy (and some others) these long guns were superseded by carronades towards the end of the First Empire period, and further carronade-armed corvettes were constructed from 1820 onwards.

(A) Corvettes in service or on order at 1 January 1786

HIRONDELLE. This vessel, built as a privateer and completed in September 1762 as the *Expédition*, was purchased for the navy on 22 October 1762 as a 12-gun corvette, and renamed *Hirondelle* on 20 December. She served as a packet for voyages to the West Indies in the 1760s, and in 1774 was converted to a training corvette at Brest.
   Dimensions & tons: 85ft 0in, 70ft 0in x 24ft 0in x 11ft 10in (27.61, 22.74 x 7.80 x 3.84m). 240/458 tons. Draught 9ft 8in/12ft 6in (3.14/4.06m). Men: 125.
   Guns: 16 x 6pdrs.
Hirondelle Nantes.
   K: 1761. L: 8.1762. C: 9.1762.
   Struck 1797.

The few 6pdr corvettes built in 1767-71 were flush-decked vessels, with a continuous orlop deck below, although the constructors at Brest complained that their size was too limited for the ordnance and stores which they were expected to stow. All on the 1785 List were allocated a complement of 200 men in wartime and 120 in peacetime.

FLÈCHE. Corvette of 18 x 6pdr guns, designed by Louis-Hilarion Chapelle. The vessel was ordered on 25 December 1767 and was named in February 1768, but on 19 February the Ministry suspended construction (until 18 March) on learning that work had begun without the design being approved. She was the most elderly of the corvettes surviving in 1786 (having been substantially refitted in 1779-80). In the 1785 List she is rated at 20 guns.
   Dimensions & tons: 108ft 0in, 93ft 0in x 27ft 6in x 13ft 8in (35.08, 30.21 x 8.93 x 4.44m). 320/550 tons. Draught 10¾/11¾ft (3.49/3.82m). Men: 200 (war) 120 (peace).
   Guns: 18 x 6pdrs (by 1794 reduced to 14 x 6pdrs).
Flèche Toulon Dyd. (Constructeur: Coulomb)
   K: 12.1.1768. L: 19.10.1768. C: 9.1769.
   Captured by the British Navy at Bastia 21.5.1794, and added as HMS *Fleche* (now rigged as brig); wrecked 12.11.1795 off Corsica.

ROSSIGNOL. Corvette of 16 x 6pdr guns, designed by Joseph-Louis Ollivier. She was ordered in 1769 and named on 25 August 1769 (although work commenced on her earlier). By 1785 she was listed as 20 guns. Of the corvettes launched in 1768, the similar (but smaller) *Perle* had been captured on 5 July 1780 by HMS *Rodney*, the *Cerf-Volant* had been sold in 1775, and the smaller *Écureuil* was converted into the transatlantic packet *Courrier de l'Amerique* in October 1783 (and struck in 1785).
   Dimensions & tons: 108ft 0in, 98ft 0in x 28ft 0in x 14ft 0in (35.08, 31.83 x 9.10 x 4.55m). 350 tons. Draught 12ft 1in/13ft 2in (3.93/4.28m). Men: 150 (war) 100 (peace).
   Guns: 16 x 6pdrs.
Rossignol Brest Dyd. (Constructeur: Joseph-Louis Ollivier)
   K: 5.6.1769. Named 25.8.1769. L: 14.11.1769. C: 11.1770.
   Helped capture HMS *Nemesis* 9.12.1795, probably deleted 1796.

ÉCLAIR. Corvette of 18 x 6pdr guns (originally a 'barque latine'), designed by Jean-Baptiste Doumet-Revest.
   Dimensions & tons: 98ft 0in, 80ft 0in x 27ft 0in x 12ft 0in (31.83, 25.99 x 8.77 x 3.90m). 230/395 tons. Draught 11ft 6in/11ft 10in (3.74/3.84m). Men: 166.
   Guns: 16 x 6pdrs.
Éclair Toulon Dyd.
   K: 4.1770. L: 5.7.1771. C: 1772.
   Refitted at Toulon 1781, listed as corvette from 1783. Captured by HMS *Leda* in the Mediterranean 9.6.1793, and added as HMS *Éclair*; hulked 4.1797 and sold at Sheerness 27.8.1806.

SERIN. Corvette of 14 x 6pdr guns, designed by Henri Chevillard.

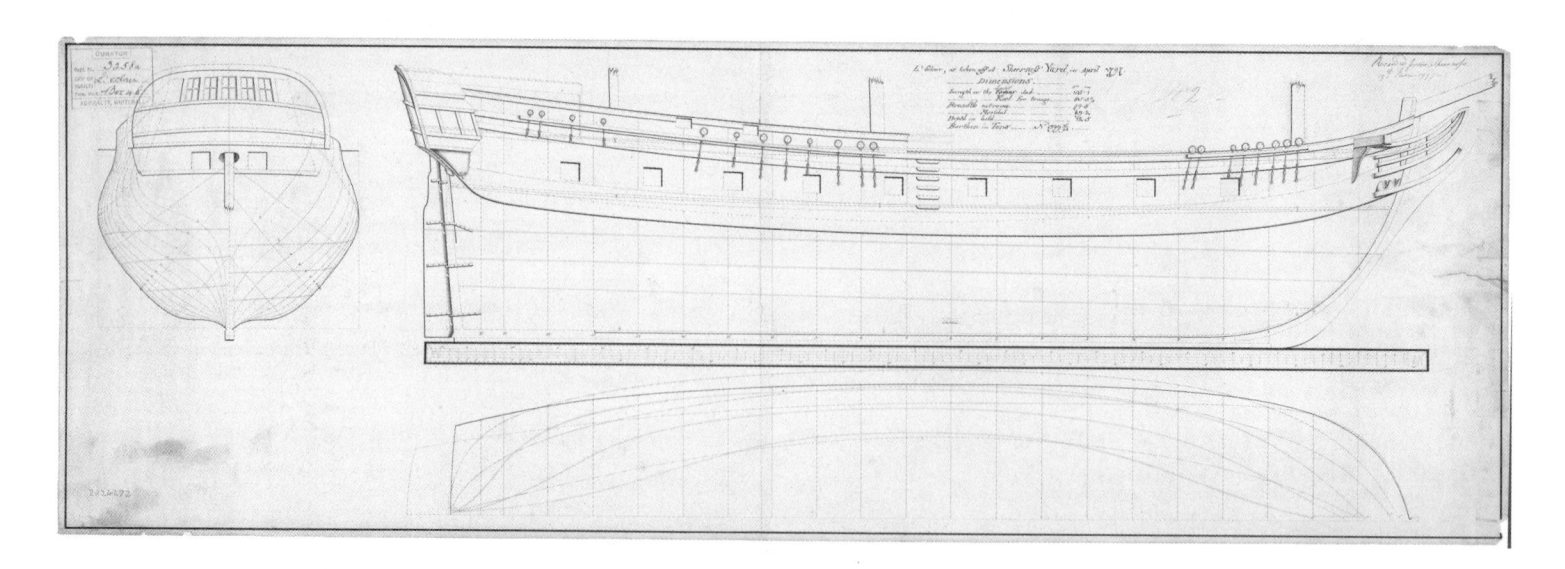

Rigged as a snow.
>Dimensions & tons: 99ft 0in x 26ft 0in x 12ft 8in (32.16 x 8.45 x 4.11m). 250/600 tons. Draught 10½/11ft 2in (3.41/3.63m). Men: 150 (war) 100 (peace).
>Guns: UD 14 x 6pdrs (in 1785 List she is shown with 20 x 6pdrs); SD nil.

Serin Rochefort Dyd.
>K: 6.1770. L: 2.3.1771. C: 5.1771.
>Refitted at Brest 1778. Renamed *Courrier de L'Europe* 9.1783, and employed as a transatlantic packet 1783-87. Sold 1.1789 at Le Havre.

SARDINE Class. Corvette of 16 x 6pdr guns (pierced for 18 ports), designed by Joseph-Marie-Blaise Coulomb. In 1785 listed as 20-gun. There may have been a sister-ship, which appears as *Suzane* in the 1785 List
>Dimensions & tons: 106ft x 27ft x 13ft 3in (34.43 x 8.77 x 4.30m). 280 tons. Draught 10ft 7in/11ft 4in (3.44/3.68m). Men: 86/100.
>Guns: 16 x 6pdrs.

Sardine Toulon Dyd. (Constructeur: Broquier)
>K: 6.1770. L: 14.7.1771. C: 1772.
>Captured by the British at Toulon in 8.1793, recovered by the French at the surrender of that port on 12.1793, but captured again by the British Navy in 3.1796 and taken into service as HMS *Sardine*; sold 1806.

After a barren few years from 1772, construction resumed in the mid-1770s with two small corvettes, *Curieuse* and *Favorite*, both built at Le Havre in 1776; these were raséed and re-classed as avisos in July/August 1780, but the first was lost in 1780 and the second was struck in 1784. Two more, somewhat larger 6pdr types were built to carry 20-gun batteries, while a pair of prototype 8pdr-armed corvettes were built at Toulon in 1779 (and soon followed by others of the same design). As 8pdr frigate construction had come to an end in the 1770s, the new corvettes could be seen to be taking on the role and duties of the small frigates.

SUBTILE Class. Corvettes of 18 x 6pdr guns (pierced for 20 guns), designed by Raymond-Antoine Haran. The second vessel – *Valeur* (launched at Saint-Malo in 1778) – had been destroyed by HMS *Experiment* at Cancale on 13 May 1779.
>Dimensions & tons: 110ft 0in x 28ft 0in x 14ft 6in (35.73 x 9.10 x

Admiralty draught of *Eclair* as taken off at Sheerness in April 1797. Although the ship has a classic French underwater form, the curious topside with a swept-up bow derives from its origin as a 'barque latine', a Mediterranean lateen-rigged type related to the xebec (see Chapter 10 for examples). After short service in the Mediterranean, the ship was sailed to Britain and reduced to a hulk about the time this draught was produced. (© National Maritime Museum J4582)

>4.71m). 320/600 tons. Men: 130.
>Guns: UD 18 x 6pdrs (on the 1785 List, 20 x 6pdrs); SD 6 x 4pdrs.

Subtile Rochefort Dyd.
>K: 4.1777. L: 7.9.1777. C: end 1777.
>Renamed *Sainte Catherine* 1.1787, but original name restored 3.1787. Condemned 12.1788 at Toulon and struck. BU probably 1791.

COQUETTE Class. Corvettes of 20 x 8pdr guns, although appearing in the 1785 List as 26-gun vessels (their SD 6 x 6pdrs being included in this count). Designed by Joseph-Marie-Blaise Coulomb, these were equivalent to (and perhaps superior in design to) the contemporary British 9pdr-armed 28-gun Sixth Rates. All eight to this design were built at Toulon; the first two of the class, *Coquette* and *Naïade* (both launched in 1779), had been both captured by the British Navy in 1783, although not added to the British Navy; both still appeared on the French 1785 List. The first four below were all ordered on 20 April 1780 and names assigned on 16 June 1780; the final pair were named on 3 March 1781.
>Dimensions & tons: 119ft 0in, 106ft 0in x 30ft 6in x 15ft 6in (38.65, 34.43 x 9.90 x 5.03m). 480/850 tons. Draught 14ft/15ft (4.55/4.87m). Men: 200 (war) 120 (peace).
>Guns: UD 20 x 8pdrs; SD 6 x 6pdrs.

Badine Toulon Dyd.
>K: 5.1780. L: 5.8.1780. C: 12.1780.
>Decommissioned and condemned at Martinique 18.3.1804 because she could no longer remain afloat. Hulk captured by the British 2.1809.

Sémillante Toulon Dyd.
>K: 5.1780. L: 11.8.1780. C: 12.1780.
>Burnt by accident at Toulon 5.1.1787.

Blonde Toulon Dyd.
>K: 8.1780. L: 6.1.1781. C: 2.1781.
>Taken by HMS *Latona* and HMS *Phaeton* off Ushant 28.11.1793. Sold 1794.

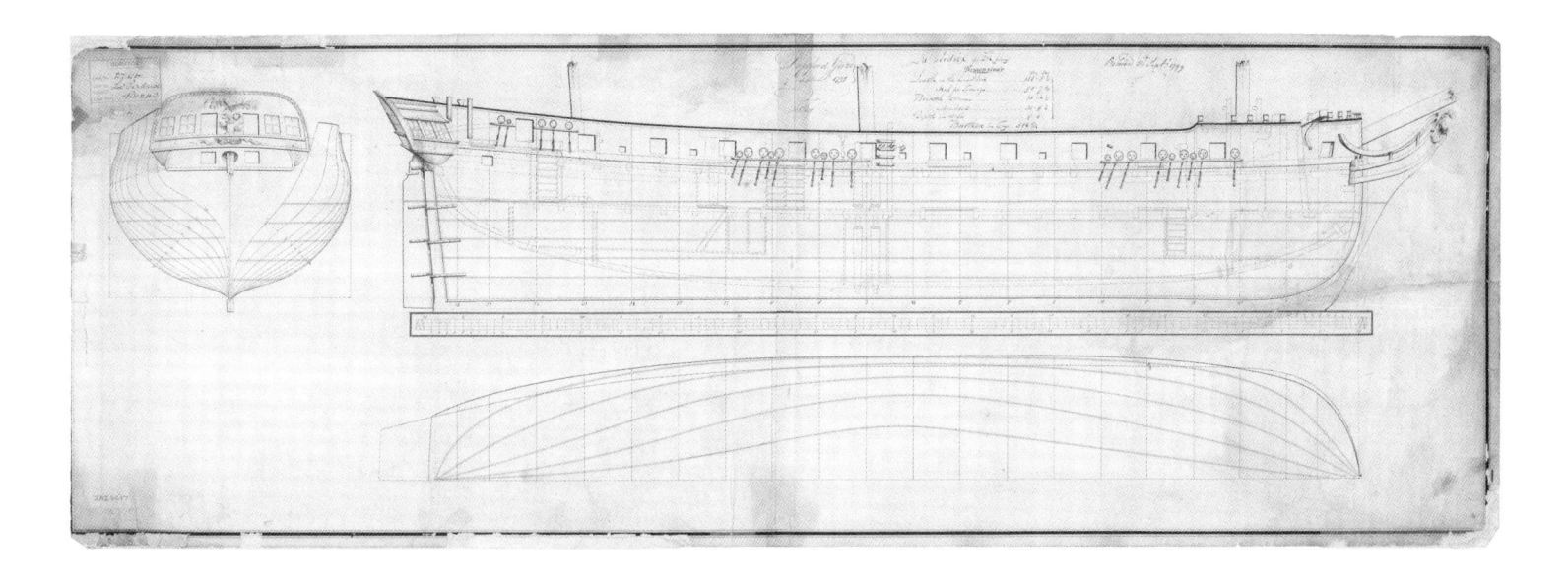

Brune Toulon Dyd.
K: 8.1780. L: 20.1.1781. C: 3.1781.
Taken by the Russians at Corfu 3.3.1799 and handed over to the Turks.

Poulette Toulon Dyd.
K: 9.1780. L: 22.3.1781. C: 30.6.1781.
Handed over by Royalists to the British at Toulon 29.8.1793, becoming HMS *Poulette*. Burnt as unserviceable at Ajaccio 20.10.1796.

Belette Toulon Dyd.
K: 10.1780. L: 5.3.1781. C: 17.6.1781.
Handed over by Royalists to the British at Toulon 29.8.1793, becoming HMS *Belette*. Burnt as unserviceable at Ajaccio 10.1796.

TOURTEREAU. Corvette of 18 x 6pdrs. Design by Jean-Denis Chevillard. The 1785 List describes this vessel as '*Tourtereaux*' (which seems to be in error) and carrying 22 UD guns (26 guns in all).
Dimensions & tons: 100ft 0in x 26ft 4in x 13ft 0in (32.48 x 8.55 x 4.22m). 320/550 tons. Draught 12/13ft (3.90/4.22m). Men: 120.
Guns: 18 x 6pdrs.

Tourtereau Calais.
K: end 1781. L: 27.3.1782. C: 8.1782.
Struck 1787 at Rochefort and BU.

FAUVETTE Class. Corvettes of 20 x 6pdr guns, designed by Charles-Étienne Bombelle (Baron de Bombelle) with technical help from Charles Segondat-Duvernet. This class had a short topgallant forecastle, and the otherwise flush upper deck had a small step-up aft to increase the headroom in the captain's cabin. As built there were ports for the 10 pairs of guns and for 12 pairs of oars. The first two were ordered at Rochefort in April 1782 and named on 13 April 1782. Two more to the same design were projected at Rochefort – *Enjouée* and *Légère* (and may have been intended to carry 18 x 8pdrs instead of their 20 x 6pdrs), but in the event these were not built. *Fauvette* was listed in 1793 with 18 x 8pdrs broadside, 2 x 24pdrs chase forward and 2 x 18pdrs aft, but within a year had reverted to 20 x 6pdrs.
Dimensions & tons: 112ft 0in, 101ft 0in x 28ft 0in x 14ft 3in (36.38, 32.81 x 9.09½ x 4.63 m.). 430/752 tons. Draught 12ft/12½ft (3.90/4.06m). Men: 160.
Guns: 20 x 6pdrs.

Fauvette Rochefort Dyd. (Constructeur: Hubert Pennevert)

Admiralty draught of *Perdrix* dated Deptford 7 September 1799, shortly before the decision was taken to break her up. It is annotated '24 guns', although the chase ports would have to be armed to mount this number of guns. This form of flush-decked corvette, popularised by the French Navy, offered considerable advantages in sailing qualities over the older quarterdecked form of sloop or corvette. *Perdrix* was not literally flush-decked, as there was a small step up to the deck aft to give the captain's cabin more headroom, while a small topgallant forecastle was added forward to facilitate handling the headsails. (© National Maritime Museum J6197)

K: 6.1782. L: 15.6.1783. C: 9.1783.
Gunnery school at Toulon 5.1795. Struck 1796 but restored to the list in 1798 and refitted at Toulon with 20 x 8pdrs, reduced by 1809 to 14 x 8pdrs. Condemned at Toulon and sale approved 16.6.1814, BU 4.1815.

Perdrix Rochefort Dyd.
K: early 1783. L: 18.6.1784. C: 2.1785.
Taken by HMS *Vanguard* off Antigua 5.6.1795, added as HMS *Perdrix*. BU at Deptford 10.9.1799.

Favorite Rochefort Dyd.
K: 1784/5. L: 8.1785. C: 10.1785.
Taken by HMS *Alfred* off Cape Finisterre 5.3.1795, but not added to RN.

Alouette Rochefort Dyd.
K: early 1785. L: 1.1786. C: 5.1786.
Renamed *Maire Guiton* from 8.1793. Taken by HMS *Hebe* 5.1794 but retaken after 4 days. Name restored to *Alouette* 5.1795. Hulk at Lorient end 1795.

VIGILANTE Class. Corvette-gabarres of 16 x 6pdrs. Designed by Jean-Joseph Perrin de Boissieu, and built by Raymond-Antoine Haran. In 1788 and 1789 respectively they became training ships at Brest, and then were converted to gabarres.
Dimensions & tons: 112ft 0in, 102ft 0in x 25ft 0in x 13ft 3in (36.38, 33.13 x 8.12 x 4.30m.). 350/500 tons. Draught 10ft 4in/10ft 4in (3.36/3.36m). Men: 156/180 men (average).
Guns: 14/16 x 6pdrs (*Vigilante* later had 4 x 36pdr obusiers added, *Sincère* had 20 guns when taken).

Vigilante Bayonne.
K: 4.1783. L: 11.1783. C: 2.1784.
Struck 1796.

Sincère Bayonne.
K: 1783. L: 4.1784. C: 8.1784.
Handed over to Anglo-Spanish forces at Toulon 29.8.1793, becoming HMS *Sincere*. Sold 1799.

Ex-BRITISH NAVAL PRIZES (1778-1782). HMS *Active* and HMS *Ariel* were captured from the British Navy in 1778 and 1779 respectively, commissioned under their British names, and initially classed by the French as frigates. These 8pdr frigates were redesignated as corvettes in January 1789, but are listed in Chapter 5. The sloop *York* (captured in 1778) had been retaken after a month but taken again in 1779. Renamed *Duc d'York*, she was struck in 1783. The sloops *Senegal*, *Zephyr* and *Helena* (also captured in 1778) had been retaken by the British in 1779 and 1780; the *Weazle* (captured in 1779) was sold in 1781. The naval sloop *Ceres* was also captured in 1778; she was retaken by the British in 1782, becoming HMS *Raven*, but was again captured in 1783, remaining in French service until 1791. The sloop *Loyalist* (originally *Restoration*), captured in July 1781, was given to the Americans in November. The sloop *Sandwich* (originally the mercantile *Marjory*), captured in August 1781, was sold a few months later. The brig-sloop *Stormont* (taken in 1782 and classed as a corvette by the French) was struck in 1786.

CÉRÈS. A one-off British naval ship-sloop ordered in 1774 to be copied from the draught of the (ex-French) prize sloop *Chevrette* (taken in 1761 and renamed HMS *Pomona*). Originally captured by the French on 17 December 1778, the *Ceres* was retaken by the British in the Mona Passage by Rodney's fleet on 9 February 1782 and reinstated as HMS *Raven*, but was again taken by the French frigates *Nymphe* and *Concorde* off Montserrat on 7 January 1783, resuming her name of *Cérès*.
Dimensions & tons: 102ft 0in x 25ft 8in (33.13 x 8.34m). 280/450 tons. Men: 150.
Guns: 18 x 6pdrs
Cérès Woolwich Dyd.
K: 27.5.1776. L: 25.3.1777. C: 1.5.1777.
Sold at Brest 1791.

***SWAN* Class.** The standard British ship-sloop class of the American War, 25 ships were built to this 1766 design by John Williams, of which *Fortune*, *Thorn*, *Cormorant*, *Bonetta* and *Alligator* were captured by the French during this period, but *Thorn* and *Bonetta* were retaken by the British during 1782, and *Cormorant* was seemingly lost. The *Fortune* and *Alligator* were converted to transatlantic packets at Lorient in 1783-84 and operated as packets between Le Havre and New York, but both were retained on the 1785 List of the French Navy, rated as 20-gun corvettes; they were transferred in 1787 to the Régie des Paquebots until their sale in 1789; they are listed below, with measurements in French units.
Dimensions & tons: 94ft 0in, 83ft 0in x 25ft 2in x 12ft 10in (30.53, 26.96 x 8.18 x 4.17m). 300/470 tons. Draught 11ft 4in/12ft (3.68/3.90m). Men: 135-150 (war) 100 (peace).
Guns: UD 16 x 6pdrs.
Fortune Woolwich Dyd.
K: 19.4.1777. L: 28.7.1778. C: 19.9.1778.
Captured by Guichen's squadron off Barbuda 26.4.1780. Renamed *Courrier de Lorient* 10.1783 and became a packet between Le Havre and New York; sold at Le Havre 1.1789.
Alligator John Fisher, Liverpool.
K: 10.1779. L: 11.11.1780. C: 5.1781.
Captured by frigate *Fée* off the Isles of Scilly 26.6.1782. Renamed *Courrier de New York* 10.1783 and became a packet between Lorient and New York; sold at Le Havre 1.1789.

Ex-BRITISH MERCANTILE PRIZES (1778-1782). Several British merchantmen or privateers were captured during the 1778-82 period and incorporated into the French Navy. Of these, the privateer *Sparrowhawk* (captured in 1778 and renamed *Épervier*) was sold for commerce in 1783; the privateer *Vulture* (captured 1782 and renamed *Vautour*) was made a hydrological research vessel in 1784-5 and was deleted in 1786. The following still remained in naval service in 1786:
Pilote des Indes (brig of 150 tons, with 100-130 men and 10 guns). Decomm. at Brest 3.1790 and struck.
David (250 tons, with 88-145 men and 18 x 12pdrs). Decomm at Brest 5.1786 and struck.
Hypocrite (100 tons, with just 6 x 4pdrs by 1787). Struck at Rochefort 1789.

PURCHASED VESSELS (1782-1785). Four merchant vessels were taken up by the French Navy in 1782-85 and operated as corvettes. Few technical details are recorded.
Duc de Chartres (brig of 80 tons, built 1779-80 at Saint-Malo as a 24-gun privateer and purchased by the navy 9.1782 at Île de France; carried 14 x 4pdrs). Renamed *Coureur* 29.9.1792 and condemned at Île de France 3.1798.
Auguste (Bordeaux merchantman of 360 tons, purchased by the navy 3.1783 in the Indian Ocean for Suffren's squadron; carried 22 x 6pdrs). Struck 1785 or 1786 at Brest.
Juliette (Nantes merchantman of 260 tons, purchased by the navy at Île de France 4.1783). Hulked at Lorient 3.1787.
Maréchal de Castries (New York built vessel of 250 tons purchased by the navy in 2.1785; carried 18 x 6pdrs). Transferred to the Régie des Paquebots in 2.1787 but reacquired by the navy 11.1788; briefly renamed *Corsaire* in 9.1792 but resumed original name in same month; delivered by her pro-Royalist officers to the Spanish at Trinidad in 1.1793.

(B) Corvettes acquired from 1 January 1786

In 1786 Jean-Charles de Borda, as Inspector of Naval Shipbuilding (*Inspecteur des Constructions*), proposed to raise the number of corvettes to sixty, including twenty of 119ft length armed with 24 x 8pdrs, and twenty of 113ft length armed with 20 x 6pdrs. The remaining twenty were to be brig-rigged vessels of between 12 and 16 guns. Unlike with the frigates of the Borda-Sané program, the constructeurs were allowed to vary the form and dimensions of the proposed corvettes. However, this program was not put into effect during the Revolutionary years, and no new corvettes were begun until 1792. The lack of suitable escorts for convoys and other duties were felt as soon as war broke out, and a large number of vessels were ordered, mainly from private contractors (as the main dockyards were occupied with ships of the line and frigates), while a variety of ships were purchased (some on the stocks) or requisitioned over the next few years.

The period from April 1793 to 1795 was dominated by the Committee of Public Safety, which exercised everyday executive power of behalf of the Convention. In August the Jacobin majority on the Committee purged Girondins and other moderate elements, and on 5 September 1793 officially introduced the Terror, which lasted until the reaction of 27 July 1794 (9 Thermidor in the Revolutionary Calendar) which overthrew Robespierre and his colleagues, and substituted an ineffective and decentralised executive, the Directorate of five members which ruled from 26 October 1795 (13 Vendemiaire) until overthrown in turn by the Napoleonic coup of 9 November 1799 (18 Brumaire), which restored a strong central executive.

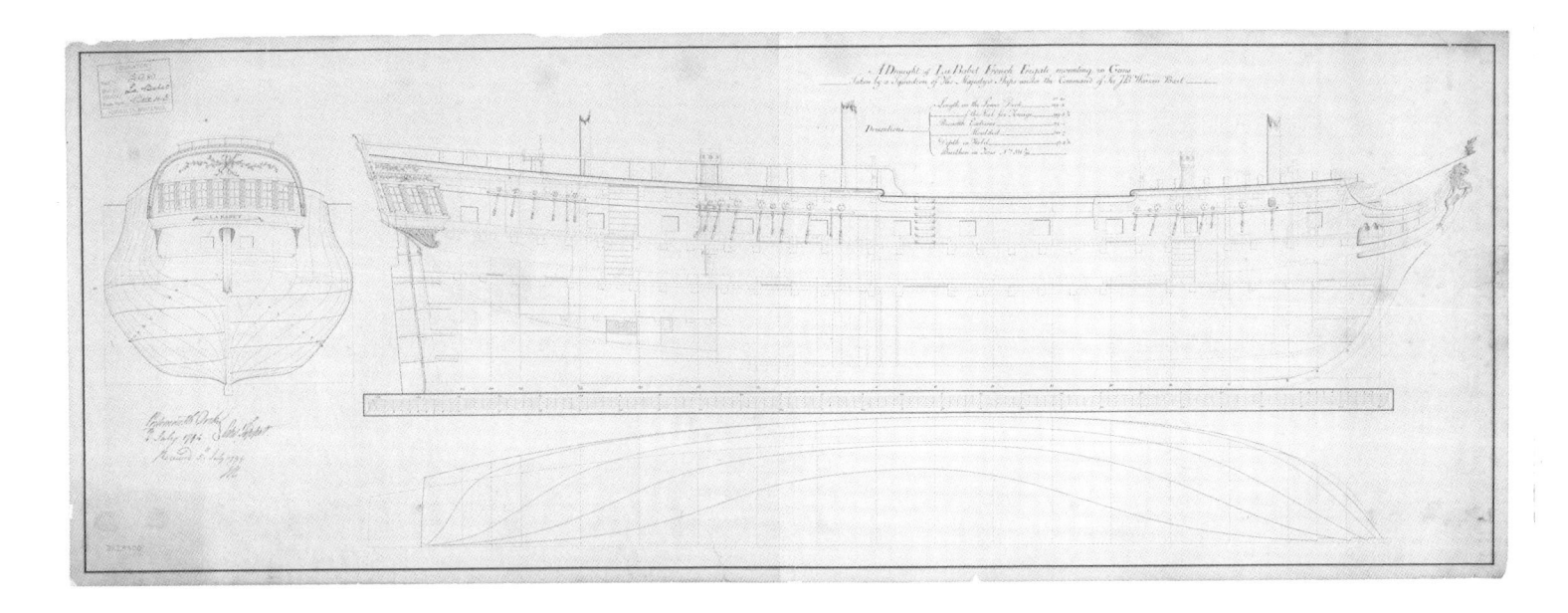

Throughout this period of chaos, accurate record-keeping was hardly a priority among officials desperate to placate both their superiors and the revolutionary mobs, in order to ensure their own survival. Reliable records of instructions issued, changed, countermanded and reissued are few and far between, and as few if any of the corvettes and smaller vessels emerged from contractors' premises in the form in which they were originally ordered, considerable uncertainties exist over the final details and even the nature of vessels acquired. This section below represents the authors' best conclusions on the procurement of corvettes during this era, but undoubtedly contains inaccuracies.

PROMPTE Class. Corvettes of 20 x 8pdr guns. Designed by Joseph-Marie-Blaise Coulomb to the reduced lines of the *Coquette* class of 8pdr corvettes built at Toulon in the early 1780s (see Section A). These two ships were built at Le Havre by Pierre Mauger, and were the only French corvettes to be built between the Revolution and the outbreak of war against the British.

Dimensions & tons: 116ft 0in, 111ft 6in wl, 98ft 0in x 28ft 6in x 14ft 5in (37.68, 36.22, 31.83 x 9.26 x 4.69m). 410/603 tons. Draught 11ft 7in/13ft 5in (3.76/4.36m). Men: 170.

Guns: UD 20/22 x 6pdrs; SD 4 x 4pdrs.

Prompte Pierre Mauger, Le Havre.
K: 1.1792. L: 30.11.1792. C: 2.1793.
Captured by HMS *Phaeton* off Cape Ortegal 18.5.1793, and added as HMS *Prompte*. Broken up at Portsmouth in 7.1813.

Babet Pierre Mauger, Le Havre.
K: 2.1792. L: 12.2.1793. C: 5.1793.
Captured by HMS *Flora* off Île de Batz 23.4.1794, added as HMS *Babet*. Lost, presumed foundered in the Caribbean during 10.1801.

Ex SARDINIAN PRIZES (1792). Corvettes of 16 x 8pdr guns. Both captured 29 September 1792 by Rear-Adm Laurent Truguet's squadron at Villefranche-sur-Mer (near Monaco) in the County of Nice, at that time a part (like Savoy and Piedmont) of the Kingdom of Sardinia, at the start of France's Sardinian campaign (October 1792 – March 1793). They were in bad condition, and *Caroline* was used as a flûte while *Auguste* became a hospital flûte. They fell into the hands of the British at the surrender of Toulon in August 1793, and at its evacuation in

Admiralty draught of *Babet* as taken off at Portsmouth, dated 4 July 1794. Alongside more weatherly flush-decked types, France continued to build quarterdecked corvettes that were effectively small frigates. So strong was this preference, which continued well into the post-war years, that they must have had a role that could not be executed by the open-battery type. This was probably related to the better habitability of the quarterdecked type, which must have made them more suitable for long cruises and distant stations. (© National Maritime Museum J6887)

December both were partially burnt and abandoned, then regained by the French.

Dimensions & tons: dimensions unknown. 350 tons (*Auguste*). Men: 125 (*Caroline*).

Guns: 16 x 8pdrs (after her repair in 1794, *Caroline* had 16 x 6pdrs).

Caroline (ex Sardinian *Carolina*)
Repaired at Toulon 1-7.1794. On sale list 10.1797, last reported 8.1802 as a sunken hulk at Toulon.

Auguste (ex Sardinian *Augusta*)
Seemingly not repaired after her recovery in 12.1793. Hospital hulk 6.1794 at Toulon, unserviceable 3.1803.

RÉVOLUTIONNAIRE Class. Corvettes of 20 x 6pdr guns. Design by Pierre Duhamel. *Tigre* was built for a private owner (Michel Delastelle), and was purchased for the French Navy in March 1794 after service as a privateer. She was probably brig-rigged.

Dimensions & tons: 88ft 0in x 27ft 4in (28.5 x 8.45m). 267/420 tons. Men: 136.

Guns: 20 x 6pdrs (*Révolutionnaire*), 18 x 6pdrs (others).

Révolutionnaire Saint-Malo.
Ord: 21.2.1793. K: 3.1793. L: 8.1793. C: 11.1793.
Captured 12.1793 in the Antilles by HMS *Blanche* (32), recaptured 5.1794. Renamed *Reprise* 5.1795. Wrecked at Aberwrac'h 18.9.1795 but refloated and repaired. Struck at Saint-Malo 5.1797, ordered BU 4.5.1797.

Jean Bart Saint-Malo.
K: 4.1793. L: 10.1793. C: 12.1793.
To have been renamed *Installée* 5.1795 but captured 28.3.1795 in the Channel by HMS *Cerberus* (32) and HMS *Santa Margarita* (36). Became HMS *Arab*. Wrecked 10.6.1796 on the Île des Gléanans.

Tigre Saint-Malo

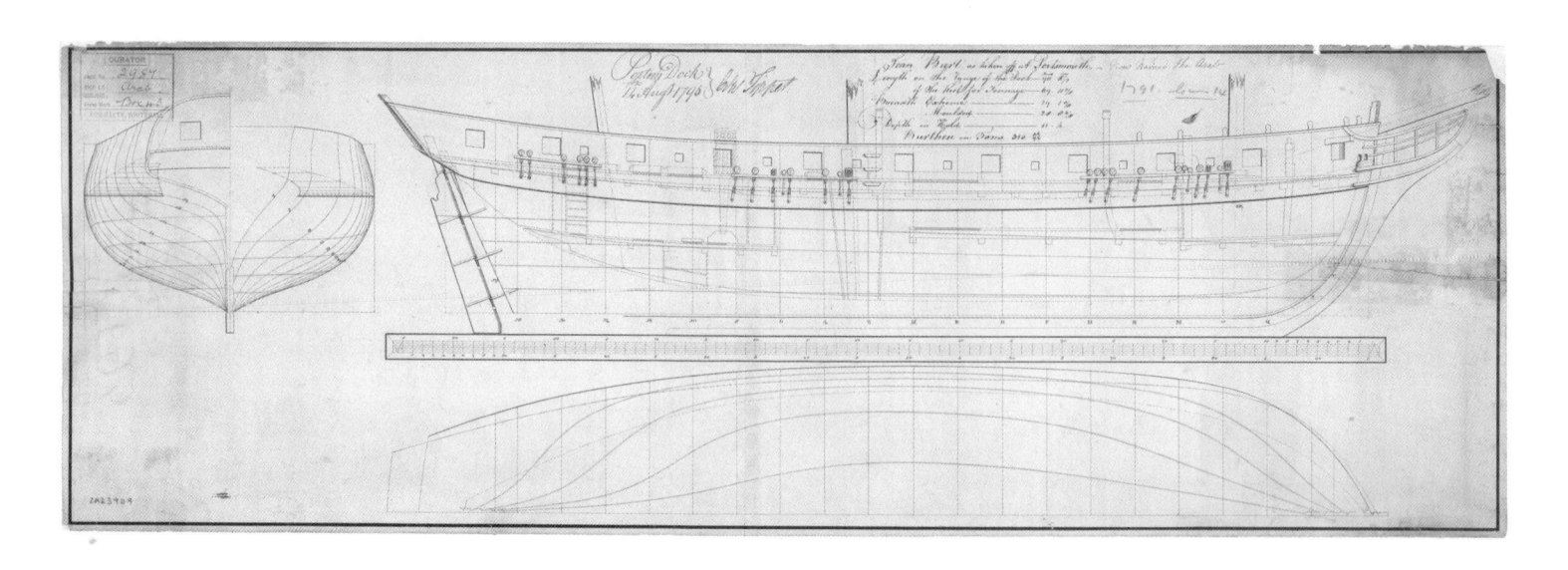

K: 2.1793. L: 5.1793. C: 6.1793. Comm: 3.1794.

Purchased 3.1794. Renamed *Tactique* 5.1795. Rearmed 1806 with 18 x 24pdr carronades and 2 x 6pdrs. Condemned at Toulon and ordered sold 16.6.1814, BU 1815.

Admiralty draught of *Arab* (ex *Jean Bart*) as taken off at Portsmouth, dated 14 August 1795. In hull form and layout this design, originally for a privateer, resembled an enlarged brig, with tiller steering on deck and limited facilities below deck. (© National Maritime Museum J4172)

NAÏADE Class Designed by Pierre-Augustin Lamothe. They were originally intended to carry an armament of 6 x 24pdrs. Two corvettes ordered on 15 April 1793 to be built at La Rochelle but neither named nor built might have been of this class; one was to carry 6 x 24pdrs and the other 12 x 12pdrs.

Dimensions & tons: 97ft 9in x 25ft 7in x 12ft 10in (31.75 x 8.31 x 4.17m), 270/461 tons. Draught 11ft/12ft (3.57/3.90m). Men: 187.

Guns: *Naïade*: 12 x 12pdrs, 4 x 6pdrs. *Festin*: 12 x 18pdrs. *Diligente*: 12 x 18pdrs, 6 x 36pdr obusiers

Naïade (*Nayade*) Brest Dyd

K: 5.1793. Named: 31.8.1793. L: 24.10.1793. C: 12.1793.

Corvette-canonnière or brig. As in other ships at this time, her armament changed frequently, becoming 16 x 8pdrs in 1798, 16 x 12pdrs in 1800, and 18 x 12pdrs in 1804. Taken 16.10.1805 in the Antilles by HMS *Jason* (32) and became HMS *Melville*. Sold 11.1808.

Fraternité Brest Dyd.

K: 5.1793. Named: 31.8.1793. L: 18.11.1793. Comm: 14.11.1793. C: 2.1794.

Renamed *Festin* 5.1795. Brig or corvette. Barracks hulk at Brest 7.1804. Recomm. 6.1806 to replace *Levrette* (see cutters) as training and station ship at Brest and listed as a corvette-brig or flûte with 8 x 6pdrs. Was stationnaire at Brest in 1808 and listed as brig with 14 x 12pdrs. Became an annex to the naval school ship *Tourville* (74) 1.1812 and was given a third mast for training duties. Struck following a light grounding on 13.6.1813 in Brest harbour.

Diligente Brest Dyd

K: 6.1793. L: 17.1.1794. C: 2.1794.

Sister to *Naïade*, originally a brig and later a corvette. Armament reduced to 12 x 18pdrs in 1795 and 12 x 12pdrs in 1797. Captured 6.1800 in the Antilles by HMS *Crescent* and placed in service in the Royal Navy as a 14-gun transport, HMS *Diligente*. Sold 8.1814.

ASSEMBLÉE NATIONALE. Originally built as a packet (*Paquebot No.2*) in 1787-88 to a design by Pierre-Alexandre-Laurent Forfait, this corvette had been employed as a slaver from May 1790 (when she was renamed) until March 1792. She was repurchased for the navy as a corvette in May 1793 and employed as a convoy escort between Cancale and Brest.

Dimensions & tons: 92ft 0in x 27ft 6in x 14ft 6in (29.89 x 8.93 x 4.71m). 362/625 tons. Draught 12ft 2in/13ft 2in (3.95/4.28m). Men: 160-192.

Guns: 14 x 8pdrs (but may have carried up to 22 x 8pdrs), + 6 swivels.

Assemblée Nationale Benjamin Dubois, Saint-Malo (Montmarin)

K: 1787. L: 1788. C: 1788.

Wrecked at Tréguier 2.9.1795 while under chase by HMS *Diamond*.

UNITÉ Class. 24 guns. Designed by Pierre-Alexandre-Laurent Forfait. The third vessel of this class was ordered as *Fidèle* and was renamed *Tourterelle* in February 1794.

Dimensions & tons: 117ft 9in, 106ft 0in x 29ft 2in x 14ft 4in (38.2 x 9.5 x 4.2 m.). 350/657 tons. Draught 11ft/13ft (3.57/4.22m). Men: 172/220.

Guns: UD 22 x 8pdrs; SD 2 x 12pdrs, 6 x 36pdr obusiers.

Unité Jean Fouache, Le Havre.

K: 8.1793. L: 16.1.1794. C: 4.1794.

Taken by HMS *Inconstant* off Bône 20.4.1796, becoming HMS *Surprise*. Sold at Deptford 2.1802.

Républicaine Le Havre.

K: 9.1793. L: 4.2.1794. C: 27.4.1794.

Taken by HMS *Tamar* off Dutch Guiana 25.8.1799, but not added to RN.

Tourterelle Honfleur

K: 9.1793. L: 18.3.1794. C: 5.1794.

Taken by HMS *Lively* off Cape Lizard 13.3.1795, becoming HMS *Tourterelle*. Burnt 1816.

Cornélie Jean-Louis Pestel, Honfleur.

K: 10.1793. L: 1.5.1794. C: 5.1794.

Renamed *Calliope* 5.1795. Destroyed in action 17.7.1797.

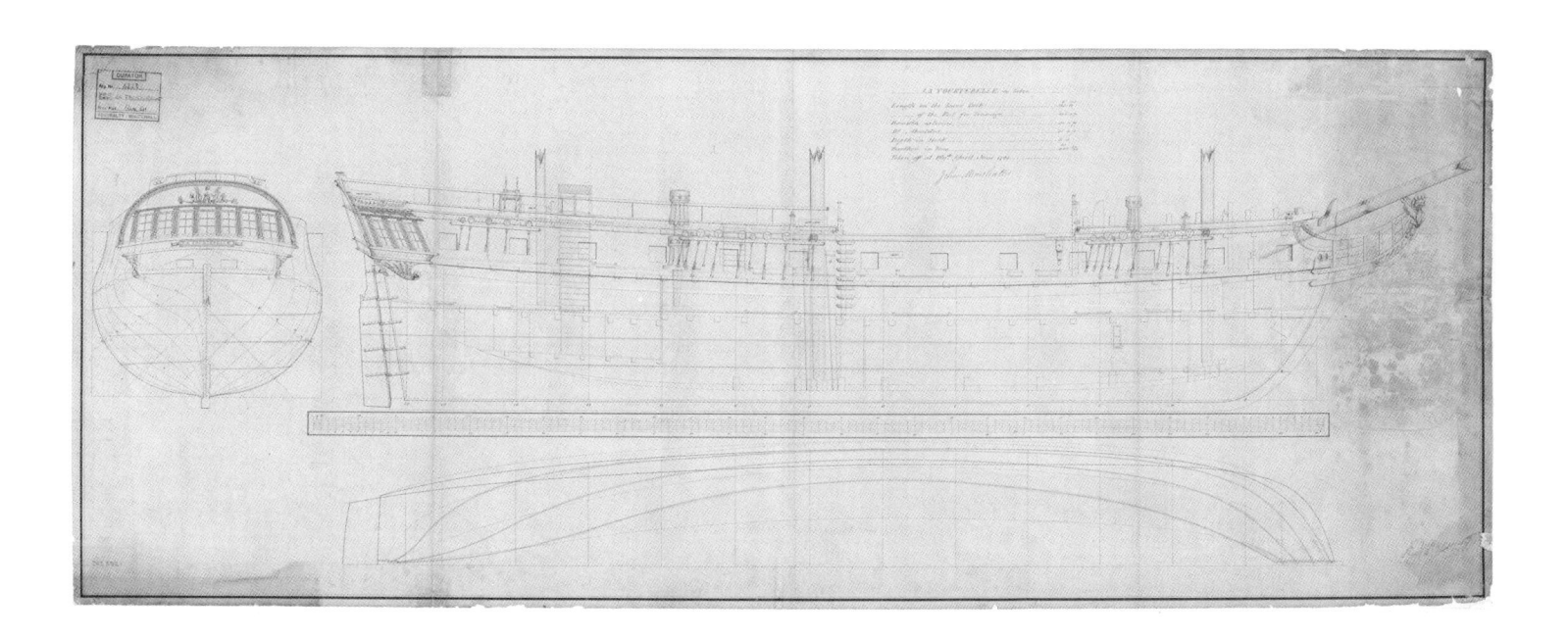

***BRÛLE GUEULE* Class**. Flush-decked corvettes of 20 x 6pdr guns. Designed by Charles-Henri Tellier. *Brûle Gueule* has also been attributed to Jean-Louis Pestel.

Dimensions & tons: 114ft 0in, 98ft 0in x 28ft 8in x 14ft 6in (37.03, 31.83 x 9.32 x 4.71m). 450/628 tons. Draught 12/13ft (3.90/4.22m). Men: 172.

Guns: (*Brûle Gueule*) 22 x 6pdrs, (*Constance*) 22 x 8pdrs (9pdrs); 24 x 8pdrs (9pdrs) when taken.

Brûle Gueule André-François and Joseph-Augustin Normand, Honfleur

K: 8.1793. L: 17.3.1794. C: 5.1794.

Wrecked 7.1.1800 in the Raz de Sein near Brest.

Constance Jean Fouache, Le Havre

K: 8.1793. L: 1.5.1794. C: 5.1794.

Captured with the frigate *Résistance* by HMS *San Fiorenzo* and HMS *Nymphe* 9.3.1797 at the mouth of the Iroise River, becoming HMS *Constance*. Grounded at Mont Saint Michel and recaptured 12.10.1806. When recaptured had 22 x 32pdr carronades in the battery, 2 x 16pdrs (British 18pdrs, carronades?) and 2 x 6pdrs on the forecastle and 1 x 16pdr (18pdr) carronade on the quarterdeck. Grounded at Solidor 12.1806, taken to Saint-Malo but found to be beyond repair and condemned 2.1807.

Admiralty draught of *Tourterelle* dated June 1795 and marked 'as taken'. Although rated as corvettes by the French, these quarterdecked ships were similar in size and layout to the old British 28-gun frigates, and captured examples were rated as such. (© National Maritime Museum J6362)

JACOBINE. Corvette of 22 x 12pdr guns. A one-off design by Pierre Degay. She was ordered as *Bonheur* but was renamed in November 1793.

Dimensions & tons: 122ft 0in x 30ft 9in (39.63 x 9.99m). Men: 223.
Guns: 22 x 12pdrs.

Jacobine Louis & Antoine Crucy and Jean Baudet, Basse-Indre

K: 8.1793. L: 30.3.1794. C: 6.1794.

Intended to be renamed *Inconstante* in 1794, but instead captured in the West Indies by HMS *Ganges* and HMS *Montagu* 30.10.1794, becoming HMS *Matilda*. Hulked 1799, BU at Woolwich 8.1810.

***SOCIÉTÉ POPULAIRE* class**. Designed by Jacques-Noël Sané. The

Admiralty draught of *Constance*, as taken off at Plymouth, dated 8 November 1799. The design was essentially flush-decked but there was a short deck over the cabin and steerage aft and a topgallant forecastle platform; the latter aided sail-handling but also served to prevent big seas breaking over the bows from washing down the length of the exposed upper deck. (© National Maritime Museum J7144)

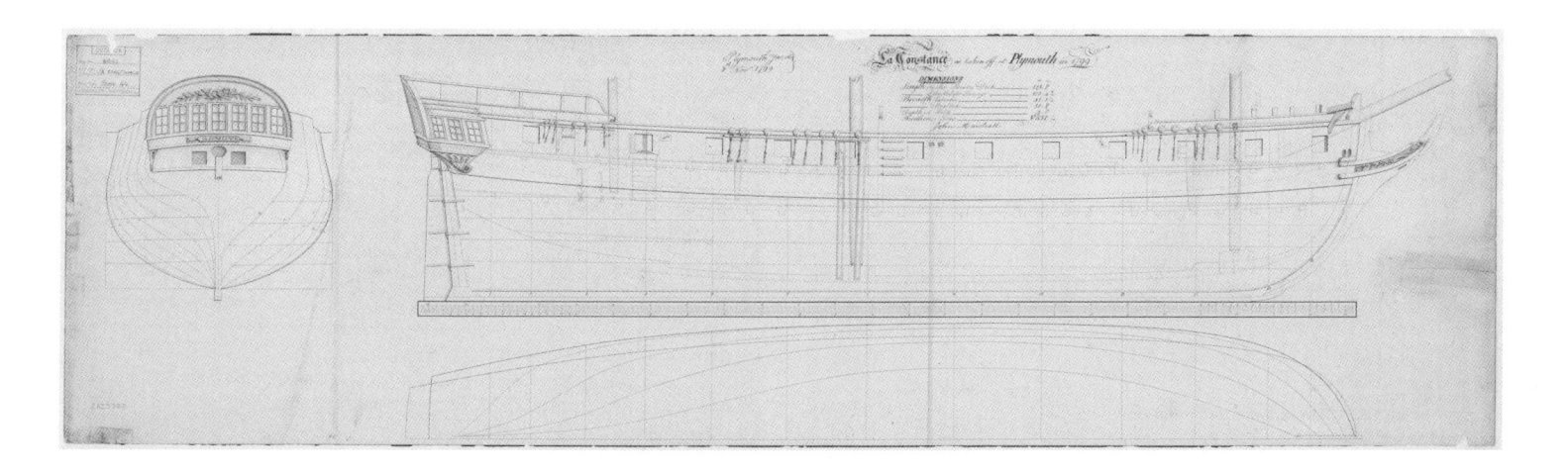

third ship (which may have been a variant from this design) was initially named *Doucereuse* on 24 March 1795, but was renamed *Décius* around the time of launch.

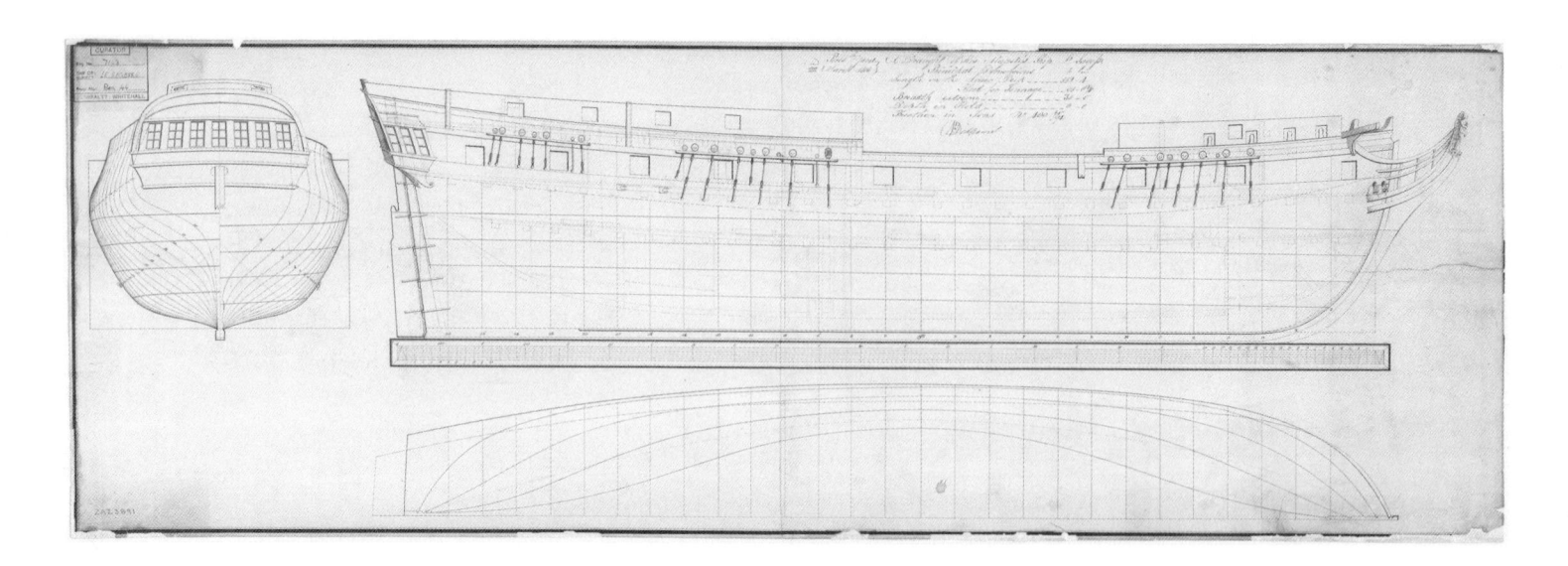

Dimensions & tons: 108ft 0in x 27ft 6in x 12ft 3in (35.08m x 8.93m x 3.98m). 300/580 tons. Draught 11ft 10in/12ft 11 in (3.84/4.20m). Men: 220

Guns: 16 x 8pdrs. *Société Populaire* (1801) 20 x 12pdrs. *Bergère* (1799) 16 x 12pdrs. *Décius* 18 x 6pdrs + 2 x 8pdrs; also 6 x 18pdr (British) carronades; when taken carried 24 x 6pdrs, 2 x 12pdr carronades.

Société Populaire Le Havre (or Brest Dyd.?)
K: 11.1793. L: 14.4.1794. C: 5.1794.
Renamed *Société* 5.1795. In 1.1807 she became a gunnery and navigation training ship replacing *Thomas Bristol*, which in turn replaced the cutter *Hoop* as a life-saving station at Port Louis near Lorient. In 4-6.1807 she was refitted as headquarters hulk at Lorient. Replaced by *Géographe* and decomm. 31.10.1811.

Bergère Brest Dyd
K: 12.1793. L: 7.1794. C: 9.1794.
Captured 17.4.1806 in the Mediterranean off the mouth of the Tiber River by HMS *Sirius* (44) and became HMS *Bergere*. BU at Blackwall 7.8.1811.

Décius Brest Dyd.
K: 8.1794. L: 8.10.1795. C: 12.1795.
Captured between 25.11.1796 and 3.12.1796 by HMS *Lapwing* in the Antilles, burned when pursued by two French frigates.

SAGESSE. Corvette of 20 x 8pdr guns. A one-off design of 1793 by Raymond-Antoine Haran. She was probably a forerunner to his *Bonne Citoyenne* design which was slightly enlarged from this vessel.

Dimensions & tons: 108ft 0in x 27ft 10in x 14ft 3in (35.08 x 9.04 x 4.63m) 280/580 tons. Draught 11ft 7in/13ft 4in (3.76/4.33m). Men: 180.

Guns: 20 x 8pdrs, 6 x 4pdrs; had 20 x 8pdrs, 8 x 4pdrs when taken.

Sagesse Bayonne
K: 8.1793. L: 15.5.1794. C: 7.1794. Comm: 11.1794.
Captured 8.9.1803 by HMS *Theseus* (74) at Port Dauphin, San Domingo, becoming HMS *Sagesse*. Hulked as prison hospital at Portsmouth 1805. Sold 7.6.1821.

***BONNE CITOYENNE* Class.** Corvettes of 20 x 8pdr guns. Designed by Raymond-Antoine Haran.

Admiralty draught of *Sagesse* as taken off at Portsmouth, dated 22 March 1805. Like many other draughts of captured minor warships, this seems to have been a record made shortly before the subject was broken up or relegated to subsidiary service, in the case of this ship to a prison hospital hulk. The forecastle and quarterdeck barricades are almost certainly British additions. (© National Maritime Museum J7087)

Dimensions & tons: 113ft 4in, 104ft 0in x 28ft 6in x 14ft 4in (36.82, 33.78 x 9.26 x 4.66m). 300/570 tons. Draught 11ft 1in/12ft 2in (3.60/3.95m). Men: 148-180.

Guns: 20 x 8pdrs.

Bonne Citoyenne Bayonne.
K: 7.1793. L: 9.7.1794. C: 5.1795.
Taken by HMS *Phaeton* 10.3.1796, becoming HMS *Bonne Citoyenne*. Sold 3.2.1819.

Perçante Bayonne.
K: 9.1793. L: 6.1795. C: 7.1795.
Captured on or before 29.2.1796 by HMS *Intrepid* off Puerto Plata, San Domingo, becoming HMS *Jamaica*. Sold 11.8.1814.

Vaillante Bayonne.
K: 7.1794. L: 1796. C: 8.1796.
Renamed *Danaë* 8.1798. Captured by HMS *Indefatigable* off Ile de Ré 7.8.1798, becoming HMS *Danae*. Restored to France at Brest after British crew mutinied 17.3.1800. Sold 1801.

Gaîté (Gaieté) Bayonne.
K: 10.1793. L: 1796. C: 2.1797.
Captured by HMS *Arethusa* off Barbuda 20.8.1797, becoming HMS *Gayette*. Sold 21.7.1808.

BERCEAU. Designed by Jacques-Noël Sané.
Dimensions & tons: 113ft 0in x 28ft 0in x 14ft 2in (33.45 x 9.10 x 4.60m). 350/650 tons. Draught 12ft 2in/12ft 7in (3.95/4.09m). Men: 180.

Guns: 22 x 8pdrs. 2 x 12pdr obusiers added 1797 and 6 more added 1800.

Berceau Lorient Dyd.
Ord: 16.2.1793. Named: 29.11.1793. K: 12.1793. L: 12.7.1794. C: 7.1794.
Captured 12.10.1800 north of Cayenne by USS *Boston* (38), returned 22.6.1801 at Boston and recommissioned. Served with the Linois division in the Indian Ocean in 1803-4. Returned in bad condition to Vigo 8/9.1804 and on 28.9.1804 the Emperor

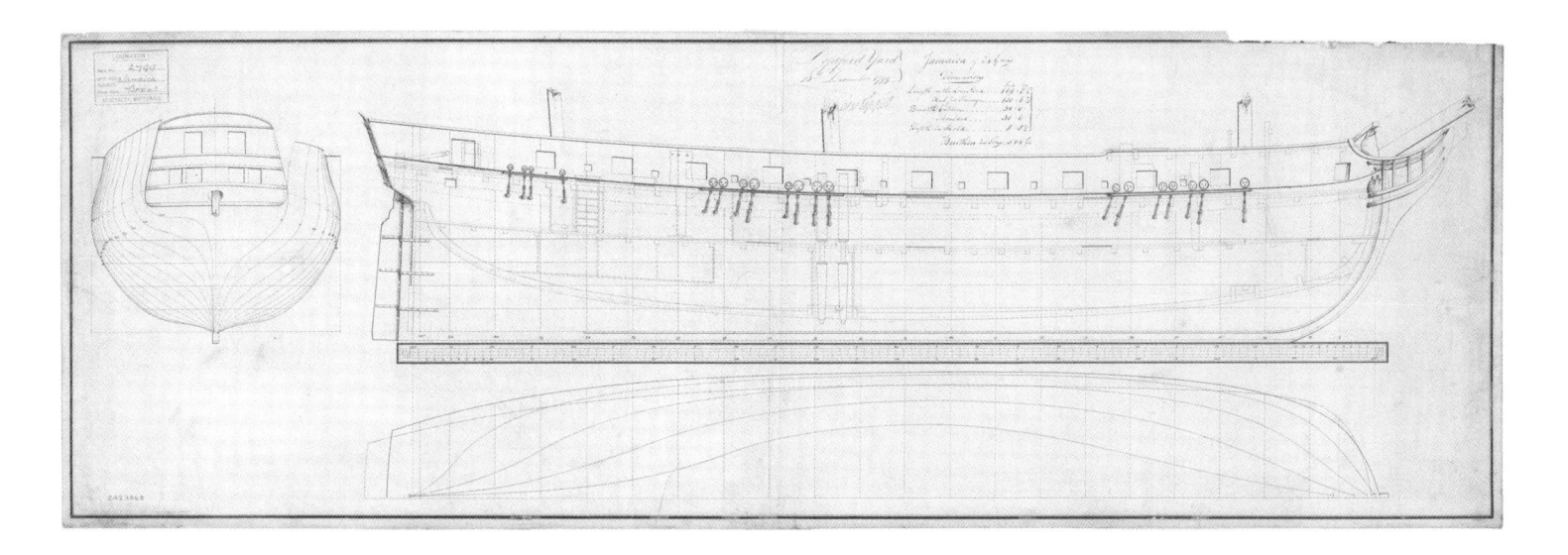

Admiralty draught of *Jamaica* (ex *Perçante*) as taken off at Deptford, dated 13 December 1799. The flush-decked layout was still rare in the Royal Navy for anything larger than a brig, and this class – all four of which were captured – made a big impression. Later, during the War of 1812, this class became the model for a new type designed to counter the big ship-sloops of the US Navy. (© National Maritime Museum J6557)

ordered her sold there. Decomm. 4.11.1804 and sold.

SANS CULOTIDE. Designed by Pierre Degay, and probably similar to *Jacobine* above (may have been to same plans).
  Dimensions & tons: probably the same as *Jacobine* above. Men: 160.
  Guns: 22 x 6pdrs (reduced from *Jacobine* ordnance).
Sans Culotide Louis & Antoine Crucy and Jean Baudet, Basse-Indre
  Ord: 31.1.1793. Named: 11.1793 (*Heureuse*). K: 12.1793. L: 8.1794. C: 11.1794.
  Originally named *Heureuse*, renamed *Sans Culotide* 3.1794. Corvette having 'novel lines'. Renamed *Soucieuse* 30.5.1795. The design was apparently unsuccessful and she was condemned in 1797 and converted to a transport. Fitted 4.1804 to store powder at Brest. Decomm. 20.7.1807 and hulked. BU in drydock at Brest 8.1816.

CIGOGNE. Designed by Pierre Degay and built at the Crucy-Baudet yard at Basse-Indre, which the government took over on 19 August 1794 and leased back to the Crucys. The ship was considerably smaller than Degay's *Jacobine* and *Sans Culotide*, was described as having 'unusual hull lines marked by a considerable forward extension of the stem' and was officially assessed as a 'sort of corvette of an uncommon form'. The original designed armament was 6 x 24pdrs and 6 x 36pdr obusiers.
  Dimensions & tons: 102ft 6in, 75ft 0in x 25ft 6in x 10ft 6in (33.29, 24.36 x 8.28 x 3.41m). 250/450 tons. Draught 12ft/12ft 9in (3.90/4.14m). Men: 168.
  Guns: 14 x 18pdrs, then (1799) 18 x 12pdrs (rated for 20 guns), then (1801) 20 x 8pdrs.
Cigogne Louis & Antoine Crucy and Jean Baudet, Basse-Indre
  Ord: 15.4.1793. K: 8.1793. L: 9.12.1794. C: 5.1795.
  Condemned 8.2.1803 at Fayal in the Azores because of an unrepairable leak.

JOIE class. *Corvette-canonnières*. Probably designed by Raymond-Antoine Haran. The measurements of *Tapageuse* differed slightly: 96ft 0in x 26ft 6in x 12ft 9in (31.18 x 8.61 x 4.14m); 190/450 tons; draught 11ft/12ft 2in (3.57/3.95m).
  Dimensions & tons: 98ft 0in x 25ft 6in x 10ft 3in (31.85 x 8.28 x 3.33m). 190/400 tons. Men: 75.
  Guns: *Joie* and *Tapageuse*: 12 x 12pdrs, *Réjouie*: 6 x 24pdrs; (1797) 8 x 18pdrs, 4 x 8pdrs; (1805) 8 x 8pdrs. *Tapageuse* (1801) 14 x 12pdrs.
Joie Bayonne
  Ord: 15.4.1793. K: 1793. L: 1.1795. C: 5.1795.
  Hauled out at Rochefort 11.1801 and converted to a 190-ton (cubic metre) gabarre, re-launched 3.8.1802, and comm. 23.9.1802. Her armament as a gabarre was 8 x 12pdrs. She was attacked on 12.7.1804 by HMS *Aigle* (36) while en route from Bayonne to the Gironde, run aground off Cordouan at the mouth of the Gironde, and burned on 24.7.1804 by her attackers.
Réjouie Bayonne
  Ord: 15.4.1793. K: 1793. L: 1795. C: 4.1795?.
  Converted to a 150/190-ton gabarre at Rochefort 4.1804 to 10.1805. Captured by the British and Spanish 10.6.1809 at the surrender of Santander, fate unknown.
Tapageuse Bayonne
  K: 7.1794. L: 19.3.1795. Comm: 21.5.1795. C: 7.1795.
  Taken 6.4.1806 at Verdun by boarding parties from the boats of HMS *Pallas* (32) while her commanding officer was ashore.

CORVETTES PURCHASED ON THE STOCKS (1793-1794). With the intensification of war, in 1793-94 France sought to purchase additional vessels of corvette size to employ as seagoing convoy escorts. In March 1793 the Ministry of Marine purchased the new ship-rigged privateer corvette *Aimable Céleste*, armed with 6pdr and 4pdrs guns while she was fitting out afloat and took over the contracts for construction of four newbuilding vessels designed for 8pdr batteries which had been ordered as privateers, and commissioned them as naval vessels.
Céleste Joseph-Augustin Normand, Honfleur (ex *Aimable Céleste*)
  K: 11.1791. L: 20.10.1792. C: 5.1793.
  Dimensions & tons: dimensions unknown. 150 tons. Men: 84-104.
  Guns: UD 2 x 6pdrs, 12 x 4pdrs; SD 8 swivels
  Purchased 3.1793 when nearly complete. Re-rigged as a brig 6.1795 at Le Havre. Struck 10.1795, fate unknown.
Républicain Bordeaux
  K: 1793. L: 9.1793. C: 11.1793.
  Dimensions & tons: Unknown. Men: 141-149.
  Guns: 18 x 8pdrs (20 ports)
  Purchased on the stocks at Bordeaux in 1793. Captured and burned

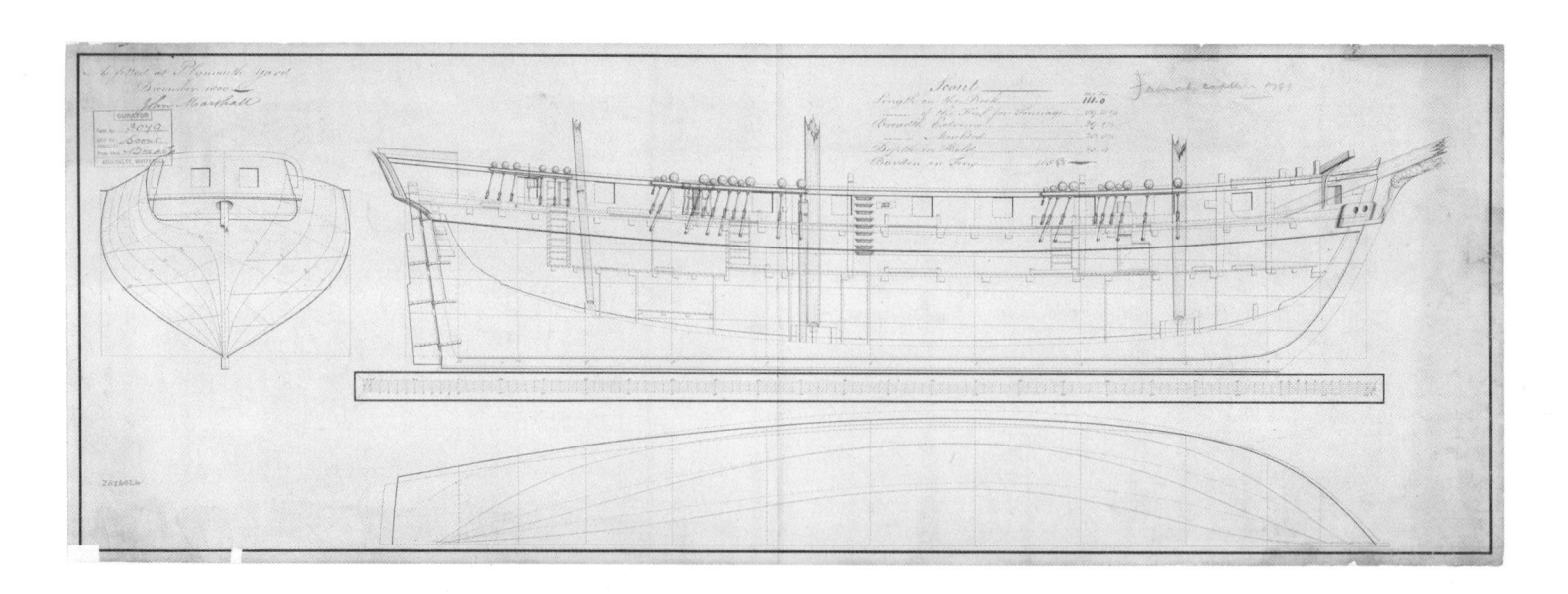

25.5.1794 by HMS *Niger* (32) off Brest.
Bayonnaise Bastiat, Dufouc & Fils, Bayonne.
K: 3.1793. L: 9.1793. C: 12.1793.
Dimensions & tons: dimensions unknown. 580 tons burthen. Men: 172-386.
Guns: UD 24 x 8pdrs; SD 8 x 4pdrs
Requisitioned before sailing in 1793 and purchased in 3.1794. Officially renamed *Brême* 5.1795 but continued to be called *Bayonnaise*. While returning from the Antilles fitted as a 6-gun flûte she was chased by HMS *Ardent* (64) and a British division on 28.11.1803, and her crew ran her aground near Cap Finistère and burned her to prevent capture.
Montagne Bordeaux.
K: 1793. L: 1.1794. C: 3.1794.
Dimensions & tons: unknown. Men: 148.
Guns: UD 20 x 8pdrs; SD 4 x 4pdrs.
Requisitioned on the ways 12.1793. Renamed *Chevrette* 5.1795. Boarded and captured at Camaret during the night of 21-22.7.1801 by boats from HMS *Beaulieu* (40), *Doris* (36), and *Uranie* (38), but not put into service with the British Navy.
Vengeance Bordeaux.
K: 1793. L: 1.1794. C: 4.1794.
Dimensions & tons: 101ft 11in x 28ft 0in x 12ft 6in (33.10 x 9.10 x 4.06m). 290/550 tons. Draught 11ft/14ft (3.57/4.55m). Men: 185.
Guns: UD 22 x 8pdrs; SD 4 x 4pdrs, 10 x 4pdrs in 7.1798.
Purchased on the ways in 1793. Renamed *Vénus* 12.1795. Captured by HMS *Indefatigable* (38) and *Fisgard* (38) off Portugal 22.10.1800, becoming HMS *Scout*. Wrecked off the Isle of Wight 25.3.1801.
Volage (built at Bordeaux, probably purchased or ordered there in 1794)
K: 6.1794. L: 7.1795. C: 9.1795.
Dimensions & tons: 115ft, 100ft x 29ft 6in x 14ft (37.36, 32.48 x 9.58 x 4.55m). 400/630 tons. Draught 11ft/12ft (3.57/3.90m). Men: 168-185.
Guns: 22 x 8pdrs (24 ports); (as privateer 12.1797) 2 x 18pdrs, 20 x 8pdrs.
Grounded 30.3.1796 in combat with a British division at Le Croisic, refloated and repaired at Nantes. Became privateer at Nantes 12.1797. Captured 23.1.1798 off the southwest coast of Ireland by HMS *Melampus* (36), became HMS *Volage* (22). BU 8.1804.

Admiralty draught of *Scout* (ex *Vénus*) as fitted at Plymouth, dated December 1800. In French service the ship had carried guns on the gaillards – 4 x 4pdrs, with 4 x 36pdr obusiers added in 1796, and later listed as '10 x 4pdrs and obusiers' – so the British had clearly cut down the upperworks. The extremely sharp lines of this corvette betray her origins as a privateer, although she had been purchased for the French Navy while building. (© National Maritime Museum J4349)

ETNA class. Corvettes of 16 x 18pdr guns. Designed by Pierre-Alexandre-Laurent Forfait and his adherent, Charles-Henri Tellier. Like most of the corvettes ordered in 1792-94, these ships underwent numerous changes between ordering and coming into service, and this list below reflects the best estimate as to which ships were completed to this design (although there were undoubtedly differences between individual ships). The vessel begun at Le Havre as *Courageuse* was renamed *Cérès* in May 1795. Another corvette, probably to the same or a similar Forfait design, with 12 or 14 x 18pdrs, was ordered built at St.Valéry-sur-Somme on 16 April 1794, but was never built or named. A brig-rigged vessel, *Colombe*, was also built at Cherbourg to plans by Forfait modified by Pierre Ozanne; she was somewhat smaller than the *Etna* class.
Dimensions & tons: 110ft 8in, 100ft 0in x 30ft 0in x 14ft 10in. (35.95, 32.48 x 9.74 x 4.82m). 350 or 420/642-719 tons. Draught 14ft 5in/15ft 11in (4.68/5.17m). Men: 122-198
Guns: UD 16 x 18pdrs (probably designed for 16 x 18pdrs and 1 x 12in mortar). *Cérès* (1798) 18 x 18pdrs. *Torche* (1798) 16 x 12pdrs, 2 x 18pdrs. *Mignonne* (1803) 10 x 18pdrs.
Etna André-François and Joseph-Augustin Normand, Honfleur
K: 6.1794. L: 4.1795. C: 5.1795.
Taken 13.11.1796 off Barfleur by HMS *Melampus* and *Childers*, becoming HMS *Cormorant*. Wrecked 20.5.1800 on the Egyptian coast.
Torche Courtois, Honfleur
K: 6.1794. L: 4.1795. C: 5.1795.
Captured 16.8.1805 north of Cape Ortegal by HMS *Goliath* and *Camilla*, becoming HMS *Torch*. BU 6.1811.
Cérès Jean Fouache, Le Havre
K: 5.1794. L: 5.1795. C: 7.1795.
May have been renamed *Enfant de la Patrie* in 1797. Wrecked 17.2.1798 on the Norwegian coast.
Vésuve Denise, Honfleur

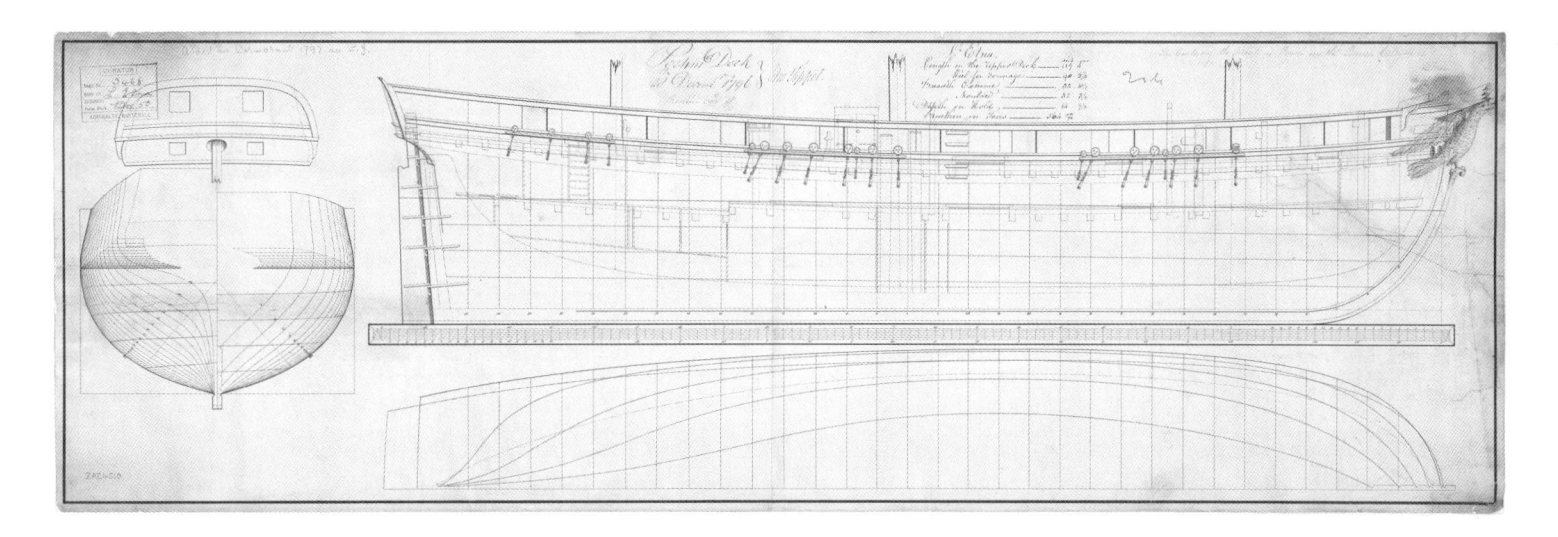

Admiralty draught of *Etna* (later renamed *Cormorant*), dated Portsmouth 28 December 1796. The design of the stem – not to mention the over-large figurehead, which presumably inspired her renaming – is very unusual. (© National Maritime Museum J4134)

K: 6.1794. L:7.8.1795. C: 10.1795.
Fitted as 346-ton or 400-ton flûte with 20 x 12pdrs at Le Havre 11.1802 to 6.1803, reclassified as a 20-gun corvette when refitted at Le Havre in 2.1807. Use as headquarters hulk at Rochefort in place of *Serpente* approved 31.10.1815. BU at Rochefort 8-9.1830.

Étonnante Fouache & Reine, Le Havre
Ord: 27.4.1794. K: 6.1794. L: 27.8.1795. C: 11.1796.
Listed at 500 tons but probably as *Etna*. Designed for 14 x 24pdrs, had 16 x 18pdrs in 1797-1803. Grounded after launching and salvaged with much difficulty. Condemned 4.7.1804 and 11.10.1804 at Brest, converted to a guard station (*corps de garde*). Last mentioned 1806.

Mignonne Cherbourg Dyd. (Constructeurs: Pierre Ozanne and from 3.1795 Jean-François Lafosse)
K: 6.10.1794. L: 15.10.1795. C: 4.1797.
Captured 28.6.1803 off Santo Domingo by HMS *Goliath* (74), became HMS *Mignonne*. Damaged in grounding 12.1804 and condemned.

MALICIEUSE. Designed by Pierre-Alexandre-Laurent Forfait, a lengthened version of his *Etna* class, and probably the prototype for the *Serpente* class, for which the design was modified by Forfait's pupil, Charles-Henri Tellier.
Dimensions & tons: 124ft x 30ft 0in x 14ft 10in (40.28 x 9.74 x 4.82m). 351/750 tons. Draught 12ft 10in/14ft 2in (4.17/4.60m). Men: 188.
Guns: UD 16 x 12pdrs, 2 x 18pdrs; (1801) 18 x 18pdrs; (1804 as gabarre) 18 x 6pdrs.

Malicieuse Jean Fouache, Le Havre
K: 6.1794. L: 4.1795. C: 7.1795.
Converted to a 260-ton gabarre at Rochefort 11.1803 to 12.1804 and re-rigged as a brig. Ran herself ashore 5.4.1806 at La Teste with *Garonne* to avoid capture by HMS *Pallas* (32). Similar if not identical to the *Serpente* class.

SERPENTE Class. Corvettes of 20 x 18pdr guns, designed by Charles-Henri Tellier. Three ships were ordered to this design at Honfleur in 1794; the first was contracted as the *Uranie* in August with Louis Deros, but he had barely begun preparing to build her when he died; the task passed to another constructor at Honfleur, Nicolas Loquet, but with the French treasury in distress he refused to launch her until he was paid. The ship was renamed from *Uranie* to *Galatée* (*Galathée*) in 1797 to avoid confusion with a frigate, but was renamed *Géographe* fifteen days after launching, for use in a scientific expedition. A fourth ship was ordered at Le Havre in 1795.
Dimensions & tons: 124ft 0in x 30ft 0in x 14ft 10in (40.28 x 9.74½ x 4.82m). 350/727 tons. Draught 11ft/11ft 10in (3.57/3.84m). Men: 188.
Guns: UD 20 x 18pdrs.

Galatée Louis Deros, then Nicolas Loquet, Honfleur
K: 9.1794. L: 8.6.1800. C: 9.1800.
Renamed *Géographe* 23.6.1800. Comm. 28.9.1800 with 24 x 12pdrs and departed Le Havre 19.10.1800 for an expedition under Capt. Nicolas Baudin with consort *Naturaliste* to map the coast of Australia. Returned 23.3.1804. On 7.5.1804 while she was under repair at Lorient the Minister of Marine approved the substitution of 24 x 8pdrs for her 12pdrs, reduced to 20 x 8pdrs in 1806 and 14 x 8pdrs in 1811. Used to store powder in the Caudran district at Lorient from 1807 and as a barracks ship there from 1808. Replaced *Société* as headquarters hulk at Lorient 10.1811. Decomm. 12.1811 and continued in use as a service craft. Reported unserviceable and struck 6.4.1819.

Serpente Jean-Louis Pestel, Honfleur
K: 10.1794. L: 1.9.1795. C: 1.1796.
Armament reduced to 18 x 12pdrs by 1.1802. Refitted at Rochefort later in 1802. Converted 6.1806 to floating battery at Verdon, replaced *Lionne* 7.9.1807 as headquarters hulk at Rochefort, condemned to be BU 31.10.1815 and replaced at Rochefort by *Vésuve* 11.1815. Her builder was the elder brother of the naval constructor François-Timothée Pestel.

Bacchante Pierre, Jacques & Nicolas Fortier, Honfleur
K: 10.1794. L: 29.12.1795. C: 1796.
Used as privateer 1797-1798. Armament reduced to 18 x 12pdrs by 4.1803. Captured off the Azores 25.6.1803 by HMS *Endymion* (40), became HMS *Bacchante*. Sold 2.7.1809.

Confiante Fouache & Reine, Le Havre.
K: 9.1795. L: 10.5.1797. C: 2.1798. Comm: 29.4.1798.
Attacked 29.5.1798 by HMS *Hydra* (38), run aground in the mouth of the Dives River and burned by the British. Designed for 16 x 18pdrs, carried 20 to 24 x 12pdrs and 6pdrs when lost.

PROJECTED MEDITERRANEAN CORVETTES. In January 1794 the construction of fourteen corvettes was planned at a range of private shipyards on the Mediterranean coast, at Sète, Marseille, La Seyne and La Ciotat. Of varying designs, these would have carried between 12 and 20 guns, some with 12pdrs and some with 8pdrs, but none were begun or even named. Another four corvettes, armed with 18 or 20 x 18pdrs, were proposed for building at Toulon, but these likewise never progressed. All of these corvettes were probably associated with a large January 1794 building program of ships of the line and frigates at Toulon, only part of which was realised.

CORVETTES PURCHASED ON THE STOCKS (1795-1798)
Insolente (origin uncertain, possibly built at Bordeaux and probably purchased there in 1795 or 1796)
    K: 9.1795. L: 6.1796. C: 9.1796
    Dimensions & tons: Unknown. Men: 120 men
    Guns: 14 to 18 x 6pdrs
    Name sometimes rendered *Insolent* and ship called a brig, but was listed as a corvette. Captured and burned by HMS *Impetuous* 5.6.1800 in a raid on Port Navalo near Quiberon.
Sans Pareille (privateer corvette, probably Spanish, built at La Ciotat and purchased there in 1797 or 1798).
    K: 1797. L: 1798. C: 12.1799.
    Dimensions & tons: 95ft 0in x 26ft 10in (30.86 x 8.72m). 250/480 tons. Men: 148.
    Guns: 18 x 8pdrs, 2 x 36pdr obusiers.
    Captured 20.1.1801 near Sardinia by HMS *Mercury* (28) while carrying despatches from Toulon to Egypt. Did not put up a serious fight, most of her crew being seasick. Became HMS *Delight* (18), sold 4.1805.

A corvette named *Érigone* armed with 20 x 8pdrs and possibly brig-rigged was ordered in 1797 at Dunkirk, probably to be built there by the naval constructor Louis Jean Baptiste Bretocq, but she had not been begun as of 4.1798 and was not built.

MUTINE Class. Corvettes of 16 x 8pdrs, designed by Charles-Henri Tellier. Ordered as *Nouvelle* and *Aurore* in 1797, but the first was renamed *Mutine* at her launch in May 1799.
    Dimensions & tons: 95ft 0in, 90ft 0in x 26ft 6in x 13ft 3in (30.86m, 29.23m x 8.61m x 4.30m). 250/379-400 tons. Draught 10ft (3.25m) mean. Men: 156.
    Guns: 16 x 8pdrs.
Mutine Le Havre
    K: 10.1797. L: 17.5.1799. C: 8.1799.
    Wrecked on the coast of Cuba 17.8.1803 after combat with HMS *Racoon* (16).
Aurore Le Havre
    K: 11.1797. L: 16.7.1799. C: 8.1799.
    Captured 18.1.1801 near Île d'Oléron by HMS *Thames* (32), became HMS *Charwell* (sloop, 16). Sold 28.4.1813.

On 30 December 1798 Napoleon ordered the construction of a corvette at Suez, probably to plans by one of the two French naval constructors in Egypt, Jean-Louis Féraud or Étienne Maillot. If begun, she was not completed before the evacuation of Egypt by the French in April 1801.

ETNA. *Corvette-canonnière.* Designed by Antoine Geoffroy
    Dimensions & tons: dimensions unknown. 150 tons. Men: 87-113.
    Guns: 6 x 18pdrs.
Etna Cherbourg Dyd. (Constructeur, Aubert)
    K: 12.1799 or 4.1800. L: 9.1800. C: 6.1801.
    Hauled out at Le Havre 8.1815, rebuilt as a brig-rigged gabarre of 160 or 220 tons, and re-launched 29.6.1816. Condemned 12.1833.

DILIGENTE Class (prototype). Corvette of 20 x 6pdr guns. Designed by Pierre Ozanne. The prototype was built at Brest on a private plan by Ozanne that was adopted by the Minister of Marine on 5 December 1800, probably after the ship was begun. She proved to be a very fast ship on a reach (12 to 13 knots), but mediocre running before the wind. Beginning in 1808 several additional ships (listed in the next session) were ordered to the same design. *Diligente* was hauled out for a refit on 22 August 1820 and re-launched on 4 January 1821. On 9 January 1821 she was ordered armed with 18 x 18pdr carronades (probably 16 x 18pdr carronades and 2 x 12pdrs), and during 1821 she was reclassified as a corvette-aviso.
    Dimensions & tons: 104ft 0in, 92ft 0in x 26ft 0in x 14ft 0in (33.78, 29.88½ x 8.45 x 4.55m). 278/476 tons. Draught 11½ft/14⅓ft (3.76/4.66m). Men: 114/141.
    Guns: 14 x 6pdrs, 6 x 12pdr British carronades.
Diligente Brest Dyd. (Constructeur: Pierre Ozanne)
    K: 20.6.1800. L: 7.11.1801. Comm: 23.9.1801. C: 12.1801.
    Condemned and struck 11.10.1854, BU.

Ex BRITISH NAVAL PRIZES (1793-1801). Six assorted Sixth Rates and ship-sloops were captured from the British Navy during the French Revolutionary War, and were classed as corvettes by the French; four were retaken by the British during the War, and one was destroyed in action. They are listed below along with a captured French privateer that was then taken from the Royal Navy by the French Navy. Measurements are in French units.

PORCUPINE Class. British 24-gun Sixth Rate post ship, built to a 1776 design by John Williams, an enlarged version of the *Sphinx* class below. Ten ships were built to this design, of which the *Hyaena* was captured by the *Concorde* off Hispaniola on 27 May 1793, and renamed *Hyène*.
    Dimensions & tons: 120ft 0in, 107ft 6in x 30ft 0in x 18ft 0in (38.98, 34.92 x 9.75 x 5.85m). 400/800 tons. Draught 14ft 8in/15ft 8in (4.76/5.09m). Men: 168.
    Guns: UD 22 x 9pdrs (British guns); SD nil in French service.
Hyène John Fisher, Liverpool.
    K: 5.1777. L: 2.3.1778. C: 1.1779 at Portsmouth Dyd.
    Sold to become a privateer at Bayonne in 12.1796. Retaken by HMS *Indefatigable* off Teneriffe 25.10.1797; sold at Deptford 2.1802.

PYLADES Class. British 16-gun ship-sloop, built to a 1793 design by Sir John Henslow. Six ships were built to this design, of which the *Alert* was captured 14 May 1794 by *Unité* off the coast of Ireland while en route to Halifax.
    Dimensions & tons: 101ft 0in, 90ft 0in x 26ft 3in x 13ft 6in (32.81, 29.24 x 8.53 x 4.39m). 280/500 tons. Draught 12ft 4in/12ft 8in (4.01/4.11m). Men: 125-150.
    Guns: UD 16 x 6pdrs; SD 4 swivels.
Alerte John Randall, Rotherhithe.
    K: 4.1793. L: 8.10.1793. C: 22.1.1794 at Deptford Dyd.
    Driven ashore and destroyed in combat against HMS *Flora* and *Arethusa* of Warren's squadron off Audierne 23.8.1794.

SPHINX Class. British 20-gun Sixth Rate post ship, built to a 1773 design by John Williams. Ten ships were built to this design, of which

the *Daphne* was captured by *Tamise* and *Méduse* in the Channel on 23 December 1794.
> Dimensions & tons: 105ft 0in, 93ft 0in x 28ft 2in x 11ft 0in (34.11, 30.21 x 9.15 x 3.57m). 350/650 tons. Draught 13/14½ft (4.22/4.71m). Men: 188-230.
> Guns: UD 20 x 9pdrs (British guns); SD 4-8 x 4pdrs (in French service).

Daphné Woolwich Dyd.
> K: 8.1774. L: 21.3.1776. C: 25.5.1776.
> Retaken by HMS *Anson* in the Bay of Biscay 29.12.1797 after sailing from the Gironde for Guadeloupe; sold at Sheerness 5.1802.

ENTERPRISE Class. British 28-gun Sixth Rate frigate, built to a 1771 design by John Williams. Twenty-seven ships were built to this design, of which the *Nemesis* was captured by *Sensible* and *Sardine* off Smyrna on 9 December 1795.
> Dimensions & tons: 116ft 0in, 104ft 0in x 31ft 6in x 17ft 0in (37.68, 33.78 x 10.23 x 5.52m). 450/850 tons. Draught 14/15ft (4.55/4.87m). Men: unknown.
> Guns: UD 24 x 9pdrs (British guns); SD 4 x 3pdrs.

Némésis Jolly, Leathers & Barton, Liverpool (finished after launching by Smallshaw & Co, Liverpool).
> K: 11.1777. L: 23.1.1780. C: 22.6.1780 at Plymouth Dyd.
> Retaken by HMS *Egmont* near Tunis 9.3.1796; sold at Plymouth 9.6.1814.

ZEBRA Class. British 16-gun ship-sloop, built to a 1779 design by Edward Hunt. Three ships were built to this design, of which the *Bulldog* was converted to a bomb vessel in 1798 but was captured by the French garrison at Ancona on 27 February 1801 when she entered the port by mistake.
> Dimensions & tons: 98ft 0in x 23ft 6in x 11ft 6in (31.83 x 7.63 x 3.73m). 200/380 tons.
> Guns: 18 x 8pdrs & 6pdrs, 2 x 24pdr obusiers or mortars.

Bull-Dog Henry Ladd, Dover.
> K: 10.1781. L: 10.11.1782. C: 27.2.1783 at Deptford Dyd.
> Retaken 24-25.5.1801 at Ancona by boats from HMS *Mercury* but recaptured next morning by the French balancelle *Furet*. Again retaken by HMS *Champion* off Gallipoli in Apulia 16.9.1801 and became a powder hulk at Portsmouth. BU there 12.1829. The French also rendered the name as *Boule-Dogue* and *Chien-Dogue*.

HOUND Class. British 16-gun ship-sloop, built with four sisters to a design by John Henslow. All were ordered 17.1.1788 and four were named 23.10.1788, of which *Hound* was renamed from *Hornet* on 9.12.1788. *Hound* was captured on 14.7.1794 by the French frigates *Seine* and *Galathée* off the Scilly Isles while en route from the West Indies and became the French *Levrette*, also being referred to as *Levrette No.2* to distinguish her from a former cutter rebuilt as a corvette in 1794.
> Dimensions & tons: 94ft, 85ft x 25ft 4in x 14ft (30.53, 27.61 x 8.23 x 4.55m). 250/480tons. Draught 12ft 2in/13ft (3.95/4.22m). Men: 136
> Guns: UD 18 x 6pdrs, 2 obusiers.

Levrette Deptford Dyd.
> K: 9.1788. L: 31.1.1790. C: 1.7.1790 at Woolwich.
> Last mentioned 7.1795 while station ship at the Île de Bréhat on the northern coast of Brittany.

ESPION. Completed at Nantes in February 1793 as the 18-gun privateer *Robert*, this vessel was taken 13.6.1793 by HMS *Syren* (32) and became corvette HMS *Espion* (16), then retaken 22.7.1794 by *Tamise* and two other French frigates south of the Scilly Isles and became the French naval corvette *Espion*.
> Dimensions & tons: 82ft 0in x 25ft 6in (26.64 x 8.28m). 250/400 tons. Men: 135-146.
> Guns: UD 18 x 6pdrs

Espion Nantes
> Taken by HMS *Lively* (32) 3.3.1795 off Brest and became HMS *Spy* on 20.5.1795. Sold 7.9.1801.

Ex BRITISH MERCANTILE AND PRIVATEER PRIZES (1793-1801)

Elise (British privateer corvette *Ellis* built in Britain, taken 7.1793 by the frigate *Gracieuse*, then taken by the Spanish and retaken 11.1793 by the French, 400 tons, 150 men, carried 22 x 6pdrs in 1795). Renamed *Espérance* 2.1794. Captured 8.1.1795 off the Chesapeake by HMS *Argonaut* (64) and *Oiseau* (36) and became HMS *Esperance* (16). Sold 6.1798.

Camphroust (British merchant corvette taken in 1793, 92 men, carried 8 x 4pdrs). Was described as old in 1793. On sale list and struck 12.1795 at Brest.

Lord Gordon (British merchant or privateer corvette *Lord Gordon* built in Britain and taken in 1793, 136 men, carried 20 x 4pdrs). Renamed *Instituteur* 1794, reverted to *Lord Gordon* 5.1795. Last mentioned 4.1798 being fitted out at Brest.

Mercury of London (British three-masted merchant or privateer corvette *Mercury* from London built in Britain and captured 5.1793 by the privateer *Patriote de Brest* (see cutter *Levrette* of 1779), 400 tons, 125 men, carried 16 x 4pdrs). Renamed *Noviciat* 1794 and *Mercure de Londres* 1796. Handed over 2.1798 at Bordeaux for use as a privateer and named *Mercure*, captured 31.8.1798 by HMS *Phaeton* (38) in the Gulf of Gascony.

Réolaise (British merchant corvette built in England 1788 and purchased or seized by the French, requisitioned at Bordeaux 8.1793, 103 men, carried 18 x 4pdrs). Ran aground while in combat against the British 17.11.1800 at Port Navalo near Quiberon and burned by the enemy.

Thétis (captured British privateer corvette *Thetis*, probably requisitioned 8.1793, 50-100 men, carried 10 x 4pdrs). Renamed *Thalie* 5.1795, last mentioned 5.1795 while in service in the roadstead of Mindin, then struck.

Phénix (British merchant corvette built in England 1779, captured by French privateers and purchased by the state in 9.1793, 150 tons, 148 men, carried 20 x 6pdrs). Converted in 1797 into a 123-ton brig-rigged transport with 4 x 4pdrs and 40 men. Decomm. 15.10.1826 at Cherbourg and condemned.

Prompt (British merchant corvette built in Britain and taken 10.1793 by *Éole* (74), 95-120 men, carried 16 x 8pdrs, 6pdrs, and 4pdrs). Captured 5.1795 by the British, fate unknown.

Scorpion (British merchant or privateer corvette *Scorpion* captured 1.1794, 250 tons, 125 men, carried 14 to 16 x 6pdrs). Grounded at Noirmoutier 9.1795 and abandoned, finally refloated and became barracks hulk at Nantes. Listed as transport 5.1799. Struck end 1799 or 1800, receiving hulk at Nantes, still there 12.1803.

Vengeur (French privateer corvette *Marseillaise* acquired 1.1794 in the Antilles, previously the British merchant corvette *Avenger*, carried 16 guns). Captured 17.3.1794 at St. Pierre, Martinique by a British squadron and became HMS *Avenger* (16), sold 1802.

Décade (British merchant corvette built in Britain and taken c2.1794 and in French Navy service on 27.3.1794, 148 men, carried 20 x 6pdrs). On convoy duty between Cherbourg and the Gironde in 1794 and between Saint-Malo and Nantes in 1795. Probably struck 7.1795 at Nantes.

Défiante (British privateer corvette *Defiance* taken 5.1794, 125 men, carried 16 x 4pdrs). Was at Rochefort in 1795, later fate unknown.

Joseph (merchant or slave trade corvette built in Britain, taken into Brest ca. 5.1794 while on a voyage from Liverpool to Africa, and in service 30.6.1794 at Verdon, 160 tons, 115 men, carried in 1794 4 x 6pdrs and 1 obusier and in 1795 14 x 6pdrs, 4pdrs and 3pdrs). Became a 160-ton transport at Bordeaux in 3.1797 with three masts and 4 x 4pdrs, struck late 1797.

Expédition (British merchant corvette built in Britain, taken c9.1794, and in service 10.1794 at Brest, 125 men, carried 16 x 6pdrs). Captured 16.4.1795 by a British frigate off Belle-Isle.

Princesse Royale or ***Princess*** (British slaver and privateer, probably *Princess Royal*, built by Wells at Deptford 1786 and captured 8.1795 by *Expériment*).

Dimensions & tons: 84ft, 76ft x 26ft x 15ft 1in (27.28, 24.69 x 8.45 x 4.90m). 322/550 tons. Draught 13ft 4in/14ft 8in (4.33/4.77m). Men: 148.

Guns: 20 x 8pdrs

Grounded 2.1800 but refloated. Renamed *Utile* 24.12.1801 and listed as a gabarre. Began major refit 12.1802 but was 'very old' and was condemned 6.1803 although the refit continued. BU 9.1806.

Alerte (British merchant or privateer corvette *Alert*, captured 12.1798)

Dimensions & tons: 80ft, 69ft 6in x 20ft x 9ft 7in (26.00, 22.56 x 6.50 x 3.00m). 150-180/300 tons. Men: 110.

Guns: 12 x 4pdrs

Was a training corvette at Antwerp in 11.1799 and was stationed at Flushing in 1800. Probably was the ship listed as a 'transport and flûte' or 'gabarre transport' that was commissioned at Antwerp 22.3.1800, made a voyage to Senegal in 1802, and was decommissioned at Lorient 24.2.1803. Recaptured 6.6.1803 near Martinique on a voyage from Lorient.

Two coast defence ships (*garde-côtes*), *Basse-Ville* and *Dragomire*, armed with 6 x 24pdrs and probably seized in Italy, were commissioned in the Adriatic in 1798. They were last mentioned in 1799 at locations near the mouth of the Po River, *Basse-Ville* at Polisella and *Dragomire* between Santa Maria and Po di Goro.

A vessel of unknown nationality captured before May 1799 was named *Thérèse* and commissioned at Nantes as a coast defence ship. She carried 20 guns, although these may have been small. In August 1799 she became station ship at Fromentine. On the night of 1-2 July 1800 she was boarded, captured and burned by boats from HMS *Fisgard* (38) and *Defence* (74) near Noirmutier.

The former Austrian corvette *Aquila*, taken over by Napoleon's Italian Navy in December 1805, is listed in Chapter 5 with the Venetian 32-gun *Cerere* class of light frigates, of which she was initially a member. She was taken by the French on the ways at the Venice Arsenal in May 1797 and sabotaged by them there in September 1797, but the Austrians salvaged her and completed her as a 32-gun corvette.

Ex SPANISH PRIZES (1793-1794)

Alcudia (privateer built in Spain 1793 and captured 10.1793 by *Uranie*, commissioned under her Spanish name with 20 x 6pdrs and 136 men) Renamed *Barra* in June 1794; reduced to 18 x 6pdrs in 1795 for convoy duties. Sold 1797.

Las Casas (mercantile vessel or privateer built in Spain 1794 and captured 7.1794; commissioned 9.1794 with 18 x 6pdrs and 136-160 men, without change in name). Sold 5.1796 to become privateer.

Ex DUTCH PRIZE (1794)

Vigilance (Noorderkwartier Admiralty corvette *Waaksaamheid*, built in 1786 at Enchuizen and captured 23.5.1794).

Dimensions & tons: 110ft 0in x 29ft 8in (35.73 x 9.64m). 370/680 tons. Men: 168.

Guns: UD 22 x 8pdrs; SD 2 x 6pdrs.

Used for service off the Guinea coast then restored to the Dutch (Batavian) Navy 1795 under original name; taken by HMS *Sirius* off Texel 24.10.1798, becoming HMS *Waaksaamheidt*; sold at Deptford 9.1802.

There was also another prize of unknown nationality, a former mercantile or privateer vessel captured in late 1794 or early 1795 and named *Allantia*, commissioned with 18 x 4pdrs and 120-130 men at Brest. She was struck at end 1795 or early 1796, her subsequent history and other details are unknown.

Ex OTTOMAN PRIZES (1798-1801).

Two corvettes were seized from the Ottoman Navy; the first had been built at Constantinople (possibly by Le Brun), while the second was originally a British fishing corvette, taken by the Ottomans in 1801. Their Turkish names are unrecorded, as are their dimensions and tonnage. The first was captured at Alexandria in July 1798 during Napoleon's invasion and armed there on 1 November 1800, while the second was taken by Ganteaume's division off North Africa in 1801.

Héliopolis (116 men, carried 12 x 6pdrs, Commissioned at Alexandria 1.9.1798). Recomm. 6.11.1800 at Toulon, made a round trip voyage to Alexandria and 'sailed well'. Returned to Alexandria 7.6.1801 as a scout for Ganteaume's squadron and was taken there by the British in the capitulation on 31.8.1801 and returned to the Ottomans in 1803.

Mohawk (148 men, carried 16 x 12pdrs, 4 x 6pdrs, taken c6.1801, commissioned at Toulon 4.7.1801). Decomm. at Toulon and ordered sold 16.6.1814.

Ex TUSCAN PRIZE (1799).

Having been forced out of Piedmont by the French, King Charles Emmanuel IV of Sardinia embarked on the small Tuscan frigate *Rondinella* at Leghorn on 24 February 1799 and arrived at Cagliari, Sardinia, on 3 March 1799. *Rondinella* was seized by the French at Leghorn later that month. The French classified this vessel as a corvette.

Rondinella (180 men, carried 18 x 12pdrs, 6 x 4pdrs, 2 x 36pdr obusiers, taken 3.1799). Refitted at Toulon in mid-1799. She was condemned as 'old' in 4.1803 at Le Havre, then served as a headquarters hulk there until 1809.

PURCHASED AND REQUISITIONED VESSELS (1793-1800).

To supplement its own escort vessels and those captured as prizes of war, the French Navy between 1793 and 1800 acquired a considerable number of assorted vessels which it classified as corvettes. Most of these were existing privateers ('corsairs'), although some were merchant vessels whose construction similarly suited naval requirements and others were of unknown origin. Acquisition of such vessels was facilitated by a ban on privateering between 22 June 1793 and 15 August 1795 to provide manpower for the navy. For many of these ships technical details are somewhat sparse or non-existent, and for these only outline details are listed below, in chronological order of their requisition. Some were returned to service as privateers after spending time in naval service.

Oiseau (corvette commissioned at Brest 2.1793, built there or elsewhere c1791-1793, 125 men, carried 16 x 6pdrs). Missions to Senegal and Cayenne 1794. Burned 7.1795 at Vannes to prevent capture.

Île de France (merchant corvette *La Fayette* from Bordeaux requisitioned

Goulu or *Goulue* (merchant corvette requisitioned c7.1793, 100 men, carried 10 x 4pdrs). Was in service at Le Havre 8.1793, having come from another Channel port. In 11.1793 participated in the defence of Granville against a Royalist army. Struck 4.1795, having probably been returned.

Chéri (merchant vessel *Fleur Royale* built at the Chantiers de la Fosse at Nantes in 1788-89, renamed *Mère Chérie* 11.1790, commissioned there as a privateer corvette or frigate in 1793, and then requisitioned there 7.1793 by the navy and renamed *Chéri*, 600 tons, 187-197 men, carried 4 x 12pdrs, 18 x 8pdrs, 4 x 6pdrs and 2 x 36pdr obusiers). Returned to her owner 3.1796 for use as a privateer, captured 5.1.1798 by HMS *Pomone* (44) off Ushant, then sank.

Citoyenne Française. See the old French frigate *Flore Américaine*, ex *Vestale*, in Chapter 5.

Brutus (merchant corvette built in 1780 at Bordeaux, commissioned as a privateer in 1793 at Bordeaux, and purchased by the navy in 9.1793 at Brest, 136 men, carried 18 x 6pdrs). Re-rigged as a brig at Brest either in 1793 or in 5.1795. Carried out two diplomatic missions to the United States during 1794. Renamed *Célère* 5.1795. Captured 10.10.1795 by HMS *Mermaid* (32) off Grenada.

Musette (merchant corvette built at Nantes in 1781, commissioned there as a 20-gun privateer 6.1793, and requisitioned there by the navy 11.1793.)
  Dimensions & tons: 97ft 0in, 86ft 0in x 25ft 8in x 15ft 0in (31.51, 27.94 x 8.34 x 4.87m). 300/460 tons. Draught 11ft/12ft 6in (3.57/4.06m). Men: 148.
  Guns: 20 x 6pdrs (+6 small guns mounted on top of the dunette).
  Returned to privateer service 5.1795, taken by HMS *Hazard* 21.12.1796, becoming HMS *Musette*; hulked 1801, then floating battery at Plymouth 1803; sold 21.8.1806.

Difficile (corvette built at Nantes in 1788, commissioned as a privateer there in 1793, and requisitioned there by the navy in 11.1793, 148 men, carried 20 x 6pdrs). Sold as worn out 10.1796 at Brest, recommissioned as a privateer corvette, captured 11-12.2.1797 in the Channel by HMS *Phoenix* (36), *Triton* (32), and *Scourge* (18).

Spartiate (1) (merchant corvette built in 1750, commissioned at Bordeaux in 1793 as a privateer, requisitioned there in 11.1793 by the navy, carried 16 x 8pdrs). Renamed *Saison* 5.1795. Returned to privateer service 1796 as *Spartiate*, condemned 1805 and hulked at Brest.

Liberté (1) (corvette acquired in late 1793, carried 14-16 guns). Captured 28.3.1794 off Jamaica by HMS *Alligator* (28). She could have been the merchant corvette *Comte de Vergennes* of 319 to 400 tons and 14 guns that entered service at Lorient in 3.1786 and was renamed *Liberté* in 4.1791.

Neptune (corvette commissioned 2.1793 at Nantes as a privateer and requisitioned there 11.1793 by the navy, carried 8 x 8pdrs, 2 x 4pdrs, 4 x 3pdrs & 2 x 2pdrs). Became a flûte in 1796. Returned to privateer service 1.1797, taken 27.3.1797 by HMS *Aurora* (28).

Citoyen (British merchant corvette *Ravenworth* built in England 1779 or 1784-5, purchased by the French East India Co. in England or at Bordeaux, refitted at Bordeaux and renamed 1789, purchased from the French East India Co. in December 1793).
  Dimensions & tons: dimensions unknown. 512 tons (British measurement). Men: 160-224.
  Guns: UD 22 x 8pdrs; SD 8 x 4pdrs, 2 x 16pdr carronades; (1800) 20 x 8pdrs, 6 x 4pdrs.
  Last mentioned 1801.

Fabius (merchant corvette built by Arnous at Lorient between 1781 and 1783, commissioned at Nantes in 1793 as a privateer, and requisitioned there in 1793 by the navy, 250/400 tons, 148 men, carried 20 x 6pdrs). Returned to her owner 1796 for use as a privateer, captured 8.9.1797 by HMS *Doris* (36) at the entrance to the English Channel.

Jean Bart (merchant corvette built at Bayonne in 1786, commissioned in Nantes in 1793 as a privateer, and requisitioned there in 1.1794 by the navy).
  Dimensions & tons: 103ft 0in x 28ft 0in (33.46 x 9.10m). 300/550 tons. Men: 177.
  Guns: 5 x 12pdrs, 19 x 8pdrs; (1795) 24 x 8pdrs.
  Also listed as *Jean Bart No.2* from 1.1794 to distinguish from the corvette *Jean Bart (No.1)* built in 1793, above. Was to have been renamed *Imposante* 5.1795 but was captured 4.1795 off Rochefort by a British squadron including HMS *Artois* (38) and became HMS *Laurel* (22). Sold 1797 at Jamaica.

Confiance or *Confiante* (privateer corvette with 20 x 8pdrs requisitioned by or given to the Republic 21.2.1794 at Nantes, 350 tons, 125 men, carried 16 x 6pdrs). May have been returned to her owners c9.1795.

Sophie (slave trade corvette launched at Nantes in 5.1790, commissioned there as a privateer in 1793, and requisitioned there by the navy on 21.2.1794).
  Dimensions & tons: 105ft 0in x 27ft 0in (34.11 x 8.77m). 226/500 tons. Men: 148.
  Guns: 20 x 8pdrs.
  Returned to her owners 1.1795 for use as a privateer, captured 9.1798 by HMS *Endymion* (40) off the Irish coast and became HMS *Sophie* (18), BU 6.1809.

Républicaine (corvette commissioned as a privateer at Bordeaux in 1793 and requisitioned 2.1794 by the navy, referred to as *Républicaine No.2* to distinguish her from several other ships with this name, carried 22 guns). Captured 3.1795 by a British squadron in the Channel.

Intrépide (corvette built in 1781, entered the slave trade at Nantes in 9.1791, commissioned there as a privateer in 1793, and requisitioned or purchased by the navy in 3.1794, 525 tons, 172 men, carried 22 x 8pdrs and 4 x 6pdrs). May have been the *Intrépide* wrecked 26.2.1795 on the Rochers de la Baleine in the Mediterranean. Otherwise struck 1796, probably having been returned to her former owner.

Spartiate (2) (merchant corvette requisitioned at Île de France in April 1794, 200 tons, 125 men, 16 guns). Renamed *Minerve* 1794. Grounded at Ushant 1795, refloated. Reportedly renamed *Magique* 5.1795, but a corvette named *Minerve* that had come from Île de France was at Roscoff in 3.1796. Her further fate is obscure, but she may have been the 'old corvette' *Minerve* (8 x 4pdrs) that was serving as station ship at Brest in 1800/1801 and that was fitted as a transport in 3.1802 and struck soon afterwards.

Duguay-Trouin (merchant corvette built in 1783 as the slave trader *Baron Bender*, commissioned as a privateer frigate at Saint-Malo 3.1793, and requisitioned at Saint-Malo 5.1794, 300-360/450 tons or 500 tons burthen 160 men, carried 22 x 6pdrs). Renamed *Calypso* 5.1795. Returned to her owners 2.1797 for service as a privateer, captured 2.2.1798 by HMS *Shannon* (32).

Félicité (corvette built in 1787-88 at Lorient for the slave trade, possibly commissioned as a privateer at Bordeaux in 1793, and requisitioned by the navy there 5.1794). Renamed *Epi* 5.1795, run ashore and destroyed at Île de Ré 7.1795 to prevent capture by HMS *Phaeton* (38).

Spartiate (3) (merchant corvette requisitioned 5.1794, 172 men, carried 26 x 8pdrs and 4pdrs). Renamed *Moineau* 1794. Stationed at Île de France until returning to France in 1796. Sold or returned to owner in 1797.

Révolution (requisitioned corvette that was in service at Saint-Malo in 7.1794, 148 men, 20 x 6pdrs). Last reported in 7.1794 departing Saint-Malo for Brest. A *Révolution* was captured on 8.10.1794 off Porto Maurizio between Nice and Genoa by HMS *Dido* (28).

Navigateur (corvette placed in merchant service at Saint-Malo in 8.1792 and requisitioned at Île de France in August 1794, 300 tons). Probably returned to merchant service at the end of 1796.

Affranchie (corvette in service in the Antilles at the end of 1794, probably a requisitioned merchantman). Fate unknown.

Assiduité (corvette, either requisitioned or hired, commissioned at Le Havre on 10.4.1795 as a training corvette for navigation and gunnery with 39 men and 74 students). Decomm. 18.10.1795 at Le Havre, fate unknown.

Liberté (2) (corvette commissioned at Bordeaux as a privateer in 2.1793, sold at Guadeloupe in 6.1793, recommissioned there as a privateer in 7.1793, and requisitioned there by the navy in early 1795, 125 men, carried 16 x 4pdrs). Sunk 30.5.1795 off Puerto Rico by HMS *Alarm* (32).

Enfant de la Patrie (merchant corvette built at Bordeaux and requisitioned in 6.1795 at Guadeloupe, 110 men, carried 12 x 6pdrs). Sold 8.1796 at Bordeaux and became a privateer, 16.4.1797 off Cape Finisterre by HMS *Boston* (32).

Sans Culotte (corvette commissioned c1795 in the Antilles, carried 18 guns). Captured and burned 22.9.1795 in the Antilles by HMS *Aimable* (32).

Républicaine (merchant corvette requisitioned 1795 at Grenada, 250 men, carried 18 x 4pdrs, name also reported as *République* and *Républicain*). Captured 14.10.1795 in the Antilles by HMS *Mermaid* (32) and *Zebra* (16), became HMS *Republican* (lugger, 18 guns, 200 tons bm, also described as ship rigged), sold 1803.

Biche (corvette commissioned 4.1796 at Rochefort). Last mentioned 7.1796.

Importune (corvette that left Rochefort on 24.5.1796 with the brig *Épervier* for French Guiana). Last mentioned 6.1798 at French Guiana. Also reported as a schooner.

Mouette (corvette that was in service on 20.7.1796 at Camaret). Later fate unknown.

Égalité (corvette commissioned 1.1797 at Guadeloupe and possibly built there, 20 guns according to the British). Carried passengers from Guadeloupe to Corunna, Spain; while continuing to France chased by HMS *Aurora* (28) and run ashore 6.1798 near Bilbao, Spain.

Bonne Aventure (corvette commissioned as a privateer at Santo Domingo in 1798, requisitioned by the navy 20.2.1799 at Cayenne, also referred to as a flûte). As of 20.11.1799 she was under orders from the authorities in French Guiana to proceed to France, her further fate is unknown.

Éole (corvette commissioned as a privateer at Bordeaux in 1797, requisitioned and commissioned by the navy at Rochefort 9.1799, probably with her privateer commander and crew).
  Dimensions & tons: 95ft 0in x 27ft 3in (30.9 x 8.85m). 300/500 tons. Men: 107.
  Guns: 16 x 8pdrs, 2 x 36pdr obusiers (according to the British)
  Captured 23.11.1799 off Cape Tiburon, Santo Domingo, by HMS *Solebay* (32), became HMS *Nimrod* (sloop, 18). Sold 2.1811.

Général Brun (corvette commissioned 14.11.1800 at Guadeloupe, 108 men, 14 guns). Captured 9.4.1801 in the Channel by HMS *Amethyst* (38). Recorded by the British as *Général Brune*, a privateer.

(C) Corvettes acquired from 25 March 1802

A 20-gun 8pdr corvette (*Érigone*) to the design of *Fauvette* (of 1783) was named on 29 September 1802 and ordered at Toulon the next day; in 1803 this order was replaced by that for *Victorieuse* (see below). Another 20 gun 8pdr corvette (*Hébé*) was ordered at Dunkirk on 19 February 1803 but was cancelled in June 1803; presumably this would have been to the same design as *Érigone*. A 30-gun corvette named *Loiret* was offered by subscription by that Département in 6.1803 but the project was abandoned.

DÉPARTEMENT DES LANDES. Corvette of 20 x 8pdr guns. Designed by Pierre Rolland (cadet), and ordered on 21 February 1803 as *Égérie*. On 13 August 1803 the Département des Landes offered a corvette to the government, and the ship was ordered the same day at Bayonne. By a decision of 20 January 1804 the order at Bayonne was cancelled and *Égérie* was renamed for the département while under construction and was completed on its account.
  Dimensions & tons: 120ft 10in x 30ft 1½in x 15ft 5in (39.25 x 9.79 x 5.00m). 368/760 tons. Draught 13¾ft/14¾ft (4.46/4.78m). Men: 157/189.
  Guns: 20 x 8pdrs (by 1805, UD 16 x 24pdr carronades, 4 x 12pdrs; Gaillards 2 x 8pdrs, 4 x 6pdrs; in 1814, the 12pdrs had been replaced by 12pdr carronades).

Département des Landes (ex *Égérie* 20.1.1804) Bayonne (Constructeur: Jean Baudrey)
  Ord: 21.2.1803 K: 5.1803. L: 19.7.1804. Comm: 10.12.1804. C: 12.1804.
  Struck a rock entering Brest 13.9.1814 and decomm. 30.11.1814. Condemned 1820 at Brest and off the list. Ordered BU 29.10.1829, BU 12.1829 – 2.1830.

VICTORIEUSE Class. Corvettes of 20 x 8pdr guns. Designed by François Poncet as altered by Jacques-Noël Sané. On 29 September 1802 the corvette *Érigone* (20 x 8pdrs) was ordered at Toulon on the plans of *Fauvette*. On 13 September 1803 the Minister of War informed the Minister of Marine that the Army of Italy under General Murat had voted funds for a corvette, and the navy decided that this vessel would be built in place of *Érigone* and would be named *Victorieuse*. On 10 January 1804 it was proposed to build her at La Ciotat, the name was formally assigned on 21 February 1804, and the contract was dated 5 April 1804. The contractor, Reyboulet, may have been the Riboulet who was part of a firm at La Ciotat that built brigs, flutes, and gabarres. Although designed for 8pdrs all were probably completed with 24pdr carronades.

The official rating of this type, 20 guns, excluded any guns on the quarterdeck and forecastle. The armament carried by individual units varied considerably as indicated below. Although the design for *Victorieuse* provided for 20 ports in the battery, *Hébé* as captured had 22 – and room to add chase ports if required. All ships of this type, as well as *Département des Landes* and the *Iris* class, probably had a long quarterdeck, which however could probably not carry guns larger than 6pdrs or small carronades, and in some ships it was not armed at all.

On 1 July 1835 the Minister of Marine noted that *Victorieuse* needed repairs and asked if her sailing qualities could be improved by raséeing her to an open battery (flush-decked) corvette. Toulon replied that it would not only improve the ship but also save two thirds of the cost of the refit, as most of the deterioration was in her gaillards. On 3 August 1835 Paris authorised Toulon to proceed with the work. She recommissioned on 11 March 1839 rated as a 24-gun corvette and with an armament of 16-30pdr carronades, 4 x 16cm shell, and 2 x 12pdrs.
  Dimensions & tons: 120ft 0in, 109ft 0in x 30ft 0in x 15ft 6in (38.98,

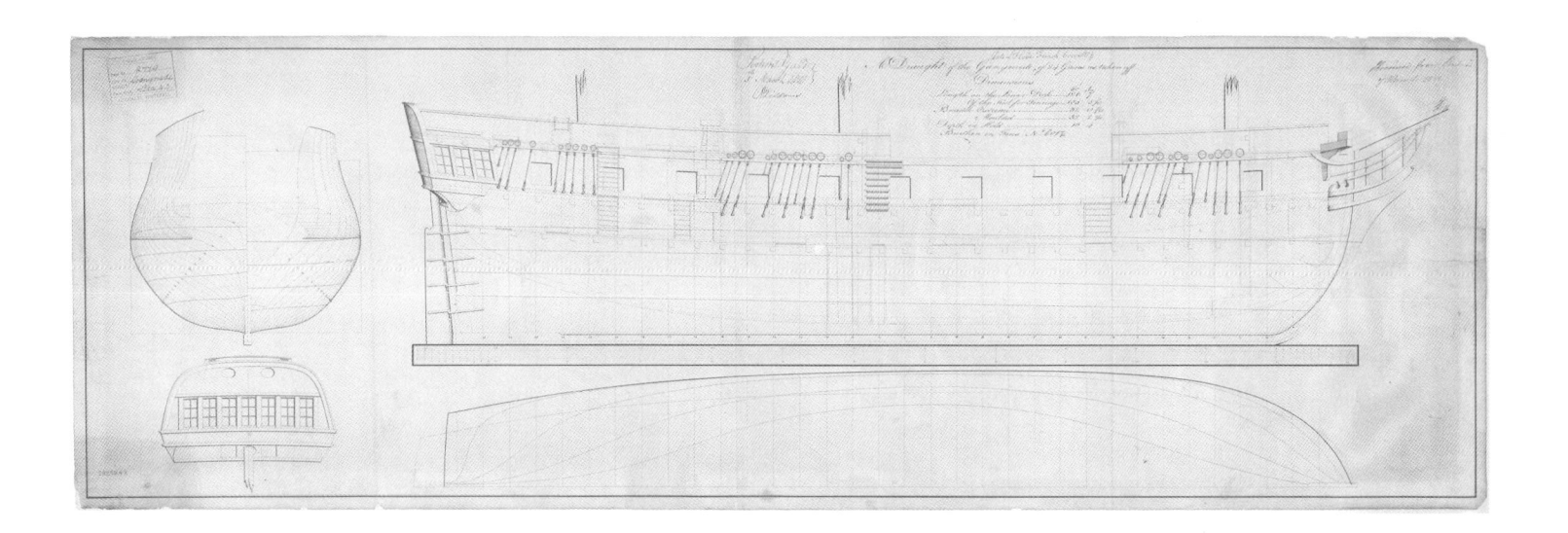

Admiralty draught of *Ganymede* (ex *Hébé*) as taken off at Portsmouth, dated 5 March 1810. The eleven ports a side was one more than required by her established armament. Unlike many French prizes, quarterdecked corvettes had a poor reputation in the Royal Navy for mediocre sailing qualities; some were even regarded as over-gunned and weapons mounted on their upperworks were often removed – despite the barricades there is no provision for guns on the forecastle and quarterdeck of this ship as fitted for British service. (© National Maritime Museum J6143)

35.40 x 9.75 x 5.03m). 380/756 tons. Draught 12¾ft/14ft (4.14/4.55m). Men: 153.

Guns: (*Victorieuse*) 20 x 24pdr carronades, 6 x 4pdrs, (1813) 20 x 24pdr carronades, 2 x 8pdrs, (1814) 10 x 24pdr carronades, 2 x 8pdrs, 6 x 6pdrs and 1 x 9pdr carronade; (20.3.1821) 22 x 24pdr carronades and 2 x 12pdrs.

(*Diane*) 14 x 36pdr carronades, 2 x 12pdrs; (1812) 18 (20 in 1814, later 22) x 24pdr carronades, 2 x 12pdrs.

(*Hébé*) 18 x 24pdr carronades, 2 x 12pdr carronades.

(*Sapho*, unchanged throughout) 18 x 24pdr carronades, 2 x 12pdrs.

(*Bayadère*) 18 x 24pdr carronades and 2 x 12pdrs; (4.1823) 22 x 24pdr carronades and 1 x 12pdr

Victorieuse Reyboulet (Riboulet?), La Ciotat
   Ord: 29.9.1802. Named: 21.2.1804. K: 10.1804. L: 17.4.1806. C: 6.1806.
   Wrecked 10.8.1847 with the frigate *Gloire* on the west coast of Korea on Ho-Hoonto Island near Gunsan.

Diane Le Havre (Constructeur: François-Toussaint Gréhan)
   Ord: 8.6.1807. K: 25.6.1807. L: 5.9.1808. Comm: 11.1.1809. C: 2.1809.
   Hauled out 11.8.1820 at Brest for refit, re-launched 4.1.1821. Struck 31.8.1831 and cut down to a careening hulk (*ponton de carène*) at Brest.

Hébé François, Jean-Baptiste, & Laurent Courau, Bordeaux (Constructeurs: Jean Chaumont and after 8.1808 Antoine Bonnet-Lescure)
   K: 1.7.1807. Named: 17.7.1807. L: 20.9.1808. Comm: 1.11.1808. C: 12.1808.
   Captured 5.1.1809 by HMS *Loire* in the Bay of Biscay, becoming HMS *Ganymede*. After 20 years as a prison ship, she capsized 1838, but was raised and BU in 2.1840. The three Couraus who built her were brothers.

Sapho François, Jean-Baptiste, & Laurent Courau, Bordeaux (Constructeurs: Jean Chaumont, later Antoine Bonnet-Lescure)
   K: 20.6.1807. Named: 17.7.1807. L: 18.1.1809. Comm: 16.3.1809. C: 4.1809.
   Missed stays and ran aground at Brest 8.8.1823, drydocked 21.8.1823 but was seriously damaged and was condemned 31.8.1823 and BU 11.1824 to 2.1825.

Bayadère Rochefort Dyd. (Constructeur: Jean-Baptiste Hubert).
   K: 10.8.1810. L: 16.6.1811. C: 3.1812. Comm: 27.6.1812.
   Struck and ordered BU 9.3.1833 at Brest, BU 5-7.1833.

IRIS Class. Corvettes of 20 x 8pdr guns. Designed by Louis Bretocq as altered by Jacques-Noël Sané. These ships were essentially similar to the *Victorieuse* class but were described as having bottom lines that were more 'pinched', i.e. with more deadrise to the floors. On 19.2.1803 corvettes named *Iris* and *Hébé* were ordered at Dunkirk. *Iris* was not begun until two years later, and *Hébé* was cancelled around June 1803. A different *Hébé* was later built at a different shipyard to the Poncet plans for *Victorieuse*, but two more corvettes were eventually ordered at Dunkirk to the Bretocq plans. Bretocq probably acted as constructeur for all three ships. A fourth unit of this class was planned in May 1815 to be built at Dunkirk, but was not named or commenced.

In 1817 *Espérance* was listed with 18 x 24pdr carronades and 2 x 12pdrs and may have had 6 more 24pdr carronades on her quarterdeck and forecastle. On 22.7.1823 this ship was ordered put into working order, and it was probably at this time that Brest raséed her quarterdeck and forecastle and converted her to a flush-deck corvette.

Dimensions & tons: 120ft 0in, 106ft 0in x 30ft 0in x 15ft 6in (38.98, 34.43 x 9.74 x 5.03m). 380/756 tons. Draught 12ft 6in/14ft 6in (4.06/4.71m). Men: 140.

Guns: (designed) 20 x 8pdrs; (1808) 18 x 24pdr carronades, 2 x 12pdrs.

Iris Dunkirk
   K: 20.2.1805. L: 11.10.1806. C: 6.1808. Comm: 1.10.1808.
   Captured by HMS *Aimable* (32) off the Dutch coast 3.2.1809, became HMS *Rainbow*. Sold 25.3.1815.

Égérie Dunkirk
   K: 15.2.1810. L: 18.11.1811. C: 2.1812. Comm: 20.5.1814.
   Struck 15.5.1826. Harbour service at Toulon 4-8.1829, BU after 6.1830.

Espérance Dunkirk
   Ord: 20.2.1812. K: 5.1812. L: 16.2.1817. C: 3.1817. Comm: 2.4.1817.
   Decomm. and condemned at Brest 31.7.1827. Struck and ordered BU 2.11.1827. BU 11.1827 at Brest.

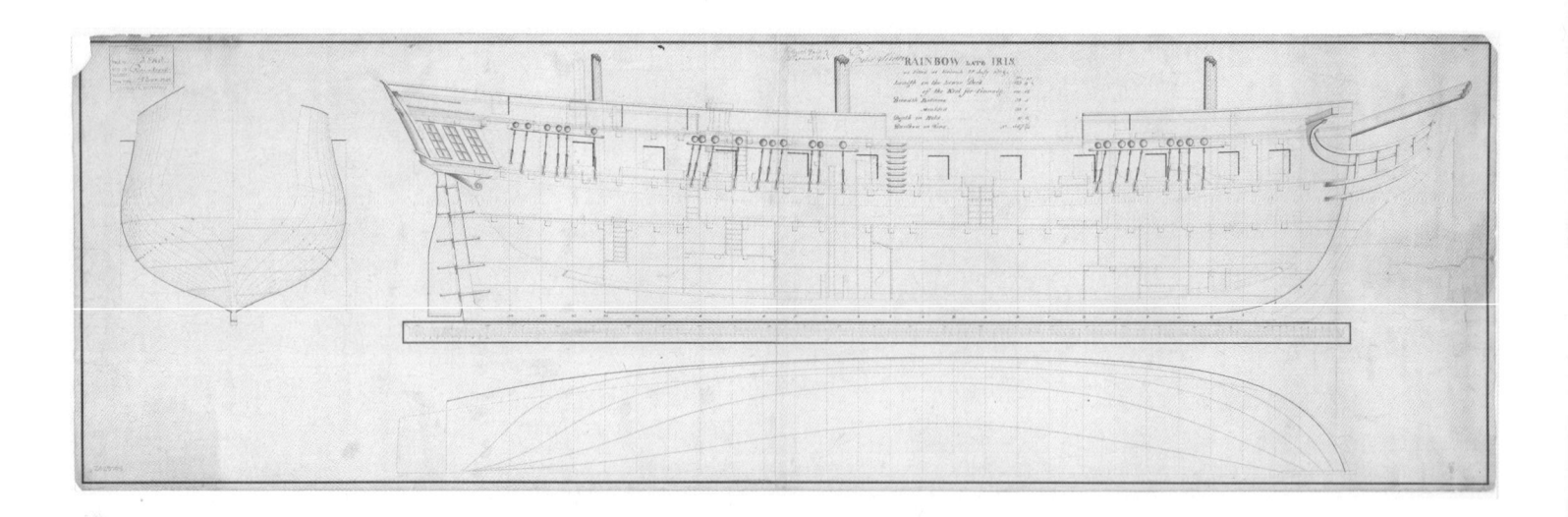

Admiralty draught of *Rainbow* (ex *Iris*) as fitted at Woolwich 28 July 1809. There is a later date of 22 March 1810 which may relate to the alterations, shown in green on the original, reducing the height of the waist rails and barricades, that on the quarterdeck also being cut off just abaft the capstan. (© National Maritime Museum J7081)

FOUDRE Class. *Corvette-canonnières* of 8 x 24pdr guns. Designed by Jean Tupinier, primarily for personal use by Napoléon during the planned invasion of England. They were brig-rigged.

  Dimensions & tons: 84ft 0in, 76ft 9in x 20ft 8in x 8ft 0in (27.28, 24.93 x 6.72 x 2.60m). 160/250 tons. Draught 6½ft/8ft (2.14/2.60m). Men: 80.
  Guns: 6 x 24pdrs, 2 x 24pdr carronades (by 1805, 6 x 18pdrs, 4 x 36pdr obusiers).

Foudre Saint-Malo.
  K: 12.1803. L: 19.3.1804. C: 5.1804. Comm: 19.3.1804 or 11.5.1804.
  Ex *Forte*, renamed 1804. May have become a training corvette at Brest in 1812. Struck 1813 (she may have been among the many vessels scuttled or burnt in early 12.1813 by the French at Willemstad before evacuating the Netherlands).

Audacieuse Saint-Servan.
  K: 12.1803. L: 4.1804. C: 5.1804. Comm: 30.5.1804.
  Decomm. 17.11.1814 at Brest and struck c1815.

TRIOMPHANTE Class. *Corvette-canonnières* of 6 x 24pdrs. Designed by Jean-François Chaumont. They may have been brig-rigged. *Décidée* was to have transported the French general officers in the invasion of England.

  Dimensions & tons: 84ft 0in, 76ft 9in x 21ft 0in x 8ft 4in (27.28, 24.93 x 6.82 x 2.71m). 170/261 tons. Draught 6½ft/9ft (2.14/2.92m). Men: 80.
  Guns: 6 x 24pdrs, 2 smaller (by 1812, the small guns were replaced by 4 swivels).

Triomphante Le Havre (Constructeur: Jean Tupinier)
  K: 12.1803. L: 5.4.1804. C: 5.1804. Comm: 14.9.1804.
  Decomm. 1.10.1814 at Dunkirk. Renamed *Isère* 9.6.1817 and hauled out at Dunkirk 6.1817, converted by Pierre Dupin to a 230-ton gabarre, re-launched 24.2.1818 and comm. 25.3.1818. As a gabarre she measured 27.93m x 7.15m x 3.57m, c300t, draught 2.60m/3.08m. Men: 34. Guns: 6 to 10 x 4pdrs. Brig-rigged. Decomm. at Rochefort 15.10.1823 and condemned, BU there 7.1826.

Official lines plan of the *Audacieuse*, designed by Tupinier to act as Napoleon's personal transport during the planned invasion of England. This brig-rigged craft was little more than a yacht but was rated as a *corvette-canonnière*. (Atlas du Génie Maritime, French collection, plate 558)

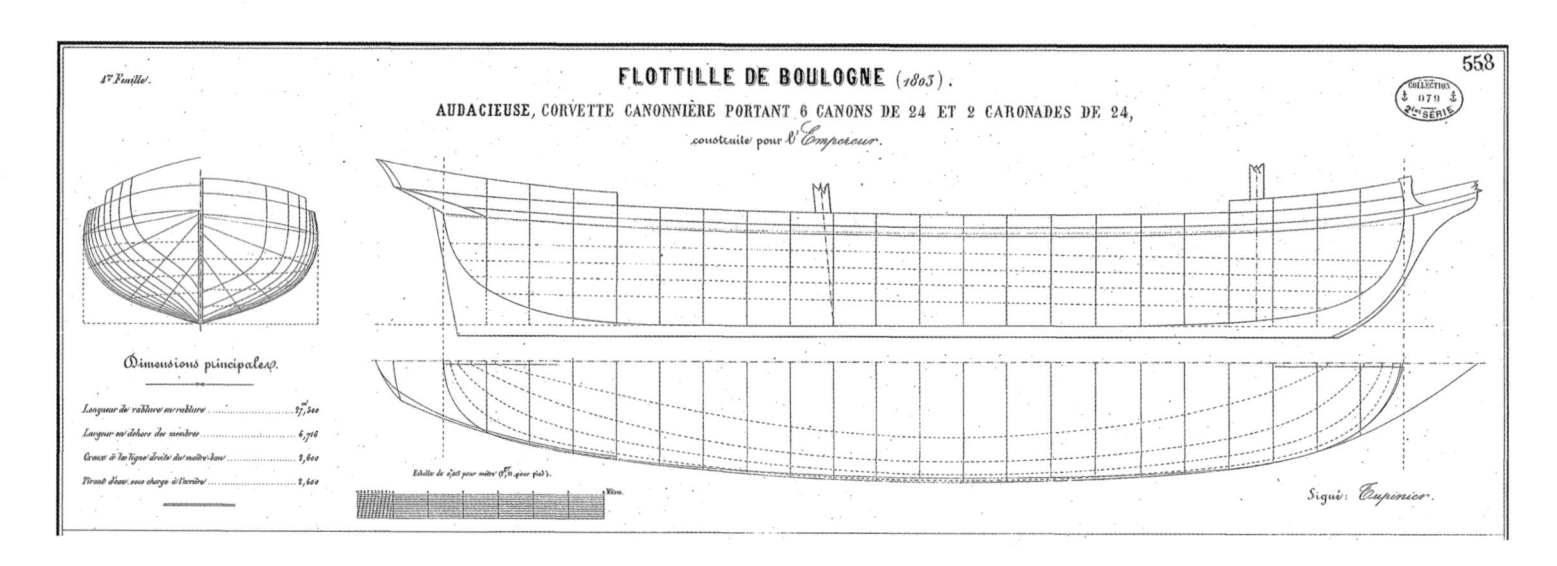

Décidée Jean-Louis Pestel, Honfleur.
K: 12.1803. L: 11.4.1804. C: 5.1804. Comm: 14.9.1804.
Decomm. 1.5.1814, seized 5.1814 at Antwerp by the Dutch and condemned.

Vaillante Jean-Louis Pestel, Honfleur.
K: 12.1803. L: 11.4.1804. C: 5.1804. Comm: 14.9.1804.
Decomm. 6.5.1814 and seized the same day in the Scheldt by the Dutch, renamed *Bruinvisch* 4.1815, sold for BU 1822. Called a brig by the Dutch.

Heureuse Le Havre (Constructeur: Jean Tupinier)
K: 12.1803. L: 20.4.1804. C: 5.1804. Comm: 14.9.1804.
Deleted at the end of 1813 (probably burnt by the French at Willemstad in early 12,1813 in the evacuation of the Netherlands).

CAROLINA Class. 32- or 34-gun corvettes, sometimes called frigates. Probably designed by the Italian chief constructor at Venice, Andrea Salvini, under the general direction of Jean Tupinier. *Carolina* was launched in the presence of Napoleon during his only visit to Venice, and both ships were commissioned in his Italian Navy.

Dimensions & tons: 124ft 0in, 113ft 11in x 31ft 6in x 14ft 6in (40.28, 37.0 x 10.23 x 4.71m). 770 tons. Draught 12ft 4in/13ft 10in (4.00/4.50m).

Guns: 22 x 12pdrs, 12 x 24pdr carronades; in French lists with 24 x 12pdrs, 8 x 6pdrs or carronades.

Carolina (ex *Speranza* 1807) Venice (constructed by Salvini and others)
K: 22.4.1807. L: 2.12.1807. C: 1808. Laid down as *Speranza*, launched as *Carolina*.
At Corfu in spring 1808. At Ancona in August 1809, on 21 June 1810 was in combat with some British sloops. Decomm. 1811. Taken over by the Austrians 25.4.1814 in the occupation of the Venice Arsenal and commissioned in the Austrian Navy on 7.7.1814 as *Carolina*. Renamed *Adria* 13.5.1815, decomm. at Venice 25.8.1815. Hauled out for repairs 12.7.1818, relaunched 20.2.1819, renamed *Carolina* 21.2.1819 after the emperor's wife. Hauled out 23.5.1832 and BU after a very active career. New corvettes named *Carolina* were begun in 1832 and 1844, officially as reconstructions of the preceding *Carolina*s.

Bellona Venice (constructed by Salvini and others)
K: 22.4.1807. L: 14.6.1808. C: 12.1808.
Taken 13.3.1811 by British forces under Commodore William Hoste at the Battle of Lissa, became troopship HMS *Dover*. Hulked 1825, sold 1836.

The final stage of the Battle of Lissa on 13 March 1811, with the *Bellona* shown striking the colours of Napoleon's Italian navy in the foreground. Aquatint engraved by Robert Dodd after his own painting. (Courtesy of Beverley R. Robinson Collection, US Naval Academy Museum)

DILIGENTE Class (series production). Corvettes of 20 x 6pdr guns. Designed by Pierre Ozanne. Although series production of the *Curieux* and *Sylphe* class brigs (see Chapter 7) beginning in 1803 provided large numbers of small cruising vessels armed with 6pdr guns, three copies of Pierre Ozanne's *Diligente* of 1800 were ordered in 1808-9 at Bayonne and Lorient, perhaps to fill a perceived need for a few three-masted vessels armed with the 6pdr. On 13 December 1810 Napoleon annexed the three Hanseatic cities of Bremen, Hamburg, and Lübeck to France, and in late 1811 the French Navy ordered two corvettes to be built in each of these three cities. The two Lübeck ships were listed as 18-gun corvettes with 18pdr carronades (specifically 16 x 18pdr carronades and 2 x 8pdrs) and were most likely a variant of the Ozanne design. The designed height of battery of this type was 1.40m at 4.20m mean draught.

Écho was assigned an armament of 20 x 24pdr carronades (18 x 24pdr carronades and 2 x 6pdrs) by a decision of 17 August 1818 and retained her classification as a corvette when *Diligente* was rearmed with 18pdr carronades and became a corvette-aviso in 1821. On 26 October 1822 *Écho*'s 24pdr carronades were ordered replaced with 18pdr carronades and the results were reported to be good. The *Diligente* design was revived in the 1820s, with a further nine corvette-avisos armed with 18pdr carronades being ordered to it (of which one was cancelled), and it was again copied in 1848 for two small corvettes with auxiliary screw propulsion (*Biche* and *Sentinelle*).

 Dimensions & tons: 104ft 0in, 92ft 0in x 26ft 0in x 14ft 0in (33.78, 29.88½ x 8.45 x 4.55m). 278/476 tons. Draught 11½ft/14⅓ft (3.76/4.66m). Men: 114/141.

 Guns: 20 x 6pdrs

Coquette Bayonne (Constructeur: Jean Baudry)
 Ord: 4.6.1808. K: 22.3.1809. L: 21.11.1809. Comm: 1.4.1810. C: 4.1810.
 Commissioning process completed 1.1.1811. Docked at Rochefort 24.11.1821 for refit and found unusable. Condemned 2.1822, struck and BU approved 4.4.1822, BU completed 5.1822.

Friponne Bayonne (Constructeur: Jean Baudry)
 Ord: 4.6.1808. Named 16.3.1809. K: 22.3.1809. L: 4.5.1810. C: 1811.
 Hauled out at Rochefort 11.4.1820 and found beyond repair. Condemned 6.1820, struck and BU approved 11.7.1820, BU completed 1.12.1820.

Écho (ex *Favorite* 23.7.1810) Lorient Dyd. (Constructeur: Aimé Le Déan)
 Ord: 1.7.1809. Named 31.7.1809 (*Favorite*). K: 12.1809. L: 3.7.1810. Comm: 8.12.1810. C: 12.1810.
 Renamed just after launching to avoid conflict with a frigate building at Venice. Refitted (12/24ths) at Brest 8-11.1822. Rated corvette-aviso 1.1826, 24-gun corvette 1.1827, and 20-gun corvette 1.1831. Decomm. 19.3.1831, struck 30.7.1844 at Toulon.

Badine Lübeck.
 K: 12.1811. Not launched.
 Was 7/24ths built when abandoned on the ways in the evacuation of Lübeck in 12.1813.

Coquille Lübeck.
 K: 12.1811. Not launched.
 Was 7/24ths built when abandoned on the ways in the evacuation of Lübeck in 12.1813.

AIGRETTE Class. Corvettes of 20 x 24pdr carronades. *Aigrette* was listed as built on plans of Jacques-Noël Sané that were described as derived from the plans of *Diligente*, the corvette built most recently at Brest. *Aigrette*'s dimensions and armament, however, were very close to those of the *Victorieuse* and *Iris* classes and she was more likely a variant of one of these designs. Like some of these ships, she was rated for 20 guns in her battery but appears to have carried 22. After annexing the three Hanseatic cities of Bremen, Hamburg, and Lübeck, the French in late 1811 ordered two corvettes in each of these cities. The four ships ordered in Bremen and Hamburg were listed as 20-gun corvettes with 24pdr carronades (specifically 18 x 24pdr carronades and 2 x 8pdrs) and were probably of the *Aigrette* type.

 Dimensions & tons: 120ft 0in, 110ft 0in x 30ft 0in x 15ft 6in (38.98, 35.73 x 9.74½ x 5.03½ m). 390/752 tons. Draught 13¼ft/15ft (4.30/4.87m). Men: ?.

 Guns: (prototype) 20 x 24pdr carronades, 2 x 12pdrs or 20 x 24pdr carronades, 2 x 8pdrs and 1 x 4pdr; (others) 18 x 24pdr carronades, 2 x 8pdrs

Aigrette Brest Dyd. (Constructeur: Charles Simon)
 K: 16.7.1810. L: 14.8.1811. C: 27.11.1811. Comm: 4.2.1812.
 Hauled out 28.7.1822 for refit but found to be in worse condition than expected. Struck 20.8.1822, to have been used as storage hulk at Brest but BU 1822.

Alouette M. Tecklembourg, Bremen (built by M. Soetezmer for the contractor)
 K: 11.1811. L: 27.11.1812. C: 10.1813.
 Contract dated 1 or 14.10.1811. Was complete but not yet commissioned when Allied armies approached Bremen in late 10.1813. The Maritime Prefect at Antwerp had her scuttled on 26.10.1813 to prevent falling into enemy hands. She may have been seized on 31.10.1813 by British boats on the Weser, her subsequent fate is unknown.

Perdrix M. Tecklembourg, Bremen
 K: 11.1811. L: ?9.1813. Never completed.
 Was 20/24ths built when Allied armies approached Bremen in late 10.1813. She may have been seized on 31.10.1813 by British boats on the Weser, her subsequent fate is unknown.

Hambourgeoise Jaunez, Hamburg
 K: 10.1811. Never completed.
 Was 13/24ths built when Hamburg was besieged in late 10.1813. Lost when French forces in Hamburg surrendered in 5.1814.

Elbine Jaunez, Hamburg
 K: 10.1811. Never completed.
 Was 11/24ths built when Hamburg was besieged in late 10.1813. Lost when French forces in Hamburg surrendered in 5.1814.

LETIZIA – 32 guns. In 1807 Napoleon directed the construction at Naples of two ships of the line and two frigates. On 17 September 1808, just 11 days after his arrival at Naples, Murat announced that a frigate (*Carolina*) would be laid down that week at Naples. *Carolina* was built as a standard 18pdr frigate but the second unit, *Letizia*, although frigate-built with two decks and a covered battery, was constructed to a smaller design and was eventually reclassified as a corvette.

 Dimensions & tons: 107ft 0in x 27ft 6in (34.76 x 8.94m). 400/762 tons. Draught 12ft 11in (4.19m) mean. Men: 360.

 Guns: 24 x 24pdrs, 2 x 6pdrs, 10 x 24pdr carronades; also reported as 24 x 24pdrs, 20 x 24pdr carronades.

(*Principessa*) *Letizia* Naples (Constructeurs: probably Jean-François Lafosse and Philippe Greslé)
 K: 1811. L: 25.12.1812. C: 5.1813. Comm: 5.6.1813.
 When on 30 May 1815 Murat defected to Napoleon during the Hundred Days, *Carolina* and *Letizia* were being blockaded in port at Brindisi by the British. The British convoyed the ships to Naples where on 1 June 1815 they declared loyalty to the Bourbon monarchy and were renamed *Amalia* and *Cristina* respectively. *Cristina* was refitted in 1828 as a corvette with an armament of 10 x 24 pdrs, 20 x 24pdr carronades, and 2 x 60pdr shell guns. She was inscribed on the list of the new Italian Navy 17.3.1861 as a 2nd Rank sailing corvette with 4 x 160pdrs and 10 x 60pdr shell guns. Decomm. 12.4.1865 after 50 years of nearly continuous active service. Struck 18.7.1866, sold for BU 10.10.1866.

NAÏADE – 20 guns. This ship was probably begun to the plans by Sané for *Aigrette*, but she appears to have been completed on Dutch plans, probably by the senior Dutch naval constructor at Amsterdam, P. Schuijt Jr.

Dimensions & tons: Unknown.
Guns: 20 x 24pdr carronades, 2 x 8pdrs.

Naïade (**Nayade**) Amsterdam (constructed by P. Schuijt Jr. supervised by Jean-François Guillemard)
K: 1.1812. L: 4.1814. C: 1814.
Was 9/24ths complete when seized on the stocks 14.11.1813 in the Dutch uprising with the other ships under construction at Amsterdam and taken into the Dutch Navy in 12.1813 as *Bellona*. Launched by the Dutch and entered Dutch service in 1814 as *Eendragt* (*Eendracht*). In 1820 she carried 20 x 12pdr carronades, 2 x 6pdrs, and 2 x 50pdr mortars. BU 1840 at Nieuwediep.

A corvette named *Chicaneur* was ordered in 1812 at Leghorn (Livorno) but was not laid down. It is not known to which class she would have belonged.

Ex BRITISH NAVAL PRIZES (1805-1808). Four assorted Sixth Rates and ship-sloops were captured from the British Navy during the Napoleonic War, and were classed as corvettes by the French; three were retaken by the British during the War, and the fourth fell into Prussian hands. They are listed below, with measurements in French units.

BITTERN Class. British 18-gun quarterdecked ship-sloop, designed in 1795 by John Henslow as an enlargement of the *Pylades* class (see Section (B) above). Five vessels were built to this design, of which the *Cyane* was captured on 12 May 1805 by *Hortense* and *Hermione* off Martinique.
Dimensions & tons: 104ft 8in x 27ft 9in (34.00 x 9.01m). 350/600 tons. Men: 190.
Guns: 18 x 6pdrs, 2 x 4pdrs, 6 x 12pdr carronades (all British guns).

Cyane John Wilson, Frindsbury,
K: 5.1795. L: 9.4.1796. C: 15.6.1796 at Chatham Dyd.
Retaken 5.10.1805 by HMS *Princess Charlotte* (36) off Tobago and became HMS *Cerf*. Sold 1.1809.

CORMORANT Class. British 16-gun quarterdecked ship-sloop, designed in 1793 by John Henslow and William Rule jointly, based on the hull form of the French *Amazon* type of 1745. Thirty-one ships were built to this design, of which the *Favourite* was captured 6.1.1806 by the division of Capitaine de Vaisseau Lhermitte off the Cape Verde Islands.
Dimensions & tons: 104ft 8in, 93ft 0in x 27ft 9in x 14ft 6in (34.00, 30.21 x 9.01 x 4.71m). 350/600 tons. Draught 12ft/12½ft (3.90/4.06m. Men: 150.
Guns: When taken had 18 x 6pdrs and 11 x 12pdr carronades. On departure for Cayenne had 16 x 6pdrs and 12 x 12pdr carronades (all British guns).

Favorite Randall & Brent, Rotherhithe.
K: 4.1793. L: 1.2.1794. C: 14.5.1794 at Deptford Dyd.
Retaken 27.1.1807 off Cayenne by frigate HMS *Jason* and became HMS *Goree*. Prison hulk 1814, BU at Bermuda 1817.

COMBATANT Class. British 18-gun flush-decked ship-sloop, designed by John Stainforth, MP in 1804. Three ships were built to this design, of which the *Dauntless* was taken by the French Army on 16 May 1807 when grounded in the River Holm during the French siege of Danzig after being damaged by shore batteries.
Dimensions & tons: 114ft 0in, 97ft 0in x 26ft 3in x 10ft 6in (37.03, 31.51 x 8.53 x 3.41m). 250/450 tons.
Guns: 20 x 24pdr carronades.

Sans-Peur John Blunt, Hull.
K: 1804. L: 11.1804. C: 29.3.1805 at Woolwich Dyd.
Her fate is uncertain, but she may have been left to the Prussians when Napoleon in 7.1807 handed the city of Danzig over to them.

LAUREL Class. British 22-gun Sixth Rate post ship, designed by Sir John Henslow in 1805. Six ships were built to this design, of which the name ship of the class was captured by the frigate *Canonnière* off Port Napoléon, Île de France (Mauritius) on 12 September 1808.
Dimensions & tons: 114ft 0in, 103ft 0in x 29ft 6in x 14ft 9in (37.03, 33.46m x 9.58m x 4.79m). 350/680 tons. Draught 12½ft/13½ft (4.06/4.39m).
Guns: 22 x 9pdrs, 4 (or 2) x 6pdrs, 6 (or 8) x 18pdr carronades.

Laurel Nicholas Bools & William Good, Bridport.
K: 6.1805. L: 2.6.1806. C: 16.11.1806 at Plymouth Dyd.
Comm. 16.9.1808 as *Laurel*, but sold into commercial service 5.1809 and renamed *Espérance*. Sailed as a naval vessel *en flûte* on 15.12.1809 from Île de France and retaken 12.4.1810 by HMS *Unicorn* off Île de Ré after 118 days at sea. Became HMS *Laurestinus*, wrecked 21.8.1813 in the Bahamas.

Ex BRITISH MERCANTILE AND PRIVATEER PRIZES (1803-1810)

Hasard (British *Hazard* captured 31.12.1803 by the schooner *Courrier*). Retaken 30.9.1804 off Bonaire by HMS *Echo* (16). Was probably a merchant or privateer and was not the Royal Navy's *Cormorant* class ship-sloop of the same name. When retaken she was described by the British as a privateer with 16 guns.

Otway (British merchant slaver and privateer, probably *Ottway* or *Otway*, taken by the Lhermitte division at the beginning of 1806, carried 4 x 12pdrs, 14 x 6pdrs, 2 x 18pdr carronades). May have been commissioned by the French but was not included in the fleet list for 1807.

Plowers (British merchant slaver and privateer, probably *Plover*, taken by the Lhermitte division at the beginning of 1806, carried 20 x 6pdrs). May have been commissioned by the French but was not included in the fleet list for 1807.

Zéphyr (British *Zephyr*, merchant corvette or privateer with 18 guns according to the British, captured in 1806 and was in service at Martinique in 9.1806). Captured 10.1809 in the Channel by HMS *Seine* (36).

Discovery (British merchant corvette, probably of the same name captured 18.1.1809 by the frigate *Canonnière* in the vicinity of Poulo-Aor in the Far East). Taken into Batavia 29.1.1809 and was left in that port. Further fate unknown.

Aurore (British East India Company sloop *Aurora*, 16 guns, built in 1809 for the Bombay Marine, captured 20.9.1810 by *Iphigénie* and *Astrée* under Bouvet and taken to Île de France). Retaken by the British 12.1810 in the surrender of that island. Last listed on 1 January 1828 as still with the Bombay Marine.

Ex NEAPOLITAN PRIZE (1806)

FAMA (Neapolitan corvette). In late 1.1806 the King of Naples was transported to Palermo by his Navy. *Fama* and the frigate *Cerere* were sent back to Naples for the queen's baggage and on 14.2.1806 were captured at Castellammare di Stabia. They became the nucleus of Murat's Neapolitan Navy.
Dimensions & tons: unknown. Men: 200-260
Guns: 22 x 8pdrs, 6 x 6pdrs or 4pdrs. Rated at 20 guns 1808-9. An Italian source gives her armament as 6 x 36pdrs (obusiers?), 2 x 18pdrs, and 22 x 18pdr carronades

Fama Castellammare di Stabia.
K: 1788, L: 15.9.1789, C: 1790.

In 12.1813 Murat abandoned Napoleon to keep his throne but, knowing that the Austrians planned to depose him, re-joined Napoleon in 1815 during the Hundred Days. *Fama* carried reinforcements to Murat's army in Romagna in 3.1815 but joined the Bourbon Neapolitan Navy in 6.1815. She was placed on the sale list on 17.10.1820 and was sold for BU on 13.2.1823.

Ex PORTUGUESE PRIZES (1807)

Andorinha (Portuguese *Andorinha*, 6th Class (28 guns), built at Lisbon)
K: 1796, L: 13.3.1797, C: 1797).
Dimensions & tons: 93ft 11in x 28ft 2in (30.5 x 9.14m). 250/450 tons. Men: 163.
Guns: (1797) 20 x 12pdrs, 8 x 6pdrs; (1801) 2 x 9pdrs, 22 x 24pdr obusiers
Seized at Lisbon 30.11.1807. May have been called *Hirondelle* by the French. Retaken in the evacuation of Lisbon early 9.1808 and returned to Portuguese service. Wrecked 1810.

Benjamin (French whaling corvette built at Bordeaux 1791-92, 347 tons, 166 men, carried 22 x 6pdrs and 2 other guns). Purchased by Benjamin Hussey 5.1792 and placed in service at Dunkirk 8.1792. Raised the American flag 1793 and listed at New Bedford 2.1794. Returned to Bordeaux and commissioned as a privateer corvette 1796. Captured by the Portuguese Navy 1797 and became a 28-gun corvette with 20 x 12pdrs and 8 x 6pdrs. Seized by the French at Lisbon 30.11.1807. Retaken in the evacuation of Lisbon early 9.1808 and returned to Portuguese service. BU 1828.

PURCHASED RUSSIAN VESSELS (1809)

Derzkiy (Merchant corvette built at Fiume in 1803 and purchased by the Russians in 1806 at Castelnuovo in Montenegro, sold to France 27.9.1809 at Venice)
Dimensions & tons: 92ft 1in x 26ft 9in x 11ft 8in (29.9 x 8.69 x 3.80m) or in Russian sources 80ft 8in x 23ft 5in x 9ft 7in (26.2 x 7.6 x 3.1m). 200/380 tons.
Guns: 28
Had served in Vice Admiral Senyavin's squadron in 1806-7 and, after the Treaty of Tilsitt led to war between Russia and England, moved to Trieste 12.1807 and to Venice 1.1808. Found by the French to be in bad condition, BU at Venice c1810.

Versona (Probable merchant corvette purchased by the Russians in 1805 at Kotor and sold to France 27.9.1809 at Corfu, 22 guns). Had served from 2.1806 as a storeship in Vice Admiral Senyavin's squadron and was left at Corfu when Senyavin's squadron returned to Russia in 1808. BU c1810.

Pavel (Converted by the Russians to a corvette from a privateer or transport at Kherson in 1804 and sold to France 27.9.1809 at Corfu, 18 guns). Had joined Vice Admiral Senyavin's squadron at Corfu in the autumn of 1806 and was left at Corfu when Senyavin's squadron returned to Russia in 1808. Probably BU c1810.

Al'tsinoye (Probable merchant corvette purchased by the Russians in 1805 at Kotor and sold to France 27.9.1809 at Corfu, 18 guns). Had served from 2.1806 as a storeship in Vice Admiral Senyavin's squadron and was left at Corfu when Senyavin's squadron returned to Russia in 1808. BU c1810.

ANNEXED DUTCH VESSELS (1810-1811).

About fifteen Dutch 24-gun small frigates (quarterdeck type) fell into the hands of the new Batavian Republic when it was proclaimed on 19 January 1795. Most of these were of a 125-foot (Dutch measurement) type that the Amsterdam Admiralty built between 1768 and 1788. By the end of 1800 all but two of these ships had been BU or taken by the British Navy, and the last two, *Zeepaard* and *Scipio,* followed in 1806-7. The Batavian Navy did not continue construction of this type but replaced it with smaller vessels that were similar except for their rig to large brigs.

AJAX Class. *Ajax* was originally one of a group of six brigs with 16 guns and 98 men, three of which were soon re-rigged as corvettes. She was built by the chief constructor of the Amsterdam dockyard in a small dockyard that had formerly built ships for the Friesland Admiralty. Her near sisters were the brig *Daphne*, launched at Rotterdam in 1796, re-rigged as a corvette in 1801 and given to Morocco in 1804; the corvette *Hippomenes*, built at Flushing in 1797 and captured by the British in 1804; the brig *Atalante*, built at Flushing in 1796 and taken by the British in 1803; the brig *Galathe*, launched at Rotterdam in 1796 and taken by the British in 1799, and the brig *Spion*, launched at Amsterdam in 1797 and also captured by the British in 1804.
Dimensions & tons: 100ft 3in x 28ft 7in x 15ft 8in (32.54 x 9.29 x 5.09m). 330/650 tons. Draught 13ft 1in/14ft 10in (4.24/4.81m). Men: 120.
Guns: 16 x 8pdrs (18 ports).

Ajax Harlingen (constructed by P. Schuijt Jr.)
K: 3.1796, L: 10.1796 or 18.11.1796, C: 1798
Raised the French flag in the Scheldt 16.8.1810, transferred to account of French Navy 1.1.1811. Stationed at Willemstadt in 1813, taken there in early 12.1813 in the Dutch uprising. Sent to the East Indies 1819, participated in the blockade of Palembang 1820. To the Colonial Navy 1822 and BU the same year.

IRIS. Designed by P. Glavimans Jnr.
Dimensions & tons: 104ft 7in, 94ft 6in x 29ft 5in x 14ft 6in (33.97, 30.70 x 9.57 x 4.74m). 340/660 tons. Draught 12ft 2in/13ft 11in (3.96/4.53m). Men: 120.
Guns: 18 x 8pdrs, 2 x 24pdr carronades; later (1812) 18 x 12pdrs, 2 x 6pdrs.

Iris Amsterdam.
K: 12.1802. L: 10.1803. C: 1804
Ex Dutch *Duifje*. Hoisted French colours 16.8.1810 in the Scheldt, transferred to account of French Navy 1.1.1811. Retaken at Hellevoetsluys 12.1813 in the Dutch uprising, Sent to the East Indies after the war, to the Colonial Navy 1816 and later BU.

LYNX Class. These two ships, which shared the same hull structure, differed only slightly from their predecessor, *Iris*.
Dimensions & tons: 104ft 7in x 29ft 5in x 14ft 6in (33.97 x 9.57 x 4.73m). 350/670 tons. Draught 12ft 4in/14ft 1in (4.01/4.58m). Men: 134-149.
Guns: 20 x 12pdrs, 2 x 6pdrs, 2 x 12pdr carronades.

Lynx (ex Dutch *Lynx* or *Lijnx*) Rotterdam (constructed by P. Glavimans Jr.)
K: 1.1806. L: 1807? C: 1807
Transferred to account of French Navy 1.1.1811. Grounded and cut up by the French near Hellevoetsluis or Willemstadt 11.1813. Taken 12.1813 in the Dutch uprising but not repaired.

Vénus (ex Dutch *Venus*) Amsterdam (constructed by P. Schuijt Jr.)
K: 1.1806. L: 5.1807. C: 1807
Transferred to account of French Navy 1.1.1811. Was in the Texel squadron in 4.1814. Turned over to the Dutch 22.4.1814 at Nieuwdiep in accordance with the capitulation of Vice Admiral Verhuell after the fall of the Empire. Carried a governor to the Guinea coast in 1815-16, then departed 1.1817 for the East Indies. Participated in the blockade of Palembang 1820, then declared unfit for the trip home and transferred to the Colonial

Navy 1.1821. BU 1823.

JAVAN. This small vessel was built in the United States in 1796-98 and was probably acquired by the Dutch in the East Indies.
    Dimensions & tons: 87ft x 29ft or 23ft x 9ft (28.26 x 9.42m or 7.47 x 2.92m). 240/400 tons.
    Guns: 14 (16 ports).
Javan (ex Dutch *Javaan*).
    Arrived at Bordeaux from Java with *Royal Hollandais* (later *Malais*) on 25.10.1810 and hoisted the French flag on 29.10.1810. In bad condition, ordered sold or BU 1.7.1811, ordered BU 12.8.1811, and BU completed 30.11.1811.

PURCHASED AND REQUISITIONED VESSELS (1803-1808)

Eure (merchant corvette *Saint Pierre* built for the slave trade at Bordeaux 1803 and purchased at Bordeaux 8 or 9.1803 while new by the Département de l'Eure for donation to the navy, 240 tons, 18 guns). Was to have been delivered 24.9.1803 but the navy found her unsuitable and returned to her original owner who restored the name *Saint Pierre*. This ship was later hired at Bordeaux in 7-9.1805 as a transport and may be the same ship that is listed as *Diligente* (1808) below.

Iéna, later *Victor* (privateer corvette *Revenant* built at Saint-Malo and commissioned at Saint-Malo 10.1806 under the privateer Robert Surcouf, who provided the specifications for the ship's design. Surcouf sailed for Île de France 4.1807 and operated there until 2.1808. His ship was requisitioned 4.7.1808 by the Captain-General of Île de France and renamed *Iéna*).
    K: 1806. L: 1806 C: 10.1806.
    Dimensions & tons: 106ft, 88ft x 28ft, 28ft 6in (34.43, 28.58 x 9.10, 9.26m). 300/550 tons
    Guns: (1806-8) 14 x 32pdr carronades, 6 x 8pdrs; (1808) 18 x 24pdr carronades; (1809) 6 x 8pdrs, 14 x 32pdr carronades.
    Sent on 14.7.1808 on a cruise with the frigates *Caroline* and *Manche*. Captured by HMS *Modeste* (36) 8.10.1808 and became HMS *Victor*. Recaptured by French frigate *Bellone* 2.11.1809 and comm. 11.1.1810. Captured by the British in the capitulation of Île de France 4.12.1810.

Vénus (corvette of unknown origins in service at Île de France 10.1808, 200 tons, carried 14 x 12pdr carronades). Sold into commercial service 3.1809 and recommissioned as a privateer. Captured near Île de France c1810 by boats from HMS *Boadicea* (38).

Diligente (ex *Saint Pierre*?) (corvette of unknown origin commissioned at Martinique c1808, 240 tons, 18 guns). Captured by the British in the capitulation of St. Pierre de la Martinique and became HMS *St. Pierre* (sloop, 18, 371 tons bm). Sold 9.1814. May be the same ship that is listed as *Eure* (1803) above.

Rossolis (corvette (or brig) of unknown origin commissioned at Martinique c1808, 18 guns according to the British). Burned 2.1809 by the French in Martinique to prevent her capture by the British.

(D) Sailing corvettes acquired from 26 June 1815

France emerged from the Napoleonic Wars with a relatively small collection of corvettes, consisting on 1 October 1816 of ten units carrying 24pdr carronades and three vessels with 6pdr guns, all with 20 guns. Most of the 24pdr group, descended from older 8pdr types, were of the generally similar *Victorieuse*, *Iris*, *Aigrette*, and *Département des Landes* classes while the smaller 6pdr corvettes were *Diligente* and two later copies. Of these only *Diligente* herself was regarded as fully successful. *Victorieuse* and possibly some others of her wartime group had a light quarterdeck with additional small guns, and the first corvettes ordered after the war were a pair of similarly fitted vessels. These not proving successful, the French during the 1820s settled on two main types of corvettes, one with 30pdr carronades and one copied from *Diligente* with 18pdr carronades, both with open batteries. However at the end of that decade a new type entered production that was essentially a miniature frigate with 30pdr carronades in a covered battery and a handful of small guns on a complete spardeck. This type accounted for all new French sailing corvette construction during the 1830s and 1840s.

POMONE Class – Quarterdecked corvettes, 28 guns. This class was designed by Jean-Michel Segondat along the lines of *Victorieuse* but with an additional 8 guns on the quarterdeck and forecastle and more men to operate them. They were described as covered battery corvettes (*corvettes à batterie couverte*). On 11 November 1823 Inspector General of the *Génie Maritime* Rolland argued that the eight additional small guns were not worth the inconvenience of adding 15 men to the crew which had recently been reduced to 145 men. The original crew of 180 men had depressed the height of the main battery above the water from 5ft to 4ft 8in. In 1826 France's quarterdecked corvettes were redesignated *corvettes à gaillards* while the open battery types were redesignated *corvettes sans gaillards* (of which only one, the recently raséed *Espérance*, remained in service) and *corvette-avisos*.
    Dimensions & tons: 38.98m x 9.82m, 10.04m ext x 5.11. 750 tons. Draught 4.35/4.66m. Men: 180, later 145.
    Guns: UD 20 x 24pdr carronades; SD 6 x 12pdr carronades, 2 x 6pdrs.
Pomone Cherbourg Dyd. (Constructeur: Jean-Michel Segondat)
    Ord: 15.2.1820. K: 1.5.1820. L: 28.8.1821. Comm: 1.11.1821. C: 12.1821.
    Condemned and struck 23.12.1830. BU 1831 at Brest due to the use of bad timber in her construction.
Hébé Le Havre (Constructeur: Charles Alexandre)
    K: 26.10.1820. L: 5.8.1822. Comm: 5.8.1822. C: 9.1822.
    Struck 11.3.1835. Cut down to a careening hulk (*ponton de carène*) at Brest 1835.

REPEAT DILIGENTE Class – Corvette-avisos, 18 guns. Pierre Ozanne's *Diligente* of 1801 had proved very successful in service, being an excellent sea boat, easy to steer, and very fast (12-13 knots) on a reach. She had been rearmed with 18pdr carronades in around 1818, and the Restoration navy soon decided to reproduce her. The armament assigned to this type in the Royal Ordinance of 10 March 1824 was 16 x 18pdr carronades and 2 x 8pdrs. These small open battery corvettes were redesignated *corvette-avisos* in 1826 when the larger corvettes were redesignated *corvettes à gaillards* (quarterdecked corvettes) and *corvettes sans gaillards* (flush-deck corvettes). The designed height of battery of this class was 1.40m at 4.20m mean draught. *Cornélie* was originally projected to be begun at Lorient in 1824 but was reassigned to Cherbourg before construction began in 1824. Another ship, *Niobé*, was projected in 1825 with *Perle* to begin construction in 1826, but she was cancelled in 1825 and her name was reassigned in 1826 to a new 2nd Class frigate at Rochefort.
    Dimensions & tons: 33.78m, 29.56m x 8.45m, 8.71m ext x 4.66m. 422 tons. Draught 3.55m/4.55m. Men: 110.
    Guns: 16 x 18pdr carronades, 2 x 8pdrs.
Isis Cherbourg Dyd. (Constructeurs: Louis Bretocq and Alexandre Liénard)

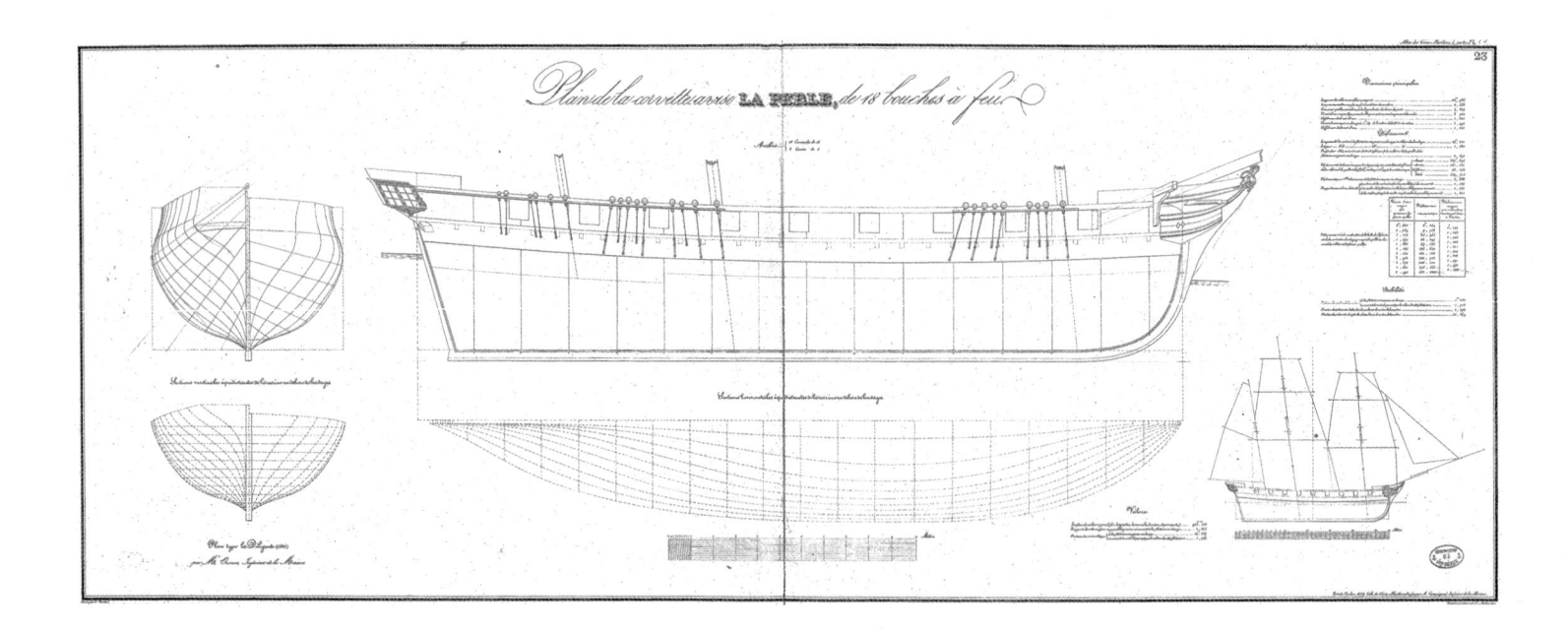

Official lines plan of the 18-gun *Perle*, one of the ships built in the 1820s to the design of the wartime *Diligente* class by Pierre Ozanne. The sail plan shows the rig reduced to that of a barque (with no square yards on the mizzen), totalling 936 sq.m. (Atlas du Génie Maritime, French collection, plate 23)

Ord: 4.12.1821. Named: 16.4.1822. K: 8.7.1822. L: 14.4.1823. Comm: 7.6.1823. C: 6.1826.
  Ordered BU and struck 26.1.1833. BU at Brest 4.1833.
Sylphide Lorient Dyd. (Constructeurs: Jean-Michel Segondat and Pierre Le Grix)
  Ord: 4.12.1821. K: 21.3.1822. L: 12.5.1823. C: 6.1823. Comm: 21.8.1823.
  Wrecked 23.2.1829 at Haiti.
Bayonnaise Cherbourg Dyd. (Constructeurs: Louis Bretocq and Alexandre Liénard)
  Ord: 10.2.1824. K: 12.3.1824. L: 2.6.1825. Comm: 25.11.1825. C: 11.1825.
  Struck 24.6.1835. BU at Brest 1835.
Cornélie Cherbourg Dyd. (Constructeurs: Louis Bretocq and Alexandre Liénard)
  Ord: 10.2.1824. K: 12.3.1824. L: 2.6.1825. Comm: 10.1.1826. C: 1.1826.
  Struck 25.11.1846.
Cérès Cherbourg Dyd. (Constructeurs: Émile Etiennez and probably others)
  K: 15.6.1825. L: 7.6.1826. C: 12.1827. Comm: 8.1.1828.
  Struck 7.10.1840. Condemned 16.10.1840. BU at Brest 10-12.1840.
Églé Cherbourg Dyd.
  K: 15.6.1825. L: 7.6.1826. C: 2.1828. Comm: 1.3.1828.
  Struck 6.11.1843 at Brest and BU.
Orythie (*Orithye*) Lorient Dyd. (Constructeurs: Jean-Michel Segondat and others)
  K: 29.9.1825. L: 14.3.1827. Comm: 24.12.1827. C: 12.1827.
  Annexe to the Naval Academy at Brest from 1834 to 1842. Struck 6.11.1843, BU at Brest 1844.
Perle Bayonne (Constructeur: Gabriel Nosereau)
  K: 11.1826. L: 1.7.1829. Comm: 22.2.1830. C: 3.1830.
  Struck 7.3.1856. Victualling hoy (*bugalet-cambuse*) at Toulon. BU 1869.
Niobé Cherbourg Dyd
  Projected in 1825 to be begun in 1826 but cancelled in 1825.

CRÉOLE Class – Flush-deck corvettes, 24 guns. In May 1822 Jean-Marguerite Tupinier, then the Deputy Director of Ports and a *Directeur des Constructions de 2ᵉ classe* in the Génie Maritime, published his *Observations on the Dimensions of the Ships of the Line and Frigates in the French Navy*, a paper that essentially defined the ship types built by the French during the Restoration and July Monarchies. After dealing at length with the larger ships he stated that the present 20-gun quarterdecked corvettes (a reference to *Victorieuse* and similar vessels) were slow and awkward to manoeuvre because their quarterdecks made them too high above the water given their relatively short length and shallow draught. He proposed renouncing quarterdecked corvettes entirely and having only open battery (flush-deck) corvettes. These would be of two types, one with the dimensions of the current quarterdecked corvettes and the other similar to Ozanne's *Diligente*. The smaller *Diligente* type was already under construction but the French had only one of the larger type, the recently raséed *Victorieuse* class ship *Espérance*. The armament assigned in the Royal Ordinance of 10 March 1824 to the larger type of flush-deck corvettes was 20 x 30pdr carronades and 4 x 18pdrs. In April 1827 Paul Leroux completed plans for a flush-deck corvette with hull dimensions similar to *Victorieuse* but with only a diminutive forecastle and poop in place of the quarterdeck. Its designed height of battery was 1.80m at 4.33m mean draught. While Tupinier's new flush-deck corvette was thus developed, his advice to abolish quarterdecked corvettes was not followed, and in 1827 Leroux also designed the enlarged quarterdecked (spardecked) corvettes of the *Ariane* class.
  Dimensions & tons: 38.22m, 38.00m wl, 35.7m x 9.70m, 9.92m ext x 5.15m. 751 tons. Draught 4.13m/4.53m. Men: 166.
  Guns: (*Créole*) 20 x 30pdr carronades, 4 x 18pdrs; (*Triomphante* as completed 1836, possibly experimental) 16 x 16cm shell, 4 x 18pdrs; (Both by c1838) 20 x 30pdr carronades, 4 x 16cm shell.
Créole Cherbourg Dyd. (Constructeur: Paul Leroux)
  Ord: 11.12.1826. K: 1.8.1827. L: 5.5.1829. Comm: 1.1.1830. C: 1.1830.

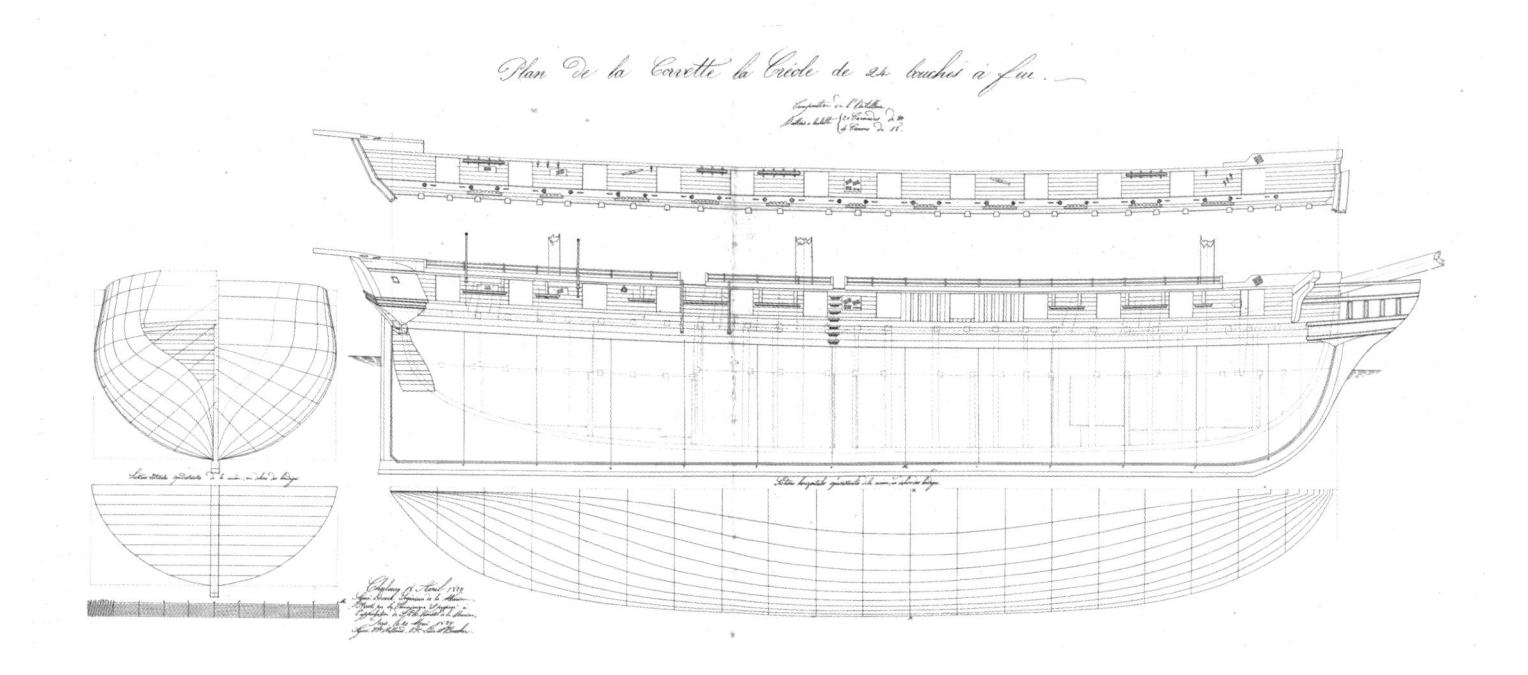

Dated Cherbourg 18 April 1827 and signed by Paul Leroux, this official lines plan of *Créole* depicts one of the new 24-gun corvettes intended to supersede the old quarterdecked type. The part elevation shows the belaying points on the inside of the bulwarks. (Atlas du Génie Maritime, Genoa collection, image 1-0012)

Struck 29.12.1845 at Brest.
Triomphante (ex *Guadeloupe* 3.8.1831) Cherbourg Dyd. (Constructeur: Jean-Baptiste François Lamaëstre)
  Ord: 16.11.1829 and named (*Guadeloupe*). K: 14.6.1830. L: 4.9.1834. Comm: 11.4.1836. C: 4.1836.
  Struck 24.5.1861, headquarters hulk at Rochefort. Renamed *Dragon* 1869. BU 1879.

FAVORITE Class – Flush-deck corvettes, 24 guns. This class was designed by Antoine-Bernard Campaignac in January 1827 using the same specifications as for *Créole* but with round instead of square sterns. *Favorite* was originally projected to be begun at Bayonne in 1827 but was reassigned to Toulon before construction began in 1827.
  Dimensions & tons: 39.00m, 38.00m wl, 34,65m x 9.70m, 9.92m ext x 5.15m. 757 tons. Draught 3.90m/4.76m. Men: 166.
  Guns: (*Favorite*) 20 x 30pdr carronades, 4 x 18pdrs; (others as commissioned) 20 x 30pdr carronades, 4 x 16cm shell.
Favorite Toulon Dyd. (Constructeurs: Campaignac and Jean-Baptiste Pironneau)
  K: 11.1827. L: 11.6.1829. Comm: 16.6.1829. C: 8.1829.
  Originally to have been built at Bayonne. Struck 2.9.1844, probably hulk at Toulon until 1853.
Brillante Toulon Dyd. (Constructeur: Campaignac)
  K: 7.1828. L: 20.8.1830. C: 1831. Comm: 22.2.1839.
  Struck 20.4.1857, turned over to the school for boys and novices at Nantes. After this school closed in 12.1859 *Brillante* became the training ship for boys at Bordeaux until at least 1874. Plans in 3.1875 to transfer her to the Maritime Academy at Arcachon fell through, the date of her scrapping is unknown.
Danaïde (ex *Île de Bourbon* 3.8.1831) Toulon Dyd.
  Ord: 16.11.1829 and named (*Île de Bourbon*). K: 9.1830. L: 13.6.1832. C: 1833. Comm: 1.1.1839.
  Struck 20.4.1857, BU before 1865.

NAÏADE – Flush-deck corvette, 24 guns. This ship was designed by Jean-Baptiste Lebas in July 1828 using the same specifications as for *Créole* and probably following Campaignac's *plan type* for *Favorite* with its round stern. In 1835 she carried her guns at 1.69m above the water at a mean draught of 4.61m.
  Dimensions & tons: 39.00m, 38.00m wl, 34.96m x 9.70m x 5.15m. 751 tons. Draught 4.12m/5.10m. Men: 166.
  Guns: 20 x 30pdr carronades, 4 x 18pdrs.
Naïade (**Nayade**) (ex *Cordelière* 3.8.1831) Lorient Dyd. (Constructeur: Lebas)
  Ord: 29.3.1828 and named (*Cordelière*). K: 13.10.1828. L: 22.5.1830. C: 11.1830. Comm: 15.11.1832.
  Condemned 7.3.1851, struck 11.3.1851, BU at Brest.

BLONDE – Flush-deck corvette, 24 guns. This ship was designed by Charles-Robert Alexandre in October 1828 using the same specifications as for *Créole* and probably following Leroux's *plan type* for *Créole* with its square stern.
  Dimensions & tons: 38.00m wl x 9.70m. 752 tons. Men: 166.
  Guns: (1839) 20 x 30pdr carronades, 4 x 16cm shell.
Blonde (ex *Jeanne Hachette* 3.8.1831) Saint-Servan. (Constructeur: Charles-Robert Alexandre)
  K: 12.10.1828. Named: 18.12.1828 (*Jeanne Hachette*). L: 12.9.1832. C: 1833. Comm: 16.3.1839.
  Wrecked 11.10.1846 in a storm at Havana, raised and returned 5.1847 to Rochefort, decomm. 15.6.1847. Repaired there 4-11.1848, then struck 11.1848 and turned over to the school for novices and boys at Bordeaux. Replaced 5.1849 by the brig *Zèbre* and BU 6-7.1849.

CAMILLE Class – Corvette-avisos, 20 guns. With this class a sequence of small ship designs came full circle. In 1824 a commission consisting of Mathurin Boucher, Pierre Lair, and Pierre Rolland had based the hull plans of the new *Cygne* class brigs on the corvette-aviso *Diligente*. In

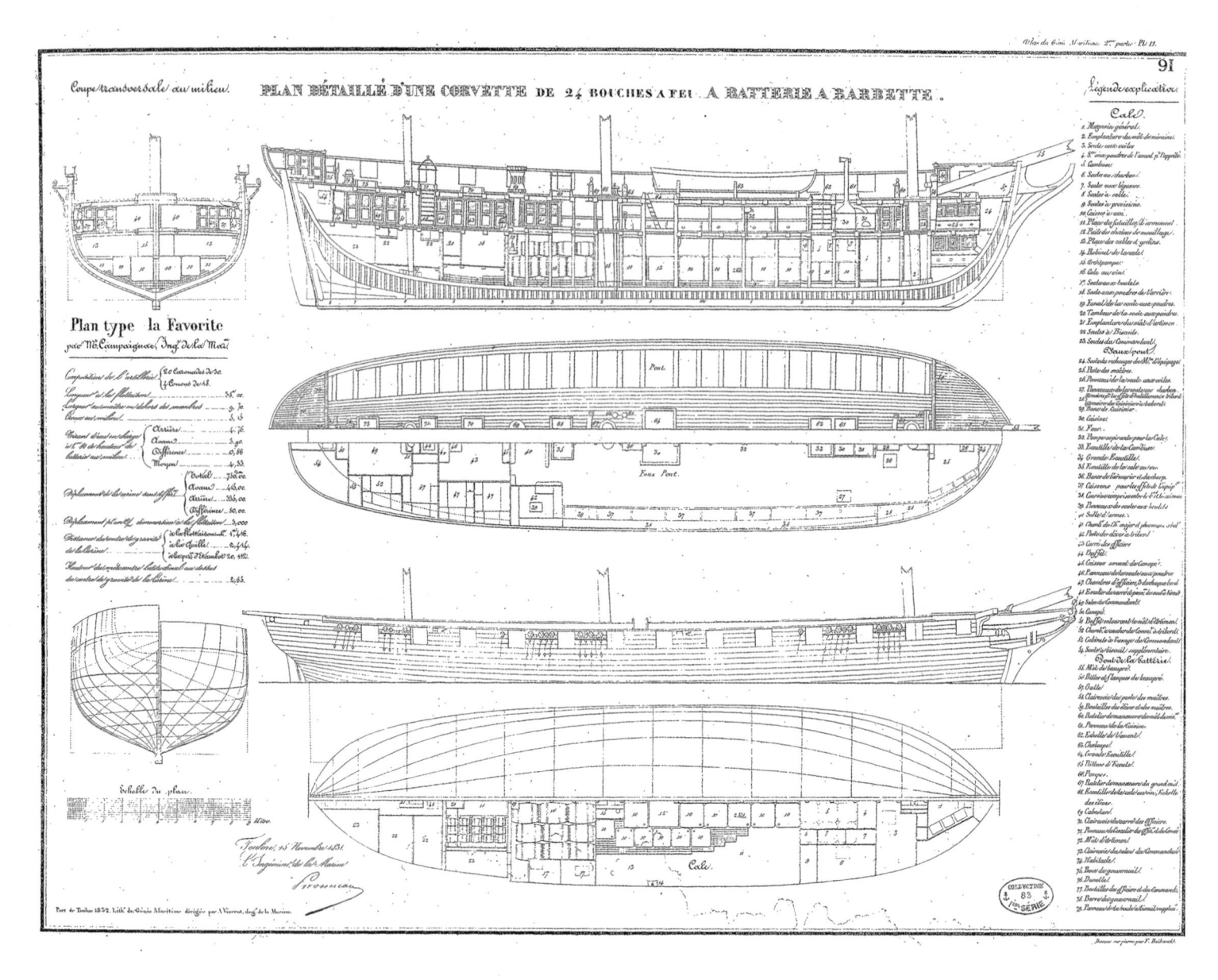

Internal arrangements of the *Favorite* by Antoine-Bernard Campaignac, a competitive 24-gun design to Paul Leroux's *Créole*; plan dated Toulon 15 November 1831. Slightly longer and narrower than Leroux's design, this ship has more space at the ends of the battery, and even contrives an extra chase port forward. (Atlas du Génie Maritime, French collection, plate 91)

October 1828 the navy laid down the first of a new class of corvette-avisos which were exact copies of the brig *Cygne* except that they had three masts. The apparent reason for the change was to upgrade the armament of corvette-avisos from 18pdr to 24pdr carronades. The second ship was laid down in July 1832 and the third was ordered in December 1833. Each ship had a small forecastle and poop but was otherwise flush-decked. On 17 May 1837 the Ministry of Marine informed the ports that because these ships carried 20 guns their previous classification as corvette-avisos had been in error and that they would henceforth be called flush-decked corvettes (*corvettes de guerre sans gaillards*).

Dimensions & tons: 34.42m, 33.60m wl, 30.20m x 9.00m x 4.69m. 548 tons. Draught 4.23m mean. Men: 110.

Guns: 18 x 24pdr carronades, 2 x 16cm shell.

Camille Bayonne (Constructeur: Gabriel Nosereau)
 K: 14.10.1828. L: 18.8.1830. C: 6.1831?. Comm: 7.9.1837.
 Struck 1.4.1851 at Rochefort and probably BU soon afterwards.

Bergère Toulon Dyd.
 K: 7.1832. L: 30.12.1833. Comm: 23.6.1836. C: 6.1836
 Struck 20.4.1857 at Toulon, BU before 1865.

Coquette Saint-Servan (Constructeurs: Joseph-Anne Daviel and Georges Allix)
 Ord: 1.12.1833. K: 1834. L: 22.6.1838. Comm: 15.8.1838. C: 8.1838.
 Struck 6.9.1852 at Brest, condemned 20.9.1852, probably BU 1853.

ARIANE Class – Spardecked corvettes, 32 guns. The advice of Jean-Marguerite Tupinier in his 1822 *Observations on the dimensions of the Ships of the Line and Frigates in the French Navy* to renounce quarterdecked corvettes was not followed. The Royal Ordinance of 10 March 1824 assigned to quarterdecked corvettes an armament of 20 x 30pdr carronades and 4 x 18pdrs in the battery and 8 x 30pdr carronades on the gaillards. In 1827 Paul Leroux designed the *Ariane* type to carry this armament. She was a new type of quarterdecked or spardecked corvette that was in essence a miniature frigate with a main armament of carronades. During construction a round stern was substituted for the

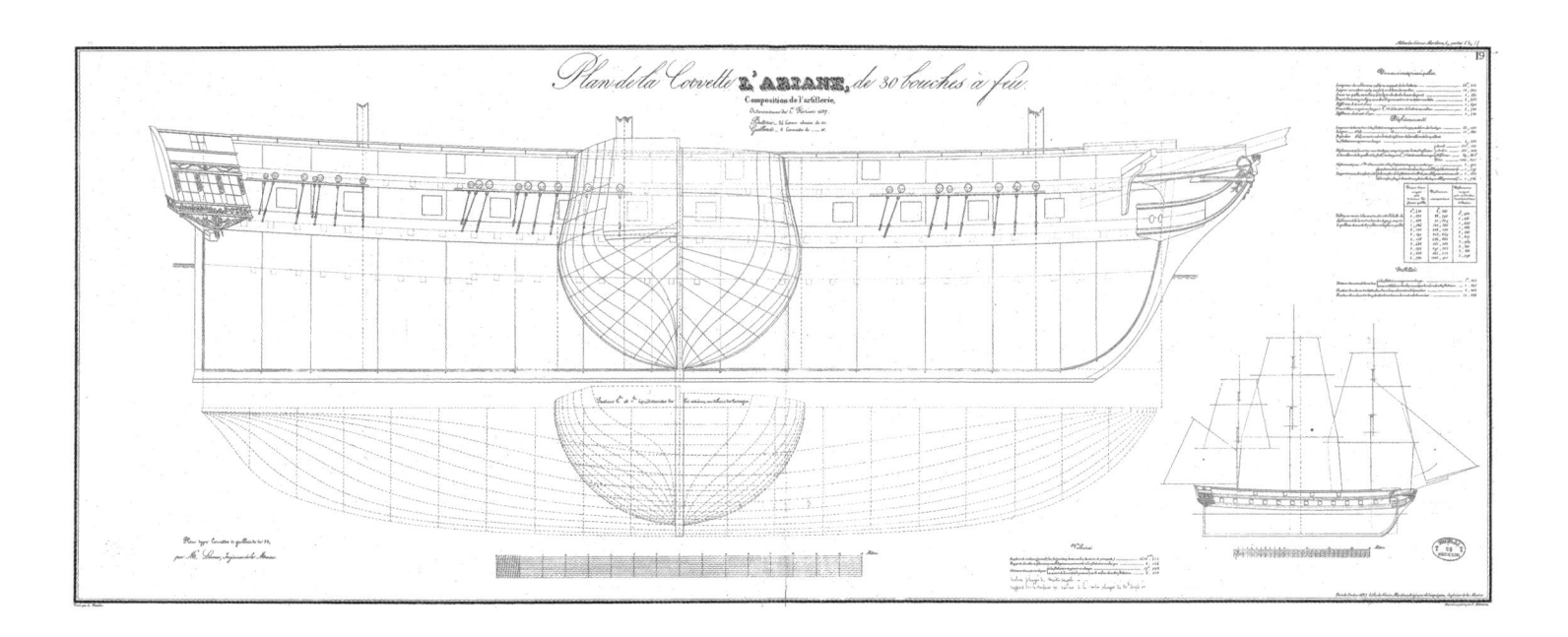

The quarterdecked corvette had been much criticised for poor sailing qualities, mainly due to the windage of the extra topside height, and after 1815 there was pressure to give up the type altogether. However, it staged a comeback in a new spardecked form with the 32-gun *Ariane* class in the late 1820s, as shown in this official plan engraved in 1837. As with larger rates of the period, the quarterdeck and forecastle were joined to form a continuous spardeck, but unlike frigates and ships of the line, in the corvettes the armament on this deck was spaced out in the middle section of the ship. The sail plan shows a total area of 1,455 sq.m. (Atlas du Génie Maritime, French collection, plate 19)

original square stern and, as in the other large vessels of the post-Napoleonic navy, the forecastle and quarterdeck were joined to form a complete spardeck. This spardeck, although fully exposed, allowed the guns at this level to be moved towards the middle portion of the ship. The type was probably designed for a height of battery of 1.80m at 4.73m mean draught but in 1842 *Sabine* managed only 1.62m at 4.97m mean draught. On 18 June 1834 *Sapho* was ordered completed with UD 20 x 30pdr carronades and 4 x 18pdrs in the battery and 6 x 18pdr carronades on the spardeck. In 1835 the armament for new spardecked corvettes was changed to 24 x 16cm shell guns and 6 x 18pdr carronades, and *Boussole* and *Embuscade* were completed in 1840 with this armament. The navy soon decided to retrofit this armament to ships already afloat, which was easy because the new artillery would fit in the existing gunports. The spardeck armament of 6 x 18pdr carronades was suppressed for this type in 1844. *Sapho* was originally projected to be begun at Toulon in 1827 but was reassigned to Saint-Servan before construction began in 1827.

Dimensions & tons: 42.28m, 42.00m wl, 39.40m x 10.70m, 10.96m ext x 5.55m. 1,015 tons. Draught 4.50m/4.73m/4.96m. Men: 229.

Guns: UD 20 x 30pdr carronades, 4 x 12pdrs or 18pdrs; SD 8 x 30pdr carronades.

Ariane Cherbourg Dyd. (Constructeur: Paul Leroux)
   Ord: 11.12.1826. K: 1.8.1827. L: 22.5.1830. C: 1831. Comm: 20.6.1832.
   Condemned 21.11.1850, struck 23.11.1850, coal hulk at Brest. Sold and BU 1866.
Sapho Saint-Servan.
   K: 25.7.1828. L: 23.8.1831. Comm: 14.4.1834. C: 4.1834.
   Construction planned for Toulon in 1826. Struck 18.12.1843 at Brest.
Boussole Cherbourg Dyd. (Constructeur: Jean-Baptiste Lamaëstre)
   Ord: 16.11.1829 and named. K: 26.8.1830. L: 21.5.1833. C: 1834. Comm: 9.5.1840.
   Wrecked 3.3.1848 on Little Curaçao Island.
Alcmène (ex *Martinique* 3.8.1831) Saint-Servan. (Constructeur: Charles-Robert Alexandre)
   Ord: 16.11.1829 and named (*Martinique*). K: 12.1.1830. L: 20.9.1834. C: 1835. Comm: 1.9.1837.
   Wrecked 3.6.1851 during a cyclone at Mocatua on the northwest coast of New Zealand.
Sabine Saint-Servan (Constructeur: Charles-Robert Alexandre)
   Ord: 28.12.1830. Named: 22.6.1831. K: 29.8.1831. L: 20.9.1834. C: 1835. Comm: 16.10.1837.
   Struck 16.10.1849, hulk at Rochefort. BU there 5-7.1854.
Embuscade Saint-Servan (Constructeurs: Charles-Robert Alexandre and Pierre Daniel)
   Ord: 24.8.1831 and named. K: 1.9.1832. L: 20.5.1837. C: 1837. Comm: 11.8.1840.
   Struck 21.2.1861, guard station (*corps de garde*) and floating barracks at Cherbourg. Renamed *Émulation* c1862. BU 1883.

HÉROÏNE – Spardecked corvette, 32 guns. Jean-Baptiste Perroy designed this ship in 1827 using the same specifications as for *Ariane* and probably following Leroux's *plan type* for that ship. She was probably ordered with *Ariane* on 11 December 1826 and was the first ship of this *plan-type* to be completed. Her designed height of battery was 1.80m at 4.73m mean draught but in 1835 she carried her guns at only 1.65m above the water at 4.98m mean draught. The spardeck artillery was suppressed in this type in 1844.

Dimensions & tons: 42,28m, 42.00m wl, 39.40m x 10.70m x 5.55m. 1,015 tons. Draught 4.81m/5.15m. Men: 229.

Guns: (1835) UD 20 x 30pdr carronades, 4 x 12pdrs; SD 8 x 30pdr carronades.

Héroïne Brest Dyd. (Constructeurs: Antoine Geoffroy and Jean-Baptiste Perroy)
   K: 21.11.1827. L: 8.5.1830. Comm: 1.7.1830. C: 7.1830.
   Condemned 28.12.1850, struck 30.12.1850, guard station (*corps de garde*) at Brest to 1866. Renamed *Plougastel* 1861, BU 1867.

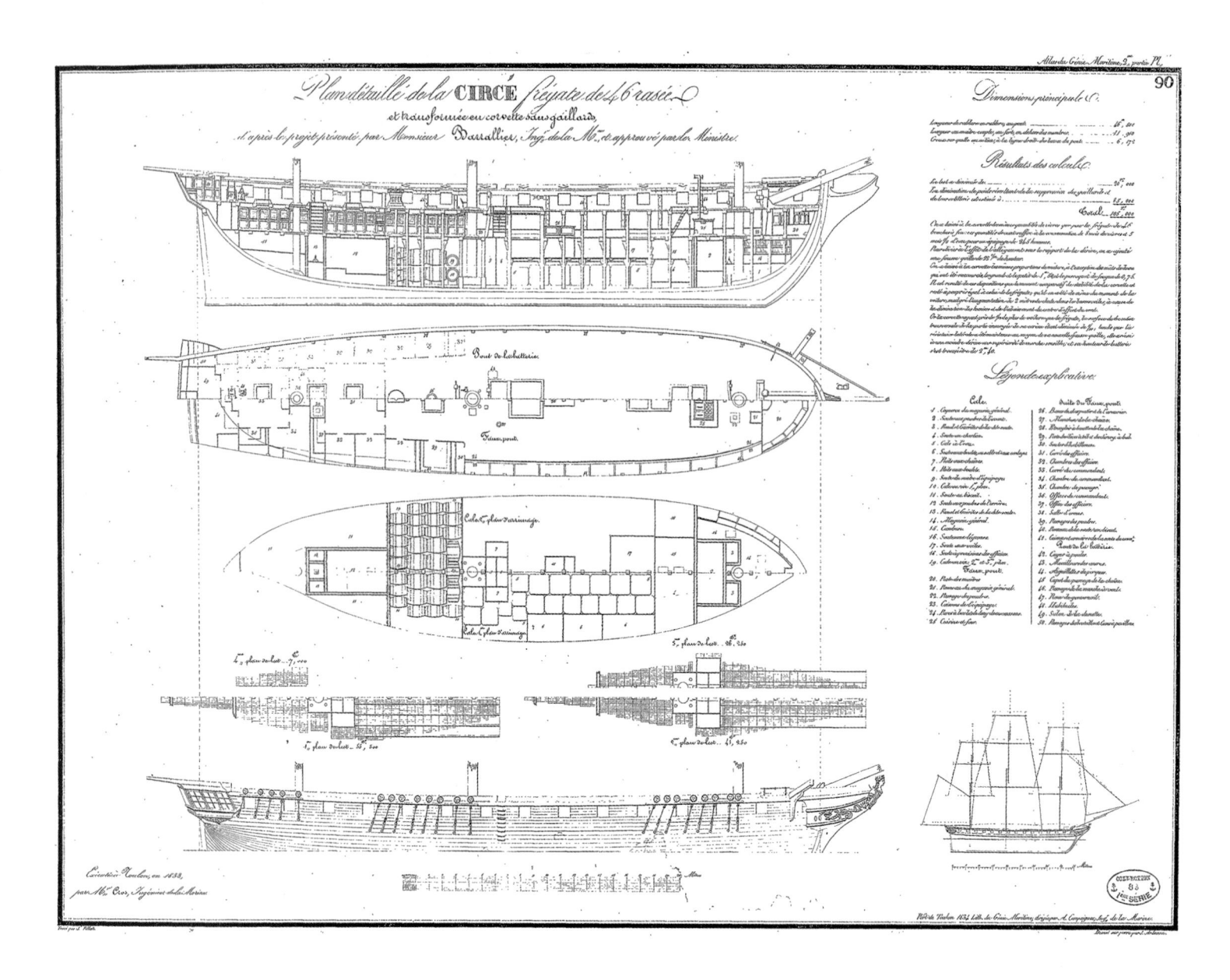

THISBÉ – Spardecked corvette, 32 guns. Jean-François Guillemard completed plans for this ship in May 1828 using the same specifications as for *Ariane* and probably following Leroux's *plan type* for that ship. She served only one period in commission, from 1 July 1832 to 26 February 1840.

   Dimensions & tons: 42.00m wl, 41.60m x 10.70m. 1,015 tons. Men: 229.
   Guns: GD 20 x 30pdr carronades, 4 x 18pdrs; SD 8 x 30pdr carronades.

Thisbé Rochefort Dyd. (Constructeurs: Guillemard and from 6.1830 by Alphonse Levesque)
   K: 6.1828. L: 21.6.1830. C: 6.1832. Comm: 1.7.1832.
   Struck 17.8.1842 at Brest, mooring hulk at Lorient. BU 1865.

CORNALINE Class – Spardecked corvettes, 32 guns. This class, designed by Jean-François Chaumont following Leroux's *plan type* for *Ariane*, incorporated a 1 metre increase in waterline length and a 10cm increase in depth of hull compared to *Ariane*. This modification was approved on 2 February 1833 because changes to the *Ariane* type during construction, notably the round stern and the joining of the gaillards by a spardeck over the waist, had increased its weight and reduced the height of its battery above the waterline. Chaumont's plans were approved on 18 August 1833.

   Dimensions & tons: 43.00m wl x 10.70m x 5.70m. 1,057 tons. Draught 4.83m mean. Men: 229.
   Guns: (*Berceau*) UD 20 x 30pdr carronades, 4 x 12pdrs; SD 8 x 30pdr carronades; (*Cornaline* as comm. 1839) UD 24 x 16cm shell; SD 6 x 18pdr carronades.

Cornaline Lorient Dyd. (Constructeurs: Jean-Michel Segondat, then Jean-François Chaumont and others)
   K: 26.9.1833. L: 29.11.1834. C: 1835. Comm: 9.3.1839.
   Condemned 13.10.1843, struck 22.4.1844, designated service craft

Just as ships of the line could be cut down by a deck to turn them into powerful frigates, so frigates could have their quarterdeck and forecastles removed to make them corvettes. This was usually driven by an escalation in the calibre of gun regarded as the norm for each class, so as frigates acquired guns of battleship size, corvettes began to carry frigate-type main batteries. The official plan of *Circé* shows the layout of a 46-gun frigate as cut down to a flush-decked corvette in 1833 but retaining her original 18pdr main armament. (Atlas du Génie Maritime, French collection, plate 90)

Official lines plan of *Iguala* dated 25 June 1840. This captured Mexican corvette was built in the United States, as evidenced by the sharp hull lines and exaggerated drag aft of the so-called Baltimore schooner style. The lines were taken off at Brest in April 1840 because there was a French Navy interest in copying the hull form for similar ships. (Atlas du Génie Maritime, French collection, plate 38)

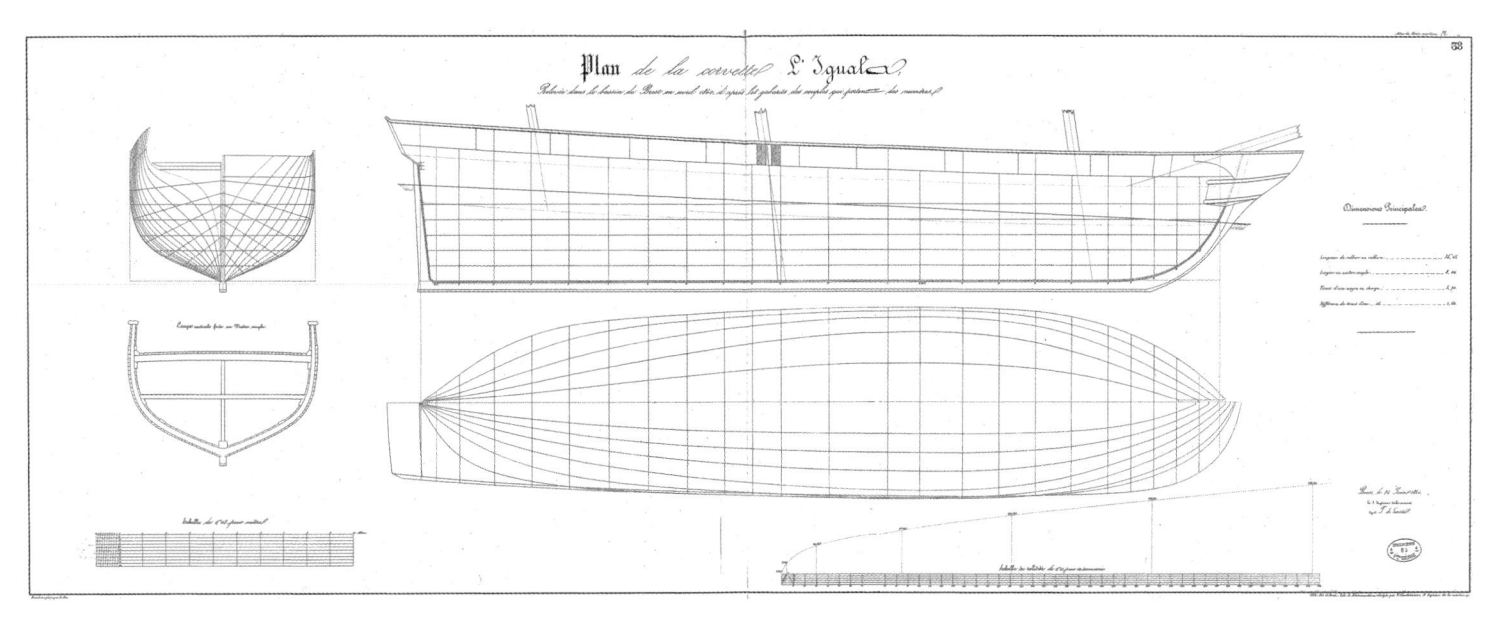

27.4.1844 as hulk at Brest. Ordered moved to Cherbourg 1849, used there from 10.1849 to 11.1869 as a headquarters and storage hulk. BU 1869-70.

Berceau Lorient Dyd. (Constructeurs: Jean-Michel Segondat, then Jean-François Chaumont and others)
  Ord: 8.12.1832 and named. K: 9.8.1833. L: 16.10.1834. C: 1835. Comm: 11.9.1840.
  Lost 13.12.1846 with all hands while leaving the harbour of St. Denis, Réunion, in a cyclone.

RASÉED FRIGATES – Flush-deck corvettes, 28 guns. On 13 August 1831 the Minister of Marine approved a proposal from Toulon to rasée two 3rd Rank frigates to flush-deck corvettes. Plans by Louis Barrallier were approved in 10.1831, and conversion of a third ship at Brest on the same plans was approved on 17 March 1832. The captain of *Circé* noted c1840 that the high speed of the ship would do an enemy much harm, but he did not recommend additional conversions because of difficulty accommodating the crew. In 1841 *Aréthuse* carried her guns at an ample 2.15m above the water at 5.38m mean draught.
  Dimensions & tons: 47.00m, 46.50m wl x 11.92m x 6.17m. ? tons. Draught 5.04m/5.38m/5.72m. Men: ?.
  Guns: (*Circé*) 28 x 18pdrs; (*Cybèle*) 24 x 18pdrs, 4-16cm shell; (*Aréthuse*, 1841) 22 x 30pdrs No.2 (28 ports).

Circé Toulon Dyd.
  Ord: 13.8.1831. K: 11.1831. L: 1833. Comm: 1.2.1833.
  Struck 26.4.1844, BU 1844 at Brest.

Cybèle Toulon Dyd. (converted by Louis Barrallier)
  Ord: 13.8.1831. K: 1833 (hauled out 4.4.1835). L: 26.1.1836. C: 2.1836. Housed over after launch and not commissioned.
  Ordered 31.7.1848 to be converted into a floating battery for the defence of Algeria, but found to be in bad shape and condemned and struck on 4.3.1850 at Toulon. Renamed *Remise* 1850 as a hulk, initially as a guard hulk, then as a careening hulk (*ponton-fosse*). Was a mooring hulk at Toulon in 1893, BU 1894.

Aréthuse Brest Dyd.
  Ord: 17.3.1832. K: 1.1833. L: (unknown). C: 1834. Comm: 11.5.1841.
  Struck 11.6.1851, coal hulk at Brest. Unserviceable 1865 and BU.

Ex MEXICAN PRIZE (1838). 16-gun corvette-aviso. *Iguala*, a three-masted ship, was launched in 1836 in Baltimore for the Mexican government. Her lines resembled the French schooner-brigs of the *Gazelle* class, which were also based on American designs. She was captured with most of the Mexican Navy on 28 November 1838 at Vera Cruz. A letter of 13 December 1841 proposed building ships like her and Boucher recommended building one. *Iguala* measured 33.50m x 8.00m compared to 33.76m wl x 8.45m for the corvette-aviso type and her lines were much like those of the 10-gun brigs. Her lines were taken off in April 1840 and were reported in the *Atlas du Memorial du Genie Maritime* as 34.15m x 8.00 x 3.70 draught. The sailing report (*devis*) for her recommissioning on 11.8.1840 gives 34.11m wl x 8.01m, while her 1839 *devis* gives 38.50m x 8.00m (the length being either overall or in error) with an armament of 16 x 16pdrs (possibly British or American 18pdrs used by the Mexicans).
  Dimensions & tons: 34.11m, 33.50m wl, 31.09 x 8.01m x 4.26m. 454 tons. Draught 2.87m/4.41m. Men: ?.
  Guns: (as recommissioned 8.1840) 14 x 18pdr carronades, 2 x 12pdrs.

Iguala (Mexican naval corvette *Iguala*)
  Captured 28.11.1838 at Vera Cruz, comm. there 20.3.1839.
  Decomm. at Brest 1.3.1843, struck 24.7.1843, and BU 1843.

BAYONNAISE Class – Spardecked corvettes, 30 guns. Plans for three new spardecked corvettes (*Bayonnaise*, *Galatée*, and *Artémise*) were requested from the ports on 31 August 1843 with the beam increased to permit carrying the armament assigned to the type in 1835 and 1838: 24 x 16cm on the gun deck and 6 x 18pdr carronades on the gaillards (joined, as in the *Ariane* type, by a spardeck over the waist). Plans by Paul Picot de Moras for *Bayonnaise* were approved on 6 June 1844. On 21 March 1846 the Council of Works discussed a proposal to give this type an armament of heavier guns to match foreign corvettes such as HMS *Carysfort* observed on foreign stations. During this discussion construction of two more ships, *Constantine* and *Eurydice*, was ordered on 28 April 1846, and to save time, the 1843 plans were reused for them as their gunports could be arranged to carry either the current or the proposed armament. On 7 May 1846 the Council of Admiralty decided that the 1843 ships should carry 22 x 16cm shell and 2 x 22cm No.2

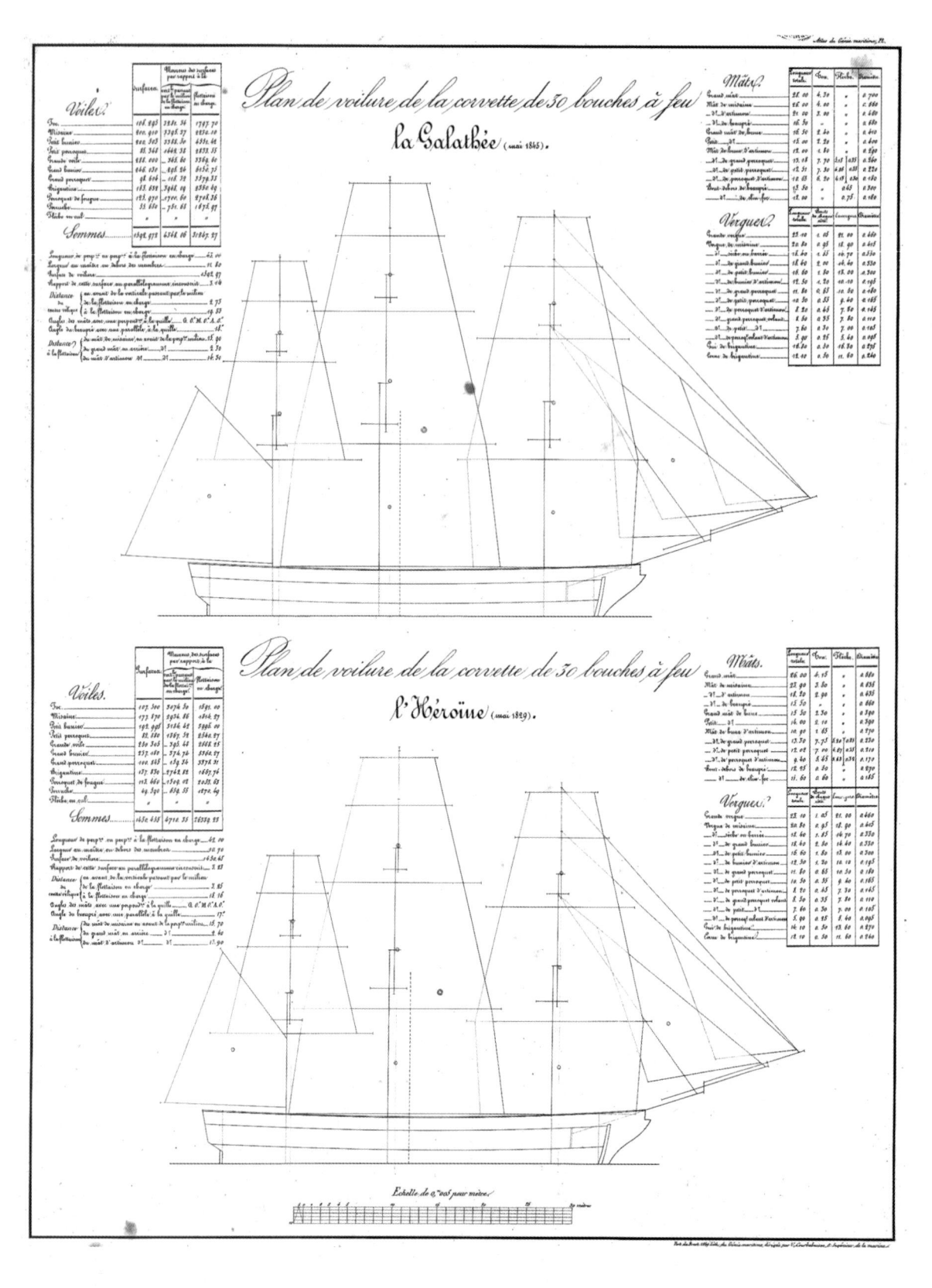

Comparative sail plans for the spardecked corvette *Galathée* (as designed, May 1845) and the earlier *Héroïne* (as designed, May 1829) of the same type. The tables contain the dimensions of all the spars shown on the plans, but the calculated sail areas – 1,593 and 1,450 sq.m. respectively – omit the royals and include only a single headsail, which seems to have been the conventional basis for determining the sail area of French warships at this time. (Atlas du Génie Maritime, Genoa collection, image 1-0042)

shell in the battery with 4 x 16cm shell on the gaillards while the two 1846 ships should carry 20 x 30pdrs No.3 and 2 x 22cm No.3 shell (both proposed new model guns) in the battery with 4 x 16cm shell on the gaillards if the new guns proved successful. As completed, the ships had slightly different armaments, some of which are shown in their listings.

Dimensions & tons: 43.90m, 43.00m wl x 11.80m x 5.85m. 1,117 tons. Draught 4.95m mean. Men: 229.
Guns: (*Bayonnaise* 1847) UD 18 x 16cm shell, 2 x 22cm shell, 2 x 30pdrs No.2; SD 6 x 16cm shell.
Bayonnaise Cherbourg Dyd. (Constructeur: Picot de Moras)
K: 31.7.1844. L: 7.9.1846. Comm: 1.2.1847. C: 2.1847.

Struck 15.11.1869, headquarters hulk at Cherbourg. Ordered BU 1.1877 but instead used as target in torpedo trials. Damaged 2.2.1877, torpedoed and sunk 3.3.1877 by two torpedo boats.

Capricieuse Toulon Dyd.
K: 10.1847. L: 5.7.1849. Comm: 1.9.1849. C: 9.1849.
Guns as completed (c1849) UD 22 x 16cm shell, 2 x 30pdrs No.1; SD 2 x 30pdrs No.1. Later the two 30pdrs on deck traded positions with two of the 16cm guns in the battery.
Condemned and struck 18.3.1865 at Toulon. BU 1868.

ARTÉMISE Class – Spardecked corvettes, 30 guns. These ships were designed by Jean-Baptiste Larchevesque-Thibaut using the same specifications as for *Bayonnaise*. The plans were requested from the ports on 31 August 1843 and approved on 10 June 1844. On 7 March 1847 *Thisbé* was ordered built to the plans of *Artémise*.
Dimensions & tons: 45.17m, 43.00m wl, 40.37m x 11.80m, 12.06m ext x 5.88m. 1,134 tons. Draught 4.81m mean. Men: 254.
Guns: (*Thisbé* 1849) UD 22 x 16cm shell, 2 x 22cm shell; SD 6 x 18pdr carronades.

Artémise (*Arthémise*) Lorient Dyd. (Constructeur: Larchevesque-Thibaut)
K: 21.8.1844. L: 19.11.1846. C: 3.1847. Comm: 5.4.1847.
Condemned and struck 7.12.1868 at Cherbourg. BU 1868.

Thisbé Lorient Dyd. (Constructeurs: Hippolyte Prétot and Camille Audenet)
K: 24.3.1847. L: 9.1.1849. Comm: 6.3.1849. C: 3.1849.
Refitted as a hospital and floating storage at Lorient 7-9.1864 and sent to Gabon. Struck 17.8.1869 at Gabon, out of service 7.1870 and BU 1871.

GALATÉE Class – Spardecked corvettes, 30 guns. These ships were designed by Antoine Roger using the same specifications as for *Bayonnaise*. The plans were requested from the ports on 31 August 1843 and approved on 9 February 1844. On 11 August 1846 *Eurydice* was ordered built to the plans of *Galatée*. Upon completion *Galatée* carried her guns at 1.91m above the water at 5.02m mean draught, a substantial improvement over the older *Ariane* class although less than the probably intended 2.10m.
Dimensions & tons: 44.25m, 43.00m wl, 40.20m x 11.80m, 12.06m ext x 5.80m. 1,179 tons. Draught 4.78m/5.02m/5.26m. Men: 254.
Guns: (*Galatée* 1846) UD 22 x 16cm shell, 2 x 22cm No.2 shell; SD 4 x 16cm shell.

Galatée (*Galathée*) Brest Dyd. (Constructeurs: Antoine Roger and Alexandre Chedeville)
K: 16.2.1844. L: 27.12.1845. C: 7.1846. Comm: 12.9.1846.
School for apprentice seamen at Brest 1865. Struck 17.8.1869, school hulk and annex to the training hulk *Borda* 1870-77, annex to *Bretagne* 1878-92. To the Domaines 17.10.1893 for sale.

Sérieuse Brest Dyd. (Constructeurs: Paul Leroux and others)
K: 24.3.1847. L: 12.8.1848. C: 1.1849. Comm: 12.3.1849.
Guns as completed (c1849) UD 22 x 16cm shell, 2 x 30pdrs No.1; SD 2 x 30pdrs No.2.
Condemned and struck 15.2.1872 after conversion between 7.1870 and 2.1872 into a disciplinary barracks hulk (*ponton-caserne des disciplinaires*) at Cherbourg. Served as such until 1881, BU 1889.

Eurydice Cherbourg Dyd. (Constructeurs: Édouard Nouet, Eugène Antoine, and Louis-Alexandre Corrard)
Ord: 14.10.1845 and named. K: 26.9.1846. L: 23.5.1849. Comm: 10.9.1849. C: 9.1849.
Converted to a 600-ton transport between 11.1862 and 8.1863 at Toulon. Fitted as hospital hulk 7-8.1876 at Brest and sent to Libreville, Gabon, 9.1876. Struck there 3.5.1877, mentioned for the last time in 1879 as a hospital warehouse at Libreville.

CONSTANTINE – Spardecked corvette, 30 guns. Initially it was proposed to build four covered battery corvettes in 1846, but the number of these ships in the new fleet plan was reduced from 30 to 20 and the number to be built was reduced to two. Plans for one of these ships, *Constantine*, were prepared by Armand Forquenot and approved on 27 July 1846. The other 1846 ship (*Eurydice*) and three begun in 1847 were built to existing designs. The intended armament of *Constantine* in late 1852 was UD 14 x 30pdrs No.3, 2 x 30pdrs No.2, 2 x 22cm shell No.2; SD 2 x 30pdrs No.1 or No.2.
Dimensions & tons: 45.74m, 44.00m wl, 41.2m x 11.50m x 6.09m. 1,142 tons. Draught 5.00m mean. Men: 254.
Guns: (5.1.1853) UD 18 x 16cm shell, 2 x 30pdrs No.1; SD 2 x 30pdrs No.3.

Constantine Rochefort Dyd. (Constructeurs: Alfred Lebelin de Dionne, Henri De Lislefeme, and Henri Denis de Senneville)
K: 17.8.1846. L: 10.10.1851. C: 9.1852. Comm: 1.12.1852.
Converted to headquarters ship for the reserves at Rochefort 2-12.1862 and served as such until 1894. Struck as a corvette 25.4.1867 and became a service craft. BU 1894.

Two corvette-avisos (2nd Class corvettes), *Écho* and *Aigrette*, were projected in the 1848 budget (presented in January 1847) to be begun in 1848 under contract, and they were listed again in the 1849 budget (presented in December 1847) to be begun in 1849. They were cancelled in 1848 before being ordered and before contractors were selected, construction of ships of the line and frigates having being given priority. The *Diligente* type was then in favour and these would probably have been similar to it.

AVENTURE Class – Spardecked corvettes, 30 guns. This class, consisting of ships begun in 1849 and 1850, was designed by Antoine Roger and was similar to his earlier *Galatée*. *Aventure*, *Cornélie*, and *Favorite* were originally projected to be begun respectively at Cherbourg, Brest, and Toulon in 1849 but were reassigned respectively to Brest, Toulon, and Rochefort before construction began in 1849. Likewise, *Cordelière* was originally projected to be begun at Toulon in 1850 but was reassigned to Lorient before construction began in 1850. Another ship, *Jeanne Hachette,* was projected in 1849 to be begun in 1850 with *Cordelière* but was deferred several times and finally cancelled around 1853.
Dimensions & tons: 43.00m wl, 40.2m x 11.80m, 12.00m ext x 5.80m. 1,192 tons. Draught 4.60m/5.24m. Men: 229.
Guns: (*Cornélie* and *Cordelière*) UD 16 x 16cm shell, 4 x 22cm No.2 shell; SD 2 x 30pdrs No.1.

Aventure Brest Dyd. (Constructeur: Louis-Auguste Silvestre du Perron)
K: 2.5.1849. L: 27.11.1852. Comm: 11.3.1854. C: 3.1854.
Lost 28.4.1855 on the reefs of the Île des Pins, New Caledonia.

Cornélie Toulon Dyd. (Constructeurs: Paul Picot de Moras and Jules Aurous)
K: 9.1849. L: 6.11.1858. Comm: 1.9.1860. C: 9.1860.
Fitted at Toulon as a station hulk and struck 17.8.1869. Boys training ship at Algiers 1869 to 1873. Refitted at Toulon 10.1873 to 1874 and reactivated as a seamen's training corvette at Brest. Struck again 9.5.1879 and became headquarters hulk and headquarters for the reserves at Rochefort. Barracks hulk and annex to *Embuscade* 1901-5, headquarters hulk for a torpedo boat flotilla 1906-7, and guard station (*corps de garde*) 1908-9. BU

1909.

Cordelière Lorient Dyd-Caudan.
- K: 26.4.1850. L: 12.6.1858. Comm: 5.7.1858. C: 7.1858.
- Reassigned from Toulon to Lorient c1850. Struck 10.3.1870 from the list of combatant ships and fitted as a station and storage hulk for Gabon. Reclassified as a service craft 1874, out of service at Gabon 10.1876 and probably BU there.

Favorite Rochefort Dyd. (Constructeurs: Henri Denis de Senneville, Auguste Boden, Bernard Chariot, and many others to Roger's plans updated by Nathaniel Lucien Villaret).
- K: 30.7.1849. L: 14.5.1870. Comm: 14.10.1878. C: 10.1878.
- Guns as completed (1878) UD 8 x 14cm No.1 MLR.
- While under construction was reclassified as a 600-ton transport 1.1864, as a corvette transport 1.1873, and back to a corvette 1.1879. Refitted as a training corvette at Brest 1-2.1887. Condemned and struck 10.2.1892, BU 1893.

Jeanne Hachette Toulon Dyd
- Projected in 1849 to be begun in 1850 but deferred, then cancelled c1853.

CONVERTED TRANSPORTS – 24 guns.

In 1845 a decision to contract out most of the navy's cargo-carrying operations left the navy with some surplus transports. The following 800-ton burthen transports (formerly called flûtes, then corvettes de charge) were reclassified as 24-gun quarterdecked corvettes: *Somme* (1840-51), *Rhin* (1841-54), *Meurthe* (1842-53), *Seine* (1845-46), and *Durance* (1847-54). All reverted to transport status between 1849-51 except for *Seine*, wrecked in New Caledonia in 1846. The following 380-ton transports (formerly gabarres-écuries) were reclassified as 14-gun flush-deck corvettes: *Émulation* (1811-45), *Lamproie* (1812-50), *Astrolabe* (1811-52), *Zélée* (1812-63), *Prévoyante* (1834-60), *Expéditive* (1834-66), *Recherche* (1834-63), *Indienne* (1835-56), *Sarcelle* (1838-57), *Prudente* (1842-55), and *Infatigable* (1843-62). *Zélée* received a steam engine in 1853 (see steam transports). Four of these former gabarres reverted to transport status between 1851-54. A few transports such as *Uranie* (ex *Ciotat*, 467 tons burthen, 1811-20) and *Astrolabe* (ex *Coquette*) had previously been called corvettes temporarily while in use for scientific expeditions.

PURCHASED VESSEL (1820)

Physicienne (three-masted American whaling ship *Mercury* pierced with 16 gunports, originally a merchant corvette or privateer launched at Venice in 1807, hired in 3.1820 by the captain of the exploration corvette *Uranie* following the loss of his ship in the Falkland Islands to carry his crew from the Falklands to Montevideo. At Montevideo he purchased the ship in 5.1820 for 18,000 Spanish piasters, placed her in commission on 9.5.1820, and renamed her).
- Dimensions (French feet) & tons: 80ft x 26ft 3.3in x 16ft (26.0 x 8.54 x 5.2m). 280 to 327t burthen, 550 tons. Men: ?.
- Guns: 6
- After repairs at Rio de Janeiro *Physicienne* returned to Cherbourg on 10.11.1820 and was decomm. 6.12.1820. Her sale was approved on 13.2.1821, and she was sold at Brest on 27.2.1821 to MM V^e. Lefèvre, Roussac, Labarraque & Cie. for mercantile use. In 11.1826 she was in merchant service between Le Havre and Brazil.

Ex PRIVATEER PRIZE (1821)

Gloriole (privateer *El Valiente Guaicurum*, an old three-masted vessel flying the flag of the Uruguayan patriot Artigas who however had ceased operations in September 1820. Captured 24.3.1821 by the frigate *Africaine* near the Ile de St. Barthelemy in the Caribbean. Judged to be a pirate ship and a legitimate prize by a court at Martinique 14.4.1821 and offered to the King by the crews of the Division of the Antilles. Commissioned at Martinique on 25.4.1821 and refitted there 5-8.1821).
- Dimensions (French feet) & tons: 101ft, 94ft (wl?) x 20ft 6in, 22ft x 10ft 6in (32.80, 30.53 x 6.66, 7.15 x 3.41m). 400 tons. Men: ?.
- Guns: 16 x 4pdrs
- After her return to Brest on 12.9.1821 she was hauled out for repairs but was found to be in bad condition. Her refit was suspended on 23.11.1821, the ship was condemned, and BU at Brest was approved on 22.1.1822.

(E) Screw corvettes

France's first screw corvettes were either experimental vessels, intended for comparison with paddle equivalents, or vessels built for special purposes. Thus *Chaptal*, *Caton*, and *Roland* evolved out of the paddle corvette building program while *Comte d'Eu* was developed as a yacht for the King and *Biche* and *Sentinelle* were designed as auxiliary screw versions of the sailing corvette *Diligente* for use in the anti-slavery patrol on the west coast of Africa. (These two ships were much more appropriately described by their final classification as 2nd Class screw avisos.) The French screw corvette took its definitive form with the open battery *Phlégéton* class of 1850, which in 1855 was adopted as the standard for future French screw corvettes (later 2nd Class cruisers) beginning with the four ships of the *Dupleix* type. The covered battery type represented by *D'Assas* and *Du Chayla* was rejected in this decision, while the two ships of the *Vénus* class, initially designed as cruising frigates for overseas stations, are best seen as successors of the 3rd Rank screw frigates, one of which, *Armorique*, was also classified as a corvette between 1862 and 1872.

CHAPTAL. 2nd Class corvette. iron hull. *Chaptal* appeared in the building program in late 1838 as a 160nhp paddle steamer to be built at Indret, became a 450nhp ship at Rochefort during 1839, and then became a 220nhp ship at Lorient in 1840, when she was one of three 220nhp paddle corvettes scheduled to be begun in 1842. Two of these were built as wooden-hulled paddle steamers in which conventional side-lever engines in *Cassini* were compared with the new type of oscillating-cylinder direct-acting engines in *Titan*. To extend the experiment, the Minister of Marine on 2 April 1842 ordered that *Chaptal* be built exactly as *Titan* but with an iron hull and a screw propeller. Mathurin Boucher's plans for the iron hull were approved on 2 July 1842, an engine identical to that in *Titan* was ordered from François Cavé by a contract approved on 8 September 1842, and the hull was ordered from Cavé by a contract approved on 13 February 1843. The expectation was that the paddle engine could be connected to a screw through gearing, but before ordering the propeller and gearing the navy sponsored experiments with various forms of screw propulsion which Cavé carried out on the Seine between February and December 1843 in his own steamer *Oise*. Cavé concluded that direct drive and a different machinery layout were preferable, and new engines were ordered from him by a contract approved on 25 October 1844. (The original engines were used in *Newton*.) He also found it necessary to depart from *Titan*'s hull plans and lengthen the stern 1.40m to provide finer lines for the screw. (The hull retained the slab sides of a paddle steamer, however.) The ship was to have had only two masts, but she was completed with an experimental three-masted rig which she retained. The design could accommodate an armament of 12 x 30pdr carronades. *Chaptal* was the first screw ship with direct drive in either

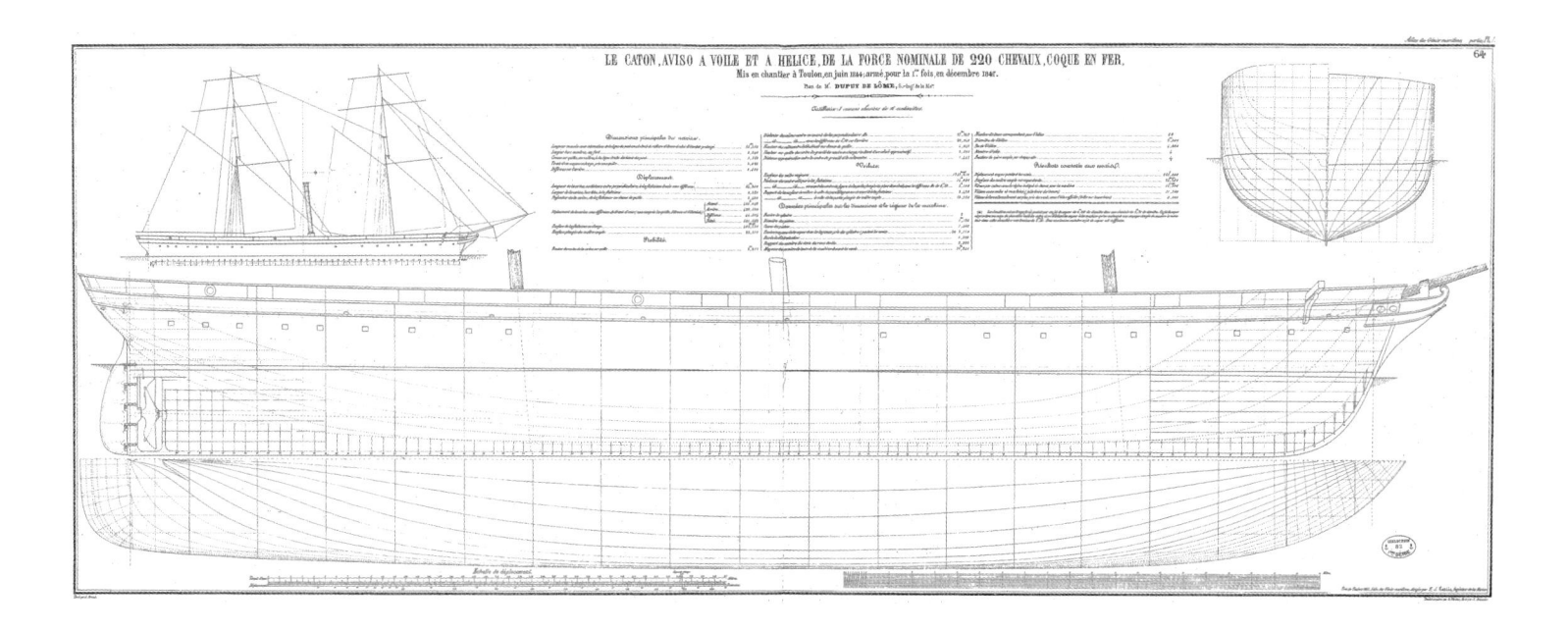

France or Britain. By 1859 this pioneering machinery was requiring excessive maintenance, and new engines were ordered for the ship from the Forges et Chantiers de la Méditerranée by a contract of 30 January 1860 and installed in 1861.

Dimensions & tons: 54.30m wl x 9.53m x 6.48m. 1,007 tons disp. Draught 3.76m mean. Men: 123.
Machinery: 220nhp. Direct, 9.8kts. Coal 260t.
Guns: (1846) 1 x 22cm No.1 shell, 1 x 22cm No.2 shell, 2 x 30pdrs No.1. Soon (1847) reduced to 1 x 22cm No.2 shell, 1 x 30pdr No.1.

Chaptal François Cavé, Asnières-sur-Seine/Cavé (Constructeurs: Georges Allix and Amédée Mangin)
Ord: 13.2.1843 (contract). K: 7.1844. L: 9.12 1845. Comm: 1.8.1846. C: 11.1846.
Blown ashore 25.10.1862 in a storm near Vera Cruz during the Mexican operation. Engine and boilers salvaged to be reused in *Linois* (1867) although they may have been used elsewhere. Struck 27.1.1863, remains sold 14.3.1863 for 405 piasters.

CATON. 2nd Class corvette, iron hull. *Caton* appeared in the building program in late 1842 as a 160nhp steamer to be begun in 1843 at Toulon. During 1842 the 26-year old Stanislas-Charles-Henri Dupuy de Lôme was sent from Toulon to England to learn the techniques for building iron-hulled ships, and after his return to Toulon on 2 May 1843 sent to Paris plans for an iron shipbuilding facility and for a 220nhp paddle steamer (*Caton*) to be built there. The Minister approved the plans on 28 August 1843 but ordered 'slight modifications' to allow the use of a screw propeller instead of paddle wheels. Dupuy de Lôme quickly found that the screw required a totally different type of hull, and submitted new plans which were approved on 29 January 1844. The hull was completed by the middle of 1845, but the engines were ordered from Schneider only by a contract approved on 31 August 1846 due to long bureaucratic delays in Paris. By this time, new engine technology made possible an increase in power from 220 to 260nhp. The ship was brig-rigged and had a sail area of 1,247 sq.m.

Dimensions & tons: 56.98m, 54.38m wl, 50.10m x 9.28m, 9.37m ext, x 5.55m. 892 tons disp. Draught 3.27/3.97m. Men: 123.
Machinery: 260nhp. Oscillating cylinders, geared, 10.30kts.
Guns: (1848) 8 x 16cm shell.

Official lines plan, engraved in 1851, for the iron screw corvette *Caton*, the French Navy's first iron warship. At that time iron ship construction was only practised by a few British commercial shipbuilders and the ship's designer, Dupuy de Lôme, had to go to England in order to study the techniques involved. The inset shows the brig sail plan; the total area of the 'major sails' (undefined) is given as 1,847 sq.m. (Atlas du Génie Maritime, French collection, plate 64)

Caton Toulon Dyd/Schneider (Constructeur: Dupuy de Lôme)
Ord: 28.8.1843. K: 20.6.1844. L: 1.5.1847. Comm: 12.7.1847. C: 12.1847.
Struck 30.1.1874, BU 1875 at Toulon.

COMTE D'EU. 1st Class corvette, iron hull. This ship was built as a yacht for the use of King Louis Philippe during his summers at Eu, on the Channel coast. She was originally to have been a replacement for the previous *Comte d'Eu* (q.v.), a 120nhp paddle steamer whose trials in 1843 had been a failure. On 28 September 1843 a ministry official proposed building at Indret a shallow draught iron steamer of about 200 tons with 120nhp paddle engines with Penn's oscillating cylinders. The Prince de Joinville, a son of the King who had made the navy his career, expressed his dissatisfaction with Indret's products and wrote the Minister on 6 October 1843 that, to get the best possible ship for the King, the navy should give the ship's specifications to France's best private firms and give them a free hand. He was probably also responsible for the fact that, by the time the King signed the order to build the ship on 9 October 1843, she had grown to be a 320nhp screw steamer. This, in turn, made her too large to fulfil her original mission of entering and leaving the port at Tréport which served Eu, a task which was eventually passed on to the smaller *Anacréon* and *Passe Partout*. The hull was ordered from Augustin Normand and the engines were ordered from Schneider by contracts approved on 30 July 1844. By this time the ship's mission was described as providing rapid communications for the King between France and England and between French ports.

Normand designed a ship with a graceful hull and a substantial rig (1,574 sq.m. on three masts with square sails on the fore and main). The Council of Works approved Normand's plans on 11 August 1845, bringing to a head a year-long quarrel between Normand and Schneider, who was already building the engines and who objected to the hull lines. The machinery was ready long before the hull was launched. Trials were interrupted in August 1847 by a serious boiler explosion and the discovery that the boilers were producing only a third of the steam called for in the contract. The boilers were finally rejected and new boilers were ordered from Schneider by a contract approved on 6 January 1852. A contract with Mazeline for new 450nhp engines for this ship was approved on 3 October 1853 but cancelled on 2 February 1854 because repairs to the existing engines had been successful. The ship saw her first active service in 1853 as the imperial yacht *Reine Hortense*. She replaced the corvette *Roland* in this duty and was in turn replaced in 1867 by the aviso *Cassard*, whose name she took. Commissioned as a cruiser on 12 March 1867, she carried 3 x 14cm rifles in 1874.

> Dimensions & tons: 64.50m, 63.00m wl x 10.96m ext x 6.22m. 919 tons disp. Draught 4.23m mean. Men: 191.
> Machinery: 320nhp. 4 cylinders, oscillating cylinders, geared, 11.33kts. Coal 120t.
> Guns: (1854 as yacht) 6 x 12cm No.2 bronze shell.

Comte d'Eu Augustin Normand, Le Havre/Schneider.
> Ord: 30.7.1844 (contract). K: 9.1844. L: 20.12.1846. Comm: 1.1.1847. C: 8.1847.
> Renamed *Patriote* 29.2.1848, *Reine Hortense* effective 1.6.1853, and *Cassard* 14.2.1867. Struck 8.4.1882, headquarters hulk for the mobile defence force (*Défense mobile*) at Toulon. Replaced 1887 by *Cérès*, torpedo-boat base ship at Port Vendres from 5.1888 to 1913. Renamed *Faune* 10.1893. BU at Cette 1914-1920.

ROLAND. 1st Class corvette. *Roland* appeared in the building program in late 1842 as a 450nhp steamer and by late 1843 had become a 320nhp ship to be begun in 1844 at Lorient. She was moved to Toulon during 1844. On 28 February 1844 Jean-Baptiste Pironneau completed two sets of plans for a steam corvette, one with paddle wheels and one with a screw propeller. The Minister approved the paddle plans on 9 December 1844 for *Roland* and *Colbert*, 320nhp corvettes that were then to be begun during 1845. On 21 May 1845 Inspector General of the Génie Maritime Jacques-Louis Bonard and Pironneau requested a review

A lithograph after a Brierly drawing showing the *Reine Hortense* joining the Anglo-French Baltic fleet at Ledsund in 1854. The imperial yacht was bringing the French General Baraguey D'Hilliers to take command of the expeditionary force destined for the attack on the Russian fortress of Bomarsund. Over the yacht's bow can be seen the British flagship HMS *Duke of Wellington* with yards manned and wreathed in smoke from the welcoming salute. The French 90 *Inflexible* is saluting in the foreground. (© National Maritime Museum PY0480)

of this decision in view of the early successes of the screw, and on 16 June 1845 the Minister approved the use of the screw plans for *Roland*. Her engines, which were similar to those in the British screw frigate *Amphion*, were ordered from Mazeline by a contract approved on 19 October 1846. In mid-1848 problems were encountered installing *Roland*'s propeller shaft because of her extremely fine lines aft, and her stern was shortened by about 3 metres. (Her original waterline length had been 56.00m.) A similar problem had caused the navy to revert to the paddle wheel in another new wooden hull, the aviso *Milan*, in May 1848. Because of the ship's light framing and fine lines fore and aft her armament was limited to two long and four shell guns. Trials in 1852, however, were regarded as a great success. *Roland* was refitted as a presidential yacht in June and July 1852 at Le Havre but was quickly converted back to a corvette after being replaced as a yacht in mid-1853 by the former *Comte d'Eu*.

> Dimensions & tons: 54.67m, 52.92m wl x 10.20m, 10.40m ext x 6.70m. 1,299 tons disp. Draught 4.13/5.03m. Men: 191.
> Machinery: 400nhp. 4 cylinders, geared, trials 988ihp = 12.2kts.
> Guns: (1852) 2 x 30pdrs No.1, 4 x 16cm shell; (c1853) 10 x 16cm shell.

Roland Toulon Dyd/Mazeline (Constructeur: Charles Auxcousteaux)
> Ord: 19.6.1845. K: 6.8.1845. L: 5.9.1850. C: 1.1851. Comm: 10.3.1852.
> Initially served briefly as a yacht, being renamed *Hortense* 14.4.1852 and *Reine Hortense* 24.4.1852. Replaced by *Comte d'Eu* and name reverted to *Roland* effective 1.6.1853. Struck 2.5.1870 at Brest, BU 1870.

BICHE. 2nd Class corvette *mixte* (with auxiliary screw), iron hull. This 120nhp ship and her half-sister *Sentinelle* were built as part of a program for the suppression of the West African slave trade (see the paddle corvette *Euménide* for details). Unlike the 120nhp screw 2nd Class avisos which they resembled in size, they were designed as mixed propulsion ships (sailing ships with auxiliary steam power) and before 1850 were classified as open-battery corvettes with 120 horsepower machinery (*corvettes à batterie barbette munie d'une machine de 120 chevaux*). Their designers were instructed to follow the hull lines of the highly successful sail corvette-aviso *Diligente* as closely as possible. Plans for *Biche* by Stanislas-Charles-Henri Dupuy de Lôme were approved on 18 July 1846 and she was built by Gaspard Malo at Dunkirk on building ways belonging to the State under a contract approved on 23 November 1846. Her engines were ordered from Mazeline by a contract approved on 17 November 1846. Both ships were completed with brig rigs. Their designed armament was 2 x 16cm shell guns, one to port and one to starboard, but on 11 January 1848 they were ordered fitted with two short 12pdrs. The position of the boats forced a change in *Biche* in mid-1849 to two bronze 4pdrs, but *Sentinelle* had higher bulwarks and her boats would not interfere with the 12pdrs. *Biche* became the first French Navy ship with water-tube boilers when she was experimentally fitted at Cherbourg in February to May 1855 with new high-pressure 200nhp engines by Charbonnier, Bourgougnan and Co. (Cavé's successors) and high-pressure water-tube boilers designed by Julien François Belleville of Saint-Denis near Paris that had been ordered by contracts approved on 6 September 1853. The boilers had vertical coiled tubes that gave much trouble. On a trial run from Cherbourg to Brest *Biche* started out with four functioning boilers, but she had only one available for the return

Sentinelle. This diminutive vessel and her near sister *Biche* were classified as auxiliary screw corvettes (*corvettes mixtes*) because they were designed using the hull lines of the sailing corvette *Diligente* modified just enough to include a small steam engine to supplement their full sailing rigs. They were given a more appropriate classification as avisos in 1859. (Marius Bar)

voyage because of tube failures. The boilers were ordered removed in late 1857. The increase in rated horsepower caused her to be reclassified as a 1st Class screw corvette in 1856; she was redesignated as a 1st Class aviso in 1859 and as a 2nd Class aviso in 1862. The original engines of *Biche* were reused in the transport-aviso *Loiret* of 1856.

Dimensions & tons: 33.85m wl x 8.71m ext. 439t disp. Draught 3.30/4.30m. Men: 81.
Machinery: 120nhp. Two fixed cylinders, geared, 8.5kts.
Guns: (1849) 2 x 4pdrs bronze.
Biche Gaspard Malo, Dunkirk/Mazeline.
Ord: 23.11.1846 (contract). K: 12.1846. L: 3.9.1848. Comm: 25.10.1848.
Struck 13.2.1868, BU 1868 at Toulon.

SENTINELLE. 2nd Class corvette *mixte* (with auxiliary screw), iron hull. *Sentinelle*, ordered with other ships to combat the West African slave trade, was designed to the same specifications as *Biche* and like her half-sister was in effect a sailing vessel modelled on the corvette-aviso *Diligente* and fitted with an auxiliary 120nhp steam engine. Plans by Victor Gervaize were approved on 18 July 1846 and she was built by Chaigneau and Bichon at Bordeaux (Lormont) under a contract approved on 23 November 1846. Her engines were ordered from Mazeline by a contract approved on 17 November 1846. She was placed in reduced commission on 27 March 1849. On trials in June 1849 she reached 8.5kts under steam and 7.6kts under sail. In service her best performance under both sail and steam was 10kts and she rarely exceeded 8.5kts. While her speed under steam was about what would have been expected from auxiliary propulsion, her speed under sail was far less than the ship whose hull lines she imitated, *Diligente*. She was fitted in 1849 with two short 12pdrs but on 19 May 1851 was ordered refitted with 6 x 12pdr carronades. New 120nhp engines were ordered from Ernest Gouin at Nantes by a contract signed on 21 June 1861. She was reclassified as a 1st Class aviso in 1859 and as a 2nd Class aviso in 1862.

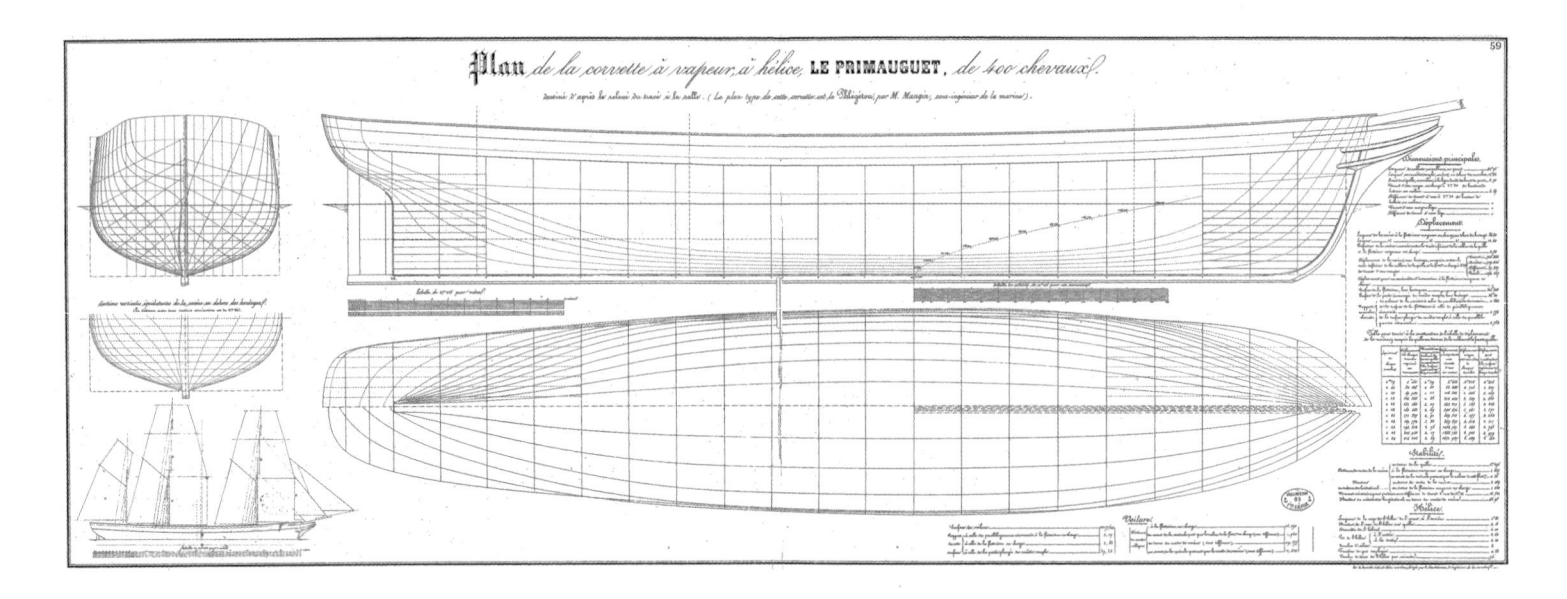

Dimensions & tons: 35.08m, 34.00m wl, 30.08m x 8.62m ext. Draught 3.20/4.40m. 457t disp. Men: 81.
Machinery: 120nhp. Fixed cylinders, geared, 8.5kts. Coal 54-56 tons.
Guns: (1850) 2 x 12pdrs (short), 4 swivels.

Sentinelle Chaigneau & Bichon, Bordeaux-Lormont/Mazeline (Constructeur: Nicolas Courtin).
Ord: 23.11.1846 (contract). K: 15.1.1847. L: 29.8.1848. C: 6.1849. Comm: 6.4.1850.
Struck 17.8.1869. Engines removed 1869, hull fitted for the transport of mules and sent to Algeria, where she became a boys training ship. Towed back to Toulon 1872 for use as a maritime school for young convicts at Tremblade. Careening hulk (*ponton-fosse*) in 1873. BU 1877 at Toulon.

PHLÉGÉTON Class. 1st Class corvettes. *Phlégéton* appeared in the building program in late 1847 as a 400nhp 1st Class corvette to be begun at Toulon during 1849. On 16 October 1848 the Minister of Marine ordered her construction at Cherbourg in 1849 as a 400nhp screw corvette. After extensive studies, plans for the hull by Amédée Mangin and for the geared engines by Victorin Sabattier at Indret were approved on 27 March 1850. Her two sisters were added to the program in 1850. The direct drive engines of *Laplace* were ordered from Schneider by a contract approved on 25 November 1850. Built on Schneider's plans, they were not sufficiently sturdy and were replaced in 1864 by a set of trunk engines initially ordered from Indret for a later but similar ship, *Decrès*. In trials in 1870 these produced 1,155ihp for 11.47kts. The engines of *Primauguet* were ordered from Mazeline by a contract approved on 23 July 1851. The sail area of *Primauguet* was 1,417 sq.m. Ships of this type were initially classified as 1st Class steam corvettes and then

Lines plan of the screw corvette *Primauguet* engraved in 1851 after the original. The sail plan shows the barque rig of 1,417 sq.m. The armament, comprising a small number of powerful guns, was carried entirely on the open upper deck, so no gunports are apparent on the draught. (Atlas du Génie Maritime, French collection, plate 59)

became screw corvettes in 1856 and screw *corvettes à barbette* (open battery) in 1862.

Dimensions & tons: 61.75m, 56.72m wl, 56.27m x 11.22m, 11.40m ext x 6.70m. 1467t. Draught 4.59/5.45m. *Laplace* same but 1436t and draught 3.86/5.46m. *Primauguet* same but 61.60m, 1658t, and draught 4.48/5.78m. Men: 191.
Machinery: 400nhp. *Phlégéton*: 2 cylinders, geared, 972ihp, 11kts. *Laplace*: 4 cylinders, direct, 975ihp, 11.5kts. *Primauguet*: 4 cylinders, direct, trials 960ihp = 9.79kts. Coal 280t (*Phlégéton* 350t).
Guns: (*Phlégéton* 1854) 6 x 30pdrs No.1, 4 x 22cm No.1 shell; (others initially) 4 x 30pdrs No.1, 2 x 22cm No.1 shell; (*Primauguet* 1854) 4 x 30pdrs No.1, 2 x 22cm No.1 shell.

Phlégéton Cherbourg Dyd/Indret (Constructeur: Mangin)
Named: 16.10.1848. K: 24.4.1850. L: 25.4.1853. Comm: 17.3.1854. C: 3.1854.
Struck 28.5.1868 at Brest, BU 1868.

Laplace Lorient Dyd/Schneider (Constructeurs: Pierre Thomeuf and Antoine Delapoix de Fréminville)
Ord: 12.4.1850. K: 26.7.1850. L: 3.6.1852. C: 11.1852. Comm: 18.11.1852.
Struck 18.3.1879 at Brest, sold or BU 1880.

Primauguet Brest Dyd/Mazeline (Constructeurs: Charles-Marc Boumard and Jules Villain)
K: 18.6.1850. L: 15.9.1852. Comm: 25.6.1853. C: 3.1854.
Struck 3.5.1877 at Brest and used in torpedo trials. Hull damaged on 25.4.1882 in trials of bottom mines in Brest harbour, placed in drydock and BU 1882 or 1884.

D'ASSAS. 1st Class corvette. On 5 April 1851 the Council of Works decided that the navy had enough ships like *Phlégéton* which it said were essentially large avisos and proposed building instead a real fighting ship: a covered-battery corvette like *Infernal* with a heavy armament in the battery, coal for 10 days, and machinery completely below the waterline. During this session the Council approved the design for

CORVETTES 199

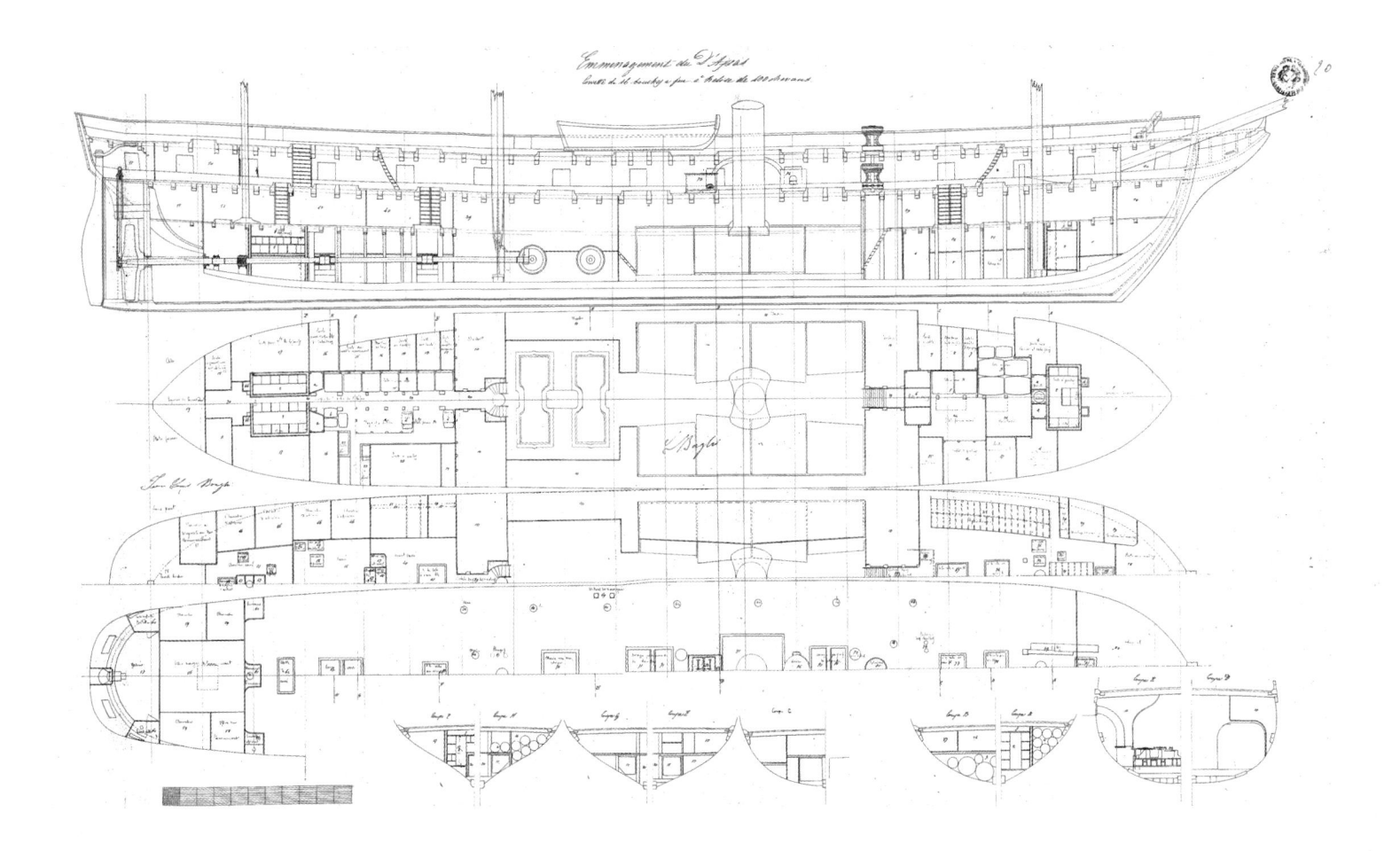

The original plans of the internal arrangements for the 16-gun covered-battery corvette *D'Assas*. With a substantial broadside armament, these vessels were intended for serious fighting rather than imperial policing roles, and as such their engines and boilers were completely below the waterline for protection. (Atlas du Génie Maritime, Genoa collection, image 2-0019)

400nhp engines for this ship by Charles Henri Moll (Indret) but specified that, because of the military functions of the ship, the boilers should be redesigned to be entirely below the waterline. Hull plans by Guillaume Masson were approved by the Council of Works on 12 November 1851. The original engines of *D'Assas* were condemned in 1860 and replaced in 1862 by 2-cylinder engines built by the Forges et Chantiers de la Méditerranée under a contract approved on 9 November 1860. On trials in 1874 these developed 1,201ihp and 9.40kts. This ship and her half-sister *Du Chayla* were initially classified as 1st Class steam corvettes and then became screw covered battery corvettes in 1856, screw 3rd Rank frigates in 1859, and screw covered battery corvettes (*corvettes à batterie*) in 1862.

Dimensions & tons: 63.65m, 61.85m wl, 59.63m x 10.70m, 10.98m ext x 5.58m. 1,945 tons disp. Draught 4.84m mean. Men: 251.
Machinery: 400nhp. 4 cylinders, 9.8kts. Coal 378t.
Guns: (1855) UD 12 x 30pdrs No.2, 2 x 22cm No.2 shell; SD 2 x 30pdrs No.2.

D'Assas Lorient Dyd-Caudan/Indret (Constructeur: Masson)
Ord: 9.12.1851. K: 2.1.1852. L: 27.4.1854. Comm: 1.11.1854. C: 11.1854.
Struck 5.6.1878, mooring hulk at Lorient. Renamed *Euphrate* 12.1893. BU at Lorient 1933.

DU CHAYLA. 1st Class corvette. The origins of this ship were the same as for *D'Assas* except that she was designed by Pierre Armand Guieysse, her plans also being approved on 12 November 1851. Her engines were designed at Lorient by Louis-Édouard Lecointre and their plans were approved by the Council of Works on 27 June 1853. Originally named *Volta*, she was renamed on 16 May 1855 for Vice Admiral Blanquet du Chayla, who was severely wounded at the Battle of Aboukir in 1798. She was selected instead of a newer unnamed ship in an effort to get the name to sea during the Crimean War. Her sail area was 1,353 sq.m. With *D'Assas* she was classified as a 3rd Rank frigate from 1859 to 1862.

Dimensions & tons: 63.52m, 60.60m wl x 10.90m, 11.14m ext x 5.86m. 1,846 tons disp. Draught 4.41/5.41m. Men: 251.
Machinery: 400nhp. Trials 979ihp = 10.36kts. Coal 360t.
Guns: (1856) UD 12 x 30pdrs No.2, 2 x 22cm No.2 shell; SD 2 x 30pdrs No.2.

Du Chayla (ex *Volta* 16.5.1855) Lorient Dyd/Lorient (Constructeurs: Guieysse and Louis De Bussy)
Ord: 9.12.1851. K: 2.1.1852. L: 19.3.1855. Comm: 12.10.1855. C: 5.1856.
Struck 4.11.1875, mooring hulk at Lorient. Coal hulk at Lorient 1886, sold for BU 1890.

DUPLEIX. Corvette. In 1855 a Superior Commission formed by the Minister of Marine to reorganise the fleet decided that it would include 30 1st Class steam corvettes of the *Phlégéton* type, 30 1st Class avisos similar to *Chaptal*, and 30 2nd Class avisos similar to *Corse*. One result of this restructuring was that all 2nd Class corvettes of 260nhp and below, including *Caton* and *Chaptal*, were reclassified as 1st Class avisos and the remaining corvettes were merged into a single corvette category (soon called simply 'corvettes') covering ships in the 300-400nhp range. On 16 October 1855 the Council of Works proposed characteristics for these three types, recommending for the corvettes an increased armament of 6 x 22cm No.1 shell guns and 8 x 30pdr No.1 long guns along with increased length and displacement and other adjustments. Plans by Louis-François Octave Vésignié for *Dupleix* were approved on 1 October 1856. Her machinery was designed by Victorin Sabattier and ordered from Indret in March 1858; its installation was completed in December 1861.

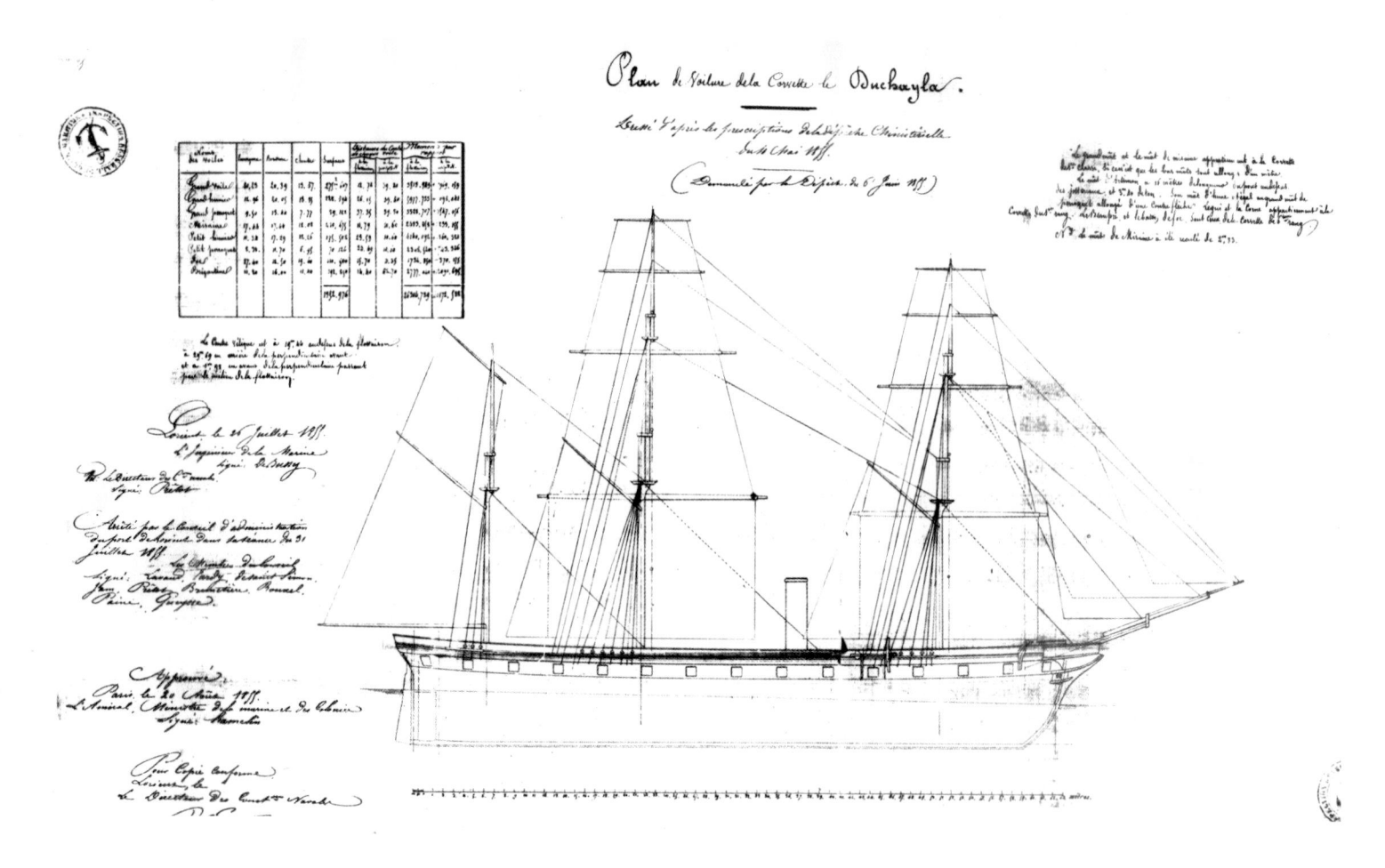

- Dimensions & tons: 66.34m, 63.80m wl x 11.40m ext x 6.60m. 1,773 tons disp. Draught 4.61/5.61m. Men: 191.
- Machinery: 400nhp. 2 cylinders, trunk, trials 986ihp = 11.66kts. Coal 340t.
- Guns: (1862) 10 x 16cm rifles M1860.

Dupleix Cherbourg Dyd/Indret (Constructeurs: Vésignié, Nathaniel Villaret, and Adrien Joyeux)

Ord: 1.10.1856. K: 9.10.1856. L: 28.3.1861. Comm: 13.6.1861. C: 26.2.1862.

After an active career in the Far East from 1862 to 1871, this vessel served on fishery protection duties off Iceland from 1876 to 1886. Struck 2.7.1887 at Cherbourg, BU 1890.

COSMAO Class. Corvettes. The origins of *Cosmao* were the same as for *Dupleix* except that she was designed by Émile Courbebaisse, her plans also being approved on 1 October 1856. Her machinery was designed by Charles Henri Moll (Indret) and its installation was completed in December 1861. *Decrès*, begun in 1861, was built to the same plans; her machinery was designed by Victorin Sabattier.

Barque rig sail plan for the 16-gun covered-battery corvette *Du Chayla* dated Lorient 26 July 1855. The calculated sail area of 1,353 sq.m. includes only one headsail and omits the royals, the fore and main spencers, and the jackyard topsail on the mizzen. (Archives de la Marine, 8-DD1-25 no. 26)

- Dimensions & tons: 64.39m, 62.84m wl x 11.80m ext x 6.60m. 1,619 tons disp. Draught 4.25/5.45m. Men: 191.
- Machinery: 400nhp. 2 cylinders, trunk, trials 1317ihp = 11.69kts. Coal 310t.
- Guns: (1862) 4 x 16cm rifles, 6 x 30pdrs No.1.

Cosmao Lorient Dyd/Indret (Constructeurs: Charles Louis Eugène Duchalard and Charles Louis Layrle)

Ord: 1.10.1856. Named: 4.10.1856. K: 26.11.1856. L: 10.6.1861. Comm: 22.7.1861. C: 7.1862.

Struck 29.6.1881 at Brest, BU 1882.

Decrès Lorient Dyd/Indret (Constructeurs: Charles Louis Layrle)

K: 23.10.1861. L: 10.9.1866. C: 4.1867. Comm: 1.5.1867.

Struck 25.6.1890, coal hulk at Rochefort 1896, sold for BU 1910.

CASSARD. Corvette. By a supplement signed on 3 December 1861 to Normand's contract of 16 November 1860 for the aviso *Talisman* the navy ordered a 1st Class aviso like *Jérôme Napoléon* (ex *Cassard*) which was given the name *Cassard*. On 24 May 1862 the Minister of Marine asked Normand to enlarge the new *Cassard* and increase the size of her machinery to give her the maximum speed suitable for her intended military service as a fast corvette. Mazeline produced a plan for installing in the ship a 3-cylinder 450nhp low-pressure engine like the one in the transport *Loiret*, and Normand then produced a new plan for the ship that called for hull dimensions of 78.00m x 10.60m and a displacement of 1600 tons. The plans were approved on 30 June 1863 and a modification to the contract was signed on 31 July 1863 to alter her hull. Another modification was signed on 8 April 1864 to further enlarge the vessel. On 14 August 1864 it was proposed to substitute the *Cassard* for the *Jérôme Napoléon* as a yacht, and in October the Emperor directed that she be put at the disposition of Prince Napoléon. The engines for the ship were ordered by a contract signed on 23 December 1864 by Mazeline under the new name of that firm after merging with Arman of Bordeaux. On 3 July 1865 Normand completed plans to complete her as a yacht, and another modification to the contract was signed on 22 December 1865. By a new contract signed on 24 November 1865 a new ship, *Coquette* (renamed *Château-Renaud* in March 1867, later rendered *Châteaurenault*) was ordered from Normand to replace the second *Cassard* as a cruiser. The former yacht retained her after deckhouse when renamed *Desaix* and converted back to a cruiser in the early 1870s.

Dimensions & tons: 79.55m wl x 10.62m ext. 1,684 tons disp. Draught 5.47m aft. Men: 159.

Machinery: 450nhp. Compound, 3 cylinders. Designed 1,800ihp, trials (1866) 14.21kts. Coal 304 tons.

Guns: (1866 as yacht) 4 x 12cm

Cassard Augustin Normand, Le Havre/Chantiers et Atéliers de l'Océan, Le Havre (Constructeurs: Eugène-Jacques-Louis De Sandfort and Achille Antoine Guesnet)

Ord: 12.1861 (contract). K: 1.1.1862. L: 20.2.1866. Comm: 16.8.1866. C: 1.9.1866.

Renamed *Jérôme Napoléon* as a yacht 16.8.1866 and *Desaix* as a corvette 19.9.1870. Condemned 1891 at Toulon as a cruiser and made into a school aviso. Struck 10.8.1894, sold 21.12.1894 at Toulon for BU.

This ship was ordered in late 1861 as a replacement for the aviso *Cassard*, then redesigned as a corvette, and completed as the yacht *Jérôme Napoléon*. She reverted to a corvette in 1870 under the name *Desaix*. Her armament was light for a corvette, being seven 12cm guns in the late 1870s (only one of which is visible here), and her two-masted rig also betrayed her yacht origins. (USN NH-74967)

VÉNUS Class. Covered battery corvettes (*corvettes à batterie*). In accordance with a decision of 27 September 1860, the Minister of Marine on 16 November 1860 sent to the ports specifications for a 22-gun frigate for use on overseas stations (*frégate de croisière*) and asked the naval constructors in the ports to submit designs for it. The ship was to serve as a station flagship in place of the old large frigates which were expensive to man. On 4 June 1861 the Council of Works reviewed seven designs and gave conditional approval to the design of Théophile Zéphyrin Compère-Desfontaines, which was the one whose construction would require the lowest expenditures. Revised plans were completed on 24 July 1861 and approved on 13 August 1861 by the Council of Works. On 26 August 1861 the Minister approved the plans of Compère-Desfontaines and signed a despatch to Brest ordering the immediate start of work on *Minerve* and *Vénus*, whose construction had been announced on 26 November 1860 as part of the building program for 1861. Their engines were ordered from Schneider by a contract signed on 6 December 1861 and were designed by the contractor. The ships were classified as screw *corvettes à batterie* (covered battery corvettes) throughout the 1860s and were then briefly classified as screw 3rd Rank frigates in 1872 and 1873 before becoming 1st Class cruisers in 1874. *Vénus* was commissioned for trials on 22 July 1865 and *Minerve* was similarly commissioned on 20 March 1866.

Dimensions & tons: 75.05m wl x 12.93m ext. 2,737 tons disp. Draught 5.26/6.48m. Men: 412.

Machinery: 500nhp. Designed 1720ihp, trials (1865) 1500ihp = 12.57kts. Coal 341 tons.

Guns: (c1865-66) UD 10 x 16cm MLR, 8 x 30pdrs No.1; SD 4 x 16cm MLR (4 x 30pdrs No.1 in *Minerve*).

Vénus Brest Dyd/Schneider (Constructeurs: Compère-Desfontaines and Édouard-Thomas Nouet)

Ord: 26.8.1861. K: 5.9.1861. L: 27.12.1864. Comm: 7.10.1865. C: 10.1865.

Vénus departing Algiers on 12 August 1886 at the end of her active career. Her 1883 armament included twelve short 14cm rifles, some of which are visible in the battery, four long 14cm rifles, not discernable here, and some smaller weapons. (USN NH-74972)

Struck 10.12.1886, mooring hulk at Rochefort. Sold 5.10.1909 for BU.

Minerve Brest Dyd/Schneider (Constructeurs: Compère-Desfontaines and Édouard-Thomas Nouet)

Ord: 26.8.1861. K: 9.1861. L: 10.7.1865. Comm: 11.7.1866. C: 7.1866.

Struck 26.10.1888 at Brest, then fitted as hospital hulk for Gabon. On sale list 1895-96. Accidentally burned 1897, wreck ceded to the colony.

7 Brigs

French naval brigs evolved in the late eighteenth century from the brigantine, a two-masted merchant vessel with a mainmast carrying a fore-and-aft mainsail (or brigantine sail) and a square main topsail, a foremast carrying a square foresail and a topsail, and a bowsprit with two or three jibs and sometimes a sprit-topsail. (The word 'brig' was probably a corruption of the word 'brigantine'; the spelling 'brick' became standard in France in the early nineteenth century.) The snow had a variant of the brigantine rig to which a square mainsail was added. The adoption by the French Navy in the 1770s of cutters and luggers led to a major increase in the hull dimensions of these types, reaching lengths of 28 metres during the war of the American Revolution. When the rigs of these vessels were scaled up proportionally the single mast and gaff mainsail of the cutter became too large to handle with safety, and much the same applied to the labour-intensive lugger rig. The solution consisted of applying the brigantine and later the snow rig to these hulls. In the resulting naval brig, which unlike the brigantine and snow was designed for speed, the rig was further developed by adding topgallant sails, royals, staysails, and more jibs and by expanding the size of most of the sails. During the Restoration the large naval brigs were sometimes called 'bricks de guerre' and after 1846 they were classed as 1st Class brigs.

In 1792 the British subdivided their brigs into two categories, brig-sloops (large) and gunbrigs (small), and proceeded to build large quantities of both. The French did not follow suit until the early 1820s, instead keeping all their brigs in one category and after around 1793 building brigs of only the larger (16-gun) size. However they also built many hundreds of gunboats, and some of these were brig-rigged. These brig-rigged gunboats are listed in Chapter 9. The French finally built a handful of gunbrigs beginning in 1823; previously their only vessels of this type came from Britain, Holland, and Italy.

The brig rig was also applied to a few avisos of the Ancien Régime and 'avisos-mouches' of the First Empire, although most 'avisos-mouches' remained schooner-rigged. These early brig-rigged avisos are listed with their schooner-rigged contemporaries in Chapter 8 as records do not always clearly indicate the rig of individual vessels. Under the Restoration a large class of 'goélette-bricks' or schooner-brigs was begun in 1821, but these vessels were soon re-rigged as brigs and designated 'bricks-avisos' or brig-avisos This type continued to be built through the 1840s, and the brig-avisos were additionally designated as 2nd Class brigs in 1846. As steam propulsion matured towards the middle of the century, the 1st and 2nd Class brigs and the few gunbrigs were gradually replaced in the fleet by 1st and 2nd Class steam avisos (see Chapter 12).

(A) Brigs in service or on order at 1 January 1786

The French Navy built no brigs before 1786. However in 1782 the cutter *Pandour* (see Chapter 8) had been re-rigged and re-classed as a brig. In 1783 the cutters *Levrette* and *Fanfaron* had also been re-rigged and re-classed as brigs (see Chapter 8); however in 1794 the *Levrette* was re-rated as a corvette and in 1797 the *Fanfaron* was re-rated as a lugger. The gabarres *Pluvier* and *Saumon* (see Chapter 13), two-masted vessels that carried 20 x 6pdrs, were also sometimes listed as brigs after briefly being fitted as bomb vessels in 1779-80.

Ex BRITISH NAVAL PRIZES (1782)

SYLPHE. British mercantile cutter *Active* purchased by the British Navy in May 1780, renamed *Sylph* and re-rigged as a brig. Taken by de Kersaint's French squadron 3 February 1782 at the surrender of Demerara.
    Dimensions & tons: 74ft, 63ft x 24ft 9in x 9ft 10in (24.04, 20.46 x 8.04 x 3.19m). 173/300 tons. Draught 8ft 2in/12ft (2.65/3.90m).
    Guns: 16 or 18 x 4pdrs.
Sylphe (HMS *Sylph*)
    Refitted at Rochefort 1785, struck there 1788.

TARLETON. This 14-gun brig had been purchased and put into service by the British Navy in 1782, but was captured in the same year by the French. She mounted 14 x 6pdrs and had 50 men, but other details are unknown. She remained in French service until August 1793, when she was handed over to Anglo-Spanish forces at the occupation of Toulon. Removed to Britain on the evacuation of Toulon in December, she was re-added as a fireship, but was deleted in 1798.

(B) Brigs acquired from 1 January 1786

In 1786 the first French naval vessels to be designed from the start to carry brig rigs were ordered, two pairs to two separate designs at Saint-Malo and at Bayonne. These were classed as 'brick-avisos' (brig-rigged advice or despatch vessels). A fifth, somewhat larger brig was ordered in the same year. A year later the two brick-aviso designs were enlarged and a further six vessels were ordered to each. No further orders were placed until after the onset of war against Britain.

PAPILLON Class. Brig-avisos, initially of 4 or 6 guns, designed by Pierre-Alexandre Forfait, and named on 13 April 1786.
    Dimensions & tons: 78ft 0in, 70ft 0in x 26ft 0in x 12ft 0in (25.34, 22.74 x 8.45 x 3.90 m.). 134/245 tons. Draught 8½ft/11ft (2.76/3.57m). Men: 67.
    Guns: (1786) 4 or 6 x 4pdrs; (1794) 12 x 4pdrs; (1797) 14 x 4pdrs.
Papillon Benjamin Dubois, Saint-Malo (Montmarin).
    K: early 1786. L: 28.4.1786. C: 6.1786.
    Refitted 8-9.1793 at Brest, and in 1795 also at Brest. Renamed *Parleur* 30.5.1795 and *Découverte* in 12.1795. Taken by the frigate HMS *Unity* in the Channel 11.10.1797, not taken into the RN.
Furet Benjamin Dubois, Saint-Malo (Montmarin).
    K: early 1786. L: 28.4.1786. C: 6.1786.
    Wrecked 11.8.1795 near St Brieuc.

GOÉLAND Class. Brig-avisos of 4 or 6 guns, designed by Raymond-Antoine Haran.
    Dimensions & tons: dimensions uncertain (but probably very close to *Papillon* class). 130 tons. Men: 65-66.

Admiralty draught of *Espiegle* as captured, dated Portsmouth 12 February 1794. This class was typical of the first generation of French purpose-built brigs-of-war, which were small and lightly armed, although the deck space allowed the increase in armament later – as captured *Espiegle* had eight ports a side. The small size of the gunports compared to the sweep ports between them indicates how light the guns were. (© National Maritime Museum J4689)

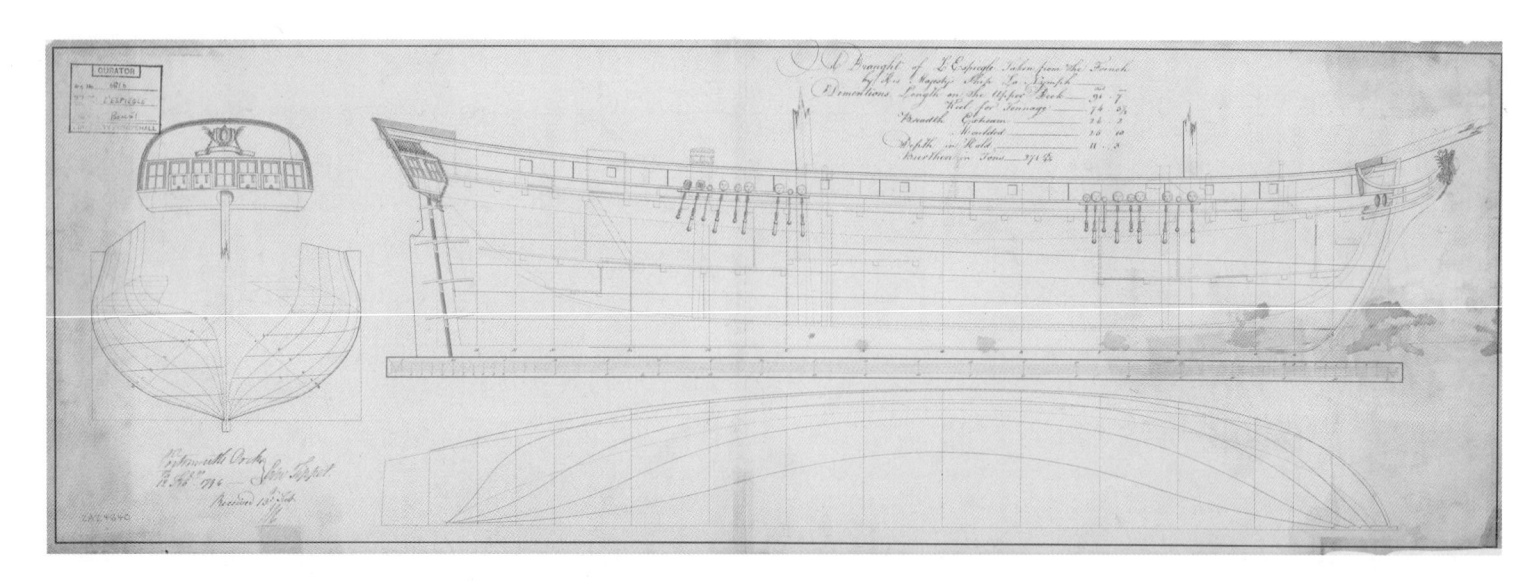

Guns: (1787) 4 x 4pdrs or 6 x 3pdrs; (1793) *Goéland* carried 10 small guns.

Goéland Bayonne.
K: 1786. L: 5.1787. C: 1787.
Taken by HMS *Penelope* 26.4.1793 off Haiti and became HMS *Goelan*. Sold 10.1794, in merchant service until at least 1813.

Mouche Bayonne.
K: 1786. L: 5.1787. C: 1787.
Sold 2/3.1797 and became a privateer.

ALERTE. Brig of 10 guns. Ordered in 1786 as *Aviso No.1*, and named on completion.
Dimensions & tons: 84ft 0in, 71ft 0in x 24ft 0in x 12ft 0in (27.29, 23.06 x 7.80 x 3.90m). 170/332 tons. Draught 7ft 11in/9ft 3in (2.57/3.00m). Men: (1786) 90; (1794) 98.
Guns: (1787-93) 10 x 4pdrs; (1794) 14 x 4pdrs.

Alerte Rochefort Dyd. (Constructeur, Hubert Pennevert)
K: 1786. L: 20.4.1787. C: 1.1788.
Handed over to the RN at the occupation of Toulon 8.1793 and became HMS *Vigilante*, but recovered (partly burnt) by French 12.1793 on the evacuation, with original name restored and repaired 1-2.1794. Refitted 6-7.1797 at Venice. Taken again by HMS *Emerald* off Toulon 18.6.1799 and became HMS *Minorca*. Sold 1802.

EXPÉDITION Class. Brig-avisos of 6 guns, designed by Pierre-Alexandre Forfait (the design was modified from the *Papillon* class).
Dimensions & tons: 83ft 0in, 80ft 0in wl, 71ft 0in x 26ft 0in x 13ft 0in (26.96, 25.98, 23.06 x 8.45 x 4.22m). 140/318 tons. Draught 10ft/12ft (3.25/3.90m). Men: 82.
Guns: (1788-91) 6 x 4pdrs; increased by 1794 to 10 to 18 x 4pdrs.

Expédition Benjamin Dubois, Saint-Malo (Montmarin).
K: 10.1787. L: 21.1.1788. C: 2.1788.
Decomm. 11.1795 at Baltimore and sold.

Curieux Benjamin Dubois, Saint-Malo (Montmarin).
K: 10.1787. L: 26.1.1788. C: 2.1788.
Captured by HMS *Inconstant* in the Windward Islands 3.6.1793.

Épervier Benjamin Dubois, Saint-Malo (Montmarin).
K: 10.1787. L: 23.2.1788. C: 3.1788.
Condemned at Cayenne 4.1797, became privateer, captured 14.11.1797 by HMS *Cerberus* off Ireland, becoming HMS *Epervoir*; sold at Plymouth 7.9.1801.

Sans-Souci Benjamin Dubois, Saint-Malo (Montmarin).
K: 10.1787. L: 23.2.1788. C: 2.1788.
Wrecked on rocks near Croisic during the night of 8/9.4.1793.

Cerf Benjamin Dubois, Saint-Malo (Montmarin).
K: 1.1788. L: 21.4.1788. C: 5.1788.
Condemned 9.1795.

Impatient Benjamin Dubois, Saint-Malo (Montmarin)
K: 1.1788. L: 21.4.1788. C: 5.1788.
Captured 29.5.1803 by HMS *Naiad* (36) in the Bay of Biscay while returning from Senegal to Brest.

HASARD Class. Brig-avisos of 6 guns, designed by Raymond-Antoine Haran (the design was modified from the *Goéland* class).
Dimensions & tons: 84ft 0in, 76ft 9in x 24ft 0in x 11ft 6in (27.29, 24.93 x 7.80 x 3.74m). 134-180/286-322 tons. Draught 9ft 4in/10ft 4in (3.03/3.36m). Men: 110.
Guns: (1788-91) 6 x 4pdrs; increased by 1794 to 10 to 16 x 4pdrs.

Hasard Bayonne.
K: 10.1787. L: 1.1788. C: 4.1788.
Wrecked on Île Saint Honorat 28.10.1796.

Lutin Bayonne.
K: 10.1787. L: 2.1788. C: 4.1788.
Taken by HMS *Pluto* off Newfoundland 25.7.1793; sold at Plymouth 26.1.1796.

Espiègle Bayonne.
K: end 1787. L: 1788. C: 1788.
Taken by HMS *Nymphe* and *Circe* off Ushant 30.11.1793. Became brig HMS *Espiegle*, sold 2.1802.

Espoir Bayonne.
K: end 1787. L: 3.1788. C: 4.1788.
Renamed *Lazouski* 1793 or 1794, reverted to *Espoir* 1795. Taken by HMS *Thalia* in the Mediterranean 18.9.1797, became HMS *Espoir*. Sold 9.1804 at Sheerness.

Serin Bayonne.
K: end 1787. L: 1788. C: 1788.

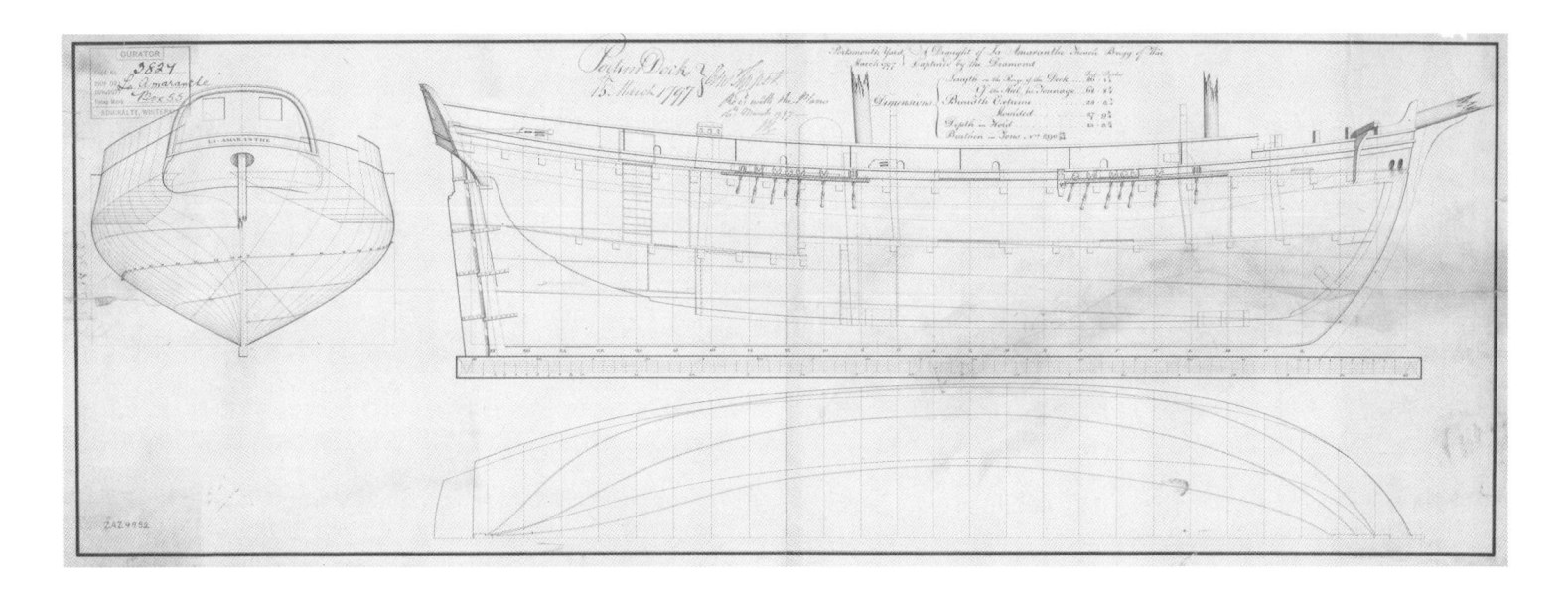

Admiralty draught of *Amaranthe* as taken off at Portsmouth, dated 15 March 1797. More heavily armed than previous brig classes, this design was broader and deeper than its predecessors, with a typical Forfait V-shaped mid-section. (© National Maritime Museum J4864)

Taken by HMS *Intrepid* and *Chichester* off San Domingo 31.7.1794; lost, presumed foundered 8.1796 in Bay of Honduras.

Éveillé Bayonne.
K: end 1787. L: 4.1788. C: 8.1788.
Taken by HMS *Thunderer* and *Pomone* 17.10.1795, becoming HMS *Eveille*; no record of disposal.

CONVERTED CHASSE-MARÉE. This vessel was built at Auray or Redon in southern Brittany in 1785 as *Chasse-Marée No.18* to support construction work at Cherbourg and was rebuilt at Cherbourg by Martin or Jacques Fabien as a 'brick de guerre' in 1793.

Dimensions & tons: 57ft 0in, 49ft 0in x 18ft 9in x 7ft 0in (18.51, 15.92 x 6.09 x 2.27m). 77/150 tons. Draught 5ft 7in/6ft 7in (1.81/2.14m). Men: 92

Guns: 8 or 10 x 4pdrs

Pourvoyeur Cherbourg Dyd. (rebuilt)
K: 3.1793. Named: 5.1793. L: 13.7.1793. C: 9.1793.
Escorted convoys and carried cargo between Cherbourg and nearby ports. To sale list and struck 3.1797 but retained as a service craft. Recommissioned 1.1807 at Cherbourg as a lugger with 6 x 4pdrs. Became a 77-ton transport with 4 x 4pdrs 1819 and carried the engine of the French Navy's first steamer, *Voyageur*, from Rouen to Lorient 6.1819 and its second steamer, *Africain*, from Paris to Lorient 7.7.1819. Reverted to a lugger 1821, decomm. 11.1826 at Cherbourg and struck.

TROMPEUSE. Brig of 16 guns, built as a privateer and requisitioned by the French Navy in April 1793 while on the stocks. One of three brigs building as privateers that were taken over by the navy in that month.

Dimensions & tons: 86ft 0in, 78ft 0in x 27ft 4in (27.94, 25.34 x 8.88m). 200/400 tons/ Men: 105-120.

Guns: 16 x 6pdrs.

Trompeuse Jean Fouache, Le Havre.
K: 3.1793. L: 17.7.1793. C: 9.1793.
Captured 13.1.1794 off Cape Clear and became HMS *Trompeuse*; bilged in Kinsale Harbour 15.7.1796.

AVENTURIER. Brig of 12 guns (14 gunports), built as a privateer to a design by Jean-Louis Pestel and requisitioned by the French Navy on 3 April 1793 while still on the stocks. Fitted out at Le Havre in November 1793 although there were problems in arming her fully. Used initially to patrol between Le Havre and Dieppe, but subsequently as convoy escort between Cherbourg and Brest, and later cruised out of Saint-Malo.

Dimensions & tons: 74ft 0in x 21ft 0in (24.04 x 6.82m). 250 tons disp. Men: 80-95.

Guns: 12 x 4pdrs.

Aventurier Honfleur.
K: 3.1793. L: 24.7.1793. C: 10.1793.
Cut out by boats from HMS *Melpomene* and *Childers* 4.8.1798 at port of Corréjou, becoming HMS *Aventurier* (gunbrig, refitted with 14 x 4pdrs + 2 x 12pdr carronades); deleted 1802.

VIPÈRE. Brig of 12 guns, built as a privateer and requisitioned by the French Navy in April 1793 while still on the stocks.

Dimensions & tons: 92ft 0in x 24ft 4in (29.89 x 7.90m). 200/370 tons. Men: 116.

Guns: 10 x 4pdrs + 2 x 6pdrs.

Vipère Michel Reine, Le Havre.
K: 3.1793. L: 8.1793. C: 10.1793.
Captured 23.1.1794 by HMS *Flora* in the Channel, becoming HMS *Viper*; wrecked in the Shannon Estuary 2.1.1797.

AMARANTE Class. Brigs of 12 guns, designed by Pierre-Alexandre-Laurent Forfait.

Dimensions & tons: 80ft 0in, 72ft 0in x 26ft 0in x 13ft 0in (25.99, 23.39 x 8.45 x 4.22m). 150/288 tons. Draught 9ft/9ft 8in (2.92/3.14m). Men: 110.

Guns: 12 x 6pdrs or 10 x 6pdrs, 2 x 8pdrs; (*Suffisante* 1795) 10 x 6pdrs, 4 x 4pdrs (12 ports)

Amarante (*Amaranthe*) Joseph-Augustin Normand, Honfleur.
K: 5.1793. L: 23.8.1793. C: 10.1793.
Taken 31.12.1796 by HMS *Diamond* off Alderney, becoming HMS *Amaranthe*. Wrecked near Cape Canaveral, Florida, 25.10.1799.

Suffisant Louis Deros, Le Havre.
K: 3.1793. L: 2.9.1793. C: 10.1793.

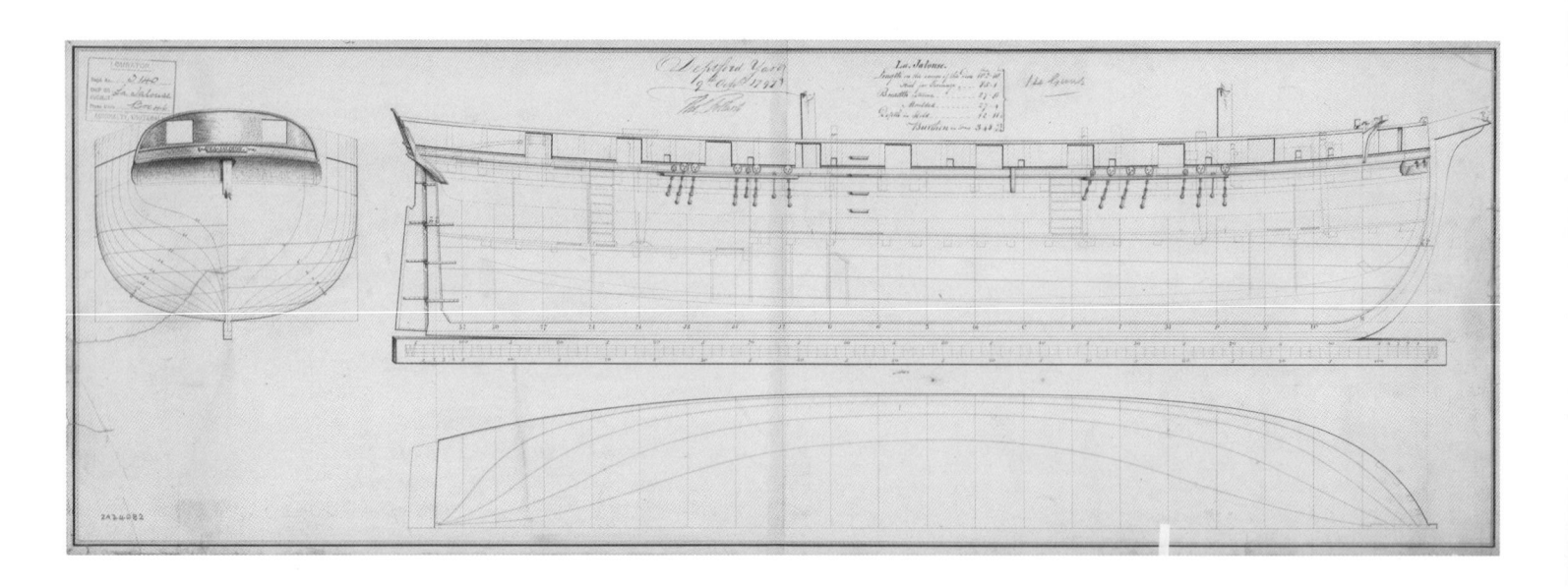

Taken 25.8.1795 by Duncan's squadron off Texel, becoming HMS *Suffisante*. Wrecked off Cork 25.12.1803.

BELLIQUEUSE Class. Brigs of 12 guns, also classed as *corvette-canonnières*, designed by Pierre-Alexandre-Laurent Forfait and all five ordered on 15 April 1793. While intended to carry 12 x 12pdrs, their actual guns varied; *Belliqueuse* and *Jalouse* carried 6 x 24pdrs (plus 2 smaller guns).

    Dimensions & tons: 96ft 9in, 89ft x 25ft 9in x 12ft 6in (31.43, 28.91 x 8.36 x 4.06m). 220-280/475 tons. Draught 9ft 4in/10ft 10in (3.03/3.52). Men: 116-140.

    Guns: UD 12 x 12pdrs (most also carried 2 smaller cannons or carronades).

Inconnue Michel Colin-Olivier, Dieppe.
    K: 5.1793. L: 30.12.1793. C: 2.3.1794.
    Captured 25.5.1794 by the RN off Brest and burned.

Belliqueuse Michel Colin-Olivier, Dieppe.
    K: 5.1793. L: 30.12.1793. C: 30.3.1794.
    Sold as a privateer 11.1797. Captured 1.1798 by the RN, becoming HMS *Belette*; sold 1801

Mutine Pierre, Jacques & Nicolas Fortier, Honfleur.
    K: 7.1793. L: 5.1.1794. C: 2.1794.
    Captured 28.5.1797 at Tenerife by HMS *Lively* and *Minerve*, becoming HMS *Mutine*.

Jalouse Pierre, Jacques & Nicolas Fortier, Honfleur.
    K: 7.1793. L: 4.2.1794. C: 4.1794.
    Captured 13.5.1797 in the North Sea by HMS *Vestal*, becoming HMS *Jalouse*; BU 1807.

Victorieuse Jean Gallon, Honfleur.
    K: 10.1793. L: 1.4.1794. C: 4.1794.
    Captured 31.8.1795 by HMS *Venerable* and *Minotaur* in the Channel, becoming HMS *Victorieuse*; BU 1805.

ZÉPHIR Class. Small brigs of 12 guns, built at Saint-Malo.
    Dimensions & tons: dimensions unknown. 120 tons. Men: 110.
    Guns: 12 x 4pdrs.

Zéphir (*Zéphyr*) Saint-Malo
    K: 2.1793. L: 6.1793. C: 7.1793.
    May have been renamed *Nord-Est* 5.1795. On sale list 4.1797 but not sold, renamed *Zéphir No.2* in 1799. Converted to a 56-ton transport for the Boulogne Flotilla at Le Havre in 1803 and renamed *Transport No.973 Zéphir* in 9.1804, and *Transport No.973* in 11.1810. Decomm. 3.1814 at Cherbourg and struck.

Espiègle Saint-Malo
    K: 1793. L: 8.1793. C: 10.1793.
    Captured 16.3.1794 in the West Indies by HMS *Iphigenia*, becoming HMS *Espiegle* (gunbrig); sold 1800.

SÉRIEUSE Class. Brigs designed for 12 guns, built at Le Havre.
    Dimensions & tons: 110ft 0in x 30ft 0in x ? (35.73 x 9.75 x ? m). 320/600 tons. Men: 116-120.
    Guns: 12 x 12pdrs intended, but *Étourdie* carried 6 x 24pdrs.

Sérieuse Le Havre
    K: 3.1793. L: 9.6.1793. C: 9.1793.
    Wrecked 25.12.1794 at Cherbourg.

Étourdie Le Havre
    K: 6.1793. L: 2.3.1794. C: 5.1794.
    Sunk 18.3.1798 in action with HMS *Diamond* in Bay of Erquy.

SUBTIL. French forces occupied the Austrian Netherlands (modern Belgium) in later 1792, and the French Navy commenced work at Ostend on a brig of 14 guns, built for cruising in the North Sea.
    Dimensions & tons: unknown.
    Guns: 14 x 4pdrs.

Subtil Ostend.
    K: 3.1793. L: 7.1793. C: 8.1793.
    Became a privateer 5.1797 at Dunkirk (12 x 4pdrs). Probably discarded 1809.

CITOYENNE. Brig of 16 guns.
    Dimensions & tons: dimensions unknown. 170t. Men: 125
    Guns: (1796) 16 x 8pdrs.

Citoyenne Saint-Malo.
    K: 5.1793. L: 5.1794. C: 7.1794.
    Renamed *Choquante* 5.1795 and *Citoyenne* or *Citoyenne No.2* in 1798.

Admiralty draught of *Jalouse* dated Deptford 9 October 1797. These flat-sheered vessels of relatively shallow draught were closer in design to coastal gunboats than conventional cruising brigs. They were intended to carry a heavy armament relative to their size, which is reflected in their designation as *corvette-canonnières*. (© National Maritime Museum J4323)

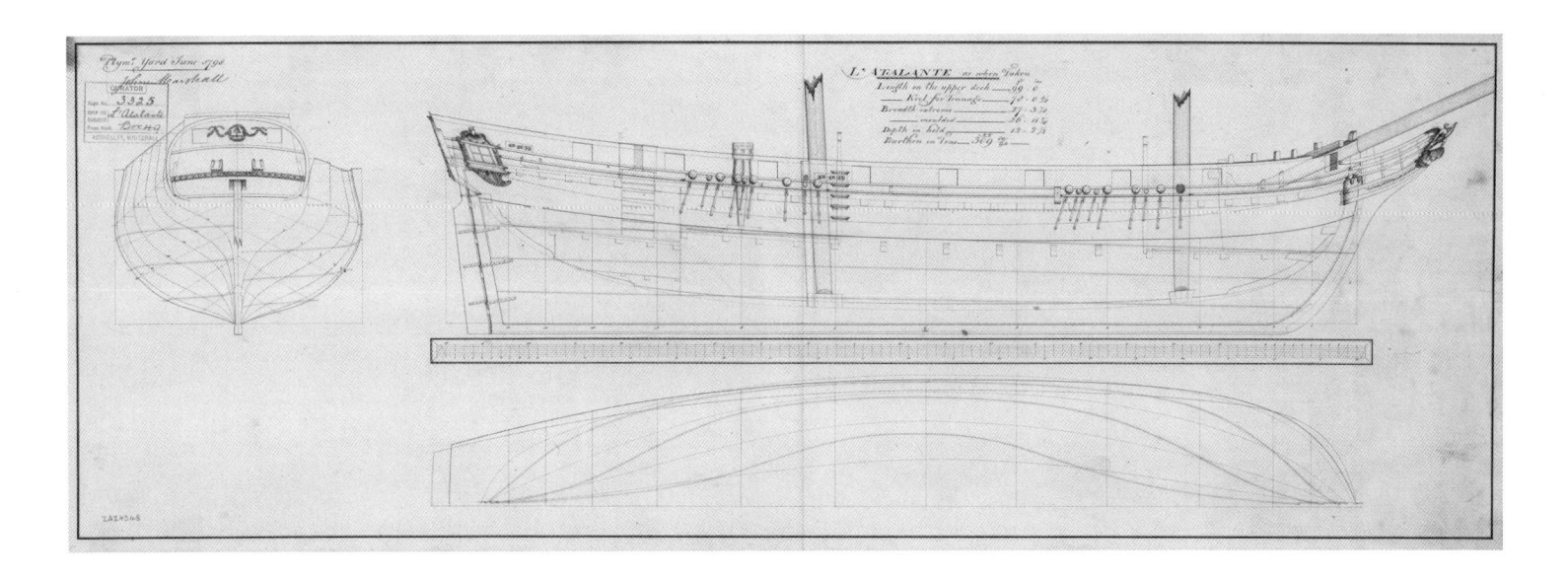

Admiralty draught of *Atalante* (renamed *Atlanta*) 'as when taken', dated Plymouth June 1798. After the outbreak of war, the French Navy began to build larger brigs, this being one of the first 16-gun designs. (© National Maritime Museum J4516)

Refitted at Antwerp in 1800 and Dunkirk in 1802. Coming from Dunkirk was wrecked 22.11.1802 at the entrance to the Goulet at Brest.

CERF-VOLANT Class. Brigs of 12 guns, built at Nantes.
  Dimensions & tons: 60ft 0in x 20ft 0in x 9ft 3in (19.49 x 6.50 x 3.00m). 87/160 tons. Draught 7ft 11in/10ft 5in (2.57/3.38m). Men: 110.
  Guns: 10 x 6pdrs or 4pdrs; (*Papillon*) 12 x 4pdrs (14 ports)
Cerf-Volant Nantes
  K: 5.1793. L: 8.8.1793. C: 10.1793.
  Captured 1.11.1796 off Santo Domingo by HMS *Magicienne* (32), not taken into the RN.
Papillon Nantes
  Ord: 16.5.1793. K: 6.1793. L: 23.8.1793. C: 10.1793.
  Sometimes referred to as *Papillon No.2*. Captured 4.9.1803 by HMS *Vanguard* off Saint-Marc, Haiti, and became the gunbrig HMS *Papillon*. Last seen in a gale 25.9.1805, her convoy arrived in Britain in mid-October.

ATALANTE Brig of 16 guns, designed by Raymond-Antoine Haran
  Dimensions & tons (tentative): 96ft, 85ft x 27ft x 15ft (31.18, 27.61 x 8.77 x 4.87m). 450 tons displ. Draught 12ft 6in/14ft 2in (4.06/4.60m). Men: 120.
  Guns: 16 x 6pdrs.
Atalante Bayonne
  K: 1793. L: 1.1794. C: 4.1794.
  Sometimes listed as a corvette. Captured 1.1797 off the Scilly Isles by HMS *Phoebe* (36) and became HMS *Atalanta*. Wrecked 2.1807, Île de Ré.

CITOYENNE FRANÇAISE. Brig of 12 guns, designed by Raymond-Antoine Haran.
  Dimensions & tons: dimensions unknown. 110 tons. Men: 100
  Guns: 12 x 4pdrs.
Citoyenne Française Bayonne.

  K: spring 1795. L: 6.1795. C: 7.1795.
  Ex *Républicaine* 5.1795. Refitted at Brest in 1798. Renamed *Citoyenne* or *Citoyenne No.1* c1800. BU at Brest 4.1805.

COLOMBE. Brig built to plans by Pierre-Alexandre-Laurent Forfait, modified by Pierre Ozanne. She may have been a reduced version of the *Etna* class corvettes that were built at the same time.
  Dimensions & tons: 103ft, 93ft x 27ft x 13ft 6in (33.45, 30.21 x 8.77 x 4.38m). 250/400 tons. Draught 9ft 8in/10ft 10in (3.14/3.52m). Men: 136.
  Guns: Designed for 6 x 24pdrs, then 12 x 18pdrs, completed with 12 x 12pdrs.
Colombe Cherbourg Dyd. (Constructeurs: Ozanne and Louis-Jacques Normand)
  K: 6.1794 (or 1.11.1794). L: 18.5.1795 (or 27. 9.1795). C: 11.1795.
  2 masts. Captured 18.6.1803 off Ushant by HMS *Dragon* (74) and *Endymion* (44) while returning from Martinique, became the brig-sloop HMS *Colombe*. BU 1811.

LIGURIENNE. Sectional brig, designed by François-Frédéric Poncet following the specifications of General Napoleon Bonaparte.
  Dimensions & tons: 80ft x 21ft 7in x 9ft 3in (25.98 x 7.01 x 3.0m). 150/300 tons. Men: 104.
  Guns: 14 x 6pdrs, 2 x 36pdr obusiers (according to the British) or 1 x 12pdr, 6 x 6pdrs (according to the French)
Ligurienne Toulon Dyd. (Constructeur: Honoré Garnier Saint-Maurice)
  K: 3.1798. L: 2.5.1798. C: 7.1798.
  Built in 8 sections so that 10 wagons could transport her by land from Alexandria to the Red Sea. Had 16 ports for guns and 7 pairs of small ports for oars. Not sent to Egypt, captured 21.3.1800 off Marseille by HMS *Petrel* (16) while escorting a convoy from Cette to Toulon.

The tartane *Albanaise* was re-classed as a brig in February 1799 and captured in August 1800. She is listed in Chapter 10. The cutter *Dragon* was re-classed as a brig in March 1798 and captured in May 1800. She is listed in Chapter 8. The cutter *Souffleur* was built at Boulogne in 1793 and re-rigged as a brig in January 1802; in 1808 she had 10 x 4pdrs and was out of commission at Lorient. She was a service craft on 1 January 1811, was hulked in 1813, and was no longer on the list of ships at Lorient in 1814. She is listed in Chapter 8.

This watercolour portrait by Antoine Roux makes the brig *Ligurienne* look conventional enough but the vessel was designed to be broken down into sections. Intended for Bonaparte's Egyptian expedition, the plan was to carry the vessel overland in eight segments to the Red Sea, but in the event the brig did not go to Egypt. (Wikimedia Commons)

ARÉTHUSE. Brig of 18 guns, designed by Jean-François Gauthier.
 Dimensions & tons: 96ft 0in, 86ft 0in x 27ft 5in x 13ft 6in (31.18, 27.93 x 8.93 x 4.38m) 250/464 tons. Draught 11ft 4in/11ft 10in (3.68/3.84m) Men: 136
 Guns: 18 x 8pdrs (designed for 20)
Aréthuse Louis & Antoine Crucy, Basse-Indre
 K: 10.1797. L: 29.4.1798. C: 1.1799.
 Captured 10.10.1799 in the Atlantic by HMS *Excellent* (74) while en route from Lorient to Cayenne, became HMS *Raven*. Wrecked 7.1804.

Two brigs named *Flore* and *Iris* armed with 18 x 6pdrs or 16 x 8pdrs were ordered in 1797 at Dunkirk, probably to be built there by the naval constructor Louis Jean Baptiste Bretocq, but they had not been begun as of April 1798 and were not built. In addition two brigs with 6 x 8pdrs

Admiralty draught of *Raven* (ex *Aréthuse*) as fitted at Plymouth, dated October 1800. The first recorded 18-gun brig built for the French Navy, and one of the first with 8pdrs, this design remained larger than the norm down to the end of the wars in 1815. (© National Maritime Museum J4139)

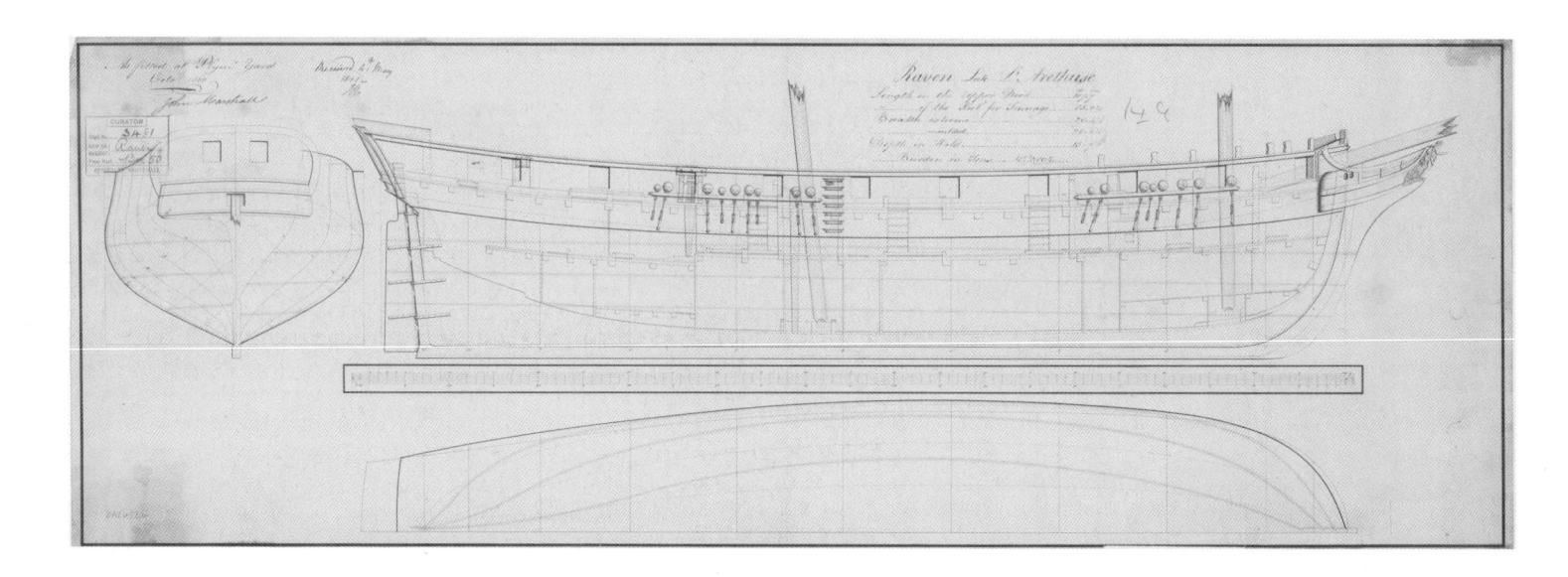

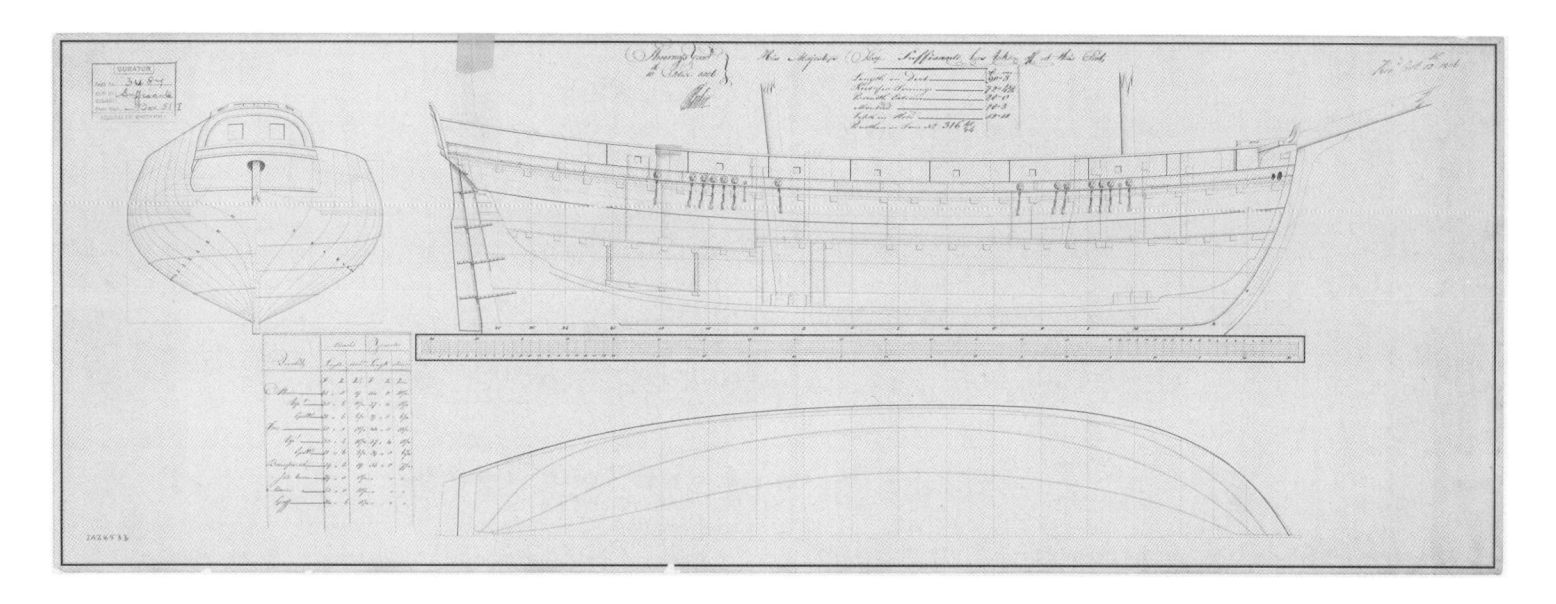

were ordered at Bayonne in 1797 and two brigs with 16 x 8pdrs were ordered at Cherbourg in September 1797 followed by a third in January 1798. The third Cherbourg brig was cancelled in April 1798 and the other four, all unnamed, had not been begun as of that date and were not built.

FLÈCHE Class. Brigs of 16 guns, built to Gauthier's plans for *Aréthuse* as modified by Pierre Degay. The Crucy yard at Nantes was established in 1796 on the Quai de la Piperie.

Dimensions & tons: 89ft 9in x 26ft 5in x 13ft 2in (29.16 x 8.58 x 4.29m) 200/500 tons. Men: 125

Guns: 16 x 8pdrs (18 ports)

Note: The naval archives in Paris hold the plan of a brig by Pierre Degay with the following characteristics: 31.67m, 27.93m x 8.90m x 4.77m. 260/500 tons. Draught 4.22/4.44m.

Flèche Louis, Antoine, & Mathurin Crucy, Nantes.
K: 7.1798. L: 20.5.1799. C: 11.1799.
Armament reduced in 1801 to 8 x 8pdrs to augment her autonomy. Burnt 5.9.1801 at Mahé in the Seychelles to avoid capture after fight with HMS *Victor* (18). Refloated 1803 and sold to a Portuguese merchant.

Curieuse Louis, Antoine, & Mathurin Crucy, Nantes.
K: 7.1798. L: 19.6.1799. C: 10.1799.
Captured 29.1.1801 off Barbados by HMS *Bordelais* (24), sank from her damage soon after capture.

VIGILANT Class. Brigs of 16 guns, designed by Pierre-Alexandre-Laurent Forfait. All built by Entreprise Thibaudier at Le Havre, for whom the Le Havre shipbuilder Jean Fouache acted as constructor until his death on 25 May 1800.

Dimensions and tons: 86 ft, 76ft x 26ft x 13ft (27.93, 24.69 x 8.45 x 4.22m). 164/349 to 373 tons. Draught 10ft 2in/10ft 10in (3.30/3.52m). Men: 105.

Guns: (Designed) 16 x 4pdrs; (*Observateur* and *Bélier*, 1803) 16 x 6pdrs; (*Surveillant*, 1805) 16 x 6pdrs, 2 x 36pdr obusiers; (*Argus*, 1805) 14 x 8pdrs (bronze); (*Observateur*, 1805) 14 x 4pdrs, 4 x 12pdr British carronades.

Vigilant (ex *No.1*, 10.1799) Jean Fouache and Entreprise Thibaudier, Le Havre
K: 6.1799. L: 20.7.1800. Comm: 21.4.1802. C: 4.1802.
Taken 30.6.1803 by the British at Santo Domingo, becoming HMS

Admiralty draught of *Suffisante* (ex *Vigilant*) as taken off at Sheerness, dated 10 October 1806. This class was effectively an enlarged version of Forfait's earlier *Amarante* class (compare draught reproduced earlier), lengthened to accommodate two extra gunports on the broadside. (© National Maritime Museum J5109)

Suffisante. Sold 5.1807.
Surveillant (ex *No.2*, 10.1799) Jean Fouache and Entreprise Thibaudier, Le Havre
K: 7.1799. L: 4.8.1800. C: 4.1801. Comm: 20.2.1802.
Reclassed as a cutter 1.1809, unserviceable at Bayonne 5.1809, decomm. 12.6.1809, condemned and ordered BU there 12.10.1811.

Argus (ex *No.3*, 10.1799) Jean Fouache and Entreprise Thibaudier, Le Havre
K: 7.1799. L: 20.7.1800. Comm: 6.5.1802. C: 5.1802.
Condemned and ordered BU at Cayenne 31.3.1807, decomm. 21.4.1807 and BU.

Observateur (ex *No.4*, 10.1799) Jean Fouache and Entreprise Thibaudier, Le Havre
K: 7.1799. L: 20.7.1800. C: 3.1802. Comm: 21.4.1802.
Taken 9.6.1806 off Bermuda by HMS *Tartar* (32), becoming HMS *Observateur*. Sold 9.1814.

Bélier (ex *No.5*, 10.1799) Jean Fouache and Entreprise Thibaudier, Le Havre
K: 8.1799. L: 22.7.1800. Comm: 9.8.1801. C: 8.1801.
Stopped at Muros near Vigo, Spain, while returning from Île de France and decomm. there 29.6.1804. Condemned there 28.9.1804 and sold 1.4.1805 to M. Papin, captain of the Bordeaux privateer *Confiance*. Captured and burnt 4.6.1805 at Muros by HMS *Loire* (40); also reported burnt by the French 7.1805.

Diligent (ex *No.6*, 10.1799) Jean Fouache and Entreprise Thibaudier, Le Havre
K: 8.1799. L: 25.6.1800. Comm: 23.9.1801. C: 9.1801.
Taken 23.5.1806 off Guadeloupe by HMS *Renard* (16), becoming HMS *Prudent*, later *Wolf*. BU 6.1811.

CURIEUX Class (prototype). 16-gun brig, designed by François-Timothée Pestel. This brig became the prototype for a large class begun in 1803, listed in the next section. The hull measurements listed here are for the 1803 group; the dimensions on the plans of *Curieux* were 29.22m

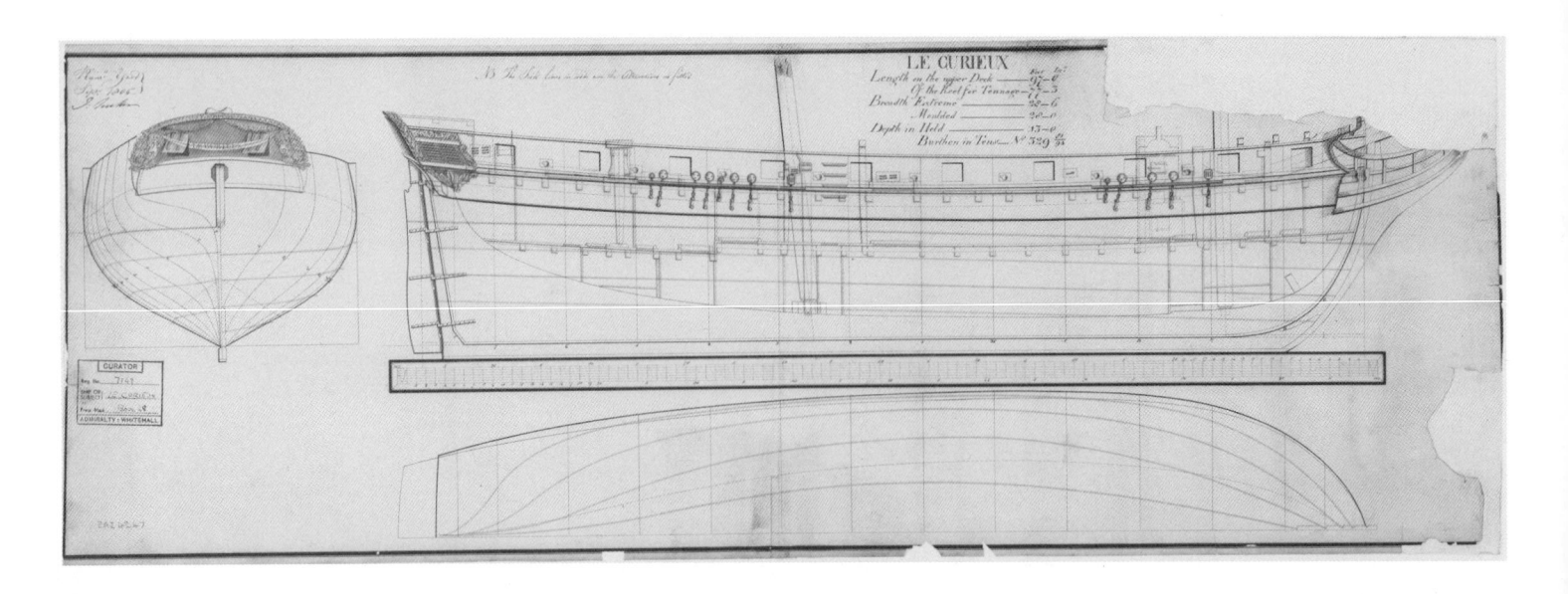

The damaged Admiralty draught dated Plymouth September 1805 of *Curieux*, substantially as captured but with minor alterations marked in dotted lines. The sharp midsection suggests speed and, indeed, the brig had just given an impressive demonstration of her capabilities by racing home from the West Indies with Nelson's dispatches, allowing the Admiralty to make the dispositions that led to the Battle of Trafalgar. Pestel's design was also highly regarded in the French Navy and *Curieux* was to become the prototype for a large class built from 1803 onwards. (© National Maritime Museum J4296)

wl, 25.80m x 8.44m x 4.22m (90ft 0in, 79ft 5in x 26ft 0in x 13ft 0in) and she reportedly actually measured 30.04m wl, 28.26m x 8.61m x 4.55m (92ft 6in, 87 0inft x 26ft 6in x 14ft 0in).

Dimensions & tons: 86ft 0in, 72ft 0in x 26ft 0in x 13ft 2in (27.93, 23.39 x 8.45 x 4.29m). 158/290 tons. Draught 10ft 0in/12ft 6in (3.25/4.06m). Men: 94.

Guns: 16 x 6pdrs

Curieux Entreprise Ethéart, Saint-Malo (Constructeur: François-Timothée Pestel)

L: 10.1799. L: 20.9.1800. Comm: 20.2.1801. C: 2.1801.

Boarded and captured at Fort-de-France, Martinique in the night of 4.2.1804 by the boats of HMS *Centaur* (74), becoming HMS *Curieux*. Wrecked off Guadeloupe 22.9.1809.

ABEILLE Class. 16-gun brigs, designed by Alexandre Notaire-Grandville. The plans were dated 2 January 1801.

Dimensions & tons: 92ft 4in, 71ft 10in x 26ft 6in x 13ft 3in (30.00, 23.35 x 8.61 x 4.30m). 164/391 tons. Draught 11/11ft 6in (3.55/3.75m). Men: 141.

Guns: (*Abeille*) 16 x 6pdrs; (1807) 16 x 8pdrs; (1808) 16 x 24pdr carronades, 2 x 6pdrs; (1818) 6pdrs removed. (Other three) 16 x 4pdrs

Abeille Toulon Dyd.

Ord: 24.12.1800. Named: 21.5.1801. K: 1.1801. L: 24.6.1801. Comm: 8.7.1801. C: 7.1801.

Struck 14.11.1844 at Brest and hulked. Renamed *Molène* c1858. Storage hulk for anchors by 1864. BU 1866.

Furet Toulon Dyd.

Ord: 24.12.1800. Named: 21.5.1801. K: 5.1801. L: 24.12.1801. Comm: 25.2.1802. C: 3.1802.

May have been named *Amaranthe* until 3.1801. Captured 27.2.1806 off Cadiz by HMS *Hydra* (38).

Mouche Toulon Dyd.

Ord: 24.12.1800 and 30.9.1802, named: 21.5.1801, not begun because of shortage of timber, order cancelled 1804.

Serin Toulon Dyd.

Ord: 24.12.1800 and 30.9.1802, named: 21.5.1801, not begun because of shortage of timber, order cancelled 1804.

ALCYON Class. 16-gun brigs. The brothers Louis, Antoine and Mathurin Crucy contracted on 6 July 1800 to build six vessels to a design by Jean-Michel Segondat, and names were assigned on 21 May 1801, although one vessel, *Épervier*, was eventually built to a different and slightly larger design produced by François Gréhan, while the last two were cancelled in November 1801.

Dimensions & tons: first three 83ft ?0in x 26ft 2in (27 x 8.50m). 150/280 tons. Men: ?

Épervier 88ft 4in, 86ft 0in wl, 75ft 9in x 26ft 6in x 13ft 10in (28.70, 27.94 wl, 24.6m x 8.61 x 4.50m). 160/320 tons. Draught 10½ft/11¾ft (3.41/3.82m).

Guns: (first two) 16 x 6pdrs; (others) 16 x 4pdrs.

Alcyon Louis, Antoine, & Mathurin Crucy, Basse-Indre

K: 6.1801. L: 2.1802. Comm: 11.4.1802. C: 4.1802.

Launching planned for 7.10.1801 delayed by high water. Captured 9.7.1803 by HMS *Narcissus* (36) west of Sardinia, becoming HMS *Halcyon*. BU 6.1812.

Goéland (*Goëlan*) Louis, Antoine, & Mathurin Crucy, Basse-Indre

K: 6.1801. L: 7.10.1801. Comm: 9.2.1802. C: 2.1802.

Captured 13.10.1803 by HMS *Pique* (36) and *Pelican* (18) at Aux Cayes, Santo Domingo, becoming HMS *Goelan*. BU 9.1810.

Colibri Louis, Antoine, & Mathurin Crucy, Basse-Indre

K: 10.1801. L: 31.5.1802. Comm: 5.7.1802. C: 7.1802.

Given to the Pope by Napoleon and renamed *Saint Pierre* 1.9.1802, departed Toulon 14.12.1802 and arrived at Civita-Vecchia 16.11.1802 for delivery as *San Pietro*. Taken by the French there 6.1806 and listed as *San Petro*. When Civita-Vecchia was annexed by the Empire 5.1809 the brig was renamed *Saint Pierre*, but in 1.1813, still at Civita-Vecchia, she was found to be unserviceable and was subsequently struck.

Épervier Louis, Antoine, & Mathurin Crucy, Basse-Indre

K: 10.1801. L: 30.6.1802. Comm: 20.7.1802. C: 8.1802.

Captured 27.7.1803 by HMS *Egyptienne* (40) in the Atlantic while returning from Guadeloupe to Lorient, became HMS *Epervier*. BU

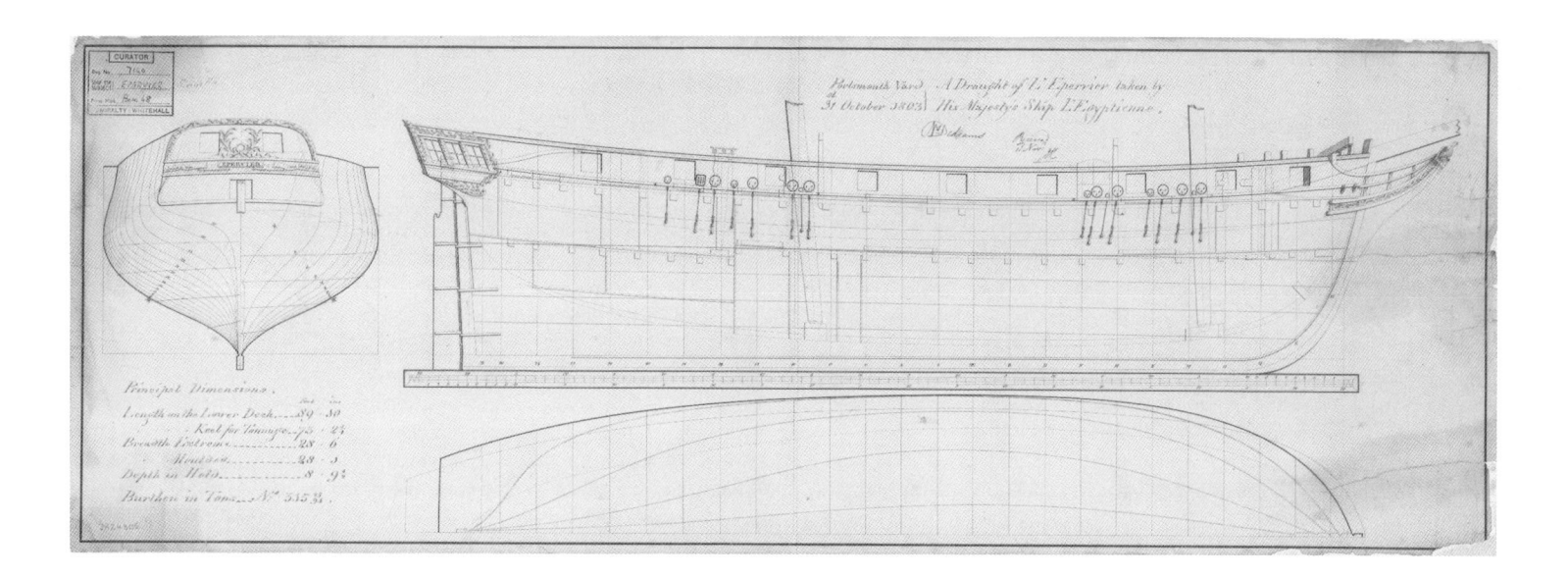

6.1811 at Chatham Dyd.
Requin Louis, Antoine, & Mathurin Crucy, Basse-Indre
Order cancelled 5 or 24.11.1801.
Sardine Louis, Antoine, & Mathurin Crucy, Basse-Indre
Order cancelled 5 or 24.11.1801.

Ex BRITISH NAVAL PRIZES (1794)

SPEEDY. 14-gun brig, designed by her builder and ordered for the British Navy on 23 March 1781. She had been captured on 11 August 1782 by *Résolue* and *Friponne*, but retaken on 6 December 1782 at Barbados. On 9 June 1794 she was captured again, by *Sérieuse* and two other French frigates off Nice.
  Dimensions & tons: 75ft 0in, 62ft 0in x 24ft 0in x 11ft 0in (24.36, 20.14 x 7.80 x 3.57m). 158/270 tons. Draught 9/11ft (2.92/3.57m). Men: 116.
  Guns: 14 x 4pdrs; (1801) 12 x 6pdrs.
Speedy Thomas King, Dover.
  K: 6.1781. L: 29.6.1782. C: 25.10.1782.
  Retaken again 3.1795 by HMS *Inconstant*. Captured a third time on 3.7.1801 by *Desaix* of Linois's squadron near Gibraltar and recommissioned. Given to the Pope by Napoleon and renamed *Saint Paul* 1.9.1802, departed Toulon 14.12.1802 and arrived at Civita-Vecchia 16.11.1802 for delivery as *San Paolo*. Struck c1806.

SCOUT. 16-gun brig, purchased by British Navy 28 March 1780 while on the stocks, and captured by frigates *Vestale* and *Alceste* off Cape Bon on 4 August 1794.
  Dimensions & tons: 77ft x 27ft 8in (25.01 x 8.99m). 160/300 tons. Draught 8ft/9ft 4in (2.60/3.03m). Men: 120.
  Guns: 16 x 4pdrs.
Scout Phineas Jacobs, Folkestone.
  L: 30.7.1780.
  Wrecked 12.12.1795 off Cadiz.

Ex BRITISH PRIVATEERS (1793-1799)

Betzy (Guernsey privateer brig *Betsy* taken 5.1793 by *Sémillante*, and put into service 7.1793, 18 guns). Became convoy escort between Brest and Lorient; captured by HMS *Amazon* off Ushant 12.6.1796, but not added to British Navy.
Actif (Liverpool privateer brig *Active*, built c.1789, taken 5.1793 by

Admiralty draught of *Epervier* dated Portsmouth 31 October 1803. This vessel was a one-off design with fine lines and a midship section whose hollow garboards seem to anticipate nineteenth-century hull forms. (© National Maritime Museum J4598)

Sémillante, 6 guns). Retaken 3.1794 in the West Indies by HMS *Iphigenia*, becoming HMS *Actif*; foundered 26.11.1794 off Bermuda while en route to Britain.
Résolution (British privateer brig *Resolution* taken 9.1793 by lugger *Hook*, 16 guns: 12pdr obusiers and 6pdrs). Taken by the Spanish in early 1794; in service at Cadiz 1795.
Cornish Hero (Malta privateer brig *Cornish Hero*, built at Venice and taken late 1797, 18 guns). Recaptured 5.1798 by HMS *Flora* off the south coast of Sicily, but not added to British Navy.
Dart (**Dard**) (British privateer brig *Dart*, built in 1796, accidentally grounded off Calais 12.1798, refloated by the French and placed in service 1.1799, 120 tons, carried 6 x 4pdrs or 2pdrs). Transported troops from Dunkirk to Senegal in 1802 to re-take possession of the island of Gorée. Recaptured 29.6.1803 by HMS *Apollo* off Cape Finisterre while returning from Martinique, becoming the 8-gun lugger HMS *Dart*; sold in 3.1808.

Ex BRITISH MERCANTILE PRIZES (1793-1799)

Caroline or *Aimable Caroline* (British merchant brig, built in Britain, seized 2.1793 at the declaration of war and commissioned at Rochefort, 100 men, carried 8 x 4pdrs, 2 obusiers). Wrecked in the Loire 1.1799 and refloated, was station ship at Mindin 8.1799, still there 8.1800 and struck soon afterwards, BU 3.1801.
Expédition (British merchant or privateer brig, built in Britain and captured 5.1794 in the Mediterranean, 115 men, carried 14 x 4pdrs). Retaken by a British frigate off Belle-Isle 16.4.1795, but not added to British Navy.
Hermione (British merchant brig of 238 tons, taken 1794, fitted with 6 x 4pdrs and 86 men). Became training ship at Ile de Ré 9.1795 and sold at Rochefort 10.1797.
Arabe (British merchant or privateer brig *Arab*, built in Britain, captured 6.1794).
  Dimensions & tons: 69ft x 19ft x 6ft (22.41 x 6.17 x 1.95m). 100/180 tons. Men: 100.
  Guns: 14 x 4pdrs
  Converted to 98-ton transport at Lorient 1-2.1803. Captured

14.6.1803 west of Sardinia by HMS *Maidstone* (36).

Surveillante (British merchant brig, taken 11.1794, with 6 x 3pdrs and 30 men) Burnt at the entrance to Saint-Malo 12.1795.

Amitié (British merchant brig *Friendship* captured in 1794, 159 tons, 40 men, 2 guns). Converted at Brest to school ship 8.1795, to aviso 1799-1800, and to schooner-transport 2.1803. Wrecked at Miquelon in a squall 13.11.1816.

Fortitude (British merchant brig *Fortitude* captured 1794, 430 tons displacement, carried 8 x 2pdrs). Recomm. 8.1795 at La Rochelle and used as an aviso. Designated as a cutter 5.1801, commissioned at Dunkirk 10.1802 as a cutter-rigged transport. Placed on sale list at Antwerp and struck 1.1808.

Rosine (British merchant brig *Rosine*, built in Britain 1791, taken at the end of 1794, 150 tons, carried 10 x 4pdrs). Training corvette at Dunkirk, offered for sale there 6.1796 but not sold and refitted as a transport at the beginning of 1797. Struck at Dunkirk 1808 and hulked, mentioned for the last time 10.1813.

Sally (British merchant brig *Sally* captured 1.1795, 90 men, carried 8 x 6pdrs in 1800). Recommissioned at Dunkirk as a privateer, cruised off Portugal in 1796. Made into a station ship at Brest in 1797. Rigged as a lugger 1800. Captured 9.1801 by the British while going from Nantes to Rochefort.

Dolphin (British merchant or privateer brig *Dolphin*, taken 7.1795 and put into service at Lorient, with 10 x 4pdrs and 92 men). Disarmed there 1.1796 and sold.

Belle London (British merchant brig taken 7.1795 and became training ship on the River Seudre, with 10 x 6pdrs and 100 men). Sold at Rochefort 10.1797.

Ex VENETIAN PRIZES (1797)

Venetian *ENEA* Class cutters, later 16-gun brigs. Six of these cutters were laid down on the slips at the Venice Arsenal during the final ten years of the Venetian Republic. The plans of these ships have inscriptions in English and measurements in both English and in Venetian feet and may have been bought in an English shipyard, as were those of the bomb vessel *Distruzion*. The first ship of the class, *Enea*, was completed by Andrea Chiribiri at the Arsenal on 28 September 1790, captured by Algerians pirates in February 1796, and taken to Algiers. The second, *Accate*, was completed by Chiribiri on 28 September 1790 and wrecked off Sicily during a great storm in 1792. The next two vessels were re-rigged as brig-cutters just before the French acquired them.

Dimensions & tons: 75ft x 24ft 7in x 10ft 9 (24.4×8.0×3.5m). 170/300 tons. Draught: 8ft 10in/11ft 9in (2.71/3.57m). Men: 94. British measurement: 81ft 5½in x 25ft.

Guns: 16 x 8pdrs; (*Polluce* 1798) 4 x 12pdrs, 12 x 6pdrs; (*Polluce* ex *Castore* 1801) 2 x 12pdrs, 16 x 6pdrs; (same 1805) 18 x 6pdrs, 2 x 3pdrs.

Pollux (Venetian *Polluce*) Venice (built by Andrea Spadon)
K: 6.1791 L: c1796. C: 6.8.1796
Part of the Division for the Defence of Venice of Admiral Leonardo Correr. Re-rigged by the Venetians as a brig-cutter with two masts in April 1797. Taken by the French (Captain Guillaume François Joseph Bourdé de la Villehuet) 16.5.1797 at the Venetian Arsenal, French name became *Pollux* until renamed *Mondovi* 6.1797. Boarded and captured 30.5.1798 in the harbour of Cerigo (now Kythira) by boats from HMS *Flora* (36), became HMS *Mendovi*. BU 5.1811.

Castor (Venetian *Castore*) Venice (built by Carlo Novello)
K: 6.1791 L: c1796. C: 6.8.1796
Part of the Division for the Defence of Venice of Admiral Leonardo Correr. Re-rigged by the Venetians as a brig-cutter with two masts in April 1797. Taken by the French (Captain Guillaume François Joseph Bourdé de la Villehuet) 16.5.1797 at the Venetian Arsenal. As the French *Castor* escorted the convoy carrying French troops that, while flying the Venetian flag, occupied the Venetian base at Corfu on 28.6.1797. Renamed *Rivoli* 11.11.1797. Captured by the Austrians at the surrender of Ancona 14.11.1799, became Austrian *Polluce*. Ceded to French Italy by the Austrians at Venice 19.1.1806 became French *Polluce*. Was at Venice out of commission in 4.1808, struck 1810, BU c1812.

The fifth and sixth cutters of this class were laid down at the beginning of 1797 on slip No.27 at the Venetian Arsenal. They were built by Iseppo Fonda and Iseppo Cason and were taken by the French on 17.5.1797 while they were only 1/12ths completed. Sabotaged by the French on 30.12.1797, they were taken by the Austrians on 18.1.1798, lengthened 6 Venetian feet (1.80 metres), and re-rigged as brigs. Original measurements were 75 Venetian feet (26.08m), 60 ft on the keel (20.86m) x 24 ft 7 in. (8.55m) x 10ft 2 in (3.54m) draught with 81 men. Completed by the Austrians and launched with the names of *Oreste* and *Pilade*, they stayed out of French hands in 1806 at Trieste, both were sold on 20.11.1809 to a Prussian merchant. (See Chapter 8 for a full listing.)

Venetian brig-cutter *GIASONE*, later 20-gun brig. This vessel was probably designed by the Venetians as a cutter but completed by them as a brig.

Dimensions & tons: 83ft 6in x 28ft 11in x 12ft (27.1 x 9.4 x 3.9m). 250/400 tons. Draught 10ft 2in/16ft (3.08/4.87m). Men: 94.

Guns: 20 x 8pdrs; (11.1797) 18 x 6pdrs; (1.1800) 14 x 6pdrs, 2 x 3pdrs, 6 x 36pdr obusiers.

Jason (Venetian *Giasone*) Venice (built by Piero Beltrame)
K: 29.8.1791. L: 29.8.1795. C: 9.1796.
Captured at Corfu 23.7.1797, name became *Jason*. Renamed *Lodi* (*Lody*) 11.11.1797. Arrived at Toulon 7.2.1798. Recaptured by boarding by HMS *Racoon* 11.7.1803 at Léogane, Santo Domingo, where she was station ship.

Ex SPANISH PRIZES (1793-1795)

Infante (Spanish *Infante*, built at Cadiz 1787, captured at Toulon Dec. 1793).

Dimensions & tons: 88ft 0in x 23ft 2in (28.59 x 7.53m). 200/350 tons. Men: 95/112.

Guns: 18 x 6pdrs.

Renamed *Liberté* 1.1794; resumed original name 5.1795, then renamed *Salamine* 10.5.1798. Taken off Toulon by HMS *Emerald* of Markham's squadron 18.6.1799, becoming HMS *Salamine*. Sold at Malta in late 1802.

Courtois (Spanish brig captured in June 1795, 116 men, carried 12 x 6pdrs). Employed as training ship at Ile de Ré from 8.1795. Sold at Rochefort 10.1797.

MISCELLANEOUS PRIZES

Concorde (108-ton polacre taken in Egypt 7.1798, 14 guns). Re-rigged as a brig 1799. Sold at Marseille 7.1802.

Saint Philippe (Neapolitan privateer brig *San Filippo*, was new when taken by *Frontin* (64) in the roadstead at Toulon in 1798/99, carried 2 x 12pdrs). By 1807 she was in use at Corfu as a transport. Taken by the British when the French evacuated Corfu 7.1814.

PURCHASED VESSELS (1793-1801)

Surveillant (Merchant cutter *Surveillant*, built at Bordeaux 1788 and requisitioned 4.1793, carried 4 x 4pdrs and 4 obusiers). Renamed *Siècle* 5.1795, re-rigged as brig 1796, as such carried 10 x 4pdrs in 1797, used as a coast defence vessel. Wrecked at Cherbourg 13.12.1804. Raised 1806, pilot cutter at Brest 1.1807. Renamed *Braque* 2.1809. Also called a sloop. Service craft at Cherbourg 1.1815. Fishery protection vessel 1822, decomm. 1.1828. Ordered commissioned for the Granville station 1829, re-rated service craft 14.11.1835. This entry may cover two or even three vessels.

Républicain (Merchant brig *Boussole*, possibly built at Saint-Malo, purchased at Toulon 6.1793, 115 men, carried 2 x 8pdrs, 12 x 6pdrs). Renamed *Railleur* 5.1795. Captured 8.1798 at Rhodes by the Turks and crew enslaved.

Voltigeur (merchant brig *Reine* built at Roscoff in 1780 and purchased in 1793, 75-86 men, carried 8 to 12 x 4pdrs). Also called a lugger and a corvette. Lost 1.1797 on the Irish coast, either wrecked or captured by the British.

Sans Culotte (Merchant brig bought at Martinique 8.1793). Taken by HMS *Blanche* 9.10.1794 in the West Indies.

Petit Jacobin (brig purchased and commissioned 9.1793 at Baltimore). Sent to Santo Domingo where she probably received another name in 1794.

Robuste (brig from Nantes that entered service in the slave trade in 3.1789 and was purchased by the navy 12.1793 and commissioned at Rochefort)
Dimensions & tons: 97ft x 27ft (31.51 x 8.77m). 350/542 tons. Men: 106
Guns: 10
Captured 16.4.1796 by HMS *Pomone* (40) southeast of Penmarch in Brittany, became the ship-sloop HMS *Scourge* (18). Sold 8.1802.

Hirondelle (aviso, ex merchant brig, probably a captured British ship built in 1784, placed in merchant service at Rochefort 4.1793 and purchased 4.1793 at Honfleur, 50 tons, 86 men, carried 6 x 4pdrs). Renamed *Fleche* 6.1799 at Antwerp and described as a schooner. Given to the postal service 1.1802.

Oiseau (brig acquired in 1794 and in service at Toulon 7.1794, 247 tons, 120 men, carried 18 x 6pdrs). Renamed *Orage* in 5.1795, school ship at Marseille 8.1795, reverted to *Oiseau* 1796. Recomm. 4.1798 at Marseille to help take the Reynier division to Egypt. Captured by the RN 7.1801 in the eastern Mediterranean and taken to Aboukir.

Nathalie (merchant brig requisitioned at Île de France 8.1794 after arriving there 7.1792 from Pondichery and Port Louis, 150 tons, 100 men, carried 10 x 4pdrs). Carried despatches and passengers from Île de France to Vigo, Spain, in 7-11.1796. Refitted at Lorient 1800. Condemned 1802 at Santo Domingo for dilapidation. Also classed as an aviso.

Léger (brig from Port Louis, Île de France, in merchant service since 1787, purchased or requisitioned by the navy and commissioned in 11.1794, 60 tons, had 16 gunports). Commanded by Lieutenant de Vaisseau Jean-Baptiste-Philibert Willaumez she arrived at Brest 3.1795 with despatches and with many passengers whom the colony desired to expatriate. (She is shown as a three-masted vessel in a watercolour by Frédéric Roux in his *Album de l'Amiral Willaumez.*). Last mentioned 2.1797 while at Batavia.

Pélagie (merchant brig built at Saint-Malo, 1790, and requisitioned or purchased 3.1795 at Île de France, 90 men, carried 8 x 4pdrs). Carried despatches from Réunion to Bordeaux 1795. Recomm. 23.9.1801 at Lorient and sent to Caribbean. Decomm. at Martinique 12.2.1804, in poor condition there and struck 1.1807.

Escaut (brig that was in service at Toulon in 5.1795, 120 men, carried 14 x 6pdrs). Struck at the end of 1795.

Pêcheur (fishing brig requisitioned or purchased and in service at Saint-Malo in 5.1795, carried 4 x 1pdrs). Struck at the end of 1795.

Athénienne (brig, probably a privateer, requisitioned and commissioned in the Antilles in 4.1796, 150 tons, 14 guns according to the British). Captured 8.5.1796 off Barbados by HMS *Albacore* (16) and became the gunbrig HMS *Athenienne*. Sold 1802 for BU.

Blonde (brig acquired c5.1796, 16 guns according to the British). Captured 6.1796 off Ushant by a British division.

Africaine (brig requisitioned and commissioned c11.1796 in the Antilles, 18 guns according to the British). Captured 12.1796 by HMS *Quebec* (32) off Santo Domingo.

Alexandre (brig commissioned 2.1799 at Ancona, 8 to 16 guns). Captured 2.3.1799 near Brindisi with despatches for Napoleon by the Russian frigate *Schastlivyy* (36) and taken into the Russian Navy as *Svyatoy Aleksandr*. Arrived at Sevastopol from the Mediterranean in 1801, collided 12.8.1804 in a storm with the wrecked ship of the line *Tolskaya Bogoroditsa* and was also wrecked.

Dorade (brig commissioned 5.1799 at Toulon, 4 guns). Sent from Toulon to look for a Spanish fleet and taken 2.6.1799 by HMS *Montagu* and another frigate off the Île de Riou near Marseille.

Sénégal (brig in service in Senegal in 1800 carried 18 guns including 6pdrs and 12pdr carronades). Captured by boarding 3.1.1801 at the mouth of the Senegal River by boats from HMS *Melpomene* (38) but then grounded on the river bank and the British could not salvage her.

Cerf (British *Stag*, ex Spanish Navy 18-gun brig *Ciervo*, built at Havana in 1794-95, purchased from her civilian British captors 15.12.1801 by the Captain-General of Guadeloupe, renamed *Cerf*, and commissioned 22.12.1801)
Dimensions & tons: 69ft 3in x 20ft 7in (22.5 x 6.7m). 90/170 tons
Guns: 6 x 18pdr carronades, 8 x 9pdrs.
Taken 30.11.1803 in the capitulation of Santo Domingo, became the gunbrig HMS *Cerf*. Sold 8.1806.

REQUISITIONED PRIVATEERS (1794). These French privateers were acquired by the navy for coastal escort and patrol purposes.

Eugénie (Nantes privateer built 1793 and requisitioned 3.1794).
Dimensions & tons: 81ft 0in, 63ft 6in x 24ft 0in (26.31, 20.63 x 7.80m). 180/300 tons. Men: 95-105.
Guns: 16 x 6pdrs + 12 swivels; from 1795 2 x 6pdrs and 14 x 4pdrs.
Returned to privateering at Nantes 2.1796 (with 16 x 6pdrs). Taken by HMS *Magnanime* 16.3.1798, becoming HMS *Pandour*; never commissioned in British Navy, but renamed *Wolf* 14.6.1800. BU at Plymouth 3.1802.

Intrépide (Nantes privateer built 1781 and requisitioned 3.1794, 530 tons, 100 men, carried 12 x 12pdrs). Returned to privateer at Nantes. Taken by the British 12.1797, but not added to British Navy.

Sans Peur (Bayonne privateer built 1788 and requisitioned 1794, 120 tons, 116 men, carried 12 x 6pdrs). Struck 1797.

Hirondelle (privateer requisitioned at Île de France 10.1794, 140 tons, 12 guns). Returned to privateer service there in 11.1794.

(C) Brigs acquired from 25 March 1802

LYNX Class. Two 16-gun brigs, designed by Pierre-Jacques-Nicolas Rolland. Both were captured by the British Navy, being re-armed for British service with 14 x 24pdr carronades. For another brig attributed to Rolland see *Requin* in the *Sylphe* class.
Dimensions & tons: 90ft 0in, 80ft 0in x 26ft 9in x 13ft 3in (29.23,

One of many incidents in the remarkable career of Thomas Cochrane, the Royal Navy's most daring frigate captain, was a clash between his small 12pdr-armed frigate *Pallas* and the 18pdr 40-gun *Minerve* supported by the 16-gun brigs *Lynx*, *Sylphe* and *Palinure* off Rochefort on 14 May 1806. Despite losing his fore topmast in a collision with the large French frigate (which had grounded on a shoal), Cochrane managed to extricate his ship, having heavily damaged one of the brigs in the action, as two more 40-gun frigates – *Armide* and *Infatigable* – were fast approaching. This print is based on a painting by the famous marine artist Nicholas Pocock, so the depiction of the frigates and brigs is likely to be very accurate. (Courtesy of Beverley R. Robinson Collection, US Naval Academy Museum)

25.98 x 8.69 x 4.30m). 240/402 tons. Draught 11ft/12ft 7in (3.60/4.10m). Men: 94.

Guns: 16 x 6pdrs

Lynx (*Linx*) Bayonne (Constructeur: Jean Baudry)

Ord: 21.2.1803. K: 5.1803. L: 17.4.1804. Comm: 14.6.1804. C: 8.1804.

Captured 21.1.1807 by boats from the 32-gun HMS *Galatea* (32) while becalmed off La Guaira (Saintes), becoming HMS *Heureux*. Sold 9.1814.

Actéon Rochefort Dyd. (Constructeur: Rolland)

Ord: 21.2.1803. K: 24.6.1803. L: 11.7.1804. Comm: 6.10.1804. C: 10.1804.

Ordered at Bayonne but built at Rochefort. Taken by HMS *Egyptienne* (40) 3.10.1805 off Rochefort or 27.9.1805 at Île d'Aix, becoming HMS *Acteon*. BU 10.1816.

ORESTE Class. 16-gun brigs, built to the design of Alexandre-Jean-Louis Notaire-Grandville for the *Abeille* class with modifications. *Favori* may have been of the original *Abeille* type.

Dimensions & tons: 85ft 0in, 79ft 0in x 26ft 0in x 13ft 0in (27.61, 25.66 x 8.45 x 4.22m). 150/352 tons. Draught 11/11ft 6in (3.55/3.75m). Men: 94.

Guns: (*Oreste*, 1805) 12 x 6pdrs and 4 x 32pdr carronades; (*Oreste*, 1807) 14-24pdr carronades, 2-8pdrs; (*Favori*) 16-24pdr carronades, 2-8pdrs.

Oreste Le Havre

K: 7.1804. L: 16.1.1805. C: 1805.

Captured 12.1.1810 by HMS *Scorpion* (18) just after sailing from Basse-terre, Guadeloupe, becoming HMS *Wellington*. Never commissioned in British Navy, and BU 8.1812.

Favori Antwerp (Constructeur: Jean-François Guillemard)

Ord: 1.6.1804. K: 29.6.1804. L: 30.7.1806. Comm: 1.9.1806. C: 9.1806.

Burned 1.2.1809 at Martinique to avoid capture by British troops.

PYLADE. 16-gun brig, a one-off small design by Jean-François Chaumont.

Dimensions & tons: 83ft 6in, 75ft 0in x 26ft 0in x 13ft 0in (27.12, 24.36 x 8.45 x 4.22m). 170/341 tons. Draught 10ft 6in/12ft 2in (3.38/3.96m). Men: 100.

Guns: 16 x 6pdrs; (1806) 12 x 6pdrs, 4 x 32pdr carronades; (1807) 14 x 24pdr carronades, 2 x 6pdrs.

Pylade (*Pilade*) Le Havre.

K: 8.1804. L: 17.4.1805. Comm: 12.11.1805. C: 11.1805.

Taken by HMS *Pompee* (74) off Martinique 20.10.1808, becoming HMS *Vimiera*. Paid off 8.1810 and sold 1.9.1814.

CURIEUX Class (series production). 16-gun brigs, designed by François-Timothée Pestel. In 1803 series production began of a design first used in 1799 for the construction of a single ship (*Curieux*), listed above. Nineteen out of the twenty-one brigs of this class that were completed (including *Curieux*) were eventually captured by the British, and fifteen subsequently found service with the British Navy. Available measurements of some of the ships of this class differ somewhat from the class figures given below. The adoption in 1804 of iron carronades permitted substituting 24pdr carronades for 6pdr guns in *Palinure* in 1804 (probably for trials) and in the ships completed in 1806 and later. Sané reportedly modified the design of *Écureuil* and *Cygne* on 13 June 1805, extending their length from 86ft to 90ft (29.24m), while the plans for *Fanfaron* and *Espiègle* were reportedly also altered, giving them a hull length of 87ft 8in (28.48m) overall. Neither design change, however, is confirmed by surviving measurements.

Dimensions & tons: 86ft 0in, 72ft 0in x 26ft 0in x 13ft 2in (27.93, 23.39 x 8.45 x 4.29m). 158/290 tons. Draught 10ft 0in/12ft 6in (3.25/4.06m). Men: 94.

Guns: 16 x 6pdrs (as designed); later 14 x 24pdr carronades, 2 x

8pdrs or 6pdrs

Palinure Lorient Dyd-Caudan, by Louis, Antoine, & Mathurin Crucy.
Ord: 19.2.1803 (and 2.1.1803 and 19.3.1803). K: 7.1803. Named: 9.6.1803. L: 12.1.1804. Comm: 20.5.1804. C: 5.1804.
Captured 31.10.1808 by HMS *Circe* (32) off Diamond Rock, Martinique, becoming HMS *Snap*. Paid off 2.1811 and BU 6.1811 at Sheerness.

Néarque Lorient Dyd-Caudan, by Louis, Antoine, & Mathurin Crucy.
Ord: 19.2.1803 (and 2.1.1803 and 19.3.1803). Named: 9.6.1803. K: 15.6.1803. L: 27.3.1804. Comm: 13.7.1804. C: 7.1804.
Captured 28.3.1806 by HMS *Niobe* (38) off Île de Groix while leaving Lorient to attack the British whaling fleet, becoming HMS *Nearque*, but never commissioned in British Navy, and sold 21.7.1814.

Phaeton Danet, Antwerp.
Ord: 18.4.1803 (contract). Named 21.4.1803 and construction ordered. K: 7.1803. L: 28.6.1804. Comm: 23.9.1804. C: 11.1804.
Captured 26.3.1806 by boarding off Santo Domingo by HMS *Pique* (44) and became HMS *Mignonne*. Renamed HMS *Musette* 7.10.1807, sold 1.9.1814.

Voltigeur Danet, Antwerp.
Ord: 18.4.1803 (contract). Named 21.4.1803 and construction ordered. K: 6.1803. L: 6.9.1804. Comm: 24.9.1804. C: 11.1804.
Captured 26.3.1806 off Santo Domingo by HMS *Pique* (44) and became HMS *Pelican*. Sold 16.4.1812.

Chasseur Danet, Antwerp
Ord: 18.4.1803 (contract). Order cancelled around 6.1803 and probably replaced with an order for prames.

Dragon Danet, Antwerp.
Ord: 18.4.1803 (contract). Order cancelled around 6.1803 and probably replaced with an order for prames.

Fanfaron Entreprise Ethéart, Saint-Malo.
Ord: 6.6.1803. K: 4.7.1803. L: 15.3.1804. Comm: 21.4.1804. C: 4.1804.
In 1809 carried 14 x 18pdr British carronades, 2 x 8pdrs. Captured 6.11.1809 by HMS *Emerald* (36) off Brest two days after leaving Brest for Guadeloupe.

Lutin Entreprise Ethéart, Saint-Malo.
Ord: 6.6.1803. K: 7.1803. L: 7.6.1804. Comm: 20.6.1804. C: 7 or 8.1804.
Captured 24.3.1806 by HMS *Agamemnon* (64) and HMS *Carysfort* (28) off Martinique, becoming HMS *Hawk*. Renamed HMS *Buzzard* 8.1.1812, paid off 10.1814, and sold 15.12.1814.

Espiègle Entreprise Ethéart, Saint-Malo.
Ord: 6.6.1803. K: 7.1803. L: 12.7.1804. Comm: 20.7.1804. C: 9.1804.
Captured 16.8.1808 by HMS *Sybille* (38) west of the Bay of Biscay, becoming HMS *Electra*. Sold 7.1816.

Pandour Louis, Antoine, & Mathurin Crucy, Basse-Indre
Ord: 22.8.1803. K: 12.1803. L: 23.6.1804. Comm: 7.11.1804. C: 11.1804.
Captured 1.5.1806 in the Atlantic by a British squadron.

Faune Louis, Antoine, & Mathurin Crucy, Basse-Indre
Ord: 22.8.1803. K: 2.1804. L: 8.7.1804. Comm: 22.12.1804. C: 2.1805.
Captured 15.8.1805 in the Atlantic by HMS *Goliath* (74) and *Camilla* (20), becoming HMS *Fawn*. Deleted late 1806.

Nisus Lerond Campion & Co., Granville.
Ord: 21.2.1804 (?). K: 31.3.1804. L: 15.2.1805. C: 3.1805. Comm: 1.2.1806.
Captured 12.12.1809 by boats from HMS *Thetis* (38) and two brigs including HMS *Pultusk* (16) while anchored at Port Deshayes, Guadeloupe. Became HMS *Guadeloupe*, sold 11.1814.

Euryale Lerond Campion & Co., Granville.
Ord: 21.2.1804. K: 31.3.1804, was listed as 8/24ths complete during 1806 but was not being worked on. Construction evidently abandoned for unknown reasons.

Endymion Murio & Migone, Genoa (Constructeur: Jean-Baptiste Lefebvre)
Ord: 6.2.1804 and named. K: 2.1804. L: 10.1.1805. Comm: 20.2.1805. C: 5.1805.
Built by Compagnia Murio & Migone in Genoa's Lazzaretto district. Originally armed with 18 x 6pdrs. The Emperor ordered on 17.9.1810 that she carry 14 x 24pdr carronades and 4 x 8pdrs. Taken 19.4.1814 by the British in the capitulation of Genoa.

Cyclope Murio & Migone, Genoa (Constructeur: Jean-Baptiste Lefebvre)
Ord: 6.2.1804 and named. K: 2.1804. L: 7.3.1805. Comm: 16.3.1805. C: 5.1805.
Original armament was 16 x 6pdrs and 2 x 8pdrs, changed in 1809 to 14 x 24pdr carronades and 2 x 6pdrs. On 14.6.1810 the Emperor transferred the brigs *Écureuil*, *Mercure*, and *Cyclope*, then at Venice, from his Imperial Navy to his Royal (Italian) Navy in exchange for the Italian frigate *Favorite*, built at Venice. Became Italian *Ciclope* 6.1810, ceded at Venice to Napoleon's Illyrian (Trieste) Navy 10.1810 and renamed *Mercurio*. Participated in the Battle of Lissa on 13.3.1811. With the Illyrian *Eridano* (16) and the Italian *Mamelucco* was escorting the 74-gun *Rivoli* when she was intercepted by the British off Venice on 22.2.1812; while engaging HMS *Weazel* (18), *Mercurio* accidentally blew up leaving only 3 survivors.

Griffon Rochefort Dyd. (Constructeurs: Jean-Baptiste Lemoyne-Sérigny, then Pierre Rolland)
Ord: 30.4.1804. K: 5.4.1805. L: 2.6.1806. Comm: 9.8.1806. C: 8.1806.
Captured 11.5.1808 by HMS *Bacchante* (20) off Cape San Antonio, Cuba. Became HMS *Griffon*, sold 3.1819.

Écureuil Toulon Dyd. (Constructeur: Jean-Baptiste Lefebvre)
Ord: 26.3.1805. K: 20.6.1805. L: 15.1.1806. Comm: 1.3.1806. C: 3.1806.
On 14.6.1810 the Emperor transferred the brigs *Écureuil*, *Mercure*, and *Cyclope*, then at Venice, from his Imperial Navy to his Royal (Italian) Navy in exchange for the Italian frigate *Favorite*, built at Venice. Ceded at Venice to Napoleon's Illyrian (Trieste) Navy 10.1810 and renamed *Eridano*. Participated in the Battle of Lissa on 13.3.1811 under the command of Giuseppe Cocumpergher and fled to Trieste. With the Illyrian *Mercurio* (18) and the Italian *Mamelucco* was escorting the new 74-gun *Rivoli* when she was intercepted by the British off Venice on 22.2.1812; *Eridano* and *Mamelucco* abandoned *Rivoli* after *Mercurio* blew up. *Eridano* was out of service at Venice in 1812, taken over by the Austrians 25.4.1814 in the occupation of the Venice Arsenal, and BU 1816.

Épervier Nantes
Ordered 2.4.1805 at Nantes, soon cancelled. A brig of the same name was ordered 8.1805 at Rochefort and either was not built or was re-ordered in 1806 as *Pluvier* of the *Sylphe* class, below.

Milan Entreprise Ethéart, Saint-Malo.
Ord: 28.12.1805. K: 3.1806. L: 6.7.1807. Comm: 20.1.1808. C: 1.1808.
Captured 30.10.1809 in the Atlantic by frigates HMS *Surveillante* (36) and *Seine* (40, ex *Ambuscade*) 50 miles west of Île de Ré while en route to Guadeloupe. Became HMS *Achates*, sold 6.1818.

Cygne (*Cigne*) Le Havre (Constructeur: Pierre Jaunez)

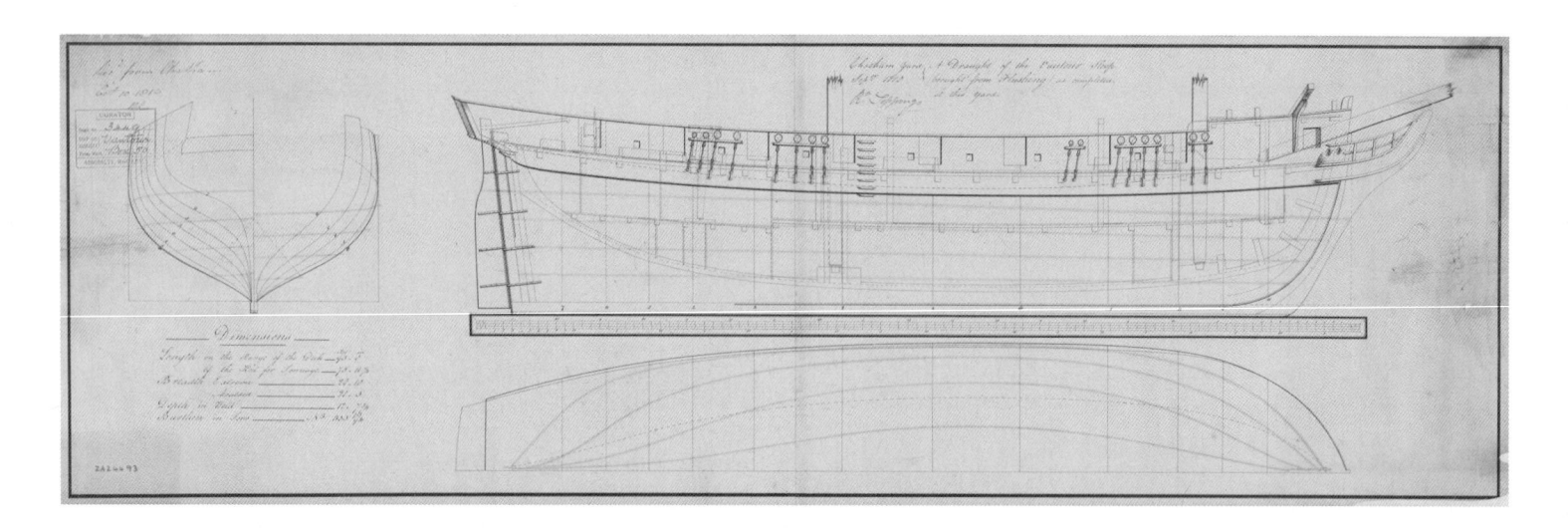

Admiralty draught of *Vautour* as completed for Royal Navy service at Chatham, dated September 1810. The ship was captured on the stocks at Flushing, completed to launching stage in less than two months and towed to Chatham for completion. The brig must have been in an advanced stage of construction when taken as the hull form is the same as that of other captured members of the class for which draughts survive, but alterations to the topsides were substantial. The broadside ports were reduced from nine to eight and rearranged (as were the sweep ports); the bulwarks must have been strengthened to allow the channels to be moved up from deck level, making them less vulnerable to damage in heavy weather; and a topgallant forecastle was added between the foremast and the stem, to keep the vessel drier in a head sea. In general the alterations were aimed at improved seaworthiness, and at a detailed level these included a less elaborate head, reduction of the steep rake aft of the transom, and the fitting of a larger and more effective rudder. (© National Maritime Museum J4132)

Ord: 21.2.1806. K: 28.4.1806. L: 12.9.1806. Comm: 22.11.1806. C: 11.1806.

Run onto rocks on 13.12.1808 near St. Pierre de la Martinique by a local pilot while under fire from seven enemy ships one day after her arrival there, rig and stores salvaged.

Serpent (ex *Rivoli* 4.6.1807) Louis & Michel-Louis Crucy, Paimboeuf

Named 4.6.1806 (*Rivoli*). Ord: 19.7.1806. K: 9.1806. L: 30.10.1807. Comm: 20.1.1808. C: 1.1808.

Captured 17.7.1808 by HMS *Acasta* (40) at La Guaira near Caracas. Named HMS *Pert* locally but renamed *Asp* by the Admiralty as *Pert* was already in use. BU 10.1813.

Colibri (*Colibry*) Le Havre (Constructeur: François-Toussaint Gréhan)

Ord: 17.11.1807. K: 15.1.1808. Named 25.2.1808. L: 8.8.1808. Comm: 1.10.1808. C: 10.1808.

Captured 16.1.1809 by HMS *Melampus* (36) off Santo Domingo, becoming HMS *Colibri*. Wrecked 22.8.1813.

Béarnais Bayonne (Constructeur: Jean Baudry).

Ord: 5.5.1808. K: 8.6.1808. Named: 13.6.1808. L: 19.11.1808. Comm: 18.1.1809. C: 1.1809.

Taken 14.12.1809 by HMS *Melampus* (36) while en route from Bayonne with *Basque* and after escaping from HMS *Druid* (32) which had taken her sister. Became HMS *Curieux*, sold 5.1814. This ship may have been of the *Sylphe* class, below.

Basque Bayonne (Constructeur: Jean Baudry).

Ord: 5.5.1808. K: 8.6.1808. Named: 13.6.1808. L: 13.2.1809. Comm: 7.4.1809. C: 4.1809.

Taken 12.11.1809 by HMS *Druid* (32) in the Atlantic while en route from Bayonne to Guadeloupe with sister *Béarnais*, becoming HMS *Foxhound*. Sold 2.1816. This ship may have been of the *Sylphe* class, below.

SYLPHE Class. 16-gun brigs, designed by Jacques-Noël Sané. The standard brig design from 1805 onwards, to which 32 vessels were built. Originally designed to have carried 16 x 6pdrs, but after the iron 24pdr carronade became available in 1804 all but the prototype *Sylphe* were completed with a battery of those weapons.

Dimensions and tons: 90ft 0in, 81ft 0in x 26ft 0in, 26ft 6in ext x 13ft 6in (29.23, 26.31 x 8.45, 8.61 ext x 4.35m). 190/374 tons. Draught 3.34/4.14m. Men: 98.

Guns: (*Sylphe*) 16 x 6pdrs; (others) 16 x 24pdr carronades or 14 x 24pdr carronades, 2 x 8pdrs.

Sylphe Dunkirk (Constructeur: Pierre-Joseph Pénétreau).

Ord: 7.3.1803 and named. K: 10.6.1803. L: 10.7.1804. Comm: 29.9.1804. C: 1.1805.

From 2.1806 carried 10 x 6pdrs and 8 x 16pdr carronades and from 1807 had 14 x 24pdr carronades and 2 x 6prs. Taken 18.8.1808 by HMS *Comet* (18) near Île d'Yeu, becoming HMS *Seagull*. Sold 7.1814.

Mercure Genoa (Constructeur: Jean-Baptiste Lefebvre).

Ord: 1.1805. K: 4.1805. L: 17.7.1806. Comm: 1.11.1806. C: 11.1806.

On 14.6.1810 the Emperor transferred the brigs *Écureuil*, *Mercure*, and *Cyclope*, then at Venice, from his Imperial Navy to his Royal (Italian) Navy in exchange for the Italian frigate *Favorite*, *Mercure* being renamed *Simplon*. Borrowed back and comm. 11.11.1810 at Trieste under her Italian name, renamed *Curieux* on 24.9.1814, *Simplon* on 22.3.1815, and *Curieux* on 15.7.1815. May have carried 16 x 18pdr carronades in 1815. Became school for apprentice seamen at Toulon in 1829. Struck 5.6.1833.

Adonis Genoa (Constructeur: Jean-Baptiste Lefebvre).

Ord: 1.1805. K: 4.1805. L: 18.8.1806. Comm: 21.11.1806. C: 11.1806.

Struck at Toulon 6.11.1822, ordered BU 20.1.1823.

Génie Dunkirk (Constructeur: Louis Bretocq)

Ord: 27.10.1806. K: 1.12.1806. L: 23.7.1808. Comm: 1.12.1808. C: 12.1808.

Had 16 vice 14 x 24pdr carronades plus 2 x 8pdrs. Seized by the Dutch 4.5.1814 at the surrender of Nieuwediep but returned to the French. Struck 1833.

Papillon Le Havre (Constructeur: François-Toussaint Gréhan)

Ord: 11.9.1806. K: 11.1806. L: 22.4.1807. C: 6.1807. Comm: 1.7.1807.

Captured 19.12.1809 by HMS *Rosamond* (18) between Guadeloupe and Montserrat. Became HMS *Papillon*, sold 10.1815.

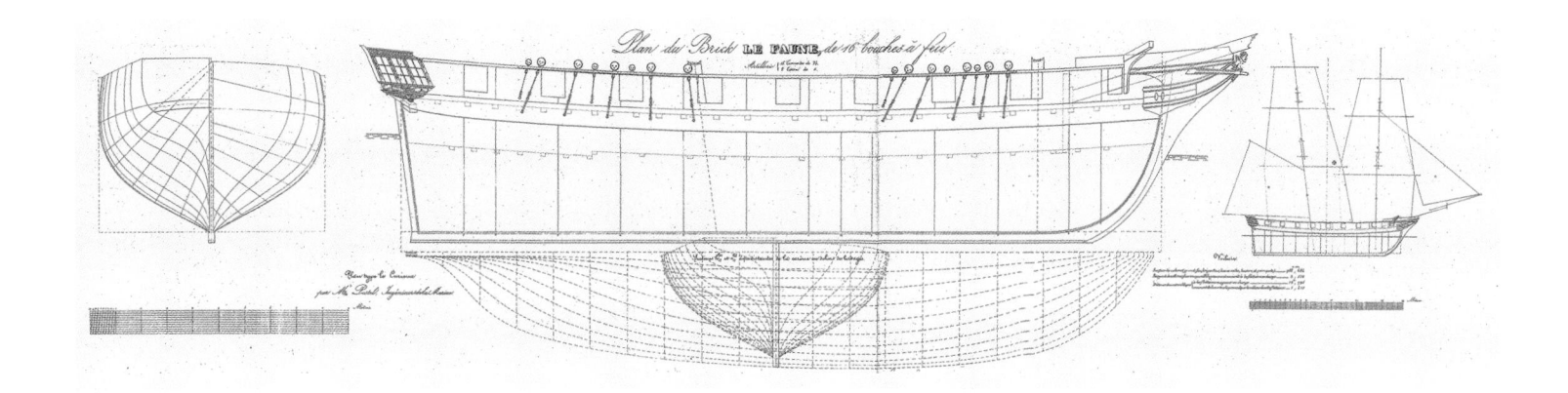

Requin Rochefort Dyd. (Constructeurs: Jean-François Chaumont and from 7.1806 Jean-Baptiste Lemoyne-Sérigny).
Ord: 26.3.1805. K: 17.10.1805. L: 8.11.1806. C: 1.1807. Comm: 2.3.1807.
Originally ordered to plans by Rolland (see *Lynx* class). Captured 28.7.1808 by HMS *Volage* (22) near Monaco, became HMS *Sabine*. Sold 29.1.1818.

Pluvier Rochefort Dyd. (Constructeur: Jean-Baptiste Lemoyne-Sérigny).
Ord: 24.11.1806. K: 10.12.1806. L: 19.10.1808. C: 3.1809. Comm: 18.4.1809.
May originally have been ordered 8.1805 as *Épervier* of the *Curieux* class. Grounded and burned 24.8.1811 near Royan in the Gironde to avoid capture in a raid by HMS *Semiramis* (36) and *Diana* (38).

Étourdi Vian, Velin, Riboulet, & Ménard, La Ciotat.
Ord: 10.10.1807. Named 15.2.1808. K: 1.3.1808. L: 6.8.1808. C: 2.1809. Comm: 1.10.1809 (sic).
Carried a non-standard armament of 10 x 8pdrs and 6 x 24pdr carronades. Chased by HMS *Pomone* (38) into a cove on Monte Cristo island near Elba and burned 14.3.1811 to avoid capture.

Coureur Vian, Velin, Riboulet, & Ménard, La Ciotat.
Ord: 10.10.1807. Named 15.2.1808. K: 1.3.1808. L: 30.8.1808. C: 1.1809. Comm: 1.11.1809 (sic).
Carried a non-standard armament of 12 x 24pdr carronades, 4 x 8pdrs and from c1811 16 x 24pdr carronades, 2 x 8pdrs. Taken 19.4.1814 by the British in the capitulation of Genoa.

Hussard Dunkirk (Constructeur: Louis Bretocq)
K: 20.8.1808. L: 26.6.1809. Comm: 21.11.1809. C: 11.1809.
Decomm. at Brest 28.1.1817, struck c6.1822 and BU 8.1822.

Alcyon Le Havre (Constructeur: François Gréhan)
K: 3.3.1809. Named: 3.4.1809. L: 11.8.1809. Comm: 3.11.1809. C: 11.1809.
Captured 17.3.1814 near the Lizard by HMS *Ajax* (74).

Vautour Flushing (Vlissingen).
Ord: 14.8.1806. K: 10.1806. L: 9.10.1809 (by the British)
Taken on the ways by the British 16.8.1809. Launched there 9.10.1809, taken to Chatham and hauled out, re-launched 15.9.1810, and completed as HMS *Vautour*. Disappeared at sea between 8.1813 and 3.1814.

Renard Genoa (Constructeurs: Mathurin Boucher and Jean-Baptiste Marestier).
K: 11.1808. L: 12.5.1810. Comm: 13.6.1810. C: 6.1810.
Taken 19.4.1814 by the British in the capitulation of Genoa.

Flibustier Bayonne (Constructeur: Jean Baudry).
Ord: 28.7.1808 and 20.2.1809. Named: 7.3.1809. K: 3.1809. L: 6.3.1810. Comm: 16.4.1811. C: 4.1811.

A postwar official plan of *Faune* of 1804. Despite the fact that this brig was captured in 1805, the draught does not relate to the later *Faune* of 1811, as the annotation clearly describes the subject as of the *Curieux* type designed by Pestel. The armament is listed as fourteen 24pdr carronades and two long 8s. The sail area as shown in the plan totalled 953 sq.m. (Atlas du Génie Maritime, French collection, plate 25)

Burned 13.10.1813 while at anchor off Biarritz to avoid capture by HMS *Constant* (22), *Challenger* (18) and *Telegraph* (12).

Épervier Bayonne (Constructeur: Jean Baudry).
Ord: 28.7.1808 and 20.2.1809. K: 20.3.1809. L: 19.5.1810. C: 3.1811.
Station ship at Île d'Aix from 1815 to 1821; on 15.7.1815 carried Napoleon and his suite to HMS *Bellerophon* (74). Decomm. 12.1821 in bad condition at Rochefort, struck and BU approved 19.2.1822, BU 5-6.1822.

Railleur Le Havre (Constructeur: François Gréhan).
K: 8.1809. L: 2.6.1810. Comm: 17.10.1810. C: 10.1810.
Struck and BU approved 12.2.1822, BU at Brest 4.1822.

Mamelouck (*Mameluck, Mamelouk*) Antoine Crucy, Basse-Indre.
K: 4.1809. L: 3.7.1810. Comm: 10.9.1810. C: 10.1810.
Renamed *Olivier* 21.4.1814, *Mamelouck* 22.3.1815, and *Olivier* 15.7.1815. Struck and BU approved 5.8.1823 at Lorient.

Zèbre Marseille.
Ord: 7.8.1809 and named. K: 10.1809. L: 1.12.1810. Comm: 1.1.1811. C: 1.1811.
Struck 12.1.1847 or 20.3.1847, hulk at Brest. Assigned 5.1849 to the school for boys and novices at Bordeaux, replacing the corvette *Blonde* (1832). Replaced 1864 by the corvette *Brillante* (1830).

Faune Vian, Velin, Riboulet, & Ménard (probably), La Ciotat
Ord: 1.7.1809 (contract). Named: 7.8.1809. K: early 1810. L: 17.1.1811. C: 3.1811. Comm: 20.3.1811.
Lost 4.5.1832 near the bar at Tuspay, Rio de la Plata.

Éclaireur Bayonne (Constructeur: Jean Baudry).
K: 14.3.1810. L: 9.4.1811. C: 1812.
Out of commission at Bayonne until departing 1.8.1814 for Rochefort where she decommissioned. In bad condition by 1821, struck and BU approved 22.5.1821. BU at Rochefort 8.1821.

Lancier Bayonne (Constructeur: Jean Baudry).
K: 3.1810. L: 22.5.1811. C: 1812.
In commission from 1.9.1814 to 26.10.1814. In bad condition at Rochefort by 1821, struck and BU approved 22.5.1821, BU 11.1821.

Laurier Dunkirk (Constructeur: Louis Bretocq)
K: 20.2.1810. L: 20.6.1811. Comm: 1.9.1811. C: 9.1811.

In bad condition at Brest after a cruise in 1817 to the Antilles, struck 15.6.1818 and hulked there. BU 1-2.1832.

Sans-Souci Rochefort Dyd. (Constructeurs: Jean-Baptiste Lemoyne-Sérigny, then Jean-Charles Rigault de Genouilly).

K: 1.2.1810. L: 20.7.1811. C: 12.1811. Comm: 20.2.1812.

Burned 7.4.1814 off Meschers in the Gironde with *Regulus* (74) and the brigs *Javan* and *Malais* to avoid capture by the approaching British.

Inconstant Leghorn (Constructeur: Jean-Baptiste Marestier).

Ord: 6.4.1809. K: 11.7.1809. L: 28.11.1811. Comm: 10.2.1812. C: 2.1812.

Construction contract signed 21.4.1809 with S^r· André but cancelled 28.1.1810 when the ship was 9/24ths complete and the navy completed her. Originally had 2 x 6pdrs instead of 2 x 8pdrs, and in 1815 had 18 x 18pdr carronades. Left Toulon 24.4.1814 in order to convey Napoleon from St. Tropez to Elba but a British frigate carried him instead. Sailed for Elba 24.5.1814, given to Napoleon on 27.5.1814, and enrolled in Napoleon's Elban Navy to maintain communications between Elba and Leghorn. Between 26.2 and 1.3.1815 transported Napoleon and his generals from Elba to Golfe Juan. Reintegrated into the French Navy 3.1815, returned to Toulon 24.5.1815 escorted by frigate *Dryade*. Condemned 17.8.1842, BU at Brest 12.1843.

Actéon Antwerp (Constructeur: André Hamart & Jean-François Guillemard)

K: 9.1810. L: 24.8.1812. Comm: 13.5.1813. C: 5.1813.

Part of a squadron sent 11.1814 to recover Guadeloupe. Mutiny in favour of Napoleon suppressed by the British, retained by the French governor at Martinique during the Hundred Days and returned to Brest 24.11.1815. Struck 12.1821, BU at Brest 5.1822.

Sapeur Antwerp (Constructeurs: André Hamart & Jean-François Guillemard)

K: 9.1810. L: 7.9.1812. C: 8.1813.

Ceded 1.8.1814 to the Allies with the frigate *Van der Werff* in accordance with the treaty of 30.5.1814 as compensation for the Allied share in four frigates and two brigs that were at Flushing on 23.4.1814, the date of the convention, and that were later sent to Brest. These vessels were *Ems*, *Érigone*, *Vistule*, *Milanaise*, *Hussard*, and *Actaeon*. *Sapeur* became the Dutch *Spion*, which made a voyage between late 1815 and 26.4.1816 from the Texel to Batavia in the East Indies and which was BU in 1817.

Zéphyr (*Zéphir*) Leghorn (Constructeur: Jean-Baptiste Marestier).

Ord: 6.4.1809. K: 17.7.1809. L: 27.6.1813. Comm: 1.8.1813. C: 8.1813.

Wrecked 2.5.1823 (or 3.3.1823) near Cape Palos on the Spanish Biscay coast.

Sphinx Genoa (Constructeur: Mathurin Boucher).

K: 2.1813. L: 21.11.1813.

Handed over to naval suppliers at Genoa 17.4.1814 when nearly completed as part-payment for debts; taken 18.4.1814 by the British in the capitulation of Genoa. Brought to the UK by the RN and purchased 1816 by the RN for North Sea service as HMS *Regent*. Later in Customs service on the Scottish coast, for sale 1.11.1824.

Euryale Lerond Campion & Co, Le Havre (Constructeur: François Gréhan).

Ord: 18.2.1811. K: 11.3.1811. L: 9.12.1813. Comm: 1.1.1815. C: 1.1815.

Built by a Granville firm at the Le Havre dockyard under the supervision of Gréhan, the senior Génie Maritime engineer there.

In 11.1829 became a school ship for apprentice seamen at Toulon, then at Algiers from 1830 to 1846. Struck 14.3.1846.

Silène Louis & Michel-Louis Crucy, Paimboeuf.

K: 5.1809. L: 17.8.1814. Comm: 17.8.1814. C: 10.1814.

Completed after the Crucy firm failed in October 1813 by Auguste Guibert and François-Michel Ronsard. Escorted the French Navy's first steamer, *Voyageur*, into Saint Louis, Senegal, on 1.11.1819. Wrecked in fog 60nm east of Algiers on 15.5.1830 with the brig-aviso *Aventure*, The crews reached shore safely but many of the men were massacred by Bedouins.

Huron Louis & Michel-Louis Crucy, Paimboeuf.

Ord: 18.1.1810. K: 5.1810. L: 29.9.1814. Comm: 25.9.1814. C: 10.1814.

Completed after 1813 by Auguste Guibert and François-Michel Ronsard. Returned to Lorient from Senegal 4.5.1822, struck 13.8.1822, condemned 10.9.1822 and hulked.

Rusé La Ciotat

K: 8.1813. L: 9.1814. C: 11.1814. Comm: 1.5.1815.

Contract dated 6.2.1813. Wrecked 24.1.1835 near Bône, Algeria, in a storm.

Two brigs were ordered built at La Spezia in May 1808 (with three 74s and two frigates), but as that yard did not yet exist the orders were moved to Genoa where they became probably *Renard* and possibly *Sphinx*. A draught for a brig signed by Mathurin Boucher at Genoa on 15 September 1812 exists in the French archives; this vessel of 230/432 tons measured 93ft 11in, 84ft 0in x 27ft 8in x 13ft 10in (30.50, 27.30 x 9.00 x 4.50m) with a draught of 11ft 1in/12ft 11in (3.60/4.20m) and carried 18 x 24pdr carronades and 2 x 8pdrs. Another draught signed by Boucher at Genoa on 20 January 1813 is for a brig with 16 x 24pdrs and 2 x 8pdrs and unknown dimensions, it was signed by Sané on 5 February 1813 and approved by Decrès. The latter draught could have been used for *Sphinx* (1813) but any differences from the standard Sané *Sylphe* design were probably minor.

IENA class. 18-gun brigs, designed by Andrea Salvini, the Italian chief constructor at Venice. The first ship of the class, *Eolo* (ex *Castore*), was launched on 12 August 1805, stayed out of French hands in 1806 at Trieste, and was sold to an American at Fiume in November 1809. She was armed with 16 x 9pdrs, 4 x 18pdr carronades, and 2 x 3pdrs. The second unit, *Sparviero*, and a sister were under construction when the French occupied Venice for the second time, on 19 January 1806, and they passed to Napoleon's Italian Navy. The Austrian names of these two brigs were changed in 1806 by petition of the people of Venice, who had resented Austrian rule.

Dimensions & tons: 95ft 5in x 26ft 6in x 13ft 10in (31.00 x 8.60 x 4.50m). 391 tons. Draught 12ft 7in (4.10m). Men: 110. *Pr. Augusta* may have been larger, at 104ft 7in x 27ft 7in (34m x 9m) and 450 tons.

Guns: (*Pr. A,* 1812) 18 x 9pdrs; (*Principessa Augusta/Sparviero,* 1814) 16 x 9pdrs, 4 x 18pdr carronades; (*Sparviero,* 1815) 16 x 24pdr carronades, 2 x 11pdrs; (*Iena,* 1815) 16 x Austrian 12pdrs, 1 x 4pdr, 4 x 1pdrs; (*Veneto,* 1826): 14 x 24pdr carronades, 2 x 12pdrs.

Principessa Augusta Venice (constructed by Josef Fonda)

K: 20.10.1805. L: 27.11.1806. Comm: 8.9.1807.

Name in French *Princesse Auguste*, ex Austrian *Sparviero* 1.1806. At Ancona 12.1807, at Corfu 1807-8, and at Ancona 6.1808. Blockaded at Corfu until 25.3.1809. Back at Ancona 8.1809, in combat with some British sloops off that city on 21.6.1810. Participated in the Battle of Lissa on 13.3.1811 under Captain Bolognini, then went to Curzola (now Corçula in Croatia). To Spalato (now Split) 19.11.1811. Met the xebec *Eugenio* and the brig *Lodola* at Zara (now Zadar), then returned to Venice in 11.1811 and decomm. 7.9.1812. Taken over by the Austrians 25.4.1814 in the occupation of the Venice Arsenal. Renamed *Sparviero* 11.6.1814. Hauled out 10.6.1820, re-launched 22.4.1826 as hospital ship for the Levant Squadron. Decomm. and hauled out 26.6.1830. Ordered BU 31.7.1836.

Iena Venice
K: 7.1805. L: 25.11.1806. Comm: 11.1807.
Name in French *Iéna*, ex Austrian *Lodola* 1.1806. At Corfu in 1808, at Ancona in June 1808. Blockaded at Corfu until 25.3.1809, at Ancona in 1810. Participated in the Battle of Lissa on 13.3.1811. At the Venice Lido in 1813 and at Venice in 1814. Taken over by the Austrians 25.4.1814 in the occupation of the Venice Arsenal, sank there while in use as a guardship 1815, renamed *Veneto* 5.5.1815 and raised 10.5.1815. Decomm. 21.6.1830, hauled out 15.9.1830 for rebuilding. The new *Veneto*, also a 31.00 x 8.60m brig, was launched 11.2.1832.

ILLYRIEN or **FRIEDLAND** Class. 18-gun Italian brigs, designed by Andrea Salvini and built at Venice by Giacomo or Francesco Coccon. Four of this class were laid down in the winter of 1806-7 for Napoleon's Italian Navy, and all were captured by the British Navy during 1808. The first of these was begun as *Illyrien*, giving the class its original name, but was renamed *Vendicare* in early 1807 and then *Friedland* in July 1807 (after launch). On 20 November 1807 *Nettuno* received the first 18 (sic) carronades made at the foundry at Venice. On 2 May 1808, HMS *Unite* began a cruise in the Gulf of Venice, capturing numerous coastal vessels and preventing the movement of shipping in the region. Three Italian brigs sent against the frigate were captured, *Ronco* on 2 May and *Nettuno* and *Teulié* on 31 May. A fourth was driven back to Venice. *Cesare* and *Montecuccoli*, begun two years after the others, were probably also of this class (their measurements were very similar), but they were still incomplete when the Austrians took Venice in 1814.

Dimensions & tons: 90ft 0in, 81ft 0in x 26ft 9in x 13ft 6in (29.23, 26.31 x 8.69 x 4.38m). 180/360 tons. Draught 10ft 9in /12ft 2in (3.50/3.96m). Men: 112.
Guns: (1812) 14 x 24pdr carronades, 2 x 6pdrs or 12pdrs; (*Montecuccoli*, 1817) 16 x 12pdrs; (*Montecuccoli*, 1826, and *Orione*, 1827) 14 x 24pdr carronades, 2 x 12pdrs.

Friedland Venice.
K: 11.1806. L: 6.1807. C: 11.1807.

Admiralty draught of *Cretan* (ex *Nettuno*) as taken off at Sheerness in August 1809. This was one of a class of large brigs built at Venice and designed by the experienced Venetian naval architect Andrea Salvini. The large gunports suggest a carronade armament, and indeed *Nettuno* was carrying 16 when captured; their calibre was recorded as 32pdrs in English sources but they were almost certainly 24pdrs. (© National Maritime Museum J5104)

At Ancona in December 1807, at Corfu in 1807-8, and at Santa Maria di Leuca in March 1808. Taken by HMS *Standard* (64) and HMS *Active* (38) off Cape Blanco 26.3.1808, becoming HMS *Delight*. Paid off 7.1810 and sold 1.9.1814.

Nettuno Venice.
K: 12.1806. L: 6.1807. C: 11.1807.
Launch attended by Viceroy Eugène de Beauharnais. At Venice in November 1807, at Lesina and then at Ancona in May 1808. Taken by HMS *Unite* (40) off Zara 1.6.1808, becoming HMS *Cretan*. Paid off 1813 and sold 29.9.1814.

Ronco Venice.
K: 6.1807. L: 4.1808. C: 1808.
Taken by HMS *Unite* (40) off Cape Promontore, Istria, 2.5.1808, becoming HMS *Tuscan*. Paid off 1813 and sold 29.1.1818.

Teulié Venice.
K: 61807. L: 4.1808. C: 1808.
Taken by HMS *Unite* (40) off Zara 1.6.1808, becoming HMS *Roman*. Paid off 1.1811 and sold 1.9.1814.

Cesare Venice
K: 18.1.1809. L: 29.1.1812. C: 1815.
Taken over by the Austrians 25.4.1814 in the occupation of the Venice Arsenal, renamed *Orione* 13.5.1815 or 10.6.1815 and in service 1815. Decomm. 9.11.1830. Hauled out at Venice 9.1831 for repair. The new ship, a 31 x 8.6m brig, was launched 21 or 27.10.1832 and named *Oreste* because of a smuggling scandal during the last commission of the old ship.

Montecuccoli Venice.
K: 18.1.1809. L: 22.3.1817. C: 1817.
Taken by Austrian forces while still on the stocks at the surrender of Venice 4.1814, retained name. Decomm. at Venice 13.2.1830 and hauled out 15.4.1830. A new *Montecuccoli*, a brig of 31 x 8.6 metres, was launched 14.7.1831.

CARLOTTA. 8-gun Italian brig-rigged *corvetta-cannoniera* or, according to a drawing, *corvetta-brig*. Probably designed by Andrea Salvini and built by him.

> Dimensions & tons: 84ft, 77ft x 21ft x 9ft (27.28, 25.0 x 6.82 x 2.92m). 110/200 tons. Draught 7ft 6in/8ft 4in (2.43/2.71m). Men: 66 (100 when taken).
>
> Guns: 8 x 8pdrs or 10 x 6pdrs. (Had 10 ports according to a drawing and had 10 guns mounted when taken).

Carlotta Venice.
> K: 6.1807. L: 2.12.1807. C: 2.1808.
>
> Originally named *Fiamma*. Launched in the presence of Napoleon. Was at Goro-Primaro in summer 1810. While sailing from Venice to Corfu on 11 December 1810 she was captured by HMS *Belle Poule*. She became the British gunbrig *Carlotta*. Paid off 2.1815 and BU 5.1815.

The French naval constructor Jean Tupinier arrived in Venice in 1807 to build three 74-gun ships of the line there, and he became the director of French naval construction in Venice in early 1808. He was given entire independence from the Italian naval construction organisation headed by Salvini, and he wrote in his memoirs that a French decision in his favour during 1808 made Salvini into a 'mortal enemy'. Although Tupinier is sometimes listed as designer or co-designer of small combatants including these brigs, he was mainly responsible for the French building program of ships of the line and frigates at Venice and probably left these smaller, primarily Italian, craft to Salvini and his organisation, exercising only general oversight over the work on them.

MAMELUCCO Class. 10-gun Italian brigs, probably designed by Andrea Salvini, constructed by Luigi Paresi for Napoleon's Italian Navy. Two more unnamed units were planned at Trieste but were not named or built. *Mamelucco* was launched on 26.8.1808 at 11am, then was taken to the fitting-out pier and, while Viceroy Eugène de Beauharnais watched, was fully rigged by 3pm. She left the Arsenal on 26.10.1808. (Eugène was in Mantua on 7.10.1808, her other reported launch date.) She was reportedly designed for 6 x short 12pdrs and to have replaced these with 6 x 24pdr carronades in 8.1810. Two other units, *Ciclope* and *Mercurio* were also reported, and a *Mercurio* was at Alberoni in 1809 and sunk by British ships near Caorle in 1810 while commanded by Giuseppe Pellicucchio, both locations being near Venice. The wreck was reportedly discovered some years ago. Alternatively these were among four more units, two unnamed, that were planned at Trieste but were not built.

> Dimensions & tons: 75ft 5in x 19ft 8in x 8ft 9in (24.50 x 6.40 x 2.85m). Men: 66.
>
> Guns: (1812) 10 x 6pdrs, (1826) 8 x 12pdr carronades and 2 x 6pdr chase guns.

Mamelucco Venice
> K: 1807. L: 26.8.1808. C: 26.10.1808.
>
> Name in French *Mameluck*. At Alberoni in 1809, at Venice in 1810, and then at Rimini. Participated in the Battle of Lissa on 13.3.1811 under a captain named Albert and fled to Trieste. At Malamocco from June 1813, participated in the defence of Venice in 11.1813. Taken over by the Austrians 25.4.1814 in the occupation of the Venice Arsenal, renamed *Ussaro* 5.5.1815. Decomm. 29.8.1828 for reconstruction as a schooner. Her material was used to build the schooner *Fenice*, which was launched on 18.2.1829. A new brig named *Ussaro* was launched on 17.6.1829.

Ciclope Venice? (see notes)

Mercurio Venice? (see notes)

LEPANTO. 8-gun Italian brig or, according to a drawing, *cannoniera-brig*, probably designed by Andrea Salvini, constructed by Luigi Paresi for Napoleon's Italian Navy. The similarity of her measurments to *Mamelucco* suggests she might have been a sister, although she was not so listed.

> Dimensions & tons: 76ft, 68ft x 20ft x 8ft 8in (24.69, 22.1, x 6.50 x 2.82m). 110/200 tons. Draught 6ft 4in/8ft (2.06/2.60m). Men: 66.
>
> Guns: 8 x 8pdrs, 8 ports.

Lepanto Venice.
> K: 4.1808. L: 1809. C: c1810.
>
> Participated in the defence of Venice in 8.1809 and was still at Venice in 2.1810. At Pesaro on July 1810. Out of service 2.1811, back in service at Venice 1813-14.

INDIANO. 12-gun Italian brig. Either laid down 1808 at the Venice Arsenal, probably as a merchant brig, or built abroad in 1808 and purchased for Napoleon's Italian Navy. May have been converted from the former Russian brig *Aleksandr* or *Letun*, both purchased at Venice in September 1809, although this appears unlikely.

> Dimensions & tons: unknown.
>
> Guns: (1815) 10 x 6pdrs, 2 x 10.5pdrs; (1820) 10 x 6pdrs, 2 x 12pdr carronades.

Indiano
> Name in French *Indien*. Participated in the defence of Venice 11.1813. Taken over by the Austrians 25.4.1814 in the occupation of the Venice Arsenal, becoming Austrian *Dalmato* 11.6.1814. She was given a taller rig at Venice for postal service on 29.4.1820 and on her first voyage capsized in a squall on 21.5.1820 in the Zara Channel between Meleda and Puntadura islands. Raised 9.1820 and BU.

OTELLO. 20-gun Italian brig, probably designed by Andrea Salvini with Tupinier's new deputy, Jean Dumonteil, for Napoleon's Italian Navy.

> Dimensions & tons: 105ft oa, 101ft 8in wl, 85ft 10in x 28ft x 14ft (34.10, 33.04, 27.9 x 9.10 x 4.55), 300/520 tons, Draught 11ft 6in/14ft (3.73/4.55m). Men 120.
>
> Guns: 18 x 36pdr carronades, 2 x 12pdrs (bronze)

Otello Venice.
> K: 17.3.1812. L: 16.5.1818. C: 5.1819.
>
> Taken over by the Austrians 25.4.1814 on the ways in the occupation of the Venice Arsenal. Renamed *Veloce* before or at launching in 1818. Re-rigged as corvette 2-5.1827. Decomm. at Venice for repairs 7.2.1832. On 5.9.1832 ordered replaced by a new ship of the same name. The new *Veloce*, a 40m corvette, was launched on 24.4.1834. Plans of 10.1836 to make the old *Veloce* into a floating battery were abandoned and she became a a coal hulk in 1837, was ordered BU 15.5.1839, and was BU 10.1839.

ENTREPRENANT. 12-gun brig. In 1808 Lieutenant Pierre-François Bouvet, having with the local shipbuilder Grisard built the felucca *Entreprenant* at Île de France and conducted a successful raid in her at the beginning of that year, supervised the construction of a larger *Entreprenant* at Île de France. Grisard's shipbuilding activities are described in the entry for the schooner *Gobe-Mouche* in Chapter 8.

> Dimensions & tons: 82ft 0in, 80ft 0in x 25ft 0in x 12ft 0in (26.63, 25.98 x 8.12 x 3.90m). 160/300t. Draught 10ft 11in/12ft 6in (3.56/4.06m). Men: 88-110.
>
> Guns: 12 x 12pdrs

Entreprenant Port-Napoléon (Port-Louis), Île de France (built by Grisard).
> K: 5.1808. L: 8.1808. C: 10.1808).

The capture of the *Alacrity* by the *Abeille* in 1811 was a notable French success in single-ship encounters, as the British brig carried 32pdr carronades to the French 24pdrs. It was a battle of manoeuvre, won by the French brig gaining a winning position on *Alacrity*'s quarter – as shown in this nineteenth-century lithograph – from whence there could be almost no return fire. All the British officers were killed or incapacitated and, despite having suffered very little damage aloft, *Alacrity* was forced to surrender. (Courtesy of Beverley R. Robinson Collection, US Naval Academy Museum)

Bouvet sailed in his new brig on 4.10.1808 for Ormuz with despatches and then cruised off the Malabar coast, taking 19 prizes and suppressing a mutiny. He returned to Île de France on 16.3.1809. After further service the brig was captured by the British in the fall of Île de France 4.12.1810.

Ex BRITISH NAVAL PRIZES (BRIGS, 1804-1813). All measurements quoted are in French units.

Victorine (HMS *Vincejo*, ex Spanish *Vinsejo*. Probably built at Port Mahon in 1797, captured by the British in 3.1799, captured by the French 8.5.1804 and renamed)
   Dimensions & tons: 86ft 7in, 80ft 9in x 23ft 7in x 12ft 5in (28.12, 26.22 x 7.67 x 4.03m). 150/290 tons. Draught 10ft 0in/10ft 7in (3.24/3.44m).
   Guns: (1797) 18 x 6pdrs; (1799) 16 x 18pdr carronades, 2 x 6pdrs.
   Sold at Lorient 1.1805.

Netley (HMS *Netley*, an experimental vessel designed by Samuel Bentham and launched at Redbridge 4.1798, may have been schooner-rigged. Taken 17.12.1806 off Guadeloupe by *Thétis* (44) and *Sylphe* (18).)
   Dimensions & tons: 81ft 3in x 20ft 2in x 10ft 6in (26.4 x 6.54 x 3.4m). 130/250 tons
   Guns: (designed) 16 x 24pdr carronades; (later?) 18 x 12pdr carronades
   Sold 1.1807 as a privateer, renamed *Duquesne*. Retaken by HMS *Blonde* 23.9.1807 and became gunbrig HMS *Unique*. Expended 31.5.1809 as a fireship in an attack on Basse Terre, Guadeloupe.

Maria (HMS *Maria*, purchased in 1807, taken 9.1808 off Guadeloupe by the corvette *Département des Landes*, 172 tons (bm?), 12 or 14 guns). Run aground at Guadeloupe 10.1808 to prevent her from sinking, then refloated. Burned 2.1809 by the French at Martinique.

Linnet (HMS *Linnet*, ex Revenue Cutter *Speedwell*, built at Cowes 1797 and purchased 1806, captured off Madeira 2.1813 by the frigate *Gloire*.)
   Dimensions & tons: 72ft 11in x 23ft 9in x 10ft 2in (23.7 x 7.72 x 3.3m). 200 tons displ. Men: 75.
   Guns: 12 x 16pdr carronades, 2 x 6pdrs.
   Sold at Brest 1813, became the American privateer *Bunkers Hill*, and retaken by HMS *Pomone* and *Cydnus* 4.3.1814.

CRUIZER **Class**. The standard 16-gun brig-sloops of the Napoleonic War, designed in 1797 by Sir William Rule. After the prototype was built in 1797-98, over 100 were built to this design between 1802 and 1815, of which three were captured by the French. The *Carnation* was taken by the *Palinure* off Martinique on 3 October 1808; the *Alacrity* by the *Abeille* off Corsica on 26 May 1811; and the *Grasshopper* by *Gloire* and *Ferreter* (former HMS) in the Texel on 25 December 1811. In French service all three were fitted as 18-gun brigs.
   Dimensions & tons: 97ft 1½in, 81ft 6in x 28ft 7in x 14ft 0in (31.55, 26.47 x 9.29 x 4.57m). 200/400 tons. Draught 9½ft/13ft (3.10/4.20m). Men: 149.
   Guns: 16 x 32pdr carronades (British guns), 2 x 8pdrs (bow) chase guns.

Carnation William Taylor, Bideford.
   K: 8.1806. L: 3.10.1807. C: 21.1.1808 at Plymouth Dyd.
   Burned 31.1.1809 at St Martin to avoid recapture.

Alacrity William Rowe, Newcastle.
   K: 5.1806. L 13.11.1806. C: 31.3.1807 at Chatham Dyd.
   Commissioned 1.7.1811 at Toulon. Struck 20.8.1822 at Toulon, ordered BU 28.8.1822, BU 9.1822.

Grasshopper Richards Brothers & John Davidson, Hythe.
   K: 4.1806. L: 29.9.1806. C: 15.12.1806 at Portsmouth Dyd.
   On capture she was first placed in Dutch service. The Minister of Marine ordered on 11.12.1812 that she be put into French Navy service instead of the former Dutch small brig *Irene* which would be sold in her place; she swapped names with *Irene* when the French Navy took possession on 20.1.1813. Taken by Dutch

partisans 12.1813 in the Dutch uprising, became Dutch *Irene*. Cruised in the West Indies 1815-16, in the Mediterranean 1816-18, and in the East Indies 1819-21. BU 1822 at Vlissingen.

Ex BRITISH NAVAL PRIZES (GUNBRIGS, 1804-1808)

The Napoleonic navy had no standard class of small brigs equivalent to the postwar brig avisos. The only true small brigs on the navy list in 1816 were four of the British gunbrigs that had been captured during the war. In French hands these retained their British names until 24 September 1814 along with their British 18pdr (rated 16pdr by the French) carronades, and were classed by the French as *brick-canonniers*. At the start of the Hundred Days on 22 March 1815 the original (British) names were restored by Napoleon, but the new names were restored on 15 July.

ARCHER **Class**. Gunbrigs designed in 1800 by Sir William Rule, to which design ten were ordered on 30 December 1800 and another 48 (the Later *Archer* class) in the first half of 1804. Of the first batch the *Conflict* ran aground off Niewport on 24 October 1804 while in combat with the prame *Ville de Montpellier*, and *Mallard* grounded off Wissant Bay near Calais on 24 December, both being taken by French land forces. Of the later batch, the *Bouncer* suffered a similar fate off Dieppe on 21 February 1805, while the *Plumper* and *Teazer* were captured on 16 July 1805 in the Chausey Isles near Saint-Malo by a division of French gunboats (six brigs, a schooner and a ketch), and were taken into Granville.

    Dimensions & tons: 77ft 10in, 73ft 10in wl, 69ft 9in x20ft 3in x 9ft 6in (25.28, 24.00wl, 22.66 x 6.58 x 3.08m). 140/210 tons. Draught 6¾ft/7ft ((2.20/2.28m).

    Guns: 10 x 18pdr carronades (British design); by c.1811 had 12 carronades and 2 x 12pdr (bow) chase guns

Conflict John Dudman, Deptford.
    K: 1.1801. L: 17.4.1801. C: 9.5.1801 at Deptford Dyd.
    Commissioned 23.10.1806 by the French Navy at Dunkirk. Renamed *Lynx* 24.9.1814, then *Conflict* 22.3.1815, and *Lynx* again on 15.7.1815. Struck 10.1834 at Rochefort, BU 11.1834.

Mallard Mrs Frances Barnard, Deptford.
    K: 1.1801. L: 11.4.1801. C: 12.5.1801 at Woolwich Dyd.
    Purchased by the French Navy 2.1805. Fitted as a gunboat (*canonnière*) in 1811, retaining her 12 (British) 18pdr carronades. Renamed *Favori* 24.9.1814, then *Mallard* 22.3.1815, and *Favori* again on 15.7.1815. Struck 1827 at Brest, rated service craft there 17.9.1831.

Bouncer William Rowe, Newcastle.
    K: 4.1804. L: 11.8.1804. C: at builder's yard. Comm: 11.1804.
    Purchased by the navy 21.2.1805. Renamed *Écureuil* 24.9.1814, then *Bouncer* 22.3.1815, and *Écureuil* again on 15.7.1815. Condemned 28.6.1827.

Plumper John Dudman, Deptford.
    K: 4.1804. L: 7.9.1804. C: 12.12.1804 at Deptford Dyd.
    Commissioned 30.8.1805 at Saint-Servan. Renamed *Argus* 24.9.1814, then *Plumper* 22.3.1815, and *Argus* again on 15.7.1815. Accompanied the frigate *Méduse* to Senegal and on 17.7.1816 discovered the famous raft with the survivors of her shipwreck. Assigned to colonial service and sent in 1818 to Galam, Senegal to reoccupy Fort St. Joseph and prepare for expeditions into the interior with the aviso *Colibri* and the colonial brig *Postillon*. Condemned 10.1822 at Saint-Louis, Senegal, struck 1827.

Teazer John Dudman, Deptford.
    K: 5.1804. L: 16.7.1804. C: 14.9.1804 at Deptford Dyd.
    Commissioned 30.8.1805 at Saint-Servan. Was station ship at Verdon in 1808. Recaptured 25.8.1811 with *Pluvier* at Verdon in the entrance to the Gironde by HMS *Semiramis* (36) and *Diana* (38), resumed service as HMS *Teazer*. Sold 3.8.1815.

BLOODHOUND **Class**. Gunbrigs designed in 1801 by Sir John Henslow. Ten were ordered to this design on 7 January 1801, of which the *Ferreter* was captured off the mouth of the River Ems on 31 March 1807 by seven Dutch gunboats, and was transferred to the French Navy in July 1810 when the Kingdom of Holland was annexed by France.

    Dimensions & tons: 80ft x 22ft x 12ft (25.98 x 7.15 x 3.90m). 100/180 tons. Draught 6ft/8ft (1.95/2.60m). Men: 71.

    Guns: 14 x 18pdr carronades (British), 2 x 12pdr (bow) chase guns.

Ferreter Perry, Wells & Green, Blackwall
    K: 1.1801. L: 4.4.1801. C: 29.4.1801 at Woolwich.
    Captured 12.1813 on the Vlie in the Dutch uprising, renamed *Daphne*. Sold 1841.

CONFOUNDER **Class**. Gunbrigs designed in 1804 by Sir William Rule with improved performance under sail. Twenty vessels were ordered to this design on 20 November 1804 (an extra one was ordered in 1805), of which the *Bustler* grounded near Cape Griz Nez on 26 December 1808 and was taken into Boulogne by the French after attempts to burn her by her crew failed.

    Dimensions & tons: 81ft 0in, 71ft 0in x 20ft 4in x 11ft 0in (26.31, 23.06 x 6.61 x 3.57m). 140/250 tons. Draught 9ft/10ft (2.93/3.23m). Men: 67.

    Guns (British): 12 x 18pdr carronades, 2 x 6pdrs (bow and stern); from 1813, 12 x 6pdrs, 2 x 18pdr carronades.

Bustler Obadiah Ayles, Topsham.
    K: 3.1805. L: 12.8.1805. C: 14.9.1806 at Plymouth Dyd.
    Purchased by the navy 18.3.1809 and commissioned 16.4.1809. Scuttled 8.12.1813 by the French while serving as station ship at Ziericksee and taken in the Dutch uprising.

Ex BRITISH MERCANTILE AND PRIVATEER PRIZES (1803-1813)

Laurel (British merchant or privateer brig *Laurel* captured 13.10.1803 by frigate *Didon*, and comm., probably on 17.10.1803, carried 6 x 6pdrs, 6 x 12pdr carronades. Unserviceable at La Rochelle 3.1806, sold 5.1806.

Créole (British merchant or privateer brig *Isabella*, originally Spanish, captured in the Indian Ocean 8 or 9.1805 under unknown circumstances and renamed *Créole* 11.1805. Alternatively, she may originally have been the transport brig *Isabelle* that was commissioned at Toulon 6.8.1805)

    Dimensions & tons: 83ft 6in, 72ft 0in x 23ft 1in, 24ft 0in ext x 15ft 0in (27.12, 23.39 x 7.50, 7.80 x 4.87m). 150/241 tons. Draught 11ft 0in/13ft 0in (3.58/4.22m). Men: 53.

    Guns: 10 x 6pdrs, 2 x 12pdr carronades (had 20 ports for 6pdrs).

    Refitted at Île de France 3.1806. Her fate is as unclear as her origins. Being in need of a refit, she was designated on 30.3.1807 to be BU at Bayonne, but she may then have become the schooner *Créole* that was taken by the Portuguese at French Guiana in 1.1809 and renamed *Lusitania*.

Rolla (British merchant or privateer brig *Rolla* taken on 22.11.1805 or 5.12.1805 by the Linois division and used by it.)

    Dimensions & tons: 75ft 5in x 19ft 8in x 10ft 6in (24.5 x 6.4 x 3.4m). 196/200 tons.

    Guns: 10 (14 ports). Probably carried 16 x 6pdrs and 4pdrs as a British privateer or merchant.

    Captured 21.2.1806 by the British at the Cape of Good Hope and became HMS *Rolla*. Sold 3.1810.

Grappler (British brig, probably the Bombay Marine's *Grappler* of 150bm launched in 1804, taken 6.9.1806 in the Indian Ocean by *Piémontaise*, carried 8 x 12pdr carronades, 2 x 6pdrs). Captured 21.9.1809 with the frigate *Caroline* by a division led by HMS *Sirius* (36) near Saint Paul, Île de Bourbon (Réunion).

Marguerite (East India Co. brig, new when taken, captured 7.2.1808 in the Indian Ocean by Pierre Bouvet in the felucca *Entreprenant*, 270 tons, carried 8 x 12pdr carronades, 2 x 9pdrs). Bouvet abandoned *Entreprenant* to the crew of the prize and brought the prize back to Port Napoleon in 4.1808. Her later fate is unclear; she may have been sold into merchant service in 11.1808.

Énéas (British brig of unknown origin, possibly ex British merchantman *Aeneas*, rigged as an 'infernal machine' [explosion vessel] and taken at Île d'Aix on 12.4.1809.)
  Dimensions & tons: 83ft 0in x 23ft 0in x 15ft 0in (26.96 x 7.47 x 4.87m). 304/450 tons. Men: 97.
  Guns: 6 x 18pdrs, 6 x 12pdrs, 6 x 8pdrs; (1814) 4 x 6pdrs
  Refitted at Rochefort 8-9.1810 and comm. 1.12.1810. Converted to transport in early 1814 and in fleet lists at Rochefort in 4.1814 as a brig-transport with 2-6pdrs and in 5.1814 as a transport with 4-6pdrs. Decomm. at Rochefort 5.7.1815 and BU 1816.

ANNEXED LIGURIAN VESSELS (1805)

Janus (Ligurian brig *Janus*, begun at Genoa in 1801 and launched 10.1802, taken by the French at Genoa following a legal decision of 6.7.1805 and commissioned 9.7.1805, carried 8 x 8pdrs). Was part of a light division led by the French corvette *Bergère* when HMS *Sirius* captured the corvette off Anzio on 17.4.1806; at that time she carried 12 x 18pdrs and 2 heavy mortars. Rated at 12 guns in 1809 and 16 guns in 1810. Handed over 17.4.1814 to navy suppliers in the port of Genoa in payment for part of the supplies furnished by them, apparently not appropriated by the British when they occupied Genoa two days later.

The end of the action of 3 May 1810 in the Bay of Naples, showing the British frigate *Spartan* and in the foreground the surrendered Neapolitan brig *Sparviero*. Oil painting by Thomas Whitcombe. (© National Maritime Museum BHC0595)

Ligurie (Ligurian brig *Ligurie* or *Liguria* built at Genoa in 1801-2, taken by the French at Genoa following a legal decision of 6.7.1805 and commissioned on 7.7.1805, carried 10 x 8pdrs). Was part of a light division led by the French corvette *Bergère* when HMS *Sirius* captured the corvette off Anzio on 17.4.1806; at that time she carried 12 x 18pdrs and 2 heavy mortars. Rated at 10 guns in 1809 and 16 guns in 1810. Decomm. 4.1813, station ship at La Spezia, scuttled 27.3.1814 during the evacuation of La Spezia to avoid capture.

Ex NEAPOLITAN PRIZE (1806)

Sparviero (Neapolitan brig or brigantine *Sparviero* launched at Naples 14.1.1782, used as a yacht by the Bourbon kings of Naples, then taken by the French at Naples 23.1.1806 and used as a yacht by Joachim Murat, carried 12 x 8pdrs). *Sparviero* joined the frigate *Cerere* and the corvette *Fama* in an engagement on 3.5.1810 against two British frigates near Procida in the Bay of Naples but was shattered by a broadside from HMS *Spartan* (38) and surrendered. The British towed her to Palermo and returned her to the Bourbons, but because of her damage she was sold for BU at Messina.

Ex PORTUGUESE PRIZE (1807)

Gaivota do Mar (Portuguese naval brig, 24 guns, launched at Lisbon in 1792)
  Dimensions & tons: 91ft 0in x 28ft 2in x 16ft 11in (29.57m x 9.14m x 5.49m). Tons unknown. Men: 154
  Guns: (1792) 20 x 12pdrs, 4 x 6pdrs.
  Seized at Lisbon 30.11.1807. Left to the Portuguese 9.1808 at the evacuation of Lisbon. Out of service in Brazil 1822.

PURCHASED RUSSIAN VESSELS (1809)

Fenice (Russian *Feniks*, a former French ship captured by the British and purchased at London 10.1805 by the Russians. Sold to France at Venice in accordance with an imperial decree of 27.9.1809).
  Dimensions & tons: 65ft 8in x 18ft 9in x 8ft 5in (21.3 x 6.1 x 2.74m). Tons unknown.
  Guns: 18 carronades (or 14 or 16 guns, 18 ports)
  Feniks had joined Vice Admiral Senyavin's squadron at Portsmouth 1.11.1805, arrived at Corfu 23.1.1806, left Corfu 24.12.1807 with the squadron of Commodore Saltanov, and was in the detachment of small craft that arrived at Venice from Trieste on 20.1.1808. She may have been re-rigged as the Italian schooner *Fenice* (q.v.) but the latter was more likely a new ship.

Alexandre (Russian *Aleksandr* purchased for the Russian Black Sea Fleet in 1804 while on the ways at Kherson from A. Perets and converted from a transport to a brig, sold to France at Venice by imperial order of 10.1809, carried 16 or 12 x 4pdrs.) *Aleksandr* had sailed from Sevastopol to Corfu 1805, won a fierce engagement at Spoleto 17.12.1806 against a French tartane and three gunboats, left Corfu 24.12.1807 with the squadron of Commodore Saltanov, and was in the detachment of small craft that arrived at Venice from Trieste on 20.1.1808. She may have been refitted as the Italian brig *Indiano*, although this appears unlikely.

Letun (Russian *Letun*, purchased by the Russians at Malta 1805, sold to France at Venice in accordance with a decree of 27.9.1809, carried 12 guns) *Letun* had joined Vice Admiral Senyavin's squadron at Messina 12.1.1806, left Corfu 24.12.1807 with the squadron of Commodore Saltanov, and was in the detachment of small craft that arrived at Venice from Trieste on 20.1.1808. She moved to the Venice Arsenal 11.1809 and decommissioned. She may have been refitted as the Italian brig *Indiano* although this appears unlikely.

ANNEXED DUTCH VESSELS (1810-1811). Several brigs smaller than those of the *Ajax* type (see corvettes, above) were on the stocks when the new Batavian Republic was proclaimed on 19 January 1795 or were laid down soon afterwards. The *Gier* of 16 guns and 87ft 2in (28.31m) in length was launched at Harlingen in 1797 and captured by the British in 1799 and a sister with 18 x 8pdrs, *Echo*, was launched there by P. Schuijt Jnr. in 1798 and captured by the British in 1804. In 1810 the French annexed five relatively small Dutch brigs that were analogous to British gunbrigs, one larger experimental vessel, and four miscellaneous acquired brigs.

ZEEMEEUW Class. *Haai* (*Haay* or *Haaij*), begun two years after *Zeemeeuw*, was listed with the same hull dimensions except for a reduced depth of hull of 7ft 10in (2.55m). *Haai* had the same hull structure and dimensions as *Cachelot*, a vessel that the French classified as a gunboat and that is listed in Chapter 9. These small brigs were only slightly larger than the nine *Bruinvis* class schooners, which the French also classified as gunboats.
  Dimensions & tons: 69ft 9in x 18ft 4in x 9ft 7in (22.64 x 5.94 x 3.11m). 70/120 tons. Draught 6ft 6in/7ft 5in (2.12/2.40m).
  Guns: (*Haai*) 3 x 18pdr carronades, 4 x 6pdrs.

Zeemeeuw Amsterdam (constructed by R. Dorsman)
  K: 1798. L: 1800. C: 1800.
  Raised the French flag in 1811. Taken 12.1813 in the Dutch uprising. Was a guardship at Rotterdam in 1814, sold there 1816. Like other brigs around 1800 this vessel was classed by the Dutch as a galjoot.

Haai Rotterdam (constructed by P. Glavimans)
  K: 3.1800. L: 5.1800. C: 1803.
  Raised the French flag in 1811. Taken 12.1813 at Rotterdam in the Dutch uprising. Left Vlissingen for the West Indies in 1815 but had to put in to Falmouth with a leak. Hulked 1825 at Medemblik.

HAVIK Class. *Havik* and *Irene*, both designed by P. Glavimans Jnr, were listed with the same hull dimensions except for a beam of 19ft 7in (6.37m) in *Irene*. *Havik* had the same hull structure as *Ketty* (*Kettij*), a vessel that is otherwise sparsely documented. *Havik* originally had ten guns. All three ships were at times described as brig avisos.
  Dimensions & tons: 65ft 4in, 57ft 6in x 19ft 4in x 10ft 5in (21.22, 18.68 x 6.28 x 3.40m). 80/140 tons. Draught 7ft 5in/8ft 9in (2.40/2.84m).
  Guns: (*Havik*) 3 x 18pdr carronades, 4 x 6pdrs; (*Irene*) 6-18pdr carronades; (*Ketty*) 6 guns.

Havik Rotterdam (constructed by P. Glavimans Jnr.)
  K: 4.1806. L: 5.1807. C: 1807.
  Raised the French flag 1811. Taken 12.1813 at Hellevoetsluys in the Dutch uprising. Left with a squadron for the Mediterranean 22.12.1814 but was forced by a storm to throw her guns overboard and take refuge at Plymouth. She left Plymouth 16.6.1815 with a squadron for the Mediterranean and returned in 1816. Sold 1828 at Hellevoetsluis.

Irene Amsterdam (constructed by P. Schuijt Jr.)
  K: 1806. C: 1806-7
  Commissioned 1811 in the Scheldt under the French flag. Attached 1.1811 to the institute at Enkhuizen. On 11.12.1812 the captured British 18-gun brig *Grasshopper* was ordered commissioned in her place, and the two ships traded names on 20.1.1813. A letter of 22.1.1813 reported this name change and stated that the former Dutch *Irene* was to be sold.

Ketty Amsterdam
  K: 1805. C: 1806.
  Retaken by the Dutch 1813 or 1814, sold 1814.

HYÈNE. This heavily-armed flat-bottomed gunvessel was fitted with three sliding keels that could be lowered through slots cut in her keel. Her design, by P. Glavimans Jnr, was based on that of the similarly-fitted HMS *Crash*, an *Acute* class gunvessel that was captured by the Dutch in 1798. She had three masts but was classed as a brig in the French Navy.
  Dimensions & tons: 87ft 2in, 76ft 1in x 23ft 6in x 8ft 0in or 9ft 2in (28.31m, 24.70m x 7.64m x 2.60 or 2.97m). 80/150 tons. Draught 5ft 2in/5ft 2in (1.67/1.67m). Men: 83 (1813).
  Guns: 12 x 36pdr carronades, 3 x 18pdrs (2 forward and 1 aft).

Hyène (ex Dutch *Hyena* or *Hijena*) Amsterdam
  K: 1806. C: 1807
  Annexed with the Dutch Navy 7.1810, raised the French flag in 1811. Taken 12.1813 in the Vlie in the Dutch uprising. Sold 1821 at Medemblik for BU.

MISCELLANEOUS Ex DUTCH BRIGS

Claudius Civilis (Dutch brig built at Amsterdam 1807-8 by P. Schuijt Jr., annexed with the Dutch Navy 7.1810)
  Dimensions & tons: 78ft 5in x 22ft 8in x 12ft 11in (25.47 x 7.38 x 4.20m). 150/280 tons. Draught 8ft 10in/10ft 0in (2.88/3.26m).
  Guns: 12 x 8pdrs, later 12 x 18pdr carronades (14 ports)
  Departed the Texel on 18.9.1810 and was at Batavia on 1.5.1811 when the French frigates *Méduse* and *Nymphe* arrived there bringing French troops. Captured by the British in the fall of Batavia in 8.1811.

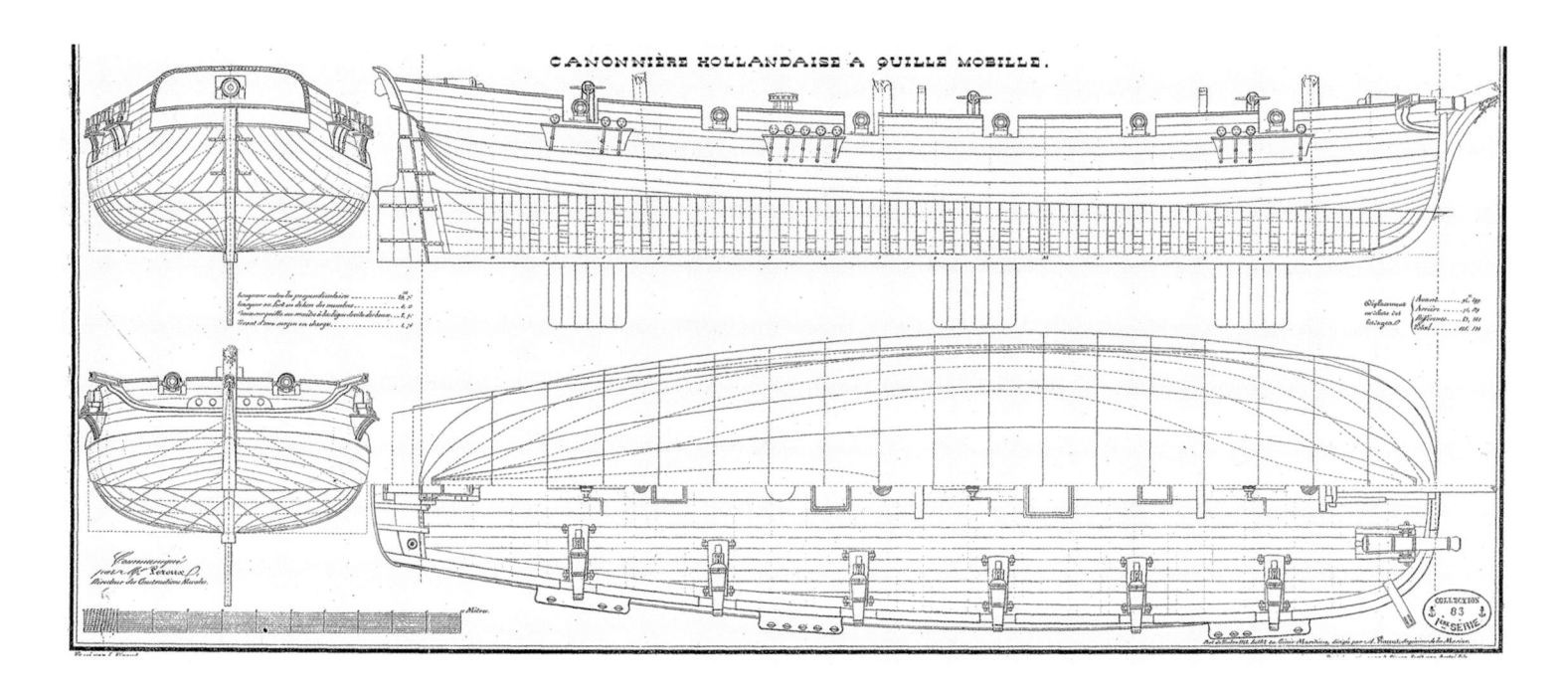

Ruby (Dutch brig, was a British mercantile brig taken after stranding on the island of Vlieland in 1799, annexed with the Dutch Navy 7.1810.)
  Dimensions & tons: 72ft 4in x 20ft 6in x 8ft 3in (23.50 x 6.65 x 2.69m). Tons unknown.
  Guns: 12 or 14.
  Last mentioned in 1810 at Onherstelbaar, fate unknown.

Royal Hollandais (ex Dutch *Koninglijke Hollander*, transport brig built of oak at New York 1800-1, arrived at Bordeaux from Java on 25.10.1810 and raised the French flag 29.10.1810.)
  Dimensions & tons: dimensions unknown. 150 tons burthen.
  Guns: 12 (12 ports plus 2 chase ports); (1813) 4 x 4pdrs.
  Sent to Rochefort 15.7.1811 and renamed *Malais* 22.8.1811. Used as a school ship and annex to *Regulus* (74) in the Gironde after 8.1813 and burned 7.4.1814 with her and the brig *Javan* to avoid capture by the approaching British.

Copenhague (Dutch transport brig built of teak at Île de France in 1809, arrived at Bordeaux from Java 28.4.1811 and raised the French flag 7.5.1811.)
  Dimensions & tons: 77ft x 20ft x 9ft (25.01 x 6.50 x 2.92m). 125/200 tons. Draught 5ft 6in/10ft 9in (1.78/3.48m)
  Guns: 4 x 4pdrs
  Comm. 24.6.1811, refitted at Rochefort, and renamed *Javan* 22.8.1811. Burned 7.4.1814 in the Gironde by the commanding officer of *Regulus* (74) with his own ship and the brig *Malais* to avoid capture.

MISCELLANEOUS PRIZES (1804-1810)

Surveillant (Prussian or British 160-ton merchant brig *Hope*, launched in 1798, arrested at Briel (Antwerp) 17.1.1804 by the stationnaire there, the prame *Ville de Coignac*, 22 men, carried 6 x 12pdr carronades, 2 x 4pdrs). Replaced *Ville de Coignac* as stationnaire at Briel under a ministerial order of 9.4.1804 that also renamed her. Renamed *Éveillé* 20.2.1809. Still there 1814 as stationnaire, decomm. 23.5.1814 and ceded to the Dutch 8.1814.

Calabrese (American merchant brig or brigantine *Emily* of 198 tons net belonging to Gordon & Rossier of New York captured 22.1.1810 by Murat's Neapolitan Navy and placed in service, carried 6 x 12pdrs).

A French plan of the ex Dutch *Hyène*, a heavily armed gunvessel listed with the brigs in the French Navy (despite her three masts). A feature of the design was the provision of three large drop keels on the centreline, designed to make shallow-draught vessels less leewardly on a wind. The British had been experimenting with similar devices since at least 1790, and installed them in a whole class of gunboats, a few of which were captured and probably provided the inspiration for this design. The British found that the cases always leaked and the drop keels often jammed, so they were eventually removed, being deemed more trouble than they were worth. (Atlas du Génie Maritime, French collection, plate 39)

When on 30.5.1815 Murat defected to Napoleon during the Hundred Days the British seized *Calabrese* at Taranto and handed her over to the Bourbons. Hauled out 6.1838 for repairs at Castellammare, recommissioned 26.9.1839 but decommissioned at the end of the year and offered for sale for BU 15.6.1842.

PURCHASED AND REQUISITIONED VESSELS (1803-1812)

Auguste (mercantile brig whose purchase at Bordeaux from citizen Bonaffé was approved by the Minister of Marine on 29.8.1803.)
  Dimensions & tons: 86ft, 78ft x 21ft 5in x 10ft 9in (27.93m, 25.34m x 6.95m x 3.49m) plus a 5ft (1.62m) tween-decks. 267/380 tons. Men: 76.
  Guns: Pierced and rated for 16 x 6pdrs but carried 6 x 6pdrs in 1806.
  Commissioned 17.10.1803. Spent her entire career at Île d'Aix, initially as station ship. Classed as a 260-ton transport (with three masts) from 1808 and a hospital ship from 5.1809. Condemned and ordered BU 11.1814.

Polasky (*Polaski*) (mercantile brig, ex prize, whose purchase on 29.8.1803 at Bordeaux from citizen Hubert Le Chevalier was approved by the Minister of Marine on 29.8.1803)
  Dimensions & tons: 65ft (21.11m). Tons unknown. Men: 57
  Guns: 14 x 4pdrs (or 10 x 4pdrs).
  Commissioned 24.9.1803. Renamed *Dragon* 28.11.1805. Stationnaire at St. Martin in 1808. Decomm. at Rochefort in bad condition 1811. Last listed in 1813 in the Charente, no longer on the list of ships at Rochefort in 1814 and the French record-keeper wrote 'What happened to her?'

César (mercantile brig or *corvette-senault* (snow-rigged corvette) launched in 1802 and whose purchase at Bordeaux from citizen Dupuch was

approved by the Minister of Marine on 29.8.1803.)
Dimensions & tons: 82ft (26.63m). Tons unknown. Men: 86.
Guns: 18 x 4pdrs.
Comm. 17.3.1804. Boarded and captured 15.7.1806 in the roadstead of Verdun by boats from HMS *Indefatigable* (44) and became HMS *Cesar*. Wrecked in the Gironde 3.1807.

Jaseur (brig commissioned c7.1806 at Île de France, rated at 14 guns, but carried only 6 carronades). Captured 12.7.1807 by HMS *Bombay* (32) in the Nicobar Islands, became the brig-sloop HMS *Jaseur*. Foundered 8.1808 en route from Bengal to Penang.

Créole (mercantile schooner built at Port-Napoléon (Port-Louis), Île de France in 1808, probably by Grisard, and purchased 12.1808 while approaching completion)
Dimensions & tons: 82ft, 76ft 6in x 21ft, 22ft ext x 10ft (26.66, 24.85 x 6.82, 7.15 x 3.25m). 190 tons. Draught 6ft 4in/10ft 4in (2.06/3.36m)
Guns: 8 x 4pdrs; (1815) 10 x 12pdr carronades.
This ship was built as a three-masted schooner on the model of an American ship, had very fine lines, and could only carry a small armament. Comm. 1.1.1809. Her rig was repaired at Île de France in 4.1811 but a lack of masts forced her to be rigged as a brig. Left Île de France 3.5.1811 and arrived at Morlaix 24.9.1811. Re-rigged at Brest as a three-masted schooner 10.1821. Left Brest 20.10.1823 for Rochefort and disappeared, presumed lost with all hands 30.11.1823 in the Gulf of Gascony.

Consolateur (brig launched 10.5.1808 at Bayonne for Spanish owners as *San Pedro*, purchased 15.5.1808 while Napoleon was at Bayonne and renamed 18.5.1808, probably comm. 20.5.1808).
Dimensions & tons: 78ft oa, 63ft x 23ft x 10ft 6in (25.34, 20.46 x 7.47 x 3.41m). 110/200 tons.
Guns: 1 x 16pdr pivot, 2 x 4pdrs (pierced for 12 x 4pdrs)
Sailed 30.5.1808 for Buenos Aires. Run ashore 10.8.1808 at Maldonado, Rio de la Plata, to avoid capture by the boats of two British ships of the line, one day after arriving there.

Améthyste (brig-aviso commissioned 1809, 14 guns). Captured 29.10.1809 by HMS *Minerva* (32).

Mercure (brig of unknown origin, possibly the 200-ton Hamburg merchantman *Mercurius* of 1803, commissioned 1.1.1811, probably at Hamburg, carried 12 x 2pdrs). Was flagship of the Elbe flotilla. Decomm. 31.12.1813 and struck 1814. Hamburg surrendered to the Allies in 5.1814 after the fall of the Empire. *Mercurius* remained in merchant service until 1819.

Sophie (brig or polacre that was in service with Napoleon's Italian Navy at Zara in 3.1811). Sale proposed in 1812. Zara surrendered to the Austrians in 12.1813.

Suappop (*Snappop?*). (brig commissioned 1.2.1812 at Hamburg, carried 12 guns, 3pdrs and smaller). Decomm. at Hamburg 9.3.1813.

David (brig commissioned 1.10.1812 at Hamburg, 131 men). Decomm. at Hamburg 31.12.1812.

(D) Brigs acquired from 26 June 1815

France on 1 October 1816 had a collection of 25 brigs, of which 19 belonged to a single class, Sané's 16-gun *Sylphe* class. Not one of the many brigs built to Pestel's comparable *Curieux* class survived to the end of the war. The collection was filled out by three smaller captured gunbrigs, all of the British *Archer* class, and three single ships. After the war the French built two sizes of brigs – large 18-gun and 20-gun successors to the wartime 16-gun classes armed with 24pdr and 30pdr carronades, and a new smaller type of schooner-brig to a design brought back to France from America and armed with 18pdr carronades. By the late 1830s these had evolved into 10-gun brig-avisos, still with 18pdr carronades. To meet specialised needs the French also built two classes of even smaller gunbrigs, one in 1823-24 with six guns and one in 1838-41 with four guns.

DRAGON Class – Brigs, 18 guns. Plans for this class, the navy's first post-Napoleonic brigs, were completed by Louis Barrallier in July 1821. Its height of battery was listed in the early 1830s as 1.62m at 3.52m mean draught.
Dimensions & tons: 33.32m, 32.50m wl, 28.60m x 8.78m, 8.97m ext x 4.26m. 398 tons. Draught 3.52m mean. Men: 107.
Guns: 16 x 24pdr carronades, 2 x 8pdrs or 12pdrs.

Cuirassier Toulon Dyd. (Constructeur: Barrallier)
Ord: 3.7.1821. K: 10.1821. L: 6.9.1822. Comm: 13.12.1822. C: 12.1822.
Struck 6.11.1843. BU at Brest 12.1843.

Dragon Toulon Dyd. (Constructeur: Barrallier)
Ord: 3.7.1821. K: 4.1822. L: 24.12.1822. Comm: 8.2.1823.
Struck 11.10.1854 at Toulon. BU before 1865.

Lancier Lorient Dyd. (Constructeurs: Jean-Michel Segondat and others)
Ord: 2.10.1821. K: 19.11.1821. L: 1.8.1822. C: 12.1822.
Struck 17.8.1842, hulk at Brest. BU 1854-55.

Endymion Lorient Dyd. (Constructeur: Jean-Michel Segondat?)
Ord: 27.8.1822. K: 29.1.1823. L: 26.7.1824. Comm: 17.5.1825. C: 5.1825.
Struck 3.10.1840. BU at Brest 12.1840.

GAZELLE Class – Schooner-brigs, 16 guns, later brig-avisos. This class was designed by Jean-Baptiste Marestier following his return from a trip to the United States to study steam navigation and naval architecture there. He used ideas from American designs and completed his plans for a class of 'schooner-brigs' with 16 x 18pdr carronades in May 1821. In April 1826 Marestier produced a plan of a schooner-brig entirely rigged as a brig, and subsequent ships were probably built with this rig and a reduced armament. (*Eclipse* was re-rigged in September 1829.) On 14 January 1830 the class was formally given the new designation brig-aviso and assigned an armament of 12 x 18pdr carronades and 2 x 12pdrs, which was reduced by another four 18pdrs on 15 August 1832. *Dunois* and *Bougainville* were fitted c1836 with 8 x 18pdr carronades and 2 x 12pdrs. The number of 18pdr guns was increased to ten on 9 September 1839 to provide officers of the newly-created grade of *capitaine de corvette* with enough suitable commands (ships with more than 10 guns). *Papillon* was completed in 1842 with 10 x 18pdr carronades and 2 x 12pdrs. The designed height of battery of the class was 1.40m at 3.27m mean draught. At least three non-naval ships were built to this design: *Sylvestre*, *Dupont de Nemours*, and *Écrevisse*.
Dimensions & tons: 30.00m, 27.57m wl, 22.00m x 8.00m, 8.15m ext x 3.85m. 320 tons. Draught 2.80/4.30m. Men: 92.
Guns: 16 x 18pdr carronades or 14 x 18pdr carronades, 2 x 12pdrs.

Gazelle Bayonne (Constructeur: probably Gabriel Nosereau)
K: 9.1821. L: 22.4.1822. Comm: 1.7.1822. C: 7.1822.
Struck c6.1837 at Brest. Probably hauled out and rebuilt as the school brig (service craft) *Gabier* (launched 4.9.1838, 35.50m x 8.00m x 3.75m, 160t disp.). Coal hulk at Brest 1853. BU 1868.

Antilope Bayonne (Constructeur: probably Gabriel Nosereau)
K: 7.1822. L: 8.6.1823. Comm: 11.6.1823. C: 7.1823.
Struck and ordered BU 4.4.1832.

Aigrette Bayonne (Constructeur: Gabriel Nosereau)
K: 9.1823. L: 13.3.1824. Comm: 8.4.1824. C: 5.1824.

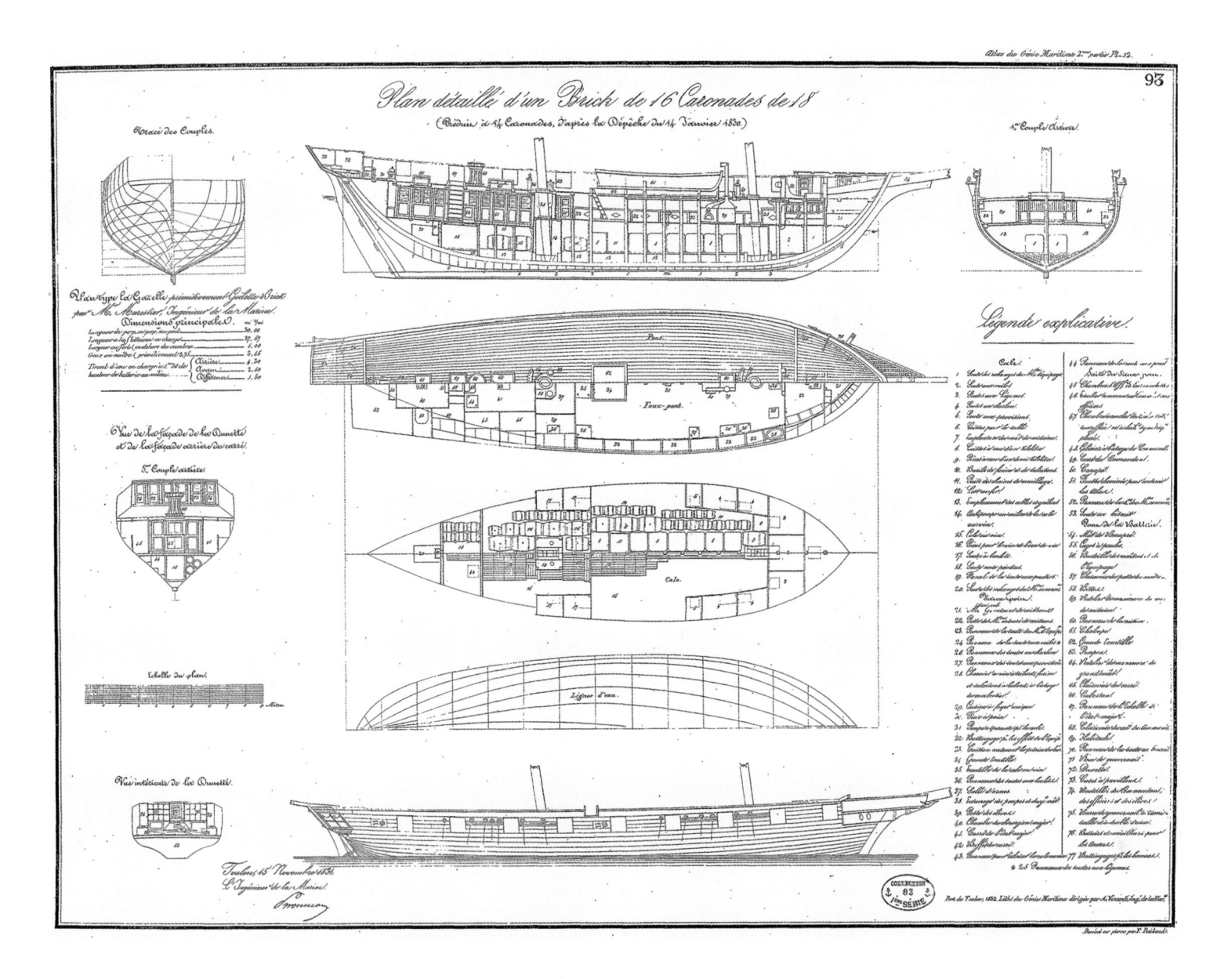

Struck and ordered BU 28.7.1832, BU 8-9.1832 at Brest.

Volage Toulon Dyd.
  K: 4.1824. L: 9.4.1825. Comm: 29.11.1825.
  Re-rigged as brig 8.1826 at Toulon. Sometimes called a bomb vessel around 1840 and may have briefly carried one or two mortars. Struck 7.3.1856, service craft at Toulon. BU before 1865.

Surprise Toulon Dyd.
  K: 4.1824. L: 22.4.1825. Comm: 23.1.1826.
  Struck 11.4.1851 at Brest. BU before 1865.

Flèche Rochefort Dyd. (Constructeurs: Bernard Chariot, then Camille-François Rougier)
  K: 4.1824. L: 1.6.1825. Comm: 1.12.1825.
  Struck 11.12.1851 at Toulon. Last mentioned 1852.

Railleuse Rochefort Dyd. (Constructeurs: Bernard Chariot, then Camille-François Rougier)
  K: 4.1824. L: 1.6.1825. Comm: 1.12.1825. C: 12.1825.
  Struck 26.1.1839, probably at Toulon.

Baucis Bayonne (Constructeur: Gabriel Nosereau)
  K: 6.1824. L: 30.6.1825. Comm: 1.10.1825. C: 10.1825.
  Struck 19.11.1829. BU 3-4.1831 at Brest.

Lines plan and arrangements of the 16-gun schooner-brig *Gazelle* dated 15 November 1831. This class was heavily influenced by American practice, to be seen in the sharp lines, substantial drag of the keel (the ship drawing far more water aft than forward) and the heavily raked masts – the designation schooner-brig at this time meant that there were no square yards crossed on the mainmast, a rig that would soon be known by the old term brigantine. (Atlas du Génie Maritime, French collection, plate 93)

Alcyone Bayonne. (Constructeur: Gabriel Nosereau)
  K: 6.1824. L: 30.6.1825. Comm: 12.9.1825.
  Struck 5.10.1853 at Brest. Sold or BU before 1865.

Comète Toulon Dyd.
  K: 1825. L: 15.4.1826. Comm: 8.6.1827.
  Struck 12.12.1853, school hulk for boys at Brest. Renamed *Ouessant* c1859. Used by the Apprentice School of the Naval Academy at Brest 1873-78. BU 1879-80.

Cigogne Bayonne. (Constructeur: Gabriel Nosereau)
  K: 6.1824. L: 20.7.1826. Comm: 26.7.1827.
  Struck 4.3.1850 at Cherbourg. BU before 1865.

Éclipse Bayonne. (Constructeur: Gabriel Nosereau)
  K: 9.6.1824. L: 20.7.1826. Comm: 24.8.1827.

Caption (right column top): Official plan of the gunbrig *Alsacienne*, engraved in 1837. Sail plan area, as shown, totalled 676 sq.m., although a later plan quotes 766 for the same sails. (Atlas du Génie Maritime, Genoa collection, image 1-0040)

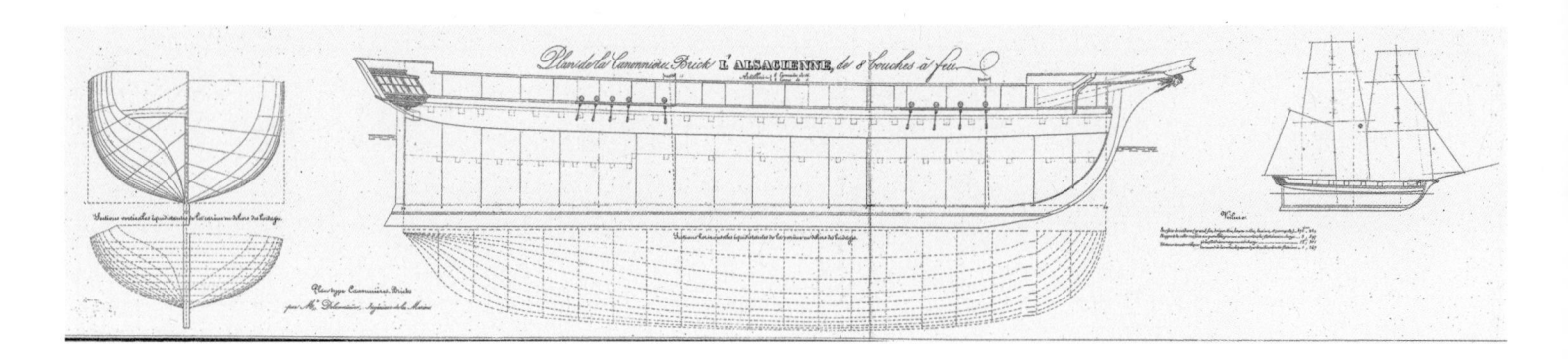

Guns as reduced (1835) 8 x 18pdr carronades, 2 x 12pdrs. Refit abandoned 1849 due to bad condition, struck 16.10.1849. BU before 1865.

Aventure Toulon Dyd.
K: 1825. L: 12.2.1827. Comm: 8.6.1827. C: 6.1827.
Wrecked in fog 60nm east of Algiers on 15.5.1830 with the brig *Silène*.

Badine Bayonne (Constructeur: Gabriel Nosereau)
K: 1.12.1825. L: 5.10.1827. Comm: 15.2.1828. C: 4.1828.
Struck 29.10.1842, BU at Brest 1842.

Capricieuse Bayonne (Constructeur: Gabriel Nosereau)
K: 1.12.1825. L: 1.3.1828. Comm: 10.3.1828. C: 4.1828.
Decomm. 1.4.1836. BU at Brest 8.1836.

Dunois Bayonne (Constructeurs: Gabriel Nosereau and Athanase-Marie Serpin-Dugué, then Nosereau and Alexandre Robiou de Lavrignais)
K: 12.1828. L: 18.4.1830. C: 6.1831. Comm: 22.6.1833.
Disappeared at sea with all hands, probably in a storm in the Bahamas Channel, and presumed lost 4.9.1842.

Sylphe (ex *Primauguet* 3.8.1831) Toulon Dyd. (Constructeur: probably Jean-Baptiste Pironneau)
K: 1828. Named: 16.11.1829 (*Primauguet*). L: 25.9.1830. C: 1831. Comm: 20.11.1833.
Struck 1854 at Toulon. BU 1857.

Dupetit Thouars Toulon Dyd. (Constructeur: probably Jean-Baptiste Pironneau)
K: 25.10.1828. L: 4.12.1830. C: 1831. Comm: 1.5.1833.
Struck 31.12.1864, school hulk for boys (*mousses*) at Brest. Renamed *Mousse* 3.1867. Renamed *Ouessant* 1878 when assigned as an annex to the school ships *Austerlitz* and *Borda* at Brest. Condemned 1881, became an oyster bed at Brest in 1881 and a hulk on the Odet River in 1884 (later moved to Brest, annex to *Perle* 1887-89 and to *Cuvier* 1890-3). BU 1893.

Bougainville Toulon Dyd.
Ord: 16.11.1829 and named. K: 26.4.1830. L: 16.5.1832. C: 1832. Comm: 24.10.1835.
Struck 7.3.1856 at Brest, service craft. BU c1865.

Argus (ex *Étienne Marchand* 3.8.1831) Toulon Dyd. (Constructeur: Jean-Baptiste Pironneau)
Ord: 16.11.1829 and named. K: 11.1830. L: 13.6.1832. C: 1832. Comm: 23.6.1836.
Reportedly fitted c1848 with a diminutive (10nhp) auxiliary steam engine and screw but this is not confirmed in official sources. (See the *Zéphyr* class, below, for another report of small steam engines in brig-avisos.) Struck 20.4.1857, school hulk at Algiers. Renamed *Argonaute* 1860. Became a careening hulk (*ponton-fosse*) at Toulon 1873, used there in torpedo trials 1877-80. Condemned 13.6.1882 and BU.

Laurier Cherbourg Dyd. (Constructeur: Jean-Félix De Robert)
Ord: 16.11.1829 and named. K: 5.6.1830. L: 28.6.1832. C: 7.1832.
Comm: 24.3.1836.
Replaced the chasse-marée *Joubert* as station ship at Pauillac 6.1842. Struck 29.8.1849 at Bordeaux. Sold or BU before 1865.

Borda Bayonne. (Constructeurs: Gabriel Nosereau, Gustave Garnier, and Jean-Baptiste Bayle)
K: 12.1828. L: 26.9.1832. C: 1.1833. Comm: 15.4.1834.
Renamed *Observateur* 18.12.1839. Struck 11.6.1849 at Rochefort and hulked. BU there 5-6.1854.

Lutin (ex *Lahire* 3.8.1831) Brest Dyd. (Constructeurs: Antoine Geoffroy, later Jean-Michel Segondat and others)
Named: 26.11.1829 (*Lahire*). K: 1830. L: 18.5.1833. Comm: 13.7.1834.
Struck 11.12.1851 at Toulon. Mentioned for the last time 1852, BU before 1865.

Fabert Rochefort Dyd. (Constructeurs: Jean-Émile Le Jouteux, Jean-Baptiste Bayle, Antoine Auriol and others)
Ord: 16.11.1829 and named. K: 26.4.1830. L: 30.12.1833. C: 27.4.1836. Comm: 3.6.1836.
Left Jamaica 8.1838 and disappeared in the Atlantic with her crew, presumed lost 16.8.1838.

Cerf Toulon Dyd. (Constructeur: Jean-Baptiste Pironneau)
K: 10.1831. L: 30.12.1833. C: 1834. Comm: 10.12.1836.
Struck 10.5.1858 at Lorient, mooring hulk there until 1874, then a life-saving station. On sale list at Bordeaux 1891, BU 1.1892.

Messager Rochefort Dyd. (Constructeurs: Charles Moll and Henri De Lisleferme)
K: 26.8.1840. L: 17.8.1841. Comm: 25.10.1841.
Struck 20.4.1857 at Toulon, sold or BU before 1865.

Papillon Rochefort Dyd. (Constructeurs: Charles Moll and Henri De Lisleferme)
K: 26.8.1840. L: 2.9.1841. Comm: 15.11.1841.
Struck 14.8.1851 at Rochefort, BU there 6-7.1851.

ALSACIENNE Class – Gunbrigs (*canonnières-bricks*), 8 guns. This class was designed by Jean-François Delamorinière in 1823. Its designed height of battery was 1.40m at 2.44m mean draught, although the ships tended to float deeper. The beam measurements below were taken at the waterline, the maximum moulded beam was 7.43m.

Dimensions & tons: 26.15m, 26.00m wl, 24.50m x 7.00m, 7.24m ext x 3.15m. 241 tons. Draught 2.91/3.27m. Men: 50.
Guns: 6 x 18pdr carronades, 2 x 8pdrs; (1837) 4 x 16cm shell

Alsacienne Cherbourg Dyd.
Ord: 4.2.1823. K: 12.2.1823. L: 13.4.1823. Comm: 27.4.1823. C:

Detailed rig and sail plan for the 20-gun brigs of the Cygne class. It is dated Toulon 1839 and signed by Pironneau, so may relate specifically to the Ducouëdic. A separate sail plan for one of this class, Hussard, calculates the sail area as 1,113 sq.m. without royals. These latter were set 'flying' on a pole extension of the topgallant masts, royals in French being designated perroquets volants *('flying topgallants'). (Atlas du Génie Maritime, French collection, plate 209)*

5.1823.
Condemned 11.4.1851.

Bressane Cherbourg Dyd.
　Ord: 4.2.1823. K: 12.2.1823. L: 13.4.1823. Comm: 10.5.1823. C: 5.1823.
　Decomm. at Lisbon 24.12.1830 and sold there 1833, struck 1833.

Malouine Lorient Dyd.
　K: 18.2.1823. L: 22.4.1823. Comm: 1.5.1823. C: 5.1823.
　Struck 10.5.1858 at Brest, mud lighter (*gabarre à clapet pour le transport de déblais*). BU 1868.

Lilloise Lorient Dyd. (Constructeurs: Joseph Fauveau and Vital-François Lesage)
　Ord: 8.2.1823 and named. K: 18.2.1823. L: 23.4.1823. Comm: 1.5.1823. C: 5.1823.
　Left Rochefort 31.5.1833 for an exploration of the polar seas, left Vapna Fjord, Iceland, for Greenland 5.8.1833 and disappeared without trace, after futile searches 1834-36 presumed crushed in the ice.

Champenoise Cherbourg Dyd. (Constructeur: Louis-Just Moissard, built in the commercial port)
　Ord: 10.2.1824. K: 8.3.1824. L: 19.6.1824. C: 10.1824. Comm: 13.3.1826.
　Struck 22.10.1834 at Rochefort, BU 11.1834.

Bordelaise Cherbourg Dyd. (Constructeur: Émile Etiennez, built in the commercial port)
　Ord: 10.2.1824. K: 8.3.1824. L: 19.6.1824. C: 10.1824. Comm: 16.10.1826.
　Struck 17.3.1841 at Montevideo.

CYGNE Class – Brigs, 20 guns. The plans for this class were completed in April 1824 by the same commission that designed the new 100-gun and 90-gun ships of the line and were approved by the Council of Works on 13 May 1824. The hull plans were based on the corvette-aviso *Diligente*, with 0.32m more beam and with the ends strengthened. The class was notable for its round stern. Its designed height of battery was 1.48m at 4.07m mean draught. The first two were initially ordered as ships of the *Cuirassier* type at Bayonne, and were reassigned to Toulon in 1823 and reordered on the new plans in 1824. *Griffon* and *Méléagre* were originally projected to be begun respectively at Toulon and Rochefort in 1829 but were instead begun at Brest and Lorient in 1828.
　Dimensions & tons: 34.15m, 33.60m wl, 30.50m x 9.00m, 9.20m ext x 4.59m. 548 tons. Draught 3.57/4.57m. Men: 113.
　Guns: 18 x 24pdr carronades, 2 x 18pdrs or 12pdrs.

Alacrity (ex *Colibri* c11.1822) Toulon Dyd. (Constructeur: Jean-Baptiste Lebas)
　Ord: 10.2.1824. K: 7.1824. L: 25.4.1825. Comm: 27.8.1825.
　Struck 16.10.1849 at Toulon. Sinking in place and ordered BU 29.7.1851.

Palinure (**Palynure**) Toulon Dyd. (Constructeur: Jean-Baptiste Lebas).
　Ord: 10.2.1824. K: 7.1824. L: 9.5.1825. Comm: 25.10.1825.
　Commissioned 7.5.1855 after conversion to a bomb vessel for the Crimea with 2 x 32cm mortars and 2 x 30pdrs No.3. Reverted to a brig 1.1856. Struck 8.11.1862, cut down to barge for Lorient c1863. BU 1887 at Lorient.

Cygne (**Cigne**) Lorient Dyd. (Constructeur: Pierre Thomeuf)
　Ord: 10.2.1824 and named. K: 26.8.1824. L: 28.7.1825. Comm: 19.10.1825.

Struck 14.8.1851 at Toulon. BU before 1865.
Faucon Rochefort Dyd. (Constructeur: Gustave Garnier)
Ord: 10.2.1824. K: 20.8.1824. L: 13.8.1825. Comm: 16.8.1827. C: 8.1827.
Struck 22.5.1847. BU 1848 at Toulon.
Grenadier Rochefort Dyd. (Constructeur: Gustave Garnier)
Ord: 10.2.1824. K: 20.8.1824. L: 13.8.1825. Comm: 4.10.1827.
Struck 19.7.1849 at Brest, service craft, used as occasional transport. Coal depot 1852, BU 1865.
Alerte Lorient Dyd. (Constructeur: Pierre Thomeuf)
Ord: 10.2.1824. K: 8.1824. L: 16.8.1825. Comm: 11.7.1827. C: 7.1827.
Struck 30.6.1845 and condemned 7.7.1845 at Brest. Reappeared, probably in error, on the list 31.12.1846 as a brig out of commission at Toulon and struck there 1847.
Alcibiade Toulon Dyd.
K: 1825. L: 27.3.1826. Comm: 11.7.1826.
Struck 8.11.1862, barge and warehouse for steam engine parts at Lorient. Condemned 16.3.1888, ordered BU 26.3.1888, BU 5.1888 to 4.1889.
Nisus Lorient Dyd. (Constructeur: Pierre Thomeuf)
K: 10.1824. L: 5.7.1826. C: 1.1827. Comm: 1.1.1828.
Struck 24.10.1844 at Brest.
Adonis Toulon Dyd.
K: 6.1825. L: 12.2.1827. Comm: 8.6.1827.
Struck 20.4.1857, storage hulk at Brest. BU 6.1865.
Actéon Lorient Dyd. (Constructeur: Pierre Thomeuf)

A coloured lithograph depicting a simulated boat attack on the brig *Voltigeur* in the roadstead of Brest on 30 August 1843. The value of the round stern in this class is apparent: without gunports bearing aft, the brig would have an entirely blind arc astern, allowing the boats to approach under no more than small-arms fire. Although less apparent in this view, there was also an oblique chase port right forward to counter attacks from ahead, and this is being employed to fire on the boats off the brig's starboard bow. Note also the anti-boarding netting rigged on poles above the deck. (© National Maritime Museum PY0839)

K: early 1825. L: 11.4.1827. Comm: 1.9.1827. C: 9.1827.
Condemned 3.3.1847, struck 22.5.1847. BU 1848 at Toulon.
Hussard Rochefort Dyd. (Constructeur: Alphonse Levesque)
K: 7.12.1825. L: 25.6.1827. Comm: 24.1.1828.
Struck 22.12.1864 at Lorient, hulk. Cut down to barge 1866, renamed *Larmor* 1876, On sale list 1898 but still hulk at Lorient 1899 (*Ponton No.1*), date BU unknown.
Voltigeur Rochefort Dyd. (Constructeur: Alphonse Levesque)
K: 26.10.1825. L: 25.6.1827. Comm: 10.2.1828.
Struck 4.3.1850 at Lorient, BU before 1865.
Griffon Brest Dyd. (Constructeurs: Antoine Geoffroy and others)
Ord: 29.3.1828 and named. K: 7.7.1828. L: 2.7.1829. Comm: 19.2.1830.
Struck 29.4.1850, hulk at Cherbourg. BU before 1865.
Ducouëdic (*Du Couëdic*) Toulon Dyd. (Constructeur: probably Jean-Baptiste Pironneau)
K: 14.3.1828. L: 26.9.1829. Comm: 1.4.1830.
Struck 5.3.1859, school hulk for boys at Lorient. Coal hulk 1866,

renamed *Charbonnier* 1867 and *Charbonnière* 1868. BU 1878.
D'Assas Rochefort Dyd. (Constructeurs: Alphonse Levesque, then Gustave Garnier)
K: 19.5.1828. L: 24.3.1830. Comm: 15.3.1830 (began to go into commission before launch, probably ready for service 4.1830).
Struck 11.6.1851 at Brest, hulk. Renamed *Kermorvant* c1852. BU 1866.
Bisson Lorient Dyd. (Constructeur: Pierre Thomeuf)
Ord: 29.3.1828. K: 5.1828. L: 5.7.1830. C: 1831. Comm: 7.10.1835.
Decomm. 6.12.1842, struck 18.4.1844, sailing lighter at Brest. Renamed *Cormorandière* c1850. BU 1914 at Brest.
Méléagre Lorient Dyd-Caudan. (Constructeur: Pierre Thomeuf)
K: 26.5.1828. L: 7.7.1830. Comm: 26.6.1832.
Struck 20.4.1857 at Brest, hulk. Coal hulk 1875. BU 1883.
Lapérouse (*Lapeyrouse*) Lorient Dyd. (Constructeurs: Jean-François Chaumont and others)
Ord: 16.11.1829 and named (*Lapeyrouse*). K: 6.10.1830. L: 30.7.1832. Comm: 3.4.1837.
Training brig for boys at Ajaccio 11.5.1864. Struck 17.8.1869, school hulk for boys at Ajaccio. Careening hulk (*ponton-fosse*) at Toulon 1873. Renamed *Lézard* 1.1875. Target ship 1877, while being towed by *Utile* was sunk 15.2.1877 off Ste. Marguerite at Toulon by a towed torpedo being tested by *Desaix*.
Cassard Lorient Dyd. (Constructeurs: Jean-François Chaumont and others)
Ord: 16.11.1829 and named. K: 6.10.1830. L: 10.9 1832. C: 1833. Comm: 7.12.1835.
Struck 23.11.1850. Probably BU 1851.
Oreste (ex *Jean de Vienne* 3.8.1831) Brest Dyd. (Constructeurs: Antoine Geoffroy, then Jean-Michel Segondat and others)
Named: 16.11.1829 (*Jean de Vienne*). K: 20.5.1830. L: 4.5.1833. Comm: 13.7.1834.
Carried two mortars in 1855. Struck 20.4.1857, school hulk for boys at Marseille. BU 1875.
Pylade (*Pilade*) (ex *Saint-Ouen* 3.8.1831) Rochefort Dyd. (Constructeurs: Jean-Émile Le Jouteux, Bernard Chariot, Alexandre Robiou de Lavrignais and others)
Ord: 16.11.1829 and named (*Saint-Ouen*). K: 26.8.1830. L: 28.12.1833. C: 5.1835. Comm: 15.11.1838.
Conducted trials of an experimental geared capstan in 1834. Struck 20.4.1857 at Brest, sold or BU before 1865.

OLIVIER – Aviso rigged as brig, 6 guns. Designed by the Commission of Brest (Duperré, Geoffroy, Gicquel des Touches, Bazoche, Mallet, and Auriol, of whom only Geoffroy and Auriol were naval constructors). Her sail area appears to have been much too large for her hull dimensions, probably accounting for her loss.
Dimensions & tons: 27.40m, 26.00m wl, 22.30m x 7.50m wl, 8.08m ext x 3.90m. 243 tons. Draught 3.07/3.85m. Men: probably 74.
Guns: 6 x 12pdrs (designed), 4 x 8pdrs (actual)
Olivier Brest Dyd. (Constructeur: Antoine Auriol)
Ord: 27.9.1828. K: 3.11.1828. Named: 20.11.1828 (and designated aviso). L: 3.6.1829. Comm: 16.10.1829. C: 10.1829.
Left Brest 14.12.1829 and disappeared on a voyage to Cuba. On 27.5.1831 was declared presumed lost.

TACTIQUE Class – Gunbrigs (*canonnières-bricks*), 4 guns. This class was designed by Mathurin Boucher. The Ordinance of 1 February 1837 established a new standard armament for this type of 4 x 30pdr *canons-obusiers*, which the existing gunbrigs could not carry. Boucher was directed to prepare new plans that would accommodate the new armament but keep the hull essentially as is because of the good qualities of the existing gunbrigs. He ended up increasing the draught by 15cm, increasing the height of the battery by 15cm, and increasing the displacement by 49 tons. Two of the guns were placed before the foremast and two aft of the mainmast. Boucher's plans were approved on 9 June 1838 and the first four ships were ordered and named four days later. According to Pierre Le Conte, *Chevrette* was ordered on 15 December 1841 in place of a 380-ton gabarre of the same name that had been ordered on 30 October 1841. She was placed in reduced commission (*commission de rade*) on 1 January 1846 and in full commission in May.
Dimensions & tons: 28.06m, 27.80m wl, 25.80m x 7.50m wl, 7.70m ext x 3.30m. 265 tons. Draught 2.59/2.83m aft. Men: 50.
Guns: 4 x 16cm shell.
Tactique Rochefort Dyd. (Constructeur: Antoine Auriol)
Ord: 13.6.1838 and named. K: 20.12.1838. L: 29.3.1839. C: 5.1839. Comm: 1.8.1839.
Struck 10.5.1858 at Brest, sailing mud lighter (*transport de déblais à voiles*). Renamed *Lochrist* c1860. BU 1888.
Vigie Rochefort Dyd. (Constructeur: Antoine Auriol)
Ord: 13.6.1838 and named. K: 24.12.1838. L: 30.3.1839. C: 5.1839. Comm: 1.8.1839.
Struck 10.5.1858 at Brest, sailing mud lighter (*transport de déblais à voiles*). Renamed *Bertheaume* c1860. BU 1888.
Églantine Lorient Dyd. (Constructeur: Jean-Baptiste Larchevesque-Thibaut)
Ord: 13.6.1838 and named. K: 2.1.1839. L: 13.6.1839. Comm: 1.9.1839. C: 9.1839.
Struck 10.5.1858 at Brest, sailing mud lighter (*transport de déblais à voiles*). Waste transport (*transport de déchets*) at Brest 1870, station hulk in the Odet River 1880. BU 1885.
Boulonnaise Lorient Dyd. (Constructeur: Jean-Baptiste Larchevesque-Thibaut)
Ord: 13.6.1838 and named. K: 12.1838. L: 16.5.1839. Comm: 17.8.1839. C: 8.1839.
Decomm. 28.7.1845 at Brest, struck 1846.
Alouette Cherbourg Dyd.
K: 2.1.1839. L: 14.5.1839. Comm: 20.8.1839. C: 8.1839.
Struck 10.5.1858 at Brest, sailing mud lighter (*transport de déblais à voiles*). BU 1868.
Vedette Cherbourg Dyd.
K: 2.1.1839. L: 14.5.1839. Comm: 20.8.1839. C: 8.1839.
Wrecked 6.10.1842 on the west coast of Miquelon.
Chevrette Cherbourg Dyd. (Constructeurs: Alexandre Robiou de Lavrignais and others)
Ord: 30.10.1841 and named. K: 5.10.1842. L: 23.9.1843. C: 1.1846. Comm: 25.5.1846.
Sunk 19.10.1846 in collision with the transport *Prévoyante* in the entrance to the Firth of Forth, Scotland.
Panthère Lorient Dyd. (Constructeur: Jean-Baptiste Larchevesque-Thibaut)
K: 17.2.1841. L: 17.2.1844. C: 3.1844. Comm: 2.10.1847.
Struck 10.5.1858 at Brest, sailing mud lighter (*transport de déblais à voiles*). BU 1888.

GÉNIE Class – Brigs, 18 guns. Mathurin Boucher reported to the Council of Admiralty on 9 March 1841 that, based on commanding officers' reports, the current *Cygne*-type brigs had good seakeeping qualities but were slow and their batteries were not high enough. They seemed too long, too narrow, and a bit unstable, and compared to similar

British ships they were inferior in firepower. He recommended that this type be abandoned for the four brigs to be built in 1841 (*Génie* and *Mercure* at Brest and *Fanfaron* and *Faune* at Toulon) and that new hull plans and a new armament be adopted for them. Specifically, the length of the ships was to be reduced, beam and depth of hull increased, and the 18 x 24pdr carronades in the armament replaced with 16 x 30pdr carronades. The Council had doubts about the reduction in length and decided to order two of the four brigs with Boucher's proposed dimensions (*Génie* and *Fanfaron*) and two with the existing length, the beam increased by 0.60m, and the hull lines of the *Cygne* type (*Mercure* and *Faune*).

Boucher completed his plans for *Génie* in May 1841. On 14 March 1848 the later ships of this class were ordered built with an armament of 16 x 16cm shell guns. *Nisus* and *Euryale* were originally projected to be begun at Rochefort and Brest respectively in 1849 but they traded dockyards before construction began in 1850. *Euryale* and *Chevert* were completed as transports and *Beaumanoir* was converted in 1869 into a transport rigged with three masts. Another ship, *Drouot*, was projected in 1849 to be begun in 1850 with *Beaumanoir* and *Chevert* but was deferred and cancelled in 1852.

Dimensions & tons: 33.00m, 32.50m wl, 29.75m x9.60m, 9.80m ext x 4.89m. 542 tons. Draught 4.05m mean. Men: 101-125.

Guns: 16 x 30pdr carronades, 2 x 16cm shell; (*Victor* 1852) 14 x 16cm shell.

Génie Brest Dyd. (Constructeur: Antoine Roger)
K: 13.7.1841. L: 23.6.1842. Comm: 1.1.1843. C: 1.1843.
Struck 8.11.1866, coal hulk at Lorient. BU 1889.

A coloured lithograph of the gunbrig *Boulonnaise* on the Antilles Station in 1841 or at Cayenne in 1844-45. (© National Maritime Museum PY0842)

Janus Toulon Dyd. (many constructors, completed by Napoléon Achille Romagnesi)
K: 8.1847. L: 21.11.1848. Comm: 10.6.1861. C: 6.1861.
Completion suspended from 1849 to 1860. Completed with 2 x 18pdr carronades. Annex to the boys' school ship *Navarin* at Toulon from 4.1865 to 5.1866 with 2 x 12cm rifles. Fitted 6.1871 as annex to the gunnery school at Toulon (in *Alexandre*) with 4 x 14cm rifles and in 5.1879 (as an annex to *Souverain*) to train apprentice gunners. Refitted at Brest 12.1881-2.1882 with a three-masted square rig (and called a 'brig with three masts') and 2 x 12cm rifles as an annex to the naval academy hulk *Borda*. Struck 22.1.1884 and continued to support *Borda* until 1897, when she was refitted as a hulk for use in calibrating compasses at Brest. Offered for sale at Brest 20.10.1913 but bids were too low, BU 1914.

Victor Brest Dyd. (Constructeur: Jules Villain)
K: 4.8.1848. L: 21.7.1849. C: 12.1850. Comm: 7.1.1852.
Struck 15.7.1867 at Brest. Became a coal hulk there in 1874 and a storage hulk (*ponton-dépôt*) in 1878, BU 1881.

Nisus Brest Dyd.
K: 11.6.1849. L: 14.5.1850. C: 1850. Comm: 16.10.1854.
Refitted 1864 for use by the Naval School at Brest. Struck 13.12.1866 and continued to serve until 1914 as an annex to the boys training hulk *Bretagne* at Brest. BU 1915.

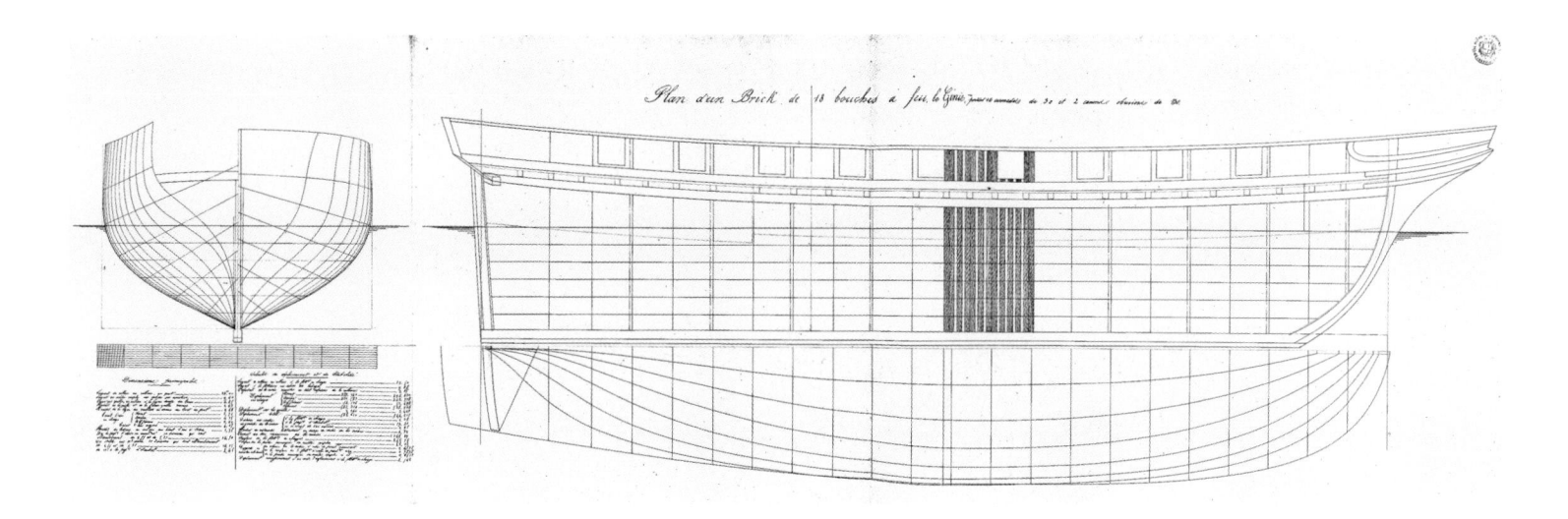

Official lines plan of the 18-gun *Génie*. A separate sail plan gives the sail area – as usual, minus royals and including only a single headsail – as 1,139 sq.m. (Atlas du Génie Maritime, Genoa collection, image 1-0011)

Beaumanoir Cherbourg Dyd. (Constructeurs: Albin Vidal and Louis Antoine)
   Ord: 5.1.1850. K: 19.1.1850. L: 2.12.1853. Comm: 3.5.1854. C: 5.1854.
   As a sailing brig in 1871 carried 4 x 12cm rifles. Converted to transport with three masts 11.1878 to 3.1879. Struck 23.10.1883 and fitted as a seamanship school ship at Cherbourg. Coal hulk c1900, sold for BU 1904.
Zèbre Lorient Dyd. (Constructeurs: Pierre Le Grix and Pierre Guieysse)
   K: 26.5.1848. L: 4.11.1854. Comm: 6.7.1857. C: 7.1857.
   Construction suspended 1851-53 and 1855-57. Did not go to sea after 9.1860. Struck 8.11.1866, headquarters hulk at Lorient. BU 1896.
Euryale Rochefort Dyd. (Constructeurs: Jean Félix De Robert, Charles Louis Jay, Achille August Zani de Ferranty, Henri De Lisleferme, and Auguste Émile Boden)
   K: 31.10.1849. L: 11.11.1863. Comm: 9.2.1864. C: 3.1864.
   Construction suspended 1853-62, completed 1863-64 as 250-ton transport on plans by E. Boden. Wrecked 5.3.1870 on Starbuck Island in the Pacific.
Chevert Rochefort Dyd. (Constructeurs: Achille Auguste Zani de Ferranty, Charles Louis Jay, Alfred François Lebelin de Dionne, Henri De Lisleferme, and Auguste Émile Boden)
   K: 4.1850. L: 26.11.1863. Comm: 12.2.1864. C: 3.1864.
   Construction suspended 1855-62, completed 1863-64 as 250-ton transport on plans by E. Boden. Harbour service at Papeete 1.1872, on sale list there 1.1873, decomm. and struck 1.8.1873.
Drouot Toulon Dyd
   Projected in 1849 to be begun in 1850 but deferred, cancelled in 1852.

OLIVIER – 18 guns. Prix-Charles Sochet completed the plans for this ship, one of three ordered with *Génie*, in April 1841.
   Dimensions & tons: 33.00m, 28.90m x 9.60m x 4.85m. 550 tons. Draught 4.05m mean. Men: 101.
   Guns: 16 x 30pdr carronades, 2 x 16cm shell.
Olivier (ex *Fanfaron* c2.1842) Toulon Dyd. (Constructeur: Sochet)
   K: 7.1843. L: 28.12.1844. C: 1845. Comm: 1.4.1848.
   Struck 7.5.1868, coal hulk at Cherbourg. BU 1887.

MERCURE – Brig, 18 guns. Hippolyte Prétot completed the plans for this ship, one of three ordered with *Génie*, in April 1841.
   Dimensions & tons: 34.00m, 33.70m wl, 29.80m x 9.40m x 4.85m. 618 tons. Draught 4.04/4.62m. Men: 101.
   Guns: 16 x 30pdr carronades, 2 x 16cm shell.
Mercure Brest Dyd. (Constructeur: Prétot)
   K: 26.6.1841. L: 25.5.1842. Comm: 1.2.1843.
   Struck 8.3.1862, coal hulk at Lorient. BU 1888.

ABEILLE – Brig, 18 guns. Jean-Baptiste Bayle completed the plans for this ship, one of three ordered with *Génie*, in April 1841. She was originally to have been built at Toulon, and Bayle's plans were completed there on 20 April 1841, but she was reassigned on 2 March 1843 to new facilities at Cherbourg. Launched as *Faune*, she was renamed when the previous *Abeille* was struck on 15 November 1844 to perpetuate the name of the brig that captured the British brig *Alacrity* on 26 May 1811. The commander of *Abeille* in 1811 was Minister of Marine in 1844.
   Dimensions & tons: 34.00m, 33.37m wl, 30.40m x 9.40m x 4.85m. 538 tons. Draught 3.75/4.35m. Men: 101.
   Guns: 16 x 30pdr carronades, 2 x 16cm shell.
Abeille (ex *Faune* 14.11.44) Cherbourg Dyd. (Constructeur: probably Alexandre De Lavrignais)
   K: 26.6.1843. L: 14.9.1844. Comm: 18.8.1845. C: 8.1845.
   Wrecked 10.12.1847 off the fort at Quita (now Keta, Ghana) in the Gulf of Benin.

AGILE – Brig-aviso, 10 guns. On 9 March 1841, in the same session of the Council of Admiralty in which he recommended new plans and armaments for large brigs, Mathurin Boucher noted that the current brig-avisos had a lot of rake to the sternpost and the stem, a very large difference in draught forward and aft, narrow beam for their length and consequently little stability, insufficient hull capacity, and speed lower than should be expected from their fine lines. He proposed for the four brig-avisos to be laid down in 1841 (*Agile* and *Rossignol* at Cherbourg and *Pandour* and *Léger* at Lorient) new lines more appropriate to their rig with reduced length and a slight increase in beam and depth of hull. He also proposed a new armament of 24pdr carronades. As it did for the larger brigs, the Council decided to order two of the four brig-avisos with Boucher's proposed changes (*Agile* and probably *Pandour*) and two with the present length and the beam increased by 0.40m (probably

Rossignol and *Léger*). Boucher completed the plans for *Agile* in April 1841.
>Dimensions & tons: 27.56m wl, 24.8m x 8.40m x 4.23m. 327 tons. Draught 3.65m mean. Men: 92.
>Guns: 8 x 24pdr carronades, 2 x 12pdrs.

Agile Cherbourg Dyd.
>Ord: 7.4.1841. K: 3.8.1841. L: 30.3.1843. Comm: 1.5.1844.
>Annex to the school for apprentice seamen (*Forte*) 5.1865. Struck 24.12.1866, coal hulk at Cherbourg. Renamed *Agilité* 1888. Sold and BU 1891.

ROSSIGNOL – Brig-aviso, 10 guns. This ship was ordered in 1841 with *Agile* in an effort to develop an improved brig-aviso design. Georges Allix completed the plans for *Rossignol* in June 1841. Her designed armament was 8 x 24pdr carronades, 2 x 12pdrs.
>Dimensions & tons: 27.60m wl, 25.2m x 8.40m x 4.23m. 291 tons. Draught 3.40m mean. Men: 92.
>Guns: (c1845) 6 x 16cm shell.

Rossignol Cherbourg Dyd. (Constructeur: Allix)
>Ord: 7.4.1841. K: 14.12.1841. L: 4.4.1843. Comm: 1.9.1845.
>Struck 3.11.1859 at Cherbourg, sold or BU before 1865.

PANDOUR – Brig-aviso, 10 guns. This ship was ordered in 1841 with *Agile* in an effort to develop an improved brig-aviso design. Jean-Baptiste Larchevesque-Thibaut completed the plans for *Pandour* in July 1841.
>Dimensions & tons: 27.45m wl, 25.2m x 8.40m. 293 tons. Men: 92.

Entreprenant was one of several brigs ordered during the 1840s and later re-rigged with three masts as transports or training ships. *Entreprenant* was modified in 1868 and served as a transport based at Rochefort until 1881. She is shown here at Algiers near the end of her seagoing service. At this stage of her career she is almost indistinguishable from a merchant ship. (USN NH-74954, from an ONI album of French warships)

>Guns: (Designed) 8 x 24pdr carronades, 2 x 12pdrs. May have carried 8 x 18pdr carronades, 2 x 8pdrs.

Pandour Lorient Dyd.
>K: 11.1841. L: 22.11.1843. Comm: 25.4.1844.
>Left Montevideo 17.7.1848 to return to France and disappeared. She was believed lost on the Rio Grande shoals off Brazil. Struck 21.7.1850.

LÉGER – Brig-aviso, 10 guns. This ship was ordered in 1841 with *Agile* in an effort to develop an improved brig-aviso design. Pierre Guieysse completed the plans for *Rossignol* in June 1841. Her designed armament was 8 x 24pdr carronades, 2 x 12pdrs.
>Dimensions & tons: 28.00m wl, 24.9m x 8.40m x 4.20m. 296 tons. Draught 3.76m mean. Men: 92.
>Guns: (c1845) 6 x 16cm shell.

Léger Lorient Dyd. (Constructeur: Guieysse)
>K: 5.3.1842. L: 20.1.1844. Comm: 17.8.1845.
>Served as school ship for apprentice seamen 1856-59. Struck 16.3.1868, fishery protection storage hulk at Arcachon. Loaned 1872 to the life-saving station at Rochefort. BU 1875.

Sail plan of the brig-aviso *Fabert*. This class was intended to carry a large spread of canvas to equip them for chasing speedy slaving vessels. Nevertheless, the calculated sail area omitted the royals and all but one headsail, for a total of 894 sq.m. (Atlas du Génie Maritime, Genoa collection, image 1-0040)

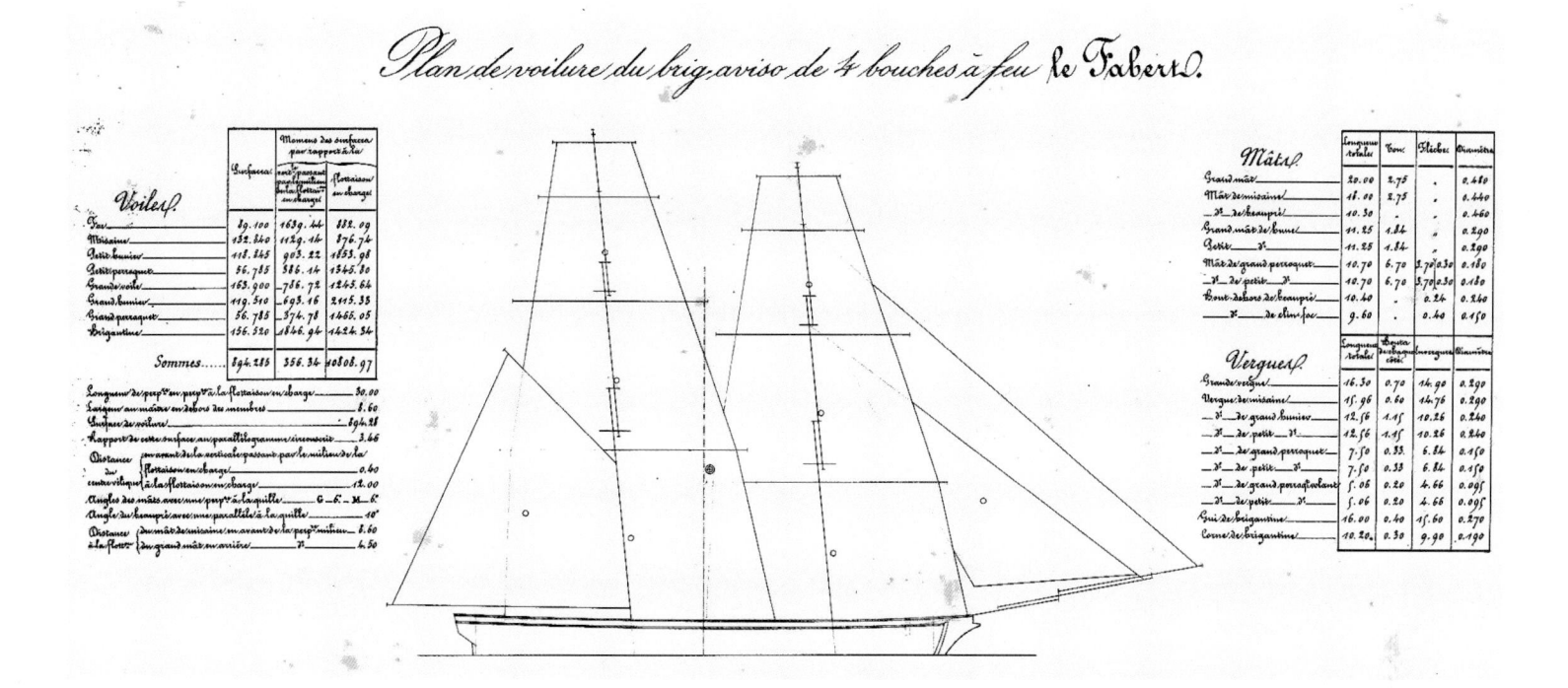

FAUNE – Brig, 14 guns. New plans were ordered 15 January 1846 for brigs to carry an armament of 16cm shell guns. Four were ultimately built, all to plans by different designers: *Faune*, *Chasseur*, *Entreprenant*, and *Obligado*. Plans by Joseph De Gasté were approved for *Faune* on 22 May 1846. New ships of the *Génie* class were also built with the new type armament.

Dimensions & tons: 32.50m, 30.3m x 9.75m x 4.95m. 537 tons. Draught 3.82/4.52m. Men: 125.
Guns: 12 x 16cm shell, 2 x 18pdrs.

Faune Brest Dyd. (Constructeur: De Gasté)
K: 5.6.1846. L: 17.4.1847. Comm: 26.2.1849.
Annex to *Borda* (Naval Academy) 1852. Refitted with three masts in 1854 for use by the school for boys at Brest. Struck 31.12.1864, hulk for the school for boys at Cherbourg. BU 1869.

ENTREPRENANT – Brig, 14 guns. This ship was designed to carry the same armament as *Faune*. Plans by Henri Denis de Senneville were approved for her on 22 May 1846. She is not to be confused with the frigate *Entreprenante*, which was also converted to a transport.

Dimensions & tons: 34.00m, 30.20m x 9.70m x 4.90m. 494m disp. Draught 4.06m. Men: 125.
Guns: 12 x 16cm shell, 2 x 18pdrs.

Entreprenant Rochefort Dyd. (Constructeur: Denis de Senneville)
K: 26.5.1846. L: 20.1.1849. Comm: 23.3.1849. C: 5.1849.
Converted to a 250-ton transport with three masts at Rochefort 2-12.1868. Became service craft at Rochefort in 1881 and torpedo-boat depot hulk at Bastia from 4.1887. Struck 2.8.1887, remained in use until BU 1909.

CHASSEUR – Brig, 14 guns. This ship was designed to carry the same armament as *Faune*. Plans for her by Pierre Guieysse were approved on 23 December 1846.

Dimensions & tons: 32.50m wl, 29.00m x 9.70m x 4.70m. 509 tons. Draught 4.12m mean. Men: 125.
Guns: 12 x 16cm shell, 2 x 18pdrs.

Chasseur Lorient Dyd. (Constructeurs: Charles Robert Alexandre and Hippolyte Prétot)
K: 26.5.1847. L: 31.7.1848. Comm: 23.5.1849. C: 5.1849.
Refitted 5.1856 as a school ship and served as annex to the brig *Faune* until 1858. Received a third mast for training duty prior 1869. Struck 31.12.1864, training brig 1865, hulk 1866, coal hulk 1875, renamed *Rose* 1876, on sale list 1886, BU 1887.

OBLIGADO – Brig, 14 guns. This ship was designed to carry the same armament as *Faune*. Plans by Émile Dorian were approved for her on 6 March 1848. She was named after a joint Franco-British action on 20 November 1845 against the Argentines.

Dimensions & tons: 33.56m wl, 29.70m x 9.60m x 5.05m. 565 tons. Draught 4.13/4.31m. Men: 125.
Guns: (1852) 14 x 16cm shell.

Obligado Cherbourg Dyd. (Constructeurs: Dorian and Achille Quesnet)
Ord: 30.11.1847 and named. K: 26.8.1848. L: 10.7.1850. Comm: 21.8.1852. C: 8.1852.
Struck 15.11.1878, school hulk for novices and annex to *Bretagne* at Brest and from 1880 boys training ship and annex to *Austerlitz* at Brest. Became a torpedo-boat depot hulk in 1889 at Morlaix and from 1895 at Aberwrach (Brest, as an annex to *Navarin*). BU 1910.

ZÉPHYR Class – Brig-avisos, 6 guns. On 10 July 1845 the Minister of Marine informed the ports that the navy did not have enough light ships to execute the anti-slavery convention of 29 May 1845 and asked the ports to provide plans for brigs for the West African patrol. The minister specified that they were to be of a new type optimised for speed in order to catch slavers, and that the designers were to be left free to choose their dimensions and lines. They were, however, to be as light as possible. These 1845 specifications also called for installing a 30nhp steam engine in several instead of some ballast and a third of their provisions as an experiment, but there is no later reference to this idea. A commission examined the plans submitted by the ports, and on 15 December 1846 the Minister of Marine approved plans by Hippolyte Prétot, Antoine Roger, and Alexandre Chedeville and directed that two ships be built to each for a total of six ships instead of the planned four. The six ships were ordered from three shipbuilders by contracts awarded on 12 April 1847 and approved on 20 April 1847. At the same time contracts were awarded for two 800-ton transports, *Durance* and *Moselle*, which may have been intended to support the six brig-avisos plus the six paddle and two screw steamers built for the anti-slavery patrols.

Alexandre Chedeville completed the plans for *Zéphyr* and *Lynx* in September 1845 and they were built by Chaigneau & Bichon at Bordeaux. Once these two ships were delivered at Rochefort they may never have left that port although they were both repaired there frequently. Plans of September 1850 to commission both were abandoned, and *Lynx* was never commissioned.

Dimensions & tons: 30.00m wl, 28.3m x 9.10m x 4.00m. 300 tons. Draught 3.12m mean. Men: 92.
Guns: 6 x 16cm shell.

Zéphyr Chaigneau & Bichon, Bordeaux-Lormont (Constructeur: Nicolas Courtin)
Ord 20.4.1847 (contract). K: 8.1847. L: 13.3.1848. C: 10.1848. Comm: 9.4.1849.
At Rochefort by 3.1849. Decomm. 1.10.1849. Struck 29.5.1858 and BU.

Lynx Chaigneau & Bichon, Bordeaux-Lormont (Constructeur: Nicolas Courtin)
Ord 20.4.1847 (contract). K: 8.1847. L: 2 or 6.6.1848. C: 12.1848.
At Rochefort by 5.1849. Condemned 3.1858, BU 3-4.1858, struck 29.5.1858.

FABERT Class – Brig-avisos, 6 guns. The origins of these two ships were as the *Zéphyr* class. Antoine Roger completed plans for them in August 1845, and they were built by Guibert at Nantes.

Dimensions & tons: 30.00m wl, 28.2m x 8.60m x 4.23m. 298 tons. Draught 3.40m mean. Men: 92.
Guns: 6 x 16cm shell.

Fabert Guibert, Nantes.
Ord 20.4.1847 (contract). K: 5.1847. L: 20.5.1848. Comm: 2.4.1849. C: 4.1849.
Commissioned 2.4.1849 for trials at Brest and found to be very unstable; rig and armament reduced. Decomm. 27.1.1853 in bad condition, struck 30.12.1854. Became a service craft at Toulon, then towed by *Brasier* 6.10.1858 to Sète for use as a merchant marine boys' training ship. Sold there for BU 12.1.1872, was completely rotten.

Inconstant Guibert, Nantes.
Ord 20.4.1847 (contract). K: 6.1847. L: 17.5.1848. C: 3.1849.
In reduced commission (*commission de port*) from 27.3.1849 to 9.11.1850 and did not go to sea after her transit from Nantes to Brest in 1849. She was probably as unsatisfactory as her sister. Struck 20.4.1857 and hulked at Brest. BU 1868.

RUSÉ Class – Brig-avisos, 6 guns. The origins of these two ships were as the *Zéphyr* class. Hippolyte Prétot completed plans for them in September 1845.

Dimensions & tons: 29.00m wl, 26.5m x 8.40m x 4.18m. 295 tons. Draught 3.45m mean. Men: 92.
Guns: 6 x 16cm shell.

Rusé Baudet, Paimboeuf.
Ord 20.4.1847 (contract). K: 6.1847. L: 3.6.1848. Comm: 16.8.1849. C: 8.1849.
Served in West Africa 5.1850 to 12.1851, inactive thereafter. Struck 20.4.1857 at Brest and BU.

Railleur Pivert, Saint-Malo.
Ord 20.4.1847 (contract). K: 7.1847. L: 16.8.1848. C: 12.1848.
Struck 20.4.1857 but restored to list as a 150-ton transport for New Caledonia 27.5.1857. Comm: 20.8.1857. Wrecked 11.1861 at Mooréa in the Society Islands, struck 17.6.1862.

Three brig-avisos (2nd Class brigs) of unknown design, *Curieux*, *Alerte*, and *Silène*, were projected in the 1849 budget (presented in December 1847) to be begun under contract in 1849. Names were assigned to them on 20 December 1847 but they were cancelled in 1848 before being ordered and before contractors were selected because of a reduction in the budget.

SMALL COLONIAL BRIGS (1818-1843)

Commandant Fleuriau or ***Fleuriau*** (old brig, origins unknown, 13 men). Commissioned in Senegal in 1819 as station vessel at Dagana on the Senegal River. Wrecked by cyclone 19.8.1821. Never appeared on Navy fleet lists and was probably carried on colonial accounts.

Postillon (ex slave brig owned by Tessier of Bordeaux seized on 28.4.1818 at Île Saint-Louis, Senegal, after sailing from Bordeaux 10.1.1818. 70 tons). Comm. by the navy 6.1818 in Senegal for colonial service. Recomm. 1.4.1819 with the crew of the aviso *Moucheron*. Decomm. 16.7.1820 and used 5.8.1820-15.10.1820 by the colonial administration with a native crew for an expedition to Galam. On the navy fleet list by 11.1820, carried out a second voyage to Galam 1821. From 12.1822 to 1824 she was used as station ship at the bar of the Senegal River with a native crew, then became unserviceable. Off fleet list 1826, struck 1828 and probably BU the same year. Carried in various naval lists as a brig, brig-aviso, schooner, and aviso.

Créole (ex Spanish 2-deck slave brig *Créole* (ex *Isis* 8.1823) owned by Louis Bureau, seized at Guadeloupe 3.1824 and confiscated by the government, 119 or 129 tons, 18 men, 2 guns). In 1826 was station brig at Pointe-à-Pitre. First appeared on the navy's fleet list in 1827, having previously probably been carried on colonial accounts. Struck 1838 at Brest. Carried in various navy lists as a brig and as a schooner

Colibri (brig purchased and comm. 12.3.1835 at St. Denis, Île Bourbon, 4 guns). On the fleet list 11.1835. Re-rated brig transport 2.1843 and aviso 4.1845. Capsized under sail and sank near the Badamo isles off the Madagascar coast 26.2.1845. Carried in various navy lists as a brig-schooner, aviso, schooner, brig-aviso, and flotilla craft

Anna (merchant vessel purchased in 1843 at Valparaiso, 200 tons, 17 men). In action on Tahiti station 1847. Annexe to frigate *Sirène* 1.1.1848 to 10.2.1850. Appeared on navy fleet lists as a 200-ton transport brig for the local service of Tahiti and the Marquises; previously she was probably carried on colonial accounts or manned and funded by the allowances given to larger ships on the station. Struck 29.2.1856. Carried in various navy lists as a gunbrig (*canonnière-brick*), 2nd Class brig, and schooner.

Ex SPANISH PRIZES (1824)

Encantador (Spanish Navy brig-schooner commissioned on 25.5.1824

at Cadiz by the French Navy. Had been built in a private shipyard and put in service in the Spanish Navy in 1819). Decomm. 23.11.1824 and probably returned to the Spanish.

Cometta (Spanish brig commissioned 28.7.1824 at Cadiz by the French Navy). Decomm. 22.11.1824 and probably returned to her owner.

Ex GREEK PRIZE (1827)

Panayoti (Greek pirate brig from Scarpento captured 10.1827 on the coast of Syria by the gabarre *Lamproie*, taken to Alexandria, and placed in service with 14 men from the frigate *Magicienne* to fight piracy in the Greek islands). Departed Alexandria 1.11.1827 under the command of Enseigne de Vaisseau Bisson, who ordered his pilot, Trémentin de Batz, to blow her up after being overwhelmed in combat near Stampali by Greek pirates 6.11.1827.

Ex ALGERIAN PRIZES (1830)

Cassauba (Algerian brig-aviso *Fath al Islam* ('Conquest of Islam'), built at Algiers in 1818, taken by the French at Algiers on 5.7.1830 and commissioned as a corvette on 24.7.1830).
  Dimensions & tons: 33.96m x 8.73m. 400 tons. Draught 3.19m. Men: about 150 when Algerian
  Guns: 12 x 18pdrs, later 10 guns. Had 22 gunports.
  Initially referred to as *No.1*, she was overhauled at Algiers in 7-9.1830 and renamed *Cassauba* in 9.1830. She was decomm. 12.10.1830, probably at Toulon. Escorted by the schooner *Bearnaise*, the 'felucca *Casauba*' carried supplies from Algiers to Bône in 2.1832. *Cassauba* first appeared on the fleet list in 1833 as a brig-aviso. On 21.10.1835 she was struck from the list at Toulon and became a service craft (*brick de servitude*).

Torre Chica (Algerian brig-aviso *Djeirein* ('Roe deer'), taken by the French at Algiers on 5.7.1830 and commissioned as a corvette on 24.7.1830).
  Dimensions & tons: 33.48m x 8.02m. 380 tons. Draught 3.04m. Men: about 140 when Algerian.
  Guns: Unknown, later 10 guns. Had 22 gunports.
  Initially referred to as *No.2*, she was overhauled at Algiers in 7-9.1830 and renamed *Torre Chica* in 9.1830. She was decomm. 12.10.1830, probably at Toulon. She first appeared on the fleet list in 1833 as a brig-aviso. On 21.10.1835 she was struck from the list at Toulon and became a service craft (*brick de servitude*).

Sidi-Ferruch (Algerian brig-schooner *Nimeti-Khouda* ('Gift of God'), taken by the French at Algiers on 5.7.1830 and commissioned on 24.7.1830).
  Dimensions & tons: 25m oa x 5.96m x 2.56m. 170 tons. Men: 110 while Algerian.
  Guns: 14 including 12pdrs, later (1833) 6 x 12pdr carronades. May have had 18 gunports.
  Initially referred to as *No.3*, she was overhauled at Algiers in 7-9.1830 and renamed *Sidi-Ferruch* in 9.1830. She was decommissioned at Toulon on 6.10.1830. Described as having 'lines and construction of great refinement', she first appeared on the navy list in 1833 as a 6-gun schooner but was not recommissioned. She was struck and re-classed in 11.1835 a service craft (*goélette de servitude*).

Pescado (Algerian brig-schooner *Mudjeres* ('Bringer of Good News'), taken by the French at Algiers on 5.7.1830).
  Dimensions & tons: 29.94m x 7.29m x 3.04m. 300 tons. Men: about 120 when Algerian
  Guns: 16 including 12pdrs. The French in 9.1830 considered her capable of carrying 16 x 18pdr carronades.
  Initially referred to as *No.4*, she was overhauled at Algiers in 7-9.1830 and renamed *Pescado* in 9.1830. She was taken to Toulon and decommissioned there on 13.10.1830. Described as having 'lines that were old and in bad taste', she was never inscribed on the fleet list and her fate is unknown.

Ex ARGENTINE PRIZES (1839-1845)

Saint Martin or *San Martin* (Argentine brig-schooner or schooner *San Martin*, built in Argentina, purchased by the Argentine Navy in 5.1838, taken off Buenos Aires 4.1839, and comm. by the French Navy at Montevideo 3.6.1839).
  Dimensions & tons: 20m x 5m x 3.6m. 75 tons. Draught 1.9m mean. Men: 46.
  Guns: 5 x 12pdrs (Argentine); 1 x 30pdr, 4 x 12pdr carronades (French, 6.1839).
  Decomm. at Montevideo 14.11.1840 and returned in accordance with the Convention of Mackau to the Argentines, struck 1841. The Argentines on 10.1841 renamed her *Republicano* and withdrew her from service 1842.

Saint Martin or *San Martin* (Argentine brig *San Martin*, probably built in France in 1839 and purchased 16.10.1844 by the Argentine Navy, taken 3.8.1845 by French forces and immediately commissioned).
  Dimensions & tons: 200 tons, 30m x 5.5m x 4.3m, mean draught 2.0m. Men: 100 (Argentine)
  Guns: 22 x 18pdrs and 6pdrs (or, according to Argentine sources, 2 x 24pdrs and 16 x 16pdrs); rearmed by the French in 1845 with 8 x 16cm canons-obusiers.
  Badly damaged in the Battle of Obligado on 20.10.1845, in which she was the French flagship, and probably abandoned soon after the battle. Last mentioned 6.1846.

Résistance (?) (Brig *Cagancha* taken by the Argentines from the 'Orientals', (Uruguayans) in 12.1841, became Argentine *Restaurador*, renamed *Echague* 1.1842, taken 3.8.1845 by Anglo-French forces).
  Dimensions & tons: 165 tons, 28m x 7m, mean draught 2.10m. Men: 120.
  Guns: 16 (24pdrs, 16pdrs, and 12pdrs).
  The French used her immediately with a Uruguayan crew and in 9.1845 she was placed under the Uruguayan flag. Damaged in collision 25.1.1847 at Montevideo and hulked.

Procida (Argentine brig-schooner *Procida*, built in Sardinia, taken or purchased in 10.1845 and commissioned by the French Navy, 71 tons, carried 3 x 18pdrs). Was in operation against the Argentines 11.1845, last mentioned 5.1846.

8 Small Sailing Patrol Vessels

(Schooners, Sailing Avisos, Cutters, Luggers, Chasse-Marées, etc.)

As in other navies, while the principal warship remained the three-masted ship-rigged vessel, there was a constant need for smaller craft for the rôle of coastal patrol and escort. While necessarily limited in operational range, these vessels were often deployed overseas, particularly to the Caribbean, as well as the Mediterranean and similar waters. There were a multitude of specialised types of sailing rig adopted for the purpose, of which the principal types by the 1770s were the schooner, cutter and lugger. While the schooners and luggers were two- or three-masted, the cutters were fast single-masted craft. The development of these types need to be separately considered, although they shared some common features.

The armed schooner seems to have first been used by the French Navy in the late 1760s, with two vessels built at Rochfort by Jean-Denis Chevillard in 1767 (*Afrique* and *Gorée*) and a smaller pair built at Brest by Joseph-Louis Ollivier in 1769 (*Abervrac'h* and *Nanon*), while others were acquired from merchant use. These and other craft taken up during the American War had all gone by 1786, and the French were not to acquire further naval schooners until after their own Revolution.

The French Navy in 1770 – much later than the British – decided to emulate their rivals and adopt their first cutters, and seven were ordered at Bordeaux, Dunkirk, Saint-Malo and Lorient (again, all these had gone before 1786). The cutter's rig, coupled with its sharp hull lines, was ideal for speed, although its single-masted sail plan required skilful handling, particularly when the concept was enlarged in an attempt to increase the armament carried, as happened with the cutters built by Denÿs during the 1778-80 period. Disillusion with their handling problems meant that many of these were completed as or converted to brig rig within a few years.

The first French naval lugger, derived from a British fast-sailing mercantile design, was the *Espiègle*, whose design was approved in December 1772 and was built in 1773 by Jacques and Daniel Denÿs, the leading constructors for these vessels. This prototype was discarded in 1783, but she was followed by over fifty similar craft over the next few decades, many likewise built by one or both of the Denÿs.

(A) Vessels in service or on order at 1 January 1786

***MUTIN* Class** – cutters. Designed by Jacques & Daniel Denÿs, the plans being dated 28 May 1778. Of the original four ships in this class, *Mutin* and *Pilote* were taken by the British in 1779 and *Clairvoyant* was wrecked in 1784. The ships of this class were similar to but slightly smaller than those of the *Cerf* class, below.
    Dimensions & tons: 75ft, 65ft x 24ft x 11ft (24.36, 21.11 x 7.80 x 3.57m). 115/212 tons. Draught 8ft/11ft 9in (2.60/3.82m). Men: 85-115.
    Guns: 14 x 6pdrs.
Pandour Jacques & Daniel Denÿs, Dunkirk.
    K: 4.1780. L: 16.6.1780. C: 9.1780. Re-rigged as brig 1782.
      Captured 31.8.1795 by HMS *Caroline* off the Texel and became HMS *Pandour* (also recorded as *Pandora*). Foundered with all hands 6.1797 in the North Sea.

***CERF* Class** – cutters. Designed by Jacques & Daniel Denÿs, and built by them at Dunkirk and to their plans at Saint-Malo. There were originally nine vessels in this class, of which four (*Hussard* and *Chevreuil* in 1780, and *Espion* and *Lézard* in 1782) had been taken by the British, while *Cerf* was struck in 1780 and *Serpent* in 1784. Their disappointing sailing characteristics when rigged as cutters meant that some were subsequently converted to brigs.
    Dimensions & tons: 81ft 0in, 68ft 6in x 25ft 10in x 11ft 6in (26.31, 22.25 x 8.38 x 3.73 m.). 130/256 tons. Men: 104-135. Draught 8ft 6in/12ft (2.76/3.90m).
    Guns: 18 x 6pdrs. (*Levrette* 1795) 18 x 6pdrs, 2 obusiers; (1800) 20 x 6pdrs; (*Fanfaron* 1796) 6 x 3pdrs.
Levrette Jacques & Daniel Denÿs, Dunkirk.
    K: 11.1778. L: 16.4.1779. C: 7.1779.
      Re-rigged as brig 1783 at Brest. Hired out as a privateer 4.1793 and renamed *Patriote de Brest* but returned to the navy 5.1793. Condemned 6.1793 at Brest, then hauled out 6.1793 at Saint-Malo, re-launched 9.1793 as a corvette, renamed *Levrette* 9.1793, and completed 3.1794. Training corvette 1799. Replaced by the corvette *Festin* and in 7.1806 became target ship for the gunnery school at Brest.
Malin Jacques & Daniel Denÿs, Dunkirk.
    K: 10.1780. L: 12.3.1781. C: 6.1781.
    Wrecked 11.1786 in Bay of Biscay.
Fanfaron Jacques & Daniel Denÿs, Dunkirk.
    K: 12.1780. L: 23.6.1781. C: 9.1781.
      Re-rigged as brig at Lorient 1783 and as lugger at Le Havre 5.1797. Scuttled in the Scheldt 21.3.1793 but salved and repaired at Antwerp. For sale at Dunkirk 1.1802.

***FACTEUR* Class** – cutters. Designed by Charles Segondat-Duvernet. The class originally consisted of six vessels, of which *Bienvenu* and *Espérance* had been captured by the British in 1781 and 1782, *Facteur* was sold in 1783 (becoming mercantile *Madagascar*), and *Lévrier* and *Téméraire* were struck in 1784. These were rated as *côtre-avisos*, but designed equally for conversion as schooners or schooner-avisos. All were built at a yard founded by the Arnous family in 1757 in a cove of the Scorff River at Lorient, upstream from the naval dockyard. On 5 August 1785 its owner, Nicolas Arnoux Dessaulsays, signed an agreement with the new Compagnie des Indes that made his 'chantier naval du Blanc' the chief shipbuilding facility for the company. The yard was requisitioned by the navy on 16 March 1794.
    Dimensions & tons: 80ft 0in, 65ft 0in x 20ft 0in x 8ft 4in (25.99, 21.11 x 6.50 x 2.71m). 150/220 tons. Men: 53/54.
    Guns: 2 x 4pdrs
Papillon Arnous, Lorient.
    K: 2.1781. L: 27.4.1781. C: 8.1781.
    Disappeared at sea 1789.

***CERF-VOLANT* Class** – luggers. Designed by Daniel Denÿs at Dunkirk, plans dated 10 December 1781. The Dunkirk vessels were constructed by Denÿs and inspected by the naval officer Baron De Bavre. An eighth vessel of this class, *Sylphe*, was built at Boulogne by Pierre Sauvage and captured by the British in October 1782.

An engraving by Jean-Jérôme Baugean of a large naval cutter originally published in 1814. Baugean's work is highly regarded for its accuracy, but some of the images represented earlier practice than their publication date suggests. This 18-gun cutter is described as Dutch – although the ensign looks French – but is comparable in overall appearance to the *Cerf* class. The cutter followed a similar arc of development in the navies of Britain, the Netherlands and France where they grew in size and power to the point where the gaff mainsail became dangerously large and difficult to handle, whereupon cutters were often rerigged as brigs or adopted other two-masted sail plans.

Dimensions & tons: 67ft 0in, 59ft 0in x 17ft 8in x 8ft 8in (21.76, 19.17 x 5.74 x 2.82m). 50/113 tons. Draught 6ft 9in / 9ft 7in (2.19/3.11m). Men: 52/70 men.
Guns: 4 x 3pdrs (later up to 10 x 3pdrs)

Cerf-Volant Jacques Rivet, Calais.
K: 2.1782. L: 9.7.1782. C: 9.1782.
Out of service at Brest 6.1786. Struck at end 1786.

Pivert Daniel Denÿs, Dunkirk.
K: 1.1782. L: 24.7.1782. C: 9.1782.
Struck 1787.

Vanneau Daniel Denÿs, Dunkirk.
K: 1.1782. L: 25.7.1782. C: 9.1782.
Taken 6.6.1793 in the Bay of Biscay, and added to RN as gunbrig.

Tiercelet Daniel Denÿs, Dunkirk.
K: 2.1782. L: 22.8.1782. C: 9.1782.
Sold at Rochefort 4.1797.

Gerfaut Daniel Denÿs, Dunkirk.
K: 2.1782. L: 24.8.1782. C: 9.1782.
Wrecked off Tunis 9.3.1796 to avoid capture by the RN.

Courrier Boulogne.
K: 3.1782. L: 7.9.1782. C: 9.1782.
Taken 23.5.1794.

Ballon Nicolas Rivet, Boulogne.
K: 3.1782. L: 21.9.1782. C: 10.1782.
Lost 11 or 12.1795.

Ex BRITISH PRIZES (1780-1783)

Chien de Chasse (British privateer cutter *Lurcher* taken c8.1780).
Dimensions & tons: 83 or 86ft, 74ft x 27ft x 12ft 6in (26.96 or 27.94, 24.04 x 8.77 x 4.06m). 200/350 tons. Draught 7ft/14ft (2.27/4.55m).
Guns: 22 x 9pdrs, 8 x 6pdr obusiers.
Also called an aviso. Condemned 6.1787 at Tobago as worn out.

Poisson Volant (probably ex HMS *Flying Fish*, a purchased cutter, wrecked 12.1782 near Calais and salvaged by the French.)
Dimensions & tons: 70ft x 24ft x 10ft. (22.74 x 7.80 x 3.25m). 100/200 tons. Men: 50-70.
Guns: 18 x 6pdrs.
Comm. 12.6.1783 at Dunkirk. Was out of commission at Santo Domingo 7.1785, struck 1785 or 1786.

Surprise (cutter taken or purchased 1783, possibly ex HMS *Surprize*, ex American privateer *Bunker Hill* taken 12.1778 and sold by the Royal Navy in 1783 at Sheerness, 106 tons, 50-70 men).
Guns: 18 x 6pdrs (original) or 8 x 4pdrs, 6 x 3pdr
Struck 1789 at Rochefort.

PURCHASED AND REQUISITIONED VESSELS (1777-1786)

Va et Vient (schooner in service at Rochefort in 1777 and 1783 as a service craft without armament). Used to carry supplies from Rochefort to ships in the roadstead at Île d'Aix. Decomm. 1787 at Brest.

Actif (schooner in service in the Antilles in 1779). Last mentioned 7.1792 while in service at Martinique.

Celeste (schooner in service at Rochefort in 5.1783). Last mentioned 1792 at Rochefort.

Levrette (schooner acquired 1784, ex *Levrette de Saint-Malo*, possibly purchased at Saint-Malo.)
Dimensions & tons: 66ft 4in x 18ft 5in x 7ft 10in (21.55 x 5.99 x 2.54m). 170 tons disp. Draught 8ft 4in/10ft 8in (2.71/3.47m)
Guns: 14 x 4pdrs.
Refitted at Brest 1790. For sale 5.1792 at Rochefort.

Légère (schooner begun at Rochefort 6.1783 and in service 1784). Off the list c1786.

Louise (schooner probably purchased in Martinique 10-11.1784). Sent to

France via Cayenne to serve as a model, last mentioned 1.1786.

Nymphe (schooner possibly purchased 10.1785, in service at Martinique 11.1786, 9-11 men). Last mentioned 1788 in the Antilles.

Surveillant (cutter in service at Guadeloupe in 2.1786). No other details known.

Légère (schooner built in North America 1784-85 and purchased 7.1785 from an American at Fort Royal de la Martinique, 62 men, carried 4 x 6pdrs in 1785 and 14 x 6pdrs in 1786). Wrecked 3.1786 at Pointe-à-Pitre, Guadeloupe.

(B) Vessels acquired from 1 January 1786

GALIBI – schooner. Name also rendered *Galiby*, ex *Goélette No.5* 1786. She was built for service at Cayenne and had ports for 13 pairs of oars.)
Dimensions & tons: 69ft, 61ft x 19ft x 6ft 6in (22.4, 19.82 x 6.17 x 2.11m). 72/120 tons. Draught 6ft/6ft 6in (1.95/2.11m).
Guns: 10
Galibi Toulon Dyd. (Constructeur, Jacques Balthazar Brun-Sainte-Catherine)
K: 8.1786. L: 18.11.1786. C: 12.1786.
Wrecked 24.5.1794 on the coast of French Guiana.

COUSINE – schooner. Built for service in Senegal.
Dimensions & tons: 55ft, 49ft x 16ft 6in x 8ft (17.86, 15.92 x 5.36 x 2.60m). 61/123 tons. Draught 7ft 6in/8ft (2.44/2.60m). Men: 17-40.
Guns: 6 x 4pdrs, 4 swivels.
Cousine Bayonne (Constructeur, Raymond-Antoine Haran)
K: 9.1786. L: 11.1786. C: 12.1786.
Departed Rochefort for Senegal 10.4.1788 with frigate *Flore*. Designated as an aviso and performed escort duty between Rochefort and Brest in 1793-94. Became service craft at Rochefort 1795. Last mentioned 1807.

LÉGÈRE class – schooners.
Dimensions & tons: Unknown
Guns: Unknown.
Légère United States
K: 1787. L: 1.1788. C: 1.1788.
Refitted at Santo Domingo 1.1791. Turned over 1.1793 to the Spanish at Trinidad by her Royalist officers.
Philippine United States
K: 1787. L: 1.1788. C: 1.1788.
Condemned 1.1791 at Santo Domingo. May have become the brig *Philippine*, which was placed in service in Santo Domingo in 9.1791 and was last mentioned as sailing 11.1791 for New Spain.

CLAIRVOYANT Class – cutters. Possibly designed by Daniel Denÿs, who had built an earlier *Clairvoyant* in 1780 and who was still active at Dunkirk as a commercial shipbuilder. *Ami du Commerce* is only possibly to same design.
Dimensions & tons: dimensions unknown. 30 tons. Men: 72
Guns: 6 x 2pdrs; (1794) 4 x 3pdrs.
Clairvoyant Dunkirk
K: 1792. L: 2.1793. C: 2.1793.
Converted to transport 2.1798 at Cherbourg. Struck 1799 or 1800.
Ami du Commerce Cherbourg Dyd. (Constructeur: Martin or Jacques Fabien)
K: 1.1793. L: 2.1793. C: 2.1793.
Converted to transport 2.1799 at Le Havre. Struck 1799 or 1800.

ENFANT – lugger, ex lugger-rigged yacht, probably built on the plans by Hubert Pennevert for the yacht *Rochefort* of 1787 but did not serve as a yacht; also called a brig.
Dimensions & tons (probably): 54ft, 48ft x 15ft x 5ft (17.54, 15.59 x 4.87 x 1.62m). 60/100 tons. Draught 5ft/6ft (1.62/1.95m).
Guns: 8 x 4pdrs.
Enfant Le Havre (Constructeur, Pierre Mauger)
K: 1.1792. L: 21.9.1792. C: 12.1792.
Captured late 1795 at Île d'Yeu by the British.

ARGUS – aviso rigged as chasse-marée.
Dimensions & tons: Unknown. Men: 43.
Guns: 2 x 6pdrs, 6 x 3pdrs; (1795) 3 x 24pdrs.
Argus Dieppe.
K: 1792. L: 1793. C: 8.1793.
Converted to *chaloupe-canonnière* at Dunkirk 1795. Last mentioned 6.1796 at Le Havre, then struck.

SENTINELLE Class – cutters, 6 guns. Lemarchand, the builder and possibly designer of these cutters, called himself a sous-ingénieur when he signed some gunboat plans at Saint-Malo on 11 February 1793. He may have been related to the Lemarchand at Saint-Malo who built the frigate *Résolue* in 1778.
Dimensions & tons: 43ft 0in, 36ft 0in x 14ft 0in x 7ft 8in (13.97, 11.69 x 4.55 x 2.49m). 30/50 tons. Draught 6ft/7ft (1.95/2.27m).
Men: 38.
Guns: 6 x 3pdrs
Sentinelle Saint-Malo (Constructeur, Lemarchand)
K: 1.1793. L: 2.3.1793. C: 3.1793.
Reclassed to 50-ton transport between 1814 and 1816. Service craft at Brest 1.1827, struck 1827.
Vigilant Saint-Malo (Constructeur, Lemarchand)
K: 1.1793. L: 4.3.1793. C: 3.1793.
Renamed *Vainqueur* 5.1795 but captured by HMS *Childers* (14) as *Vigilant* in early 9.1795 off north Brittany near St Brieuc or the Île de Batz, not taken into the Royal Navy.

MONTAGNE Class – cutters, 10 guns. Designed by Daniel Denÿs.
Dimensions & tons: 60ft, 53ft x 20ft x 9ft 3in (19.49, 17.21 x 6.50 x 3.00m) 80/135 tons. Draught 7ft 6in/10ft 3in (2.43/3.33m).
Men: 63.
Guns: 10 x 4pdrs; (*Narcisse*) 6 x 6pdrs, 2 x 4pdrs; (*Aiguille* ex *Montagne* c1800) 10 x 6pdrs; (*Souffleur* 1802) 4 x 6pdrs, 6 x 4pdrs; (same 1804) 10 x 4pdrs.
Montagne Cherbourg Dyd. (Constructeur, Martin or Jacques Fabien)
K: 3.1793. L: 7.1793. C: 8.1793.
Renamed *Aiguille* 5.1795. Captured 2.7.1803 by a British squadron off Santo Domingo, probably BU.
Pelletier (*Lepeletier*) Cherbourg Dyd. (Constructeur, Martin or Jacques Fabien)
K: 3.1793. L: 7.1793. C: 8.1793.
Renamed *Printemps* 30.5.1795. Captured 19.7.1815 in the harbour of Correjou, Finistère, by the British.
Marat Cherbourg Dyd. (Constructeur, Martin or Jacques Fabien)
K: 6.1793. L: 12.1793. C: 1.1794.
Renamed *Anguille* 5.1795 and *Aspic* 12.1795. Captured 10.3.1796 at the entrance to St. George's Channel by HMS *Quebec* (32).
Narcisse Calais
K: 6.1793. Named: 12.8.1793. L: 6.12.1793. C: 2.1794.

Captured 18.6.1794 off the Shetlands by HMS *Aurora* (28).
Souffleur Boulogne
   K: 5.1793. Named: 12.8.1793. L: 4.2.1794. C: 4.1794.
   Re-rigged as brig 1.1802. Service craft at Lorient 6.1810, hulk 1813, BU 1814.
Poisson Volant Boulogne
   K: 5.1793. Named: 12.8.1793. L: 18.2.1794, C: 4.1794.
   Loaned as Dunkirk privateer *Président Parker* 9.1797, captured 4.10.1798 by HMS *Flora* (36) and *Caroline* (36), became British privateer. Recaptured 9.1800 and reverted to *Poisson Volant*. Condemned and BU 2.1802 at Rochefort.
Père Duchèsne Saint-Malo
   Ord: 18.5.1793. K: 6.1793. L: 9.1793. Comm: 2.11.1793. C: 11.1793.
   Renamed *Terreur* 4.1794 after the fall of the Hébertistes. Captured 18.3.1804 off Jacmel, Haiti, by HMS *Pique* (40).
Bonnet Rouge Saint-Malo
   Ord: 18.5.1793 and named. K: 6.1793. L: 10.1793. C: 12.11.1793.
   Renamed *Abeille* 30.5.1795. Captured 2.5.1796 off the Lizard by HMS *Dryad* (36). Became HMS *Abeille*, BU 1798.
Trois Couleurs Saint-Malo
   Ord: 18.5.1793. K: 6.1793. L: 10.1793. C: 1.1794.
   Renamed *Saint Pierre* 5.1795 but captured as *Trois Couleurs* 11.6.1796 by HMS *Indefatigable* (38) and *Amazon* (36) off Ushant, became British privateer *St. Peter*. Recaptured 20.5.1797 by the Nantes privateer *Vengeance*. Taken 20.6.1798 as *Trois Couleurs* (4) off Trinidad by HMS *Victorieuse* (14) or wrecked 6.1798 at Santo Domingo.

GRANVILLE – cutter, 4 guns.
   Dimensions & tons: unknown. Men: 72-95
   Guns: 4 x 2pdrs; (c1795) 4 x 4pdrs.
Granville Granville
   K: 7.1793. L: 4.11.1793. 1.1794.
   Re-rigged as a lugger in early 1795 at Le Havre or Cherbourg. Decomm. for the last time 3.10.1815 at Brest, struck 1820.

PETIT DIABLE Class – cutters, 12 guns. May have been designed by Raymond-Antoine Haran.
   Dimensions & tons: unknown. Men: 42-65.
   Guns: 12 x 4pdrs.
Petit Diable Bayonne
   K: 5.1793. L: 17.10.1793. C: 11.1793.
   Ashore 27.8.1797 near Arcachon after combat with HMS *Pomone* (44) and lost.
Serpentin Bayonne
   K: 5.1793. L: 25.11.1793. C: 2.1794.
   Unserviceable at Bayonne 4.1802, struck 1803.

COURRIER – cutter (or *Courrier de Nantes*).
   Dimensions & tons: Possibly as the lugger *Écureuil* (1794). Men: 84.
   Guns: 10 to 14 x 4pdrs.
Courrier Nantes.
   K: 5.1793. L: 8.8.1793. C: 10.1793.
   Renamed *Chercheur* 5.1795. Captured 5.1795 in the Antilles by HMS *Thorn* (16), her name then being reported as *Courrier National*.

DRAGON – cutter, rerigged as brig 3.1798 at Bayonne. A cutter named *Fendant* was also ordered at Bordeaux in 1793 but was not built.
   Dimensions & tons: Unknown. Men: 60-75.
   Guns: 10 x 4pdrs.
Dragon Bordeaux.
   K: 5.1793. L: 8.8.1793. C: 17.10.1793.
   Captured 5.5.1800 in the Channel by HMS *Cambrian* (40) and *Fishguard* (44).

REQUIN – cutter, re-rigged as brig early 1795. Designed by Daniel Denÿs, plans dated 4.2.1793.
   Dimensions & tons: 68ft 6in, 57ft x 22ft x 10ft 3in (22.25, 18.52 x 7.15 x 3.33m). 110/171 tons. Draught 7ft 10in/10ft 10in (2.54/3.52m).
   Guns: 12 x 6pdrs, 2 x 12pdr obusiers (14 ports).
Requin Boulogne.
   K: 5.1793. Named: 12.8.1793. L: 3.1794. C: 4.1794.
   Captured 20.2.1795 off Dunkirk by HMS *Thalia* (36), became gunbrig HMS *Requin*. Wrecked near Quiberon 1.1.1801.

RENARD – lugger, 10 guns.
   Dimensions & tons: 95ft x 26ft 6in (30.86 x 8.61m). 200/400 tons.
   Men: 110.
   Guns: 4 x 6pdrs, 6 x 4pdrs; (1795) 12 x 6pdrs.
Renard Michel Colin-Olivier, Dieppe
   K: 3.1793. L: early 6.1793. C: 6.1793.
   Purchased on the ways 4.1793. Re-rigged as a schooner 1800-1803. Captured 25.11.1803 by HMS *Cameleon* (16) off Corsica, became HMS *Renard*. Taken 9.3.1807 by three Spanish privateers near Gibraltar but apparently recaptured and sold 1.1809 to BU.

COURAGEUX – lugger, purchased on the ways.
   Dimensions & tons: Unknown. Men: 43.
   Guns: 8 x 2pdrs.
Courageux Dunkirk.
   K: 1793. L: 8.1793. C: 9.1793.
   Blew up 13.8.1797 in combat with the large merchantman *Exeter* in the Kattegat.

SANS QUARTIER – lugger.
   Dimensions & tons: Unknown.
   Guns: 6 x 3pdrs.
Sans Quartier Rouen.
   K: 1793/94. L: 5.1794. C: 6.1794.
   Captured 4.4.1799 north of the Chausey Islands by HMS *Danae* (20).

ACTIF – aviso.
   Dimensions & tons: Unknown.
   Guns: 2 x 2pdrs, 2 x 1.5pdrs.
Actif Dunkirk.
   K: 1793. L: 1794. C: 1794.
   Last mentioned 10.1795 while in service at Calais.

ARGUS – chasse-marée (later cutter, then lugger), 6 guns.
   Dimensions & tons: unknown. Men: 22 to 40.
   Guns: 2 x 4pdrs, 4 x 12pdr obusiers
Argus Martin or Jacques Fabien, Cherbourg
   K: 2.1793. L: 5.1793. C: 6.1793.
   Re-rigged as cutter 1795. Renamed *Titus* 5.1795. Converted to transport and re-rigged as lugger at Cherbourg 12.1798. Sold 1.1816 at Cherbourg.

AMI DES LOIS – chasse-marée (later lugger), 6 guns
   Dimensions & tons: unknown. Men: 17-38
   Guns: 6 x 4pdrs.

Ami des Lois Lorient Dyd
K: 1793. L: 6.1793. C: 7.1793.
Re-rigged as lugger c1797. In bad conditions at Lorient 6.1813, struck and BU.

ESPIÈGLE – cutter.
Dimensions & tons: Unknown.
Guns: 6 x 2pdrs; (1795) 4 x 3pdrs.
Espiègle Saint-Malo.
K: 1794. L: 1795. C: 1795.
For sale at Saint-Malo 5.1796 or 5.1797.

HARDI Class – cutters, 6 guns. May have been designed by Pierre-Alexandre Forfait and built under contract by Jean Fouache.
Dimensions & tons: unknown. Men: 33
Guns: (*Hardi*) 6 x 6pdrs; (*Sans-Souci*) 6 or 8 x 3pdrs; (same 1799) 8 x 4pdrs..
Hardi (*Hardy*) Jean Fouache, Le Havre
K: 6.1794. L: 9.1794. C: 12.1794.
Sold 1.1803 at Le Havre.
Sans-Souci Jean Fouache, Le Havre
K: 6.1794. L: 9.1794. C: 12.1794.
Sold 2.1803 at Le Havre.

ÉCUREUIL – lugger. Designed by Pierre Degay.
Dimensions & tons: 83ft 5in, 72ft x 21ft 8in x 10ft 8in (27.10, 23.39 x 7.04 x 3.47m). 100/180 tons. Draught 9ft/11ft (2.92/3.57m). Men: 105-110.
Guns: 14 x 4pdrs.
Écureuil Louis & Antoine Crucy and Jean Baudet, Basse-Indre.
Ord: 28.2.1794. K: 3.1794. L: 10.1794. C: 12.1794.
Chased ashore while escorting three merchant vessels and burned 24.4.1796 by HMS *Niger* (32) in the inlet at Guilvinec near Penmarch.

BELLISLOIS – lugger, 6 guns
Dimensions & tons: 57ft 8in x 16ft 8in x 7ft 0in (18.73 x 5.42 x 2.27m). 71/110 tons. Draught 6ft 9in/7ft 2in (2.19/2.32m). Men: 33-78.
Guns: 2 x 8pdrs, 4 x 6pdrs; (1801) 10 x 6pdrs.
Bellislois (*Bellilois*) Nantes
K: 1794. L: 6.1795. C: 8.1795.
Re-rigged as brig 1820 at Brest. Wrecked 1823 on the beach at Coloye, Cape Finisterre. The lugger *Ami de Lorient* was also briefly named *Bellislois* in 1806-7.

AFFRONTEUR Class – luggers, 16 guns. Probably designed by Pierre-Alexandre Forfait.
Dimensions & tons: unknown. Men: 87-120.
Guns: 16 x 6pdrs.
Affronteur Michel Colin-Olivier, Dieppe
K: 1794. L: 18.7.1795. C: 11.1795.
Captured 18.5.1803 off Ushant by HMS *Doris* (36), became gunbrig HMS *Caroline*. BU 1807.
Vautour Michel Colin-Olivier, Dieppe
K: 1794. L: 8.1795. C: 11.1795.
Captured 25.11.1803 off Cape Finisterre by HMS *Boadecia* (38) while returning from Santo Domingo.

SAUMON – lugger, 2 guns. Designed by Pierre-Alexandre Forfait, probably jointly with Joseph-Marie Sganzin, an *ingénieur des ponts et chaussées*. This vessel was designed to navigate on rivers, and she could lower her masts and sails for passing under bridges. Forfait and Sganzin used this special lugger in 1797 to survey possible routes for a canal between Paris and Le Havre. By 1803 Sganzin was *inspecteur general des ponts et chaussées* and was also the senior officer of that service assisting the navy with its construction work.
Dimensions & tons: 78ft, 75ft, 68ft x 18ft x 8ft 6in (25.34 oa, 24.36, 22.09 x 5.85 x 2.76m). 150/200 tons. Draught 5ft 4in to 6ft 6in (1.73m to 2.11m) mean. Men: 28-52.
Guns: 2.
Saumon Rouen
K: 12.1794. L: 23.4.1795. C: 8.1795.
Sold 1.1803 at Le Havre.

PASSE-PARTOUT – schooner, 4 guns
Dimensions & tons: unknown. Men: 70
Guns: 4 x 3pdrs or 4pdrs.
Passe Partout Saint-Malo
K: 1794. L: 1.1795. C: 5.1795.
Also designated aviso. Re-rigged as cutter 1800 at Saint-Servan. Decomm. for the last time there 11.2.1805, struck at Saint-Malo 1815.

FOUDRE – aviso, 6 guns. Brig-rigged.
Dimensions & tons: unknown. Men: 52
Guns: 6 x 4pdrs (8 ports).
Foudre Toulon Dyd.
K: 9.1795. L: 1796. C: 6.1796.
Captured 3.1799 on the Syrian coast by a British division, gunbrig HMS *Foudre*. Retaken 9.4.1799 by the French frigate *Courageuse* and returned to service. Recaptured 1800 by the British, again HMS *Foudre*. Sold 1801.

BEAULANÇON – lugger, 4 guns
Dimensions & tons: unknown. Men: 22
Guns: 4 x 2pdrs.
Beaulançon (*Beau-Lançon*) Le Havre.
K: 1796. L: 1797. C: 1797.
For sale at Dieppe 4.1802.

GLOBE – lugger, 8 guns
Dimensions & tons: unknown. Men: 38.
Guns: 8 x 4pdrs.
Globe Brest Dyd
K: 1797. L: 1797. C: 9.1797.
Sometimes listed as a schooner. Listed 1814 as a 20-ton lugger-rigged transport at Brest (no guns). Service craft at Brest 1826, struck 1827.

AGILE Class – schooners, 8 guns.
Dimensions & tons: 80ft, 77ft wl, 64ft 8in x 20ft 2in, 17ft 7in x 7ft. (25.98, 25.01wl, 21.01 x 6.55, 5.71wl x 2.27m) 65/112 tons. Draught 6ft 4in/7ft 10in (2.06/3.25m).
Guns: 8 x 4pdrs.
Agile Brest Dyd
K: 1797. L: 22.5.1797. C: 7.1797
Captured by the British at the end of 1797 but recaptured by the French. Capsized 9.7.1798 in a squall in the Antilles.
Biche Brest Dyd
K: 4. 1798. L: 18.8.1798. C: 9.1798.
Probably rebuilt or replaced at Brest 1801 (see below) after the loss of

SMALL SAILING PATROL VESSELS

This unnamed model of an 8-gun French lugger from about 1800 depicts the kind of vessel much used in both the French Navy and by privateers. Heavily canvassed, they were fast and very weatherly but required large, highly skilled crews. (© National Maritime Museum F2925-3)

Agile.
Découverte Brest Dyd
  K: 5.1798. L: 10.9.1798. C: 10.1798.
  Last mentioned 4.1800 while at Ferrol, Spain. Probably rebuilt or replaced at Brest 1800 (see below) after the loss of *Agile*.

ÉCUREUIL – lugger, 12 guns
  Dimensions & tons: dimensions unknown. 70 tons. Men: 51.
  Guns: 12 x 4pdrs; (1802) 10 x 4pdrs.
Écureuil Michel Colin-Olivier, Dieppe
  K: 1798. L: 8.3.1799. C: 3.1799.
  Left Havana 12.11.1802 for Guadeloupe carrying 500,000 francs and disappeared with all hands.

CÉLÈRE – aviso, 2 guns
  Dimensions & tons: unknown.
  Guns: 2 x 6pdrs.
Célère Toulon Dyd
  K: 1798. L: 7.1798. C: 8.1798.
  Her seakeeping qualities were unsatisfactory. Decomm. 11.1800 at Toulon and struck.

TÉLÉGRAPHE Class – schooners, 18 small guns. Designed by Pierre Ozanne and built by the Crucy brothers (Mathurin, Louis, and Antoine) at Nantes.
  Dimensions & tons: 77ft, 74ft wl x 10ft x 7ft 7in (25.01, 24.04 x 6.17 x 2.46m). 67/107 tons. Draught 7ft/8ft 4in (2.27/2.71m). Men: 55.
  Guns: 18 swivels; (*Vigie* 1804 and *Agile* 1806) 6 x 4pdrs, 6 swivels;
  (*Télégraphe* 1805) 1 x 8pdr, 2 x 4pdrs.
Télégraphe Louis, Antoine, & Mathurin Crucy, Nantes.
  K: 4.1799. L: 6.1799. C: 7.1799.
  Decomm. 31.3.1814 at Quimper or Lorient. Struck 1.1815. BU 8.1815.
Agile Louis, Antoine, & Mathurin Crucy, Nantes.
  K: 4.1799. L: 6.1799. C: 7.1799.
  Captured 18.6.1815 by the British off Guadeloupe and sent to Martinique. Condemned there 8.1815.
Vigie Louis, Antoine, & Mathurin Crucy, Nantes.
  K: 5.1799. L: 7.1799. C: 9.1799.
  Wrecked 30.12.1810 on an unknown rock near the Pointe des Pilours in the Vendée. Her six bronze guns were recovered.
Tricolore Louis, Antoine, & Mathurin Crucy, Nantes.
  K: 5.1799. L: 7.1799. C: 4.1800.
  Captured 14.10.1803 by the British off Santo Domingo, subsequent fate unknown.
Courrier Louis, Antoine, & Mathurin Crucy, Nantes.
  K: 5.1799. L: 19.7.1799. C: 10.1799.
  Captured the British merchantman or privateer *Hazard* 31.12.1803 (see corvettes), took her into Havana, still there 2.1804 and not struck until 1807. The *Courrier de Nantes* captured by HMS *Vanguard* (74) on 5.9.1803 was probably another vessel.
Éclair Louis, Antoine, & Mathurin Crucy, Nantes.
  K: 5.1799. L: 23.9.1799. C: 11.1799.
  Captured 18.1.1801 at Trois-Rivières, Guadeloupe, by HMS *Garland* (24), became HMS *Eclair* and in 1809 HMS *Pickle*. Sold 1818.

DÉCOUVERTE Class – schooners, 12 small guns. These were probably the schooners of the same names of 1798 rebuilt after the capsizing of sister *Agile* in 6.1798.
  Dimensions & tons: 77ft, 64ft 8in x 19ft 8in (25.0, 21.0 x 6.4m). 60/110 tons. Draught 6ft 4in/7ft 10in (2.06/2.54m).
  Guns: 12 swivels; (*Découverte*, 1803) 8 x 4pdrs
Découverte Brest Dyd.
  K: 1799. L: 22.8.1800. C: 9.1800.
  Captured 22-23.9.1803 by boats from HMS *Bellerophon* (74) and *Elephant* (74) at Santo Domingo, became HMS *Decouverte* and served on the Jamaica station until 1806, then sold.
Biche Brest Dyd.
  K: 1800. L: 19.8.1801. C: 10.1801. Comm: 23.9.1800 (1801?).
  Decomm. 11.1803 at Martinique. Condemned 4.1807 at Fort de France, BU 5.1807.

FINE Class – schooners, 18 small guns. Designed by Pierre Ozanne, all built by the Crucy Bros. (Mathurin, Louis, and Antoine) at Nantes under a contract dated 26 October 1799.
  Dimensions & tons: 78ft, 63ft x 20ft 2in x 7ft 7in (25.33, 20.46 x 6.55 x 2.46m). 67/107 tons. Draught 7ft/8ft 3in (2.26/2.68m).
  Guns: 18 x 1pdr swivels; (*Aventurière* 1808) 6 x 4pdrs; (*Aventurière* 1810-14) 3 x 24pdr carronades, 1 obusier
Fine Louis, Antoine, & Mathurin Crucy, Nantes.
  K: 2.1800. L: 4.1801. C: 6.1801. Comm: 10.4.1802.
  Unserviceable 7.1807 at Martinique, burned 1.1809 to avoid capture there.
Légère Louis, Antoine, & Mathurin Crucy, Nantes.
  K: 2.1800. L: 4.1801. C: 6.1801. Comm: 21.4.1802.
  Captured 6.1803 in the Channel by the British privateer *Alarm* (or captured by the British 28.6.1802).
Oiseau Louis, Antoine, & Mathurin Crucy, Nantes.
  K: 2.1800. L: 4.1801. C: 6.1801 (but construction reported 8/10ths

A French naval foretopsail schooner of 12 guns as depicted in an engraving by Baugean.

complete 23.9.1801).
Captured 25.7.1803 with *Duquesne* (74) near Santo Domingo by HMS *Bellerophon* (74), *Vanguard* (74), and *Tartar* (32).

Volage Louis, Antoine, & Mathurin Crucy, Nantes.
K: 2.1800. L: 5.1801. C: 6.1801. Comm: 7.9.1801.
In 8.1810 was at Lorient in need of repairs. Struck there c1816.

Aventurière Louis, Antoine, & Mathurin Crucy, Nantes.
K: 2.1800. L: 5.1801. C: 7.1801 (but construction reported 8/10ths complete 23.9.1801).
In 9.1813 was at Dunkirk in need of repairs. Sold there 1816.

Coureuse Louis, Antoine, & Mathurin Crucy, Nantes.
K: 2.1800. L: 6.1801. Comm: 11.4.1802. C: 4.1802
Wrecked 5.3.1804 at Martinique.

Ex BRITISH NAVAL PRIZES (1795-1801)

Cygne or *Swan* (cutter HMS *Swan* built in 1792 for the Revenue Service at Cowes and taken off Brittany 14.10.1795 by *Forte* (50), 14 guns). Captured 5.1796 off the Scillies by HMS *Doris* (36). May have become the British merchant cutter *Cygnet* which operated from 1796 to 1799.

Vengeur (schooner HMS *Charlotte*, purchased 1797, 60 men, 8 guns, carried 8 x 6pdrs). Captured 16.10.1798 by the schooner *Enfant Prodigue* off Cap Français, Santo Domingo. Recaptured 24.11.1799 off Cape Tiburon by HMS *Solebay* but not recommissioned and instead BU.

Goze (schooner HMS *Gozo*, previously the Spanish *Malta*, built in America in 1797 and taken by the British in 1800).
Dimensions & tons: 75ft 5in x 20ft 4in (24.51 x 6.60m). 100/180 tons.
Guns: 10 x 4pdrs.
Seized by the French after her mutinous crew took her into Brindisi in 8.1801 and comm. at Toulon 23.12.1801. Wrecked near Ajaccio 19.4.1803.

Ex BRITISH MERCANTILE AND PRIVATEER PRIZES (1793-1801)

Étoile du Matin (British merchant ship *Morning Star* seized 2.1793 and commissioned 9.1793 at Cherbourg as an aviso, carried 2 x 2pdrs). Struck at Cherbourg at the end of 1795.

Fanny (British merchant ship seized 2.1793 at Le Havre and commissioned as an aviso, 25 tons, carried 1 x 2.5pdr and 4 swivels). Fitted as headquarters ship at Le Havre 2.1794 but the headquarters ship at Le Havre was ordered suppressed on 10.7.1794 and she was struck.

Bon Espoir (British mercantile cutter *Good Hope* taken 3.1793 and in service 4.1793 with 6 x 4pdrs). Struck 12.1795 at Rochefort.

Actif (British merchant vessel taken 5.1793, in service 6.1793 as an aviso, carried 2 x 2pdrs). Refitted at Le Havre as a 48-ton transport 3.1798 and renamed *Transport No.21 Actif*, sold 9.1800 at Cherbourg.

Ark (British mercantile cutter *Ark*, taken 5.1793 and commissioned at Lorient 6.1793, 12 men, carried 4 guns). Captured 20.2.1801 in Quiberon Bay by boats from HMS *Excellent* (74). Name also rendered in French records as *Arc*, *Lark*, and *Larck*.

Henri (British lugger *Henry* taken 5.1793 and commissioned 6.1793, 50 men, carried 4 x 3pdrs and 2 swivels). Burned 7.1795 at Vannes to prevent capture.

Succes (British cutter taken 5.1793, loaned as a privateer 6.1793 at Calais, and in service there by 5.1794, 35 tons, carried 6 x 3pdrs or 4pdrs). Given 3.1797 to a French shipowner to replace a lost vessel.

Angélique (British privateer lugger captured by a French privateer, taken into La Rochelle, and requisitioned 6.1793 34-70 men, 2 x 3pdrs, 2 obusiers) Renamed *Accès* 5.1795 but reverted to *Angélique* later that year. Became a service craft at Rochefort 1815, later fate unknown.

Portland (British merchant sloop taken 6.1793 and in service at Brest 7.1793 as a cutter-rigged aviso, carried 6 x 1pdrs). Hulked at Lorient 3.1798, last mentioned 1799.

Charlotte (British lugger, captured 1793 and commissioned at Rochefort 7.1793, carried 6 x 3pdrs). Renamed *Cancer* 5.1795 (order never executed) and *Charlotte* 1796. Unserviceable at Rochefort 5.1803 and to be sold or BU.

Deux Colombes (British merchant ship, possibly *Two Doves*, taken in 1793 and commissioned as an aviso, carried 14 x 4pdrs) Refitted at Brest 1794, decomm. 10.1796 at Lorient and struck 1797.

Royal Charlotte or *Charlotte* (British lugger built at Dover and taken in 1793, 30 men, carried 4 x 3pdrs). Mentioned for the last time 3.1797 while at Calais.

Hirondelle (British privateer cutter *Swallow* built in Britain and taken in 1793, 127 men, carried 16 x 4pdrs). Captured 20.11.1798 in the Channel by HMS *Phaeton* (38), *Ambuscade* (32), and *Stag* (32).

Jean Bart (British lugger taken 8.1793 and commissioned 8.1793 at Cherbourg, probably 50 tons, 22 men, carried 8 swivels). Renamed *Joyeux* 5.1795, refitted as an aviso at Cherbourg 10-11.1795. Renamed *Jean Bart* 1796. Decomm 11.1800 at Cherbourg and struck.

Martinet (British lugger *Angenoria* taken before 9.1793 and commissioned at Brest in 1794, 30-70 men, carried 4 x 3pdrs). Renamed *Angenoria* 5.1795, BU early 1796 as worn out, probably at Verdon.

Hook (British lugger taken 9.1793, 106 men, carried 16 x 4pdrs). Wrecked off Saint-Malo 8.11.1794.

Hoop or *Hope* (British privateer or mercantile cutter *Hoop* boarded and captured 6.9.1793 by the French lugger *Hook* (above), commissioned 11.1793 at Brest, 90 tons, 40-60 men, carried 8 x 8pdrs, 2 x 6pdrs, 2 x 4pdrs). Renamed *Lutin* 24.9.1814, *Hoop* 22.3.1815, and *Lutin* 15.7.1815. Converted to 50-ton transport 1.1815 at Brest. Sold 12.1820 at Le Havre.

Surveillant (British privateer lugger *Coureur* taken by a French privateer, requisitioned 10.1793 at Granville and renamed 11.1793, 70 tons, 92 men, carried 4 x 4pdrs and 4 obusiers). Renamed *Satyre* 5.1795. Wrecked near Vannes 27.12.1795. Also reported as renamed *Surveillant* in 1796 and wrecked near Vannes 1.1798.

Pensée (British mercantile cutter taken 10.1793 and in service at Dunkirk 2.1794, 60-120 men, carried 8 x 3pdrs). Renamed *Montagne* 1.1794, *Pensée* 1.1796, and *Vedette* 7.1796. Captured 10.2.1800 off Brest by HMS *Triton* (32), became HMS *Vidette*. Deleted 1802.

Épervier (British mercantile or privateer cutter built in Britain in 1792 and possibly named *Sparrowhawk*, in service in 11.1793 and in 12.1794 as *Cutter No.2*, named *Épervier* 1.1795, carried 6 to 8 x 4pdrs in 1794). Decomm. 4.1797 at Saint-Malo and sold. An otherwise unidentified *Cutter No.3* (3 x 3pdrs, 2 x 2pdrs) was in service at Dieppe in late 1794 and was last mentioned at Saint-Malo in 11.1795.

Aigle (British privateer schooner *Eagle* taken in 1793 or 1794, carried 4 x 3pdrs). Condemned 7.1795 at Rochefort.

London (British mercantile cutter, possibly *London*, taken 1.1794, carried 10 x 4pdrs). Renamed *Granville* 2.1794 and *London* 5.1795, sold at Cherbourg 10.1797.

Brilliant (British lugger, possibly *Brilliant*, taken 1.1794 and commissioned 2.1794 at Rochefort, 120 men, carried 12 x 3pdrs and 2 obusiers). To Cayenne 1798, condemned 1.1799 at Guadeloupe.

Rutland (British privateer lugger taken 6.12.1793 by the gunboat *Île d'Yeu* in the Bay of Bourgneuf and purchased 2.1794 at Nantes, 8 guns). Served at Saint-Nazaire and on the Basque coast during 1794, then at Rochefort. Went to sea 22.10.1796 and disappeared. A former British privateer lugger named *Rutland* or *Rusland* was also mentioned at Le Havre in 5.1795 with an armament of 1 x 4pdr and 7 x 2pdrs.

Courrier (British cutter taken 3.1794 and in service 4.1794 with 6 guns). In the Scheldt in 1795, struck late 1795 or 1796.

Surprise (British cutter, possibly a privateer, taken between 2.1794 and 4.1794, in service at Brest 4.1794 with 70 men and 10 x 4pdrs and 4 swivels). Captured 9.9.1794 by HMS *Pallas* (32) and *Aquilon* (32) off Ushant.

Union (British cutter taken at Martinique 3.1794 and at Brest in 1795, 82 men, carried 4 x 2pdrs). Renamed *Visible* 5.1795 and *Union* in 1797. Decomm. 19.2.1801 at Dunkirk and struck.

Six Soeurs (British schooner *Six Sisters* built in 1791, taken 4.1794 and commissioned 5.1794 at Lorient). Struck 6.1795 at Nantes.

Somerset (British lugger built in Britain in 1782, taken in 1794 and commissioned 4.1794 at Lorient, 60 men, carried 2 x 3pdrs). Struck at Lorient between 5.1795 and 9.1795.

Monro or *Munro* (British-built chasse-marée taken in 1794 and commissioned 5.1794 at Lorient, carried 2 x 2pdrs). Struck late 1795 at Lorient.

Steck (British lugger *Sterk* from Jersey, built in England in 1791, taken 5.1794 by the frigate *Proserpine*, 35-80 men, carried 6 x 2pdrs, name also rendered in French lists as *Steeck* and *Esteck*). Sold 9.1802 at Lorient.

Assistance (British cutter taken 6.1794 and commissioned 7.1794 at Lorient with 1 gun). Last mentioned 1.1797 while in service at La Rochelle.

Ranger (British cutter *Ranger* taken off Brest 28.6.1794 by *Railleuse* (32); had been the revenue cutter *Rose* purchased by the Royal Navy in 2.1787.)

  Dimensions & tons: 70ft x 24ft (22.96 x 8.02m). 100/180 tons. Men: 107.

  Guns (French): 16 x 4pdrs, 6 swivels.

  Re-rigged as a brig 6-7.1795 at Lorient. Captured 13.10.1797 off the Canaries by HMS *Indefatigable* (44), retaken 2.11.1797 by the French privateer *Vengeance*, taken again 6.11.1797 by HMS *Galatea* (32) off the Gironde and became HMS *Venturer*, sold 10.2.1803.

Surveillante (British schooner taken 6.1794 and in service at Toulon 7.1794 with 6 x 3pdrs and 2 x 2pdrs). Struck 6.1795 at Toulon.

Talbot (Spanish or British lugger built in Britain, taken 1794, 45-69 men, carried 8 x 4pdrs). Re-rigged as cutter 1796 or 1797, refitted as transport 1799. Sold at Cherbourg 2.1803.

Quartidi (British privateer cutter taken by French privateers and purchased 6.1794 at Nantes, 60 men, carried 10 x 4pdrs and 4 pierriers). Captured 7.9.1794 near the Scillies by a British division.

Ariel (British schooner taken 10.1794 and commissioned at Brest in late 1794 with 60-90 men and 8 x 3pdrs). Sold at Rochefort 16.9.1796.

Attentive (coast defence vessel or *garde-côtes* built in Britain in 1792, captured and in service at Lorient in 11.1794, carried 2 swivels). Last mentioned 5.1795 while coast defence vessel at Lorient, then struck.

Malin (cutter commissioned at Flushing 15.5.1795, built at Dover and taken from the British in 1793, previous name possibly *Actif*, carried 2 x 2pdrs). Decomm. 18.8.1803 at Dunkirk, struck 8.1805 and sold 4.1806.

Alcion (*Alcyon*) (British cutter belonging to the Duke of York, built in Britain in 1786, taken 5.1795, carried 2 x 2pdrs). Taken back by the British and recaptured by the French 12.1796, grounded at Zuydcoote 28.4.1803, refloated and repaired 5.1803. Placed on sale list and struck at Flushing 9.1805.

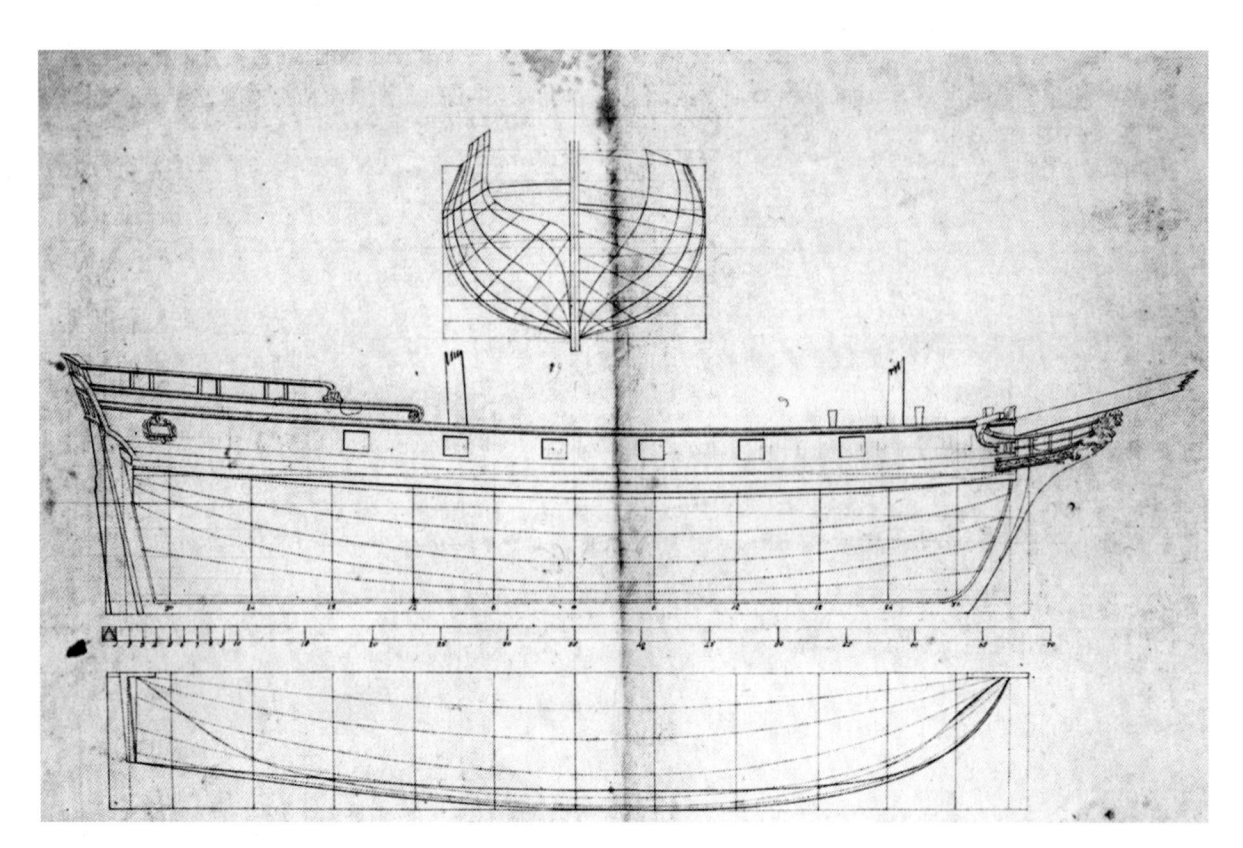

Original draught of the Venetian *Cibelle* class schooners. They were unusual in having substantial bulwarks and even a short quarterdeck in contrast to the minimal upperworks in the schooners of other nations. (Biblioteca Civica, Trieste)

Wendor (British cutter *Wendor* taken in 12.1796 or 1.1797 in Bantry Bay by the frigate *Sirene*, carried 8 x 4pdrs). Last mentioned 4.1798 while at Brest.

Sally (cutter of uncertain nationality, possibly the British *Sally*, taken at Corfu 7.1797, 44 men, 6 guns). Renamed *Torride* end 1797 or early 1798, arrived at Toulon 4.1798 and received 2 x 18pdrs and 4 swivels. Captured 25.8.1798 off Aboukir by boats from HMS *Goliath* (74), recaptured 18.3.1799 and returned to service but retaken the same day by HMS *Tigre* off St. Jean d'Acre. In Royal Navy service as a ketch until 1802.

Renau (Renaud) (British cutter taken in the Antilles 1.1798 and comm. 2.1798 at Guadeloupe, 59 men, carried 4 x 3pdrs). Decomm. 16.1.1813 at Rochefort, struck c1815.

Loterie (British privateer lugger *Lottery* captured in 1-2.1798 and in service at Lorient 3.1798, carried 6 x 2pdrs). Placed on sale and struck at Lorient 9.1801.

Actif (British cutter, possibly a privateer, taken 24.3.1799, 24 men, carried 4 x 2pdrs). Refitted 1815 at Rochefort as a yacht for the Duc d'Angoulême. Converted back to a lugger there 6.1819 and re-rigged as a cutter there 1.1824. Service craft at Rochefort 1.1827, condemned and struck 4.3.1830. Another cutter *Actif* (below) was in Senegal from 1821 to 1836.

Peggy (British *Peggy*. probably the Royal Navy cutter *Peggy* hired on 16.6.1795 and listed as foundered in the Channel 8.4.1799 but captured on that date by the cutter *Souffleur* and in service at Saint-Malo 6.1799, 50 tons, carried 8 x 3pdrs). Decomm. at Brest 2.1802, BU 11.1805.

Favori (British cutter taken 1798 by French privateers and purchased 6.1799 at Ostende, carried 4 swivels). Condemned 8.1805 at Dunkirk and sold there 4.1806.

Sandwich (Royal Navy cutter *Sandwich* hired 23.5.1798, taken 14.6.1799 by *Créole* (44) and/or the lugger *Affronteur* near Barcelona and in service at Lorient 8.1799, 111 tons (bm), carried 8 x 4pdrs).

Recaptured by the British at Aux Cayes in the Antilles 15.10.1803 and returned to her former British owner.

Anne (British privateer lugger *St. Ann* taken 7.1799 by *Réolaise*, carried 4 x 3pdrs). Recaptured and burned by the British 6.6.1800 at Port Navalo.

Plymouth (British lugger *Plymouth* taken 18.7.1799 by the frigate *Sirène*, carried 6 x 2pdrs, 1 x 1pdr, 4 swivels). Placed on sale at Lorient 10.1801.

Succes (British cutter, possibly a privateer, taken 7.1801 at Algesiras, 70 men). In 1805 first carried 1 x 12pdr, 3 x 3pdrs and then 12 x 4pdrs. Captured by HMS *Volage* (22) 6.11.1807 near La Galite.

Ex VENETIAN PRIZES (1797)

Venetian *CIBELLE* Class schooners. Laid down at Venice in 1775 and completed as schooners by Andrea Spadon in 1790-91. Like the bomb vessel *Distruzion* and the *Enea* class cutters (later brigs), their plans had measurements in both British and Venetian feet and may have been purchased in Britain. They were pierced with 12 ports in high bulwarks on the upper deck and also had a quarterdeck with 6 smaller ports. A third sister, *Cimodecca*, launched the same day as *Cibelle*, was lost off Malonta near Cattaro in 1793.

Dimensions & tons: 70ft, 63ft x 21ft, 21ft 6in ext x 9ft 3in (22.74, 20.46m x 6.82, 6.98m x 3.00m). 100/180 tons. Draught 7ft/9ft (2.27/2.92m). Men: 64

Guns: 12 x 8pdrs (12 x 6pdrs in *Mérope*). (*Cibele* ca 1800) 14 x 6pdrs; (1801) 18-9pdrs; (1802) 12 x 6pdrs.

Cybèle (Venetian *Cibelle*) Venice (built by Andrea Spadon) K: 10.1775. L: 17.5.1790. C: 22.5.1790.

Taken by the French 17.5.1797 at Venice, name became *Cybèle*. Accompanied the French ships that hoisted the Venetian flag to occupy the Venetian base at Corfu. Captured 14.11.1799 by the Austrians at Ancona, name became *Cibele*. In service 1800, refitted

In April 1796 boats from the British frigate *Diamond*, commanded by Sir Sidney Smith, cut out the lugger *Vengeur* from the anchorage off Le Havre, but were trapped by the wind dying away. This allowed the French to counter-attack – as shown in this coloured aquatint based on an eyewitness sketch – led by the lugger *Renard* (the largest vessel to the left) and three gunboats. The surviving British crews were all captured, including Smith. (© National Maritime Museum PY7893)

1801, decomm. at Venice 9.8.1803. In 1805 was to be sunk as unusable and used as a barrier in the lagoon. To Italy 1.1806 and probably sold. On 1.8.1806 a hired schooner named *Cibelle* was used in the salvage operation of a brig named *Dalmato*.

Mérope (Venetian *Merope*) Venice (built by Andrea Chiuribiri)
K: 10.1775. L: 25.6.1791. C: 7.1791.
Was at Venice when the French took the city 17.5.1797 but was among the commercial vessels and the French only found and seized her in 12.1797. Captured 3.1799 by the Russians at the surrender of Corfu, subsequent fate unknown.

AGILE (Venetian schooner)
Dimensions & tons: 57ft 10in x 15ft. (18.78 x 4.87m), 30/50 tons. Draught 4ft 10in (1.57m). Men: 37.
Guns: 8 x 3pdrs; (1801) 6 x 6pdrs.

Agile (Venetian *Agile*) Venice
L: 1791
Not listed as part of the Venetian Navy. Taken by the French 5.1797 at Venice and scuttled there 12.1797. Refloated by the Austrians, in comm. 5.1798. Last mentioned 1.8.1805 at the Lido at Venice, probably sold as unseaworthy.

Venetian unnamed cutters, later Austrian PILADE class brigs.
Both laid down as cutters on building way No.27 at Venice. Taken by the French 17.5.1797 while 1/12th complete, sabotaged by them 30.12.1797. Taken by the Austrians 18.1.1798, lengthened 6ft (1.80m), and re-rigged as brigs. Original length was 75ft (60 ft on keel).
Dimensions & tons: (1799) 81ft, 66ft? x 24ft 7in x 10ft 2in (26.3, 21.44? x 8.0 x 3.6m). 120/210 tons. Draught 6ft 5in/11ft (2.09/3.57m). Men: 81 (Austrian)
Guns: (1797) 18 x 9pdrs, 2 x 3pdrs; (1799) 18 x 6pdrs, 2 x 3pdrs; (1804) 18 x 6pdrs, 2 x 9pdrs, 2 x 3pdrs.

Pylade (Austrian *Pilade*) Venice (slip No.27)
K: 30.4.1797. L: 6.4.1799. Comm. 1800 and 1.8.1803. C: 4.1801.
Launched and completed by the Austrians. Stayed out of French hands in 1806 at Trieste, sold 20.11.1809 to a Prussian merchant.

Oreste (Austrian *Oreste*) Venice (slip No.27)
K: 30.4.1797. L: 30.3.1799. Comm. 27.5.1803. C: 5.1803.
Launched and completed by the Austrians. Stayed out of French hands in 1806 at Trieste, sold 20.11.1809 to a Prussian merchant.

MISCELLANEOUS PRIZES (1793-1799)
Anonyme (lugger, possibly a prize, commissioned at Granville 6.1793, carried 2 x 6pdrs and 6 swivels). Wrecked 20.5.1795, struck 8.1795.

Cornelia (merchant ship taken 8.1793 and commissioned as an aviso 3.9.1793). Decomm. 10.10.1794, last mentioned 12.1794.

Sans Culotte (merchant ship built in New England, taken 9.1793, and commissioned as an aviso 10.1793 at Bordeaux, carried 8 x 4pdrs, 6 obusiers, and 10 swivels). Renamed *Fortuné* 5.1795. Sold 6.1797 at Lorient.

Martinet (British lugger taken in 1793 and commissioned at Rochefort in 1794, carried 4 x 2pdrs). Renamed *Microcosme* 5.1795, struck at the end of 1795.

Neptune (Spanish lugger *Neptuno* taken 1794, carried 1 obusier and 10 swivels but listed as a 20-gun ship when taken in 1798). Renamed *Trompeur* 1794 and *Neptune* 1796. Captured 12.8.1798 by HMS *Hazard* (18) off Ireland with 52 crew and 270 troops from Île de France, then described as pierced for 20 guns and carrying 10.

Espagnol (Spanish cutter taken in 1794 or early 1795, carried 8 x 4pdrs). Was at Bayonne 5.1795 but could not be commissioned, struck 12.1795.

Magicienne (U.S. Navy schooner *Retaliation* taken by *Insurgente* and *Volontaire* on 20.11.1798 off Guadeloupe, ex French privateer *Croyable* of Santo Domingo built in Maryland and taken by USS *Delaware* on 7.7.1798 off New Jersey, 100 tons, carried 4 x 6pdrs and 10 x 4pdrs in U.S. service and 12 or 14 x 6pdrs in French service). Captured

6.1799 by USS *Merrimack* (24) but not returned to U.S. service.

Mère Duchèsne (Portuguese schooner, probably mercantile, taken c9.1799 by a division of 3 frigates under C.V. Landolphe and incorporated into that division, carried 4 guns). Fate unknown.

PURCHASED AND REQUISITIONED LUGGERS AND CHASSE-MARÉES (1792-1799)

Bellislois (chasse-marée, built 1785, requisitioned 10.1792 at Lorient, 20 men, carried 2 x 12pdrs). Struck c1802. Not to be confused with the lugger of the same name of 1795-1823.

Oiseau (chasse-marée commissioned 3.1793 at Lorient, 24 men, 6 swivels). Captured 6.1793 by the British.

Aimable Adélaide (mercantile lugger hired 4.1793 at Rochefort and then purchased, 30-90 men, carried 6 x 4pdrs and 4 swivels). Renamed *Aglaé* 16.5.1795, decomm. at Rochefort 7.1795, sold there 12.1795.

Chargeur (lugger, built 1782, requisitioned 4.1793 at Lorient, 48 tons, 30 men, carried 2 x 12pdrs and 2 x 3pdrs or 4pdrs). Decomm. 5.11.1801 at Rochefort, sold there 10.1803.

Rafleur (lugger requisitioned 5.1793 at Granville, carried 5 swivels). Last mentioned 9.1794 while at Saint-Malo.

Loi (mercantile lugger or chasse-marée, requisitioned 5.1793 at Lorient and in service there 6.1793, 50 men, carried 6 x 8pdrs). Decomm. 23.12.1801 at Lorient and struck.

Liberté (chasse-marée commissioned 6.1793 at Lorient, 20 men, carried 2 x 12pdrs and 2 x 4pdrs). Was lugger-rigged in 1795-96, struck at Lorient as a transport in late 1796.

Égalité (chasse-marée or lugger commissioned 6.1793 at Lorient, 20 men, carried 2 x 12pdrs and 2 x 4pdrs). Last mentioned 9.1796 as a transport at Bordeaux.

Lézard (lugger commissioned 6.1793 at Rochefort, 80 men, carried 6 x 4pdrs). Struck at Rochefort at the end of 1795.

Cerbère (lugger that was in service at Île d'Aix in 9.1793, carried 10 x 4pdrs). Renamed *Contrariant* 5.1795, reverted to *Cerbère* 1795. Condemned 1796 at Santo Domingo.

Républicain (privateer lugger built at Cherbourg and requisitioned 10.1793, 41 men, carried 12 x 3pdrs and 2pdrs). Renamed *Rayon* 5.1795. Burned 17.3.1796 to prevent capture but repaired. Last mentioned 5.1798 while at Cherbourg.

Hirondelle (privateer lugger requisitioned at Saint-Malo in late 1793, 25 tons, 30 men, carried 4 x 1pdrs and 4 swivels). Wrecked 24.12.1794 near Rothéneuf.

Oiseau (lugger requisitioned 6.1794 and comm. at Rochefort, carried 2 x 3pdrs and 4 swivels). Renamed *Olympe* 5.1795. Returned to her owners 12.1795.

Républicaine (lugger requisitioned from the slave trade 10.1794 and comm. at Rochefort). Renamed *Receleur* 5.1795. Wrecked 6.9.1795 near Royan.

Patriote (chasse-marée commissioned 12.1794 at Lorient, 28 men, carried 4 x 6pdrs). Used as a gunboat on the Loire 1-2.1796. Last mentioned 9.1796 as a transport at Bordeaux.

Rusé (lugger requisitioned at the end of 1794, carried 8 x 4pdrs). Sunk 1.1795 in combat near Fécamp.

Creutzen (Dutch lugger taken by French privateers and requisitioned c1794, 2 guns). Was in service at Dunkirk 5.1795 and at Flushing 8.1795, then struck.

Chasseur (lugger commissioned at Bayonne in 1794 or early 1795, carried 8 x 4pdrs). Last mentioned 7.1797 while at Jennary.

Résolue (lugger in service in the Mediterranean in early 1795, 8 guns). Was at Villefranche on 26.5.1795 and may have been renamed *Reflex* 5.1795, later fate unknown. The *Résolue* that was captured 26.8.1795 by Nelson's squadron in the Bay of Alassio was probably a different vessel (see the xebec *O Hydra*).

Oiseau (lugger that was a health vessel at Cherbourg in 5.1795). Renamed *Chardonneret* 5.1795, at Saint-Malo 1.1796 under the name *Oiseau*, then struck.

Providence (lugger that was in service at Brest in 1.1796, 30 tons, 4 guns). Returned to her owner and commissioned as a privateer at Saint-Malo 10.1796, captured in early 11.1796 in the Channel by HMS *Dover* (44).

Neptune Fortuné (lugger that was in service at La Teste on 6.4.1796, carried 1 x 24pdr and 8 swivels). Was unserviceable at Rochefort in 11.1798 and struck. May have been the lugger *Neptune* that escorted a convoy along the Biscay coast in 6.1795.

Carnac (chasse-marée belonging to the State that was in service at Belle-Isle in 9.1796). No further information known.

Fouine (lugger *Furet* commissioned at Bordeaux and renamed around late 1796, 26 men, carried 6 x 4pdrs). In service at Brest 1.1797. Was escorting a convoy to Brest in 8.1798, captured 17.11.1798 off Brest by HMS *Sylph* (16).

Libérateur d'Italie (lugger or tartane requisitioned at Ancona 3.1797, 45-52 men, carried 4 x 12pdrs, 4 x 8pdrs, and 2 swivels). Sent by Napoleon into the port of San Nicolò at Venice which was closed to foreign warships, refused to leave when ordered and boarded and taken 20.4.1797 by the Venetian galliot or galley *Bella Chiaretta* (also referred to as *Annetta Bella*), the resulting loss of life providing the pretext for the first French occupation of Venice. Retaken at Venice 5.1797 by the French, returned to her owners 7.1797.

Bonaparte (lugger also called an aviso requisitioned at Ancona 3.1797, 40 men, carried 6 x 6pdrs). Wrecked 21.11.1799 on the Île du Levant near Hyères.

Éveillé (lugger that was in service at Le Havre in 7.1797, possibly a former numbered *bateau canonnier*, 13-34 men, 2 guns). Struck early 1798.

Cormoran (lugger commissioned 17.7.1798 at Saint-Malo). Decomm. 10.1798, no further record.

Hoche (lugger comm. at Brest 10.1798). Last mentioned 8.1799 while returning to Brest.

Rebecca (chasse-marée commissioned at Brest in 3.1799 or 4.1799, 8 men, 4 swivels). Sent to sea with false despatches about a planned landing attempt in Ireland by Vice-Adm. Étienne Eustache Bruix and captured as intended on 27.4.1799 off Ushant by the hired cutter HMS *Black Joke* (10); the despatches caused Adm. Lord Bridport to wait for Bruix off Ireland while Bruix left Brest on 26.4.1799 with 24 of the line to reinforce French forces in Corfu, Malta, and Egypt.

Orage (lugger commissioned 3.1799 at Cherbourg, carried 6 swivels). Fate after 1799 unknown.

Vedette (chasse-marée, origin unknown, comm. 10.1799 at Cherbourg, 70 tons, carried 4 x 2pdrs). Decomm. 12.1800 at Cherbourg, last mentioned 2.1804.

PURCHASED AND REQUISITIONED CUTTERS (1786-1799)

Hirondelle (packet cutter acquired at Dunkirk 1-6.1786, carried 4 x 3pdrs). Struck 1787 at Brest and converted to gabarre, condemned at Brest 11.1788.

Montagne (cutter or lugger requisitioned at Dunkirk 1793, carried 8 x 3pdrs). Renamed *Pivert* 5.1795, re-rigged as chasse-marée 1795, struck 1796.

Éclair (cutter or lugger built at Quimper 1792 and purchased there 8.1793, carried 3 x 4pdrs). Decomm. 7.1796 at Lorient, then struck.

Actif (cutter built 1789 and requisitioned 9.1793 at Lorient, carried 2 to 4 x 3pdrs). Renamed *Affranchi* 5.1795. Returned 1796 to her owner at Lorient.

Forcalquier or *Fort-Calquier* (cutter or chasse-marée, built in Nantes in 1785 or 1791 and requisitioned c10.1793, 41 men, carried 4 x 3pdrs). Renamed *Morbihan* 11.1793 and *Messager* 5.1795. Re-rigged as lugger 1800 at Lorient. Captured 16.8.1803 off Ushant by boats from HMS *Ville de Paris* (110).

Courrier de Lorient (cutter built at Lorient and requisitioned 12.1793, 35 men, carried 8 x 4pdrs). Renamed *Circulateur* 5.1795, struck 1796.

Neptune Hardi (cutter *Petit Neptune* launched at Dunkirk 3.1786 and requisitioned 4.1794, carried 1 x 1pdr, also called aviso). Burned 17.3.1796 at Serquy (Saint Brieuc) to prevent capture.

Aldudes (cutter commissioned 5.1794 at Bayonne, carried 8 x 3pdrs, 2 x 2pdrs, and 5 swivels). Captured 4.7.1794 by the Spanish frigate *Santa Teresa* off Ferrol and named *Alduides* in the Spanish navy.

Expédition (cutter commissioned 10.1794 at Brest, 30 tons, 15 men, carried 6 swivels, also called sloop). Renamed *Extraordinaire* 5.1795. Struck 1796, commissioned 11.1797 at Saint-Malo as a privateer.

Renommée (cutter, built at Bayonne 1792-93, requisitioned and comm. 12.1794 at Lorient then purchased, 22 men, carried 4 x 3pdrs). Renamed *Ravisseur* 5.1795 and *Renommée* 1796. For sale at Lorient 9.1801 and struck. An unidentified *Renommée* was in service in French Guiana in 1803.

Loyauté (privateer cutter built at Bayonne 1793 and purchased 6.1795, carried 10 x 4pdrs). Wrecked 17.2.1798 near Arcachon on voyage from Bayonne to Bordeaux.

Bruiteux (cutter that was in service 2.1796 at Brest). Fate unknown.

Pensée (cutter in service at Brest in 2.1796 or at Dunkirk in 11.1796, 70 tons, carried 4 x 2pdrs). Renamed *Vedette* 11.1796. Decomm. at Dunkirk 22.4.1801. (See also the 8-gun *Pensée/Vedette* captured from the British in 10.1793.)

Vigilant (cutter commissioned 11.1797)
Dimensions & tons: 60ft x 20ft 8in (19.49m x 6.71m). Tons unknown.
Guns: 1 x 18pdr
Later classed as *bateau canonnier*. Decomm. 7.1801 at Ostende or Dunkirk.

Fulminante (cutter in service in 1798)
Dimensions & tons: 41ft x 14ft 3in (13.32 x 4.63m). Tons unknown.
Guns: 8 x 4pdrs
Captured 29.10.1798 in the Mediterranean by HMS *Espoir* (16) and became HMS *Fulminante*. Captured by French privateer *Deux Frères* 2.6.1800, recaptured 9.1800. Wrecked 24.3.1801 while providing fire support to landings at Aboukir.

Furet (cutter in service at Cherbourg 10.1799, carried 4 x 2pdrs). Decomm. 19.2.1801 at Flushing or Dunkirk and struck 1801.

PURCHASED AND REQUISITIONED SCHOONERS (1786-1800)

Coureur (schooner built in North America, acquired c1786, and in service in the Antilles 6.1787). Renamed *Élisabeth* 10.1792. Taken to Trinidad 1.1793 and handed over to the Spanish by her Royalist officers.

Iphigénie (schooner placed in service 5.1786 at Martinique). Sunk 3.1791 in collision in the harbour of Fort-Royal de la Martinique.

Aglaé (schooner commissioned 1789 at Toulon). Not further mentioned.

Bigotte (schooner that was in service at Martinique in 9.1791). Taken 1791 by 'rebels' (probably revolutionaries), retaken 10.11.1791 by the Royalist *Ferme* (74), probably retaken by the Republicans in the 1.1793 revolt at Martinique, last mentioned 7.1793 while in the Antilles.

Hirondelle (schooner commissioned in France that arrived at Santo Domingo in 1.1792). Last mentioned 3.1792 departing Port-au-Prince for Léogane.

Jeannette (schooner that was in service in the Antilles c1792). Captured 6.1793 by the British at Tobago.

Armande (fishing schooner laid down 1.1793, launched, requisitioned, and placed in service as an aviso for convoy escort duty 4.1793 at Le Havre, 25 tons, 21 men, carried 2 x 2pdrs). Renamed *Eurydice* 5.1795. Returned to her owners 4.1796.

Guadeloupienne (schooner purchased as a brig 4.1793 at Pointe-à-Pitre, 60-120 men, carried 16 x 6pdrs). Captured by the British at Guadeloupe 4.1794, retaken by the French along with Pointe-à-Pitre 6.1794 and renamed *Guadeloupe* 6.1794. Temporarily classed as a fireship in 1795. Re-rigged as a schooner at Rochefort 8-9.1796. Decomm. 26.6.1805 at Rochefort, condemned 8.1806.

Boston or *Petit Boston* (schooner of North American origin placed in service 1793 at Toulon, 10 men, carried 2 x 4pdrs and 4 swivels). Taken 8.1793 by the British at Toulon and commissioned by the Royal Navy, retaken by the French 12.1793, subsequent fate unknown.

Sainte Croix (schooner that was in service at Toulon in 1793). Taken 8.1793 by the British at Toulon and served with 8 men and 4 swivels as HMS *St. Croix* until 1794.

Convention Nationale (mercantile schooner *Marie Antoinette* requisitioned 1793 at Santo Domingo)
Dimensions & tons: 80ft x 21ft 7in (26.07 x 7.01m). 80/150 tons
Guns: 10 x 4pdrs
Captured 9.1793 by a British division at Cap St. Nicolas at Santo Domingo, became HMS *Marie Antoinette*. Returned to the French 9.1797 in the Antilles by her mutinous crew, later fate unknown.

Carmagnole (schooner commissioned 1793 in Guadeloupe, carried 10 guns). Taken 30.11.1794 off St. Lucia by HMS *Zebra* (16).

Carmagnole (schooner-rigged service craft placed in service 4.1794 at Rochefort). Last mentioned 8.1794 while at Rochefort.

Coureuse (schooner built at New York in 1788 or 1785, purchased at Cayenne 4.1794 and commissioned 6.1794 at Lorient)
Dimensions & tons: 52ft 4in, 35ft x 14ft 9in x 6ft 7in (17.00, 11.37 x 4.79 x 2.14m). 18/33 tons. Draught 4ft 4in/7ft 6in (1.41/2.43m). Men: 23.
Guns: 8 x 2pdrs.
Captured 26.2.1795 near the Île de Groix by HMS *Pomone* (44), became HMS *Coureuse*. Sold 13.4.1799.

Heureuse Rencontre (privateer schooner requisitioned and commissioned 6.1794 at Bayonne, 80 men, carried 6 x 3pdrs and 6 swivels). Sold 10.1797 at Brest.

Coureur (schooner built in Bermuda and in service at Brest in 10.1794, 42 men, carried 8 x 3pdrs). Was at Santo Domingo in 1.1795. Renamed *Enjouée* 5.1795. Struck c1796.

Liberté (coast defence schooner purchased 12.1794 at Santo Domingo by Toussaint-Louverture and commissioned 12.1794 at Gonaïves with 25 men). Probably returned to privateering in 1795 or 1796.

Dorade (schooner that was in service at Dunkirk in 3.1795, carried 12 x 4pdrs). Condemned 7.1797 at Dunkirk, BU late 1798.

Espérance (schooner captured 5.1795 and commissioned at Santo Domingo, carried 6 x 1pdrs). Re-rigged as a brig or lugger at Rochefort 1800-1. Grounded 13.12.1801 in the bay of Concarneau after springing a leak, refloated 1.1802 but wrecked near Lorient.

Alerte (corsair schooner requisitioned 7.1796 at Île de France, had 16 ports with 8 to 14 guns). Left Île de France with a division under Rear Admiral Sercy for a raiding cruise in the Indian Ocean, while off the Coromandel coast during the night of 19.8.1796 attacked HMS *Carysfort* (28) which she mistook for a merchantman and was captured.

Volante (schooner built at Cayenne and purchased there from American owners 9.1796, carried 8 x 6pdrs). Operated in the Caribbean through at least 8.1797. Capsized and wrecked 2.1800 near Croisic (Loire).

Enfant Prodigue (schooner, built in America in 1790 and purchased in 1796 at Bordeaux)
  Dimensions & tons: 72ft or 71ft 1in x 20ft 6in x 7ft 8in (23.39 or 23.09 x 6.66 x 2.49m). 70/120 tons. Men: 59.
  Guns: 12 x 4pdrs; (1803) 16 x 4pdrs.
  Captured 24.6.1803 off St. Lucia by HMS *Emerald* (36), became gunbrig HMS *Saint Lucia*. Retaken 23.3.1807 near Guadeloupe by the French privateer schooners *Vengeance* (12) and *Friponne* (5), subsequent fate unknown.

Arabe (schooner built in Bermuda c1788, date of acquisition unknown, perhaps 1797)
  Dimensions & tons: 59ft, 47 ft x 17ft 9in x 8ft 7in (19.17, 15.27 x 5.76 x 2.79m). 50/90 tons. Draught 6ft/8ft 4in (1.95/2.71m).
  Guns: 4 to 8.
  Captured 6.1797 by the British, became HMS *Ant*. Sold 23.4.1815.

Cisalpine (schooner or schooner-rigged gun launch requisitioned 4.1798 at Genoa for the expedition to Egypt, then purchased, 28 men, carried 1 x 8pdr). Captured by the Austrians 13.11.1799 in the fall of Ancona and incorporated in the Austrian Navy as a gun launch. Fate unknown.

Providence (ex-British schooner hired in 1798 or 1799, 132 tons, 22 men, 2 guns). Captured 4.7.1803 off the Île de Sein near Brest by boats from HMS *Naiad* (38). When captured she was carrying a cargo of 36pdr, 24pdr, and 18pdr guns.

Étourdie (schooner acquired in French Guiana in early 1799 and commissioned at Cayenne 4.1799, 95 men, carried 8 x 4pdrs). Departed Cayenne 5.1799 with passengers for Bayonne. Placed on sale list at Rochefort 4.1802.

Curieuse (schooner or biscayenne commissioned 5.1799 at Lorient, 6 tons, 24 men, carried 1 x 36pdr obusier). Captured 6.1800 at Port Navalo by the British.

Victoire (schooner, origin unknown, in service at Cayenne in 8.1799). Mentioned 2.1807 as still in service at Cayenne. One of three acquired schooners named *Victoire* on the list at about this time.

Suffren (schooner that was in commission for four months in 1799 during the Egyptian campaign). Fate unknown.

Victoire (schooner-aviso, origin unknown, commissioned at Toulon 23.9.1800, 132 tons, 22 men, carried 6 x 6pdrs). Classified as bombarde in 1806-7 and a gunboat in 1814. Station ship at Villefranche in 1808. Turned over to the Prince of Monaco 20.8.1814 with the xebec *Syrène* in exchange for the corvettes *Carolina* and *Augusta*, which had been taken at Nice.

PURCHASED AND REQUISITIONED AVISOS (1792-1800)

Entreprise (British-built aviso commissioned 11.1792 at Dunkirk, carried 6 swivels). Apparently lost in the Scheldt in the autumn of 1793 and recovered c10.1795 in Belgium, later fate unknown.

Hirondelle (aviso, ex British merchant brig built in 1784, captured, purchased from her French owner and comm. 4.1793 at Rochefort, 50 tons, 86 men, carried 6 x 4pdrs). Renamed *Flèche* 6.1799 at Antwerp and described as a schooner. Given to the postal service 1.1802.

Aimée (schooner-rigged aviso, a new vessel built at Honfleur in 1792 but damaged in a grounding and purchased 4.1793 at Honfleur, 25 tons, 37 men, carried 4 x 4pdrs). Sold 1.1803 at Le Havre. Repurchased or requisitioned 8.1803 as *Transport No.231 Aimée* for the Boulogne Flotilla and redesignated *Transport No.222* in 2.1804. Decomm. 3.1807.

Vedette (aviso requisitioned and commissioned 5.1793 at Dunkirk, carried 6 x 6pdrs and 2 swivels). Last mentioned 6.1794 while at Dunkirk.

Espérance (privateer galiote *Belle en Cuisse* loaned without payment 6.1793 to the state as an aviso, 19 tons, 8 men). Returned to her owner 4.1795, resumed privateering (6 guns), captured 4.1799 by the fleet of Admiral Parker.

Petite Victoire (brig-rigged aviso commissioned 7.1793 at Toulon, carried 2 x 6pdrs). Captured 8.1793 by the British at Toulon, lost in Royal Navy service 1793 off Cap Corse.

Républicain (aviso that was in service 10.1793). Last mentioned 12.1793 while on escort duty on the Atlantic coast.

Société Populaire (newly-built privateer requisitioned at Bordeaux 1793 as an aviso, carried 12 x 3pdrs). Renamed *Savant* 30.5.1795. Returned to her owner 2.1796.

Double Marin (aviso commissioned 6.1794 at Rochefort, 229 tons, carried 2 x 6pdrs, 2 obusiers, and 2 swivels). Fate unknown.

Tricolore (aviso commissioned 6.1794 at Rochefort, carried 4 x 6pdrs, 2 obusiers, and 2 swivels). Fate unknown.

Rutlan (aviso commissioned 6.1794 at Rochefort, carried 1 x 3pdr and 2 swivels). Fate unknown.

Utile (aviso, origin unknown, commissioned 12.1794 at Cherbourg, carried 4 x 2pdrs). Renamed *Verseau* 5.1795, reverted to *Utile* 1796. Decomm. at Cherbourg 2.1804.

Épervier (requisitioned and commissioned as an aviso at Toulon in early 1795, carried 6 x 6pdrs and 4pdrs). Renamed *Espion* 5.1795. Returned 1.1797 to owner at Toulon but again requisitioned 5.1798 as *Épervier*. Last mentioned 7.1798 when en route to Corsica.

Sophie (aviso, arrived at Lorient 6.1795 from New York, carried 2 guns). Became transport 1.1797, last mentioned 9.1797, then struck.

Faisceau (aviso that was in service at Saint-Malo in 1.1796 and 1.1797). Struck 1797.

Paix (aviso that was in service at Saint-Malo in 1.1796). Struck 1797.

Galatée (cutter-rigged aviso that was in service at Saint-Malo in 1.1796, 25 men). Also used as transport. Last mentioned 1.1797 while at Saint-Malo.

Marie-André (aviso that was in service at Saint-Malo in 1.1796). Fate unknown.

Surveillante (mouche commissioned at Lorient c8.1796). Last mentioned 9.1796 in service in the Vilaine.

Colombe (cutter-rigged aviso that was in service at Dunkirk in 10.1796, 50 tons). Wrecked 11.1796 near Fort Risban at Calais, BU 1797-98.

Dragut (aviso commissioned at Guadeloupe c3.1797). Last mentioned 10.1797 leaving Lorient for Guadeloupe.

Droits de l'Homme (aviso or 'small corvette' in service at Santo Domingo at the beginning of 1798). Last mentioned 7.1798 in service at Cap François.

Vif (aviso, origin unknown, presumably requisitioned, commissioned 5.1798 in Corsica, 6 guns). Decomm. 11.1800, struck and probably returned to her owner.

Félicité (aviso, origin unknown, commissioned 1798 at Toulon). Captured 6.1801 by the British.

Menzaleh (aviso or gunboat commissioned in Egypt in 1798). Last mentioned 23.6.1799 while at Om-Fareg in Egypt. An aviso with this name was in the Damietta flotilla with the avisos *Cerf*, *Sainte Marthe*, and *Amoureuse* plus the gunboat *Sans Quartier* and cange *Surveillante* when the ships of this flotilla were burned, sunk, or captured by the Turks near Rosetta on 10.4.1801.

Reconnaissant (aviso commissioned in early 2.1799 at Ancona and sailed 10.2.1799 for Egypt). Probably lost in Egypt 8.1801, although she might have been the chasse-marée *Reconnaissance* that was in

The build up of small craft for Napoleon's planned invasion of England occasioned many clashes outside the Channel ports between the small craft of both sides. This aquatint celebrates one such engagement – too small to warrant a mention in most histories, but highly dramatic nonetheless. On 31 October 1803 the British hired cutter *Admiral Mitchell* attacked a French gunbrig that was supported by five cutters and a schooner; in the action which followed the gunbrig and one of the cutters were driven ashore, while the *Admiral Mitchell* escaped with some damage. This aquatint by R Livesay gives a good impression of the naval small craft involved. (Courtesy of Beverley R. Robinson Collection, US Naval Academy Museum)

service at Toulon in 10.1802.

Isis (aviso commissioned at Genoa in 4.1799). Captured 5.1799 by the British near Sardinia.

Audacieux (cutter-rigged aviso, origin unknown, commissioned 4.1799 or 4.1800 at Cherbourg, carried 4 swivels). Wrecked 4.2.1802 (or 4.2.1800?).

Subtile (aviso commissioned at Toulon in 1799). Went to Malta 1799, fate unknown. She may have been the speronare that crossed from Malta to Nice in 6.1800.

Étourdi (aviso hired then commissioned at Toulon in 1799/1800, carried 4 x 4pdrs). Decomm. 9.1801 at Toulon and returned to her owner.

Three coast defence vessels (*garde-côtes*) were in service in October 1799, *Pérou* at Cartaret, *Protecteur* at Becquet, and *Stationnaire* at Étel. Nothing more is known about these vessels.

(C) Vessels acquired from 25 March 1802

JOUBERT –chasse-marée, 2 guns.
Dimensions & tons: dimensions unknown. 30/50 tons. Men: 23
Guns: 2 x 8pdr carronades
Joubert Saint-Malo.
K: 1803. L: 8.1803. C: 9.1803. Comm: 2.9.1803.
Commissioned at Lorient or Saint-Servan in 1803 but was probably rated as a service craft while two other avisos named *Joubert* were on the fleet lists, a xebec taken at Leghorn (1800-9) and an ex-Russian bomb vessel (1809-14). The 1803 chasse-marée appeared on fleet lists in 1816 and 1818 as out of commission at Brest. Refitted at Brest in 4.1819, she was listed in 11.1819 as an aviso. Decomm. 24.8.1822, she was re-rigged as a schooner in 3.1823 at Rochefort and was in commission from 29.5.1823 to 22.1.1824. She continued to be listed as an aviso until demoted to a service craft at Rochefort in 1.1827. Back in commission by 1.1.1829 as a depot ship, she was assigned to Bordeaux from 11.12.1830 as station ship at Pauillac (probably still schooner-rigged) until she was decomm. there on 1.1.1842 and struck. She had reappeared on the fleet list briefly in 1834-35 as an aviso, was reported as struck in 1835, and reappeared in 1837-41 as a chasse-marée. The brig-aviso *Laurier* replaced her at Pauillac in 6.1842 and was assigned to Bordeaux for that purpose on 1.1.1843.

GOBE-MOUCHE – schooner, 8 guns. Designed and/or built by Grisard. Grisard was a local shipbuilder, and in the absence of a representative of the Génie Maritime at Île de France the Colonial Prefect, General Decaen, assigned him much naval construction work. Impressed by the results, Decaen in 1808 requested for him the title of *ingénieur-constructeur*. Grisard did not have his own shipyard, and this little vessel may have been built at a yard owned by Rondeaux or one owned by Piston. His later work included design and construction of the felucca *Entreprenant* in 1807, a brig of the same name in 1808, and the schooner-aviso *Lutin* in 1810.
Dimensions & tons: unknown. Men: 32.
Guns: (1808) 8 x 12pdr carronades.
Gobe-Mouche Île de France.
K: 1805. L: 1806. Comm: 1.4.1806. C: 9.1806.
Captured 20.12.1808 near Réunion by the British. Sometimes called a brig.

PSICHE Class – schooners, 10 guns. Probably designed by the chief Italian constructor at Venice, Andrea Salvini, and built by Luigi Paresi. All served in Napoleon's Italian Navy.
Dimensions & tons: 85ft x 21ft x 9ft 7in (27.61m x 6.82m x 3.01m). 100/177 tons. Men: 62.
Guns: 8 or 10 x 6pdrs; (*Gloria*) 2 x 8pdrs, 6 x 12pdr carronades; (*Vigilante* 1815) 6 x 12pdrs.

Psiche (in French *Psyché*) Venice.
K: 12.1806. L: 1807. C: 2.1808.
Captured 5.1808 while crossing between Lesina (now Hvar in Croatia) and Ancona.

Ortensia (in French *Hortentia*) Venice.
K: 12.1806. L: 1807. C: 2.1808.
Captured 16.7.1808 by HMS *Minstrel* (18) at Brioni, became HMS *Ortenzia*, sold 1812.

Gloria Venice.
K: 12.1806, L: 12.1807 (or 7.3.1807), C: 2.1808 (or 12.1807)
Taken over by the Austrians 25.4.1814 in the occupation of the Venice Arsenal, renamed *Vigilante* 20.5.1815. Hauled out 24.9.1836 and ordered BU and replaced by a new *Vigilante*. The new *Vigilante*, a schooner of about 26 metres, was laid down 30.11.1837 but was still on the ways when she was renamed *Arethusa* 18.11.1849.

CERF Class – schooners, 10 to 12 guns. Designed by François-Frédéric Poncet, plans reviewed by Jacques-Noël Sané.
Dimensions & tons: 79ft 11in, 74ft 0in x 22ft 4in x 12ft 2in (25.95, 24.04 x 7.26 x 3.95m). 150/273 tons. Draught 9ft 8in (3.15m) mean. Men: 86.
Guns: 2 x 8pdrs or 6pdrs, 8 or 10 x 24pdr carronades.

Cerf Toulon Dyd. (Constructeurs: Antoine Arnaud and Poncet)
Ord: 11.5.1807. K: 6.1807. Named: 2.7.1807. L: 11.1807. Comm: 17.1.1808. C: 1.1808.
Decomm. and condemned 30.6.1821 at Martinique, became careening hulk (*ponton de carène*) and lighter 10.1821.

Flèche Toulon Dyd. (Constructeur: Jean-Nicolas Guérin)
Ord: 11.5.1807. Named: 2.7.1807. K: 1.1808. L: 13.10.1808. C: 1.1809. Comm: 6.12.1809.
Captured 23.12.1813 off Vintimilles by HMS *Alcmene* (38) while escorting *Lybio* and *Baleine* with troops for Corsica.

Antilope Toulon Dyd. (Constructeur: Antoine Arnaud)
K: 1809. L: 5.1.1810. Comm: 27.2.1810.
Captured 6.7.1815 off Sardinia by HMS *Alcmene* (38).

MOUCHE No.2 Class – schooner-avisos, 1 gun. Designed by Jean Baudry on the plans of *Villaret* (ex *Kingfish*, see captured vessels) that he took off himself. He probably was also *constructeur* of the vessels built at Bayonne. *Mouches Nos.2-7* were ordered on 16 May 1808.
Dimensions & tons: 56ft 9in, 46ft 0in x 16ft 3in x 6ft (18.43, 14.94 x 5.28 x 1.95m). 38/60-80 tons. Draught 4ft 9in/7ft 8in (1.54/2.50m). Men: 12-25.
Guns: 1 x 4pdr (in most) or 1 x 6pdr, on pivot

Mouche No.2 Bayonne.
K: 5.1808. L: 4.6.1808. C: 6.1808. Comm: 13.6.1808.
Departed Bayonne 14.6.1808 for Île de France and disappeared at sea.

Mouche No.3 Bayonne.
K: 14.5.1808. L: 5.6.1808. C: 6.1808. Comm: 25.6.1808.
Captured 19.9.1808 in the Antilles, probably by HMS *Cossack* (22).

Mouche No.4 Bayonne.
K: 14.5.1808. L: 23.6.1808. C: 7.1808. Comm: 8.7.1808.
Captured 26 or 28.2.1809 a month after being refitted at Bayonne.

Mouche No.5 Bayonne.
K: 14.5.1808. L: 25.6.1808. C: 7.1808. Com: 12.7.1808.
Destroyed 9.3.1809 at Borneo to prevent capture.

Mouche No.6 Bayonne.
K: 15.5.1808. L: 6.1808. C: 7.1808. Comm: 4.8.1808.
Seized 24.5.1809 near Manila by the Spanish, who had sided with the British. Crew rescued in early 9.1809 by Lieutenant Pierre-François Bouvet in his brig *Entreprenant*.

Mouche No.7 Bayonne.
K: 14.5.1808. L: 8.7.1808. C: 7.1808. Comm: 19.7.1808.
Captured 10.6.1809 at Santander by HMS *Amelia* (38), HMS *Statira* (38), and the Spanish.

Mouche No.8 Bayonne.
K: 9.8.1808. L: 5.9.1808. C: 9.1808. Comm: 5.10.1808.
Renamed *Serin* 4.6.1817 and recomm. 28.6.1817, probably for colonial service. Left Brest 9.1817 with an expedition to retake French Guiana from the Spanish, lost 16.10.1817 with all hands in a squall en route to Cayenne via Senegal. Struck 10.11.1817.

Mouche No.9 Rochefort Dyd. (Constructeur: Jean-Baptiste Lemoyne-Sérigny)
K: 10.8.1808. L: 10.9.1808. C: 11.1808. Comm: 1.11.1808 (?)
Condemned 3.1817 at Rochefort, BU 4.1817.

Mouche No.10 Rochefort Dyd. (Constructeur: Jean-Baptiste Lemoyne-Sérigny)
K: 10.8.1808. L: 10.9.1808. C: 11.1808. Comm: 15.1.1809.
Condemned 3.1817 at Rochefort, BU 4.1817.

Mouche No.11 Mathurin & Antoine Crucy, Basse-Indre
K: 8.1808. L: 19.9.1808. Comm: 16.11.1808.
Burned at Guadeloupe 2.1810 when the British took the island.

Mouche No.12 Lorient Dyd.
K: 7.1808. L: 22.9.1808. C: 10.1808. Comm: 14.3.1809.
Guns: 1 x 4pdr, 4 x 12pdr carronades (1814-16).
Renamed *Rossignol* 24.3.1817 and recomm. 9.4.1817, probably for colonial service. Lost with all hands 21.10.1817 in a hurricane near Martinique.

Mouche No.13 Brest Dyd.
K: 8.1808. L: 5.11.1808. Comm: 9.11.1808.
Captured 8.3.1809 near the Azores by HMS *Reindeer* (18).

Mouche No.14 Boulogne (Constructeur: Jean-Charles Garrigues)
K: 8.1808. L: c10.1808. C: 11.1808.
Captured 11.8.1815 by the British at Guadeloupe, fate unknown.

Mouche No.15 Boulogne (Constructeur: Jean-Charles Garrigues)
K: 8.1808. L: c10.1808. C: 11.1808. Comm: 16.11.1808.
Renamed *Éclair* 1.1818, recomm. 1.5.1818, and rated aviso for colonial service. To Martinique 1818-19. Decomm. 10.6.1825 at Martinique and struck.

Mouche No.16 Dunkirk (Constructeur: Louis Bretocq)
K: 8.1808. L: 13.9.1808. C: 12.1808. Comm: 1.1.1809.
Renamed *Colibri* 3.1817, recomm. 1.5.1817, and probably rated aviso for colonial service. In Senegal by 1818, schooner-rigged. On fleet list 1825 as an aviso. Decomm. and condemned at Senegal 1.8.1832, off fleet list 1832 and sold and BU at Senegal. Another *Colibri* (see below) was in service at Île Bourbon from 1825 to 1833.

Mouche No.17 (*Goélette No.17*) Flushing.
K: 8.1808. L: c15.9.1808. C: 9.1808.
Decomm. 16.2.1814 at Antwerp and struck there 5.1814. Probably ceded to the Netherlands 8.1814.

Mouche No.18 (*Goélette No.18*) Flushing.
K: 8.1808. L: c15.9.1808. C: 9.1808.
Decomm. 1.3.1814 at Antwerp and struck there 5.1814. Probably ceded to the Netherlands 8.1814.

Mouche No.19 (*Goélette No.19*) Flushing.
K: 8.1808. L: c15.9.1808. C: 9.1808.
Decomm. 15.2.1814 at Antwerp and struck there 5.1814. Probably ceded to the Netherlands 8.1814.

Mouche No.20 Toulon Dyd.
K: 8.1808. L: 24.3.1809. Comm: 25.3.1809.

A large French naval schooner in an etched portrait by Antoine Léon Morel-Fatio. The vessel is about the size of the Levrette *class. (© National Maritime Museum PU6147)*

Renamed *Ramier* 1.1818, recomm. 25.3.1818, and rated aviso. Decomm. 5.12.1826, condemned 10.3.1828 at Toulon and struck.

Mouche No.21 Toulon Dyd.
K: 8.1808. L: 24.3.1809. Comm: 25.3.1809. C: 4.1809.
Renamed *Moucheron* 1.1818, recomm. 17.4.1818, and rated aviso for colonial service. To Senegal, manned by an entirely Senegalese crew from 1823, last mentioned operationally 1826. Off fleet list and to colonial accounts 9.1830.

Mouche No.22 Genoa (Constructeur: François Pestel)
K: early 1809. L: 15.7.1809. C: 9.1809. Comm: 18.9.1809.
Ceded 17.4.1814 to the navy's creditors at Genoa one day before the city fell to the British, who appear not to have seized her.

Mouche No.23 Bayonne.
K: 26.7.1809. L: 2.8.1809. Comm: 4.8.1809. C: 8.8.1809.
Captured 2.6.1810 off Île de France by HMS *Nereide* (36). Retaken 30.8.1810 by the French frigate *Astrée*. Recaptured 2.12.1810 by the British when they took the colony.

Mouche No.24 Bayonne (Constructeur: Jean Baudry)
K: 26.7.1809. L: 12.8.1809. Comm: 17.8.1809. C: 18.8.1809.
Renamed *Papillon* 4.1817, recomm. 12.5.1817, and probably rated aviso for colonial service. Disappeared 21.10.1817 with all hands at Martinique in a hurricane.

Mouche No.25 Bayonne.
K: 9.8.1809. L: 15.3.1810. Comm: 16.8.1809. C: 26.8.1809.
Captured 15.3.1810 at or near Guadeloupe by the British.

Mouche No.26 Bayonne.
K: 17.8.1809. L: 29.8.1809. Comm: 16.9.1809.
Captured 8.1.1810 in the Atlantic by HMS *Indefatigable* (44), then wrecked 12.1.1810 on Mona Island near Puerto Rico.

Mouche No.27 Bayonne.
K: 14.9.1809. L: 20.10.1809. C: 11.1809. Comm: 1.4.1810.
Captured 12.1.1811 at the entrance to Port Napoléon (Port Louis, Île de France) by a British frigate flying the French flag.

Mouche No.28 Bayonne.
K: 19.9.1809. L: 11.1809. C: 11.1809. Comm: 1.4.1810.
Captured c11.1810 by the British near Île Bonaparte (Réunion) and recommissioned by them for the attack on Île de France.

Mouche No.29 Antoine Crucy, Nantes
Ord: 23.9.1809. K: 10.1809. L: 19.2.1810. C: 3.1810. Comm: 6.8.1811.
Refitted at Lorient 3-5.1815, departed for Île Bourbon 16.5.1815. Probably became the *Lys* that was in service at Île Bourbon in 6.1815, grounded in 1825 on Providence Atoll in the Indian Ocean, but remained in service at Bourbon in 10.1827. (This *Lys* was never on fleet lists.)

VEDETTA No.1 Class – schooner-avisos, 1 gun. Listed in French sources as identical to the *Mouche No.2* class above except that they were built at Venice and served in Napoleon's Italian (Venetian) Navy. They may be the four 'paranze cannoniere' named *Vedetta, Superiore, Fortelligente* (or *Sorvegliante*), and *Staffetta* listed in Italian sources. These sources also describe *Vedetta* as a schooner-rigged gunboat and *Staffetta* as a *mosca* (mouche). On 27 March 1813 *Superiore* distinguished herself in combat against British launches that made an incursion at Cortellazzo.

According to Austrian sources *Vedetta* was taken over by the Austrians at Trieste in 1813 and served primarily as a transport until ordered BU 6.10.1825, while *Superiora* (sic) was taken over in 1814 and BU in December 1827. The fate of the other two is unknown. An aviso-mouche named *Vedetta* with one 24pdr carronade and a crew of 29 men was reported in service at Venice in October 1813 and lost in April 1814 in the fall of the city; she might have been one of this class.

Vedetta No.1 Venice (Constructeur: Jean Tupinier)
    K: 8.1808. L: 4.10.1808. C: 11.1808. See notes above.

Vedetta No.2 Venice (Constructeur: Jean Tupinier)
    K: 9.1808. L: c15.11.1808. C: c12.1808. See notes above.

Vedetta No.3 Venice (Constructeur: Jean Tupinier)
    K: 1808. L: 1809. C: 1809. See notes above.

Vedetta No.4 Venice (Constructeur: Jean Tupinier)
    K: 1808. L: 1809. C: 1809. See notes above.

LEVRETTE Class – schooners, 10 guns. Designed by François Pestel (plans reviewed by Jacques-Noël Sané).
    Dimensions & tons: unknown. Men: 59-111.
    Guns: 10 x 8pdrs

Levrette Genoa (Constructeur: Jean-Baptiste Marestier)
    K: 2.1808. L: 26.7.1808. C: 10.1808.
    Hauled out at Toulon 1.1821, re-launched 11.4.1821. Wrecked 5.3.1823 on reefs of the Île d'Ayre near Port Mahon.

Biche Genoa (Constructeur: Jean-Baptiste Marestier)
    K: 2.1808. L: 8.1808. C: 10.1808.
    Built with timber from a warship begun at Genoa by the Ligurian government and dismantled on the ways. Decomm. 11.11.1817 at Toulon, condemned there 1.1828 and hulked. BU after 2.1830.

FENICE – schooner, 10 guns. The origins of this ship are obscure: she is said to have been the Russian brig *Feniks* (purchased 9.1809, q.v.) re-rigged as a schooner, although this seems unlikely and she might instead have been a sister to *Leoben* and/or *Aretusa*, below. An unidentified schooner named *Fenice* was reported to have been active in February 1811.
    Dimensions & tons: 83ft 1in x 20ft 7in x 9ft 10in (27.00 x 6.70 x 3.20m). 214 tons. Men: 59. French records show her at 90ft x 28ft 7in x 11ft 10in (29.26 x 9.30 x 3.85m) and 250/400 tons.
    Guns: (1814) 10 x 6pdrs; (1815) 8 x 10.5pdr carronades; (1821) 2 x 6pdrs.

Fenice Venice.
    K: 1808 or 1811. L: 26.3.1812 (?). Comm: 19.11.1813 (?).
    Participated in the defence of Venice 6.1813. Taken over by the Austrians 25.4.1814 in the occupation of the Venice Arsenal. Hauled out 13.11.1828 to be replaced by a new *Fenice*, a 27m schooner that was built with material from the brig *Ussaro* (ex *Mamelucco*) and launched 18.2.1829.

LEOBEN. – schooner, 10 guns. Designed by Andrea Salvini, built by Luigi Paresi. Served in Napoleon's Italian Navy. Called a *goletta-balaou* on a drawing.
    Dimensions & tons: 78ft 8in x 20ft 8in x 8ft 6in (25.56 x 6.72 x 2.76m). Draught 7ft 0in (2.27m). Men: 60
    Guns: 2 x 12pdrs No.2 (French) in the bow, 8 carronades on the sides. (10 ports)

Leoben Venice.
    K: 18.2.1809. L: 1810.
    In service in the Adriatic by 7.1810 (10 guns). Was sailing along the Albanian coast from Venice to Corfu with a cargo of ordnance stores when on 30.1.1811 HMS *Belle Poule*, *Leonidas*, *Victorious* and *Imogen* caught her. Her own crew set her on fire and she subsequently blew up. The French date of 5.3.1811 for her loss is probably incorrect.

ARETUSA. – schooner, 10 guns. Probably designed by Andrea Salvini, built by Luigi Paresi. Served in Napoleon's Italian Navy.
    Dimensions & tons: 80ft, 73ft x 21ft x 9ft 6in (25.98, 23.71 x 6.82 x 3.08m). 100/180 tons. Draught 11ft 6in (3.74m) aft. Men: 36.
    Guns: (design) 3 pivot guns (1 forward, 2 aft) and six small guns; (later) 8 x 12pdrs, 2 x 6pdrs; (1822) 10 x 6pdrs; (1838) 16 x 6pdrs, 4 x 12pdr carronades.

Aretusa Venice.
    K: 1810 (or 10.11.1811). L: 4.11.1811. C: 1812.
    Was out of commission in 1813, either inactive or incomplete. Taken over by the Austrians 25.4.1814 in the occupation of the Venice Arsenal, name became *Arethusa*. Major repair 1836-38, ordered BU and replaced by a new *Arethusa* 22.11.1842 and hauled out. The name *Arethusa* was eventually assigned to a new ship on 18.11.1849 (see *Gloria*, above).

PRINCIPESSA DI BOLOGNA. schooner. Taken by Napoleon's Italian Navy in the port of Lissa on 22 October 1810. Her origin is unknown.
    Dimensions & tons: 76ft 7in x 19ft 1in x 9ft 3in (24.90 x 6.20 x 3.00m). Men: 25
    Guns: 8 x 12pdr carronades, 2 x 6pdrs.

Principessa di Bologna
    Part of Dubordieu's squadron in the Battle of Lissa 13.3.1811, went to Spalato after the battle. Renamed *Aurora* c3.1811 to free the name for a frigate. Taken over by the Austrians 25.4.1814 in the occupation of the Venice Arsenal. Briefly on the sale list 1814, hauled out 1816, returned to service 1820. Again hauled out and repaired 1830-33. Ordered BU 22.4.1844, BU by 7.1844.

ROSE – schooner, 12 guns. Designed by Jacques-Noël Sané.
    Dimensions & tons: 79ft x 22ft 4in x 11ft 2in (25.66 x 7.26 x 3.62m). 80/150tons. Draught 3ft 10in/6ft 6in (1.24/2.12m). Men: 95.
    Guns: 2 x 6pdrs, 10 x 24pdr carronades

Rose Toulon Dyd. (Constructeur: Jean-Nicolas Guérin)
    K: 2.1810. L: 9.6.1810. C: 8.1810.
    Wrecked 1.4.1815 at Porto de Fero on the island of Chios in a squall.

ESTAFETTE Class – schooners, 7 guns. Designed by François-Frédéric Poncet.
    Dimensions & tons: 78ft, 62ft 6in x 19ft 8in x 9ft (25.33, 20.30 x 6.39 x 2.93m). 85/145 tons. Draught 5ft 4in/11ft 8in (1.73/3.79m). Men: 59-80.
    Guns: 1 x 8pdr pivot, 6 x 4pdrs.

Estafette Toulon Dyd.
    K: early 1810. L: 21.7.1810. C: 8.1810.
    Sunk to avoid capture 11.12.1813 at Agay near St-Raphaël while transporting a cargo of rifles from Toulon to Genoa with the gunboat *Air* (which was taken); soon refloated. Hauled out and repaired at Toulon 8-9.1826. Departed Toulon 7.2.1836 and disappeared on a voyage to Cayenne, struck 18.7.1836.

Momus Toulon Dyd. (Constructeur: Jean-Nicolas Guérin)
    K: 7.1810. L: 11.1810. Comm: 28.11.1810. C: 12.1810.
    Decomm. 17.7.1837 at Guadeloupe, struck end 1837. Sold or BU 1838.

Bacchante Mancini shipyard, Leghorn (Constructeur: Jean-Baptiste Marestier)

SMALL SAILING PATROL VESSELS

A large armed lugger of 10 or 12 guns at anchor, engraved by Baugean. Although such craft were popular with privateers, the headgear of the crew suggests a naval vessel. Note the sweeps (long oars) lashed to the quarters; these could be used in calms to close with a target or escape from a more powerful foe.

Ord: 16.4.1811 (contract). K: 5.1811. L: 21.3.1812. C: 5.12 at Leghorn, probably 11.1812 at Toulon. Comm: 1.1.1813 at Toulon. Loaned to Napoleon 4-5.1814 pending the arrival of *Inconstant*, returned to Toulon 7.6.1814 manned by that brig's crew. Decomm. 4.5.1824 at Île Bourbon, struck c10.1824.

Cabriole Leghorn (Constructeur: Jean-Baptiste Marestier)
K: c10.1813, not launched. Construction abandoned c3.1814 when 9/24ths complete upon the evacuation of Leghorn by the French.

LUTIN – schooner-aviso. Designed and/or built by Grisard on the order of General Decaen. Grisard's activities are described in the entry for the schooner *Gobe-Mouche*, above.
Characteristics unknown.

Lutin Île de France.
K: 1809/1810. L: c7.1810. C: 8.1810.
Captured 2.12.1810 by the British in the surrender of Île de France. She was probably inspired by *Mouche No.6* and *Mouche No.23* which called at the colony in late 1808 and early 1810. She was considered to be a fast vessel.

VIGILANT Class – luggers, 10-15 guns. Designed by Jacques-Noël Sané. On 23 December 1817 these two ships were ordered to be re-rigged as brigs, 'which was more suitable to their hulls'.
Dimensions & tons: 70ft 10in x 20ft 4in x 10ft 2in (23.01 x 6.61 x 3.30m). 156/200 tons. Draught 7ft 3in/8ft 3in (2.36/2.68m). Men: 46-98.
Guns: (*Vigilant*) 1 x 12pdr, 6 x 4pdrs, 8 x 12pdr carronades; (*Oiseleur*) 6 x 8pdrs, 4 x 12pdr carronades; (same 1819-26) 10 x 16pdr carronades.

Vigilant Lorient Dyd. (Constructeur: Paul Leroux)
Ord: 18.1.1810. Named: 3.1810. K: 2.1810 or 19.5.1810. L: 7.1810.
C: 8.1810.
Refitted with brig rig at Lorient 1-6.1818, became 150-ton transport at Lorient 1819. Last refitted at Rochefort 5.1824, decomm. 20.4.1826, condemned and struck 4.1826, and probably hulked as a receiving ship (*cayenne*).

Oiseleur Lorient Dyd.
Ord: 18.1.1810. K: 4.1810. Named: 23.7.1810. L: 30.10.1810. C: 12.1810.
Station ship at Lorient 1816. Refitted with brig rig at Lorient 4.1818. Decomm. 3.12.1823. Became service craft at Lorient 1.1827, unserviceable there 4.1834 and condemned 9.1834.

MESSAGER – schooner, 7 guns. Designed by Jacques-Nöel Sané.
Dimensions & tons: Unknown. Men: 47-87.
Guns: 1 x 8pdr amidships, 6 x 4pdrs.

Messager Brest Dyd. (Constructeur: Charles Simon or Mathieu Traon)
K: 2.1811. L: 8.6.1811. Comm: 14.8.1811. C: 8.1811.
Described as a transport 1811-12, a *corvette de pêche* 1813-17, and an aviso 1818-21. Decomm. 23.2.1821. Hulked 6.1821 at Martinique, BU there 6.1822.

TORCHE Class – schooners, 6 guns. Designed by Honoré-Louis Jobert.
Dimensions & tons: 77ft 11in oa, 75ft 10in wl, 64ft x 20ft 3in x 9ft 10in (25.3, 24.63, 20.8 x 6.58 x 3.20m). 100/200 tons. Draught 7ft 7in/11ft 10in (2.46/3.84m). Men: 59-61.
Guns: 6 x 4pdrs, 10 x 12pdr carronades

Torche Civita Vecchia (Constructeur: Honoré-Louis Jobert)
K: 10.1811. L: 6.9.1812. C: 1.1813. 10 x 12pdr carronades (1816-26).
Probably (re)comm. 1.1.1814 at Toulon. Decomm. 18.5.1836 at Toulon, struck there 1837.

Étincelle Civita Vecchia.
K: c1.1813. Not launched, was 9/24ths complete when the Neapolitans took Civita Vecchia on 14.3.1814.

SOTERNE – lugger or chasse-marée, 2 guns.
Dimensions & tons: Unknown. Men: 9.
Guns: 2 x 12pdr carronades.
Soterne (Sauterne) Arnaud Chaigneau, Bordeaux-Lormont (Constructeur: Antoine Bonnet-Lescure)
K: 6.1813. L: 8.1813. C: 9.1813. Cost of construction 5,700 francs.
Station ship at Bordeaux 1816. During the night of 22.6.1819 at Pauillac the transport *Élan* collided with this small vessel which sank almost immediately, the crew having just enough time to save themselves.

BRESTOISE – schooner, 4 guns. Designed by Jacques-Nöel Sané.
Dimensions & tons: 62ft 2in oa, 58ft 6in, 53ft 7in x 18ft 4in x 6ft 8in (20.20, 19.00, 17.4 x 5.96m x 2.17m). 70 tons disp. Draught 5ft 6in/6ft 9in (1.78/2.20m). Men: 36.
Guns: 4 x 8pdr carronades.
Brestoise Brest Dyd.
K: 1.1.1815. L: 12.3.1815. Comm: 27.4.1815. C: 4.1815.
Decomm. 1.1.1845. Struck 1.9.1845, probably at Saint-Pierre & Miquelon.

MIQUELONNAISE – schooner, 2-4 guns. Designed by Jacques-Nöel Sané.
Dimensions & tons: 55ft 9in oa, 52ft 4in, 47ft 9in x 16ft 4in x 6ft 0in (18.10 oa, 17.00, 15.5 x 5.31 x 1.95m). 50 tons disp. Draught 4ft 10in/6ft 0in (1.57/1.95m). Men: 36.
Guns: 2 or 4 small guns.
Miquelonnaise Brest Dyd. (Constructeur: Jean-Baptiste Marestier)
K: 1.1.1815. L: 12.3 1815. Comm: 27.4.1815.
Decomm. 12.11.1818 at Saint-Pierre & Miquelon, struck 1819.

CONSTANCE – sloop rigged as cutter. Rated 25-ton transport until 1824.
Dimensions & tons: Dimensions unknown. 40 tons. Men: 10 to 20.
Guns: (1824) 4.
Constance Le Havre.
K: 1815. L: 3.8.1815. C: 12.1815. Comm: 15.12.1815.
Used 1822 for fishery protection. Reclassed sloop-aviso 1824. Classed among the service craft 15.10.1836, struck (condemned) 19.11.1836 at Cherbourg or Brest. BU at Brest 8.1843.

Ex BRITISH NAVAL PRIZES (1803-1807)
Redbridge (Red-Bridge) (experimental schooner-gunboat HMS *Redbridge*, ex *Advice Boat No.2* 1796, built at Redbridge in 1796 by Hobbs to plans of Samuel Bentham, captured 4.8.1803 by a Toulon division.)
Dimensions & tons: 75ft 1in, 69ft 3in x 20ft 10in (24.38, 22.50 x 6.76m). 80/150 tons. Men: 107.
Guns: 12 x 16pdr (18pdr) carronades.
Comm. 5.8.1803. Decomm. at Leghorn 1813, sold there 1.1814. Also listed by the French as a corvette with 14 x 22pdr carronades (British 24pdrs?).
Cumberland (HMS *Cumberland*, schooner. Had been purchased by the Royal Navy at Port Jackson, Australia, in 1803, seized by the French at Île de France in 1804. May have been identical to *Casuarina*, which was also purchased in Australia in 11.1802.)
Dimensions & tons: Dimensions unknown. 30 tons burthen.

Captured by the British and returned to Royal Navy service, sold 1810.
Napoléon (HMS *Dominica*, previously a French schooner purchased by the British in 1805 and delivered 21.5.1806 at Guadeloupe by her mutinous crew and seized.).
Dimensions & tons: Dimensions unknown. 40/75 tons.
Guns: 1.
Recaptured 24.5.1806 by HMS *Wasp* (14) and again became HMS *Dominica*. Deleted and BU 1808.
Villaret (Captured 3.7.1806 by the Willaumez squadron, probably at or near Nevis). French accounts identify her as HMS *King Fish* and indicate that she had been ordered by Admiral Alexander Cochrane, commander of the Leeward Islands Station, as a *mouche* for his flagship. However British reports indicate that HMS *King Fish* (or *Flying Fish*), a *Ballahoo* class small schooner or aviso built in Bermuda in 1803-4, was captured either by prisoners on board in 9.1805 or by a French privateer in 1.1808, became the Guadeloupe-based privateer *Tropard*, and on 5.4.1808 was recaptured in the western Atlantic by HMS *Pheasant* (18). As this chronology is incompatible with that of the French vessel, below, the original identity of both Admiral Cochrane's *mouche* and the French *Villaret* is unresolved. The Bermuda schooners were similar in size to the French *mouches*, their British measurements being about 16.8m x 5.5m.
Dimensions & tons: 57ft 10in x 15ft 9in x 5ft 10in (18.78 x 5.12 x 1.89m). 38/70 tons. Draught 3ft 11in/6ft 11in (1.27/2.25m). Men: 35-38.
Guns: (1806) 1 x 6pdr, 2 x 12pdr carronades; (1807) 1 x 6pdr.
Named for the captain-general of Martinique, and used in the Antilles until departing for Bayonnne 7.1807. Renamed *Rapide* 4.11.1807 soon after arriving, then out of commission 11.11.1807 to 14.5.1808 while her lines were taken off by Jean Baudry for use in building a series of numbered *Mouches*. Renamed *Mouche No.1* on 16.5.1808 when the first six copies, *Nos.2-7*, were ordered. Sailed from Bayonne 21.5.1808 for Cayenne and Vera Cruz, captured 17.8.1808 near Barbados. Subsequent fate unknown.
Magpie (HMS *Magpie*, a *Cuckoo* class schooner with 4 x 12pdr carronades and 20 men, launched at Newcastle on 17.5.1806 on Bermudan plans, handed over 18.2.1807 to the French near Perros-Guirec, Brittany, because of a storm that threatened to sink her and seized).
Dimensions & tons: 57ft 6in, 54ft 2in x 17ft 3in x 7ft 4in (18.67, 17.60 x 5.60 x 2.38m). 50/95 tons. Draught 6ft 1in/8ft 9in (1.98/2.84m). Men: 78.
Guns: 6 x 4pdrs, 3 x 12pdr carronades, 2 x 12pdr obusiers; (1808) 12 x 12pdrs.
Comm. by the French 16.5.1807. Renamed *Colombe* 24.9.1814, *Magpie* 22.3.1815, and *Colombe* 15.7.1815. Decomm. 20.8.1815, recomm. 5.4.1816 for Senegal as an 80-ton transport. Reverted to schooner (6 x 12pdr carronades) 1823, service craft 1.1827, and BU 8.1828 at Rochefort.

Ex BRITISH MERCANTILE AND PRIVATEER PRIZES (1803-1810)
Georges (British mercantile cutter *George* of 125 tons, 40 men, and 12 guns, built c1781 and hired by the Royal Navy between 6.1798 and 11.1801, captured or seized c8.1803).
Dimensions & tons: Dimensions unknown. 87/130 tons.
Guns: 10 x 4pdrs.
Initially comm. 6.9.1803 by the French as *Transport No.714* (*Georges*), from 1806 listed as combatant vessel *Georges*. Unserviceable 9.1813 at Dunkirk, struck c1816.
Aurore (British cutter or sloop, probably mercantile, seized 15.8.1803 at

SMALL SAILING PATROL VESSELS

As neutral traders in a world at war, American shipowners had developed a breed of fast schooners that had a good chance of escaping the unwanted attention of belligerent navies. Later generically known as 'Baltimore clippers', they were a recognisable – and highly regarded – type. This Baugean engraving shows an American schooner at anchor drying her vast spread of canvas. A number of such vessels were captured or purchased for use by the French Navy.

Bayonne and comm. 22.8.1803).
  Dimensions & tons: 28ft 10in, 24ft 10in x 9ft 6in x 5ft 8in (9.37, 8.07 x 3.08 x 1.84m). 14/22 tons. Draught 2ft 6in/5ft 5in (0.81/1.75m). Men: 21.
  Guns: 1 x 6pdr carronade (deleted by 1805), 5 swivels.
  Briefly designated *Cotre No.3* in 1803. Decomm. at Saint-Brieuc or Brest 28.8.1812, struck c1819.
Mars (British mercantile cutter, grounded off Granville 23.11.1804 and refloated and captured by the French, 46-53 men, carried 8 x 3pdrs). Decomm. at Cherbourg 20.6.1823, unserviceable 12.1832 and struck.
Elisa (*Eliza*) (British privateer schooner *Eliza*, captured 20.1.1804 off Nice by the corvette *Fauvette* and immediately commissioned by the French at Villefranche, carried 12 x 9pdr and 6pdr carronades). Recaptured 8.2.1805 near Leghorn (Livorno) by two British privateers. Probably became the *Elisa* that was purchased by the French in 2.1807 and renamed *Sentinelle*, see under purchased vessels.
Santander (British lugger, probably mercantile, captured 10.1808, 23-46 men, carried 2 x 4pdrs, 4 x 6pdr carronades). Overhauled 1.1809 at Bayonne. Last mentioned 1811, struck 1811 or 1812.
Lion (British mercantile cutter *Lion* of 87 tons and 8 guns hired by the Royal Navy between 6.1804 and 8.1805, captured 15.5.1808 (?) off the Sables d'Olonne by French *péniches*, 50/90 tons, carried 8 x 12pdr carronades). Sold c1809.
Idas (British mercantile cutter *Idas* of 102 tons and 10 guns built in 1808 and hired by the Royal Navy in 4.1809 for the Scheldt expedition, grounded in the mouth of the Scheldt 3.6.1810, refloated and commissioned by the French the next day).
  Dimensions & tons: 58ft 8in x 19ft 8in x 9ft 0in (19.06 x 6.40 x 2.92m). 110/180 tons. Draught 5ft 0in/10ft 4in (1.62/3.36m).
  Guns: 12 x 9pdrs (14 ports).

Ceded to the Netherlands at Antwerp 8.1814, unserviceable 3.1815.

Ex PORTUGUESE PRIZE (1807)
Curiosa (Portuguese schooner, probably mercantile, built before 1799, 43 men, captured late 1807-early 1808, carried 10 or 12 guns). Reportedly recomm. by French Navy, fate unknown.

Ex AMERICAN PRIZES (1808-1810)
Fama (American schooner *Fame*, built at Boston in 1804, seized in the Marseille roadstead by the tartane *Provençale* on 20.1.1808 or possibly 6.7.1808).
  Dimensions & tons: 63ft 0in x 18ft 5in x 6ft 5in (20.46 x 6.01 x 2.11m). 50/80 tons. Draught 2ft 0in/8ft 2in (0.66/2.60m). Men: 56.
  Guns: 8 x 4pdrs.
  Run ashore near Bastia 26.4.1811 to avoid capture, recovered intact the next day. Placed on sale at Toulon 1815, sold 1816.
Élizabeth (American schooner *Elizabeth* from Baltimore, built in 1809, confiscated at Trieste in 1810).
  Dimensions & tons: 81ft 0in x 20ft 0in x 9ft 0in (26.31 x 6.50 x 2.92m). 155/220 tons. Draught 5ft 2in/11ft 3in (1.67/3.65m).
  Guns: 1 x 12pdr, 4 x 4pdrs.
  Used as yacht or coast defence vessel. Decomm. at Trieste 12.1812, taken there by the Austrians 8.11.1813.
Postillon (American schooner *Post Boy* from Baltimore or Philadelphia, seized on 11.10.1810 at Bayonne).
  Dimensions & tons: 80ft 0in x 22ft 0in x 9ft 6in (26.0 x 7.15 x 3.1m). 143 tons burthen. Men: 23.
  Guns: many espingoles.
  Renamed *Balaou No.1* in 12.1810. Captured 17.3.1811 in the Atlantic by two British frigates two days after leaving Bayonne for

Batavia.

Faune (American schooner *Fawn*, seized 11.10.1810 at Bayonne).
Dimensions & tons: 77ft 0in, 61ft 7in x 20ft 0in (25.0, 20.0 x 6.50m). 119 tons burthen. Men: 44.
Guns: (1812) 2 x 4pdrs, 2 x 9pdr carronades.
Renamed *Balaou No.2* in 12.1810. On 12.5.1813 her commander deserted in her with 11 of her crew to raid commerce in Louisiana, fate unknown.

Léger (American schooner *Hawk* from Baltimore or Philadelphia, seized on 11.10.1810 at Bayonne).
Dimensions & tons: 77ft 7in, 62ft 2in x 20ft 1in x 8ft 4in (25.20, 20.2 x 6.53 x 2.71m). 83/210 tons. Men: 35-40.
Guns: 4 x 4pdrs.
Renamed *Balaou No.3* in 12.1810. Renamed *Lévrier* 10.1816 for colonial service, made a hydrographic voyage from Cayenne to the Para River (Brazil) in 1819-20. Condemned at Martinique 8.1821, BU 6.1822.

Moustique (American schooner *Trim* or *Trimmer* from Baltimore seized on 11.10.1810 at Bayonne, 143 tons, 53 men, carried 6 x 6pdrs, 4 x 4pdrs). Renamed *Balaou No.4* in 1.1811. Wrecked on 16.11.1811 when, returning from Batavia, her cables parting one hour after her arrival at San Sebastian, Spain.

Sans-Façon (American schooner *Exchange* from Baltimore seized on 11.10.1810 at Bayonne, 163 tons, 28 men, carried 2 x 6pdrs, 10 swivels) Renamed *Balaou No.5* in 1.1811 and comm. 15.2.1811. Seized by the Americans at Philadelphia 7.1811, released 5.1812. Burned 15.3.1814 at La Teste de Buch near Bordeaux to avoid capture.

Gabier (American schooner *Prosper* from New York seized on 11.10.1810 at Bayonne, 184 tons, 25 men, carried 6 x 6pdrs, 4 x 4pdrs). Renamed *Balaou No.6* in 1.1811. Captured 20.10.1813 near La Teste de Buch near Bordeaux by HMS *Andromache* (38).

Rapide (American three-masted schooner *Hawk* from Philadelphia seized on 11.10.1810 at Bayonne, 415 tons, carried 4 x 4pdrs). Renamed *Balaou No.7* in 1.1811. Inscribed on the fleet list but not commissioned by the French. Placed on sale 6.1813 at Bayonne, finally sold 30.7.1814.

Lama (American schooner *Eleanor* seized on 11.10.1810 at Bayonne, 34 men). Renamed *Balaou No.8* in 1.1811. Unserviceable 2.1814 at Bayonne and BU.

PURCHASED AND REQUISITIONED LUGGERS AND CHASSE-MARÉES (1802-1803)

Deux Amis or *Lougre No.9* (mercantile lugger or chasse-marée acquired 12.1802 and comm. at Bayonne 22.8.1803, 40 tons, 78 men, carried 4 x 4pdrs, 10 espingoles). Refitted 5.1806 at Brest as fireship. Renamed *Dauphin* 1.1809 and refitted as a *lougre garde-côte* (coastal escort). Decomm. at Brest 5.4.1814, struck between mid-1818 and 10.1819.

Passe-Partout (mercantile and privateer chasse-marée hired 11.1803 at Île de France and comm. 8.11.1803, 36 men, 2 guns). Captured 14.1.1804 off Goa by boats from HMS *San Fiorenzo* (40).

Ami National (mercantile lugger or chasse-marée hired 12.1803, 70 tons, 48 men, carried 6 x 6pdrs, 2 x 12pdr obusiers). Purchased 3.1807 by the navy and renamed *Alouette*. Wrecked 10.9.1807 in fog near Étel while going from Brest to Nantes.

Pont d'Arcole (mercantile lugger or chasse-marée comm. at Nantes 5.1803, then purchased 9.1803, 38-61 men, carried 2 x 8pdrs, 4 x 6pdrs, 4 x 1pdr swivels). In bad condition at Lorient 10.1815 and sold c1816.

Lougre No.1, later *Rapace* (mercantile lugger purchased 8.1803 at Bayonne from Dufourq & Cie., 88 men, carried 1 x 12pdr, 6 x 4pdrs). Wrecked 26.1.1804 on the Sables d'Olonne in a squall, refloated and repaired 8-9.1804. Renamed *Rapace* 8.1804. Decomm. 10.8.1815, recomm. 27.5.1823, decomm. 9.12.1823. Became service craft at Rochefort in 1.1827, fate unknown.

Lougre No.2, later *Uranie* (mercantile lugger acquired 8.1803 at Bayonne, 40/90 tons, 88 men, carried 4 x 6pdrs, 10 espingoles). Renamed *Uranie* 1805. Converted to transport at Brest 1.1815. Wrecked and sunk 2.3.1816 at the entrance to Perros-Guirec.

Lougre No.3, later *Chasseur* (mercantile lugger purchased 8.1803 at Bayonne, 35-41 men, carried 6 x 12pdr carronades). Renamed *Chasseur* 1805. Decomm. 20.7.1821, rated as service craft 1821-23, recomm. 20.3.1823. Decomm. 1.9.1829, unserviceable 1833 at Toulon, struck 1834.

Marie-Joseph (*Marie-Josephe*) or *Lougre No.6* (mercantile lugger acquired 8.1803 at Bayonne, 40/70 tons, 68 men, carried 4 x 4pdrs, 10 espingoles). Renamed *Requin* 9.1808 as a coast defence vessel (*garde-côtes*), then as coastal transport. Reclassified transport 1819. Struck 1822, probably at Brest.

Ami de Lorient (mercantile (?) lugger or chasse-marée built at Nantes, may have been purchased from the merchant marine in 9.1803).
K: 7.1803, L: 8.1803, C: 9.1803.
Dimensions & tons: 45ft 3in x 14ft x 6ft (14.70 x 4.55 x 1.95m). 40/70 tons. Men: 53.
Guns: 4 x 4pdrs, 2 x 12pdr obusiers; (1807) 4 swivels.
Renamed *Bellislois* (*Bellilois*) 1806. Refitted 9-10.1807 as combatant at Lorient and renamed *Alerte* 10.1807, probably because there was another *Bellislois* on the list. Became service craft at Rochefort 12.1815, fate unknown.

Lodi (*Lody*) (mercantile lugger or chasse-marée laid down at Lorient or Nantes 8.1803, launched and purchased from the merchant marine 9.1803, 47-66 men, carried 6 x 6pdrs, 2 x 12pdr obusiers, 6 swivels). Was in bad condition at Lorient 10.1815, sold and struck.

PURCHASED AND REQUISITIONED CUTTERS (1803-1812)

Amitié (mercantile cutter purchased 3.1803 at Santo Domingo from the American Nathan Haley for the service of the colony). Captured at Santo Domingo 14.10.1803 by HMS *Racoon* (18).

Mars (mercantile cutter comm. 4.1803 at Le Havre, 39 men, 8 guns). Decomm. at Antwerp 7.11.1805, last mentioned 1807.

Jeune Sophie (mercantile cutter comm. 11.1803 at Honfleur, 54 or 83 tons, carried 2 x 4pdrs, 4 x 12pdr carronades). Decomm. at Caen 25.12.1804, struck 1805 or 1806.

Strela (18-gun cutter built for the Russian Navy at Kronshtadt by V. D. Vlasov, launched 1804, sold by Russia to France at Venice 27.9.1809). Had sailed from Kronshtadt to Corfu 1806 and joined the squadron of Adm. D. N. Senyavin, operated in Adriatic until arriving at Venice 20.1.1808. Not comm. by either the French or the Italian Navy. Left to the Austrians at Venice 4.1814, sold 8.1814.

Principe Achille or *Achille* (Auxiliary cutter, probably ex-mercantile, in the Neapolitan Navy of Murat comm. 4.1810, 80 men, 8 guns). Last mentioned 5.1810 as being in combat near the island of Ischia.

Courrier (mercantile cutter comm. 1.2.1811 at Hamburg, 40 men, carried 12 x 8pdrs and 2pdrs). Decomm. at Hamburg 16.3.1813.

Frédéric (mercantile cutter comm. 1.2.1812 at Hamburg, 27 men, carried 12 x 6pdrs, 4pdrs, or 2pdrs). Decomm. 9.5.1813, probably in a Baltic port.

Gustave (Hamburg merchant cutter *Gustav*, built in 1805 and comm. 1.2.1812 at Hamburg, 160 tons, 17 men, carried 12 x 6pdrs and 4pdrs). Decomm. at Hamburg 9.3.1813, resumed merchant service 1814.

PURCHASED AND REQUISITIONED SCHOONERS (1802-1814)

Victoire (vessel acquired 6.1802 and in service in the Ponant 7.1802, may have been a former 50-ton decked lighter (*gabarre pontée*) from Brest re-rigged as a schooner or a schooner that arrived in a French Atlantic port from French Guiana in 1802, 40 tons, carried 12 x 4pdrs). Commissioned 6.10.1809 at Rochefort as a hydrographic schooner. Station ship at Pauillac in 11.1813. Off the list by 4.1814.

Abeille (probable mercantile schooner built at Le Havre c1799-1800, comm. at Cherbourg 30.7.1802, 75-100 tons, 47 men, carried 6 x 4pdrs, 2 x 36pdr obusiers). Station ship at Saint-Malo 17.6.1803. Decomm. there 10.8.1815, condemned 22.12.1815, sold there 13.2.1816.

Estelle (schooner that was in service 11.1802, 60-100 tons, 43 men, carried 10 x 3pdrs). Sold at Le Havre 1.1815 but not decomm. there until 20.12.1815.

Casuarina (Australian 30-ton mercantile schooner, built of casuarina wood at Port Jackson or Sidney in 1800-2 and purchased 11.11.1802 in Australia as an exploration ship without armament, 30 tons, measured 9.42m on keel). Possibly a sister of *Cumberland* (see prizes). Decomm. 12.1803 at Île de France.

Téméraire (American-built mercantile schooner purchased 9.1803 at Cap-Français, Santo Domingo, 66 men, carried 4 x 4pdrs, 2 x 36pdr obusiers). Placed on sale at Lorient 10.1815, sold 1817.

Océan (mercantile schooner purchased and in service at Santo Domingo c1803).
  Dimensions & tons: 71ft, 55ft x 18ft (23.06, 17.86 x 5.85m). 80/150 tons. Draught 8ft 3in (2.68m).
  Arrived at Vigo from New York 3.1804, sold at Vigo 8.1804.

Musette (mercantile schooner-aviso purchased c1803 at Senegal by the governor of French Guiana, Victor Hughes; carried 6 x 4pdrs). Probably captured 1.1809 by the Portuguese at the surrender of French Guiana.

Département du Nord (mercantile schooner purchased c1803 at Santo Domingo and in service there 1.1804, carried 1 x 12pdr). Last mentioned on the fleet lists in 1807, may have been the 7-gun schooner sunk 9.4.1805 by HMS *Gracieuse* (12).

Mousquito or *Musquito* (mercantile schooner probably purchased at Cap Français at Santo Domingo and in operation on 1.1.1804, carried 8 guns according to the British). Captured 23.8.1807 in the Antilles by HMS *Lark* (18) and *Ferret* (18).

Vertu (mercantile schooner comm. c5.1803 at Santo Domingo, 2 guns). Captured 7.6.1803 off Santo Domingo by HMS *Racoon* (18).

Deux Amis (mercantile schooner comm. c7.1803 in the Antilles, 3 guns). Captured 8.1803 off Cuba by HMS *Racoon* (18).

Amitié (mercantile schooner purchased at Santo Domingo and in service by 11.1804, carried 1 x 16pdr — or 14 guns according to the British). Captured 10.6.1805 in the Antilles by HMS *Blanche* (36), not struck from the fleet lists until 1807.

Trimeuse (American-built mercantile schooner purchased at Pointe-à-Pitre, Guadeloupe, in 4.1805).
  Dimensions & tons: 63ft x 16ft 8in x 6ft (20.46 x 5.42 x 1.95m). 67/110 tons. Draught 7ft/10ft (2.27/3.25m). Men: 35.
  Guns: 1 x 6pdr, 2 x 9pdr carronades.
  Captured 12.3.1807 in Antilles by HMS *Wolverine* (18).

Impérial (*Impériale*) (mercantile schooner-aviso comm. in Guadeloupe 23.9.1805, 3 guns). Captured 24.5.1806 off Dominica by HMS *Cygnet* (18), became HMS *Vigilant* and later (11.1806) HMS *Subtle*. Wrecked at Bermuda 10.1807.

Perle (mercantile schooner *Jalouse* of St. Pierre de la Martinique requisitioned c3.1805 to serve as a coast defence vessel in Martinique, 75 men and 4 guns as privateer). Last mentioned 6.1805, probably became the privateer *Jalouse* that was captured 23.8.1808 in the Antilles by HMS *Belette* (18).

Aurore (probable mercantile schooner or cutter, perhaps a former *corvette de pêche*, that was in service in 1806 and comm. at Brest 20.5.1807; 21-71 men, carried 5 x 1pdrs). Renamed *Vedette* late 1808 (then carried 2 x 4pdrs, 8 x 12pdr carronades, 6 x 1pdr espingoles). Decomm. 31.5.1814 at Lorient, sold there 8.1817.

Dauphin (mercantile schooner *Deux Amis* comm. in the Antilles in early 1807, 3 guns). Captured 14.2.1807 off Santo Domingo by HMS *Bacchante* (20), used by the British under her French name 2.1807 to clear out a nest of pirates in Samana Bay, Santo Domingo.

Sentinelle (British privateer schooner *Elisa* taken 3.10.1806 by 12 French and Neapolitan prisoners on board, then purchased by the Imperial Navy on 16.2.1807, 112/200 tons, 33 men, carried 10 x 4pdrs). Station ship at Genoa 1808. Burned 22.8.1810 after combat with the frigate HMS *Seahorse* to avoid capture. Was probably previously the *Eliza* or *Elisa* under prizes.

À Propos (mercantile schooner purchased at Île de France in 7.1807 and comm. 31.7.1807, 120/200 tons, 70 men, carried 4 x 12pdr carronades). Run ashore 13.3.1808 at Viveiro, Spain, to avoid capture and burned there by HMS *Emerald* (36).

Éclair (mercantile schooner *Nostra Señora del Carmina*, built in North America in 1802 and purchased 9.1808 at Leghorn).
  Dimensions & tons: 68ft x 21ft 8in x 9ft 4in (22.09 x 7.04 x 3.03m). 146/250 tons. Men: 93.
  Guns: 14 x 6pdr carronades.
  Sold at Leghorn 2.1814.

Goéland (privateer schooner *Prince d'Essling* launched at Toulon in 4.1811 and purchased and renamed 25.4.1811, 53 men, carried 4 x 6pdrs, 4 x 12pdr carronades). Decomm. at Martinique 20.1.1819 and condemned, BU c2.1819.

Poméranienne (schooner, origin unknown, acquired c3.1812 and comm. at Hamburg 1.4.1812, 34 men, carried 1 x 18pdr, 2 x 12pdr). Was in service in the Baltic in 1.1813. Decomm. 16.3.1813, then struck.

Étoile (mercantile schooner purchased at Leghorn by Napoleon c12.1814 and comm. by him in his Elban Navy on 1.1.1815, 80/150 tons, 43-66 men, carried 6 x 4pdrs). Taken over by the French Navy after Napoleon's return to France in 1815. Decomm. at Toulon 13.6.1845, condemned and struck there 9.11.1848, BU there 1-2.1849.

(D) Vessels acquired from 26 June 1815

ASTROLABE Class – hydrographic schooners, 4 guns. Designed by Pierre Rolland with changes by Jacques-Nöel Sané. They were later called *goélettes-mouches*.
  Dimensions & tons: 17.98m oa, 17.54m wl x 5.20m x 2.27m. 50 tons disp. Draught 1.64m mean. Men: 14 (*Astrolabe*) and 33 (both 1822).
  Guns: 4 x 12pdr carronades; (*Recherche*) 4 x 8pdr carronades.

Astrolabe Brest Dyd. (Constructeur: Charles-Léger Desmarest)
  Ord: 9.1.1816. K: 26.1.1816. L: 30.3.1816. Comm: 1.5.1816. C: 5.1816.
  Used by Beautemps-Beaupré from 1816 to survey the Gulf of Gascony. On blockade duty 1823 during the war with Spain. Decomm. 11.9.1826, struck 1827 at Brest.

Recherche Brest Dyd. (Constructeur: Charles-Léger Desmarest)
  Ord: 9.1.1816. K: 1.1816. L: 30.3.1816. Comm: 1.5.1816. C: 5.1816.
  Surveyed the region around Brest in 1816-18 and the Breton and

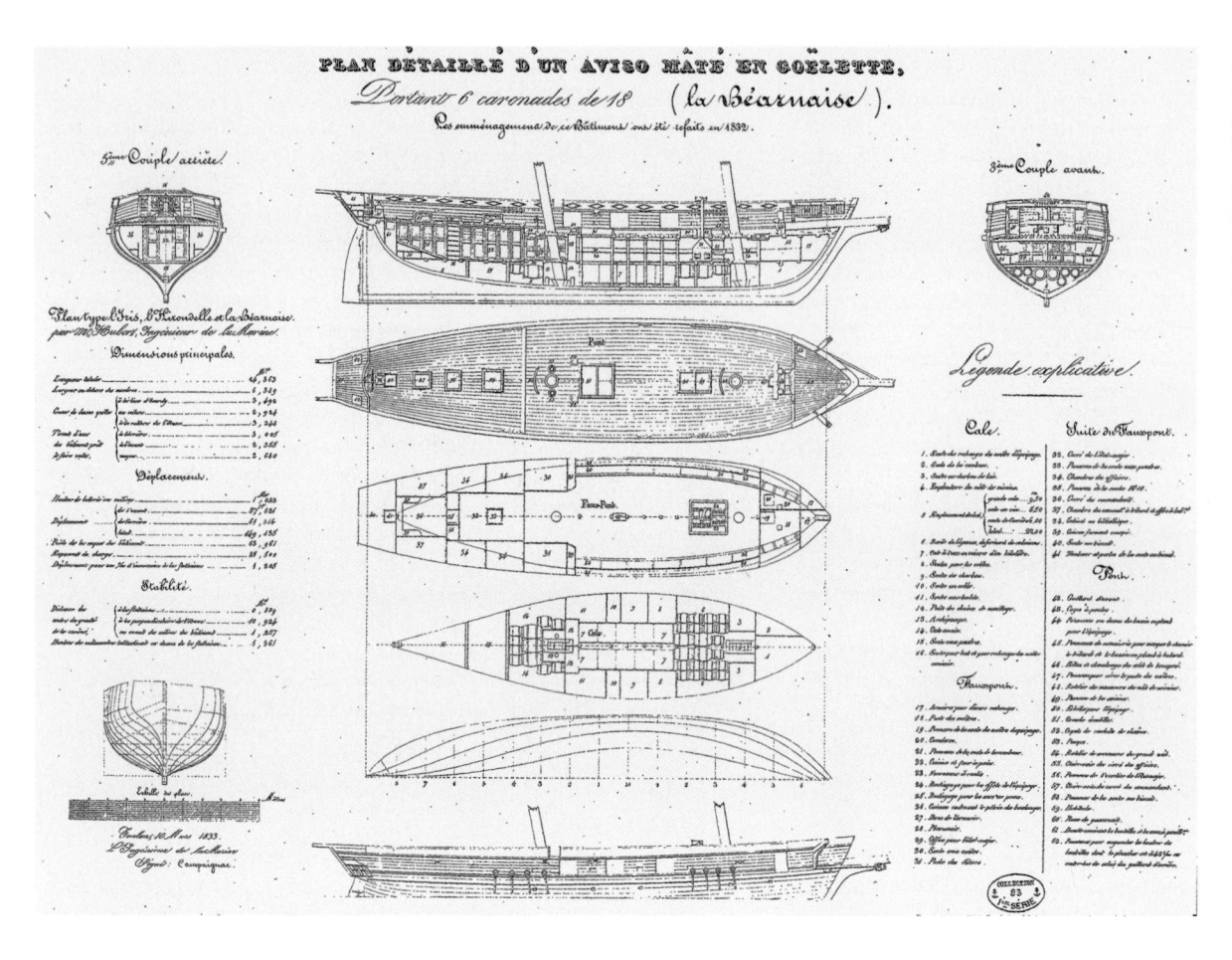

The internal arrangements for the 6-gun schooners of the *Iris* class (specifically *Béarnaise*), as established in 1832, dated Toulon 10 March 1833. A separate sail plan shows square topsails and topgallants on both fore and main masts. (Atlas du Génie Maritime, French collection, plate 26)

French Biscay coasts in 1819-22. After blockade duty in 1823 during the war with Spain, surveyed the region of Île d'Aix and Landes 1824-26. Decomm. 17.5.1826, struck 1827 at Brest.

SAUTERELLE Class – schooners, 6 guns. *Sauterelle* designed by Jean-Baptiste Lefebvre. *Amarante* is believed to have been similar to *Sauterelle* although they may not have been exact sisters.

Dimensions & tons: 29.4m oa, 24.36m wl x 6.39m ext x 2.92m. 110 tons disp. Draught 2.28/2.92m. Men: 50
Guns: 6 x 24pdr carronades

Sauterelle Brest Dyd. (Constructeur: Lefebvre)
Ord: 3.9.1816. K: 12.1816, L: 28.7.1817. Comm: 2.8.1817. C: 8.1817.
Wrecked 15.3.1819 at the mouth of the Corentin River near Dutch Guiana.

Amarante (*Amaranthe*) Lorient Dyd.
Ord: 3.9.1816. K: 5.1817. L: 25.8.1817. Comm: 20.3.1818. C: 3.1818.
Struck 1.6.1833.

IRIS Class – schooners, 6 guns. This class was designed by Jean-Baptiste Hubert. Its designed height of battery was 1.05m at 2.77m mean draught. On 24 October 1835 the Director of Ports reported that among the 6-gun schooners there were few that would last much longer. Vessels of this type were perfectly suited for local service in the colonies and it was necessary to plan for replacements. He proposed building four 6-gun schooners along with four 4-gun avisos (the *Biche* class, below), also for colonial service. Two of each type were to be built at Saint-Servan and two at Lorient. On 25 November 1835 he recommended approving the plans of Pierre Rolland for the 6-gun schooners, which were to be copies of the *Iris* type of which the Ministry had had nothing but good reports. The schooners were named *Daphné* (name reused), *Levrette*, *Fine*, and *Doris*. On 19 March 1842 the Director of Ports reported that the Governor of Martinique needed to replace the schooners *Toulonnaise* and *Antilope* and that the navy generally needed more schooners. He recommended building four new 6-gun schooners similar to *Toulonnaise*, two at Brest and two at Toulon. They became *Estafette*, *Gazelle*, *Hirondelle* (name reused), and *Topaze*.

Dimensions & tons: 25.18m, 24.68m wl, 22.80m x 6.39m, 6.41m ext x 2.92m. 157 tons disp. Draught 2.00/3.30m. Men: 61.
Guns: (1st 6 units) 6 x 24pdr carronades; (others) 6 x 18pdr carronades.

Iris Rochefort Dyd. (Constructeur: Hubert)
K: 7.1817. L: 6.4.1818. Comm: 21.4.1818.
Struck 14.11.1844, service craft at Toulon. BU before 1865.

Béarnaise Bayonne (Constructeurs: Jean Delamorinière, later Gabriel Nosereau)
K: 7.1819. L: 17.5.1820. Comm: 1.8.1820. C: 9.1820.
Completed by Hubert at Rochefort 10.1820. Decomm. at Martinique 1.3.1837, having been condemned as worn out.

Hirondelle Bayonne (Constructeurs: Jean Delamorinière, later Gabriel Nosereau)
K: 7.1819. L: 31.5.1820. Comm: 1.8.1820. C: 9.1820.
Completed by J.-B. Hubert at Rochefort 10.1820. Condemned at Rochefort 4.1837, BU 7.1837.

Lyonnaise Bayonne (Constructeur: Gabriel Nosereau)
K: 17.9.1820. L: 31.5.1821. Comm: 6.6.1821. C: 8.1821.
Boys' school ship at Brest 1832. Struck 21.3.1838 at Brest, BU 3-4.1838.

SMALL SAILING PATROL VESSELS

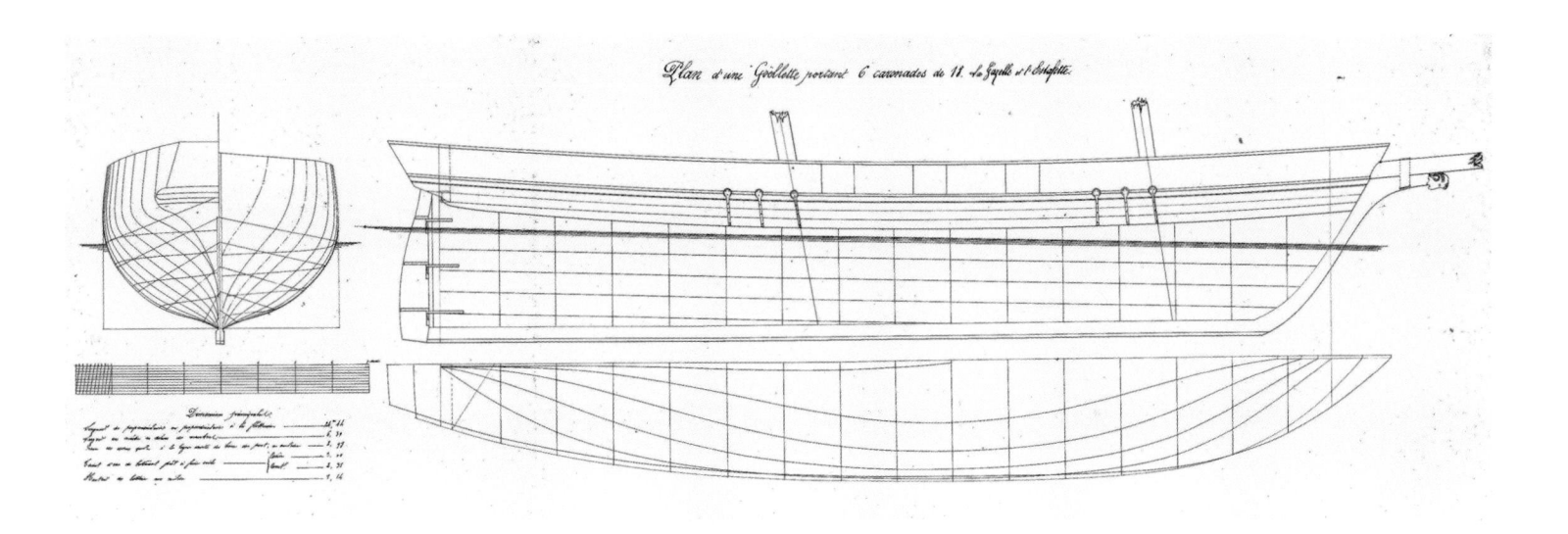

Lines plan for the last two 6-gun schooners of the *Iris* class, *Gazelle* and *Estafette* of 1842. Compared with the earlier ships, the hull is much plainer and does not carry the false quarter galleries but has a plain transom. The height of the barricades has been reduced and there are fewer shrouds. (Atlas du Génie Maritime, Genoa collection, image 1-0009)

Provençale Bayonne (Constructeur: Gabriel Nosereau)
K: 9.1820. L: 14.6.1821. Comm: 23.6.1821. C: 9.1821.
Struck 6.1827 at Rochefort, BU 3.1828.

Philomèle Bayonne (Constructeur: Gabriel Nosereau)
K: 2.1822. L: 2.8.1822. Comm: 13.11.1822. C: 12.1822.
Struck 31.12.1834 at Brest. BU 2.1836.

Gloriole Bayonne (Constructeur: Gabriel Nosereau)
K: 2.1822. L: 2.8.1822. Comm: 1822. C: 1.1823.
Wrecked 12.7.1823 on the coast of Portugal.

Dauphinoise Bayonne (Constructeur: Gabriel Nosereau)
K: 2.1823. L: 25.6.1823. Comm: 17.7.1823. C: 8.1823.
Decomm. 11.12.1837 at Toulon and struck 1837. Probably BU 1851.

Artésienne Bayonne (Constructeur: Gabriel Nosereau)
K: 2.1823. L: 25.6.1823. Comm: 27.7.1823. C: 9.1823.
Struck 1836 at Toulon.

Toulonnaise Toulon Dyd. (Constructeurs: Jacques-Louis Bonard and others)
K: 5.1823. L: 4.1823. Comm: 16.8.1823. C: 9.1823.
Struck 18.12.1843 at Martinique.

Mésange Toulon Dyd. (Constructeurs: Jacques-Louis Bonard and others)
K: 4.1823. L: 24.7.1823. Comm: 25.7.1823. C: 8.1823.
Struck 17.7.1851 at Brest.

Fauvette Bayonne (Constructeur: Gabriel Nosereau)
K: 9.1823. L: 13.3.1824. Comm: 19.4.1824. C: 4.1824.
Struck 1836 at Toulon.

Turquoise Bayonne (Constructeur: Gabriel Nosereau)
K: 9.1823. L: 16.3.1824. Comm: 19.4.1824. C: 4.1824.
Lost with all hands 11.2.1829 near Île Bourbon in a cyclone.

Daphné (1) Lorient Dyd.
K: 3.1824. L: 9.8.1824. Comm: 6.12.1824. C: 12.1824.
Struck 1833 at Toulon (or at Oran?).

Daphné (2) Lorient Dyd.
K: 15.12.1835. L: 17.3.1836. Comm: 9.4.1836. C: 4.1836.
Struck 6.2.1843, barracks hulk at Lorient. BU 1866.

Levrette Lorient Dyd.
Ord: 23.12.1835. Named: 30.1.1836. K: 1.1836. L: 21.3.1836. Comm: 22.4.1836. C: 5.1836.
Wrecked 14.1.1846 off La Guaira, New Granada (Venezuela).

Fine Saint-Servan (Constructeur: Joseph Daviel)
K: 3.1836. L: 26.8.1836. Comm: 5.9.1836. C: 9.1836.
Struck 6.3.1850 at Cherbourg.

Doris Saint-Servan (Constructeur: Joseph Daviel)
K: 3.1836. L: 26.8.1836. C: 11.1836 and 6.6.1837. Comm: 6.6.1837.
Capsized and sank 14.9.1845 when hit by a squall while mooring in Brest harbour after a three-year cruise. Refloated, taken into Brest, and struck 1846.

Estafette Brest Dyd.
K: 4.4.1842. L: 23.7.1842. Comm: 1.8.1842. C: 8.1842.
Struck 18.7.1856, hulk. Storage hulk for fishery protection vessels at Brest 1864. Renamed *Mollusque* 1.1.1868. BU 1871-72.

Gazelle Brest Dyd.
K: 1.4.1842. L: 31.10.1842. Comm: 26.1.1843. C: 2.1843.
Struck 24.9.1855 at Brest, hulk. Renamed *Toulinguet* c1859. Storage hulk for fishery protection vessels at Brest 1865. BU 1875.

Hirondelle Toulon Dyd.
K: 10.1842. L: 9.9.1843. C: 2.1844. Comm: 22.8.1845.
Struck 20.4.1857 but restored to list 21.10.1857 effective 11.9.1857 and recomm. 21.9.1857 for local service at Guadeloupe. Struck 26.10.1865.

Topaze Toulon Dyd.
K: 4.1843. L: 29.6.1844. C: 1845.
Struck 20.4.1857, sold or BU before 1865. This schooner seems never to have been commissioned.

AUTRUCHE – schooner, 8 guns. Designed by Gabriel Nosereau following specifications of C. V. Lecoupé dated 16.2.1820. She appeared on annual navy lists between 1826 and 1829, during which time she served in Senegal; previously she was probably on colonial accounts. Her name means Ostrich.

Dimensions & tons: 29.00m oa, 25.98m wl, 22.60m x 7.80m x 2.92m. 266 tons disp. Draught 2.60/2.60m. Men: 34
Guns: 6 x 18pdr carronades, 2 x 4pdrs

Autruche Bayonne (Constructeur: Nosereau)
K: 10.1821. L: 24.4.1822. Comm: 1.5.1822. C: 5.1822.
Arrived in Senegal 1.7.1822 for service on the Senegal River, on fleet lists there 1825, off the list and to colonial accounts 1830.

Lines plan for the 6-gun cutters *Furet* and *Rôdeur* designed to protect the oyster fisheries. (Atlas du Génie Maritime, Genoa collection, image 1-0008)

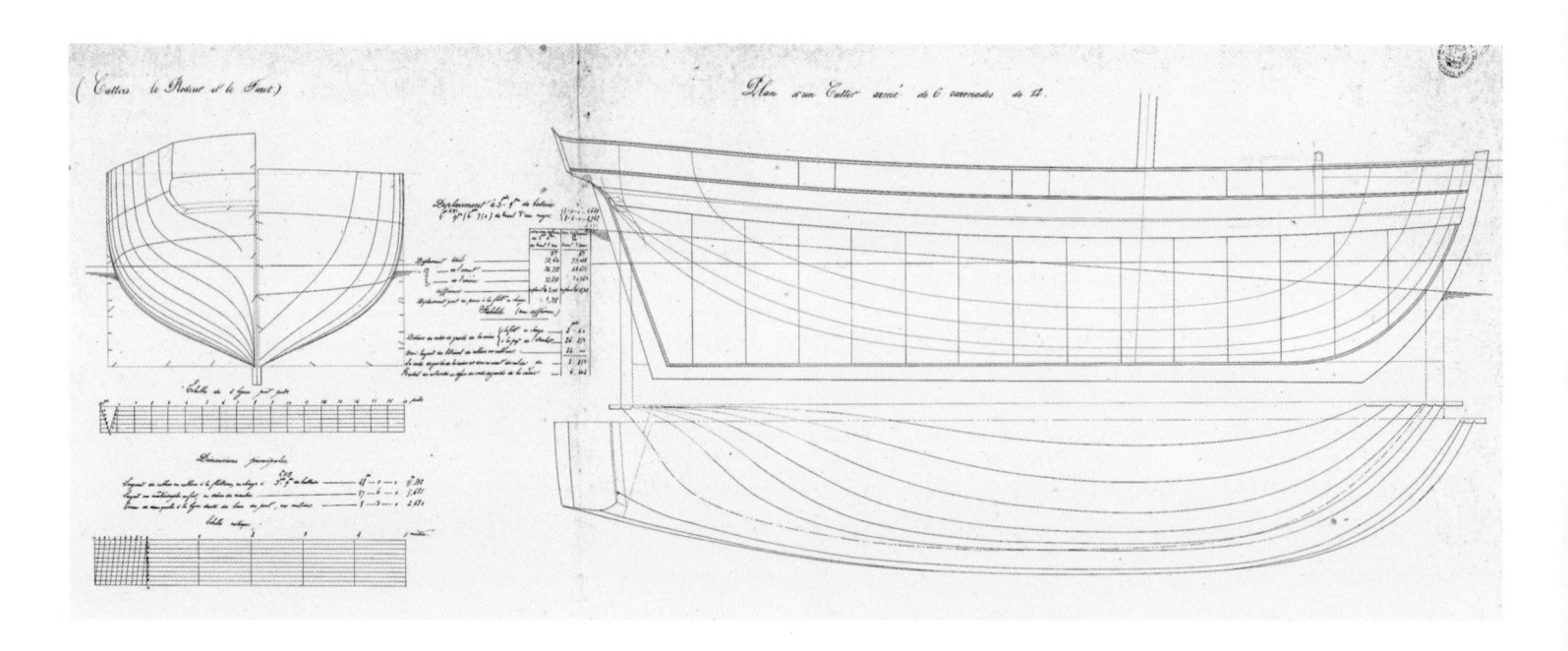

Recomm. 1.4.1830 as station ship at the bar of the river, condemned 8.1832 as unsafe and decomm. 1.9.1832 at Saint-Louis, Senegal.

TURBOT – sloop, 4 guns. Rated as a 60-ton transport until 1824. Also described as cutter.
Dimensions & tons: unknown. Men: 30.
Guns: 4
Turbot Cherbourg Dyd.
K: 4.9.1821. L: 6.7.1822. Comm: 4.9.1823. C: 9.1823.
Struck 1835 at Cherbourg.

FURET Class – cutters, 6 guns. Designed by Louis Bretocq. She was ordered for the protection of oyster fisheries.
Dimensions & tons: 18.00m oa, 15.59m wl, 13.73m x 5.69m x 2.68m. 73 tons disp. Draught 1.78/2.64m. Men: 31
Guns: 6 x 12pdr carronades
Furet Cherbourg Dyd. (Constructeur: Bretocq)
Ord: 24.12.1821. K: 21.1.1822. L: 6.5.1822. Comm: 1.7.1822. C: 7.1822.
Rebuilt at Toulon 12.1835 to 11.1836. Ceded to Ministry of Finance in 7.1848 or 1.1849. Struck 30.8.1850.
Rôdeur Cherbourg Dyd. (Constructeur: Bretocq)
K: 21.1.1822. L: 6.5.1822. Comm: 4.7.1822. C: 7.1822.
Struck 12.4.1850 at Cherbourg.

DORADE Class – schooners, 6 guns. Designed by Jean-François Delamorinière. *Dorade* was built at Bayonne in 1822 for use in Senegal. In January 1836 the colonial administration forwarded to the navy a letter from the governor of Senegal that requested two schooners like *Dorade* for river service. On 30 January 1836 the Director of Ports noted that Saint-Servan had lots of small pieces of timber and recommended that they be built there.
Dimensions & tons: 18.65m oa, 17.00m wl, 15.05m x 4.50m x 2.30m. 57 tons disp. Draught 1.60/2.00m. Men: 11
Guns: (*Dorade*) 6 espingoles; (others) 1 x 4pdr bronze and 4 espingoles
Dorade Bayonne (Constructeur: Gabriel Nosereau)
K: 9.1822. L: 15.10.1822. Comm: 1.11.1822. C: 11.1822.
Struck 1844 at Brest after serving in Senegal.
Cigale Saint-Servan (Constructeur: Georges-Baptiste Allix)
K: spring 1836. L: 1.6.1836. Comm: 14.6.1836. C: 1836.
Struck 1846 in Senegal, hulk.
Belette Saint-Servan (Constructeur: Georges-Baptiste Allix)
K: spring 1836. L: 1.6.1836. Comm: 14.6.1836. C: 7.1836.
Struck 1846 in Senegal, hulk.

JACINTHE Class – schooners, 2 guns. Designed by Jean-François Delamorinière. *Jacinthe* was fully described in a 1989 monograph by Jean Boudriot.
Dimensions & tons: 23.20m oa, 21.00m wl, 18.10m x 5.80m x 2.36m. 88 tons disp. Draught 1.74/2.56m. Men: 32 to 40.
Guns: 2 x 12pdr carronades
Jacinthe Toulon Dyd. (Constructeurs: Jacques-Louis Bonard and others)
K: 3.1823. L: 20.5.1823. Comm: 1.6.1823. C: 6.1823.
Struck 5.6.1841 at Guadeloupe.
Jonquille Toulon Dyd. (Constructeurs: Jacques-Louis Bonard and others)
K: 3.1823. L: 20.5.1823. Comm: 1.6.1823. C: 6.1823.
Served at Cayenne, condemned 1830 after grounding in the Antilles 17.2.1830.
Émeraude Cherbourg Dyd.
Ord: 22.2.1823. K: 1.3.1823. L: 24.5.1823. Comm: 5.7.1823. C: 7.1823.
Struck 13.10.1843 at Martinique and BU there.
Topaze Cherbourg Dyd.
Ord: 22.2.1823. K: 1.3.1823. L: 24.5.1823. Comm: 12.7.1823.
Decomm. 11.6.1838 at Martinique, probably after being wrecked.
Rose Bayonne (Constructeur: Gabriel Nosereau)
K: 3.1823. L: 8.6.1823. Comm: 19.6.1823. C: 7.1823.
Decomm. 21.10.1843 at Guadeloupe, probably after being damaged in an earthquake on 8.2.1843. Struck and sold 1844, in mercantile use until 1850.
Anémone Bayonne (Constructeur: Gabriel Nosereau)
K: 3.1823. L: 8.6.1823. Comm: 1.7.1823. C: 7.1823.

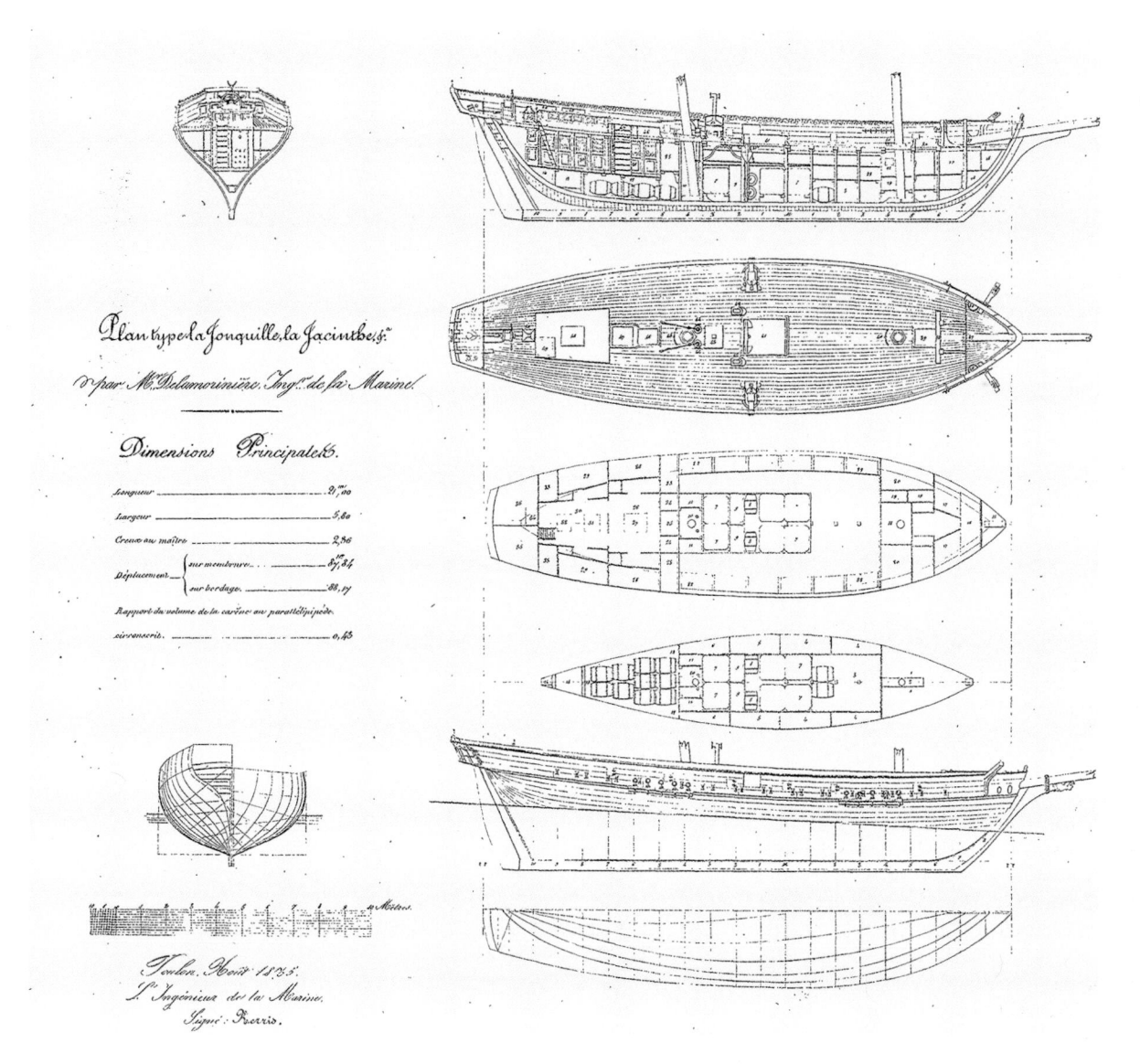

Official internal arrangement plan for the schooners of the *Jacinthe* class, specifically *Mutine*, dated Toulon August 1835. (Atlas du Génie Maritime, French collection, plate 95)

Wrecked 8.10.1824 at Les Saintes near Guadeloupe in a hurricane.
Mutine Lorient Dyd. (Constructeur: Pierre Thomeuf)
  Ord: 23.12.1823. K: 12.1.1824. L: 7.10.1824. Comm: 6.4.1825. C: 4.1825.
  Struck 1841 at Guadeloupe.
Légère Lorient Dyd. (Constructeur: Pierre Thomeuf)
  Ord: 23.12.1823. K: 1.1824. L: 3.2.1825. Comm: 24.4.1826. C: 4.1826.
  Capsized in a squall near Martinique 13.6.1850.

GOËLAND – cutter, 2 guns. Designed by Paul Leroux.
  Dimensions & tons: 13.00m oa, 11.60m, 11.07m wl, 9.40m x 4.50m, 4.68m ext x 1.86m. 40 tons disp. Draught 1.50/2.14m. Men: 17
  Guns: 2 x 12pdr carronades, 4 swivels
Goëland Cherbourg Dyd. (Constructeur: Leroux)
  K: 12.2.1827. L: 12.4.1827. Comm: 12.4.1827. C: 4.1827.
  Struck 14.11.1844, service craft at Rochefort, wrecked 11.1845 near Le Havre.

VIGILANT – sloop, 1 gun. Designer unknown.
  Dimensions & tons: 15.5m x 4.80m. 50 tons disp. Men: 26.
  Guns: 1
Vigilant Pierre-François Vandenbussche, Dunkirk.
  K: 1827. L: 30.4.1828. C: c6.1828.
  Struck 6.7.1842 at Cherbourg, service craft. Disposal unknown.

ÉCUREUIL Class – cutters, 6-8 guns. Designed by Louis Bretocq. On 27 May 1840 the Director of Ports recommended that *Mirmidon* be built to replace *Écureuil* on fishery protection duty at La Hogue. The schooner *Écureuil No.2* (below) was acquired in 1846, causing the original *Écureuil* to become *Écureuil No.1*. The cutter reverted to her original name when the schooner was struck in the late 1850s.
  Dimensions & tons: 15.56m oa, 13.00m, 11.92m x 4.75m x 2.28m. 41 tons disp. Draught 1.46/2.26m. Men: 21.
  Guns: 8 swivels. *Écureuil* may have had 8 x 12pdr carronades in 1831-34.
Écureuil Cherbourg Dyd. (Constructeur: Bretocq)
  Ord: 29.1.1829. Named: 12.2.1829. K: 26.2.1829. L: 8.7.1829. Comm: 3.2.1831. C: 2.1831.
  Renamed *Écureuil No.1* 1849, replaced 7.3.1852 by *Capélan* as fishery protection vessel and became *bâtiment de servitude*, struck 6.8.1858.

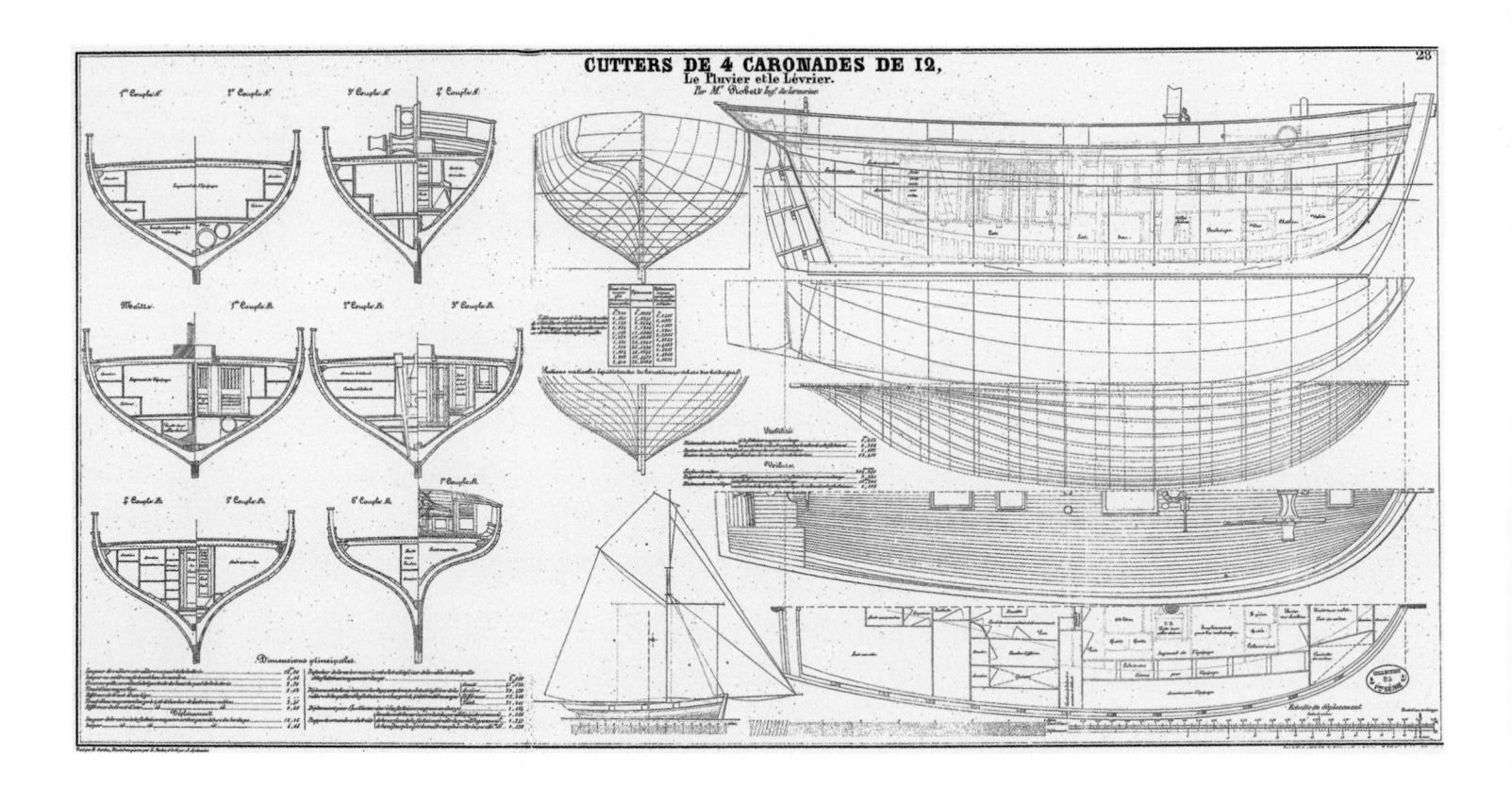

Back on list 1859 as *Écureuil* (2 guns) and in Senegal by 2.1861. Struck 1872 at Brest and BU.
Mirmidon Cherbourg Dyd. (Constructeur: Jean-Baptiste Lefebvre)
K: 6.10.1840. L: 25.3.1841. Comm: 13.9.1841. C: 9.1841.
Struck 24.10.1860 at Cherbourg, became storage hulk in the Îles Chausey near Granville. BU or sold 1882.

RENARD Class – cutters, 6-8 guns. Designed by Louis Bretocq.
Dimensions & tons: 20.76m oa, 18.00m wl, 16.50m x 6.57m x 3.15m. 126 tons disp. Draught 2.18/3.10m. Men: 43.
Guns: (*Renard*) 2 guns; (*Renard*, 1836) 8 x 12pdr carronades; (others) 6 guns
Renard Cherbourg Dyd. (Constructeur: Bretocq)
Ord: 29.1.1829. Named: 12.2.1829. K: 26.2.1829. L: 8.7.1829. Comm: 1.1.1830. C: 1.1.1830.
Struck 9.3.1847 at Cherbourg and ordered BU.
Éperlan Cherbourg Dyd.
K: 9.2.1837. L: 7.5.1837. Comm: 16.5.1837. C: 6.1837.
Struck 12.1850. On sale list 20.8.1851.
Passe-Partout Cherbourg Dyd.
K: 9.2.1837. L: 7.5.1837. Comm: 16.5.1837. C: 6.1837.
Renamed *Mutin* 3.11.1845. Struck 30.12.1850, converted to 54-ton water barge at Cherbourg and renamed *Ondine* in 1851, BU before 1865.

ESPIÈGLE Class – cutters, 6 guns. On 26 December 1832 the Director of Ports reported that *Furet* had been sent to Constantinople and that the navy was short of this type of vessel, which was needed for fishery protection off Cherbourg. He recommended building two cutters on the plans of *Furet*. They were designed by Charles Robert.
Dimensions & tons: (*Espiègle*) 19.60m oa, 16.80m, 16.00m wl, 15.24m x 5.80m x 2.80m. 77 tons disp. Draught 2.00/2.64m. Men: 20; (*Moustique*) 18.00m oa, 17.12m wl, 16.20m keel x 6.20m x 3.04m; 120 tons disp; draught 2.43/3.23m.
Guns: 6 x 12pdr carronades
Espiègle Cherbourg Dyd.
K: 26.9.1833. L: 26.4.1834. Comm: 26.11.1835. C: 11.1835.
Struck 12.8.1872 at Cherbourg, cut down to lighter. BU 1888.
Moustique Cherbourg Dyd.
K: 26.9.1833. L: 26.4.1834. Comm: 1.12.1835. C: 12.1835.
Struck 9.5.1882 at Brest, hulk (*ponton-marégraphe* 1887). BU 1893.

Official general arrangement drawing of the *Lévrier* class 4-gun cutters. (Atlas du Génie Maritime, French collection, plate 28)

BICHE Class – avisos, 4 guns. On 24 October 1835 the Director of Ports reported that among the 6-gun schooners there were few that would last much longer. Vessels of this type were perfectly suited for local service in the colonies and it was necessary to plan for replacements. He proposed building four 6-gun schooners along with four 4-gun avisos, also for colonial service, that were very similar to the navy's old *mouches*. Two of each type were to be built at Saint-Servan and two at Lorient. On 25 November 1835 he recommended approving the plans of Pierre Rolland for the 6-gun schooners, which were to be copies of the Iris type of which the Ministry had had nothing but good reports. The schooners, *Daphné*, *Levrette*, *Fine*, and *Doris*, are listed with the Iris class above. The *Biche* class avisos were probably schooner-rigged. *Antilope* was initially to have been named *Basilic*.
Dimensions & tons: 23.00m oa, 21.25m, 20.67m wl, 17.65m x 6.20m x 2.68m. 104 tons disp. Draught 1.87/2.70m.
Guns: 4 x 12pdr carronades
Biche Lorient Dyd. (Constructeur: Jean-Baptiste Larchevesque-Thibaut)
Ord: 2.12.1835. Named: 30.1.1836. K: 21.3.1836. L: 10.8.1836. C:

10.1836. Comm: 19.10.1836.
Struck 8.12.1845 at Brest after service at Cayenne and Guadeloupe. Converted to barge at Cherbourg, named *Chevrette* c1846 and *Allège No.4* in 1866. BU 1878.

Colombe Lorient Dyd.
K: 5.1836. L: 12.8.1836. C: 1836. Comm: 14.1.1839.
Struck 22.5.1847 at Cherbourg after service at Cayenne and Guadeloupe.

Antilope Saint-Servan (Constructeurs: Joseph Daviel and Henri Lapparent)
K: 3.1836. L: 11.1836. Comm: 26.1.1837. C: 1.1837.
Decomm. 28.12.1842 and struck 1843 at Martinique.

Épervier Saint-Servan (Constructeurs: Joseph Daviel and Henri Lapparent)
K: 3.1836. L: 11.1836. Comm: 26.1.1837. C: 1.1837.
Decomm. 21.9.1841 and struck 1841 at Martinique.

LÉVRIER Class – cutters, 4 guns. On 29 January 1837 the Minister of Marine ordered from Cherbourg two cutters for fishery protection duty off Iceland. They were designed by Charles Robert.
Dimensions & tons: 19.50m oa, 16.90m, 16.08 wl, 15.20m x 5.95m (or 5.68m wl) x 2.70m. 71 tons disp. Draught 2.08/2.70m. Men: 20
Guns: 4 x 12pdr carronades

Lévrier Cherbourg Dyd. (Constructeurs: Robert, probably then Alexandre Robiou de Lavrignais)
K: 8.5.1837. L: 17.10.1837. Comm: 1.12.1837. C: 12.1837.
Struck 12.11.1886 at Cherbourg. Sold or BU 1887.

Pluvier Cherbourg Dyd. (Constructeurs: Robert, probably then Alexandre Robiou de Lavrignais)
K: 8.5.1837. L: 17.10.1837. Comm: 1.12.1837. C: 12.1837.
Struck 5.4.1869 at Cherbourg and BU.

BAUCIS Class – schooners, 4 guns. On 28 August 1839 the Director of Ports proposed building four schooners for local service in the colonies. The navy had few of these craft, some of which needed replacement. He proposed building two large ones (4 guns) at Lorient and two small ones (1 gun) at Cherbourg. The large ones, *Baucis* and *Turquoise*, were designed by Jean-Baptiste Larchevesque-Thibaut. On 1 August 1840 the Minister ordered two more 4-gun schooners, *Décidée* at Lorient and Jouvencelle at *Cherbourg*, the latter to a different design.
Dimensions & tons: 28.10m oa, 25.30m, 24.90m wl, 21.55m x 6.24m x 2.83m. 150 tons disp. 2.12/3.70m. Men: 20 (1860).
Guns: 4 x 24pdr carronades

Baucis Lorient Dyd. (Constructeur: Larchevesque-Thibaut)
K: 16.3.1840. L: 27.8.1840. Comm: 1.11.1840. C: 11.1840
Struck 20.4.1857 at Brest and hulked. Was store hulk for fishery protection vessels 1865-72 and torpedo workshop at Brest 1874-78. BU 1880.

Turquoise Lorient Dyd. (Constructeur: Larchevesque-Thibaut)
K: 16.3.1840. L: 11.9.1840. Comm: 1.11.1840. C: 11.1840.
Departed Brest 10.3.1856 to replace *Estafette* as station ship at Réunion, assigned to Mayotte 1857. Back to Réunion 10.1862 and struck 19.3.1863. Turned over to the colonial service 29.8.1864 for use as a storage hulk at Nossi-Bé.

Décidée Lorient Dyd. (Constructeur: Alexandre Robiou de Lavrignais)
K: 11.8.1840. L: 21.12.1840. Comm: 16.1.1841. C: 2.1841.
Struck 10.5.1858 at Lorient, cut down to barge. Renamed *Danois* c1861, BU 1868.

JOUVENCELLE – schooner, 4 guns. Built to plans drafted by Pierre Rolland in January 1836 shortly before his death.
Dimensions & tons: 22.90m oa, 21.25m, 20.80m wl, 17.70m x 6.20m x 2.84m. 199 tons disp. Draught 1.90/2.70m. Men: 36
Guns: 4 x 12pdr carronades

Jouvencelle Cherbourg Dyd. (Constructeur: Joseph De Gasté)
Ord: 1.7.1840. Named: 5.8.1840. K: 8.9.1840. L: 11.1.1841. Comm: 1.2.1841. C: 2.1841.
Struck 5.2.1858 at Guadeloupe. BU 1867.

MIGNONNE Class – schooners, 1 gun. On 28 August 1839 the Director of Ports proposed building four schooners for local service in the colonies. The navy had few of these craft, some of which needed replacement. He proposed building two large ones (4 guns) at Lorient and two small ones (1 gun) at Cherbourg. The small ones, *Mignonne* and *Mouche*, were designed by Mathurin Boucher. On 15 April 1840 the Minister approved construction of a third unit, *Gentille*, and a fourth followed later.
Dimensions & tons: 19.20m oa, 17.00m, 16.70m wl, 14.35m x 4.80m x 2.40m. 59 tons disp. Draught 1.60/2.10m. Men: 34.
Guns: (1st three) 1 carronade, later 4 swivels; (*Fauvette*) 6 swivels.

Mignonne Cherbourg Dyd. (Constructeur: Victor Prouhet-Kérambour)
K: 8.1.1840. L: 5.5.1840. Comm: 11.5.1840. C: 6.1840.
Decomm. 24.10.1848 and struck 1849 at Cayenne.

Mouche Cherbourg Dyd. (Constructeur: Victor Prouhet-Kérambour)
K: 8.1.1840. L: 5.5.1840. Comm: 11.5.1840. C: 6.1840.
Struck 21.12.1872 at Saint-Pierre & Miquelon, sold there 1873.

Gentille Cherbourg Dyd.
Ord: 15.4.1840. K: 5.1840. Named: 3.6.1840. L: 11.8.1840. Comm: 12.8.1840. C: 9.1840.
Struck 30.3.1868 at Saint-Pierre & Miquelon, cut down to lighter. BU 1876.

Fauvette Cherbourg Dyd.
Ord: 25.12.1841. K: 10.1.1842. L: 13.4.1842. Comm: 13.4.1842. C: 5.1842.
Struck 30.3.1868 at Saint-Pierre & Miquelon, cut down to lighter. BU 1875-76.

CAPÉLAN – cutter, 4 guns. Designed by Charles Robert or Jean De Robert. Built for fishery protection in the bay of Saint-Brieuc.
Dimensions & tons: 17.80m oa, 16.90m, 15.30m x 5.95m x 2.70m. 104 tons disp. Draught 2.34/3.00m. Men: 20
Guns: 4 carronades

Capélan (ex *Papillon* 22.5.1841) Cherbourg Dyd. (Constructeur: Victorin Sabattier)
Ord: 5.5.1841 and named (*Papillon*). K: 26.6.1841. L: 29.12.1841. Comm: 7.3.1842.
Struck 13.6.1892, probably at Brest.

FAVORI – cutter, 4 guns. Designed by Georges Allix and Victorin Sabattier. Built for fishery protection off Iceland.
Dimensions & tons: 19.20m, 18.35 wl, 16.60m x 6.70m. 6.74m ext x 3.26m. 139 tons disp. Draught 2.23/3.33m. Men: 30.
Guns: 4 x 12pdr carronades

Favori Cherbourg Dyd. (Constructeur: Allix and Sabattier)
Named: 22.9.1841. K: 30.11.1841. L: 13.4.1842. Comm: 13.4.1842.
Struck 17.6.1857, converted to sailing water barge. Renamed *Citerne No.1c* c1860 and *Réservoir* by 1865. Sold or BU at Cherbourg 1869.

JONQUILLE Class – schooners, 6 guns. Probably built to new plans by Victor Gervaize.
Dimensions & tons: dimensions unknown. 90 tons disp. Men: 62 (1860)

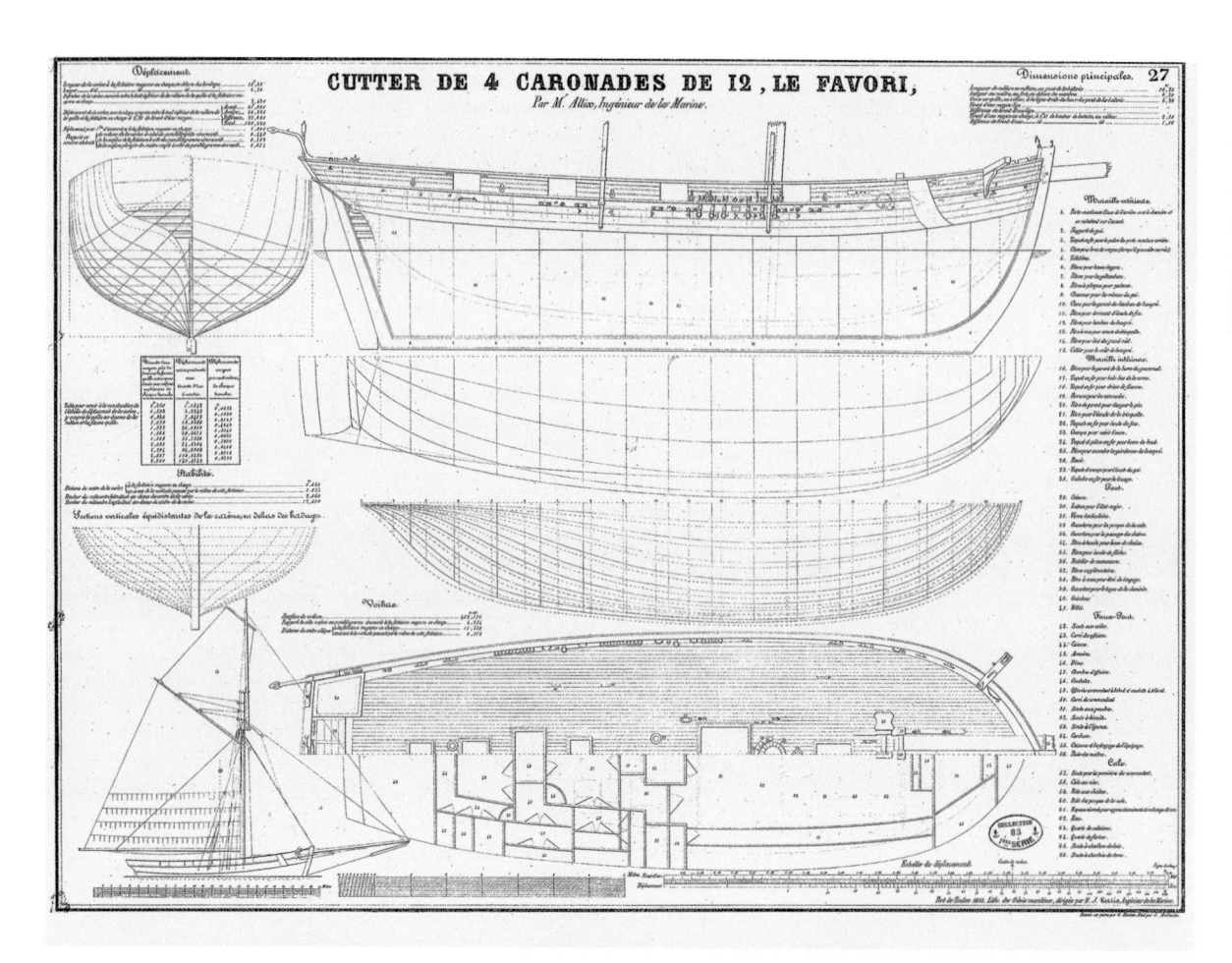

Official general arrangement drawing of the 4-gun fishery-protection cutter *Favori*. Note that the vessel has twice the number of gunports required by the established armament, and the fitting of davits for a large boat abreast the main shrouds. (Atlas du Génie Maritime, French collection, plate 27)

Guns: 6 swivels

Jonquille Lorient Dyd.
K: 30.5.1843. L: 20.8.1845. Comm: 1.9.1845. C: 10.1845.
Struck 20.4.1857 at Toulon.

Amarante (*Amaranthe*) Lorient Dyd.
K: 1.6.1843. L: 16.9.1845. Comm: 17.9.1845. C: 10.1845.
Struck 31.5.1869 at Martinique.

ÉGLÉ Class – schooners, 2 guns. In April 1846 two schooners were ordered for Mayotte from private builders to their own plans. *Églé* was designed and built by Louis-Auguste Guibert at Nantes and *Iris*, probably identical to *Églé*, was built by Arnaud & François Chaigneau et Jean Bichon at Bordeaux. A third vessel was planned for Martinique but it was held up by problems with contract negotiations.

Dimensions & tons: 24.40m oa, 21.50m, 20.50 wl, 16.80m x 6.12m x 3.10m. 140 tons disp. 2.50/3.38m.
Guns: 2

Églé Auguste Guibert, Nantes.
K: 11.1845. L: 20.8.1846. Comm: 24.11.1846. C: 11.1846.
Struck 26.12.1859 at Réunion, out of service there 7.1860.

Iris Chaigneau & Bichon, Bordeaux-Lormont.
K: 1.1846. L: 8.7.1846. Comm: 12.8.1846. C: 9.1846.
Briefly classed as transport 1851-52. Wrecked in Mozambique 18.7.1855 (drifted ashore while waiting for a pilot).

AGATHE – schooner, 4 guns. Probably designed by Victor Gervaize.
Dimensions & tons: dimensions unknown. 90 tons disp.
Guns: 4

Agathe (*Agate*) Brest Dyd.
K: 1846. L: 9.1846. Comm: 1.10.1846. C: 10.1846.
Listed 1.1.1847 on the Brazil and Plata station. Decomm. 22.5.1849 at Montevideo. Classed as gunboat 1.1851, back to schooner 1.1852. Struck at Montevideo 1852.

SOURIS – schooner, 4 guns. Probably designed by Victor Gervaize, possibly as a yacht.
Dimensions & tons: dimensions unknown. 90 tons disp.
Guns: 4

Souris Brest Dyd?
K: 1846. L: c7.1846. Comm: 4.8.1846.
Comm. at Brest. Listed 1.1.1847 on local service in Senegal. Decomm. there 16.8.1849, struck 7.4.1855 and BU 1855.

ÉCUREUIL No.2 – schooner, 2 guns. Her origin is unknown.
Dimensions & tons: unknown.
Guns: 2

Écureuil No.2
Acquired and on fleet list late 1846. Rated cutter 1848, back to schooner 1849. To Senegal from Brest 1848-49. was out of commission at Senegal in 4.1849. Comm. there 7.3.1852 and classed as cutter 1853. Struck at Senegal 19.6.1859.

ÎLE D'OLÉRON – 50 tons. Schooner rig.
Dimensions & tons: 15.00m wl, 14.45m x 4.68m x 2.26m. 80 tons disp. Draught 2.36m mean.
Guns: none.

SMALL SAILING PATROL VESSELS

Most of the last sailing cutters built for the French Navy were designed as fishery protection vessels. For this purpose they carried large boats to facilitate boarding and inspecting fishing vessels, as shown in this engraving by A L Morel-Fatio (published in *La Marine Française*, 1865).

Île d'Oléron Rochefort Dyd. (Constructeur, Achille-Auguste Zani De Ferranty)
  K: 8.1846. L: 6.10.1846. Comm. 6.10.1846. C: 11.1846.
  Listed 1.1.1847 as a schooner on local service in Senegal, by 1.1.1848 was listed as a 50-ton transport. Replaced a chasse-marée (*bâtiment de servitude*) built at Rochefort by Alphonse Levesque in 1824 and decommissioned on 22.11.1845, may have been that ship rebuilt as a schooner. Decomm. 21.1.1849 at Saint-Louis de Senegal. Listed as schooner instead of a transport from 1855. Struck 13.9.1858 at Gorée.

ÎLE MADAME Class – schooners, 2 guns. Three small schooners were built at Rochefort, apparently of one class for which *Île Madame* was the lead ship or *plan-type*. *Île Madame* and *Île d'Énet* were initially listed as *goélettes* (*bâtiments de la flotte*) and replaced two *goélettes de servitude* (not listed here) of the same names that had been built in 1828 and decommissioned in 1852-53. *Île d'Aix* was initially listed simply as a *goélette* as were the other two by 1855. *Île d'Aix*, which may have replaced a *goélette de servitude* built around 1815, was listed as built on plans by Alfred François Lebelin de Dionne with Henri De Lisleferme as *constructeur*. Her dimensions, shown below, match those of the *plan-type*.
  Dimensions & tons: 18.40m oa, 17.82m, 16.67m x 5.28m, 5.44m (ext?) x 2.47m. 95/60 tons. Draught 2.15/2.29m. Men: 14
  Guns: 4 swivels
Île Madame Rochefort Dyd.
  K: 1851. L: 1851. Comm: 29.7.1851. C: 7.1851.
  Departed Rochefort 6.1852 to serve as *citerne à voiles* at Cayenne. She could carry 30 tons of fresh water. Decomm. 1.10.1860 and condemned 9.1.1861.
Île d'Aix Rochefort Dyd.
  K: 9.1852. L: 8.4.1853. Comm: 28.5.1853. C: 6.1853.
  Assigned to the French Guiana station. Condemned 29.1.1866, decomm. 1.4.1866 at Cayenne and BU.
Île d'Énet Rochefort Dyd.
  K: 6.1853. L: c7.1853. Comm: 8.8.1853. C: 8.1853.
  Decomm. at Cayenne 23.5.1862, condemned 8.11.1862.

LABORIEUSE Class – schooners, 2 guns. Designed by Alfred François Lebelin de Dionne
  Dimensions & tons: 21.5m oa, 20.00m, 18.8m x 5.75m, 5.84m ext x 2.68m. 113 tons. Draught 2.20/2.56m. Men: 14
  Guns: 2 espingoles
Laborieuse Rochefort Dyd. (Constructeurs: Henri De Lisleferme and Jean Adrien Bayssellance)
  K: 9.2.1855. L: 20.6.1855. Comm: 17.7.1855. C: 7.1855.
  Struck 1.8.1871 at Cayenne.
Pourvoyeuse Rochefort Dyd. (Constructeurs: Henri De Lisleferme and Jean Adrien Bayssellance)
  K: 9.2.1855. L: 20.6.1855. Comm: 17.7.1855. C: 7.1855.
  Condemned 22.2.1874 at French Guiana, used there as storage hulk until sold or BU 1880.
Vigilante Rochefort Dyd. (Constructeurs: Henri De Lisleferme and Jean Adrien Bayssellance)
  K: 9.2.1855. L: 20.6.1855. Comm: 17.7.1855. C: 7.1855.
  Wrecked 24.2.1869 on the Roches Noires of Îlet La Mère near Cayenne. Struck 2.6.1870.

ALCYONE – cutter, 2 guns. This cutter was built to replace *Mirmidon* at Granville. She was designed by either Victor Pierre Legrand or Augustin Normand.
>Dimensions & tons: 17.80m oa, 16.90m, 16.25m wl, 14.68m x 5.10m x unk. 78 tons. Draught 1.97/2.73m. Men: 28
>Guns: 2 obusiers and 4 espingoles

Alcyon (*Alcyone*) Cherbourg Dyd. (Constructeur: Victor Pierre Legrand)
>K: 16.6.1858. Named: 4.10.1858. L: 24.12.1858. Comm: 21.2.1859. C: 3.1859.
>Struck 16.5.1892.

CALÉDONIENNE Class – schooner-transports, 2 guns. In September 1857 the Minister of Marine approved the plans of Jean-Baptiste Pastoureau-Labesse for a schooner for French Oceania. At the same time he decided to build her at Brest, and on 21 September 1857 he named her *Calédonienne*. This vessel was first classified as a 60-ton transport, then (from 1873) as a schooner, the others were classified as schooners from the beginning but were built to the plans of *Calédonienne*. A second *Perle* was built to the same design in 1875 and lasted until 1892.
>Dimensions & tons: 37.5m oa, 32.70m wl, 25.4m x 7.06m, 7.30m ext x 3.20m. 245 tons disp. Draught 2.48/3.18m. Men: 29. *Perle* and *Gazelle* measured 38m oa, 33m wl, 25.5m x 7.15m, 7.32m ext x 3.25m, 245 tons, draught 2.96/3.16m.
>Guns: 2 x 12pdr carronades

Calédonienne Brest Dyd
>K: 25.9.1857. L: 12.5.1858. Comm: 6.9.1858. C: 9.1858.
>Struck 3.2.1883 at New Caledonia.

Perle Arnaud, François, & Charles Chaigneau, Bordeaux-Lormont.
>Ord: 25.11.1859 (contract). K: 1.12.1859. L: 20.6.1860. C: 8.1860. Comm: 20.11.1860.
>Wrecked 13.5.1863 in the Seychelles.

Gazelle Arnaud, François, & Charles Chaigneau, Bordeaux-Lormont.
>Ord: 25.11.1859 (contract). K: 12.1859. L: 1860. Comm: 1.9.1860. C: 9.1860.
>Struck 3.2.1883 in New Caledonia.

Ex SPANISH PRIZES (1823)

Maria (schooner, probably a Spanish prize, that was in service in the French Navy in 8.1823.) Commissioned 28.6.1824 after repairs at Cadiz, decommissioned 19.11.1824.

Santo Christo (schooner, probably a Spanish prize, that was in service in the French Navy on 20.9.1823.) Later fate unknown.

Ex SLAVERS (1829-1835)

Cupidon (shallow draught slave schooner in service at Guadeloupe in 1828, nearly new when captured 1.1829 in the Rio Pongo by the brig *Bordelaise*, 49 tons, 16-21 men, 2 guns). Purchased by the colonial administration of Senegal 29.5.1829, on fleet list 1830. Decomm. and crew to *Bonne Marie* (below) 1.1.1834. Reportedly condemned 10.1833 and sold at Darmancours on the Senegal River. However this or another *Cupidon* was in service at Gorée at the end of 1833 and participated in the war against the Maures and the Wales in 1833-35. This *Cupidon* was decomm. in 1838 and again in 1841 and struck at Senegal in 1843.

Aglaé (American built slave schooner in service at Guadeloupe in 1831, captured 29.1.1832 by the brig *Cigogne* and taken to Senegal, 62 tons displacement, 35 men). Purchased by the government for the Senegal river flotilla 3.8.1832. Accountability shifted from the colony to Brest 1.8.1834 and on the fleet list 1835. Decomm. in Senegal 20.9.1836, struck in Senegal 13.11.1843.

Aigle d'Or (*Aguila de Oro*, American slave schooner under Spanish flag, taken 2.1834 by the corvette-aviso *Bayonnaise* near Saloum, Senegal, 31-48 men, 4 guns). Purchased in 4.1834 by the colonial administration of Senegal. Comm. 7.5.1834 on the account of Rochefort and on the fleet list 1835. Struck 1.8.1846, decomm. and sold 10.11.1846.

Ex ALGERIAN PRIZES (1830)

Oran (Algerian schooner *Tougarda* or *Tongarda* taken by the French in the port of Algiers 5.7.1830).
>Dimensions & tons: 25.5m oa x 6.24m x 2.59m. 180 tons. Men: 80 when Algerian.
>Guns: (1825) 14; (1830) 12; (8.1830) none.
>This vessel was in service in the Algerian Navy by 1825. Initially referred to as *No.5*, she was overhauled by the French at Algiers in 7-8.1830 and renamed *Oran* in 9.1830. She was decomm. at Toulon on 6.10.1830, being described as of a 'disgraceful form', and was probably condemned c1831 without ever being inscribed on the fleet list.

Bona (Algerian schooner *Sureuna* or *Sureira* ('Pleiades'), taken by the French in the port of Algiers on 5.7.1830).
>Dimensions & tons: 21.02m x 5.20m x 2.40m. 120 tons.
>Guns: 12.
>This vessel was in service in the Algerian Navy by 1825 and was fitted as a fireship in 6.1830. Initially referred to as *No.6*, she was overhauled at Algiers in 7-8.1830 and renamed *Bona* in 9.1830. She was decomm. at Toulon on 8.10.1830, being worn out and in need of major repairs, and was probably condemned c1831 without ever being inscribed on the fleet list.

Mers el Kebir (Algerian schooner *Chaini Deria*, 'Sea Falcon', built at Leghorn and taken by the French in the port of Algiers on 5.7.1830).
>Dimensions & tons: 23.62m x 5.94m x 2.10m. 130 tons.
>Guns: 6 x 12pdr carronades.
>This vessel was in service in the Algerian Navy by 1825 and was fitted as a fireship in 6.1830. Initially referred to as *No.7*, she was overhauled at Algiers in 7-8.1830 and renamed *Mers el Kebir* 9.1830. Although her lines promised speed, she was decomm. at Toulon on 6.10.1830 and was probably condemned c1831 without ever being inscribed on the fleet list.

VESSELS PURCHASED OR TAKEN FOR THE RIO DE LA PLATA BLOCKADE (1838-1840)

Vigilante (Argentine mercantile schooner *Casas Blancas* or *Casablanca*, probably built at Montevideo, purchased there for the Brazil Station and comm. 28.4.1838)
>Dimensions & tons (Argentine): 22m x 5.5m (or 8m?) x 3m height of hull. 70 tons disp. Draught 1.6m. Men (Argentine): 49-70.
>Guns: 3 x 12pdrs, 2 x 24pdr carronades.
>Decomm. at Montevideo 14.11.1840, struck 1841. Was to have been sold to the Uruguayan government but was ultimately turned over by the French to the Argentines in accordance with the Convention of Mackau of 10.1840 in replacement of the gun-launch *Porteña*. Burned under the Argentine flag in the Battle of Obligado 20.11.1845.

Campechana (Mexican mercantile schooner taken as a prize during the Plata blockade in 1838 and comm. by the French in 1839). Wrecked 1840.

Cérès (On fleet list 1839, type and origin unknown, would have been acquired in the Plata region in 1838.) Deleted 1840, not in any other sources and probably did not exist.

Fils Unique (Mexican mercantile schooner, possibly *Hijo Único*, taken as a prize during the Plata blockade in late 1838 and comm. by the

French in 1839). Struck 1840.

Forte (mercantile schooner purchased 12.1838 at Montevideo from Brazilians for the blockade of the Plata and on the fleet list in 1839). Her expenses were charged to the larger ships that provided her crew. Comm. 1.1.1839 and again on 1.1.1840. Decomm. at Montevideo 1.12.1840 and struck there 1841.

Actif (Argentine mercantile cutter, probably ex *Luz*, an Argentine prize purchased around 2.1839 in Brazil for the blockade of the Plata and on the fleet list in 1839, 11 men). Her expenses were charged to the larger ships that provided her crew. Lost with all hands 4.1.1842, struck 11.6.1842.

Ana (Argentine mercantile schooner, possibly an Argentine prize, purchased around 2.1839 in Brazil for the blockade of the Plata and on the fleet list in 1839, 28 tons, 2 guns). Her expenses were charged to the larger ships that provided her crew. Comm. 1.1.1840 at Montevideo, decomm. 1.12.1840. Struck 11.6.1842.

Firmesa (Argentine mercantile schooner, possibly ex *Firmeza* and possibly an Argentine prize, purchased around 2.1839 in Brazil for the blockade of the Plata and on the fleet list in 1839). Her expenses were charged to the larger ships that provided her crew. Decomm. 1.12.1840 and again (?) in 1842, struck 1842.

Fortune (Argentine mercantile schooner *Fortuna*, possibly an Argentine prize, purchased around 2.1839 in Brazil for the blockade of the Plata and on the fleet list in 1839). Comm. 1.1.1840 at Montevideo. Decomm. 1.12.1840. Struck 1842.

Labrador (Argentine mercantile schooner, possibly an Argentine prize, purchased around 2.1839 in Brazil for the blockade of the Plata and on the fleet list in 1839). Her expenses were charged to the larger ships that provided her crew. Comm. 1.1.1840 at Montevideo. Decomm. 1.12.1840. Struck 1842 and sold at Montevideo.

Martin Garcia (schooner built at Buenos Aires and purchased in 1830 by the Argentine Navy to maintain communications between the island of Martin Garcia and Rio de Janeiro, purchased as a prize around 2.1839 in Brazil for the blockade of the Plata and on the fleet list in 1839).

Dimensions & tons: 16m x 5.75m x 3m. 60 tons disp. Draught 1.6m mean. Men: 15-25 (Argentine).

Guns: 1 x 12pdr pivot.

Her expenses were charged to the larger French ships that provided her crew. Comm. 1.1.1840 at Montevideo. Decomm. 1.12.1840. Struck 1842 and reverted to the Argentines who kept her in service until 1845. The island of Martin Garcia was taken by the French and Uruguayans on 10.10.1839.

Esperanza (schooner acquired by the Argentine Navy in 1838, captured and commissioned by the French in 1839, 3 guns). Struck 10.1840 and eventually returned to the Argentines who did not return her to naval service. Off the French fleet list in 1843.

Éclair (mercantile schooner *Relampago* purchased 12.1838 at Montevideo from Brazilians for the blockade of the Plata and comm. by the French 1.1.1840). Her expenses were charged to the larger ships that provided her crew. Retained on the Brazil Station after war, struck 1845 but restored to fleet list 1846, decomm. 21.5.1846, struck 1848, off fleet list 1849. (An earlier *Éclair*, a former bomb vessel, was decommissioned at Brest on 24.8.1839.)

Ex ARGENTINE PRIZES (1845)

Palmar (built at Baltimore as the American schooner *William Jenkins*, became the 'Oriental' (Uruguayan) *Palmar*, taken by the Argentines 5.1841 and renamed *Nueve de Julio,* and taken by the French 2.8.1845.)

Dimensions & tons: 20m x 5.7m x 3m. 70 tons. Draught (mean) 1.70m. Men: 42-44 (Argentine)

Guns: 1 x 18pdr pivot, 2 x 8pdrs.

By 1847 she had been abandoned by the French in South America. Argentine sources claim the French renamed her *Vénus* but this is not supported by French sources.

Obligado (Argentine schooner taken by an Anglo-French squadron 2.8.1845 and commissioned by them). In 11.1845 her commander was English but she does not appear on the British Navy Lists. Last mentioned 2.1846, later fate unknown.

Ex HAWAIIAN PRIZE (1851)

Kaméhaméha (Hawaiian government schooner seized by the French from the Hawaiian government in 1851 and placed in service, 21 men and 2 guns). May have been the vessel reported as *Kamchatka* that left Valparaiso on 1.11.1851 for Callao and then the Marquises. Was in commission by 1.1.1855. Decomm. 15.12.1858 at Papeete, struck 23.12.1859.

SMALL COLONIAL VESSELS (1825-1860)

Utile (aviso, probably cutter-rigged, that was in service at Senegal in 1819 and assigned to the Senegal (River) Flotilla at its establishment on 18.5.1820, 19.6 tons 11-15 men, carried 3 swivels). On fleet list 1825. Condemned 10.5.1830 at Saint-Louis de Senegal as worn out and sold for BU. See the listing for a probable second *Utile* (1831-35) below.

Virginie (schooner in service at Île Bourbon from 1823). On fleet list 1825 to 1830. Transferred to the account of the colony in 9.1830. A different *Virginie*, a former slave brig, was used in Senegal as a colonial vessel from 1830 to 1832 but never appeared on Navy fleet lists.

Général Magallon (lugger in service at Île Bourbon from 1821). Re-rigged as schooner 1825, on fleet list 1825 to 1830. Transferred to the account of the colony in 9.1830.

Colibri (schooner probably built at Bayonne in 1824, captured by the British as a 45-ton slaver in 1825, sold by them 12.1825, purchased by the French and comm. at Île Bourbon in 1825 for local service, 88 tons, 16-25 men, carried 2 x 12pdr carronades). Participated 7.1829 with *Terpsichore* in the expedition to retake the French posts in Madagascar. On fleet list as a schooner 1830 to 1833. Struck 1833 at Île Bourbon. Another *Colibri* appeared on the fleet list in 11.1835; she is listed under small colonial brigs. An aviso named *Colibri* (ex *Mouche No.16*) was in colonial service at Senegal from 1820 to 1832.

Actif (cutter comm. in Senegal 12.1821, 15 tons displacement, 9 men and 2 espingoles). On fleet list 1826. Off fleet list and to colonial accounts 1830, struck after 1836. Another cutter named *Actif*, captured from the British on 24.5.1799, was in service at Rochefort until 1830.

Deux Amis (cutter or sloop purchased by the Administration of Senegal 6.9.1824, 8.6 tons, 7-9 men and 2 espingoles). On fleet list 1826. Off fleet list and to colonial accounts 1830, decomm. 7.1835 and struck. She had been a slaver in 1821, possibly from Cherbourg.

Espérance (schooner acquired near the end of 1825 and comm. at Martinique 1.1.1826, 11-17 men and 2 guns). On fleet list 1827. Decomm. 18.11.1835 and again in 1841. Struck 1843.

Utile (aviso, origin unknown). An aviso named *Utile* remained on the fleet list in 1831-33 without an indication of her location after the aviso of that name in Senegal was struck in 1830. In 1.1834 this *Utile* was listed as a sloop at Martinique, her probable location. By 11.1835 she had been struck.

Bonne Marie (schooner hired in Senegal 11.1833 for the Walo war). Comm. in Senegal 1.1.1834 with the crew of *Cupidon* (q.v.). Returned to her owner 6.8.1835 after peace signed, charter ended 12.1835.

Back on fleet list 1838, also reported out of service c1838. Struck 1844.

Clémentine (schooner that on 17.4.1844, assisted *Phaéton*, *Uranie*, and *Embuscade* in landing troops at Mahaena against Tahitian insurgents). Wrecked on reefs in French Polynesia 5.10.1844. In response to a question in Parliament in 7.1850 the navy stated that she had not been a warship, leaving her naval status uncertain.

Ibis (schooner launched in Cayenne, French Guiana in 8.1845 and on the fleet list in 1846, 2 guns). Comm. 1.1.1848. Wrecked 17.5.1857 on rocks near the mouth of the Oyapock River in French Guiana.

Papeïti (mercantile schooner with a length of 11 to 12m purchased at Papeete late 1847, 20 men and 2 guns). On fleet list 1848/49. Was annexe to corvette *Galatée* 1.1.1848 to 30.3.1850, annexe to corvette *Artémise* 21.6.1852 to 30.6.1854 and to the corvette *Aventure* from 1.7.1854. In commission from 1.1.1855 to 1.3.1856 and 1.11.1857 to 15.11.1858 (service craft 11.1857). Struck 23.12.1859.

Sultane (mercantile schooner purchased at Papeete late 1847). On fleet list 1848/49. Annexe to frigate *Sirène* 1.1.1848 to 6.12.1849. Struck end 1854, last mention 1855.

Clémentine (mercantile schooner purchased at Papeete c1848 — a replacement was possibly purchased in 1851). On fleet list 1851. Off the list 1854.

Nu-Hiva (mercantile schooner purchased at Papeete 1.1851, 19 men and 2 guns). On fleet list 1851. Annexe to corvette *Artémise* 21.6.1852 to 30.6.1854, to corvette *Aventure* from 1.7.1854. Comm. in the Marquises for local service 1854. Struck 30.11.1865.

Hydrographe (mercantile schooner purchased at Papeete in 1851, 20 men and 2 guns). Listed as a *goélette (service local de remorqueur)*, this vessel was annexe to the corvette *Artémise* from 21.6.1852 to 30.6.1854 and then to the corvette *Aventure* from 1.7.1854. Listed in 1855 as a flotilla craft (*bâtiment de flottille*), she was decomm. 1.1.1859 and struck 23.12.1859. An earlier *Hydrographe* may have been purchased in 1846, probably at Papeete, but did not appear on fleet lists.

Tane Manou (mercantile schooner or schooner-brig purchased at Valparaiso 12.1852 for local service in the Marquises, 16 men and 2 guns). Annexe to the corvette *Artémise* 1853. Grounded 17.2.1854 at New Caledonia but refloated. Recomm. 29.2.1856 as a flotilla craft, lost on 27.5.1858 on a reef near Port de France, New Caledonia, and struck 8.9.1859.

Sakalave (mercantile (?) schooner built at Nossi-Bé. K: 1.1855. L: 4.1855. C: 10.1856. 20 men, 2 guns). Comm. 1.10.1856. Commissioned as annexe to the hulk (ex transport) *Indienne* at Mayotte. Struck 16.11.1860. Back in service 25.3.1864, *ponton-stationnaire* at Mayotte 1865, out of service and off list 1.1869. Was a service craft during part or all of her career.

Aurore (68-ton mercantile schooner built at Salem, Mass., and purchased 3.1860 in French Guiana from a merchant named Fabius.)
Dimensions & tons: 21.50m, 20.50m wl, 20.7m? x 5.80m ext x 2.35m. 150 tons (capacity 84 tons). Draught 1.80/2.80m. Men: 13.
Guns: (1861) 2
Comm. 1.4.1860. Condemned 7.3.1867, out of service 24.7.1867.

Fine (mercantile (?) schooner built in New Caledonia and purchased in late 1860, 20 men, 2 guns). Comm. 1.1.1861. Decomm. 5.10.1869 at Nouméa, struck 20.11.1871.

Mirage (mercantile schooner purchased in China 6.1860 and fitted (at Shanghai?) as a *goélette-citerne*. 20 men, 1 gun). Comm. 1.11.1861. Decomm. 16.12.1867 in China, struck 30.1.1868, sold with the steamer *Déroulède* at Shanghai 25.3.1868.

9 Sailing Gunboats and Coastal Vessels

(Including the Boulogne Invasion Flotilla)

This chapter lists the gunboats and other small craft built by the French Navy for coastal patrol and defence service as well as for offensive use in the English Channel. These were usually built in wartime and generally did not have a long existence, being removed from service in peacetime. The gunboats (*chaloupes-canonnières*, often shortened to *canonnières*) built during the 1779-82 conflict had largely gone before 1786.

Beginning in 1793 the French built huge numbers of small craft for coastal and inshore warfare and for planned cross-channel invasions, including hundreds of *chaloupes-canonnières* and smaller flotilla craft (especially *bateaux-canonniers* or artillery boats and *péniches* or pinnaces) as well as a few heavily-armed larger troop-carrying vessels (*prames* or converted *bateaux-plats*, which broadly speaking were shallow-draught corvettes). The *chaloupes-canonnières* were often brig-rigged (and sometimes called *bricks-canonniers*) while the smaller vessels were schooner or lugger-rigged and were designed primarily to transport troops plus some field guns and their horses. These vessels formed the core of the invasion flotilla of the late 1790s and the 'Boulogne Flotilla' of 1803-5.

Numbered vessels without names are generally outside the scope of this volume but the main building programs for numbered flotilla craft between 1793 and 1805 are summarised here. For information on individual numbered craft after 1800 plus over 2,000 other flotilla vessels, small craft and service craft not on the regular fleet lists the reader is referred to Cdt. Alain Demerliac's *Nomenclature des navires français de 1800 à 1815* (see Bibliography).

(A) Vessels in service or on order at 1 January 1786

CHALOUPES-CANONNIÈRES (GUNBOATS)

Between 1778 and 1783, France had built twenty-two *chaloupes-canonnières* or gunboats on the Channel and Atlantic coasts, primarily for harbour defence and coastal escort duties. Most were armed with three heavy guns, two mounted forward and one aft, and carried what was basically a two-masted schooner rig. By 1786 just seven of these remained extent.

VIOLENTE Class. A class of three, both survivors built at Brest in 1778, designed by Antoine Geoffroy, and refitted at Le Havre in 1782. A third of this class, the Lorient-built *Vautour*, was sold in 1783. Two more (simply called *Premier Batiment* and *Second Batiment*), assembled at Cayenne after being prefabricated either at Nantes or at Rochefort, had been disposed of by 1786. They carried 20 pairs of oars.
   Dimensions & tons: 100ft 0in, 80ft 0in x 17ft 0in x 5ft 3in (32.48, 25.99 x 5.52 x 1.71m). 60/100 tons. Men: 45-63.
   Guns: 3 x 24pdrs originally, 1 x 24pdr only from 1781, then 2 x 24pdrs from 1792.
Violente Brest Dyd
   K: 3.1778. L: 21.5.1778. C: 8.1778.
   Struck 2.1793 at Antwerp.
Rusée Brest Dyd
   K: 3.1778. L: 20.5.1778. C: 8.1778.
   Struck 2.1793 at Antwerp.

IMPUDENTE Class. A class of seven built in 1778-79 (all at Rochefort, except *Lynx* built at Bordeaux), designed by Raymond-Antoine Haran. Of this class, the *Impudente*, *Embuscade*, *Panthère* and *Cyclope* were sold in 1783. Two vessels of a similar design by Henri Chevillard – *Levrette* and *Méfiante* – were built at St. Malo but were struck in 1785 or 1786, as were four designed and built by Daniel Denys at Dunkirk – *Bruyante*, *Couleuvre*, *Cerbère* and *Furieuse*. They carried 14 pairs of oars.
   Dimensions & tons: 60ft 0in, 53ft 0in x 16ft 6in x 6ft 0in (19.49, 17.22 x 5.36 x 1.95m). 42/80 tons. Men: 39-50. Draught 5ft 0in/5ft 8in (1.62/1.84m).
   Guns: 3 x 18pdrs and 8 swivels.
Mégère Rochefort Dyd
   K: 10.1778. L: 16.1.1779. C: 2.1779.
   Renamed *Méridienne* 5.1795. Struck 1797 at Cherbourg.
Nantaise Rochefort Dyd
   K: 11.1778. L: 16.2.1779. C: 3.1779.
   May have been named *Arrogante*. Struck 2.1792 at Rochefort, ordered BU 1.5.1792.
Lynx Bordeaux
   K: 5.1779. L: 10.7.1779. C: 8.1779.
   Struck 1797 at Saint-Malo.

MARTINIQUE Class. A class of two built at Le Havre in 1779-80, designed by Jean-Joseph Ginoux, but modified in 1780 by Antoine Groignard. They carried 20 pairs of oars. Two similar ships, the St. Malo-built *Lionne* and *Querelleuse*, were struck in 1784.
   Dimensions & tons: 81ft 0in, 71ft 0in x 17ft 0in x 5ft 0in (26.31, 23.06 x 5.52 x 1.62m). 70/100 tons. Draught 4/5ft (1.30/1.62m). Men: 52-63.
   Guns: 3 x 24pdrs (*Sainte Lucie* 1 x 24pdr and 2 x 18pdrs from 1797).
Martinique Le Havre
   K: 2.1779. L: 4.5.1779. C: 6.1779.
   Wrecked 10.1792 off Dunkirk.
Sainte Lucie Le Havre
   K: 2.1779. L: 4.5.1779. C: 6.1779.
   Sold 12.1801 at Dunkirk.

(B) Vessels acquired from 1 January 1786

(i) PRAMES and BATEAUX-PLATS

CHAMEAU Group – *Bateaux-Plats*. *Éléphant* was originally built as a dogger to carry cavalry (see Chapter 10). These shallow-draught cargo vessels were not necessarily to a common design.
   Dimensions & tons: dimensions unknown. 200 tons burthen. Men: 12
   Guns: 6 x 6pdrs.

Chameau Le Havre.
   K: 12.1794. L: 23.5.1795. C: 5.1795.
   Taken 24.1.1804 off Cap de la Hague near Cherbourg by HMS *Cerberus* (32), not taken into the RN.

Éléphant Le Havre.
   K: 12.1794. L: 1795. C: 1796.
   Hauled out in 1801 and rebuilt as a *prame* with 12 x 18pdrs to plans by Pierre Lair. L: 8.1.1802. C: 6.1802. In commission at Le Havre from 20.6.1802 to 29.3.1803. Renamed *Ville de Brest* 6.10.1803 and commissioned at Calais for Admiral Bruix on 2.11.1803 and at Boulogne from 23.9.1804 to 31.12.1806. As of 21.2.1804 she could carry 51 troops in addition to a crew of 38. Not recommissioned, struck before 1814.

Mulet Le Havre.
   K: 12.1794. L: 2.7.1795. C: 7.1795.
   As of 2.1802 could only be used on the Seine. She may have become the *ponton armé Mulet* listed at Brest between 5.1807 and 8.1808.

Smaller *bateaux-plats* in the 1790s included *Actif* (ex Dutch galiote *Wrou Maria*, seized 1795 at Nantes as a *bateau-canonnier*, renamed 12.1795, decomm. 6.1796 after the civil war in the west, fitted as transport 10.1796), *Diligent,* and *Prudent* (or *Prudence*), possibly former *bateaux-canonniers* that were at Dieppe in 1795-97, and *Bateaux-Plats Nos.1-12* (or *Bateaux-Canonniers Nos.1-12*) built at Rochefort in 1798 and last mentioned in 1802.

FOUDROYANTE – 500 tons. Designed by Pierre-Alexandre-Laurent Forfait. Flat-bottomed. In contemporary lists as a corvette or a *corvette-prame*.
   Dimensions & tons: 131ft 0in, flat portion 123ft 0in x 35ft 0in (42.55, flat portion 39.95 x 11.37m). 500/950 tons. Draught 16ft (5.20m). Men: 88 (capacity 250, presumably including troops).
   Guns: 16 x 24pdrs, 1 x 12-inch mortar on pivot (the mortar gone by 1798).

Foudroyante Nicolas Loquet, Honfleur
   K: 5.1794. L: 11.12.1794. C: 7.1795.
   Condemned 4.7.1804 at Brest, was to serve as a guard station (*corps de garde*) but instead was converted to a flûte at Dunkirk in 5.1805. Struck 5.1806 and BU in drydock at Brest.

VULCAIN – 450 tons. Designed by Pierre-Alexandre-Laurent Forfait. Flat-bottomed. In contemporary lists as a corvette or a *corvette-prame*.
   Dimensions & tons: 124ft 4in, flat portion 115ft 0in x 32ft 0in x 15ft 0in (40.39, flat portion 37.35 x 10.39 x 4.87m). 450/950 tons. Draught 11ft 8in/16ft (3.80/5.20m). Men: 112 (capacity 250, presumably including troops).
   Guns: 14 or 16-24pdrs, 1 x 12-inch mortar on pivot. Had 20-18pdrs in 1801.

Vulcain Jean-Baptiste Gallon, Honfleur
   K: 11.1794. L: 5.1795. C: 7.1795.
   Re-rated corvette 9.1803 and armed with 16 x 12pdrs. Floating hospital at Brest 12.1808. Condemned at Brest and ordered BU 16.6.1810, BU in drydock.

SANS-PITIÉ Class. Designed by Pierre-Alexandre-Laurent Forfait. The *Sans-Pitié* is believed to be to the same design as the *Foudroyant* of 1799 whose dimensions are given below.
   Dimensions & tons: 100ft 0in x 24ft 0in x 7ft 0in (32.48 x 7.80 x 2.27m). 200/360 tons. Draught 6ft 6in/7ft 6in (2.11/2.33m). Men: c120, 46 + 51 soldiers in 1804.
   Guns: (*Sans-Pitié*) 18 x 18pdrs, (*Foudroyant*) 12 x 24pdrs, 12 x 18pdrs in 1801.

Sans-Pitié Le Havre (Constructeur, Charles-Henri Tellier)
   K: 1797. L: 5.1798. C: 6.1798.
   Re-rated transport 6.1802 and gunboat (with 6 x 12pdrs) 1803. Reduced to 6 x 8pdrs by 1812. Gunboat in 1814. Decomm. at Brest 5.1815 and then struck.

Foudroyant Le Havre (Constructeur, Charles-Henri Tellier)
   K: 1798. L: 3.1799. C: 4.1799.
   Renamed *Ville de Lille* 24.8.1803, had 10 x 24pdrs in 1.1804. Decomm. 31.3.1807 at Dunkirk, struck before 5.1814.

Ex VENETIAN PRIZES (1797)

Venetian floating battery (*prama*) IDRA. This unusual vessel was laid down by order of Jacopo Nani, *Provveditore delle Lagune e Lidi* at Venice, on the advice of Gianmaria Maffioletti, headmaster from 1777 of the Venetian school of *Studi fisico-matematici relativi alla Naval Architettura*. She was ordered by a decree of the Venetian Senate on 2 June 1796 and built by Andrea Salvini in only 110 days, being completed at the beginning of 1797. Her design was based on a plan dated 1760 by the Swedish architect Fredrik Henrik Af Chapman. Chapman's plan had a conventional hull; while Salvini's design had a hull with a 'W' cross-section to give the ship better stability. *Idra* (the Italian equivalent of the Latin *Hydra* and French *Hydre*) had two masts and 12 pairs of oars.
   Dimensions & tons (French feet): 96ft 11in keel x 27ft 6in max x 6ft 6in *puntale* (depth) (31.48 x 8.93 x 2.11m). 207 tons burthen. Draught 4ft 2in (1.35m). The length of the hull without the bowsprits was 97 Venetian feet (33.73m). Fitted with oars which the oarsmen rowed while standing.
   Guns: (1797, Venetian) 7 Venetian 50pdrs on pivots on the centreline; (1797, French) 7 French 36 pdrs; (1798, Austrian) 7 Austrian 24pdrs, 12 x 3pdrs; (1804) 7 Austrian 26pdrs, 4 x 3pdrs; (1809, French) 11 French 18 pdrs; (1814) 7 French 36 pdrs, 12 x 3 pdrs; (from 1815, Austrian) 3 x 36 pdrs, 1 x 6 pdr, 3 x 36pdr carronades.

The Venetian floating battery *Idra*, which became the French *Hydre* in 1797. An unusual vessel whose main armament was on centreline pivot mountings that could fire on either broadside, the concept was inspired by the ingenious gunvessels specially designed in the 1760s by Fredrik Henrik af Chapman for the Swedish Inshore Fleet, a force optimised for what is now called littoral warfare. The schooner-rigged *Idra* could also be rowed by standing oarsmen, a technique familiar to all Venetian boatmen. (Archivio di Stato, Venice; by courtesy of Guido Ercole)

Hydre (Venetian *Idra*) Venice
K: 8.1796. L: 1.1797 C: 31.1.1797
Taken afloat 5.1797 by the French, name became *Hydre*. Sabotaged by the French 12.1797 in the Venice Arsenal. Refloated by the Austrians and returned to service 4.1798 as *Idra*. Annexed 1.1806 at Venice by the French as *Hydre*. Retaken 4.1814 at Venice by the Austrians as *Idra*. BU 1822.

Venetian ceremonial state galley *BUCINTORO*. This vessel was ordered on 15 March 1704 to replace the previous *Bucintoro* (launched 1606), designed and begun by Stefano Conti (d. 1707), launched in 1719 after the end of the Second Morean War, in service without ornaments in 1727, and fully ornamented for the Ascension Day celebrations of 28 May 1729. She had 21 oars per side with four seated oarsmen per oar and had a single mast aft to display the pennant of the Doge. She was still in excellent condition in May 1797 when the French took her on her slip at the Venice Arsenal. The French renamed her *Bucentaure* and on 9 January 1798, by personal order of Napoleon, removed and burned her decorations in order to take the gold with which they were plated (about 3kg, delivered to Napoleon in Milan) and to symbolise the destruction of the Venetian Republic. The Austrians cut down the damaged hull to its first deck beginning in 1802 and made it seaworthy, and in 1805 they installed twelve Austrian 9pdrs along her sides for use as a *prama* in defending the city.

   Dimensions & tons (Venetian feet): 120 ft oa without the bow spurs and rudder, 100 ft keel x 21 ft max x 10ft (41.73, 34.77 x 7.30m x 3,46m). 200 tons disp.
   Guns: (1805, Austrian) 12 x 9pdrs; (1806, French) 15 x 20pdrs; (1814, French) 22 x 18pdrs; (from 1815, Austrian) 15 x 12 pdrs.

Bucentaure (Venetian *Bucintoro*) Venice
K: 1704. L: 6.1719. C: 5.1729
Reverted to the Austrians 1.1798 as *Bucintoro* and transformed into a 'prama' (floating battery) in 1802-5. Annexed 1.1806 at Venice by the French as *Bucentaure*. Retaken 4.1814 at Venice by the Austrians. BU 1824.

(ii) *CANONNIÈRES* (GUNBOATS)

From the start of 1793, a considerable number of gunboats were begun in northern French ports to a variety of designs. There were variously described as *bricks-canonniers*, *chaloupes-canonnières*, or simply *canonnières* (the terms were generally interchangeable) and they were all two-masted craft, seemingly brig-rigged. They initially carried three 24pdr guns, usually two mounted as bow chasers and the third fitted amidships or aft, as well as smaller weapons; however the armament of individual vessels necessarily varied from time to time.

***TEMPÊTE* Class.** *Brick-canonniers*. These vessels were designed by Charles-Henri Tellier and carried 21 pairs of oars. The Havre pair were begun as *Chaloupes-canonnières Nos 1* and *2*, but were named in March 1793. The two built at Honfleur were not necessarily to the same plans, but had similar dimensions and armament. *Éclatante* was described as schooner-rigged.

   Dimensions & tons: 90ft 0in, 83ft 0in x 20ft 0in x 6ft 6in (29.24, 26.96 x 6.50 x 2.11m). 50-80/170 tons. Draught 5/5¼ft (1.62/1.71m). Men: 46-61.
   Guns: 3 x 24pdrs, + 12 swivels.

Tempête Fouache & Reine, Le Havre.
K: 1.1793. L: 30.3.1793. C: 5.1793.
Renamed *Canonnière No.5* in 6.1803. Decomm. 19.1.1805.

Fulminante Fouache & Reine, Le Havre
Ord: 29.10.1792. K: 1.1793. L: 2.5.1793. C: 5.1793.
Last mentioned 1796 on escort duty at Fécamp.

Éclatante Michel Colin-Olivier, Dieppe.
Ord: 17.2.1793. K: 4.1793. L: 7.1793. C: 9.1793.
Renamed *Canonnière No.7* in 6.1803. In commission at Antwerp 9.1811, struck before 1814.

Terrible Michel Colin-Olivier, Dieppe.
K: 4.1793. L: 7.1793. C: 9.1793.
Renamed *Trombe* 5.1795, reverted to *Terrible* 1795. Redesignated *Canonnière No.328* in 2.1804. Left Boulogne for Ostend 8.1809, no further mention.

Inquiète Fouache & Reine, Honfleur.
K: 5.1793. L: 7.8.1793. C: 9.1793.
Redesignated *Canonnière No.21* in 3.1803. Captured 19.7.1815 by HMS *Fly* (18), *Fury* (8), and *Sealark* (10) in the channel at Correjou.

Etna Fouache & Reine, Honfleur.
K: 5.1793. L: 23.8.1793. C: 9.1793.
Renamed *Effroyable* 5.1795, reverted to *Etna* 1796. Last mentioned 7.1797 at Le Havre.

***BRAVE* Class.** *Canonnières* or *corvette-canonnières*, designed by Pierre-Alexandre Forfait in 1793. Begun as *Corvette-canonnières Nos.1* and *2* respectively, they were named in March 1793. Both brig rigged. On 5 July 1794 Forfait proposed the construction of a similar vessel at Fécamp but she was neither named nor built.

   Dimensions & tons: 84ft 0in, 69ft 0in x 24ft 0in x 11ft 0in (27.28, 22.41 x 7.80 x 3.57m). 110/288 tons. Draught 8ft 11in/9ft 1in (2.90/2.95m). Men: 94.
   Guns: 4 x 24pdrs (6 ports). *Citoyenne* later had 5 x 24pdrs, 2 x 8pdr obusiers; in 1797 she had 12 x 4pdrs.

Brave Le Havre
K: 1.1793. L: 26.4.1793. C: 5.1793.
Renamed *Arrogante* 5.1795. Taken 23.4.1798 in the raz de Sein off Brest by HMS *Jason* (36) and *Naiad* (38). Initially classed in the RN as a gunbrig under her French name (*Arrogante*) but renamed HMS *Insolent* on 31.8.1798 and re-rated in 10.1811 as a brig-sloop, when she was described as 'nearly the same as the *Crocus* and the other 252-ton brigs'. Sold 6.1818.

Citoyenne Le Havre
K: 2.1793. L: 27.5.1793. C: 6.1793.
Renamed *Citoyenne No.2* in 1798 and *Citoyenne* in 1803. Probably became a numbered gunboat in the Boulogne Flotilla in 1804, number and fate unknown. .

***VESUVE* Class.** *Brick-canonniers* (although *Cruelle* was described as schooner-rigged). A plan of a *chaloupe canonnière* (this class) carrying 4 x 24pdrs and brig-rigged was signed by Lemarchand, sous-ingénieur, at Saint-Malo on 11 February 1793; Lemarchand probably built as well as designed the ships.

   Dimensions & tons: 70ft 0in, 60ft 0in x 20ft 0in x 7ft 8in (22.74, 19.49 x 6.50 x 2.49m). 80/140 tons. Draught 5ft 6in/7ft 4in (1.79/2.38m). Men: 53.
   Guns: 4 x 24pdrs (+ 2 swivels).

Vésuve Saint-Malo
K: 2.1793. L: 5.1793. C: 6.1793.
Renamed *Vedette* 30.5.1795 but change not implemented. Taken 3.7.1795 by HMS *Melampus* (36) and *Hebe* (36) off Cap Fréhel, becoming HMS *Vesuve* (brig-rigged gunboat).

Vaillante Saint-Malo (probably)

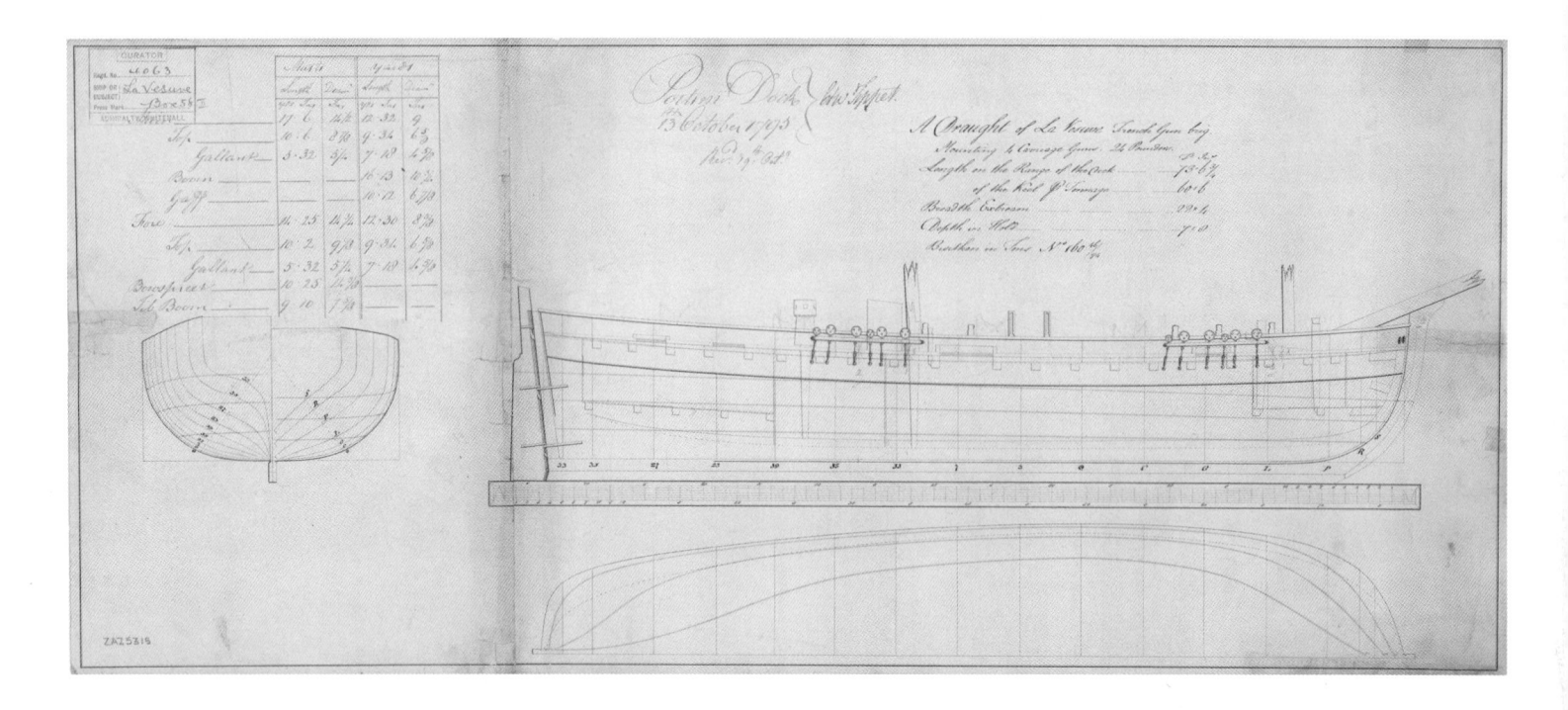

K: ca.3.1793. L: 1793. C: 6.1793.
Renamed *Violente* 5.1795, reverted to *Vaillante* 1796. Destroyed 25.11.1796 by HMS *Lapwing* (28) after being chased ashore on St Martin (Antilles).

Volage Saint-Malo
K: 3.1793. L: 5.1793. C: 6.1793.
Renamed *Venteux* 5.1795. Taken 27.6.1803 by boats from HMS *Loire* (38) off Morlaix, became gunbrig HMS *Eclipse* (ex *Eagle*). The *Volage* that was renamed *Verité* in 5.1795 was probably an acquired vessel.

Cruelle Saint-Malo (probably)
K: ca.3.1793. L: 7.1793. C: 8.1793.
Taken 12.4.1800 by HMS *Mermaid* (32) off the Îles d'Hyères, becoming HMS *Cruelle* (schooner-rigged gunboat).

Protectrice Saint-Malo
K: 3.1793. L: 8.1793. C: 9.1793.
Renamed *Canonnière No.9* in 6.1803. Decomm. 31.3.1807.

Hargneuse Saint-Malo
K: ca.3.1793. L: 10.1793. C: 11.1793.
Renamed *Canonnière No.14* in 6.1803 and *Canonnière No.11* in 9.1803. Decomm. 28.2.1810 at Brest.

Foudre Saint-Malo
Ord: 14.2.1793. K: 1793. Named: 12.8.1793. L: 1.1794. C: 2.1794.
Renamed *Fantôme* 5.1795 but change not implemented. Struck 12.1798 at Saint-Valéry en Caux.

INSOLENTE. Lugger-rigged gunboat. May have been converted from a chasse-marée in addition to the ten conversions at Cherbourg listed below.
Dimensions & tons: unknown. Men: 43.
Guns: 2 x 24pdrs; (1795) 3 x 24pdrs; (1803) 3 x 18pdrs.

Insolente Granville.
K: 1793. L: 4.1793. C: 5.1793.
Name spelled *Insolent* in 1797. Refitted at Dunkirk 4.1803 and renamed *Canonnière No.3* in 6.1803 (or on 24.8.1803). Decomm. 25.3.1805.

Admiralty draught of *Vesuve* as taken off at Portsmouth, dated 13 October 1795. Described on the draught as a 'gun brig', the mast and spar dimensions for the vessel's brig rig, including topgallants on both fore and main, are also listed. (© National Maritime Museum J6857)

DÉDAIGNEUSE Class. *Brick-canonniers*, brig-rigged. Designed and built by Hubert Penevert or Jean-Denis Chevillard. *Île d'Yeu* was sometimes written as *Île Dieu*.
Dimensions & tons: 68ft, 64ft x 20ft x 7ft 6in (22.09, 20.79 x 6.50 x 2.43m). 166 tons. Draught 5ft 6in/6ft (1.78/1.95m). Men: 24-66.
Guns: 3 x 24pdrs, + 10 swivels.

Dédaigneuse Rochefort Dyd
K: 4.1793. L: 6.6.1793. C: 6.1793.
Renamed *Deplaisante* 5.1795, reverted to *Dédaigneuse* 1797. Struck at Rochefort 1826.

Subtile Rochefort Dyd
K: 4.1793. L: 6.6.1793. C: 6.1793.
Struck at Rochefort 1826.

Gironde Rochefort Dyd
K: 5.1793. L: 7.1793. C: 8.1793.
Renamed *Bec d'Ambez* 1793 or 1794, reverted to *Gironde* 16.5.1795. Struck 1797.

Île de Ré Rochefort Dyd
K: 5.1793. L: 7.1793. C: 7.1793.
Renamed *Île Républicaine* 6.1794, reverted to *Île de Ré* 5.1795. Wrecked in Arcachon Basin (Landes) 5.1797.

Île d'Yeu Rochefort Dyd
K: 6.1793. L: 9.8.1793. C: 8.1793.
Renamed *Indienne* 1.1794, reverted to *Île d'Yeu* 9.1794. Struck at Rochefort 1820 or 1821.

Noirmoutier Rochefort Dyd
K: 6.1793. L: 9.8.1793. C: 8.1793.
Grounded and lost 10.1793 in combat against the Chouans near Gois on the coast of the Île de Noirmoutier.

CROCODILE. Schooner-rigged gunboat, possibly designed by Pierre

Rolland. She is also reported as the British vessel *Alligator* captured in 5.1794 and fitted as a gunboat at Rochefort in 1795.
> Dimensions & tons: 75ft x 18ft x 6ft 3in (24.36 x 5.85 x 2.03m). 72/130 tons. Draught 5ft 3in/6ft 3in (1.70/2.03m). Men: 42-80.
> Guns: 3 x 18pdrs.

Crocodile Brest Dyd.
> K: 5.1793. L: 28.8.1793. C: 10.1793.
> Renamed *Colère* 5.1795. Sailed from Rochefort for Cayenne 1795, BU there c1796.

ARDENTE Class. *Chaloupes-canonnières*. All were ordered in February 1793, and named on 12 August 1793. An additional unit named *Inconnue* was listed as built at Dunkirk in 1793-94 but there is no record of her service and the listing probably resulted from confusion with a 12-gun brig of the same name built at Dieppe at the same time. Another unit named *Maringouin* was listed as built at St. Valéry-sur-Somme in 1793 but she was probably a chasse-marée of the same name that was converted to a gunboat at Cherbourg at the same time.
> Dimensions & tons: 75ft 0in, 69ft 0in x 18ft 0in x 6ft 3in (24.36, 22.38 x 5.85 x 2.03m). 70/130 tons. Draught 4ft/5ft 8in (1.30/1.84m). Men: 51-53.
> Guns: 3 x 24pdrs.

Ardente Dunkirk
> K: 4.1793. Named: 12.8.1793. L: 30.8.1793. C: 1.1794.
> At Senegal in 1807, probably struck before the British took the colony in 7.1809.

Enflammée Dunkirk
> Ord: 2.1793. K: 3.1793. Named: 12.8.1793. L: 5.1794. C: 7.1794.
> Renamed *Canonnière No.6* in 6.1803. Decomm. 31.3.1807.

Incommode Dunkirk
> K: 3.1793. Named: 12.8.1793. L: 5.1794. C: 7.1794.
> Renamed *Canonnière No.4* in 6.1803 (or on 24.8.1803), decomm. 21.3.1805. The '*Commode*' taken by the British on 14.6.1803 was her sister *Méchante*.

Chiffonne St. Valéry-sur-Somme
> Ord: 14.2.1793. K: 3.1793. Named: 12.8.1793. L: 11.1793. C: 12.1793.
> Renamed *Curieuse* 5.1795, reverted to *Chiffonne* 1796. Redesigned *Canonnière No.329* in 2.1804, decomm. 22.9.1804.

Méchante Boulogne
> K: 4.1793. Named: 12.8.1793. L: 17.6.1793. C: 3.1794.
> Chased ashore with sister *Inabordable* near Boulogne 14.6.1803 by HMS *Immortalité* (36), *Jalouse* (18), and *Cruizer* (18), captured and refloated by the British Navy but not added to the RN. British accounts of the action give her name as *Commode*, French accounts identify her as *Méchante*.

Surprise Boulogne
> K: 4.1793. Named: 12.8.1793. L: 5.2.1794. C: 3.1794.
> Renamed *Canonnière No.2* in 6.1803 (or *No.1* on 24.8.1803, see *Énigme* ex *Etna*). Wrecked 21.7.1804 off Boulogne.

Inabordable Calais
> Ord: 2.1793. K: 12.1793. Named: 12.8.1793. L: 4.3.1794. C: 5.1794.
> Chased ashore with sister *Méchante* near Boulogne 14.6.1803 by HMS *Immortalité*, *Jalouse*, and *Cruizer*, captured and refloated by the British Navy but not added to the RN.

Brûlante Calais
> Ord: 2.1793. Named: 12.8.1793. K: 12.1793. L: 21.3.1794. C: 5.1794.
> May have been renamed *Canonnière No.15* in 6.1803 and *Canonnière No.12* in 9.1803. *Brûlante* decomm. 19.5.1814 at Le Havre, *Canonnière No.12* decomm. 2.8.1815 at Brest, struck before 1820.

VOLCAN. Brig-rigged gunboat, originally with one large gun but sent overseas with twelve smaller.
> Dimensions & tons: unknown. Men: 38-80.
> Guns: 1 x 18pdr; (1796) 12 x 4pdrs.

Volcan Lorient.
> K: 12.1792. L: 1793. C: 1.1794.
> Captured 4.5.1796 off Bermuda by HMS *Spencer* (18).

MONTAGNE. Brig-rigged gunboat.
> Dimensions & tons: unknown. Men: 43.
> Guns: 3 x 24pdrs.

Montagne Lorient.
> K: 1793. L: 2.1794. C: 3.1794.
> Renamed *Autruche* 16.5.1795. Last mentioned 9.1796 while in the Vilaine.

RUDE. Brig-rigged gunboat.
> Dimensions & tons: unknown. Men: 46-70.
> Guns: 3 x 24pdrs.

Rude Paimboeuf.
> K: 4.1793. L: 15.11.1793. C: 1.1794.
> Armed with guns taken from local fortifications. Participated in the reconquest of the island of Noirmutier 1-8.1794. Beached and burned 25.9.1795 on Noirmutier to prevent capture by HMS *Pomone* (44).

CHALIER Class. *Brick-canonniers*, designed by Pierre-Alexandre Forfait. The first (its name was sometimes noted as *Chaslier*) was ordered on 19 March 1793.
> Dimensions & tons: 77ft 0in, 69ft 8in x 18ft 6in x 6ft 6in (25.01, 22.63 x 6.01 x 2.11m). 70/130 tons. Draught 4ft 8in/6ft (1.52/1.95m). Men: 43.
> Guns: 3 x 24pdrs (2 bow chasers, 1 midships) + 1 x 8pdr.

Chalier Cherbourg Dyd
> K: 8.1793. L: 4.1.1794. C: 2.1794.
> Renamed *Cerbère* 5.1795. Taken 29.7.1800 by boats of HMS *Amethyst* (36) and cutter *Viper* (12) while at anchor at Larmor-Plage becoming HMS *Cerbere* (brig-rigged gunboat); wrecked off Beachy Head 20.2.1804.

Barra Cherbourg Dyd
> K: 10.1793. L: 2.1794. C: 3.1794.
> Renamed *Folle* 5.1795. Last mentioned 6.1795 at Cherbourg.

Crachefeu Cherbourg Dyd
> K: 10.1793. L: 2.1794. C: 3.1794.
> Captured by Strachan's squadron (HMS *Melampus*, *Diamond*, *Hebe*, *Niger*, and *Siren*) in Cartaret Bay 9.5.1795, becoming HMS *Crache Feu* (brig-rigged gunboat); BU 1797.

Brutale Cherbourg Dyd
> K: 10.1793. L: 3.1794. C: 4.1794.
> Took the name of a converted chasse-marée that had been wrecked off Granville 8.10.1793. Renamed *Canonnière No.8* in 7.1803. Departed Dunkirk for Flushing 12.4.1809, no further mention.

Etna Cherbourg Dyd.
> K: 3.1794. L: 12.1794. C: 1.1795.
> Renamed *Énigme* 5.1795 and *Canonnière No.1* on 6.1803 (or *No.2* on 24.8.1803, see *Surprise*). Decomm. 31.3.1807.

CONVERTED CHASSE-MARÉES. In 1785 twenty numbered chasse-marées were built under contract in southern Brittany for use as service craft in harbour construction at Cherbourg. Details of these are to be found in Chapter 14. *Nos.1-11* and *Nos.14-20* were at Cherbourg when in 1793 ten of them (original numbers unknown) were rebuilt there as *chaloupes-canonnières* by Martin or Jacques Fabien. The name *Insolente* was reported for an eleventh conversion, but as she was produced at Granville she was more likely new construction.

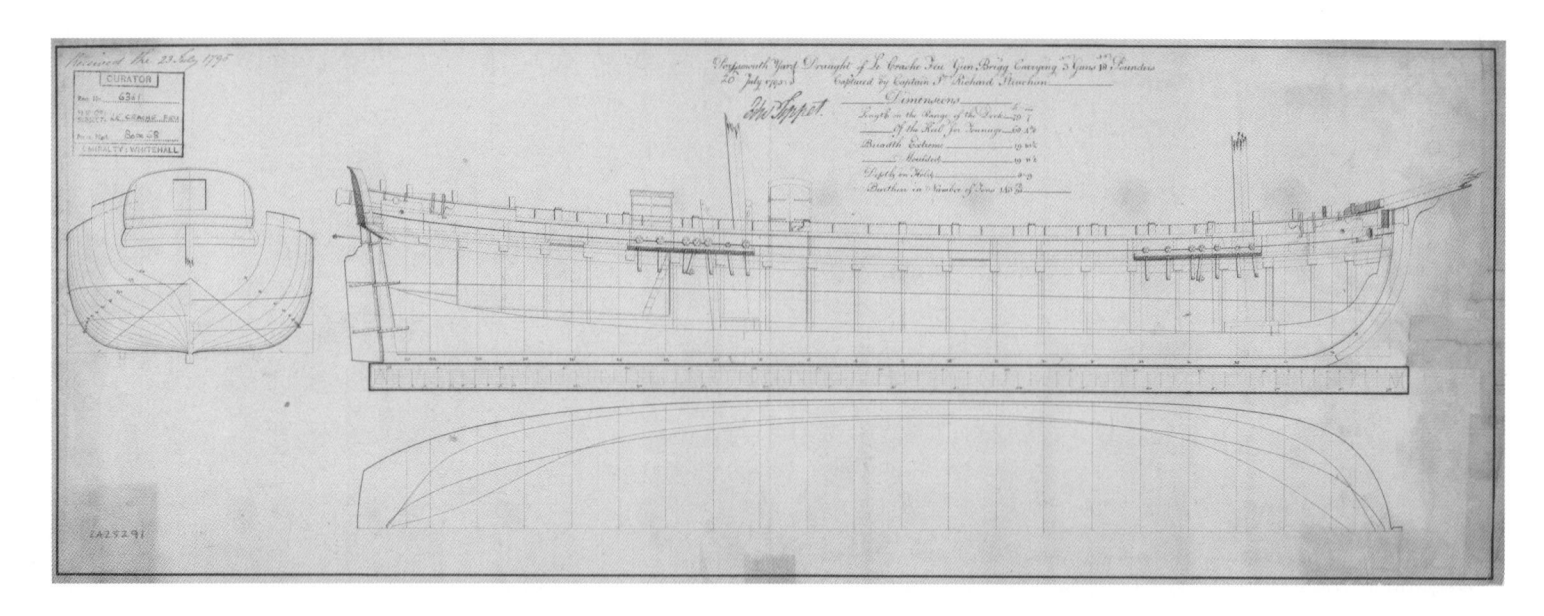

Dimensions & tons: 57ft, 49ft x 18ft 9in x 7ft (18.52, 15.92 x 6.09 x 2.27m). 90/150 tons. Draught 5ft 7in/6ft 7in (1.81/2.14m). Men: 35-53.

Guns: 3 x 24pdrs or 18pdrs.

Brutale. Converted 4-5.1793 at Cherbourg, comm. 5.1793.
  Wrecked off Granville 8.10.1793, name reused for a new gunboat.
Tonnerre. Converted 4-5.1793 at Cherbourg, comm. 5.1793.
  Renamed *Rivale* 5.1795. Last mentioned 9.1795 navigating on the Seine as a transport.
Mouche Sans Raison. Converted 4-5.1793 at Cherbourg, comm. 5.1793.
  Ex *Mouche* 1793. Renamed *Maritime* 5.1795, reverted 1795 to *Mouche Sans Raison*. Fitted 1798 as lugger-rigged transport of 77 to 90 tons. Name shortened to *Mouche* 1803, rigged as schooner 1805 at Cherbourg. Struck 1822 at Le Havre and sold.
Moustique. Converted 4-5.1793 at Cherbourg, comm. 5.1793.
  Fitted as lugger-rigged transport 11.1800 at Cherbourg. Became a service craft at Cherbourg 11.1826 and struck.
Furet. Converted 4-5.1793 at Cherbourg, comm. 5.1793.
  Renamed *Farceur* 5.1795. Returned 4.1797 to her former operator for construction work at Cherbourg.
Maringouin. Converted 4-5.1793 at Cherbourg, comm. 5.1793.
  Fitted 1795 at Brest as a lugger-rigged transport. Decomm. 5.1808.
Éclair. Converted 9-11.1793 at Cherbourg, comm. 11.1793. Lugger-rigged.
  Captured by Strachan's squadron (HMS *Melampus*, *Diamond*, *Hebe*, *Niger*, and *Siren*) in Cartaret Bay 9.5.1795. Fitted as a schooner 4.1796 (HMS *Eclair*?), hulked and renamed *Safety* 1802. Listed as a guardship in the West Indies in 1808 and as a prison ship in 1810, then reappeared as a receiving hulk at Tortola in 1841. BU 1879.
Sinon. Converted 9-11.1793 at Cherbourg, comm. 11.1793.
  Fitted 3.1794 at Cherbourg as an 80-ton coal transport, reconverted 5.1798 at Cherbourg to a lugger-rigged gunboat, again fitted as a transport 9.1804 at Cherbourg. Decomm. 10.1815 at Cherbourg, sold 1816.

Admiralty draught of *Crache Feu* dated Portsmouth 20 July 1795; the armament is noted as three 18pdrs, (two forward and one aft). In general the Admiralty did not show much interest in French naval small craft – most surviving draughts taken off cutters, schooners and the like are privateers of extreme hull forms – but they made an exception for coastal gunboats and other types that might be used in an invasion attempt. (© National Maritime Museum J0020)

Chat. Converted 9-11.1793 at Cherbourg, comm. 11.1793.
  Lost with all hands 4.1799 near Saint-Marcouf.
Souris. Converted 10.1793-1.1794 at Cherbourg, comm. 2.1794.
  Captured 26.2.1798 off the Saint-Marcouf Islands by HMS *Badger* (4) and *Sandfly* (4), not taken into the RN.

PURCHASED AND REQUISITIONED GUNBOATS (1793-1796)

Jean Bart (tartane purchased or requisitioned in 1792 or 1793 and commissioned at Toulon as a gunboat, carried 2 x 8pdrs, 2 x 6pdrs). May have been the tartane *Saint-François* of 1792 (see Chapter 10) renamed after 2.1793. Taken by the British and Spanish at Toulon 8.1793, appears to have been taken to Cadiz by the Spanish in 12.1793 under the name *Jean Var*.
Pavillon National (Bordeaux merchant vessel requisitioned at Pointe-à-Pitre, Guadeloupe, in 1.1793 and modified as a gunboat by Jean-François Landolphe, 60 men, carried 1 x 18pdr). Probably returned 2.1793 to her owner.
Laurette (merchant corvette hired 6.1793 at Le Havre and commissioned as a gunboat 7.1793, 200 tons, 49 men, carried 4 x 24pdrs and 4 x 4pdrs). Charter terminated 1.1794, ship fitted 6.1795 as a gunnery and navigation school at Le Havre. Subsequent fate unknown.
Dorade (merchant tartane built at Toulon and purchased 6.1793 as a gunboat, 46 men, carried 2 x 12pdrs and 2 x 6pdrs). Renamed *Département du Var* in 1793 or 1794 and *Assaillante* 5.1795. Redesignated aviso 1.1797. Captured 1.1799 by the Tunisians but apparently recovered. Sailed for Egypt 8.1800, subsequent fate unknown and struck.
Convention (gunboat that was in service at Toulon 1.1794, carried 1 x 24pdr and 4 swivels). Renamed *Cocyte* 5.1795. Decomm. 7.1795 at Toulon, then struck.
Marguerite (galiote commissioned at Cherbourg 3.1794 and classified as

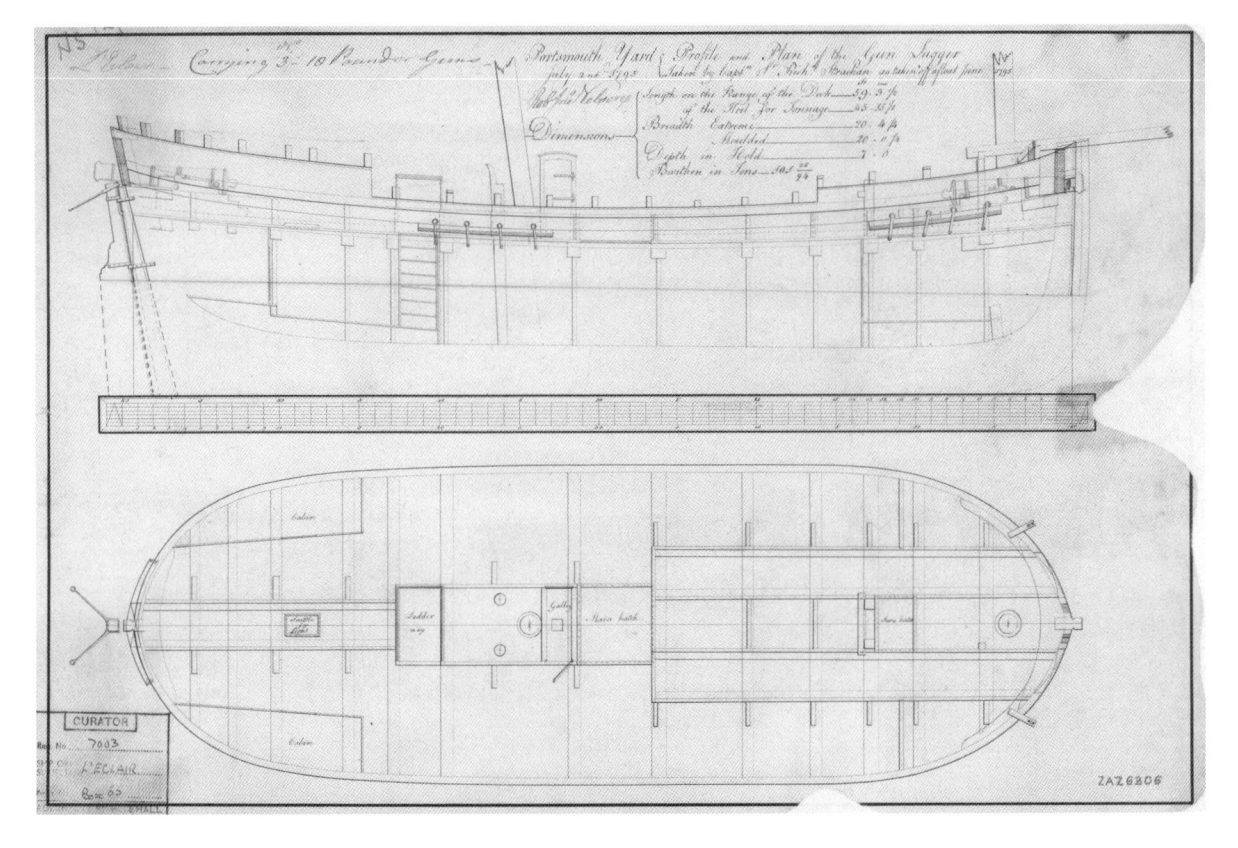

Admiralty draught of *Éclair* dated Portsmouth 2 July 1795. There is no lines plan because the draught was taken off afloat, but the interest seems to have been in the arrangement of guns – the deck view shows the slide mountings for the two forward and one after guns (noted as 18pdrs). Described as a 'gun lugger' on the draught, the mercantile appearance of the hull is explained by the vessel's origins as a chasse-marée built to support the construction of the breakwater at Cherbourg. (© National Maritime Museum J0576)

a gunboat in 1797-98, 140 tons, 18-49 men, carried 2 x 24pdrs). Was a station gunboat at Le Havre 3.1800. Fitted as a transport for the Boulogne Flotilla 11.1803 and renamed *Transport No.950 Marguerite*. Decomm. 3.1807.

Ça Ira (gunboat commissioned in the Mediterranean 6.1794 or 7.1794, 3 guns). Captured 8.1794 by the British in the surrender of the port of Calvi.

Saint-Jacques or ***Jacques*** (merchant brig or dogger requisitioned 6.1794 at Nantes and fitted as a gunboat, carried 1 x 36pdr and 2 x 8pdrs). Renamed *Inévitable* 5.1795 and *Saint-Jacques* 1796. Captured 9.1799 off Lorient by HMS *Triton* (32).

Blanche (gabarre or dogger requisitioned 6.1794 at Nantes and fitted as a gunboat, carried 2 x 18pdrs and 2 x 12pdrs). Last mentioned 5.1795 while in service at Saint-Malo, probably returned to her owner in 1796.

Madeleine (Dutch mercantile dogger or lugger requisitioned 6.1794 at Nantes as a gunboat with 2 x 6pdrs and 1 x 36pdr obusier). Renamed *Mélodieux* 5.1795, reverted to *Madeleine* or *Dame Madeleine* in 1796. Refitted as transport 1798. Wrecked 1.1802 at Mardick.

Gotiche (merchant dogger requisitioned 12.1793 at Nantes and fitted as a gunboat c6.1794, carried 1 x 36pdr and 2 x 8pdrs). Last mentioned 5.1795 while out of service at Saint-Malo, probably returned to her owner.

Légère (gunboat commissioned 10.1794 at Brest, 3 guns). Renamed *Latitude* 5.1795, reverted to *Légère* 1796. Was in service in 1799 in Guadeloupe, later fate unknown.

Volage (gunboat commissioned 10.1794 at Brest, 43-60 men, carried 3 x 24pdrs). Renamed *Vérité* 5.1795 while at Guadeloupe, later fate unknown. Another *Volage* (above) was renamed *Venteux* in 5.1795.

Bonne Intention (galiote commissioned 1.1796 as a gunboat in the Loire estuary, 200 tons, 22 men, carried 2 x 18pdrs, 4 x 6pdrs, and 2 x 2pdrs). Last mentioned 3.1797 while at Bordeaux, then struck.

MISCELLANEOUS PRIZES (1793-1794)

Pauline (Dutch galiote seized 2.1793 at Le Havre and fitted as gunboat in 6.1793, 80 tons, 53 men, carried 4 x 24pdrs). Fitted as a transport in 1796, renamed *Transport No.28 Pauline* in 1798, last mentioned 1798 while at Le Havre.

Sainte-Marie (Spanish merchant vessel *Santa Maria* built in Spain, probably a tartane, taken in early 1794 and fitted in 4.1794 at Agde as a gunboat, 43-60 men, carried 3 x 24pdrs). Renamed *Nivôse* 4.1794. Last mentioned 7.1797 while at Toulon.

Crocodile (British merchant ship or privateer *Alligator* taken 5.1794 and fitted as a gunboat at Rochefort in 1795, carried 7 x 12pdrs and 4pdrs). Last mentioned 5.1795 while at Rochefort.

TARTANES ACQUIRED NEAR TOULON IN 1794 AS GUNBOATS.

Between March and June 1794 the French acquired 28 merchant tartanes at Sète and Agde west of Toulon and fitted them as gunboats. Each was manned by about 40 men and generally carried three large guns, often 18pdrs and sometimes 12pdrs or 24pdr. The former tartane that was in service the longest was *Force* (name rendered as *Forte* from 1800), which was redesignated as an aviso in 1.1797 and decommissioned in 9.1802 at Toulon. Also of note was *Génie*, which was captured on 31.5.1796 off Oneglia near Genoa. She has been identified as the gunbrig HMS *Venom* that was deleted from the Royal Navy in 1800 after service in the West Indies, although *Venom* may have been captured in 1794. The British measurements of *Venom* were 65ft 1in x 22ft 8in x 9ft 0in and 128 tons.

Commissioned at Sète in March 1794 was *Gasparin* (renamed *Guêpe* 5.1795 but captured as *Gasparin* 24.5.1795 by HMS *Romulus* off Mahon). Acquired at Sète or Agde in May 1794 were *Récompense* (ex *Aimable Émilie* 5.1794, last mentioned 5.1798 at Toulon), *Travail* (ex *Vigne* 5.1794, captured with *Gasparin* 24.5.1795), *Union* (renamed *Torride* 5.1795 and *Union* 9.1797, sold 10.1797 to the Bey of Tunis in part for rotten wheat), *Foudre* (renamed *Fantôme* 5.1795, last mentioned 5.1795 at Toulon), *Etna* (renamed *Étonnante* 5.1795, last mentioned 5.1795 at Toulon), *Messidor* (struck 1796), *Fructidor* (returned to her owner 1796), *Germinal* (last mentioned 1.1796 departing Toulon, then returned to her owner), *Pluviôse* (last mentioned 5.1795 in service at Toulon), *Ventôse* (last mentioned 4.1796 departing Toulon), *Volcan* (renamed *Torpille* 5.1795, struck 1796), *Hecla* or *Éclat* (last mentioned 5.1795 at Toulon), *Opinion* (struck 1796), *Force* (see above), *Terreur* (renamed *Tourmente* 5.1795, last mentioned 26.5.1795 operating near the eastern Pyrenees and later struck), and *Vipère* (renamed *Tortue* 5.1795 and last mentioned 5.1798 at Toulon).

Purchased or requisitioned at Agde in June 1794 were *Prairial* (last mentioned 1.1797 departing Toulon), *Floréal* (last mentioned 6.1796 departing Toulon), *Frimaire* (decomm. 30.12.1798 at Corfu and captured there 3.1799), *Brumaire* (last mentioned 5.1795 in service at Toulon), *Thermidor* (last mentioned 5.1795 in service at Toulon), *Vendémiaire* (name uncertain, struck late 1794 or early 1795), *Dune Libre* (renamed *Arrimeuse* 5.1795, last mentioned 5.1795 in service at Toulon), *Génie* (see above), *Mégère* (struck 1796), *Vertu* (renamed *Urne* 5.1795, last mentioned 5.1795 in service at Toulon), and *Vésuve* (renamed *Vive* 5.1795, last mentioned 5.1795 out of service at Toulon).

CHALOUPES-CANONNIÈRES BUILT AT TOULON IN 1794.
While acquiring the above tartanes the navy in 1794 and early 1795 also built 12 gunboats, *Nos.1-9* and *Nos.12-14*, at Toulon. No specifications are available for these except that they were manned by 35 men and carried either 1 x 12pdr or 1 x 18pdr plus a few swivels. In May 1795 *Nos.6, 9, 12* and *14* were renamed *Nuit, Nue, Négligente*, and *Négative*, *No.9* soon reverting to her number. *No.7* and *No.8* were struck before 5.1795, *Négligente* (*No.12*) was wrecked near Genoa in 5.1795, *Nuit* (*No.6*) was decomm. 7.1795 at Toulon, *No.13* and *Négative* (*No.14*) were last mentioned in 1.1797 and 7.1797 respectively in service at Toulon, *Nos.1-5* were decommissioned 6.1798 at Malta, while *No.9* was still in service at Toulon in 7.1798.

BATEAUX-CANONNIERS ACQUIRED AT NANTES 1794.
During the Royalist uprising in the Vendée that began in March 1793 and the related Chouan peasant revolts Nantes remained loyal to the Republic, and after an attack on the city was repelled in June 1793 it became a centre for operations against the insurgencies. In 1795 the navy acquired the following private French vessels at Nantes and fitted them as *bateaux-canonniers*: *Annibal, Argus, Aventure, Brave, Ça-Ira, Carmagnole, Cassard, Caton, Citoyen, Colomb, Duquesne, Fabius, Forbin, Fort, Intrépide, Invincible, Jean-Bart, Lapeyrouse, Pompée, Résolution,, Révolutionnaire, Thémistocle, Tourville*, and *Vengeur*. The following Dutch vessels were also seized or taken at Nantes and similarly fitted: *Actif* (ex *Wrou Maria* 12.1795), *Aristide* (ex *Voorsiggoge* 12.1795), *Catherine-Élisabeth* or *Vieux Catharina* (ex *Wrou Catharina* 10.1795), *Courageux* (ex *Staad Amsterdam* 12.1795), *Curieux* (ex *Jonge Hond k Belle* 12.1795), *Fanfaron* (ex *Wrou Elisabeth* 12.1795), *Imposant* (ex *Fortuyne* 12.1795), *Karsus* (ex *Anna-Louisa* 2.1796), *Prévoyant* (ex *Petite Fortune* 12.1795), *Ruither*, and *Surveillant* (ex *Twege Justerud* 12.1795). One British merchant ship, *Cook*, was similarly taken and converted.

Specifications are sparse, but the vessels of French and British origin tended to have crews of 20 to 36 men and armaments of 2 to 6 x 4pdrs or 4 x 6pdrs. The ex-Dutch vessels were rated at from 65 to 200 tons and had crews and armaments similar to those of the French vessels. The French craft were returned to their owners in around June 1796 after the end of the civil war in the west, and the others were decommissioned then and probably disposed of later that year except *Actif, Fanfaron* and *Imposant* which became transports and *Courageux* which became a barge.

Fanfaron was decommissioned at Nantes in 8.1799. *Cook* was a service craft at Lorient in 1802 rigged as a chasse-marée.

BATEAUX-CANONNIERS BUILT IN 1795-1797 FOR OPERATIONS IN WESTERN FRANCE.
In January 1795 24 *bateaux-canonniers* were ordered at Nantes and Basse-Indre and six more were ordered at Paimboeuf, all to counter the insurgencies in the region. Probably designed by Pierre Degay, they were 50-ton vessels with a crew of 25 men and a designed armament of 1 x 24pdr (in service 2 x 18pdrs were often carried). Ten units launched in late 1795 at Nantes and Basse-Indre were named *Caroline, Désirée, Émilie* (or *Émile*), *Fanny, Françoise, Henriette, Lise, Nanine, Rosette*, and *Zoé*. Two vessels named *Boudeuse* and *Lutine* were launched at Paimboeuf in 1796 (probably as barges), while five more craft, *Adèle, Belette, Biby* (or *Bibi*), *Fourmi* and *Mutine* were launched at Nantes and Basse-Indre in 1797. Nine vessels at Nantes and Basse-Indre and four at Paimboeuf were never completed, the four at Paimboeuf still being on the ways in August 1799. These vessels quickly became service craft and none was mentioned after 1804.

VESSELS BUILT IN 1795-1796 IN NORTHERN PORTS

Bateaux-canonniers No.1 type. At the beginning of 1795 the French ordered 192 *bateaux-canonniers* in northern ports to a design by Pierre-Alexandre Forfait: 60 at Le Havre, 20 at Dieppe, 12 at Fécamp, 20 at Rouen, 40 at Paris, 30 at Honfleur, and 10 at Caen. These included *Nos.1-7* and *No.11* built at Le Havre by Jean Fouache, *Nos.61-66* built at Dieppe by Michel Colin-Olivier, *Nos.93-97* built at Rouen, and *Nos.113-117* built at Paris. The Rouen and Paris boats were to be sent to Le Havre upon completion. *Bateau canonnier No.1* was launched on 8.3.1795 and launchings may have continued into 1796. *Nos.8-10* were converted during construction into *Bateaux-bombardiers Nos.8-10* with 1 x 12-inch mortar and renamed *Bateaux-bombardiers Nos.1-3* in 7.1797; these were decommissioned around 1800-1. The 33 gunboats that remained in service in 1.1798 at Le Havre were renumbered *Bateaux-canonniers Nos.25-57* and the few that survived to 1803 were incorporated into the Boulogne Flotilla.
   Dimensions & tons: 57ft, 52ft x 14 ft x 4ft 10in (18.52, 16.89 x 4.55 x 1.57m). 50 tons (displ.). Draught 3ft 6in/4ft (1.14/1.30m). Men: 28.
   Guns: 1 x 24pdr

BELETTE Class *péniches*. *Belette, Furet*, and *Marthe* were built between May and July 1796 at Le Havre while a fourth unit, *Libre*, was commissioned in 1798 or 1799. They had three masts and 14 to 16 pairs of oars and were also called *double-péniches*. *Belette* decommissioned in 4.1801, *Marthe* decommissioned in 1800, and *Libre* was last mentioned in 8.1799 in service at Le Havre. Some or all of these may later have seen service in the Boulogne Flotilla. *Furet* left service in 11.1812.
   Dimensions & tons: 60ft, 53ft x 10ft x 4ft 8in (19.49, 17.22 x 3.25 x 1.52m). 20 tons. Draught 2ft 11in/3ft 10in (0.95/1.24m). Men: 8 to 13 plus about 30 oarsmen.
   Guns: 2 x 1pdrs except *Furet*, 4 x 2pdrs.

VESSELS BUILT IN 1796-1798 FOR THE INVASION OF ENGLAND.
In early 1796 the Directory authorised Lieutenant Joseph-Augustin-François Muskeyn, an officer of Flemish origin who had served with the Swedes and gained much experience in the military use of small craft, to form a flotilla at Dunkirk for an assault on Yarmouth and Newcastle. He built gunboats and procured troopships for an expedition of 5,000 men but the troops deserted in large numbers at the prospect of going to sea in small boats. After a major French effort during 1797 to

SAILING GUNBOATS AND COASTAL VESSELS

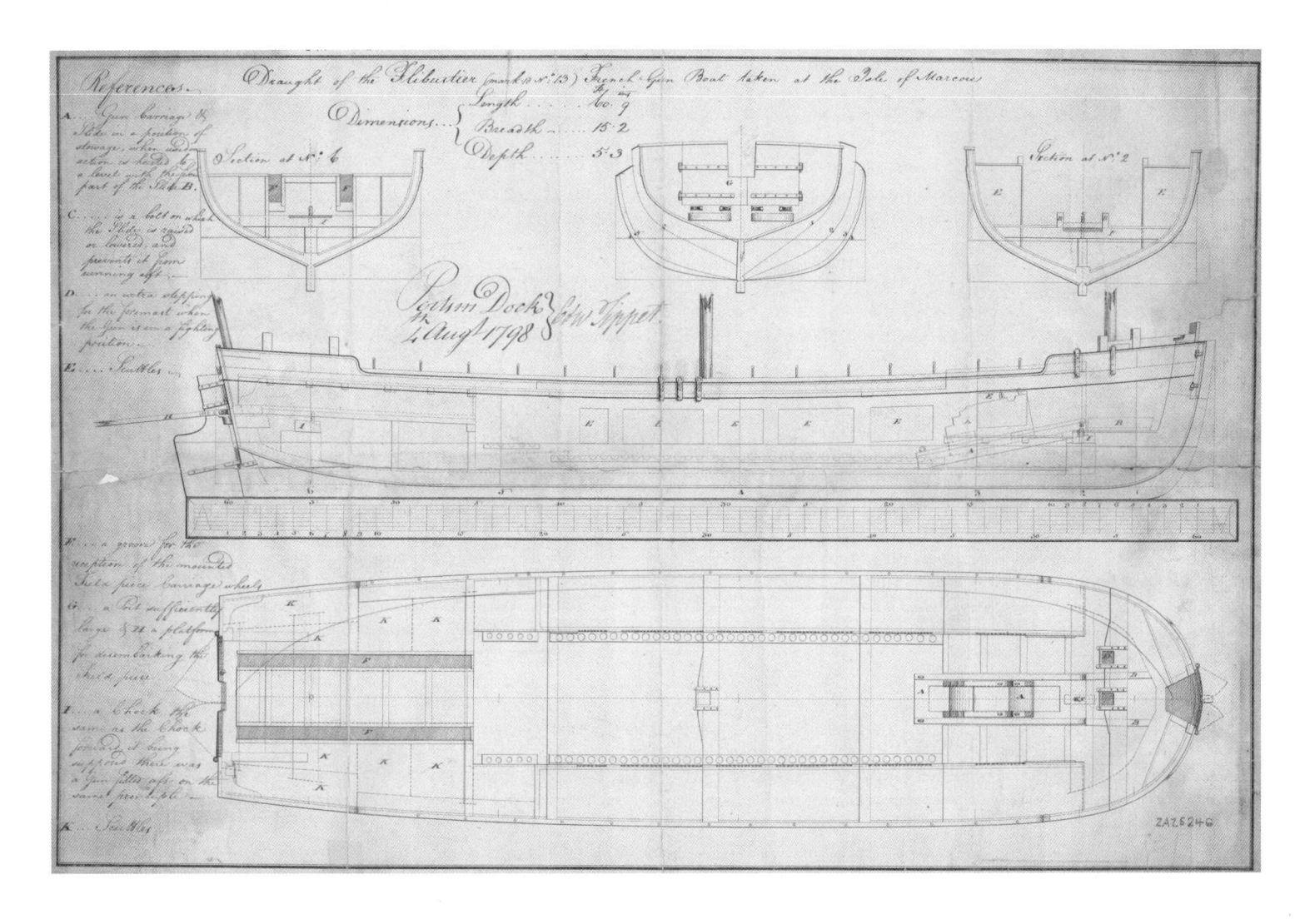

support an Irish uprising, preparations were begun in October 1797 along the French coasts for an invasion of the English mainland in the spring of 1798. While these efforts were dwarfed by the huge construction effort of 1803-5 they did result in the construction of some assault craft including the following.

1. Twelve *bateaux-canonniers*, *Nos.1* to *12*, built at Dunkirk between March and September 1796 on plans by Muskeyn. These were of 40/60 tons and measured 59ft 9in, 53ft, x 16ft x 5ft 2in (19.40, 17.21 x 5.20 x 1.67m) with a draught of 4ft/4ft 6in (1.30/1.46m). They had one 18pdr, one 6pdr, three masts, and 14 banks of sweeps. They were soon named *Guerrier, Soldat, Marin, Tout-Coeur, Abordant, Qui-Vive, Loup de Mer, Hussard, Grenadier, Coulebas, Incendiaire,* and *Bruletout*. The last reference to any of these vessels was in 1799.

2. Twelve more *bateaux-canonniers*, also numbered *1* to *12*, built at Dunkirk between 1796 and May 1797. These were identical to the previous group except that they carried only one 12pdr. They were named (order unknown) *Pas-de-Charge, Chevreuil, Feu Roulant, Maraudier, Cerf, Coq, Crachefeu, Flibustier, Hardi, Sans-Peur, Surveillant* and *Vigilant*.

3. Around 180 *bateaux-canonniers* including 60 built at Dunkirk, 31 at Le Havre, 13 at Honfleur, 16 at Dieppe, 40 at Saint-Malo, and 20 at Granville. These were built between January and August 1798 on plans by Muskeyn and had a mobile deck for putting troops ashore. Their measurements and other characteristics were very similar to those of the 1796 vessels except that some had a 24pdr forward

Admiralty draught of *Flibustier*, which it identifies as 'Flibustier (mark'd No 13)', dated Portsmouth 4 August 1798. This is one of the Muskeyn designs, inspired by experience with the Swedish Inshore Fleet, and intended for the first planned invasion of England in 1798. It was sufficiently unusual to warrant this very detailed and keyed drawing, the most significant feature being the railed ramp aft designed to quickly land a wheeled field gun – an idea borrowed directly from a Swedish design. *Flibustier* was captured during the repulse of an attack on the small English garrison occupying the St Marcouf islands off the Normandy coast. Led by Muskeyn himself, the assault was regarded as a small-scale rehearsal for the invasion of England: it ended in disaster for the attackers. (© National Maritime Museum J0012)

instead of an 18pdr. Some were returned to service in 1803 for the Boulogne Flotilla with different numbers.

4. Five *bateaux bombardiers*, *Nos.69, 71, 72, 73,* and *78*, built at Le Havre between January and November 1798 on plans by Muskeyn. These were of 30/50 tons and measured 56ft 4in, 50ft x 16ft x 5ft 2in (18.30, 16.24 x 5.20 x 1.68m) with a draught of 4ft/4ft 6in (1.30/1.46m). They had one 12-inch mortar, three masts, and 14 banks of sweeps. The survivors were redesignated *bateaux-canonniers* in 1801.

5. Ten *chaloupes-canonnières*, *Nos.74* to *83*, built at Le Havre in March and April 1798. These were of 30/50 tons and measured 61ft 4in, 57ft 9in x 16ft 3in x 5ft 4in (19.92, 18.76 x 5.28 x 1.73m) with a draught of 3ft 4in/3ft 8in (1.08/1.19m). They had a 24pdr gun forward, a 3pdr aft, and two masts. *Nos.74* to *81* were redesignated *bateaux-canonniers* in 1801.

6. Fifty *péniches* ordered, of which at least *Nos.1* to *12, 18, 20,* and *23* were built at Dunkirk between 1798 and July 1800. They were of about 20 tons and measured 60ft, 53ft x 10ft x 4ft 8in (19.49, 17.22 x 3.25 x 1.52m) with a draught of 2ft 11in/3ft 10in (0.94/1.23m). Lightly armed with 2 x 1pdrs (4 x 2pdrs in the first few), they had three masts and 14 to 16 banks of sweeps.

VENETIAN PRIZES (1797). The French took eight gun launches at Venice in 5.1797 and of these two, named *Contente* and *Enjouée* by the French, were included in the Second French Division of the Adriatic under Bourdé that occupied Corfu on 28.6.1797.

Dimensions & tons: 51ft (Venetian) x 14ft 11in x 5ft 4in (17.73 x 5.18 x 1.84m). Draught 2ft 2in/3ft 2in (0.75/1.10m). Men: 40
Guns: (Venetian) 1 x 28pdr; (French) 1 x 22pdr, 2 x 6pdr.
Later fate unknown.

Ex BRITISH NAVAL PRIZE (1798)
Growler (HMS *Growler*, gunboat of the *Courser* class launched 10.4.1797 by Pitcher, Northfleet, captured 21 December 1797 off Dungeness by the French privateers *Espiègle* and *Rusé*, and purchased by the French Navy in November 1798)

Dimensions & tons: 76ft 0in, 71ft 0in x 21ft x 8ft 4in (24.69, 23.06 x 6.82 x 2.71m). 132/200 tons. Men: 37-47.
Guns: 2 x 32pdr carronades forward, 10 x 16pdr carronades, 2 x 8pdrs.
Found by the British 1.8.1809 in a very decayed state at Veere on the island of Walcheren.

GUNBOATS BUILT IN 1798-1799 IN EGYPT. On 30 December 1798 four gunboats were ordered to be assembled at Suez for use in the Red Sea. Designed and/or built by Jean-Louis Féraud or Étienne Maillot, they had been prefabricated at Cairo and their parts were carried to Suez on camelback. The first, *Castiglione*, was launched on 14 January 1799 and completed on 15 January. *Millesimo* and *Tagliamento* were launched on 20 January, *Isonzo* followed at the end of January, and all three were completed on 1 February 1799. Three of them returned to Suez on 19 February 1799 after a sortie into the Red Sea but *Tagliamento* blew up with the loss of her entire crew on 7 February 1799 after firing three shots in combat at Kosseir. The survivors were probably scuttled when the French evacuated Suez in April 1801. Three were listed with one 6pdr or 4pdr and two 2pdrs while the ill-fated *Tagliamento* was listed with one 8pdr and two 2pdrs.

Féraud or Maillot also designed and/or built one gunboat named *Petite Cisalpine* or *Cisalpine* at Alexandria. She was launched and completed in October 1798 and was last mentioned in January 1799 on Lake Menzaleh in Egypt. She was armed with one 12pdr and four 2pdrs. The same engineer was responsible for two *bateaux-canonniers* or *barques-canonnières*, probably named *Saône* and *Garonne*, that were built at Boulak and Damietta in October and November 1798. These may have been prefabricated at Toulon in March 1798. Each carried one 12pdr gun.

LOIRE-INFÉRIEURE. Gunboat. She may have been the 'bombarde' with 4 x 24pdrs and 1 x 12-inch mortar ordered from Mathurin, Louis, and Antoine Crucy in 1794.

Dimensions & tons: unknown.
Guns: unknown.
Loire-Inférieure Nantes or Paimboeuf.
K: 1797. L: 1798. C: 10.1798.
Wrecked 12.1798 on a bar between Pont d'Yeu and Saint-Jean de Monts near Île d'Yeu.

PARISIENNE. Gunboat rigged as a *gribane* (a working craft on the lower Seine), also called a *cange*.

Dimensions & tons: unknown. Men: 11-25.
Guns: unknown.
Parisienne Paris, quai de La Rapée.
K: 1798. L: 9.1798. C: 10.1798.
Refitted as an 80-ton transport at Rouen in 12.1803 and designated *Transport No.336 Parisienne*. Decomm at Le Havre 6.1814 and sold 8.1814.

VOLCAN. Gunboat designed and/or built by Jean-François Lafosse and launched under the name *Canonnière No.1*.

Dimensions & tons: 80ft x 18ft 6in x 6ft 3in (25.99 x 6.01 x 2.03m). 60/146 tons.
Guns: 3 x 24pdrs.
Volcan Le Havre.
K: 10.1799. L: c21.1.1800. C: 3.1800.
Wrecked near Shoreham 4.12.1802.

ETNA. Gunboat. Another *Etna*, a *corvette-canonnière*, was built at about the same time at Cherbourg.

Dimensions & tons: unknown. Men: 42-47.
Guns: 3 x 24pdrs.
Etna Toulon Dyd.
K: 1800. L: c6.1801. Comm: 4.7.1801. C: 7.1801.
Condemned at Toulon c7.1814, BU there 1815.

PURCHASED AND REQUISITIONED GUNBOATS (1798-1799)
Négresse (tartane requisitioned 3.1798 at Marseille and fitted as a gunboat, 53 men, carried 2 x 18pdrs and 2 x 6pdrs). Captured 18.3.1799 off the Syrian coast by a British division and taken into RN service as a gunboat with 6 guns, sold 1802.
Étoile (tartane requisitioned 3.1798 at Marseille and fitted as a gunboat or aviso, 55 men, carried 2 x 18pdrs and 2 x 6pdrs). Sent from Toulon to Egypt 1.8.1800 and captured by a British brig off Cape Bon.
Éclair (tartane requisitioned 3.1798 at Marseille and fitted as a gunboat, 55 men, carried 2 x 18pdrs and 2 x 6pdrs). Last mentioned 1.1799 while in Egypt at Rosetta.
Marguerite (tartane requisitioned 3.1798 at Marseille and fitted as a gunboat, 55 men, carried 2 x 12pdrs and 2 x 6pdrs). Captured 8.1798 by the Turks in the Mediterranean.
Hirondelle (tartane requisitioned 3.1798 at Marseille and fitted as a gunboat, 55 men, carried 2 x 12pdrs and 2 x 6pdrs). Arrived at Marseille from Egypt 29.9.1799 and probably returned to her owner.
Espérance (gunboat requisitioned at Civita-Vecchia in 3.1798, carried 1 x 36pdr). Burned or sunk on 16.4.1801 with *Hélène, Saint Jean-Baptiste,* and *Thébaïde* by British and Turkish gunboats, probably during the assault on Fort Julien near Rosetta. No other information is available on *Saint Jean-Baptiste* and the djerme *Thébaïde*.
Sainte-Hélène or *Hélène* (gunboat or djerme probably requisitioned at Civita-Vecchia in 3.1798, carried 1 x 18pdr). Mentioned 11.1799 en route to Burlos in the Nile Delta. Burned or sunk on 16.4.1801 with *Espérance, Saint Jean-Baptiste,* and *Thébaïde* by British and Turkish gunboats, probably during the assault on Fort Julien near Rosetta.
Constance (gunboat requisitioned at Civita-Vecchia in 3.1798, carried 1 x 36pdr). Left at Malta 6.1798, unserviceable there 8.1798.
Expédition (tartane requisitioned and commissioned 4.1798 at Toulon as a gunboat, 55 men, carried 2 x 18pdrs and 2 x 6pdrs). Captured 3.1799 by the Russians in the capitulation of Corfu and became *Ekspedition* in the Russian Navy. Described in Russian sources as a three-masted polacre. The Russians operated her in the Black Sea until 1821.

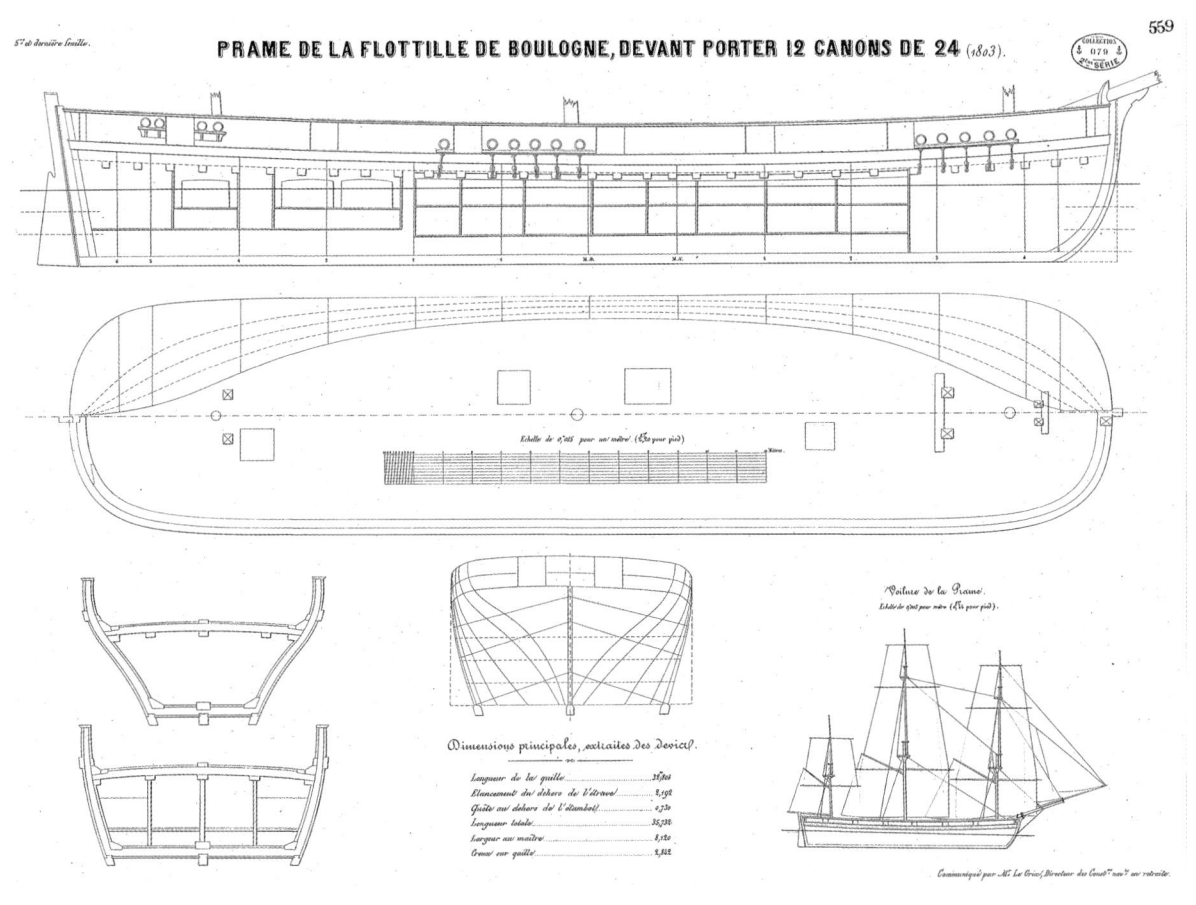

PRAME DE LA FLOTTILLE DE BOULOGNE, DEVANT PORTER 12 CANONS DE 24 (1803)

Official general arrangement plan of the Boulogne Flotilla *Prame* design. The sections show the flat-bottomed hull with skids at each bilge to keep it upright when beached. The type was ship rigged, but the mizzen was far smaller than usual in proportion to the rest of the sail plan. (Atlas du Génie Maritime, French collection, plate 559)

Victoire (gunboat commissioned during the Egyptian expedition, possibly requisitioned 4.1798 at Civita-Vecchia, carried 1 x 36pdr and 4 x 2pdrs). Operated on the Nile, captured 8.3.1801 by the British.

Utile (gunboat that was at Toulon in 5.1798 out of commission). Later fate unknown.

Bourlos (gunboat that was in service on the Nile in 1798). Last mentioned 1799 in Egypt.

Terrible (gunboat that was in service at Toulon in 1799, 4 guns). Refitted at Toulon 7.1803, possibly BU at Brest 7-8.1804.

(C) Vessels acquired from 25 March 1802

VESSELS BUILT FOR THE BOULOGNE FLOTILLA (1803-1805)
(*Prames, Chaloupes-Canonnières, Bateaux-Canonniers, Péniches* and other vessels)

Following the collapse of the Treaty of Amiens, on 13 May 1803, Napoleon as First Consul decided that he needed to finish with Britain. At this date, in addition to 23 ships of the line, 25 frigates and 107 corvettes and similar combatant vessels in commission, the navy still included 167 flotilla craft retained from the invasion flotilla of 1800. Napoleon's planned offensive against Britain initially envisaged a total force of 310 small, shallow-draught armed vessels to operate in support of a vast collection of requisitioned fishery and other craft transporting 100,000 troops across the Straits of Dover. The scale of the project was swiftly increased from the initial 310 armed vessels to 1,410 by July and 2,008 by August.

Under his energetic direction, plans advanced rapidly with the establishment of the Army of the Ocean Coasts, and 160,000 soldiers and 10,000 horses were concentrated on camps established at Boulogne and other ports scheduled as embarkation points for the invasion – Étaples, Ambleteuse and Wimereux. Napoleon's Boulogne Flotilla, which was to carry his invading army to England, consisted of several thousand small craft of many types. Most of them were fishing vessels and other coastal craft, over 500 of which were requisitioned or purchased in French ports. These purchased vessels are outside the scope of this study, but fortunately a detailed alphabetical list of them is contained in Cdt. Alain Demerliac's *Nomenclature des navires français de 1800 à 1815* (see Bibliography).

A massive new construction program of some 1,300 vessels was also undertaken in support of the flotilla, primarily consisting of dozens of *prames* ('flat-bottomed' troop transports with heavy gun batteries) and hundreds of vessels of the three smaller types shown below. All of these were designed with shallow draughts (which inhibited their seaworthiness) for landing amphibious forces directly upon British beaches, and a parallel can be drawn with the numerous landing ships and landing craft of the modern era. The *prames* were named, while the smaller types were designated only by numbers and did not receive names; the reader is referred to Demerliac for individual listings. Two specialised types of corvettes built primarily for use with the Boulogne Flotilla, *corvettes-canonnières* and flat-bottomed corvettes, are listed with the other corvettes in Chapter 6.

(i) *PRAMES*

VILLE DE GAND Class – 450 tons. Designed by Pierre-Alexandre-Laurent Forfait, who had been Minister of Marine under the Consulate, and from June 1803 was Inspector-General for the Boulogne Flotilla (the prospective invasion force). The *prames* combined a very heavy gun armament with the ability to put ashore a contingent of over 100 troops. At least 61 *prames* were planned in 1803, of which 20 were completed (3 as gabarres) and 16 were named but not completed. Construction of the latter and at least 15 unnamed units was abandoned in early 1804. The unnamed units included eight to be built under contract at Antwerp by Danet after the two listed below, two at Calais after the two listed below, two at St. Valéry, and three at Honfleur. Of the thirteen ports in northern France and Belgium that built these vessels, only Le Havre produced more than two units. Available records for many of these *prames* show periods of service from commissioning to 31 March 1807 and then again from mid-late 1811 to 31 December 1812; these service records may not be complete. Another listing, probably in error, includes a *Ville de La Mayenne* (reflecting confusion with *Ville de Mayence*?) and a *Ville de Paris* while omitting *Ville de Perpignan*.

The vessels were rigged as corvettes, but with a minimal sail area, and had a curved keel on each side separated from the centreline keel by 3.00 metres amidships and joining it at each end intended to stabilise the vessel when beached. Their shallow draught, built with a view to landing troops on beaches, made them extremely leewardly and difficult to sail close-hauled. The twelve broadside ports for 24pdrs were staggered port and starboard to allow each gun adequate space to recoil; there were also additional pairs of ports at bow and stern to allow guns from the broadside to be deployed as bow or stern chasers. When fitted as horse transports they could carry 50 horses.

Dimensions & tons: 110 ft 0in wl x 25ft 0in, 25ft 6in ext x 8ft 9in (35.73 x 8.12, 8.30 x 2.84m). 230/450 tons. Draught 8ft 4in (2.70m) aft. Men: 38 plus 120 soldiers.

Guns: 12 x 24pdrs.

Ville de Gand Ghent.
K: 7.1803. Named: 17.9.1803. L: 10.1803. Comm: 11.10.1803 at Ostend. C: 3.1804.
Decomm. 31.12.1812 at Boulogne, probably struck 3.1814.

Ville de Montpellier Ghent.
Named: 17.9.1803. K: 10.1803. L: 4.2.1804. Comm: 29.3.1804 at Ostend. C: 5.1804.
Decomm. 31.12.1812 at Boulogne, probably struck 3.1814 then BU.

Ville de Clermont-Ferrand Ghent.
Named: 17.9.1803. K: 2.1804. Construction abandoned in 3.1804.

Ville de Cognac or *Ville de Coignac* Liège or elsewhere on the Meuse?
K: 1803. L: 1.1804. C: 2.1804. Probably was a *prame* identical to *Ville de Gand* but this is not certain.
She was in service on 17.1.1804 at Brielle near Rotterdam at the mouth of the Meuse as a station ship when, under the name *Ville de Coignac*, she arrested the Prussian brig *Hope*. The brig was taken into the navy as *Surveillant* (later *Éveillé*) and replaced her captor as station ship under a ministerial order of 9.4.1804. *Ville de Coignac* does not appear to have rejoined the flotilla at Boulogne and her fate is unknown.

Ville de Bruxelles Ostend.
K: 8.1803. Named: 17.9.1803. L: 9.2.1804. Comm: 16.2.1804. C: 3.1804.
Decomm. 31.12.1812 at Boulogne, probably struck 3.1814 then BU.

Ville de Tours Ostend.
K: 8.1803. Named: 17.9.1803. L: 3.1804. Comm: 2.3.1804. C: 4.1804.
Decomm. 31.12.1812 at Boulogne, probably struck 3.1814 then BU.

Ville d'Ostende Ostend (probably).
K: end 1803. Construction abandoned in 1804.

Ville de Mayence Dunkirk (Constructeur, probably Jean-Charles Garrigues)
K: 20.7.1803. Named: 17.9.1803. L: 13.2.1804. C: 5.1804. Comm: 1.6.1804 at Ostend.
Decomm. 31.12.1812 at Boulogne, probably struck 3.1814 then BU.

Ville de Poitiers Dunkirk.
K: 8.1803. Named: 17.9.1803. Construction abandoned 1.1804 at 4/24ths completion.

Ville d'Avignon Dunkirk.
K: 8.1803. Named: 17.9.1803. Construction abandoned 1.1804 at 3/24ths completion.

Ville de Rennes Dunkirk.
Named: 17.9.1803. K: 1.1804. Construction abandoned 1.1804 at 1/24th completion.

Ville d'Angers Dunkirk.
Named: 17.9.1803. Not laid down. Construction ordered abandoned 22.10.1803 to hasten the construction of *péniches*.

Ville de Reims Dunkirk.
Named: 17.9.1803. Not laid down. Construction ordered abandoned 22.10.1803 to hasten the construction of *péniches*.

Ville de Turin Dunkirk (probably).
Named: 17.9.1803. Not laid down. Construction ordered abandoned 22.10.1803 to hasten the construction of *péniches*.

Ville d'Anvers Danet, Antwerp
K: 8.1803. Named: 17.9.1803. L: 10.3.1804. Comm: 3.3.1804. C: 4.1804.
Refitted as gabarre (4 x 8pdrs) in 8.1811 at Boulogne and recomm. 1.10.1812. Renamed *Bretonne* 24.9.1814, *Ville d'Anvers* 23.3.1815, and *Bretonne* 15.7.1815. Condemned 3.2.1815 or c9.1815 at Le Havre and BU there approved 10.10.1815.

Ville d'Aix Danet, Antwerp
K: 8.1803. Named: 17.9.1803. L: 10.3.1804. Comm: 3.3.1804 (sic). C: 4.1804.
Decomm. 31.12.1812 at Boulogne, probably struck 3.1814 then BU.

Ville de Genève Bruges.
K: 8.1803. Named: 17.9.1803. L: 3.1804. Comm: 22.3.1804 at Ostend. C: 7.1804.
Refitted as gabarre (450 tons, 4-8pdrs) at Boulogne in 8.1811 and recomm. 23.8.1811. Renamed *Flamande* 24.9.1814, *Ville de Genève* 23.3.1815, and *Flamande* 15.7.1815. Sailed for Brest 16.1.1815 and used as barracks at Brest (Kerhuon). Listed as transport 1819-26. Struck 1826, last mentioned 1827.

Ville d'Aix La Chapelle Calais.
K: 8.1803. Named: 17.9.1803. Construction ordered abandoned 10.9.1804 at 5/24ths completion and incomplete hull left to her builder.

Ville de Grenoble Calais.
K: 8.1803. Named: 17.9.1803. Construction abandoned 1.1804 at 3/24ths completion.

Ville de Dijon Gravelines.
K: 8.1803. Named: 17.9.1803. Construction abandoned 1.1804 at 3/24ths completion.

Ville de Toulouse Gravelines.
Named: 17.9.1803. K: 8.1803. Construction abandoned 1.1804 at 1/24th completion. Name may have been spelled *Toulouze*.

Ville de Metz Bruges.
Named: 17.9.1803. K: 10.1803. Construction abandoned in 2.1804.

Ville de Pau Rouen.
K: 11.1803. L: 25.3.1804. Comm: 12.4.1804. C: 6.1804.
Decomm. 30.9.1813 at Boulogne, probably struck 3.1814 and then BU.

Ville de Limoges Rouen.
K: 11.1803. Not launched, construction stopped 2.1804 when at 10/24ths completion. Decided in 4.1804 to complete her as a gabarre (probably modified as *Ville d'Amiens*, below) but this was apparently not done.

Coloured aquatint published in 1812 depicting the action off Boulogne in which a British squadron comprising the frigate *Naiad* and three brigs fought seven prames and fifteen gunboats on 20 September 1811, resulting in the capture of the prame *Ville de Lyons*. The engraving gives a good overall impression of the low, flat profile of a prame, but the mizzen carries a topgallant not present on the plan. (Courtesy of Beverley R. Robinson Collection, US Naval Academy Museum)

Ville de Perpignan Rouen.
K: 12.1803. Construction abandoned in 2.1804.

Ville de Strasbourg Fécamp.
K: 11.1803. L: 26.3.1804. Comm: 21.4.1804. C: 5.1804.
Decomm. 31.12.1812 at Boulogne, probably struck 3.1814 then BU.

Ville de Besançon Le Havre (Constructeur, Jean Chaumont)
K: 11.1803. L: 26.3.1804. Comm: 26.4.1804. C: 5.1804.
Decomm. 31.12.1812, Service craft by 5.1814 (no longer on fleet lists), struck 1819 at Dunkirk.

Ville de Rouen Le Havre (Constructeur, Jean Chaumont)
K: 10.1803. L: 12.3.1804. Comm: 17.4.1804. C: 4.1804. Later armed with 2 x 8pdrs and 12 x 24pdr carronades.
Refitted as gabarre (450 tons) 4.1814 at Boulogne or Le Havre and recomm. 1.4.1814. Decomm. 1.3.1816. Unserviceable at Le Havre 7.1816. Sold 24.1.1818 at Le Havre.

Ville de Caen Le Havre (Constructeur, Jean Chaumont)
K: 10.1803. L: 26.3.1804. Comm: 21.4.1804. C: 5.1804.
Refitted as gabarre (450 tons) 8.1811 at Boulogne and recomm. 10.8.1811. Decomm. 20.8.1814. Condemned 17.10.1814 and became service craft at Brest. Entered a drydock at Brest 22.8.1816 to be BU, BU completed 9.1816.

Ville de Lyon Le Havre (Constructeur, Jean Chaumont)
Named: 24.8.1803. K: 12.1803. L: 10.4.1804. Comm: 21.4.1804. C: 6.1804.
Boarded and captured 20.9.1811 off Boulogne by HMS *Naiad* (38), with brigs *Rinaldo*, *Redpole* and *Castillian*. The British recorded her dimensions as 117 x 26 British feet (35.66 x 7.92m).

Ville de Cambrai Le Havre (Constructeur, Jean Chaumont)
K: 12.1803. L: 24.4.1804. Comm: 21.4.1804 (sic). C: 5.1804.
Decomm. 31.12.1812 at Boulogne, probably struck 3.1814 then BU.
A list dated 2.11.1803 may show two *prames* named *Ville de Cambrai*, one at Le Havre at 3/24ths and one at Rouen at 1/6th.

Ville du Havre Le Havre (Constructeur, Jean Chaumont)
K: 12.1803. L: 5.1804. Comm: 15.5.1804. C: 6.1804.
Decomm. 31.12.1812 at Boulogne, probably struck 3.1814 then BU.

Ville d'Amiens Le Havre-Ingouville (constructed and modified by Jean Chaumont)
K: 10.1803. L: 13.6.1805. Comm: 15.11.1805. C: 11.1805.
Re-rated gabarre 5.1804, lifted on her building ways 4-5.1805 to add a hull with conventional lines under her flat bottom and convert her to a gabarre. As modified: 225/430 tons, 38 men, 4-8pdrs (1805), 14-36pdr carronades and 4-36pdr obusiers (9.1811), 14-6pdrs (1813). Could carry 225 tons of shipbuilding timber. Captured 26.5.1815 near Guernsey by HMS *Désirée* (36) and taken to Plymouth.

Ville d'Orléans Le Havre-Ingouville (constructed and modified by Jean Chaumont)
K: 11.1803. L: 28.6.1805. C: 1805.
Re-rated gabarre (450 tons) 5.1804, converted in the same manner as *Ville d'Amiens* 4-5.1805. Used as barracks at Cherbourg 1815. Listed as transport 1821-26. Struck 1826 and hulked at Cherbourg, last mentioned in 1827. Armaments: 4-8pdrs (1806), 14-6pdrs (1811).

Ville de Liège Le Havre-Ingouville (constructed and modified by Jean Chaumont)
K: 11.1803. L: 5.3.1806. C: 1806.
Converted to a gabarre (450 tons) in the same manner as *Ville d'Amiens* in 1805. Renamed *Picarde* 24.9.1814, *Ville de Liège* 23.3.1815, and *Picarde* 15.7.1815. Listed as transport 1819-26. Struck at Cherbourg 1826 and hulked, last mentioned in 1827. Armaments as *Ville d'Orléans*. Name sometimes reported as *Picardie* but official lists show *Picarde*.

CANONNIÈRE DE LA FLOTTILLE DE BOULOGNE (1803).

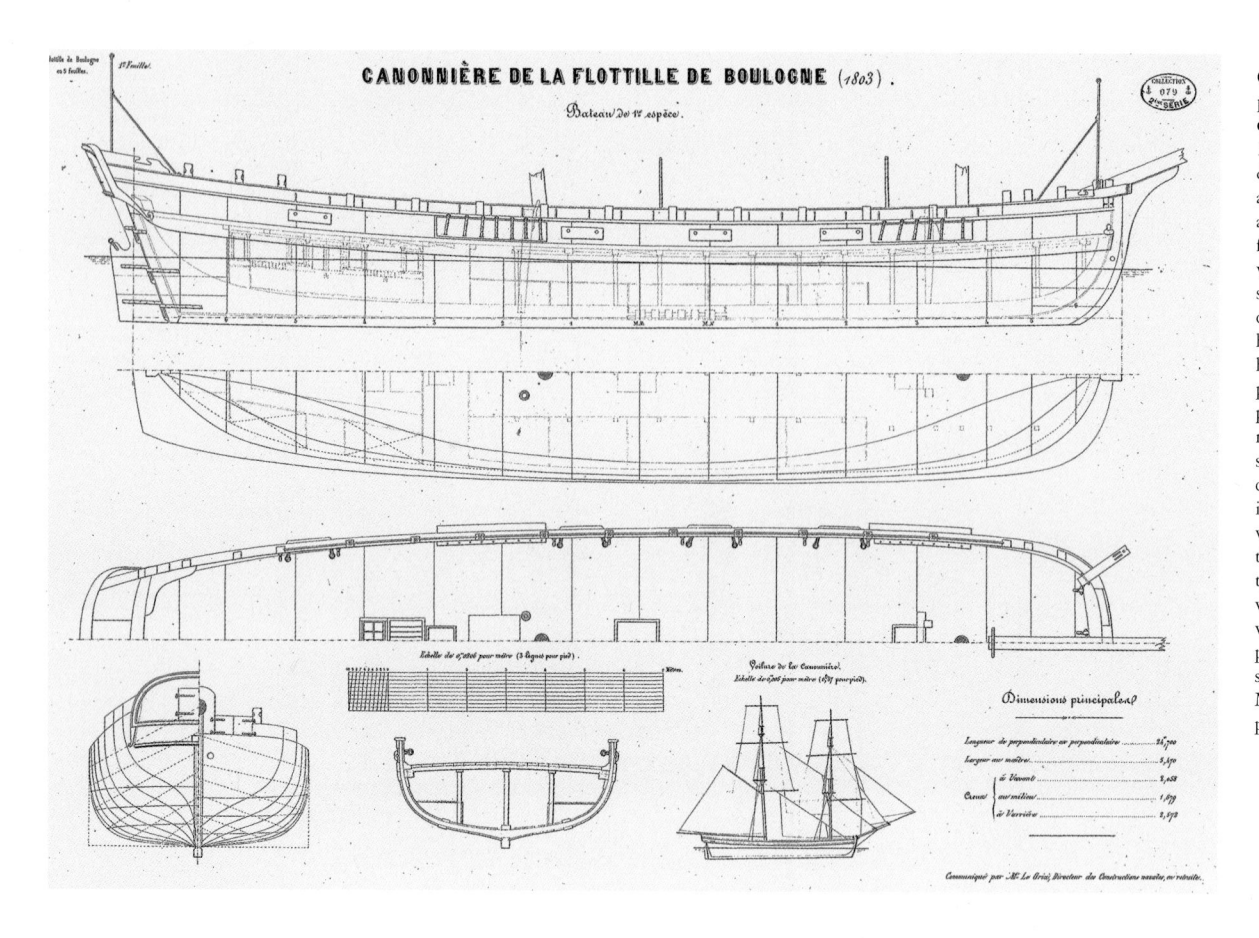

Official general arrangement plan of the Boulogne Flotilla *Canonnière* design (*bâtiments de 1ère espèce*). The gunports were disposed two facing forwards and one aft. Although they had a rather more sea-kindly hull form than the prames, they were still flat enough to allow safe beaching. However, the combination of this shallow hull and the brig rig would have meant a very poor performance to windward – in practice they could do little more than sail downwind – severely constraining the conditions under which an invasion could be mounted with any chance of success. As the second and third main types of the Boulogne Flotilla were equipped with far more weatherly lug rigs, this is a particularly curious choice of sail plan. (Atlas du Génie Maritime, French collection, plate 555)

Ville de Chambéry Le Havre.
K: 11.1803. Construction abandoned 2.1804 at 6/24ths completion.

(ii) CHALOUPES-CANONNIÈRES (BÂTIMENTS DE 1ère ESPÈCE)

Canonnière No.22 Class. These *bâtiments de 1ère espèce* ('vessels of the first type'), usually simply called *canonnières*, were generally similar to the gunboat classes of the 1790s. Designed by Pierre-Alexandre-Laurent Forfait, they combined a serious gun armament with the ability to carry a company of infantry (130 men) without undue crowding. Some 330 of this type were initially intended, but nearly a hundred additional units were added subsequently. *Canonnière No.21* was probably the prototype for the class, although she was renumbered No.98 in February 1804. As built, the class consisted of *Nos.22* to *No.445* less some cancelled. They had 11 pairs of sweeps and were brig-rigged. The locations below are those where each batch was commissioned (not necessarily the place of construction, although probably so). Typically each cost 30,000 francs including armament. *Canonnières No.1–No.13* were gunboats from 1793-94 that exchanged their names for numbers. *Canonnières No.14–No.20* were commissioned at Brest, Rouen, and Lannion between 9.1803 and 2.1804; their origin is unknown and they may have been purchased.

Dimensions & tons: 76ft 1in, 70ft 6in x 16ft 10in x 5ft 0in (24.72, 22.90 x 5.47 x 1.62m). 70/131 tons. Draught 4ft 4in/4ft 11in (1.40/1.60m). Men: 62, or 22 crew and 106-130 soldiers.
Guns: 3 x 24pdrs, 2 x 36pdr or 1 x 8in. obusiers.

No.21	See *No.98* below. (The number was reused for the *Inquiète* of 1794.)
No.22 to *No.23*	Lançon (comm. 9-11.1803)
No.24 to *No.56*	Saint-Servan and Saint-Malo (comm. 11.1803-3.1804)
No.57 to *No.65*	Granville (comm. 1-2.1804, *No.66* to *No.68* cancelled 3.1804)
No.69 to *No.72*	Lorient (comm. 10-11.1803)
No.73 to *No.94*	Nantes (comm. 9.1803-3.1804)
No.95 to *No.97*	Rochefort (comm. 11-12.1803)
No.98 to *No.119*	Le Havre (comm. 9.1803-4.1804)
No.120 to *No.122*	Fécamp (comm. 12.1803-1.1804)
No.123 to *No.124*	St. Valéry en Caux (comm. 11.1803)
No.125 to *No.129*	Dieppe (comm. 10-12.1803)
No.130 to *No.140*	Rouen/Paris (comm. 8.1803-1.1804)
No.141 to *No.159*	Le Havre (comm. 9.1803-4.1804)
No.160 to *No.162*	Caen (comm. 12.1803-4.1804)
No.163 to *No.182*	Bordeaux (comm. 7.1803-2.1804, some built by André Guibert)
No.183 to *No.194*	Bayonne (comm. 11.1803-3.1804)
No.195 to *No.197*	Nantes (comm. 1-2.1804)
No.198 to *No.200*	Redon (comm. 12.1803, built by Claude Donat)
No.201 to *No.213*	Dunkirk (comm. 12.1803-6.1804, *No.208* probably not completed)
No.214	Bergues (comm. 5.1804)
No.215 to *No.220*	St. Valéry sur Somme (comm. 1-5.1804)
No.221 to *No.232*	Calais (comm. 2-6.1804, *No.225* and *232* abandoned 1 and 17.1.1804)
No.233 to *No.237*	Étaples (comm. 1-2.1804, *No.237* abandoned 10.3.1804)
No.238 to *No.248*	Boulogne (comm. 11.1803-3.1804)
No.249 to *No.257*	Liège (comm. 10-12.1803)
No.258 to *No.259*	Gravelines (comm. 5.1804)
No.260 to *No.266*	Le Havre (comm. 1-5.1804)
No.267 to *No.269*	St. Valéry en Caux (comm. 11.1803-3.1804)

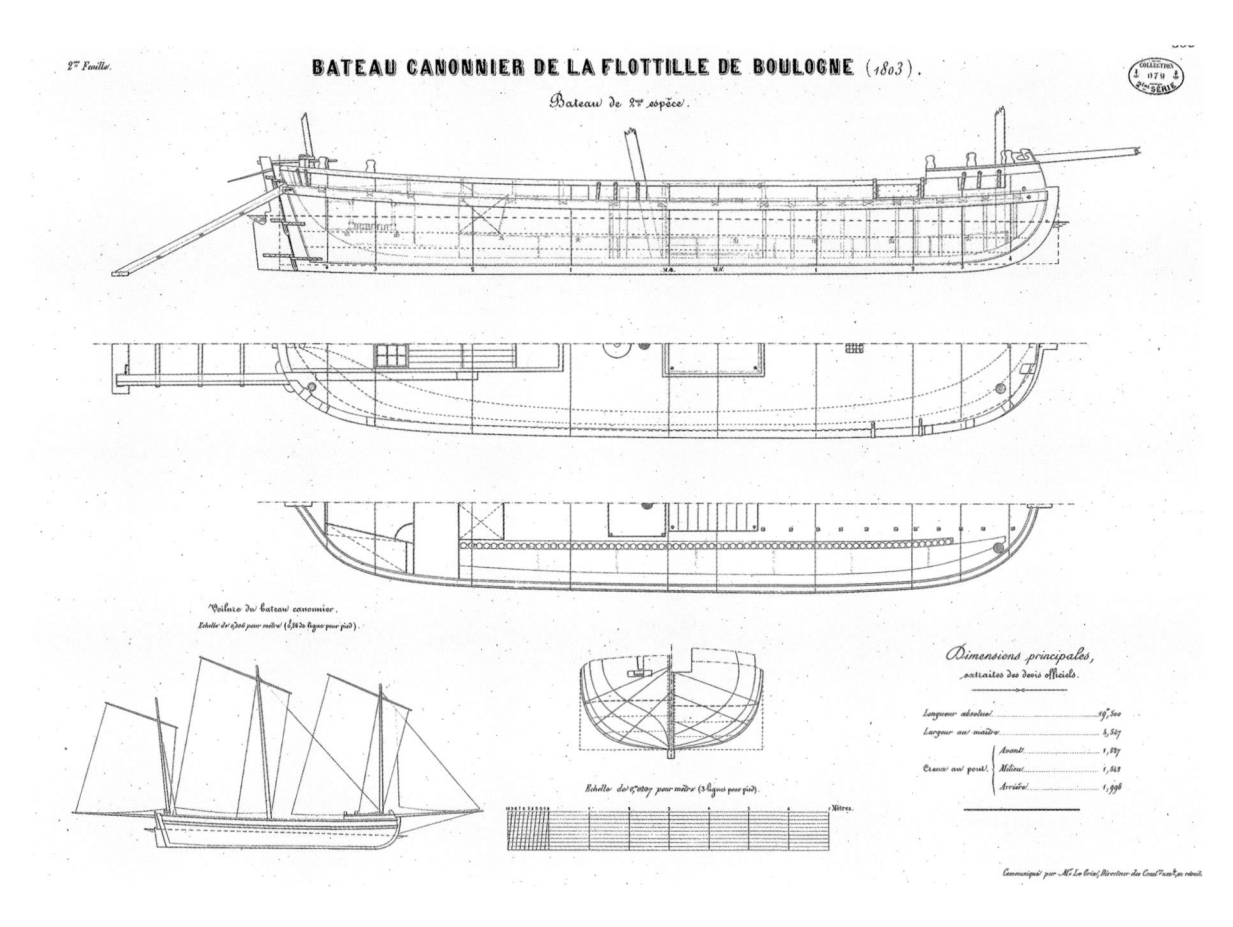

BATEAU CANONNIER DE LA FLOTTILLE DE BOULOGNE (1803).

Official general arrangement plan of the Boulogne Flotilla *Bateau-canonnier* design (*bâtiments de 2ème espèce*). This was a specialist artillery transport, intended to carry a field gun or howitzer, its ammunition limber, and the two horses to draw it. The ramp at the stern would be used to land the gun. Not shown is the 24pdr bow gun, but the offset to starboard of the fore and mizzen masts to make way for this gun and the stern ramp is indicated. (Atlas du Génie Maritime, French collection, plate 556)

No.270 to *No.271*	Rouen (comm. 11.1803-3.1804, *No.271* became *No.77* in 1804)
No.272 to *No.273*	Cherbourg (comm. 10-11.1803, ex *Foudre* and *Infernale* 6.1803)
No.274	Caen (comm. 4.1804)
No.275	La Hogue (comm. 2.1804)
No.276	Le Havre (comm. 4.1804)
No.277 to *No.278*	Rouen (comm. 3.1804)
No.279	Bergues (comm. 6.1804)
No.280	Antwerp (comm. 4.1804)
No.281 to *No.283*	Nantes (comm. 2-3.1804)
No.284 to *No.286*	Le Havre (comm. 11.1803-3.1804)
No.287 to *No.309*	Rouen (comm. 1-4.1804)
No.310 to *No.313*	Mézières (comm. 3-5.1804)
No.314 to *No.323*	Colmar (comm. 4.1804-11.1805, *No.322* and *323* probably abandoned in 3.1804)
No.324 to *No.327*	Strasbourg (comm. 12.1803)
No.328 and *No.329*	These were the *Terrible* and *Chiffonne* of 1793 redesignated in 2.1804.
No.330	Le Havre, Chantier de 'La Barre' (comm. 10.1804)
No.331 to *No.400*	May have been projected but were not built.
No.401 to *No.402*	Cherbourg (comm. 12.1803)
No.403 to *No.435*	May have been projected but were not built.
No.436	Le Havre (comm. 2.1804)
No.437 to *No.443*	Honfleur (comm. 3-5.1804)
No.444 to *No.445*	Dieppe (comm. 1-2.1804)

The Boulogne Flotilla had 118 of these *canonnières de 1ère espèce* in July 1804 and increased rapidly to 259 in July 1805. Numbers then fell off; the flotilla returning to 118 gunboats in January 1813 and declining to 59 on 30 May 1814. Only the following ten remained on the fleet list on 1 November 1819.

No.29, comm. 7.12.1803 at Saint.Malo, decomm. 31.5.1814 at Cherbourg, struck 1821.

No.71, comm. 14.11.1803 at Lorient (4 x 24pdrs), decomm. 7.1815 at Brest, struck 1821.

No.74, comm. 7.12.1803 at Nantes, struck late 1820.

No.88, comm. 23.9.1804 at Nantes, wrecked 11.11.1810 at Yport but refloated, at Cherbourg 6.1811, struck there 1821.

No.97, comm. 12.12.1803 at Rochefort (3 x 24pdrs), decomm. 29.7.1815 at Brest, struck 1821.

No.171, comm. 12.7.1803 at Bordeaux, refitted 1-6.1812 at Rochefort (70 men, 3 x 24pdrs, 2 x 4pdrs), refitted 1819 (28 men, 3 x 24pdrs) station ship at Pauillac 8.1819, decomm. 31.12.1826, condemned early 1831. Dimensions & tons in 9.1819: 78ft 10in, 68ft 6in x 17ft 9in x 4ft 10in (25.61, 22.25 x 5.76 x 1,57m). 50/165 tons. Draught 5ft 4in/6ft 10in (1.73/2.22m). Guns: 2 x 24pdrs, 4 swivels.

No.179, comm. 24.9.1803 at Bordeaux, listed in 1813 at St.Malo with 108 men and 1 x 12pdr, 4 x 4pdrs, decomm. 31.7.1815, struck 1821.

No.180, comm. 24.9.1803 at Bordeaux, listed in 1813 at St.Malo with 80 men and 3 x 18pdrs, 2 x 12pdrs, decomm. 31.7.1815, struck 1821.

No.192, comm. 8.3.1804 at Bayonne, listed in 1812 with 130 men and 4 x 12pdrs, decomm. 10.7.1814 at Brest, listed in 1820 with 4 x 24pdrs, struck 1821 at Brest.

No.*282*, comm. 22.3.1804 at Nantes, listed in 1806 with 2 x 24pdrs and 8 x 12pdrs, listed in 1812with 132 men and 4 x 12pdrs, decomm. 1.8.1815 at Brest, struck 1821.

(iii) *BATEAUX-CANONNIERS (BÂTIMENTS DE 2ème ESPÈCE)*

Bareau-canonnier No.98 Class. These *bateaux-canonniers* (artillery boats) or 'vessels of the second type' were designed by Pierre-Alexandre Forfait specifically to carry some of the expedition's horses, artillery, and ammunition. They were three-masted lug-rigged vessels, with a total sail area of 2,540 sq.ft (268 sq.m) and 14 pairs of sweeps. Each had a stable fitted in the hold with stalls for two artillery horses. On deck was a fully-loaded artillery wagon, and the howitzer or field artillery piece on the stern was intended to be put ashore during the landing. Some 450 of these were planned initially, and about 312 of these were built in 1803-4 (numbered from 98 to 476, with some gaps in the numbering). The locations below are those where each batch was commissioned (not necessarily the place of construction, although probably so). Typically each cost 20,000 francs including armament. Individual disposals are not given below, but most were decommissioned during the post-Trafalgar period and disposed of. None remained on the list in 1819.

Dimensions & tons: 60ft 0in, 54ft 0in x 14ft 0in x 4ft 9in (19.50, 17.54 x 4.55 x 1.54m). 35/52-68 tons. Draught 4ft/4ft 2in (1.30/1.35m). Men: 6 crew, + 64-94 soldiers and 2 horses.
Guns: 1 x 24pdr siege piece, plus a howitzer and a field gun

No.98 to *No.104*	Cherbourg (comm. 9.1803)
No.105 to *No.111*	St. Malo (comm. 9.1803)
No.112 to *No.116*	Granville (comm. 9.1803)
No.117 to *No.125*	St. Malo (comm. 9-10.1803)
No.126	Granville (comm. 9.1803)
No.127 to *No.135*	These were pre-1802 vessels renumbered
No.136 to *No.137*	Granville (comm. 3.1804)
No.138 to *No.146*	Le Havre (comm. 8-10.1803)
No.147	St Valéry en Caux (comm. 3.1804)
No.148 to *No.151*	Rouen (comm. 9-12.1803)
No.152 to *No.158*	Le Havre (comm. 11.1803-1.1804)
No.159 to *No.165*	Fécamp (comm. 11-12.1803
No.166 to *No.174*	St Valéry en Caux (comm. 11.1803-3.1804)
No.175 to *No.182*	Dieppe (comm. 10-12.1803)
No.183 to *No.225*	Rouen/Paris (comm. 8.1803-3.1804)
No.226 to *No.228*	Le Havre (built at Nantes, comm. at Le Havre 10.1803-1.1804)
No.229 to *No.234*	Honfleur (comm. 1-5.1804)
No.235 to *No.250*	Le Havre (comm. 10.1803-6.1804, *No.238* not built)
No.251	Cherbourg (comm. 2.1804)
No.252 to *No.255*	Caen (comm. 1-4.1804)
No.256 to *No.258*	Cherbourg (comm. 12.1803-4.1804)
No.259 to *No.269*	Thsese were pre-1802 vessels renumbered
No.270 to *No.274*	Rochefort (comm. 12.1803-9.1804)
No.275 to *No.316*	Jean-Baptiste and Laurent Courau, Bordeaux (comm. 9.1803 except *No.278*, 4.1804)
No.317 to *No.320*	Rochefort (comm. 11-12.1803)
No.321 to *No.322*	Bayonne (comm. 2-3.1804)
No.323 to *No.324*	Not completed.
No.325 to *No.339*	Mathurin, Louis & Antoine Crucy, Nantes (comm. 9.1803-3.1804)
No.340 to *No.343*	Lorient (comm. 12.1803)
No.344 to *No.350*	Auray (comm. 1-2.1804)
No.351	Hennebon (comm. 2.1804)
No.352 to *No.354*	Claude Donat, Redon (comm. 12.1803)
No.355 to *No.357*	Auray (comm. 1-2.1804)
No.358 to *No.361*	Vannes (comm. 1-2.1804)
No.362	Dunkirk (comm. 12.1803)
No.363 to *No.364*	Boulogne (comm. 12.1803-1.1804, probably built at Dunkirk)
No.365 to *No.366*	Antwerp (comm. 1.1804)
No.367 to *No.373*	Dunkirk (comm. 4-5.1804)
No.374	Antwerp (comm. 1.1804)
No.375 to *No.379*	Dunkirk (comm. 4-5.1804)
No.380 to *No.385*	Bergues (comm. 2-3.1804)
No.386	Ostend (comm. 4.1804, built at Bruges)
No.387 to *No.396*	Calais (comm. 2-5.1804, *No.393-396* abandoned 1.1804)
No.397 to *No.409*	St. Valéry sur Somme (comm. 11.1803-2.1804)
No.410 to *No.414*	Nantes (comm. 10.1803-3.1804)
No.415 to *No.424*	Saint-Malo (comm. 9.1803-4.1804)
No.425	Rouen (comm. 2.1804, possibly built at Le Havre)
No.426 to *No.427*	St. Valéry en Caux (comm. 3.1804)
No.428 to *No.430*	Le Havre (comm. 2-4.1804)
No.431	Not completed.
No.432	Unknown (captured 1.1804)
No.433	Dunkirk (comm. 2.1804)
No.434 to *No.436*	These were probably earlier vessels renumbered
No.437	Antwerp (comm. 3.1804)
No.438	Le Havre (comm. 2.1804)
No.439 to *No.458*	Rouen (comm. 12.1803-5.1804)
No.459	Boulogne (comm. 5.1804)
No.460	Rouen (comm. 4.1804)
No.461	Ostend (comm. 4.1804)
No.476	Le Havre (comm. 1.1804)

(iv) *PÉNICHES (BÂTIMENTS DE 3ème ESPÈCE)*

Péniche No.1 Class. These péniches (pinnaces) or 'vessels of the third type' were designed by Pierrre-Alexandre-Laurent Forfait to carry the bulk of the troops of the expedition. These slender three-masted craft were lug-rigged and had 13 pairs of oars. They carried only one or two small guns and used most of their modest capacity to transport 55 to 60 soldiers with their rations, weapons, and baggage. Some 460 of these péniches were built in 1803-4 for the planned invasion of Britain in numerous ports between Antwerp through Northern France and down the Atlantic coast as far as Bayonne. The craft were numbered Péniches No.1 to No.542 (one probably later being renumbered No.584), the numbers originally being followed by a 'bis' that was soon omitted from the lists. These numerous vessels began to leave service soon after 1805, and by 1819 none remained on the fleet list.

Dimensions & tons: 60ft 0in, 53ft 8in x 10ft 0in x 4ft 0in (19.49, 17.43 x 3.25 x 1.31m). 20/39 tons. Draught 3ft 11in/4ft (1.27/1.31m). Men: 6 (including an officer), 60 soldiers
Guns: 1 x 4pdr plus a 6in obusier or an 8in mortar

Forfait also prepared a design for smaller caiques for use where facilities would not permit the 60ft péniches to be built. These vessels were of 13/25 tons, and measured 42ft 0in x 8ft 6in x 3ft 0in (13.64 x 2.76 x 0.97m); they are also recorded as 12/22 tons and 43ft 3in, 37ft 3in x 10ft 6in x 4ft 0in (14.05, 12.10 x 3.41 x 1.30m) with a draught of 2ft 11in (0.94m). The type was not successful and construction was abandoned after about 48 were built.

The losses to the battle fleet at Trafalgar did not end Napoleon's aim of invading Britain. The Treaty of Tilsit with Russia contained secret text, articles by which the two powers agreed to compel Denmark, Sweden and Portugal to join the war against Britain; among other consequences the forty ships of the line in these navies would be added to the forces ranged against the British Navy. Returning from Tilsit, Napoleon instructed Decrès to keep the Boulogne Flotilla ready for invasion, and pressed for increased shipbuilding efforts. In May 1808 the Emperor decreed another 'immense project' which revived the schemes of 1803-5, with expeditionary forces to be readied at Brest, Lorient, Rochefort,

PÉNICHE DE LA FLOTTILLE DE BOULOGNE (1803).

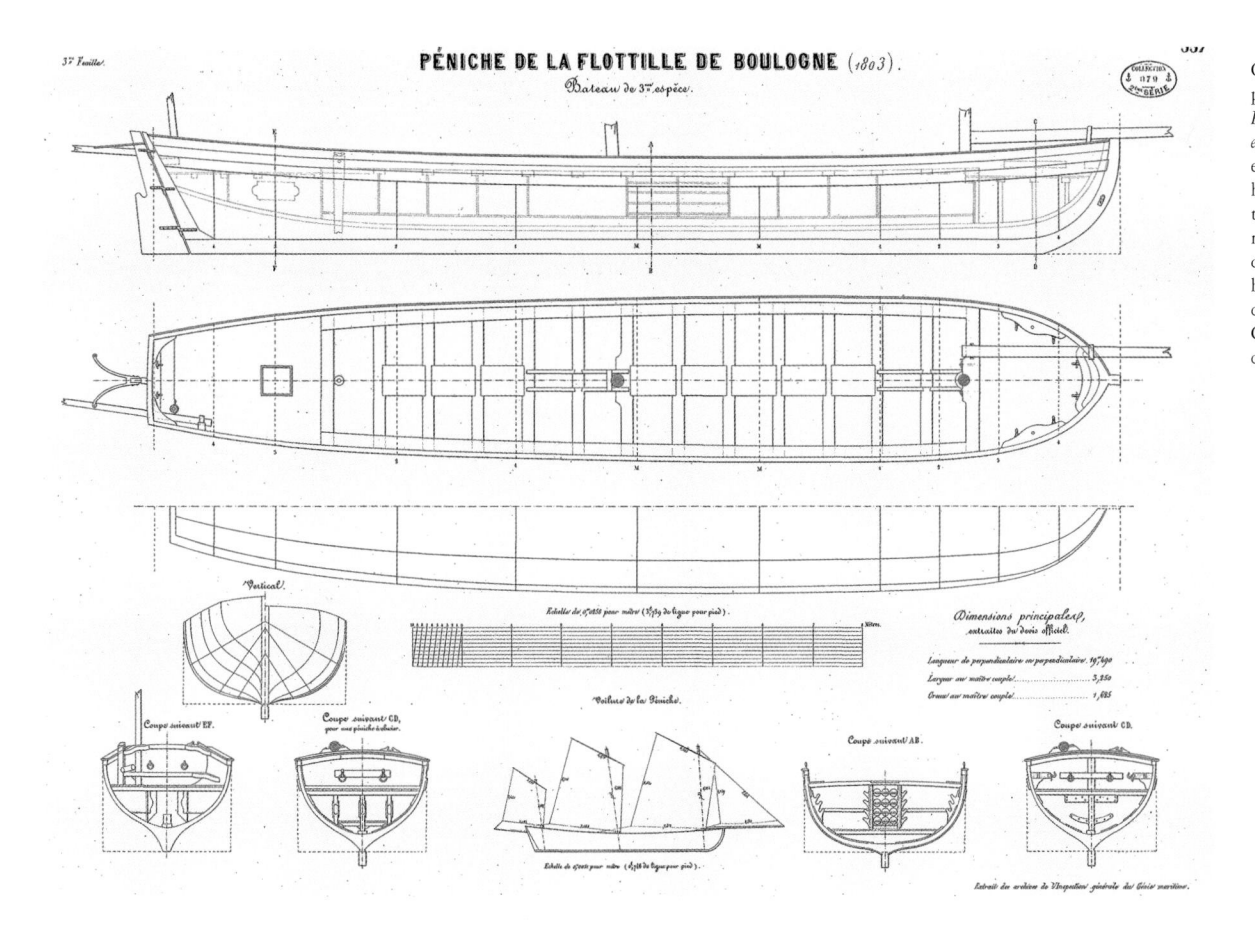

Official general arrangement plan of the Boulogne Flotilla *Péniche* design (*bâtiments de 3ème espèce*). Little more than an enlarged ship's boat, it would have been optimistic to expect troops to endure a passage of many hours in such confined conditions – especially if they had to row – and still be in a condition to fight. (Atlas du Génie Maritime, French collection, plate 557)

Ferrol, Nantes and Toulon, to attack Britain from every quarter. The Spanish insurrection quickly negated this project, and in June Napoleon told Decrès to scale down his preparations. In practice, the dream of invasion was finally abandoned.

ITALIAN (VENETIAN) GUNBOATS (1806-1811)

The following six gun launches belonged to classes that probably entered service between 1793 and 1800. They were in service when Napoleon took Venice for the second time in January 1806. They were manned by 22 to 29 men.

Diana - in service in 11.1793 at Venice.
Dea - laid down 9-1794. 1 x 24pdr, 2 x 3pdrs. Still in service 11.1813.
Incorruttibile - laid down 2-1795, struck in 1807.
Ninfa - laid down 10-1800. 7 guns. Captured 19.4.1809 at Rovigno by the Austrians.
Belle-Poule - 1 x 24pdr, 2 x 3pdrs. still in service in 11.1813.
Comachiese - was in service in 5.1806 at Venice, lost between 8.1807 and 1812.

Sixteen gun launches or small gunboats designed by Andrea Salvini in 1805 for the Austrians were laid down at Venice in 6-7.1805 and completed in 1806-7 for Napoleon's Italian (Venetian) Navy. They were under construction when Napoleon took Venice in 1.1806. They had a single mast with a lateen sail and 12 pairs of oars.

Dimensions & tons: 54ft 0in x 15ft 0in x 5ft 8in (17.54 x 4.87 x 1.84m). 48/90 tons. Draught 5/6ft (1.62/1.95m). Men: 21-56. Guns: 1 x 24pdr, 2 x 3pdrs, 2 x 1pdrs.
Bella Veneziana - Venice, 6-1805/1806. Still in service in 11.1813.
Bresciana - Venice, 6-1805/1806. Still in service in 11.1813.
Mantovana - Venice, 6-1805/1806. Captured 1.1814 at Zara by the Austrians. Last mentioned 1817 at Budua.
Milanese - Venice, 6-1805/1806. At Venice in 1813 out of commission.
Trevigiana - Venice, 6-1805/1806. Struck between 1808 and 1813. Left to the Austrians at Chioggia in April 1814, stranded 1818.
Veronese - Venice, 6-1805/1806. Still in service in 11.1813.
Vittoria - Venice, 6-1805/1806. Still in service in 11.1813.
Capricciosa - Venice, 7-1805/1807. Still in service in 11.1813.
Coraggiosa - Venice, 7-1805/1807. At Venice in 11.1813. Left to the Austrians at Zara in April 1814, BU 1819.
Folgore - Venice, 7-1805/1807. At Venice in 11.1813 out of commission.
Modenese - Venice, 7-1805/1807. Lost between 1808 and 1813.
Padovana - Venice, 7-1805/1807. Captured 1.1814 by the Austrians.
Prodigiosa - Venice, 7-1805/1807. At Venice in 11.1813 out of commission.
Sovrana - Venice, 7-1805/1807. Captured by the Austrians 1.1814 at Zara, at Ragusa 1817 and soon BU.
Tempesta - Venice, 7-1805/1807. Struck between 1808 and 1813.
Vicentina - Venice, 7-1805/1807. Struck between 1808 and 1813.

Ten more similar vessels were launched circa 1807-11, also designed/built by Andrea Salvini.
Calipso - Venice, 7-1806/1808. 1 x 24pdr, 3 x 3pdrs. Was still in service in 11.1813. Left to the Austrians at Venice or Zara in April 1814, Austrian *Calypso*, gone 1831
Ferrarese - Placed in service about 1810, at Venice in 11.1813 out of commission.
Medusa - Placed in service about 1810. 1 x 24pdr, 2 x 3pdrs. Lost 1-1814 at Zara.

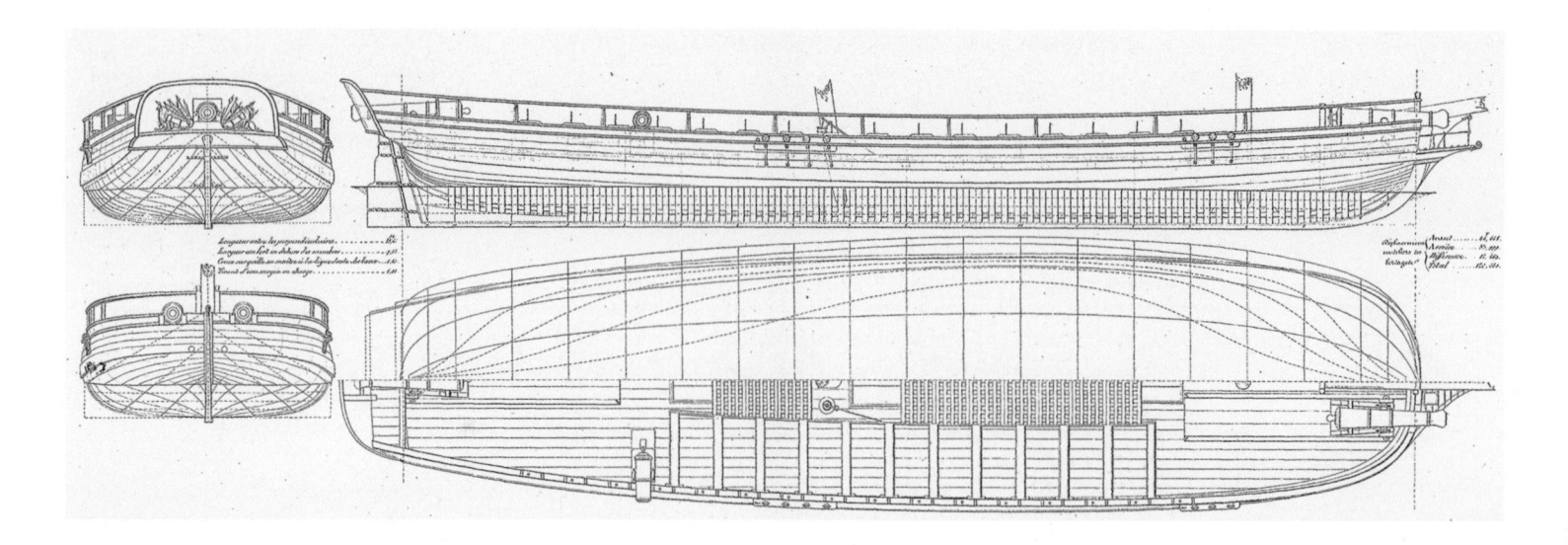

Baccante – 1 x 24pdr, 2 x 3pdrs. Was in service in 11.1813 at Venice. Captured 1.1814 at Cattaro by the British and became Austrian, gone by 1819.

Bolognesa - Was in service in 11.1813 at Venice.

Comachiese (2) - 1 x 24pdr, 2 x 4pdrs. Was in service in 11.1813 at Venice.

Egida - 1 x 24pdr, 1 x 3pdr. Was in service in 11.1813 at Venice. Left to the Austrians at Venice or Zara in April 1814, gone 1821.

Elvetia - 1 x 18pdr, 2 x 4pdrs. Was in service in 11.1813 at Venice.

Orevizana - Was in service in 11.1813 at Venice.

Volpe - 1 x 25pdr, 1 x 7pdr (sic). Was in service in 11.1813 at Venice.

ANNEXED DUTCH GUNBOATS (1810)

Dutch Schooner-gunboats. In 1800 the Dutch dockyard at Rotterdam (P. Glavimans senior constructor) built nine small schooners (*schoeners*), later called schooner-gunboats (*kanonneerschoeners*). Additional units were probably built at Amsterdam and elsewhere but information on them is lacking. Of the nine Rotterdam ships, *Knorhaan*, *Rob*, *Horsel*, and *Krekel* appear in French sources as gunboats (*canonnières*) annexed in July 1810 and are listed below. The other Rotterdam ships were named *Bruinvis*, *Snoek*, *Wesp*, *Sprinkhaan*, *Hagedis*, and *Tor*. *Brak* and *Circe* are shown in French sources as built at Rotterdam but they do not appear on the Dutch list of ships built at the dockyard there and were probably either built at Amsterdam or renamed. *Cachelot* was a sister to the brig-aviso *Haai* but was classified by the French as a gunboat.

Dimensions (Dutch, *Bruinvis* class): 75ft x 19ft x 7ft (21.23 x 5.38 x 1.98m)

Guns: 7. Later armaments from French sources include *Krekel* with 2 x 8pdrs, 4 x 6pdrs;

Horsel, built at Rotterdam in 1800, retaken c12.1813 in the Zuiderzee by the Dutch, sold for BU 1814.

Krekel, built at Rotterdam in 1800, renamed *Canonnière* No.13 1.1814. Retaken in 4.1814 by the Dutch, sold for BU 1814 at Antwerp.

Knorhaan, built at Rotterdam in 1800, retaken c12.1813 in the Zuiderzee by the Dutch, sold for BU 1822 at Nieuwediep.

Rob, built at Rotterdam in 1800, retaken in 12.1813 or in 1814 by the Dutch, sold for BU 1814.

Cachelot, launched in 1800 at Rotterdam, retaken c1813 in the Vlie by the Dutch, sold 1817 at Medemblik.

Crocodil, launched at Amsterdam (?) in 1799, retaken c12.1813 in the Vlie by the Dutch, sold 1823 at Nieuwediep.

Official general arrangement plan of the type of Dutch gunboat taken over by France in 1810. The armament shown comprises three long guns (two on slides facing forward, and one aft) and two small carronades on the broadside. There are thole pins for 16 pairs of oars. (Atlas du Génie Maritime, French collection, plate 39)

Beschutter, built at Amsterdam in 1800, retaken c12.1813 in the Zuiderzee by the Dutch, BU 1815.

Brak, built at Rotterdam (?) in 1800, retaken c12.1813 in the Vlie by the Dutch, sold for BU 1814.

Circe, built at Rotterdam (?) in 1800, retaken c12.1813 in the Zuiderzee by the Dutch, BU 1815 at Amsterdam.

Named Dutch gunboats. In 1803-4 the Batavian Republic built at least 45 gunboats named mostly after admirals. These included 18 *schoeners* built at Rotterdam. Of this type 36 appear in French sources as gunboats (*canonnières*) annexed in July 1810; these are listed below. Thirty of these 36 appear in Dutch sources as recovered in 1813-14. A French source also lists a *Wachtschip ou Stationnaire*, built in 1803, retaken in May 1814 at Nieuwediep by the Dutch, which may have been a functional designation for one of these vessels. She was listed with 3 x 18pdrs, 2 x 8pdrs, and 2 x 24pdr carronades. *Schout-bij-nacht* is the Dutch equivalent of Rear Admiral.

Dimensions (Dutch) & tons: 85ft 7½in, 80ft 10in x 21ft x 9ft 7in (24.23, 22.90 x 5.94 x 2.72m). 80/150 tons. Draught 6ft 10in/7ft 1in (1.95/2.00m). Men: 36-63

Guns: 1 x 18pdr, 2 x 12pdr, 4 x 24pdr carronades. Later armaments from French sources include *Banker*, *Gaad*, *Schram*, *Van Galen* and *Van Wassenaar* with 3 x 12pdrs, 2 x 24pdr carronades; *Schrijver* with 3 x 12pdrs, 6 x 12pdr carronades; *Van der Does* with 3 x 12pdrs; and *Van Nes*, *Verschoor*, *Vlack* and *Waterhoud* with 1 x 18pdr, 2 x 12pdrs, 2 x 24pdr carronades.

Banker, retaken in 12.1813 at Rotterdam by the Dutch, not listed 1814.

Bloys (Vice-admiraal), built at Amsterdam in 1803, retaken c12.1813 by the Dutch, in service 1814.

Brakel (Kapitein), built in 1803, retaken in 12.1813 or in 1814 by the Dutch, sold for BU 1823.

Crul (Schout-bij-nacht), built in 1804, retaken in 12.1813 or in 1814 by the Dutch, sold for BU 1814.

Das, built in 1803, retaken in 12.1813 or in 1814 by the Dutch, sold for BU 1814.

De Gelder (Admiraal), built in 1803, retaken in 12.1813 or in 1814 by

The boarding and capture of four French gunboats off the North Sea island of Nordeney by the boats of a British squadron on 2 August 1811. It is not clear to what class the gunboats belonged, but they were all the same and according to British reports were brig-rigged with a single long 12pdr in the bow, plus two 6pdrs, and a crew of 25 each. (Courtesy of Beverley R. Robinson Collection, US Naval Academy Museum)

the Dutch, sold 1819.

De Haan (Admiraal), retaken c12.1813 in the Vlie by the Dutch, in service 1815.

De Haas (Schout-bij-nacht), retaken c12.1813 in the Vlie by the Dutch, sold for BU 1815.

De Liefde (Admiraal), built in 1803, retaken c12.1813 in the Vlie by the Dutch, sold for BU 1827.

Evertsen (Admiraal), built in 1803, retaken in 12.1813 or in 1814 by the Dutch, sold for BU 1814.

Floris, retaken in 12.1813 in the Vlie by the Dutch, not listed 1814. May be *Pieter Florisz*, below.

Gaad (or *Haac*?), retaken in 12.1813 at Rotterdam by the Dutch, not listed 1814.

Gijzel or *Gyssel (Vice-admiraal Arnoud)*, built in 1804, retaken c12.1813 in the Vlie by the Dutch, sold for BU 1814.

Heemskerk (Admiraal), built at Amsterdam in 1803, retaken c12.1813 in the Vlie by the Dutch, was still at Hellevoetsluis in 1819.

Hulst (Vice-admiraal), built in 1803/1804, retaken in 12.1813 or in 1814 by the Dutch, sold for BU 1814.

Kemphaan, built in 1803/1804, retaken in 12.1813 or in 1814 by the Dutch, sold for BU 1814.

Pieter Floriszoon or *Pieter Florisz (Schout-bij-nacht)*, launched at Amsterdam in 1803, retaken in 12.1813 or in 1814 by the Dutch, sold 1825 at Hellevoetsluis.

Reynst (Admiraal), built in 1803/1804, retaken in 12.1813 or in 1814 by the Dutch, sold for BU 1814.

Roemer Vlack, built in 1803/1804, retaken in 12.1813 or in 1814 by the Dutch, sold for BU 1814.

Schram (Vice-admiraal), built in 1803/1804, retaken in 12.1813 at Rotterdam by the Dutch, sold for BU 1815.

Schrijver (Admiraal), built at Amsterdam in 1803, retaken in 1813 in the Vlie by the Dutch, sold 1817 at Medemblik.

Staghouwer (Schout-bij-nacht), built in 1803/1804, retaken in 12.1813 or in 1814 by the Dutch, sold for BU 1814.

Tjerk Hiddes de Vries (Vice-admiraal), built in 1803, retaken in 12.1813 or in 1814 by the Dutch, sold for BU 1814.

Triton, built in 1803/1804, retaken in 12.1813 or in 1814 by the Dutch, was still at Hellevoetsluis in 1819.

Tromp (Admiraal Cornelis), built in 1803, retaken in 12.1813 in the Vlie by the Dutch, sold for BU 1826 at Rotterdam.

Van der Does (Vice-admiraal), built in 1803/1804, retaken in 12.1813 by the Dutch, sold for BU 1814.

Van Galen (Commandeur), built in 1804, retaken in 12.1813 at Rotterdam by the Dutch, sold for BU 1815.

Van Gendt (Schout-bij-nacht), built in 1803, retaken in 12.1813 or in 1814 by the Dutch, sold 1826 at Hellevoetsluis.

Van Nes (Vice-admiraal), built in 1803, retaken in 12.1813 at Rotterdam by the Dutch, sold for BU 1814.

Van Wassenaar (Luitenant-admiraal), built at Rotterdam in 1803, retaken in 12.1813 at Rotterdam by the Dutch, sold for BU 1827.

Verschoor, built at Amsterdam, retaken in 12.1813 at Rotterdam by the Dutch, not listed 1814.

Vlack, retaken in 12.1813 at Rotterdam by the Dutch, not listed 1814.

Vlug or *Vlugh (Vice-admiraal)*, built in 1803/1804, retaken in 12.1813 at Rotterdam by the Dutch, sold for BU 1814.

Warmond or *Warmont (Vice-admiraal)*, launched at Amsterdam in 1803, retaken in 12.1813 by the Dutch, sold 1817 at Medemblik.

Waterhoud, retaken in 12.1813 at Rotterdam by the Dutch, not listed 1814.

Witte Cornelisz de With (Vice-admiraal), built at Amsterdam in 1803/1804, retaken in 12.1813 or in 1814 by the Dutch, sold for BU 1814.

Numbered Dutch gunboats. Some 100-foot schooner-rigged gun-galleys designed by Wichers and armed with 3 guns and 4 carronades were built in 1800, as were some 70-foot gun launches with one gun. In

The boats of the British brig-sloop *Procris* attacking a squadron of French (ex Dutch) colonial gunboats off the coast of Java on 30 July 1811. Five of these lateen-rigged craft were captured and the sixth blew up. (Courtesy of Beverley R. Robinson Collection, US Naval Academy Museum)

1803 the Dutch dockyard at Rotterdam under P. Glavimans built 50 small gunboats (*kanoneerboten*, later *kanonneerschoeners*) numbered from *No.81* to *No.130*, and in 1804 Rotterdam built 28 more numbered from *No.189* to *No.216*. Additional units were probably built at Amsterdam and elsewhere, but information on them is lacking. The Dutch dimensions of the Rotterdam vessels were 50ft x 20feet x 6½ft (14.15 x 5.66 x 1.84m).

Dutch colonial gunboats. In late 1810 the French annexed at least eight Dutch gunboats at Java. These vessels, whose names if any are unknown, had lateen rigs, crews of 60 men, and armaments of 1 x 32pdr carronade and 1 x 18pdr carronade. In 1811 two of them were at Fort Marrack at the northwest tip of Java and six were at the mouth of the Indramayu River between Batavia (Jakarta) and Semarang. Of the latter, one blew up and five were captured in action on 30 July 1811 with boats from HMS *Procris* (18).

LATER NAMED GUNBOATS

CORFU GUNBOATS. The following six gunboats were built at

Corfu-Govino between 1809 and 1811, the last three by Pierre-Charles Dupin. Four of the six vessels were listed with an armament of 1 x 12pdr and 1 x 4pdr while *Bellone* was listed with 1 x 24pdr. It is not known if they were all built to the same design.

Bellone Corfu-Govino.
K: 1809. L: 1809. Comm: 1.1.1810.
Seized 21.6.1814 at Corfu by the British.

Diligente Corfu-Govino.
K: 1809. L: 1810. Comm: 25.6.1810.
Wrecked and taken during combat 6.1.1813 off Otranto with boats from HMS *Bacchante* (38) and *Weazle* (18).

Vigilante Corfu-Govino.
K: 1809. L: 1810. Comm: 1811-12.
Guns: 1 x 14pdr and 3 carronades or 3 swivels.
Wrecked in 1813-14, or taken 14.2.1813 by HMS *Bacchante* (38).

Furieuse Corfu-Govino.
K: 1810. L: 1810. Comm: 1.1.1811.
Captured 15.12.1812 near Otranto by the British.

Arrogante Corfu-Govino.
K: 1810. L: 1811. Comm: 5.3.1811.
Captured 6.1.1813 off Otranto by boats from HMS *Bacchante* (38) and *Weazle* (18).

Indomptable Corfu-Govino.
K: 1810. L: 1811. Comm: 28.3.1811.
Captured 6.1.1813 off Otranto by boats from HMS *Bacchante* (38) and *Weazle* (18).

SURVEILLANTE and **OBSERVATEUR**. It is not known if these *canonnières* were built to the same design.
Dimensions & tons: unknown. Men: 30-40.
Guns: 1 x 36pdr carronade.

Surveillante Toulon Dyd.
K: 1807. L: 1807. Comm: 1.1.1808.
Renamed *Flamme* 20.2.1809. Struck 1826 at Toulon.

Observateur Toulon Dyd.
K: 1807. L: 1808. Comm: 24.5.1808.
Also reported as built at Toulon in 1803. Struck 1826 at Toulon.

AIR Class. *Canonnières* (some designated *bombardes-canonnières*) designed by François-Frédéric Poncet, and probably all schooner-rigged. Those not built at Toulon were built in private shipyards. The last five units were ordered in 1812 and laid down in late 1813 or early 1814 at La Seyne-sur-Mer near Toulon but were abandoned incomplete in April 1814. Of these *Fulminante* was to be cutter-rigged.
Dimensions & tons: 77ft 0in x 18ft 11in x 5ft 11in (25.01 x 6.15 x 1.92m). 80/141 tons. Draught 6ft 1in (1.98m) aft. Men: 72.
Guns: 4 x 18pdrs. Some also had 4 swivels and 2 or 4 espingoles. *Eau* carried 2 x 12pdrs & 4 swivels in 1820; 4 x 6pdrs in 1827. By 1820 most probably carried 4 x 6pdrs and lighter weapons only.

Air Toulon Dyd.
K: 1810. L: 9.1810. Comm: 8.10.1810.
Boarded and captured 11.12.1813 at Agay (near St-Raphaël) by boats from the British (privateer?) *Warwick* while transporting a cargo of rifles from Toulon to Genoa with the schooner *Estafette*.

Eau Toulon Dyd.
K: 1810. L: 10.1810. Comm: 1.11.1810.
Renamed *Foudre* 3.1820, for hydrography duties off Corsica. Condemned 5.4.1837 at Toulon and struck.

Feu Toulon Dyd.
K: 4.1811. L: 8.1811. Comm: 31.8.1811.
Renamed *Surveillante* 11.1819. Condemned 1837 at Toulon and struck.

Volcan La Seyne.
K: 5.1811. L: 9.1811. Comm: 14.10.1811.
Condemned 1829 and became service craft at Toulon. Last mentioned 9.1830.

Arquebuse La Seyne.
K: 5.1811. L: 9.1811. Comm: 1.11.1811.
Condemned 10.1829 at Toulon and converted to a mud lighter of 70t to 80t capacity.

Salpêtre La Ciotat.
K: 5.1811. L: 21.9.1811. C: 12.1811. Comm: 1.1.1812.
Condemned 1837 at Toulon and struck.

Cerbère La Seyne.
K: 5.1811. L: 10.1811. C: 1812. Comm: 14.12.1812.
Condemned 10.1829 at Toulon and converted to a mud lighter of 70t to 80t capacity.

Tocsin La Seyne.
K: 5.1811. L: 11.1811. C: 1812. Comm: 16.12.1812.
Condemned 1837 at Toulon and struck.

Averne Toulon Dyd.
K: 8.1811. L: 12.1811. Comm: 21.3.1812.
Condemned 10.1829 at Toulon and converted to a mud lighter of 70t to 80t capacity.

Euménide Toulon Dyd. Built by Roustan.
Named: 17.3.1813. K: 7.1813. L: 21.4.1814. C: 1814.
Was 20/24ths built in 4.1814, possibly never commissioned, but might have been the French *bombarde* severely damaged by Spanish gunfire off Cadiz on 23.9.1823. Condemned at Toulon 1825 and struck.

Pétillante La Seyne.
Named: 17.3.1813. Not launched, was 4/24 complete when construction abandoned in 4.1814.

Fournaise La Seyne.
Not launched, was 5/24 complete when construction abandoned in 4.1814.

Alecton La Seyne.
Named: 17.3.1813. Not launched, was 2/24 complete when construction abandoned in 4.1814.

Fulminante La Seyne.
Not launched, was 1/24 complete when construction abandoned in 4.1814.

Furie La Seyne.
Not launched, was 1/24 complete when construction abandoned in 4.1814.

BOMBE Class. These *bombardes-canonnières* were designed by François-Frédéric Poncet. The last two were originally ordered at Toulon, but were built as shown below; the vessel at La Seyne was named *Boutefeu* on 17 March 1813 following the loss of the previous vessel of that name at Tampan. By 1814 all had lost their mortars and were listed with the gunboats, above, which they closely resembled. They were probably all schooner-rigged.
Dimensions & tons: 77ft 0in x 18ft 11in x 5ft 11in (25.01 x 6.14 x 1.92m). 90/141 tons. Draught 5ft 6in/5ft 8in (1.80/1.84m). Men: 67.
Guns (designed): 1 x 12-inch mortar, 4 x 18pdrs; (*Encelade*) 1-12-inch mortar, 2-18pdrs, 2-33pdr carronades; (same, 1814) 4 x 18pdrs.

Bombe Toulon Dyd.
K: 1.1811. L: 7.1811. C: 9.1811.
Condemned 10.1829 at Toulon and converted to a mud lighter of 70t to 80t capacity.

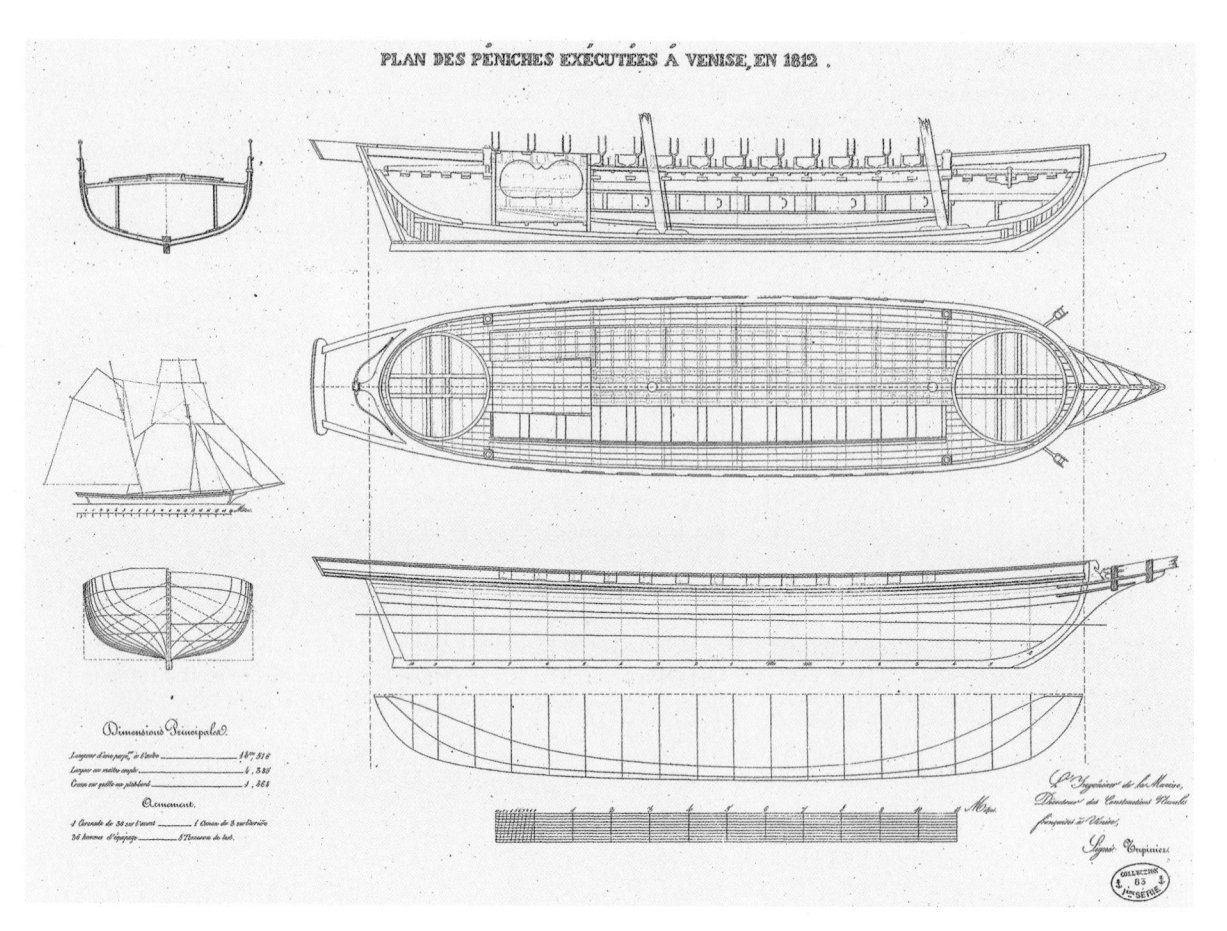

Official general arrangement plan of the *péniches* designed or approved by Tupinier and built in Venice in 1812. They were rigged as topsail schooners. Note the turntables for the pivot guns fore and aft. (Atlas du Génie Maritime, French collection, plate 35)

Encelade Toulon Dyd.
  K: early 1811. L: 17.7.1811. Comm: 6.9.1811. C: 9.1811.
  Listed as brig-rigged in 1826. Fitted 1844 as a boys' training ship at Toulon, listed as schooner-rigged in 1848-51. Struck there 1854.
Grenade Toulon Dyd.
  K: early 1811. L: 17.7.1811. Comm: 23.8.1811. C: 8.1811.
  Decomm. at Toulon 18.5.1836, struck there 1837.
Terre Toulon Dyd.
  K: early 1811. L: 17.7.1811. Comm: 28.8.1811. C: 8.1811.
  Renamed *Agile* 11.1819. Condemned 5.4.1837 at Toulon and struck.
Boutefeu (1) La Ciotat.
  K: 1811. L: 3.9.1811. Comm: 10.9.1811. C: 9.1811.
  Attacked 29.4.1812 by three British frigates including HMS *Undaunted* (38) in the Gulf of Saintes Maries de la Mer, west of Marseille, beached at Tampan and blown up.
Boutefeu (2) La Seyne.
  K: 12.1812. Named: 17.3.1813. L: 21.4.1814. C: 4.1814.
  Listed as in commission from 16.2.1813 (sic) to 18.5.1814. Condemned 1837 at Toulon and struck.

ACHÉRON Class. *Bombardes-canonnières* designed by Louis Dubois. By 1814 they had lost their mortars and were listed with the gunboats, below, which they closely resembled. In contrast to the *Bombe* and *Air* classes, these two vessels were listed as brig-rigged.
  Dimensions & tons: 76ft 6in x 20ft 4in x 8ft 0in (24.84 x 6.61 x 2.60m). 90/140 tons. Draught 6¾ft (2.20m) aft. Men: 66.
  Guns: (designed) 1 x 12-inch mortar, 2 x 24pdrs, 2 x 18pdrs (*Achéron*), 1 x 12-inch mortar, 4 x 18pdrs (*Incendiaire*).
Achéron Toulon Dyd.
  Named: 17.3.1813. K: early 1813. L: 7.1813. C: 1813.
  Condemned 24.12.1825 at Toulon and converted to *citerne flottante*. BU c1847.
Incendiaire Toulon Dyd.
  Named: 17.3.1813. K: early 1813. L: 8.1813. Comm: 25.11.1813. C: 11.1813.
  Renamed *Liamone* 3.1821. Re-rigged as a schooner 1834. Station ship at Algiers 6.1845. Decomm. there 1.1.1847, condemned and struck 22.5.1847.

PURCHASED AND REQUISITIONED NAMED GUNBOATS (1810-1813)
Tonnante (half-galley rebuilt as a gunboat at Corfu-Govino by Pierre-Charles Dupin, K: 3.1810, L: 6.1810, C: 7.1810, carried 1 x 18pdr). Captured 24.8.1813 between Otranto and Corfu by HMS *Weazle* (18).
Salamine (felucca or trincadour built or acquired at Corfu, 37 men, carried 1 x 4pdr, 1 x 24pdr carronade). Comm. at Corfu in 1812 or 1.1.1813. Captured 6.1.1813 off Otranto by boats from HMS *Bacchante* (38) and *Weazle* (18).
Alcinous (built or acquired at Corfu, 32-45 men, carried 3 x 4pdrs). Comm. at Corfu 16.1.1813. Captured and destroyed 14.2.1813 near Otranto by boats from HMS *Bacchante* (38).

Ex BRITISH PRIVATEER PRIZE (1808)
Actif (British privateer *Active* captured 18.2.1808 by the frigates *Thémis* and *Pénélope*, carried 1 x 9pdr). Refitted 5.1809 and comm. 21.5.1809 as aviso. Refitted again 1.1811, renamed *Active* 1.1811, and comm. 1.1.1811 as a gunboat or a *courrière*. Retaken 14.2.1813 near Corfu by the British.

LATER NAMED *PÉNICHES*

DILIGENTE Class. *Péniches* built by Quoniam at a cost of 5,450 francs each.
- Dimensions & tons: 52ft 0in x 10ft 6in x 4ft 8in (16.89 x 3.41 x 1.52m). 18/35 tons. Men: 31-36.
- Guns: 1 x 12pdr.

Diligente Cherbourg Dyd.
- K: 8.1808. L: 9.1808. C: 2.1809.
- Decomm. 8.2.1814.

Mutine Cherbourg Dyd.
- K: 8.1808. L: 9.1808. C: 2.1809.
- Decomm. 3.2.1814.

Adèle Cherbourg Dyd.
- K: 8.1808. L: 9.1808. C: 2.1809.
- Condemned 22.5.1834 (decision of 17.5.1834).

CORFU *PÉNICHES*. Six *péniches* were probably built at Corfu in around 1810 by Pierre-Charles Dupin. Of these, *Morlaque, Gliata, Ragusaise, Rovignoise,* and *Salona* were lost 1.1814 at Zara while *Boccaise* was captured 12.1813 in the Bay of Cattaro between Perzagno and Dobrota by Bocca rebels. They were manned by 33 to 36 men and armed with 1-8pdr and 1-12pdr carronade.

ITALIAN (VENETIAN) *PÉNICHES*. Six *péniches* were built at Venice around 1811-12 by Jean Tupinier. They were commissioned by Napoleon's Italian Navy under the names *Fiamma, Tartaria, Bionda, Forte, Elena,* and *Bianca*. All were left to the Austrians in 4.1814 in the evacuation of Venice but all were gone by 1819 except *Bionda* (1824) and *Elena* (1833).
- Dimensions & tons: 55ft 0in x 13ft 0in x 4ft 6in (17.86 x 4.22 x 1.46m). About 30t burthen, 50t displ. Draught 3ft 3½in/3ft 11in (1.07/1.27m). Men: 37-40. 13 pairs of oars, 2 masts.
- Guns: 1 x 36pdr carronade forward on pivot, 1 x 3pdr aft on pivot.

TRIESTE *PÉNICHES*. Five *péniches* were built at Trieste in 1811-12 (*Arsa* in 1812-13) by Jean-Baptiste Lefebvre and probably also Vincenzo Fanvilli to plans by Jean Tupinier. Of these *Triestine, Laybach,* and *Narenta* were lost 1.1814 at Zara, *Brenta* was captured 12.1813 in the Bay of Cattaro between Perzagno and Dobrota by Bocca rebels, and *Arsa* was burned 8.9.1813 near Trieste to avoid capture. They were either identical to *Fiamma*, above or differed in having a draught of 4ft (1.30m) fore and aft and an armament of 1 x 24pdr carronade forward on pivot and 1 x 12pdr carronade or 1 x 6pdr aft on pivot.

The numerous unnamed gunboats and pinnaces built between 1805 and 1814 included 50 *canonnières* built at Naples in 1806 to 1808 in addition to the 45 taken from the Bourbons there in February 1806, 15 *péniches* (*Nos.1-15*) built at Lorient in 1808, 12 *péniches* (*Nos.1-12*) and 12 *caiques* (*Nos.1-12*) built at Rochefort in 1809, 15 *canonnières* (*Nos.1-15*) built at Corfu-Govino between 1809 and 1812, 48 *canonnières* (*Nos.1-48*) and 55 péniches (*Nos.1-55*) built at Rota, Spain, in 1810 for the Spanish campaign, 12 *péniches* (*Nos.1-12*) built at Toulon in 1813, 21 *canonnières* (*Nos.1-21*, of which *Nos.19-20* may not have been completed) plus 18 *bateaux-canonniers* (*Nos.1-18*) built at Bayonne between October 1813 and February 1814, and an unknown number of *canonnières* built at Mayenne on the Rhine in December 1813 and January 1814. Some Portuguese *canonnières* including *No.1* (captured by the British on 13 February 1808) were taken at Lisbon in November 1807.

(D) Vessels acquired from 26 June 1815

After European peace returned in 1815 the French Navy built no further sailing gunboats, and the few small sailing coastal craft that it built or acquired after that date were mostly ships with Mediterranean rigs that are listed in Chapter 10. It was not until the outbreak of the Crimean War that the French again built gunboats, but these were screw propelled and are listed in Chapter 12.

10 Miscellaneous Sailing Vessels
(Lateen-rigged vessels, bomb vessels, floating batteries, hydrographic vessels, and yachts)

Lateen-rigged vessels (xebecs, half-xebecs, tartanes, feluccas, brigantines, trincadours, galleys, half-galleys, etc.)

Vessels carrying lateen sails (triangular sails, attached to a long yard or boom set diagonally fore-and-aft) had been historically prominent in the Mediterranean for centuries. Many of these were built for or taken into service with the French naval forces in the Mediterranean (the 'Levant fleet') and use of this type continued into the nineteenth century. The most common types used by France (and also by the Spanish and Italian navies) were the tartane and the felucca. The former was a small – the name literally means 'small ship' – two-masted vessel which carried a prominent forward-projecting bluff bow, and were lateen-rigged on both pole masts, with the foremast raked sharply forward; however a single-masted version later developed. A number were acquired by the French Navy during the Revolutionary Era, but had all gone by 1800. The felucca was similar but was also fitted with oars as an alternative to sail; again most were in existence only during the Revolutionary War, but some occurred later and a few were added in the 1830s.

The xebec (*chébec*) was a somewhat larger vessel with three masts, carrying a lateen sail on each; it was adopted by the French during the Napoleonic Wars, but did not survive beyond them, although three appeared in the 1820s. There was also a smaller version of this, termed the half-xebec (*demi-chébec*).

(A) Vessels in service or on order at 1 January 1786

Although a number of lateen-rigged vessels had been used by the French during the eighteenth century, and some had even been acquired during the American War, none was in service at 1786 or were added until the 1790s.

The French galley fleet at Marseille was merged with the sailing fleet at Toulon by an ordinance of 27 September 1748, and by 1768 all of the remaining galleys had become prison hulks at Toulon or Marseille except for *Brave* and *Duchesse*, which followed in 1776 and 1778. However in the summer of 1798 *Duchesse*, which had been renamed *Patience* in October 1792, was put in condition for a last trip to sea, being fitted with 1 x 24pdr for the occasion. *Patience* was BU in 1814 along with the other remaining old galley, *Ferme*, while *Brave* was last mentioned in October 1802.

The identification of small fore-and-aft rigged types is afflicted by the vague and varied terminology applied by different nations in various time periods, which explains why many of the vessels listed in this chapter have more than one designation. In this Jean-Jérôme Baugean engraving, originally published in 1814, the two vessels in the foreground – probably privateers – carry lateen sails and would probably be described as a pinque (nearest) and a tartane. Both can also set square canvas in suitable conditions: the tartane has a fidded topmast with topsail and topgallant sails that can be set simultaneously with the lateen; the pinque has two square sails slung from the mainmast for drying, but these could only be set in lieu of the lateen sails, in a following wind.

(B) Vessels acquired from 1 January 1786

ALBANAISE. Tartane designed by Ricaud du Temple with the plans being dated 23 September 1789 and approved 23 October 1789. She was built for the purpose of transporting lumber for shipbuilding from Albania and Italy, but the project was abandoned and she was employed as an ordinary transport. In late 1792 she served as a powder magazine for four small frigates converted into bomb vessels, and she then served out of Agde and Sète under Enseigne de Vaisseau Bernard. In 1795 the French Navy converted her to a gunboat, of eight guns, and between 1798 and February 1799 they converted her to a 12-gun brig.
  Dimensions & tons: 80ft 0in, 60ft 0in x 23ft 6in x 11ft 0in (25.99, 19.49 x 7.63 x 3.57m). 200/359 tons. Draught 10¼/10¾ft (3.33/3.49m).
  Guns: originally 4, from 1795 had 4 x 12pdrs + 4 x 6pdrs; re-armed 1799 with 12 x 8pdrs.
Albanaise Toulon Dyd.
  K: 4.1790. L: 30.7.1790. C: 3.1792. Rated *canonnière* 1795, then brig 2.1799.
  Captured 3.6.1800 off Cape Fano by HMS *Phoenix* and *Port Mahon*, becoming HMS *Albanaise*; seized by mutineers 23.11.1800 and handed over to the Spanish at Malaga the next day, and restored to France, but not returned to service there.

CARMAGNOLE – Tartane or aviso.
  Dimensions & tons: unknown. Men: 35
  Guns: 2 x 12pdrs, 2 x 6pdrs.
Carmagnole Toulon Dyd.
  K: 1792. L: 7.1793. C: 7.1793.
  Renamed *Capricieuse* 30.5.1795. Captured 1.9.1801 off Corsica by HMS *Termagant* (18) after departing Toulon for Egypt.

PELLETIER – Tartane or aviso.
  Dimensions & tons: unknown. Men: 40-45
  Guns: 2 x 12pdrs, 2 x 6pdrs.
Pelletier (*Peltier*) Toulon Dyd.
  K: 1794. L: 4.1794. C: 5.1795.
  Renamed *Pluvier* 30.5.1795. Captured 9.1801 at Alexandria by the British or by the Turks.

TURBULENT – Tartane or aviso.
  Dimensions & tons: unknown. Men: 39
  Guns: 4 x 8pdrs, 4 x 6pdrs.
Turbulent Toulon Dyd.
  K: 1794. L: 5.1794. C: 6.1794.
  Lost in Egypt 1801 and struck.

CHIEN DE CHASSE – Tartane or aviso
  Dimensions & tons: unknown. Men: 45.
  Guns: 2 x 8pdrs, 4 x 4pdrs.
Chien de Chasse Toulon Dyd.
  K: 1794. L: 5.1794. C: 6.1794.
  Captured 22.9.1798 near Rhodes by a Turkish privateer, crew enslaved.

SANS PEUR – Tartane or aviso
  Dimensions & tons: unknown. Men: 63.
  Guns: .
Sans Peur Toulon Dyd.
  K: 1794. L: 5.1794. C: 6.1794.
  Renamed *Sans Crainte* 5.1795. Last mentioned 1.1797 while at Toulon out of service.

ENCOURAGEANTE – Felucca
  Dimensions & tons: unknown. Men: 30
  Guns: 2 x 6pdrs.
Encourageante Toulon Dyd
  K: 1794. L: 1794. C: 1794.
  Named in early 1795, previously *Felouque No.5*. Also called a trincadour. Sunk 22.3.1800 near Porto-Vecchio, Corsica, after a collision with the pink *Indépendant* (ex *Intrépide*).

PIERRE – Xebec
  Dimensions & tons: unknown. Men: 60.
  Guns: 6 x 6pdrs.
Pierre Toulon Dyd.
  K: 1795. L: 8.1795. C: 9.1795.
  Captured 7.5.1798 near Toulon south of Cape Sicié by HMS *Terpsichore* (32).

HIRONDELLE – Felucca
  Dimensions & tons: unknown. Men: 27
  Guns: 1; (1801) 2 x 4pdrs or 2pdrs; (1814-16) 2 x 4pdrs
Hirondelle La Seyne
  K: 1796. L: 1796. C: 1.1797.
  Refitted 1803 at Toulon. Wrecked at Bastia 22.1.1805 but immediately refloated. Decomm. 27.5.1814, for sale 7.1814 at Toulon, back in commission 27.5.1816 to 23.6.1816, struck 1816, BU 1818.

EXPÉDITIF Class – Half-xebecs built on the specifications of Pierre-Alexandre Forfait. May have been built in sections for the Egyptian expedition like the brig *Ligurienne*.
  Dimensions & tons: unknown.
  Guns: (*Expéditif*) 2 x 12pdrs, 2 x 4pdrs; (*Osiris*) 6 x 4pdrs.
Expéditif Toulon Dyd
  K: 4.1798. L: 5.1798. C: 6.1798.
  Decomm. 8.10.1800 at Alexandria and probably taken there in 9.1801 by the British or Turks in the surrender of that port.
Osiris Toulon Dyd.
  K: 12.1798. L: 1.1799. C: 1.1799.
  Left Toulon 2.11.1800 for Egypt, wrecked 13.11.1800 near Bizerte, Tunisia. Another half-xebec named *Osiris* (1800-13) is listed below.

TEMPÊTE Class – Half-galleys
  Dimensions & tons: unknown. Men: 34
  Guns: 1 x 18pdr.
Tempête Toulon Dyd
  K: 11.1798. L: 1799. C: 9.1799. Comm: 23.9.1799.
  Decomm. at Toulon 19.1.1805, service craft, last mentioned 2.1807.

Tonnante Toulon Dyd.
  K: 11.1798. L: 1799. C: 7.1801. Comm: 5.7.1801.
  Struck 1809, rebuilt 1810 as a gunboat (q.v.) at Corfu, captured 24.8.1813.

REVANCHE Class – Felucca-gunboats, designed by Pierre-Alexandre Forfait. *Romaine* is also reported as a *chaloupe-canonnière* built at the same time and place as was a sister named *Cisalpine*. These were schooner-rigged with one gun. *Cisalpine* was taken by the Austrians at Ancona in November 1799. An ex-Papal half-galley named *Romaine* (q.v.) was completed for the French at Civita-Vecchia in 1798 and lost in Egypt in 1801, while a frigate of this name was in service from 1794 to 1816.
  Dimensions & tons: 43ft, 38ft x 10ft 6in (13.97, 12.34 x 3.41m).

5/10 tons. Men: 46.
Guns: 1 x 12pdr.
Revanche Toulon Dyd.
K: 4.1798. L: 4.1798. C: 5.1798.
Decomm. 26.7.1809 at Toulon, BU there 1.1813.
Romaine Toulon Dyd.
K: 4.1798. L: 4.1798. C: 5.1798.
Last mentioned at Rosetta in 2.1799 and probably lost in Egypt.

GUERRIER – Half-xebec
Dimensions & tons: unknown.
Guns: 4.
Guerrier Toulon Dyd
K: 1799. L: 1800. C: 1800. Comm: 23.9.1800.
Captured by the British 12.12.1800, probably en route to Egypt from Toulon and possibly by HMS *Termagant* (18).

PURCHASED AND REQUISITIONED VESSELS (1792-1801)

Saint François (tartane acquired c1792). Last mentioned returning to Toulon in 2.1793. In 6.1793 may have become the tartane-gunboat *Jean Bart* (2 x 8pdrs, 2 x 6pdrs) that was taken 8.1793 by the British and Spanish at Toulon.

Annonciation (brigantine hired in late 1792 in the Mediterranean and purchased 6.1793). Renamed *Biscayenne* 6.1793. Taken by the British and Spanish 8.1793 at Toulon, became Spanish *Anunciacion*.

Liberté (felucca purchased 12.1792 and in service in the Mediterranean 2.1793). Taken by the British and Spaniards at Toulon 8.1793, subsequent fate unknown.

Vigilante (felucca acquired in late 1792 and in service in the Mediterranean 2.1793, carried 2 x 1pdrs). Taken by British and Spanish at Toulon 8.1793, retaken by the French 12.1793. May have been renamed *Vogue* 5.1795. Captured 26.8.1795 by Nelson's squadron in the Bay of Alassio west of Genoa with *Hydra, République,* and *Constitution*.

Bonne Aventure (xebec comm. 5.1793 at Toulon, 60 tons, 86 men, carried 6 x 6pdrs and 4 x 4pdrs). Renamed *Jacobin* 1793 and *Bonne Aventure* 30.5.1795. Offered 6.1795 to the Bey of Tunis (or Algiers) who refused her. On sale list at Le Havre 3.1797 but not sold, converted there to 60-ton transport in 1797 and renamed *Transport No.16 Bonne Aventure* 1798, decomm. 4.1798 and struck.

Brave Sans Culotte or *Petit Sans Culotte* (xebec or tartane comm. 5.1793 or purchased 7.1793 at Toulon, 100 men, carried 14 x 6pdrs). Taken by the British at Toulon 8.1793 and named *Petite Victoire* with a crew from HMS *Victory*, retaken by the French 12.1793. Renamed *Citoyen* 30.5.1795. Struck at Toulon 12.1795.

Général Biron (felucca or tartane in service in the Mediterranean 4.1793, 24 men, carried 1 x 3pdr, 2 swivels). Renamed *Constitution de 1793* late 1793, *Constitution* 1794, *Calcul* 5.1795, may also have been named *Caressante* in 1795. Captured 26.8.1795 by Nelson's squadron in the Bay of Alassio west of Genoa with *Hydra, Vigilante,* and *République*.

Amazone, Buse or *Buze, Commode, Effronté, Émeraude,* and *Venturie* (tartanes or small merchant craft, among 14 purchased 7.6.1793 at Toulon). *Commode, Effronté*, and *Venturie* were ex *Jésus-Marie-Joseph, Carmagnole,* and *Marie-Catherine* respectively while *Amazone, Buze,* and *Émeraude* were all recorded as ex *Vierge de Miséricorde*. Presumably taken by the Allies 8.1793 at Toulon and struck 1793.

Révolutionnaire (tartane or or small merchant craft purchased 7.6.1793 at Toulon, former name retained). Capsized 3.5.1794 while being chased by an enemy vessel.

Amitié (tartane purchased 7.6.1793 at Toulon, 48 men, carried 6 x 4pdrs). Refitted at Genoa 1796-97, last mentioned 1797.

Joyeuse (tartane, ex *Sans-Quartier*, purchased 7.6.1793 at Toulon with 13 other small vessels, 54 men, carried 2 x 8pdrs, 4 x 6pdrs). Renamed *Syzygie* 5.1795. She may have been the aviso named *Sans-Quartier* in the Damietta flotilla with the avisos *Cerf, Sainte-Marthe, Menzaleh* and *Amoureuse* and the cange *Surveillante*, all of which were burned, sunk, or captured by the Turks near Rosetta on 10.4.1801. Another *Sans-Quartier*, a lugger (q.v.), was taken off Saint-Malo 2.4.1799 by HMS *Danae*.

Providence (brigantine commissioned 6.1793 at Rochefort, 4 guns). Captured 10.8.1794 by the British in the port of Calvi.

Trompette (ex *Fortunée*, tartane or small merchant craft purchased at Toulon 7.6.1793, 4 guns). May have been the tartane *Fortunée* captured 10.1793 at Genoa by a British squadron, otherwise she was taken at Toulon in 8.1793.

Union (tartane probably purchased 6.1793 at Toulon, 4 guns). Captured 10.1793 at Genoa by a British squadron.

Sans-Culotte (brigantine in service at Toulon in 7.1793). Taken at Toulon 8.1793 by the British and Spanish, retaken there 12.1793 by the French. Renamed *Soigneux* or *Sougneuse* 5.1795. Struck late 1795.

Société d'Ayeau (brigantine in service at Toulon in 7.1793). Taken at Toulon 8.1793 by the British and Spanish, burned 12.1793 by the British at Toulon.

Révolutionnaire (xebec comm. 10.1793, carried 2 x 12pdrs, 2 x 8pdrs, and 2 x 4pdrs). Renamed *Téméraire* 1794, captured 13.4.1795 by HMS *Dido* (28) off Leghorn but renamed *Tympan* 5.1795 and not struck at Toulon until late 1795.

Républicaine (Customs felucca commissioned 12.1793 at Villefranche, carried 4 x 1pdrs, 2 swivels). Renamed *Reptile* 5.1795. Returned to Customs 5.1795 and reverted to *Républicaine*.

Auguste (brigantine commissioned in the Mediterranean in 1793 or 1794, 4 guns). Captured 8.1794 by the British in the port of Calvi.

République Française (tartane requisitioned in late 1793 or early 1794 in the Mediterranean as an aviso, 48 men, carried 2 x 12pdrs, 2 x 6pdrs). Renamed *Ruisselante* 5.1795, also called *République*. Captured 26.8.1795 by Nelson's squadron in the Bay of Alassio west of Genoa with *Hydra, Vigilante,* and *Constitution*.

Général Stuart (balancelle built in 1793 or 1794 and in service at Toulon in 1799, carried 1 x 3pdr). Last mentioned 9.1802 while in service at Toulon.

Duguay-Trouin (tartane commissioned 5.1794 as an aviso, 23 men, carried 2 x 8pdrs, 2 x 4pdrs). Renamed *Dangereuse* 5.1795 or 2.3.1796. Captured 3.1799 on the Syrian coast by a British division and reportedly used as a gunboat by the Royal Navy until sold in 1800 or 1802.

Baleine (trincadour commissioned 6.1794 at Bayonne, carried 1 x 4pdr obusier, 2 swivels). Last known in service at Bayonne 5.1795.

Cincinnatus (tartane commissioned 6.1794 as an aviso, 60 men, carried 2 x 6pdrs, 2 x pdrs, 4 swivels). Renamed *Anémone* 5.1795. Run ashore near Alexandria 2.9.1798 while carrying despatches from Malta to avoid capture by HMS *Seahorse* (38) and *Emerald* (36).

Courrier d'Italie (half-xebec built at Genoa 1793/94, ex *Vierge du Rosaire*, acquired 6.1794, probably at Genoa, carried 6 x 6pdrs). Renamed *Cassius* 1795. Decomm. 5.11.1801, unserviceable at Toulon 7.1802 and struck.

Exterminateur (felucca comm. at Toulon 6.1794, 4 swivels). Was at Toulon 7.1795 out of service, struck.

Furet (felucca requisitioned 6.1794 at Marseille, 30 men, carried 2 x 2pdrs). Renamed *Fertile* 5.1795. Returned to her owners 12.1796 at Marseille.

Intrépide (pink or half-xebec comm. in the Mediterranean 6.1794, 45 men, carried 4 x 4pdrs). Renamed *Indépendant* 5.1795. Captured 17.9.1800 south of Sardinia by the British while en route from Toulon to Egypt. French records name her captor as *Theresa* or *Sainte Therese*.

Levrier (xebec built at Nantes in 1793-94, requisitioned there 6.1794 and in service as a xebec 7.1794, 96 men, carried 6 x 4pdrs). Re-rigged as a schooner 1795 and as a lugger in early 1798. Captured 11.1799 off Cape Tiburon, Santo Domingo, by HMS *Solebay* (32).

Petit Jacobin or *Jacobin* (tartane commissioned 6.1794 as an aviso, carried 2 x 4pdrs, 6 swivels). Renamed *Loup* 30.5.1795. Was in service out of commission at Toulon 7.1795, struck 8.1795.

Sardine (trincadour commissioned 6.1794 at Bayonne, carried 1 x 4pdr obusier, 2 swivels). Renamed *Spongeux* 5.1795. Last known in service at Bayonne 5.1795.

Abondante (felucca comm. 1794). Struck in early 1795.

Jeune Émilie (privateer brigantine built in America and requisitioned at Saint-Malo before 7.1794, 60 tons, 80 men, carried 5 x 4pdrs, 7 x 3pdrs, 7 swivels). Renamed *Isolé* 5.1795, reverted to *Jeune Émilie* 1796. Returned to owner 1796 and resumed privateering, captured 2.1797 by HMS *Triton* (32).

Alerte (felucca in service 7.1794 at Toulon, 24 men, carried 2 x 4pdrs, 2 swivels). Renamed *Argo* 5.1795. Last mentioned 5.1795 while at Toulon.

Amitié (brigantine commissioned 1794 at Le Havre). Fate unknown.

Légère (felucca comm. 6.1794 at Toulon, 20 men, 1 x 6pdrs, 10 swivels). May have been renamed *Lente* 5.1795. Captured 22.8.1798 off Alexandria by HMS *Alcmene* (32) and became gunvessel HMS *Legere*. Struck 1801.

Saint Ramond (xebec comm. 1794 at Toulon, 6 guns). Renamed *Régénéré* 1794 and *Réformateur* 5.1795. struck at Toulon 12.1795.

Constance (felucca comm. at Lorient 11.1794, 24 men, 2 guns). Renamed *Cacique* 5.1795. Struck 9.1795 at Brest.

Aventurière (felucca comm. at Toulon 12.1794, 1 gun). Was at Toulon 7.1795 out of service, struck.

Consolante (felucca comm. at Toulon 12.1794, 2 guns). Renamed *Canicule* 5.1795. Was at Toulon 7.1795 out of service, struck.

Fidèle (felucca comm. in the Mediterranean 12.1794). Renamed *Fée* 5.1795. Last mentioned 5.1795 while in service at Nice.

François de Paule (tartane commissioned in late 1794 as an aviso, carried 4 x 4pdrs). Renamed *Flottante* 5.1795. Wrecked on the Hyères Islands 28.10.1796 while supporting the Army of Italy.

Jeune Barra (felucca comm. in the Mediterranean 12.1794, 2 guns). Renamed *Inondée* 5.1795 when in service at Antibes, struck c1796.

Pourvoyeuse (felucca comm. in the Mediterranean 12.1794, 4 guns). Last mentioned 1798.

Petite Colette (brigantine in service at Saint-Valéry sur Somme in early 1795). Renamed *Permuteur* 5.1795, struck late 1795.

Petit Barra (felucca comm. mid-1795). Renamed *Montesquieu* 5.1795 or 9.10.1795, later fate unknown.

Corse (xebec requisitioned at Ancona 3.1797 for the Egyptian expedition, 10 guns). Ready on 29.7.1798 to depart with Napoleon's despatches for France, captured by the British.

Deux Frères (tartane requisitioned 3.1798 at Marseille and commissioned as a transport, 23 men, 4 guns). Captured 18.3.1799 off Syria by a British division.

Marie or *Marie-Rose* (tartane requisitioned 3.1798 at Marseille and commissioned as a transport, 22 men, 4 guns). Captured 3.1799 off Syria by a British division and served as the gunbrig HMS *Marie Rose* until 1800.

Courageux (brigantine requisitioned or purchased 4.1798 in the Mediterranean, carried 10 x 4pdrs). Was at Toulon in 12.1799. Struck 1800.

Nativité (tartane requisitioned 4.1798 and commissioned as a transport for the expedition to Egypt). Arrived 12.1798 at Ancona and probably returned to her owner.

Sentinelle (felucca comm. at Toulon 4.1798, 20 men, carried 1 x 3pdr). Unserviceable at Toulon 9.1803 and BU. Other small craft named *Sentinelle* included an aviso or felucca (1795-98) and a transport (ex *Mélanie*, 1803-14).

Vierge de la Garde (tartane requisitioned 4.1798 and commissioned as a transport for the expedition to Egypt). Captured 1.1799 by the British in the Mediterranean.

Caroline (biscayenne or trincadour commissioned at Lorient 6.1798, 6 tons, 24 men, carried 1 x 36pdr obusier). Sent from Egypt with despatches, taken 24.2.1801 in the Bay of Tunis by a British brig.

Actif (pink in service 7.1798 at Toulon). Unserviceable at Toulon 10.1802 and BU.

Requin (felucca comm. 26.7.1798 at Bastia). Captured 4.1.1799 by a Turkish privateer, crew taken to Tunis as slaves, then freed.

Nil (felucca in service 11.1798 at Rosetta in Egypt, 65 men). Last mentioned 6.1799 in combat on the Nile.

Curieuse (biscayenne in service at Lorient in 5.1799, 6 tons, 23 men, carried 1 x 36pdr obusier). Last mentioned 10.1799 while in service at Lorient.

Terreur (felucca comm. 5.1799 at Toulon). In 8.1799 carried to Toulon the body of General Joubert, killed at the Battle of Lodi. Captured 10.8.1801 off the coast of Piombino, Tuscany, by the boats of two British frigates.

Égyptien (half-xebec launched 1800 in Sicily and comm. 10.7.1800 at Toulon, carried 4 or 6 x 3pdrs). Decomm. 27.4.1802. Converted 4.1804 to water barge *Joie* at Toulon. Last mentioned 1807.

Osiris (half-xebec purchased 11.1800 at Tunis, three masts, carried 8 x 6pdrs). Condemned 1812, BU at Toulon 1813. Another half-xebec named *Osiris* (1798-1800) is listed above.

Entreprenant (bateau or aviso built at Toulon in 1800 and comm. 23.9.1800 at Toulon, 10 men and 10 passengers). While en route to Alexandria ran onto the beach at Riva near Genoa 29.7.1801 and taken by two British privateers including a xebec.

Merle (balancelle or pink comm. 23.9.1801 at Toulon, 10 men, carried 2 x 4pdrs). Decomm. at Toulon 11.12.1814, Fleet lists for 4.1814 and 5.1814 contain both this vessel (as a balancelle) and the half-xebec *Merle* listed below, a fleet list for 10.1816 contains only the half-xebec. BU 1818.

Ex VENETIAN PRIZES (1797)

Venetian xebecs

Cerf (Venetian *Cervo*) Venice
  Dimensions & tons: 86ft 2in x 15ft 0in x 4ft 10in (28.00 x 4.87 x 1.56m). 40/85 tons. Draught 4ft 8in (1.51m) aft. Men: 70-82.
  Guns: 12 x 8pdrs
  Taken 20.5.1797 at Venice. While escorting 60 ships with the xebec *Lejoille* (escaped) and the brig *Ligurienne* (captured), ran ashore at Les Tignes near Marseille 22.3.1800 to avoid capture by HMS *Mermaid* (32) and *Peterel* (16).

Mincio (Venetian name unknown) Venice
  Dimensions & tons: as *Cerf*.
  Guns: 12 x 8pdrs, 6pdrs, and 4pdrs
  Taken 5.1797 or 6.1797 in Dalmatia and renamed by the French for a French victory. May have participated in the occupation of Corfu although not on the list of Bourde's division. May have been the Venetian *Diocleziano*, built 1771 at Venice (28.50 x 5.10 x 2.0m.

100 tons), taken over by the Austrians in Dalmatia 8.1797, prison ship 4.1801, BU 1803.

Bon Destin (Venetian *Buon Destino*) Venice
Dimensions & tons: as *Cerf*.
Guns: (1805) 2 x 6pdrs, 8 x 3pdrs.
K: 8.1794. L: 5.1796. C: 6.1796.
Also called a *galeotta da corso* (fast galliot) and a *mezza galera* (half galley). Taken 5.1797 or 6.1797 in Dalmatia. Taken over by Austria c8.1797 in Dalmatia as *Buon Destino*. In Istria at the end of 1805. To Napoleon's Italian Navy 1.1806. At Venice 4.1808 out of service, struck c1810.

Venetian half-xebecs

Lonato (Venetian name unknown) Venice
Dimensions & tons: 68ft 8in x 13ft 9in x 5ft 8in (22.31 x 4.46 x 1.84m). 30/50 tons. Draught 3ft 5in/4ft 7in (1.11/1.49m). Men: 85.
Guns: 12 x 6pdrs, 2pdrs
Built 1790-95.
Taken at Venice 5.1797 and renamed by the French for a French victory. Was part of the Second French Division of the Adriatic under Bourdé that occupied Corfu on 28.6.1797. On 11.11.1797 the French reused the name *Lonato* for a frigate. *Lonato* or *Tyrol* may have been the Venetian *Ardito il Grande*, built 1790 or 1794 at Venice (21.81 x 4.74 x 2.53 m, 80 tons, 67 men, 16 guns in1797, 6 x 3pdr in 1798), taken over by the Austrians in Dalmatia 3.7.1797 and struck at Venice in 1805.

Tyrol (Venetian name unknown) Venice
Built 1790-95, probable sister or near-sister to *Lonato*.
Taken at Venice or in the Gulf of Venice 5.1797 and renamed by the French for a French victory. Was part of the Second French Division of the Adriatic under Bourdé that occupied Corfu on 28.6.1797. *Tyrol* or *Lonato* may have been the Venetian *Emilio*, built at Venice (20.10 x 4.45 x 1.6 m, 60 tons, 30 men, 12x 3pdr in 1798), taken over by the Austrians at Zara 8.1797 and struck 7.1803.

Saint Georges (Venetian name unknown) Venice
Dimensions & tons: 48ft 2in x 9ft 1in x 2ft 10in (15.64 x 2.95 x 0.92). Draught 1ft 6in/2ft (0.48/0.65m). Men: 60.
Guns: 6 x 6pdrs, 2pdrs
Built 1790-93.
Taken in the Gulf of Venice 5.1797 or 6.1797 and renamed by the French for a 1796 French victory. May have participated in the occupation of Corfu although not on the list of Bourde's division. May have been the Venetian *Prudente*, built 1793 at Venice, 17.00 x 4.10 x 1.40m, 50 tons, 30 men, 8 x 3pdr in 1798), taken over by the Austrians at Zara 8.1797 and sunk 7.1805 as a blockship at Venice.

Mantoue (Venetian name unknown) Venice
Built 1790-93, probable sister or near-sister to *Saint Georges*.
Taken in the Gulf of Venice 5.1797 or 6.1797 and renamed by the French for a French victory. Was part of the Second French Division of the Adriatic under Bourdé that occupied Corfu on 28.6.1797. On 11.11.1797 the French reused the name *Mantoue* for a frigate. May have been the Venetian *Ardito il Piccolo*, built 1791 at Venice (16.44 x 3.60 x 1 m, 25 tons, 30 men, 8 guns in 1798, 4 x 6pdr in 1801), taken over by the Austrians in Dalmatia 8.1797 and sunk 7.1805 as a blockship at Venice.

Énea (Venetian xebec or half-xebec *No.28*) Venice
Dimensions & tons: 62ft 10in x 16ft 0in x 6ft 5½in (20.4 x 5.2 x 2.1m). 40/70 tons. Draught 4ft 10in (1.26m) mean. Men: 30.
Guns: (1801) 2 x 9pdrs, 6 x 6pdrs; (1805) 2 x 6pdr, 8 x 3pdr
K: ?. L: 1799. C: 1800.
On slip No.28 at the Venice Arsenal during the first French occupation in 1797. Completed by the Austrians as *Enea*. Annexed 1.1806 with the city of Venice, French *Énea*. Was at Venice out of commission in 4.1808, may have been rebuilt as the xebec *Eugenio* listed below in 1809-10. A Venetian cutter named *Enea* was laid down in 1790 and captured by the Algerians in 1796.

Venetian Galleys. All were built at Venice.

Gloire (Venetian *Gloria,* flagship galley, 30 banks of oars)
Dimensions & tons: 172ft 9in x 23ft 4in x 7ft 6in (56.11 x 7.58 x 2.43m). 380 tons (displ.) Draught 6ft 5in/7ft 6in (2.09/2.43m). Men: 170.
Guns: 1 x 36pdr, 2 x 8pdrs.
Taken 5.1797 at Venice and commissioned by the French. Was part of the Second French Division of the Adriatic under Bourdé that occupied Corfu on 28.6.1797 and was then called a *mezza galera* (half galley) with three guns. At the same time the French seized the Venetian ship of the line *Gloria Veneta* in the Arsenal and renamed her *Gloire*; this *Gloire* also carried troops to Corfu in the Bourdé division. The subsequent history of the galley is unknown; she may have remained at Corfu.

Junon, Merope, Paix (ex *Pace*)*, Phénix, Sémiramis, Vénus* (Venetian galleys, *Pace* class, *Merope* launched 1791)
Dimensions & tons: 143ft 1in x 19ft 7in x 6ft 5in (46.48 x 6.36 x 2.09m). 250/300 tons. Draught 6ft 9in/7ft 10in (2.19/2.54m).
Guns: (*Junon*) 1 x 36pdr; (others) 1 x 20pdr (Venetian), 2 x 8pdrs (6pdrs in *Paix*).
Taken 5.1797 at Venice. Not commissioned by the French, all sabotaged by the French 12.1797 before handing the city over to the Austrians. Wrecks BU 1798.

Zaire (Venetian *Zaira*, *Pace* class, built in 1787)
Guns: (1797) 1 x 20pdr, 2 x 9pdrs, 10 x 6pdrs, and 2 x 2pdrs. Men: 337 in 1801.
At Zara in 6.1797 her Venetian commander volunteered to the Austrians and assisted in the Austrian occupation of Dalmatia. Became Austrian *Zaira*, prison ship 4.1801, to Venice from Zara 1802, struck 1803, hulk to the Italian navy 1806. A possible sister, *Diana* (same hull dimensions but called a *galeotta da corso* or fast galliot after completion), that was incomplete on the ways at Venice and called *galera novissima* (new galley) in 1797 was allocated to the Italian navy at Venice in 1.1806 but does not appear in French lists and seems instead to have passed to the Austrians at Trieste.

Cheval Marin (Venetian galley, *Pace* class, taken in Dalmatia 5.1797, carried 8 x 6pdrs). Fate unknown.

Proserpine (Venetian galley, *Pace* class, taken at Venice 5.1797 or at Corfu 6.1797). Fate unknown. The Austrians took over a xebec or felucca with 3 x 3pdrs named *Proserpina* in 1798 and used her as a hospital ship in Dalmatia until 1803.

Andromaque (Venetian *Andromaca*). This or *Proserpine*, above, was probably the *mezza galera* (half galley) with three guns named *Rose* taken at Venice 5.1797 and immediately commissioned as part of the Second French Division of the Adriatic under Bourdé that occupied Corfu on 28.6.1797; there is no further record of this *Rose*.
Dimensions & tons: 155ft 3in x 22ft 11in x 7ft 2in (50.43 x 7.45 x 2.32m). 200/330 tons. Draught 6ft 2in/7ft 3in (2.0/2.4m).
Guns: 2 x 12pdrs, 8 x 4pdrs.
Taken by the French at Venice 5.1797 or at Corfu 6.1797. On 26.9.1797 in Porto Olivetto during a voyage from Corfu to Venice

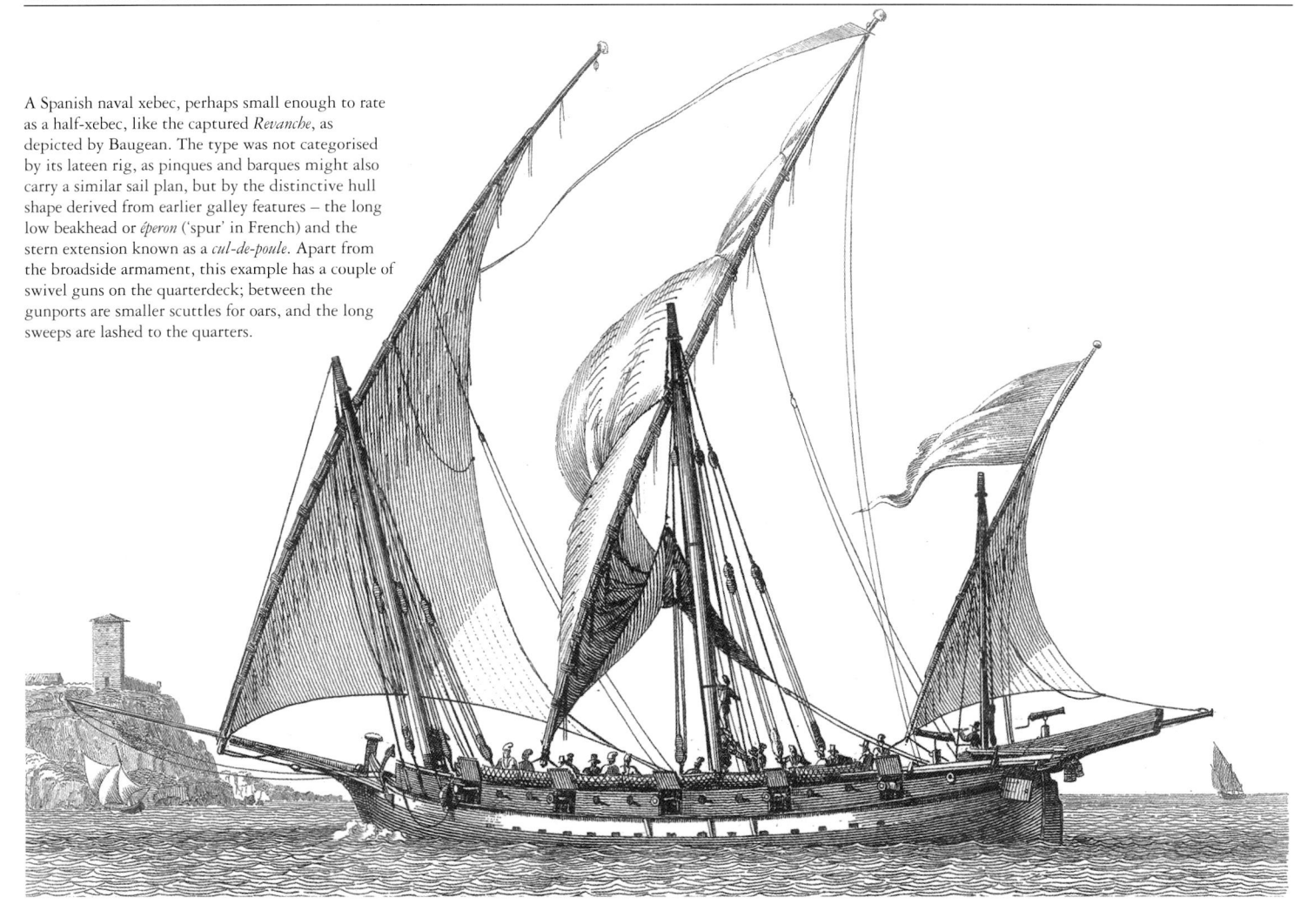

A Spanish naval xebec, perhaps small enough to rate as a half-xebec, like the captured *Revanche*, as depicted by Baugean. The type was not categorised by its lateen rig, as pinques and barques might also carry a similar sail plan, but by the distinctive hull shape derived from earlier galley features – the long low beakhead or *éperon* ('spur' in French) and the stern extension known as a *cul-de-poule*. Apart from the broadside armament, this example has a couple of swivel guns on the quarterdeck; between the gunports are smaller scuttles for oars, and the long sweeps are lashed to the quarters.

her officers decided to turn the ship over to the Austrians, which they did at Zara the next day. Later fate unknown.

Medusa, *Fusta*, and *Chiaretta* or *Bella Chiaretta* (Venetian galleys, *Medusa* class, all taken at Venice 5.1797)
Guns: 6 x 3pdrs. Men: 154.

On 20.4.1797 *Bella Chiaretta* (also referred to as *Annetta Bella*) boarded and took the French lugger or tartane *Libérateur d'Italie* which had entered Venice and refused orders to leave, providing the pretext for the first French occupation of Venice. None commissioned by the French, all ceded intact to the Austrians 1.1798. *Fusta* was struck 13.4.1801 and became a prison hulk. *Medusa* and *Chiaretta* were struck in 1802 and became prison hulks. *Fusta* and *Chiaretta* passed to Italy in 1806 as hulks. These two were laid down 8.1794.

MISCELLANEOUS PRIZES (1793-1800)

Alexandrine (British brigantine built in Britain, 'recent' when seized 2.1793 at Le Havre, 150-180 tons, 60 men, carried 8 x 4pdrs, 4 x 1pdrs). Listed as an aviso escorting merchant ships between Le Havre, Brest, and Lorient in 1793-4, as a *gabarre de port* at Brest in 1797, and as a brig commissioned at Brest 23.9.1800. Wrecked 11.1805.

Good Intent (British xebec *Good Intent* built in 1792 and captured 1793, carried 4 x 18pdrs). Renamed *Montagne* 1793, reverted to *Good Intent* 5.1795. Used at Dunkirk as a transport 1794-1801, decomm. there 20.9.1801 and struck. She was not a former Royal Navy vessel as sometimes reported, the only *Good Intent* in the RN during this period being a hired gun barge in 1801.

Notre Dame de Grace (tartane from Marseille seized 7.1793 at Genoa by a squadron of the French Republic). Probably renamed, no further information.

Surveillante (British felucca captured 9.1793 and taken to Marseille, in service 10.1793, 24 men, carried 2 x 1pdrs, 6 swivels). Used by the customs service at Antibes. Renamed *Resplendissante* 5.1795. out of service at Toulon 9.1795 and soon struck.

Revanche (Spanish half-xebec built in Spain and taken in early 1794, 46 men, carried 4 x 6pdrs, 2 x 4pdrs). Renamed *Réjouissant* or *Revanche* 5.1795. *Revanche* was captured 17.6.1800 between Toulon and Malta by HMS *Phoenix* (36) and capsized the next day.

Angélique (schooner-rigged fireship or aviso built in Britain and taken in early 1794, 18 x 6pdrs and 60 men as fireship, 6 x 6pdrs and 38 men as aviso). Commissioned 4.1794, headquarters ship at Rochefort 6.1795 to 2.1797.

London (British felucca taken in 1794 and commissioned 7.1794 at Lorient, 24 men, 2 x 1pdrs). Was in service at Lorient 5.1795, struck soon afterwards.

Léonidas (Spanish felucca or half-galley taken 12.1794, 26-45 men, carried 2 x 4pdrs). Sailed from Ancona 2.1799, then struck, became the corsair *Léonide*.

Montagne (half-xebec taken 12.1794, 43 men, carried 4 x 3pdrs). Renamed *Merle* 30.5.1795 while in service at Toulon. Placed in use by the Customs Service 3.1797. Service craft at Toulon 9.1802 to 11.1804. Recomm. 20.11.1804 and restored as a combatant ship 11-12.1804. Fleet lists for 4.1814 and 5.1814 contain both this vessel and the balancelle *Merle* listed above. Decomm. 29.5.1814 but recomm. at Toulon 19.6.1815 and taken by the British 15.7.1815. Evidently the French got her back, as she appears in a fleet list for 10.1816 and was listed as BU 1818.

O Hydra (Spanish xebec built in Spain and taken 12.1794, 65 men, carried 6 x 12pdrs and 3pdrs). Reamed *Résolue* 1.1795, reverted to *O Hydra* 30.5.1795. Captured 26.8.1795 by Nelson's squadron in the Bay of Alassio west of Genoa with *République*, *Vigilante*, and *Constitution*, became gunbrig HMS *Resolue*, deleted 1802. (O Hydra means 'the hydra' in Portuguese.)

Platon (Spanish polacre built in Spain and taken in early 1795, being commissioned at Toulon 5.1795, 30 men). Later fate unknown.

Postillon (Venetian polacre built in Spain, taken 5.1795, and immediately commissioned at Toulon as an aviso; 30 men, carried 6 x 4pdrs). Captured 9.3.1796 with the corvettes *Némésis* and *Sardine* by a British force including HMS *Egmont* (74) at Tunis, the lugger *Gerfaut* being destroyed in the same engagement.

Betzy (*Betsy*) (brigantine captured c1796, 80-99 tons, 4 guns). Was in service at Dunkirk 3.1797. Captured 3.6.1803 by HMS *Russel* (74) while returning from Martinique and destroyed. A transport named *Betzy* or *Betsy* (1796-1826) was renamed *Aimable Bristol* in 1803.

Fortanatus (British privateer xebec *Fortunatus* built at Venice in 1788-89 as *Fortunato Jacob* and commissioned at Malta, rigged as a corvette, taken by frigate *Justice* 12.1797 and arrived at Toulon 2.4.1798, 150 tons, 70-90 men, carried 18 x 6pdrs). Captured 8.1798 off the Nile Delta by HMS *Swiftsure* (74) and became HMS *Fortunatus*, retaken 5.1799 by the French brig *Salamine*, then sank off Jaffa.

Amoureuse (Papal half-galley built at Civita-Vecchia 1796-98, seized there 3.1798 and completed 5.1798, sister to *Romaine*, same armament). Sunk 10.4.1801 near Rosetta and captured by the Turks.

Coquette (Papal half-galley built at Civita-Vecchia and seized there 3.1798)

By the late eighteenth century the galley had long ceased to be an effective weapon of war. In France the galley fleet was formally abolished in 1748, and only lasted that long because galley service was a convenient punishment for criminals, dissidents and heretics. However, galleys lived on in a few conservative navies like those of the Pope and the Knights of Malta, and a handful of these were taken into French naval service. This Baugean engraving shows a small half-galley like those taken from the Papal States in 1798.

Dimensions & tons: 92ft 1in x 17ft 10in (29.9 x 5.8m). Tons unknown.
Sunk 1801 in Egypt.

Romaine (Papal half-galley built at Civita-Vecchia 1796-98, seized there 3.1798 and completed 5.1798, sister to *Amoureuse*)
Dimensions & tons: 92ft 4in x 18ft 6in (30 x 6m). Tons unknown.
Guns: 1 x 24pdrs, 2 x 12pdrs.
Lost 1801 in Egypt. Had 20 pairs of oars. This name is also reported for a felucca (q.v.) built in 1798 at Toulon and last mentioned in Egypt in 1799 and was also carried by a frigate from 1794 to 1816.

Victoire (Papal galley taken 3.1798 at Civita-Vecchia, 6 guns). BU at Malta 1800.

Aventurière (Maltese half-galley taken on the ways 6.1798 at Valletta, L: 1799, C: 11.1799. Had 14 pairs of oars, 2 men per oar, and three masts. 68 men, carried 1 x 8pdr, 2 x 6pdrs). Comm. 24.11.1799. Decomm. 29.5.1814. BU at Toulon 1818.

Décidée (Maltese half galley, taken on the ways 6.1798 at Valletta, L: 1800, C: 9.1800, sister of *Aventurière*, carried 1 x 8pdr, 2 x 6pdrs). Comm. 3.9.1800. Decomm. 29.5.1814. For sale at Toulon 6.1814 but not sold and BU 1818.

Saint Hilaire (xebec built at Port Mahon and taken at Ajaccio 1798, 64 men, carried 10 x 8pdrs). Renamed *Espérance* 8.1802. Given by the First Consul 9.1802 to the Pasha of Tripoli. Decomm. 4.11.1802.

Santa Ferma (Maltese galley completed at Civita-Vecchia 9.1796 and taken at Valletta 6.1798, manned by 22 chevaliers and 280-320 men, 25 banks of oars, carried 1 x 48pdr, 2 x 24pdr, and 2 smaller). Two others were also taken, probably *San Nicola* and *Vittoria*. None commissioned by the French, all probably BU 1799.

Santa Lucia (Maltese galley built between 10.1795 and 4.1796 and taken at Valletta 6.1798, manned by 22 chevaliers and 280-320 men, 25 banks of oars, carried 1 x 48pdr, 2 x 24pdr, and 2 smaller). Not commissioned by the French. Captured 9.1800 by the British and Portuguese at the surrender of Valletta.

Fortune (half-xebec called *Chébec Turc No.2* taken in 1798 while on the ways in Egypt, L: 3.1799, C: 4.1799, 87 men, carried 8 x 4pdrs). Named *Fortune* 29.10.1798. Recomm. at Elba 14.8.1807. Scuttled 16.5.1813 at Cavalaire-sur-Mer near Saint-Tropez to avoid capture by boats from HMS *Berwick* (74) and *Euryalus* (36).

Thévenard (xebec called *Chébec turc No.1* taken on the ways at Damietta 7.1798, L: 8.1798, C: 9.1798). Probably captured 4.1799 by HMS *Lion* (64) in the Mediterranean, described then as a 16-gun corvette.

Vaubois (galley captured and commissioned in Sardinia 10.1798). Captured 11.1798 by the British while en route from Sardinia to Malta.

Éole (British privateer xebec taken while new by a French privateer and purchased 1.1799 at La Ciotat, 120 men, carried 16 x 6pdrs). Re-rigged as corvette 1.1803. Wrecked in the Antilles 21.4.1803.

Éléphantine (Egyptian felucca, half-galley, or djerme probably captured 2.2.1799 from the Mamelucks at Aswan and in service by 9.2.1799). Lost in Egypt 1800 or 1801.

Good Union (British privateer xebec built at Port Mahon and captured 2.1799, carried 4 x 8pdrs, 8 x 4pdrs). Left Alexandria 19.5.1801 to carry back to France General François-Étienne Damas, who had been placed under arrest, but was taken by a British frigate and corvette 31.5.1801 near Crete.

Joubert (xebec built at Monaco in 1793 and taken 3.1799 at Leghorn, 70 men, carried 2 x 8pdrs, 4 x 1pdrs). Captured 31.5.1809 at Sainte-Maure (Lefkada) Island near Corfu by five boats from HMS *Topaze* (36).

Légère (felucca taken 3.1799 at Leghorn, 22 men, 4 swivels). Reported taken off Villefranche 4.8.1799 by a British brig while en route from Toulon to Corsica, but also reported as refitted at Toulon in 1801 and 1807 and as a service craft at Toulon 1811. Subsequent fate uncertain. May have been renamed *Hirondelle* in 1812 although that name was already in use by another felucca and 1814 fleet lists only show one *Hirondelle*. Not to be confused with the balancelles *Légère* or *Léger* of

---

Lateen sails were tricky to handle in heavy weather and were inefficient for downwind sailing. Xebecs traditionally carried some square canvas that could, if such conditions pertained, replace the lateen sails, whose long yards would then be struck down on deck. However, in the eighteenth century some xebecs began to adopt something closer to a conventional ship rig, while retaining the xebec hull. As demonstrated by this big Genoese example, the fore and main were usually 'polacca' masts, in a single piece as opposed to the usual fidded lower mast–topmast–topgallant structure. Most later naval xebecs probably carried this sort of rig, as shown here by Baugean.

1814.

Lejoille (xebec built at Leghorn and taken there 3.1799, 50 men, carried 10 x 4pdrs). Grounded with *Cerf* at Les Tignes near Marseille 23.3.1800 when their convoy was attacked by the British but later refloated. Last mentioned in 8.1804 as a service craft at Toulon. Struck c1805.

Postillon (felucca taken 3.1799 at Leghorn, 2 swivels). Service craft at Toulon 1811. BU 2.1813 at Toulon.

Raggio or *Prima* (Genoese galley seized or acquired c1799)
Dimensions & tons: 149ft x 22ft (48.40 x 7.15m). Men: 257 + 300 rowers on 26 benches.
Guns: 1 x 36pdr, 2 x 24pdrs.
Captured 5.1800 off Genoa by the British who sold her to Sardinia where she was renamed *Santa Teresa* in 1804.

Fortuné or *Fortunée* (half-xebec or tartane or felucca of Maltese origin captured 8.8.1800 by the half-xebec *Merle*, carried 2 x 4pdrs). Condemned and BU 1810.

Reprise (felucca or bateau 'retaken' in 1800 and recomm. at Toulon 23.9.1800, any previous history unknown, carried 1 x 4pdr, 5 swivels). Wrecked 11.12.1805 on Cape Taillat on the Côte d'Azur.

(C) Vessels acquired from 25 March 1802

GAULOISE Class – tartane-gunboats, 5 guns.
Dimensions & tons: 50ft 0in x 14ft 11in x 6ft 4in (16.24 x 4.84 x 2.06m). 50/85 tons. Men: 39-45.
Guns: 1 x 18pdr, 4 x 4pdrs.

Gauloise Aguillon fils, La Seyne.
K: spring 1804. L: 25.8.1804. Comm: 23.9.1804.
Sunk 10.12.1808 with *Julie* in Cadaques Bay, Catalonia, by HMS *Imperieuse* (38), then raised and taken with her 11-ship supply convoy.

Provençale Aguillon fils, La Seyne.
K: spring 1804. L: 25.8.1804. Comm: 23.9.1804.
Decomm. at Toulon 29.1.1814, sold 1816.

Gentille Aguillon fils, La Seyne.
K: spring 1804. L: 9.1804. Comm: 14.11.1804.
Burned 14.4.1811 off Palamos in Catalonia to avoid capture.

Jalouse Aguillon fils, La Seyne.
K: spring 1804. L: 9.1804. Comm: 22.11.1804.
Decomm. at Toulon 12.2.1814, sold 1816.

TURLURETTE Class – feluccas, 5 guns. First two designed by Jean-Louis Féraud, others (also built in private yards) were probably nearly identical. May have had 13 pairs of oars. *Linotte* was called a half-xebec by her commander in 1814.
Dimensions & tons: 56ft 0in x 14ft 2in x 5ft 6in (18.19 x 4.60 x 1.78m). 30/50 tons. Draught 4ft 8in (1.52m) aft. Men: 45.
Guns: 1 x 12pdr (forward), 4 x 3pdrs.

Turlurette Aguillon fils, La Seyne.
K: spring 1804. L: 9.1804. Comm: 23.9.1804.
Captured 24.6.1808 at Port San Felice by insurgent Spanish ships. Retaken by the French a few months later but burned 31.8.1809 at Valamos in Catalonia to avoid recapture.

Linotte Aguillon fils, La Seyne.
K: spring 1804. L: 9.1804. Comm: 1.12.1804.
Decomm. at Toulon 27.5.1814, sold 1816.

Julie Blaise, Ménard, Marseille.
Ord: 8.6.1806 (contract). K: 1806. L: 9.9.1806. Named: 15.9.1806.
Comm: 24.10.1806.
Sunk 10.12.1808 with *Gauloise* in Cadaques Bay, Catalonia, by HMS *Imperieuse* (38), then raised and taken with her 11-ship supply convoy.

Thisbé (*Thysbé*) Blaise, Ménard, Marseille.
Ord: 5.11.1806 (contract 5.1.1807). Named: 10.11.1806. K: 1807. L: 10.4.1807. Comm: 2.5.1807.
Decomm. at Leghorn 22.4.1814, sold there 1818.

TISIFONE – Felucca in Napoleon's Italian Navy. This *Tisifone* apparently replaced a felucca of the same name built in 1796 that was one of 15 feluccas assigned to French Venice in the division of the Austrian fleet there in January 1806. None of these older units appears to have remained on the list much beyond 1806 although one, *Mora* was taken from the Austrians c1809.
Dimensions & tons: unknown. Men: 28.
Guns: 3 x 3pdrs or 1 x 6pdr and 2 x 3pdrs.

Tisifone Venice Arsenal
K: 11.1806. L: 1807.
Name in French *Tisiphone*. In service in Dalmatia in 6.1808 and 8.1809 and at Trieste 1.1810. Captured 2.9.1812 or 31.8.1812 in the Lim Channel (fjord), Istria, by HMS *Bacchante* (38).

PROSERPINA Class – Feluccas in Napoleon's Italian Navy. The felucca *Proserpina* first appears in the Corfu division in June 1808. The construction of 6 (more?) feluccas of the *Proserpina* class was approved on 12 August 1810 for the defence of Corfu; two of these apparently became *Volpe* and *Curiosa* while the others did not materialise. All three were assigned to the defence of the lagoons in 1812. In 1813 *Proserpina* and *Volpe* participated in the defence of Venice while *Curiosa* was at Ancona.
Dimensions & tons: unknown. Men: 24.
Guns: 1 x 24pdr, 2 x 3pdrs.

Proserpina Venice Arsenal
Built 1807.
At Corfu in June 1808, at Senigallia in mid-1810. Accompanied six '*peniche*' (rafts armed with a cannon) to defend the construction of coastal batteries at Lignano, Porto Buso and Punta Sdobba. Captured an enemy ship near Rovigno 12 December 1810. To Corfu 23 December 1810 carrying provisions. At Goro in June 1813 commanded by Francesco Bandiera, who became an Admiral of the Austrian Navy in the 1840s. Taken over by the Austrians 4.1814, sold without entering Austrian service.

Volpe Venice Arsenal
K: 11.1811. L: 1812.
At Ravenna in June 1812, at Goro in June 1813, at Venice from November 1813. Taken by the Austrians as *Volpe* 20.4.1814 in the occupation of Venice. Austrian active service primarily in Dalmatia 1815-22 with an armament of 1 x 24pdr and 2 x 3pdrs. BU 1823.

Curiosa Venice Arsenal
K: 11.1811. L: 1812.
At Venice in 1812, at Ravenna from June 1812, and at Ancona in 6.1813 as part of Napoleon's Italian Navy. No further record as *Curiosa*. Austrian historians list the *Mora* (see below) that was taken by the Anglo-Austrians in the surrender of Zara on 5.12.1813 as a new ship built in 1811-12, in which case she was most likely ex-*Curiosa*. This *Mora* was listed in Austrian service with 1 x 12pdr, served in Dalmatia in 1815, and was struck 18.4.1817.

ENTREPRENANT – Felucca or patmar, 1 gun. Built by Grisard and

A Baugean engraving of a Neapolitan felucca at anchor, with the main yard acting as a ridge-pole for the awnings, which may be the vessel's sails. The similarity with the xebec is evident in the hull – which is why feluccas are called half-xebecs in some lists. Vessels of generally similar design were to be found all around the Italian peninsula, and large numbers were either captured or built for Napoleon's navy.

Lieutenant Pierre-François Bouvet. This vessel had two masts sharply raked forward at an angle of 23 degrees with the vertical. She had 15 pairs of oars. Grisard's activities are described in the entry for the schooner *Gobe-Mouche* in Chapter 8.
    Dimensions & tons: 66ft 0in x 15ft 0in (21.44 x 4.87m). Tons unknown. Men: 40.
    Guns: 1 x 12pdr forward.
Entreprenant Île de France (built by Grisard).
    K: 9.1807. L: 10.1807. C: 11.1807.
    In 1807 the former privateer and now navy lieutenant Pierre Bouvet requested the construction of a patamar or 'brig gourable' at Île de France to raid commerce on the Indian coast. A 'gourable' was an Indian type vessel with a high massive stern and a low pointed bow, probably the same type the English called a 'grab'. The little ship was named and commissioned 30.11.1807 and sailed for Indian waters on 7.12.1807. On 8.2.1808 she captured the British mercantile packet brig *Marguerite*, upon which Bouvet gave *Entreprenant* to the crew of the captured vessel and returned to Île de France in his larger prize.

EUGENIO – Venetian xebec.
    Dimensions & tons: unknown. Men: 79.
    Guns: 6 x 8pdrs, 4 x 10pdr carronades.
Eugenio Possibly built at Venice in 1809-10 or rebuilt from the *Énea* of 1799 (see above).
    A *Eugenio* was in Albania from July 1806 to June 1808. This or another *Eugenio* (see *Énea* above) was comm. at Venice c1810 by Napoleon's Italian navy. Participated in the Battle of Lissa 13.3.1811 and went to Spalato after the battle. On 19.5.1811 with *Paranza No.1* (a light Adriatic ship type) was in combat with two light enemy ships off Meleda. At the Venice Lido in 1813-14. Left to the Austrians at Venice 4.1814, sold 29.8.1814.

CALYPSO Class – spéronares or galiotes built at Corfu. The known details of *Nausicaa* match *Calypso* and they may have been sisters. *Nausicaa* was said to be fast both when sailing and when rowing.
    Dimensions & tons: The usual specifications for spéronares at this time were 47ft 9in x 13ft 7in (15.50 x 4.40m), 12/22 tons. Men: 23.
    Guns: 1 x 10pdr carronade (British 12pdr).
Calypso Corfu (Constructeur, Pierre-Charles Dupin).
    K: 1812. L: 17.8.1812. Comm: 17.8.1812. C: 9.1812.
    Departed Corfu for Otranto 1.1813 with the trincadour *Salamine* and the gunboats *Indomptable*, *Arrogante*, and *Diligente*. All the vessels were captured 6.1.1813 by HMS *Bacchante* (38) and *Weazle* (18) except *Diligente* which was wrecked in the action.
Nausicaa Corfu (Constructeur, Pierre-Charles Dupin?)
    K: early 1813. L: 4.1813. C: 5.1813.
    Seized 6.1814 at Corfu by the British.

TRINCADOUR No.1 class – trincadours. Designed and built by Jean Baudry. Had two masts and 10 pairs of oars.
    Dimensions & tons: 37ft 4in x 8ft 3in x 4ft 3in (12.13 x 2.68 x 1.37m). 9/15tons. Draught 3ft 1in/3ft 4in (1.00/1.12m). Men: 11.
    Guns: 10 espingoles de ½ (*No.1*), 4 swivels (*No.2*).
Trincadour No.1 Bayonne.
    K: 20.8.1813. L: 9.1813. C: 9.1813.
    Decomm 10.1823 for the last time. Unserviceable at Bayonne in early 1832 and stricken there.
Trincadour No.2 Bayonne.
    K: 20.8.1813. L: end 10.1813. C: 11.1813.
    Decomm 10.1823 for the last time. Unserviceable at Bayonne in early 1832 and stricken there.

PURCHASED AND REQUISITIONED VESSELS (1804-1814)

Redoutable (half-xebec launched at Bastia in 1803 and comm. 23.9.1804 at Bastia for convoy protection in Corsica). Wrecked at Bastia 22.1.1805 in a squall.

Adèle (felucca-gunboat launched 6.1804, probably at Toulon, and comm. 6.6.1804 at Toulon, 19 men, carried 1 x 8pdr). Decomm. at Toulon 18.2.1813 and struck 1813.

Gazelle (Genoese felucca, probably built in Genoa, purchased there and comm. 29.6.1806)
  Dimensions & tons: 47ft 0in x 11ft 0in (15.27 x 3.57m). Tons unknown. Men: 29-40.
  Guns: 2 x 8pdrs; (1814) 2 x 6pdrs.
  Ceded 17.4.1814 at Genoa to Navy suppliers in payment of debts.

Légère (balancelle, felucca, or aviso in service at Elba in 1806 and commissioned on 1.1.1807, 26-53 men, carried 1 x 10pdr, 2 x 3pdr, 2 swivels). Put at the disposition of Napoleon at Elba 4-5.1814 pending the arrival of the brig *Inconstant*. Departed Elba 4.6.1814, decomm. 20.6.1814 at Toulon and sold in 1816. Not to be confused with the contemporary balancelle (ex half-xebec) *Léger*.

Deux Amis (mercantile bateau or British 'bow' sequestered at San Stefano 1806 and placed in service by the French Navy at Leghorn in 1808)
  Dimensions & tons: 50ft 0in x 13ft 0in x 4ft 10in (16.24 x 4.22 x 1.57m). 33/50 tons. Men: 61.
  Guns: 4 x 16pdr carronades.
  Given 4.1814 at Genoa to Navy suppliers in payment of debts.

Abeille and *Mouche* (mercantile feluccas purchased at Leghorn at the end of 1814 by Napoleon I for his Elban Navy and used as avisos, 10 men, no guns). Arrived 3.1815 at Antibes coming from Elba, further fate unknown.

Ex BRITISH MERCANTILE AND PRIVATEER PRIZES (1803-1813)

Léger (British mercantile half-xebec *Jesus-Maria-Joseph* seized at Marseille late 5.1803, 21 men, carried 1 x 32pdr obusier, 6 swivels). Decomm. 11.2.1813. Listed as a balancelle in 1814-16. Placed on sale at Toulon 6.1814, not sold and BU 1818. Not to be confused with the contemporary balancelle *Légère*.

Caroline (British mercantile spéronare or felucca rigged as a schooner and equipped with oars, built 1786 at Genoa and captured 8.1803 from the British by a division of frigates from Toulon and taken to Toulon).
  Dimensions & tons: 36ft 2in x 7ft 6in x 2ft 4in (11.75 x 2.44 x 0.75m). 7/12 tons. Draught 2ft 3in (0.73m) aft. Men: 18.
  Guns: (1807) 1 x 3pdr, 2 swivels.
  Recomm. 1.1.1807 by the French at Elba, decomm. 30.6.1808. Taken apart at Elba 9.1811, rebuilt 1811-12 at a private yard in Elba (K: 10.1811. L: 2.1812. C: 28.2.1812). Dimensions changed but not recorded, roughly same crew size and armament. Arrived 3.1815 at Antibes from Elba as part of the flotilla of Napoleon I

Neptune (British privateer xebec or half-xebec, built in Italy 1799/1800, captured 23.5.1805 off Cape Roux (Côte d'Azur) by the corvettes *Mohawk* and *Tactique* and comm. 24.9.1805)
  Dimensions & tons: 54ft 0in x 17ft 0in x 9ft 0in (17.54 x 5.52 x 2.92m). 88/120 tons. Men: 59-61.
  Guns: 4 x 6pdrs, 4 x 10pdr carronades (British 12pdrs).

The balancelle was of Neapolitan origin but was taken up by the Spanish, the two states having close contacts as their rulers were drawn from the same royal family. The balancelle was widely used for gunboat duties, and a number found their way into French naval service. This Baugean engraving shows one at anchor and another under sail; note the small lateen set from what the anchored example is using as an ensign staff.

MISCELLANEOUS SAILING VESSELS

Decomm. 30.6.1814, probably at Sète. Sold 1816.

Bamberg (*Bambery*) (British privateer half-xebec *Passe-Partout-Alexandre* or *Passe-Tout* captured 13.9.1806 at Leghorn by the half-xebec *Fortune* and comm. 1.1.1807)
  Dimensions & tons: 54ft 4in x 15ft 4in x 4ft 0in (17.65 x 4.98 x 1.30m). 34/55 tons. Draught 5ft 3in (1.70m) aft. Men: 42.
  Guns: 2 x 6pdrs, 2 x 4pdrs, 6 swivels.
  Left at Leghorn 2.1814 during the evacuation of the city with orders to sell her.

Sirène (*Syrène*) (British privateer xebec or half-xebec *Syrene* captured 25.3.1808 off Ajaccio by the frigates *Thémis* and *Pénélope* and comm. 1.1.1810).
  Dimensions & tons: 62ft 0in x 18ft 2in x 7ft 3in (20.14 x 5.90 x 2.35m). 70/120 tons. Draught 7ft 9in (2.51m) aft. Men: 85.
  Guns: 4 x 8pdrs, 6 x 8pdr carronades; (5.1814) 6 x 8pdr carronades
  Stationed at Bastia 1810-14. Decomm. 22.5.1814. Turned over 8.1814 to the Prince of Monaco with the aviso *Victoire* as indemnity for the corvettes *Carolina* and *Augusta*, which had been seized in 9.1792.

Envie (*Invidia*) (British privateer half-xebec *Invidia*, built in 1804-5 and captured 25.7.1808 near Ajaccio by the brig *Requin*).
  Dimensions & tons: 47ft 0in x 15ft 0in x 5ft 0in (15.27 x 4.87 x 1.62m). 38/60 tons. Draught 5ft 6in (1.78m) aft. Men: 46.
  Guns: 4 x 6pdrs, 2 x 12pdr carronades; (1814) 4 x 4pdrs, 2 x 12pdr carronades.

Comm. or recomm. 2.3.1810. Captured 15.7.1815 near Elba by a British frigate.

Joseph (British felucca, possibly privateer, comm. in early 1809 at Santo Domingo, 3 guns). Captured 10.3.1809 on the coast of Santo Domingo by the boats of HMS *Argo* (44).

Delphine (British half-xebec, felucca or brigantine, taken in 1810 by a Neapolitan privateer and purchased 7.1811 by the French Navy)
  Dimensions & tons: 47ft 7in x 12ft 11in x 4ft 0in (15.46 x 4.20 x 1.30m). 26/35 tons. Men: 60.
  Guns: 4 x 4pdrs; (1816) 2 x 4pdrs.
  Sold 10.1817 to the French customs service, mentioned for the last time in 1822.

Aigle (British mercantile xebec captured 2.8.1813 from the British by three French gunboats and one péniche, carried 1 x 4pdr, 4 x 6pdr carronades). Chased, boarded, and taken 27.5.1814 while going from San Stefano to Corfu by the brig HMS *Wisler* (sic) and four boats from HMS *Elizabeth* (74) because she was flying the tricolour despite the end of the war and was thus a pirate.

Ex AUSTRIAN (VENETIAN) PRIZES (1806-1809)

Obusiera (Venetian felucca, laid down at Venice 1795, annexed 1.1806 with the city of Venice and served in Napoleon's Italian navy)
  Dimensions & tons: 48ft 2in x 10ft 0in x 3ft 2in (15.65 x 3.25 x 1.04m). 10/18 tons. Draught 1ft 8in/2ft 0in (0.54/0.64m). Men: 10-15.
  Guns: 1 or 2 x 3pdrs.
  At Venice in 4.1808 out of commission, at Treporti in August 1809, struck soon afterwards.

This heavily armed lateen-rigged privateer looks like a xebec but the artist, Jean-Jérôme Baugean, describes the vessel as a barque, possibly because of its flat stern without the characteristic extension (assuming the vessel in the background is just a different view of the same subject, in the common convention of ship portraiture). By no means all Mediterranean privateers operated under French letters of marque; many, sailing out of British-occupied ports like Malta, flew British colours, and some were captured and taken into the French Navy.

Vittoria (Venetian felucca, laid down at Venice 1795 as a sister of *Obusiera*, above, annexed 1.1806 with the city of Venice and served in Napoleon's Italian navy). In Dalmatia in July 1806, attacked a Russian brig off Spalato on 28 December 1806 without result. At Venice in 4.1808 out of commission, struck soon afterwards.

Vigilanza (Austrian felucca, built at Venice in 1805, annexed 1.1806 with the city of Venice, 12 men, carried 2 x 3pdrs). Name in French *Vigilante*. Struck before 1813.

Mora (Venetian felucca taken by the Austrians in Dalmatia in 7.1797, in the Austrian fleet at Venice in 11.1804, and the only former Venetian felucca that remained Austrian in 1.1806 because she was then at Trieste. Sold by the Austrians 7.11.1809 at Fiume to a private buyer, may have become the *Mora* that was a French station vessel at Trieste in 1.1811. 14-22 men, carried 3 x 3pdrs in 1809). A *Mora* was in commission in the French Navy 1.1.1813 to 6.12.1813 and was taken by the Anglo-Austrians in the surrender of Zara on 5.12.1813. Austrian historians list this *Mora* as a new ship built in 1811-12, in which case she was most likely ex-*Curiosa*, above. This *Mora* was listed in Austrian service with 1 x 12pdr, served in Dalmatia in 1815, and was struck 18.4.1817.

Ex PAPAL STATES PRIZES (1806)

Poisson Volant (Papal States balancelle seized 6.1806 at Civita Vecchia, 26 men, carried 2 x 4pdrs). Comm. by the French Navy 1.1811. Captured 14.3.1814 by the Neapolitans at the surrender of Civita Vecchia.

Petit Page (Papal States felucca or balancelle seized 6.1806 at Civita Vecchia, 17 men, carried 1 x 4pdr). Recomm. by the French Navy in 1.1811. Listed in 1814 as an aviso and in 1814-16 as a felucca. Decomm. at Toulon 14.6.1814, BU 1818.

Ex SICILIAN PRIZES (1807)

Bretonne (Sicilian xebec or half-xebec *Saint Jean-Baptiste Sainte Marguerite*, built in 1800 and confiscated following the decree of 7.12.1805, taken into French Navy service 8.12.1807 and renamed *Bretonne* 12.1807).
Dimensions & tons: 47ft 7in x 16ft 1in x 8ft 0in (15.46 x 5.23 x 2.60m). 65/100 tons. Men: 56.
Guns: 2 x 24pdr carronades, 2 x 16pdr carronades
Decomm. at Toulon 25.5.1814, sold 1816.

Languedocièrne (Sicilian xebec *Sainte Vierge de Trepany* confiscated following the decree of 7.12.1805, taken into the service of the French Navy 8.12.1807 and renamed *Languedocièrne* 12.1807)
Dimensions & tons: 61ft 4in x 21ft 6in x 10ft 10in (19.92 x 6.98 x 3.52m). 159/200 tons. Draught 8ft 6in (2.76m) mean.
Guns: 8 x 6pdrs, 2 swivels.
While serving as a gabarre was captured with the transport *Castor* 4.11.1811 near Cap Corse, Corsica, by HMS *Sultan* (74).

MISCELLANEOUS PRIZES (1808-1811)

Saint Antoine or *Antoine* (Portuguese felucca *San Antonio* captured 11.2.1808 by the frigates *Thémis* and *Pénélope*, and comm. 21.6.1809 at Toulon). Subsequent fate unknown.

Entreprise (Austrian galeotta or half-galley *Intrapresa* designed by Andrea Salvini and built at Venice, was to have been the first ship of a new class. Had three masts with a lateen rig, the main yard was 30m long. Hauled out at Porto Ré by the Austrians in 1807, destruction ordered 12.5.1809 but taken by the French)
Dimensions & tons: 103ft 1in x 20ft 4in x 6ft 6in (33.50 x 6.60 x 2.10m). Men: 49-84. Draught 5ft 6in (1.8m).
Guns: 2 x 18pdr, 2 x 12pdr
K: 10.11.1804 (construction approved). L: 21.5.1805. C: 6.1805.
Was station vessel under the French flag at Trieste in 1.1811. Burned 8.9.1813 or 23.9.1813 in the port of Duino to avoid capture by the British.

Colombe (felucca *Saint Antoine* from Port Mahon, built on Majorca or Minorca, captured 7.1809 by the gunboat *Observateur*).
Dimensions & tons: 37ft 7in x 10ft 6in x 3ft 8in (12.20 x 3.40 x 1.20m). 15/22 tons.
Guns: 1 x 3pdr.
Was probably in the convoy destroyed on 29.4.1811 off Marseille by five boats from HMS *Volontaire* (38), *Undaunted* (38), and *Blossom* (18).

Sirène (*Syrène*) (half-xebec privateer from Port Mahon captured 9.8.1809 by the brig *Étourdi*, carried 2 x 4pdrs, 2 espingoles). Renamed *Trompeuse* 11.1809. In commission at Toulon 21.11.1809 to

Official general arrangement plans of the trincadours (or trincadoures) built in 1823 for operations on the coast of Spain. They were based on a traditional Biscay fishing boat type that was designed to sail very close to the wind. They were widely employed in the Basque region on both sides of the Franco-Spanish border. (Atlas du Génie Maritime, French collection, plate 34)

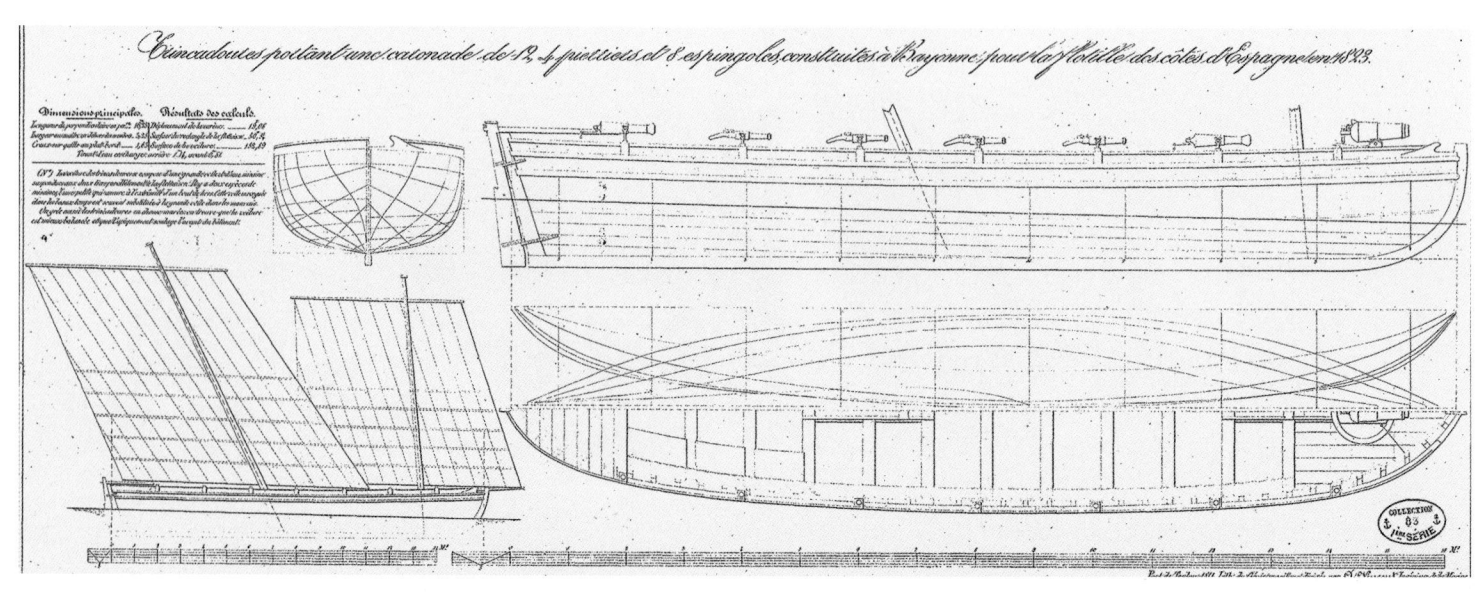

1.10.1810. Converted to *péniche* at Toulon 2.1813 and renamed *Péniche No.6*. Captured 19.8.1813 by the British between Toulon and Genoa.

Vengeance (Spanish insurgent half-xebec privateer from Port Mahon, possibly named *Venganza*, captured 20.7.1810 by the frigate *Pénélope* and comm. 1.10.1810, 42 men, carried 2 x 6pdrs, 2 x 4pdrs). Decomm. 29.9.1815, condemned and BU 1818.

Bon Patriote (Spanish half-xebec, balancelle or pink possibly named *Buen Patriota* captured 5.5.1811 by the felucca *Colombe*)
Dimensions & tons: 33ft 10in x 9ft 1in x 3ft 7in (11 x 2.95 x 1.16m). 12/20 tons. Men: 29.
Refitted at Toulon 8.1811, renamed *Troubadour* 8.1811, comm. 9.8.1811. Listed as balancelle in 1814. Decomm. at Toulon 7.3.1815 and sold 1816.

(D) Vessels acquired from 26 June 1815

TRINCADOUR No.3 Class – trincadours. Designed by Jean Delamorinière or Gabriel Nosereau. The dimensions shown for this class were normal for Bayonne trincadours at this time. *Trincadours No.1–No.2* (see above) were built at Bayonne in 1813 and were decomm. in 1823 and stk. in early 1832 with *Nos.3-5*.
Dimensions & tons: 13.0m x 2.7m x 1.3m. 10 tons disp. Draught 0.7/0.9m. Men: 11-12.
Guns: about 12 swivels or espingoles.

Trincadour No.3 Bayonne.
L: c1819. Decomm. at Bayonne 21.10.1823, refitted there 1826, and stk. there in early 1832.
Trincadour No.4 Bayonne.
L: c1819. Decomm. at Bayonne 21.10.1823, refitted there 1826, and stk. there in early 1832.
Trincadour No.5 Bayonne.
L: c1819. Decomm. at Bayonne 21.10.1823, refitted there 1826, and stk. there in early 1832.

TRINCADOUR No.6 Class – trincadours. Built on plans of Gabriel Nosereau,
Dimensions & tons: 16.35m x 3.25m x 1.63m. 19 tons disp. Draught 0.81/1.14m. Men: 14.
Guns: 1 x 6pdr or 1 x 12pdr carronade (preferred) plus 4 swivels and 2 espingoles (all on pivots).

Trincadour No.6 Bayonne
L: 30.6.1823. Hauled out 1831, renamed *Sentinelle* 7.1831, rebuilt, re-launched and comm. 22.8.1831. Decomm. 24 Nov 1844, stk. at Bayonne 1845.
Trincadour No.7 Bayonne
L: 30.6.1823. Blew up 4.8.1823 in combat in the bay of Santoña after being hit by a bomb from Fort Saint-Charles.

CHORIA Class. – trincadours. Built on plans of Jean-Baptiste Bayle. Had 10 pairs of oars.
Dimensions & tons: 14.54m x 3.40m x 1.77m. 29t disp. Draught 1.30m aft. Men: 24.
Guns: 12 swivels.

Choria Bayonne.
L: 23.10.1834. Decomm. 26 Feb 1842, struck at Bayonne 1842.
Araïna (Arraïna) Bayonne.
L: 12.11.1834. Decomm. 24 Nov 1842, struck at Bayonne 1845.

Variously spelled as mistic, mystique or misticou, this small lateen-rigged type was another cousin of the xebec. This example is a Spanish privateer, two of which were captured in 1823. The engraving by Baugean was originally published in 1819.

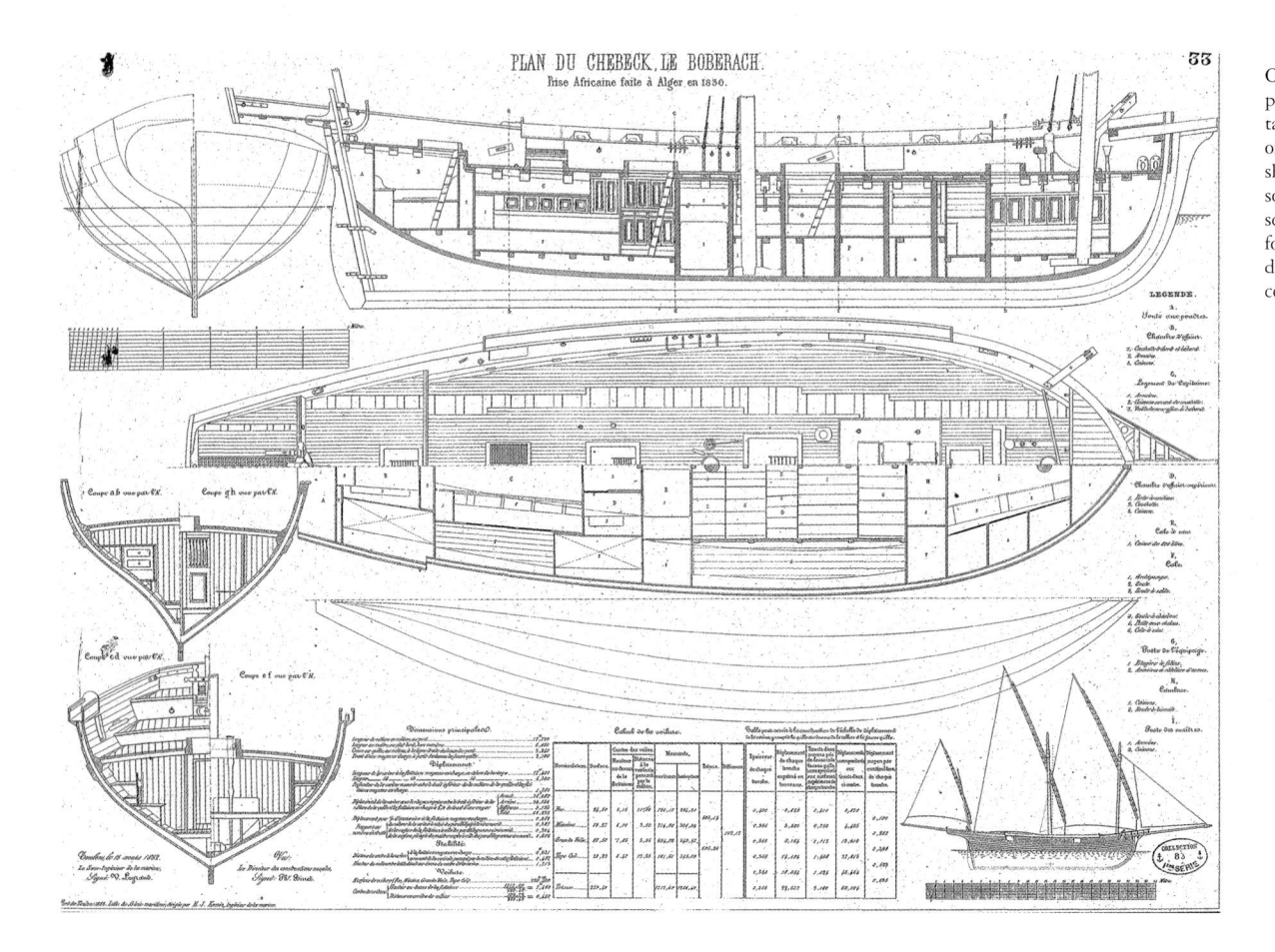

Official general arrangement plans of the xebec *Bobérach*, taken at Algiers in 1830 – one of the final descendants of a ship-type that had made the so-called Barbary corsairs a scourge of the Mediterranean for over two centuries. (Atlas du Génie Maritime, French collection, plate 33)

PURCHASED AND REQUISITIONED VESSELS (1819-1838)

Africaine (balancelle or bateau comm. at Toulon 16.4.1827, 14-22 men). Decomm. 11 Nov 1833, struck at Toulon 1835.

Marianne (trincadour launched or purchased at Bayonne, comm. 1.8.1834). Decomm. 15.6.1837, later struck.

Ernéa (trincadour launched or purchased at Bayonne, comm. 4.8.1834). Decomm. 1 Nov 1839, struck at Bayonne 1842.

Eugénie (trincadour, origin unknown, comm. at Bayonne 16.6.1837). Decomm. 17.11.1844. Struck 1850 at Rochefort, BU there 1851.

Belle Hélène (trincadour, origin unknown, in service at Bayonne 1837). Decomm. 1.12.1844. Struck 1850 at Rochefort or Bayonne and BU.

Seybouse (balancelle comm. at Toulon 20.4.1837). Wrecked at La Calle in Algeria 23.11.1839.

Tafna (balancelle or possibly trincadour, origin unknown, comm. at Toulon 20.4.1837). Decomm. 17.8.1848, struck at Toulon 1852.

Raschgoun (balancelle or possibly bateau launched at Toulon 8.1832 as service craft and comm. there 27.9.1837). Called lugger in 1844. Decomm. at Toulon 1.10.1844 and struck. Name also rendered *Rasgouhn* and *Rachgoun*.

Colombi (bateau or probably balancelle like *Raschgoun* launched at Toulon 8.1832 as service craft and comm. there 27.9.1837). Called lugger in 1842. Wrecked on the Algerian coast 25.3.1842.

Arach (balancelle probably built at Toulon and comm. there 24.11.1838). Struck 1845 and became service craft at Algiers, decomm. 1.8.1846 at Stora.

Massafran (balancelle probably built at Toulon and comm. there 24.11.1838). Decomm. at Toulon 1.12.1843 and struck there 1844.

Ex SPANISH PRIZES (1823)

Lévrier (Spanish aviso or xebec *Galgo* or *Lebrel*? taken 1823 and comm. 14.7.1823 at Toulon, 16-22 men, carried 1 x 12pdr). Decomm. 30.11.1825, off fleet list 1826 but restored 1827, struck at Toulon 1833.

Chamois (Spanish xebec or mistic *Gamuza*? taken 6.1823 and comm. at Toulon 28.10.1823, 19-23 men, 2 guns). Decomm. 1.12.1825, struck 1826 but recomm. 1.2.1828 after being hauled out 10.1827 at Cadiz and relaunched 3.1828. Service included fishery protection in the Mediterranean. Thrown onto the jetty at Grau du Roi by a squall 24.7.1849 and wrecked.

Étincelle (Spanish balancelle or bateau *Chispe*? taken 1823, possibly at Cadiz, 11-16 men, 1 gun). Decomm. 11 Nov 1833, unserviceable at Toulon in 1836 and struck

Ex ALGERIAN PRIZE (1830)

Bobérach (Algerian xebec *Majorca* or *Majorce* taken by the French in the port of Algiers 5.7.1830).

Dimensions & tons: 17.72m, 17.40m wl x 6.20m ext, 5.30m x 3.24m. 68 tons disp. Draught 2.10/2.26m. Men: 29-30.

Guns: 4 x 8pdr carronades and 4 other guns (4 ports). three masts.

This vessel was built at Algiers c1825/1827. Initially referred to as *No.8*, she was comm. 1.8.1830, refitted at Algiers 8.1830, and renamed *Bobérach* in 9.1830. She was decomm. at Toulon on 6.10.1830. Described as 'new and of an advantageous form', she was recomm. on 18.7.1831 and appeared on the fleet list in 1833. She was wrecked on 26.5.1858 and was decomm. and struck on 28.7.1858. *Bobérach* was the only Algerian prize that saw extensive French service. Three others, the brigs *Cassauba* (*No.1*), *Torre Chica* (*No.2*), and *Sidi Ferruch* (*No.3*), made it onto the fleet list briefly in 1833-35 while four others, the brig *Pescado* (*No.4*) and the schooners *Oran* (*No.5*), *Bona* (*No.6*), and *Mers el Kebir* (*No.7*), never did.

Bomb (mortar) vessels

The idea of using large mortars at sea for high-trajectory bombardment originated with Bernard Renau d'Elicagary, a Basque whose first purpose-built vessels in 1681 had provided the French Navy with a broad-beamed and stable weapon platform. The French designated these vessels as *galiotes à bombes* or as *bombardes*.

(A) Bomb vessels in service or on order at 1 January 1786

ARDENTE Group. Survivor of a trio of vessels built at Toulon in the 1720s, *Tempête* was designed and built by François Coulomb in 1725. Her sister *Foudroyante* had been captured off Ushant by a British privateer in February 1746, and the similar *Ardente* had been hulked at Toulon in August 1745 and struck in 1757.
  Dimensions & tons: 80ft 0in, 67ft 0in x 26ft 6in x 10ft 11in (25.99, 21.76 x 8.61 x 3.55m). 180/350 tons. Draught 9ft 6in/11ft (3.09/3.57m). Men: 55 -76.
  Guns: 8 x 6pdrs, plus 2 x 12in mortars.
Tempête Toulon Dyd.
  K: 1725. L: 24.8.1726. C: 1728.
  Struck at Toulon 1786 and ordered to be sold 15.7.1786.

SALAMANDRE Group. Two similar vessels built at Toulon and ordered on 16 November 1752, the first designed by Joseph Coulomb and the second by François Chapelle, but essentially successors to the *Ardente* Group. Two slightly larger vessels designed and built in 1753-55 by Jacques-Luc Coulomb at Brest, *Terreur* and *Vésuve*, were struck in 1762.
  Dimensions & tons: 81ft 0in, 69ft 0in x 25ft 0in x 11ft 2in (26.31, 22.41 x 8.12 x 3.63m). 180/350 tons. Draught 9ft 11in/11ft 10in (3.22/3.84m). Men: 66-80.
  Guns: 8 x 6pdrs, plus 2 x 12in mortars.
Salamandre Toulon Dyd. (Constructeur, Joseph Coulomb)
  K: 5.1753. L: 30.3.1754. C: 8.1754.
  Struck at Toulon 1785 or 1786, but survived as harbour craft until 1791.
Etna Toulon Dyd. (Constructeur, François Chapelle)
  K: 6.1753. L: 13.4.1754. C: 8.1754.
  Struck at Toulon 1785 or 1786.

(B) Bomb vessels acquired from 1 January 1786

LOUISE. Designed by Jean-Denis Chevillard or Hubert Penevert and described as a *bateau-plat* when ordered (plans for a 110-ton *bateau-plat* are still at Rochefort) and later as a dogger, a *galiote à bombes,* and a *canonnière-bombarde*.
  Dimensions & tons: 68ft 0in, 64ft 0in x 20ft 0in x 7ft 6in (22.09, 20.79 x 6.50 x 2.43m). 166 tons. Draught 5ft 6in/6ft 0in (1.78/1.95m). Men: 24-66.
  Guns: 6 x 4pdrs, 1 x 12in mortar; (1802-15) 6 x 12pdrs.
Louise Le Havre (Constructeurs, Charles-Henri Tellier and Jacques Fabien)
  K: 1.1792. L: 19.9.1792. C: 1.1793.
  Renamed *Longitudinale* 5.1795. Station ship at Bénodet 1804. Decomm. and struck 31.8.1815.

ROUSSE. Rated as *galiote-canonnière* or transport, also described as a chatte, probably built to plans by Hubert Pennevert dated 25 August 1791 (these are still at Rochefort).
  Dimensions & tons: 62ft 0in, 52ft 6in x 18ft 0in x 9ft 6in (20.14, 17.05 x 5.85 x 3.08m). 100/171 tons. Draught 7/8ft (2.27/2.60m). Men: 44.
  Guns: 4 x 16pdrs, 2 x 4pdrs (from 5.1801 re-armed with 4 x 24pdrs and 4 x 6pdrs).
Rousse Le Havre (Constructeur, Jacques Fabien)
  K: 9.1792. L: 22.5.1793. K: 6.1793.
  Built as a *chatte* (lighter), probably for use at Rochefort, but named *Rousse* in 1793 and served as station ship at Le Havre 1793-95. Re-rigged as a brig and refitted 1801, reclassified and re-armed as a gunboat, and renamed in 5.1803 as *Canonnière No.13* (or *Treizième*). Wrecked 2.1804 at Audierne.

SALAMANDRE Class. 400-ton bomb vessels or *galiotes à bombes* constructed and probably designed by Pierre-Alexandre Forfait (plans dated 14 January 1793). They became flûtes or gabarres in 1796.
  Dimensions & tons: 120ft 0in, 111ft 0in x 27ft 0in x 13ft 6in (38.98, 36.05 x 8.77 x 4.38m). 350-400/650-687 tons. Draught 11ft/11ft 4in (3.57/3.68m). Men: 86-150.
  Guns: 10 x 8pdrs, 2 x 12-inch mortars on the centreline; (1806) 22 x 8pdrs plus 4 x 24pdr carronades in *Salamandre*
Salamandre Le Havre
  K: 2.1793. L: 8.8.1793. C: 1.1794.
  Refitted as a flûte 1796. Chased 12.10.1806 by a British division while en route from Saint-Malo to Brest and ran into shallow water near Mont St-Michel. Taken by HMS *Constance* (ex French corvette) which took her in tow but then ran aground and was taken by French troops. *Salamandre* was either burned or towed to Saint-Malo, but she did not return to service.
Menaçante Le Havre
  K: 8.1793. L: 12.9.1795. C: 2.1796.
  Completed as a gabarre. Renamed *Naturaliste* 23.6.1800, designated as a corvette, and sailed from Le Havre 19.10.1800 with *Géographe* on an expedition under Nicholas Baudin to map the coast of Australia. Detached from the expedition at Tasmania in 12.1802 to bring the first collections home, returned to Le Havre 7.6.1803, and decomm. 23.6.1803. Reclassified gabarre c1807. Condemned 12.1810, sold 25.1.1811 at Le Havre.

BOMBARDIER Class, *bombardes* or *bateaux-bombardiers*.
  Dimensions & tons: unknown.
  Guns: 2 x 12pdrs, 2 x 36pdr obusiers, 1 mortar.
Bombardier Brest Dyd. (?)
  K: 1793. L: 1794. C: 1794.
  Was for sale at Brest in 12.1801, last mentioned under repair there 5.1803 under the name *Bombe*. May have been renamed *Canonnière No.10* in 6.1803, in which case she was in commission at Boulogne from 23.9.1804 to 9.1805.
Mortier Brest Dyd. (?)
  L: c1795
  Redesignated as a transport 5.1801, redesigned as a gunboat and refitted at Brest 5.1803. May have been renamed *Canonnière No.15* in 8.1803. May have become the *Canonnière No.12* that was in commission at Boulogne from 9.1804 to 7.1811. *Canonnière No.12* was at Antwerp in 1.1813 and was decomm. 2.1815 at Brest.

DUPETIT-THOUARS Class. Rated as *bombardes* or *chaloupes-bombardières*, cutter-rigged. Constructed and probably designed by

Antoine Bonjean.
- Dimensions & tons: 70ft 0in, 65ft 10in x 20ft 0in x 6ft 0in (22.74, 21.38 x 6.50 x 1.95m) 70/142 tons. Draught 6ft 2in/6ft 5in (2.00/2.08m)
- Guns: 2 x 24pdrs (1 fore, 1 aft), 1 x 12-inch mortar with 50 projectiles in the magazine.

Dupetit-Thouars Toulon Dyd
- K: 11.1798. L: summer 1799. C: 9.1799.
- Little used because her seakeeping qualities were very poor. Service craft at Toulon 1804, later fate unknown.

Thévenard Toulon Dyd
- K: 11.1798. L: summer 1799. C: 9.1799.
- Service craft at Toulon 5.1803, later fate unknown.

Ex VENETIAN PRIZES (1797)

Venetian bomb vessel DISTRUZION. *Distruzion* and a sister named *Polonia* were built in Venice as copies of the British *Infernal* class bomb vessels (of which the first was begun at Southampton in 1756 and six others followed in 1758). In the late 1760s the Venetian ambassador in London bought the building plans from the Deptford yard, and *Distruzion* was built at Venice in 1770-72. The British ships of this type carried a 13-inch (396mm) mortar and one of 10 inches (305mm), while the Venetian ships had a 500 libbre (332mm) mortar and one of 300 libbre (280mm). Like other contemporary bomb vessels they were ketch rigged (with main- and mizzen masts but no foremast). *Distruzion* was the prototype Venetian ship built with the new structural method of the 'double frame' (*con struttura a ordinate doppia*) that was used in French and English vessels, and her construction was used to train the workmen of the Venetian Arsenal in this new method. The 'double frame' method, however, was more expensive than the old working method of the 'single frame' (*con struttura a ordinate singola*) that had been developed in the middle ages to build galleys, and the Venetian Senate authorised its general use only on 8 May 1778. Both ships participated in the Venetian bombardments of Tunis, Susa, Bizerte and Sfax in 1785-86; there is no record of *Polonia* after 1786.
- Dimensions & tons: Length 97ft (31.51m). Tons unknown.
- Guns: 12 x 18pdrs, 2 mortars; (1800) 2 x 60pdrs, 14 x 3pdrs; (1801) 12 x 6pdrs; (1805) 10 x 18pdrs

Destruction (Venetian *Distruzion*) Venice.
- K: 2.1770. L: 1784. C: 1784.
- Taken by the French at Venice 17.5.1797 while hauled out for repairs, name became *Destruction*. Sabotaged by them 30.12.1797 on slip No.30, taken by the Austrians 18.1.1798 and rebuilt 1801-2 by Andrea Salvini as the Austrian brig *Orione*. Ceded to French Italy by the Austrians at Venice 19.1.1806. Was at Venice out of commission 4.1808, struck c1810.

Venetian mortar boats. The French took 31 *barques obusières* at Venice in 5.1797 and named and commissioned three of them, *Montenotte* and *Dego* in 1797, and *Passage du Po* in 1797/98. In 1.1798 they sabotaged 18 of them before turning the city over to the Austrians. On 20.2.1802 the Austrians returned to service 16 of these as *Nos.1-16* with armaments of 2 x 40pdr or 50pdr Venetian guns and 4 x 6pdrs and crews of 18 to 23 men. They all passed to Napoleon's Italian Navy in 1.1806.

Ex PORTUGUESE PRIZE (1798)

Portugaise (captured Portuguese vessel requisitioned and comm. at Marseille 13.4.1798 and fitted as a bomb vessel at Toulon for the Egyptian expedition, 92 men, carried 1 x 12-inch mortar and 6 x 6pdrs). Survived the Battle of Aboukir with *Oranger*, below, decomm. 1.1799 at Alexandria, subsequent fate unknown.

PURCHASED AND REQUISITIONED BOMB VESSELS (1793-1801)

Canada (Purchased by the Navy 9.1782 as a gabarre, was probably a British merchant ship taken by privateers; struck 4.1785 and lay as a hulk at Cherbourg until reinstated on the list in 4.1793 as a bomb vessel. 422 tons burthen, 120 men, carried 4 x 24pdrs and 1 mortar). Decomm. 11.1796, BU 11.1797 at Cherbourg.

Galiote Hollandaise or *Frédéric Guillaume* (Dutch galiote seized 2.1793 and refitted at Cherbourg 7-9.1793, 230 tons, 40-100 men, carried 1 mortar and 4 x 24pdrs). Renamed *Révolution* 10.1793. Station ship at Cherbourg 1793-95. Redesignated as a transport 5.1795, renamed *Rustique* 5.1795 and *Frédéric* 5.1795. Bombarde, transport in 1800. Wrecked 3.1801.

Espérance (sailing barge requisitioned or hired 5.1793 at Le Havre and fitted there as a bomb vessel, 38 tons, carried 1 x 12-inch mortar and either 4 x 4pdrs or 2 x 8pdrs). Returned to her owners 4.1795.

Marguérite Adélaïde (merchant dogger requisitioned 4.1794 at Nantes and fitted there 6.1794 as a bomb vessel, carried 1 x 8-inch mortar and 2 x 12pdrs). Renamed *Meilleur* 5.1795. Last mentioned 5.1795 while at Saint-Malo, probably returned to her owner.

Victoire Sophie (merchant gabarre or dogger requisitioned 6.1794 at Nantes and fitted there as a bomb vessel, carried 1 x 8-inch mortar and 2 x 12pdrs). Renamed *Vérificateur* 5.1795. Last mentioned 5.1795 while at Saint-Malo, probably returned to her owner.

Hercule (merchant ship requisitioned at Marseille, comm. 1.1798 at Toulon, and fitted there as a bomb vessel in 3-4.1798, 92 men, carried 1 x 12-inch mortar and 6 x 6pdrs). Grounded 1.8.1798 under British fire near the fort at Aboukir after cutting her cable, wreck burned by the French 15.8.1798.

Aglaé (merchant ship requisitioned 3.1798 at Marseille and fitted as a bomb vessel at Toulon in 4-5.1798, 92 men, carried 1 x 12-inch mortar and 6 x 6pdrs). Last mentioned 10.1798 while at Alexandria.

Oranger (merchant ship requisitioned and commissioned 13.4.1798 at Marseille and fitted as a bomb vessel at Toulon in 4-5.1798 for the Egyptian expedition, 92 men, carried 1 x 12-inch mortar and 6 x 6pdrs). Survived the Battle of Aboukir with *Portugaise*, above, decomm. 9.1799 at Alexandria, later fate unknown.

Patriote (vessel of unknown origin and characteristics comm. 23.9.1799 at Toulon) Decomm. 23.9.1800 at Toulon.

Pulvérisateur or *Pulvériseur* (*bombarde* or *galiote à bombes* comm. at Boulogne 8.9.1801, probably came from Le Havre, manned by 37 men and 34 soldiers). Out of commission 10.1801, fate unknown.

(C) Bomb vessels acquired from 25 March 1802

INFERNALE. The only purpose-built *bombarde* acquired by the French Navy during the Napoleonic regime.
- Dimensions & tons: 59ft 5in, 55ft 5in x 20ft 7in x 10ft 1in (19.30, 18.00 x 6.68 x 3.28m). 90/160 tons. Draught 6ft 2in (2.00m) mean. Men: 50.
- Guns: 1 x 12-inch mortar, 6 x 8 small guns.

Infernale Le Havre.
- K: 2.1804. L: 2.8.1804. Comm: 23.10.1804. Rigged as lugger. Decomm. and struck at Boulogne early 1814.

PURCHASED AND REQUISITIONED BOMB VESSELS (1803-1809)

MISCELLANEOUS SAILING VESSELS

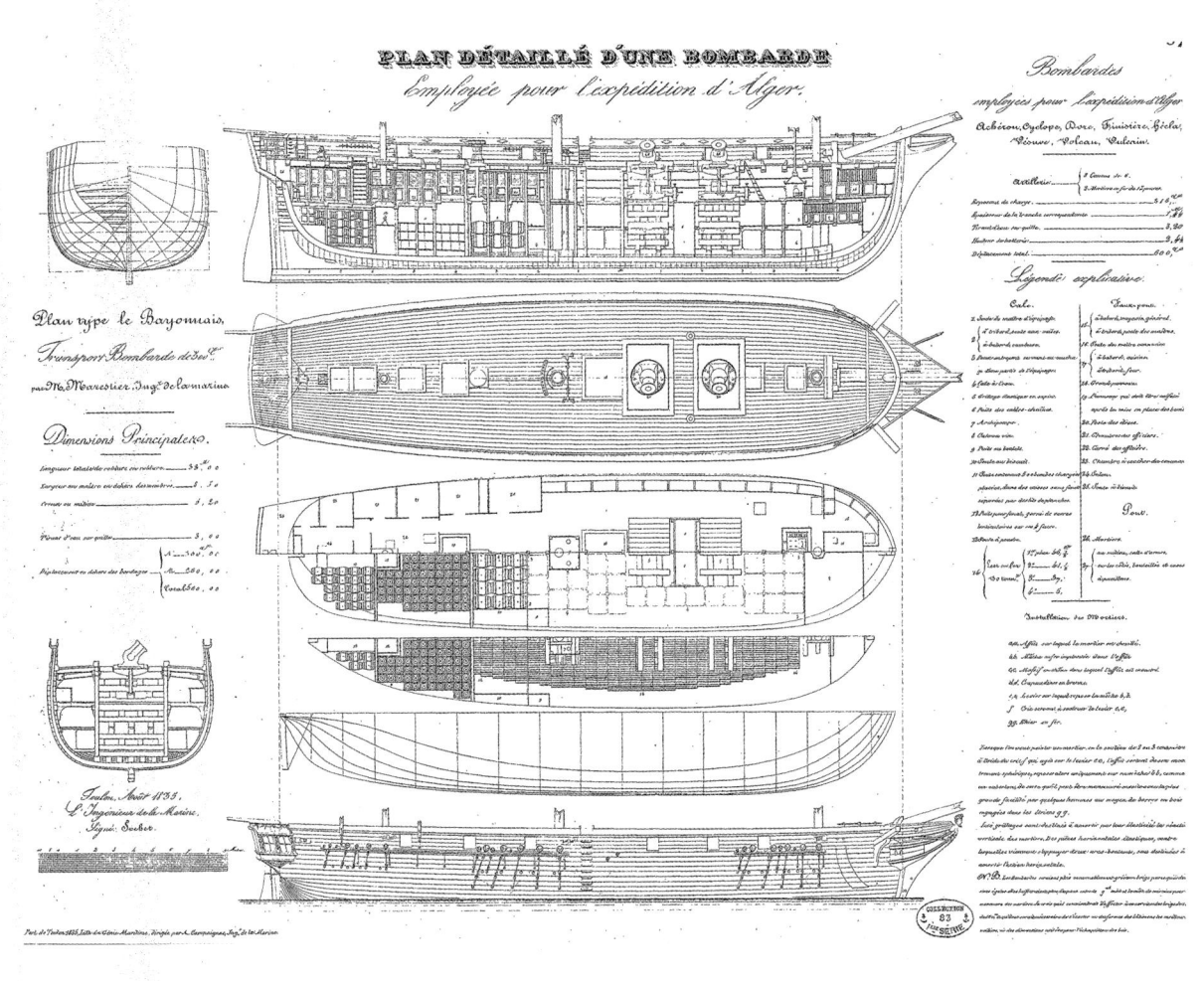

Official general arrangement plans of the *Vésuve* class bomb vessels, based on the design of the *Bayonnaise* type transports. They were used in the attack on Algiers. (Atlas du Génie Maritime, French collection, plate 97)

Hercule (purchased 25.11.1803 at Boulogne and comm. there 23.9.1804, 50 men, carried 2 x 4pdrs, 2 swivels, and probably 1 mortar that was not in place in 2.1804). Last mentioned departing Dunkirk 24.6.1814 for Cherbourg.

Amélia (acquired c1.1804 and in service at Boulogne 2.1804, 50 men, carried 2 x 4pdrs, 2 swivels, and probably 1 mortar that was not in place in 2.1804). Decomm. 31.3.1807.

Joubert (Russian bomb vessel *Tynder-Otregoc* built in 1806 at Monte Santo near Salonica, not on Russian navy lists and probably of Greek mercantile origin, acquired 12.1809 at Corfu and comm. 1.1.1810)
  Dimensions & tons: 49ft 7in x 17ft 3in x 9ft 3in (16.10 x 5.60 x 3.00m). 84/120 tons. Men: 54-61.
  Guns: 4 x 12pdrs, 6 x 3pdrs.
  Refitted as aviso at Corfu 1810. Seized by the British there 21.6.1814.

Ex PRUSSIAN PRIZES (1807)

Pintade (Prussian merchant vessel *Güte Hoffnung* seized 10.1806 at Bordeaux, renamed 24.8.1807, refitted at Bordeaux and comm. 20.11.1807).
  Dimensions & tons: 70ft 6in x 21ft 6in x 10ft 9in (22.90 x 6.98 x 3.49m). 173/300 tons.
  Guns: 2 x 18pdrs, 1 long-range mortar.
  Converted to bomb vessel at Rochefort 4-5.1809 and recomm. 1.7.1809. Decomm. 24.1.1811, struck c1816.

Tortue (Prussian merchant vessel *Jonge Vrouw Tella* seized 10.1806 at Bordeaux, renamed 24.8.1807, refitted at Bordeaux and comm. 16.1.1808)
  Dimensions & tons: 74ft 8in x 21ft 8in x 11ft 8in (24.26 x 7.04 x 3.79m). 159/300 tons.

  Guns: 2 x 18pdrs, 2 short-range mortars.
  Converted to bomb vessel at Rochefort 4-5.1809. Struck at Rochefort 11.1814 and BU.

(D) Bomb vessels acquired from 26 June 1815

VÉSUVE Class. This class was designed by Jean-Baptiste Marestier, who practically duplicated his plans for a 300-ton gabarre (transport) of 1817, *Bayonnais*. The class was designed to carry two mortars on rotating platforms on the centreline between the foremast and the mainmast and firing on the beam. Its designed height of battery was 2.24m at 3.68m mean draught. *Bayonnais* and her sister *Garonne* also were fitted to carry mortars, but were never classified as mortar vessels. The *Vésuve* class ships were originally designated as bombardes and were redesignated transport-bombardes in 11.1824, 300-ton gabarres in 1827, bombardes in 1829, gabarres in 1.1838, and 300-ton transports in 1.1846. *Dore* and *Finistère* were originally to have carried 16 x 24pdr carronades (18 ports) but were completed with 8 x 24pdr carronades and had 2 x 12-inch mortars added in 1829. *Cyclope* and *Vulcain* still had their two mortars in 1838.
  Dimensions & tons: 34.30m, 33.00m wl, 29.90m x 8.82m, 8.90m ext x 5.20m. 669-695 tons disp. Draught 4.09/4.45m. Men: 88-101 as bombardes, 64-66 as gabarres.
  Guns: 2 x 12-inch mortars, 8 x 8pdrs (24pdr carronades in *Dore* and *Finistère*) as bombardes, 4 or 6 x 8pdrs or 6pdrs as gabarres.

Vésuve Bayonne (Constructeur, Gabriel Nosereau)
  Ord: 10.2.1824. K: 6.1824. L: 28.7.1825. C: 10.1825. Comm: 22.11.1825.

Struck 1840. Ceded to Marseille as a barracks hulk for the school for boys there.

Hécla Bayonne (Constructeur, Gabriel Nosereau)
K: 6.1824. L: 22.5.1826. Comm: 1.6.1826. C: 8.1826.
Struck 30.8.1850 at Toulon, last mentioned 1851.

Volcan Bayonne (Constructeur, Gabriel Nosereau)
K: 6.1824. L: 22.5.1826. Comm: 15.6.1826. C: 8.1826.
Struck 1850, barracks hulk at Martinique. BU 1856.

Dore Bayonne (Constructeur, Gabriel Nosereau)
K: 9.1827. L: 15.4.1828. Comm: 13.4.1828. C: 7.1828.
Station ship at Toulon 1839. Decomm. 23.12.1850 at Toulon and struck, BU 1851.

Finistère Bayonne (Constructeur, Gabriel Nosereau)
K: 9.1827. L: 15.4.1828. Comm: 19.5.1828. C: 7.1828.
Struck 21.3.1838 and became tender (*patache*), later guard hulk at Toulon. Renamed *Ponton* 1865. Struck 13.8.1874 from the list of service craft. BU 8.1874-2.1875 at Toulon.

Cyclope Toulon Dyd. (Constructeur, Prix Sochet)
K: 10.1827. L: 19.4.1828. C: 1828. Comm: 22.2.1830.
Station ship at Toulon from 1850 to 1865. Struck 10.8.1874 at Noumea, guard hulk until BU 1879.

Vulcain Toulon Dyd.
K: 1827. L: 10.5.1828. C: 1828. Comm: 8.6.1829.
Struck 15.7.1851 at Toulon, careening hulk (*ponton-fosse*). Renamed *Dépôt* 1865. BU 1875.

Achéron Toulon Dyd.
K: 1827. L: 15.3.1828. C: 3.1829. Comm: 1.3.1829.
Renamed *Éclair* 1835. Struck 1846, school hulk for boys at Nantes. Condemned and BU 1858.

TOCSIN Class. These ships were designed for Crimean War service by Jean-Baptiste Pastoureau-Labesse and were inspired by British plans dated 6 October 1854. They were rigged as brig-schooners and were designed to be towed into action by steam gunboats. Their two mortars fired to starboard.
Dimensions & tons: 24.00m, 23.40m wl, 22.43m x 6.10m, 6.24m ext x 2.25m. 183 tons disp. Draught 1.98/1.98m. Men: 21.
Guns: 2 x 12-inch mortars.

Tocsin Lorient Dyd. (Constructeur, Louis De Bussy)
K: 22.11.1854. L: 3.4.1855. Comm: 16.4.1855. C: 5.1855.
Ordered 12.8.1857 converted to sailing water barge, struck 29.8.1857, converted to *Citerne No.1* at Cherbourg 8-11.1857 by Jules Lemaire. Name reverted to *Tocsin* 1.1861 after refit at Brest. Was at Gabon in 1864-73 and Senegal in 1873-75. Struck 1875.

Bombe Lorient Dyd. (Constructeur, Louis De Bussy)
K: 11.1854. L: 18.4.1855. Comm: 8.5.1855. C: 5.1855.
Listed as a schooner 1858. Struck 21.10.1859. Converted to sailing water barge *Citerne No.5* at Cherbourg in 5-9.1860, then converted to sailing hoy *Bugalet No.2* at Cherbourg in 1865 and renamed *Fort* in 1.1866. In use at Cherbourg until 1920.

Fournaise Lorient Dyd. (Constructeur, Louis De Bussy)
K: 12.1854. L: 24.4.1855. Comm: 21.5.1855. C: 5.1855.
Struck 29.6.1858, converted to sailing water barge *Citerne No.2* or *2R* at Cherbourg in 1858-59. At Rochefort by 4.1865, renamed *Jouvence* 2.1866. Struck 1885 at Rochefort, BU c1886.

Torche Lorient Dyd. (Constructeur, Louis De Bussy)
K: 12.12.1854. L: 2.5.1855. Comm: 21.5.1855. C: 5.1855.
Struck 29.6.1858, converted to sailing water barge *Citerne No.1* or *1R* at Cherbourg 1858-59. Renamed *Lupin* in 2.1866, was at Rochefort by 1869. Unserviceable there 1887.

Trombe Lorient Dyd. (Constructeur, Louis De Bussy)
K: 12.12.1854. L: 5.5.1855. Comm: 29.5.1855. C: 6.1855.
Ordered 12.8.1857 converted to sailing water barge, struck 29.8.1857, converted to *Citerne No.2* at Cherbourg 8-11.1857. Name reverted to *Trombe* c1859. Was in Senegal 1860 through 1869 or 1872, struck 1870.

Floating batteries

(A) Floating batteries in service or on order at 1 January 1786

The French Navy had no floating batteries between 1759 and 1793. In 1759 a hexagonal craft named *Diable* and a sister were hastily built for the defence of Quebec and then broken up for use as firewood.

(B) Floating batteries acquired from 1 January 1786

PURCHASED AND REQUISITIONED FLOATING BATTERIES
(1793). In February 1793 the French seized four Dutch galiotes at Dunkirk and converted them into floating batteries for the defence of Dunkirk. Another was seized at Le Havre, and two more were seized later in 1793 at Dunkirk. They were manned by 40 men and carried two or four 24pdrs and a few smaller guns. Their dimensions and tonnages are unknown.

Liberté (2 x 24pdrs, 2 x 6pdrs). Refitted at Dunkirk 5.1793. Unserviceable 5.1797 and BU at Dunkirk.

Égalité (2 x 24pdrs, 2 x 6pdrs). Refitted at Dunkirk 5.1793. Struck 1795 at Dunkirk.

République (4 x 24pdrs, 2 x 12pdrs, 2 x 8pdrs). Refitted at Dunkirk 5.1793 and stationed there 7.1793 to 6.1795. Fought a British division in the Dunkirk roadstead 7.8.1800. Wrecked 9.11.1800 near Dunkirk, wreck sold 16.11.1800.

Constitution (4 x 24pdrs, 2 x 8pdrs). Refitted at Dunkirk 5-6.1793. Struck late 1794 or early 1795.

Deux Amis (350 tons, 4 x 24pdrs). Seized 2.1793 and refitted at Le Havre. Called a *galiote-canonnière*, also used as a transport. Struck 1796.

Carpe (ex Dutch *Jacoba Catharina* seized at Dunkirk 1793 and refitted there 1-2.1794, carried 4 x 24pdrs, 4 x 12pdrs). Originally called *Batterie Flottante No.1*, renamed *Carpe* late 12.1794 and *Jacoba Catharina* 7.1795. Burned accidentally 9.1796 in Dunkirk harbour and blew up.

Brochet (ex Dutch *Jonker Slewig* or *Joncker Slewigh*, built c1786-87, seized at Dunkirk 1793 and refitted there 1-2.1794, carried 4 x 24pdrs, 4 x 8pdrs). Originally called *Batterie Flottante No.2*, renamed *Brochet* 12.1794 and *Jonker Slewig* (*Joncker Slewigh*) 7.1795. Fought a British division in the Dunkirk roadstead 7.8.1800. Struck 10.1801, sold 1.1802 at Dunkirk.

(C) Floating batteries acquired from 25 March 1802

PURCHASED OR REQUISITIONED FLOATING BATTERY
(1803)
Triton (origin unknown, possibly the old 24-gun Dutch corvette *Triton*

of 1789, comm. at Flushing 9.4.1803, 46 men, carried 8 x 8pdrs, 2 x 4pdrs). Decomm. at Flushing 10.4.1807. May have become the transport *Triton* which was comm. at Antwerp 1.1.1811 and decomm. 17.6.1814.

Hydrographic vessels

(A) Hydrographic vessels acquired from 25 March 1802

Marc (probably mercantile, schuyt (scuts) or double schuyt comm. 15.12.1803 at Ostende, 11 men, probably no guns as hydrographic vessel, 1 x 4pdr, 2 x 2pdr carronades, and 4 x 1pdr swivels in 1807). Recomm. under the name *Recherche* 26.2.1804 to survey the North Sea coasts of the French Empire (including Dunkirk and Ostende) under the direction of Beautemps-Beaupré. Departed 14.3.1804, returned and decomm. 23.9.1804. Renamed *Marc* c1805. Abandoned 6.1814 at Ostende where she had been station vessel.

Boussole (mercantile schuyt or cutter *Jean-Baptiste* comm. 26.2.1804 to survey the North Sea coasts of the French Empire under the direction of Beautemps-Beaupré, 10 men, probably no guns). Decomm. 1.10.1814, probably at Brest.

Espérance (mercantile schuyt or cutter *Jacques* comm. 21.2.1804 to survey the North Sea coasts of the French Empire under the direction of Beautemps-Beaupré, 10 men, probably no guns). Decomm. 5.2.1805. Refitted at Antwerp 6.1805. Captured 4.1808 by the British.

(B) Hydrographic vessels acquired from 26 June 1815

See the *Astrolabe* class (1816) in Chapter 8 for two schooners specifically designed for hydrographic work. As in previous years, many other ships including corvettes and gabarres were temporarily assigned to duty as hydrographic vessels.

Yachts

(A) Yachts in service or on order at 1 January 1786

YACHT DE LA REINE.
Built at Paris or Saint-Cloud in 1785, sold at Paris 2.1793, no other information.

(B) Yachts acquired from 1 January 1786

ROCHEFORT Class. Designed by Hubert Pennevert. The lugger *Enfant* was probably built to her plans in 1792.
  Dimensions & tons: 54ft, 48ft x 15ft x 7ft (17.54, 15.59 x 4.87 x 2.27m). 55-60/90 tons. Draught 5ft/6ft (1.62/1.95m).
  Guns: (*Rochefort*) none; (*Enfant*) 8 x 4pdrs, later 8 x 6pdrs.
Rochefort Rochefort Dyd
  K: 4.1787. L: 2.8.1787. C: 8.1787.
  Fate unknown.

(C) Yachts acquired from 25 March 1802

BONAPARTE. Yacht or *corvette de rivière*.
  Launched c1801? Was in service at Paris in 1802. Given in 1802 by

Official general arrangement plans of the *Canot Royal de Brest* (ex *Canot Impérial d'Anvers*) in the 1830s. (Atlas du Génie Maritime, French collection, plate 114)

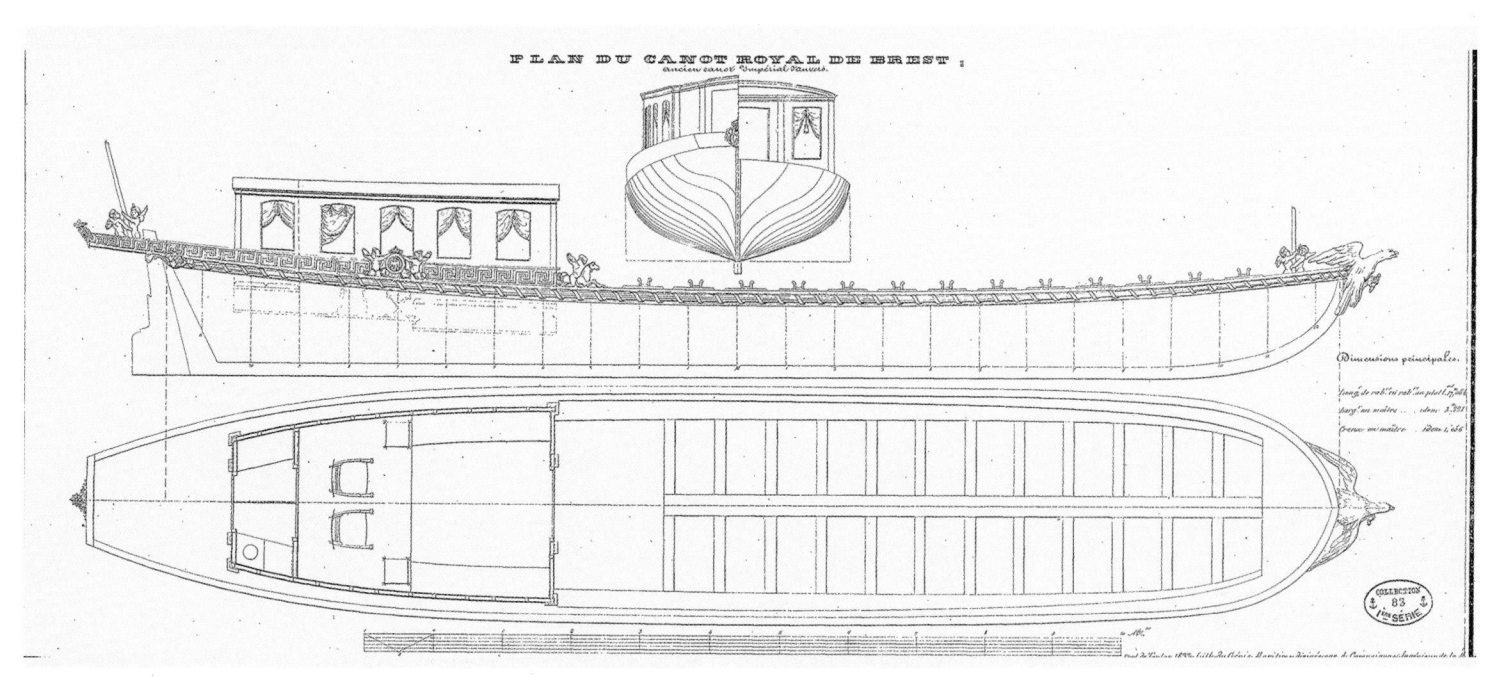

the First Consul to Charles-François Lebrun, who sold her to Lucien Bonaparte.

HEUREUX. Yacht.
   Dimensions & tons: 70ft 10in x 19ft 6in (23.00 x 6.33m).
Heureux Flushing
   Purchased at Flushing 7.1803, named 21.7.1803, refitted at Antwerp 4.1805 and comm. there 25.4.1805.
   Reassigned to Brest 1.1.1810. Condemned at Brest at the end of 1831, struck in early 1832.

VOLTEGGIATORE. Yacht with two masts probably designed by Andrea Salvini, part of Napoleon's Italian Navy..
   Dimensions & tons: 69ft 0in x 19ft 0in x 7ft 6in (22.41 x 6.17 x 2.43m). 93/133 tons disp. Draught 6ft 9in (2.19m) aft.
   Guns: 10 ports.
Volteggiatore Venice
   K: 1806, L: 1807. C: 1808.
   At Venice June 1808, at Goro or Maestro (Po River) in mid-1810, at Venice 1813-14. Left to Austria 4.1814 at the surrender of Venice and renamed *Drogone* (*Dragone?*), later became the brig *Cesarea* (?). Struck 1829.

CANOT IMPÉRIAL D'ANVERS. River yacht built at Antwerp by Le Theau of Granville to plans by Jean-François Guillemard inspired by Fredrik Henrik af Chapman. Had 12 to 14 pairs of oars.
   Dimensions & tons: 53ft 0in x 10ft 6in x 3ft 3in height of hull (17.21 x 3.40 x 1.06m). 18 tons. Draught 2ft 2in/2ft 6in (0.70/0.80m).

Canot Impérial d'Anvers Antwerp
   K: 7.4.1810, L: 28.4.1810. C: 30.4.1810.
   Was at Dunkirk in 10.1813. Renamed *Canot Royal de Brest* in 1815 and *Canot de l'Empereur* in 1848. Rebuilt and redecorated at Brest in 7-8.1858. Underway for the last time in 1922 at Brest. Preserved since 1943 at the Musée de la Marine at Paris and on display there.

(D) Yachts acquired from 26 June 1815

REINE AMÉLIE. Yacht designed by Jean-Félix De Robert. Brig-rigged. May have had positions for 6 pairs of oars.
   Dimensions & tons: 22.50m wl, 20.70m x 6.25m x 3.30m. 139 tons disp. Draught 2.3/2.4m. Men: ?.
   Guns: 12 swivels (designed), 8 brass guns in 1844
Reine Amélie Cherbourg Dyd. (Constructeur: Robert)
   K: 26.1.1835. L: 12.9.1835. C: 6.1836. Initially comm. 16.6.1836, definitively comm. 7.11.1838.
   Stationed every summer in 1836-48 at Tréport while the royal family stayed at the Château d'Éu. On fleet list 1844 as schooner, 4 guns, although was brig-rigged during royal visit to Portsmouth on 8.10.1844. Renamed *Parisien* 29.2.1848 and redesignated cutter, decomm. 1.4.1848. By this time she may have had one mast with two square sails. Not recommissioned although designated second class *brick-aviso* or cutter 1852 and schooner 1853. Struck 28.2.1853 and ordered BU.

11 Paddle Vessels

France adopted the marine steam engine not long after it became viable, first for use in the colonies, then to provide tugs for its major dockyards, and finally for military use. From the late 1820s to the early 1840s a single pattern of low-pressure condensing engine developed by James Watt dominated. This mechanism except in its smallest applications had two cylinders of equal power mounted side by side that acted as two independent engines connected through large side-levers to the shaft of the paddle wheels. The cylinders were double acting, meaning that steam was admitted alternatively at the top and the bottom of the cylinder to power both the upward and downward stroke of the piston. During each stroke steam from the boiler at barely above atmospheric pressure was on one side of the piston, while on the other side was a vacuum produced by the condenser into which the spent steam vented. The entire engine rested on a heavy metal foundation plate that contained the condenser, and the paddle shaft and the two side-levers, one on each side of the engine assembly, supported by an often ornately-decorated large metal frame. Except at the bottom these engines were entirely independent of the hull structure of the ship. The main competition to the Watt engine during the early years came from the high pressure engine, which dispensed with the vacuum and the condenser and worked solely by the pressure of steam above the atmosphere, which was somewhat higher than in the Watt engines. A few engineers advocated this type, but the higher temperatures and pressures caused problems with fabrication and reliability and high pressure engines ended up being used mainly in small or specialised applications.

After the late 1820s the French primarily used two patterns of boilers. One, developed by Fawcett, consisted of a single large shell containing several compartments with furnaces, the compartments sharing piping for water supply and steam exhaust. The other, developed by Maudslay, consisted of two or four independent boilers; this soon became the French standard. These were all flue boilers, meaning that the hot combustion gases passed through the water in large rectangular ducts, producing steam with a pressure of about 7.5 pounds above atmospheric pressure. In the mid-1840s flue boilers were replaced by tubular boilers in which the combustion gases passed through the water in many small-diameter tubes; the steam pressure in these boilers in French applications ranged from 15 to 22 pounds. These boilers took their feed water from the sea, the water impurities being manageable at the low pressures of the day. Also in the 1840s the heavy side-lever engines were replaced with various types in which the pistons were connected directly to the shaft, the most successful for paddle steamers being those in which the cylinders oscillated on trunnions as the paddle shaft turned. Water tube boilers, in which water replaced combustion gases in the boiler tubes, began to appear only at the very end of our period.

Early paddle vessels

VOYAGEUR Class – 32nhp steam vessels. These two ships, the first steamers associated with the French Navy, were built to support an ambitious effort under Colonel Julien-Désiré Schmaltz to reoccupy Senegal after the Napoleonic wars and extend French influence to farming regions up the Senegal River. The steamers were to provide communications on the river and to keep the local population under control. They were designed by a naval constructor, Clément-Marie Lebreton, to carry comparatively large artillery on a hull high enough to command the river banks. Their plans were signed on 24 June 1818 and the ships were ordered at Lorient by a ministerial decree of 31 August 1818. The contract for the engines was signed by Scipion Périer on 1 September 1818 and approved by the Minister of Marine on 8 September 1818. The engine of *Voyageur* was delivered at Rouen in June 1819 and then transported to Lorient by the brig *Pourvoyeur*, which then delivered the engine of *Africain* to Lorient on 7 July 1819. The single piston of the engine had a diameter of 30 inches (engineers used British measurements), the stroke was the same, and the diameter of the paddle wheels was 11ft 10in. The engines were connected to the paddle shaft by gearing. The two iron boilers were 14ft long with ends 5.5ft square. The single funnel was 25ft tall but was articulated at 3ft above the deck to permit lowering it. The ships also had a brig rig and were sometimes called *bricks à vapeur*. They made the voyage to Senegal under sail with their paddle wheels on deck. Their designer died around 10 December 1819, probably on board *Voyageur* in Senegal.

The engines of both ships remained in very good condition despite extensive service, but by late 1822 the boilers of *Africain* needed replacement. New copper boilers were ordered for her in 1823 and were installed between November 1823 and July 1824. By late 1823 the boilers of *Voyageur* were entirely unserviceable, but the high cost of the new boilers for *Africain* and problems with *Voyageur*'s hull caused the colony to propose sending the ship back to France in exchange for a new, smaller ship. The engines of *Voyageur* were sent back to Brest in February 1825 and may have been used in *Requin*, below, but the hull stayed in the colony.

Dimensions & tons: 33.24m wl, 31.00m x 7.15m x 3.57m. 277 tons disp. Draught 1.88m. Men: 26-44.
Machinery: 32nhp, 4.50 to 4.73kts. Side-lever, 1 cylinder, 2 boilers. Coal 63 tons.
Guns: (Designed) 6 x 12pdr carronades, 4 x 4pdrs.

Voyageur Lorient Dyd/Scipion Périer, Chaillot, Paris (Constructeur, François Chanot)
Ord: 31.8.1818. K: 29.9.1818. L: 24.2.1819. Comm: 10.7.1819. C: 8.1819.
Launched as *No.2*, named 16.3.1819. Installation of engine began 11.7.1819, trials 23.9.1819 (3.80 knots against the wind). Sailed for Senegal 16.10.1819 escorted by the brig *Silène*, arrived 1.11.1819. Decomm. 24.9.1823. Engines removed and left Senegal for France 26.2.1825 on the merchant brig *Jupiter*; hull fitted as a stationary hulk at the bar at Saint-Louis du Senegal. Condemned 12.1830 and replaced by the schooner *Autruche*, offered for sale 20.1.1831.

Africain Lorient Dyd/Scipion Périer, Chaillot (Constructeur, François Chanot)
Ord: 31.8.1818. K: 21.9.1818. L: 8.2.1819. Comm: 1.1.1820. C: 1.1820.

Launched as *No.1*, named 16.3.1819. Installation of engine began 26.9.1819, first trials 24.1.1820 (3 knots). Left Lorient for Senegal 21.4.1820 escorted by the gabarre *Infatigable*, arrived 12.5.1820. Returned from an expedition up the Senegal River to Galam on 25.9.1825, judged unfit to make the same voyage in 1826. Condemned 2.1827 at Saint-Louis du Senegal, hull sold 9.1827. Engine removed but attempts to send it back to France in late 1827 on the schooner *Autruche* and then on the corvette de charge *Rhône* failed.

COUREUR Class – 80nhp steam vessels. In early 1821 a steamer to tow the king's ships on the Charente River between Rochefort and the Île d'Aix was added to a program for a steam floating battery at Rochefort (see the Postscript). Preliminary design work by François Chanot led to the adoption of two 40nhp engines for the tug. On 10 September 1822 the Director of Ports reported to the Minister of Marine that Jean-Baptiste Marestier had completed hull plans for the ship based on his observations during a trip to America and recommended that he be sent to Rouen to negotiate a contract for the construction of two tugs. Rouen was selected because it would minimise transportation coasts for the engines, which would be built near Paris. Marestier was also to contract for the engines and then shuttle between Rouen and Paris to supervise the work on the ships. The Minister approved this report on the same date, thereby ordering construction of the two ships. Marestier reported the characteristics of the ships to the Minister on 14 September 1822 and also listed identical characteristics for a third ship to be built for French Guiana (see *Caroline*, below). The hulls of the two 80nhp tugs were ordered from Bataille at La Maillerayne near Rouen by a contract signed on 11 October 1822 and approved on 22 October 1822. The engines for all three ships were ordered from Manby, Wilson, Henry & Cie. of Charneton by a contract approved on 24 December 1822. All three vessels were schooner-rigged and sometimes called *goélettes à vapeur*, although *Caroline* was also called a *brick à vapeur*.

Coureur arrived at Cherbourg on 4 April 1824 for machinery trials. The trials board reported on 1 July 1824 that *Coureur* could tow one 800-ton transport out of Brest against wind and tide, and that two steamers like her could tow out a frigate. *Coureur* was withdrawn from service at Rochefort in October 1827 and was sent to Toulon to help resupply ships stationed off Algiers, but she soon had to be taken out of service for boiler repairs. She joined the Morea expedition with an augmented armament at the end of 1828.

Rapide arrived at Cherbourg for machinery trials on 21 March 1825 and then proceeded to the Île d'Aix, arriving on 18 June 1825. She operated as a tug there until on 28 October 1826, after towing the corvette de charge *Ariège* from Rochefort to the Île d'Aix and the gabarre *Vésuve* back into the port, she stopped her paddle wheels and the boilers exploded, ripping off the deck above them, toppling the funnel, damaging the engines, and killing or gravely injuring 11 men. Jean-Baptiste Hubert was sent from Rochefort to London in December 1827 to buy new boilers for *Rapide* and obtained a contract from Maudslay. Maudslay boilers soon became the standard type in French naval steamers. After *Rapide* was condemned in 1840 a new hull was ordered from Indret for her engines.

Dimensions & tons: 36.00m, 35.00m wl x 7.00m x 3.25m. 269 tons normal disp. Draught 1.75m normal, 2.05m max. Men: 33-69.
Machinery: 80nhp. 2 cylinders (0.915m diameter).
Guns: 2 to 6 x 12pdr carronades; (*Coureur*, 1828) 8 x 18pdr carronades.

Coureur Bataille, La Maillerayne/Manby, Henry, Wilson & Co., Charenton
Ord: 10.9.1822. K: 1.1823. L: 24.8.1823. Comm: 1.3.1824. C: 28.3.1824.
Refitted at Rochefort in 1824 and 1827 and at Toulon in 1828. Struck 15.3.1837, reclassified as a service craft, and continued to serve as a tug at Toulon. Received boilers removed from *Vedette* in 1844. BU 1849.

Rapide Bataille, La Maillerayne/Manby, Henry, Wilson & Co., Charenton
Ord: 10.9.1822. K: 1.1823. L: 21.9.1823. Comm: 1.1.1825. C: 26.3.1825.
Refitted at Rochefort in 1825 and 1830, at Toulon in 1831, and at Cherbourg in 1835. Struck and reclassified as a service craft (tug) 10.9.1834, used to tow barges of stones for the breakwater at Cherbourg. Out of service 7.1839, condemned 4.1.1840.

CAROLINE – 50nhp steam vessel. In 1819 France embarked on an effort to create a community of European farmers in French Guiana. The plan called for a steamer to provide communications along the coast and on the rivers. The hull plans by Jean-Baptiste Marestier for this ship were identical to those of the 80nhp tugs of the *Coureur* class except for the engines. He gave the colonial ship two 50nhp engines for a total of 100nhp, but the colony requested instead two 25nhp engines for a total of 50nhp. When on 22 October 1822 the Minister of Marine approved Bataille's contract for the two tugs he added this third ship to it, but it was soon determined that Bataille could not build three ships and the third was reordered from the unsuccessful October bidder, Armand Malleux of Rouen, by a contract signed on 28 November 1822 and approved on 7 December 1822. Her engines, ordered with those of the two tugs, were built in Britain by Manby's firm, which also supplied the parts for the engines of the other two ships. Trials began on 15 July 1824 and the machinery was accepted on 28 July 1824. The ship was renamed *Caroline* after transporting Dutchess Marie Caroline de Berry from Rouen to La Maillerayne on 24 July 1824. Her machinery was reused in a tug built at Brest in about 1837.

Dimensions & tons: as *Coureur*.
Machinery: 50nhp, 7kts. 2 cylinders (0.740m diameter, 0.915m stroke).
Guns: 6.

Caroline (ex *Galibi* 29.7.1824) Armand Malleux, Rouen/Manby, Henry, Wilson & Co., Charenton.
Ord: 22.10.1822. K: 1.1823. L: 23.8.1823. Comm: 10.7.1824. C: 28.7.1824.
In Cayenne 1824-27. Renamed *Louise* 12.7.1828. Refitted at Brest in 1824, at Le Havre in 1827 and at Brest in 1829. Departed Brest for Cayenne 26.4.1829. Decomm. 21.11.1832 at Izacombo in French Guiana. Struck 20.7.1833, sold 23.1.1834 in French Guyana.

SERPENT – 40nhp steam vessel. The Minister of Marine on 18 October 1824 ordered construction of this ship to replace *Voyageur* in Senegal. Jean-Baptiste Marestier designed her in response to experience with *Voyageur* and *Africain*, which suggested that the colony needed shorter, smaller steamers with smaller crews and less coal consumption. (The earlier ships were expensive to operate, had difficulty negotiating some river bends, and were vulnerable to crosswinds because of their high sides.) His plans were dated 20 November 1824. The ship was given a schooner rig and was sometimes called a *goélette à vapeur*. Her hull was ordered from Emmanuel Thibault at Rouen by a contract signed on 22 February 1825 and approved on 4 March 1825, and her engines were ordered from Manby, Wilson & Co., Charenton, by a contract signed on 8 January 1825 and approved on 20 January 1825. Machinery trials were successfully completed on 25 July 1826 and the ship was sent to Senegal. She received the boilers of *Voyageur* between September and

November 1829 at Saint-Louis du Senegal. Her replacement, the second *Africain* was ordered in 1830 and arrived in Senegal in 1833.
  Dimensions & tons: 30.00m x 7.00m x 3.00m. 257-292 tons disp. Draught 2.25/2.45m. Men: 23-50.
  Machinery: 40nhp, 6.81kts. 2 cylinders. 2 copper boilers. Coal 96 tons.
  Guns: 6 x 18pdr carronades.
Serpent Thibault, Rouen/Manby, Wilson & Co., Charenton.
  Ord: 18.10.1824. K: 2.1825. L: 11.3.1826. Comm: 14.6.1826. C: 9.1826.
  Engine failed 1831, made station ship at the bar in Senegal 8.1832 in place of the schooner *Autruche*, struck 1833. Probably remained in use until BU 1839.

The budget for 1826 (presented in March 1825) contained three new steamers of 160nhp each (*Nageur*, *Souffleur*, and *Pélican*) plus the smaller *Requin*. On 31 October 1825 a commission that included some of the French Navy's leading naval constructors and experts on steam propulsion (Pierre Rolland, Pierre Lair, Mathurin Boucher, Charles Dupin, Jean-Baptiste Marestier, and Jean Delamorinière) was formed to develop hull plans for the three large steamers. These plans were completed on 18 January 1826. The designed armament for this class (probably never carried) was two large guns forward, one aft, and three carronades on each side. The navy determined not to continue the de facto monopoly of Manby, Wilson & Co. on marine steam engines and ordered the three sets of engines from three different firms. *Nageur*, *Souffleur*, and *Pélican* had identical hulls but are presented here separately as their machinery was radically different.

NAGEUR – 160nhp steam vessel. This ship's engines were ordered from Manby, Wilson & Cie. by a contract signed on 1 July 1826 and approved on 13 July 1826. This ship was given eight boilers, four forward of the engines and four aft, presumably giving her two widely-spaced funnels. *Nageur* left Cherbourg in October 1827 to receive her machinery at Rouen, returned to Cherbourg in April 1829 and departed in May 1829 under sail with a temporary three-masted rig for Toulon where she was a limited success. It was soon determined that six boilers were sufficient for her and two were removed and used to re-boiler *Coureur*. *Nageur* was rigged as a brig or a schooner-brig. The beam over the paddle boxes was 13.50m.
  Dimensions & tons: 48.00m oa, 45.00m wl, 41.00m x 8.40m x 4.00m. 615 tons disp. Draught 2.50m mean. Men: 58-72.
  Machinery: 160nhp. 2 cylinders (80nhp each, 1.28m diameter, 1.29m stroke). 8 boilers (2 furnaces each).
  Guns: (*Nageur* 1829) 4 x 24pdrs.
Nageur Cherbourg Dyd/Manby, Wilson & Co., Charenton.
  Ord: ca.12.1825. K: 31.8.1826. L: 11.9.1827. Comm: 10.1827. C: 3.1829.
  To Toulon 1829. Struck 21.2.1838 at Toulon. Machinery removed for use in *Ténare* and hull BU.

SOUFFLEUR – 160nhp steam vessel. *Souffleur* was initially ordered at Lorient on 8 December 1825 but because no building way was available there she was built at Cherbourg. Her engines were ordered from Aitken & Steel by a contract approved on 20 July 1826. Aitken & Steel built the engines to their own model, which was similar to the British 'crank-bell' system and which they claimed could generate up to 200nhp. The two cylinders were arranged fore and aft of the paddle shaft instead of side by side and were connected to the shaft by a complex system of iron bars instead of by side-levers. The boilers were to port and starboard of the engines, suggesting that she had two funnels side by side. *Souffleur* went to Rouen in 1828 to receive her machinery, arrived at Cherbourg in November 1829 after its installation and departed for Toulon under sail in January 1830. She was schooner-rigged. Her machinery, of a type already abandoned in Britain, failed to satisfy the terms of the contract and the ship performed poorly. She arrived at Brest on 1 September 1834 for use as a tug and was downgraded to a service craft ten days later, but she was in bad condition and did not complete repairs until 10 September 1835. Even then she gave only mediocre results as her boilers could not provide the steam required by her engines. She was sent to Cherbourg under sail on 26 September 1836 to get new boilers and, although still considered unreliable, then served as a tug at Brest until 1843.
  Dimensions & tons: as *Nageur*.
  Machinery: 160nhp. 2 cylinders (80nhp each, 1.28m diameter), 2 boilers.
  Guns: 6 (designed).
Souffleur Cherbourg Dyd/Aitken & Steel, Gare d'Ivry, Paris.
  Ord: 8.12.1825. K: 31.8.1826. L: 14.4.1828. Comm: 5.1828? C: 11.1829.
  Struck and reclassified as a tug (service craft) 10.9.1834, placed in service at Brest 7.11.1834. Out of service 23.7.1843, engines ordered BU 12.1843, hull converted to coal hulk at Brest. BU 1865.

PÉLICAN – 160nhp steam vessel. This ship's engines were ordered from Philippe Gengembre by a contract signed on 7 July 1826 and approved on 17 July 1826. Gengembre fitted her with a steam plant possibly unique among seagoing paddle steamers with four paddle wheels, a pair forward and a pair aft, each pair driven by its own pair of 40nhp engines. Each pair of engines had its own boiler with its own funnel. In 1827 Gengembre was appointed the first director of the navy's new steam engine factory at Indret, partly so he could install the engines of *Pélican* there. *Pélican* duly went there for her engines in November 1828. The beam outside *Pélican*'s paddle wheels was 13.50m and she was schooner-rigged. By late 1830, following experience with all three ships during the Algerian expedition, the navy became disillusioned with *Pélican*'s machinery arrangement, which took up a lot of space and caused the engines to operate unevenly in heavy seas. Her after pair of engines was removed in 1836 and put in the aviso *Flambeau*, and when her hull wore out in the early 1840s her remaining machinery was put in a tug (service craft) named *Boyard*, which was begun at Rochefort in January

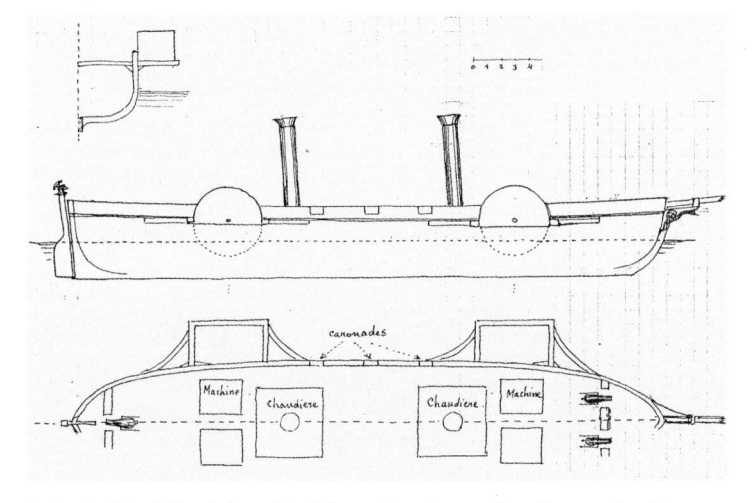

A sketch of the *Pélican* in her original form with twin sets of machinery and paddle wheels. (Archives de la Marine (Brest), Sous-série 9-S, Fonds Adam)

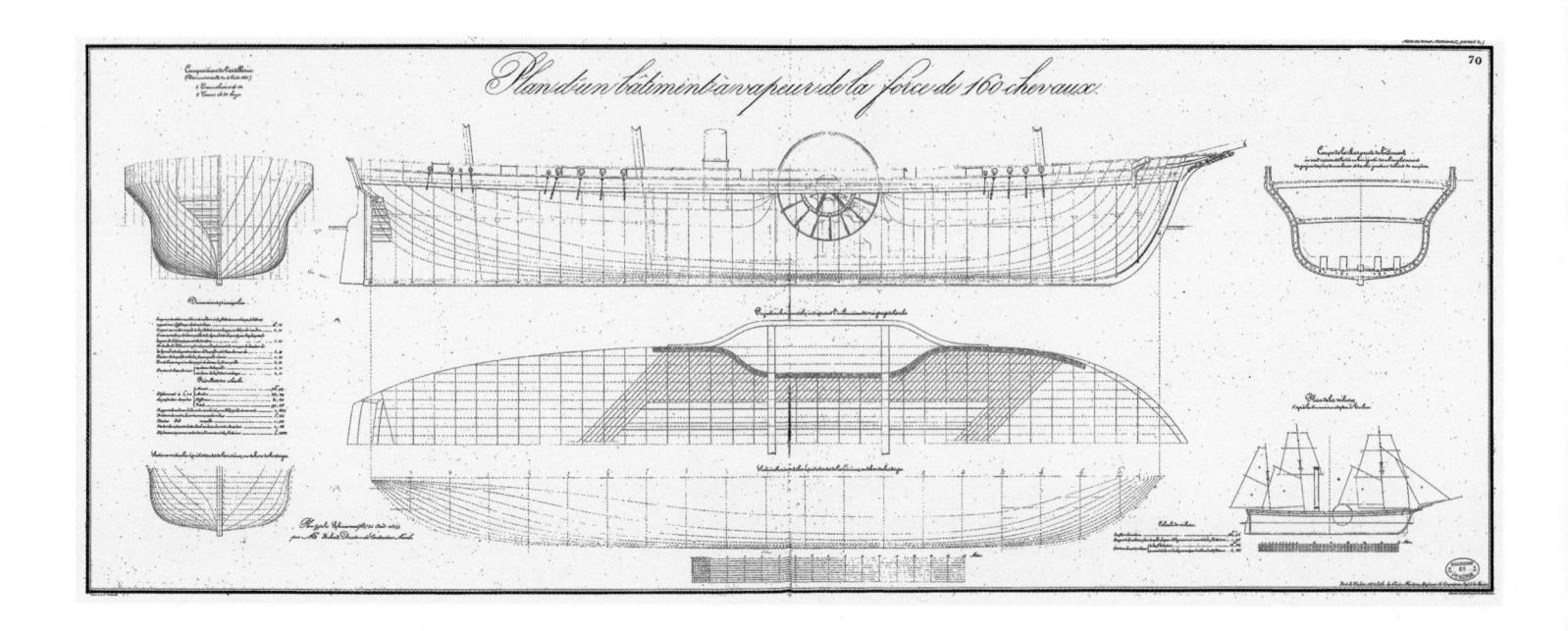

Official general arrangement plans of the *Sphinx* dated 24 August 1830. This successful design became the prototype of a large series of similar ships that followed. The small sail plan shows the impact of the machinery on a three-masted rig, which requires the mainmast to be further aft than optimum for a balanced spread of sail; total area was 745 sq.m. The fore-and-aft mizzen defines this as a barque rig. (Atlas du Génie Maritime, French collection, plate 70)

1843, launched on 28 July 1843, and completed in December 1843 for use primarily in the construction of Fort Boyard. This 80nhp tug was constructed by Charles-Louis Duchalard to his plans and served at Rochefort until condemned in 1879 and BU in 1880.

    Dimensions & tons: as *Nageur*.
    Machinery: 160nhp. 4 cylinders (40nhp each, 0.915m diameter, in two pairs), 2 boilers.
    Guns: 6 (designed).

Pélican Lorient Dyd/Philippe Gengembre
    Ord: 8.12.1825. K: 1826. L: 6.10.1828. Comm: 8.11.1828. C: 5.1829.
    Struck and reclassified as a service craft (tug) 10.9.1834. After set of engines removed at Rochefort 2.1835 to 3.1836, resumed service 7.1836 as an 80nhp tug on the Charente. Remaining machinery removed c1843, hull became a mooring hulk at Rochefort, BU 1865.

REQUIN – 32nhp steam vessel. This ship was probably ordered 1 December 1826 and may have received the engines of *Voyageur*. She served as a tug towing barges of stones for the new breakwater at Cherbourg. Her characteristics are largely unknown.

    Machinery: 32nhp.
    Guns: probably none.

Requin Brest Dyd/from *Voyageur?*
    Ord: 1.12.1826? K: 1827. L: 15.2.1828. C: 1829.
    In commission from 9.4.1830 to 11.12.1830 at Cherbourg. Classified as service craft (tug) at Cherbourg 21.10.1835, struck 28.10.1835, BU 1837.

COMMERCE DU HAVRE – 100nhp steam vessel. Ex mercantile *Commerce du Havre*, completed in March 1826. Although built for a route between Le Havre and London, which she could travel in about 30 hours at an average of 5.5 knots, she only made a few voyages and then served as a tug until acquired by the navy. In 1828 the navy needed a steamer for logistic support of the expedition to the Morea, and because *Coureur* was out of service for boiler repairs it purchased *Commerce du Havre* at Le Havre from the Société anonyme des bâtiments en vapeur en fer on 8 September 1828. After repairs at Cherbourg she departed on 29 October 1828 for Toulon, where her deck was reinforced and six or eight guns were installed. She had three masts and was schooner-rigged. Her builders and owners rated her at 80nhp but the navy increased the rating to 100nhp.

    Dimensions & tons: Dimensions about the same as *Coureur*. 190 tons disp. Men: 64.
    Machinery: 100nhp (rated 80nhp in civil service.).
    Guns: (1828) 8 x 18pdr carronades.

Commerce du Havre Fouache, Le Havre/Manby, Wilson & Co., Charenton.
    K: 1825. L: 1.1826. Comm: 1.12.1828.
    Renamed *Ville du Havre* 22.6.1829. Found unsuitable for use under sail 1837, struck 15.7.1837 and ordered converted to a water barge. Sold 1843.

Early SPHINX Class – 160nhp steam vessels, later paddle 1st Class avisos. The budget for 1827 (presented in March 1826) contained four new steamers to be begun in 1827 to follow the four in the 1826 budget. These were *Castor* at Cherbourg, *Crocodile* at Brest, *Sphinx* at Rochefort, and *Vautour* at Toulon. None was begun, and the budget for 1828 (of March 1827) contained the same four ships, now to be started in 1828, *Crocodile* and *Vautour* being reassigned to Saint-Servan and Lorient respectively. During 1828 *Sphinx* was begun at Rochefort, but the hulls of the other three were again deferred. Problems with the machinery of the French Navy's early steamers had led the navy to want to get an example of the best British technology before building more steamers. In 1827 one of the senior engineers at Rochefort, Jean-Baptiste Hubert, was ordered to design a steamer on the lines and dimensions of the British merchantman *Leeds*, which had just visited Bordeaux. At the same time, he was ordered to go to Britain to purchase a set of engines to power the ship and to serve as a model for engines to be built in France. Hubert purchased engines of 160nhp from Fawcett, Preston & Co. of Liverpool while he was in Britain between 1 November 1827 and 5

April 1828 and completed the plans for the ship to receive them, *Sphinx*, soon after returning to France. *Sphinx* proved to be completely successful, and she also became famous when she brought the first news of the conquest of Algiers in 1830 back to France and a few years later towed to France the Egyptian obelisk that is now in the Place de la Concorde at Paris.

In 1828 the navy decided to consolidate most of its steamer construction at its new steam engine facility at Indret (which also had slipways left over from the Napoleonic period), and in the 1829 budget (presented in April 1828) the three steamers that had been deferred from 1828 were reassigned to Indret to be laid down in 1829 along with three more steamers, *Ardent*, *Chimère*, and *Salamandre*. The last two were initially 80nhp steamers and were only upgraded to 160nhp when the Minister decided on 2 July 1831 not to put the two 80nhp pairs of engines of *Pélican* into them. The 1830 budget (of April 1829) added two more, *Fulton* and *Phénix*. However Indret was slow to get into production, and the two 1830 ships, now named *Fulton* and *Styx*, were only ordered and begun in 1832 (*Fulton* at Rochefort). Indret was also slow in beginning production of engines, and some of the hulls built at Indret and at Rochefort were engined by two leading private French firms, François Cavé of Paris and Alexis Hallette of Arras. *Crocodile* was the first to receive 160nhp engines of the Fawcett type built at Indret, which were fully successful. Their beam over the paddle boxes was around 14m.

Two early ships of this class, *Ardent* and *Vautour*, received high pressure engines and another, *Castor*, received British-built machinery of 120nhp. Because of their substantially different machinery these three ships are described in separate listings below. The ships built after regular series production of the class began in 1832 are listed below as the Later *Sphinx* class, while the final ship of the class, *Ténare*, was lengthened slightly to accommodate an old engine and is also described separately.

Dimensions & tons: 47.26m, 46.25m wl, 44.00m x 8.00m, 8.18m ext x 5.40m. 910-934t disp. Draught 3.75m mean. Men: 77-93.
Machinery: 160nhp, 320ihp, 8kts. Side-lever, 2 cylinders (48in/1.22m diameter, 57in/1.45m stroke), 1 Fawcett flue boiler with 4 compartments or 2 Maudslay flue boilers, low pressure. Coal 170 tons.
Guns: Designed for 3 x 24pdr long guns and 6 or 8 x 24pdr carronades, typically carried 6 x 24pdr carronades.

Sphinx Rochefort Dyd/Fawcett, Preston & Co., Liverpool (Constructeur, Hubert)
Ord: c11.1827. K: 26.6.1828. L: 31.8.1829. C: 2.1830. Comm: 1.3.1830.
Engine contract 29.1.1828. Ran first trials 25.2.1830. Wrecked 6.7.1845 in fog at Cape Matifou on the Algerian coast. Wreck discovered 25.6.2005.

Crocodile Indret/Indret (Constructeur, Pierre Le Grix)
Ord: c11.1829. K: 9.1829. L: 10.10.1832. Comm: 5.12.1832. C: 2.1833.
Struck 3.3.1856, hulked 11.1856 in the Antilles. BU before 1865.

Chimère Indret/Cavé, Paris (Constructeur, Pierre-Félix Le Grix)
Ord: 16.11.1829 and 25.1.1830. K: 7.1831. L: 29.10.1833. Comm: 16.1.1834. C: 1.1834.
Engine contract approved 11.7.1832. Struck 9.1.1861, prison hulk in French Guiana, BU 1871.

Salamandre Indret/Cavé, Paris (Constructeur, Pierre-Félix Le Grix)
Ord: c11.1829. K: 1831. L: 26.12.1833. Comm: 15.3.1834. C: 3.1834.
Engine contract approved 11.7.1832. Wrecked 26.12.1835 on the Algerian coast near Mostaganem.

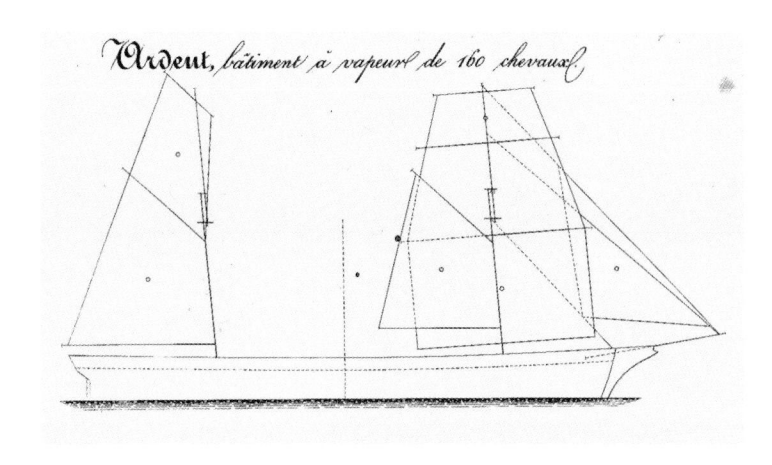

In early steamers sail remained an important element in the propulsion mix, but the space needed for the funnel and paddle boxes often complicated, or even prohibited, a conventional spar plan. As a result there was a tendency to adopt what were then termed hermaphrodite rigs, combining some square canvas forward for driving power with fore-and-aft sails for simpler rigging. The sail plan of *Ardent* shows what at the time would have been called a brigantine rig, with square foremast and fore-and-aft main (total area 652.35 sq.m.). From about the second quarter of the nineteenth century the gaff topsail was usually hoisted from a separate spar called a jackyard, as shown here. (Atlas du Génie Maritime, Genoa collection, image 2-0038)

ARDENT – 160nhp steam vessel, *Sphinx* class, later paddle 1st Class aviso. In 1829 Jacques Frimot, an engineer of the Ponts et Chaussées from Landernau near Brest, succeeded in persuading the Minister of Marine to order by a contract of 19 February 1829 a 160nhp engine on his system for the second ship of the *Sphinx* type, *Ardent*. Frimot's system was untested, and he first built a vessel named *Éclair* in which to trial his prototype engines before beginning the engines for *Ardent*. *Éclair* proved to be severely underpowered and Frimot got the navy's approval to give *Ardent* three engines instead of two. These were ready for comparative trials with *Castor* at Brest in late 1832 and with *Sphinx* in February 1834. In the latter trials *Ardent*'s coal consumption was 7/8ths that of *Sphinx*'s instead of the promised half, *Ardent* was unable to make the trial speed, her speed declining as the trial proceeded, and her engines lacked the required solidity. The navy rejected the machinery on 12 July 1834. Frimot, however, was an advanced theoretician who attracted support from leading French scientists including François Arago in the Chamber of Deputies who launched intense political attacks on the navy. The navy finally accepted the machinery in late 1838 simply to be done with Frimot. It had become rusted scrap at Brest by 1841. New experimental four-cylinder low-pressure engines on the system of Pierre Jean-Baptiste Rossin that had been given the proportions of a 225nhp engine by Frédéric Reech were ordered from Indret for *Ardent* in 1841 and three experimental low-pressure tubular boilers totalling 160nhp were ordered from Charles Beslay at Paris on 24 March 1841. *Ardent* was recommissioned on 7 June and towed to Indret by *Archimède* on 28 June 1843 to receive her new machinery. Beslay had to change the boilers in 1845 and trials resumed only in May 1848 when the boilers were found still to be too difficult to operate. Decommissioned on 21 October 1848, *Ardent* received the engines of a sister, *Phaéton*, and finally performed successful commissioned service between 18 March 1852 and 1 July 1860.

Dimensions & tons: 47.00m, 46.00m wl, 44.00m x 8.00m, 8.15m ext x 5.51m. 913 tons. Draught 3.40/3.50m. Men: 100.
Machinery: 160nhp, 8.10kts. High pressure
Guns: 6 x 24pdr carronades

Ardent Brest Dyd/Frimot, Landerneau (Constructeur, Jean-Baptiste Hubert)
Ord: 28.9.1829. K: 12.10.1829. L: 22.5.1830. Comm: 21.3.1831. C: 6.1833.
Hull completed without engines 3.1831. Refitted at Brest 10.1848 to 3.1852 and engines replaced with those of *Phaéton*. Struck 24.10.1860, mooring hulk at Lorient, BU 6.1881.

CASTOR – 160nhp steam vessel, *Sphinx* class, later paddle 1st Class aviso. The third ship of the *Sphinx* type, *Castor*, was ordered before Indret was ready to build engines, and in order to encourage French industry the navy ordered her machinery from Émile Martin of Fourchambault, Nièvre, by a contract approved on 26 February 1829. On 4 December 1828 Martin had proposed two engines of 60nhp instead of 80nhp, noting that good models were available in Britain for 60nhp engines but not for those of 80nhp and concluding that 120nhp was enough for a steamer intended for use as a packet and as a tug. After his submission was approved by the navy on 26 February 1829, Martin went to Britain and decided to copy engines made by Maudslay, which he told the navy would require buying the critical parts from them. The trial report dated 17 October 1831 noted that not just some but all the major parts of the engine (tanks, cylinders, condensers, side-levers, pistons, etc.) had been made in Britain and that only the paddle wheels and boilers had been built at Fourchambault. However the report contained no complaints of low power or speed and the ship appears to have been a success in service. Her 120nhp engines, however, led her to be reclassified from a 1st to a 2nd Class aviso in 1849.
Dimensions & tons: 46.25m, 45.50m wl x 8.20m x 5.30m. 750 tons. Draught 3.33m mean. Men: 59-73.
Machinery: 120nhp. 2 cylinders (1.09m diameter, 1.22m stroke)

A detailed and convincing lithographic portrait of the paddle aviso *Castor*. Like her half-sister *Sphinx*, she has three masts, but the absence of a fore and main course turns this into a form of schooner rig. The big gaff-headed fore-and-aft trysails, known to the British as spencers, replaced staysails in many navies in the first half of the nineteenth century and were particularly useful in steamers as they did not foul the funnel. The French Navy referred to them as a *goëlette* ('schooner') sail. (© National Maritime Museum PY0864)

Guns: 6; (1840s) 4 x 16cm shell
Castor Indret/Émile Martin, Fourchambault (Constructeur, Pierre-Félix Le Grix)
Ord: 29.11.1827. K: 1.7.1829. L: 26.5.1831. Comm: 16.9.1831. C: 9.1831
Struck 22.10.1853, engines removed at Lorient 10.1853 to 12.1854, and arrived under sail at Cayenne 4.1855 for service as a hospital and prison ship. Decomm. 22.4.1855, BU before 1865.

VAUTOUR – 160nhp steam vessel, *Sphinx* class, later paddle 1st Class aviso. In early 1830 Gengembre proposed to build engines at Indret that would weigh much less than those of *Sphinx* and be capable of operation at both low pressure as in *Sphinx* and at a higher pressure. He was authorised on 22 April 1830 to build one set of engines to this design. They had free-swinging side-levers, tubular boilers, and several other advanced features. A trials commission was ordered on 6 August 1834 to carry out comparative trials of *Vautour* and the conventionally-engined *Styx*, and it reported that the engines of *Vautour* weighed 18 percent less, were well built, and produced speeds faster than *Styx* in calm water (though not in rough water) at low pressure. The engines were also easier to operate, but their high pressure features produced wear and vibrations that nullified the expected fuel economy and raised concerns about durability. On 20 October 1836 the Council of Works reviewed a report from Toulon on repairs made to these engines and decided to renounce the use of this type of machinery for future ships. In around 1844 she received new tubular boilers by Fawcett, among the first in the French Navy. On 6 July 1854 *Vautour* was ordered converted to a steam bomb vessel with 2 x 32cm mortars and 2 x 30pdrs No.3. The conversion was carried out in July 1854 by Jules Aurous and the ship participated in the bombardment of Kinburn in October 1855 with *Sésostris*, *Cassini*, and *Ténare*..

Dimensions & tons: as *Sphinx* class.
Machinery: 160nhp. High pressure, 2 cylinders (1.22m diameter), 6 cylindrical boilers.
Guns: 6 x 24pdr carronades

Vautour Indret/Indret (Constructeur, Pierre-Félix Le Grix)
Ord: 16.11.1829 and 25.1.1830. K: 10.1830. L: 7.7.1834. Comm: 11.7.1834. C: 12.1834.
Rated as *bombarde à vapeur* 1854-55. Struck 9.5.1863 and converted to a careening hulk (*ponton carénage*) or mooring hulk at Martinique. BU 1866.

REMORQUEUR – 40nhp steam vessel. Machinery of an experimental type (*à réaction*) was ordered from the French physician Pierre Pelletan and his friend Doctor de la Barre by a contract approved on 24 June 1830. The high-pressure engine consisted of one horizontal cylinder and was placed between two pipes running the length of the ship from bow to stern and open at the ends. The two boilers were outboard of the pipes and the ship had no funnels, the exhaust gases being used to help propel the ship. The ship was assigned the generic name *Remorqueur* (tug) on 1 December 1830 and was soon (1831 or 1832) reclassified as a service craft. After trials the machinery was rejected on 7 February 1835 and the builder was invited to substitute paddle wheels for the experimental system. This move was unsuccessful, the machinery was definitively rejected on 7 April 1838, and the navy finally sold it in 1841 to recover some of its money.

Dimensions & tons: 30.00m x 5.00m. ? disp. Draught 1.16/1.26m.
Machinery: 40nhp. 1 cylinder, 2 boilers
Guns: probably none.

Remorqueur Cherbourg Dyd/Pelletan & de la Barre, built at Chaillot
Ord: 24.6.1830 (contract). K: 16.11.1830. L: 18.1.1832. Not commissioned.
Machinery rejected 7.4.1838 and sold in 1841. Hull became barge *Allège No.3* at Cherbourg, a designation later given to *Rameur* in 1866.

At least two other ships were listed under the generic name *Remorqueur*. One of 50nhp and 50 tons was begun at Brest in November 1834, launched on 10 August 1835, renamed *Actif* on 11 June 1836, and placed in service 23 August 1836 as a tug at Cherbourg. Renamed *Érèbe* 1861 and BU 1869. She appeared briefly on the navy list in 1854 as a 50nhp aviso, but reverted to service craft status on 1 January 1855 after plans to send her to the Crimea were cancelled. The other *Remorqueur*, soon named *Boyard*, was launched at Rochefort on 28 July 1843 to use the forward engines of *Pélican* (q.v.). A larger (120nhp) tug was requested by the public works service (*Ponts et Chaussées*) and originally assigned to Bayonne for construction but transferred to Rochefort on 27 April 1839. Intended to tow ships in the mouth of the Adour river, she was named *Adour* and built at Rochefort between November 1839 and March 1841 by Gustave Garnier to plans by Jean-Baptiste Hubert. She was either launched on 15 July 1840 or begun in July 1840 and launched on 13 February 1841. She measured 350 tons and 38.16m (wl) x 7m x 4.54m with a draught of 2.60/2.82m and engines of 100-120nhp. She may have received a 120nhp engine ordered from Maudslay in England by Pierre Jean-Baptiste Rossin when he ordered the 320nhp engine of *Cuvier*. She was last recorded when under refit at Rochefort between July and December 1846. These steam tugs never appeared on the navy list because of their status as service craft.

AFRICAIN – 40nhp steam vessel. This ship, a replacement for *Serpent*, was named and probably ordered (hull and engines) on 8 July 1830. She was designed by Lieutenant de Vaisseau William Lelieur de Ville sur Arce, the former commander of *Serpent*. Instead of standard low-pressure engines, Philippe Gengembre, the first director of Indret, gave her medium-pressure engines with no condenser and no side-levers. Her boilers consisted of four cylindrical sections in which water circulated unevenly and salt built up rapidly, leading to 'deplorable' results. The arrival of *Africain* in Senegal was reported on 19 May 1833. She was schooner-rigged and was sometimes called a *goélette à vapeur*.

Dimensions & tons: 35.00m x 7.00m. 300 tons disp. Draught 2.5/2.5m. Men: 64-80.
Machinery: 40nhp, 5.8kts. 2 cylinders, 2 boilers
Guns: 6 x 18pdr carronades (6 ports).

Africain Indret/Indret (Constructeur, Pierre-Félix Le Grix)
Ord: 8.7.1830. K: 12.1830. L: 14.5.1832. Comm: 15.10.1832. C: 10.1832.
Left Brest 5.1833 under tow by a corvette, lit fires only to cross the bar at Senegal as the boilers leaked when the ship rolled and she could only steam in calm waters. After the arrival of *Érèbe* the Minister on 22.8.1837 approved using *Africain* as station ship at the bar at Senegal. Engines removed 7.3.1838 to be sent back to France, decomm 1.7.1838, and struck.

RAMEUR – 60nhp steam vessel. On 9 July 1830 G. Dumoulin of Paris proposed to build 40nhp engines (soon increased to 60nhp) for a ship that was needed to tow barges carrying stones for construction of the breakwater at Cherbourg. The engines, of an experimental high-pressure type, were ordered from Dumoulin by a contract approved on 15 September 1830. The hull for these engines was ordered and named 23 December 1830 and was designed by Jean-Baptiste Marestier. On trials conducted on 12 September 1831 the ship made a maximum of 3.26 knots. She was accepted on 15 November 1831 but Dumoulin was removed from the list of qualified contractors.

Dimensions & tons: 33.00m x 6.00m. 140? tons disp.
Machinery: 60nhp. 2 cylinders (30nhp each), 1 copper boiler with 3 compartments
Guns: probably none.

Rameur Cherbourg Dyd/Dumoulin
Ord: 23.12.1830. K: 20.1.1831. L: 28.6.1831. Not commissioned.
Struck 2.3.1850 and converted to a barge at Cherbourg. Renamed *Allège No.3* 1866, BU 1878 at Cherbourg

Later SPHINX Class – 160nhp steam vessels, later paddle 1st Class avisos. The January 1832 orders to begin the hulls of *Fulton* and *Styx* were the beginning of series production of the *Sphinx* class following the tentative period of 1828-31 during which *Sphinx* ran her successful trials and the ship and engine building facility at Indret overcame problems starting up production. On 2 October 1830 the Minister of Marine approved improved plans for the *Sphinx* type submitted on 24 August 1830 by Hubert that reduced the hull weight by 22 to 24 tons for for *Vautour* and later ships, *Crocodile* and *Chimère* having already been begun. The builder of the engines of *Fulton*, Alexis Hallette of Arras, chose boilers on the Maudslay pattern, which soon became the preferred though not only type in French naval steamers.

This contemporary lithograph gives a stern view of the *Fulton* as completed with three masts. She provided communications services between Toulon and Algeria in the late 1830s and appears to be arriving in the new colony with a high dignitary, as she is flying a special (possibly royal) flag at the main truck and the ships in the harbour are dressed overall. (© National Maritime Museum PY0882)

At the beginning of 1834 the navy received a proposal from the British firm of Fenton, Murray, & Jackson at Leeds to provide engines that, while firmly based on Watt's principles, were lighter, more solid, smaller, and less expensive than those of *Sphinx*. The French sent an engineer to Leeds to investigate this proposal and on 8 October 1834 the Minister decided to buy a pair of Fenton's 80nhp engines for *Papin*. Comparative trials with *Cerbère* in 1836 showed that the manufacturer's claims were fully justified. The only problem was that the placement of the machinery would require moving the mainmast 2.5 metres aft, which could be accomplished by deleting the mizzen mast and moving the foremast aft by the same amount. This was not considered a problem as the *Sphinx* class ships had rarely been able to use sails on their mizzen masts. The original rig of the class had been three masts with a sail area of 745 sq.m. but *Ardent, Castor, Fulton,* and others were later modified or completed with two masts.

On 14 August 1835 the standard armament for 160nhp steamers was set at 2 x 30pdr long guns and 3 x 22cm shell guns. Although many ships of this class carried relatively light armaments some were given more ambitious artillery. One of these was *Météore*, which in 1835 was given 3 x 22cm shell guns and 6 x 24pdr carronades for surveillance duty on the Spanish coast. Others, including *Tonnerre, Cerbère,* and *Papin,* were listed with the new standard of 2 x 30pdrs No.1 and 3 x 22cm shell guns. In the 1840s most reverted to lighter armaments appropriate to their role as avisos, generally 2 or 4 x 16cm shell. A few continued to be armed as combatants – *Tonnerre* received 2 x 22cm and 4 x 16cm shell in a major refit in 1844 during which she also received a brig rig in place of her original ship rig.

The main results of the navy's steamer program in the 1830s were a large homogeneous class of ships and the development of three substantial steam engine builders in France, the private firms of Cavé and Hallette and the navy's own facility at Indret. A final ship of the class, *Ténare*, was lengthened slightly to accommodate an old engine and is described here in a separate listing below.

Dimensions & tons: 47.26m, 46.28m wl, 44.00m x 8.00m, 8.20m ext x 5.44m. 894-910t disp. Draught 3.52/3.62m. Men: 77-93.

Machinery: 160nhp, 320ihp, 8kts. Side-lever, 2 cylinders (48in/1.22m diameter, 57in/1.45m stroke), 1 Fawcett flue boiler with 4 compartments or 2 Maudslay flue boilers, low pressure. Coal 170 tons.

Guns: (Fulton 1833) 2 x 18pdrs, 2 x 24pdr carronades; see above for later variations.

Fulton Rochefort Dyd/Hallette, Arras (Constructeur, Jean-Georges Clarke)

Ord: 18.1.1832. K: 21.2.1832. L: 6.4.1833. Comm: 27.11.1833. C: 11.1833.

Engine contract approved 18.11.1831. Struck 7.3.1867 at Brest, BU 1867.

PADDLE VESSELS

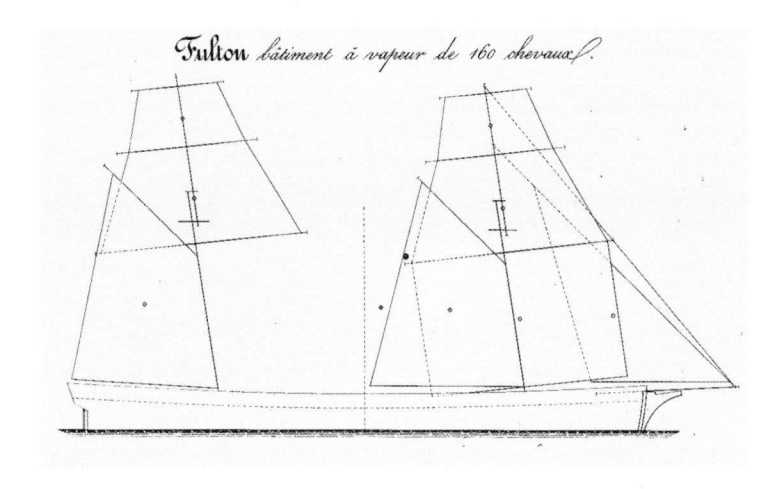

Official sail plan of *Fulton* rerigged as a brig in 1844. Although reduced from a three to two masts, sail area increased from 745 to 862 sq.m. as the original barquentine rig had no square canvas on main or mizzen. (Atlas du Génie Maritime, Genoa collection, image 2-0040)

Styx Indret/Indret (Constructeur, Pierre-Félix Le Grix)
   Ord: 18.1.1832. K: 6.1832. L: 17.9.1834. C: 12.1834. Comm: 1.1.1835.
   Struck 25.7.1867 at Brest and BU 1867.
Météore Rochefort Dyd/Hallette, Arras (Constructeurs, Jean Clarke and Claude Jobart-Dumesnil)
   Ord: 8.12.1832. K: 1.1.1833. L: 28.10.1833. Comm: 1.3.1834. C: 7.1834.
   Engine contract approved 1.8.1832. Struck 15.4.1867 at Toulon, sent to Gabon 7.1867 and fitted as a floating hospital, BU 1874.
Phare Indret/Indret (Constructeurs, Pierre-Félix Le Grix and Alexandre Robiou de Lavrignais)
   Ord: 8.12.1832. K: 6.1833. L: 14.3.1835. Comm: 14.3.1835. C: 4.1835.
   Used as a hydrographic ship in 1853-54. Struck 29.4.1865 at Lorient,

Machinery arrangement drawings for the *Papin*, showing the lightweight, improved version of Watt-type engines supplied by the British firm of Fenton, Murray and Jackson. The company made the drawing, which is annotated in English and dated Leeds October 1833. The so-called 'violin' shape of the weather deck of this type is very evident. (Archives de la Marine, 1-DD1-32)

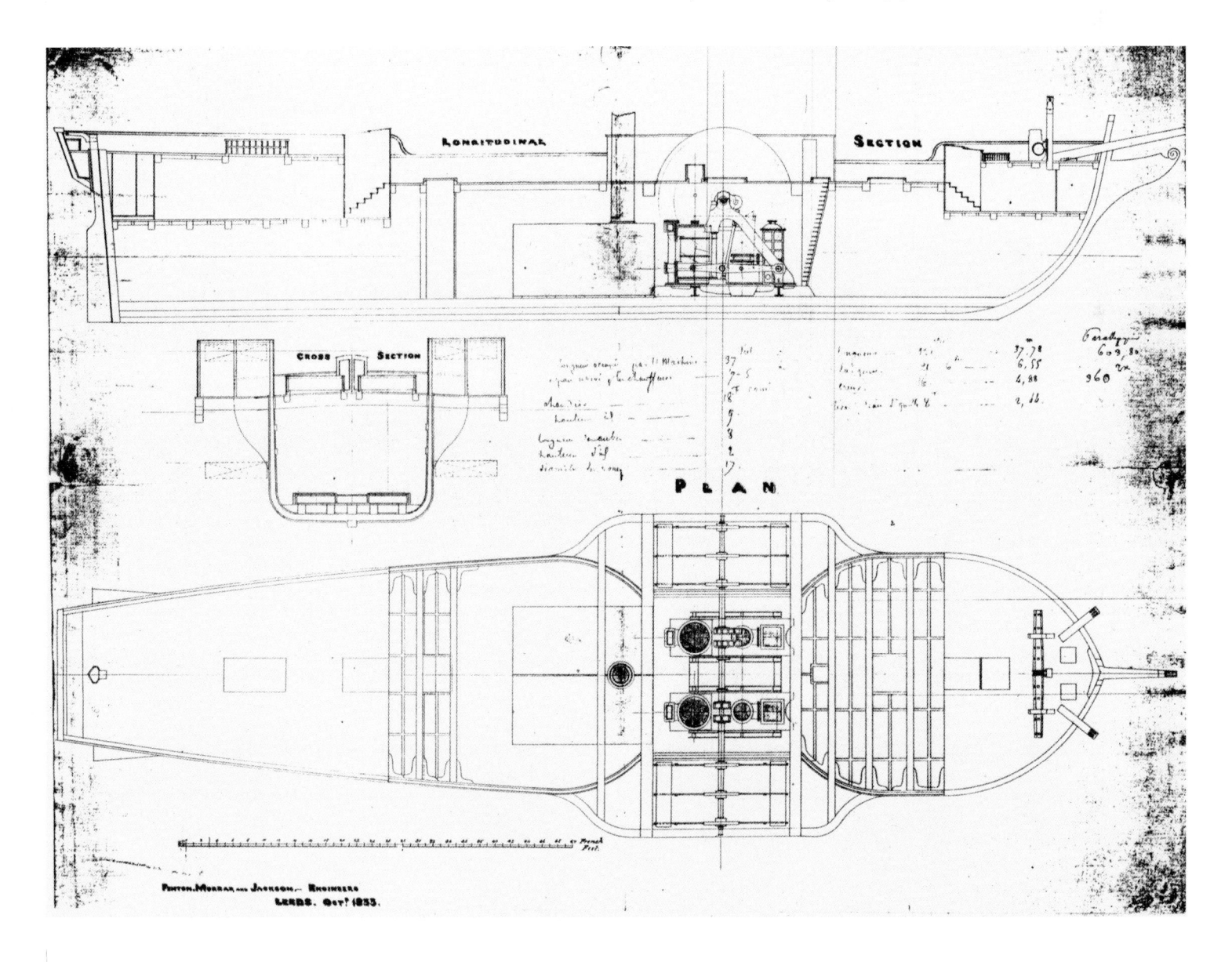

BU 1866.

Cerbère Indret/Indret.
　Ord: 23.1.1834. K: 2.1834. L: 16.2.1836. Comm: 17.2.1836.
　Initially fitted as a hospital ship for the repatriation of sick troops from North Africa. Struck 22.12.1864 at Toulon and fitted as a storage hulk. Renamed *Gardien* 4.1865, sold 1866 and BU 1867.

Papin Indret/Fenton, Murray, & Jackson, Leeds, U.K..
　Ord: c1.1834. K: 2.1834. L: 3.2.1836. Comm: 3.2.1836.
　Engine contract approved 3.12.1834. Wrecked 6.12.1845 at Mazagran on the Moroccan coast.

Tartare Indret/Cavé, Paris (Constructeurs, Pierre-Félix Le Grix and Alexandre Robiou de Lavrignais)
　Ord: c1.1834. K: 5.1834. L: 14.7.1836. Comm: 15.7.1836. C: 12.1836.
　Engine contract approved 10.9.1834. Struck 15.7.1867 at Cayenne and BU 1867.

Achéron Rochefort Dyd/Hallette, Arras (Constructeurs, Jean Clarke and Antoine Auriol, then Gustave Garnier)
　Ord: c1.1835. K: 21.1.1835. L: 18.12.1835. Comm: 5.10.1836. C: 10.1836.
　Engine contract approved 10.9.1834. Struck 15.11.1869 at Lorient and hulked, BU 1872.

Etna Indret/Cavé, Paris.
　Ord: c1.1835. K: 2.1835. L: 28.7.1836. Comm: 29.7.1836. C: 8.1836.
　Engine contract approved 10.9.1834. Wrecked 20.1.1847 near Cape Ténès, Algeria.

Cocyte Indret/Indret (Constructeur, Pierre Le Grix)
　Ord: 7.1.1835. K: 2.1835. L: 7.4.1837. Comm: 14.4.1837. C: 5.1837.
　Engines removed and converted at Lorient to a 500-ton sail transport 9.1858 to 8.1859. Struck 31.1.1867, storage hulk at Guadeloupe. BU 1875.

Phaéton Indret/Hallette, Arras (Constructeur, Alexandre Robiou de Lavrignais)
　Ord: 23.12.1835. K: 4.1836. L: 28.10.1837. Comm: 1.11.1837. C: 11.1837.
　Engine contract approved 28.5.1836. Sent to the Marquesas Islands in 1843. Boilers worn out by 1846. Struck 18.12.1849. Engines removed 1850-51 and sent to France for use in *Ardent*, hull converted to coal hulk. Renamed *Charbonnier* 1859. Sold or BU before 1865.

Tonnerre Indret/Cavé, Paris (Constructeur, Alexandre Robiou de Lavrignais)
　Ord: 23.12.1835. K: 9.3.1836. L: 24.2.1838. Comm: 24.2.1838. C: 7.1838.
　Engine contract approved 3.8.1836. Blown ashore 10.10.1846 at Havana in a hurricane, refloated 1847 and returned to service. Refitted as transport 3.1854. Struck 21.10.1859 and converted to careening hulk at Lorient. Coal hulk at Lorient 1872-76, renamed *Charbonnier* 5.2.1873, BU 1878.

Euphrate Indret/Indret (Constructeurs, Alexandre Robiou de Lavrignais and Pierre Le Grix)
　Ord: 25.9.1836. K: 15.1.1837. L: 28.4.1839. Comm: 1.5.1839. C: 10.1839.
　Original engine reassigned to *Grondeur*. Struck 27.2.1862 at Cherbourg, sold or BU before 1865.

Brandon (1) Lorient Dyd/Renaud de Vilback (Cie. des Forges et Fonderies), Charenton, completed at Indret.
　Ord: 10.12.1836 and named. K: 1837. L: 20.12.1839. Comm: 16.1.1841. C: 3.1841.
　Engine contract approved 6.12.1837 for *Grégeois*, builder failed, incomplete engines sent to Indret and reassigned. Installation of engines completed 3.1841, trials completed 8.1841, wrecked 21.12.1841 on the St. Philippe rocks near the entrance to Port Mahon, Minorca, crew rescued 25.4 to 3.5.1842.

Grondeur Lorient Dyd/Sudds, Adkins & Barker, Rouen.
　Ord: 14.12.1836. K: 9.6.1837. L: 16.3.1839. Comm: 22.6.1839. C: 6.1839.
　Engine contract approved 25.10.1837 for *Euphrate*, soon reassigned. Refitted as transport 3.1853. Struck 8.6.1860, fitted as paddle tug, and placed in service as a service craft at Brest 9.1861. Out of service 3.1862 at French Guiana and fitted as a prison hulk. BU 1875.

Grégeois Cherbourg Dyd/Indret (Constructeurs, Alexandre Robiou de Lavrignais and others)
　Ord: c12.1836. K: 20.2.1838. L: 17.1.1839. Comm: 1.11.1839. C: 11.1839.
　Received engines begun at Indret for *Brandon*. Fitted as hospital ship 1.1841 at Lorient. Struck 26.10.1865 at Toulon and BU.

BRASIER – 100nhp steam vessel, later paddle 2nd Class aviso. Two 80nhp steamers, *Brasier* and *Flambeau*, appeared in the building program in August 1831 to be begun at Toulon in 1832. The hull of *Brasier* was designed by Jean Antoine Vincent. The Minister of Marine decided on 26 December 1832 that Louis-Just Moissard, then in Britain, would in addition to his other assignments negotiate the purchase of 100nhp engines for *Brasier*. He obtained proposals from Maudslay and Fawcett, and the engines were ordered from Fawcett by a contract approved on 18 February 1833. The ship was lengthened at Brest between December 1838 and July 1839 to increase her coal capacity. She was subsequently listed as a 120nhp steamer, probably because of increased boiler power.
　Dimensions & tons: 36.00m wl x 6.70m. Lengthened 1839: 43.20m wl x 6.70m x 3.86m. 385 tons disp. Draught 2.85/2.89m. Men: 41-59.
　Machinery: 100nhp. Flue boilers.
　Guns: (1839) 2 x 12pdr carronades.

Brasier Toulon Dyd/Fawcett, Preston & Co., Liverpool
　Ord: c8.1831. K: 10.1831. L: 29.8.1833. Comm: 2.11.1833. C: 11.1833.
　Used as tug at Toulon 1849. Struck 1854.

FLAMBEAU – 80nhp steam vessel, later paddle 2nd Class aviso. On 22 June 1831 the navy agreed to purchase from the builder of the 160nhp engines of *Ardent*, Frimot, the engines of his experimental steamer *Éclair*, and a ship to receive them, *Flambeau*, was one of two 80nhp steamers that appeared in the building program in August 1831 to be begun in 1832. . Her hull was laid down at Brest in February 1832 on plans by Polydore Alexis Vaneechout, but the engines had been irreparably damaged when *Éclair* collided with the 90-gun *Suffren* on 17 June 1831 and the deal with Frimot fell through. *Flambeau* languished until a decision was made on 24 April 1835 to give her the after set of engines from *Pélican*. She was finally placed in reduced commission on 10 June 1839. *Flambeau* was lengthened at Cherbourg in May-November 1844 (re-launched 1 August 1844) and fitted with new engines built there.
　Dimensions & tons: 40.40m oa, 36.00m wl x 6.50m x 4.45m. Draught 2.70m. As rebuilt 1844: 42.00m wl x 6.50m x 4.45m. 512 tons disp. Draught 3.03m. Men: 64.
　Machinery: 80nhp. New engines 1844: 120nhp (Cherbourg), 8.5kts, flue boilers.
　Guns: (1840s) 4 x 8pdrs.

Flambeau Brest Dyd/from *Pélican*.
   Ord: 20.8.1831. K: 20.2.1832. L: 3.6.1837. C: 6.1839. Comm: 27.4.1840.
   Struck 21.12.1861 as an aviso and used as a tug (service craft). Station ship at Brest 1865-79. Condemned and BU 1880.

ÉCLAIREUR Class – 150nhp steam vessels, *Ramier* later designated 1st Class paddle aviso. These ships were built as *Gironde* and *Garonne* for a Bordeaux–Le Havre steam packet line being established by Iñigo Ezpeleta & Cie. of Bordeaux. *Gironde* made the first sailing on the new line on 6 February 1833 and *Garonne* followed on 21 March 1833. The enterprise was apparently abandoned almost immediately, for on 21 August 1833 the Minister of Marine approved a contract for the purchase of the two ships, which were commissioned in February 1834.
   Dimensions & tons: 45.45m wl x 8.30m x 5.28m. 600 tons disp. (as mercantile). Draught 3.47m mean. Men: 56.
   Machinery: 150nhp. Flue boilers.
   Guns: 2 x 18pdr carronades.
Éclaireur Bordeaux/Seaward & Capel, London
   L: 1832. Comm: 25.2.1834.
   Ex mercantile *Gironde* 3.1834. Wrecked 12.2.1835 in a storm in the harbour of Algiers. Wreck refloated and BU 1836, engine reused in sister *Ramier*.
Ramier Bordeaux/Seaward & Capel, London
   L: 1832. Comm: 13.2.1834.
   Ex mercantile *Garonne* 3.1834. Engine and boilers replaced with those of *Éclaireur* at Toulon 1836 to 12.1837. Struck 17.11.1847 and BU. The barge 'ex-*Ramier*' at Cherbourg in 1.1865 was probably actually ex-*Rameur* of 1831.

COURSIER – 60nhp steam vessel. This ship was built to replace *Louise* (ex *Caroline*) in French Guiana. Plans by Pierre Le Grix were approved on 9 December 1835.
   Dimensions & tons: 39.38m oa, 35.00m wl x 6.40m x 3.44m. ? tons disp. Draught 1.90m. Men: 49.
   Machinery: 60nhp.
   Guns: 3.
Coursier Indret/Indret.
   Ord: 19.7.1834. K: 10.1835. L: 8.11.1836. C: 12.1836. Comm: 1.1.1837.
   At Cayenne by 1841, decomm. there 16.5.1843 and struck.

ÉRÈBE – 60nhp steam vessel, later paddle 2nd Class aviso. Engines of 60nhp for a ship to be built at Indret were ordered from Maudslay, one of the best British engine builders, by a contract approved on 27 July 1836. The contract had been negotiated in Britain by Jean-Georges Clarke while he was there to buy 220nhp engines for *Véloce*. In approving this contract on 27 July 1836 the Minister of Marine directed Pierre Félix Le Grix at Indret to draw plans for a hull to receive the engines. The ship was named *Érèbe* in late 1836. While under construction she was designated to replace the second *Africain* in Senegal, where she served for a decade. After she was struck her engines were sent back to Brest and reused in *Marabout* (below).
   Dimensions & tons: 43.43m oa, 39.00m wl x 5.50m x 3.35m. 252 tons disp. Draught 2.20m. Men: 47-49.
   Machinery: 60nhp. 2 cylinders (0.82m diameter, 0.91m stroke)
   Guns: 4 x 18pdr carronades.
Érèbe Indret/Maudslay, London (Constructeur, Alexandre Robiou de Lavrignais)
   Ord: 27.7.1836. K: 3.1837. L: 30.12.1837. Comm: 9.1.1838. C: 12.1838.

Was at Saint-Louis de Senegal by 11.1839. Struck 16.10.1849 because she could no longer go to sea. The colony hoped to use her as a river transport, but her hull sank in the Senegal River in a storm around September 1850.

TÉNARE – 160nhp steam vessel, modified *Sphinx* class, later paddle 1st Class aviso. This, the last ship of the *Sphinx* class, was built to plans of Jean-Baptiste Hubert lengthened slightly to receive the engines from *Nageur*. In 1853-4 these were replaced with the engines from the corvette *Espadon* which, with new smaller boilers, were rerated at 180nhp. She was ordered converted into a steam mortar vessel with two mortars similar to *Vautour*, probably on 12 January 1855, and she participated in the bombardment of Kinburn in October 1855 with *Vautour*, *Cassini*, and *Sésostris*.
   Dimensions & tons: 48.00m wl x 8.00m x 5.34m. 906 tons disp. Draught 3.63m mean. Men: 100.
   Machinery: 160nhp.
   Guns: 4 x 16cm shell.
Ténare Toulon Dyd/from *Nageur*.
   Ord: 27.12.1837. K: 7.1838. L: 3.3.1840. Comm: 16.5.1840. C: 6.1840
   Struck 2.5.1861 at Lorient, sold or BU before 1865.

Paddle frigates and corvettes

On 4 March 1842 a royal ordinance enlarged and restructured the French steam navy. The previous fleet structure had been defined by a royal ordinance of 1 February 1837 which included among its total strength of 310 ships 40 steam vessels of 150nhp and above. Steamers below 150nhp were not considered part of the navy's military strength. In 1842 this lower limit for military steamers was raised to 220nhp and three categories were defined using for the first time terminology drawn from the sailing navy: steam frigates of 540nhp, steam frigates of 450nhp, and steam corvettes of 320 to 220nhp. The 40 military steamers in the 1837 program were now all to be of these larger types (20 frigates and 20 corvettes). In addition the navy was to maintain 30 steam vessels of 160nhp and below, not as combatants but for use as packets and in local service at the navy's ports and in the colonies. This increased the overall size of the French steam navy to 70 vessels. A royal ordinance of 22 November 1846 that again restructured the navy redesignated the smaller steamers, which now included vessels up to 200nhp, as steam avisos (in contrast with the larger ships which were 'war vessels'). It also subdivided the corvettes and avisos into two classes each based on their nominal horsepower, 1st Class corvettes having 400 to 320nhp, 2nd Class corvettes having 300 to 220nhp, 1st Class avisos having 150 to 200nhp, and second class avisos being of 120nhp and below.

VÉLOCE Class – 220nhp steam vessels, later paddle 2nd Class corvettes. On 28 June 1833 the Minister of Marine ordered the director of Indret, Philippe Gengembre, to draft plans for 220nhp machinery following as closely as possible the design of the successful 160nhp engines in the aviso *Sphinx*. Gengembre wanted to build more innovative machinery and did not produce plans acceptable to Paris until March 1835. A steamer of over 160nhp first appeared in the building program in the budget of 1837, presented in January 1836, in the form of a 200nhp *Lavoisier* to be begun at Indret during 1836.

Perhaps anticipating trouble with Gengembre's designs, the navy decided on 23 April 1836 to send Jean-Georges Clarke to Britain to buy a set of 220nhp engines for *Véloce*, a ship added to the building program in early 1836 for construction at Rochefort. Clarke ordered the engines

A model, now in the Musée de la Marine at Paris, of the paddle corvette *Véloce* as completed. (USN NH-55797, from an unidentified old book)

from Fawcett and Preston of Liverpool, the company that had built the engines of *Sphinx*, by a contract approved on 6 July 1836. By December 1836 a third 220nhp ship, *Caméléon*, had been added to the program to begin construction at Indret in 1837, and by December 1837 *Gassendi* and *Pluton* had been added, the first already begun at Indret in 1837 and the second to be begun at Brest in 1838. The hull plans for the class by Jean-Baptiste Hubert were approved on 29 September 1836 and followed *Sphinx* very closely. The beam over the paddle boxes varied from 15.60m in *Véloce* to 16.02m in *Pluton*. The class was completed with a three-masted rig with a sail area of up to 1,388 sq.m, but *Pluton* was re-rigged with two masts in 1844 with a sail area of 1,114 sq.m. and others may have followed her.

Véloce with her British machinery was an immediate success, the engines running smoothly and producing a trial speed of around 9 knots. The engines of *Pluton*, ordered from Schneider by a contract approved on 30 October 1839 as exact copies of those in *Véloce*, delivered a trial speed of 8.9 knots. In contrast, two of the three ships engined by Indret were disappointing. The poor performance of *Lavoisier*, Gengembre's first ship, which recorded only 7.95 knots on her initial trials on 22 April 1839, was blamed on numerous unauthorised modifications made to the engine plans by Gengembre and on badly built boilers. Her speed rose to 9 knots when her boilers were replaced in 1841. *Gassendi* began to go into commission a day before her launch but did not run trials until 2 April 1842 when she made only 8 knots. In 1843 her boilers were judged to be too small and were replaced, and in 1854 her engines were replaced with engines taken out of *Élan*. *Caméléon*, on the other hand, delivered the best trial speed of the class with 9.5 knots in 1840.

Dimensions & tons: First four: 59.40m, 58.05m wl, 55.91 x 9.00m, 9.16m ext x 5.97m. 1,334 tons disp. Draught 4.23/4.23m. *Pluton*: 60.25m x 9.24m ext x 6.11m. 1,509 tons disp. Draught 4.22/4.60m. Men: 123.

Machinery: 220nhp, 440ihp, 8 to 9.5kts. Side-lever, 2 cylinders (1.41m diameter, 1.68m stroke in *Véloce*, 1.52m stroke in *Lavoisier* and *Caméléon*), 1 Fawcett flue boiler with 4 compartments in *Véloce*, 1 flue boiler with 6 compartments in *Lavoisier* and *Caméléon*, 2 flue boilers in others. Coal 380 tons.

Guns: 3 x 22cm shell, 4 x 16cm shell, of which often only the 16cm guns were embarked; (*Pluton* as completed 1841) 2 x 22cm shell, 4 x 30pdrs.

Véloce Rochefort Dyd/Fawcett, Preston & Co., Liverpool (Constructeurs, Gabriel Nosereau, then Gustave Garnier)
  Ord: 6.4.1836. K: 15.9.1836. L: 12.3.1838. Comm: 1.7.1838. C: 8.1838.
  Collided with and sank the paddle gunvessel HMS *Lizard* 24.3.1843. Struck 16.11.1860 at Toulon, BU before 1865.

Lavoisier Indret/Indret (Constructeurs, Pierre Le Grix and Alexandre Robiou de Lavrignais)
  K: 16.8.1836. L: 4.10.1838. Comm: 1.1.1839. C: 1.1839.
  Struck 29.4.1865 at Lorient, coal hulk at Lorient. Mooring hulk in 1878, sold and BU 1885-86.

Caméléon Rochefort Dyd/Indret (Constructeurs, Gustave Garnier, Joseph Cros, and Antoine Auriol)
  Ord: 8.7.1837. K: 17.7.1837. L: 20.11.1839. C: 6.1840. Comm: 1.8.1840.
  Refitted as headquarters ship for the reserves at Brest 9.1856 to 9.1857 and struck 15.2.1858. BU 1865 at Brest.

Gassendi Indret/Indret (Constructeur, Paul-Émile Masson)
  K: 15.6.1837. L: 27.9.1840. Comm: 26.9.1840. C: 1.1841.
  Struck 14.2.1865, coal hulk at Brest, BU 1866.

Pluton Brest Dyd/Schneider (Constructeur, Hippolyte Prétot)
  Ord: 21.10.1837. K: 26.2.1838. L: 22.4.1841. Comm: 11.8.1841. C: 9.1841.
  Blown ashore 14.11.1854 in a storm while at anchor at Eupatoria in the Crimea in company with the sailing ship of the line *Henri IV*.

As of December 1838 the building program contained only one projected steamer with more than 220nhp (*Cuvier* at Rochefort of 300 to 400nhp) to be begun in 1840. Other ships to be begun in 1840 included a 220nhp *Asmodée* at Lorient and a 220nhp *Infernal* and a 160nhp *Gomer* at Rochefort. By December 1839 *Infernal* had become a 320nhp ship,

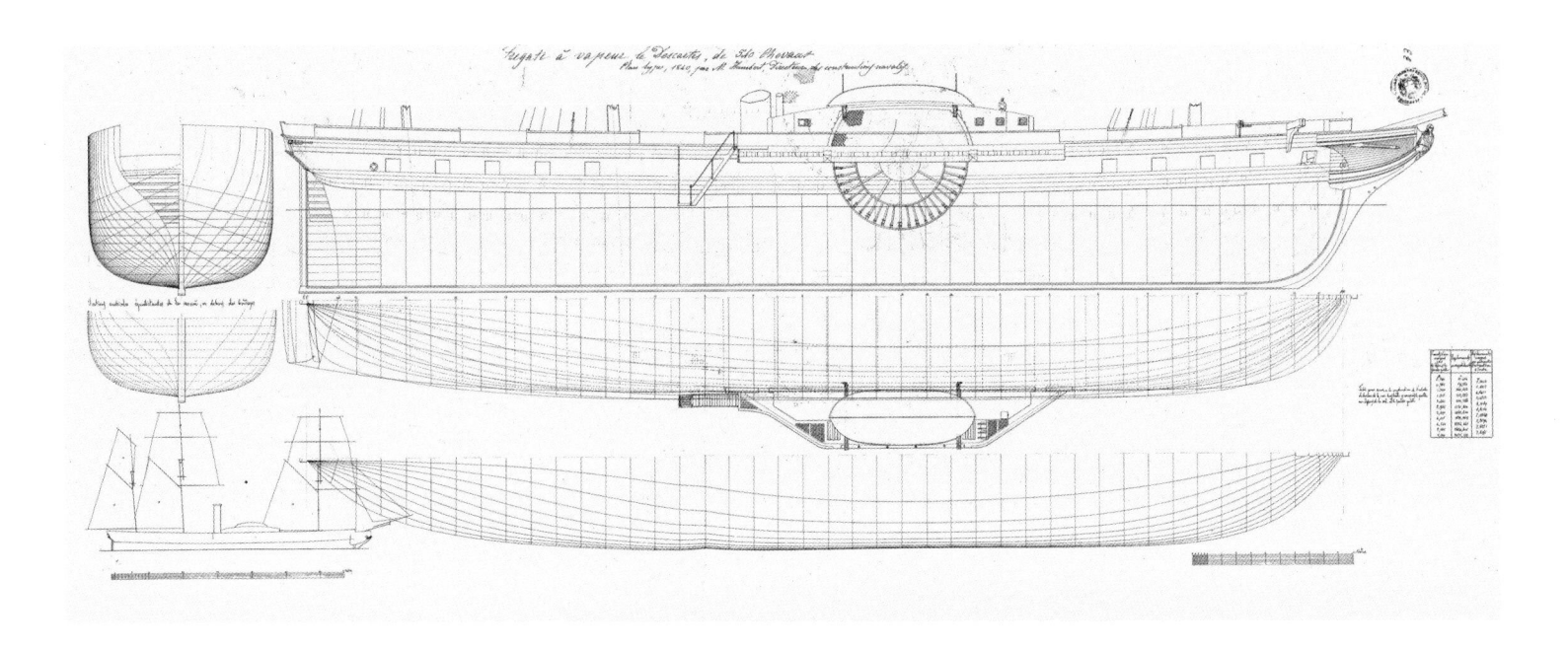

Official general arrangement plans of the paddle frigate *Descartes*, the first of a new type with powerful 540nhp machinery. Unlike earlier steamers, whose guns were confined to the weather deck, this ship carried a battery between decks, as revealed by the row of gunports before and abaft the paddle boxes. Note also the *canot-tambour* or paddle box boat, a large metal barge inverted over the paddle box to double as its cover. (Atlas du Génie Maritime, Genoa collection, image 5-0032)

Asmodée and *Gomer* were 450nhp ships, and three more 450nhp ships (including *Cuvier*, now at Rochefort) and another 320nhp ship were projected. The hulls and engines of *Asmodée* and *Gomer* were ordered between November 1839 and May 1840. In March 1841 the names *Asmodée* and *Gomer* were reassigned to former packet hulls and the hulls that formerly had these names were completed respectively as the 540nhp *Vauban* and *Descartes*.

INFERNAL – 450nhp paddle frigate. *Infernal* appeared in the building program in late 1837 as a 220nhp steamer to be begun in 1838 at Rochefort. However the appearance of larger steamers in Britain led to a ministerial order of 30 January 1839 to design a paddle frigate similar to the British *Gorgon*, and on 15 May 1839 Boucher and Tupinier recommended to the Minister that this *Infernal*, then only 1/24th complete, be abandoned and replaced by a 320nhp ship then being designed by Jean-Baptiste Hubert that would be given the same name. In the meantime Pierre Jean-Baptiste Rossin was sent to Britain in April 1839 to buy a set of 320nhp side-lever engines similar to those in HMS *Gorgon*, and he ordered the engines from the firm of Miller, Ravenhill & Co. by a contract approved on 8 June 1839. Jean-Baptiste Hubert's plans for her hull were approved on 8 January 1840.

In late 1840 Mathurin Boucher realised that the engines were too small to give such a large ship the desired speed, and on 9 December 1840 the Minister of Marine approved his recommendation to build a new, smaller hull under the name *Cuvier* for the original 320nhp engines and assign to the original hull (soon named *Infernal*) experimental 450nhp engines under construction at Indret that had originally been intended for *Asmodée*. *Infernal*'s new engines, among the earliest that could be called direct-acting, were built on a system developed simultaneously by Pierre Jean-Baptiste Rossin at Indret and by the famous British engine builder Maudslay which connected four small cylinders directly to the paddle shaft instead of linking two large ones to it by means of a large, heavy side-lever.

Infernal was commissioned on 27 May 1843 at Rochefort within a month of launching and was taken to Paimboeuf in June 1843 to receive her engines. On trials they did not develop as much power as expected and they were not repeated. *Infernal* was designed in 1840 with a brig rig in imitation of HMS *Gorgon* but was later assigned three masts. In 1845 Joinville recommended reverting to the two-masted rig. On 5 May 1846 accountability for the ship passed to Toulon, and she was recommissioned there on 1 October 1846. She was re-rated as a 400nhp 1st Class corvette on 1 January 1847. In June 1855 her engines were ordered removed and she was sent to the Pacific as a sail transport and hulked upon arrival at Valparaiso.

    Dimensions & tons: 63.85m, 62.00m wl, 60.00m x 10.80m, 11.00m ext x 5.78m. 2,034 tons disp. Draught 4.65/5.15m. Men: 200.
    Machinery: 450nhp, 837ihp, 10.2kts. direct-acting, 4 cylinders (1.5m diameter, 1.75m stroke), 4 flue boilers. Coal 475 tons.
    Guns: (Designed, 1840) UD 12 x 30pdrs No.2; SD 2 x 22cm shell pivots, 4 x 16cm shell; (As completed, 1846) UD 2 x 30pdrs No.1, 2 x 22cm No.1 shell; SD 2 x 30pdrs No.1, 2 x 22cm No.1 shell.

Infernal Rochefort Dyd/Indret (Constructeurs, Antoine Auriol, Charles Moll, and Armand Forquenot)
    Ord: 7.12.1839. K: 13.1.1840. L: 1.5.1843. Comm: 27.5.1843. C: 11.1845.
    Decomm. 12.6.1855 as steamer and simultaneously recomm. as sail transport. Decomm 1.7.1857 at Valparaiso and simultaneously recomm as a storage hulk. Caught fire at Valparaiso 1.10.1861 two days after returning there, after six hours the blazing wreck was sunk by detonating her powder magazine. Struck 14.12.1861.

DESCARTES – 540nhp paddle frigate. In late 1839 Firmin-Isidore Joffre was sent to Britain to buy a set of engines of 450nhp to serve as a model for large paddle frigate machinery to be built in France, and he ordered the engines from Fawcett, Preston & Co. by a contract approved on 13 November 1839. The hull for these engines was ordered on 7 December 1839 to be begun in 1840 under the name *Gomer*. Jean-Baptiste Hubert designed the ship with a beam and depth of hull very close to those of sail 3rd Class frigates, although the length had to be much greater in order to accommodate the engines. His plans were approved on 15 February 1840. The designed armament was UD 18 x 30pdrs No.2, 2 x 22cm shell forward; SD 14 x 16cm shell, 2 x 22cm shell; this was changed on 27 June 1840 to match that of her half-sister *Asmodée* (later *Vauban*).

The original engines and name were reassigned to a smaller hull on 27 February 1841 (see the *Gomer* class below) and the original hull was renamed *Descartes* and designated along with *Vauban* to receive a 540nhp engine. Because neither Indret nor French industry had built such a large engine the Minister of Marine decided on 23 June 1841 to order the engines for these ships from Gerhard-Moritz Roentgen (Röntgen), director of the Nederlandsche Stoomboot Maatschappij at Fijenoord. On 20 July 1841 Roentgen signed a contract to furnish two traditional side-lever engines of 540nhp for the two ships. After it was decided to provide a different type of engine for *Vauban* the July contract was cancelled and a new contract for both ships was approved on 20 October 1841. The plans for the engines for *Descartes* were approved on 23 March 1842 but completion of the ship was slowed by the transatlantic packet program. The beam of *Descartes* outside her paddle boxes was 20.00m and her sail area was 1,785 sq.m.

> Dimensions & tons: 70.45m, 70.14m wl, 68.00m x 12.40m, 12.65m ext x 6.40m. 3,037 tons disp. Draught 5.37/5.97m. Men: 304.
> Machinery: 540nhp, 1200ihp. Side-lever.
> Guns: (1845) UD 6 x 30pdrs No.1, 2 x 22cm No.1 shell; SD 6 x 22cm No.1 shell, 2 x 30pdrs No.1.

Descartes (ex *Gomer* 3.3.1841) Rochefort Dyd/Roentgen, Fijenoord (Constructeurs, Gustave Garnier and Armand Forquenot)
> Ord: 7.12.1839. K: 11.2.1840. L: 5.3.1844. Comm: 8.5.1844. C: 5.1845.
> Struck 15.7.1867. BU 1867.

VAUBAN – 540nhp paddle frigate. On 29 August 1839 the Minister of Marine decided to have Indret build a set of four-cylinder engines of 450nhp to an experimental plan by Pierre Jean-Baptiste Rossin. A hull for these engines was ordered on 7 December 1839 to be begun in 1840 under the name *Asmodée*. On 27 February 1840 the Council of Works decided that the Indret design was too daring and should be tried on a 60nhp ship (*Rapide*) first, but as the 1841 budget (prepared in late 1839) included two 450nhp steamers and no engines of this size had yet been built in France, Mathurin Boucher was sent to Britain to buy 450nhp engines for *Asmodée* there. After many discussions he ordered a duplicate of *Gomer*'s engines from Fawcett by a contract approved on 13 May 1840. While in Britain Boucher learned that the hull of Hubert's ship was heavier than its British equivalents. Boucher's plans, approved on 27 June 1840 and used to build the ship, had a hull 140 tons lighter than Hubert's and slightly finer lines but retained the cross-sectional dimensions of a 3rd Class frigate. The designed armament in June 1840 was UD 18 x 30pdrs No.2, 2 x 22cm shell; SD 10 x 16cm shell, 2 x 22cm shell.

Hulls and engines were reallocated on 27 February 1841 as in the case of *Descartes*, the original hull of *Asmodée* becoming *Vauban*. On 20 July 1841 Gerhard-Moritz Roentgen signed a contract for two traditional side-lever engines of 540nhp for this ship and *Descartes*, but he then came to Paris and pointed out that the hulls of the ships had been designed for 450nhp engines and that his 540nhp engines would be heavier than those, requiring a reduction of about 80 tons in coal and stores. He proposed instead an early form of direct-acting engines in which the cylinders were inclined to permit their direct connection with the paddle shaft. The navy adopted this model engine for *Vauban* (which had finer lines than *Descartes*), the July contract was cancelled, and a new contract for both ships was approved on 20 October 1841. The plans for the engines for *Vauban* were approved on 25 May 1842 but completion of the ship was slowed by the transatlantic packet program. The new model engines worked well, but were as bulky as conventional side-lever engines and were not duplicated. The beam of *Vauban* outside her paddle boxes was 20.00m.

> Dimensions & tons: 70.50m, 69.94m wl x 12.50m, 12.77m ext x 6.40m. 2,873 tons disp. Draught 5.55m mean. Men: 304.
> Machinery: 540nhp, 1,313ihp, 9.5kts. Inclined direct-acting. Coal 565 tons.
> Guns: (1847) UD 6 x 30pdrs No.1, 2 x 22cm No.2 shell; SD 6 x 22cm No.2 shell, 2 x 30pdrs No.1.

Vauban (ex *Asmodée* 3.3.1841) Lorient Dyd/Roentgen, Fijenoord (Constructeurs, Charles-Robert Alexandre (?) and Hippolyte Prétot)
> Ord: 7.12.1839. K: 10.7.1840. L: 8.3.1845. *Comm de rade*: 1.4.1845. C: 10.1846. Comm: 23.2.1847.
> Struck 8.6.1865 at Toulon. Sunk by an experimental spar torpedo at Toulon 28.2.1866, wreck beached for further experiments and then BU.

GOMER Class – 450nhp paddle frigates. The hulls of these ships were ordered on 23 August 1840 under a program to build fourteen 450nhp steamers for service on new French transatlantic packet lines. Plans by six naval engineers were approved on 26 September 1840 and 16 January 1841: Antoine Bernard Campaignac (Packets Nos.1-2 at Cherbourg), Alexandre Chedeville (Nos.3-4 at Brest), Louis-Just Moissard (No.5 at Brest), Mathurin Boucher (Nos.6-8 at Lorient), Jean-Baptiste Hubert (Nos.9-12 at Rochefort), and Firmin-Isidore Joffre (Nos.13-14 at Toulon). The French soon realised that these packet designs were far too heavy to compete economically with contemporary British packets like *President* and *British Queen*, and on 27 February 1841 new plans were ordered for the packets and the four hulls whose construction was furthest along were reallocated to the navy as a head start on its steam frigate program. The first two of these, *Gomer* and *Asmodée* (packet hulls Nos.9 and 10), had their engines and names reassigned from the even larger frigates ordered at the end of 1839 and, because they were built quickly, became France's prototype paddle frigates. *Gomer* received the Fawcett engines ordered on 13 November 1839 while *Asmodée* received those ordered on 13 May 1840; both sets of engines performed well on trials. Construction of the other two reallocated ships, *Mogador* and *Sané* (packets Nos.11 and 1), proceeded more slowly. Of the other packets, No.12 was barely begun (0.5/24ths) at Rochefort in mid-December 1840 and her materials were used in *Groenland* (the new No.9). Nos.6 and 7 were begun at Lorient in late 1840 and were ultimately completed to new plans as *Caraïbe* and *Cacique*.

The armament of *Asmodée* reflected the navy's early experience with the new large paddle frigates. The original design for the converted packets called for the same armament of 32 guns that was assigned to *Vauban*, which imitated the armament of 3rd Class sailing frigates. The designed armament in June 1841 was UD 18 x 30pdrs No.2, 2 x 22cm shell; SD 10 x 16cm shell, 2 x 22cm shell. When *Asmodée* was commissioned in 1842 this armament had already been reduced somewhat, but she had a heavy square rig and the combination was still too much for her. When recommissioned in 1845, she still had essentially the same armament but her rig was lightened. In 1845 a commission under the Prince de Joinville studied the question of the missions and armament of naval steamers, and concluded that, since paddle steamers were vulnerable on the broadside, they should be configured for end-on fighting and armed with a smaller number of the heaviest guns available. They were also given armoured bulkheads forward and aft of the machinery. *Descartes* and *Infernal* were the prototypes for this concept, and *Asmodée* was rearmed along their lines in

A watercolour by T S Robins celebrating the state visit of King Louis-Philippe to Britain in 1844. The French king arrived at Portsmouth in the paddle frigate *Gomer* (centre left), and was greeted by HMS *Victory* with yards manned and dressed overall. The main French ships from left to right are *Caiman*, *Gomer*, *Pluton* (behind *Gomer*), and the sailing royal yacht *Reine Amélie*. (© National Maritime Museum PX9823)

1846. The beam of both ships outside their paddle boxes was 19.83m and their sail area was 1,762 sq.m. on three masts.

Dimensions & tons: 72.75m, 70.95m wl, 68.00m (67.10 in *Asmodée*) x 12.20m, 12.45m ext x 6.05m. 2,736 tons disp. Draught 5.14/5.54m. Men: 267.

Machinery: 450nhp, 900ihp, 10.8kts (*Gomer*), 11.7kts (*Asmodée*). Side-lever, 2 cylinders (1.93m diameter, 2.93m stroke), 4 flue boilers. Coal 498 tons.

Guns: (Both 1841-2) UD 12 x 30pdrs No.2; SD 4 x 22cm No.2 shell, 4 x 16cm shell; (*Asmodée* 1846-52) UD 4-22cm No.1 shell, 4-30pdrs No.1; SD 2-22cm No.1 shell, 4-30pdrs No.1; (*Gomer* 1848) 6-16cm shell, 8-30pdrs No.2.

Gomer (ex *Asmodée* 13.3.1841) Rochefort Dyd/Fawcett, Preston & Co., Liverpool (Constructeurs, Antoine Auriol and Gustave Garnier)
Ord: 23.8.1840. K: 25.9.1840. Named (*Asmodée*) 3.3.1841. L: 19.7.1841. Comm: 15.12.1841. C: 4.1842.
Struck 30.3.1868, BU 1868 at Brest.

Asmodée (ex *Monge* 13.3.1841) Rochefort Dyd/Fawcett, Preston & Co., Liverpool (Constructeur, Gustave Garnier)
Ord: 23.8.1840. K: 19.10.1840. Named (*Monge*) 3.3.1841. L: 30.10.1841. Comm: 1.7.1842. C: 7.1842.
Struck 18.12.1865 at Toulon, BU 1866.

SANÉ – 450nhp paddle frigate. This ship, formerly hull No.1 in the first group of packets ordered in August 1840 and designed by Antoine Bernard Campaignac, was built slowly. She received a side-lever engine initially ordered from Indret for the packet program and subsequently reassigned. Her beam outside her paddle boxes was 19.83m.

Dimensions & tons: 72.02m, 71.00m wl x 12.40m, 12.65m ext x 6.15m. 2,650 tons disp. Draught 5.26/5.54m. Men: 264.

Machinery: 450nhp, 10.17kts (trials 21.9.1848). Side-lever, tubular boilers. Coal 576 tons.

Guns: (1849) UD 4 x 30pdrs No.1, 4 x 22cm shell; SD 4 x 30pdrs No.1, 2 x 22cm shell.

Sané Cherbourg Dyd/Indret (Constructeur, Louis-Alexandre Corrard)
Ord: 23.8.1840. K: 26.10.1840. L: 15.2.1847. Comm: 25.6.1848. C: 2.1849.
Wrecked 23.9.1859 on the Chaussée du Sein, probably due to compass error.

MOGADOR – 650nhp paddle frigate. This ship was hull No.11 in the first group of packets ordered in August 1840 and her hull, designed by Jean-Baptiste Hubert, was identical to the *Gomer* class. She was named *Monge* in March 1841 but construction was suspended on 22 December 1843 with a few exceptions. She was renamed *Mogador* on 28 November 1844 to commemorate the deeds of the Prince de Joinville who commanded the French bombardment of that Moroccan port in August.

On 28 November 1844 the Minister decided to exploit new engine technology to give this ship's machinery substantially more power than in her half-sisters. Her original 450nhp engines were reassigned to the smaller *Caffarelli* and after consideration of many options including a screw propeller, new 650nhp engines were ordered for her from Schneider by a contract approved on 31 August 1846. These were built on one of the most successful patterns of direct-acting paddle engines, popularised by the British engine builder Penn, in which the cylinders were mounted on trunnions and oscillated as their connecting rods drove the paddle shaft. On a trial run on 17 August 1849, she averaged 9.82kts from Toulon to Algiers and 10.25kts on the return trip. Indret and some other leading French engine builders made extensive use of this type of machinery after abandoning the traditional side-lever engines. The beam of *Mogador* outside her paddle boxes was 20.21m.

Dimensions & tons: 72.75m, 70.95m wl, 68.00m x 12.20m, 12.45m ext x 6.05m. 2,750 tons disp. Draught 5.14/5.54m. Men: 305.

Machinery: 650nhp, 1,695ihp, 10kts. Oscillating, 2 cylinders (1.8m diameter, 3m stroke), 6 tubular boilers. Coal 630 tons.

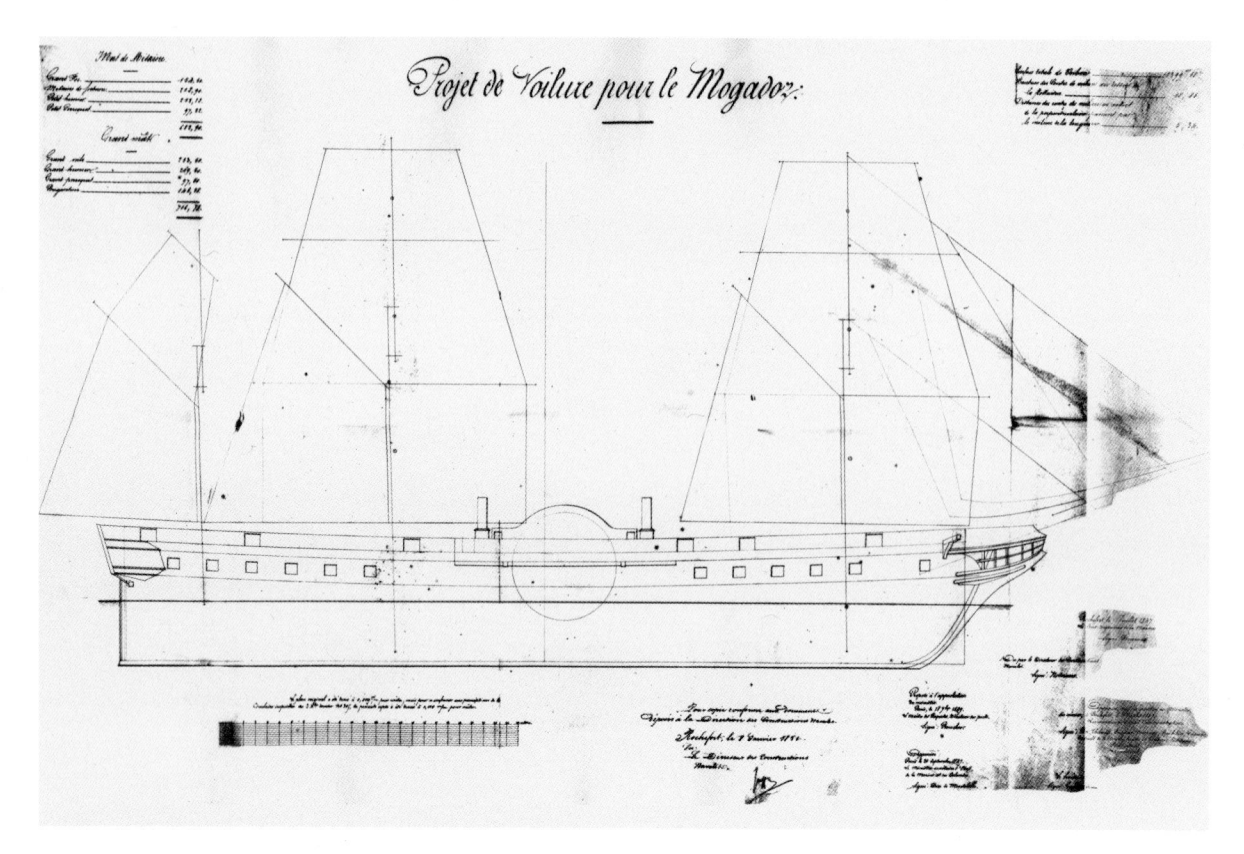

Official barque sail plan for the paddle frigate *Mogador* as approved at Rochefort on 6 July 1847 and at Paris on 21 September 1847. The machinery arrangement was probably soon altered, as later views show her with a single large funnel as in the other large French steamers. (Archives de la Marine, 8-DD1-18 no. 24)

Guns: (1847) UD 12 x 30pdrs No.1; SD 4 x 22cm shell.
Mogador (ex *Monge* 28.11.1844, ex *Gomer* 13.3.1841) Rochefort Dyd/Schneider (Constructeurs, Antoine Auriol and Nicolas Courtin, then Charles Duchalard, Armand Forquenot, and Victorin Sabattier)
    Ord: 23.8.1840. K: 16.11.1840. Named (*Gomer*) 3.3.1841. L: 19.2.1848. Comm: 22.8.1848. C: 1.1849.
    Struck 20.4.1878 at Toulon, BU 1880.

CUVIER – 320nhp paddle corvette, later 1st Class. Plans by Mathurin Boucher were approved on 31 December 1840 for a ship to receive the 320nhp engines ordered in Britain for the frigate *Infernal* (q.v.). The new ship was given the same beam as *Infernal*, but was shorter and had finer lines. The beam over her paddle boxes was 17.32m. Her engines were not completed on time, and when the navy threatened to cancel the contract the builder came to Paris and agreed in a new contract approved on 18 December 1841 to substitute direct-acting engines for the traditional side-lever engines originally specified. In these engines the connecting rod from the cylinder was connected directly to the paddle shaft – an elementary form of direct action which became popular in small ships but was not repeated in the navy's larger steamers. The armament in the battery was quickly abandoned and in 1845 she had an armament, all on deck, of 4 x 22cm shell sides, 2 x 30pdrs ends.
    Dimensions & tons: 60.00m, 60.00m wl x 10.76m, 11.00m ext x 5.35m. 1,656 tons disp. Draught 4.35/4.75m. Men: 180.
    Machinery: 320nhp, 618ihp, 8kts sustained. Direct-acting.
    Guns: (1843) UD 8 x 30pdrs No.2; SD 4 x 22cm shell.
Cuvier Lorient Dyd/Miller and Ravenhill (Constructeur, Pierre Félix Le Grix)
    Ord: 31.12.1840. K: 20.1.1841. L: 5.9.1842. Comm: 1.1.1843. C: 1.1843.
    Burned off Mahon, Majorca 25.1.1848 following the spontaneous combustion of the coal in her bunkers.

ARCHIMÈDE – 220nhp paddle corvette, later 2nd Class. Mathurin Boucher submitted copies of his 20 February 1841 plans for the four 220nhp packets of the *Phoque* class (below) and proposed that they be used to build *Archimède*. This proposal was approved on 10 March 1841. Engines identical to those of *Pluton* were ordered from Schneider by a contract approved on 3 December 1840. *Archimède* had two masts and a sail area of up to 1,173 sq.m.
    Dimensions & tons: 56.90m, 55.20m wl, 52.20m x 9.20m, 9.36m ext x 6.18m. 1,309 tons disp. Draught 4.25m mean. Men: 123.
    Machinery: 220nhp, 9kts. Side-lever, 2 cylinders (1.41m diameter, 1.68m stroke), 2 flue boilers. Coal 220 tons.
    Guns: 2 x 22cm shell, 4 x 16cm shell.
Archimède Brest Dyd/Schneider (Constructeur, Jean-Émile Le Jouteux)
    Ord: 13.3.1841. K: 12.4.1841. L: 25.4.1842. Comm: 1.9.1842. C: 9.1842.
    Struck 25.4.1853, mooring hulk at Rochefort. Renamed *Alligator* c1859, BU 1868.

DARIEN Class – 450nhp paddle frigates, converted packets. On 16 July 1840 the French passed a law forming four transatlantic steam packet lines to free France from dependence on Britain for steam communications with the New World. After a false start (see the *Gomer* class), the navy built fourteen 450nhp steamers for transatlantic service and four 220nhp steamers for three satellite lines in the Americas. (The ships' program numbers are shown after their names in the tables – note that *Canada* may have been No.4 and *Christophe Colomb* No.3.) All 14 packets were named on 23 March 1842. It soon became clear that the proposed lines would not be viable, and the ships found their way into the navy, more or less in the three groups indicated below. The ships in the first group had received all of their luxury passenger fittings during construction and were kept in reserve at Cherbourg and Brest until being turned over to the Société Hérout et Handel (Compagnie Générale des

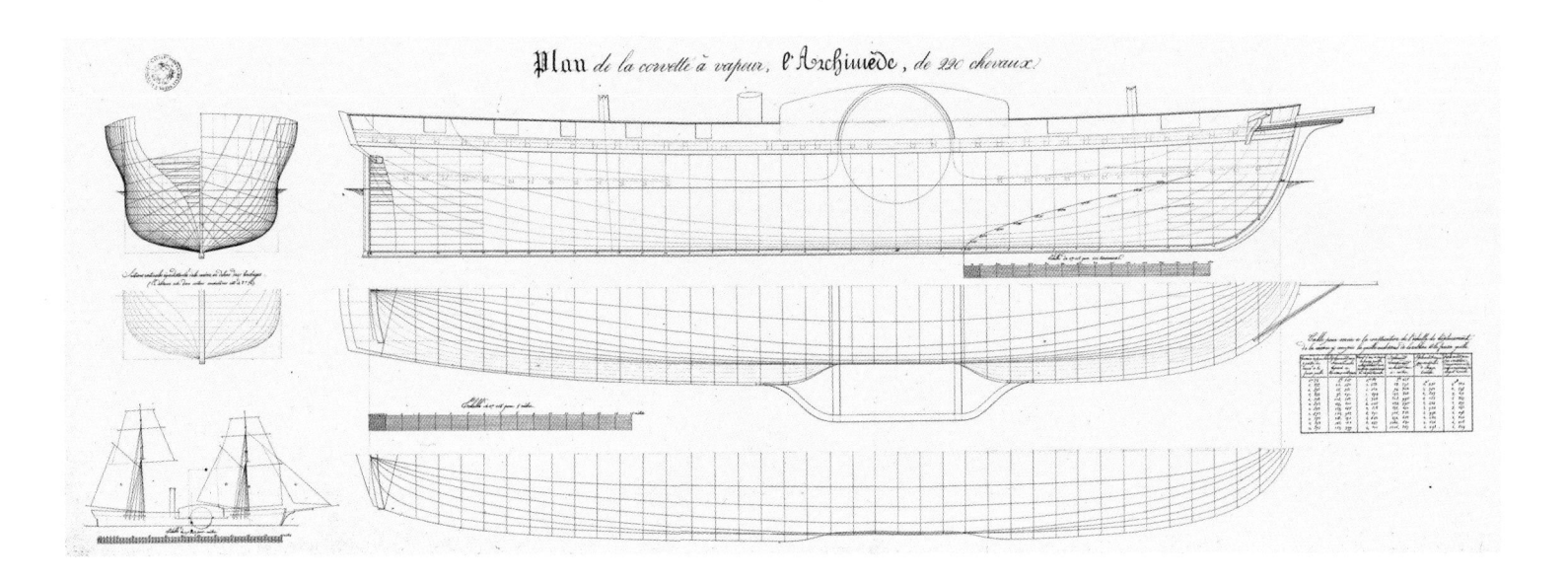

Official general arrangement plans of the paddle corvette *Archimède*. The French Navy was closely involved with the national effort to develop steam packet services, including designing the vessels, many of which they later took over when the companies proved commercially unviable. Although intended as a naval corvette from the start, *Archimède* was based on a design for a packet; the vessel was rigged as a brig. (Atlas du Génie Maritime, Genoa collection, image 5-0008)

Paquebots Transatlantiques) under a law of April 1847 for transatlantic operations under the names *New York*, *Missouri*, *Philadelphie*, and *Union*. The ships were renamed on 12 May 1847 and ceased to belong to the navy on 12 June 1847. *Missouri* (ex *Ulloa*) could carry 85 passengers in 1st Class, 200 in 2nd Class, and 200 tons of merchandise while *New York* (ex *Darien*) could take 104 passengers in 1st Class cabins. This enterprise suspended service in January 1848 due to financial losses and the ships were returned to the navy on 12 April 1848 and reverted to their original names on 23 June 1848. In the second group, *Caraïbe* was taken over in July 1845 as flagship of the West Africa station (where she was lost), *Magellan* and *Cacique* were transferred in March 1846 to support military operations in Algeria, and *Eldorado* was taken over around September 1846. The ships in the third group never received their passenger fittings. *Orénoque* and *Labrador* were attached to the fleet by a decision of 23 December 1843 and all were used to support the navy's expedition against Morocco in 1844. *Groenland* was wrecked during this operation, and the other five were assigned to the navy in July 1845 to provide packet and transport services in the Mediterranean. The sail area of *Orénoque* was 1,496 sq.m.

All of these ships were built to different plans and technically form separate classes, but their dimensions were so similar that they are consolidated here into one group. Their beam over their paddle boxes was about 19.4m. The plans for the ships were approved on 24 March and 21 and 28 April 1841. Nine engines on plans by Schneider were ordered from private builders by contracts approved on 17 October 1840. These, along with four engines ordered from Indret, provided for all but one of the ships. Two of the Indret engines were later reassigned to the navy frigate program (*Sané* and *Monge*) because they would not be ready in time for the packets (the other two went to *Cacique* and *Eldorado*), and additional engines were ordered for *Magellan*, *Albatros*, and *Orénoque* by contracts approved on 13 May 1842. The Schneider-designed engines were successful, *Labrador* being considered a very good ship that still ran well in 1861. The engines of *Cacique* were ordered removed 25 May 1865 and she became a sail transport.

Dimensions & tons: 69.60m to 70.72m, 69.00m wl, 63.40 to 65.76m x 11.80m, 12.05m ext x 5.95m to 6.05m. 2,591 tons disp. Draught 5.30m mean. Men: 267.

Machinery: 450nhp, 900ihp, trials 9.78kts (*Magellan*) to 11.4kts (*Canada*). Side-lever, 2 cylinders (1.93m diameter, 2.28m stroke), 4 flue boilers. Coal 655 tons max.

Guns:

Group 1: 2 small; (*Darien*, 1850) 4 x 30pdrs No.2; (*Canada*, 1.1854) UD forward: 2 x 30pdrs No.2, 2 x 22cm No.2 shell; UD aft: 2 x 22cm No.2 shell, 2 x 30pdrs No.2; SD 2 x 30pdrs No.1, 4 x 22cm shell; (*Darien*, 1854) UD 4 x 22cm No.2 shell, 4 x 30pdrs No.2; SD 4 x 22cm No.1 shell, 2 x 30pdrs No.1.

Group 2: (*Magellan*, *Caraïbe*, and *Cacique*, 1846) UD 2 x 22cm shell forward, 4 x 30pdrs No.2 aft (No.1 in *Magellan*); SD 2 x 22cm shell, 2 x 30pdrs No.1; (*Eldorado*, 1847) UD 6 x 30pdrs No.2; SD 4 x 22cm No.2 shell, 2 x 30pdrs No.1.

Group 3: 4 x 16cm shell; (*Labrador*, 1854) UD 4 x 22cm shell No.2, 4 x 16cm shell; SD 4 x 22cm shell No.1, 2 x 16cm; (*Panama*, *Magellan* and *Cacique* in late 1850s) UD 8 x 30pdrs No.1; SD 6 x 22cm No.2 shell.

Group 1.
Darien (1) Cherbourg Dyd/Cavé (Designer and constructeur, Anne-François Besuchet)
Ord: c8.1840. K: 26.8.1841. L: 6.10.1842. Comm: 1.8.1843. C: 12.1843.
Handed over 6.8.1847 as mercantile *New York*, left Le Havre for New York 24.10.1847. Returned to Navy 12.4.1848, comm. 15.4.1848. Struck 15.7.1869, BU 1869 at Brest.

Ulloa (2) Cherbourg Dyd/Cavé (Designer, Georges Allix; Constructeur, Alexandre Robiou de Lavrignais)
Ord: c8.1840. K: 12.5.1841. L: 7.8.1842. Comm: 10.7.1843. C: 7.1843.
Known as *Ulua* 1842-47. Mercantile *Missouri* 12.5.1847, left Le Havre for New York 31.7.1847. Returned to Navy 12.4.1848, comm. 15.4.1848. Struck 8.6.1865 at Rochefort, mooring hulk and sheer hulk. BU approved 2.12.1887, BU 1888 by M. Février.

Canada (3) Brest Dyd/Schneider (Designer, Alexandre Chedeville; Constructeur, Jean-Michel Segondat)
Ord: c8.1840. K: 13.4.1841. L: 15.3.1843. Comm: 1.7.1843. C: 7.1843.

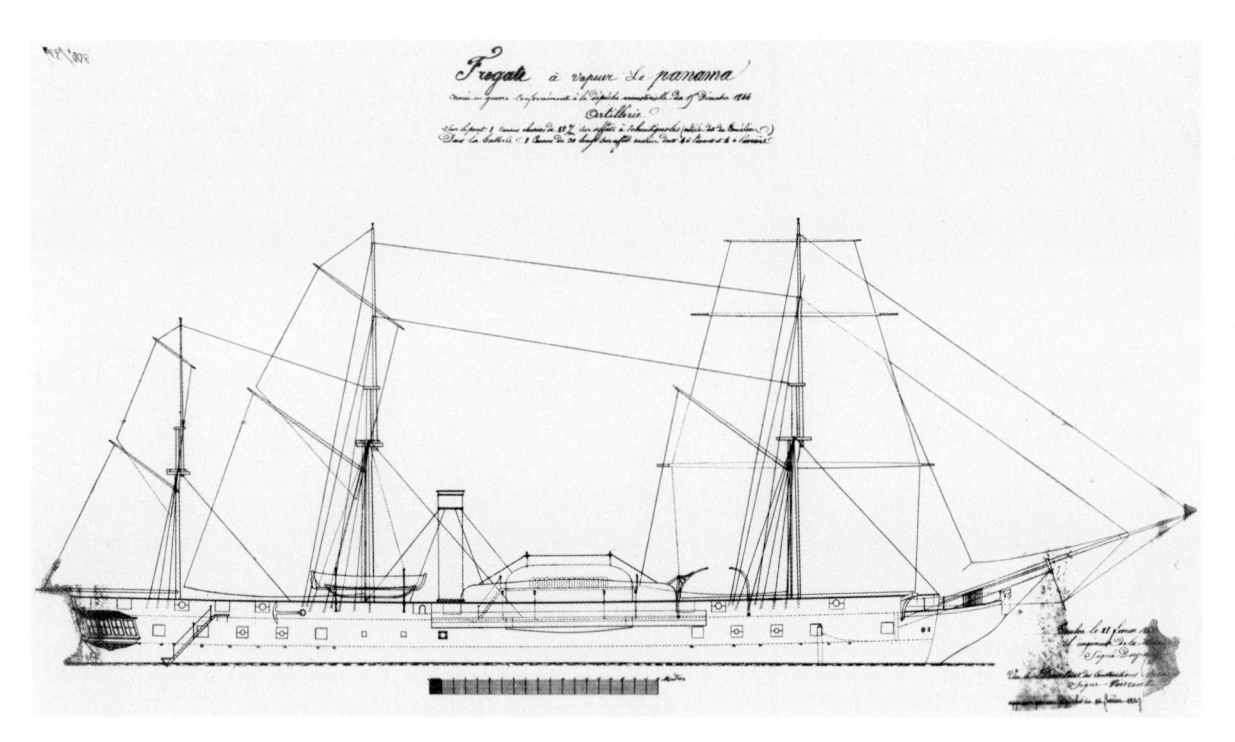

The barquentine sail plan of *Panama* as designed, dated Toulon 28 February 1847. According to a note on the plan, the ship was to carry eight 22cm shell guns on the weather deck on *affuts à echantignoles* (mountings with chocks instead of rear wheels to limit the recoil of the guns); the eight 30pdrs on the battery deck were disposed four forward and four aft. (Archives de la Marine, 8-DD1-24 no. 56)

Mercantile *Union* 12.5.1847, left Le Havre for New York 22.6.1847. Returned to Navy 12.4.1848, in reduced commission 6.5.1848. Struck 20.11.1871, hulk at Toulon. BU 1878.

Christophe Colomb (4) Brest Dyd/Cavé (Designer, Hippolyte Prétot; Constructeurs, Jean-Michel Segondat and others)

Ord: c8.1840. K: 26.5.1841. L: 15.3.1843. Comm: 21.3.1843. C: 4.1843.

Mercantile *Philadelphie* 12.5.1847, left Cherbourg for New York 15.7.1847. Returned to Navy 12.4.1848, comm. 1.6.1848. Struck 4.6.1868 at Toulon, school hulk for engineers. Ordered BU 15.6.1877, BU 1878 by M. Schmuck.

Group 2.

Magellan (5) Brest Dyd/Cavé (Designer, Louis-Just Moissard; Constructeur, Antoine Roger)

Ord: 20.8.1840. K: 26.5.1841. L: 15.5.1843. Comm: 16.1.1844. C: 3.1846.

Struck 9.5.1879 at Toulon, hulked, sold for BU 1884.

Caraïbe (6) Lorient Dyd/Schneider (Designer, Mathurin Boucher; Constructeur, Pierre Guieysse)

Ord: 20.8.1840. K: 1.10.1840. L: 2.12.1842. Comm: 21.9.1843. C: 20.4.1844.

Wrecked 11.1.1847 at Indiago near St. Louis, Senegal.

Cacique (7) Lorient Dyd/Indret (Designer, Boucher; Constructeur, Pierre Guieysse)

Ord: 20.8.1840. K: 2.12.1840. L: 9.9.1843. C: 10.1844. Comm: 21.12.1844.

Converted to sail transport at Rochefort 1-8.1865, transported female convicts to Cayenne, French Guiana, 9-10.1865, then became one of three prison hulks there. Sank suddenly 26.12.1868. Struck 31.5.1869.

Eldorado (8) Lorient Dyd/Indret (Designer, Pierre Félix Le Grix)

Ord: 20.8.1840. K: 10.5.1841. L: 7.12.1843. C: 1.1844. Comm: 1.1.1845.

Struck 20.11.1871 at Toulon, hulked. BU 1875.

Group 3.

Groenland (9) Rochefort Dyd/Hallette (Designer, Jean-Baptiste Hubert; Constructeur, Antoine Auriol)

Ord: c8.1840. K: 6.1841. L: 13.5.1843. Comm: 8.7.1843. C: 7.1844.

Wrecked 26.8.1844 in fog near Larache, Morocco. Wreck burned 27.8.1844.

Montézuma (10) Rochefort Dyd/Hallette (Designer, Hubert; Constructeur, Antoine Auriol)

Ord: 20.8.1840. K: 26.6.1841. L: 28.6.1843. Comm: 9.8.1843. C: 7.1844.

Grounded 17.7.1863 at the mouth of the Coatzacoalcos river in Mexico, abandoned and burned 27.7.1863.

Panama (11) Rochefort Dyd/Hallette (Designer, Gustave Garnier; Constructeurs, Garnier and Henri Denis de Senneville)

Ord: 20.8.1840. K: 26.8.1841. L: 21.11.1843. Comm: 1.4.1844. C: 11.1844.

Struck 20.11.1871, hulk at Toulon. Careening hulk 1874, barracks hulk 1875, target ship 7.1895 for a mortar installed on the torpedo-aviso *Dragonne*, sunk off Toulon 3.2.1897.

Albatros (12) Rochefort Dyd/Schneider (Designer, Garnier; Constructeurs, Garnier, Armand Forquenot, and Henri Denis de Senneville)

Ord: 20.8.1840. K: 3.12.1841. L: 15.7.1844. Comm: 25.10.1844. C: 3.1845.

Struck 9.5.1879 at Toulon, BU 1880. May have been used as a barge at Brest until 1891 under the name *Saint Mathieu*.

Labrador (13) Toulon Dyd/Schneider (Designer, Firmin-Isidore Joffre)

Ord: 20.8.1840. K: 1.1841. L: 7.8.1842. Comm: 1.1.1843. C: 4.1843.

Struck 20.11.1871 at Toulon. Storage hulk for artillery 1873, BU 1878.

Orénoque (14) Toulon Dyd/Schneider (Designer, Jean-Baptiste Pironneau)

Ord: 20.8.1840. K: 7.1841. L: 19.8.1843. Comm: 7.9.1843. C: 9.1843.

Struck 20.4.1878, storage hulk at Toulon. BU 1880.

PHOQUE Class – 220nhp paddle corvettes (later 2nd Class), converted

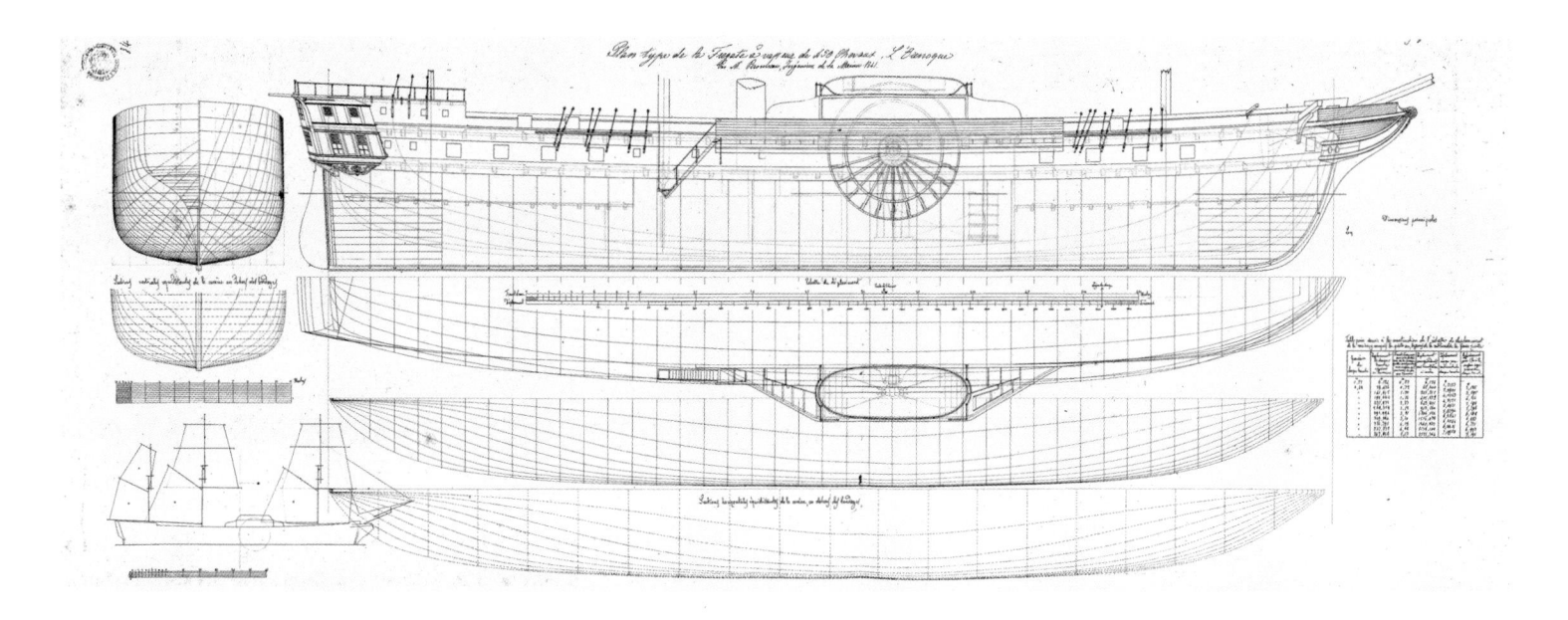

Official general arrangement plans of the paddle frigate *Orénoque*, dated 1841. Generally similar to *Panama*, the most obvious difference was the addition of a poop and with it a second set of stern galleries; this ship had a hybrid sail plan – a barque but without a square main course. (Atlas du Génie Maritime, Genoa collection, image 5-0033)

packets. This and the next class were ordered on 23 August 1840 as part of the 1840 packet program to provide branch lines in the New World in support of the transatlantic 450nhp packets. The engines of all four ships were ordered in contracts approved on 7 November 1840 by relatively small engine builders, two from Stehelin and Huber of Bitschwiller, Haut Rhin, and two from Antoine Pauwels at La Chapelle, Saint-Denis, near Paris. Stehelin copied Fawcett's engines for *Véloce*, while Pauwels copied engines of Miller & Ravenhill. Plans by Mathurin Boucher intended for all four ships and used for the first two were approved on 20 February 1841. All four ships were allocated to the navy permanently in July 1845 for use on the West Africa station. The beam over the paddle boxes was 15.80m. They originally had three masts with square sails on the foremast only and a sail area of 1,154 sq.m. *Phoque* was rerigged in 1850 as a brig with 1,820 sq.m. of sails. The increase was due to the fact that her new mainmast was further from the funnel and could carry a full set of square sails.

Dimensions & tons: 56.05m, 55.20m wl, 52.50m x 9.20m, 9.48m ext x 6.10m. 1,196 tons disp. Draught 4.00m mean. Men: 123 (est.).

Machinery: 220nhp, 8.88kts (*Phoque*), 9.06kts (*Espadon*). Side-lever, 2 cylinders (1.45m diameter, 1.50m stroke), 2 flue boilers. Coal 263 tons max.

Guns: 6 x 16cm shell.

Phoque (15) Indret/Stehelin (Constructeur, Paulin Masson)
Ord: 23.8.1840. K: 2.3.1841. L: 7.8.1842. Comm: 1.11.1842 and 7.4.1843. C: 4.1843.
Struck 28.9.1855 at Brest, mooring hulk at Rochefort 1856, renamed *Pingouin* c1859, BU 1878.

Espadon (16) Indret/Pauwels (Constructeurs, Amédée Laimant and others)
Ord: 23.8.1840. K: 2.3.1841. L: 4.10.1842. Comm: 1.4.1843. C: 3.1844.
Struck 16.12.1852 at Brest, last mentioned 1854. Her early demise was attributed to rapid construction and continuous use on foreign stations. Her engines were reused in the aviso *Ténare*.

ÉLAN Class – 220nhp paddle corvettes (later 2nd Class), converted packets. As in the case of the 450nhp packets, an attempt was made to lighten the designs of the 220nhp ships. Revised plans by Mathurin Boucher for the two ships which had not yet been begun were approved on 17 July 1841.

Dimensions & tons: 57.40m, 54.08m wl, 52.50m x 9.00m x 6.05m. 1,035 tons disp. Draught 3.85m mean. Men: 123 (est.).

Machinery: 220nhp, 8.8kts (*Élan*), 9.22kts (*Caïman*). Side-lever, 2 cylinders (1.45m diameter, 1.50m stroke), 2 flue boilers. Coal 240 tons.

Guns: 6 x 16cm shell.

Élan (17) Indret/Stehelin (Constructeur, Amédée Laimant)
Ord: 23.8.1840. K: 15.8.1841. L: 30.3.1843. Comm: 11.4.1843. C: 6.1843.
Struck 28.10.1851 at Rochefort. Her rapid demise was attributed to the use of bad timber in her construction. Her engine was reused in *Gassendi*.

Caïman (18) Indret/Pauwels (Constructeurs, Amédée Laimant and others)
Ord: 23.8.1840. K: 8.1841. L: 28.6.1843. Comm: 20.7.1843. C: 15.10.1843.
Grounded 1.4.1854 in poor visibility and lost 2.4.1854 near Aden.

TITAN – 220nhp paddle corvette, later 2nd Class. *Titan* appeared in the building program in late 1840 at Brest and was moved to Toulon in 1842. On 2 April 1842 the Minister decided that two of the three 220nhp steamers planned for construction in 1842 (*Titan*, *Cassini* and the screw *Chaptal*) would became experiments with new types of machinery. The engine builder François Cavé was an early advocate of direct-acting engines with oscillating cylinders, and he produced his own variations on a standard pattern developed by Penn in Britain. On 8 September 1842 the Minister approved two contracts with Cavé for two early examples of this type of machinery, paddle engines for *Titan* and identical ones for the iron-hulled *Chaptal* with minimal alterations to drive a screw propeller. The engine built for *Chaptal* was ultimately used to drive paddle wheels in *Newton*. On 2 April 1842 the Minister also decided to include special internal arrangements for use as a hospital ship, because a new ship was needed to replace converted steamers like the 160nhp *Cerbère* then supporting the army in Algeria. Mathurin Boucher modified the hull plans of *Archimède* for this purpose. His plans, approved on 2 July 1842, provided for rapid conversion back to an armed steamer. The beam over *Titan*'s paddle boxes was 15.79m.

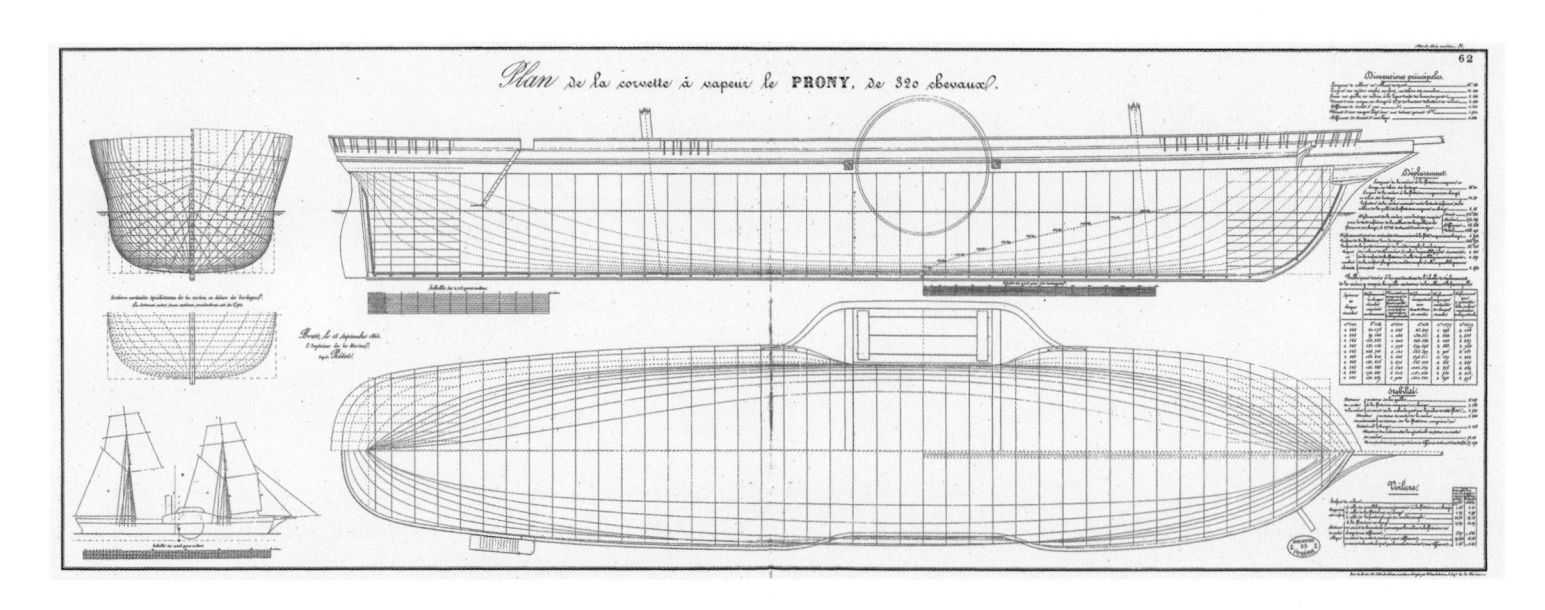

Titan was one of the first large French naval steamers designed with only two masts. This rig was proposed on 6 July 1843 to avoid problems in fitting her engines, but by this time the navy was also dissatisfied with the three-masted rig of its steamers because the sails on the mizzen mast had proven to be practically useless and the mainmast could not carry square sails because of its proximity to the funnel. The French were also influenced by the fact that nearly all British steamers in the 220-320nhp range had two masts.

    Dimensions & tons: 53.87m, 53.20m wl x 9.30m, 9.45m ext x 6.00m. 1,049 tons disp. Draught 3.77/3.93m. Men: 123.
    Machinery: 220nhp, 9kts. Oscillating, 2 cylinders. Coal 175 tons.
    Guns: 4 x 16cm shell.

Titan Toulon Dyd/Cavé (Constructeur, Stanislas-Charles-Henri Dupuy de Lôme)
    Ord: 6.4.1842. K: 11.10.1842. L: 19.3.1844. Comm: 1.6.1844. C: 6.1844.
    Struck 4.5.1868, coal hulk at Lorient and later a hulk there. Sold for BU 1896.

CASSINI – 220nhp paddle corvette, later 2nd Class. *Cassini* appeared in the building program in late 1839 as a 320nhp steamer at Toulon and was changed in the following year to a 220nhp steamer at Lorient. She became one of three 220nhp steamers planned for construction in 1842, and engines identical to those of *Archimède* were ordered for her from Schneider by a contract approved on 25 May 1842. Hull plans by Pierre Félix Le Grix, who modified the plans of *Archimède* for the new ship, were approved on 3 December 1842. *Cassini* was built with conventional side-lever engines for comparison with the direct-acting machinery installed in her contemporary, *Titan*. On 12 January 1855 *Cassini* was ordered converted into a steam mortar vessel. She received 2 mortars and 2 smoothbores and served at the bombardment of the forts at Kinburn with *Vautour*, *Sésostris*, and *Ténare*.

    Dimensions & tons: 54.00m wl x 9.40m, 9.60m ext x 6.20m. 1,175 tons disp. Draught 4.35m mean. Men: 123.
    Machinery: 220nhp, 440ihp, 10.80kts. Side-lever.
    Guns: 2 x 22cm No.2 shell, 2 x 30pdrs No.1.

Official lines plan of the paddle corvette *Prony*, dated Brest 15 September 1844. This corvette was rigged as a brig, with a total sail area of 977 sq.m. (Atlas du Génie Maritime, French collection, plate 62)

Cassini Lorient Dyd/Schneider (Constructeurs, Alexandre Auguste Robiou de Lavrignais and Louis Corrard)
    Ord: 21.7.1841. K: 10.4.1843. L: 22.4.1845. Comm: 1.5.1845. C: 10.1845.
    Struck 9.11.1863, storage hulk at Toulon. BU 1869.

The 1844 budget (produced in late 1842) contained a new paddle frigate program of one ship of 540nhp (*Tamerlan* at Rochefort) and four of 450nhp (*Roland* and *Godefroi* at Lorient and *Coligny* and *Catinat* at Rochefort). Following the transfer of some of the 450nhp packets to the navy only two of these (*Tamerlan* and *Godefroi*, now both of 540nhp) remained in the 1845 budget (produced in late 1843), the other names being reused for smaller ships. *Tamerlan* and *Godefroi* increased in power to 700 to 800nhp during 1844 but they were deferred on 28 November 1844 and did not appear in the 1846 budget (produced at the end of 1844). No further paddle frigates were ordered by the French except *Caffarelli*, a 320nhp corvette altered to use the last 450nhp engine left over from the two packet programs of the early 1840s.

CAFFARELLI – 450nhp paddle frigate. *Platon* (later *Caffarelli*) appeared in the building program in late 1842 as a 220nhp steamer and by late 1843 had become a 320nhp ship to be begun in 1845. On 28 November 1844 the Minister decided to put one of the engines built at Indret for the packet program (the one originally allocated to *Mogador* ex *Monge*) into a hull significantly lighter than the *Gomer* group. *Platon*, scheduled to be laid down at Brest in 1845, was selected and upgraded to 450nhp on 9 December 1844. This was possible because of the recent development of tubular boilers, which were smaller than their predecessors and of which hers were among the first built by the French Navy. On 24 February 1845 the Minister of Marine renounced the further use of flue boilers in new ships, noting that tubular boilers had proven their superiority, though flue boilers already under construction were to be completed. In contrast with the larger ships, the new one was to carry only eight guns and have a light rig of two masts. Alexandre Chedeville's plans were approved and the ship was ordered on 10 April 1845. A miscalculation was made during the design process and her beam had to be augmented 80cm by additional planking (adding 110 tons to her displacement) to correct stability problems. She was briefly rated as a 400nhp corvette around 1848-49.

Dimensions & tons (after modification): 66.70m, 64.00m wl, 58.55m x 10.70m, 11.80m ext x 6.15m. 2,000 tons disp. Draught 4.98m mean. Men: 267.

Machinery: 450nhp, 11.3kts. Side-lever, 4 tubular boilers (5 furnaces each). Coal 325 tons.

Guns: (1850) UD 4 x 22cm shell, 2 x 30pdrs No.1; SD 2 x 30pdrs No.1.

Caffarelli (ex *Platon* 11.11.1846) Brest Dyd/Indret (Constructeur, Chedeville)

Ord: 10.4.1845. K: 17.4.1845. L: 29.5.1847. Comm: 16.1.1848. C: 2.1848.

Struck 7.3.1867, mooring hulk at Rochefort. BU 1883.

PRONY – 320nhp paddle 1st Class corvette. *Socrate* (later *Prony*) appeared in the building program in late 1842 as a 220nhp steamer and by late 1843 had become a 320nhp ship to be begun in 1844. Plans by Hippolyte Prétot were approved on 9 December 1844 for this ship, which was now to be begun during 1845. Her engines were of the double traverse type with articulated guides, which combined some of the improvements of direct-acting engines with a connecting mechanism resembling the traditional side-lever. This ship, the smaller *Anacréon* and possibly *Dauphin* appear to have been the only French naval ships with this type of machinery: both did well on trials, but the machinery was almost as large and heavy as traditional side-lever engines. The beam outside her paddle boxes was 17.02m. She had two masts.

Dimensions & tons: 60.80m, 58.00m wl, 53.70m x 10.00m, 10.16m ext x 6.61m. 1,365 tons disp. Draught 3.85/4.15m. Men: 136.

Machinery: 320nhp, 853ihp, 12.2kts. Direct-acting, double traverse, tubular boilers.

Guns: (1849) 3 x 22cm shell, 2 x 16cm shell; (1851) 3-16cm shell, 2-30pdrs No.2.

Prony (ex *Socrate* 11.11.1846) Brest Dyd/Indret (Constructeurs, Paul Leroux and others)

Ord: 9.12.1844. K: 2.1.1845. L: 23.9.1847. Comm: 16.2.1849. C: 3.1849.

Wrecked 5.11.1861 in Ocracoke Inlet near Cape Hatteras in a storm.

COLBERT – 320nhp paddle 1st Class corvette. *Colbert* appeared in the building program in late 1842 as a 220nhp steamer and proposals were made to order 220nhp engines for her in November 1842 from Pauwels at Paris and February 1843 from Cherbourg. By late 1843 she had become a 320nhp ship to be begun in 1844. On 28 February 1844 Jean-Baptiste Pironneau completed two sets of plans for a steam corvette, one with paddle wheels and one with a screw propeller. The Minister approved the paddle plans on 9 December 1844 for *Roland* and *Colbert*, both of which were now to be begun during 1845. In the meantime the Minister had asked Indret on 13 May 1844 to prepare plans for 320nhp engines similar to the British engines in *Cuvier*, and Jean-Baptiste Lamaëstre responded with two designs, one for standard side-lever engines on Fawcett's pattern and one imitating Seaward's *Cyclops*. On 28 February 1845 the Minister selected the Fawcett design. *Roland* was later reprogrammed as a screw corvette but *Colbert* was built to the paddle plans. The designed armament was 2 x 22cm No.1 shell, 4 x 30pdrs No.1. The ship consumed a large amount of coal, 40 tons per day at full power, and her small sail rig gave her only 5.7kts with wind astern. The beam over her paddle boxes was 17.16m. She had two masts.

Dimensions & tons: 61.05m, 57.70m wl x 10.20m, 10.35m ext x 6.85m. 1,294 tons (later 1,566 tons) disp. Draught 4.22m mean (later 4.53/4.71m). Men: 136.

Machinery: 320nhp, 8 to 9kts in service. Side-lever, 4 tubular boilers. Coal 275 tons.

Guns: (1849) 2 x 22cm No.1 shell, 6 x 16cm shell.

Colbert Cherbourg Dyd/Indret (Constructeurs, Émile Dorian and Achille Guesnet)

Ord: 9.12.1844. K: 5.6.1845. L: 5.5.1848. Comm: 1.7.1849. C: 7.1849.

Struck 15.4.1867 at Rochefort, BU 1867.

NEWTON – 220nhp paddle 2nd Class corvette, iron hull. *Newton* appeared in the building program in late 1842 as a 220nhp steamer and by late 1843 had become a 320nhp ship to be begun in 1844. On 5 December 1844 the Minister of Marine decided to begin this ship in 1845 and give her the 220nhp engines that had been ordered on 8 September 1842 for the screw corvette *Chaptal* but found unsuitable during extensive experiments in 1843. Hull plans by Louis-Just Moissard, a naval engineer who specialised in designing post office packets, were approved on 17 January 1845. The use of an iron hull resulted in a substantial saving in weight compared to earlier 220nhp ships. The beam over her paddle boxes was 15.60m.

Dimensions & tons: 57.95m, 54.20m wl x 8.96m ext x 5.67m. 924 tons disp. Draught 3.48/3.48m. Men: 123.

Machinery: 220nhp. Oscillating, tubular boilers. Coal 190 tons.

Guns: (1856) 6 x 16cm shell.

Newton Cherbourg Dyd/Cavé.

Ord: 21.2.1845. K: 3.11.1845. L: 14.10.1848. Comm: 1.9.1849. C: 9.1849.

Wrecked 10.6.1857 at Port-au-Choix, Newfoundland.

CATINAT – 400nhp paddle 1st Class corvette. *Catinat* appeared in the building program in late 1842 as a 450nhp steamer and by late 1843 had become a 320nhp ship to be begun in 1844. Hull plans for her were approved on 13 February 1845 after her designer, Joseph Cros, reduced her tonnage to 1,331 tons from the 1,619 tons in his initial design. The plans were otherwise similar to those that had recently been approved for *Prony* and *Colbert*. In mid-1846 the navy decided to exploit new engine technology to raise her horsepower from 320nhp to 400nhp without increasing her size. Unfortunately, when the engines were ordered from Schneider by a contract approved on 11 September 1848, the navy supplied the original 1,619-ton plans, and the engines were designed too large for the ship. When the error was discovered on 26 December 1848, the Schneider engines were reassigned to *Berthollet* (below) and the engines proposed for that ship were designed to fit in *Catinat*. Those engines were designed by Joseph Cros and built at Rochefort by Victorin Sabattier. The beam of *Catinat* over her paddle boxes was 17.50m. She had two masts.

Dimensions & tons: 59.60m, 57.00m wl, 54.40m x 10.24m ext x 7.00m. 1,440 tons disp. Draught 4.65m mean. Men: 163.

Machinery: 400nhp, 10.8kts. Oscillating, 4 tubular boilers. Coal 306 tons max.

Guns: 2 x 30pdrs No.1, 4 x 16cm shell.

Catinat Rochefort Dyd/Rochefort (Constructeurs, Jean De Robert, Victorin Sabattier, and Antoine Auriol)

Ord: 28.8.1843. K: 15.3.1845. L: 11.10.1851. C: 8.1852. Comm: 10.10.1852.

In 12.1872 became annex to the transport *Messager*, the torpedo school at Rochefort. Moved to Lorient 1875 and then to Gabon. Struck 11.5.1880, storage hulk at Gabon, BU 3.1885.

COLIGNY – 300nhp paddle 2nd Class corvette, iron hull. *Coligny* appeared in the building program in late 1842 as a 450nhp steamer to be begun in 1844, but on 7 August 1843 side-lever engines of 220nhp like those in *Véloce* were ordered from Rochefort to give that yard experience in engine building and these engines were eventually assigned to *Coligny*. Plans by Jean-Baptiste Hubert for *Coligny* were approved on 1 September 1845. On 3 July 1846 Rochefort reported that the 220nhp engines were almost completed, but the navy felt it unwise to put these older type engines in a ship for which high speed was the main objective and instead opted to use the latest technology to increase the horsepower of *Coligny* to 300nhp and to put the 220nhp engines into a tug, which was later built under the name *Laborieux*. The 300nhp engines of *Coligny* were built at Rochefort by Victorin Sabattier to plans that were approved by the Council of Works on 25 November 1846. The ship was brig-rigged.

    Dimensions & tons: 54.90m, 52.48m wl, 48.55m x 9.02m ext x 6.10m. 1,032 tons disp. Draught 3.76/4.28m. Men: 128.
    Machinery: 300nhp, 10.43kts. Direct-acting, 4 tubular boilers. Coal 215 tons.
    Guns: (1856) 4 x 16cm shell.

Coligny Rochefort Dyd/Rochefort (Constructeurs, Antoine Auriol, Henri De Lisleferme, Jean De Robert, and Victorin Sabattier)
    Ord: 30.6.1845. K: 27.11.1845. L: 5.11.1850. Comm: 7.4.1851. C: 4.1851.
    Struck 19.11.1888 at Cherbourg, BU 1889.

On 29 May 1845 France signed a treaty with Britain committing each country to maintain 26 ships, including a substantial number of steamers, on the West Africa station to eradicate the slave trade. The navy did not have enough steamers to fulfill this obligation, and eight new ones were built under a special law of 19 July 1845. These ships all had iron hulls and were all built by contract to encourage the development of the French steam engine and shipbuilding industries. They included two paddle corvettes of 300nhp (*Euménide* and *Gorgone*), four paddle avisos of 200nhp (the *Mouette* group), and two screw 'corvettes-mixtes' (*Biche* and *Sentinelle*). Six sailing brig-avisos of the *Zéphyr* group and possibly two 800-ton transports of the *Durance* class were also built for the same purpose.

EUMÉNIDE – 300nhp paddle 2nd Class corvette, iron hull. This ship and her half sister *Gorgone* were the largest of the eight ships built to combat the slave trade under the special law of 19 July 1845. Plans by Stanislas-Charles-Henri Dupuy de Lôme were approved for *Euménide* on 9 January 1846. The designed armament was 2 x 30pdrs No.1, 4 x 16cm shell. The hull was ordered from Chaigneau & Bichon at Bordeaux by a contract approved on 15 May 1846 and the engines were ordered from Hallette by a contract approved on 31 August 1846. Hallette was one of the navy's earliest major French suppliers of steam machinery and followed the successful pattern of Penn in designing his direct-acting engines. His firm went bankrupt while building the engines, however, and machinery trials in October 1849 were a failure, giving only 247nhp and 8 knots. The firm was penalised for imperfections in the machinery and failure of the boilers to produce enough steam. The ship remained idle at Rochefort, where in April 1853 the machinery was modified and repaired with good results. She left Rochefort for the first time in 1854. A poop was added before 1867. She had two funnels and two masts. The beam over her paddle boxes was 16.18m.

    Dimensions & tons: 59.74m, 56.00m wl, 52.65m x9.30m, 9.32m ext x 5.55m. 936 tons disp. Draught 2.84/3.36m. Men: 128.
    Machinery: 300nhp, 8kts. Oscillating, 2 cylinders, 4 tubular boilers. Coal 140 tons (238 max).
    Guns: (1854) 4 x 16cm shell.

Euménide Chaigneau & Bichon, Bordeaux-Lormont/Hallette (Constructeur, Nicolas Courtin)
    Ord: 15.5.1846 (contract). K: 1.10.1846. L: 23.3.1848. C: 3.1849. Comm: 24.5.1849.
    Struck 2.2.1887, mooring hulk at Lorient. Sold for BU 1907.

GORGONE – 300nhp paddle 2nd Class corvette, iron hull. This ship was built under the same program as her half sister *Euménide*. Plans by Charles Sochet were approved for her on 9 January 1846. The hull was ordered on 15 May 1846 with that of *Euménide* and the engines were ordered from Louis Benet of La Ciotat by a contract approved on 21 September 1846. On 14 February 1847, however, Benet informed the navy that his British engineer, John Barnes, had not yet started to draw the plans for the engines, and as Benet did not know when the delay would end he asked that the contract be cancelled. The Minister approved the cancellation on 9 March 1847 and decided to reorder the engines from Hallette in an effort to help that struggling firm stay in business. A copy of the machinery of *Euménide* was ordered from him by a contract approved on 8 June 1847. The rescue effort failed, however, and the machinery suffered from the same problems as that of *Euménide* and developed only 240nhp on initial trials. It was fixed at Rochefort in May and June 1853, and the ship saw her first active service in 1854. She had two funnels and was schooner-rigged on two masts.

    Dimensions & tons: 63.78m, 60.00m wl, 56.25m x 9.50m, 9.52m ext x 5.45m. 990 tons disp. Draught 3.22m mean. Men: 128.
    Machinery: 300nhp, 8kts. Oscillating, 2 cylinders, 4 tubular boilers. Coal 175 tons.
    Guns: (1848) 4 x 16cm shell.

Gorgone Chaigneau & Bichon, Bordeaux-Lormont/Hallette (Constructeur, Nicolas Courtin)
    Ord: 15.5.1846 (contract). K: 1.10.1846. L: 14.8.1848. Comm: 16.10.1849. C: 1.1851.
    Wrecked 19.12.1869 on the Black Rocks at Brest, all 93 hands lost.

LABORIEUX – 220nhp paddle 2nd Class corvette. This ship was built to use 220nhp engines ordered for *Coligny* in 1843. These engines were designed by Joseph Cros and built at Rochefort by Victorin Sabattier. *Laborieux* was classified as a corvette but was designed and used as a tug in the vicinity of Rochefort. Her hull, designed by Henri Denis de Senneville, was originally to have been iron but was changed to wood at Rochefort's request. The plans were approved on 24 May 1847.

    Dimensions & tons: 48.40m, 45.00m wl, 41.00m x 8.35m, 8.50m ext x 6.12m. 849 tons disp. Draught 3.85/4.17m. Men: 123.
    Machinery: 220nhp, 11kts. Side-lever engine, one tubular boiler. Coal 120 tons max.
    Guns: (1853) 2 carronades.

Laborieux Rochefort Dyd/Rochefort (Constructeur, Denis de Senneville)
    Ord: 1.6.1847. K: 6.1847. L: 29.7.1848. Comm: 3.5.1849. C: 5.1849.
    Provided towing services between Rochefort and Brest, replaced the sail brig-aviso *Alcyone* as station ship at Ile d'Aix 1853, served in the Baltic 1854. Struck 5.12.1861 at Rochefort, mooring hulk 1865, BU 1879.

SOUFFLEUR – 220nhp paddle 2nd Class corvette, iron hull. This ship was built to use a 220nhp engine ordered at Indret for *Éclaireur* in 1843. She was classified as a corvette but was designed as a tug for use in the vicinity of Brest. It was originally planned to build her at Brest but was reassigned to Indret on 30 December 1846 in exchange for the wooden-hulled corvette *Tanger*. Plans by Victor Charles Gervaize drafted at Brest

The iron-hulled *Souffleur* serving as a tug at Brest in the 1870s or early 1880s. Although officially listed as a corvette, the ship was only ever intended for employment as a tug. (Marius Bar)

were approved on 25 January 1847. She had two masts. Hers was the last hull to be built at Indret, which thereafter only built steam machinery.
    Dimensions & tons: 49.20m, 46.00m wl x 8.32m x 4.80m. 700 tons disp. Draught 3.36/3.40m. Men: 123.
    Machinery: 220nhp, 12kts. Side-lever. 2 boilers. Coal 150 tons.
    Guns: (1856) 2 x 12pdr carronades.
Souffleur Indret/Indret.
    Ord: 25.1.1847. K: 6.1847. L: 17.9.1849. Comm: 22.2.1850. C: 7.1850.
    Replaced *Robuste* (service craft) as tug at Brest 1850. Served in the Baltic 1854. Struck 12.7.1887 at Brest, coal hulk. BU 1900.

TANGER Class – 300nhp paddle 2nd Class corvettes. These two ships appeared in the building program in late 1844 as 220nhp steamers to be begun in 1846, *Tanger* at Indret and *Tisiphone* at Lorient. They were planned with iron hulls, but unfavorable artillery experiments against iron hulls in both Britain and France and problems with fouling in French ships caused the French to revert around December 1846 to wooden hulls for combatant ships. As a result of this decision the wood-hulled *Tanger* was reassigned to Brest on 30 December 1846 while the iron-hulled *Souffleur* and a 100nhp iron aviso that was not built moved from Brest to Indret. The engines of both corvettes were built on plans drafted at Indret and approved on 22 June 1846 using Penn's pattern of oscillating cylinders. Hull plans by Victor Gervaize were approved for *Tanger* on 5 July 1847 and applied to *Tisiphone* on 17 September 1847. The sail area of *Tanger* was 882 sq.m. on two masts.
    Dimensions & tons: 56.20m, 55.00m wl, 51.65m x 9.28m, 9.45m ext x 6.09m. 1,119 tons disp. Draught 3.80m mean. Men: 128.
    Machinery: 300nhp, 10.5kts (*Tanger*), 10.32kts (*Tisiphone*). Oscillating, 4 tubular boilers. Coal 220 tons max.
    Guns: 4 x 16cm shell (*Tanger*).
Tanger Brest Dyd/Indret (Constructeur, Gervaize)
    Ord: 5.7.1847. K: 6.8.1847. L: 26.3.1849. Comm: 6.6.1850. C: 7.1850.
    Struck 29.12.1874, depot and barracks hulk at Toulon. BU 1889.
Tisiphone Lorient Dyd/Lorient (Constructeurs, Louis De Bussy, Charles Duchalard, and Louis Lecointre)
    Ord: 17.9.1847. K: 9.11.1847. L: 27.8.1851. Comm: 21.4.1854. C: 4.1854.
    Struck 22.7.1872, hulk at Brest. BU 1875.

A large steamer named *Monge* was projected to be begun at Lorient in the 1847 budget (prepared in December 1845) and was moved to Toulon as a 600nhp steam frigate in the 1848 budget (January 1847). She was reduced to a 1st Class paddle corvette of 400nhp at Toulon in the 1849 budget (December 1847) and disappeared from the building program in the 1850 budget (August 1849).

BERTHOLLET – 400nhp paddle 1st Class corvette. *Berthollet* appeared in the building program in late 1847 as a 400nhp 1st Class corvette to be begun at Rochefort during 1849. Had it not been for the mistake over the engines of *Catinat* (q.v.), this ship might have been a screw corvette. When Victorin Sabattier at Rochefort was ordered on 4 September 1848 to design a new corvette, he drew plans for a 1,900-ton 10-knot quarterdecked corvette similar to *Infernal* but with a screw. On 6 December 1848 he was asked to produce plans for a 1,400-ton 11-knot flush-deck screw corvette similar to *Phlégéton*. On 26 December 1848 *Berthollet* was assigned *Catinat*'s paddle engines, which had been ordered from Schneider by a contract approved on 11 September 1848, and new hull plans to accommodate these engines were drawn by Armand Forquenot and approved on 13 June 1849. *Berthollet*'s beam over her paddle boxes was 17.64m.

> Dimensions & tons: 61.30m, 58.00m wl, 53.10m x 10.40m, 10.60m ext x 6.92m. 1,509 tons disp. Draught 4.54m mean. Men: 163.
> Machinery: 400nhp, 1,046ihp, 10.90kts. Direct-acting, 4 tubular boilers. Coal 319 tons max.
> Guns: 2 x 30pdrs No.1, 4 x 16cm shell.

Berthollet Rochefort Dyd/Schneider (Constructeurs, Henri Denis de Senneville and Joseph Dreppe)
> Ord: 13.6.1849. K: 7.1849. L: 7.7.1850. Comm: 1.11.1850. C: 5.1851.
> Struck 15.3.1866 at Rochefort, BU 1866.

Larger paddle avisos

COMTE D'EU (VEDETTE) – 120nhp steam vessel, later paddle 2nd Class aviso. This ship was designed by Victor Gervaize as a yacht for the use of the King during his summers at Eu. Her four-cylinder engines, designed by Pierre Jean-Baptiste Rossin, were similar in design to those in the frigate *Infernal*. They were installed in July 1842. In her trials in August and October 1842 her maximum speed was around 7 knots (attributed to insufficient steam from the original flue boilers) and her stability was found to be not completely satisfactory. She was decommissioned at Indret, her royal furnishings were removed, and she was renamed *Vedette* on 1 April 1844. In February 1845 her original boilers were replaced with new tubular boilers by Penn (among the first in the French Navy) for service as an aviso.

> Dimensions & tons: 47.70m, 44.10m wl, 41.73m x 6.50m. 6.80m ext x 4.65m. 375 tons disp. Draught 2.65m. Men: 64.
> Machinery: 120nhp. 4 cylinders, 2 tubular boilers. Coal 60 tons.
> Guns: 4 x 12pdr carronades.

Comte d'Eu Indret/Indret (Constructeur, Gervaize)
> Ord: 30.10.1841. K: 11.1841. L: 22.6.1842. Comm: 11.10.1843. C: 10.1843.
> Renamed *Vedette* 1.4.1844. Struck 2.7.1856 at Toulon.

BRANDON – 160nhp steam vessel, later paddle 1st Class aviso. This ship was added to the building program on 27 July 1842 to replace the first *Brandon*, lost in December 1841 and was ordered on 6 August 1842 for construction in 1843. Plans by Frédéric Reech for her hull were approved on 15 June 1843 and approval of his machinery plans followed on 27 June 1843. The order for the engines went to the maintenance facility at Lorient, which had over time developed the capability to build new engines and needed work. Reech advocated different proportions between engines and boilers that did other engineers, and he gave the ship boilers for 160nhp and cylinders for 220nhp. The capacity of her hold was enlarged somewhat compared to the *Sphinx* class to accommodate the engines. Tubular boilers were ordered for her from Mazeline by a contract approved on 11 May 1846 and she ran trials on 16 June 1847.

> Dimensions & tons: 50.00m wl x 8.50m ext x 5.47m. 752 tons disp. Draught 3.81m mean. Men: 100.
> Machinery: 160nhp, 10kts. Side-lever, 2 tubular boilers.
> Guns: 4 x 16cm shell.

Brandon (2) Lorient Dyd/Lorient (Constructeurs, Frédéric Reech and Louis Alexandre Corrard)
> Ord: 6.8.1842. K: 26.1.1844. L: 11.4.1846. Comm: 11.11.1846. C: 7.1847.
> Struck 15.7.1867 at Lorient, BU 1867.

SOLON – 160nhp steam vessel, later paddle 1st Class aviso, iron hull. This ship appeared in the building program in late 1842 to be begun in 1844. Engines were ordered for her from Indret on 15 September 1843, but hull plans by Henri De Lisleferme were approved only on 9 December 1844. On 28 November 1844 the Minister of Marine had decided to give her engines of 260nhp with oscillating cylinders to be purchased from Penn at Greenwich, England, but this did not occur. The beam over *Solon*'s paddle boxes was 13.46m.

> Dimensions & tons: 51.37m, 48.00m wl x 7.92m ext x 5.32m. 565 tons disp. Draught 2.84/3.16m. Men: 78.
> Machinery: 160nhp. Side-lever, 2 tubular boilers.
> Guns: 2 x 12cm bronze shell.

Solon Indret/Indret (Constructeurs, Jean-Baptiste Lamaëstre and Victorin Sabattier)
> Ord: 11.9.1843 and 13.5.1844. K: 10.5.1845. L: 8.8.1846. Comm: 7.12.1846. C: 12.1846.
> Struck 22.3.1867, coal hulk at Rochefort. BU 1879.

ANACRÉON – 100nhp steam vessel, later paddle 2nd Class aviso, iron hull. A 60nhp paddle steamer named *Anacréon* appeared in the building program in late 1842 to be begun at Indret in 1844. By late 1843 she had become an 80nhp ship to be begun in 1845. By February 1845 she had been renamed *Passe Partout*, and as such she was designed by Firmin Joffre to fulfill the mission as royal yacht for which *Vedette*, ex *Comte d'Eu*, had been designed and which *Var* was then fulfilling. (The name, chosen by the King, referred to her ability to 'go anywhere', specifically the port of Tréport, near Eu, which required a draught under 2 metres.) On 1 September 1845 the King noted with approval the 13-knot speed of HMS *Fairy*, a tender for the British royal family which was one of the

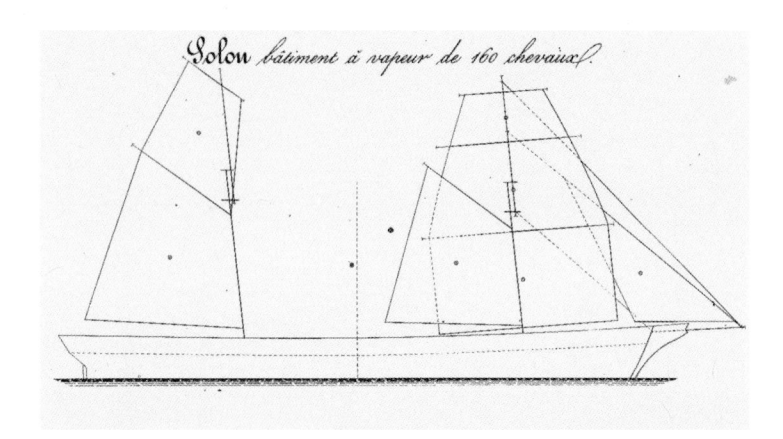

Official brigantine sail plan of the paddle aviso Solon. Total sail area was 607 sq.m. (Atlas du Génie Maritime, Genoa collection, image 2-0040)

earliest screw steamers. The navy lost no time examining the possibility of substituting a screw for the paddle wheels in *Passe Partout*, but on 4 October 1845 decided to build an entirely new ship for the screw. The paddle steamer reverted to the name *Anacréon* and was completed as an aviso after the delivery of the screw *Passe Partout*. She had the same type engines as the corvette *Prony* (their installation was completed in March 1847). The beam outside her paddles was 11.04m.

Dimensions & tons: 42.65m, 40.00m wl x 6.26m x 3.30m. 297 tons (originally 236 tons) disp. Draught 2.08/2.28m. Men: 64.

Machinery: 100nhp, 254ihp, 9.75kts. Direct-acting, double traverse, 2 tubular boilers.

Guns: (1847) 8 swivels.

Anacréon (ex *Passe Partout* ex *Anacréon*) Indret/Indret (Constructeurs, Jean-Baptiste Lamaëstre and Victorin Sabattier).

Ord: 11.9.1843 and 13.5.1844. K: 17.6.1845. L: 2.11.1846. Comm: 22.11.1846. C: 3.1847.

Struck 3.11.1859 at Lorient, BU 1860.

NARVAL Class – 160nhp steam vessels, later paddle 1st Class avisos, iron hulls. On 17 January 1843 the Minister of Marine decided to build an iron-hulled 160nhp steamer to provide communications with and around the Marquesas Islands, which the French had just occupied. She was to replace *Phaéton*, sent there in 1843. On 24 January 1843 the Minister decided to negotiate a contract for the ship and her engines with Louis Benet, who had submitted plans for an iron-hulled version of the postal packets *Périclès* and *Télémaque*, designed by Louis-Just Moissard. By April 1843 a second ship had been added to the program because of recent events at Tahiti. The hull and engines of *Narval* were ordered from Benet of La Ciotat by a contract approved on 26 May 1843. The hull was to follow Benet's *Périclès* plans and the engines were to be exactly as those of *Périclès*. In approving this contract the Minister decided to contract for the second ship on the same conditions with a Bordeaux shipbuilder and with François and Adolphe Mazeline frères of Le Havre, a firm that soon became one of France's leading engine builders. The hull of *Australie* was duly ordered from Chaigneau & Bichon by a contract approved on 29 May 1843 and the engines were ordered from Mazeline by a contract signed on 1 June 1843. The two ships were named on 1 June 1843 and were funded by a special law of 23 July 1843. Moissard drew the plans for the new class to specifications by Stanislas-Charles-Henri Dupuy de Lôme. They were brig-rigged.

Dimensions & tons: 51.45m, 48.80m wl, 45.01m x 7.92m, 8.00m ext x 5.11m. 699 tons disp. Draught 3.06m mean. Men: 78.

Machinery: 160nhp, 9.3kts (*Narval*), 8.8kts (*Australie*). Side-lever, 2 cylinders, flue boiler with 3 compartments. Coal 120 tons max.

Guns: 4 x 16cm shell.

Narval Louis Benet, La Ciotat/Benet

Ord: 26.5.1843 (contract). K: 5.1843. L: 29.9.1844. Comm: 1.12.1844. C: 12.1844.

Struck 24.6.1875 at Toulon, BU 1877.

Australie Chaigneau & Bichon, Bordeaux-Lormont/Mazeline

Ord: 29.5.1843 (contract). K: 20.6.1843. L: 17.8.1844. Comm: 12.12.1844. C: 12.1844.

Struck 15.4.1867, coal hulk at Rochefort. BU 1876.

DAUPHIN Class – 180nhp paddle 1st Class avisos, iron hulls. *Dauphin* was one of three 180nhp ships whose construction was directed on 1 July 1844 using resources made available by curtailing the construction of sailing transports (corvettes de charge and gabarres). Her hull was ordered from Auguste Guibert at Nantes by a contract approved on 6 November 1844, and her engines were ordered from Vincent Gâche aîné & Jean-Simon Voruz aîné at Nantes by a contract approved on 20 October 1845. *Épervier* was added to the program on 22 January 1846 to keep her builder's yard occupied. Her hull was ordered from Guibert by a contract approved on 24 April 1846 and her engines were ordered from Jean-Alexandre Baboneau at Nantes by a contract approved on 10 November 1846. These two ships were designed by Alexandre Robiou de Lavrignais. They represented an effort to bring the latest technology to the 160nhp type: iron hulls, tubular boilers, and direct-acting engines all helped increase the engine power while reducing the size of the ship. The coal supply and armament were also reduced, the latter because the 160-180nhp type was now considered strictly an aviso, not a fighting ship. The designed rig was two light masts. In the engines of *Dauphin*, direct action was achieved through the use of articulated guides on the system of Oliver Evans rather than fixed guides, while *Épervier*'s engines used Penn's system of oscillating cylinders. Both patterns were subsequently used in numerous French Navy steamers, even though *Épervier* only developed 160nhp on trials.

Dimensions & tons: 49.23m, 46.00m wl, 42.66m x 7.61m x 4.95m. 502 tons disp. Draught 2.95m mean. Men: 93.

Machinery: *Dauphin*: 180nhp, 9.00kts. Direct-acting, 2 tubular boilers. *Épervier*: 180nhp, 9.50kts. Oscillating, 2 tubular boilers. Coal 100 tons.

Guns: 2 x 18pdr carronades (2 x 12cm bronze shell in *Épervier*).

Dauphin Auguste Guibert, Nantes/Gâche & Voruz, Nantes

Ord: 9.11.1844. K: 7.5.1845. L: 23.6.1846. Comm: 27.5.1847. C: 6.1847.

Struck 16.3.1868 at Cherbourg, BU 1868.

Épervier Auguste Guibert, Nantes/Baboneau, Nantes

Ord: 24.4.1846 (contract). K: 13.5.1846. L: 19.6.1847. Comm: 20.3.1848. C: 5.1848.

Wrecked 15.4.1857 at Capbreton (near Bayonne) because of a leak.

PÉTREL – 180nhp paddle 1st Class aviso, iron hull. *Pétrel* was the second of the three 180nhp ships whose construction was directed on 1 July 1844. She was designed by Firmin Joffre. Her hull was ordered from Gaspard Malo of Dunkirk by a contract approved on 6 November 1844 and her engines were ordered from Baboneau by a contract approved on 20 October 1845. Her oscillating-cylinder engines, probably similar to those of *Épervier*, only developed 172nhp on trials.

Dimensions & tons: 52.50m, 46.50m wl, 42.20m x 8.00m x 4.90m. 505 tons disp. Draught 2.83m mean. Men: 93.

Machinery: 180nhp. Oscillating, two cylinders, 2 tubular boilers. Coal 122 tons max.

Guns: (1847) 2 x 18pdr carronades.

Pétrel Gaspard Malo, Dunkirk/Baboneau, Nantes (Constructeur, Georges Allix)

Ord: 9.11.1844. K: 1.1845. L: 20.12.1846. 15.3.1847. C: 3.1847.

Wrecked 5.11.1855 while under control of a pilot at Kristiansand, Norway, crew brought to Portsmouth by HMS *Ajax*.

REQUIN – 180nhp paddle 1st Class aviso, iron hull. *Requin* was the third of the three 180nhp ships whose construction was directed on 1 July 1844. She was designed by Alexandre Chedeville. Her hull was ordered from Courau & Arman at Bordeaux by a contract approved on 6 November 1844 and her engines were ordered from Gâche & Voruz by a contract approved on 15 January 1846. After launching she was completed at Rochefort by Nicolas-Émile Courtin and Victorin Sabattier. Her direct-acting engines were probably similar to those in *Dauphin*.

Dimensions & tons: 45.00m wl, 40.80m x 7.50m x 5.45m. 500 tons disp. Draught 2.80m mean. Men: 93.

Machinery: 180nhp. Direct-acting, 2 tubular boilers. Coal 100 tons.

Guns: 2 x 8pdrs (brass).

Requin Courau & Arman, Bordeaux-Lormont/Gâche & Voruz, Nantes
Ord: 9.11.1844. K: 15.1.1846. L: 18.3.1847. Comm: 12.4.1848. C: 7.1850.
Struck 8.11.1862, lighter at Cherbourg or Rochefort, BU 1874.

As noted earlier, France did not have enough steamers to fulfill the treaty obligation with Britain committing each country to maintain 26 ships, including a substantial number of steamers, on the West Africa station to eradicate the slave trade. A special law of 19 July 1845 provided funds to build seven more, all with iron hulls. These were one screw steamer of 400nhp, two paddle steamers of 300nhp (*Euménide* and *Gorgone*), two paddle steamers of 180 to 200nhp (the *Mouette* group), and two screw 'corvettes-mixtes' of 90 to 100nhp (*Biche* and *Sentinelle*). After the law was passed the Minister of Marine assigned the 450nhp former transatlantic packet *Caraïbe* to this duty (where she was lost), allowing the construction of two more 200nhp steamers with the funds provided for the one 400nhp steamer.

MOUETTE – 200nhp paddle 1st Class aviso, iron hull. This ship and her three half-sisters, *Héron*, *Goéland*, and *Phénix*, were built for the West Africa station under the same program as the corvettes *Euménide* and *Gorgone*. Plans by Paul Marie Étienne Picot de Moras were approved for *Mouette* on 9 January 1846. Her hull was ordered from Philip Taylor at La Seyne by a contract approved on 2 July 1846 and her engines were ordered from Taylor by a contract approved on 31 August 1846. In service she displaced 550 tons at a mean draught of 2.95m. She received new 192nhp engines from Forges et Chantiers de la Méditerranée, La Seyne (the successor to Philip Taylor) in 1857-8 under a contract approved on 17 June 1857.
  Dimensions & tons: 52.00m wl x 8.50m x 4.94m. 514 tons disp.

The iron-hulled paddle aviso *Mouette* enjoyed a moment of fame when she rescued Francis II, destined to be the last king of the Two Sicilies, and his queen Maria Sophie, at the fall of the Neapolitan fortress of Gaeta in 1861, one of the final acts in the process of Italian unification. (Courtesy of Beverley R. Robinson Collection, US Naval Academy Museum)

  Draught 2.60m mean. Men: 93.
  Machinery: 200nhp. Side-lever, tubular boilers, 10.16kts.
  Guns: 2 x 16cm shell.
Mouette Philip Taylor, La Seyne/Taylor
  Ord: 6.7.1846. K: 8.10.1846. L: 14.8.1847. Comm: 1.1.1848. C: 1.1848.
  Struck 11.6.1867 at Toulon, BU 1867.

HÉRON – 200nhp paddle 1st Class aviso, iron hull. *Héron* was built for the West Africa station under the same program as *Mouette*. Plans for her by Joseph Cros were approved on 9 January 1846. Her hull was ordered from Louis-Auguste Guibert at Nantes by a contract approved on 2 July 1846 and her engines were ordered from François Cavé by a contract approved on 13 October 1846. The engines worked well on trials in July 1850 but only developed 190nhp.
  Dimensions & tons: 51.05m, 48.60m wl, 45.70m x 7.60m x 4.79m. 512 tons disp. Draught 2.64m mean. Men: 93.
  Machinery: 200nhp, 9.37kts. Oscillating, 2 tubular boilers. Coal 117 tons.
  Guns: ?
Héron Auguste Guibert, Nantes/Cavé (Constructeurs, Charles Brun and Paulin Masson)
  Ord: 6.7.1846. K: 8.1846. L: 6.11.1847. Comm: 20.5.1848. C: 5.1848.
  Struck 4.8.1871, hulk at Toulon. BU 1874.

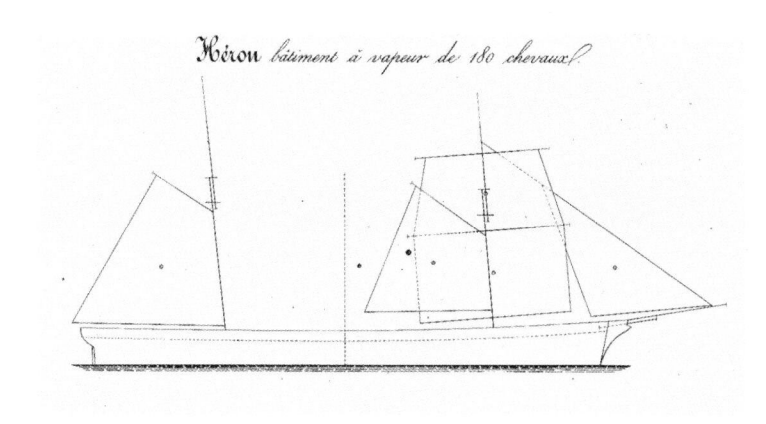

Official brigantine sail plan of the paddle aviso *Héron*. There was no fore topgallant and no gaff topsail on the main; total sail area was 439 sq.m. (Atlas du Génie Maritime, Genoa collection, image 2-0040)

GOÉLAND – 200nhp paddle 1st Class aviso, iron hull. *Goéland* was built for the West Africa station under the same program as *Mouette*. Plans by Stanislas-Charles-Henri Dupuy de Lôme and Louis Sanial-Dufay were approved on 9 January 1846 and one of these was used for *Goéland*. Her hull was ordered from Louis-Auguste Guibert by a contract approved on 2 July 1846 and her engines were ordered from Gâche and Voruz by a contract approved on 31 August 1846. In service she displaced 559 tons.
  Dimensions & tons: 48.00m wl x 7.90m x 4.80m. 480 tons disp. Men: 93.
  Machinery: 200nhp. Direct-acting, tubular boilers, 482ihp.
  Guns: 4.
Goéland Auguste Guibert, Nantes/Gâche & Voruz (Constructeur, Guillaume Masson).
  Ord: 6.7.1846. K: 8.1846. L: 3.6.1848. *Comm. de port*: 9.11.1849. C: 11.1849. Comm: 7.6.1852.
  Struck 22.7.1872, mooring and depot hulk at Rochefort, renamed *Cormoran* 1880. Condemned 8.1886, sold for BU 11.1887.

PHÉNIX – 200nhp paddle 1st Class aviso, iron hull. *Phénix* was built for the West Africa station under the same program as *Mouette*. Plans for her by Charles Sochet were approved on 9 January 1846. Her hull was ordered from Gaspard Malo at Dunkirk by a contract approved on 2 July 1846 and her engines were ordered from Charles-Michel Nillus at Le Havre by a contract approved on 31 August 1846. In service she displaced 620 tons at a mean draught of 2.76m.
  Dimensions & tons: 50.60m, 50.00m wl, 47.70m x 8.02m x 4.75m. 482 tons disp. Draught 2.20m mean. Men: 93.
  Machinery: 200nhp, 11.70kts. Oscillating, 2 tubular boilers. Coal 125 tons.
  Guns: 1 x 16cm shell, 2 x 12cm bronze shell.
Phénix Gaspard Malo, Dunkirk/Nillus (Constructeur, Georges Allix)
  Ord: 6.7.1846. K: 8.1846. L: 8.1.1848. Comm: 27.5.1848. C: 3.1849.
  Struck 4.8.1871, hulk at Toulon. BU 1874.

ÉCLAIREUR Class – 200nhp paddle 1st Class avisos, iron hulls. *Éclaireur* appeared in the building program in late 1842 as a 160nhp steamer at Toulon and was moved to Indret during 1843 but not begun. In late 1845 she was listed as a 220nhp ship to be begun in 1846 while *Prométhée* appeared in the program for the first time. On 10 July 1846 the navy decided to build *Éclaireur* as a 200nhp aviso with new type engines and put her older type 220nhp engines into a tug, which was later built under the name *Souffleur*. Plans for the two avisos were completed by Charles-Henri Moll in October 1846. The beam over the paddle boxes was 14.30m. In service, *Prométhée* displaced 703 tons at a mean draught of 3.25m.
  Dimensions & tons: 51.76m, 48.50m wl, 45.00m x 8.32m x 5.09m. 541 tons disp. Draught 2.16/3.32m. Men: 93 (*Éclaireur*), 105 (*Prométhée*).
  Machinery: 200nhp; (*Éclaireur*) 646ihp, 11.65kts; (*Prométhée*) 11.14kts. Oscillating, 4 tubular boilers. Coal 160 tons.
  Guns: 2 x 16cm shell. (*Prométhée* originally had 4 x 12cm bronze shell instead).
Éclaireur Indret/Indret.
  Ord: 13.10.1846. K: 11.1.1847. L: 24.9.1847. Comm: 17.10.1847. C: 11.1847.
  Decomm. 1.10.1863, probably at Toulon. Struck 13.2.1868. Reports that she then became Peruvian probably refer to *Marañon*, a 73.8m, 2,015-ton iron steamer bought by Peru in 1868 to tow a monitor from the United States to Peru and then used to house the Peruvian naval school.
Prométhée Indret/Indret (Constructeur, Paulin-Jean Montety)
  Ord: 13.10.1846. K: 12.1846. L: 11.10.1848. Comm: 1.1.1849. C: 1.1849.
  Struck 13.2.1868 at Toulon, BU 1868.

AVERNE – 100nhp paddle 2nd Class aviso, iron hull. This ship at Indret, the screw aviso *Ariel* at Toulon, and a 100nhp iron ship at Brest that became *Daim* were added to the building program on 22 June 1846 because of a shortage of small steamers in the 100 to 120nhp range. *Averne* was built on Firmin Joffre's plans for *Anacréon*. Her engines, designed by Charles Moll, were slightly modified copies of those in *Pélican* and *Passe Partout* and used Penn's pattern of oscillating cylinders. Though rated at 100nhp, they developed 120nhp. Her boilers and paddle wheels were copies of those in *Anacréon*.
  Dimensions & tons: 42.68m, 40.00m wl, 37.31m x 6.26m x 3.30m. 236 tons disp. Draught 2.08m. Men: 64.
  Machinery: 100nhp, 11.69kts. Oscillating, 2 tubular boilers. Coal 57 tons.
  Guns: 2 x 12cm shell.
Averne Indret/Indret (Constructeur, Charles-Marc Boumard)
  Ord: c6.1846. K: 2.1847. L: 17.6.1848. Comm: 19.6.1848. C: 9.1848.
  Struck 15.11.1878 at Brest, BU 1880.

MILAN – 200nhp paddle 1st Class aviso. On 30 November 1847 the Minister of Marine ordered Cherbourg to prepare plans for a 200nhp aviso named *Milan* whose construction had been ordered at that dockyard. On 11 January 1848 the Minister specified that this ship would be screw propelled, but this was changed to paddle on 29 March 1848 after problems were encountered installing the propeller shaft in the corvette *Roland*, which also had a wooden hull. Émile Dorian's modified plan was approved on 3 May 1848. The engines, ordered from François Mazeline, Le Havre by a contract approved on 9 October 1848, used Penn's pattern of oscillating cylinders. The beam over the paddles was 15.10m and the designed displacement was 650 tons. She ran machinery trials in May 1850 without being put in full commission.
  Dimensions & tons: 51.34m, 49.20m wl x 8.86m, 9.00m ext x 5.40m. 794 tons disp. Draught 3.59/3.87m. Men: 123.
  Machinery: 200nhp, 9.50kts. Oscillating, 2 tubular boilers.
  Guns: 4 x 16cm shell.

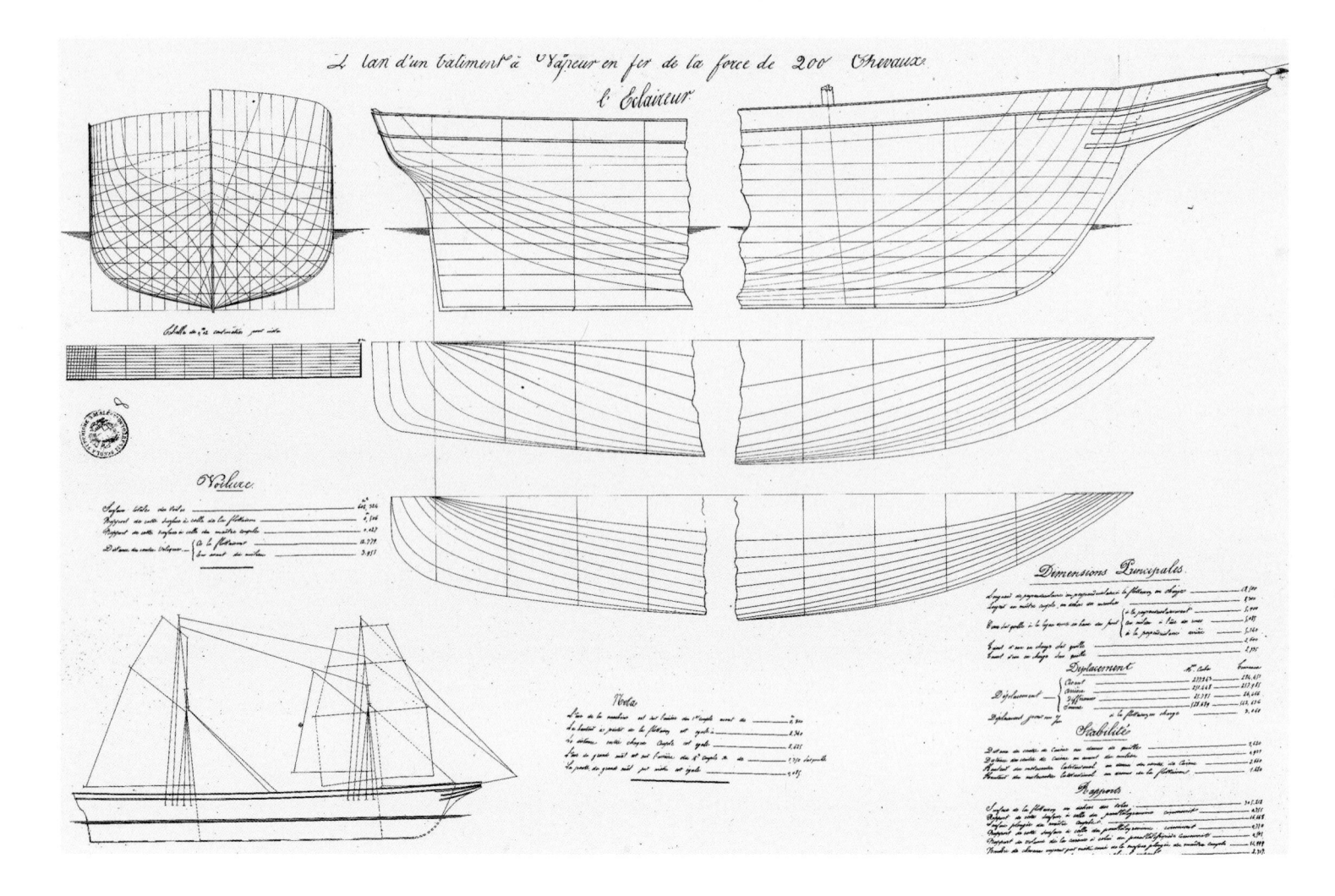

Official lines and body plan of the paddle aviso *Éclaireur*. The sail plan shows a brigantine rig totalling 602 sq.m. in area. (Atlas du Génie Maritime, Genoa collection, image 5-0007)

Milan Cherbourg Dyd/François Mazeline, Le Havre.
  Ord: 30.11.1847. K: 7.11.1848. L: 4.10.1849. Comm: 7.1.1851. C: 1.1851.
  Struck 11.2.1865 at Lorient. Replaced *Souffleur* 5.6.1865 as a coal hulk at Brest, BU approved 16.7.1866.

DAIM Class – 120nhp paddle 2nd Class avisos. An iron paddle aviso of 100-120nhp at Brest was added to the building program on 22 June 1846 along with the paddle *Averne* at Indret and the screw *Ariel* at Toulon because of a shortage of small steamers in the 100 to 120nhp range. The aviso at Brest was reassigned to Indret on 30 December 1846 with the 220nhp tug *Souffleur* in exchange for the wooden-hulled corvette *Tanger*, and in January 1847 the aviso appeared in the budget for 1848 under the name *Daim*. Plans for this ship by Victor Gervaize drafted at Brest were reviewed by the Council of Works on 6 January 1847 but Indret then drafted new plans for an iron hull that the Council rejected on 7 July 1847. In late 1847 another small aviso, *Flambart*, was added to the building program to be begun in 1848, and she and *Daim* were now to be built by contract with wooden hulls probably because Indret had ceased to build hulls. Hull plans by Prix Charles Jean-Baptiste Sochet for these two ships were approved on 26 April 1848 and 17 August 1848. The hull and engines of *Daim* were ordered from Vincent Gâche and Jean-Simon Voruz by a contract approved on 21 August 1848, while the hull of *Flambart* was ordered from Gaspard Malo and Eugène Antoine of Dunkirk by a contract approved on 21 September 1848 and her engines were ordered from Charles-Michel Nillus at Le Havre by a contract approved on 16 October 1848. The engines of *Flambart* were based on a pattern developed by Penn, and after *Flambart* was struck in 1856 these engines were adapted to the screw and reused in the aviso *D'Entrecasteaux*.

  Dimensions & tons: 41.15m, 40.00m wl, 37.69m x 6.60m, 6.74m ext x 3.60m. 339 tons disp. Draught 2.52m. Men: 64.
  Machinery: 120nhp. *Daim*: 367ihp, 10.13kts Direct-acting, 2 tubular boilers. *Flambart*: Oscillating, 2 cylinders, 2 tubular boilers. Coal 53 tons.
  Guns: 2 x 12cm bronze field shell guns (*obusiers de campagne de 12*)

Daim Gâche & Voruz/Gâche & Voruz, Nantes.
  Ord: 17.8.1848. K: 14.9.1848. L: 5.7.1849. Comm: 1.11.1849. C: 12.1849
  Struck 2.11.1877, hulk for the breakwater station (*poste de digue*) at Toulon. BU 1885.

Flambart Gaspard Malo, Dunkirk/Nillus, Le Havre (Constructeur, Charles Louis Duchalard)
  Ord: 17.8.1848. K: 10.1848. L: 20.10.1849. Comm: 5.3.1850.
  Struck 7.3.1856, coal hulk at Rochefort. BU 1865.

GALILÉE Class – 120nhp paddle 2nd Class avisos. These two small

Official general arrangement drawings of the Mediterranean postal packets *Ajaccio* and *Bastia*, dated 1841. The former was acquired by the navy in 1850. The brigantine rig set 572 sq.m. of sail. Note the feathering paddle wheel. (Atlas du Génie Maritime, French collection, plate 75)

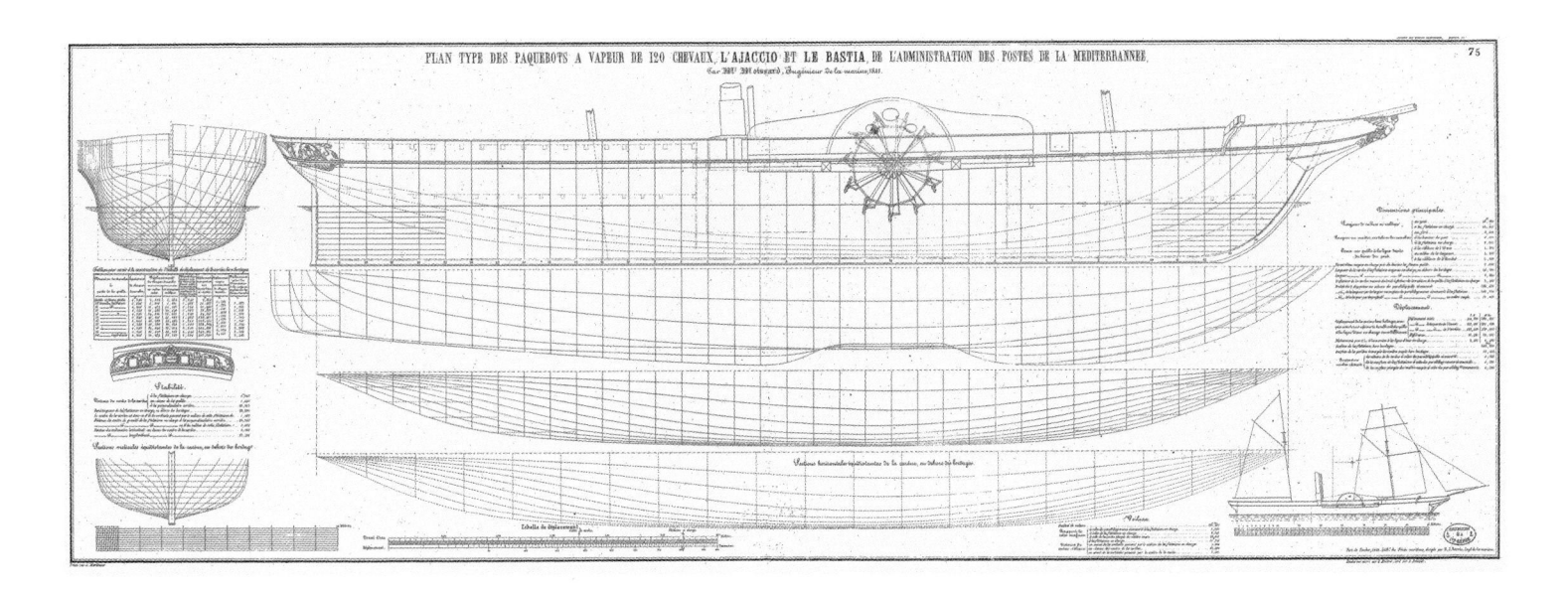

avisos were added to the building program in late 1847 along with *Flambart* to be begun during 1849 by contract. Plans for their wooden hulls by Antoine Joseph Delapoix de Fréminville were approved on 26 May 1849. Their engines were originally to be exact copies of those in *Averne*. As built, they were identical except that one of *Galilée*'s two cylinders used chloroform vapor instead of steam, on a system developed by Enseigne de Vaisseau Louis Charles Lafond and the engineer Louis Édouard Lecointre. The beam outside their paddle boxes was 11.60m. Both were placed in reduced commission on 21 March 1853; *Bisson* was placed in full commission on 3 May 1853 but installation of *Galilée*'s machinery was completed only in December 1853 and there is no record of her going into full commission. The engine of *Bisson* was replaced between September 1860 and July 1861 at Lorient with a two-cylinder Indret 120hp engine designed by Louis Édouard Lecointre, also with oscillating cylinders.

> Dimensions & tons: 42.05m, 40.00m wl, 38.94m x 6.58m, 6.70m ext x 3.50m. 304 tons disp. Draught 2.56/2.70m. Men: 64.
> Machinery: 120nhp. Oscillating, 312ihp. 1 tubular boiler with 4 furnaces in *Bisson*. Coal 61 tons.
> Guns: (1853) 2 x 18pdr carronades.

Galilée Lorient Dyd/Lorient (Constructeur, Delapoix de Fréminville)
> K: 26.7.1849. L: 12.8.1851. Comm. de port: 21.3.1853. C: 3.1853. Converted to sail transport 1867-68 at Lorient, then struck 24.4.1868 and became sailing barge for the transportation of provisions and spare parts. Sold for BU 1890.

Bisson (ex *Tantale* 18.7.1850) Lorient Dyd/Lorient (Constructeur, Delapoix de Fréminville)
> K: 26.7.1849. L: 25.7.1850. Comm: 3.5.1853. C: 5.1853. Struck 2.6.1871 at Toulon, BU 1871-72.

AJACCIO – 120nhp paddle 2nd Class aviso. This postal packet was transferred from the Ministry of Finance to the navy on 26 November 1850. She and her sister *Bastia*, which was not acquired, were designed by Louis-Just Moissard and built under a law of 14 June 1841 for a postal line between Marseille and Corsica that was operated between 1843 and 1850 by the Ministry of Finance and then turned over to private industry. *Ajaccio*'s engines were built in Paris on plans by Mazeline. The law also authorised a third ship, the pioneer French screw steamer *Napoléon* (later *Corse*). *Ajaccio*'s sail area was 571 sq.m.

> Dimensions & tons: 45.96m, 44.44m wl, 41.60m x 6.80m, 6.94m ext x 4.29m. 529 tons disp. Draught 3.20m mean. Men: 64.
> Machinery: 120nhp, 8kts.
> Guns: (1860) 2 x 12cm shell.

Ajaccio La Ciotat/Pihet, Paris (Constructeur, Charles Brun)
> K: c1842. L: 4.1843. C: 4.11.1843. Comm: 26.11.1850. Struck 23.5.1871 at Toulon, BU 1871.

SESOSTRIS – 160nhp paddle 1st Class aviso. *Sesostris* was one of ten *Mentor* class 160nhp postal packets designed by Louis-Just Moissard and built under a law of 2 July 1835 establishing a postal packet line between France and the Levant. Purchased from the Ministry of Finance on 29 December 1851, she was the only one of the ten to see naval service. On 12 January 1855 she was ordered converted into a steam mortar vessel similar to *Vautour*. She participated in the bombardment of the forts at Kinburn in October 1855 with *Vautour*, *Cassini*, and *Ténare*.

> Dimensions & tons: 51.30m, 50.00m wl, 46.10m x 8.00m, 8.18m ext x 5.34m. 771 tons disp. Draught 3.33/3.33m. Men: 100.
> Machinery: 160nhp.
> Guns: 2 x 16cm shell.

Sesostris Cherbourg Dyd/Hallette (Constructeurs, Jean-Baptiste Lefebvre and others)
> K: 21.8.1835. L: 27.8.1836. C: 25.9.1836. Comm: 11.1.1852. Struck 25.4.1861, headquarters hulk for the reserve at Lorient. Workshop for the reserve 1885, BU 1896.

CHAMOIS – 150nhp paddle 1st Class aviso, iron hull. Built under a law of 4 August 1844 as the postal packet *Daim* for the Calais-Dover route, this ship was designed by Louis-Just Moissard and built by Jean-Baptiste and Laurent Coureau and Lucien Arman. The government turned this service over to private industry in early 1855, idling two screw packets (*Faon* and *Passe Partout* and two paddle packets, *Daim* and *Biche*). *Daim* was purchased from the Ministry of Finances on 7 May 1855 and renamed *Chamois* on 16 May 1855. After being refitted in 1855-56 at Cherbourg she was placed in commission for trials on 20 April 1856 and commissioned definitively on 5 July 1856. She had two funnels and four boilers.

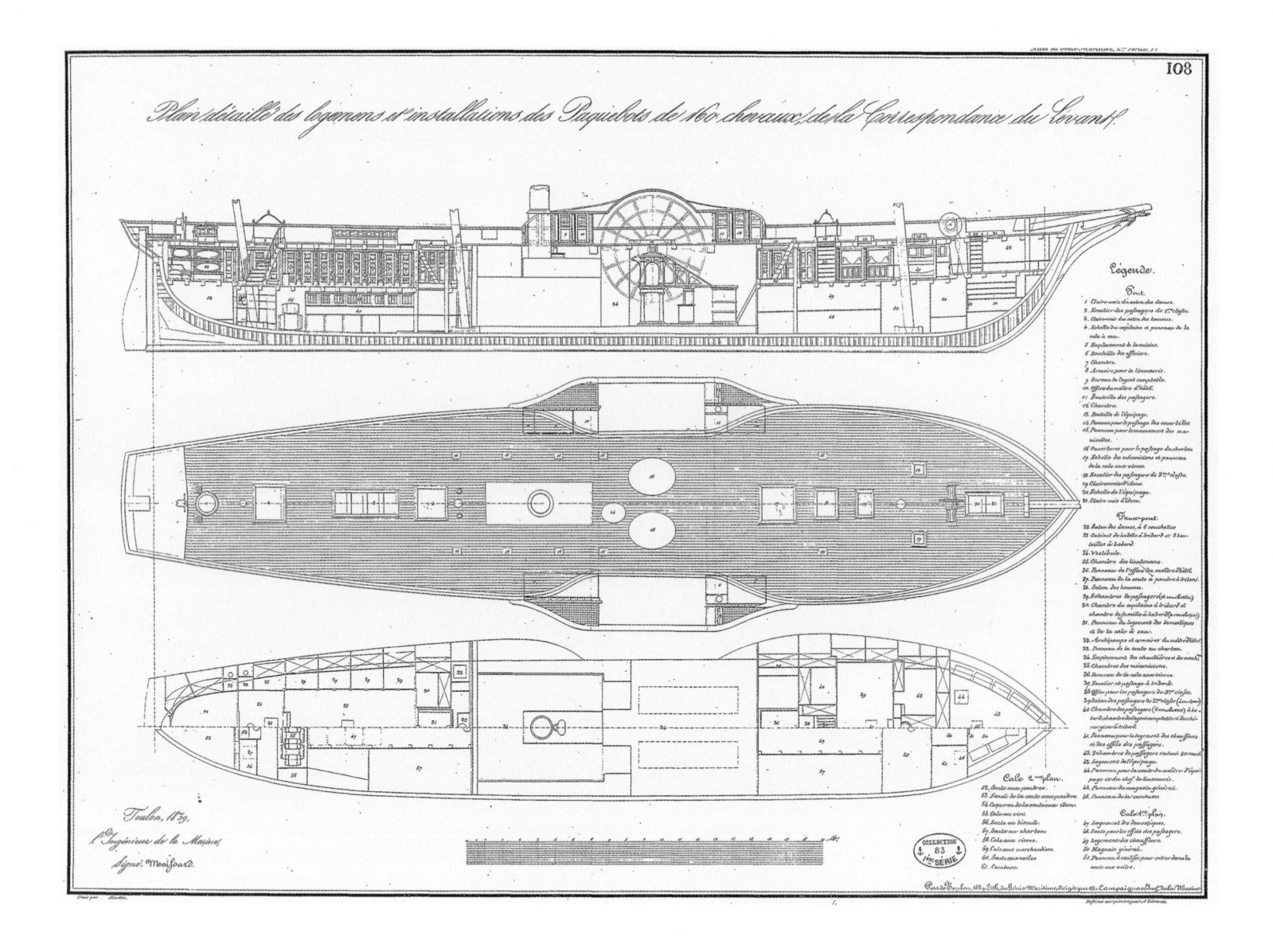

Dimensions & tons: 40.70m, 39.80m wl, 38.65m x 6.30m ext x 3.72m. 334 tons disp. Draught 2.36/2.40m. Men: 64.
Machinery: 150nhp, 8kts. 2 engines of 2 cylinders, 4 boilers, 2 funnels. Coal 28 tons.
Guns: (1856) 2 x 12pdr carronades.
Chamois Courau & Arman, Bordeaux-Lormont/Schneider
K: 12.1845. L: 1846. C: 4.1848. Comm: 20.4.1856.
Struck 15.11.1878 at Rochefort, BU 1878.

ANTILOPE – 150nhp paddle 1st Class aviso, iron hull. This ship was one of three small postal packets built under a law of 4 August 1844 for the Calais-Dover route and made redundant in 1855 when that service was turned over to private industry. Named *Biche* while a packet, she was purchased from the Ministry of Finance on 7 May 1855 and renamed on 16 May 1855. She was refitted in 1855-56 at Cherbourg.
Dimensions & tons: 41.80m, 41.00m wl, 39.90m x 6.00m x 3.30m. 290 tons disp. Draught 2.20/2.34m. Men: 64.
Machinery: 150nhp. 2 engines with 2 cylinders, 4 boilers, 2 funnels. Coal 28 tons.
Guns: (1856) 2 x 12cm bronze shell.
Antilope Chaigneau & Bichon, Bordeaux-Lormont/Schneider

Official general arrangement drawings of the ten 160nhp postal packets for the Levant service, dated Toulon 1839. One of this class, *Sesostris*, was purchased for the Navy in 1851. (Atlas du Génie Maritime, French collection, plate 108)

K: 12.1845. L: 11.8.1846. C: 1847. Comm: 10.2.1856.
Wrecked 15.12.1858 on the Senequet 20 miles north of Granville while aiding a grounded merchant ship in the fog.

ABEILLE Class – 100nhp paddle 2nd Class avisos. These two ships were designed by Charles Brun for use on the Danube River but served in Senegal. Their construction was directed on 3 August 1857 and their plans were approved on 9 February 1858. The engines were designed by Charles Henri Moll. The ships were named on 16 August 1857. On 24 February 1859 the Council of Works recommended adopting the *Étoile* type, probably with an increase in size, for use on the Danube; the result was the *Alecton* class (1859, 160nhp).
Dimensions & tons: 51.12m, 49.82m wl, 48.87m x 7.38m ext x 3.68m. 578 tons disp. Draught 2.55m mean. Men: 64.
Machinery: 100nhp, 8kts. 1 boiler. Coal 105 tons

Guns: 2 x 16cm shell.

Abeille Rochefort Dyd/Indret (Constructeurs, Brun and Alfred Lebelin de Dionne)
- K: 4.1858. L: 22.10.1858. Comm: 20.4.1859. C: 5.1859.
- Struck 26.11.1868, hulk for the torpedo school at Boyardville. Traded names 27.2.1871 with the former screw aviso *Lutin* (1861); both hulks were BU 3-5.1871.

Étoile Rochefort Dyd/Indret (Constructeurs, Alfred Lebelin de Dionne and Léon De Gérando)
- K: 1.5.1858. L: 30.12.1858. Comm: 1.5.1859. C: 6.1859.
- Struck 20.4.1878 at Rochefort, BU 1879.

CASABIANCA – 160nhp paddle 1st Class aviso. This ship was designed to transport supplies to the penal colonies in French Guiana. This required a ship with not over 3.00m draught, coal for 6 days, and capacity for 160 tons of cargo, and no ship then in the navy met these specifications. The Minister of Marine ordered her construction on 5 February 1858 and plans for her prepared by Nicolas Marie Julien Le Moine were approved on 20 April 1858. The engines were designed by Charles Henri Moll.
- Dimensions & tons: 56.49m 53.01m wl, 47.01m x 9.00m ext x 5.23m. 979 tons disp. Draught 3.38/3.50m. Men: 74.
- Machinery: 160nhp, 9.79kts. 2 cylinders, 2 boilers. Coal 193 tons max.
- Guns: (Designed) 2 x 16cm shell.

Casabianca Lorient Dyd/Indret.
- K: 14.5.1858. L: 15.8.1859. Comm: 20.4.1860. C: 5.1860.
- Served in French Guiana. Struck 3.5.1877 at Lorient, BU 1884.

ALECTON Class – 160nhp paddle 1st Class avisos. Designed by Amédée Mangin (modified *Étoile* type) with engines designed by Philip Taylor. On 24 February 1859 the Council of Works had recommended adopting the *Étoile* type (100nhp, 1858) for use on the Danube, although it was noted that the *Étoile* type was not large enough for this duty. The *Alecton* class was the result. Their hulls were ordered from the Forges et Chantiers de la Méditerranée (FCM) at La Seyne by a contract signed on 30 November 1859, their names were assigned on 26 December 1859, and their engines were ordered from FCM by a contract signed on 11 May 1860. Two more units of this type slightly modified, *Pétrel* and *Antilope*, were launched in 1872.
- Dimensions & tons: 50.92m, 49.92m wl, 49.15m x 7.38m ext x 3.68m. 592-632 tons disp. Draught 2.54/2.60m. Men: 64.
- Machinery: 120nhp, 320ihp designed, trials (*Magicien*, 1869) 392ihp = 9.68kts. Oscillating, two cylinders, 1 boiler. Coal 92 tons max.
- Guns: 2 x 12cm rifles

Alecton Forges et Chantiers de la Méditerranée, La Seyne/FCM
- Ord: 30.11.1859. K: 1859. L: 29.1.1861. Comm: 24.6.1861. C: 6.1861
- Served in French Guiana from 1861 to 1870 and 1875-78. Struck 10.8.1883, sold for BU 1884 at Lorient.

Castor Forges et Chantiers de la Méditerranée, La Seyne/FCM
- Ord: 30.11.1859. K: 3.1860. L: 23.2.1861. Comm: 9.9.1861. C: 9.1861.
- Served in multiple locations in France, West Africa, and the Caribbean. Struck 19.4.1886 and stationed at Arcachon as a tug. Condemned 7.1894, sold for BU 9.1894.

Magicien (ex *Pollux* 1859) Forges et Chantiers de la Méditerranée, La Seyne/FCM
- Ord: 30.11.1859. K: 3.1860. L: 11.4.1861. Comm: 1.12.1861. c: 12.1861.
- Served on the Danube until 1868 and then in the West Indies and Senegal. Struck 17.12.1889 at Toulon, on sale list there 1890.

ACQUIRED

Saïgon (paddle 1st Class aviso, ex mercantile built in New York and purchased in the Far East)
- Dimensions: 230ft x 32ft. Men: 30
- Machinery: 220nhp
- Guns: 1
- Purchased c3.1860 for 200,000 piastres. Renamed *Écho* c8.1860. Grounded 13.6.1865 in the Saigon River and lost. Struck 21.9.1865.

Smaller paddle avisos (90nhp and less)

GALIBI – 80nhp steam vessel, later paddle 2nd Class aviso. This ship was ordered for use as a tug at Brest, but was sent to Senegal when completed. She was designed by Alphonse Levesque. The engines were ordered from Sudds, Adkins & Barker by a contract approved on 16 November 1839.
- Dimensions & tons: 37.50m wl x 6.00m, 6.17m ext x 3.40m. 307 tons disp. Draught 2.35/2.43m. Men: 36-49.
- Machinery: 80nhp, 2 flue boilers.
- Guns: 4 swivels.

Galibi Brest Dyd/Sudds, Adkins & Barker.
- Ord: 7.9.1839. K: 26.2.1840. L: 21.5.1841. Comm: 14.3.1842. C: 3.1842.
- Struck 31.12.1854 in Senegal. Fitted as a sail transport on the Senegal River 1855, out of service 5.9.1860, BU 1865.

ALECTON – 80nhp steam vessel, later paddle 2nd Class aviso. Designed by Pierre-Félix Le Grix, this ship was ordered on 18 July 1840 to receive a 60nhp experimental engine with inclined cylinders built by Sudds, Adkins & Barker of Rouen. The British engineer who was to have built this engine, Turner, left Sudds, however, and a normal 60nhp engine was ordered from Lorient for the ship at the end of 1840. This engine was reassigned to *Éridan* in 1842 and new experimental high-pressure 80nhp engines and boilers were ordered for *Alecton* from Charles Beslay by a contract approved on 23 April 1842. In 1843 the ship was modified by the addition of 40 tons (including 25 tons of coal) for service as a fishery protection ship instead of a tug. Trials in September 1843 produced a maximum speed of

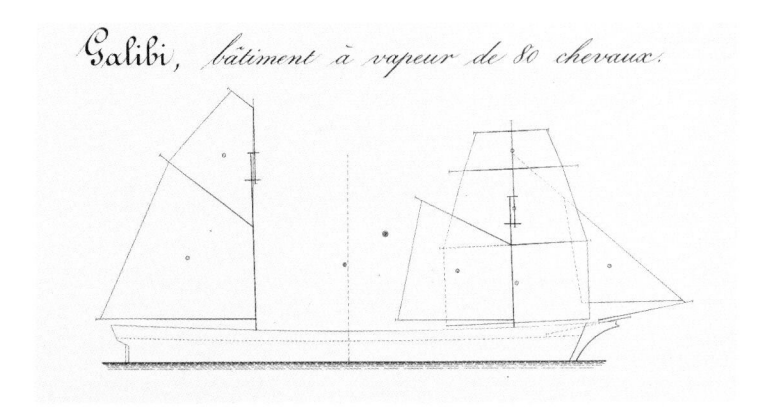

Official brigantine sail plan of the paddle aviso *Galibi*. Sail area is given as 414 sq.m. The fore-and-aft sails are designated: *misaine goëlette* (gaff sail on the foremast), *brigantine* (main gaff sail) and *flèche en cul* (main topsail). (Atlas du Génie Maritime, Genoa collection, image 2-0037)

only 6.7kts, a fact initially ascribed to excessive draught resulting from the modifications. She continued trials configured as a tug, but these were not successful and she was towed to Cherbourg in 1846 for new Beslay boilers that had been ordered by a contract approved on 3 March 1845. These also failed, and on 8 November 1847 the Council of Works renounced further trials with high pressure engines and rejected the boilers of *Alecton*. In 1848 *Alecton* was given the engines salvaged from *Éridan*, and when she was struck these engines were removed for use in *Rubis*.

Dimensions & tons: 40.40m, 39.00m wl x 5.70m, 5.90m ext x 3.45m. 300 tons disp. Draught 2.15/2.45m. Men: 47.
Machinery: 80nhp. High pressure, 2 boilers.
Guns: 4.

Alecton Cherbourg Dyd/Beslay, Paris (Constructeur, Amédée Mangin)
Ord: 12.7.1840. K: 2.10.1840. L: 31.3.1843. Comm: 21.9.1843. C: 9.1843.
Struck 5.10.1853 at Brest, BU 1854.

RAPIDE – 60nhp steam vessel, later paddle 2nd Class aviso. This ship was designed by Guillaume Masson to replace the old *Rapide* as a tug at Cherbourg. She was to receive the 80nhp engines of the old *Rapide*, but during construction she traded engines with a ship under construction on the same plans, *Voyageur*. The four-cylinder engines she received were experimental ones of 60nhp built by Pierre Jean-Baptiste Rossin on the same system as his much larger engines built for the paddle frigate *Infernal* and to a 450nhp design proposed by him for *Asmodée* (later *Vauban*) but rejected in early 1840. The beam over her paddles was 11.00m. She was used as a tug in the construction of the breakwater at Cherbourg until 1854, when she was sent to French Guiana. She returned to Cherbourg in 1856 and became a station ship.

Dimensions & tons: 41.10m wl x 6.02m. 201 tons disp. Draught 2.08/2.32m. Men: 33-44.
Machinery: 60nhp. 4 cylinders.
Guns: 2 x 12pdr carronades, 2 x 4pdrs.

Rapide Indret/Indret (Constructeurs, Amédée Laimant and others)
K: 10.6.1840. L: 21.7.1841. Comm: 1.7.1841. C: 8.1841.
Struck 21.10.1859 at Lorient, BU 1860.

VOYAGEUR – 80nhp steam vessel, later paddle 2nd Class aviso. This ship was intended to replace *Coursier* in French Guiana. She was built on plans drafted by Guillaume Masson for *Rapide* (1841), shortened slightly. She was to have received experimental engines of 60nhp being built at Indret, but during construction she swapped machinery with the new *Rapide*, thereby receiving the engines of the old *Rapide* (1823). Her trials with the old machinery were unsatisfactory and she was relegated to port service at Rochefort as a tug. She was rebuilt at Rochefort with new oscillating-cylinder engines from July 1848 to August 1849 and sailed for French Guiana later that year. The data given below are for the ship as rebuilt – her original designed displacement was 225 tons and length 39 metres.

Dimensions & tons: 46.15m oa, 40.95m wl x 6.10m x 3.46m. 337 tons disp. Draught 2.30m mean. Men: 64.
Machinery: 80nhp. New machinery 1849: 100nhp (built at Rochefort by Victorin Sabattier), oscillating, 2 tubular boilers. Coal 60 tons.
Guns: 4 x 12pdr carronades; (1849) 2 x 12cm shell.

Voyageur Indret/from *Rapide* (Constructeur, Masson)
Ord: 21.3.1841. K: 3.1841. L: 30.9.1841. Comm: 1.10.1841. C: 10.1841.
Struck 31.12.1864 in French Guiana and used as a tug. BU 1872 at Cayenne.

ÉRIDAN – 60nhp steam vessel, iron hull. This ship was built to replace *Coursier* in French Guiana after *Voyageur* was found unsuitable. The colony's need for a ship with a maximum draught of 5ft (1.52m) was met by using an iron hull – the first one in the French Navy. Engines under construction at Lorient for *Alecton* were appropriated to speed completion. The hull was ordered from François Cavé at Saint-Ouen by a contract approved on 8 September 1842. Soon afterwards Cavé moved his shipyard across the Seine to Asnières-sur-Seine. After *Éridan*'s loss her engines were reused in *Alecton* and later in *Rubis*.

Dimensions & tons: 40.00m oa, 39.00m wl x 7.00m x 3.60m. 203 tons disp. Draught 1.75m. Men: 48.
Machinery: 60nhp.
Guns: 2.

Éridan François Cavé, Saint-Ouen (Paris)/Lorient.
Ord: 8.9.1842 (contract). K: c1842. L: 3.11.1843. Comm: 15.5.1844. C: 5.1844.
Struck a rock and sank in the Oyapock River 28.8.1846. Wreck abandoned 14.11.1846 after engines recovered. Struck 20.3.1847.

SERPENT Class – 30nhp steam vessels, later paddle 2nd Class avisos, iron hulls. In 1842 Senegal indicated that it needed, in addition to one or two steamers in the 60-80nhp range, two small iron steamers for use in the small tributaries of the Senegal River. The hulls and engines were ordered from François Cavé by a contract approved on 2 February 1843 and the ships were named on 10 April 1843. These two ships, designed by their builder, were built on standard river boat plans with flat bottoms (their proposed draught was 18in or 0.46m) and were sent out together to Senegal on 23 July 1844. *Serpent* and *Basilic* wore out and were decommissioned in Senegal 14 September 1851 and 1 August 1853 respectively. Their engines were returned to France for installation in new hulls with the same dimensions and names.

Dimensions & tons: 42.00m, 40.00m wl? x 5.00m x 2.50m. c100 tons disp. Men: 32.
Machinery: 30nhp. Oscillating, flue boilers
Guns: 2 or 4. *Serpent* reported with 4 x 16cm shell (6 ports).

Serpent François Cavé, Saint-Ouen (Paris)/Cavé (Constructeur, Georges Allix).
Ord: 2.2.1843 (contract). K: 3.1843. L: 3.11.1843. Comm: 16.5.1844. C: 5.1844.
Struck 11.1.1853 in Senegal. Hull used a horse transport and hulk until 1865.

Basilic François Cavé, Saint-Ouen (Paris)/Cavé (Constructeur, Georges Allix).
Ord: 2.2.1843 (contract). K: 3.1843. L: 3.11.1843. Comm: 16.5.1844. C: 5.1844.
Struck 31.12.1854. Hull used a horse transport until 1865.

CHACAL Class – 60nhp steam vessels, later paddle 2nd Class avisos. In August 1844 Regny Bernadac offered to sell the steamers *Océan* and *Méditerranée*, then laid up at Marseille, to the navy. The offer was accepted and the ships were renamed *Chacal* and *Antilope* on 2 September 1844. The two ships had been built by the Compagnie des Bateaux à Vapeur de l'Océan et de la Méditerranée (or Compagnie Cartairade of Paris) for a service from Marseille to Naples, which *Océan* inaugurated upon completion on 5 February 1834, but they were sold in 1838 to the Société Regny of Marseille and thereafter operated between Marseille and Spain. The engines of *Antilope* were converted to screw and reused 1853 in the former sailing gabarre (transport) *Zélée* (built in 1812).

Dimensions & tons: 31.42m x 5.47m x 3.84m. 253 tons disp. Draught 3.00m. Men: 48.
Machinery: 60nhp, 6.7kts. 2 boilers.
Guns: 2 x 12pdr carronades.

Official general arrangement drawings of the three small postal packets built in 1830 for the Toulon–Corsica service. Two of the class, *Liamone* and *Var*, were acquired by the French Navy in 1844, but the drawing applies specifically to the *Golo*, which was never purchased. (Atlas du Génie Maritime, French collection, plate 82)

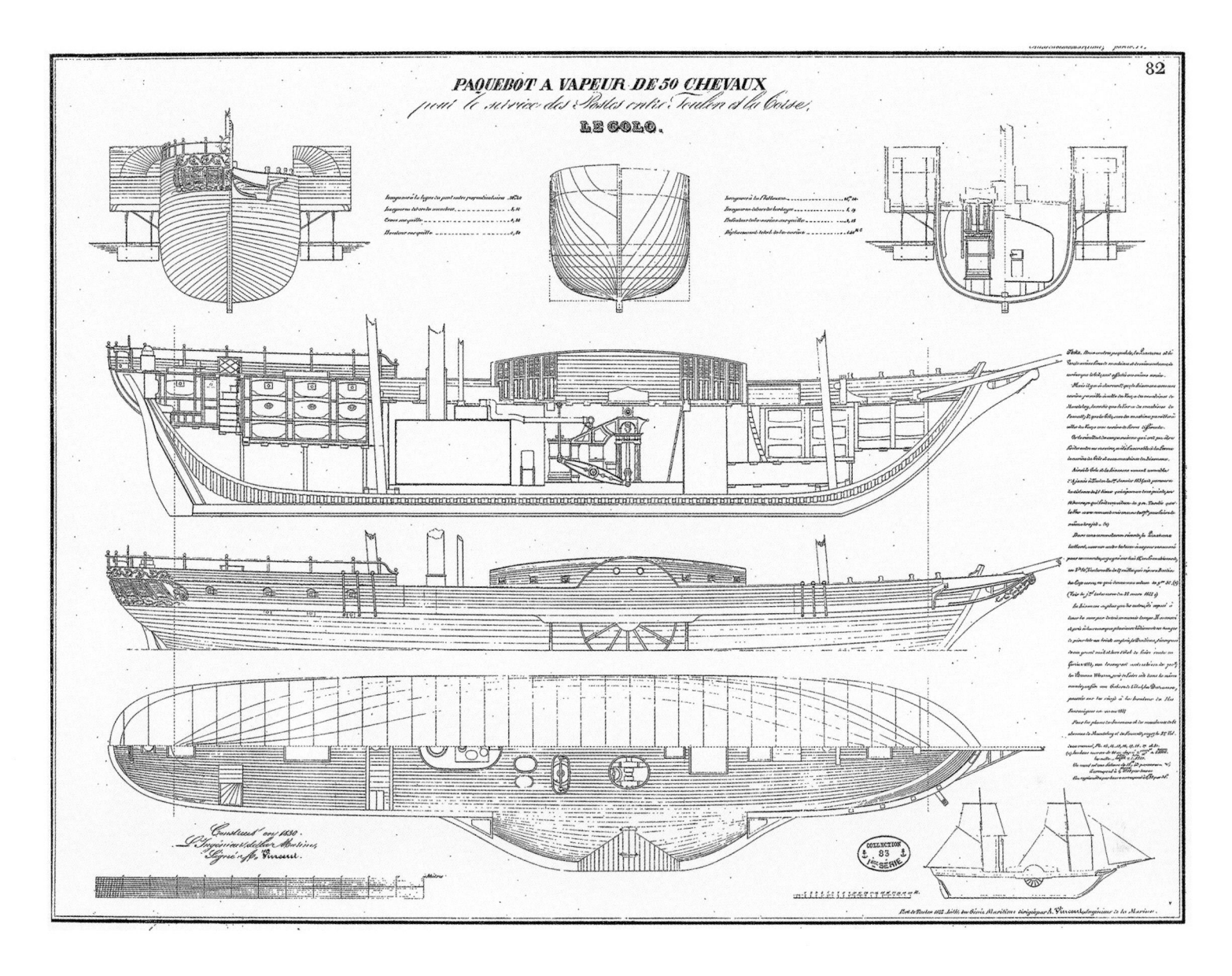

Chacal Paimboeuf/Maudslay
K: 1833 C: 1.1834. Named 2.9.1844, ex mercantile *Océan*. Comm: 16.4.1845.
Struck 5.4.1862 at Toulon, sold or BU before 1865.

Antilope Paimboeuf/Maudslay
K: 1834. C: early 1835. Named 2.9.1844, ex mercantile *Méditerranée*. Comm: 1.2.1845.
Struck 14.8.1851 at Toulon.

RUBIS – 70nhp steam vessel, later paddle 2nd Class aviso. 2nd On 11 June 1844 the Minister of Marine authorised the purchase of *Rubis* from Chappon & Cie. for use in Algeria. The purchase was completed on 17 August 1844. She and a sister, *Saphir* had been built by Louis Benet to serve Chappon's coastal line between Toulon and Marseille. *Saphir* was quickly sold to Tunisia and was wrecked on the North African coast in 1841. Benet's original machinery for *Rubis* was replaced in 1854 by machinery used previously in *Éridan* and then *Alecton*. Benet's engine may then have been used in the sawmill at the Brest arsenal.
  Dimensions & tons: 36.30m, 34.40m wl x 5.95m ext x 3.88m. 260 tons disp. Draught 2.40/2.60m. Men: 44.
  Machinery: 70nhp (rated 80nhp in civil service.).
  Guns: (1847) 2 x 12pdr carronades.

Rubis Louis Benet, La Ciotat/Benet
  K: 1840. C: 1841. Comm: 14.6.1844.
  Decomm. 5.12.1859 at Saint Louis du Senegal, service craft (tug) there by 1.1.1861. Struck 8.11.1862 and hulked. BU 1865.

LIAMONE Class – 60nhp steam vessel, later paddle 2nd Class aviso. On 6 July 1844 the Minister of Marine authorised the purchase of two former postal packets named *Liamone* and *Var* from Gérard & Fils, and the purchase was completed at Toulon on 2 September 1844. These ships were believed to be more suitable and economical for service on the North African coast than the ones then there. They had been designed by Jean-Antoine Vincent and built at the Toulon dockyard in 1830 with a sister (*Golo*, launched 19 June 1830, Fawcett engines, not acquired) to carry out a postal packet service between Toulon and Corsica for which Gérard had won a 9-year contract from the government. He stopped providing this service in 1843.

    Dimensions & tons: 28.00m wl, 25.00m keel x 5.10m ext x 3.30m. 169 tons disp. Draught 2.20/2.30m. Men: 44.
    Machinery: 60nhp (rated 50nhp by their builders), 2 cylinders (0.75m diameter, 0.84m stroke), flue boilers
    Guns: (*Liamone*) 4 swivels; (*Var*) 1 shell gun and 2 swivels.
Liamone Toulon Dyd/Maudslay.
    K: 1830. L: 15.6.1830. C: 12.1830. Comm: 8.7.1844.
    Struck 3.5.1862, coal hulk at Brest. BU 1867.
Var Toulon Dyd/Fawcett, Preston & Co., Liverpool.
    K: 1830. L: 10.7.1830. C: 1830. Comm: 8.7.1844.
    Used as a royal yacht at Tréport in 1844-45. Hauled out 1852 at Toulon and rebuilt as a tug 1852-54. Struck 1854, service craft (tug) at Cherbourg. Renamed *Haleur* c1860. BU 1882.

GUET N'DAR – 20nhp paddle 2nd Class aviso, iron hull. On 12 May 1847 the Governor of Senegal requested a small ship to provide communications between the three fortified French posts in the Gulf of Guinea (particularly Grand-Bassam and Assinie). He argued that the recommended dimensions of 18m x 5m x 0.65m could not be exceeded because of the configuration of the rivers but his representative subsequently agreed to small increases. She had a rudder at each end. The ship was ordered from Auguste Guibert at Nantes by a contract approved on 8 December 1847. The hull wore out and she was decommissioned in the Ivory Coast 21 October 1853. Her engines were returned to France for use in a replacement hull of the same name (see *Akba* class below).

    Dimensions & tons: 20.00m x 4.80m. 60 tons disp. Draught 0.65m.
    Machinery: 20nhp, 7.34kts. Direct-acting, fixed vertical cylinders, 1 tubular boiler.
    Guns: 2.
Guet N'Dar Auguste Guibert, Nantes/Gâche & Voruz, Nantes.
    Ord: 8.12.1847 (contract). K: 12.1847. L: 24.5.1848. Comm: 5.10.1848. C: 10.1848.
    Struck 31.12.1854.

MARABOUT – 60nhp paddle aviso, 2nd Class, iron hull. This ship was built to replace *Érèbe*, above, in Senegal and used her engines. Plans by Jules-Philibert Guède were approved on 16 November 1850.

    Dimensions & tons: 44.65m, 42.00m wl x 6.00m ext x 3.30m. 238 tons disp. Draught 1.86/1.92m. Men: 44.
    Machinery: 60nhp, 8kts.
    Guns: (1852) 4 x 12cm No.2 shell.
Marabout Brest Dyd/from *Érèbe*.
    Ord: 16.11.1850. K: 11.3.1851. L: 1.7.1852. Comm: 15.7.1852. C: 8.1852.
    Struck 31.12.1864, service craft (tug) at Brest. Coal hulk 1.1866, renamed *Soute* 12.1869, BU 1871.

OYAPOCK – 20nhp paddle 2nd Class aviso. This ship was built for use as a tug on the Rivière de la Comté in French Guiana. Plans by Émile Courbebaisse were approved on 4 June 1851. In service her shallow draught permitted her to go practically anywhere but her engine power was insufficient for use as a tug, leading to construction of the *Économe* class below.

    Dimensions & tons: 22.00m x 5.06m. 96 tons disp. Draught 1.34m. Men: 25.
    Machinery: 20nhp. Direct-acting, 1 tubular boiler.
    Guns: 2 mountain howitzers (*obusiers de montagne*).
Oyapock Brest Dyd/Brest.
    Ord: 18.10.1850. K: 18.6.1851. L: 3.5.1852. Comm: 15.7.1852. C: 8.1852.
    Struck 31.12.1864 in French Guiana. Sold or BU 1865.

SERPENT Class – 30nhp paddle 2nd Class avisos, iron hulls. These ships, designed by Paul Marie François Soulery, were built to replace the old *Serpent* and *Basilic* in Senegal. The new hull of *Serpent* was ordered from François Cavé by a contract approved on 4 July 1851. On 1 December 1851 the Cherbourg arsenal asked for work for its shops and on 12 December 1851 the Minister ordered from this yard the 60nhp *Rôdeur* and a sister to *Serpent*. *Serpent* was taken to Cherbourg in April 1852 for fitting out. The ships used the Cavé engines of their predecessors with new boilers, and their hulls were built on their predecessors' plans slightly modified. On 24 February 1859 the Council of Works recommended adopting the *Serpent* type with modifications for use in the upper portions of the Senegal River; the result was the *Phaéton* class.

    Dimensions & tons: 42.30m, 40.40m wl x 5.00m x 2.34m. 161 tons disp. Draught 1.10m. Men: 25.
    Machinery: 30nhp, 6.3kts. Coal 43 tons.
    Guns: 2 x 12cm No.2 shell.
Serpent François Cavé, Asnières-sur-Seine/Cavé
    Ord: 4.7.1851 (contract). K: 7.1851. L: 20.1.1852. Comm: 20.3.1853.
    Struck 18.11.1863, hulk for horses at Senegal. Sold or BU 1865.
Basilic Cherbourg Dyd/Cavé (Constructeurs, Soulery and Pierre Honoré Carlet)
    Ord: 12.12.1851. K: 20.9.1852. L: 26.9.1854. Comm: 18.3.1855. C: 5.1855.
    Struck 3.6.1873, probably in Senegal.

GRAND BASSAM Class – 40nhp paddle 2nd Class avisos. These ships were built to operate in the lagoons of the Ivory Coast and support the French posts there. The ships and the engines were designed by Victorin Sabattier. The engine of *Grand Bassam* was reused in the paddle aviso *Serpent* launched at Nantes on 2 February 1871.

    Dimensions & tons: 34.35m, 33.50m wl x 5,60m, 5.72m ext x 2.75m. 206 tons disp. Draught 1.91m mean. Men: 25.
    Machinery: 40nhp, 6.70kts. Direct-acting. 1 boiler (large tubes). Coal 37 tons.
    Guns: 4 x 12cm shell.
Grand Bassam Rochefort Dyd/Rochefort (Constructeurs, Sabattier and Joseph De Gasté)
    K: 2.1852. L: 1.7.1852. Comm: 29.7.1852. C: 8.1852.
    Struck 16.3.1868, probably in Senegal. BU 1868.
Ébrié Rochefort Dyd/Rochefort (Constructeur, Sabattier)
    Ord: 28.5.1853. K: 2.6.1853. L: 10.10.1853. Comm: 21.10.1853. C: 11.1853.
    Struck a rock and foundered 15.4.1856 in the Akba River after only 16 months in commission.

AKBA Class – 20nhp paddle 2nd Class avisos, iron hulls. These ships were built to the design of the first *Guet N'Dar* on plans by their builder, Charles Michel Nillus of Le Havre. They were double-ended ships with identical ends. *Akba* was ordered from Nillus by a contract approved on 23 August 1853 and the new *Guet N'Dar* (named on 1 September 1853) was added by a contract approved on 10 October 1853. *Guet N'Dar* received the engines of her predecessor with new boilers, while *Akba* received new machinery built by Nillus to the same plans. *Guet N'Dar* arrived at Cherbourg under tow on 7 May 1855 to receive her engines.

They were probably intended for use in the fortified French posts in the Gulf of Guinea, but they served instead in Senegal. On 24 February 1859 the Council of Works recommended adopting the *Guet N'Dar* type for use in the marshes of the Senegal River and in French Guiana; the result was the *Protée* class.

Dimensions & tons: 20.30m, 20.00m wl x 4.80m x 2.40m. 48 tons disp. Draught 0.80m mean. Men: 15-25.
Machinery: 20nhp.
Guns: 2 shell.

Akba Charles-Michel Nillus, Le Havre/Nillus.
Ord: 23.8.1853 (contract). K: 1.9.1853. L: 15.4.1854. Comm: 21.6.1854. C: 7.1854.
Struck 26.12.1859 at Gorée, Senegal.

Guet N'Dar Charles-Michel Nillus, Le Havre/from the previous *Guet N'Dar*.
Ord: 10.10.1853 (contract). K: 10.10.1853. L: 10.8.1854. C: 5.1855. Comm: 16.8.1855.
Grounded on a rock 14.11.1856 at Diakandapé in the upper Senegal River, manned by her crew as a river fort until refloated 6.1857, proceeded towards Médine but attacked and again grounded 7.1857, crew rescued 16.7.1857 by *Podor* and *Basilic*. Her engine was recovered.

ÉCONOME Class – 25nhp paddle 2nd Class avisos. These ships were built to tow barges on the Rivière de la Comté in support of the penal colony in French Guiana. They were to have greater speed than *Oyapock*, above, with only slightly increased length. The Minister instructed Rochefort on 14 July 1854 to prepare plans for the ships and engines and these, by Victorin Gabriel Sabattier, were approved by the Minister on 25 September 1854. The ships were named on 9 November 1854. They performed well in service but their wooden hulls were of very light construction and in 1859 the Council of Works noted that wood did not

The paddle aviso *Arabe* at Lorient before her departure for Senegal on 2 August 1858. Painted white for tropical service, the ship has a long row of ventilation scuttles between decks. (Marius Bar)

last long in that climate and recommended that their replacements have iron hulls and be of the modified *Guet N'Dar* type.

Dimensions & tons: 24.00m wl x 4.10m ext x 2.30m. 69 tons disp. Draught 1.20m. Men: 25.
Machinery: 25nhp, 7kts. Coal 15 tons.
Guns: (1855) 4 espingoles.

Économe Rochefort Dyd/Rochefort (Constructeur, Sabattier)
Ord: 25.9.1854. K: 17.10.1854. L: 3.4.1855. Comm: 1.6.1855. C: 6.1855.
Struck 7.11.1873 at Cayenne, BU 1874.

Surveillant Rochefort Dyd/Rochefort (Constructeur, Sabattier)
Ord: 25.9.1854. K: 17.10.1854. L: 3.4.1855. Comm: 1.6.1855. C: 6.1855.
Struck 13.2.1868 at Cayenne, BU.

PODOR Class – 60nhp paddle *avisos de flottille*. Plans for these ships by Émile Courbebaisse were first discussed by the Council of Works on 27 May 1854 and were approved by it on 8 July 1854. On 24 February 1859 the Council of Works recommended adopting the *Podor* type with modifications for use in the lower portions of the Senegal River; the result was the *Espadon* class. The beam over their paddles was 12.00m.

Dimensions & tons: 41.75m, 40.00m wl x 7.16m ext x 3.36m. 340 tons disp. Draught 1.88/1.88m. Men: 44.
Machinery: 60nhp. Coal 36 tons.
Guns: (1857) 4 x 12cm shell.

Podor Brest Dyd/Brest.

K: 10.3.1855. L: 14.8.1855. Comm: 1.2.1856.

Struck 10.11.1864, coal hulk at Brest. The hulks of *Podor* and the gunboat *Salve* were reported on 11 February 1871 to have been scuttled off Brest with the carcasses of 550 diseased cattle from a herd assembled at Landerneau for the replenishment of Paris, but *Podor* remained on the list until 1875.

Dialmath Brest Dyd/Brest.
K: 10.3.1855. L: 14.8.1855. Comm: 1.2.1856. C: 2.1856.
Struck 16.5.1865 at Gabon, BU.

CROCODILE Class – 20nhp paddle *avisos de flottille*, iron hulls. These ships were built for use in Senegal and their design by Jean Antone Vincent was based on that of *Guet N'Dar*. The Minister of Marine ordered construction of one ship on 7 May 1857 and added the second on 3 August 1857. They were named on 16 August 1857 and ordered from the Forges et Chantiers de la Méditerranée at La Seyne by a contract approved on 1 September 1857. Upon arrival in Senegal they were found to draw too much water (1.30m instead of the desired 0.80m) because of their 'exaggerated' hull scantlings.

Dimensions & tons: 21.20m, 20.00m wl x 4.80m x 2.20m. 80 tons disp. Draught 1.10/1.30m. Men: 25.
Machinery: 20nhp. Coal 10 tons.
Guns: (1858) 2 x 12cm No.2 shell.

Crocodile Forges et Chantiers de la Méditerranée, La Seyne/FCM
Ord: 7.5.1857. K: 9.1857. L: 2.1.1858. Comm: 20.4.1858. C: 4.1858.
Struck 25.3.1869 in Senegal, BU.

Griffon Forges et Chantiers de la Méditerranée, La Seyne/FCM
Ord: 3.8.1857. K: 9.1857. L: 4.1.1858. Comm: 20.4.1858. C: 4.1858.
Struck 25.3.1869 in Senegal, BU.

AFRICAIN Class – 60nhp paddle *avisos de flottille*. These ships were built for Senegal on the same plans as *Podor*. Their construction was directed on 3 August 1857 and the hulls and engines were designed by Émile Courbebaisse. They were designed for a draught of 1.60m at a displacement of 281 tons. They were named on 16 August 1857.

Dimensions & tons: 41.75m, 40.00m wl x 7.12m wl, 7.16m ext x 3.36m. 376 tons disp. Draught 1.88/1.95m. Men: 44.
Machinery: 60nhp, 7kts. 2 cylinders, 1 boiler. Coal 60 tons.
Guns: (*Arabe*, 1858) 2 x 12cm rifles, also reported with 2 x 4pdr 8.6cm rifles M1857.

Africain Lorient Dyd/Indret.
Ord: 3.8.1857. K: 8.1857. L: 15.4.1858. Comm: 5.6.1858. C: 6.1858.
Struck 19.2.1878, barracks hulk at Dakar. Sold or BU 1879.

Arabe Lorient Dyd/Indret (Constructeur, Charles-Louis Layrle)
Ord: 3.8.1857. K: 18.8.1857. L: 15.4.1858. Comm: 12.6.1858. C: 7.1858.
At Toulon for engine repairs 1864-66. Struck 20.5.1879, barracks hulk. Renamed *Africain* as a hulk 1879. Moved to the upper river 1881 and reverted to *Arabe*. Last mentioned 1882.

ARCHER Class – 20nhp paddle *avisos de flottille*, iron hulls. These ships were built for Senegal. Designed by Jean Antoine Vincent, they appear to have been slightly enlarged versions of *Guet N'Dar* with a draught approaching that of the *Crocodile* class. They were ordered from the Forges et Chantiers de la Méditerranée at La Seyne by a contract approved on 21 December 1858.

Dimensions & tons: 24.82m, 24.00m wl x 5.00m x 2.00m. 91 tons disp. Draught 1.16/1.20m. Men: 25.
Machinery: 20nhp. Coal 18 tons.
Guns: (1860) 2 x 12cm No.2 shell.

Archer Forges et Chantiers de la Méditerranée, La Seyne/FCM
Ord: 21.12.1858 (contract). K: 2.1859. L: 5.1859. Comm: 1.7.1859. C: 7.1859.
Struck 1.3.1866, barracks hulk in Senegal. BU 1871.

Pionnier Forges et Chantiers de la Méditerranée, La Seyne/FCM
Ord: 21.12.1858 (contract). K: 10.2.1859. L: 18.5.1859. Comm: 4.6.1859. C: 6.1859.
Struck 31.10.1872 in Gabon. BU 1873.

In early 1859 the Minister of Marine noticed the multiplicity of ship types that had been created for particular services, specifically local service in the colonies, for fishery protection, and on the special station on the Danube. He ordered the Council of Works to define the types of ships that could perform as many of these services as possible. The Council on 24 Feburary 1859 reduced the current eleven types to seven, discarding the *Économe*, *Oyapock*, *Crocodile*, and *Grand Bassam* types and retaining the *Casabianca*, *Podor*, *Serpent*, *Guet N'Dar*, *Labourdonnaye*, *Abeille*, and *Rôdeur* types. On 1 July 1859 the Minister of Marine directed the Council of Works to determine characteristics for the new types for special service, as it had previously done for ships for general service. At the same time he decided in principle that eight iron steam avisos would be ordered from the former Guibert yard at Nantes, operated since 1856 by Ernest Gouin. The eight ships were one screw aviso of the *Pélican* type, three paddle avisos of the *Podor* type, two paddle avisos of the *Serpent* type, and two paddle avisos of the *Guet N'Dar* type. Six plans for steam avisos for special service by Victorin Sabattier and Amédée Mangin were approved on 11 July 1859. The navy's contracting agency was told on 16 August 1859 to proceed with the contract, which was approved on 12 September 1859. The results were *Cuvier* (screw) and the *Espadon*, *Phaéton*, and *Protée* classes below.

ESPADON Class – 80nhp paddle *avisos de flottille*, iron hulls. On 24 February 1859 the Council of Works had recommended adopting the *Podor* type for use in the lower portions of the Senegal River but recommended increasing the engine power from 60 to 80nhp without increasing draught or length. The best way to accomplish this would be to shift to iron hulls. The *Espadon* class was the result. The hulls and engines were designed by Victorin Sabattier (*Podor* type modified). These ships were among eight ordered from Ernest Gouin by a contract approved on 12 September 1859. Their names were assigned on 11 November 1859.

Dimensions & tons: 42.25m, 40.00m wl, 38.70m x 7.17m ext x 3.36m. 318-379 tons. Draught 1.49/2.09m. Men: 44.
Machinery: 80nhp, 280ihp designed, trials (1860) 254ihp = 8.27kts. Oscillating, two cylinders, 1 boiler. Coal 93 tons max.
Guns: 2 x 4pdr 8.6cm mountain rifles.

Espadon Ernest Gouin, Nantes/Indret (Constructeur, Charles Auxcousteaux)
Ord: 1.7.1859. K: 10.1859. L: 4.6.1860. Comm: 1.7.1863. C: 7.1863.
Struck 29.6.1880, barracks hulk. at Saint-Louis de Senegal. Renamed *Africain* 1881. BU 1883.

Phoque Ernest Gouin, Nantes/Indret (Constructeur, Charles Auxcousteaux)
Ord: 1.7.1859. K: 10.1859. L: 6.6.1860. Comm: 22.7.1861. C: 7.1861.
Annex to the transport *Messager*, the torpedo school at Rochefort, 1879-84. Struck 9.7.1886.

Archimède Ernest Gouin, Nantes/Indret (Constructeur, Charles

Auxcousteaux)
　Ord: 1.7.1859. K: 10.1859. L: 1.8.1860. Comm: 22.7.1861. C: 7.1861.
　Became annex to the hospital at Saint-Louis du Senegal 1878. Struck 29.7.1881, sold for BU 8.1883.

PHAÉTON Class – 50nhp paddle *avisos de flottille*, iron hulls. On 24 February 1859 the Council of Works had recommended adopting the *Serpent* type for use in the upper portions of the Senegal River but recommended increasing the engine power by 10 or 20nhp without increasing draught or length. An increase of beam, however, was acceptable and was adopted along with iron hulls. They were designed by Victorin Sabattier (*Serpent* type modified). These ships were among eight ordered from Ernest Gouin by a contract approved on 12 September 1859. Their names were assigned on 11 November 1859.
　Dimensions & tons: 40.00m wl x 7.15m ext. 241 tons disp. Draught 1.24m aft. Men: 44.
　Machinery: 50nhp. Trials (1860) 148ihp = 6.91kts.
　Guns: 2 x 4pdr 8.6cm mountain rifles

Phaéton Ernest Gouin, Nantes/Indret? (Constructeur, Charles Auxcousteaux)
　Ord: 1.7.1859. K: 10.1859. L: 19.7.1860. C: 1861. Comm: 1.3.1864.
　Served in Senegal. Struck 19.2.1878 at Senegal, barracks hulk. Sold or BU 1879.

Sphinx Ernest Gouin, Nantes/Indret? (Constructeur, Charles Auxcousteaux)
　Ord: 1.7.1859. K: 10.1859. L: 18.7.1860. C: 1861. Comm: 1.3.1864.
　Ended her career in Senegal. Struck 31.1.1873 at Saint-Louis de Senegal.

PROTÉE Class – 25nhp paddle *avisos de flottille*, iron hulls. On 24 February 1859 the Council of Works had recommended adopting the *Guet N'Dar* type for use in the marshes of the Senegal River and in French Guiana as replacements for the *Économe* class and the *Protée* class was the result. Hulls and engines were designed by Victorin Sabattier (*Guet N'Dar* type modified). These ships were among eight ordered from Ernest Gouin by a contract approved on 12 September 1859. Their names were assigned on 11 November 1859. The beam outside their paddle boxes was 8.20m.
　Dimensions & tons: 25.05m, 24.00m wl x 5.00m ext x 2.40m. 125 tons disp. Draught 1.34/1.34m. Men: 25.
　Machinery: 25nhp. 2 cylinders, 1 boiler. Coal 18 tons.
　Guns: 2 x 4pdr 8.6cm mountain rifles

Protée Ernest Gouin, Nantes/Indret (Constructeur, Charles Auxcousteaux)
　Ord: 1.7.1859. K: 10.1859. L: 19.6.1860. C: 8.1860 (trials). Comm: 1.5.1864.
　Struck 15.6.1868 at Gabon (lost?).

Pygmée Ernest Gouin, Nantes/Indret (Constructeur, Charles Auxcousteaux)
　Ord: 1.7.1859. K: 10.1859. L: 21.6.1860. Comm: 18.9.1861. C: 9.1861.
　Served in Senegal, then in Gabon. Struck 8.5.1873 in Gabon.

ACQUIRED

Lily (paddle *aviso de flottille*, ex mercantile purchased in the Far East. Built c1857-58, possibly in China or the USA.)
　Dimensions & tons: unknown. Men: 30-44.
　Machinery: 90nhp (re-rated 60nhp 1867)
　Guns: 4
　Purchased 3.1858, was in service 3.1858 under the French flag at Canton. Refitted in 1860, 1864, and at Saigon in 1870. Struck 31.5.1875 at Saigon, sold 1876 for BU. .

Shamrock (paddle *aviso de flottille*, ex mercantile purchased in the Far East. Built c1858, possibly in China or the USA.)
　Dimensions & tons: unknown. Men: 25-36.
　Machinery: 40nhp (re-rated 30nhp 1867)
　Guns: 1
　Purchased 1859. Refitted in 1860 and 1863. Struck 31.5.1875 at Saigon, BU there 1876. .

Déroulède (paddle *aviso de flottille*, ex mercantile *Tahn-Wan* or *Than-Wan* built in 1852, purchased at Hong Kong or Manila)
　Dimensions & tons: unknown. Men: 30-44
　Machinery: 90nhp (re-rated 60nhp 1867)
　Guns: 2, later 3
　Purchased c3.1860, comm. 1.4.1860. Struck 31.12.1867, decomm. 10.3.1868. Either BU at Saigon 1868 or sold with the schooner *Mirage* at Shanghai 25.3.1868. .

Kien-Chan (paddle *aviso de flottille*, ex mercantile *Tory-Wan* or *Toey-Wan*, purchased in the Far East. Built possibly in China or the USA.)
　Dimensions & tons: unknown. Men: 30-44
　Machinery: 80nhp (re-rated 60nhp 1867)
　Guns: 2, later 4
　Purchased c3.1860, comm. 20.3.1860. Hospital ship in the China expedition of 1860. Boiler replaced or repaired 1862. Struck 30.10.1873 at Saigon, BU there 1876. .

Hong Kong (paddle *aviso de flottille*, ex mercantile *Hong Kong* purchased in the Far East.)
　Dimensions & tons: unknown. Men: 30
　Machinery: 90nhp
　Guns: 2
　Purchased c3.1860, comm. 1.4.1860. Struck 18.12.1865, decomm. 1.3.1866 at Saigon, BU there 1869. .

Ondine (paddle *aviso de flottille*, ex mercantile. Launched at Hong Kong 4.1.1859. Hull made of teak, schooner-rigged.)
　Dimensions & tons: 42.20m x 5.90m. 70 tons. Men: 36-44.
　Machinery: 70nhp (re-rated 50nhp 1867), 10 to 11kts.
　Guns: 2 carronades
　Purchased 2.12.1860 for 254,659 francs from the Hong Kong merchant Douglas Lupruck, for whom she had been built. She was bought to replace the *Rose*, 'a vessel of the same time leased very expensively'. Participated in the occupation of Cochinchina 1860-63, then became yacht for the naval commander there. Decomm. 1.6.1870 at Saigon, struck 12.2.1871 with instructions to send her engine to France.

Paddle yacht (later paddle corvette)

AIGLE – imperial yacht. Emperor Napoleon III was a yachting enthusiast, and during the exchange of building plans with the British during the Crimean War he obtained the plans of Queen Victoria's brand new 91m paddle yacht *Victoria and Albert*. After visiting Queen Victoria at Osborne in August 1857 and comparing the Queen's yacht with his own *Reine Hortense* (ex *Comte d'Eu*), Napoleon III ordered a new yacht for himself. However he rejected the idea of copying the British yacht, wanting a French-designed ship for both prestige and economic reasons. The task was assigned to Stanislas-Charles-Henri Dupuy de Lôme. After the Emperor approved his plans, the Minister of Marine on 14 December

A superb lithographic portrait by Louis Le Breton of the imperial yacht *Aigle*. The vessel's rig is a three-masted schooner with no standing square yards, although there is a fore yard struck down on deck from which a square fore course might be set in suitable weather conditions. (© National Maritime Museum PY8741)

1857 signed them, ordered the immediate construction of the ship at Cherbourg, and approved negotiations with Mazeline for the engines, which were ordered by a contract approved on 20 January 1858. The Emperor was disappointed that his yacht was a bit smaller and 2.6 knots slower than *Victoria and Albert*, but she was a very comfortable vessel at sea and the Imperial couple consoled themselves by minutely supervising the choice, installation, and modification of her extensive internal luxury fittings.

Dimensions & tons: 83.00m, 82.00m wl, 76.80m x 10.50m ext x 4.85m. 2,047 tons disp. Draught 4.47/4.67m. Men: 180.
Machinery: 500nhp. Trials (1859) 1,927ihp = 14.24kts. 6 boilers. Coal 270 tons.
Guns: 2 x 12cm bronze shell.

Aigle Cherbourg Dyd/Mazeline (Constructeurs, Prix-Charles Sochet and Jules Toussaint Villain)
  K: 18.12.1857. L: 23.12.1858. Comm: 8.2.1859. C: 9.1859.
  Classed as a paddle corvette and imperial yacht (paddle corvette from 1870). Used by Napoleon III in 1860 and 1865 and by Empress Eugénie in 1869 to attend the opening of the Suez Canal. Renamed *Rapide* 31.5.1873 but saw no further service. Struck 29.1.1891 at Cherbourg, sold 6.10.1891 and BU.

12 Screw Avisos and Screw Gunboats

In the sailing navy, an *aviso* was (according to the 1848 *Nautical Glossary* of A. Jal) 'a small ship that was sent to find the enemy or that was used to carry orders, advice, or news'. Avisos were intended to carry out these functions and only incidentally fight. The closest contemporary British equivalent was 'advice boat'. This functional term did not describe the ships' hull configuration or rig, and sailing vessels that fit into standard categories like corvettes, brigs, or schooners were generally classified as such with the word aviso occasionally appended. The main groups of sailing vessels given the primary classification of avisos or *mouches* (small vessels with similar missions) during our period were some miscellaneous avisos acquired during the 1790s and the 28-ship *Mouche No.2* class of 1808, small schooner-rigged vessels with one gun that were also called schooner-avisos and, when sent to the colonies after 1815, simply avisos.

Steam vessels were originally classified by their nominal horsepower, and in 1842 the rapidly expanding steam navy was subdivided into frigates, corvettes, and 'steamers of inferior rank'. In 1846 the term aviso was applied to these smaller steam vessels with relatively minor combat capabilities, which in turn were subdivided into 1st Class avisos (200 to 160nhp) and 2nd Class avisos (120nhp and below). In this chapter we insert another subdivision at 90nhp, as the vessels above and below this level were of quite different character. In 1854 the Crimean War brought about the revival of additional functional types, gunboats (*canonnières*) and gun launches (*chaloupes-canonnières*) that the French had not built since the days of the Boulogne Flotilla.

Screw 1st and 2nd Class avisos

SALAMANDRE – 120nhp, screw 2nd Class aviso, iron hull. On 2 November 1842 the Minister of Marine included in the building program for 1843 at Toulon an iron steamer of 60nhp for colonial service. On 30 November 1842 he noted that the construction of this ship would be assigned to Stanislas-Charles-Henri Dupuy de Lôme, who had studied iron ship construction in a recent trip to Britain and was to establish a new iron shipbuilding facility at Toulon. Construction was to take about 8 months and the engines were to be built at Cherbourg. By late 1843 *Salamandre* had become an 80nhp steamer that was to be begun in 1845. On 26 February 1844 hull plans by Prix Charles Sochet were approved, but his proposal to substitute experimental high pressure 160nhp engines for the planned 80nhp ones led to more delays. The Minister decided on 1 July 1844 to proceed with her hull and on 28 November 1844 decided to order engines of 120 to 130nhp for her from a French manufacturer. 120nhp engines were finally ordered for her from Louis Benet by a contract approved on 11 November 1846. The dates below (which come from different sources) suggest she began to go into commission for trials while still on the ways; she ran trials in March 1848.

Dimensions & tons: 35.00m wl x 6.50m x 3.60m. 242 tons disp. Draught 2.73m mean. Men: 74.
Machinery: 120nhp (designed by John Barnes). Trials 9.5kts sustained.
Guns: 2 x 12cm bronze shell.
Salamandre Toulon Dyd/Benet (Constructeur, Sochet)
Ord: 28.8.1843. K: 11.1844. L: 2.10.1847. Comm: 14.9.1847. C: 11.1847.
Rated *aviso de flottille* 1869. Struck 2.6.1871 at Toulon. BU 1871.

PASSE PARTOUT – 120nhp, screw 2nd Class aviso, iron hull. In 1841 a new 120nhp paddle steamer was named *Comte d'Eu* and designed as a yacht for the use of the King during his summers at the Chateau of Eu. She failed her machinery trials in early 1844 and reverted to the navy as *Vedette*. By February 1845 another paddle steamer under construction, *Anacréon*, had been renamed *Passe Partout* and designed by Firmin Joffre, the director of Indret, to fulfill the mission for which *Comte d'Eu* had been intended and which the ex postal packet *Var* was then fulfilling. (The name, chosen by the King, referred to her ability to 'go anywhere', specifically the port of Tréport, near Eu, which required a draught under two metres.) While this ship was still under construction, however, the King informed the Minister of Marine on 1 September 1845 that the new British screw-propelled *Fairy* had exceeded 13 knots, and the navy decided on 4 October 1845 to build a new screw *Passe Partout* for him.

Like the paddle *Passe Partout*, which reverted to the navy as *Anacréon*, the screw yacht was designed by Firmin Joffre. The dimensions of the ship were limited by the need to pass through the canal locks at Tréport to reach the King's summer chateau at Eu. Joffre's final plans were approved on 12 January 1846 after construction began. On 8 August 1846 the King wrote of his delight with *Passe Partout*, which finally fulfilled the mission for which the navy had designed three ships since 1841. A year and a half later the revolution of February 1848 eliminated the need for royal yachts, and on 16 January 1851 *Passe Partout* was transferred to the Ministry of Finance for use as a postal packet between Calais and Dover in partial exchange for *Corse* and *Ajaccio*. The navy reacquired her on 7 May 1855 in another deal with the Ministry of Finance in which it also acquired the screw *Faon* and the paddle *Antilope* and *Chamois*. Her screw engines, designed by Jean-Baptiste François Lamaëstre, as well as those of *Pélican* and the *Marceau* class (below), used Penn's successful system of oscillating cylinders.

Dimensions & tons: 39.15m, 37.57m wl, 35.82m x 6.35m, 6.40m ext x 3.56m. 238 tons disp. Draught 2.10/2.26m. Men: 74.
Machinery: 120nhp. Oscillating cylinders, geared, 11.5kts. Coal 35 tons.
Guns: (1855) 2 x 12pdr carronades.
Passe Partout Indret/Indret (Constructeurs, Charles Brun and Charles Antoine)
Ord: 4.19.1845. K: 12.1845. L: 26.3.1846. Comm: 27.3.1846. C: 5.1846.
Struck 4.6.1868 at Toulon. BU 1870.

PÉLICAN – 120nhp, screw 2nd Class aviso, iron hull. This ship was ordered on 15 September 1845 to be built as a platform for conducting experiments with different screw propellers, beginning with one proposed by Lieutenant de Vaisseau Siméon Bourgois. The ship was designed by Charles Marie Brun in consultation with Bourgois, and Brun's plans were approved on 15 December 1845. *Pélican* tested over

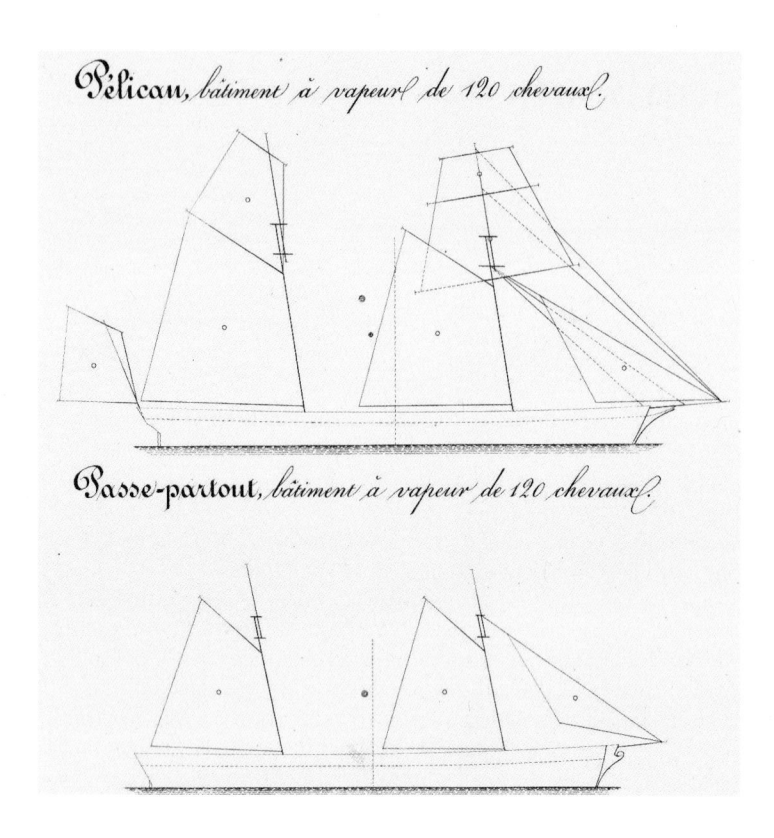

The sail plans for *Pélican* and *Passe Partout* both show schooners, although *Pélican*'s rig is actually a topsail schooner, with square topsail and topgallant on the fore and a jackyard topsail on the main. The difference in total sail area was 495 to 187 sq.m.). *Pélican*'s curious little lug sail carried right aft on a spar no bigger than an ensign staff was known in French as the *tap-cul*; it was also carried on some nineteenth-century British cutters, when it was known as a dandy rig. (Atlas du Génie Maritime, Genoa collection, image 2-0038)

Official lines and machinery drawings for the iron screw aviso *Ariel* as completed in February 1849. The details show the twin-cylinder oscillating engines, the boilers, and a brig sail plan of 408 sq.m. total area. (Atlas du Génie Maritime, French collection, plate 76)

100 different screw propellers before being assigned to general service.
  Dimensions & tons: 41.00m, 40.00m wl x 6.80m x 3.86m. 258 tons disp. Draught 2.25/2.89m. Men: 74.
  Machinery: 120nhp. Oscillating cylinders, geared, 10.84kts.
  Guns: (1848) 4 swivels (53mm bronze).
Pélican Indret/Indret (Constructeur, Brun)
  Ord: 15.9.1845. K: 4.1846. L: 1.6.1847. Comm: 16.6.1847. C: 7.1847.
  Rated *aviso de flottille* 1869. Struck 21.3.1873 at Lorient, tug (service craft). Sold 1885 to M. Degoul for BU.

ARIEL – 120nhp, screw 2nd Class aviso, iron hull. *Ariel*, the paddle *Averne*, and a third ship that became *Daim* were added to the building program on 22 June 1846 due to a shortage of small steamers in the 100 to 120nhp range. On 18 July 1846 the Minister asked Toulon for plans for *Ariel*, and of five submitted he approved those of Stanislas-Charles-Henri Dupuy de Lôme on 9 October 1846. Her engines were ordered from Louis Benet at La Ciotat by a contract approved on 11 January 1848. They were installed between 1 November and 15 December 1848 and the ship ran trials in February 1849. On 10 February 1849 the Council of Works decided that the ship should carry two bronze 12cm field shell guns (*obusiers de campagne de 12*) as had just been selected for *Flambart* and *Daim*, or, if their recoil was too great, two 12cm mountain howitzers (*obusiers de montagne de 12*). Her 1849 sailing report (*devis*) however, shows her with only two 1pdrs.
  Dimensions & tons: 42.40m, 40.00m wl, 36.80m x 6.42m, 6.62m ext x 3.60m. 261 tons disp. Draught 2.00/3.28m. Men: 74.
  Machinery: 120nhp (designed by John Barnes). Oscillating cylinders, 11.84kts. Coal 45 tons.
  Guns: (1849) 2 x 1pdr swivels.
Ariel Toulon Dyd/Benet.
  Ord: 13.10.1846. K: 1.1847. L: 1.8.1848. Comm: 20.8.1848. C: 2.1849.
  Rated *aviso de flottille* 1869. Struck 31.7.1873 at Cherbourg. BU 1875.

CORSE – 120nhp, screw 2nd Class aviso. This famous ship was laid down as *Napoléon* under a contract of 20 July 1841 between the French inventor of the screw propeller, Frédéric Sauvage, and Messrs. Augustin

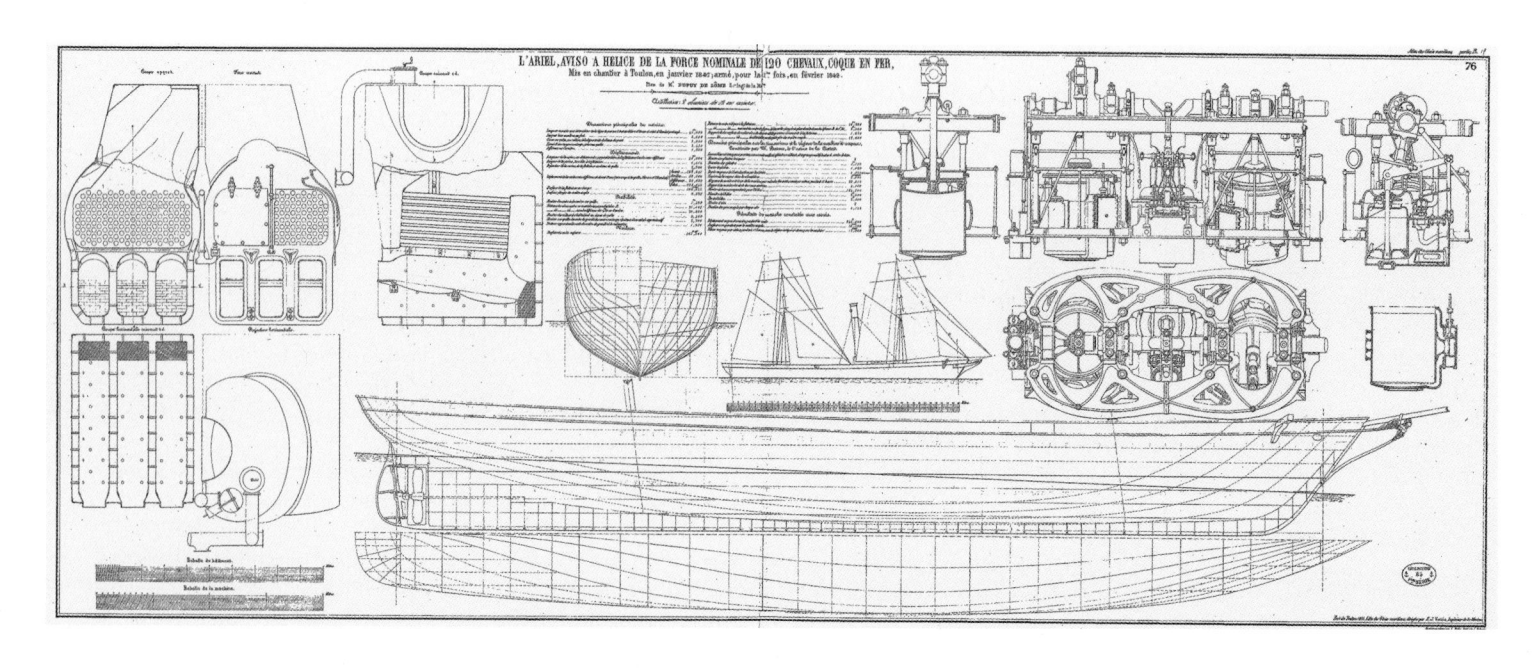

Corse shown in two views, once on the starboard quarter and once on the broadside, in a common convention of ship portraiture. The painting may be the work of François Roux. (USN NH-55796, from an unidentified old book).

Normand (hull) and John Barnes (machinery), the funds and the hull plans being provided by Normand. Barnes had the machinery built in England, possibly at his old firm which had become Miller and Ravenhill. The Ministry of Finance decided to acquire the ship for a new postal service between Marseille and Corsica if her trial speed exceeded 8 knots. She maintained over 10.5 knots, assuring the success of the screw propeller in France. Between 1843 and 1850 she saw very active service on the Marseille to Corsica postal line. She had three masts and a schooner rig. She was transferred to the navy at Toulon on 26 November 1850 with the paddle *Ajaccio* in exchange for the former royal yacht *Passe Partout,* and her name was changed to *Corse* on 18 December 1850 as the navy already had a *Napoléon*. She served at Cherbourg until the early 1870s and then at Toulon until 1890. She received new machinery in 1865.

Dimensions & tons: 48.00m, 45.90m wl, 44.42m x 8.36m, 8.52m ext x 4.13m. 506 tons disp. Draught 2.25/3.59m. Men: 73.
Machinery: 120nhp. Steeple engines, 2 cylinders, geared, 120nhp, 10.5kts. Coal 75 tons.
Guns: (1851) 4 x 4pdrs bronze.

Corse Augustin Normand, Le Havre/John Barnes.
K: early 1842. L: 6.12.1842. C: 6.1843. Comm: 6.1.1851.
Condemned 26.12.1890 and struck 31.12.1890 at Toulon. Converted to a coal hulk by M. Hoirs Curet under a contract of 26.11.1891. Sold by the Domaines 15.1.1903 to M. Martin for BU.

MARCEAU Class – 120nhp, screw 2nd Class avisos. On 15 October 1849 the Minister of Marine ordered the construction at Cherbourg of a 120nhp screw aviso, and on 14 December 1849 he requested specifications for ships of this type able to serve overseas. The Council of Works produced them on 5 January 1850, and on 30 January 1850 the Minister ordered a second ship of this type at Cherbourg. Plans by Amédée Paul Mangin for two ships were approved on 20 March 1850. They were designed with two vertical masts and hoisting screws. The engines reproduced most of the features of those of *Pélican* and *Passe Partout*. *Marceau* was placed in reduced commission on 1 February 1853 and *Duroc* on 1 December 1852.

Dimensions & tons: 43.21m, 39.94m wl x 7.67m, 7.80m ext x 4.07m. 450 tons disp. Draught 2.06/3.22m. Men: 73.
Machinery: 120nhp. 2 oscillating cylinders (vertical), geared, trials 9.09kts (*Marceau*), 9.55kts (*Duroc*). Coal 81 tons.
Guns: (1850) 2 x 24pdrs; (1860) 4 x 12pdrs; (1861) 4 x 16cm shell.

Marceau Cherbourg Dyd/Indret (Constructeur, Paul Marc Soulery)
Ord: 15.10.1849. K: 20.4.1850. L: 19.5.1852. Comm: 5.3.1853. C: 3.1853.
Struck 1.8.1871 and converted to a boys' school ship (hulk from 1874) for the merchant marine at Cette (Sète), renamed *Hérault* c12.1880, replaced by *Gabès* 1902, for sale at Cette 1903.

Duroc Cherbourg Dyd/Cherbourg.
Ord: 30.1.1850. K: 29.4.1850. L: 17.6.1852. Comm: 16.1.1853. C: 1.1853.
Wrecked 13.8.1856 on the Mellish reef, 160 leagues from New Caledonia. Her crew built the pinnace *Déliverance* from the ship's timbers and in her and three of the ship's boats made their way to Timor.

LUCIFER Class – 200nhp, screw 1st Class avisos. In December 1847 two new steamers were scheduled to be begun in 1849: a 300nhp corvette at Cherbourg named *Lucifer* and a 200nhp aviso at Rochefort named *Mégère*. They were cancelled in 1848 due to budget cutbacks, but the names were reused for two ships that the Minister of Marine on 19 February 1851 added to the 1851 building program at Rochefort. Because the Minister did not specify the functions of the ships, the Council of Works on 22 March 1851 followed specifications for transports developed by a special commission in 1845 modified for wooden instead of iron hulls. The resulting characteristics were close to those of the well-regarded 220nhp paddle packet *Périclès*, itself a development of the 160hp paddle avisos of the *Sphinx* class. Victorin Gabriel Sabattier's hull plans for *Lucifer*, approved on 22 October 1851, retained the overhanging upper decks of the paddle ships to facilitate their use as transports. *Mégère* was built on the same plans as *Lucifer* but using the composite wood and iron construction system developed by the Bordeaux shipbuilder Lucien Arman. Her hull was said to be 25 tons lighter than the all-wood *Lucifer*. Sabattier's plans for the machinery of the two ships were approved by the Council of Works on 23 February 1852 after two earlier efforts were rejected.

    Dimensions & tons: 51.64m (51.48m in *Mégère*), 49.74m wl, 47.20m x 8.00m, 8.15m ext x 5.03m. 820 tons disp. Draught 2.86/3.78m. Men: 93.

    Machinery: 200nhp. Trunk (Penn system), trials 9.8kts (*Lucifer*), 9.1kts (*Mégère*). Coal 150 tons.

    Guns: (1856-8) 2 x 30pdrs No.1, 2 x 16cm shell.

Lucifer Rochefort Dyd/Rochefort (Constructeurs, Sabattier, Antoine Auriol, and Joseph De Gasté)

    Ord: 19.2.1851. K: 12.2.1852. L: 24.5.1853. Comm: 24.2.1854. C: 3.1854.

    Struck 29.10.1874, coal hulk at Cherbourg 21.10.1875, sold for BU 1887.

Mégère Rochefort Dyd/Rochefort (Constructeurs, Sabattier and Joseph De Gasté)

    Ord: 19.2.1851. K: 7.4.1852. L: 19.7.1853. Comm: 1.4.1854. C: 4.1854.

    Converted from 3.1871 at Toulon to a 420-ton sail transport. Struck 28.9.1875, school hulk at Marseille. BU 1901.

AIGLE – 200nhp, screw 1st Class aviso. On 26 December 1851 the Director of Works (formerly called the Director of Ports and soon to become the Director of Matériel) recommended that, because Lorient had just received the order to lay down in 1852 two 400nhp corvettes (*D'Assas* type), the order for a 200nhp *corvette-transport* that was to have been built at Lorient in 1852 should be moved to another port. Cherbourg needed the work, and the order was moved there on 31 December 1851, with the plans to be provided by that port. The ship was to be of the same type as the two 200nhp 1st Class avisos in the 1851 program. Ships of this type were needed because, of the 34 avisos of 160 to 200nhp then in the navy, 14 had iron hulls and could not be used on distant service while the wooden-hulled ones were over 12 years old and needed frequent repairs. Additional ships of this type were needed for station duty at Senegal, the Antilles, the Plata, and in Oceania. Plans by Amédée Mangin for a *corvette-transport* similar to the *Lucifer* class avisos received final approval in October 1852. The ship featured a wide deck, borrowed from her paddle predecessors, for carrying 30pdr No.1 guns or troops. She was named on 22 June 1852.

A proposal to build two sisters was rejected in September 1852 because the type had become a jack of all trades and master of none and had neither the speed nor armament to be of much military use in wartime. Probably as a result of this decision, the first two ships of a new type, the transport-avisos *Loiret* and *Somme*, were laid down at Cherbourg in late 1855 to take over the more mundane duties of the old 1st Class paddle avisos.

    Dimensions & tons: 51.96m, 49.93m wl x 8.40m, 8.56m ext x 5.05m. 773 tons disp. Draught 2.81/3.57m. Men: 93.

    Machinery: 200nhp.

    Guns: 4, then 6 x 16cm shell, changed at Toulon 4.1855 to 4 x 30pdrs No.2.

Aigle Cherbourg Dyd/Cherbourg (Constructeurs, Jean-Baptiste Pironneau and others)

    Ord: 31.12.1851. K: 16.9.1852. L: 17.9.1853. Comm: 13.4.1854. C: 4.1854.

    Renamed *Épervier* 8.3.1858 to make the name *Aigle* available for a new imperial yacht, but the aviso had already been wrecked on 11.1.1858 in the Como River in Gabon. Struck 8.5.1858.

FAON – 120nhp, screw 2nd Class aviso, iron hull. This ship was one of three packets built under a law of 4 August 1844 for postal service on the Calais-Dover route, the others being the paddle *Biche* and *Daim* (later the navy's *Antilope* and *Chamois*). Louis-Just Moissard based her plans on the British *Fairy* of 120nhp which attained speeds as high as 13 knots. After the cross-channel postal service was turned over to contractors the navy purchased *Faon*, the two paddle packets, and *Passe Partout* (above) from the Ministry of Finance on 7 May 1855.

    Dimensions & tons: 41.00m, 40.50m wl x 6.00m x 3.25m. 196 tons disp. Draught 1.71/2.19m. Men: 74.

    Machinery: 120nhp. Oscillating cylinders, 12kts. Coal 24 tons.

    Guns: 2 x 4pdrs.

Faon Augustin Normand, Le Havre/Penn.

    K: early 1846. L: 1.2.1847. C: 5.1847. Comm: 16.8.1855.

    School ship for the École de Pilotage du Nord (Honfleur, then Saint-Servan) 1865-77. Rated as a flotilla craft (*bâtiment de flottille*) in 1869 and a flotilla aviso (*aviso de flottille*) in 1874. Struck 7.5.1878, barracks and headquarters hulk for the mobile defence force (*Défense mobile*) at Cherbourg, ordered BU 5 July 1881.

MONGE – 250nhp, screw 1st Class aviso. The four 1st Class avisos ordered in 1856 were initially based on the design of the 2nd Class corvette *Chaptal*. They were classified 1st Class avisos rather than 2nd Class corvettes, however, because of a major review of the role of steam in the fleet. In September 1852 the Council of Admiralty decided that the existing 1st Class avisos, from the *Sphinx* to the *Aigle* classes, no longer met its military requirements. On 11 August 1854 the Council of Admiralty concluded it needed three types of avisos: one to scout for the fleet, one for foreign stations, and one for subsidiary duties in European waters such as fishery protection. The avisos for the fleet were to have the highest possible speed along with sufficient endurance to stay with the fleet for extended periods. The Minister hoped to keep these small (150nhp), but the specified speed and endurance forced the Council of Works to increase them to 250nhp on 16 October 1855. As of 1 January 1856 the 1st Class aviso category was redefined to include all ships in the 200-260nhp range, making the new ships notional successors to both the *Chaptal* and *Lucifer* groups.

On 19 February 1856 the Council of Works accepted two sets of plans for the new fleet avisos based on the *Chaptal* design. The original building program for 1856 included two 1st Class avisos of 250nhp (*Monge* and *Forbin*) at Rochefort and two 2nd Class avisos of 150nhp (*Surcouf* and *D'Entrecasteaux*) at Cherbourg. These ships were ordered and named on 24 October 1855, but on 31 March 1856 the Minister doubled this program because the old 160nhp avisos were becoming too old to satisfy the needs of the colonial stations and other requirements. The assignments to building yards were also reversed to get the navy-built ships closer to near sisters to be built by contractors (Normand and Arman). On 2 July 1856 the specifications were modified to enhance performance under sail so the ships could operate on the foreign stations as well as with the fleet, and four different plans for 250nhp avisos were approved on 1 October 1856 of which three were used, including those for *Monge* by Jean-Baptiste Pastoureau-Labesse. The engines were ordered from Mazeline by a contract approved on 11 July 1856.

    Dimensions & tons: 66.60m, 62.40m wl x 10.20m, 10.40m ext x 5.00m. 1,154 tons disp. Draught 3.58/4.68m. Men: 136.

    Machinery: 250nhp. 2 cylinders, return connecting rod, 815ihp, 11.63kts.

    Guns: (1859) 4 x 16cm rifles.

Monge Brest Dyd/Mazeline (Constructeur, Anselme De Roussel)
 Ord: 24.10.1855. K: 10.7.1857. L: 19.3.1859. Comm: 16.4.1859. C: 6.1859.
 Lost with all hands on 4.11.1868 after leaving Saigon for Hong Kong and Japan, probably off the Annam coast in a typhoon.

FORBIN – 250nhp, screw 1st Class aviso. The origins of this ship were the same as for *Monge* except that she was designed by Jean Félix De Robert. The engines were ordered from Mazeline by a contract signed on approved on 11 July 1856.
 Dimensions & tons: 63.20m, 61.00m wl, 59.25 x 10.04m ext x 5.60m. 1,154 tons disp. Draught 3.64/4.44m. Men: 136.
 Machinery: 250nhp. 2 cylinders, return connecting rod, trials 813ihp = 11.17kts. Coal 220 tons.
 Guns: (1859) 4 x 30pdr No.1.
Forbin Brest Dyd/Mazeline (Constructeur, Jean Félix De Robert)
 Ord: 24.10.1855. K: 27.8.1857. L: 4.5.1859. Comm: 10.7.1859. C: 10.1859.
 Damaged in collision 4-5.5.1880 and decommissioned at Toulon. Struck 28.7.1884, stokers' school hulk at Lorient, renamed *Fournaise* 1885, on sale list at Lorient 1896.

FORFAIT – 250nhp, screw 1st Class aviso. The origins of this ship were the same as for *Monge* except that she was built to plans by Louis Dutard that were modified by Jean Félix De Robert and Victor Legrand. The hull was ordered with that of *Cassard* from Augustin Normand at Le Havre by a contract approved on 5 May 1856, and the engines were ordered from Mazeline by a contract signed on approved on 11 July 1856. The names were assigned on 13 May 1856.
 Dimensions & tons: 67.65m, 65.35m wl, 58.75m x 9.69m ext x 5.72m. 1,237 tons disp. Draught 3.80/4.62m. Men: 136.
 Machinery: 250nhp. 2 cylinders, return connecting rod, trials 792ihp = 11.59kts. Coal 239 tons.
 Guns: (1859) 4 x 16cm rifles.
Forfait Augustin Normand, Le Havre/Mazeline.
 Ord: 5.5.1856 (contract). K: 12.1856. L: 28.12.1859. Comm: 27.7.1860. C: 7.1860.

The 1st Class screw aviso *Forfait*, designed for fleet duties, combined relatively high speed and good endurance, for which she carried a substantial barque rig. The ironclad behind her bow is *Richelieu*, launched in 1869. (Author)

 Rammed and sunk 21.7.1875 by the ironclad *Jeanne d'Arc* during fleet exercises off Corsica, entire crew saved.

CASSARD – 250nhp, screw 1st Class aviso. The origins of this ship were the same as for *Monge*. Her hull was ordered with that of *Forfait* from Augustin Normand at Le Havre by a contract approved on 5 May 1856, and the engines were ordered from Mazeline by a contract approved on 11 July 1856. After July 1856 Normand proposed his own design for the two ships. It did not follow the navy's specifications, but the navy recognised that the proposed ship would probably be an excellent sea boat and that it was a 'veritable clipper' which should have very good speed under sail and sufficient speed under steam. Plans by Normand with Adrien Joyeux and Victor Legrand were approved on 1 October 1856 for one ship. Because of her special design, *Cassard* was selected on 30 March 1860 for use as a yacht for Prince Napoléon and was commissioned as such. Replaced in this duty in 1866 by a new *Cassard* (see corvettes) with which she traded names, she then replaced the former corvette *Comte d'Eu* as the yacht *Reine Hortense* in 1867.
 Dimensions & tons: 68.20m wl x 10.21m x 5.44m. 1,223 tons disp. Draught 3.49/4.58m. Men: 136.
 Machinery: 250nhp. 2 cylinders, return connecting rod, trials 828ihp = 12.23kts.
 Guns: (1861, as yacht) 2 bronze 12cm.
Cassard Augustin Normand, Le Havre/Mazeline.
 Ord: 5.5.1856 (contract). K: 12.1856. L: 13.12.1859. Comm: 15.7.1860. C: 7.1860.
 Renamed *Jérôme Napoléon* 30.7.1860 as a yacht, reverted to *Cassard* as an aviso 16.8.1866, renamed *Reine Hortense* as a yacht 14.2.1867, and finally became *Kléber* as an aviso 19.9.1870. Her armament as such by 1873 was 2 x 14cm No.2 MLR. Struck 23.5.1879, repair hulk for torpedo boats at Toulon, later torpedo school hulk at Bizerte, BU 1891.

Kléber was laid down as the aviso *Cassard* but was used as a yacht during the 1860s under the names *Jérôme Napoléon* and *Reine Hortense* and reverted to an aviso in 1870 under a new name. This image, undated but captioned as *Kléber*, shows her with her luxury deckhouse aft and an armament including two guns close together to starboard amidships and a smaller one aft. (USN NH-74808, from an ONI album of French warships)

BOUGAINVILLE – 120nhp, screw 2nd Class aviso. This ship was designed by Nicolas Marie Julien Le Moine to serve as a sail and steam training ship for the students at the Naval Academy at Brest. She was ordered on 3 May 1858 and named on 11 June 1858, and her plans were approved on 3 August 1858. She was relieved in 1889 as training ship at Brest by the transport-aviso *Allier*, which assumed her name.
Dimensions & tons: 57.30m, 55.50m wl, 54.90m x 9.68m x 5.45m. 737 tons disp. Draught 3.25/4.45m. Men: 85.
Machinery: 120nhp. Trunk, trials 443ihp = 9.3kts. Coal 100 tons.
Guns: (1859) 6 x 16cm shell.
Bougainville Lorient Dyd/Indret (Constructeur, Le Moine)
Ord: 3.5.1858. K: 14.10.1858. L: 30.5.1859. Comm: 17.6.1859. C: 7.1859.
Struck 15.10.1889 at Brest. BU 1890.

SURCOUF Class – 150nhp screw 2nd Class avisos. This new type of aviso grew out of the review of the role of steam in the fleet carried out in 1852 and 1854 and described under the *Monge* class, above. Avisos for the foreign stations were to be small wooden-hulled ships with a complete sail rig, auxiliary steam power of 150nhp, and one large gun and a few small ones. (Cruiser warfare requiring speed would be left to large corvettes of the *Phlégéton* type.) As of 1 January 1856 the 2nd Class aviso category was redefined to include all ships in the 100-180nhp range, making the new ships notional successors to both the *Corse* and *Sphinx* groups.

Specifications for this type were drawn up on 16 October 1855 based on Normand's highly successful screw postal packet *Napoléon* (acquired by the navy in 1850 as the 2nd Class aviso *Corse*). The speed of the design was increased somewhat over the 7 to 8 knots originally planned to make them usable with the fleet as well. Three sets of plans were approved by the Council of Works on 4 March 1856 of which two were used, including those for two ships by Louis-François Octave Vésignié. Their hulls were built on the composite wood and iron construction system developed by Lucien Arman. *D'Entrecasteaux* was built with the 120nhp engines of the paddle aviso *Flambart* re-rated to 150nhp. She later received the engines of *Tancrède* at Cherbourg in 1866-67. The engines of *Surcouf* were ordered with those of the *Prégent* class from Mazeline by a contract approved on 11 July 1856.
Dimensions & tons: 53.06m, 49.50m wl, 50.12m x 8.12m x 4.15m. 628 tons disp. Draught 3.10/3.80m. Men: 65.
Machinery: 150nhp. *Surcouf*: 2 cylinders, return connecting rod, 10.05kts. *D'Entrecasteaux*: trials 290ihp = 9.40kts.
Guns: 2 x 30pdrs.
Surcouf Rochefort Dyd/Mazeline (Constructeurs, Victorin Sabattier, then Charles Brun, Henri Denis de Senneville, and Alfred-François Lebelin de Dionne in that order)
Ord: 24.10.1855. K: 9.1856. L: 16.3.1858. Comm: 26.4.1858. C: 6.1858.
Struck 15.11.1878, headquarters hulk for torpedo boats at Brest to 1884, then a coal hulk and renamed *Charbonnier* 9.5.1885. Sunk 15.5.1902 as a gunnery target off Brest.
D'Entrecasteaux Rochefort Dyd/from *Flambart* (Constructeurs, as *Surcouf*)
Ord: 24.10.1855. K: 10.10.1856. L: 26.7.1858. Comm: 31.12.1858. C: 1.1859.
Given 18.8.1876 to the Emperor of Annam and struck on the same date (promulgated 11.10.1876). Renamed *Loi Dat*. Was unserviceable when France occupied Annam in 1884.

PRÉGENT Class – 150nhp screw 2nd Class avisos. The origins of these ships were the same as for *Prégent* and *Renaudin* except that they were designed by Marie-Pierre Honoré Carlet. The hulls of these two ships were ordered from Lucien Arman by a contract approved on 5 May 1856

Surcouf at Brest, where she was in commission for the last time between 1875 and 1877. These 2nd Class avisos were designed for foreign stations, and despite their relatively small size carried a full ship rig. (Marius Bar)

and were built on the composite wood and iron construction system developed by their builder. The engines were ordered from Mazeline by a contract approved on 11 July 1856. Both ships were placed in reduced commission (*commission de port*) on 16 May 1857 and they were transferred from Bordeaux in June and July 1857 respectively to Rochefort where they were completed by Charles Brun. The initial full commissioning date of *Prégent* is not on record.

Dimensions & tons: 54.00m, 49.50m wl, 49.70m x 8.35m x 4.45m. 615 tons disp. Draught 3.06/3.94m. Men: 65.
Machinery: 150nhp. 2 cylinders, return connecting rod, trials (*Prégent*) 480ihp = 9.9kts.
Guns: 2 x 16cm shell.

Prégent Lucien Arman, Bordeaux/Mazeline.
Ord: 5.5.1856 (contract). K: 6.1856. L: 22.4.1857. C: 10.1857.
Struck 29.10.1874, coal hulk (*charbonnière à vapeur*) at Cherbourg 21.10.1875, BU 1887.

Renaudin Lucien Arman, Bordeaux/Mazeline.
Ord: 5.5.1856 (contract). K: 7.1856. L: 19.5.1857. Comm: 1.1.1858. C: 1.1858.
Towed from Bordeaux to Rochefort for completion 29.6 – 3.7.1857 by *Laborieux*. Struck 8.5.1873 at Brest, retained for torpedo experiments. On sale list 1877, BU 1879.

D'ESTAING Class – 150nhp screw 2nd Class avisos. Construction of this pair and the first two ships of the *Lamotte-Picquet* class was directed on 3 August 1857 and they were named on 16 August 1857. They were intended both for foreign stations and for miscellaneous duties in European waters, including fishery protection. The two ships at Toulon were designed by Louis Dutard, who had been told to use the hull of Vésigné's *Lamotte-Picquet* class, below. Their engines were ordered from the Forges et Chantiers de la Méditerranée (FCM) by a contract approved on 4 June 1858.

Dimensions & tons: 54.20m, 53.00m wl, 51.86m x 8.32m, 8.40m ext x 4.45m. 695 tons disp. Draught 2.86/3.66m. Men: 65.
Machinery: 150nhp. Trials (*D'Estaing*) 390ihp = 10.18kts. Coal 112 tons.
Guns: (1860) 2 x 16cm shell.

D'Estaing Toulon Dyd/FCM.
Ord: 3.8.1857. K: 25.3.1858. L: 26.5.1859. Comm: 26.4.1859. C: 10.1859.
Decommissioned 1.8.1876 and given at Saigon to Annam on 4.8.1876 with the gunboat *Scorpion*. Struck 4.8.1876.

Latouche-Tréville Toulon Dyd/FCM (Constructeur, Napoléon Romagnesi and Dutard)
Ord: 3.8.1857. K: 6.1858. L: 16.2.1860. Comm: 7.5.1860. C: 5.1860.
Struck 5.6.1886 at Toulon. Sold and BU 1887.

LAMOTTE-PICQUET Class – 150nhp screw 2nd Class avisos. Construction of the first two was directed by the Minister of Marine with the *D'Estaing* class on 3 August 1857 and they were named on 16

A lithographic portrait by Le Breton of the *Adonis*, a 2nd Class aviso of the *Lamotte-Picquet* class. The ship was one of a pair built in Corsica, largely as a result of political lobbying, but despite the navy's reservations about the experience of the yard, *Adonis* enjoyed a long career. (© National Maritime Museum PU6228)

August 1857. They were built on plans by Louis-François Octave Vésignié that were approved by the Council of Works on 16 March 1858. Their engines were ordered from Mazeline by a contract approved on 4 June 1858. Of the privately-built ships, the construction of the first five was ordered by the Minister on 28 October 1859 and they were named on 26 December 1859. *Curieux* was built at Honfleur, the next four at Bordeaux, and the last two at Ajaccio – all, in part, to keep private yards employed. They were ordered from four different shipbuilders by contracts signed on 18 November 1859 (25 November 1859 for *Curieux*). The engines of *Diamant, Lutin, Lynx,* and *Tancrède* were ordered from FCM by a contract approved on 18 May 1860 while those of *Curieux* were ordered from Mazeline by a contract signed on 27 April 1860. The last two ships, *Adonis* and *Amphion*, were ordered from Lucien Arman by a contract signed on 16 November 1860 and approved on 27 November 1860 after the navy tried unsuccessfully to turn down the petition for the order from Arman, who was a deputy in the *Corps legislative*, on the grounds that it lacked personnel to supervise work in private yards, particularly in Corsica. The engines for these two ships were ordered from FCM by a contract signed on 23 November 1860. Dimensions varied slightly – those given here are representative of the class. This type was described as a little longer than *Latouche-Tréville* but with a little less displacement. The hulls of *Lynx* and *Tancrède* were badly built (*Tancrède* suffering from unseasoned timber and tropical humidity) and the boilers of *Lynx* were in bad condition, leading to their rapid demise, while the early end of *Lutin* may have been caused by nearly continuous overseas service (from Feburary 1862 to October 1867 except for the first half of 1865). The engines of *Lutin* were reused in *Boursaint*

(1872, 750 tons), those of *Tancrède* went into *D'Entrecasteaux* (above), and *Bruat* (1867, 677 tons) got the engines of *Lynx*.

Dimensions & tons: 56.50m, 54.55m wl, 52.55m x 8.30m, 8.50m ext x 4.45m. 672 tons disp. Draught 2.62/3.82m. Men: 65.

Machinery: 150nhp (Mazeline in *Lamotte-Picquet*, *Coëtlogon*, and *Curieux*; FCM 2-cylinder return connecting rod in others). Trials 7.90 to 11.25kts (570ihp). Coal 100 tons.

Guns: 2 x 16cm shell. *Adonis* and *Amphion* completed with 4 x 12cm bronze field MLR.

Lamotte-Picquet (*La Motte-Picquet*) Cherbourg Dyd/Mazeline (Constructeur, Vésignié)

Ord: 3.8.1857. K: 21.4.1858. L: 18.5.1859. Comm: 24.11.1859. C: 1.1860.

Struck 26.2.1881, barracks hulk and headquarters hulk for torpedo boats at Lorient, on sale list 1892.

Coëtlogon Cherbourg Dyd/Mazeline (Constructeur, Vésignié)

Ord: 3.8.1857. K: 21.4.1858. L: 4.6.1859. Comm: 10.2.1860. C: 2.1860.

Struck 2.11.1877 at Rochefort. BU 1879.

Curieux Émile Cardon, Honfleur/Mazeline (Constructeur, Adrien Joyeux)

Ord: 28.10.1859. K: c6.1860. L: 13.12.1860. Comm: 13.2.1861. C: 6.1861.

Struck 14.2.1879 at Brest. BU 1879.

Diamant Lucien Arman, Bordeaux/FCM (Constructeurs, Joseph De Gasté and Joseph Piedvache)

Ord: 28.10.1859. K: 15.12.1859. L: 8.5.1861. Comm: 1.8.1861. C: 15.10.1861.

Struck 7.5.1878 at Rochefort. BU 1879.

Lutin Lucien Arman, Bordeaux/FCM.

Ord: 28.10.1859. K: 15.12.1859. L: 25.4.1861. Comm: 1.8.1861. C: 3.10.1861.

To Rochefort 6.1861 for completion by Louis-Marc Willotte. Struck

The small iron-hulled *Cuvier* served for many years as a fishery protection vessel and is probably shown here clearing the breakwater in one of the Channel ports. (Marius Bar)

13.2.1868 at Rochefort, BU begun 5.1868, then suspended and retained as unassigned hulk. Traded names 27.2.1871 with the former paddle aviso *Abeille* (1858); both hulks were BU 3-5.1871.

Lynx Moulinié & Labat, Bordeaux/FCM.
  Ord: 28.10.1859. K: 1.12.1859. L: 10.5.1861. Comm: 16.10.1861. C: 12.3.1862.
  Towed to Rochefort 5.1861 for completion. Struck 21.6.1866 at Rochefort. BU completed 9.8.1866.

Tancrède Jean, Gustave, & Arnaud Bichon, Bordeaux-Lormont/FCM.
  Ord: 28.10.1859. K: 1.12.1859. L: 25.5.1861. Comm: 17.10.1861. C: 5.1862.
  Towed from Bordeaux to Rochefort 13.12.1861 by the tug *Boyard*. Struck 21.6.1866 at Rochefort. BU 11.1866 to 1.1867.

Adonis Lucien Arman, Ajaccio/FCM (Constructeur, Charles-Lamy Nettre)
  Ord: 27.11.1860 (contract). K: 1860. L: 15.1.1863. Comm: 18.7.1863. C: 10.1863.
  Struck 27.3.1883, mooring hulk at Rochefort, sold 1907 and BU.

Amphion Lucien Arman, Ajaccio/FCM (Constructeur, Charles-Lamy Nettre)
  Ord: 27.11.1860 (contract). K: 1860. L: 9.5.1863. Comm: 12.10.1863. C: 10.1863.
  Wrecked 21.4.1866 at Vera Cruz.

CUVIER – 120nhp, screw aviso, iron hull. Designed by Amédée Mangin as a modified *Pélican*, she was ordered along with seven paddle avisos (the *Espadon*, *Protée*, and *Phaéton* classes) from Ernest Gouin, who after 1856 operated the former Guibert yard at Nantes, by a contract approved on 12 September 1859. All eight vessels in this contract had iron hulls. Their names were assigned on 11 November 1859.
  Dimensions & tons: 41.50m wl, 40.10m x 6.82m, 7.02m ext x 3.86m. 341 tons disp. Draught 2.56/3.16m. Men: 75
  Machinery: 120nhp. Designed 400ihp, trials (1872) 364.9ihp = 10.82kts.
  Guns: 2 x 4pdr mountain guns.

Cuvier Ernest Gouin, Nantes/Indret (Constructeur, Charles Auxcousteaux)
  Ord: 1.7.1859. K: 10.1859. L: 15.9.1860. Comm: 21.4.1861. C: 4.1861.
  Rated as a flotilla craft (*bâtiment de flottille*) in 1869. Struck 5.11.1892. Hull damaged 3.12.1892 in a test explosion of a 80kg charge of nitrocellulose. On sale list at Brest 1893.

ACTIF – 120nhp, screw aviso, iron hull. On 17 February 1860 the Minister of Marine approved the proposal of the Council of Works to order for trial purposes from John Scott & Co. of Greenock an iron ship of their design equipped with a high pressure steam engine similar to the one that Scott had placed in the British vessel *Thetis* and which had been recommended by the naval engineer Armand Forquenot for its fuel economy. The engine had six cylinders, of which two operated at high pressure and four at low pressure. The ship was ordered from Scott by a contract signed on 3 July 1860.
  Dimensions & tons: 41.48m, 40.84m wl, 38.30m x 6.80m ext x 4.14m. 391 tons disp. Draught 2.80/3.60m. Men: 75

Machinery: 120nhp. Designed 400ihp, trials (1870) 419ihp = 10.41kts.
Guns: 2 x 4pdr mountain guns.

Actif Scott, Greenock/Scott.
   Ord: 17.2.1860. K: summer 1860. L: autumn 1861. Comm: 20.1.1862. C: 1.1862.
   Rated as a flotilla craft (*bâtiment de flottille*) in 1869. Struck 7.5.1892 at Rochefort and converted to a tug (service craft). Still at Rochefort 2.8.1919.

TALISMAN – 250nhp, screw 1st Class aviso. On 16 October 1860 the Minister of Marine directed that a contract be negotiated with Augustin Normand for a 250hp screw aviso on his design similar to *Jérôme Napoléon* (ex *Cassard*). The contract was approved on 16 November 1860 and the name *Talisman* was assigned to the ship on the same date. The engines were ordered from Mazeline by a contract signed on 8 February 1861.

   Dimensions & tons: 68.60m, 68.52m wl x 10.25m ext x 5.29m. 1,334 tons disp. Draught 3.53/4.83m. Men: 154.
   Machinery: 250nhp. Horizontal, trials (1863) 800 ihp = 12.38 kts.
   Guns: (Designed) 2 x 16cm rifles, 4 x 12cm rifles.

Talisman Augustin Normand, Le Havre/Mazeline. Ord: 9.11.1860
   Ord: 16.10.1860. K: 4.1861. L: 24.9.1862. C: 6.1863. Comm: 9.1863.
   Struck 7.7.1893 at Rochefort, headquarters hulk. Base ship and repair hulk for the *Défense Mobile* at Bizerte 10.1896 replacing *Guêpe*, depot hulk for torpedo boats at Oran 1906, on sale list 1908-9.

Small screw avisos (90nhp and less)

PINGOUIN – 30nhp, mixed propulsion 2nd Class aviso, iron hull. On 12 July 1843 the first governor of the *Établissements français de l'Océanie* (Tahiti and environs), while outbound to his new post, wrote home to request two iron hulled steamers of 16nhp each for communications within the Marquises Islands based on his observations of shipping in the harbour of Rio de Janeiro. When authorities in Paris studied this request they all agreed that 16nhp was not enough and decided to build instead one 30nhp ship, to be fitted with a screw propeller. Even with this enhancement her steam machinery remained an auxiliary to her sail propulsion, making her a mixed propulsion vessel. On 18 January a contract with Chaigneau fils frères & Bichon of Bordeaux for the design and construction of the ship was approved, a contract for the engines with a leading French mechanical firm, Mazeline, was approved, and the name *Pingouin* was assigned to the ship. Mazeline opted to use tubular (fire tube or locomotive) boilers in the ship, which also initially had a 6-bladed Ericsson screw. After trials Mazeline asked on 9 June 1845 to be allowed two months to replace the ship's boilers, which did not make enough steam because of a miscalculation and because the firm had increased the engines from the 30nhp in the contract to 50nhp because of their unfamiliarity at the time with tubular boilers. (The 50nhp rating has not been found in any Navy records other than this correspondence from the builder.) The ship was taken to Rochefort in July 1845 for completion by the constructeur Nicolas Courtin. Her administrative home port was changed on 1 January 1846 from Bordeaux to Cherbourg and she remained administratively assigned to that port until she decommissioned on 17 July 1855 at Toulon. With three experimental technologies on board (she also had high pressure engines), she may never have left Cherbourg for the Marquises, instead joining other Cherbourg-based small sailing and steam craft in fishery protection and coast guard operations near that port.

   Dimensions & tons: 34.45m, 33.00m wl, 30.68m x 5.50m x 2.75m. 161 tons disp. Draught 1.95m mean. Men: 51.
   Machinery: 30nhp. High pressure, oscillating cylinders. Tubular boilers. Coal 25 tons.
   Guns: None.

Pingouin Chaigneau & Bichon, Bordeaux-Lormont/Mazeline.
   Ord: 18.1.1844 (contract). K: 2.1844. L: 13.12.1844. Comm: 21.3.1845. C: 8.1845.
   Struck 21.1.1856 at Toulon, BU before 1865.

RÔDEUR Class – 60nhp, screw 2nd Class avisos, iron hulls. On 1 December 1851 the Cherbourg arsenal asked for work for its shops. On 12 December 1851 the Minister ordered from this yard one wooden hull with 60nhp engines (*Rôdeur*) and one iron hull like the one ordered from Cavé (*Basilic*). *Rôdeur* was intended for service on the coasts of southern France and Algeria (coast guard and fishery protection) or for local service in the colonies. She was named on 12 May 1852. Plans by Paul Marie François Soulery, now with an iron hull, were approved on 27 June 1853. A second iron ship (*Croiseur*) was soon added for fishery protection duty as were two 40nhp non-naval fishery protection iron steamers, *Guetteur* and *Pêcheur*, that were to be built and engined by Charles-Michel Nillus on plans by Soulery similar to *Rôdeur* furnished by Cherbourg. In service *Rôdeur* was assessed to be 'perfect' for her assigned duties because of her slight draught, low cost of operation, and relatively high speed. They were redesignated *avisos de flottille* in January 1859.

   Dimensions & tons: 36.34m, 35.00m wl, 33.50m x 5.85m, 6.02m ext x 3.02m. 175 tons disp. Draught 1.60/2.20m. Men: 51.
   Machinery: 60nhp (designed by Soulery), 9.4kts.
   Guns: 2 x 12cm No.2 bronze shell.

Rôdeur Cherbourg Dyd/Cherbourg (Constructeurs, Soulery and Louis Nicolas Sollier)
   Ord: 12.12.1851. K: 19.11.1853. L: 5.2.1855. C: 8.1855. Comm: 6.9.1855.
   Boilers replaced 1861 at Toulon with one from the service tug *Adolphe*, this condemned 12.1865. Struck 19.4.1866 at Toulon, ordered BU 9.1866.

Croiseur Cherbourg Dyd/Cherbourg.
   K: 4.7.1854. L: 31.7.1855. Comm: 6.11.1855. C: 11.1855.
   Struck 5.11.1868, probably at Toulon.

LABOURDONNAYE – 35nhp, screw aviso. This ship was a mixed propulsion schooner or aviso (with sails and weak screw machinery) designed by Émile Courbebaisse for service in Mayotte and Madagascar. She had been requested by Rear Admiral Nicolas-François Guérin, who commanded the station of Réunion and Madagascar between 1849 and 1852. Her plans were approved by the Council of Works on 27 March 1855, the order to build her was received at Brest on 17 April 1855, and her name was assigned on 19 May 1855. The only vessel of her type in the navy, she was found to meet the station's needs while being less expensive to operate than equivalent ships in the general navy. She became an *aviso de flottille* in January 1859.

   Dimensions & tons: 34.89m, 32.00m wl, 33.20m x 6.52m x 3.00m. 247 tons disp. Draught 2.21/3.11m. Men: 51.
   Machinery: 35nhp. Coal 26 tons.
   Guns: (1856) 4 x 12cm shell.

Labourdonnaye (*La Bourdonnais*) Brest Dyd/Cherbourg (Constructeurs, Courbebaisse and Victor Gervaize)
   Ord: 17.4.1855. K: 13.8.1855. L: 17.7.1856. Comm: 26.7.1856. C: 8.1856.

Struck 10.3.1870, station hulk at Nossi-Bé. Renamed *Mahé* 1873 to free name for a new aviso. To Mayotte 1873, on sale list 1874, BU 1876.

VIGIE – screw *aviso de flottille*, iron hull. This vessel was ordered from Gustave & Arnaud-Frédéric Bichon frères at Bordeaux by a contract signed on 23 September 1859 as an addition to the program of one screw (*Cuvier*) and seven paddle iron-hulled avisos (*Espadon*, *Protée*, and *Phaéton* classes) ordered earlier in the month from Ernest Gouin at Nantes. Designed by Amédée Mangin, *Vigie* duplicated *Rôdeur*, which had been assessed to be 'perfect' for her assigned duties. Her name was assigned on 11 November 1859. Her engines were ordered from FCM by a contract approved on 18 May 1860.
- Dimensions & tons: 37.15m, 35.00m wl, 33.70m x 6.16m ext x 3.38m. 240 tons disp. Draught 2.10/2.84m. Men: 51.
- Machinery: 60nhp. Trials (1867) 73ihp = 8.50kts.
- Guns: 2 x 4pdr mountain guns.

Vigie Gustave & Arnaud-Frédéric Bichon, Bordeaux-Lormont/FCM.
- Ord: 9.1859 (contract). K: 11.1859. L: 3.12.1861. Comm: 1.4.1862. C: 5.1862.
- Struck 8.4.1881 at Toulon, on disposal list 1882, BU 1885.

ARGUS – screw *aviso de flottille*, iron hull. On 3 February 1860 the Minister of Marine approved the construction of an aviso of the *Rôdeur* type to conduct experiments with the water tube boilers of Julien-François Belleville. The navy had previously tested Belleville boilers in the 'corvette mixte' *Biche* in 1855-56, but *Argus* received a new model with horizontal tubes instead of the earlier vertical tubes. The plans of *Argus* by Amédée Paul Théodore Mangin differed from the *Rôdeur* type only enough to permit installation of the different boilers. The hull of the ship was ordered from Durenne at Asnières-sur-Seine by a contract signed on 17 February 1860, her engines were ordered from Gouin's facility at Paris by a contract signed on 30 March 1860, and two Belleville boilers were ordered from the Belleville firm at Saint-Denis by a contract signed on 2 April 1860. *Argus* received Lagrafel boilers in 1875 and new trials in 1877 produced 176ihp and 8.93kts.
- Dimensions & tons: 37.20m, 35.00m wl, 33.85m x 6.12m ext x 3.38m. 239 tons disp. Draught 2.10/2.90m. Men: 50
- Machinery: 60nhp. Oscillating cylinders. Trials (1871) 80ihp = 6.57kts.
- Guns: 2 x 4pdr mountain guns.

Argus Durenne, Asnières-sur-Seine/Gouin, Paris.
- Ord: 3.2.1860. K: 3.1860. L: 26.11.1860. Comm: 5.1862 (?).
- School ship for the École de Pilotage de l'Ouest at La Rochelle with the pinnace *Mesquier* as annex, but unreliable experimental boilers caused her to be replaced frequently by *Chamois*, *Pélican*, or *Phoque*. Permanently replaced 1880 by the gunboat *Oriflamme*. Struck 6.5.1884 and BU.

SYLPHE Class – 15nhp, screw *avisos de flottille*, iron hulls. On 30 July 1860 plans by Amédée Mangin were submitted for an iron-hulled *chaloupe à vapeur* for fishery protection duty on the French coast. Two of these 15nhp vessels were to be built at Lucien Arman's yard at Paris. Arman's main yard was at Bordeaux, and the little craft are usually listed as having been built there. The ships were ordered from Arman by a contract signed on 5 August 1860. Each had a fish tank forward of the engine room.
- Dimensions & tons: 20.67m, 20.00m wl, 18.90m x 4.62m ext x 2.14m. 75 tons disp. Draught 1.32/1.92m. Men: 15.
- Machinery: 15nhp Trials (*Sylphe*) 38ihp = 6.41kts.
- Guns: (*Sylphe*) none; (*Favori*) 2 espingoles.

Sylphe Lucien Arman, Paris/Mazeline (Constructeur, Joseph Alexandre De Gasté)
- Ord: 8.1860 (contract). K: 9.1860. L: 22.7.1861. Comm: 1.1.1862. C: 1.1862.
- Struck 9.4.1878 at Brest, BU 1879.

Favori Lucien Arman, Paris/Mazeline (Constructeur, De Gasté)
- Ord: 8.1860 (contract). K: 9.1860. L: 5.8.1861. Comm: 9.1.1862. C: 1.1862.
- Struck 19.2.1878 at Toulon, barracks hulk at Marseille. Sold and BU 1887.

ACQUIRED

Norzagaray (screw *aviso de flottille*, ex mercantile)
- Length: 44m. Men: 30
- Machinery: 50nhp, also reported as 80nhp
- Guns: 2, including 1 x 12cm.
- Purchased c4.1859 at Manila, was in service in Indochina on 7.5.1859. Decomm. 1.3.1864. Struck 6.8.1866, probably in Indochina. .

Alon-Prah (screw *aviso de flottille*, ex mercantile. May have been built at Bordeaux in 1857-58. Rigged as brig-schooner.)
- Dimensions & tons: 32.11m x 7.22m. Draught 3.20m to 3.50m. Men: 45-50
- Machinery: 80nhp (re-rated 60nhp 1867)
- Guns: 2
- Purchased 11.1.1860 in the Far East. Decomm. 1.5.1868 at Saigon. Struck 11.5.1869 and fitted as floating storage at Saigon. BU 1879 at Saigon. .

Peï-Ho (screw steamer reportedly built at New York before 1859)
- Machinery: 90nhp?
- Reportedly requisitioned 12.1858 in the Far East. Nominally part of the *Division Navale des mers de Chine* in 8.1860. Last recorded in 2.1861 on the list of ships in service in Indochina, possibly returned to her owner. All details of this ship, including her reported existence in French hands, are uncertain.

Screw gunboats

ÉTINCELLE Class – 1st Class gunboats. On 21 June 1854 the Minister of Marine asked the French commander in the Black Sea to recommend characteristics for steam gunboats for operations in shallow parts of the Black Sea and the Danube River. Their wartime missions were to carry out shore bombardment and protect armoured floating batteries against enemy boat attacks. On 18 August the Minister invited plans from Cherbourg, Brest, and Rochefort for plans for steam gunboats for operations in the Baltic. On 2 September 1854 Toulon forwarded plans by Anselme De Roussel for the Black Sea gunboats, in which a relatively low speed (8 knots) was accepted because the shallow draught of these vessels would give them mediocre seagoing qualities. Separate plans were drawn up for ships for the Baltic, but on 27 October the Minister approved the use of De Roussel's plans for both theatres. On 22 November 1854 the Minister decided that 12 gunboats of this larger type would be built, allocated them to building yards, and assigned names to them and to eight smaller gunboats (see below) and five sailing bomb vessels. Four of the vessels were ordered from Normand by a contract approved on 27 November 1854, the others being built in naval dockyards, and the engines for all twelve were ordered from Schneider by a contract of the same date. The armament originally proposed for the Black Sea gunboats was 2 x 30pdrs No.1, 2 x 22cm No.1 shell, and 2 x

An engraving by Le Breton of the 1st Class gunboat *Dragonne*, showing the protective 'shields' or casemates for the forward and after gun batteries. These later had armour plates added. (Courtesy of Beverley R. Robinson Collection, US Naval Academy Museum)

16cm shell. Most of the ships were commissioned within a few days of their launchings and before their machinery was embarked; machinery installation began in May 1855 and was completed between June and July 1855.

The navy hoped the class would be useful after the war for tasks in which shallow draught and economy were more important than speed: for coast guard duties on the French coast, on naval stations (such as Spain) near France, and on colonial service. After the war these ships were typically given an armament of 2 x 16cm M1855 MLR, 2 x 16cm shell, and 2 x 12cm No.2 bronze shell on forecastle and poop. In 1858, however, the navy decided that this type was unsatisfactory, and its functions were reassigned to the new 2nd Class avisos of the *Surcouf* and following classes. At about the same time a false keel averaging half a metre in depth was added to two ships at Cherbourg and five at Toulon (*Aigrette, Fulminante, Étincelle, Éclair, Flamme, Flèche,* and *Grenade*), increasing their displacement and draught. The Cherbourg ships also received a 'primitive shield [*masque*] with removable bulwarks' with 5cm of armour plate, and in May the five Toulon ships were ordered to be similarly fitted after the other modifications were completed. On 28 May 1859 Toulon proposed adding another 6cm of armour plate to the shields, which would be pierced with ports for the two forward guns, for operations in the Adriatic. Typical figures as modified were the 536 tons and draught of 2.65m forward and 3.37m aft of *Flèche* in 1861.

Dimensions & tons: 45.40m (Toulon ships 44.38m, Brest ships 44.80m), 43.94m wl, 43.10m x 7.76m x 2.99m. 484 tons disp. Draught 2.27/2.47m. Men: 79.
Machinery: 110nhp. High pressure. Coal 41 tons.
Guns: (1855) 4 x 50pdrs SB.

Étincelle Cherbourg Dyd/Schneider.
  Ord: 22.11.1854. K: 26.11.1854. L: 18.3.1855. Comm: 25.4.1855. C: 5.1855. Engines installed 5.1855 to 12.7.1855.
  To Constantinople 12.7.1855, in reserve at Toulon 7.9.1855, to the Adriatic 18.6.1859. Lost 19.3.1862 (last seen on 15.3.62, 60 leagues from her destination of Mayotte, and probably lost with all hands in a cyclone in the Mozambique Channel). Struck 18.4.1864.

Éclair Cherbourg Dyd/Schneider.
  Ord: 22.11.1854. K: 26.11.1854. L: 18.4.1855. Comm: 25.4.1855. C: 5.1855.
  To the Black Sea 2.7.1855, to the Adriatic 18.6.1859, in Mexico 1861-63, to French Guiana 1865. Struck 20.11.1871 in French Guiana, sold there for BU 1872.

Flamme Brest Dyd/Schneider.
  Ord: 22.11.1854. K: 22.11.1854. L: 7.5.1855. Comm: 1.5.1855 and 15.6.1855. C: 5.1855. Engines installed 28.5.1855 to 26.6.1855.
  To the Black Sea (Kamysh) 2.7.1855, to the Adriatic 15.6.1859, to China 29.12.1857. Struck 24.3.1872 at Saigon, became a lightship on the Mekong River. Sold 1878.

Grenade Brest Dyd/Schneider (Constructeur, Édouard Nouet)
- Ord: 22.11.1854. K: 22.11.1854. L: 7.5.1855. Comm: 1.5.1855 and 15.6.1855. C: 5.1855. Engines installed 21.5.1855 to 29.6.1855.
- To the Black Sea 27.7.1855, to the Adriatic 15.6.1859, in Mexico 1861-63. Grounded at Cette (Sète) 1869 while on fishery patrol duty, refloated. Struck 2.5.1871, BU 1871 at Toulon.

Alarme Toulon Dyd/Schneider (Constructeur, De Roussel)
- Ord: 22.11.1854. K: 11.1854. L: 3.5.1855. Comm: 3.5.1855. C: 5.1855. Engines installed 5-6.1855.
- To the Black Sea (Kamysh) 2.7.1855, to China 29.12.1857, then to Cochinchina 1859. Struck 29.11.1871 at Saigon. BU 1872.

Flèche Toulon Dyd/Schneider (Constructeur, De Roussel)
- Ord: 22.11.1854. K: 11.1854. L: 9.5.1855. Comm: 9.5.1855. C: 5.1855. Engines installed 15.5.1855 to 13.6.1855.
- To the Black Sea 2.7.1855, to the Adriatic 18.6.1859, in Mexico 1863-64. Struck 11.2.1865 at Brest, coal hulk, BU 1883.

Fusée Toulon Dyd/Schneider (Constructeur, De Roussel)
- Ord: 22.11.1854. K: 11.1854. L: 16.5.1855. Comm: 16.5.1855. C: 5.1855.
- To the Black Sea 6.7.1855, to China early 1857, then to Cochinchina 1859. Struck 5.11.1868 at Saigon. BU 1869.

Mitraille Toulon Dyd/Schneider (Constructeur, De Roussel)
- Ord: 22.11.1854. K: 11.1854. L: 24.5.1855. Comm: 24.5.1855. C: 6.1855.
- To the Black Sea from Toulon 2.7.1855, arrived at Kamysh 27.7.1855. To China 17.12.1856, then to Cochinchina 1859. Struck 5.11.1868 at Saigon. BU 1869.

Dragonne Normand, Le Havre/Schneider.
- Ord: 22.11.1854. K: 12.1854. L: 12.5.1855. Comm: 12.5.1855. C: 5.1855.
- To the Baltic 18.7.1855, to China from Cherbourg 17.12.1856 with the corvette *Phlégéton*, then to Cochinchina 1859. Struck 7.3.1867 at Saigon. BU 1867.

Aigrette Normand, Le Havre/Schneider.
- Ord: 22.11.1854. K: 12.1854. L: 15.5.1855. Comm: 14.5.1855. C: 5.1855. Engines installed 6.1855.
- To the Baltic 18.7.1855, to the Adriatic 18.6.1859. Sunk 17.8.1859 by boiler explosion off Antivari in the Adriatic.

Fulminante Normand, Le Havre/Schneider.
- Ord: 22.11.1854. K: 12.1854. L: 20.5.1855. Comm: 20.5.1855. C: 6.1855.
- To the Baltic 18.7.1855, to the Adriatic 18.6.1859, on the Brazil station 1860-63. Struck 11.2.1865 at Brest, coal hulk, BU 1879.

Avalanche Normand, Le Havre/Schneider.
- Ord: 22.11.1854. K: 12.1854. L: 26.5.1855. Comm: 27.5.1855. C: 6.1855.
- To the Baltic 18.7.1855, to China early 1857, then to Cochinchina 1859. Struck 16.11.1866 at Saigon. BU 1867.

TEMPÊTE Class – 2nd Class gunboats. As part of the Anglo-French naval cooperation during the Crimean War, the French supplied the British with the plans of the *Dévastation* class floating batteries and the British gave the French the plans of the *Dapper* class gunboats. The Council of Works examined the British plans and concluded that they did not have sufficient displacement for their armament or enough space for crew accommodations. The British had already lengthened the ships from the 100 British feet (30.48m) of the *Pelter* class to 106ft 2in (32.36m), and the Council lengthened them again to 35 metres. The Minister of Marine approved this action on 21 November 1854 and ordered that eight of the vessels be built. On 22 November 1854 two of these were assigned to Rochefort, four to Nantes (Auguste Guibert), and two (*Redoute* and *Poudre*) to Bordeaux (probably Lucien Arman), but ultimately six gunboats including *Redoute* and *Poudre* were ordered from Guibert by a contract approved on 25 November 1854. The engines for *Redoute* and *Poudre* were ordered from Charbonnier, Bourgougnan and Co. (Cavé's successors) by a contract approved on 23 December 1854 while the engines for Guibert's other four ships were ordered from Ernest Gouin & Cie. by a contract approved on 12 January 1855. (Gouin took over the Guibert yard in 1856.) The plans were produced at Rochefort, probably by Victorin Sabattier. The armament originally proposed for Black Sea operations was 2 x 30pdrs No.1 and 2 x 16cm shell. The vessels built by Guibert at Nantes were commissioned and had their engines installed at Lorient between May and July 1855.

These ships were modified around 1859 by the addition of a forecastle and poop and provision of a false keel and lateral keels. Their armament was changed to 2 x 16cm rifles. The changes raised their tonnage to around 296t and draught to around 2.26m forward and 2.72m aft. In May 1859 the forward bulwarks of some units of this class including *Lance* and *Sainte Barbe* were fitted with armour plates for operations in the Adriatic. The early demise of this class was blamed on poor supervision of the private shipbuilder. The engines of *Poudre*, *Redoute*, *Arquebuse*, and *Salve* were removed and sent to China for use in the four units of the *Kenney* class, which were built at Ningpo by French engineers in 1863-64.

Dimensions & tons: 36.36m, 35.38m wl, 34.98m x 6.72m x 2.58m. 289 tons disp. Draught 2.18/2.47m. Men: 59.
Machinery: 90nhp. High pressure, 8.4kts.
Guns: (1855) 2 x 50pdrs SB.

Tempête Rochefort Dyd/Rochefort (Constructeur, Sabattier)
- Ord: 22.11.1854. K: 7.12.1854. L: 4.4.1855. Comm: 12.4.1855. C: 5.1855.
- To the Baltic 9.6.1855, to the Adriatic 18.6.1859, to Mexico 23.9.1862. Struck 15.10.1866 at Vera Cruz because of yellow fever on board and BU in situ.

Tourmente Rochefort Dyd/Rochefort (Constructeur, Sabattier)
- Ord: 22.11.1854. K: 7.12.1854. L: 4.4.1855. Comm: 21.4.1855. C: 5.1855.
- To the Baltic 9.6.1855, to Mexico 30.10.1862. Struck 2.3.1868 at Brest, BU 1869.

Poudre Auguste Guibert, Nantes/Charbonnier, Bourgougnan and Co..
- Ord: 22.11.1854. K: 12.1854. L: 30.4.1855. Comm: 28.5.1855. C: 6.1855.
- To the Baltic 14.6.1855, to the Adriatic 18.6.1859. Struck 31.12.1864 at Brest. Engine replaced with one of 60nhp and became a paddle tug. Condemned 1881, BU 1884.

Sainte-Barbe Auguste Guibert, Nantes/Gouin.
- Ord: 22.11.1854. K: 12.1854. L: 30.4.1855. Comm: 6.6.1855. C: 6.1855.
- To the Baltic from Lorient 25.7.1855, to the Adriatic 18.6.1859, to Mexico 1.9.1862. Decomm. at Vera Cruz 31.7.1865, the hull being badly eaten by shipworm. Struck 31.12.1865 and BU.

Lance Auguste Guibert, Nantes/Gouin.
- Ord: 22.11.1854. K: 12.1854. L: 1.5.1855. Comm: 9.5.1855 (at Nantes?). C: 5.1855.
- To the Baltic from Lorient 24.7.1855, to the Adriatic 5.5.1859, to Mexico 15.9.1862. Grounded 22.1.1863 in the Bay of Tampico, ordered burned 24.1.1863.

Redoute Auguste Guibert, Nantes/Charbonnier, Bourgougnan and Co..
- Ord: 22.11.1854. K: 12.1854. L: 1.5.1855. Comm: 6.6.1855. C: 5.1855.
- To the Baltic from Lorient 1.8.1855, to the Adriatic 18.6.1859.

Struck 25.11.1862 at Brest, coal hulk, BU 1879.
Salve Auguste Guibert, Nantes/Gouin.
   Ord: 22.11.1854. K: 1.1855. L: 4.5.1855. Comm: 1.7.1855. C: 6.1855.
   To the Baltic from Lorient 25.7.1855, to the Adriatic 18.6.1859. Struck 25.11.1862 at Brest, coal hulk. Reported scuttled off Brest with the paddle aviso *Podor* on 11 February 1871 with the carcasses of 550 diseased cattle from a herd assembled at Landerneau for the replenishment of Paris but remained on the list until BU 1875.
Arquebuse Auguste Guibert, Nantes/Gouin.
   Ord: 22.11.1854. K: 1.1855. L: 4.5.1855. Comm: 1.7.1855. C: 7.1855.
   To the Baltic from Lorient 1.8.1855, to the Adriatic 18.6.1859. Struck 25.11.1862 at Brest, coal hulk. Station hulk in the Odet 1878, back to Brest 1880, BU 1882.

COMÈTE – 1st Class gunboat. On 29 April 1858 the Ministry of Marine issued requirements for a light draught 11-knot gunboat that could also carry 1,000 troops with their equipment short distances. Lucien Arman of Bordeaux responded with a proposal to build two such vessels and submitted plans for them that were turned down by the Council of Works on 20 July 1858. Without awaiting the Council's report he submitted a second set of plans and claimed that a Ministerial despatch of 30 August 1858 exempted him from needing the Council's approval. The Director of Naval Construction on 5 October 1858, without expressing an opinion on the quality of the plans, recommended that the Minister of Marine sign a contract for one of the two vessels, Arman assuming responsibility for meeting the navy's requirements. The ship was ordered from Arman by a contract approved on 13 December 1858 and she was named on 17 January 1859. Her hull was built on the Arman composite wood and iron construction system. Her engines were installed between September and December 1859.
   Dimensions & tons: 75.80m, 73.30m wl, 72.02m x 8.76m, 8.90m ext x 3.80m. 820 tons disp. Draught 2.01/2.65m. Men: 79.
   Machinery: 120nhp. 10.67kts.
   Guns: 4 x 16cm rifles.
Comète Lucien Arman, Bordeaux/Schneider.
   Ord: 13.12.1858 (contract). K: 12.1858. L: 29.9.1859. Comm: 7.11.1859. C: 1.1860.
   Placed in reserve after completion. To Senegal and Gabon 27.8.1867, arrived at Lorient from Gabon 20.9.1870. Prison ship and transport for Communards at Rochefort 1871-72. Struck 1.7.1872 at Rochefort, converted 11-12.1874 to a steam transport (service craft) to carry convicts to the Île de Ré. BU 1880 at Rochefort.

PIQUE Class – 2nd Class gunboats. On 12 December 1859 the Minister of Marine ordered the five ports to prepare plans for four 2nd Class gunboats, which were to be generally similar to the Crimean War type. Plans by Jules Aurous were accepted in April 1860 for the construction of four ships at Toulon, but it was then proposed that the ships be a little smaller than their predecessors and be given an armoured bulwark in the bow for fighting head on. This idea was retained for a separate ship (*Diligente*, below) and on 1 October 1860 revised plans by Aurous were approved and names were assigned to the four ships. The type was defined as one with relatively powerful artillery, great mobility, restrained dimensions, and shallow draught. The final design included no armour. A flat bottom and two lateral false keels permitted the ships to beach themselves and remain high and dry for the duration of a low tide. The ships were intended for coastal operations in European waters, but were also to be useful for river operations in the colonies. They had three masts with square sails on the foremast. The engines were ordered from Schneider by a contract signed on 7 June 1861.
   Dimensions & tons: 39.56m, 38.84m wl, 34.89m x 6.72m x 2.86m. 359 tons disp. Draught 2.10/2.58m mean. Men: 59.
   Machinery: 60nhp. 2 cylinders, direct connecting rod, geared, trials (*Décidée*) 184ihp = 8.19kts. Coal 30 tons.
   Guns: (1863) 2 x 16cm M1858 MLR.
Pique Toulon Dyd/Schneider (Constructeurs, Marc-Eugène Demouy and Hyacinthe De Coppier)
   Ord: 4.1860. K: 7.1861. L: 16.10.1862. Comm: 27.1.1863. C: 2.1863.
   Struck 13.11.1886 at Nossi-Bé, coal hulk. Sold for BU 1895.
Décidée Toulon Dyd/Schneider (Constructeurs, Marc-Eugène Demouy and Hyacinthe De Coppier)
   Ord: 4.1860. K: 9.1861. L: 11.12.1862. Comm: 12.2.1863. C: 2.1863.
   Struck 8.11.1884 at Toulon. BU 1885.
Surprise Toulon Dyd/Schneider (Constructeur, Marc-Eugène Demouy)
   Ord: 4.1860. K: 3.1862. L: 19.2.1863. Comm: 1.10.1863. C: 10.1863.
   Struck 5.11.1885 in Indochina, hulk *Kep* at Haiphong until replaced 4.1887 by *Nagotna* (1884). Sold 13.9.1887 for BU.
Tactique Toulon Dyd/Schneider (Constructeur, Marc-Eugène Demouy)
   Ord: 4.1860. K: 6.1862. L: 19.3.1863. Comm: 1.10.1863. C: 10.1863.
   Struck 28.1.1886 at Buenos Aires. BU 1886.

DILIGENTE – 2nd Class gunboat. This ship was a 2nd Class gunboat with an armoured 'masque' forward to protect both the ship and its crew while fighting head on. The concept for the 'masque', initially proposed for the *Pique* class, above but not adopted for them, called for a vertical shield 5 metres aft of the stem, 10cm thick at the top and 9cm at the bottom, extending down to the keel. The hull forward of it was to be filled during wartime with cork to above the waterline. The armoured shield was composed of nine plates of wrought iron and weighed 24 tons. The ship had two schooner masts with a square sail on the foremast. The design was completed by Nicolas Le Moine in May 1861. Her engines were ordered from Schneider by a contract signed on 10 October 1862 and nine armour plates were ordered from Mariel frères by a contract approved on 17 August 1863. Four similar gunboats with armoured shields were ordered from Lorient in 1866: *Frelon*, *Aspic*, *Scorpion*, and *Couleuvre*.
   Dimensions & tons: 37.40m, 36.80m wl, 36.65m x 6.36m, 6.50m ext x 2.72m. 283 tons disp. Draught 2.20/2.38m. Men: 59.
   Machinery: 50nhp 2 cylinders, direct connecting rod, geared, trials 135ihp = 9.03kts.
   Armour: 10cm bulwark shielding gun.
   Guns: 1 x 16cm M1858 MLR forward.
Diligente Lorient Dyd/Schneider (Constructeur, Charles-Louis Layrle)
   K: 21.5.1861. L: 2.9.1864. Comm: 1.12.1864. C: 3.1865.
   Struck 15.11.1878. Served as *poste de la digue* for the Toulon breakwater until 1884. Barracks hulk at Toulon 1886, then at Marseille. BU 1893.

KENNEY Class – 2nd Class gunboats. These ships were ordered on 2 September 1862 and built in an occupied Chinese yard using engines removed from Crimean War-vintage gunboats with worn-out hulls. Their plans, by the French naval constructor in charge at Ningpo, François Verny, were similar to other 2nd Class gunboats but had lower upperworks as they were not intended for the open sea. The names of the last two were originally *Aigrette* and *Aventure*; they were renamed on 25

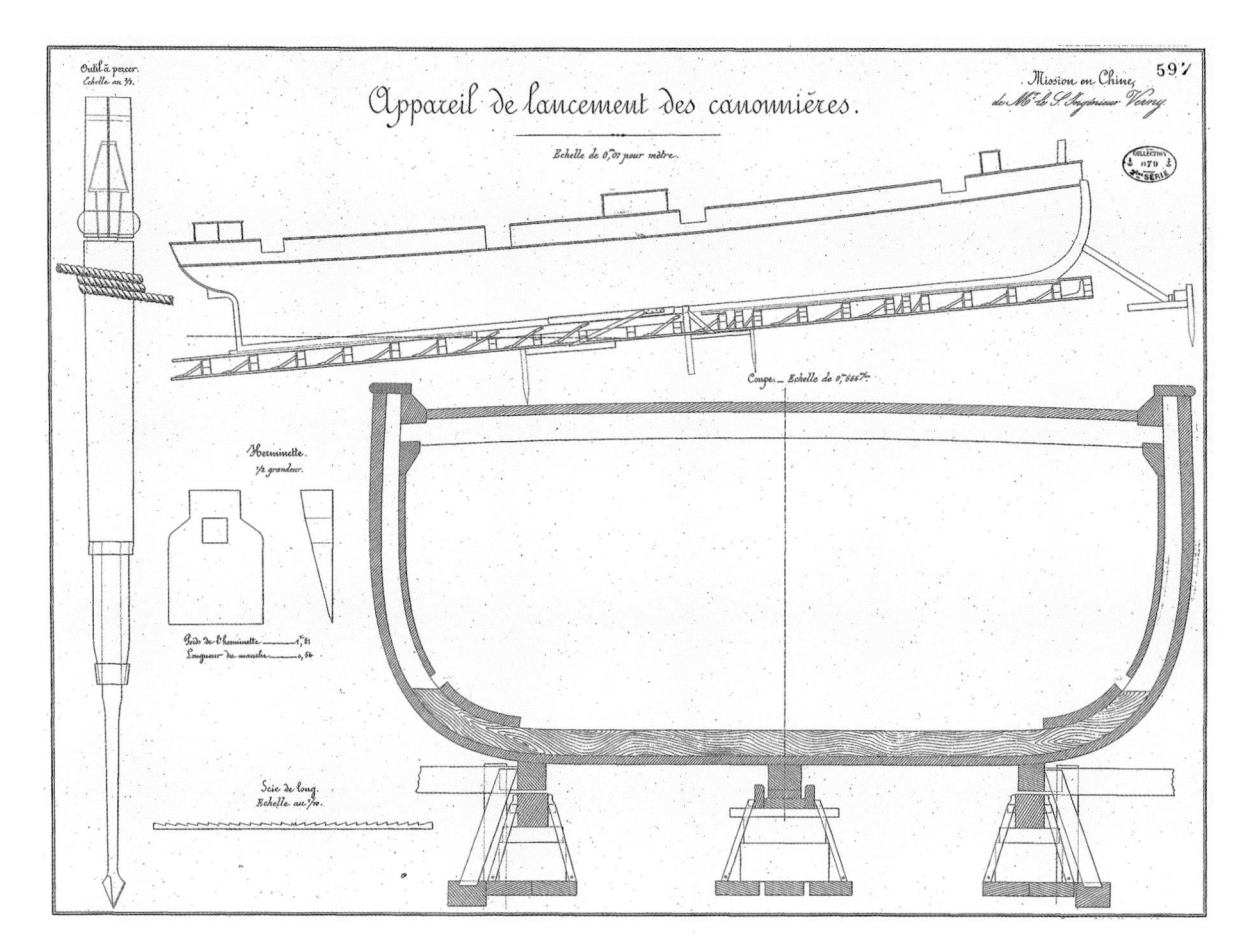

Launching ramp for the *Kenny* class gunboats built in an occupied Chinese shipyard at Ningpo. It provides some idea of the shape and structure of the gunboats themselves. (Atlas du Génie Maritime, French collection, plate 597)

September 1863. Their short service was probably due to the poor quality of timber available and perhaps to the reported tendency of the Chinese workers to steal nails and other fastenings.

Dimensions & tons: 36.04m, 35.38m wl, 32.00m x 6.72m x 2.70m. 253 tons disp. Draught 1.94/2.14m. Men: 59.
Machinery: 90nhp, 8.4kts.
Guns: (1864) 1 x 16cm rifle, 2 x 12cm bronze rifles.

Kenney Ningpo/from *Poudre* (Constructeur, Verny)
Ord: 2.9.1862. K: 5.2.1863. L: 31.10.1863. Comm: 1.12.1863. C: 12.1863.
Decomm. at Saigon 3.4.1865, could not be repaired. Struck 7.7.1868 at Saigon. BU 1869.

Bourdais (*Commandant Bourdais*) Ningpo/from *Redoute* (Constructeur, Verny)
Ord: 2.9.1862. K: 25.4.1863. L: 20.5.1864. Comm: 18.6.1864. C: 6.1864.
Struck 7.7.1868 at Saigon. BU 1869.

Le Brethon (*Lebrethon*) Ningpo/from *Salve* (Constructeur, Verny)
Ord: 2.9.1862. K: 20.7.1863. L: 17.9.1864. Comm: 9.11.1864. C: 11.1864.
Struck 19.4.1869 at Saigon and sold for BU.

Tardif Ningpo/from *Arquebuse* (Constructeur, Verny)
Ord: 2.9.1862. K: 15.11.1863. L: 14.12.1864. Comm: 26.1.1865. C: 1.1865.
Struck 7.7.1868 at Saigon, replaced lorcha *Donai* as lightship 30.7.1869. (The junk-rigged *Donai* became a lightship in 1866 and was struck on 31.5.1869.)

Screw gun launches and sectional gun launches

RAFALE Class – screw gun launches. These wooden-hulled craft were designed for Crimean War service by Hyacinthe Joseph De Coppier, who also acted as their constructeur. The engines were ordered from the Forges et Chantiers de la Méditerranée by a contract approved on 28 February 1855. In May 1859 *Mutine* and possibly *Tirailleuse* were fitted with armoured shields forward similar to those in some *Étincelle* class gunboats for operations in the Adriatic.

Dimensions & tons: 31.03m, 30.90m wl, 30.85m x 6.20m x 1.64m. 144 tons disp. Draught 1.20/1.46m. Men: 40.
Machinery: 25nhp. 2 cylinders. 6kts. Coal 12t
Armament: 1 x 16cm rifle (30pdr No.1) forward, 2 x 18p carronades on sides.

Rafale Toulon Dyd/FCM
K: 2.1855. L: 3.5.1855. Comm: 17.6.1855. C: 6.1855.
To the Black Sea 2.7.1855 with *Flèche*. Left Toulon for Senegal 27.4.1857. Struck 8.11.1862, engine removed and converted to floating depot at Grand Bassam. Sunk 24.1.1865.

Tirailleuse Toulon Dyd/FCM
K: 2.1855. L: 4.5.1855. Comm: 16.6.1855. C: 6.1855.
To the Black Sea 6.7.1855, to the Adriatic 15.6.1859. Left Toulon 31.7.1867 for Senegal under tow by the transport *Charente*. Struck 24.4.1876 in Gabon.

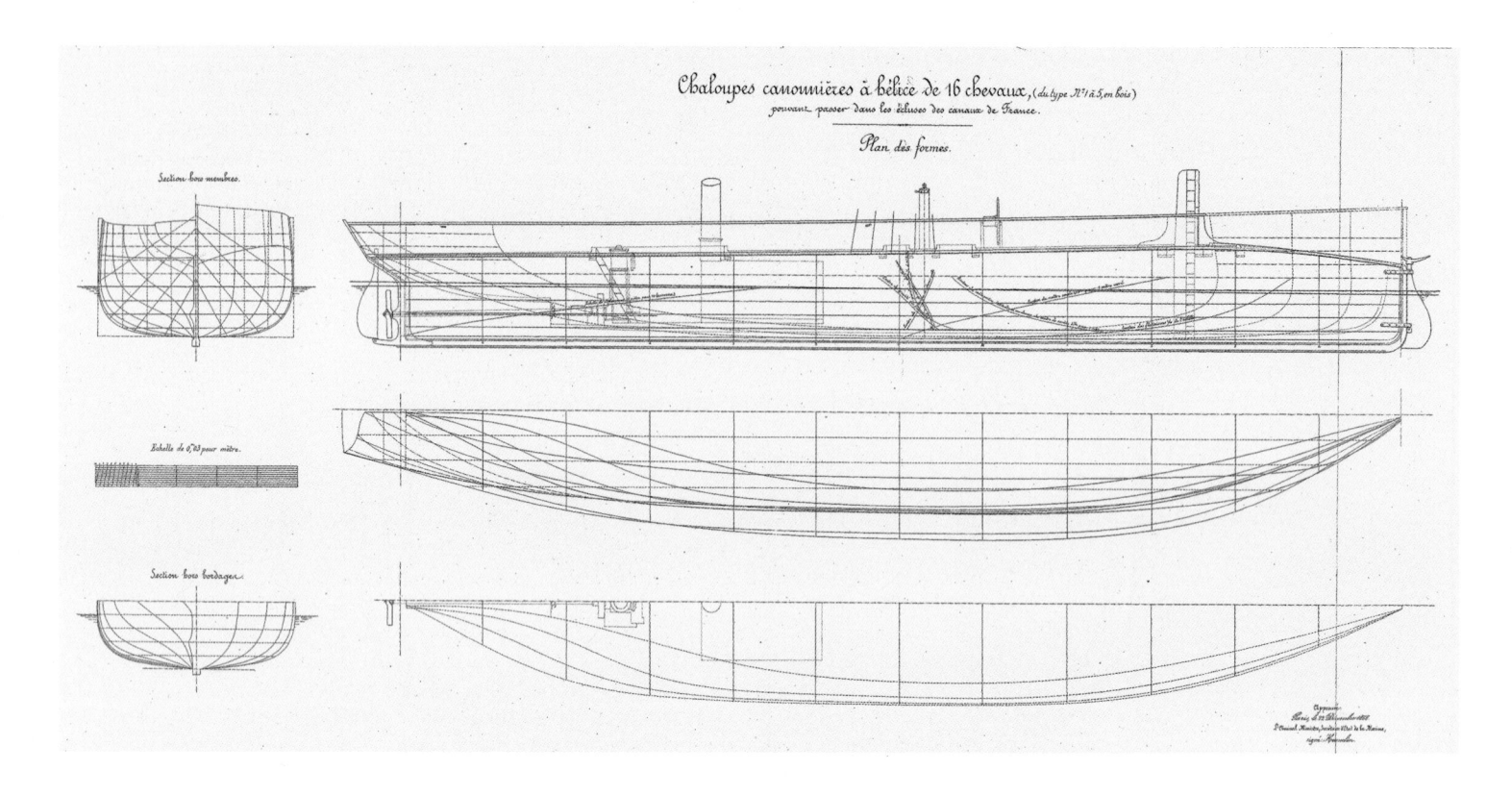

Alerte Toulon Dyd/FCM
   K: 2.1855. L: 9.5.1855. Comm: 16.6.1855. C: 6.1855.
   To the Black Sea 2.7.1855, to the Adriatic 15.6.1859. Struck 29.12.1874, lighter at Cherbourg. BU 2.1884.

Bourrasque Toulon Dyd/FCM
   K: 2.1855. L: 12.5.1855. Comm: 16.6.1855. C: 6.1855.
   To the Black Sea 7.1855, to Senegal 8.1857. Struck 20.6.1867 in Senegal.

Couleuvrine Toulon Dyd/FCM
   K: 2.1855. L: 16.5.1855. Comm: 1.6.1855. C: 6.1855.
   To the Black Sea 11.7.1855. Left Toulon for Senegal 7.4.1857. Struck 16.3.1868 in Senegal.

Mutine Toulon Dyd/FCM
   K: 2.1855. L: 23.5.1855. Comm: 1.6.1855. C: 6.1855.
   To the Black Sea 1.7.1855, to the Adriatic 6.1859. Struck 29.12.1874, lighter at Cherbourg. Ordered BU 1.2.1883.

Stridente Toulon Dyd/FCM
   K: 2.1855. L: 27.5.1855. Comm: 1.6.1855. C: 6.1855.
   To the Black Sea 1.7.1855. From Toulon to Senegal 27.4.1857. Washed ashore in a tidal wave at Rufisque, Senegal, on 31.8.1859. Struck 26.12.1859, engine returned to Toulon by transport *Yonne*.

Meurtrière Toulon Dyd/FCM
   K: 2.1855. L: 30.5.1855. Comm: 1.6.1855. C: 6.1855.
   To the Black Sea 11.7.1855. Left Toulon 3.4.1857 for the station at the mouths of the Danube. Struck 30.4.1868 at Galatz, sold 1868.

No.1 Class – screw gun launches. On 22 December 1858 the Minister ordered that ten wooden-hulled steam gun launches be built on an urgent basis for the Northern Italian campaign. They were to carry one rifled gun behind an armoured bulwark and were to be able to pass through the locks in French canals and be disassembled. They were given rudders at both ends. The first one was to be delivered assembled for trials on 25 March 1859, the second was to be delivered dismantled for transportation on 30 May 1859, and the others were to follow at a rate of two per week. Plans by Stanislas-Charles-Henri Dupuy de Lôme were approved on 22 December 1858, and the launches were ordered from the Forges et Chantiers de la Meditérranée at La Seyne by a contract approved on 7 January 1859. Iron plating and wood screws to fasten it were ordered for these launches from Schneider by a contract approved on 24 January 1859. The numerical designations were promulgated on 17 January 1859.

No.6 to *No.10* were commissioned as a group under a single commanding officer in May 1859, completed in June, transported by rail from Genoa to Lake Garda in July, and assembled at Desenzano beginning in August 1859 by the Toulon constructeur Auguste Émile Boden. They were to have participated in an attack on the fortress of Peschiera on Lake Garda, but the armistice of Villafranca intervened on 11 July 1859 and on 27 July Napoleon III informed the navy that he intended to give these five vessels, fully fitted out, to the King of Sardinia (Piedmont). They were duly transferred later in 1859.

On 7 September 1865 *Chaloupes canonnières Nos.1-5* were struck from the fleet list on the grounds that they had been in use for a long time as service craft and could not reasonably be restored to military use. They were to be inscribed on the list of service craft (an action taken on 1 October) and the choice of their names was left to their Maritime Prefects.

   Dimensions & tons: 24.70m wl, 24.45m x 4.90m x 2.00m. 101 tons disp. Draught 1.45/1.75m. Men: 18.
   Machinery: 16nhp. 1 cylinder, 7.25kts. Coal 10 tons.
   Guns: 1 x 16 cm rifle M1858 (30pdr No.1) behind an armoured bulwark.

Official lines and general arrangement plans, approved in Paris on 22 December 1858, for the wooden-hulled screw gun launches *Chaloupes canonnières Nos.1–5*. The armoured bulwark can be seen forward in the profile drawing, while amidships the outlines of five shrouds and a hinge-topped mast stump suggests a folding mast. (Atlas du Génie Maritime, French collection, plate 588)

No.1 FCM La Seyne/FCM.
Ord: 22.12.1858. K: 12.1858. L: 10.3.1859. Comm: 16.3.1859. C: 3.1859.
To the Adriatic 18.6.1859. Struck 7. 9.1865, listed 1.10.1865 as tug (service craft) *Poulmic* at Brest. BU 1896.

No.2 FCM La Seyne/FCM.
Ord: 22.12.1858. K: 1.1859. L: 4.1859. Comm: 3.5.1859. C: 5.1859.
To the Adriatic 18.6.1859. Struck 7.9.1865, listed 1.10.1865 as tug (service craft) *Précieuse* at Rochefort. BU 3.1876.

No.3 FCM La Seyne/FCM.
Ord: 22.12.1858. K: 1.1859. L: 10.4.1859. Comm: 16.4.1859. C: 5.1859.
To the Adriatic 18.6.1859. Struck 7.9.1865, listed 1.10.1865 as tug (service craft) *Va-et-Vient* at Lorient. Assigned to Gâvres 1894-1908. Hulk at Lorient 1909, sold for BU 1919.

No.4 FCM La Seyne/FCM.
Ord: 22.12.1858. K: 1.1859. L: 20.4.1859. Comm: 23.4.1859. C: 5.1859.
To the Adriatic 18.6.1859. Struck 7.9.1865, listed 1.10.1865 as tug (service craft) *Modeste* at Rochefort. Condemned 1882, BU 1883.

No.5 FCM La Seyne/FCM.
Ord: 22.12.1858. K: 1.1859. L: 20.4.1859. Comm: 23.4.1859. C: 5.1859.
To Genoa 5.6.1859 for the 'Flottille de l'intérieur de l'Italie'. Annex to hulk *Uranie* at Brest 1.12.1862. Struck 7.9.1865, listed 1.10.1865 as personnel transport (service craft) *Minou* at Brest for service as a shuttle between the training ship *Borda* and the shore. Also used in 1874 to test a torpedo tube for launching on the broadside. BU 1905.

No.6 FCM La Seyne/FCM.
Ord: 22.12.1858. K: 1.1859. Comm: 21.5.1859. C: 6.1859. L: autumn 1859.
To Genoa 28.6.1859 for the *Flottille de canonnières du lac Majeur* and assembled on Lake Garda. Decomm. 20.8.1859. Transferred to Sardinia 1859 as *Frassineto*, in service with the Italian Navy 17.3.1861, ceded to the Società per le Ferrovie dell'Alta Italia (Upper Italian Railways) 1867, definitively struck 13.12.1878.

No.7 FCM La Seyne/FCM.
Ord: 22.12.1858. K: 1.1859. Comm: 21.5.1859. C: 6.1859. L: autumn 1859.
To Genoa 28.6.1859 and assembled on Lake Garda. Decomm. 20.8.1859. Transferred to Sardinia as *Sesia*, sunk by accident 8.10.1860.

No.8 FCM La Seyne/FCM.
Ord: 22.12.1858. K: 1.1859. Comm: 21.5.1859. C: 6.1859. L: autumn 1859.
To Genoa 28.6.1859 and assembled on Lake Garda. Decomm. 20.8.1859. Transferred to Sardinia 1859 as *Torrione*, in service with the Italian Navy 17.3.1861, struck 3.12.1878.

No.9 FCM La Seyne/FCM.
Ord: 22.12.1858. K: 1.1859. Comm: 21.5.1859. C: 6.1859. L: autumn 1859.
To Genoa 28.6.1859 and assembled on Lake Garda. Decomm. 20.8.1859. Transferred to Sardinia 1859 as *Castenedolo*, in service with the Italian Navy 17.3.1861, struck 1867.

No.10 FCM La Seyne/FCM.
Ord: 22.12.1858. K: 1.1859. Comm: 21.5.1859. C: 6.1859. L: autumn 1859.
To Genoa 28.6.1859 and assembled on Lake Garda. Decomm. 20.8.1859. Transferred to Sardinia 1859 as *Pozzolengo*, in service with the Italian Navy 17.3.1861, probably struck 1867.

No.11 screw gun launch. The construction of one gunboat with a wooden protective bulwark forward on plans by Capitaine de Vaisseau Dupouy was ordered on an urgent basis from Lucien Arman at Bordeaux by a contract approved on 17 December 1858. The vessel was to be delivered on 13 March 1859, the navy providing the engines and armour to be placed on the bulwark. Her engine was added in a supplement to the contract with FCM for *Nos.1-10* when that contract was approved on 7 January 1859. She was designated *No.11* on 17 January 1859. She was designed to be capable of being dismantled for transportation.
Dimensions & tons: 26.40m wl x 6.34m x 1.90m. 127 tons disp. Draught 1.25/1.80m. Men: 18.
Machinery: 16nhp. 1 cylinder. Coal 16 tons.
Guns: 1 x 16cm M1858 (30pdr No.1) MLR behind armoured bulwark.

No.11 (Guêpe) Lucien Arman, Bordeaux/FCM.
Ord: 17.12.1858 (contract). K: 12.1858. L: 3.1859. Comm: 5.3.1859. C: 4.1859.
To the Adriatic 15.6.1859. Named *Guêpe* 1.1.1867. Struck 15.1.1878 and converted to a tug for use at Saint-Mandrier. In 1888 became a port service craft for the *Défense Mobile* at Bizerte, annex to *D'Estrées* 1889-90 and to *Hirondelle* 1891-92. Sold 1.1898 in Tunisia.

No.12 Class – screw sectional gun launches, iron hulls. On 15 October 1859 the Minister of Marine directed the construction of 20 gun launches for an expedition to China, and they were designated *chaloupes canonnières Nos.12-31* on 21 October 1859. Plans by Stanislas-Charles-Henri Dupuy de Lôme were approved on 17 October 1859 and the launches were ordered from the Le Havre yard of the Forges et Chantiers de la Méditerranée (FCM) by a contract approved on 26 December 1859. They had rudders at both ends. For shipping to the Far East they were disassembled into 15 rail-transportable sections, although these were of fairly large size and took up a lot of space because of their shape. The transports *Weser*, *Européen*, and *Japon* were purchased in England to ship them and the merchantmen *Louise*, *Léonie*, and *Pomone* were hired for the same purpose. Upon arrival the vessels were assembled and launched by the Toulon constructeur Arthur François Alphonse Bienaymé. Those that survived received names on 1 January 1867. Nine later units of the same class, *Nos.32-40*, were ordered from FCM in November 1863 for an expedition to Cochinchina. Another ten, *Arbalète*, *Biscaïen*, *Boutefeu*, *Mousquet*, *Fronde*, *Javelot*, *Dard*, *Epieu*, *Pertuisane*, and *Flambant* were ordered by a foreign government from FCM, but conditions in 1866 made delivery impossible and the navy took them over. A further ten, the *Baïonnette* group, were ordered from Claparède in 1867, still on the 1859 plans. *No.12* was first launched in January 1860 and was in commission from 23 January to 18 March 1860, probably for class trials.
Dimensions & tons: 24.70m, 24.30m wl, 24.10m x 4.90m x 2.10m. 89 tons disp. Draught 1.50/1.69m. Men: 20.
Machinery: 20nhp.8.0kts.
Guns: 1 x 16cm rifle.

No.12 (Arc) FCM Le Havre/FCM.
Ord: 15.10.1859. K: 10.1859. L: 1.1860. C: 1.1860. To Chefoo (Zhifu), China, 4.1860 in transport *Japon*. L: 8.1860. Comm: 19.8.1860.
Foundered 14.10.1873 in a storm while under tow by the aviso *D'Estrées* (1867) after leaving Saigon 11.10.1873 for Tourane (Da Nang).

No.13 (Carabine) FCM Le Havre/FCM.
Ord: 15.10.1859. K: 11.1859. C: 2.1860. To Chefoo 3.1860. L: 9.1860. Comm: 6.10.1860.
Struck 23.4.1889 at Haiphong, sold for BU.

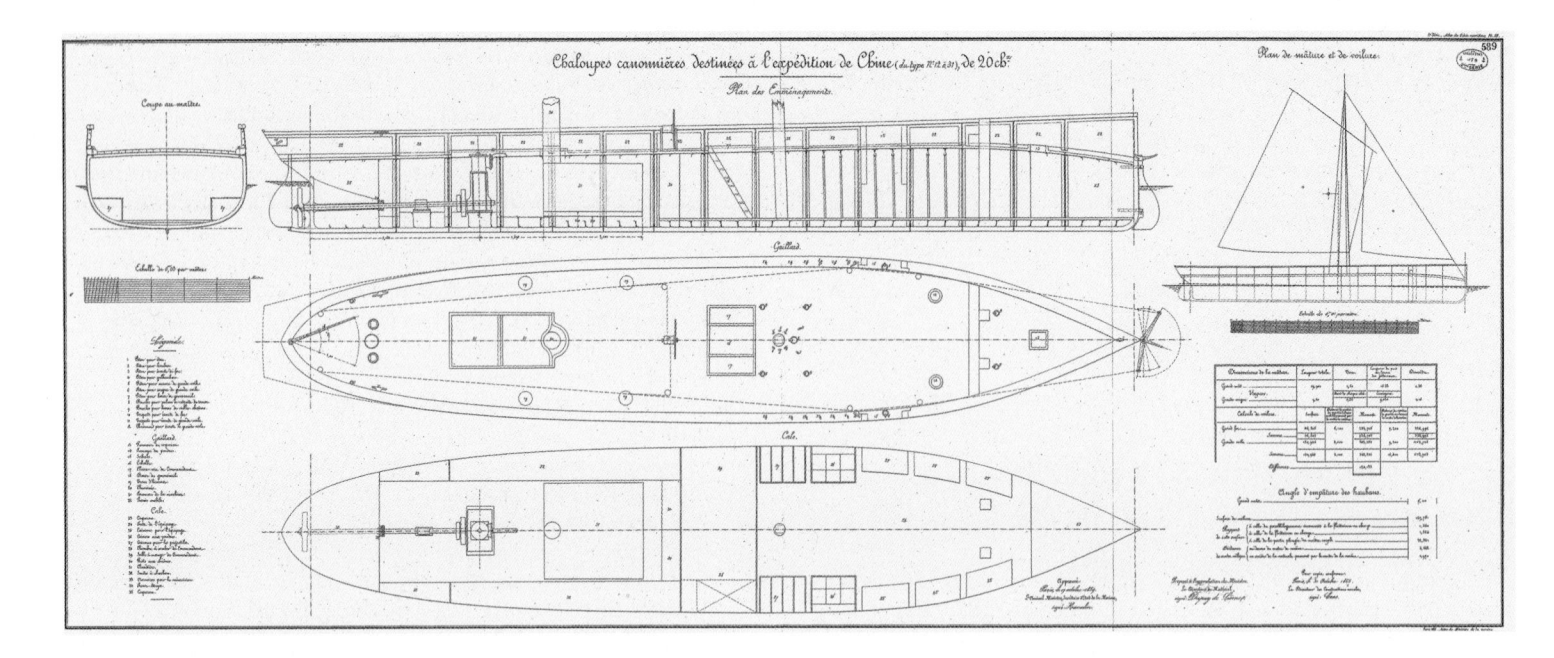

Official lines and general arrangement plans, approved in Paris on 17 October 1859, for the iron-hulled screw gun launches *Chaloupes canonnières Nos.12–31*. They were very similar to their wooden-hulled predecessors but had a fixed single-masted rig setting a large lug main. They had a similar stout bulkhead forward to secure the guns, but no protective shield. The working of the bow rudder can be seen in the deck view, the run of the tiller ropes suggesting that the wheel operated both rudders together. (Atlas du Génie Maritime, French collection, plate 589)

No.14 (***Sainte Anne***) FCM Le Havre/FCM.
  Ord: 15.10.1859. K: 11.1859. C: 2.1860. To storage at Toulon 3.1860.
  In service 1861 at Saint-Mandrier. Comm. 11.5.1865, to Cayenne 16.10.1865. Struck 20.6.1872 at Cayenne and BU.
No.15 (no name) FCM Le Havre/FCM.
  Ord: 15.10.1859. K: 11.1859. C: 2.1860. To Chefoo 3.1860. L: 9.1860. Comm: 4.10.1860.
  Sunk 14.10.1863 at Shanghai by boiler explosion. She had unofficially carried the name *Étoile* on the Yangtse in 1862-63 but this was repudiated by all authorities in 1864.
No.16 (***Casse-Tête***) FCM Le Havre/FCM.
  Ord: 15.10.1859. K: 11.1859. C: 2.1860. To Chefoo 3.1860. L: 9.1860. Comm: 19.9.1860.
  Sunk 7.5.1867 in the Mekong River by boiler explosion caused by crew error.
No.17 (no name) FCM Le Havre/FCM.
  Ord: 15.10.1859. K: 11.1859. C: 3.1860. To Chefoo 4.1860 in merchantman *Pomone*. L: 12.1860. Comm: 13.1.1861.
  Foundered 6.2.1861 while under tow by the aviso *Écho* from Chefoo to Saigon.
No.18 (***Cimeterre***) FCM Le Havre/FCM.
  Ord: 15.10.1859. K: 11.1859. C: 3.1860. To Chefoo 4.1860 in transport *Japon*. L: 8.1860. Comm: 20.8.1860.
  Struck 7.8.1870 in Indochina.
No.19 (***Coutelas***) FCM Le Havre/FCM.
  Ord: 15.10.1859. K: 11.1859. C: 3.1860. To Chefoo 4.1860 in transport *Européen*. L: 4.1861. Comm: 19.5.1861.
  Struck 21.4.1885 at Saigon. BU 1889.
No.20 (***Dague***) FCM Le Havre/FCM.
  Ord: 15.10.1859. K: 11.1859. C: 3.1860. To Chefoo 4.1860 in merchantman *Pomone*. L: 12.1860. Comm: 17.1.1861.
  Struck 24.12.1878 at Saigon, sold 1879 for BU.
No.21 (***Sainte Marie***) FCM Le Havre/FCM.
  Ord: 15.10.1859. K: 11.1859. L: 2.1860. C: 3.1860. Remained at Toulon. Comm: 28.6.1860, decomm. 13.9.1860.
  Served the hospital at Saint-Mandrier 1861-67. To Cayenne 12.6.1867 in transport *Amazone*, comm. 1.10.1867. Struck 2.4.1872 at Cayenne, BU 1872.
No.22 (***Epée***) FCM Le Havre/FCM.
  Ord: 15.10.1859. K: 11.1859. C: 3.1860. To Chefoo 4.1860 in transport *Japon*. L: 8.1860. Comm: 22.8.1860.
  Sunk 25.1.1867 near Mytho by boiler explosion.
No.23 (***Espingole***) FCM Le Havre/FCM.
  Ord: 15.10.1859. K: 11.1859. C: 3.1860. Remained at Toulon. To Saigon late 1862. L: 12.1862. Comm: 1.1.1863.
  Struck 24.12.1878 at Saigon, on sale list 1879.
No.24 (***Fauconneau***) FCM Le Havre/FCM.
  Ord: 15.10.1859. K: 11.1859. C: 3.1860. To Chefoo 4.1860 in transport *Européen*. L: 1861. Comm: 25.6.1861.
  Struck 7.8.1870 at Saigon and sold for BU.
No.25 (no name) FCM Le Havre/FCM.
  Ord: 15.10.1859. K: 11.1859. C: 3.1860. To Chefoo 4.1860 in transport *Européen*. L: 1861. Comm: 23.5.1861.
  Sunk 3.3.1862 at Rach-Dam near Mytho by a 'criminal' boiler explosion.
No.26 (no name) FCM Le Havre/FCM.
  Ord: 15.10.1859. K: 11.1859. C: 3.1860. To Chefoo 3.1860 in transport *Weser*. L: 7.1860. Comm: 26.7.1860.
  Sank 28.1.1861 off Annam while under tow by the transport *Rhône* from Woosung to Saigon.
No.27 (***Faulx***) FCM Le Havre/FCM.
  Ord: 15.10.1859. K: 11.1859. C: 3.1860. To Chefoo 3.1860 in transport *Weser*. L: 7.1860. Comm: 27.7.1860.
  Struck 24.12.1878 at Saigon, BU 1879.
No.28 (***Flamberge***) FCM Le Havre/FCM.
  Ord: 15.10.1859. K: 11.1859. C: 3.1860. Remained at Toulon. To Saigon 1862. L: late 1862. Comm: 21.1.1863.
  Struck 21.4.1885 at Saigon and BU.

No.29 (*Fleuret*) FCM Le Havre/FCM.
  Ord: 15.10.1859. K: 11.1859. C: 3.1860. To Chefoo 4.1860 in transport *Européen*. L: 6.1861. Comm: 14.7.1861.
  Struck 1.3.1878 at Saigon, BU 1886.
No.30 (*Framée*) FCM Le Havre/FCM.
  Ord: 15.10.1859. K: 11.1859. C: 3.1860. To Chefoo 4.1860 in merchantman *Pomone*. L: 12.1860. Comm: 24.1.1861.
  Struck 5.6.1891 at Saigon. Sold 1892.
No.31 (*Glaive*) FCM Le Havre/FCM.
  Ord: 15.10.1859. K: 11.1859. C: 3.1860. To Chefoo 3.1860. L: 7.1860. Comm: 1.8.1860.
  Struck 21.4.1885 in Cochinchina, BU 1886.

Screw sectional armoured floating batteries

No.1 **Class** – Screw sectional armoured floating batteries, iron hulls. In response to instructions from Napoleon III, the Minister of Marine on 10 June 1859 ordered the immediate construction of five armoured floating batteries for use against the Austrians on the Po River. Because of the need for haste the Minister accepted the offer of FCM La Seyne to build them at cost plus 12 percent without a formal contract. The batteries were designed by Stanislas-Charles-Henri Dupuy de Lôme to carry 2 x 24cm BLR, but these were not ready and older 16cm (30pdr) rifles were used. The 5cm armour was designed to be proof against Austrian 12pdr field guns (their largest). The vessels consisted of 14 sections which were bolted together with bands of rubber in between; they could be dismantled in 45 hours and reassembled in 87 hours; 32 rail cars were needed to transport one battery with its equipment. Names were proposed on 12 June 1859 but it was decided instead to use only numbers. On 2 December 1859 the Director of Naval Construction reported that the first one had been delivered on 4 July 1859 and the other four on 25 August 1859, but *Nos.1-3* are also listed as commissioned on 8 July 1859 and decommissioned on 21 July. *Batterie flottante démontable No.1* was embarked on the paddle steamer *Cacique* on 7 July 1859 in sections and transported to Genoa. She arrived by rail at

Official lines and general arrangement plans, approved in Paris on 1 June 1859, for the iron-hulled sectional *Batterie flottante démontable Nos.1–5*. They were little more than self-propelled rafts with an armoured battery forward, but to have designed and built such a craft that could be readily dismantled and re-assembled in such a short time was a creditable achievement. (Atlas du Génie Maritime, French collection, plate 795)

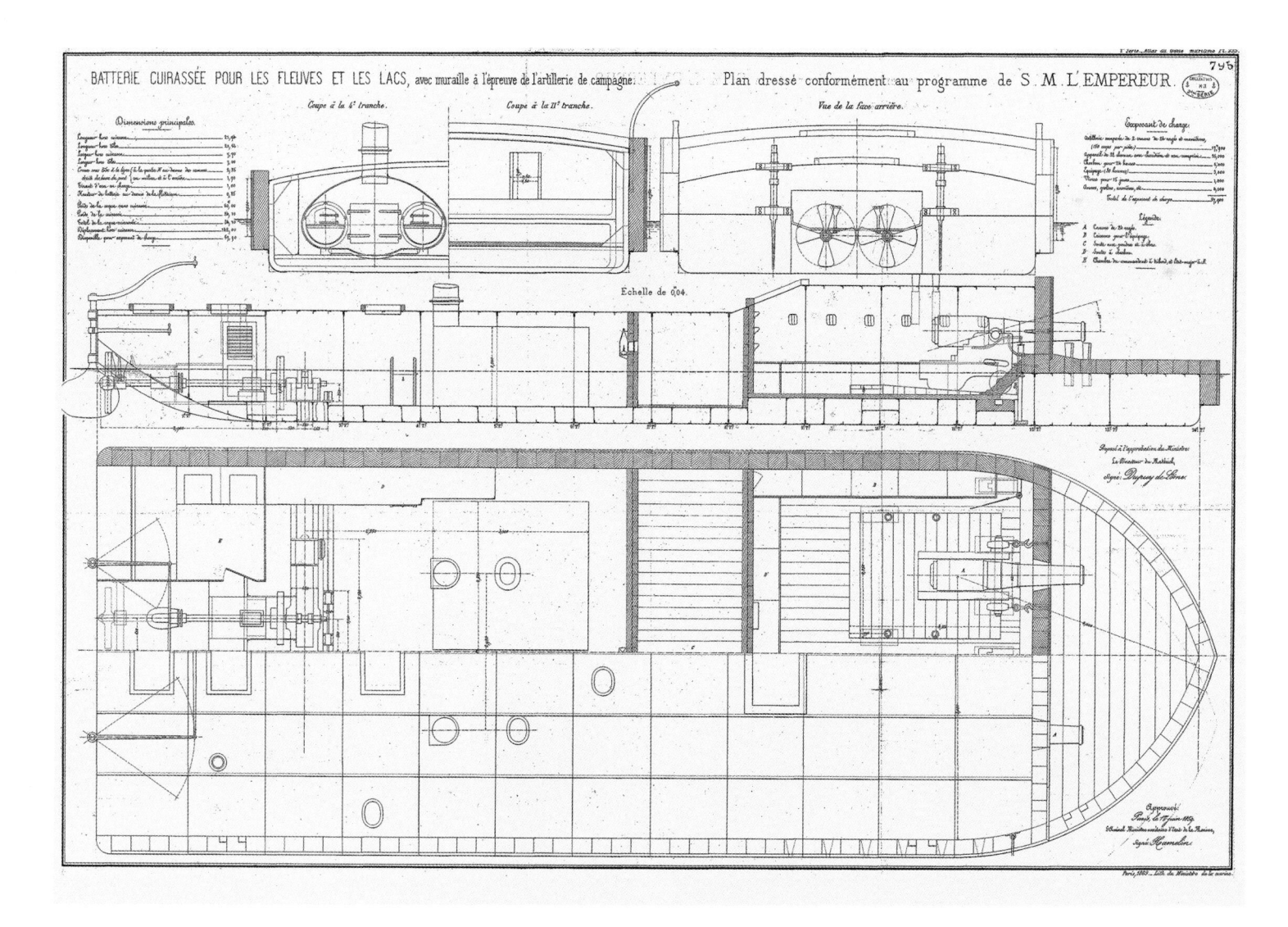

Sampierdarena just west of Genoa on 8 July 1859, the day on which the armistice of Villafranca was signed. Sent back to France still in sections, she was assembled at Toulon on 6 August 1859 in 87 hours, launched on 10 August, tried successfully in the harbour on 11 August, disassembled on 26-27 August in 30 hours, and put in storage at Mourillon. The others were sent directly to storage. All five were sent from Toulon to Paris in August 1870 (having initially been routed to Strasbourg for use on the Rhine but then diverted), and they were assembled at the Claparède yard at Saint-Denis and participated in the siege as part of the flotilla of Capitaine de Vaisseau Thomasset. Six more slightly larger and faster units, *Nos.6-11*, were ordered in 1864 for a planned campaign on the Rhine; *Nos.6-7* were lost in 1870-71 and the others were struck in 1886-88.

> Dimensions & tons: 21.94m, 18.3m keel x 7.00m hull, 7.70m outside armour x 1.70m (2.35m under the guns). 142 tons disp. Draught 1.00/1.10m. Men: 30.
>
> Machinery: 32nhp. Two boilers and two funnels. Two screws, two rudders. Trials 95ihp = 4.21kts. Coal 6 tons (24 hours)
>
> Armour: 5cm. on 30cm backing, 5cm on battery.
>
> Guns: 2 x 16cm rifles firing forward.

No.1 FCM La Seyne/FCM.
> Ord: 10.6.1859. K: 6.1859. Comm: 8.7.1859.
> Assembled 24.8.1870 and launched 2.9.1870 at Saint-Denis. Seized by the Paris Communards 18.3.1871, sunk by Government artillery or scuttled at Saint-Denis 4 or 5.1871. Struck 10.7.1871.

No.2 FCM La Seyne/FCM.
> Ord: 10.6.1859. K: 6.1859. Comm: 8.7.1859.
> Assembled 24.8.1870 and launched 2.9.1870 at Saint-Denis. Seized by the Paris Communards 18.3.1871, not used and recovered by Government forces 27.5.1871. Struck 3.7.1871, BU 1872 at Cherbourg.

No.3 FCM La Seyne/FCM.
> Ord: 10.6.1859. K: 6.1859. Comm: 8.7.1859.
> Assembled 21.8.1870 and launched 25.8.1870 at Saint-Denis. Hit a piling of the Pont Notre-Dame 8.2.1871 and sank, refloated probably after Government forces retook the city in May 1871. Struck 3.7.1871, BU 1872 at Cherbourg.

No.4 FCM La Seyne/FCM.
> Ord: 10.6.1859. K: 6.1859. C: 8.1859.
> Assembled 24.8.1870 and launched 2.9.1870 at Saint-Denis. Seized by the Paris Communards 18.3.1871, not used. Scuttled 5.1871 at Saint-Denis. Struck 10.7.1871.

No.5 FCM La Seyne/FCM.
> Ord: 10.6.1859. K: 6.1859. C: 8.1859.
> Assembled 24.8.1870 and launched 12.9.1870 at Saint-Denis. Seized by the Paris Communards 18.3.1871 and placed in service, renamed *Commune* 4.1871. Retaken 27.5.1871 near the Pont de la Concorde by Government forces, name reverted to *Batterie flottante démontable No.5*. Struck 29 10.1874 at Cherbourg, floating workshop in 1877, coal hulk in 1897. Sold 1923 at Cherbourg for BU.

13 The Larger Transports

In addition to its combatant warships, the French Navy contained large numbers of purpose-built and acquired transport vessels of various sizes and types, especially during wartime. The number of French transport ships was generally larger than that in Britain's Royal Navy, in part because the French Navy had to assume the functions that in Britain were carried out by the Transport Board (until 1817) and in part because the French did not have the large merchant marine that the Royal Navy relied on to carry out some of its transportation and supply functions.

During the period after 1786 most of the larger French transports fell into two categories, *flûtes* and *gabarres*, which are covered in this chapter. In general *flûtes* were larger vessels, frigate-built, and designed to carry both cargo and personnel long distances while *gabarres* were less substantial craft optimised for carrying cargo, often on coastal routes. Both were generally larger than *transports*, a term used before 1815 almost exclusively for small acquired vessels (covered in the next chapter). At the end of this chapter a few unusually large ships classed as transports (all after 1815) are covered, followed by the steam screw transports that were the successors of both the *flûtes* and *gabarres*.

Flûtes (corvettes de charge from 1821, transports from 1846)

Flûtes were large three-masted vessels used to carry provisions, rations, munitions, and sometimes troops to an overseas colony, to a fleet, or to a single vessel on a long voyage. The word is from the Dutch *fluijt* or *fluyt*, a dedicated cargo vessel designed to facilitate transoceanic delivery with the maximum of space and crew efficiency. Navies often commissioned old ships of the line or frigates *en flûte*, landing many of their guns and the crews that served them, to carry out distant supply missions, and the French also built ships especially for this purpose. These seaworthy ships had covered gun batteries and orlop decks like frigates but did not have either the strength of armament, size of crew, or speed to serve as warships except in emergencies.

(A) Flûtes in service or on order at 1 January 1786

***BALEINE* Class** – 500 tons. A class of four designed by Jean-Joseph Ginoux, 1778-79, all built at Le Havre. They were classed as gabarres when built, but reclassed as flûtes from 1785. Of the second pair built in 1780, the *Abondance* was captured by the British on 12 December 1781 (and sold in 1784) and the *Nourrice* was struck in early 1783 (she was sold at Brest in June 1787 for commerce).
Dimensions & tons: 112ft 0in, 112ft 0in x 28ft 8in x 11ft 7in (39.63, 36.38 x 9.31 x 3.76m). 500/920 tons. Draught 12ft 8in/13ft 0in (4.11/4.22m), Men: 93-150.
Guns: UD 20 x 8pdrs (pierced for 11 pairs of gunports); SD nil.
Baleine Le Havre.
K: 7.1778. L: 3.2.1779. C: 4.1779.
Struck in 1786 at Rochefort.
Outarde Le Havre.
K: 7.1778. L: 5.3.1779. C: 4.1779.
Struck in 1788 at Brest (used as a hulk until 6.1796).

***DROMADAIRE* Class** – 500 tons. A class of eight designed by Jean-Joseph Ginoux, 1778-79, six built at Le Havre (ordered in pairs) and two at Bayonne. They were classed as gabarres when built, but reclassed as flûtes from 1784.

Admiralty draught of *Abondance* as fitted at Plymouth in December 1782. Although this ship was captured in 1781, two of her sisters survived into the period covered by this book. It gives a good idea of the general appearance of the naval flûte – a combination of a frigate-like topside layout with a capacious underwater hull form. (© National Maritime Museum J6830)

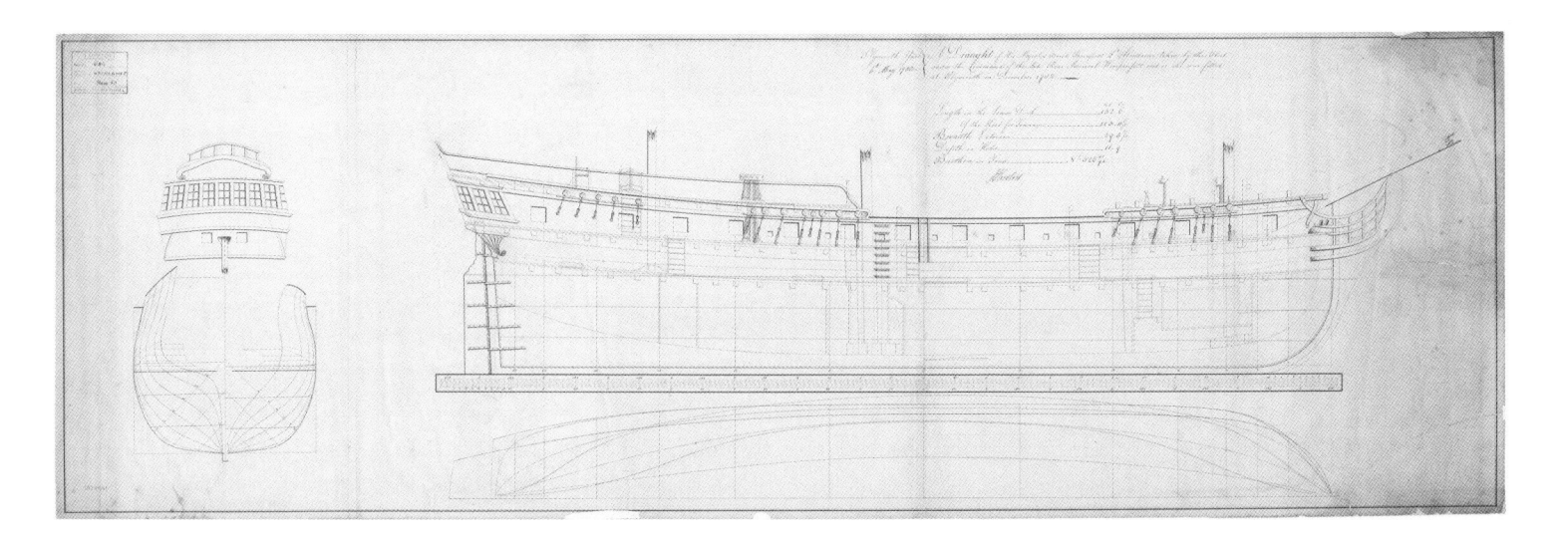

The ships built as *Autruche* and *Portefaix* were renamed *Boussole* and *Astrolabe* in May 1785, and redesignated as frigates, but these two then exchanged names on 28 May; after a refit, each with 112 men and re-armed with 12 x 6pdrs, 3 x 1pdrs and 20 swivels, they sailed from Brest on 1 August 1785 with Comte de Lapérouse's round-the-world scientific expedition, but were both lost with all hands in the Solomon Islands in early 1788 (although not officially declared lost until 14 February 1791); interestingly, a 16-year-old new 2nd Lieut, 'Napolionne' (as then spelt) Buonaparte, was provisionally selected to serve on this voyage, but was finally not appointed.

> Dimensions & tons: 127ft 0in, 112ft 0in x 27ft 3in x 15ft 6in (41.25, 36.38 x 8.85 x 5.04m). 500/970 tons. Draught 13ft 10in/14ft 7in (4.49/4.74m). Men: 84-210.
> Guns: UD 20 x 8pdrs or 6pdrs (pierced for 11 pairs of gunports); SD nil.

Dromadaire Le Havre.
> K: 10.1780. L: 10.5.1781. C: 7.1781.
> Grounded 11.1798 at Paimboeuf but refloated. Became powder hulk at Brest 1.1800. Condemned 9.1805 and BU.

Chameau Le Havre.
> K: 10.1780. L: 8.6.1781. C: 8.1781.
> Struck in 1788 at Brest (used as a hulk until 6.1796).

Astrolabe (ex-*Autruche*) Le Havre.
> K: 6.1781. L: 12.1781. C: 2.1782.
> Renamed 1785 (see note above). Wrecked off Vanikoro (Solomon Islands) in early 1788.

Lourde Le Havre.
> K: 6.1781. L: 12.1781. C: 2.1782.
> Wrecked 18.5.1797 near San Domingo.

Mulet Bayonne.
> K: 10.1781. L: 5.1782. C: 7.1782.
> Handed over to Anglo-Spanish forces at Toulon 18.8.1793, becoming HMS *Mulette*, deleted 1796.

Boussole (ex-*Portefaix*) Bayonne.
> K: 10.1781. L: 1782. C: 5.1783. Renamed 1785 (see note above). Wrecked off Vanikoro (Solomon Islands) in early 1788.

Lamproie Le Havre.
> K: 12.1781. L: 15.5.1782. C: 7.1782.
> Handed over to British Navy at Toulon 8.1793, but turned over to and removed by the Neapolitan Navy in 12.1793; renamed *Lampreda* in their service, burnt 1.1799.

Barbeau Le Havre.
> K: 12.1781. L: 28.5.1782. C: 7.1782.
> Wrecked in the West Indies 10.1791.

SEINE Class – 670 tons. A class of four designed by Antoine Groignard in November 1781, two built by Jean-Joseph Ginoux at Le Havre and two at Bayonne.

> Dimensions & tons: 132ft 6in, 117ft 6in x 30ft 0in x 14ft 0in (43.04/38.17 x 9.75 x 4.55m). 670/1,200 tons. Draught 14½ft/15¾ft (4.71/5.12m). Men: 48-86.
> Guns: UD 20 x 8pdrs or 6pdrs (pierced for 10 pairs of gunports); SD 4 x 4pdrs.

Seine Le Havre.
> K: 5.1782. L: 3.1783. C: 4.1783.
> Struck in 1788 at Rochefort.

Désirée Le Havre.
> K: 5.1782. L: 23.3.1783. C: 5.1783.
> Grounded accidentally 6.1784 but refloated. Condemned 1788 at Rochefort.

Nécessaire Bayonne.
> K: 1782. L: 5.1783. C: 7.1783.
> In bad condition and condemned 14.3.1792 at Teneriffe, also mentioned 12.1792 in the Antilles.

Étoile Bayonne.
> K: 1782. L: 6.1783. C: 7.1783.
> Captured by British 20.3.1796 off Audierne, but not added to RN.

PURCHASED AND REQUISITIONED FLÛTES (1770-1785)

Isle de France (flûte launched at Lorient 3.9.1766 for the French East India Co. and purchased 10.1770 after the company was dissolved, ex *Marquis de Sancé* 8.1772)
> Dimensions & tons: 115ft, 103ft x 31ft x 12ft 4in (37.36, 33.46 x 10.07 x 4.00m). 535/950 tons. Draught 16ft (5.20m). Men: 88-148.
> Guns: 22 or 24 x 8pdrs or 6pdrs.
> Struck 8.1789 at Lorient, hulk there 6.1790.

Pérou (flûte built at Bordeaux 1774-75 and purchased 1.1781).
> Dimensions & tons: 112ft, 92ft x 28ft x 12ft 6in (36.38, 29.88 x 9.10 x 4.06m). 400-450/896 tons. Draught 14ft 6in/15ft (4.71/4.87m). Men: 74-140
> Guns: 22 or 24 x 8pdrs or 6pdrs.
> Loaned 6.1786 to the Compagnie d'Owhère et de Bénin with a three-year monopoly on trade with Benin, returned 5.1788. Last mentioned 5.1792 at Rochefort.

Nouvelle Entreprise de Dantzig (flûte built in Danzig 1781 and purchased 11.1782, 680 tons). Also called *Nouvelle Entreprise*. Struck 1786, hulk 8.1787 at Lorient, last mentioned 1789.

Fille Unique (flûte built at Bordeaux 1782-83 and purchased 1785, 700 tons, 135-150 men, carried 24 x 8pdrs). Gunnery school at Brest 11.1794 with 26 x 12pdrs. Renamed *Faveur* 1.1795, reverted to *Fille Unique* 1796. Expedition to Ireland 11.1796. Hulk at Brest 3.1797. On sale list 28.5.1797 but not sold, powder hulk 9.1800, BU 4.1804.

(B) Flûtes acquired from 1 January 1786

BIENVENUE – 700 tons. One-off design by Pierre-Alexandre Forfait, plans dated 18 October 1787.

> Dimensions & tons: 130ft 0in, 122ft 0in x 31ft 0in x 15ft 7in (42.23, 39.63 x 10.07 x 5.06m). 700/1,230 tons. Draught 12ft/14½ft (3.90/4.71m). Men: 86.
> Guns: 20 x 8pdrs.

Bienvenue Jean-François Gouel and Louis Deros, Le Havre.
> K: 11.1787. L: 5.7.1788. C: 6.1788.
> Renamed *Royaliste* 10.1792, but restored to *Bienvenue* 1.1793. Prison hulk at Martinique 7.1793. Captured 17.3.1794 by Jervis's fleet off Martinique, becoming HMS *Undaunted*; sold 7.1795.

NORMANDE – 750 tons. Designed by Pierre-Alexandre Forfait. The design of this single ship was used after 1800 to build large numbers of similar ships, all rated at 800 tons burthen. The rated tonnage of *Normande* was later listed at 600 tons, while her displacement was also listed at 1,713 tons. Fabien was a *premier maître charpentier* (first master carpenter) who built this ship for Forfait.

> Dimensions & tons: 134ft, 124ft x 32ft x 16ft 7in (43.52, 40.28 x 10.39 x 5.39m). 750/1,380 tons. Draught 14ft 8in/15ft (4.77/4.87m). Men: 86.
> Guns: 20 to 26 x 8pdrs; (1795) 12 x 8pdrs, 10 x 6pdrs; (1810) 10 guns.

Normande Le Havre (Constructeur: Fabien)
K: 10.1788. Named: 14.3.1789. L: 23.7.1789. C: 8.1789.
Renamed *Nécessité* 5.1795. Captured 21.2.1810 by HMS *Horatio* (38) west of Funchal after a long chase while en route from Brest to Île de France.

NOURRICE Class – 700 tons. Designed and constructed by Raymond-Antoine Haran, plan dated 28 December 1789. These were the only new-construction flûtes built during the tumultuous years between 1792 and 1799. Two-deckers with 10 ports in a lower battery, probably never used, and 24 ports in the upper battery.
Dimensions & tons: 134ft 0in, 123ft 0in x 32ft 0in x 14ft 2in (43.52, 39.95 x 10.39 x 4.60m). 700/1,200 tons. Draught 14ft/15ft 2in (4.55/4.72m). Men: 100-194.
Guns: 24 x 8pdrs (in 1807 the 8pdrs in *Nourrice* were replaced by 6pdrs).

Nourrice Bayonne.
K: 2.1790. L: 3.8.1792. C: 10.1792.
Attacked with *Girafe* 1.5.1811 in the Gulf of Sagone, Corsica, by HMS *Unity* and boats from HMS *Pomone* and *Scout*, burned to prevent capture.

Prévoyante Bayonne.
K: 1791. L: 5.1793. C: 8.1793.
Captured 17.5.1795 in the Chesapeake by HMS *Thetis* and *Hussard*, becoming 12pdr frigate HMS *Prevoyante*; Hulked 1809 and BU 1819.

ESCAUT Class – 800 tons. Designed by Pierre-Alexandre Forfait. The 800-ton flûte was one of the ship types standardised during the Napoleonic Wars. It was one of three exceptionally long-lived designs in the French Navy, the others being 74-gun ships of the line and 18pdr frigates. The first ship of this type was *Normande*, designed by Forfait in 1788. In 1800 Forfait, by then Minister of Marine, revived these plans to build these two ships, and the design was then used between 1805 and 1847 to build the much larger *Var* class (below). Both of the *Escaut* class flûtes were reclassified corvettes de charge (cargo-carrying corvettes) on 13 November 1821.
Dimensions & tons: 136ft 1½in, 123ft 9in x (44.22m, 43.52m wl, 40.19m x 10.39m, 10.56m ext x 5.39m). 800/1,380 tons.

Nicholas Pocock's sketch showing the end of the action between the British frigates *Thetis* and *Hussar* and five French storeships off the Chesapeake on 17 May 1795. The dismasted *Prévoyante* can be seen at centre while the acquired *Raison* is at the extreme right. Note what appear to be three large loading ports on *Prévoyante*'s lower deck. (© National Maritime Museum PU0403)

Draught 14ft/16ft (4.56/5.20m). Men: 107-154.
Guns: 26 x 8pdrs (26 ports, ships rated for 24 guns); (*Escaut*, 1816) 10 x 24pdr carronades

Escaut Le Havre.
Ord: 5.1800. K: early 1801. L: 23.5.1803. C: 6.1803.
Renamed *Seine* 26.7.1814 or 24.9.1814, *Escaut* 22.3.1815, and *Seine* 15.7.1815. Struck at Brest 9.9.1835 and BU.

Rhône Le Havre (Constructeur: François Gréhan)
Ord. 3.7.1802. K: 10.1802. L: 4.5.1805. C: 2.1807.
Wrecked 12.1.1836 near Agde (Hérault) after losing her rudder in a storm the previous day.

Ex BRITISH MERCANTILE PRIZES (1793-1799)

Henri or *Henry* (British merchant ship *Helena* taken or seized and comm. at Bordeaux 3.1793, 500 tons, 40-50 men, carried 10 x 4pdrs). Renamed *Helena* 5.1795. Last mentioned 4.1798 while at Santo Domingo, struck 1799.

Thomas of Bristol (British merchant brig *Thomas of Bristol* captured 1793, 250-300 tons, 172 men, carried 16 x 4pdrs). Rated as flûte and later as transport. Training corvette at Lorient 11.1798. Sold 8.1802 at Lorient but hired in 1803 for the war's duration. Was a receiving ship (*cayenne*) at Lorient and may also have been a gunnery and seamanship school there. In 1.1807 she was replaced by the corvette *Société* and herself replaced the cutter *Hoop* as a lifesaving station in the harbour of Port Louis near Lorient. Her name was shortened to *Thomas Bristol* c1808. Decomm. 5.1814 and returned to her owner.

Tirone or *Tyronne* (British merchant ship built in Britain in 1789, taken in 1793, and comm. at Lorient as a flûte 6.1794, 300 tons, 182 men, carried 20 x 4pdrs). On sale list at Lorient 5.1797 but not sold, powder hulk there 10.1799, unserviceable 12.1801 and struck.

Anna Suzanna (British merchant ship taken in 1793 by the frigate

Proserpine and comm. as a flûte, 500 tons, 8 guns). Burned by accident 9.1795 in the roadstead at Brest after a refit.

Catherine-Marguerite (British merchant vessel built in Holland 1786, captured in 1793 or 1794 and in service at Lorient in 7.1794, carried 12 x 12pdrs). Name shortened to *Catherine* c1796. Struck and converted to powder hulk at Brest 1800, last mentioned 1801.

Hannach or *Hamach* (British merchant ship built in Britain 1784, taken and comm. 5.1794 at Lorient as a flûte, 260 tons, 2 x 3pdrs). Became a storage hulk at Nantes 10.1796, struck 1797.

Belmont (British 758-ton (bm) Indiaman *Bellmont* completed 1780 and taken 7.1794, 850 tons, 194 men, 18 x 8pdrs and 8 other guns). Sold 10.1795 at Brest.

Harcourt (British merchant ship *Harpy* from London taken 10.1794 on the west coast of Africa, 400 tons, 172 men, 20 guns). Renamed *Harpie* 5.1795. Struck 1796.

Exange or *Exauge* (British merchant ship *Exchange* (?) built in Britain in 1789, taken and comm. 10.1794, 2 or 4 x 1pdrs). At Glénans 5.1795, struck late 1795.

Esther (British merchant ship built in Britain in 1789, taken and comm. 10.1794 at Lorient as a flûte). Struck late 1795.

Peggy de Greenock or *Peggy de Grenoch* (British merchant ship built in Britain, taken by a French privateer, and requisitioned 10.1794, 40 men, 2 x 2pdrs) Was in service at Brest 3.11.1794. Returned 8.1795 to her privateer owners.

Hirton (British merchant ship captured 1794 and taken to Nantes, carried as a flûte on the 1795 fleet list). Stationed at Donges, transported wood, coal, artillery and iron between Brest and Indret. Struck c7.1795.

Sultan or *Sultana* (Portuguese merchant ship built in Portugal and captured 1794, 183 men, carried 20 x 6pdrs or 4pdrs). Renamed *Sénateur* or *Sultana* 5.1795. In poor condition at Brest in 3.1798 and struck there c8.1801.

Lydia (British merchant ship built in Britain, taken 1.1795 and comm. as a flûte, 18 guns). Sold 7.1797 at Lorient.

Caledonia (British merchant ship taken and at Brest 8.1795, carried 26 x 8pdrs). Struck 1797.

Triton (British 800-ton Indiaman completed in 1787, taken 1.1796 by the privateer Robert Surcouf, and seized 4.1796 by the authorities at Île de France because Surcouf did not yet have a letter of marque, carried 26 x 12pdrs). Sold 10.1796 to an American or Danish shipowner.

Cérès (British merchant ship taken 1.1796 by French privateers and purchased by the navy 3.1796 at Saint-Malo, 172 men, carried 14 x 6pdrs and 2 obusiers). Captured 4.1798 by the British.

Reine (British merchant ship *Queen* captured in 1798 and commissioned at Brest 11.1798, 400 tons, 28 men). Condemned 1.1804 at Lorient and BU.

Osterley (British Indiaman of 755 to 775 tons placed in service 3.1781 and captured 1799 by the frigate *Forte*, 800 tons). Retaken by the British 1800.

MISCELLANEOUS PRIZES

Pelopidas (Spanish merchant ship built in Spain in 1786, taken and comm. 7.1794 at Lorient as a flûte). Struck c1796.

Bonne Aventure (Spanish merchant ship *Buenaventura* built in Spain in 1788, taken and comm. 7.1794 at Lorient as a flûte , carried 2 x 2pdrs). Probably struck or sold 1796.

Hendrick (merchant ship, possibly Dutch, built in Britain and taken c1794, carried 2 x 2pdrs). Sold at Brest late 1795 as the privateer *Heureuse Nouvelle* (22 guns). Captured 2.1798 by HMS *Indefatigable* (44).

Imperial or *Ymperial* (merchant ship built in the Netherlands, taken in 1794 and comm. as a flûte). Was at Pasajes 5.1795, struck late 1795.

PURCHASED AND REQUISITIONED FLÛTES (1793-1799)

Société (merchant ship *Duc de Normandie* built at Lorient by François Caro at the Chantiers Arnous in 1784-6, hired by the French East India Company 3.1787, purchased by them 1789, renamed *Normandie* 1791 and *Société* 1792, and purchased by the navy at Lorient 2.1793. The new Compagnie des Indes had been established on 14.4.1785 but despite commercial success the revolutionary government decided in 10.1792 to liquidate it).
Dimensions & tons: dimensions unknown. 813 tons burthen. Men: 136-182.
Guns: 20 x 8pdrs (24 ports)
Renamed *Normandie* in 1793 or 1794 and *Nicodème* 5.1795. Sold 1801 at Brest.

Tigre (*Élisabeth*) (French East India Co. flûte *Royale Élisabeth* built at Chantiers Arnous in Lorient by François Caro and purchased at Lorient by the navy in 2.1793 after the company was ordered liquidated, 813 tons, 136-182 men, carried 16 x 4pdrs in a battery with 24 ports). Renamed *Élisabeth* 1793 or 1794 and refitted 1794 with 20 x 8pdrs. Captured 28.8.1796 off Cape Henry by a British division and taken to Halifax. She was a sister to *Société*, above.

Suffren (French East India Co. flûte launched at Nantes 29.5.1786 and purchased at Lorient 2.1793, 472 tons, 84 men, 6 to 12 guns). Hulked at Lorient in late 1794, sold there 2.1808.

Miromesnil (merchant ship *Miromesnil* built at Lorient 1784, hired by the French East India Company 3.1786, purchased by them 1788, requisitioned by the navy 6.1793).
Dimensions & tons: 120ft x 32ft x 15ft (38.98 x 10.39 x 4.87m). 529/1,000 tons. Men: 164.
Guns: 24 x 6pdrs, 4 x 4pdrs.
Renamed *Espérance* 3.7.1793 and *Coche* 23.7.1793. Returned 2.1799 to her owners who did not accept her, placed on sale 7.1802 at Rochefort. Alternatively *Espérance* was not the Indiaman *Miromesnil* but was a merchantman purchased from sieur Guerard on 3.7.1793 and commissioned on 7.8.1793.

Achille (flûte built at Lorient in 1783 and purchased there 6.1793, 1,200 tons, 205 men, carried 26 x 8pdrs). Station ship at Santo Domingo 1796-1801.

Ville de Lorient (merchant vessel *Ville de Lorient* built in 1784 and purchased 7.1793 at Lorient, 177 men, carried 20 x 6pdrs). Renamed *Ville de Lorient No.2* 10.1794 and *Zone* 5.1795. Wrecked 29.10.1798 in a storm off Paimboeuf.

Ville de Lorient (French East India Co. flûte *Bretagne* built at Lorient in 1787 and requisitioned at Philadelphia 12.1793 by the French representative there, then bought by the navy, 525/1,000 tons, 175 men, carried 2 x 12pdrs, 22 x 6pdrs, and 4 x 3pdrs). Renamed *Ville Commune de Lorient* 5.1794, *Ville de Lorient No.1* 10.1794, *Voyageur* 5.1795 but reverted to *Ville de Lorient*. Captured 1.1797 off Ireland with 431 soldiers by HMS *Doris* (36), *Unicorn* (32), and *Druid* (22), then wrecked on the Irish coast.

Belle Angélique (flûte built at Le Havre in 1790 and requisitioned there 4.1793, 350/700 tons, 84-131 men, carried 10 x 8pdrs, 3 x 6pdrs, and 3 x 4pdrs). Renamed *Balance* 5.1795, reverted to *Belle Angélique* 1796. Wrecked 12.1796 at Sainte-Croix de Ténériffe, wreck abandoned 3.1797.

Trajan (flûte launched at Nantes 10.1787 for Bordeaux owners and requisitioned in 1793, 400 tons, carried 4 x 8pdrs, 14 x 6pdrs, and 4 x 4pdrs). Renamed *Truite* 5.1795. Returned 4.1796 to her owner at Bordeaux.

Superbe (merchant ship from Nantes, built in 1788, requisitioned 1.1794 and commissioned as a flûte at Rochefort)
  Dimensions & tons: 116ft x 32ft 10in (37.68 x 10.66m). 450-600/1,226 tons. Men: 182.
  Guns: 20 x 6pdrs (22 ports)
  Captured 1.10.1795 off Barbados by HMS *Vanguard* (74) and made into a prison hulk at Martinique by the Royal Navy. Sold 1798.

Suffren (merchant ship *Suffren* requisitioned 12.2.1794 at Lorient, 600 tons, 194 men, carried 24 x 8pdrs). Renamed *Saisissante* 5.1795 but reverted to *Suffren*. Captured 1.1797 with 202 soldiers on board by HMS *Jason* (38), then retaken by the French frigate *Tartu* (ex *Uranie*), then sunk off Ushant by HMS *Majestic* (74), *Daedalus* (32), and *Incendiary* (14).

Antifédéraliste (Bordeaux merchant ship *Commerce de Montpellier* built at Bordeaux in 1788 and requisitioned 2.1794, 183-194 men, carried 24 x 8pdrs). Renamed *Chameau* 16.5.1795. Returned to her owner 1.1796 at Bordeaux.

Éclatant (merchant ship built at Bordeaux in 1779 and requisitioned there 2.1794, carried 4 x 8pdrs, 16 x 6pdrs, 2 x 4pdrs). Burned 7.1796 near Audierne south of Brest to prevent capture by a British division.

Deux Associés (Nantes merchant ship with three masts requisitioned 2.1794 at Rochefort to deport 450 prisoner priests to Madagascar; 550 tons, 118/136 men, carried 16 x 4pdrs). Sailed only to Île d'Aix, then used as prison ship from April to November 1794, 397 priests died on board. The last priests were removed from the ship in 3.1795 and she was reclassified as a flûte, refitted, and renamed *Écrevisse* 5.1795. Last mentioned 12.1796 as hulk at Rochefort.

Destin (merchant ship *Comte d'Estaing*, built at Saint-Malo 1782, purchased by the French East India Company at Bordeaux 1787, renamed *D'Estaing* or *Destin* 1793, and requisitioned by the navy 3.1794).
  Dimensions & tons: dimensions unknown. 331 tons burthen. Men: 70
  Guns: 10 x 4pdrs.
  Renamed *Temps* 5.1795. Sold 1800, probably at Brest.

Lambert (277-ton merchant ship *Lambert*, purchased by the French East India Company 1787 at Bordeaux, requisitioned by the navy 3.1794 and fitted as a 400-ton flûte).
  Dimensions & tons: dimensions unknown. 277-400 tons burthen.
  Men: 75
  Guns: 2
  Renamed *Licorne* 5.1795. To have been returned to her owners 2.1799, not done due to lack of rigging. Sold 7.1804 at Rochefort and BU.

Duras (East India Company ship built at Lorient in 1779 and requisitioned 3.1794 at Lorient, 534/1,000 tons, 70-160 men, carried 20 x 6pdrs). Captured 5.1.1795 with 400 soldiers on board in the Antilles by HMS *Bellona* (74) and *Alarm* (32). Renamed *Devin* 5.1795 after loss.

Raison (East India Company's *Necker* built at Lorient in 1787 and requisitioned there 3.1794, 363 tons, 127/147 men, carried 14 x 8pdrs). Captured 17.5.1795 by HMS *Thetis* (38) and *Hussar* (28) in the Chesapeake and became HMS *Raison* (26). Sold 5.1802.

Quartier Morin (Bordeaux merchant ship requisitioned there 3.1794 to deport 400 priests, 600 tons). The deportation was abandoned 4.1794, the ship being in need of major repairs, and she was returned to her owner.

Malabar (East India Company ship built before 1785 and requisitioned 4.1794 at Lorient, 500 tons). Became barracks hulk at Lorient in early 1795, sold 3.1809 for BU.

Morbihan (East India Company ship requisitioned 4.1794 at Lorient, 144 men, carried 18 x 6pdrs). In service at Brest from May to October 1794 when she returned to Lorient, later fate unknown. May have become the hulk *Pondichéry* at Lorient (sold 3.1809 for BU) or the hulk *Malabar* (above).

Breton (merchant ship placed in service 3.1786 at Nantes and requisitioned there 4.1794, 400 tons, carried 22 x 8pdrs). Returned to her owner late 1794 or early 1795, became privateer in 1797.

Jeune Charles (merchant ship requisitioned 4.1794 at Nantes, carried 22 x 8pdrs). Returned to her owner late 1794 or early 1795.

Sincère (merchant ship requisitioned 4.1794 at Nantes, carried 22 x 8pdrs). Returned to her owner late 1794 or early 1795.

Alexandre (merchant ship probably launched at Nantes in 1783 and requisitioned there 4.1794, 500 tons, carried 20 x 8pdrs). Returned to her owner late 1794 or early 1795.

Tyrannicide (merchant ship requisitioned 4.1794 at Nantes, carried 22 x 8pdrs). Returned to her owner late 1794 or early 1795.

Gentil (former slave ship commissioned as a flûte at Rochefort 4.1794 to deport 254 priests from Bordeaux to Africa or French Guiana, 600 tons, 47 men). The priests were embarked in 10.1794 but were only carried to Port-des-Barques on the Charente. The ship was probably returned to her owner around 4.1795.

Washington (merchant ship with three masts from La Rochelle requisitioned 5.1794 to deport 350 priests to Africa or French Guiana, 600 tons, 126-142 men, 8 guns). Sailed only to Île d'Aix, prison ship from July to November 1794, 138 prisoners died on board. The last prisoners were removed from the ship in 3.1795 and she was reclassified as a flûte. Wrecked 3.1796 on the reefs of the Tour des Baleines at Île de Ré.

Indien (Bordeaux merchant ship built at Bayonne in 1788 and requisitioned 7.1794 at Rochefort, 304 tons, 22 men, carried 12 x 12pdrs, 4 x 6pdrs). Purchased by the navy definitively in 5.1797. Sold 1.1798 at Corunna, Spain.

Républicain (merchant ship or privateer probably requisitioned 8.1794). Wrecked 26.9.1795 near Royan at the mouth of the Gironde.

Harmonie (flûte of unknown origin with three masts in service at Brest 3.11.1794, 8 guns). Renamed *Historique* 5.1795. Struck late 1795.

Hernoux (flûte built at Bayonne in 1780-81, probably requisitioned and in service at Brest in 9.1794, 172 men, carried 16 x 6pdrs). Decomm. 11.1795 at Île d'Aix.

Ferme (merchant ship requisitioned and comm. as a flûte at Brest 10.1794, 150 men, carried 14 x 6pdrs). Chased ashore 1.1795 in the Baie St. François at Guadeloupe and burned by the British.

Cléomène (merchant ship built at Nantes in 1759, requisitioned 10.1794 and commissioned at Brest, 350 men as school ship, 14 x 6pdrs). Served as gunnery school at Roscanvel from 11.1794 to 2.1796. Last mentioned 11.1796 out of commission at Brest.

Félix Méritis (flûte probably commissioned at Rochefort 10.1794 and in service at Pasajes on 23.11.1794). Captured 7.6.1795 by the enemy.

Soeurs (merchant ship requisitioned 1794 at Dunkirk, 500 tons). Returned to her owner in 1794 or early 1795.

Réciproque (Bordeaux merchant ship built there in 1791-92 and requisitioned and commissioned as a flûte at Brest in 1794, 700 tons, 182 men, carried 20 x 6pdrs). Sailed 4.1795 from Brest for the Indies, no further news, struck 1797.

Duquesne (merchant ship commissioned as a flûte in 1794, may have had 36 guns and 40 gunports). Captured 1.1795 in the Antilles by HMS *Bellona* (74).

Républicaine (flûte of unknown origin in service at Brest 4.1795, 180 men, carried 18 x 4pdrs). Renamed *Raffermie* 5.1795. Was at Santo

Domingo in 4.1798, struck c1799.
Africain (flûte of uncertain origin in service at Pasajes in 5.1795, 1 gun). Struck 9.1795, probably after being returned to her owner.
Fort (flûte of unknown origin in service at Cherbourg in early 1796, 4 guns). On sale list 10.1796 at Cherbourg but not sold, BU at Cherbourg 12.1797.
Justine (merchant ship commissioned in 11.1796, possibly the 309-ton *Justine* that traded from Nantes between 1785 and 1790 or perhaps a larger ship, carried 1 x 8pdr, 1 x 4pdr, 1 x 10-inch and 2 x 8-inch mortars). Captured 30.12.1796 off Ireland by HMS *Polyphemus* (64) while carrying 465 soldiers, then wrecked and lost with all hands.
Allègre (flûte of unknown origin comm. 11.1796 at Brest, carried 2 x 12pdrs, 1 x 4pdr, and 1 x 6pdr obusier). Captured 12.1.1797 off Ushant by HMS *Spitfire* (16) while carrying 552 soldiers.
Jardin de la Paix (flûte of unknown origin in service at Dunkirk in 1797, 600 tons). Last mentioned 1799 at Dunkirk, was not on the 4.1798 fleet list.
Jumeaux or *Les Jumeaux* (flûte with three masts in service at Dunkirk in 1797, 600 tons). Last mentioned 1799 at Dunkirk, was not on the 4.1798 fleet list.
Agathe-Marie (flûte of unknown origin in service at Dunkirk in 1797, 500 tons). Last mentioned 1799 at Dunkirk, was not on the 4.1798 fleet list.
Nouvelle Entreprise (flûte of unknown origin commissioned in 1797 or early 1798). Wrecked at Ténériffe 1798, her masts were used in 8.1798 to repair battle damage to the frigate *Régénérée*.
Patriote (merchant ship requisitioned at Marseille in 5.1798 and commissioned as a flûte for the Egyptian expedition, 550-580 tons). Wrecked 7.1798 at Alexandria.
Ville de Marseille (merchant flûte requisitioned c5.1798 at Marseille, 650 tons, 24 gunports). Also listed as a 12-gun prame or corvette. After sailing from Toulon *en flûte* to carry supplies to French forces in Malta, she was captured 18.2.1800 by HMS *Alexander* south of Sicily.
Cormoran (flûte of unknown origin in service at Saint-Malo 7.1798). Operated along the coast of Brittany 7-10.1798. Station ship at Saint-Malo 4.1799, decomm. 6.1799, struck c1800.
Jean-Jacob (flûte of unknown origin, 900 tons, 77 men, carried 4 guns). Was in service at Lorient in 5.1799. Sold at Lorient 11.1801 or 8.1802.

(C) Flûtes acquired from 25 March 1802

LOIRE Class – 800 tons. Designed by François-Louis Etesse and built under a contract dated 5 November 1802.
    Dimensions & tons: 133ft 6in, 123ft 6in x 33ft 0in x 17ft 3in (43.36, 40.11 x 10.72 x 5.60m). 800/1,382 tons.
    Guns: 20 x 8pdrs (24 ports).
Loire Louis, Antoine, & Mathurin Crucy, Basse Indre.
    Ord: 10.1802 (contract 5.11.1802). K: 11.1802. L: 15.10.1803. C: 11.1803.
    Attacked at anchor with sister *Seine* and burned 18.12.1809 by her crew in the Anse de la Barque, Guadeloupe, to avoid capture by HMS *Blonde* (38, ex *Hebe*), *Thetis* (38), *Freya* (36), and *Sceptre* (74).
Seine Louis, Antoine, & Mathurin Crucy, Basse Indre.
    Ord: 10.1802 (contract 5.11.1802). K: 11.1802. L: 17.9.1806. C: 3.1808.
    Attacked at anchor with sister *Loire* and burned 18.12.1809 by her crew in the Anse de la Barque, Guadeloupe, to avoid capture by HMS *Blonde* (38), *Thetis* (38), *Freya* (36), and *Sceptre* (74).

DYLE Class – 600 tons. Probably designed by Pierre Lair.
    Dimensions & tons: 129ft 1in, 114ft 6in x 29ft 8in x 16ft 2in (41.94, 37.20 x 9.63 x 5.25m). 600/1,040 tons. Draught 12ft 6in/15ft 6in (4.06/5.04m).
    Guns: Unknown.
Dyle Dunkirk.
    Ord: 19.2.1803. Named 7.3.1803. Decision 7.4.1803 to build two frigates instead of *Dyle* and *Meuse*, order cancelled c6.1803.
Meuse Dunkirk.
    Ord: 19.2.1803. Named 7.3.1803. Decision 7.4.1803 to build two frigates instead of *Dyle* and *Meuse*, order cancelled c6.1803.
Oise Toulon Dyd.
    Ord: 19.2.1803. Order cancelled c6.1803.

Two flûtes, design unknown, named *Chameau* and *Dromadaire* were ordered at Nantes on 2.4.1805 but not built.

VAR Class – 800 tons. This class was a continuation of the standard 800-ton design that originated with the *Normande* designed by Pierre-Alexandre Forfait in 1788 and that was reproduced more recently in the *Escaut* class of 1801-2. *Var* was built to plans of Forfait as reviewed by Jacques-Noël Sané (probably the plans of *Escaut*), while the others were credited only to Sané. Of the 22 ships ordered and 21 built, 18 were built by contract, 10 at La Ciotat and 8 at Marseille, making this one of the French sailing navy's larger contracting efforts. The contractors in 1808 were Vian, Velin, Riboulet, & Ménard at La Ciotat and Chicallat & Jouvin at Marseille, and these firms most likely also received the later orders. At Marseille records show a contract dated 2 October 1810 for *Golo*, a contract approval date that is probably 6 October 1810 for *Ariège*, a contract date of 6 October 1810 for *Hippopotame*, and no information on *Bonite*; all four were most likely covered by a single contract signed on 2 and approved on 6 October 1810. In 1810 the navy also ordered two flûtes each at its small dockyards at Saint-Malo and Bayonne, but these languished on the ways until and beyond the end of the war. (Two of these, *Tarn* and *Adour*, are recorded with slightly different dimensions, including a waterline length of 43.68m and a moulded beam of 10.44m.) All surviving 800-ton flûtes were reclassified corvettes de charge (cargo-carrying corvettes) on 13 November 1821.
    Dimensions & tons: 135ft 9in, 134ft 0in wl, 123ft 8in x 32ft 0in, 32ft 11in ext x 16ft 7in (44.10, 43.52, 40.17 x 10.39, 10.70 x 5.39m). 800/1,380 tons. Draught 14ft 0in/15ft 10in (4.56/5.14m). Men: 101-159.
    Guns: 22 x 8pdrs, 2 x 6pdrs (26 ports). *Var* also had 2 x 24pdr carronades. In 3.1811 all 800-ton flûtes were ordered armed with 24 x 24pdr carronades and 2 x 18pdrs, and *Cornaline* was recorded with this armament in 1814.
Var La Ciotat.
    Ord: 26.3.1805. K: 7.1805. L: 8.9.1806. Comm: 3.10.1806. C: 12.1806.
    Captured 15.2.1809 while at anchor at Valona by HMS *Belle Poule* (38) and became the 777-ton storeship HMS *Chichester*. Wrecked 5.1811 near Madras.
Baleine La Ciotat.
    Ord: 26.3.1805. K: 7.1805. L: 21.9.1807. Comm: 13.10.1807.
    Wrecked 23.12.1813 and broke up on a reef near Calvi after being chased with *Lybio* and *Flèche* by HMS *Berwick* (74), *Armada* (74). and *Alcmene* (38) and combat with boats from *Berwick* and *Euryalus* (36).
Caravane Vian, Velin, Riboulet, & Ménard, La Ciotat.
    Ord: 16.3.1808 (contract). Named: 23.5.1808. K: 6.1808. L: 10.6.1809. Comm: 10.9.1809. C: 9.1809.

THE LARGER TRANSPORTS

The destruction of the storeships Girafe *and* Nourrice *in the Gulf of Sagone, Corsica on 1 May 1811. This anonymous aquatint shows the boats of the British frigates* Unite *and* Pomone *and the sloop* Scout *about to launch a cutting-out expedition, with the French storeships in the background set on fire to avoid capture.* (© National Maritime Museum PX7117)

Blown ashore and demolished 21.10.1817 at Martinique in a hurricane.

Girafe (*Giraffe*) Vian, Velin, Riboulet, & Ménard, La Ciotat.
  Ord: 16.3.1808 (contract). Named: 23.5.1808. K: 8.1808. L: 30.8.1809. Comm: 10.11.1809. C: 11.1809.
  Burned with *Nourrice* and blown up 1.5.1811 in the Gulf of Sagone, Corsica, to avoid capture by HMS *Unité* (38) and boats from HMS *Pomone* (38) and *Scout* (18).

Persane Chicallat & Jouvin, Marseille.
  Ord: 16.3.1808 (contract). Ord: 25.4.1808. Named: 23.5.1808. K: 1.6.1808. L: 9.1809. Comm: 15.10.1809. C: 12.1809.
  Captured 29.11.1811 in the Adriatic near Langousta Is. by HMS *Unite*, *Alceste*, and *Active* (all 38). The British sold her to the Bey of Tunis.

Lybio (ex *Paon* 18.8.1808) Vian, Velin, Riboulet, & Ménard, La Ciotat.
  Ord: 16.3.1808 (contract). Named: 23.5.1808 (*Paon*). K: 9.1808. L: 17.5.1810. Comm: 12.7.1810. C: 7.1810.
  Renamed at the request of inhabitants of Corsica where the forest of Lybio provided shipbuilding timber. On 23.12.1813 survived the engagement in which *Baleine* was lost. Decomm. 1831 and crew transferred to *Bonite*. Struck 1836 and hulked at Toulon. BU 1842.

Dromadaire Chicallat & Jouvin, Marseille.
  Ord: 16.3.1808 (contract). Named: 23.5.1808. K: 6.1808. L: 6.1810. C: 7.1810. Comm: 1.10.1810.
  Captured 31.3.1811 off Elba by HMS *Ajax* (74) and *Unité* (38).

Mérinos (ex *Ambitieuse* 1810) Chicallat & Jouvin, Marseille.
  Ord: 16.3.1808 (contract). Named: 23.5.1808 (*Mérinos*). K: 6.1810.

  L: 24.1.1811. Comm: 23.3.1811. C: 3.1811.
  Captured 13.2.1812 off northern Corsica by HMS *Apollo* (38).

Salamandre (possibly ex *Normande* 1810) La Ciotat.
  Ord: 1.7.1809 (contract). Named 7.8.1809 (*Salamandre*). K: 10.1809. L: 21.3.1811. Comm: 30.3.1811. C: 5.1811.
  Grounded 13.1.1826 on the Île de Ré, lost 16.1.1826.

Éléphant Marseille.
  Ord: 19.6.1809 (contract 1.7.1809). Named 7.8.1809. K: 8.1810. L: 5.5.1811. Comm: 1.6.1811. C: 6.1811.
  Struck 1.1827, powder hulk at Lorient. In commission as such 1.8.1831 to 18.6.1833 when last mentioned.

Licorne La Ciotat.
  Ord: 18.1.1811 (contract 2.10.1810). K: 4.1811. L: 15.11.1811. Comm: 12.1.1812. C: 1.1812.
  Condemned 2.1826 at Rochefort, BU there 6.1826.

Golo Marseille.
  Ord: 2.10.1810 (contract). K: 18.2.1811. L: 28.11.1811. Comm: 1.1.1812. C: 2.1812.
  Decomm. 22.9.1821 at Toulon in need of major repairs which were not done. Condemned 1825 and hulked at Toulon. Training hulk

11.1829. Date BU unknown.
Égyptienne La Ciotat.
   Ord: 18.2.1811 (contract 2.10.1810). K: 3.1811. L: 7.1.1812. Comm: 8.5.1812. C: 5.1812.
   Renamed *Normande* 24.9.1814, *Égyptienne* 22.3.1815, and *Normande* 15.7.1815. Condemned 1824 at Sainte Marie de Madagascar, struck before 1.11.1824, and decomm. 21.2.1825. Used as a storage hulk until 1833.
Rhinocéros La Ciotat.
   Ord: 18.2.1811 (contract 2.10.1810). K: 4.1811. L: 18.3.1812. Comm: 2.5.1812. C: 5.1812.
   Blown ashore in a storm 30.10.1815 in the harbour at Cherbourg and broke in half.
Cornaline La Ciotat.
   Ord: 18.2.1811 (contract 2.10.1810). K: 3.1811. L: 4.1812. C: 9.1812. Comm: 1.1.1813.
   Wrecked in a storm 2.2.1823 on the rocks at Ericeira, Portugal while carrying troops.
Ariège (*Arriège*) Marseille.
   Ord: 18.2.1811 (contract 2.10.1810). K: 2.1811. L: 16.5.1812. Comm: 25.9.1812. C: 9.1812.
   Decomm. at Cherbourg 24.4.1829, condemned 1833. After being struck *Ariège* was an 'annexe' at Cherbourg until ordered scrapped on 9.6.1849.
Bonite Marseille.
   Ord: 18.2.1811 (contract 2.10.1810). K: 2.1811. L: 2.8.1813. C: 10.1815. Comm: 2.11.1818.
   Voyage around the world 1836-37. Decomm. 26.11.1842 at Brest, struck 19.12.1842. BU 1843.
Hippopotame Marseille.
   Ord: 18.2.1811 (contract 2.10.1810). K: 5.1811. Not launched, was 16/24ths complete when ordered finished 7.5.1814. Still at 16/24ths in a fleet list dated 1.10.1816, no longer listed by mid-1818. Either abandoned or sold into merchant service c1817.
Two unnamed Saint-Malo (Constructeur: Antoine Bonjean)
   Ord: 2.9.1810. K: 11.1810. Not launched. Both were 4/24 complete when construction was suspended soon before 1.4.1814. By 6.1814 it had been decided to take down their frames and transport them to Cherbourg to be completed. These materials were used to build *Moselle* (below).
Tarn (ex *Dordogne* c1811) Bayonne (Constructeurs: Jean Baudry and after 5.1816 Jean-Baptiste Marestier)
   K: 14.11.1810. L: 7.4.1818. Comm: 18.5.1818. C: 7.1818.
   Decomm. 6.11.1842, probably struck 19.11.1842.
Adour Bayonne (Constructeurs: Jean Baudry, after 5.1816 Jean-Baptiste Marestier, then Gabriel Nosereau)
   K: 14.11.1810. L: 25.3.1819. Comm: 1.3.1820. C: 7.1820.
   Used from 12.1845 as hospital ship at Gorée, Senegal and after c1849 at Gabon. Struck there 22.4.1851 as unfit to return to France, decomm. 24.9.1853, replaced by *Oise* in 1854 and probably BU then.
Moselle Cherbourg Dyd. (Constructeurs: Louis Bretocq and Joseph Daviel)
   K: 6.10.1814. L: 13.5.1820. Comm: 1.8.1820. C: 8.1820.
   Built using materials from two unnamed flûtes (listed above) begun at Saint-Malo in 11.1810 and dismantled in mid-1814. Renamed *Abondance* 15.4.1833. Assigned to the school for boys at Brest between 1.5.1836 and 1.10.1854, initially as training ship. Boys' barracks hulk at Brest 1.1849, struck 30.10.1851, condemned 18.7.1856 and BU.

In addition two unnamed 800-ton flûtes were ordered at Leghorn and two at Genoa in July 1810 but not built. Two more were ordered at Le Havre in September 1810 but the contract was cancelled at the beginning of 1811 and probably transferred to Saint-Malo. Another was ordered at Paimboeuf and another at Basse-Indre in September 1810 but these were cancelled in 1811 because of a dispute over the price. The unit at Paimboeuf was laid down in November 1810, built to 2.4/24ths by January 1811, and then dismantled.

Ex BRITISH MERCANTILE PRIZES (1805-1810)

Brunswick (East Indiaman of 1,219 tons built at Blackwall in 1792 for Thos. Newte and captured 10.7.1805 by the ship of the line *Marengo*).
   Dimensions & tons (approx.): 153ft 11in x 39ft 5in (50 x 12.8m). 1,200 tons burthen. Men: 250.
   Guns: 30 (64 ports including 28 in the lower battery).
   Wrecked 8.1805 or 9.1805 in Simons Bay and lost.
Olive (British merchantman, probably a former 900-ton Spanish merchant vessel from Cadiz, captured 19.6.1806 by the frigate *Sémillante* and commissioned *en flûte* 6.12.1806 at Île de France, 600/900 tons). Decomm. 3.1807.
Warren Hastings (East Indiaman of 1,356 tons built at Blackwall in 1802-3 by George Green and William Wells and captured 21.6.1806 by the frigate *Piémontaise*)
   Dimensions & tons (approx.): 157ft 0in x 40ft 0in (51 x 13m). 1,200/2,100 tons. Men: 190.
   Guns: 26 x 18pdrs (28 ports), 14 x 18pdr carronades, 4 x 12pdr carronades.
   Recaptured 1810 by the British at the fall of Île de France, returned to the East India Co. and operated in the China trade until BU in 1829.
Streatham (East Indiaman of 850 tons built at Deptford in 1804-5 by Dudman and captured 31.5.1809 by the frigate *Caroline*).
   Dimensions & tons (approx.): 132ft 4in x 33ft 10in (43 x 11m). 800/1,400 tons.
   Guns: 20 x 18pdrs, 10 carronades.
   Recaptured 9.1809 at Île Saint Paul by the British who used her until 1819.
Europe or *Europa* (East Indiaman of 820 tons built at Liverpool c1801-2 by Humble and Hurry or at Blackwall in 1803, captured 31.5.1809 by the frigate *Caroline*).
   Dimensions & tons: 131ft 2in, 120ft 1in x 33ft 10in x 18ft 6in (42.6, 39 x 11 x 6m). 800/1,350 tons. Draught 4.5/4.9m.
   Guns: 20 x 18pdrs, 10 x 18pdr carronades.
   Recaptured 9.1809 at Île Saint Paul by the British who used her until 1817.
Charlton (East Indiaman of 818 tons built at Liverpool 1798-99 by Humble and Hurry and captured 19.11.1809 by the frigates *Manche* and *Vénus* and the corvette *Créole*).
   Dimensions & tons (approx.): 129ft 3½in x 33ft 10in x 18ft 6in (42 x 11 x 6m). 800/1,350 tons.
   Guns: 20 x 18pdrs, 6 x 18pdr carronades.
   In 1810 was a prison ship at Île de France. Retaken 3.12.1810 by the British at the surrender of Île de France, fate unknown.
United Kingdom (East Indiaman of 820 tons built at Blackwall in 1801-2 by George Green and John and William Wells and captured 19.11.1809 by the frigates *Manche* and *Vénus* and the corvette *Créole*).
   Dimensions & tons (approx.): 131ft 2in, 120ft 1in x 33ft 10in x 18ft 6in (42.6, 39 x 11.0 x 6m). 800/1350 tons. Draught 4.5/4.9m.
   Guns: 20 x 12pdrs, 6 x 6pdrs.
   In 1810 was a prison ship at Île de France. Retaken 3.12.1810 by the

The French frigate Piémontaise bearing down to attack the East Indiaman Warren Hastings on 21 June 1806, as depicted in this print by Robert Dodd. Although warlike in appearance – and occasionally mistaken for warships – East Indiamen were too lightly armed and manned to take on a frigate, or even a large privateer, with any chance of success. Nevertheless, Warren Hastings put up a four-hour resistance before, with much of her top-hamper shot away, she was forced to surrender. (Courtesy of Beverley R. Robinson Collection, US Naval Academy Museum)

British at the surrender of Île de France, fate unknown.

Windham (East Indiaman of 823 tons built at Blackwall in 1800-1 by George Green and John and William Wells and captured 22.11.1809 by the frigate *Vénus*).
  Dimensions & tons: Identical to *United Kingdom*, above.
  Guns: 20 x 8pdrs, 6 x 9pdrs.
  Recaptured 29.12.1809 near Île Rodrigues by HMS *Magicienne* (36). Captured again 3.7.1810 by the French frigate *Bellone*. Recaptured again 21.8.1810 near Île de France by HMS *Sirius* (36). The British used her until 1816.

Ceylon (East Indiaman of 818 tons built in England in 1802-3 and captured 3.7.1810 by the frigate *Minerve*).
  Dimensions & tons: About the same as *United Kingdom*, above.
  Guns: 26 x 30 (34 ports).
  Sometimes called *Ceylan* in French service. In c9.1810 was a prison ship at Île de France. Retaken 3.12.1810 by the British at the surrender of Île de France, fate unknown.

Ex PORTUGUESE PRIZES (1807)

Princesa Real (Portuguese flûte launched at Pará, Brazil, in 1797 and captured at Lisbon 11.1807).
  Dimensions & tons: 126ft 8in x 30ft 11½in x 23ft 0in depth (41.15 x 10.06 x 7.47m). 700/1,200tons. Men: 144.
  Guns: 12 to 24 (42 ports).
  Retaken by the Portuguese 9.1808 at the evacuation of Lisbon.

Belem (Portuguese merchant vessel launched at Pará, Brazil, 26.3.1767 and captured at Lisbon 11.1807). Retaken by the Portuguese 9.1808 at the evacuation of Lisbon.

Généreux (Portuguese merchant vessel *Ovidor*, built of teak with iron bolts and copper sheathing, captured 20.10.1809 by the brig *Entreprenant* off Singapore with 230,000 piastres on board).
  Dimensions & tons: 115ft 0in x 30ft 0in x 15ft 1in (37.35 x 9.74 x 4.90m). 559/900 tons. Draught 13ft 2in/13ft 3in (4.27/4.30m). Men: 35-130.
  Guns: 18 x 12pdrs; (1812) 6 x 8pdrs, 6 x 4pdrs; (1814) 20 x 8pdrs; (1827) 10 x 18pdr carronades, 2 x 6pdrs.
  Renamed *Généreux* 9.1810, refitted at Île de France 9-10.1810, recommissioned there 5.10.1810. Sent to Rochefort as a cartel (prisoner exchange ship) soon before the British took Île de France in 12.1810. Recommissioned at Rochefort 2.3.1812 as a gabarre (name recorded, probably in error, as *Généreuse*). Renamed *Loire* 8.1814 and recommissioned 25.9.1814 as a flûte. Redesignated corvette de charge with the other flûtes on 13.11.1821 but listed as gabarre by 12.1822. Decomm. at Brest 1.7.1838 and crew to *Aube*. Struck 8.8.1838 and BU.

PURCHASED RUSSIAN VESSELS (1809)

Cherson (or *Herzon* or *Kerson*) (Russian Black Sea Fleet transport *Kherson*, built at Kherson, Ukraine, by M. I. Surovtsov. K: 10.7.1804. L: 28.7.1805. Refitted as 24-gun corvette at the end of 1805, joined Vice Admiral Senyavin's squadron at Corfu in 1806, sold to France 27.9.1809 at Venice).
  Dimensions & tons: 112ft 8in x 32ft 0in x 11ft 5in depth (36.6 x 10.4 x 3.7m). 723/1,200 tons.
  Guns: 12.
  Probably sold early 1811 at Corfu.

Diomède (Russian Black Sea Fleet transport *Diomid*, built at Kherson by V. I. Potapov. K: 30.1.1804. L: 29.10.1804. Transported troops to Corfu in 1805 and returned to Sevastopol, refitted as 24-gun corvette at the end of 1805, joined Vice Admiral Senyavin's squadron at Corfu in 1806, sold to France 27.9.1809 at Trieste.)
  Dimensions & tons: 131ft 7in x 37ft 6in x 15ft 1in depth (42.74 x

12.18 x 4.9m). 800/1,400 tons.

Guns: 22 x 8pdrs (24 ports)

Decomm. 4.1812 at Trieste. Taken over 4.1813 or 10.1813 by the Austrians who did not put her back into service.

PURCHASED AND REQUISITIONED FLÛTES (1807-1812)

Étoile (built by Grisard at Île de France. K: 1806, L: 1807, C: 19.6.1807, Comm: 2.8.1807. Carried 14 guns according to the British). Captured 11.1809 off Cherbourg by HMS *Euryalus* (36). French records show her as decommissioned on 6.6.1808.

Indien (merchant ship purchased 4.7.1808 on the ways at Toulon and comm. there 20.5.1809).

Dimensions & tons: 117ft 6in, 105ft 8in x 29ft 3in x 12ft 10in (38.16, 34.32 x 9.50 x 4.17m) plus a 4ft 11in (1.59m) tween-decks. 723/1,200 tons.

Guns: 14 x 6pdrs.

Decomm. 30.5.1812, condemned 15.6.1812, prison hulk at Toulon 7.1812, last mentioned 1813.

Diligente or *Flûte Impériale* (origin unknown, comm. 14.2.1810 at Île de France, previous ships there named *Diligente* included a schooner in 1804 and a 120-ton merchant brig in 1800). Scuttled or wrecked 24.8.1810 during the Battle of Grand Port, Île de France.

Constitutie (32-gun frigate of the Dutch East India Co. annexed 7.1810 with the Batavian Navy). Considered irreparable, fitted as a stable or a horse transport (*écurie*) 10.1811. Fate unknown.

Johanna-Anna (Dutch merchant ship built in 1788 and purchased 20.4.1812 at Amsterdam)

Dimensions & tons: 126ft 6in x 28ft 5in x 12ft 2in (41.02 x 9.22 x 3.96m) plus a 6ft 6in (2.11m) tween-decks. 880/1200 tons. Draught 4.55/5.11m.

Guns: probably none

Used as hospital ship for the Texel fleet. Was 'being commissioned' in 4.1814, when she was listed as 800 tons. Was a flûte and hospital ship out of commission at Nieuwediep in 1814 and was either returned to the Dutch with the Texel Squadron on 22.4.1814 or taken by them 4.5.1814 at the surrender of Nieuwediep. Became a hospital ship in the Dutch Navy, sold 1819 at Nieuwediep.

(D) Flûtes and corvettes de charge acquired from 26 June 1815

MEUSE Class – 800 tons. This class was a continuation of the standard 800-ton design that dated back to the *Normande* designed by Pierre Alexandre Forfait in 1788. The plans of *Oise*, *Allier*, *Caravane*, *Agathe*, *Rhin*, *Meurthe*, and *Fortune* were attributed to Forfait ('*Normande* type') and were very close if not identical to those of *Tarn* (one of the last of the *Var* class, above), while *Aube* was built to new plans (probably a minor update of Forfait's plans) signed by Pierre Rolland on 27 March 1829. The designed height of battery of this type was 1.50m at 4.82m mean draught. The order for *Allier* was transferred from Cherbourg to Brest in 1826 and the order for *Aube* was shifted from Brest to Saint-Servan in 1828 before construction began. *Somme*, *Rhin*, *Meurthe*, and *Seine* were reclassified 24-gun quarterdecked corvettes in 1846. *Rhin* and *Meurthe* were reclassified *corvettes à batterie barbette* in 1849; they and *Somme* reverted to transports in 1850. In late 1844 the navy's senior naval constructor, Boucher, noted that this type was designed for both transport and combat duty and, while very useful on overseas stations in peacetime, could not defend itself against smaller but faster combatant ships (like large brigs) and, despite its 800-ton rating, could carry only around 300 tons as a transport when carrying its full armament.

Dimensions & tons: 44.10m, 43.60m wl, 40.80m x 10.40m, 10.70m ext x 5.70m. 800/1347 tons. Draught 4.45/5.35m. Men: ?.

Guns: 20 x 24pdr carronades, 2 x 8pdrs (22 ports). When used exclusively as transports they could carry as few as 2 x 12pdrs. *Somme*, *Rhein* and *Seine* were completed with updated armaments as shown below.

Meuse Cherbourg Dyd. (Constructeur: Joseph Daviel)
Ord: 10.2.1824. K: 21.5.1824. L: 4.5.1825. Comm: 17.4.1826. C: 4.1826.
Unserviceable 6.1836 at Toulon and struck.

Oise Toulon Dyd.
Ord: 10.2.1824. K: 5.1824. L: 31.5.1825. Comm: 16.2.1826. C: 2.1826.
Replaced *Adour* as hospital ship at Gabon 1854, condemned 11.11.1862, beached in the Como River and burned by Africans 3.1863. Struck 2.4.1863.

Marne Toulon Dyd.
K: 6.1825. L: 29.5.1826. Comm: 27.6.1826. C: 7.1826.
Blown ashore 25.1.1841 in a storm in the anchorage of Stora, Algeria.

Caravane Toulon Dyd.
K: 6.1826. L: 17.1.1828. Comm: 22.3.1828. C: 3.1828.
Struck 29.10.1864.

Nièvre Brest Dyd. (Constructeurs: Antoine Geoffroy and others)
K: 26.7.1826. L: 12.6.1828. Comm: 1.12.1828. C: 12.1828.
Struck 8.8.1838 at Brest and BU 1838.

Allier Brest Dyd. (Constructeurs: Antoine Geoffroy and others)
K: 20.7.1826. L: 21.10.1828. Comm: 10.2.1829.
Struck 21.1.1856. Became a boys' training ship at Algiers 28.6.1856, probably renamed *Dragon* 3.1.1865, sold or BU at Algiers 1869.

Dordogne Bayonne (Constructeurs: Gabriel Nosereau with after 6.1828 Athanase-Marie Serpin-Dugué)
K: 9.1826. L: 9.12.1828. C: 10.1829. Comm: 1.1.1830.
Sent to Nossi-Bé 11.1841, in bad condition when taken from Réunion to Mayotte 1843-44, struck 1844 and hulk there 11.1844, lost 1844-45.

Saône Brest Dyd. (Constructeur: Hippolyte Prétot)
K: 2.11.1828. L: 4.9.1830. Comm: 20.2.1832. C: 2.1832.
Renamed *Agathe* (or *Agate*) 20.4.1833. Decomm. 10.5.1844, became boys' training ship at Toulon and in comm. as such 25.9.1845 to 12.6.1850. Struck 21.1.1856, condemned 15.3.1856, *caserne ambulance* or hospital hulk at Toulon replacing *Chameau* (ex gabarre, 1818) from 1857 to 1873. BU 1874-76.

Lozère Bayonne (Constructeurs: Gabriel Nosereau and from 7.1831 Gustave Garnier)
K: 2.12.1828. L: 10.10.1832. Comm: 9.8.1833. C: 8.1833.
Renamed *Égérie* 4.1834. Struck 17.8.1869 at Valparaiso, storage hulk there until 1871, BU 1873.

Var Toulon Dyd. (Constructeurs: Jacques Bonard and Claude-Marie Jobart-Dumesnil)
K: 4.1829. L: 1.5.1832. Comm: 10.1.1833. C: 1.1833.
Renamed *Fortune* 7.1833. Struck 17.8.1869 at Montevideo and retained there as a storage hulk until 1872, BU 1873-74.

Isère Lorient Dyd. (Constructeur: Pierre Thomeuf)
K: 10.6.1829. L: 12.7.1832. C: 1.1835. Comm: 1.2.1835.
Struck 2.12.1848, guard hulk at Brest. BU 1865.

Aube Saint-Servan (Constructeur: Charles Alexandre)
K: 5.1829. L: 13.9.1832. C: 9.1835. Comm: 4.2.1836.
Struck 6.9.1852 and condemned 20.9.1852 at Brest.

Somme Cherbourg Dyd. (Constructeur: Anne-François Besuchet)
K: 23.4.1839. L: 29.8.1840. Comm: 26.8.1841. C: 8.1841.

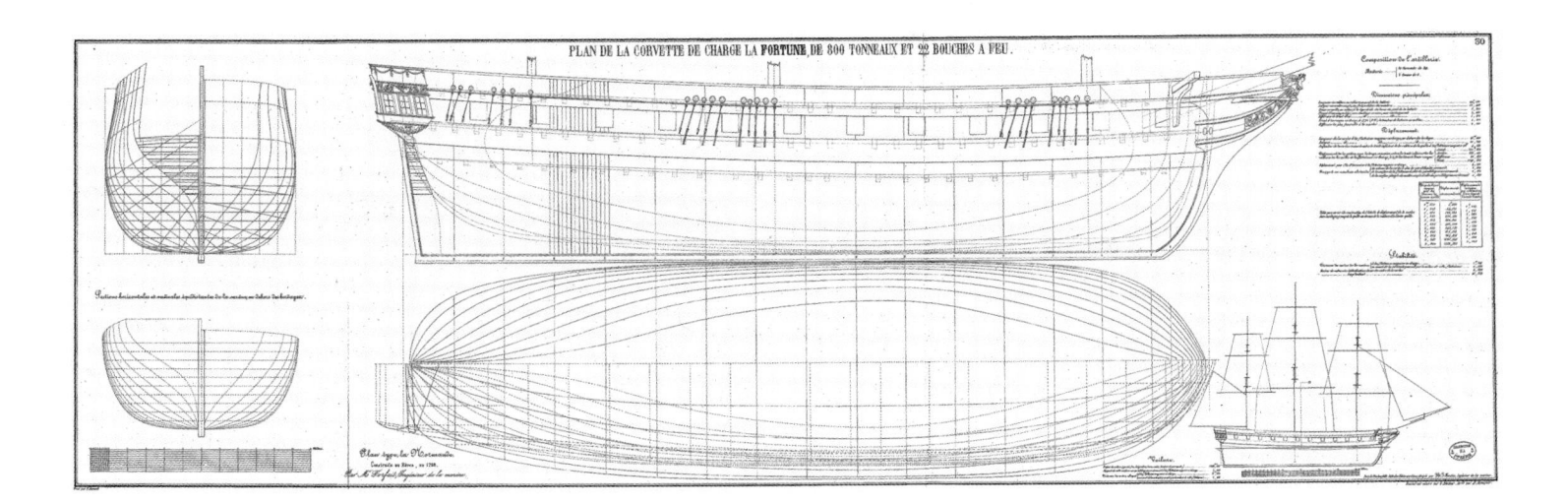

Official lines and general arrangement plans of the 'corvette de charge' *Fortune*, described as of the *Normande* type (1788) designed by Forfait. The ship carried a full ship rig, all plain sail amounting to 1,400 sq.m. (Atlas du Génie Maritime, French collection, plate 30)

sister *Zélée* on a second expedition in 1837-40. Gabarres sometimes had merchant marine crews. Harbour service and mud lighters (*gabarres portuaires*, *gabarres plates*, and *gabarres à vase*) are not listed here.

Guns as completed as *Rhin*, below.
Drydocked at Brest 9.7.1850, struck 21.11.1850, BU 1850-51.
Rhin Rochefort Dyd. (Constructeur: Charles Moll)
K: 15.4.1840. L: 21.5.1841. Comm: 1.8.1841. C: 9.1841.
Guns as completed: 18 x 24pdr carronades, 4 x 16cm shell (24 ports including 2 chase).
Struck 30.12.1854 at Toulon. Became the service craft *Depôt No.1* there.
Meurthe Lorient Dyd. (Constructeur: Pierre Thomeuf)
K: 12.5.1840. L: 2.11.1842. Comm: 18.11.1842. C: 1.1843.
Struck 6.9.1852 at Brest, hulk. Last mentioned 1854.
Seine Rochefort Dyd. (Constructeur: Bernard Chariot)
K: 26.5.1842. L: 21.2.1845. Comm: 1.3.1845. C: 3.1845.
Guns as completed (1845) 22 x 16cm shell, 4 x 8pdrs.
Wrecked 4.7.1846 in the port of Balade, New Caledonia.

The captured British frigate *Proserpine* was reclassified as an 800-ton corvette de charge in 1841 and converted in 1842. Built in 1807 and captured in 1809, she was recommissioned in 1844 and lasted until 1865. The French frigate *Aurore* (1809) was reclassified at about the same time but was not recommissioned.

Gabarres (transports from 1846)

The word *gabarre* (often spelled *gabare*) was used for river cargo barges (which today carry tourists) and also for seagoing vessels designed to carry bulky cargo. The navy often used seagoing gabarres to carry shipbuilding timbers and, beginning in the 1820s, new steam engines to its dockyards. The larger gabarres differed from flûtes primarily in that they did not have an orlop deck and carried their guns in open rather than covered batteries. They were slow but their large cargo capacity, robust hulls, and good seakeeping qualities made them (notably the *gabarre-écurie* type of 1811-12) suitable for overseas use, including on major exploration expeditions. Thus the 380-ton gabarre *Coquille*, renamed *Astrolabe* and redesignated as a corvette, was used by Dumont d'Urville on his circumnavigation voyage of 1825-29 and was joined by

(A) Gabarres in service or on order at 1 January 1786

DORADE – 250 tons. Her sister *Dorothée* was wrecked in December 1768.
  Dimensions & tons: 90ft 6in x 22ft x 11ft. 250/400 tons. Men: 21-38.
  Guns: 12 x 4pdrs.
Dorade Brest Dyd. (Constructeurs, Rolland and his son Gaspard-Séraphin Rolland)
  K: 5.1764. Named: 9.7.1764. L: 10.8.1764. C: 8.1764.
  Hulk at Brest 7.1787. Last mentioned 1789.

ÉCLUSE – 400-450 tons. Her sister *Digue* was sold in September 1771. Her original measurement of 450 tons was reduced to 400 tons in 1775 and to 350 tons in 1783.
  Dimensions & tons: 112 or 118ft, 100ft x 25ft x 13ft 3in. 400-450/700 tons. Draught 12ft 6in/13ft 6in. Men: 31-86.
  Guns: 8 to 20 x 6pdrs (pierced for 24 x 6pdrs and 8 x 4pdrs).
Écluse Le Havre (Constructeur, Jean-Joseph Ginoux)
  Named: 26.3.1764. K: 4.1764. L: 8.1764. C: 11.1764.
  Burned 5.1779 by the British at Cancale but repaired. Decomm. 5.1788 at Rochefort and condemned.

OFFICIEUSE Class – 350 tons. Two-masted vessels sometimes described as snows (*senaults*). Originally to have been a class of ten designed by Jean-Joseph Ginoux, 1776-77, but the design was lengthened for the last seven, which became the *Truite* class (see below). Of the three built to the original design, *Officieuse* (built at Havre) was wrecked in 1781 while *Pluvier* and *Saumon* were rearmed in 1779 as bomb vessels with 8 x 8pdrs and 2 x 12-inch mortars. They soon reverted to 6pdr armaments without the mortars and were sometimes listed as brigs.
  Dimensions & tons: 113ft 2in, 100ft 0in x 25ft 0in x 12ft 6in (36.76, 32.48 x 8.12 x 4.06m). 350-400/700 tons. Draught 12/13ft (3.90/4.22m). Men: 50-76.
  Guns: 20 x 6pdrs; later reduced to 16 x 6pdrs + 4 obusiers in *Pluvier*. *Saumon* carried 8 x 8pdrs + 2 x 12in mortars as bomb vessel.
Pluvier Rochefort Dyd.

K: 4.1776. L: 26.9.1776. C: 12.1776.
Converted to a bomb vessel 5-7.1779 (fitted with 2 mortars). Refitted 3-4.1780 at Brest. Taken by Allies on occupation of Toulon 8.1793, but restored 9.1793. Renamed *Commission* 12.1793. Wrecked at Pasajes 19.6.1795.
Saumon Rochefort Dyd.
K: 4.1776. L: 26.9.1776. C: 12.1776.
Converted to a bomb vessel 5-7.1779 (fitted with 2 mortars). Refitted 3-4.1780 at Brest. Struck 1787 at Rochefort.

TRUITE Class – 350 tons. A class of seven designed by Jean-Joseph Ginoux, lengthened from the *Officieuse* design. *Truite* had been transferred to the South Carolina State Navy in 1779 for use as a frigate, *Compas* was struck in 1781 at Brest and *Négresse* was struck in 1785 or 1786. The last pair were built as *Paysanne* and *Villageoise*, but renamed *Bayonnaise* and *Pintade* at launch.
Dimensions & tons: 116ft 0in, 100ft 0in x 25ft 0in x 12ft 6in (37.68, 32.48 x 8.12 x 4.06m). 350/700 tons. Draught 12/13¼ft (3.90/4.30m). Men: 46-182.
Guns: 20 x 6pdrs; later reduced to 16 x 6pdrs.
Barbue Le Havre.
K: 8.1776. L: 24.5.1777. C: 6.1777.
Hulked 1787 at Brest, condemned 20.2.1794 and BU 1796.
Guyane Benjamin Dubois, Saint-Malo.
K: 6.1777. L: 8.9.1777. C: 9.1777.
Sold 10.1788 for commerce.
Bayonnaise Bayonne.
K: 1.1779. L: 10.1779. C: 12.1779.
Training ship at Brest from 2.5.1787. Struck 1790.
Pintade Bayonne.
K: 1.1779. L: 10.1779. C: 11.1779.
Wrecked 1787 in the Loire Estuary.

BOULONNAISE – 100 tons. A small one-off design by Pierre Ozanne. Brig-rigged from 1788.
Dimensions & tons: 65ft 0in, 56ft 0in x 17ft 0in x 9ft 6in (21.11, 18.19 x 5.52 x 3.09m). 100/180 tons. Draught 7/8ft (2.27/2.60m). Men: 16-20.
Guns: 2 x ?pdrs.
Boulonnaise Nicolas Rivet, Boulogne.
K: 6.1777. L: 3.9.1777. C: 9.1777.
Struck 1791 at Brest.

LOIRE Class – 350 tons. A class of two designed by Charles Segondat-Duvernet.
Dimensions & tons: 110ft 0in x 25ft 0in x 13ft 6in (35.73 x 8.12 x 4.39m). 350/600 tons. Men: 77-90.
Guns: 20 x 6pdrs.
Loire Lorient Dyd.
K: 2.1780. L: 13.9.1780. C: 10.1780.
Struck 1793 at Brest.
Bretonne Lorient Dyd.
K: 3.1780. L: 25.11.1780. C: 12.1780.
Handed over 8.1793 to British Navy at Toulon, retaken by French 12.1793. Struck 1796 at Toulon, and sold 1803 for BU.

FORTE – 200 tons. A small one-off design by Charles Segondat-Duvernet.
Dimensions & tons: Dimensions unknown. 200 tons. Men: 42-70.
Guns: 12 x ?
Forte Lorient Dyd.
K: 12.1780. L: 5.1781. C: 6.1781.
Struck 1787 at Brest.

RHÔNE Class – 350 tons. A class of two designed by Joseph-Marie-Blaise Coulomb, named on 16 June 1780 and built by Entreprise Aguillon, commercial contractor at Toulon.
Dimensions & tons: 114ft 0in x 25ft 6in x 14ft 0in (36.98 x 8.28 x 4.55m). 350/750 tons. Draught 12/13ft (3.90/4.22m). Men: 90-100.
Guns: 20 x 6pdrs.
Rhône Toulon Dyd.
K: 6.1780. L: 21.7.1781. C: 30.10.1781.
Wrecked 12.1790 off Toulingue Rocks.
Durance Toulon Dyd.
K: 6.1780. L: 14.8.1781. C: 30.10.1781.
Renamed *Espérance* 7.1791. Seized 10.1793 by the Dutch at Surabaya, Java, recovered by French 2.1794 but ceded to the Dutch 28.10.1794 and sold 12.1794 at Batavia (Jakarta).

ADOUR Class – 350 tons. A class of five designed by Jean-Joseph Ginoux, of which *Adour* herself was wrecked on February 1784.
Dimensions & tons: 112ft 0in, 96ft 6in x 25ft 0in x 14ft 0in (36.38, 31.35 x 8.12 x 4.55m). 350/700 tons. Draught 12/13ft (3.90/4.22m). Men: 78-100.
Guns: 16 x 6pdrs.
Chèvre Rochefort Dyd.
K: 1780. L: 1782. C: 12.1782.
Struck 1.1788 at Rochefort.
Dordogne Bayonne.
K: 1.1781. L: 1781. C: 1781.
Sold at Rochefort 10.1788.
Gave Bayonne.
K: 8.1781. L: 12.1781. C: 1.1782.
Struck 1792 at Rochefort.
Cigogne Bayonne.
K: 9.1781. L: 2.1782. C: 4.1782.
Struck 1791 at Rochefort.

UTILE Class – 350 tons. Designed by Jean-Joseph De Boissieu, plans dated 13.2.1783.
Dimensions & tons: 112ft, 102ft x 27ft x 13ft 6in (36.38, 33.13 x 8.77 x 4.38m). 350/600 tons. Draught 10ft 6in/12ft (3.41/3.90m). Men: 100.
Guns: 18 x 6pdrs (*Lionne* also had 4 x 4pdrs in 1800).
Utile Bayonne
K: 1783. L: 1.1784. C: 4.1784.
Renamed *Zibeline* 5.1795 but change not implemented. Captured in the Hyères Islands 9.6.1796 by HMS *Southampton*, but not added to the RN; sold 6.1798.
Lionne Bayonne (Constructeur: Raymond-Antoine Haran)
K: 1783. L: 4.5.1784. C: 16.8.1784.
Decomm. 22.10.1802 and condemned at Rochefort, headquarters hulk. Replaced 7.9.1807 by the corvette *Serpente*, BU 1808.

A small (150-ton) brig-rigged gabarre or galiot named *Porteuse* was built by Jean-Laurent Beauvoisin at his yard at Le Havre between July 1785 and the autumn of 1785 for use in the harbour works at Cherbourg. She had a crew of 20 to 45 men and carried no guns. She was struck and placed on sale at Brest in March 1797.

Ex BRITISH MERCANTILE PRIZE (1780)

Aventure (British vessel captured 1780 by the d'Estaing squadron and purchased by the King in 1782, 200/350 tons, carried 6 x 3pdrs). Struck 1786 at Brest.

PURCHASED AND REQUISITIONED GABARRES (1781-1782)

Deux Hélènes (merchant ship purchased 3.1781 at Lorient, 255/350 tons, 14 men, pierced for 20 ports and carried 8 guns). Captured 4.1783 by a British squadron off Trincomalee but returned as peace had been signed, struck 1785 or 1786 at Brest.

Sirène (merchant ship purchased 6.1.1782 or 3.1782 at Toulon, 473 tons, carried 12 x 6pdrs, 2 x 2pdrs). Named *Comte de Stokelberg* between July and October 1785. Grounded 3.1787 at Cherbourg, refloated and loaned 7.1787 for a few months to M. Anthoine at Marseille to obtain masts at Kherson in the Crimea.

Amitié (British merchant ship *Friendship*? taken by corsairs, hired by the navy at Saint-Malo 12.4.1779 and then purchased by the King at Granville 4.1782)
Dimensions & tons: 52ft 6in x 15ft 10in x 10ft. 85/140 tons. Men: 10-20. No guns.
Designated *Amitié No.2* during 1781 and *Amitié No.3* during 1782. Struck at Brest 1791, having been destroyed by the British.

Marquis de Castries (gabarre built at Lorient-Bois du Blanc 1-11.1781 for an owner in La Rochelle, requisitioned 9.1781 then purchased 4.1782, 340-350 tons, 71-80 men). Condemned 3.1789 at Pondicherry, being rotten and sunken, last mentioned 1791.

Amphitrite (merchant ship built at Le Havre, at sea in 2.1777 and purchased by the navy 1782, 286/400 tons, 20 gunports). Conducted a hydrographic mission in 1785 in the Comoro Islands and the Persian Gulf. Struck 1785 or 1786, decomm. 7.1787 at Île de France.

Petit Cousin (gabarre of unknown origin purchased 1782, 133 tons). Struck 1785 or 1786 at Lorient, probably sold into merchant service.

Dauphin Royal or *Royal Dauphin* (merchant ship purchased at Marseille 9.1782, 325 or 350 tons, carried 12 x 6pdrs). Struck 1787 at Rochefort and sold into merchant service.

(B) Gabarres acquired from 1 January 1786

ESPÉRANCE – 400 tons. Designed by Pierre-Joseph Pénétreau, plans signed 1 December 1786.
Dimensions & tons: 115ft, 109ft x 26ft x 13ft 3in. 400/682 tons. Men: 73.
Guns: 6 x 6pdrs, 4 x 4pdrs (20 ports).
Espérance Lorient Dyd
K: 12.1786. L: 15.6.1787. C: 3.1788.
Renamed *Archimède* 7.1791. Was at Nantes 5.1795, was unaccounted for in 1796.

MARSOUIN Class – 400 tons. Designed by Raymond-Antoine Haran, 1787.
Dimensions & tons: 112ft 0in, 104ft 6in x 28ft 0in x 14ft 0in (36.38, 33.95 x 9.10 x 4.55m). 400/700 tons. Draught 11ft 4in/12ft (3.68/3.90m). Men: 73-102.
Guns: UD 20 x 6pdrs (22 x 8pdrs in *Marsouin*).
Marsouin Bayonne.
K: 1786 or 1787. L: 1787. C: 1788.
Captured 11.3.1795 by HMS *Beaulieu* at Guadeloupe, becoming HMS *Marsouin* but never commissioned; deleted 1799.
Truite Bayonne.
K: 3.1787. L: 10.1787. C: 11.1787.
In May 1791 was converted to a research ship, rated *corvette de recherche et d'exploration* and in July 1791 was renamed *Recherche*; she was sold to Holland in November 1794.
Moselle Bayonne.
K: 4.1787. L: 24.1.1788. C: 7.1788.
Handed over to Anglo-Spanish forces 29.8.1793 at Toulon; retaken 1.1794 off Toulon by the French. Captured again 23.5.1794 off the Hyères by HMS *Aimable*, becoming Sixth Rate HMS *Moselle*; sold 9.1802.

TRUITE Class – 300 tons. Designed by Pierre-Alexandre Forfait, 1789. Two gabarres of 400 tons were projected at the Montmarin yard near Saint-Malo in early 1789, but the project was reduced to one 300-ton ship.
Dimensions & tons: dimensions unknown. 300 tons.
Guns: 10 x 6pdrs (+ 2 swivels).
Truite Benjamin Dubois, Saint-Malo (Montmarin).
K: 1789. L: 1791 or 1792. C: 1792.
Handed over to Anglo-Spanish forces at Toulon 29.8.1793; retaken 12.1793 by the French at the evacuation of Toulon. Deleted late 1794 or early 1795

RHINOCÉROS – 400 tons. Designed by Pierre-Alexandre Forfait. She was sometimes called a flûte or a corvette.
Dimensions & tons: 120ft 0in, 111ft 0in x 27ft 0in x 13ft 6in (38.98, 36.05 x 8.77 x 4.38m). 400/790 tons. Draught 11ft 6in (3.73m) mean. Men: 86.
Guns: 22 x 8pdrs.
Rhinocéros Jean-Louis Pestel, Honfleur
K: 9.1793. L: 29.6.1794. C: 7.1794.
Condemned 8.7.1807 at Toulon and ordered converted to prison hulk there, used as such from 10.10.1807 to 1816.

FARDEAU – 200-250 tons.
Dimensions & tons: dimensions unknown. 200 to 250 tons burthen.
Men: 29
Guns: 2 x 8pdrs; (1794) 4 x 6pdrs.
Fardeau Lorient Dyd
Ord: 2.1793. K: 1793. L: 1794. C: 10.1795.
Struck c1806, hulk at Brest. Last mentioned 8.1815.

ROCHEFORT (cutter-rigged gabarre).
Launched at Rochefort 1797; no other information. Probably became the privateer *Rochefort* c1798.

ADOUR Class – 350 tons. Designed by Jean-Charles Garrigues. The *Charente* was ordered 19 February 1801 (and *Adour* probably at same time).
Dimensions & tons: 113ft 7½in, 107ft 5in x 27ft 7in x 14ft 6in (36.91m, 34.90m x 8.96m x 4.40m). 350/600 tons. Draught 3.65/3.75m. Men: 64-100.
Guns: Designed for 18 x 6pdrs (18 plus 2 chase ports). *Adour* actually carried 18 x 4pdrs while *Charente* carried 16 x 6pdrs.
Adour Bayonne (Constructeur: Jean Baudry)
K: 12.1801. L: 9.10.1802. C: 7.12.1802.
Captured 17.7.1803 by HMS *Endymion* in the Atlantic while returning to Rochefort from Martinique.
Charente Bayonne (Constructeur: Jean Baudry)
K: 1.1802. L: 6.2.1803. C: 3.1803.
Attacked by HMS *Aigle* 12.7.1804 while en route from Bordeaux to Pasajes, was run aground off Cordouan to avoid capture and burned 13.7.1804 by the British.

Ex BRITISH MERCANTILE PRIZE (1793)
Argo (ex British merchant brig *Argo* captured in 1793 and commissioned as a gabarre the same year at Dunkirk, 226 tons, 44 men, carried 12 x 4pdrs). Was considered 'old' in 1795. Refitted 1.1802 at Dunkirk, lost 7.1803 in Louisiana.

PURCHASED AND REQUISITIONED GABARRES (1786-1801)
Aurore or *Petite Aurore* (merchant ship from Saint-Malo purchased 11.1786 by the navy at Pondicherry)
  Dimensions & tons: 92ft, 80ft x 26ft. 350/500 tons
  Guns: 14 x 4pdrs.
  Captured by the British and Spanish 8.1793 at Toulon and taken into the Spanish Navy.
Céleste Union (merchant ship with three masts purchased 2.1788 by the navy at Pondicherry, 250 tons). Last mentioned 5.1788 at Pondicherry.
Juste (gabarre built at Lorient for the East India Company, possibly their *Boullongne* of 1785, requisitioned and in service by 6.1794, 250 tons, 40 men, carried 2 x 4pdrs). Struck late 1794 or early 1795.
Égyptien (gabarre or flûte of unknown origin commissioned at Rochefort 9.1799, 137 men, carried 18 x 12pdrs, 2 x 36pdr obusiers according to the British). Captured 11.1799 off Cape Tiburon, Santo Domingo, by HMS *Solebay*.
Catherine (gabarre of unknown origin acquired 1801?). Was at Toulon out of commission in 10.1802 and in 9.1803, struck before 1807.

(C) Gabarres acquired from 25 March 1802

POURVOYEUSE Class – 200 tons (brig-rigged). Built under a contract with the brothers Mathurin, Louis, and Antoine Crucy for four gabarres, probably on plans by Francois Etesse. They could carry 188 cubic metres of shipbuilding timber. *Prévoyante* was originally rated at 260 tons while *Désirée* was later rated at 170 tons.
  Dimensions & tons: 23.06m x 7.23m x 4.17m. 200/360 tons. Draught 3.57/3.73m. Men: 9-18.
  Guns: 6 x 4pdrs, later 2 x 6pdrs.
Pourvoyeuse Louis, Antoine, & Mathurin Crucy, Nantes.
  Ord: 6.12.1802 (contract). K: 12.1802. Named: 3.1.1803. L: 14.7.1803. C: 9.1803.
  Captured 24.6.1815 near the Glénans Islands off southwest Brittany. She arrived at Portsmouth on 7.7.1815 (after Waterloo and Napoleon's second abdication), most likely making her the last naval vessel captured in the Napoleonic Wars. She was recorded by the French as captured by HM brig *Sylphe*, but the brig of that name had been wrecked on Long Island in 1.1815; HM brig *Cephalus* (18) is another candidate.
Bienvenue Louis, Antoine, & Mathurin Crucy, Nantes.
  Ord: 6.12.1802 (contract). K: 12.1802. Named: 3.1.1803. L: 20.7.1803. C: 9.1803.
  No record after leaving Nantes for Lorient 12.8.1809. Last mentioned in 1812, struck before 1.1813.
Prévoyante Louis, Antoine, & Mathurin Crucy, Nantes.
  Ord: 6.12.1802 (contract). K: 12.1802. Named: 3.1.1803. L: 20.7.1803. C: 5.1804.
  Wrecked 30.1.1817 on the Cardinals rocks at the mouth of the Loire, all hands lost.
Désirée Louis, Antoine, & Mathurin Crucy, Nantes.
  Ord: 6.12.1802 (contract). K: 12.1802. Named: 3.1.1803. L: 18.8.1803. C: 9.1803.
  Listed as 170 tons in 1814. Wrecked 27.12.1838 on the Pointe des Baleines, Île de Ré, all hands lost.

GARONNE Class – 350 tons. Designed by Jacques-Noël Sané, they could carry 110 cubic metres of shipbuilding timber.
  Dimensions & tons: dimensions unknown. 350/600 tons. Draught 3.90m. Men: 120.
  Guns: 18 x 6pdrs (rated) or 10 x 4pdrs.
Garonne Bayonne (Constructeur: Jean Baudry)
  Ord: 23.9.1802. K: 11.1802. L: 2.8.1803. Comm: 22.8.1803. C: 2.1804.
  With *Malicieuse* (a corvette of 1795 rerigged as a brig and in use as a gabarre) and *Dordogne*, run ashore 6.4.1806 at La Teste-de-Buch on the coast south of the mouth of the Gironde to avoid capture by HMS *Pallas* (32), then destroyed by the sea.
Dordogne Bayonne (Constructeur: Jean Baudry)
  Ord: 23.9.1802. K: 12.1802. L: 16.10.1803. Comm: 23.12.1803. C: 5.1804.
  Run ashore 6.4.1806 with *Garonne* and *Malicieuse* at La Teste-de-Buch to avoid capture by HMS *Pallas* (32), then destroyed by the sea.
Moselle Bayonne (Constructeur: Jean Baudry)
  K: 25.7.1804. L: 24.8.1805. Comm: 23.9.1805. C: 10.1805.
  Wrecked 12.12.1808 in a storm at Mimizan near La Teste on the coast south of the mouth of the Gironde.

LAMPROIE Class – 467 tons. Designed by Jean-Louis Féraud, plans reviewed by Sané. These two were built under a contract approved on 24 June 1803. They could carry 350 troops. The *Lamproie, Expéditive,* and *Prudente* classes were probably very similar despite small differences in specifications.
  Dimensions & tons: 36.56m, 34.10m x 9.16m x 4.55m. 467/760 tons. Draught 4.02/4.38m. Men: 100-110.
  Guns: 14 x 8pdrs (20 ports); (*Durance*, 1821) 2 x 8pdrs, 12 x 24pdr carronades.
Lamproie (*Lamproye*) Vian, Velin, Riboulet, & Ménard, La Ciotat.
  Ord: 4.1.1803. K: 12.1803. L: 9.1804. Comm: 17.3.1805. C: 3.1805.
  Left Toulon in a convoy to resupply the Army of Catalonia at Barcelona, captured by boats from Collingwood's fleet 1.10.1809 at Rosas, Catalonia, with 9 merchant vessels from the convoy and burned.
Durance Vian, Velin, Riboulet, & Ménard, La Ciotat.
  Ord: 4.1.1803. K: 11.1803. L: 11.1804 or 9.1805. C: 3.1806.
  Decomm. at Toulon 20.1.1838, struck there 21.3.1838.

PANTHÈRE – 350 tons (gabarre without tween-decks). Designed by Léon-Michel Guignace.
  Dimensions & tons: 36.38m x 8.17m x 4.22m. 350/600 tons. Draught 3.73/4.06m. Men: 62-87.
  Guns: 16 x 6pdrs (18 ports).
Panthère Bayonne (Constructeur: Jean Baudry)
  Ord: 22.10.1804. K: 19.11.1804. L: 30.5.1806. C: 3.1807.
  Captured 24.6.1815 off Plymouth by the British, returned early 8.1815. Used around 1825 to store the oakum of the Toulon arsenal. Struck 5.6.1833 at Toulon as unserviceable.

CIGOGNE Class – 250 tons. Designed by Paul Filhon. Construction of *Dorade* was suspended in September 1806 at 11/24ths due to a lack of iron and probably resumed about a year later.
  Dimensions & tons: 29.56m, 28.26m x 7.80m x 3.90m. 250/406 tons. Draught 3.22/3.28m. Men: 43-82.

This engraving by Jean-Jérôme Baugean, originally published in 1819, is captioned as a 'gabarre' but the description of the type as frigate-like and the twenty-six ports on the gundeck suggest that the engraver had in mind one of the big flûtes of the Napoleonic era.

Guns: 4 x 6pdrs (16 plus 2 chase ports); (*Dorade*, 1810) 8 x 6pdrs.
Cigogne Bayonne (Constructeur: Jean Baudry)
Ord: 22.10.1804. K: 9.1805. L: 14.8.1806. C: 4.1807. Comm: 21.5.1807.
Wrecked 20.11.1807 between the Pointe de Graves and the Vieux Soulac near the mouth of the Gironde.
Dorade Bayonne (Constructeur: Jean Baudry)
Ord: 22.10.1804. K: 9.1805. L: 20.7.1807. C: 8.1808.
Captured 6.1812 by 6 boats from HMS *Medusa* (32) while at anchor near Arcachon but then grounded, burned by the British and blew up.

JEANNE Class – 200 tons (brig-rigged). These two ships were ordered at the same time as the *Babet* class below but appear to have been begun earlier. They could carry 171 cubic metres of shipbuilding timber.
  Dimensions & tons: 22.41m x 7.15m x 3.44m. 169(?)/250-300 tons (rated at 200 tons burthen). Draught 3.08/3.40m. Men: 9.
  Guns: 2 espingoles.
Jeanne Louis, Antoine, & Mathurin Crucy, Indret.
  Ord: 19.7.1806 and named. K: 5 or 7.1806. L: 5.8.1806. C: 12.1806.
  Lost 11.1823, circumstances unknown.
Louise Louis, Antoine, & Mathurin Crucy, Indret.
  Ord: 19.7.1806 and named. K: 5 or 7.1806. L: 5.8.1806. C: 12.1806.
  Wrecked 24.8.1816 on the La Chèvre rock in the Bay of Dinan while en route from Nantes to Brest.

BABET Class – 170-200 tons (probably cutter-rigged). These four ships were probably ordered from Louis, Antoine & Mathurin Crucy but were built by Mathurin and Antoine after the Crucy brothers split their firm in 1806. They were ordered at the same time as the *Jeanne* class, above. *Babet* and *Chloé* were listed at 170 tons burthen in 1814 and *Gertrude* was listed at 200 tons.
  Dimensions & tons: 21.11m x 6.72m x 3.14m. 135(?)/220 tons (rated at 170-200 tons burthen). Draught 2.76/2.92m. Men: 1 master and 7 men.
  Guns: none (8 ports?).
Babet Mathurin & Antoine Crucy, Indret.
  Ord: 19.7.1806. K: 8.1806. L: 10.2.1807. C: 9.1807.
  Sold 20.12.1814 at Nantes.
Chloé (*Cloé*) Mathurin & Antoine Crucy, Indret.
  Ord: 19.7.1806 and named. K: 22.8.1806. L: 18.3.1807. C: 5.1807.
  Sold 20.12.1814 at Nantes.
Gertrude Mathurin & Antoine Crucy, Indret.
  Ord: 19.7.1806 and named. K: 29.11.1806. L: 30.5.1807. C: 6.1807.
  Sold 20.12.1814 at Nantes.
Marie Mathurin & Antoine Crucy, Indret.
  Ord: 19.7.1806 and named. K: 7.12.1806. L: 9.1807. C: 11.1807.
  Refitted, armed with 8 x 3pdrs, and rated combatant cutter (*côtre de guerre*) 1813. Foundered 8.7.1816 under sail at the Pointe de Penmarc'h near Brest en route from Nantes.

SARCELLE Class – 200 tons (brig-rigged). The first two were built by the brothers Mathurin and Antoine Crucy, and may have been designed by Antoine Geoffroy. The designer of the third is unknown but this 200-

ton gabarre built by the third Crucy brother and his son was likely identical to the first two. These vessels could carry 205 cubic metres of shipbuilding timber.

    Dimensions & tons: dimensions unknown. 200/360 tons.

    Guns: none?

Sarcelle Mathurin & Antoine Crucy, Indret.

    Ord: 5.11.1807. K: 11.1807. L: 6.7.1808. C: 1.1809.

    Condemned 31.8.1829 at Lorient and ordered BU.

Nathalie Mathurin & Antoine Crucy, Indret.

    Ord: 5.11.1807. K: 15.12.1807. L: 7.7.1808. C: 1.1809.

    Captured 12.1814 or in 1815 by the British, circumstances unknown.

Porteuse Louis & Michel-Louis Crucy, Paimboeuf.

    K: 5.1809. L: 15.5.1810. C: 6.1810.

    Foundered 6.11.1810 in a storm near the Île de Groix.

GIRONDE Class – 250 tons. Designed by Jacques-Noël Sané (probably reviewing a plan by Filhon).

    Dimensions & tons: 30.00m x 7.80m x 3.90m. 250/470 tons. Draught 3.60/3.88m. Men: 62-79.

    Guns: 6 x 6pdrs (plus 2 x 2pdrs in *Gironde*).

Gironde Bayonne (Constructeur: Jean Baudry)

    Ord: 8.12.1806. K: 1.9.1807. Named: 1.10.1807. L: 23.6.1808. C: 1.1809.

    Station ship at Île d'Aix 1829-31, decomm. 28.2.1831 and became headquarters hulk at Rochefort. Struck 1833, hulk, condemned 9.1837.

Charente Bayonne (Constructeur: Jean Baudry)

    K: 9.1807. L: 12.7.1809. C: 9.1811.

    Was station ship in the Brest roadstead from 1.4.1828 to 1.9.1836 when replaced by *Robuste* (although not renamed *Robuste* as indicated by Vichot). Struck 6.2.1839 at Brest.

GIROUETTE Class – 170 tons (brig-rigged). Designed by François Gréhan.

    Dimensions & tons: 23.71m, 22.10m x 6.82m x 3.41m. 170/270 tons. Draught 2.98/3.14m. Men: 29.

    Guns: 4 x 4pdrs.

Girouette Le Havre (Constructeur: François Gréhan)

    Ord: 26.12.1807. K: 1.4.1808. L: 5.8.1808. Comm: 19.9.1808. C: 9.1808.

    Condemned 1826 at Lorient, then became a storage hulk at Cadiz. Last mentioned 9.1828.

Héron Le Havre (Constructeur: François Gréhan)

    Ord: 26.12.1807. K: 1.4.1808. L: 6.8.1808. Comm: 19.9.1808. C: 10.1808.

    Captured 18.8.1811 off the coast of Calvados by HMS *Hawk* (16) and British launches.

PETIT GABARRE ÉCURIE NO. 1 Class – 262 tons (brig-rigged). The first three were designed by Jean-Pierre Vincent and built by contract at La Seyne (though they are shown in some lists as built at nearby Toulon). The fourth was probably also designed by Vincent, built at La Seyne although listed as Toulon, and identical to the first three although listed as a 200-ton gabarre. At La Seyne the two biggest shipyards at this time were operated by the Lombard and Abran families. These gabarres were specially designed to transport horses, of which they could carry 30 in the hold. *Lézard* was reclassified as a 262-ton transport in 1846. All were originally designated only by number; the three survivors received names in July 1814.

    Dimensions & tons: 26.63m, 23.50m x 8.12m x 3.90m. 262/430 tons. Draught 3.15/3.57m. Men: 56-78.

    Guns: (*No.2*) 2 x 6pdrs, 12 x 16pdr British carronades (14 ports?); (*No.3*) 6 x 6pdrs; (*Portefaix* 1822) 2 x 18pdrs, 10 x 18pdr carronades.

Petit Gabarre Écurie No.1 (*Lézard*) La Seyne

    K: 10.1808. L: 9.1809. C: 1810.

    Renamed *Lézard* 7.1814. Designated 18.10.1834 to replace the brig (ex lugger) *Oiseleur* as station ship at Lorient. Decomm. as such 28.1.1852, condemned 18.12.1852, mooring hulk at Lorient, BU 1866-67.

Petit Gabarre Écurie No.2 (*Marsouin*) La Seyne.

    K: 10.1808. L: 9.1809. C: 1810.

    Renamed *Marsouin* 7.1814. Rebuilt 1822 at Le Havre as a combatant brig (*brick de guerre*) with 2 x 6pdrs and 10 x 18pdr carronades and recomm. 1.1.1823. Grounded 30.12.1833 in bad weather on the Île du Levant (Hyères), lost 1.1.1834.

Petit Gabarre Écurie No.3 (*Portefaix*) La Seyne.

    K: 10.1808. L: 9.1809. C: 1810.

    Renamed *Portefaix* 7.1814 and *Loiret* 14.11.1820. Decomm. 8.11.1836 at Toulon. Struck there 14.11.1844 and became service craft.

Petit Gabarre Écurie No.4 Toulon Dyd. (probably La Seyne).

    K: 12.1809. L: 9.1810. C: 1811.

    Grounded 15.1.1814 near San Remo after being chased by an enemy frigate and burned by her crew to prevent capture.

EXPÉDITIVE – 467 tons. Designed by Jean-Louis Féraud, plans reviewed by J.-N. Sané. The *Lamproie, Expéditive,* and *Prudente* classes were probably very similar despite small differences in specifications.

    Dimensions & tons: 36.05m x 9.29m x 4.60m. 467/700 tons. Draught 3.70/4.04m. Men: 88-124.

    Guns: 16 x 18pdrs, 2 x 6pdrs.

Expéditive Chicallat & Jouvin, Marseille.

    Ord: 16.3.1808 (contract). Named 23.5.1808. K: 6.1808. L: 28.12.1809. Comm: 22.2.1810.

    Condemned 5.7.1824 at Rochefort, BU there 7-8.1824.

PRUDENTE Class – 467 tons. Designed by Jacques-Noël Sané. The contracts for these ships were awarded at the same time as contracts for some 800-ton flûtes. The *Lamproie, Expéditive,* and *Prudente* classes were probably very similar despite small differences in specifications.

    Dimensions & tons: 36.38m x 9.10m x 4.55m. 467/750 tons. Draught 3.98/4.46m. Men: 42-100.

    Guns: 16 x 24pdr carronades; (both 1812-14) 16 x 8pdrs, 2 x 6pdrs; (*La Ciotat* 1817) 2 x 6pdrs, 10 x 24pdr carronades.

Prudente Vian, Velin, Riboulet, & Ménard, La Ciotat.

    Ord: 16.3.1808 (contract). Named 23.5.1808. K: 8.1809. L: 15.9.1810. C: 3.1811.

    Converted to mooring hulk at Rochefort 7-11.1826, BU there 3-4.1844.

La Ciotat La Ciotat.

    Ord: 1.7.1809 (contract). Named: 7.8.1809. K: 1.1810. L: 4.4.1811. C: 10.1811.

    Renamed *Uranie* and reclassified corvette 30.12.1816, refitted 12.1816-3.1817 for use in a circumnavigation expedition led by Louis de Freycinet. Recomm. 3.3.1817, departed Toulon 17.9.1817, struck a rock in the Falkland Islands 14.2.1820, and run aground there the next day. Crew returned to Le Havre 13.11.1820 in the purchased *Physicienne* (ex-American merchantman *Mercury*). Wreck located 2001.

GRANDE GABARRE ÉCURIE NO. 1 Class – 380 tons. Designed by

THE LARGER TRANSPORTS

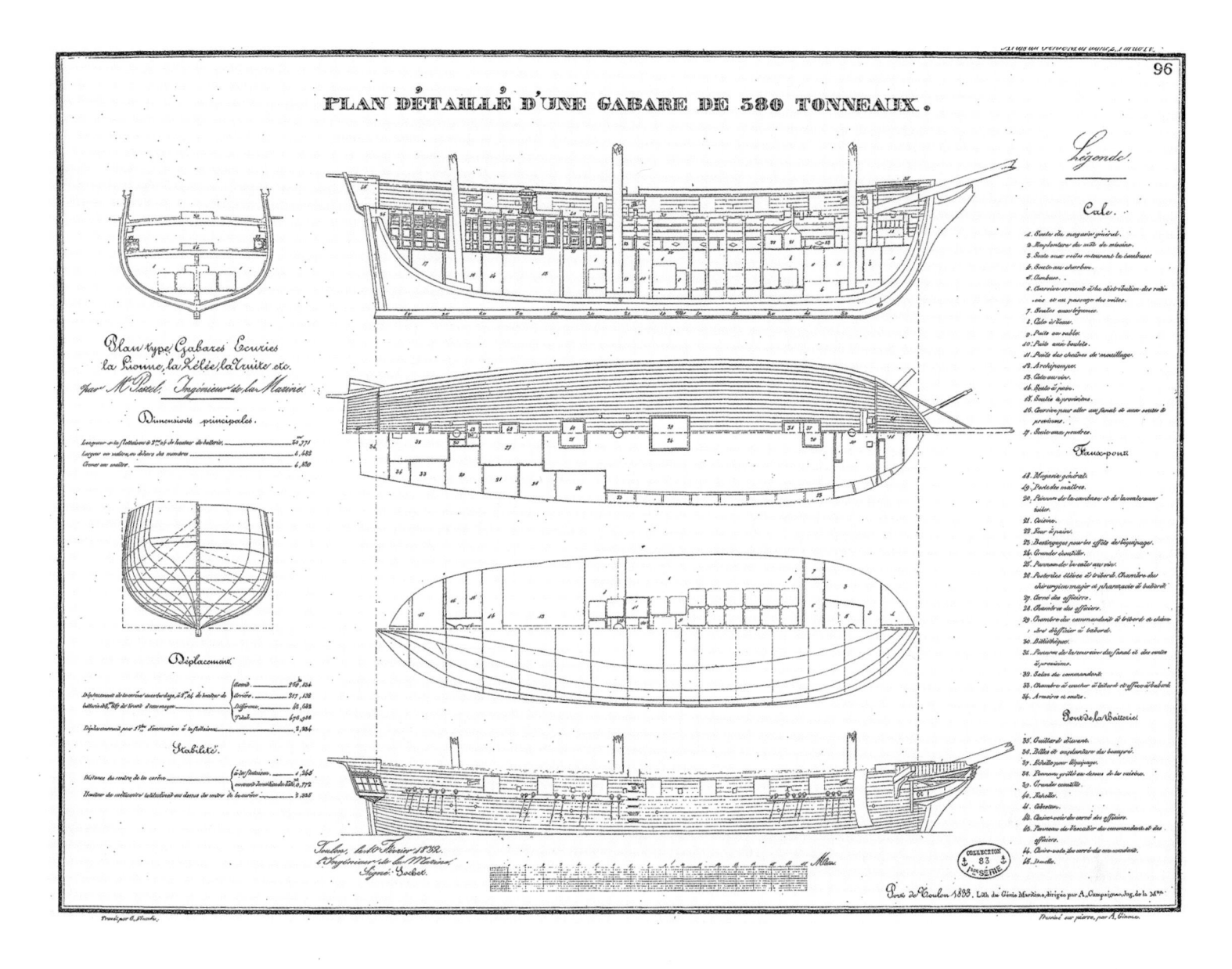

Official general arrangement plans, dated Toulon 10 February 1832, for the 380-ton *gabarre-écurie* type, like the *Lionne*, *Zélée*, *Truite*, etc, designed by Pestel. (Atlas du Génie Maritime, French collection, plate 96)

François Pestel. These 12 ships were probably built under four contracts, one dated 3 December 1810 at Toulon for *Nos.1-2* and *Nos.7-8*; one dated 1 December 1810 at La Seyne for *Nos.3-6*, one dated 1 December 1810 at La Ciotat for *Nos.9-10*, and one dated 3 December 1810 at Marseille for *Nos.11-12*. (The often-repeated attribution of *No.2* [later *Coquille* and *Astrolabe*] to La Seyne and the contract date of 3 December 1810 for *No.5* are believed to be in error.) The 'contract' at Toulon was probably an order to the dockyard; the four ships it covered were constructed there by their designer, Pestel. At La Seyne the two biggest shipyards at this time were operated by the Lombard and Abran families, and Joseph Lombard reportedly built a new yard there in 1810. At La Ciotat the firm of Vian, Velin, Riboulet, & Ménard was building brigs, flûtes and gabarres, and at Marseille the firm of Chicallat & Jouvin was building flûtes. These gabarres had three masts and were specially designed to transport horses, of which they could carry 46. All were originally designated only by number; those that had not already been named as training ships in 1812-13 received names in July 1814. Pestel's design was reused beginning in 1833 for eight ships of the *Prévoyante* class (below). *Émulation, Lamproie, Astrolabe,* and *Zélée* were designated 14-gun open-battery corvettes in 1846 along with seven units of the *Prévoyante* class.

Dimensions & tons: 31.57m, 30.86m wl, 27.60m x 8.45m, 8.52m ext x 4.71m. 380/520 tons. Draught 3.70/4.18m. Men: 51-98.

Guns (designed): 10 x 18pdr carronades, 2 x 12pdrs (18 ports). Armaments carried in 7.1814 included (*Chevrette*) 1 x 12pdr, 10 x 9pdrs, 2 x 4pdrs; (*Lionne*) 6 x 12pdr carronades, 2 x 4pdrs; and (*Infatigable* and perhaps *Églantine*) 6 x 6pdrs. In 1826 *Émulation* carried 12 x 4pdrs.

Grande Gabarre Écurie No.1 (*Chevrette*) Toulon Dyd.
Ord: 3.12.1810. K: 12.1810. L: 7.1811. C: 1812.
Renamed *Chevrette* 9.7.1814. Wrecked 20.3.1830 at the entrance to Tintingue, Madagascar.

Grande Gabarre Écurie No.2 (*Coquille*) Toulon Dyd.
Ord: 3.12.1810. K: 12.1810. L: 8.1811. C: 1.1812.
Renamed *Coquille* 9.7.1814. Made a circumnavigation of the globe between 8.1822 and 3.1825 under Duperrey with Dumont d'Urville as second in command (carried 14 x 18pdr carronades).

An anonymous lithographic depiction of the *Astrolabe* tackling Antarctic ice during the 1837 expedition. This ship and her sister *Zélée*, seen in the background, were horse transports whose small but capacious hulls made them ideal conversions for exploration voyages, most famously those of Dumont d'Urville. (© National Maritime Museum PY0878)

Renamed *Astrolabe* 15.12.1825 and reclassified corvette for a second circumnavigation, this time under Dumont d'Urville, between 4.1826 and 4.1829 (carried 12 x 12pdr carronades). A voyage to Antarctica under Dumont d'Urville with sister *Zélée* followed between 8.9.1837 and 8.11.1840. Condemned 14.8.1851, hauled out at Toulon 22.5.1852 and BU.

Grande Gabarre Écurie No.3 (***Églantine***) La Seyne.
  Ord: 1.12.1810 (contract). K: 2.1811. L: 2.1812. C: 1812.
  Renamed *Églantine* 9.7.1814. Condemned 2.1828 at Rochefort and BU 4-6.1828.

Grande Gabarre Écurie No.4 (***Marguerite***) La Seyne.
  Ord: 1.12.1810 (contract). K: 2.1811. L: 3.1812. C: 1812.
  Renamed *Marguerite* 9.7.1814. Wrecked 21.10.1817 in the bay of Fort Royal de la Martinique in a hurricane. Wreck sold 29.12.1817 or 12.1818.

Grande Gabarre Écurie No.5 (***Active***) La Seyne.
  Ord: 1.12.1810 (contract). K: 3.1811. L: 3.1812. C: 1812.
  Renamed *Active* 20.5.1813 and served as annex to the Naval Academy at Toulon in the ship of the line *Duquesne* from 5.1813 to 1.8.1815 (carried 10 x 6pdrs and 6 x 12pdr carronades). Wrecked 5.1.1827 on the rocks of Île d'Yeu at the mouth of the Loire.

Grande Gabarre Écurie No.6 (***Alouette***) La Seyne.
  Ord: 1.12.1810 (contract). K: 3.1811. L: 4.1812. C: 1812.
  Renamed *Alouette* (*Allouette*) 9.7.1814. Wrecked 6.6.1817 at the Cape of Good Hope on a voyage from Île d'Aix to Île Bourbon.

Grande Gabarre Écurie No.7 (***Zélée***) Toulon Dyd.
  Ord: 3.12.1810. K: 7.1811. L: 4.1812. C: 1812.
  Renamed *Zélée* 3.12.1812 and served as school for conscript seamen at Toulon from 12.1812 to 1.1814 (carried 20 x 12pdr carronades and 2 x 6pdrs.). Refitted at Brest 1834-35 and reclassified corvette 1835 for a voyage of exploration to Antarctica under Dumont d'Urville with sister *Astrolabe* between 9.1837 and 11.1840. Converted 1853-54 to a screw transport (q.v.).

Grande Gabarre Écurie No.8 (***Lamproie***) Toulon Dyd.
  Ord: 3.12.1810. K: 8.1811. L: 5.1812. C: 1812.
  Renamed *Lamproie* 9.7.1814. Reclassified corvette 1.1846. Struck 16.10.1849 at Toulon, BU 1850.

Grande Gabarre Écurie No.9 (***Truite***) La Ciotat.
  Ord: 1.12.1810 (contract). K: 3.1811. L: 20.8.1811. C: 1812.
  Renamed *Truite* 9.7.1814. Wrecked 13.12.1832 near Cape Sounion in the Greek islands.

Grande Gabarre Écurie No.10 (***Lionne***) La Ciotat.
  Ord: 1.12.1810 (contract). K: 1.1811. L: 20.7.1811. C: 1812.
  Renamed *Lionne* 9.7.1814. To the Île Bourbon station 1841, hulk at Nossi-Bé 15.3.1844 to 1849, last mentioned 1852.

Grande Gabarre Écurie No.11 (*Infatigable*) Marseille.
  Ord: 3.12.1810 (contract). K: 2.1811. L: 23.9.1811. C: 1812.
  Renamed *Infatigable* 3.12.1812 and served as school for registered seamen (*inscrits maritimes*) at Toulon from 12.1812 to 1.1814. Escorted the French Navy's second steamer, *Africain*, into Saint Louis, Senegal, on 12.5.1820. Decomm. 8.3.1832 at Toulon, struck there 1837.

Grande Gabarre Écurie No.12 (*Émulation*) Marseille.
  Ord: 3.12.1810 (contract). K: 3.1811. L: 12.1811. C: 5.1812.
  Renamed *Émulation* 9.6.1812 and served as annex to the Naval Academy at Toulon in the ship of the line *Duquesne* from 6.1812 to 1.8.1815. Station ship in Algeria 1838-45. Decomm. 25.9.1845 at Toulon, struck 8.12.1845.

NANTAISE – 200 tons. This single ship was ordered in 1812, probably soon after Antoine Crucy retired and rented the family's Basse-Indre yard to his nephew. Five more vessels of this type were built after 1815 as the *Bretonne* class (below).
  Dimensions & tons: dimensions unknown. 200 tons burthen. Men: 21-48.
  Guns: 4 x 4pdrs.

Nantaise Michel-Louis Crucy, Basse-Indre.
  Ord: 25.3.1812 (contract). K: 5.1812. L: 25.9.1813. C: 6.1814.
  Left Rio de Janeiro 22 May 1828 and disappeared. Presumed lost rounding Cape Horn en route Valparaiso.

(D) Gabarres acquired from 26 June 1815

BRETONNE Class – 200 tons. Designed by Charles-Robert Alexandre. *Nantaise* (1813-31) was a war-built sister ordered in 1812. *Pintade* and *Mayenne* were listed as brig-rigged.
  Dimensions & tons: 22.74m, 19.65m x 7.47m x 3.73m. 200/332 tons. Draught 3.16/3.38m. Men: 40-50.
  Guns: 2 x 4pdrs except 8 x 24pdr carronades in *Mayenne*.

Bretonne Lorient Dyd. (Constructeur: Alexandre)
  Ord: 20.8.1816. K: 28.8.1816. Named: 28.4.1817. L: 16.5.1817. Comm: 15.7.1817. C: 7.1817.
  Left Cayenne 2.9.1830 and disappeared at sea. Declared lost with all hands 27.5.1831.

Cauchoise Le Havre (Constructeur: Alexandre)
  Ord: 26.11.1816. K: 30.10.1816 (sic). L: 28.10.1817. Comm: 14.4.1818. C: 4.1818.
  Struck 1833 at Rochefort, used as a floating station (*poste flottant*). BU there 9.1838.

Pintade Lorient Dyd
  Ord: 26.11.1816. K: 22.5.1818. L: 24.10.1818. Comm: 1.8.1820. C: 8.1820 (Constructeurs: Hippolyte Prétot and others)
  Struck 29.11.1871. Coal hulk at Cherbourg 1875, BU 1887.

Ménagère Le Havre (Constructeur: Alexandre)
  Ord: 7.4.1817. K: 4.1817. L: 26.4.1819. Comm: 23.8.1819. C: 8.1819.
  Decomm. 7.8.1856 and struck 15.9.1856 or 11.10.1856, probably at Algiers.

Mayenne Bayonne (Constructeur: Gabriel Nosereau)
  Ord: 7.1820. K: 10.10.1820. L: 17.4.1821. Comm: 4.5.1821. C: 8.1821.
  Decomm. 10.5.1837 after being replaced as station ship at Rochefort by brig *Borda*. Fitted as a floating station (*poste flottant*) at Rochefort 1.1838. Ordered struck 14.11.1844 at Rochefort, BU 11.1845.

BAYONNAIS Class – 300 tons. *Bayonnais* was designed by Jean-Baptiste Marestier to carry timbers to the port of Rochefort and was listed with three masts. Her plans became the model for the design of the seven *Vesuve* class bomb vessels, which served for most of their careers as 300-ton gabarres. *Bayonnais* and *Garonne* were also fitted to carry mortars but were never classified as mortar vessels. *Chameau* is believed to have been a sister of the two Bayonne-built ships.
  Dimensions & tons: 33.00m, 30.20m x 8.50m x 5.70m. 300/560 tons. Draught 3.50/3.70m. Men: 60.
  Guns: None listed for first pair, *Garonne* had 12 x 18pdr carronades.

Bayonnais Bayonne (Constructeur: Marestier)
  K: 1.1817. L: 19.5.1817. Comm: 22.7.1817. C: 8.1817.
  Condemned 5.6.1833 and struck 1.1834 at Toulon.

Chameau Lorient Dyd.
  Ord: 3.9.1816. Named: 28.4.1817. K: 8.1817. L: 4.8.1818. Comm: 5.10.1818. C: 10.1818.
  Struck 1837, hospital hulk at Toulon. Condemned 11.11.1857, replaced by *Agathe*, and BU.

Garonne Bayonne (Constructeur: Gabriel Nosereau)
  Ord: 15.2.1820. K: 12.6.1820. L: 13.8.1821. Comm: 8.8.1822. C: 8.1822.
  Condemned 11.3.1837 at Toulon and BU.

MADAGASCAR – 450 tons. Designed by Louis-Just Moissard. She was originally listed as a cattle transport (*transport de boeufs*) but was redesignated as a gabarre in 1829 or 1830.
  Dimensions & tons: dimensions unknown. 450/800? tons. Men: 67 to 80.
  Guns: ?.

Madagascar Lorient Dyd. (Constructeur: Moissard)
  Ord: 5.4.1827. Named: 30.7.1827. K: 10.1827. L: 30.4.1828. Comm: 8.5.1828. C: 5.1828.
  Participated in 1829 with the frigate *Terpsichore* in an expedition to retake the French posts in Madagascar, which included the bombardment and occupation of Tamatave on 11.10.1829, then served at Île Bourbon. Struck 20.8.1836, headquarters hulk at Lorient. Unserviceable there 1866 and BU.

ROBUSTE Class – 550 tons. Designed by Jean-Baptiste Marestier.
  Dimensions & tons: 40.30m oa, 38.00m wl, 35.50m x 9.50m x 6.00m. 550/950 tons. Draught 4.05/4.45m. Men: 40-80
  Guns: 2 x 8pdrs, 2 x 18pdr carronades, 4 swivels (*Girafe* lacked the carronades, *Chandernagor* had only the carronades, while *Mahé* had 2 x 6pdrs and 4 x 18pdr carronades).

Robuste Bayonne (Constructeur: Gabriel Nosereau)
  K: 9.10.1826. L: 6.12.1828. Comm: 6.6.1829. C: 6.1829.
  Struck 7.6.1853, stores hulk at Brest. Renamed *Camaret* 1865 (1861?), BU or sold 1866.

Vigogne Bayonne (Constructeur: Gabriel Nosereau)
  K: 10.1826. L: 6.12.1828. Comm: 6.6.1829.
  Conversion to careening hulk (*ponton de carénage*) for Martinique ordered 28.11.1835, probably at Brest. Struck 26.8.1836, decomm. at Fort Royal 1.9.1836.

Baleine Bayonne (Constructeur: Gabriel Nosereau)
  K: 7.1828. L: 16.10.1830. C: 6.1831. Comm: 19.5.1833.
  Struck 11.1836 at Rochefort, service craft there. Condemned and BU 1850

Girafe (*Giraffe*) Bayonne (Constructeurs: Gabriel Nosereau, then Gustave Garnier)
  K: 10.7.1828. L: 7.6.1834. Comm: 8.8.1835. C: 8.1835.
  Hired out for commercial service c12.1840, returned prior 8.1845.

Struck 8.12.1864 at Toulon, may have been hospital at Toulon to 1868.

Mahé Bayonne (Constructeur: Gabriel Nosereau)
K: 5.1831. L: 26.8.1835. Comm: 23.9.1835. C: 10.1835.
Hired out from 1.1840 to 11.1842 to the Cie. Nanto-Bordelaise to transport 53 colonists to Akaroa, New Zealand, probably named *Comte de Paris* during the charter. Renamed *Dromadaire* 3.11.1845, commissioned 12.11.1845 as hospital ship for Mayotte. Struck 1849 as hospital hulk, restored to list 1851 as service craft and careening hulk (*ponton de carénage*) at Mayotte, struck 24.10.1856, again hospital hulk at Mayotte from 5.10.1861 until BU or sold 1870.

Chandernagor Bayonne (Constructeur: Gabriel Nosereau)
K: 16.5.1831. L: 11.7.1835. Comm: 17.10.1835. C: 10.1835.
Struck 21.9.1870, hulk at Toulon. Was a careening hulk (*ponton-fosse*) in 1873 and a mooring hulk in 1893. BU 1895.

BUCÉPHALE Class – 300 tons. Designed by Gabriel Nosereau.
Dimensions & tons: 37.9m oa, 35.00m wl, 32.20m x 9.00m x 4.70m. 300/694 tons. Draught 3.90 mean. Men: 39-61.
Guns: 2 x 6pdrs, 8 x 18pdr carronades

Bucéphale Bayonne (Constructeur: Nosereau)
K: 12.11.1829. L: 23.4.1834. Comm: 18.10.1835. C: 11.1835.
Was a school for boys at Cherbourg in 1846. Struck 17.8.1869 at Gabon, station hulk. BU 1873

Licorne Bayonne (Constructeur: Nosereau)
K: 12.10.1829. L: 9.5.1834. Comm: 25.8.1835. C: 8.1835.
Training corvette for the Naval Academy and annex to *Borda* at Brest 1842 (grounded 28.7.1846, refloated, cruise to Cherbourg 1852). Recomm. 20.4.1854 for Crimean War duty. Struck 15.7.1867 at Brest, hulk. Coal hulk 1876, BU 1894.

PRÉVOYANTE Class – 380 tons. This class consisted of reproductions of the highly successful 380-ton *gabarres-écuries* designed by François Pestel and built in 1810-12. The plans of most were attributed directly to Pestel ('*Zélée* type'). The plans of *Infatigable* were attributed to Mathurin Boucher and those of *Prudente* to Antoine Campaignac, both of whom probably replicated Pestel's plans with minor adjustments. *Recherche* was rated as a corvette when completed and conducted two scientific expeditions to Arctic and Scandinavian waters between 1835 and 1840. All seven surviving units were redesignated as 14-gun open-battery corvettes in 1846. *Indienne* was redesignated as a 350-ton transport in 1851. By a ministerial decree of 1.1855 *Expéditive* and *Recherche* were 'déclassés' as corvettes and listed among the transports of 380 tons. *Infatigable* was similarly redesignated at about the same time. The actual cargo capacity of this type, when fully armed, was less than 160 tons. For more information on the cancelled ships see the note below on changes in policy regarding transports during the 1840s.
Dimensions & tons: 31.57m, 30.85m wl, 27.70m x 8.48m, 8.88m ext x 4.84m. 380/428 tons. Draught 3.37/3.95m. Men: ?.
Guns: (first four) 12 x 18pdr carronades, 2 x 6pdrs; (*Sarcelle* and probably *Active*, and *Prudente*) 10 x 18pdr carronades, 2 x 12pdrs; (*Infatigable*) 8 x 18pdr carronades, 2 x 12pdrs When used exclusively as transports in peacetime they could carry as few as 2 x 12pdr carronades or 2 x 8pdrs.

Prévoyante Lorient Dyd.
K: 11.3.1833. L: 6.8.1834. Comm: 21.3.1835. C: 3.1835.
Struck 24.10.1860, sheer hulk at Cherbourg. BU 1886.

Expéditive Toulon Dyd.
K: 7.1833. L: 13.11.1834. Comm: 9.4.1835. C: 4.1835.
Struck 16.11.1866, sheer hulk to 1868, seamanship training hulk 1872-82. BU 1884.

Recherche (ex *Pourvoyeuse* 21.1.1835) Cherbourg Dyd. (Constructeur: Antoine Campaignac)
K: 8.1833. L: 2.12.1834. Comm: 13.4.1835. C: 4.1835.
Struck 2.4.1863 at Gabon, storage hulk. Sold or BU 1868.

Indienne Toulon Dyd.
K: 9.1833. L: 1.4.1835. Comm: 25.4.1836. C: 4.1836.
Struck 18.7.1856 at Mayotte, hulk. Sank in the harbour at Nossi-Bé 19.10.1863.

Sarcelle Rochefort Dyd. (Constructeurs: Jean Clarke, then Louis Lambert, then Charles Moll)
K: 26.8.1833. L: 23.5.1838. Comm: 7.7.1838. C: 7.1838.
Struck 20.4.1857 at Brest. Sold 1.1860 to B. Kerros for commercial service under her original name, still active as a 293-ton three-masted barque in 1866.

Active (ex *Mérinos* 24.10.1838) Rochefort Dyd. (Constructeurs: Jean Clarke, then Louis Lambert, then Charles Moll)
K: 8.1833. L: 18.10.1838. Comm: 1.3.1839. C: 4.1839.
Wrecked 6.8.1839 on Lobos Island in the Rio de la Plata.

Prudente Rochefort Dyd. (Constructeurs: Henri De Lisleferme, then Nicolas Courtin)
K: 3.1842. L: 18.11.1842. Comm: 1.12.1842. C: 2.1843.
Struck 28.9.1855.

Infatigable Brest Dyd. (Constructeur: Jean-Michel Segondat)
K: 24.6.1842. L: 26.8.1843. Comm: 1.1.1845. C: 1.1845.
Struck 18.8.1862 at Brest, BU before 1865.

Garonne Lorient Dyd.
Planned in 1842 as a 380-ton gabarre to begin in 1843, to 360-ton gabarre 1843. Not laid down. Suspended 1844, last listed 5.1845.

Rance Rochefort Dyd.
Planned in 1842 as a 380-ton gabarre to begin in 1844, to 360-ton gabarre 1843. Not laid down. Suspended 1844, last listed 5.1845.

Providence Brest Dyd.
Planned in 1842 as a 380-ton gabarre to begin in 1844, to 360-ton gabarre 1843. Not laid down. Suspended 1844, last listed 5.1845.

PERDRIX Class – 600 tons. On 24 August 1837 the Council of Works examined plans for a 1,200-ton transport. proposed by Vice Admiral Jurien de la Gravière for the transportation of troops and recommended that two 600-ton transports be built for each of the planned 1,200-ton ships. Mathurin Boucher, the Inspector-General of the Génie Maritime, preferred to use corvettes de charge for this purpose but recommended having two of the 600-ton type built at Toulon on plans by Firmin Joffre. Names were recommended for them on 13 June 1838. A third ship (*Loire*, below) was soon added at Brest to a different design. These were ships with a covered battery deck like the 800-ton corvettes de charge but smaller and optimised for carrying troops and cargo. For more information on the six cancelled ships that probably were of this type see the note below on changes in policy regarding transports during the 1840s.
Dimensions & tons: 41.60m, 41.09m wl, 37.20m x 10.10m, 10.33m ext x 5.40m. 600/1,030 tons. Draught 4.52/4.82m. Men: 43-67.
Guns: 16 x 24pdr carronades, 4 x 30pdrs shell (20 ports).

Perdrix Toulon Dyd. (Constructeur: Joffre)
K: 9.1838. L: 29.7.1840. Comm: 18.4.1842. C: 4.1842.
Struck 19.8.1872 at Toulon. Was a careening hulk (*ponton-fosse*) there in 1873 and a guard hulk in 1877-1900. Sold or BU 1901.

Provençale Toulon Dyd. (Constructeur: Joffre)
K: 9.1838. L: 29.7.1841. Comm: 1.11.1842. C: 11.1842.
Struck 17.8.1869, station hulk at Toulon. BU 1892.

Meuse Rochefort Dyd.

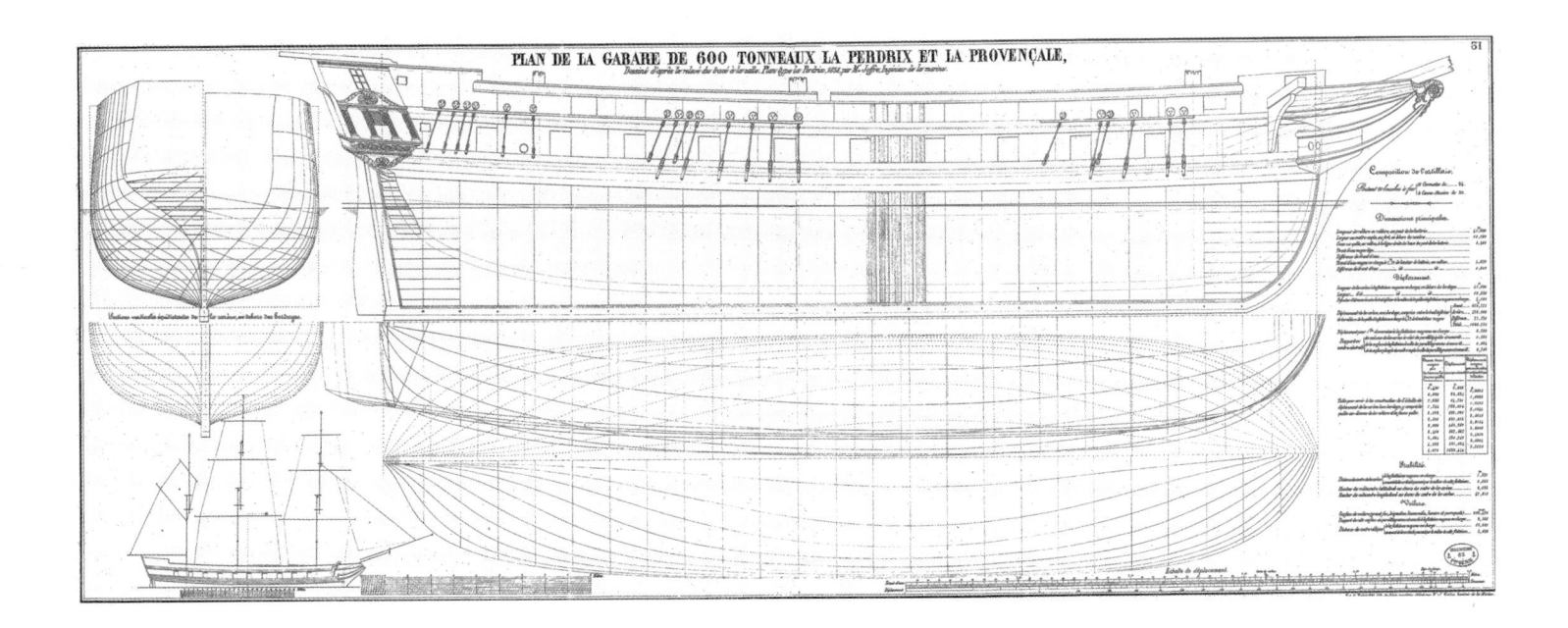

Official lines and general arrangement plans of the 600-ton gabarres of the *Perdrix* class. The vessels carried a barque rig with a total area of 992 sq.m. For such workaday vessels they had surprisingly elaborate stern decoration; the small poop cabin or dunette may have been for the senior officer of the troops when embarked. (Atlas du Génie Maritime, French collection, plate 31)

Planned in 1842 as an 800-ton corvette de charge to begin in 1843, to 600-ton gabarre 1843. Not laid down. Suspended 1844, last listed 1.1847.

Rhône Cherbourg Dyd.
Planned in 1842 as an 800-ton corvette de charge to begin in 1843, to 600-ton gabarre 1843. Suspended 12.8.1844, last listed 1.1847.

Durance Brest Dyd.
Planned in 1842 as a 380-ton gabarre to begin in 1843, to 600-ton gabarre 1843. Not laid down. Suspended 1844, last listed 1.1847.

Moselle Brest Dyd.
Planned in 1842 as an 800-ton corvette de charge to begin in 1844, to 600-ton gabarre 1843. Not laid down. Suspended 1844, last listed 1.1847.

Lozere Toulon Dyd.
Planned in 1842 as a 600-ton gabarre to begin in 1844. Not laid down. Suspended 1844, last listed 1.1847.

Vigogne Toulon Dyd.
Planned in 1842 as a 600-ton gabarre to begin in 1844. Not laid down. Suspended 1844, last listed 4.1846 at Toulon and then 1.1847 at Brest.

LOIRE – 560, later 600 tons. Similar to the *Perdrix* class above, designed by Alexandre Chedeville.
Dimensions & tons: 38.06m oa, 37.00m wl, 32.30m x 9.88m, 10.00m ext x 5.26m. 560-600/977 tons disp. Draught 4.70/4.80m. Men: ?.
Guns: unknown (18 ports).
Loire Brest Dyd. (Constructeur: Chedeville)
K: 6.5.1839. L: 28.8.1840. Comm: 21.11.1840. C: 11.1840.
Grounded in fog and wrecked 18.1.1852 between Ste.-Marie and La Goyave, Guadeloupe.

CORMORAN – 480 tons. *Cormoran* was built on the request of France's senior naval constructor, Mathurin Boucher, for a ship to transport large steam engines from the navy's engine factory at Indret or from private factories to shipyards. Plans for her by Alexandre Chedeville were approved on 4 July 1840. Her first cargo was the engine of the paddle frigate *Asmodée*, which she carried from Liverpool to Rochefort. *Cormoran* was re-rated as a 500-ton transport before 1847 and her rating was further increased to 550 tons before 1860. She transported the engine of *Austerlitz* from Indret to Cherbourg in December 1852.
Dimensions & tons: 41.23m oa, 36.00m, 36.15m wl, 33.60m x 9.40m, 9.50m ext x 5.20m. 480/795 tons. Draught 3.57/3.67. Men: 40.
Guns: 2 x 12pdr carronades.
Cormoran Brest Dyd. (Constructeur: Chedeville)
K: 27.7.1840. L: 22.3.1841. Comm: 28.4.1841. C: 4.1841.
Struck 22.7.1872 at Lorient, hulk. BU 2.1875.

MARSOUIN – 480 tons. On 10 March 1842 Mathurin Boucher asked for two more ships like *Cormoran* but slightly larger, of which one could be built at Brest. (He hoped to acquire the other ship, although this apparently did not happen.). She was probably built to Chedeville's plans for *Cormoran* lengthened by about two metres. *Marsouin* was re-rated as a 500-ton transport before 1847 and her rating was further increased to 600 tons before 1853. Among many other cargoes she transported parts of the engine of *Napoléon* and the engines of *Montebello* and *Jean Bart* between 1850 and 1852.
Dimensions & tons: 38.00m wl x 9.40m. 480 tons burthen. Men: 98.
Guns: 2.
Marsouin Brest Dyd.
K: 22.3.1842. L: 3.11.1842. Comm: 25.1.1843. C: 1.1843.
Struck 22.12.1864 at Toulon. On sale list 11.5.1865 but not sold, renamed *Caserne* as barracks hulk and/or careening hulk (*ponton-fosse*) at Toulon 1865. BU 1869.

At the end of 1842 the Minister of Marine (Vice Admiral Baron Duperré) planned to use corvettes de charge and large gabarres not only to transport troops but also to carry all stores and munitions to France's colonies and overseas stations. In the budget for 1844 (prepared in late 1842) he therefore provided for two new 800-ton corvettes de charge

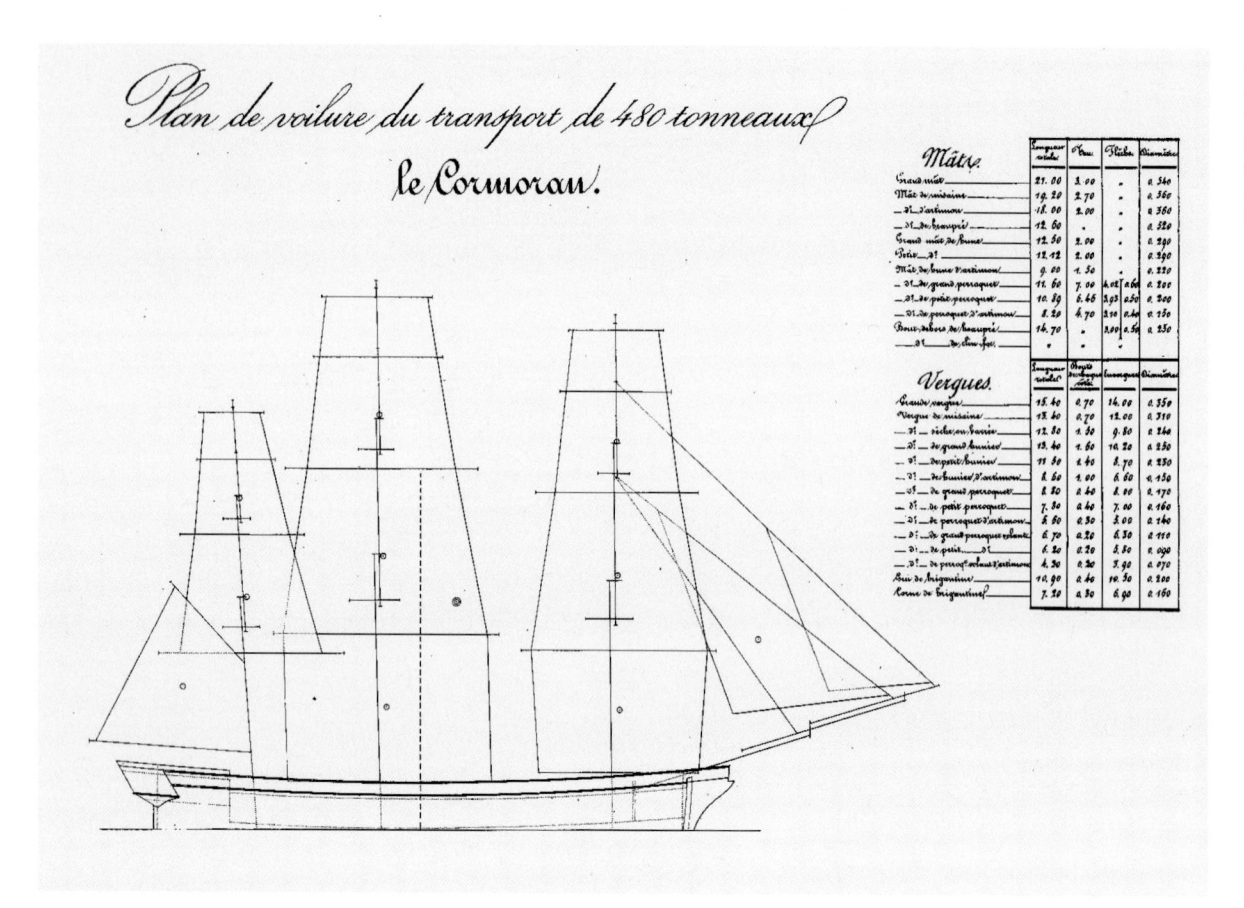

Official sail plan *Cormoran* when still rated as 480 tons. The ship rig carries a total sail area of 832 sq.m., excluding the royals. (Atlas du Génie Maritime, Genoa collection, image 1-0038)

(*Meuse* and *Rhône*) and two new 380-ton gabarres (*Durance*, and *Garonne*) to begin construction in 1843 and included beginning in 1844 one more 800-ton ship (*Moselle*), two 600-ton gabarres (*Lozère* and *Vigogne*), and two more 380-tonners (*Providence* and *Rance*). A new Minister of Marine (Vice Admiral Baron Mackau) took office in July 1843, and in his 1845 budget, drafted at the end of 1843, all three new 800-ton corvettes de charge plus the 380-ton *Durance* were listed as 600-ton gabarres while the remaining three 380-tonners became 360-ton gabarres. No details of the new 600 and 360-ton types have been found, but it seems most likely that the 600-ton ships were to have been of the *Perdrix* class or similar to it, while the 360-ton type was a minor adjustment of the 380-ton design. Under the 1845 budget the 600-ton *Rhône*, *Moselle*, *Durance*, *Lozère*, and and *Vigogne* and the 360-ton *Providence* were to be begun in 1844 while the 600-ton *Meuse* and 360-ton *Garonne* and *Rance* were to commence construction in 1845, for a total of nine new transport-type ships in two years.

In early 1844 Mackau faced a budget crisis with political implications when work on new construction authorised by the legislature fell severely behind schedule because of the diversion of manpower and funds to operational and maintenance work. By June 1844 he, with the concurrence of the legislature, had decided to hire out the transportation of stores and munitions to the colonies and overseas stations. This made the new ships unnecessary, and the Director of Ports therefore recommended on 24 June 1844 that the laying down of new corvettes de charge and gabarres be cancelled and that resources be used for more useful ship types, notably steamers.

On 21 October 1844 Mackau noted that the navy still had too many transports and recommended that the nine newest 800-ton corvettes de charge and the seven newest 380-ton gabarres be armed and fitted as combatant ships. (In the event, only the four most recent corvettes de charge and all 11 remaining 380-ton gabarres were reclassified.) He pointed out that this recommendation would lead to the abolition of corvettes de charge and 380-ton gabarres as ship types and, since this contradicted earlier directives, he recommended submitting the matter to the navy's highest advisory board, the Council of Admiralty. The Council approved the conversion of the existing ships but was reluctant to renounce in an absolute manner the construction of types known to have good qualities before ships of the proposed new types were built and tested.

During 1846 all corvettes de charge and gabarres not converted to combatant ships were redesignated transports, possibly in part because the designation 'gabarres' had prompted numerous criticisms in the legislature. Mackau's restructuring of the fleet, approved by a royal ordinance of 22 November 1846, contained only 16 transport ships, all of about 600 tons, leaving little room for new construction. No replacement design was prepared for the 380-ton gabarres, and the ships begun in 1847 as 600-ton transports, the *Moselle* class (see below), turned out to be updated copies of the 800-ton corvettes de charge.

Large transports

Vessels acquired from 26 June 1815

Into the early nineteenth century the designation *transport* was used primarily for small cargo- and troop-carrying auxiliaries, the larger ones being designated *flûtes* or *gabarres*. In the November 1819 fleet list the flûtes were 800-ton (burthen) ships except for one captured vessel of 559

THE LARGER TRANSPORTS

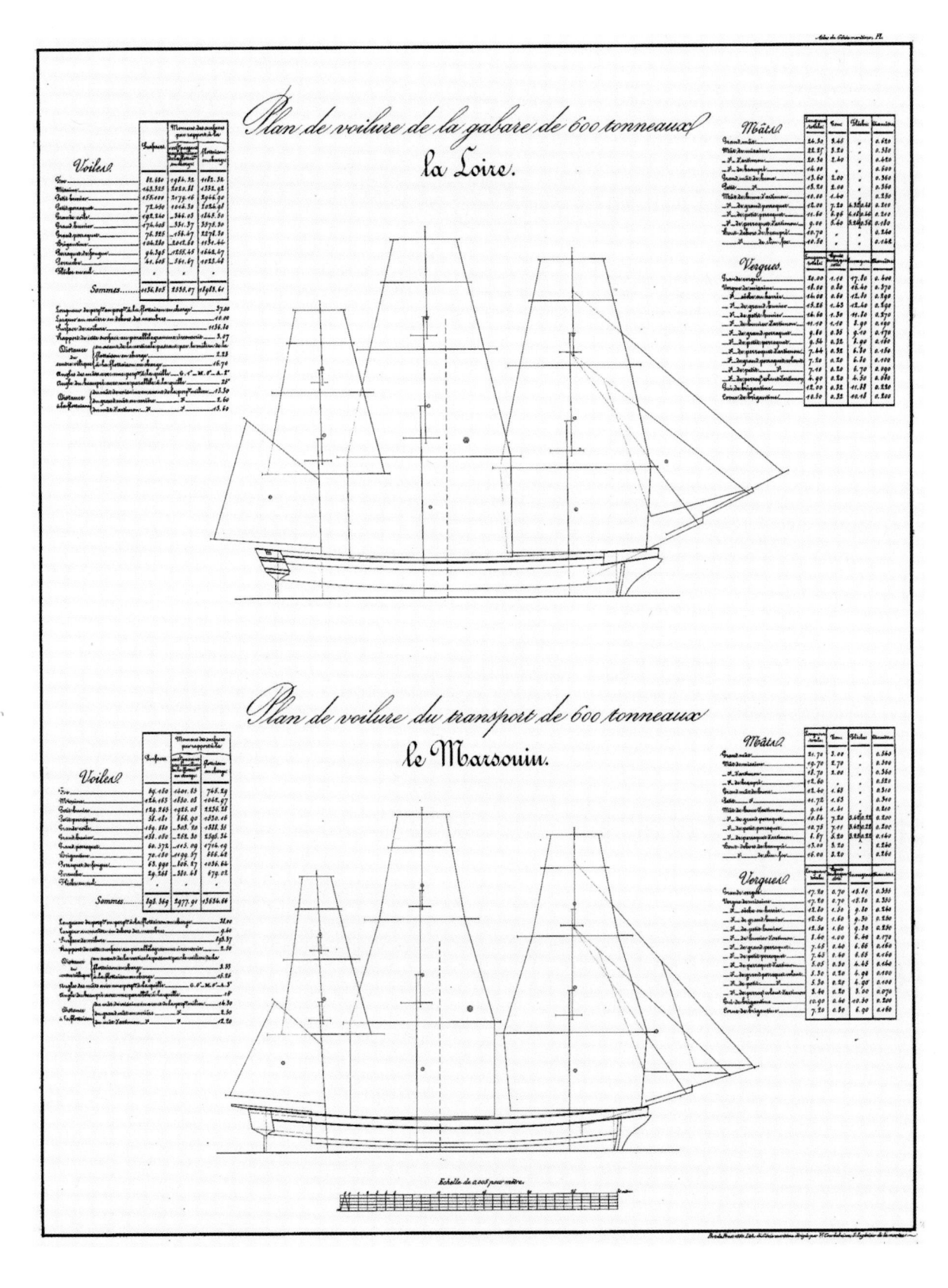

Official sail plans, engraved in 1850, comparing *Loire* and *Marsouin* (in her later rating at 600 tons). They are both ship-rigged but the narrower cut of the latter's sails makes a big difference in total area: 893 sq.m. to *Loire*'s 1136. In neither case does the calculation include royals, even though these are depicted on the plans. (Atlas du Génie Maritime, Genoa collection, image 1-0039)

tons, the gabarres ranged from 467 down to 170 tons, while the transports (listed in the next chapter), with the exception of one or two former 450-ton *prames*, ranged from 150 down to 20 tons. In 1819 this pattern was broken by an order for two 925-ton specialised vessels classified as transports, and another smaller specialised vessel followed in 1830. Otherwise the trend after 1815 was to reduce the number of transports on the fleet list. By 1826 this number was down to fifteen, and in January 1827 it was reduced to four by reclassifying most of the others as service craft. In January 1844 the transport category disappeared altogether when the two 925-ton units listed below were struck and the other two on the list were redesignated as gabarres.

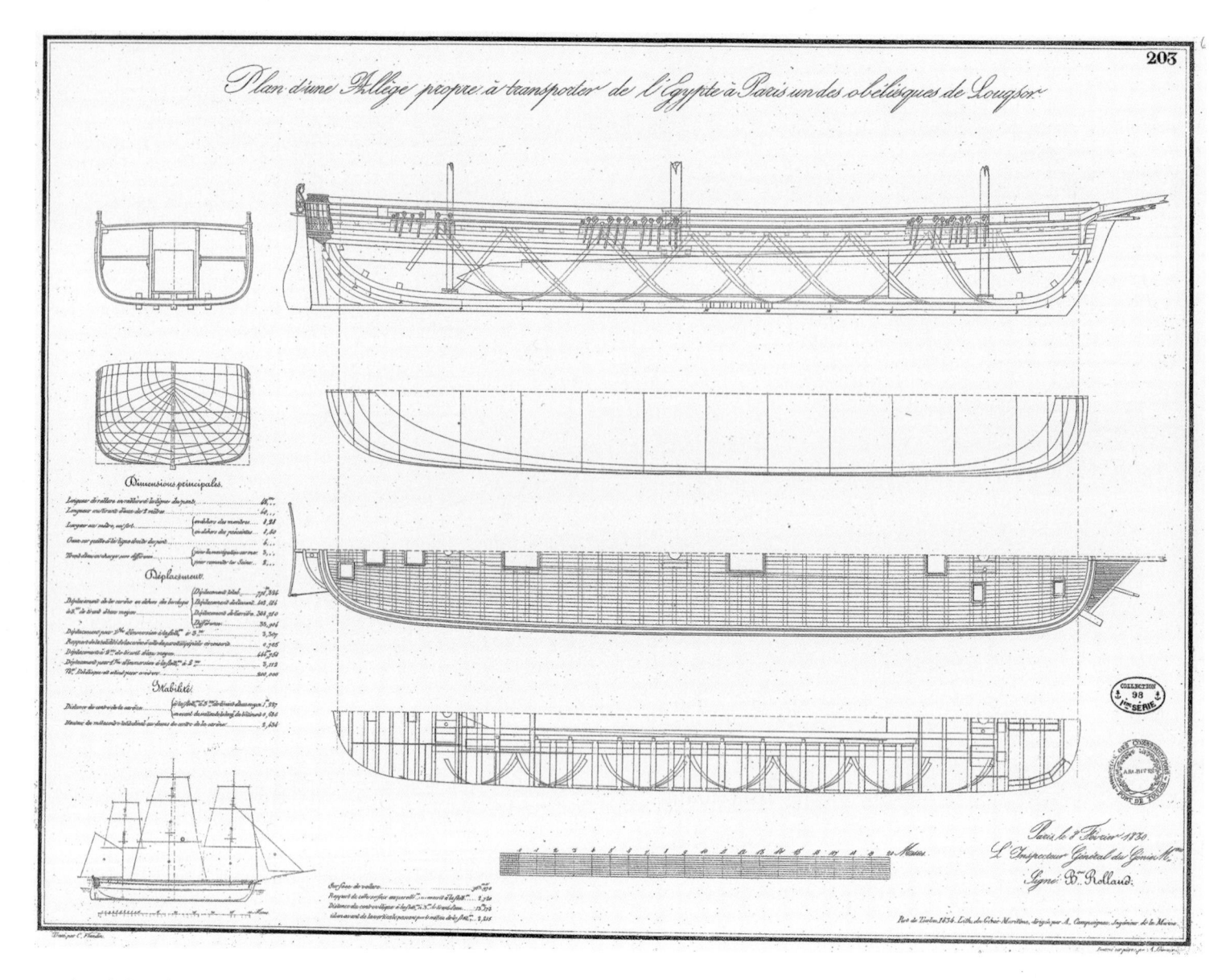

The term 'transports' quickly returned to the fleet list, however, when in 1846 all of the flûtes (now called corvettes de charge) and gabarres that were not converted into corvettes under Minister of Marine Mackau's force restructuring were redesignated as transports. On 1 January 1847 the list showed 36 transports, of which 12 were former corvettes de charge and 22 were former gabarres. However, with steam offering obvious advantages for military transport ships, the navy avoided the acquisition of any more large sail transports other than two taken from the Russians in 1854 and three acquired in 1859-60 to carry coal to Napoleon III's steam battle squadron in northern Italy.

DROMADAIRE Class – 925 tons. Designed by Jean-Baptiste Marestier. These large ships were built especially to transport timbers and were classified as transports, not gabarres. (They were listed as flûtes until 8 March 1820.) They were based at Toulon.

Dimensions & tons: 40.00m, 39.25m wl x 11.00m x 6.75m. 925/1,420 tons. Draught 4.82/4.88m. Men: 90-120.

Guns: 6 or 8 x 24pdr carronades (20 ports).

Dromadaire Toulon Dyd. (Constructeurs: Jean-François Lafosse and others)

Official lines and general arrangement plans for the *allège* (barge) that became the *Luxor*, dated Paris 8 February 1830. The Egyptian obelisk it was designed to transport is shown in the profile view; it was to be loaded by beaching the vessel bow-first, removing the bow section and hauling the obelisk into the hold. This operation dictated the very flat shape and shallow draught of the hull, which was strengthened with curved diagonal riders to support the 230-ton weight of the obelisk. The vessel duly carried out this mission and delivered the obelisk to Paris in November 1833. Despite the minimal seaworthiness of the design, it still carried a full ship rig of 956 sq.m. in total sail area. (Atlas du Génie Maritime, French collection, plate 203)

K: 8.1819. L: 22.2.1821. Comm: 20.3.1821. C: 3.1821.
Decomm. 16.8.1831 at Toulon, struck there 13.11.1843.

Rhinocéros Le Havre (Constructeur: Charles-Robert Alexandre)
K: 7.1819. L: 17.7.1821. Comm: 12.1821. C: 12.1821.
Decomm. 20.2.1832 at Toulon, struck there 13.11.1843.

LUXOR – c300 tons. Designed by Pierre Rolland, whose plans were approved in February 1830. This transport or *allège* (barge) was built to transport from Egypt to France the 230-ton obelisk that is now in the Place de la Concorde at Paris.

Dimensions & tons: 43.00m, 42.00m wl, 40.3m (middle keel of five)

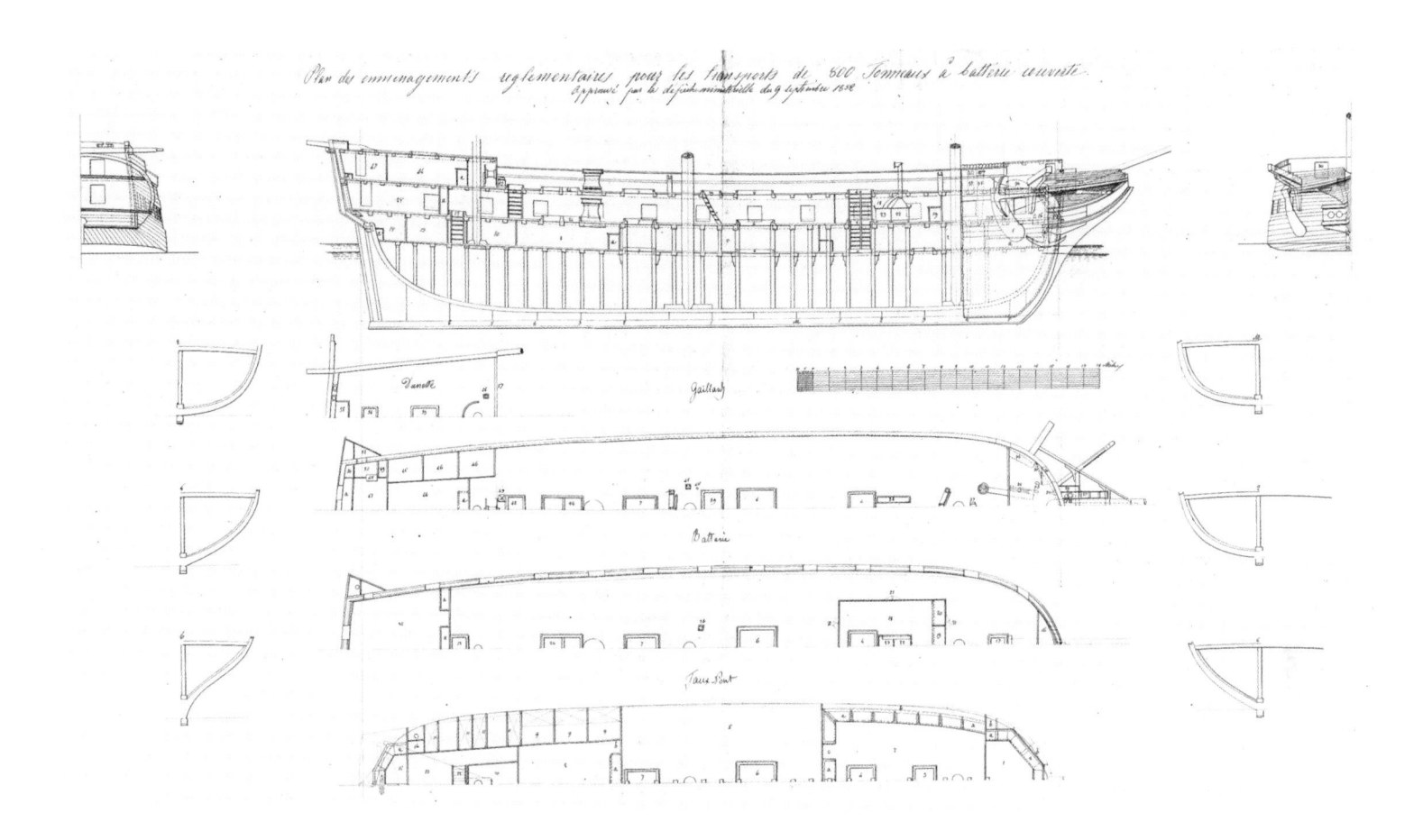

x 8.28m, 8.50m ext x 4.00m. 300/650 tons. Draught 3.00/3.00m at sea, 2.00/2.20m on the Nile. Men: 117-130.
Guns: 2 swivels

Luxor (*Louqsor*) Toulon Dyd. (Constructeurs: Jacques Bonard, Armand Mimerel, and others)
K: 3.1830. L: 26.7.1830. Comm: 23.8.1830. C: 10.1830.
Bow removed, obelisk loaded, and bow replaced on the Nile 8-12.1831. Decomm. at Paris 5.9.1834 and loaned to the Ministry of the Interior. Struck 1837. BU 5-7.1837 at Paris.

MOSELLE Class –800 tons. The plans for *Moselle* and *Durance*, labelled 800-ton corvettes de charge, were approved by the Minister of Marine in April 1847. They were attributed to Pierre-Alexandre Forfait with modifications by Jacques-Louis Bonard, suggesting that they were very similar to Forfait's classic 800-ton corvettes de charge. The ships were listed as 600-ton transports when scheduled for construction in 1847 and while under construction in early 1848, but the two ships that were built were soon re-rated 800-ton transports. All four ships were to be built by contractors, although the last two were never ordered. *Durance* was ordered from Auguste Guibert at Nantes by a contract awarded on 12 April 1847 and approved on 20 April (Guibert being notified on 7 May), and *Moselle* was ordered from Chaigneau & Bichon of Bordeaux by a contract awarded and probably approved at the same time. Contracts for six brig-avisos for the West African anti-slavery patrol were awarded and approved on the same dates, and it is possible that the transports were intended to support them along with the six paddle and two screw steamers that were built for the West African patrol. *Durance* was reclassified a 24-gun corvette in 1849, a 14-gun corvette in 1850, and a transport in 1851. She was struck in 1854 because her hull was found to be rotten and she needed a refit of 18/24ths of her structure. *Moselle*,

Official plan of internal arrangements for the 800-ton covered-battery transports of the *Moselle* class, approved by the ministry on 9 September 1852. (Atlas du Génie Maritime, Genoa collection, image 1-0027)

completed later, served as a transport throughout her equally short career.

Dimensions & tons: 44.10m, 40.40m x 10.40m x 5.70m. 800/1,250 tons (*Moselle*), 1,340 tons (*Durance*). Draught 4.68m (4.87m in *Durance*). Men: ?.
Guns: (*Durance*) 18 x 24pdr carronades, 2 x 12pdrs; (*Moselle*) 18 x 24pdr carronades, 4 x 16cm shell (24 ports).

Moselle Chaigneau & Bichon, Bordeaux-Lormont (Constructeur, Nicolas-Émile Courtin)
Ord 20.4.1847 (contract). K: 15.7.1847. L: 29.7.1848. C: 6.1849. Comm: 3.6.1851.
Repaired at Rochefort four times between 12.1849 and commissioning in 6.1851. Struck 18.7.1856 at Tahiti and hulked. Sold or BU before 1865.

Durance Auguste Guibert, Nantes.
Ord 20.4.1847 (contract). K: 7.1847. L: 27.9.1848. C: 6.1849. Comm: 6.7.1849.
Struck 12.4.1854 at Brest and renamed *Gardien* the same day (or on 9.11.1857) as a hulk. Converted to floating depot 11.1854. Recomm. 1.1855 and sent to Cayenne. BU from 7.1862.

Lybio Contractor not selected.
Scheduled to begin construction in 1848 but not ordered, cancelled 1849.

Gironde Contractor not selected.

Scheduled to begin construction in 1848 but not ordered, cancelled 1849.

Ex RUSSIAN PRIZES (1854).
Hérault (Russian mercantile *Aleksandr I*, built 1850, possibly originally a screw steamer, taken 1854 by the paddle frigate *Descartes*, purchased for the navy in 1855 as *Alexandre 1er*, comm. 1.6.1855 and renamed 6.1855).
  Dimensions & tons: dimensions unknown. 370/1,372 (?) tons. Men: 39
  Guns: 2, later 4.
  Transport in Black Sea 1855, voyage to Australia and Oceania in 1858. Struck 24.4.1862, decomm. 26.9.1862 (sic).
Orione (Russian three-masted merchant ship *Orione*, possibly the 432-ton barque *Orion* built in Finland in 1849, taken 11.7.1854 by the aviso *Averne* while under the Tuscan flag near Mamora (Mehdya), Morocco. She was considered to be a Russian ship re-registered under lax Tuscan regulations upon the outbreak of war. Purchased for the navy in 1855, comm. 1.6.1855).
  Dimensions & tons: dimensions unknown. 420 tons burthen. Men: 36.
  Guns: 2.
  Transport in the Black Sea during the Crimean War. Decomm. 17.6.1868 at Cherbourg, struck 31.1.1870, coal hulk. BU 1883.

PURCHASED LARGE TRANSPORTS
Ménagère (mercantile *Adéline* acquired 5.1859 and comm. 11.5.1859).
  Dimensions & tons: dimensions unknown. 420 tons burthen. Men: 41.
  Guns: 2.
  Decomm. 9.11.1866. Struck 31.10.1867 at Brest, coal hulk, BU 1889. *Ménagère*, *Abondance*, and *Truite* may have been sisters laid down as merchant vessels at Toulon 1.1859 and completed 5.1859; a Navy memo of 6.5.1859 stated that the Minister of Marine had just authorised their acquisition at Marseille and recommended their Navy names.
Abondance (mercantile *Lahore* acquired 5.1859 and comm. 11.5.1859)
  Dimensions & tons: dimensions unknown. 420 tons burthen. Men: 41.
  Guns: 2.
  Arrived at Venice 30.5.1859 under tow by *Algésiras* with coal for the French naval division there. She was one of 16 vessels that were wrecked on 22.9.1866 in the harbour of Saint-Pierre in a storm. Wreck sold and BU there. Probably sister to *Ménagère*.
Truite (mercantile *Gange* acquired 5.1859 and comm. 11.5.1859)
  Dimensions & tons: dimensions unknown. 420 or 460 tons burthen. Men: 41.
  Guns: 2.
  Arrived at Venice 30.5.1859 under tow with coal for the French naval division there. Decomm. 1.12.1866 at Toulon, condemned 26.8.1872, then sent to French Guiana for use as a *ponton-stationnaire* at Cayenne. Sank there 1898 from deterioration. Probably sister to *Ménagère*.

Screw transports

For screw transports converted from line of battle ships and frigates after completion as combatants see the listings for those types.

ZÉLÉE – 200 tons, 60nhp. On 28 August 1852 the Minister of Marine ordered Toulon to draw plans for the conversion of a *corvette à batterie barbette* to a 50nhp transport for service on the west coast of Africa. Toulon recommended selecting the former gabarre *Zélée*, which had been built with slight modifications in 1811-12 (launched in February 1812) on the standard gabarre-écurie plans produced by François Pestel. The Toulon naval constructor Marc Delacour produced plans and proposed using the Maudslay engines of *Antilope* (an aviso acquired in 1844 and condemned on 4 June 1851). These plans were not accepted, but subsequent plans by Charles Schlumberger, another Toulon engineer, were adopted in 1853. The ship was converted between November 1853 and late 1854. Reclassified in December 1854 as a 200-ton screw transport, she was actually a *transport mixte* (mixed propulsion or auxiliary screw transport) whose small steam engine augmented her ability to operate under sail.
  Dimensions & tons: 31.90m x 8.77m. 200/540 tons. Draught 3.95m. Men: 39.
  Machinery: 60nhp, 5.2kts.
  Guns: 12 x 18pdr carronades (maximum); 2 guns (normally).
Zélée Toulon Dyd/from *Antilope*.
  Conversion began: 11.1853. L: 1854. Comm: 1.1.1855.
  Struck 31.12.1863, mooring hulk at Lorient. Powder hulk 1876, BU 1887.

LOIRE Class – 1,200 tons, 160nhp. On 6 April 1854 the Minister of Marine asked the ports for plans for *bâtiments de charge* (cargo ships) capable of filling the role taken by the sailing corvettes de charge and flûtes before the advent of the steam navy. On 11 July 1854 the Council of Works proposed approving the plans by Louis-Clément Lebouleur de Courlon and ordering construction to them of a *transport mixte* (mixed propulsion or auxiliary screw transport) at Lorient. The plans were approved on 17 July 1854. By 4 August 1854 the Minister of Marine had ordered the construction of four *transports mixtes* (then also called *corvettes transports*), two at Lorient (*Loire* and *Durance*) on the plans of Lebouleur (type *Loire*) and two at Bordeaux (*Gironde* and *Dordogne*) by Lucien Arman, using his proprietary system of composite iron and wood construction. The two Bordeaux ships were ordered from Arman by a contract approved on 1 August 1854, and the 160nhp engines of all four ships were ordered from Mazeline by a contract approved on 30 August 1854. By 23 October 1854 the Minister had ordered construction of 11 ships of this type. On 10 November 1854 the Minister was asked to approve construction of a 12th ship (*Yonne*) at Cherbourg on the ways being vacated by the ship of the line *Arcole*, and it was noted that it might be possible to add a 13th at Toulon during 1855. Engines for three of these additional ships plus the iron-hulled *Seine* (below) were ordered from Charles-Michel Nillus by a contract approved on 20 November 1854 while Mazeline's earlier engine contract was replaced by one for six ships approved on 24 November 1854. As in many auxiliary propulsion ships with small steam engines, the boiler and funnel were located aft of the mainmast. They had a single battery deck (*entrepont*) for carrying troops. *Meuse* received a second battery deck in 1863, and plans for a similar modification to *Nièvre* were approved on 23 February 1865.
  Dimensions & tons: 73.00m, 71.00m wl, 66.90m x 12.88m ext x 7.63m. 1,200/2,750 tons. Draught 4.78/5.38m. Men: 150.
  Machinery: 160nhp. 920ihp (designed). Trials: 915.5ihp = 10.17kts (*Rhin*, 1871), 695ihp = 9.22kts (*Marne*, 1869), 501ihp = 7.38kts (*Yonne*, 1866). Coal 160 tons.
  Guns: 4 x 12cm shell.
Loire Lorient Dyd/Mazeline (Constructeur, Charles-Louis Duchalard)
  K: 1.8.1854. L: 15.6.1855. Comm: 16.8.1855. C: 10.1855.
  Struck 12.8.1872 at Cherbourg. Renamed *Dromadaire* 5.2.1873 as school hulk. BU 1877.
Durance Lorient Dyd/Mazeline (Constructeur, Charles-Louis Duchalard)

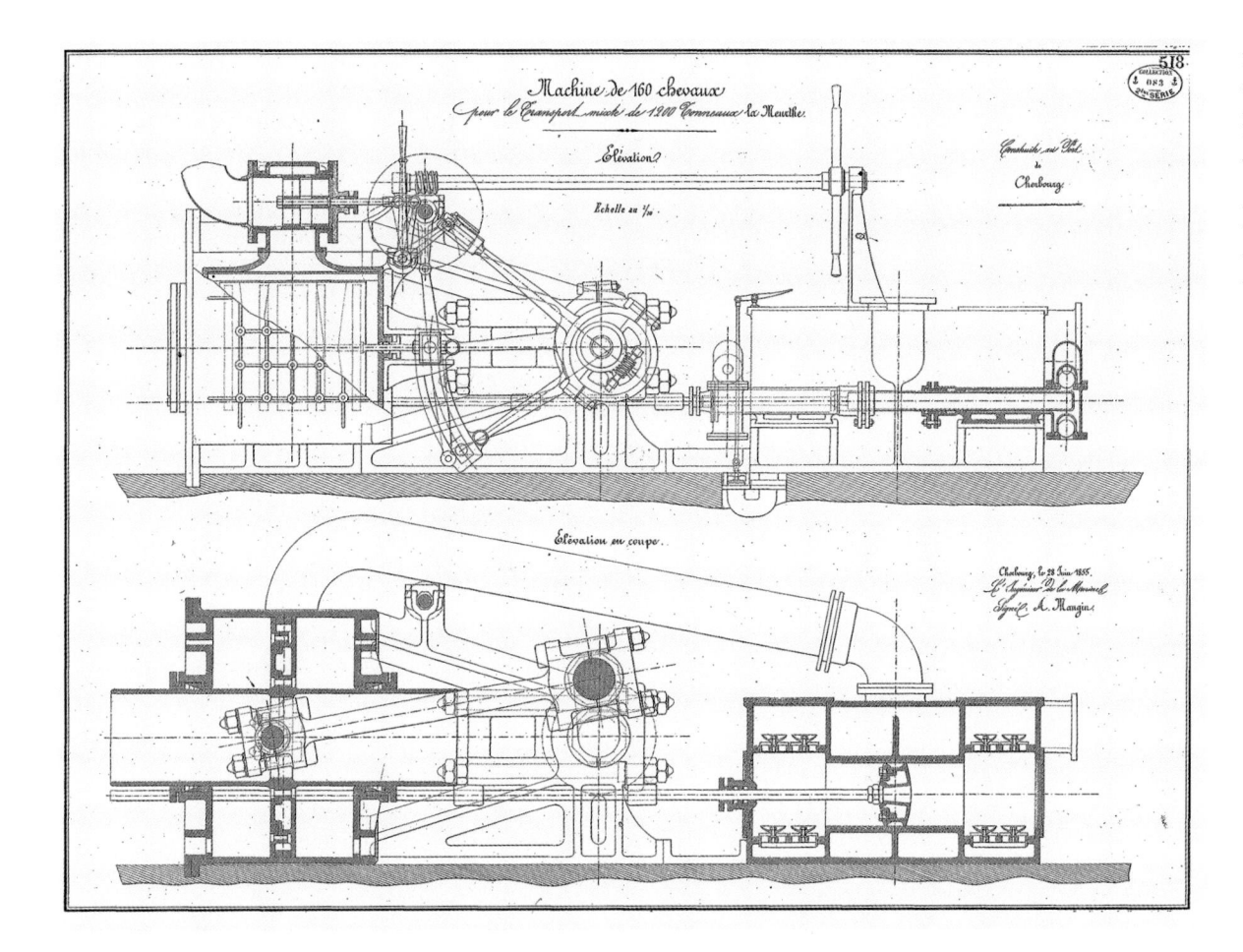

Drawings of the 160nhp single-cylinder trunk engine manufactured at Cherbourg Dockyard for the transport *Meurthe*. Dated 28 June 1855, it is signed by A Mangin, Ingénieur de la Marine, who designed it. (Atlas du Génie Maritime, French collection, plate 518)

Ord: 26.7.1854. Named: 25.8.1854. K: 8.8.1854. L: 16.7.1855. Comm: 17.9.1855. C: 11.1855.
Struck 12.8.1872 at Cherbourg. BU 1875.

Gironde Lucien Arman, Bordeaux/Mazeline (Constructeur, Henri Paul Denis de Senneville)
K: 8.1854. L: 30.5.1855. Comm: 1.9.1855. C: 9.1855.
Wrecked 9.2.1867 at Kingston, Jamaica.

Dordogne Lucien Arman, Bordeaux/Mazeline (Constructeur, Henri Paul Denis de Senneville)
K: 8.1854. L: 14.6.1855. Comm: 25.6.1855. C: 9.1855.
Engines removed 2-9.1883 at Toulon, sail transport for transporting convicts to New Caledonia. Hospital ship at Diego-Suarez 1886. Struck 24.2.1892, sold for BU 1893 at Diègo Suarez.

Rhin Rochefort Dyd/Nillus (Constructeur, Henri De Lisleferme)
K: 2.11.1854. L: 27.8.1855. Comm: 25.9.1855. C: 9.1855.
Raised by a deck 4.1869-7.1870 at Brest and given the 300nhp engines of *Allier* (1861). Struck 5.6.1886 at Brest, coal hulk and headquarters for torpedo boats as annex to *Navarin* at Lézardrieux near Brest. BU 1909-10.

Isère Rochefort Dyd/Nillus (Constructeur, Henri De Lisleferme)
K: 6.11.1854. L: 27.8.1855. Comm: 11.10.1855. C: 1.1856.
Blown onto a rock in the harbour of Amoy 17.5.1860 and lost, struck 17.8.1860.

Marne Brest Dyd/Indret (Constructeurs, Bernard Charles Chariot and Émile Marie Victor Courbebaisse)
K: 21.10.1854. L: 16.4.1855. Comm: 1.5.1855. C: 7.1855.
Struck 15.9.1878 at Brest, barracks hulk. BU 1894.

Saône Brest Dyd/Indret (Constructeurs, Émile Courbebaisse and L. C. Antoine)
K: 21.10.1854. L: 17.4.1855. Comm: 1.5.1855. C: 7.1855.
Struck 24.5.1872 at Cherbourg, BU 1875.

Meuse Lorient Dyd/Mazeline (Constructeur, Charles Lamy Nettre)
Ord: 13.10.1854. Named: 30.10.1854. K: 26.10.1854. L: 24.11.1855. Comm: 1.2.1856. C: 2.1856.
Raised by a deck 8.1862-7.1865 at Brest. Struck 29.6.1881 at Lorient, mooring hulk. Coal hulk 1894, on sale list at Lorient 1904.

Nièvre Lorient Dyd/Mazeline (Constructeur, Nicolas Marie Julien Le Moine)
K: 26.10.1854. L: 26.10.1855 at Cherbourg. Comm: 8.12.1855. C: 1.1856.
Raised by a deck 3-9.1865 at Cherbourg. Struck 29.11.1871 at Cherbourg after running aground, BU 1874.

Meurthe Cherbourg Dyd/Cherbourg (Constructeur, Achille Antoine Guesnet)
K: 25.10.1854. L: 3.5.1855. Comm: 21.5.1855. C: 6.1855.
Struck 14.5.1866 at Saigon, repair hulk. Sold or BU 1872.

Yonne Cherbourg Dyd/Nillus (Constructeur, Adrien Charles Joyeux)
K: 28.4.1855. L: 12.11.1855. Comm: 4.3.1856. C: 4.1856.
Struck 24.2.1885 at Lorient, barracks hulk. Headquarters hulk for the the mobile defence force (*Défense mobile*) at Lorient 4.1896. On sale list 1914, sold or BU 1914-18.

SEINE – 1,200 tons, 160nhp, iron hull. On 12 July 1854 the Minister of Marine asked for studies of plans for a 1,200-ton transport similar to the wooden-hulled ones then being ordered but built of iron. Because of the number of wooden-hulled ships subsequently ordered and difficulties encountered in building iron ships, the Council of Works recommended constructing only one iron-hulled ship of this type, which would use an engine that had been ordered from Charles-Michel Nillus for a 13th ship of the *Loire* class. The Council went along with the selection of plans by Achille Antoine Guesnet for this ship, which were less risky and less expensive than the experimental plans by Jean-Baptiste Pastoureau-Labesse that the Council had preferred. The hull was ordered from Auguste Guibert at Nantes by a contract approved on 15 February 1855, and the engines were ordered from Nillus by a contract approved on 20 November 1854. (She has been attributed to Gustave Guibert, Auguste's nephew, but he built in Bordeaux.) Nillus had to provide new boilers under a supplement to this contract approved on 3 March 1856. *Seine* was first commissioned on 1 January 1857, probably to ferry the ship from the contractor's yard at Nantes to the naval dockyard at Lorient for completion of fitting out. She was then decommissioned on 22 January 1857 and recommissioned on 12 March 1857.

Dimensions & tons: 78.29m, 72.71m wl, 67.20m x 11.80m ext x 7.30m. 1,200/2,150 tons. Draught 4.30/4.90m. Men: 150.
Machinery: 160nhp. Coal 171 tons.
Guns: 4 x 12cm shell.

Seine Auguste Guibert, Nantes/Nillus (Constructeur, Jules Aurous)
Ord: 12.2.1855 (contract). K: 6.1855. L: 10.12.1856. Comm: 12.3.1857. C: 4.1857.
Sank 29.8.1882 during torpedo trials in Laninon Bay, refloated. Struck 8.11.1884 at Brest, BU 1885.

ADOUR Class – 900 tons, 120nhp, iron hulls. On 9 August 1854 the Minister of Marine asked the Council of Works to prepare specifications for an iron-hulled transport with a capacity of 500-600 tons and a speed of 8 knots. The specifications were sent to the ports on 27 September 1854 with a request that engineers there propose plans. The design was later lengthened by 11.90m to produce a 900-ton transport. The Council of Works noted on 23 January 1855 that the Minister now wanted to have Philip Taylor at La Seyne and Auguste Guibert at Nantes each build two of these ships, and it recommended adopting plans by Anselme De Roussel for use by Taylor. De Roussel's plans had been completed on 8 November 1854 and approved by the Minister of Marine on 23 January 1855. Taylor was to build the engines for his ships. They were described as *transports de matériel*, making them functional successors of the sailing gabarres. Taylor's shipyard soon became the Forges et Chantiers de la Méditerranée. *Adour* was initially commissioned on 18 January 1857 and *Ariège* was initially commissioned on 21 March 1857, decommissioned on 16 March 1858, and recommissioned on 25 January 1859. *Ariège* became known as one of the worst sea boats in the fleet. She was hauled out at Lorient in 1870 and was modified in 1873 by Francis-Joseph Barba to plans by Louis Marc Willotte with engines taken out of the frigate *Zénobie*, although plans for her reconfiguration had been prepared as early as 1866.

Dimensions & tons: 71.45m, 69.10m wl, 68.00m x 10.25m ext x 8.11m. 900/2,089 tons. Draught 4.50/5.50m. Men: 125.
Machinery: 120nhp. 720ihp (designed). Trials: 788.8ihp = 10.365kts (*Ariège*, 1873). Coal 156 tons.
Guns: (*Adour*, 1873) 2 x 14cm rifles No.1.

Adour Philip Taylor, La Seyne/Taylor.
K: 21.6.1855. L: 31.5.1856. C: 3.1857. Comm: 4.1859.
Converted to floating workshop 1872 at Brest. Struck 26.2.1886, repair hulk at Haiphong until 1895, sold there for BU 1905.

Ariège Philip Taylor, La Seyne/Taylor (Constructeur, De Roussel)
K: 7.1855. L: 31.7.1856. C: 4.1857. Comm: 25.1.1859.
Struck 13.5.1895 at Diégo Suarez, sold 1896 for BU.

SÈVRE Class – 900 tons, 120nhp, iron hulls. On 9 August 1854 the Minister of Marine asked the Council of Works to prepare specifications for an iron-hulled transport with a capacity of 500-600 tons and a speed of 8 knots. The specifications were sent to the ports on 27 September 1854 with a request that engineers there propose plans. The Council of Works noted on 23 January 1855 that the Minister now wanted to have Taylor at La Seyne and Guibert at Nantes each build two of these ships, and it recommended adopting plans by Henri Denis de Senneville for use by Guibert. The hulls were ordered from Guibert by a contract approved on 15 February 1855 and were completed by Ernest Gouin, who took over Guibert's yard in 1856. Gâche & Voruz were to build the engines for Guibert's ships but they were soon reassigned to Indret. They were described as *transports de matériel* and were intended to carry cargo but not troops. *Sèvre* first commissioned on 25 August 1857, decommissioned on 1 February 1858, and recommissioned on 7 January 1859, and *Mayenne* first commissioned on 22 October 1857, decommissioned on 23 April 1858, and recommissioned on 1 March 1859.

Dimensions & tons: 78.35m, 71.98m wl, 68.40m x 10.44m ext x 5.62m. 900/1,841 tons. Draught 3.62/4.96m. Men: 117.
Machinery: 120nhp. 346ihp (*Mayenne*). Coal 150 tons.
Guns: (*Sèvre* 1868) 2 x 14cm rifles.

Sèvre Auguste Guibert, Nantes/Indret (Constructeur, Jules Aurous)
Ord: 15.2.1855 (contract). K: 1.6.1855. L: 22.6.1857. C: 11.1857. Comm: 7.1.1859.
Driven aground by the Raz Blanchard, a strong tidal current between France and the Channel Islands, and lost 6.2.1871.

Mayenne Auguste Guibert, Nantes/Indret (Constructeur, Jules Aurous)
Ord: 15.2.1855 (contract). K: 1.6.1855. L: 18.9.1857. C: 12.1857. Comm: 1.3.1859.
Transferred 1.9.1876 to the Empire of Annam (Indochina) and struck on the same date (promulgated 11.10.1876).

LOIRET Class – 300 tons, 100nhp. On 14 July 1855 Achille Antoine Guesnet completed plans for a wooden *transport mixte* of 120nhp and 300 tons with hoisting screw propellers, and the plans were approved by the Minister of Marine on 24 August 1855 for two ships to be built at Cherbourg. The ships were ordered and named on 24 October 1855. *Loiret* received the Mazeline engine that had been removed from the 'corvette mixte' *Biche*, while a new 100nhp engine was built at Cherbourg for *Somme*. New three-cylinder engines for *Loiret* were ordered from Mazeline by a contract signed on 8 February 1861. These two ships were the antecedents of the many wooden-hulled small *transports-avisos* beginning with *Cher* and *Indre* built between 1862 and 1890, although the hull dimensions of the later ships were closer to those of the somewhat larger *Moselle*, below.

Dimensions & tons: 59.40m, 57.52m wl, 53.60m x 8.96m, 9.08m ext x 5.60m. 300/1,139 tons. Draught 3.58/4.68m. Men: 44.
Machinery: 100nhp. Trials: 323ihp = 8.10kts (*Loiret*, 1868). Coal 200 tons.
Guns: (*Somme*) 2 x 16cm shell; (*Loiret* 1868-81) 2 x 12cm rifles, 1 x 8.6cm rifle.

Loiret Cherbourg Dyd/from *Biche* (Constructeur, Louis François Vésignié)
Ord: 24.10.1855. K: 16.10.1855. L: 15.9.1856. Comm: 29.6.1857. C: 7.1857.
Struck 4.1.1882 at Rochefort, BU 1883.

Somme Cherbourg Dyd/Cherbourg.
Ord: 24.10.1855. K: 16.10.1855. L: 15.10.1856. Comm: 1.8.1857. C: 6.1858.

Struck 27.6.1872, headquarters hulk at Brest replacing *Nymphe*. Replaced by *Renommée* and became hulk at Kervallon 10.9.1882. Sold for BU 9.1886, BU 1887.

JURA Class – 1,200 tons, 250nhp. These six ships were ordered and named on 24 October 1855. They were of the *transport-écurie* (horse or cavalry transport) type and were designed to carry in addition to personnel 300 horses in two battery decks illuminated through small ports and equipped with a ventilation system. *Aube* could carry 362 horses or mules, 92 in the upper battery (*spardeck*), 174 in the lower battery (*faux-pont*), and 96 in the hold. She also carried a large landing barge for the horses. On 7 January 1856 the Council of Works recommended ordering eight steam engines from Mazeline, two for line of battle ships and six for *transports-écuries*: two each at Rochefort, Lorient, and Brest. This recommendation was approved on 16 January 1856. On 15 February 1856 the Council approved plans by Achille Antoine Guesnet for these six *transports-écuries mixtes* of 200nhp and 1,200 tons. The plan to order the engines from Mazeline fell through and 250nhp engines for all six ships were ordered from Schneider by a contract approved on 6 June 1856. These ships had larger steam engines than the *Loire* class and the funnel and boiler were moved to the usual position forward of the mainmast.

Dimensions & tons: 82.70m, 79.43m wl, 76.50m x 12.95m ext x 8.00m. 1,200/3,230 tons. Draught 5.10/6.00m. Men: 200.
Machinery: 250nhp. 800ihp (designed). Trials: 714ihp = 9.62kts (*Rhône*, 1867, no cargo), 612ihp = 8.83kts (*Jura*, 1871, fully loaded). Coal 232-349 tons.
Guns: 4 x 16cm shell.

Finistère was one of six transports for carrying horses in addition to troops ordered in 1855 and built with two complete battery decks with small ports for light and air. The sponson amidships housed the latrines for the troops. She was photographed at Brest around the early 1880s by Emile Mage, who was active there from 1860 to 1900. (USN NH-88813, from an ONI album of foreign warships dated about 1900.)

Jura Lorient Dyd/Schneider (Constructeur, Nicolas Marie Julien Le Moine)
  Ord: 24.10.1855. K: 21.4.1856. L: 13.7.1858. Comm: 19.7.1858. C: 4.1859.
  Struck 18.7.1883 at Toulon, barracks hulk for the naval infantry at Toulon. Sold for BU 1888.

Calvados Lorient Dyd/Schneider (Constructeur, Nicolas Marie Julien Le Moine)
  Ord: 24.10.1855. K: 26.4.1856. L: 14.8.1858. Comm: 23.8.1858. C: 4.1859.
  Struck 5.6.1886 at Toulon, sold for BU 1887.

Garonne Brest Dyd/Schneider (Constructeurs, Jules-Philibert Guède and Charles Frédéric Peschart-d'Ambly)
  Ord: 24.10.1855. K: 2.5.1856. L: 22.10.1858. Comm: 25.4.1859. C: 6.1859.
  Struck 2.4.1891 at Brest, BU 1891.

Rhône Brest Dyd/Schneider (Constructeur, Jules-Philibert Guède and Théophile Zéphyrin Compère-Desfontaines)
  Ord: 24.10.1855. K: 2.5.1856. L: 18.4.1859. Comm: 1.10.1859. C: 12.1859.
  Prison ship at Cherbourg 1871. Struck 29.10.1874 at Cherbourg,

towed to Rochefort for use as a mooring hulk. Sold for BU 1899.
Finistère Rochefort Dyd/Schneider (Constructeur, Henri Paul Denis de Senneville)
 Ord: 24.10.1855. K: 30.5.1856. L: 1.8.1859. Comm: 29.10.1859. C: 2.1860.
 Struck 18.10.1886 at Lorient, barracks hulk. Coal hulk 1898, mooring hulk 1900. Sold 19.3.1921.
Aube Rochefort Dyd/Schneider (Constructeur, Henri Paul Denis de Senneville)
 Ord: 24.10.1855. K: 15.4.1856. L: 31.8.1859. Comm: 12.1859. C: 3.1860.
 Struck 22.7.1872 at Brest. BU 1875.

DRYADE – 1,250 tons, 250nhp. This 50-gun 2nd Rank sailing frigate was laid down on 26 March 1847 and was still on the ways when it was decided in 1856 to convert her to a mixed propulsion transport. For this purpose she was lengthened by about 20 metres (6 gunports) and given 250nhp engines by Mazeline. Her conversion plans were by Louis-Édouard Lecointre. Three 250nhp engines for *Dryade, Amazone,* and *Entreprenante* were ordered from Mazeline by a contract approved on 11 July 1856.

A ministerial circular dated 7 January 1859 noted that the frigates *Amazone, Cérès, Dryade,* and *Entreprenante* had been converted to transports by lengthening the hulls and by increasing the height of the upperworks, presumably by adding a second battery deck. It stated that this mode of conversion combined with the use of low-powered propulsion machinery made these vessels unsuited to be used later as combatant frigates and directed that they henceforth be referred to as *transports à batterie*. The specially-built transports of 1,200 tons and below, which had previously used this name, would henceforth be known simply as transports, with indication of their tonnage. Other converted frigates such as *Danaé, Renommée,* and *Pandore,* while some were fitted as transports, would continue to be called *frégates mixtes*.
 Dimensions & tons: 72.80m, 71.55m wl x 14.43m ext. 1,250/2,890 tons. Draught 6.38m aft. Men: 200.
 Machinery: 250nhp. Trials (1870) 855ihp = 9.61kts. Coal 243-290 tons.
 Guns: (1859) 2 x 30pdrs No.2; (1860, for mission to China) 12 x 30pdrs No.2
Dryade Lorient Dyd/Mazeline (converted by Lecointre)
 Conversion began: 6.1856. L: 29.12.1856. Comm: 15.3.1858. C: 6.1858.
 Struck 13.2.1883, reserve headquarters hulk at Toulon. Renamed *Iéna* 1886. Sold 24.12.1896, BU 1897.

CÉRÈS – 1,100 tons, 200nhp. This 40-gun 3rd Rank sailing frigate was laid down on 2 January 1847 and was still on the ways when it was decided in 1856 to convert her to a mixed propulsion transport. For this purpose she was lengthened by about 22 metres (5 gunports), fitted with a second battery deck, and given 200nhp engines built at Lorient. Her conversion plans were by Louis Édouard Lecointre.
 Dimensions & tons: 71.75m, 70.25m wl x 13.44m ext. 1,100/3,139 tons. Draught 5.93m aft. Men: 200
 Machinery: 200nhp. Trials (1872) 724ihp = 9.32kts.
 Guns: (1859) 2 x 30pdrs
Cérès Lorient Dyd-Caudan/Lorient (converted by Charles Lamy Nettre)
 Conversion began: 5.1856. L: 26.3.1857. Comm: 27.4.1859. C: 4.1859.
 Struck 8.11.1884, headquarters hulk for the the mobile defence force (*Défense mobile*) at Toulon, BU 1896.

AMAZONE – c1,500 tons, 250nhp. This 50-gun 2nd Rank sailing frigate was laid down on 2 January 1845 and was still on the ways when it was decided in 1856 to convert her to a mixed propulsion transport. For this purpose she was lengthened by about 20 metres and given 250nhp engines by Mazeline. Her 250nhp engines were among three sets ordered from Mazeline by a contract approved on 11 July 1856. Her conversion plans were by Charles Auxcousteaux, who then submitted additional plans to fit her for transportation of convicts that were approved by the Council of Works on 2 November 1858. Her machinery was installed between 1 July and 15 December 1858.
 Dimensions & tons: 72.85m, 71.70m wl x 14.06m ext. c1,500/3,155 tons. Draught 6.75m aft. Men: 200
 Machinery: 250nhp.
 Guns: 4 x 30pdrs No.2
Amazone Brest Dyd/Mazeline (converted by Auxcousteaux and Anselme De Roussel)
 Conversion began: 1.1857. L: 30.3.1858. Comm: 2.4.1859.
 Disabled in a hurricane in the Antilles off Saint Thomas 10.10.1871, condemned 30.10.1871 at Fort de France, struck there 15.2.1872, decomm. there 15.8.1872, BU 1873.

ENTREPRENANTE – 1,300 tons, 250nhp. This 60-gun 1st Rank sailing frigate was laid down on 5 October 1829 and was still on the ways when it was decided in 1856 to convert her to a mixed propulsion transport. For this purpose she was lengthened by about 23 metres (5 ports), fitted with a second battery deck, and given engines of 250nhp by Mazeline. Conversion plans by Louis Édouard Lecointre were approved by the Council of Works on 13 September 1856 and plans for finer lines at the bow were approved on 3 February 1857. Her 250nhp engines were among three sets ordered from Mazeline by a contract approved on 11 July 1856. She is not to be confused with the brig *Entreprenant*, which was converted to a transport after serving as a 14-gun brig (q.v.).
 Dimensions & tons: 78.10 deck, 77.00m wl x 14.44m ext. 1,300/4,063 tons. Draught 7.20m aft. Men: 200.
 Machinery: 250nhp. Designed 960ihp, trials (1859) 826.2ihp = 10.21kts. Coal 246-300 tons.
 Guns: (1859) 2 x 30pdrs No.2.
Entreprenante Lorient Dyd/Mazeline
 Conversion began: 1856. L: 4.11.1858. Comm: 11.11.1858.
 Struck 6.7.1885, barracks hulk at Toulon until 1893, sold for BU 18.6.1896.

MOSELLE – 900 tons, 120nhp, iron hull. *Elizabeth Jane*, an iron-hulled 160nhp mixed propulsion (auxiliary screw) merchant ship completed in 1857 by J. & G. Thompson, Govan, Scotland, (their hull No.31) was purchased by the French Navy on 25 May 1859 as a *transport de matériel*. She had no passenger accommodation. Until then sailing gabarres had been used for this purpose. The name *Moselle* was recommended for this ship on 27 May 1859. The French liked her enough to build two iron-hulled copies in the early to mid-1860s, *Vienne* and *Isère*, and the iron *Caravane* of the early 1870s was also based on the plans of *Moselle*.
 Dimensions & tons: 63.70m, 62.20m wl, 59.62m x 9.34m, 9.40m ext x 5.80m. 900/1,971 tons. Draught 4.80/5.00m. Men: 48.
 Machinery: 120nhp. Trials (1867): 262ihp = 6.56 knots (in heavy weather and fully loaded). Coal 151-190 tons.
 Guns: 2 x 4pdr (8.6cm) mountain.
Moselle J. & G. Thompson, Govan.
 L: 11.12.1856. Comm: 26.5.1859.
 Struck 9.2.1887.

ARDÈCHE Class – 1,200 tons, 300nhp. On 28 October 1859 the Minister of Marine ordered two *transports-écuries* similar to *Jura* and *Calvados* from Cherbourg and two from Rochefort. On the same date the Director of Naval Construction wrote that the Minister had ordered him to prepare to lay down ten new ships of this type, including the four at the two dockyards and six to be ordered from private firms. He proposed to order three hulls from Arman, one from Bichon frères, and one from Moulinié, all at Bordeaux, plus one from Ernest Gouin at Nantes. The five ships at Bordeaux were ordered from three shipbuilders by contracts signed on 18 November 1859, and the single Nantes ship was ordered by a contract signed on 25 November 1859. The engines for all six ships were ordered from Schneider by a contract signed on 3 February 1860. The Director of Ports asked Achille Antoine Guesnet to modify his plans for the *Jura* type based on experience with them, and on 25 November 1859 the Minister approved Guesnet's new plans (type *Ardèche*, based on *Rhône*), which were a little longer and wider. The names for the ships were recommended on 26 December 1859. The four dockyard ships were increased to 500 HP, making them a separate class (see below). They had two battery decks like other horse transports and could carry 440 horses and 400 cavalry personnel.

Dimensions & tons: 86.13m, 80.33m wl, 77.18m x 13.00m ext x 7.74m. 1,200/3,200 tons. Draught 5.40/6.00m. Men: 200.
Machinery: 300nhp. 920ihp (designed). Trials: 982ihp = 10.41kts (*Var*, 1872), 692ihp = 9.09kts (*Ardèche*, 1871). Coal 200-380 tons.
Guns: 4 x 16cm shell.

Ardèche Lucien Arman, Bordeaux/Schneider (Constructeur, Joseph Alexandre De Gasté)
 K: 31.1.1860. L: 4.12.1861. Comm: 1.4.1862.
 Struck 11.11.1875 at Toulon, gunnery storage hulk. Sold for BU 1887.

Drôme Lucien Arman, Bordeaux/Schneider (Constructeur, Joseph Alexandre De Gasté)
 K: 1859. L: 25.10.1862. Comm: 11.2.1863. C: 5.1863.
 Struck 22.7.1872 at Brest. BU 1875.

Var Lucien Arman, Bordeaux/Schneider (Constructeur, Joseph Alexandre De Gasté)
 K: 31.1.1860. L: 12.12.1863. Comm: 25.3.1864. C: 4.1864.
 Struck 31.12.1879 at Toulon, hulk not used. Sold for BU 1896.

Allier Ernest Gouin, Nantes/Schneider (Constructeur, Charles Marie Hippolyte Auxcousteaux)
 K: 1859. L: 11.12.1861. Comm: 3.7.1862. C: early 1863.
 Not renamed *Dragon* 3.1.1865 as sometimes reported, was still named *Allier* in late 1.1866 when she called at Martinique with a battalion of zouaves who mutinied when put ashore. Struck 26.11.1868 at Brest, probably BU 1869. Engines transferred to *Rhin* (*Loire* class, above) 1869.

Eure Moulinié & Labat, Bordeaux/Schneider (Constructeurs, Joseph Alexandre De Gasté, Joseph Eugène Piedvache, and Nathaniel Lucien Villaret)
 K: 16.12.1859. L: 16.4.1862. Comm: 22.5.1862. C: 8.1862.
 Struck 22.7.1872 at Brest. BU 1877.

Orne Gustave & Arnaud-Frédéric Bichon, Bordeaux-Lormont/Schneider (Constructeurs, Joseph Alexandre De Gasté, Joseph Eugène Piedvache, and Nathaniel Lucien Villaret)
 K: 12.1859. L: 26.9.1862. Comm: 1.1.1863. C: 3.1863.
 Struck 5.6.1891 at Rochefort, BU 1891.

SARTHE Class – 1,500 tons (first two 1,530 tons), 500nhp. On 28 October 1859 the Minister of Marine ordered two *transports-écuries* similar to *Jura* and *Calvados* from Cherbourg and two from Rochefort. On the same date the Director of Naval Construction wrote that the Minister had ordered him to prepare to lay down ten new ships of this type, including the four at the two dockyards and six to be ordered from private firms. The four dockyard ships were increased to 500 HP, making them a separate class and causing them to be described as high-speed cavalry transports (*transports-écuries à grande vitesse*). Like earlier horse transports they had two battery decks. Plans for the ships by Achille Antoine Guesnet were approved by the Minister and sent to the ports on 23 March 1860 and their names were approved on 4 April 1860. *Tarn* was probably added to the class in 1860, and plans by Dutard for modifications to her stern were approved on 28 September 1860. All five engines were probably built at Indret. All five were built up aft at Toulon in 1871-73 by the addition of a poop deck and roundhouse.

Dimensions & tons: 87.20m, 82.00m wl, 78.80m x 13.52m ext x 8.14m. 1,530/3,607 tons. Draught 5.85/6.55m. Men: 211.
Machinery: 500nhp. 1720ihp (designed). Trials: 1634ihp = 14.0kts (*Tarn*, 1865), 1618ihp = 11,65kts (*Tarn*, 1874), 1249ihp = 10.66kts (*Sarthe*, 1872). Coal 310-600 tons.
Guns: 4 x 16cm shell.

Sarthe Cherbourg Dyd/Indret
 Ord: 28.10.1859. K: 8.4.1860. L: 25.11.1862. Comm: 9.7.1863. C: 10.1863.
 Struck 11.12.1896 at Toulon, barracks hulk. Renamed *Vem* 1901, sold for BU 1911.

Aveyron Cherbourg Dyd/Indret (Constructeurs, Jean Félix De Robert and others)
 Ord: 28.10.1859. K: 5.7.1860. L: 3.9.1864. Comm: 6.7.1865. C: 10.1865.
 Driven by high winds onto the wreck of another ship (*Mekong*, lost in 1877) off Cape Guardafui on 21.8.1884. Could not be saved and was burned by her crew, who with 254 passengers were rescued by passing merchant ships.

Creuse Rochefort Dyd/Indret (Constructeurs, Henri-Paul Denis de Senneville and Auguste Émile Boden)
 Ord: 28.10.1859. K: 11.4.1860. L: 29.8.1863. Comm: 1.5.1864. C: 9.1864.
 Struck 2.4.1891 and BU.

Corrèze Rochefort Dyd/Indret (Constructeurs, Alfred François Lebelin de Dionne, Henri De Lisleferme, Jean Baron, and Henri Paul Denis de Senneville)
 Ord: 28.10.1859. K: 1.9.1861. L: 23.5.1868. Comm: 1869. C: 6.1869.
 Hospital ship at Diego Suarez 1885. Engines removed at Toulon 1889-92, Struck 5.2.1892 at Toulon, then sent back under sail to Diego Suarez as hospital hulk. BU 1896.

Tarn Toulon Dyd/Indret (Constructeurs, Louis Dutard and others)
 K: 8.1860. L: 10.12.1863. Comm: 2.9.1864. C: 9.1864.
 Struck 4.11.1889 at Toulon, barracks hulk. Hospital at Toulon 1897, barracks for 'isolés' 1901, BU 1905.

EUROPÉEN – 2,350 tons, 500nhp, steel hull. In 1855 Scott & Co., Greenock, Scotland, completed the steel-hulled passenger and cargo ship *European* (their hull No.23). On 2 November 1859 the Minister of Marine ordered that a commission be sent to Britain to buy three steamers to transport to China as many as possible of the 20 screw *chaloupes canonnières* (*Nos.12-31*) that were under construction for a forthcoming China expedition. The purchase contract for *Européen* was concluded on 14 November 1859 and the purchase was completed on 18 November 1859. The three ships retained the French versions of their mercantile names. *Européen* could carry 850 tons of cargo.

Dimensions & tons: 93.20m, 89.14m wl, 85.00m x 11.90m x 8.35m.

Européen at Algiers around the early 1880s while she was assigned to the Algerian station. This large British-built steel-hulled merchant ship was one of three purchased by the French to transport gun launches and other cargo to the Far East for operations against China in 1860. (USN NH-74878, from an ONI album of French warships)

2,350/3,747 tons. Draught 5.70/6.30m. Men: 119.
Machinery: 500nhp. Trials (1872): 1206ihp = 11.25kts. Coal 600-645 tons.
Guns: 2 x 14cm.

Européen Greenock.
K: 1854. L: 24.4.1855. Comm: 25.12.1859 at Glasgow.
Headquarters ship of the mobile defence force (*Défense mobile*) at Toulon and annex to *Japon* 1887 (made trips to Salins d'Hyères and back). Commissioned 20.9.1891 to replace *Loire* as barracks hulk at Saigon. Struck 2.4.1895 at Saigon, coal hulk 1896-1907, BU 1911.

WESER – 2,500 tons, 600nhp, steel or iron hull. *Weser* was built by Palmer Bros. & Co., Jarrow-on-Tyne, England, for the North German Lloyd in 1858. She was one of the first four ships built for this firm, the others being her sister *Hudson* by Palmer and *Bremen* and *New York* by Caird, Greenock. *Weser* had a clipper stem, two funnels, and three masts rigged for sail. There was accommodation for 70 1st, 100 2nd and 450 3rd Class passengers. She sailed from Bremen on her maiden voyage to New York on 4 December 1858 but had to put back to Cork for repairs after being damaged by heavy seas. She sailed from Cork on 6 March 1859 and arrived in New York on 18 March 1859. She started her third and last Bremen–Southampton–New York voyage on 1 July 1859. On 2 November 1859 the Minister of Marine ordered that a commission be sent to Britain to buy three steamers to transport to China as many as possible of the 20 screw *chaloupes canonnières* (*Nos.12-31*) that were under construction for a forthcoming China expedition. The purchase contract for *Weser* was concluded on 17 November 1859 and the purchase was completed on 24 November 1859. The three ships retained the French versions of their mercantile names.

Weser's sister *Hudson* was launched on 12 June 1858 and started her maiden voyage on 11 September 1858. After this voyage she was damaged by fire in dock at Bremerhaven on 2 November 1858 and was towed to Palmer's yard where she was rebuilt and had one funnel removed. She was sold and renamed *Louisiana* in 1862 and was scrapped in 1894.

Dimensions & tons: 99.8m pp x 12.1m. 2,500/4,000 tons. Draught 7.8m. Men: 150.
Machinery: 600nhp. 10kts.
Guns: ?

Weser Palmer Bros., Jarrow.
K: 1857. L: 21.10.1858. Comm: 17.12.1859.
Wrecked 16.1.1861 at the mouth of the Mekong River 27 miles southwest of Vung Tau, 400 passengers and most of the crew being rescued by the paddle aviso *Shamrock*. Struck 25.4.1861.

JAPON – 2,300 tons, 400nhp, steel hull. In 1857 the Caird shipbuilding firm at Greenock, Scotland, completed the steel-hulled cargo ship *Japan* (their hull No.57). On 2 November 1859 the Minister of Marine ordered that a commission be sent to Britain to buy three steamers to transport to China as many as possible of the 20 screw *chaloupes canonnières* (*Nos.12-31*) that were under construction for a forthcoming China expedition. The purchase contract for *Japon* was concluded on 3 December 1859 and the purchase was completed on 5 December 1859. The three ships retained the French versions of their mercantile names. *Japon* could carry 900 tons of cargo at a draught of 6.25 metres and had two enclosed decks (*entreponts*). Plans for embarking torpedo launches on this ship were drafted in 1880. She was attached to the torpedo school at Toulon in 1884 and served as a torpedo training and depot ship. In 1898 she was converted to a collier and fitted with Temperley equipment that allowed her to transfer coal to ships of the fleet while underway at 10 knots. She could carry 2,500 tons of coal in addition to her own supply.

Dimensions & tons: 100.00m, 94.50m wl, 90.50m x 12.30m ext x 8.28m. 2,300/4,017 tons. Draught 5.20/5.80m. Men: 150.
Machinery: 400nhp. 1200ihp (designed). Trials (1869): 1671.4ihp = 12.41kts. Coal 634-726 tons.
Guns: 2 x 14cm.

Japon Caird, Greenock.
L: 1857. Comm: 19.1.1860.
Torpedo school and torpedo boat transport at Toulon (Salins d'Hyères) 1884-92. Headquarters ship of the mobile defence force (*Défense Mobile*) at Toulon 1896. Converted 1898 to collier for Mediterranean Fleet (rig reduced to two masts fitted with Temperley system for coaling ships underway). Struck 22.11.1902. BU at Marseilles 1903 (broke in half during demolition).

14 The Smaller Transports

This chapter includes a variety of smaller naval auxiliaries used for the transportation of troops, stores and other material. In general, all these were sailing vessels of below 200 tons, but they had a range of different designations. Ship types included sloops, galiotes, doggers, and a few chasse-marées. Larger naval auxiliaries were normally called *flûtes* or *gabarres* and are listed in Chapter 13.

(A) Smaller transports in service or on order at 1 January 1786

Three British prizes taken in 1778-82 were put into service as small transports, as were three other vessels fitted out at Brest in 1780-81 for naval service; several others were acquired in 1779-82, and another was acquired in 1783 for service in the Indian Ocean. The only ones which seem to have survived beyond 1785 were the chasse-marées *Cormoran* and *Turbot*, built at Brest in 1776, *Marie-Françoise* and *Grondin* (ex-*Saint Esprit*) placed in service at Brest in May 1778; the *Saint François* launched at the Chantier du Blanc just upriver from the dockyard at Lorient in November of that year; and the *Saint Guillaume* acquired at Brest in 1784 (all six still in existence in 1789), and the *Félicité* acquired in 1781, which (renamed *Fabuleux* in May 1795) survived to September 1796 at Lorient. A *Saint Jean* was placed in service at Brest in 1789 but left no further record. All were small unarmed service craft of about 30 burthen tons each.

Numbered chasse-marées built in 1785. 20 of these vessels, all of 90/150 tons, were built at Lorient (*Nos.1-12*), Auray (*Nos.13-16*) and

The vessel in the foreground of this engraving by Jean-Jérôme Baugean is identified as a dogger as understood at the time (1814). Originally fore-and-aft ketch-rigged North Sea fishing vessels, operating on and around the Dogger Bank, they became larger coastal cargo carriers (up to about 250 tons), at the same time acquiring square canvas. The mainmast remained stepped relatively far aft and in this example sets a course, topsail and topgallant. The mizzen carries a gaff course and a square topsail. According to Baugean, those from North Sea ports tended to retain the round stern whereas those from the Atlantic coasts had developed a flat transom.

The vessel in the background is a chasse-marée. These were rigged like luggers, but the term was usually applied to local fishing and coasting types with fuller hull forms than the kind of luggers used by the navy and privateers.

Redon (*Nos.17-20*) to help in construction works at Cherbourg. The Lorient vessels were built by four different builders, all under the supervision of Charles Segondat-Duvernet; the Auray and Redon building was supervised by C.-B. Selve (and there may have been a further eight of these, *Nos.21-28*, built at Redon but records are unclear). Originally numbered but not named, ten of the twenty (numbers unknown) were converted to gunboats at Cherbourg in 1793-94 and given names; details of these are to be found in Chapter 9. Of the unconverted units, *No.2* was wrecked 9.3.1812, *No.5* and *No.6* (or *No.8?*) were decommissioned as coast guard vessels at La Hogue in 1802, *No.16* was lost in 1.1794, and *No.18* became the 77-ton lugger *Pourvoyeur* in 1807 and lasted until 1826.

Dimensions & tons: 57ft 0in, 49ft 0in x 18ft 9in x 7ft 0in (18.52, 15.92 x 6.09 x 2.27m). 90/150 tons. Draught 5ft 7in/6ft 7in (1.89/2.14m).

(B) Smaller transports acquired from 1 January 1786

Sloops built at Honfleur in 1786. 35 of these vessels, all of between 28 and 36 tons, were constructed at Honfleur in 1786 on the orders of Pierre Derubé for help in construction works at Cherbourg, using seven different builders:

Pierre & Jacques Fortier (4 of 30 tons) – *Minerve, Protée, Thémis,* one other.
Jean Gallon (10 of 30 to 35 tons) – *Amphitrite, Bonne Société, Castor, Danae, Galathée, Orphée, Pluton, Pollux, Triton, Urbins.*
Nicolas Loquet (2 of 32 and 36 tons) – *Amis Réunis, Vraye Humanité.*
Joseph-Augustin Normand (8 of 28 tons) – *Aurore, Céres, Circé, Diane, Hébé, Junon, Médée, Vénus.*
Louis-François Normand (3 of 28 tons) – *Annapolis, Lévrier, Makalos.*
Pierre Paysant (3 of 30 tons) – *Adonis, Astrée, Cerbere.*
Louis Pestel (5 of 30 to 32 tons) – *Amis Fideles, Conception, Elus, Pérou, Triple Alliance.*

ÉLAN Group – doggers (*dogres*). Doggers were two-masted vessels, not dissimilar to ketches (from which the type derived). Initially employed as fishing vessels, when they were gaff-rigged on the mainmast, and carried a lugsail on the mizzen, with two jibs on a long bowsprit. They were sturdy workboats, and thus were often used for auxiliary naval purposes, being relatively short and wide-beamed.

Four doggers were taken up from mercantile service at Nantes and commissioned as gunboats or bomb vessels in June 1794 with 3 guns each – *Gotiche* (requisitioned in December 1793), *Blanche, Saint Jacques* and *Victoire Sophie* (the last two renamed *Inévitable* and *Vérificateur* respectively in May 1795). *Gotiche, Blanche* and *Saint Jacques* are listed in Chapter 9 as gunboats while *Victoire Sophie* is listed in Chapter 10 as a bomb vessel.

Three more doggers (see below) were built in 1794-96. These may have been to a common design, but this is not certain. *Oreste* and *Pylade* should not be confused with the Venetian cutters of the same names, seized on the stocks in 1797. A fourth dogger built at this time, *Éléphant*, was listed as a bateau-plat and then as a prame, she is described in Chapter 9.

Dimensions & tons: dimensions unknown. 111-150/200 tons. Men: 15-19 (*Pilade* 48 in 1799).
Guns: *Oreste* carried 4 x 4pdrs, while *Pilade* seemingly mounted 2 x 24pdrs. *Élan* was unarmed.

Élan Le Havre
K: 1794. L: 6.7.1795. C: 12.1795.
Converted 12.1821 to hulk at Rochefort, then sent to Bordeaux for use by the medical service there. Struck 1.1822.

Oreste Le Havre
K: 1795. L: 22.4.1796. C: 6.1796.
Became service craft at Brest after 5.1814; struck soon after 10.1816.

Pilade (*Pylade*) Rouen.
K: 1795. L: 8.1797. C: 9.1797.
Was a gunboat in 1799 with 2 x 24pdrs, probably disarmed by 1801. Captured 5.1803 or 9.1803 by the British.

LABORIEUSE Class – 70 tons (brig-rigged). These small vessels were officially rated as gabarres.
Dimensions & tons: dimensions unknown. 70/180 tons. Men: 21 as transport, 96 as gunboat (1803).
Guns: 2 x 1pdr swivels as transport, 6 x 8pdrs as gunboat (1803).

Laborieuse Le Havre
K: 1795. L: 11.4.1796. C: 5.1796.
Converted to a gunboat at Brest in 9.1803, a transport at Antwerp in 7.1810 (designated *Transport No.619 Laborieuse*), and a gunboat at Brest in 1812. By 11.1819 she was again listed as a transport, having been absent from the list in 1816 and 1818. Service craft at Brest 12.1826, struck 2.1827, BU 3.1827.

Portefaix Le Havre
K: 1795. L: 11.4.1796. C: 5.1796.
Became receiving ship (*cayenne*) at Rouen 4.1804, recommissioned 1806 as transport. Sold 8.1814 at Le Havre.

Porteuse Le Havre
K: 1795. L: 7.1796. C: 21.8.1796.
Offered for sale 3.1798 at Le Havre but not sold and refitted 2.1801 for further service. Also known as *Brick No.2* around 1802 and in 1814. Sold 8.1814 at Le Havre.

PURCHASED AND REQUISITIONED TRANSPORTS (1793-1801). This was a miscellaneous collection of small vessels, procured to meet the needs of the day including those of successive military campaigns beginning in 1794 with the revolutionary French advance into the Austrian Netherlands and the suppression of the Royalist counter-revolution in the Vendée. The amount of details available on these vessels is limited, sometimes to little more than a name on a manuscript list. They are listed chronologically in estimated order of entering service. Hired vessels are generally excluded.

Acquired 1793

Union (sloop hired or requisitioned at Le Havre in early 1793). Wrecked 7.1793 while returning from Martinique.

Neptune (former slave ship in service at Le Havre in 11.1790, hired there 5.1793, and requisitioned 3.1794, 242 tons). Captured 9.1794 by the British.

Découverte (sloop built at Dunkirk and probably requisitioned and commissioned there in 5.1793 to defend the roadstead, carried 6 x 3pdrs and 2 x 12pdr obusiers). Last mentioned in early 1795 at Dunkirk and struck before 5.1795.

Aimable Henriette (Requisitioned 12.1793 at Le Havre to transport material from Brest to Cherbourg via Saint-Malo under a merchant captain). Decomm. 3.1794 and probably returned to her owner.

Adelaide (whaling ship completed in 2.1792 and requisitioned at Lorient in 1793, 200 tons, 29 men, carried 2 x 6pdrs). Returned to her owner 1.1795 and placed under the American flag.

Deux Amis (merchant brig requisitioned 1793 at Le Havre, 108 tons, 20 men, 4 guns). Renamed *Amis* 5.1795. Struck late 1795 and probably returned. Other ships named *Deux Amis* included an ex-Dutch floating battery (see Chapter 10), an otherwise unidentified transport captured in 8.1800 off Malta by the British, and several privateers.

Diligente (requisitioned at Le Havre 1793). Probably returned 1793-94.

François-Marie (cutter requisitioned at Le Havre 1793). Probably returned 1793-94.

Hercule (requisitioned at Le Havre 1793). Probably returned 1793-94.

Jeanne (brig requisitioned at Le Havre 1793). Probably returned 1793-94.

Septentrion (requisitioned at Le Havre 1793). Probably returned 1793-94.

Acquired 1794 at Le Havre and Dunkirk

Mélomane (merchant vessel requisitioned 1.1794 at Le Havre, 305 tons). Returned to her owner in 1794. Was a hulk at Cherbourg in 10.1799.

Quatre Frères (Dutch-built galiote requisitioned early 1794 at Le Havre, 70 tons, carried 2 x 1pdrs). Was in service 8.1794 at Dinard, struck at the end of 1794 and probably returned.

Bon Père (merchant vessel requisitioned 2.1794 at Le Havre, 268 tons, 20 men, carried 2 x 4pdrs). Struck late 1795 and probably returned.

Bon Frère (sloop requisitioned 2.1794 at Le Havre). Fate unknown.

Jeune Louis (merchant vessel requisitioned 2.1794 at Le Havre and commissioned as a transport, 330 tons). Commissioned as 'corvette' *Émulation* in late 1794, struck 7.1795 and returned to her owner in need of extensive repairs.

Républicain (merchant vessel *Saint-Esprit* requisitioned 2.1794 at Le Havre, 180 tons, carried 1 x 4pdr). Last mentioned 8.1794 at Dinard, then struck and probably returned.

Anonyme (requisitioned 2.1794 at Le Havre, 270 tons). Returned before the end of 1794. A transport named *Anonyme* made a voyage from Lorient to Paimbœuf in 2.1795 and a requisitioned or hired brig of the same name was wrecked off Treffiagat on 6.6.1795.

Jeune André (requisitioned 2.1794 at Le Havre, 276-289 tons). Returned before the end of 1794.

Nouvelle Étoile (requisitioned 2.1794 at Le Havre, 179 tons). Returned before the end of 1794.

Paix (brig requisitioned 2.1794 at Le Havre, 224 tons). Returned before the end of 1794. Served as an aviso in 1-2.1796.

Perrier or *Le Perier* (requisitioned 2.1794 at Le Havre, 200 tons). Returned before the end of 1794.

Phoenix or *Phénix* (requisitioned 2.1794 at Le Havre, 235 tons). Returned before the end of 1794.

Prudent (requisitioned 2.1794 at Le Havre, 199 tons). Returned before the end of 1794.

Saint-Pierre (merchant lugger requisitioned 3.1794 at Le Havre, 180 tons, 15 men). Renamed *Stoïcien* 5.1795. Struck late 1795 and probably returned.

Jeune Auguste (former slave ship from Le Havre completed 12.1791 and requisitioned 3.1794, 170 tons, carried 12 x 4pdrs). Renamed *Intercepté* 5.1795 while in service at Cherbourg. Struck late 1795 and probably returned.

Suzanne (merchant vessel requisitioned 3.1794 at Le Havre, 221-266 tons). Returned late 1794, requisitioned again 1795, returned 1796.

Transports requisitioned in 3.1794 at Le Havre. *Ajax* (340 tons) *Concorde*, *Espérance*, *Gentille* (315 tons), *Jeune Eugénie* (346 tons), *Jeune Victoire*, *Louise* (280 tons) *Mentor* (349 tons), *Turgot*. Struck before the end of 1794 or in early 1795.

Other transports requisitioned in 1794 at Le Havre. *Akim* (510 tons), *Alexandre*, *Alliance* (galiote),*Amazone*, *Amérique* (274 tons), *Ami des Lois* (367 tons), *Annette* (367 tons), *Astrée* (16 tons), *August-Félicité*, *Aziz*, *Belle-Françoise*, *Bergère* (304 tons), *Bien-Aimé* (441 tons), *Bien-Aimé* (140 tons), *Bienfaisant* (brig, 188 tons), *Bonne Aventure* (brig), *Brutus* (250 tons), *Catherine* (120 tons), *Cécile-Charlotte* (372 tons), *Charles* (300 tons), *Charmante-Rose* (218 tons), *Cultivateur*, *Conquête de l'Amérique* (150 tons), *David* (sloop), *Deux* Frères (galiote, 62 tons), *Deux Soeurs Créoles* (359 tons), *Étoile-Brillante* (200 tons), *Europe* (271 tons), *Fort-Samson* (127 tons), *Galathée* (330 tons), *Gange* (462 tons), *Guillaume-Tell* (76 tons, from Nantes), *Héros* (287 tons, former slaver completed 7.1784), *Jeune-Adélaïde*, *Jeune Alexandrine* (235 tons), *Jeune-Camille*, *Jeune-Robert*, *Jeune-Sophie*, *Juste* (352 tons), *Magdelaine* or *Madeleine*, *Marguerite-Unie* (180 tons), *Marie* (brig), *Marie-Françoise-Providence*, *Marie-Joseph* (320 tons), *Marie-Louise* (184 tons), *Marthe* (281 tons), *Mercure* (100 tons), *Minerve*, *Pétronille*, *Phocéen* (131 tons), *Quatre-Soeurs*, *Rose-Éléonore* (280 tons), *Sans-Culotte de Calais*, *Thémistocle* (370 tons), *Union* (brigantine, 265 tons), *Ville d'Arcangel*, *Ville de Rouen* (brig, 199 tons), and *Zéphir* (300 tons). Struck before the end of 1794 or in early 1795. Several were later hired, including in 1796-97 for use as cartel (prisoner exchange) ships.

Pallas (former slave ship from Le Havre completed in 7.1789 and requisitioned there in 1794, 435 tons, 25 men). Returned to her owner in late 1794, hired 4-7.1797 as a cartel ship.

Élisabeth-Judith or *Jeune Élisabeth* (vessel requisitioned 6.1794 at Le Havre to carry shipbuilding timbers). Later fate unknown.

Frères or *Deux Frères* (merchant vessel built in Britain requisitioned 1794 at Dunkirk, 300 tons, 6 guns). Last mentioned 10.1795 while in service at Dunkirk, then returned.

Caton (brig commissioned 1794 at Dunkirk, carried 16 x 6pdrs). Renamed *Cygne* 5.1795. Sold at Dunkirk in early 1796.

Alerte (three-masted ship commissioned late 1794 at Dunkirk, carried 14 x 14pdrs). May have been renamed *Absolu* 5.1795. Struck 1796. May have been the 14-gun brig *Alerte* that was captured 3.1796 near Santo Domingo by HMS *Cormorant* (18).

Acquired 1794 at Brest and Saint-Malo

Stanislas (merchant vessel commissioned 3.1794 at Saint-Malo). Decomm. 7.1794.

Merchant vessels commissioned as transports in 7.1794 at Saint-Malo. *Adelaide*, *Anne-Émilie*, *Caboteur*, *Castries* (300 tons, 1 x 4pdr), *Colombe*, *Décade*, *Éole*, *Jean*, *Joséphine*, *Liberté*, *Lys*, *Marie-Angélique*, *Marie-Françoise*, *Marie-Jeanne*, *Marie-Thérèse*, *Maure*, *Mesnil* (540 tons, 4 x 4pdrs), *Pique*, *Révolutionnaire*, and *Sophie*. Decomm. before the end of 1794.

Glorieux (in service 10.1794 as a transport at Brest, 46 men, 2 x 3pdrs). Renamed *Grondeur* 5.1795. Struck late 1795.

Émilie (merchant vessel built in 1790 and comm. 11.1794 at Brest for the school of student gunners, 200 tons, 2 x 4pdrs). Transport 5.1795, struck late 1795.

Sans Culotte (in service as a transport at Brest in early 1795, 2 x 3pdrs in 18 ports). Renamed *Sans Abus* 30.5.1795. Burned 9.1795 in the Antilles by HMS *Aimable* (32).

Granval (in service as a transport at Brest in early 1795). Struck late 1795.

Bec d'Ambez (comm. as a transport c1794 at Brest). Renamed *Buveur* 5.1795 and *Basilic* 7.1795. Struck early 1796.

Belle Suzanne (transport, probably requisitioned, commissioned in 1794). Was at Guetaria in 11.1794. Renamed *Bucentaure* 5.1795. Struck late 1795, probably returned.

Acquired 1794 in the Biscay ports and elsewhere

Dordogne (commissioned 4.1794 at Rochefort as a troop transport). Participated in landings at Guadeloupe. Struck late 1795.

Neptune (requisitioned 4.1794 at Nantes, 200 tons, 14 x 4pdrs). Later fate unknown.

Voltigeant (requisitioned 4.1794 at Nantes, 14 x 6pdrs). Later fate unknown.

Citoyen (slave ship in use as such from 9.1789 to 6.1791 and requisitioned 6.1794 at Nantes, 430/694 tons, carried 4 x 6pdrs). Wrecked 10.1794 at Saint-Servan.

Utilité (brig requisitioned 6.1794 in the Seychelles, 50-60 tons, 47 men). Released 8.1794 at Île de France.

Angélique (vessel built in 1783 and in service in 7.1794, 20 men, 2 x 4pdrs). Renamed *Plume* 5.1795. Struck 1795.

Dunkerque (Bordeaux merchant vessel requisitioned 10.1794, 59 men). In 11.1794 embarked 150 priests for deportation to Africa or French Guiana but sailed only to Port-des-Barques on the Charente River. Probably returned 4.1795.

Républicain (Bordeaux merchant vessel requisitioned 10.1794, 79 men). In 11.1794 embarked 201 priests for deportation to Africa or French Guiana but sailed only to Port-des-Barques on the Charente River. Probably returned 4.1795.

Aimable Lucile (merchant vessel requisitioned 11.1794 at Lorient, 10 x 4pdrs). Renamed *Angerone* 5.1795, reverted to *Aimable Lucile* 6.1795. Returned 1.1797 to her owner at Bordeaux.

Alerte (prize purchased in late 1794, probably at Nantes, 160 tons, 20 men). May have been renamed *Aborigène* 5.1795. Was out of commission at Lorient in 10.1796, then struck.

René-Marie (in service at Nantes in early 1795). Renamed *Ressouvenir* 5.1795. Struck late 1795.

Tancrède (in service at Bordeaux in early 1795, probably requisitioned late 1794). Struck late 1795.

Conquête (commissioned late 1794, probably requisitioned). Struck late 1795, probably de-requisitioned at Pasajes.

Industrie (commissioned late 1794, probably requisitioned). Struck late 1795, probably de-requisitioned at Pasajes.

Saint-Vincent (commissioned late 1794, probably requisitioned). Renamed *Surprenant* 5.1795. Struck late 1795, probably de-requisitioned at Pasajes.

Notre Dame des Carmes (commissioned late 1794, probably requisitioned). Renamed *Désintéressé* 5.1795. Struck late 1795, probably de-requisitioned at Pasajes.

Thomas or *Thames* (commissioned late 1794, probably requisitioned, perhaps British-built). Renamed *Traineau* 5.1795. Probably de-requisitioned at Pasajes.

Notre Dame des Douleurs (commissioned late 1794, probably requisitioned). Renamed *Novateur* 5.1795. Probably de-requisitioned at Pasajes.

Acquired 1795

Alerte (privateer sloop built at Honfleur in 1793 by Jean-Louis Pestel and commissioned as a transport sloop at Le Havre in late 1794 or in 1795, 16 tons). Last mentioned in late 1796 or in 1797.

Invincible (Dutch-built sloop that was in service at Dunkirk in early 1795). Struck in late 1795.

Hirondelle (merchant vessel requisitioned 1795 at Le Havre). Soon returned to owner.

Jeune Émilie (merchant vessel requisitioned 1795 at Le Havre, 180 tons). Soon returned to owner.

Pingre de Tesdal (merchant vessel requisitioned 1795 at Le Havre). Soon returned to owner.

Acquired 1796

Entreprise (merchant brig requisitioned 2.1796 at Nantes, 90 tons). Scuttled at Saint-Jean de Luz 8.1796 to prevent capture by the British. Also called a chasse-marée.

Convention (lugger commissioned as a transport 3.1796 at Brest). Later fate unknown.

Saint Jean-Baptiste (chasse-marée comm. 6.1796 at Rochefort). Decomm. 2.1802.

William-Anna (captured sloop that was in service at Dunkirk in 9.1796 and 3.1797, 90 tons). To commercial operation 5.1797.

Albo or *Albro* (brig commissioned 9.1796 at Dunkirk). Lost at sea 11.1796 off Dunkirk.

Saint Nicolas (commissioned in 1796 at Le Havre). Later fate unknown.

Acquired 1797

Belle Angélique (American merchant brig *Betsy* purchased 3.1797 at Sainte-Croix de Ténériffe, 150 tons). On sale list 8.1798 at Fécamp.

Charles (sloop of unknown origin that was in service at Dunkirk in 3.1797, 90 tons). Last mentioned 9.1799 while at Dunkirk.

Fraternité (galiote of unknown origin that was in service at Dunkirk in 3.1797, 250 tons). To commercial operation 5.1797.

Unité (galiote of unknown origin that was in service at Dunkirk in 3.1797, 180 tons). To commercial operation 5.1797.

Trois Amis (vessel, probably requisitioned, commissioned at Le Havre in late 1797, 28 tons). Redesignated *Transport No.5 Les Trois Amis* 3.1798 for the expedition to Britain. Probably de-requisitioned 3.1799. A *Trois Amis* was wrecked at Saint-Nazaire on 22.2.1800.

Jeune Émile (merchant vessel commissioned 12.1797 at Bordeaux, 12-17 men). Decomm. 4.1800 at Le Havre.

Charles (vessel, probably requisitioned, commissioned 1797 at Le Havre). Probably became a numbered transport in 2.1798 for the Expedition to Britain, either *Transport No.9* (54 tons), *No.30* (29 tons), or *No.39*.

Jean-Baptiste (brig that was in service in 1797 at Dunkirk, 80 tons). Last mentioned 1799.

Régénérée (was in service 1797). Later fate unknown.

Vaillante Hirondelle (merchant vessel comm. 9.1797 at Rochefort). Decomm. 9.1801.

Acquired 1798 for the Expedition to Britain

Requisitioned transports. Between February and April 1798, 52 merchant vessels were requisitioned at Le Havre for use as transports in the planned invasion of Britain and numbered *Transports Nos.1-52*. One more, *Clémentine*, was requisitioned in 3.1798 but returned in 4.1798 before receiving a number. Eleven more merchant vessels were requisitioned at Nantes but were not assigned numbers. Similarly unknown numbers of fishing vessels were requisitioned at Dunkirk, Boulogne, and Dieppe in February 1798 for the same expedition. The merchant vessels at Le Havre ranged from 20 to 80 tons burthen in size except *Transport No.34 Jeune Édouard* (110 tons) and *Transport No.51 Diane* (100 tons). Some of the Nantes vessels were larger, one (*Lowlay* or *Cowley*) being a captured British merchantman of 400 tons. The fishing vessels ranged from 14 to 60 tons burthen and could embark between 45 and 150 soldiers each. The fishing vessels were returned to their owners in April 1798 and the larger merchant vessels followed between then and March 1799. *Transports No.4 Marie-Flore* (1798, below), *Transport No.5 Trois Amis* (1797, above), *Transport No.16 Bonne Aventure* (Chapter 10), *Transport No.21 Actif* (Chapter 8), *Transport No.28 Pauline* (Chapter 9), and *Transport No.50 Dame-Alida* (ex-Dutch, below) also performed other service and are listed individually (where indicated).

Transport No.4 Marie-Flore (merchant vessel built at Honfleur, requisitioned and comm. 2.1798 at Le Havre). Renamed *Marie-Flore* and refitted as aviso at Le Havre 2.1799. Decomm. 3.1800, then struck.

Acquired 1798 for the Expedition to Egypt

Requisitioned transports. In April 1798 31 transports of between 119 and 282 tons were hired or requisitioned to carry the Reynier division to Egypt and another 223 to 237 transports were hired or requisitioned to carry the remainder of the force and its supplies. Many of the ships were hired for a two month period at 250 francs per ton. The foreign merchantmen were released from their charters at Alexandria on 13.9.1798 but the French, Spanish, and Ligurian vessels were held there; 103 were still in Egypt in September 1799 and 50 were captured by the British and Turks in September 1801 in the capitulation of Alexandria. Two of the Reynier division ships also performed other service and are listed here individually, *Oiseau* (Chapter 7, first acquired in 1794), and *Union* (below).

Union (merchant vessel hired or requisitioned 4.1798 for the Egyptian expedition, 148 tons, carried 4 x 2pdrs). Participated in the transportation of the Reynier division to Egypt. Wrecked 6.1802 at Toulon.

Bérouse (?) (probably the former Papal corvette *San Giovanni* or *San Pio* built at Civita-Vecchia in 1780-81 and seized and requisitioned there in 3.1798 for the expedition to Egypt). Fate unknown. Her sister was also seized in 3.1798 but was not used for the Egyptian expedition and was returned to the Pope c1799.

Marianne or *Marie-Anne* (mercantile brig requisitioned or purchased 4.1798 and commissioned as an artillery transport, 140 tons, 6 guns). Captured 18.3.1799 by HMS *Tigre* (74), retaken mid-1799, refitted at Alexandria 9.1799, recaptured 11.1799 off Provence while carrying a report from Kléber on the situation in Egypt. Became gunbrig HMS *Marianne*, sold 9.1801.

Dame de Grace or *Vierge de Grace* (merchant brig requisitioned 4.1798, 90 tons, 35 men, 4 guns). Left Damietta with 7 other small vessels transporting artillery for the siege of Acre, all were captured 18.3.1799 by boats from HMS *Tigre* (74) off Haifa on the Syrian coast and placed in service with the siege artillery that they carried. Became the gunbrig HMS *Dame de Grace* (87 tons bm), retaken 8.5.1799 by the French brig *Salamine* and scuttled.

Madone de Grace de Saint Antoine de Padoue (Genoese merchant barque requisitioned 4.1798). Reportedly captured 4.1800 off Toulon by the British *Dorothea* details uncertain.

Notre Dame des Carmes (requisitioned 4.1798). Refitted at Alexandria 3.1799 as a transport for the wounded, returned to Toulon 4.1799 and probably returned.

Sainte Anne (requisitioned 4.1798). Refitted at Alexandria 3.1799 as a transport for the wounded, returned to Toulon 4.1799 and probably returned.

Saint Jean-Baptiste (merchant bombarde requisitioned 4.1798). Refitted 2.1799 at Alexandria, arrived 4.1799 at Saint-Tropez and probably returned.

Vierge du Rosaire (requisitioned 4.1798 at Genoa). Refitted 2.1799 at Alexandria, departed Alexandria 6.3.1799, later fate unknown.

Étoile (requisitioned 4.1798). Fate unknown

Marie (a small vessel requisitioned 4.1798). Captured 1798 by HMS *Tigre* (74).

Républicain (merchant brig, probably requisitioned, commissioned as a transport 5.1798 at Toulon). Fate unknown.

Saint-Esprit (merchant brig, probably requisitioned, commissioned as a transport 5.1798 at Toulon). Fate unknown.

Santa Marina (merchant brig requisitioned 6.1798 at Valletta, Malta). Fate unknown.

Belle Maltaise (merchant brig requisitioned 6.1798 at Valletta, Malta). Returned to Taranto 1799, later fate unknown.

Honoré or *Charles-Honoré* (brig comm. 12.1798 at Toulon for general service, 6 guns). Captured 23.9.1800 by the British.

Acquired 1799

Île de la Réunion (commissioned at Île de France 2.1799 to carry deportees to Madagascar). Sunk 3.1799 by a British frigate.

Marie-Jeanne (merchant vessel commissioned at Lorient 5.1799, 300 tons, 32 men, 2 guns). Decomm. 9.1803 at Brest.

Marie-Thérèse (merchant vessel that was in service at Lorient in 5.1799, 11 men). Decomm. 5.1801 at Nantes.

Républicaine (vessel that was in service at Lorient in 5.1799, 7 men). Fate unknown.

Fructueux (brig that was in service at Cherbourg in 10.1799). Fate unknown.

Dix-Huit Fructidor (lugger that was in service at Cherbourg in 10.1799). Fate unknown.

Diligence (brig that was in service between Cherbourg and Brest in 10.1799). Probably captured 1803-4 by the British and renamed HMS *Incendiary* 5.1804 as a fireship. Sold 4.1812.

Malo (brig that was in service between Cherbourg and Brest in 10.1799). Fate unknown

Momus (brig that was in service between Cherbourg and Brest in 10.1799). Fate unknown

Alliance (brig commissioned in 1799 at Le Havre). Fate unknown.

Fortune (brig comm. 1799 at Brest, 160 tons). Sold 1.1803 at Brest.

Acquired 1800

Marie-Anne Guillemette (brig comm. at Brest 23.9.1800, 65-69 tons, 42 men). Became service craft at Brest 1.1827 and struck.

Deux Soeurs (sloop, probably mercantile, comm. at Brest 23.9.1800, 20 tons, 39 men). Decomm. at Brest 20.12.1814. Listed for the last time c7.1818. Not to be confused with the 114-ton dogger *Deux Soeurs* at Le Havre, below.

Rebecca or *Cutter No.2* (sloop, probably mercantile, comm. 23.9.1800 at Brest, 15 tons). Decomm. 30.6.1809. *Sloop de servitude* at Brest after 1809. Last mentioned 1815.

Unité (sloop, probably mercantile, comm. 23.9.1800 at Brest, 25 tons). Decomm. 3.11.1807. *Sloop de servitude* at Brest after 1807. Still there 1815, fate unknown.

Acquired 1801

Ami de la Vertu (three-masted merchant vessel purchased 2.1801 and comm. 12.2.1801 at Toulon, 135 tons, 33-35 men). Re-rigged as brig 10.1802. Decomm. 1.6.1807. Struck 7.1808 and used as floating *citerne*. Last mentioned 1814.

Lapin (merchant vessel purchased 2.1801 and comm. 21.2.1801 at Toulon, 150 tons, carried 2 x 4pdrs). Became service craft at Toulon 1811, struck 1812.

Marie (mercantile brig purchased 2.1801 and comm. 12.2.1801 at Toulon, 189 tons). Captured early 1802 by the Algerians, then returned. Decomm. 18.10.1803, struck c1804. May have become the transport *Marie* commissioned 4.1806 at Le Havre, see below.

Necker Immortel or *Immortel* (merchant vessel purchased or chartered and comm. 23.9.1801 at Toulon, 212 tons). Captured early 1802 by the Algerians, then returned. Decomm. 13.9.1803, struck c1804.

Ex BRITISH PRIZES (1793-1800).

James (British merchant brig captured and commissioned in 1793 at Le Havre as a 100-ton transport). Decomm. and struck 1795 or 1796.

Nancy de Lins (British merchant brig, possibly from Leeds, captured 3.1794 and comm. at Rochefort 5.1794, 45 men, carried 6 x 4pdrs, 6 x 1pdrs). Renamed *Nancy* 1797. Recaptured 6.1803 by the British.

Swift No.1 and *Swift No.2* (British merchant vessels taken 3.1794 and commissioned 4.1794 at Lorient as transports, 20 men, *Swift No.1* carried 2 x 3pdrs). Both struck late 1795 at Brest.

Triton (British merchant ship built in Britain in 1785, captured, then commissioned 7.1794 at Lorient as a transport) Last mentioned 1.1797 while at La Rochelle, then struck.

Mercurius (British merchant ship built in Britain, captured and placed in service c1794 at Brest). Struck late 1795 at Brest.

Nancy de Greenock (British merchant ship built in Britain in 1791, captured, then commissioned 11.1794 at Lorient as a transport, 20 men, carried 2 x 3pdrs). Offered for sale 5.1794 at Saint-Malo and struck.

Marie Graty or *Mary Graty* (British mercantile brig taken by French privateers and purchased early 1795 at Nantes, 150-180 tons, 57 men). Renamed *Rouget* 9.1814. Captured 19.7.1815 in the harbour of Correjou.

Betsy (French galiote *Aimable Bristol* built on the Aber Ildut in northwestern Brittany in 1786 and recorded as operating along the French coast in 1787, later captured by the British, retaken from the British c1795 and in service at Brest 2.1796, 70-90 tons, 22 men). Listed as a dogger at Dunkirk in 1797-99 and a transport-brig at Le Havre in 1803-5. Renamed *Aimable Bristol* 10.1803 and *Grondin* 1.1815. Struck 4.1820 and became a service craft at Brest. Out of service 3.1822, BU 1826.

Athalante (British merchant vessel taken by privateers and purchased in early 1796 at Nantes, 179 tons). Was in service at Brest in 3.1796, last mentioned 10.1796.

Apollon (British merchant brig taken by French privateers from Nantes and purchased 1.1796 as a transport, 150-200 tons, 20 men, carried 2 x 4pdrs behind 16 ports). Used as aviso 9.1800 to 11.1801 when decomm. at Lorient and struck.

Hunter (British merchant vessel with three masts taken c1796 that was in service at Bordeaux in 3.1797 as a 280-ton transport, carried 10 x 4pdrs). Subsequent fate unknown.

William (British merchant brig taken c1796 that was in service at Dunkirk in 3.1797 as a 90-ton transport). Last mentioned 9.1799 at Dunkirk.

Wilding (British merchant vessel captured, then commissioned as a transport in 1798). Captured 12.1798 in the Gulf of Gascony by HMS *Spitfire* (20).

Fame of Pool (British merchant vessel captured 2.1798 and commissioned 5.1798 at Lorient as a transport, 180 tons carried 4 x 3pdrs). Decomm. 2.1802 at Martinique, struck 12.1806.

Hoope (brig, possibly a British merchantman named *Hope*, captured c1798 and comm. 20.11.1798 at Lorient). Decomm. 12.1807 at Lorient.

Alexander (galiote probably captured from the British in early 1798 and comm. at Bordeaux 9.1798, 26 men). Decomm. 2.1803 at Rochefort, struck and hulked.

Elisa (British mercantile brig *Elisa* captured 1799 and comm. 5.12.1799 at Nantes). Decomm. 21.11.1801 at Nantes and struck.

Hercule (British mercantile brig captured c1799 and in service at Brest in 1800). In 1801 was a guard station (*bâtiment servant d'arrière-garde*) at Brest. Wrecked 11.1801 in the Camaret roadstead. Apparently raised, listed as hulk until 1804.

The terminology of small craft varied from place to place and, like the vessels themselves, changed over time. Baugean describes this as a Dutch galiot (or galiote); it resembles the dogger in hull form, and the rig is close to the fore-and-aft sail plan of earlier doggers. Like many Dutch craft designed for shallow-water sailing, this example carries leeboards – pivoting flat panels designed to reduce leeway, on the same principle as a modern sailing dinghy's centreboard; when going to windward, the downwind board was lowered, and hauled up again when the vessel changed tack. Larger coastal galiots, with deeper hulls, dispensed with leeboards.

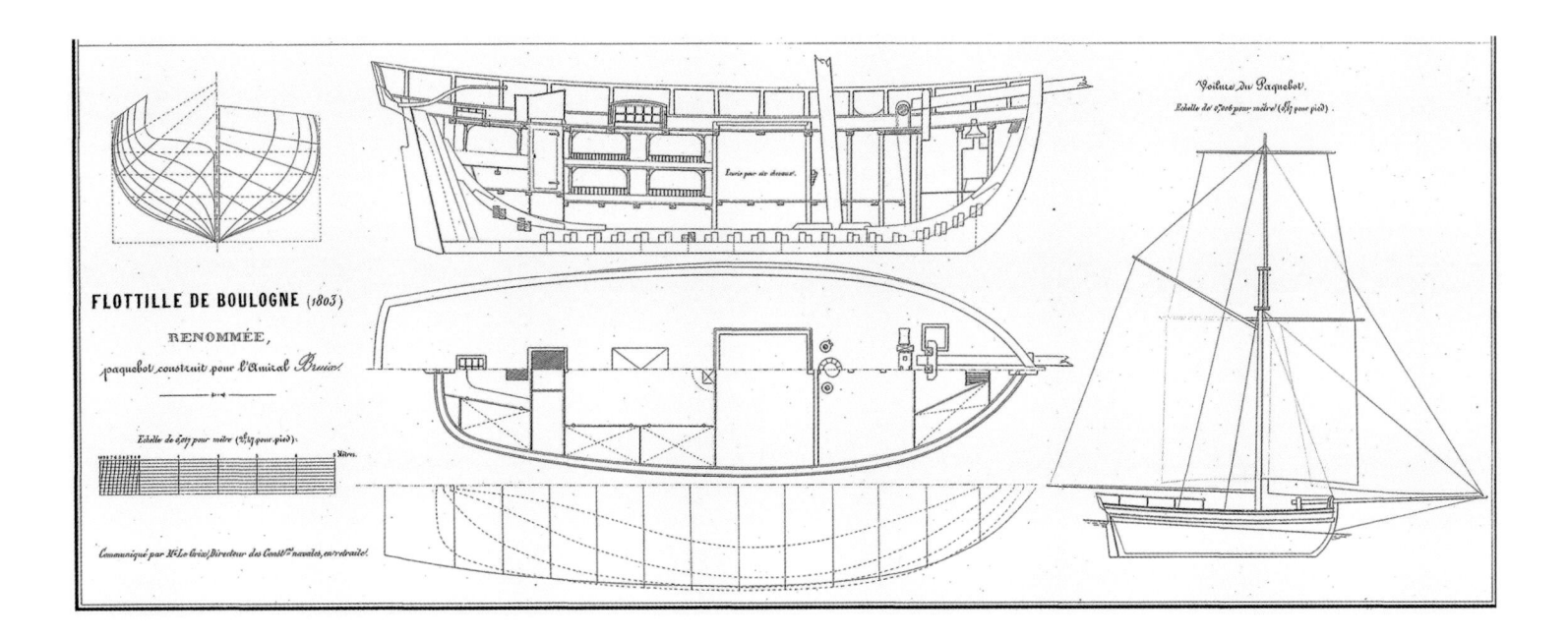

FLOTTILLE DE BOULOGNE (1803) RENOMMÉE, paquebot construit pour l'Amiral Bruix

Official general arrangement drawing of *Renommée*, designed in 1803 as a dispatch vessel for the commander of the Boulogne Flotilla. From 1803 until his death in 18 March 1805, this post was held by Vice-Adm. Étienne Eustache Bruix; on his death his deputy, Rear-Adm. Jean Raimond Lacrosse, took over responsibility. This cutter-rigged vessel could carry six horses in the hold, presumably for dispatch riders. (Atlas du Génie Maritime, French collection, plate 558)

Ex DUTCH PRIZES (1793-1795). These former Dutch galiotes were seized or captured in 1793-95.

Ange (Dutch galiote built in 1792-3, taken by French privateers in 1793 or 1794, and purchased c1796; 176-180 tons, 20 men, 2 guns). Renamed *Jeune Ange* 1799. Sold 9.1814 at Dunkirk.

Baleine, ex *Marie-Dorothée* (Dutch galiote captured by a French privateer and purchased 1793, 120-160 tons, 15-18 men, 1 to 4 guns). Renamed *Marie-Dorothée* 5.1795 and *Baleine* in 1796. Captured 5.1803 by the British in the Baie d'Audierne near Brest.

The following fourteen Dutch galiotes were built in the Netherlands and seized 2.1793 or captured in 1793-94. All were out of commission at Bordeaux in 3.1797 and had been struck: *Abraham-Jouanes* (300 tons), *Cecilia-Anna* (180 tons), *Dame Anna* (300 tons), *Dame Arentina* (110 tons), *Dame-Elsina* (120 tons, captured in 1795 by the Spanish but evidently recovered), *Dame-Francina* (240 tons), *Dame-Gertrude* (300 tons), *Dame-Girardina* (250 tons), *Dame Petronilla* (300 tons), *Jeune-Jouwerc* or *Jonk-Jouwert* (250 tons), *Juriam-William* (140 tons), *Leander* or *Jonk Cleander* (300 tons, 24-38 men, back in commission at Bayonne in 9.1802 and 1.1803), *Marie Fibrick* (250 tons), *Marie Vaudelours* or *Marie Vandelaar* (240 tons).

Dame-Catherine (Dutch galiote built in the Netherlands and seized 2.1793 or captured in 1793-94, tons unknown). Captured 1795 by the Spanish.

Jean-Johannes or *Jean-Jouannez* (Dutch galiote built in the Netherlands and seized 2.1793 or captured in 1793-94, 160/230 tons). Struck 7.1800 at Rochefort.

Nouvelle Révolution or *Nouvelle Résolution* (Dutch galiote built in the Netherlands and seized 2.1793 or captured in 1793-94, 124/250 tons). Struck 7.1800 at Rochefort.

Dame Marie (Dutch galiote built in the Netherlands and seized 2.1793 or captured in 1793-94). Unserviceable at Le Havre 2.1802.

Girardina-Maria or *Gerardina-Maria* (Dutch galiote built in the Netherlands and seized 2.1793 or captured in 1793-94, 250 tons). Converted to barge at Brest 10.1802 and struck.

Bonne-Espérance (Dutch galiote *Goedy Wartgteiger* seized 2.1793, 105 tons). Out of commission at Nantes 8.1799.

Emilia-Louisa (Dutch galiote captured in 1793, 90 tons, 30 men, carried 4 x 8pdrs and 2 x 4pdrs). Prison hulk at Nantes 8.1793, restored to service as a galiote 10.1795, barge at Nantes 11.1796.

Deux Soeurs (Dutch galiote captured or seized and commissioned in 1793 as a customs tender on the Loire, 200 tons). In service against the Chouans at Noirmoutier 10.1793. At Bordeaux 3.1797, had been struck.

Six Frères (captured Dutch galiote requisitioned in 1794 at Le Havre, 87 tons). Fate unknown.

Espérance (captured Dutch galiote purchased in 1795 at Cherbourg). Fate unknown.

Amsterdam (Dutch galiote captured in early 1795 and in service at Dunkirk in 3.1797, 200 tons). Was at Dunkirk in 9.1799 and had been struck.

Wrou-Madalena (Dutch galiote captured in early 1795 and in service at Dunkirk in 3.1797, 150 tons). To commercial operation at Dunkirk 4.1797.

Dame-Angelina (Dutch galiote captured in early 1795 and in service at Dunkirk in 3.1797, 120 tons, 11 men). Decomm. 7.1807 at Antwerp or Flushing and struck.

Dame-Alida (Dutch galiote captured in early 1795 and commissioned at Le Havre in 1795, 80 tons, 12-15 men) Renamed *Transport No.50* in 3.1798, reverted to *Dame Alida* in 8.1798. Classed as dogger from 1800. Unserviceable 2.1802 at Le Havre and struck.

Ex SPANISH PRIZES (1794)

Béarnois or *Béarnais* (Spanish merchant vessel built in Spain, name unknown, taken near the end of 1794, 20 men, carried 2 x 3pdrs). Struck late 1795 at Brest.

Perola (Spanish merchant vessel built in Spain and taken c1794, was in service as a transport at Pasajes in 5.1795). Struck late 1795.

Sorro (Spanish merchant vessel built in Spain and taken c1794, was in service as a transport at Pasajes in 5.1795). Struck late 1795.

(C) Smaller transports acquired from 25 March 1802

RENOMMÉE – 80 tons. Single-masted vessel, could embark 6 horses. She was the *paquebot* of Vice-Adm. Eustache Bruix (commander of the Boulogne Flotilla until he died on 18.3.1805, to be succeeded by his former Assistant, Vice-Adm. Jean-Raymond Lacrosse).
Dimensions & tons: 53ft 0in x 17ft 0in x 8ft 8in (17.22 x 5.52 x 2.82m). 80/120 tons. Draught 6ft 10in (2.22m) mean.
Guns: none.
Renommée Calais.
K: 12.1803. L: 8.1804. Comm: 23.9.1804.
Struck c1816.

TURBOT – Sloop, 40 tons.
Dimensions & tons: dimensions unknown. 40 tons.
Turbot Bordeaux (probably).
K: 1804. L: 1804. C: 1804.
In commission at Bordeaux and Rochefort from 7.3.1806 to 31.12.1806 and at Cherbourg from 23.1.1808 to 31.12.1814. Struck 11.1812 and became service craft at Cherbourg. Listed as in commission at Cherbourg from 1.1.1817 to 31.12.1817. Placed on sale 15.5.1821.

BAUDET – Sloop, 55 tons.
Dimensions & tons: dimensions unknown. 55 tons.
Baudet Cherbourg Dyd. (probably).
K: 1804. L: 1804. C: 1804.
In commission at Cherbourg from 2.12.1805 to 31.5.1811. Became service craft at Cherbourg 11.1811, condemned 1814.

ZÉLÉ CONSCRIT or *CONSCRIT* – Sloop, sometimes called a *péniche*, 20 tons. Built voluntarily by conscript workers.
Dimensions & tons: dimensions unknown. 20 tons.
Guns: 1 x 4pdr.
Zélé Conscrit or *Conscrit* Cherbourg Dyd.
K: 5.1804. L: c12.1804. C: 1.1805.
In commission at Cherbourg from 21.1.1805 to 31.10.1806 and from 21.6.1808 to 20.10.1810. Became service craft at Cherbourg 7.1813. Struck there early 1814.

DIGUE – Sloop
Dimensions & tons: unknown. Men: 7-9.
Digue Cherbourg Dyd. (probably).
K: 1805. L: c11.1805. Comm: 5.12.1805.
Wrecked 2.3.1807.

TJALQUE VLYT – Tjalk, 115 tons.
Dimensions & tons: dimensions unknown. 115/200 tons.
Tjalque Vlyt (Galiote Vlyt) Amsterdam.
K: 10.1810. L: 4.1811. C: 5.1811.
Taken 12.1813 by the Netherlands at Amsterdam. A *tjalk* is a type of Dutch sailing cargo barge while *vlijt* means industry or diligence.

TRANSPORTS FOR THE BOULOGNE FLOTILLA. Between August 1803 and January 1804 an estimated 709 small craft of 10 to 110 tons, mostly fishing vessels, were purchased as transports to support the flotilla being assembled at Boulogne for the invasion of England. 81 more small craft were purchased as *corvettes de pêche*. 117 transports were purchased at Antwerp, Malines, and Ghent, 175 at Ostende, Bruges, Nieuport, Blankenberges and Heist, 62 at Dunkirk, 7 at Boulogne, 217 at Le Havre, 35 at Saint-Malo, 71 at Brest, 14 at Lorient, and 11 at Bayonne (although the Bayonne and perhaps the Lorient contingents were unable to join the flotilla). They were designated by numbers between *1* and *1165* (with gaps), first assigned provisional numbers for the trip to Boulogne and there receiving their definitive numbers. They also retained their original names, and were listed under these in the navy's list of flotilla craft (which was distinct from the regular fleet list). In July 1804 there were 856 of these transports, which were purportedly able to carry 15,000 men and over 5,500 horses. Nearly all of these numbered transports were decommissioned on 31 March 1807, and in January 1813 there remained only 88 transports at Boulogne and 8 at Calais. A few of them were on the main fleet list by 1814, some under their transport numbers and some under their mercantile names, and these are listed here individually.

Jeune Thérèse or *Transport No.301* (mercantile, built at Rouen in 1787 and comm. 2.9.1803 at Le Havre, 60-80 tons, 10-21 men). Sold 8.1814 at Le Havre.

Aimable Eulalie or *Transport No.330* (mercantile sloop built in 1785 at Honfleur by Nicolas Loquet and comm. 18.11.1803 at Rouen, 80-90 tons, 20 men). Decomm. 15.10.1819, sold 1822.

Transport No.274 (mercantile sloop *Saint François* comm. 4.11.1803 at Brest, 35-40 tons). Decomm. 22.10.1815 at Dunkirk. On fleet list 1820, struck 1821.

Transport No.281 (mercantile, may have been ex *Péniche No.281* which was comm: 2.1804 or 3.1804 at Ostende). Decomm: after 4.1809. On fleet list 1819, struck 1821.

Batave or *Transport No.460* (built at Paris and comm. at Rouen 21.4.1804 as *Bateau-canonnier No.460*, 50 tons, 22-24 men). Named *Batave* (*Transport No.460*) 1808. Decomm. 14.6.1814 at Le Havre, sold 8.1814 at Le Havre.

Transport No.639 (mercantile galiote *Droiture* comm. 10.11.1803 at Ostende, 123 tons). Wrecked 3.5.1814 on the rocks of Gatteville near Harfleur.

Transport No.665 (mercantile *Jeune Marguerite* comm. 24.10.1803 at Boulogne, 90 tons). Sold in 1814 at Le Havre.

Transport No.698 (mercantile *Jeanne* comm. 24.8.1803 at Boulogne, 91 tons). Sold in 1814 at Le Havre.

Transport No.703 (mercantile galiote *Aimable Marguerite* comm. 20.8.1803 at Le Havre as a horse transport, 95 tons). Decomm. 14.3.1814 at Le Havre and sold.

Volontaire or *Transport No.749* (mercantile brig comm. 13.12.1803 at Dieppe, 110/200 tons). Decomm. 31.3.1807. Recomm. at Cherbourg as *Sorcier* 17.6.1808. Decomm. 27.6.1813 and not in 1814 fleet lists but reported as captured 17 or 27.6.1815, probably by the British.

Victorieux or *Transport No.960* (merchant vessel comm. 23.12.1803 at Le Havre, 66 tons). Renamed *Plongeon* 1.1817. Sold 3.1817 at Cherbourg.

Transport No.964 (mercantile brig *Rouennais* comm. 20.7.1804 at Brest, 83 tons). Decomm. 11.1810 at Cherbourg. On an 1816 fleet list as out of commission.

PURCHASED AND REQUISITIONED TRANSPORTS. As for the previous period, this miscellaneous collection of vessels was procured to meet the needs of the day. They are listed chronologically in order of entering service.

Acquired 1802-1803

Alexandrine (sloop-rigged merchant vessel comm. 23.9.1802 at Brest, 15 tons, 36 men probably including passengers). Renamed *Coureur* 23.9.1804. Service craft at Brest 5.1814.

Mélanie (cutter-rigged merchant vessel comm. 12.7.1803 at Brest, 20 tons, 31 men). Decomm. 20 Dec 1814. Probably replaced as a commissioned transport by the old (1793) cutter *Sentinelle,* which was listed in 10.1816 and 7.1818 as a 50-ton transport. *Mélanie* struck 1820 at Brest, BU there 3.1823. *Sentinelle* struck 1827.

Diligent (mercantile brig comm. 25.7.1803 at Brest, 76 tons, 43 men). Decomm. 25.3.1816 at Brest. Struck c1817 and became service craft.

Trois Amis (mercantile lugger purchased 8.1803 at Bayonne, 40 tons, 49 men). Also known in 1803 as *Lougre No.10*. Decomm. at Brest 3.1816, struck at Brest 12.1820 or early 1821.

Julie (mercantile brig purchased at Granville c8.1803 and comm. at Le Havre 2.9.1805, 50-70 tons, 10 men). Wrecked 2.3.1807 at La Hogue.

Jeune Édouard (sloop-rigged merchant vessel comm. 20.8.1803 at Le Havre, 47-50 tons, 14-17 men). Wrecked 15.11.1807 at Barfleur.

Deux Soeurs (mercantile dogger comm. 14.9.1803 at Le Havre, 114 or 50 tons, 16-26 men. Run ashore 20.8.1811 to avoid capture by a British corvette, refloated 22.8.1811 and repaired. Listed in 1814 and 1818 as a 114-ton gabarre and in 1816 as a 114-ton transport. Decomm. 15.2.1819. Sold 8.1822 at Le Havre. Not to be confused with the 20-ton sloop *Deux Soeurs* at Brest, above.

Aimable Rose-Désirée (mercantile sloop built in 1787 at Le Havre and comm. 4.9.1803 at Le Havre, 50/80 tons, 24 men, could transport 15 men and 6 horses). Decomm. 28.2.1814. Sold 9.1814 at Le Havre.

Corvette de pêche No.10 Poisson-Volant (merchant vessel comm. 28.9.1803 at Dunkirk). Decomm. 22.9.1805. Recomm. 15.6.1806 at Ostende as *Cutter No.10 Poisson-Volant*, soon changed to *Paquebot No.10 Poisson-Volant*. Decomm. 31.3.1807. Recomm. at Brest 21.10.1809. Decomm. 1.2.1814, then struck.

Virginie (mercantile cutter or chasse-marée comm. 17.10.1803 at Honfleur, 27 tons, 8 men). Captured 4.3.1808 by the British in the Channel and burned.

Charlotte (Swedish mercantile packet *Charlotte-Caroline* purchased 22.11.1803 at Boulogne and comm. there 23.9.1804 as a *transport paquebot*). Decomm. 1814 at Calais, then struck.

Acquired 1805-1806

Jean Leep (mercantile, ex *corvette de pêche*, comm. 23.9.1805 at Ostende, 72 men, carried 2 x 3pdrs, 2 x 1pdr swivels). Station vessel at Ostende from 1808 to 1814. Renamed *Sardine* 9.1814. Wrecked 20.1.1815 near Zuidcoote (Dunkirk).

Sardine (merchant vessel comm. 1.3.1806 at Bordeaux, 167 tons, 27-29 men). Run ashore during combat on 5.6.1807 near Saint Nicolas.

Marie (mercantile brig comm. 21.4.1806 at Le Havre, may have been the *Marie* purchased in 1801, see above, 105 or 120/200 tons, 15-19 men). Wrecked 4.10.1807 at the entrance to Port Diélette.

Transport No.1 (merchant vessel purchased and comm. 6.5.1806 at Toulon, 98 tons, 22 men). Captured 13.3.1809.

Transport No.2 (Sicilian pink *Saint Michel* built in 1801, sequestered at Toulon 12.1805 and purchased and comm. there 6.5.1806)
Dimensions & tons: 62ft 7in x 19ft 4in x 10ft 3in (20.33 x 6.28 x 3.33m). 132/200 tons. Men: 37.
Guns: 6 x 8pdrs, 2 swivels.
Renamed *Champenoise* 12.1807. Captured 4.5.1809 between Cap Couronne and Bouc west of Marseille by HMS *Renown* (74).

Transport No.3 (mercantile brig *Vierge de Trépany* purchased and comm. 6.5.1806 at Toulon, 150/250 tons, 22 men). Recomm. as *Castor* 1.11.1808, refitted at Genoa 11.1811. Captured 4.12.1811 near Cap Corse on voyage from Bastia to Sagone by HMS *Sultan* (74), then wrecked off Bastia.

Transport No.4 (merchant vessel or gabarre purchased and comm. 6.5.1806 at Toulon, 124/200 tons, 22 men). Burned 15.1.1814 by the French near San Remo to prevent capture.

Transport No.5 (mercantile *Fortune* purchased and comm. 27.5.1806 at Toulon, 48 tons, 21 men). Decomm. 1.2.1807 at Toulon and struck.

Transport No.6 (mercantile *Hirondelle* purchased and comm. in 5.1806 at Toulon, 65 tons). Last mentioned 2.1807.

Transport No.7 (merchant vessel purchased and comm. 27.5.1806 at Toulon, 50 tons, 21 men). Decomm. 1.1807.

Acquired 1808-1812

Grondin (mercantile brig purchased 7.1808 at Toulon, 350 tons, carried 6 x 6pdrs). Refitted at Toulon 3.1809. Captured 1.11.1809 off Rosas by the British.

Véloce (mercantile galiote comm. 1.1.1809 as a gunboat at Toulon, 21 men, 1 x 16pdr carronade). Captured 29.1.1813 (according to the British) or 13.3.1813 (according to the French) near Otranto by HMS *Cerberus* (32).

Dnepr (Russian naval transport built in Russia 1804, 16 guns and 18 ports, sold to France 27.9.1809 at Venice). Had been sent by the Russians to Corfu 1805 and attached to the squadron of Vice Admiral D. N. Senyavin 1.1806, went to Trieste 8.1807 and to Venice 1.1809. Probably sold early 1811 at Corfu.

Nini (mercantile decked chaloupe comm. at Le Havre 23.11.1809, 14 tons). Decomm. 30.10.1814.

Ulysse (mercantile galiote comm. 25.6.1810 at Toulon, 40 men, carried 2 x 12pdrs, 2 x 4pdrs). Captured 20.9.1812 near Corfu by HMS *Apollo* (38).

Courageuse (mercantile galiote comm. at Corfu 1.1.1811, 30 men, carried 1 x 9pdr, 2 x 4pdrs). Captured 11.6.1813 near Corfu by the British.

Bernardus (mercantile galiote comm. 9.9.1811 at Hamburg). Decomm. 31.12.1811.

Christiana (mercantile sloop comm. 1.2.1812 at Hamburg, 70 tons). Decomm. 31.3.1812.

Ex BRITISH PRIZES (1803-1811)

Concorde (Royal Navy sloop-rigged tender *Brighton*, captured 12.11.1796 according to the French or 24.2.1797 according to the British and comm. at Le Havre 23.9.1804, 87 tons, 14 men, had 14 gunports). Retaken 18.8.1811 by British pinnaces near the rocks of Calvados, her French crew escaping ashore.

Amalthéa (British mercantile brig seized on the Atlantic coast 6.1803 and comm. 27.9.1803, 135-150 tons, 15 men, carried 2 x 4pdrs). Service craft at Rochefort in 1814, struck before 1819.

Comète (British mercantile *Comet*, built at New Shoreham in 1800, captured 2.7.1803 by the division of Rear Admiral Bedout in *Argonaute* (74) while returning from Santo Domingo, and taken into La Corogne (Corunna), Spain).
Dimensions & tons: 89ft 8in x 24ft 6in x 9ft 11in (29.14 x 7.97 x 3.23m). 350/450 tons.
Guns: 16 x 12pdr carronades.
Also listed as a corvette. Sold 6.1804, probably through a Spanish intermediary, to the Royal Navy and became HMS *Spy*. Initially rated by the RN as a 16-gun sloop, she became a transport in 1810 and was sold in 12.1813. The otherwise unknown transport named *Comète* commissioned on 16.4.1803 was probably not this vessel.

Ressource (British three-masted merchant vessel captured 5.12.1805 at Luanda by the Linois division, 340 tons, 32 men). Sent to the Cape of Good Hope where she was recaptured 8.1.1806 by the British. Evidently retaken by the French, she was commissioned at Île de France on 11.12.1807 and sent as a cartel (prisoner exchange ship) to Brest, where she was decommissioned on 22.9.1808. Evidently recommissioned, she was captured 3.1809 in the Sunda Strait by the British privateer *Bic*.

Polacre No.3 (British polacre built at Malta in 1802, captured early 1811 by the gunboat *Diligente*, taken to Corfu, and commissioned 27.3.1811, 130 tons, 18 men, carried 2 x 4pdrs). Seized 6.1814 by the British at Corfu.

Fauçon (British merchant vessel taken by French privateers, purchased 5.1811 at Sète, and comm. 1.6.1811).
Dimensions & tons: 87ft 8in x 21ft 8in x 14ft 8in (28.49 x 7.05 x 4.77m). 320/480 tons. Men: 12.
Guns: 2 x 8pdrs, 6 x 6pdrs.
Decomm. 13.1.1813. Converted to *citerne flottante* 3-5.1813 at Toulon. Struck 1814-19.

Ex SWEDISH PRIZES (1805). The following four mercantile vessels were all seized in November 1805.

Jason (Swedish merchant vessel seized 11.1805 and comm. 14.1.1806 at Rochefort).
Dimensions & tons: 77ft 0in x 21ft 4in x 11ft 5in (25.01 x 6.93 x 3.71m). 150-180/300 tons. Men: 31.
Decomm. 22.1.1819. Unserviceable 5.1819, condemned at Rochefort and BU.

Saumon (Swedish mercantile brig seized 11.1805 at Bordeaux and comm. 27.1.1806, 160 tons). Decomm. 16.6.1809. Unserviceable 3.1813 at Rochefort and struck.

Turbot (Swedish merchant vessel seized 11.1805 at Bordeaux and comm. 7.3.1806, 92 tons). Described as very old, decomm. 31.12.1806. Unserviceable 6.1811 at Rochefort, condemned and BU.

Charlotte (Swedish merchant vessel seized 11.1805 at Bordeaux and comm. 20.1.1806, 133 tons, 24 men). Decomm. 11.1.1809 and became service craft at Rochefort 2.1809. Unserviceable in 1812.

Ex SICILIAN PRIZES (1805). The following four mercantile vessels were all seized in December 1805.

Alsacienne (Sicilian half-xebec *Jésus-Maria-Joseph,* built in 1798, sequestered at Toulon 12.1805, renamed *Alsacienne* 12.1807, refitted at Toulon 6-7.1808, and comm. 19.6.1809).
Dimensions & tons: 44ft 9in x 13ft 10in x 7ft 5in (14.53 x 4.49 x 2.40m). 49/70 tons. Draught 5ft 6in (1.78m) mean.
Burned 1.11.1809 off Rosas by the British.

Bourguignonne (Sicilian half-xebec *Notre Dame des Carmes et les Âmes du Purgatoire*, built in 1802, sequestered at Toulon 12.1805, renamed *Bourguignonne* 12.1807, refitted at Toulon 6-7.1808, and comm. 19.6.1809 as a gunboat).
Dimensions & tons: 46ft 11in x 15ft 4in x 6ft 5in (15.24 x 4.98 x 2.08m). 48/80 tons. Draught 5ft 8in (1.84m) mean. Men: 36.
Guns: 2 x 3pdrs.
Put on sale list at Toulon and struck 9.1814, sold 1816.

Gasconne (Sicilian pink *Jésus-Maria-Joseph* sequestered at Toulon 12.1805, renamed *Gasconne* 12.1807, refitted at Toulon 6-7.1809, and comm. 19.6.1809 as a gunboat).
Dimensions & tons: 55ft 3in x 18ft 3in x 9ft 3in (17.94 x 5.93 x 3.00m). 98/140 tons. Draught 6ft 3in (2.03m) mean. Men: 8 (1813).
Decomm. 31.12.1812, condemned 6.1814, sold at Toulon 1816.

Normande (Sicilian pink *Jésus-Maria-Saint Pierre* seized in 12.1805, renamed *Normande* 12.1807, refitted at Toulon 3-4.1808, and comm. 16.4.1808).
Dimensions & tons: 65ft 1in x 18ft 3in x 9ft 2in (21.14 x 5.93 x 2.97m). 107 tons.
Guns: 6 x 4pdrs, 4 swivels.

Captured 19.11.1809 off Rosas by the British.

Ex PRUSSIAN PRIZES (1806-1807). The following seven mercantile vessels were all seized in October 1806 (and an eighth in May 1807).

Balance (Prussian mercantile brig-rigged dogger seized 10.1806 at Cherbourg, renamed *Balance* 1.1807, and comm. 20.4.1807).
Dimensions & tons: 71ft 11in x 23ft 2in x 10ft 6in (23.36 x 7.52 x 3.41m). 130/250 tons. Men: 31-36.
Guns: 2 x 12pdr carronades.
Wrecked 23.3.1816 northwest of Guernsey.

Chameau (Prussian mercantile *Catharina Elisabeth Swart* seized 10.1806 at Bordeaux, renamed *Chameau* 24.8.1807, and comm. 16.1.1808, 251 tons). Decomm. 5.10.1809. Began a refit in 1812 at Rochefort but was found in 1813 to be in too poor condition and was condemned.

Ida (Prussian mercantile *Ida* seized 10.1806 at Bordeaux, Prussian name retained 24.8.1807, and comm. 26.8.1807).
Dimensions & tons: 72ft 0in x 20ft 0in x 10ft 0in (23.39 x 6.50 x 3.25m). 165-175/270 tons.
Decomm. 5.10.1809 and 17.9.1811, recomm. 1.1.1818, decomm. 30.11.1818. Began a refit 4.1819 at Rochefort but was found in 5.1819 to be unserviceable and was condemned.

Industrie (Prussian mercantile *Industrie* seized at Bordeaux 10.1806, Prussian name retained 24.8.1807, 413 tons). In 1809 was headquarters ship and sheer hulk at Bordeaux. Barracks hulk there 1813 and in commission there as a cayenne 11.3.1814 to 31.12.1814, when last mentioned.

Mulet (Prussian mercantile *Jaffrow Grietje Pieperberg* seized at Bordeaux 10.1806, renamed *Mulet* 24.8.1807, and comm. 1.9.1807, 176 tons). Captured 25.8.1811 in the Gironde by HMS *Diana* (38) and *Semiramis* (36).

Neptune (Prussian mercantile *Neptunus* seized at Bordeaux 10.1806, Prussian name modified to *Neptune* 24.8.1807, 258 tons). Condemned 11.1814 at Rochefort and BU, although a 130-ton *Neptune*, probably the same vessel, was listed in 1816 as out of commission at Rochefort.

Patiente (Prussian mercantile *Catharina Tholen* seized at Bordeaux 10.1806, comm. 5.5.1807 as *Catharina Tholent*, and renamed *Patiente* (not *Patience*) 24.8.1807, 241 tons). Decomm. 20.2.1808. Condemned 11.1814 at Rochefort and BU.

Autruche (Prussian mercantile *Caroline Wilhelmine* seized at Bordeaux 5.1807, renamed *Autruche* 24.8.1807, and comm. 12.1.1808, 170 tons). Went ashore 12.3.1808 near Avert to avoid capture and was then burned.

Ex PORTUGUESE PRIZES (1807) On 14 August 1807 Napoleon ordered Portugal to close her ports to British shipping and to confiscate British goods. When Portugal refused the French seized the Portuguese merchantmen that were then in French ports, including the following which came under navy control during 1808.

Crac or *Craak* (Portuguese mercantile *San Severino*, also called a gabarre, seized 8.1807 at Nantes, renamed *Crac* or *Craak* 4.1808, and refitted at Nantes 4.1808).
Dimensions & tons: 57ft 0in x 17ft 0in x 7ft 6in (18.51 x 5.52 x 2.43m). 77/150 tons. Men: 9.
Captured 1.7.1813 off Vannes by the British while going from Bénodet to Nantes.

Gavotte (Portuguese yacht *Nassa Senhora da Carma e Livramento* seized 8.1807 at Nantes, renamed *Gavotte* 6.1808, and refitted at Nantes 6.1808).
Dimensions & tons: 72ft 0in x 19ft 6in x 9ft 8in (23.39 x 6.33 x 3.14m). 144/260 tons.

Forced ashore 5.4.1811 by a British frigate at Port Manech; the British burned her after trying unsuccessfully to refloat her.

Guêpe (Portuguese snow or brig *Rainha dos Anjos* seized 8.1807 at Nantes, renamed *Guêpe* 3.1808, and refitted at Nantes 4.1808).
  Dimensions & tons: 63ft 0in x 18ft 6in x 8ft 3in (20.46 x 6.01 x 2.68m). 102/150 tons. Men: 8 (1813).
  Was a depot ship at Mindin in 6.1811, back at Nantes 1.1812. Struck and ordered sold 2.1814.

Loutre (Portuguese snow *Purificao* seized 8.1807 at Nantes, renamed *Loutre* 5.1808, and refitted at Nantes 5.1808)
  Dimensions & tons: 63ft 0in x 17ft 6in x 10ft 0in (20.46 x 5.68 x 3.25m). 117/200 tons.
  Unserviceable 12.1811 at Lorient, sold 1.1812 at Nantes.

Marmotte (Portuguese yacht *Sociedad* seized 8.1807 at Nantes, renamed *Marmotte* 5.1808, and refitted at Nantes 5.1808).
  Dimensions & tons: 63ft 0in x 17ft 0in x 8ft 0in (20.46 x 5.52 x 2.60m). 91/140 tons.
  Burned 12.4.1809 by two British fireships at the entrance to the Charente while assisting the frigate *Elbe*.

Mécontent (Portuguese schooner *Flor do Mar* seized 8.1807 at Nantes, renamed *Mécontent* 10.1808, refitted at Nantes 12.1808-1.1809, and comm. 21.1.1809).
  Dimensions & tons: 73ft 0in x 21ft 0in x 8ft 6in (23.71 x 6.82 x 2.76m). 130/200 tons.
  Captured 2.3.1809 by HMS *Sirius* (36) while en route to Senegal.

Navalo (Portuguese snow *Concordia* seized 8.1807 at Nantes, renamed *Navalo* 4.1808, and refitted at Nantes 4.1808).
  Dimensions & tons: 62ft 0in x 18ft 0in x 9ft 0in (20.14 x 5.85 x 2.92m). 106/150 tons.
  Had to put in to Belle-Île 11.1810 in bad condition, sold there 1.1811.

Mathilde or *Marie* (Portuguese mercantile brig *Maria* seized 8.1807 at Nantes, renamed *Mathilde* 3.1808, and refitted at Nantes 5.1808).
  Dimensions & tons: 53ft 9in x 18ft 0in x 10ft 0in (17.45 x 5.85 x 3.25m). 88/150 tons.
  May have been the *Marie* that was comm. at Nantes 1.12.1809 and decomm. 26.1.1811. Became station ship at Port Navalo 6.1811, unserviceable 9.1811 and struck.

Oenone (Portuguese schooner *Bon Conceito* seized 8.1807 at Nantes, renamed *Oenone* 5.1808, and refitted at Nantes 5.1808).
  Dimensions & tons: 72ft 0in x 19ft 5in x 9ft 7in (23.39 x 6.31 x 3.11m). 143/220 tons.
  Sold 12.1811 at Nantes.

Perche (1) (Portuguese mercantile brig *Triumpho do Mar* seized 8.1807 at Nantes and renamed *Perche* 5.1808).
  Dimensions & tons: 61ft 0in x 19ft 0in x 9ft 0in (19.81 x 6.17 x 2.92m). 110/160 tons.
  Her masts and rigging being in too poor condition, she was turned over on 16.6.1808 to the *Service des Domaines*, presumably for disposal.

Perche (2) (Portuguese mercantile snow *Flor do Mar* seized 8.1807 at Nantes, renamed *Perche* 6.1808, and refitted at Nantes 6.1808).

A patache, a characteristic Portuguese type used for a number of paramilitary roles like revenue protection and customs duties. According to Baugean, who published this engraving in 1814, their numbers were declining, but it might stand as a representative of the Portuguese vessels captured by France in 1807.

Dimensions & tons: 75ft 0in x 20ft 0in x 10ft 0in (24.36 x 6.50 x 3.25m). 163/250 tons. Men: 9.

Was at Nantes 11.1814 when the government ordered her to be returned to her former Portuguese owner.

Poulette (Portuguese yacht *Bon Successo & Unio* seized 8.1807 at Nantes, refitted at Nantes 4.1808, and renamed *Poulette* 6.1808), 108 tons.

Dimensions & tons: 66ft 0in x 19ft 0in x 8ft 10in (21.44 x 6.17 x 2.87m). 108/160 tons.

While en route from Nantes to Rochefort on 5.4.1811 was captured and burned by the British near the Île d'Aix.

Ruche (Portuguese schooner *Flor d'Aveiro* seized 8.1807 at Nantes, renamed *Ruche* 3.1808, and refitted at Nantes 4.1808).

Dimensions & tons: 68ft 0in x 19ft 0in x 9ft 0in (22.09 x 6.17 x 2.92m). 80-123/160 tons. Men: 9.

Was at Nantes 11.1814 when the government ordered her to be returned to her former Portuguese owner, who sold her.

Sorcier (Portuguese mercantile brig *Diligente* or *Diligent* seized 8.1807 at Cherbourg, renamed *Sorcier* 6.1808, refitted at Cherbourg 6.1808, and comm. 17.6.1808).

Dimensions & tons: 70ft 10in x 20ft 2in x 14ft 0in (23.01 x 6.55 x 4.55m). 150/250 tons.

Guns: 2 x 4pdrs.

Decomm. 27.6.1813 at Cherbourg, condemned 7.1813 to be BU.

Souris (Portuguese schooner-rigged yacht *Nossa Senhora de Almar* seized 8.1807 at Nantes, renamed *Souris* 5.1808, and refitted at Nantes 5.1808).

Dimensions & tons: 63ft 7in x 20ft 0in x 8ft 6in (20.65 x 6.50 x 2.76m). 100 or 123/170 tons. Men: 9.

Wrecked 13.1.1813 while being pursued by a British corvette on the Pointe de la Garenne in the roadstead of St. Gilles.

Tanche (Portuguese mercantile brig *Americano* seized 8.1807 at Nantes, refitted at Nantes 4.1808, and renamed *Tanche* 6.1808).

Dimensions & tons: 52ft 0in x 17ft 0in x 7ft 0in (16.89 x 5.52 x 2.27m). 65/110 tons.

Found unsuitable and turned over 10.1808 to the *Service des Domaines*, presumably for disposal.

Victorine (Portuguese schooner *Sao Jose & Sao Joao*, also called gabarre, seized 8.1807 at Nantes, renamed *Victorine* 3.1808, and refitted at Nantes probably in 4.1808).

Dimensions & tons: 63ft 0in x 18ft 6in x 8ft 0in (20.46 x 6.01 x 2.60m). 105/160 tons. Men: 9.

Was at Nantes 11.1814 when the government ordered her to be returned to her former Portuguese owner.

Puce (Portuguese galiote *Tejo*, seized 8.1807 at Nantes, renamed *Puce* 5.1808, and comm. 1.1.1810 or before).

Dimensions & tons: 60ft 0in x 15ft 0in x 7ft 3in (19.49 x 4.87 x 2.35m). 69/120 tons. Men: 53 (1.1813).

Guns: 2 x 8pdrs, 2 x 4pdrs.

Listed in 1.1809 as a 80-ton transport and in 8.1809 as a galiote serving as station ship at Nantes. Unserviceable at Nantes and decomm. 31.5.1814. Returned 11.1815 to her former Portuguese owner.

Abondance (Portuguese mercantile schooner *Baa Fortuna* seized 9.1807 at Nantes, renamed *Abondance* 3.1808, and refitted at Nantes 4.1808).

Dimensions & tons: 64ft 6in x 18ft 0in x 8ft 0in (20.95 x 5.85 x 2.60m). 90-98/150 tons. Men: 9.

Ordered sold at Nantes 2.1814.

Active (Portuguese mercantile *Palma* seized 9.1807 at Nantes, renamed *Active* 3.1808, and refitted at Nantes 4.1808).

Dimensions & tons: 72ft 0in x 18ft 6in x 8ft 0in (23.39 x 6.01 x 2.60m). 113/180 tons.

Put on sale list and struck 10.1810.

Barbue (Portuguese yacht *Nostra Senora d'Adjuda & Boofe* seized 9.1807 at Nantes, renamed *Barbue* 3.1808, and refitted at Nantes 4.1808).

Dimensions & tons: 73ft 10in x 22ft 3in x 9ft 3in (23.99 x 7.23 x 3.00m). 160/210 tons.

Wrecked 15.11.1808 on Kikerick Rock.

Bonne (Portuguese schooner *Vénus* seized 9.1807 at Nantes, renamed *Bonne* 5.1808, and refitted at Nantes 5.1808).

Dimensions & tons: 77ft 8in x 20ft 0in x 8ft 6in (25.23 x 6.50 x 2.76m). 80-139/200 tons. Men: 9.

Was at Nantes 11.1814 when the government ordered her to be returned to her former Portuguese owner who sold her.

Nossa Senhora da Solidao (Portuguese mercantile galiote *Nossa Senhora da Solidao* probably seized in 1807, commissioned 4.4.1808 at Antwerp). Renamed *Lacrosser, Senhora da Solidao* 1.1.1810 (at Boulogne) and *Solide* 1.1.1811 (at Antwerp). Decomm. 17.6.1814, probably at Antwerp, and struck.

MISCELLANEOUS PRIZES (1808-1810)

Cados (American mercantile three-masted half-xebec from New York built in America and captured 2.2.1808 off Marseille by the tartane *Jalouse*).

Dimensions & tons: 71ft 7in x 24ft 0in x 10ft 0in (23.25 x 7.80 x 3.25m) plus 4ft 7in (1.50m) tween-decks. 260/400 tons. Draught 12ft 9in (4.15m) aft.

Sold 3.1812 at Barcelona.

Ragusas (Tunisian three-masted mercantile *Madzuka* built in America c1795/1800 and confiscated 12.1810 at Trieste).

Dimensions & tons: 87ft 6in x 24ft 0in x 10ft 6in (28.42 x 7.80 x 3.41m). 232-300/400 tons.

Guns: 4 x 4pdrs.

Captured 10.1813 by the Austrians in the surrender of Trieste.

Triestin (three-masted mercantile *Vierge de Turlani* built in Greece 1806/1807 and confiscated 12.1810 at Trieste).

Dimensions & tons: 74ft 6in x 23ft 0in x 6ft 0in (24.20 x 7.47 x 1.95m). 180 tons burthen.

Guns: 4 x 3pdrs.

Captured 10.1813 by the Austrians in the surrender of Trieste. May have been the *Triestina* that served the Austrians at Venice, Zara, and Ancona until BU 1826 at Venice.

(D) Smaller transports acquired from 26 June 1815

Into the early nineteenth century the designation *transport* was used primarily for small cargo- and troop-carrying auxiliaries of 150 tons or less, the larger ones being designated *flûtes* or *gabarres*. The general trend after 1815 was to reduce the number of these small transports on the fleet list. By 1826 the number of transports was down to 15, and in January 1827 this number was reduced to four (the large *Dromadaire* and *Rhinocéros* and the smaller navy-built *Cormoran*, and *Saumon*) by reclassifying most of the others as service craft. (*Dromadaire*, *Rhinocéros*, and *Cormoran* are listed in Chapter 13.) In January 1843 the number was still four (*Dromadaire*, *Rhinocéros*, *Saumon*, and the new 150-ton *Pourvoyeur*), but in January 1844 the transport category disappeared altogether after the two large units were struck and the other two were redesignated as gabarres. Small sailing transports quickly reappeared on the fleet list in 1847 with the 90-ton *Pilote* and the 50-ton *Île d'Oléron*

THE SMALLER TRANSPORTS

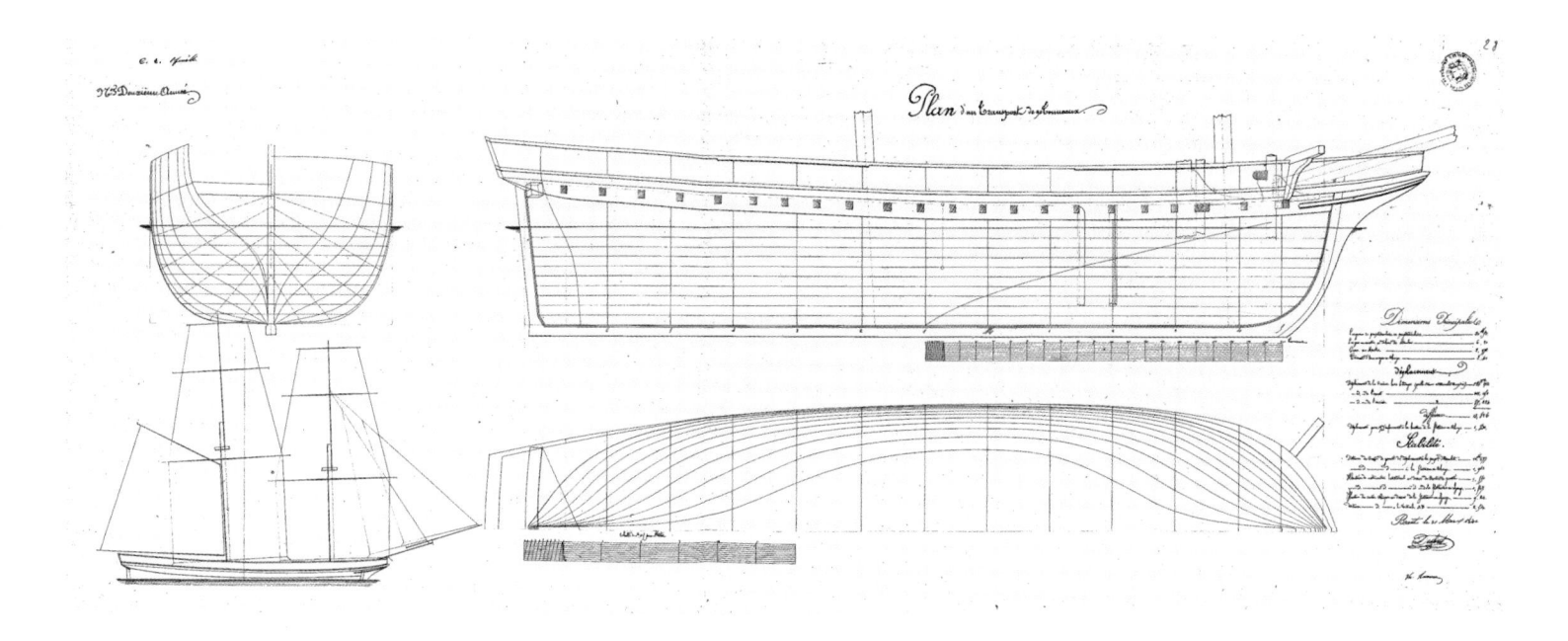

and were followed by others in subsequent years, but for the remainder of the nineteenth century most small support ships and cargo craft were carried on the fleet list as service craft rather than as naval vessels. After 1846 the term 'transports' was used primarily to refer to the larger former flûtes and gabarres and their screw-propelled successors.
Note: See also *Autruche* (1822), *Turbot* (1822), and *Calédonienne* (1858), listed here under schooners and sloops but often listed as transports. Also often classed as transports were *Autruche* (1822), *Turbot* (1822), and *Calédonienne* (1858), listed here under schooners and sloops in Chapter 8.

SAUMON – 150 tons. Probably designed by Louis Bretocq. Brig-rigged.
  Dimensions & tons: dimensions unknown. ca 250 tons disp. Men: 40-53.
  Guns: 6
Saumon Cherbourg Dyd
  K: 9.1821. L: 6.7.1822. Comm: 12.6.1824.
  Struck 8.5.1847 and BU.

POURVOYEUR – 150 tons, brig rig. On 27.3.1839 the Director of Ports reported that Cherbourg had recently lost the services of the brig *Saumon*, which was to become a training ship. He recommended building two new brigs like her for transport service. In December 1839 the Minister ordered the construction at Cherbourg of one brig-transport to serve that port, and the name *Pourvoyeur* was selected. She was designed by Victor Prouhet-Kérambour. Re-rated 200 tons in 1847, she reverted to 150 tons before 1853.
  Dimensions & tons: dimensions unknown. 150/250 tons. Men: 21-34.
  Guns: 6 x 6pdrs.
Pourvoyeur Cherbourg Dyd
  K: 11.1839. L: 30.9.1840. C: 4.1841 (Constructeur: Prouhet-Kérambour)
  Struck 29.11.1871, sailing lighter (*bugalet*) at Brest. Renamed *Divette* 10.1875 as a coal hulk at Cherbourg. BU 1887.

VIGILANT – 130 tons, brig rig. Designed by Alexandre Chedeville, initially as a *gabarre à clapet de 80m³* or mud lighter with one mast. Re-rated 150 tons c1845, 200 tons in 1847, and 90 tons in 1849, when she

Official lines plan for a 90-ton transport dated 31 March 1840. This vessel became the *Pilote*. (Atlas du Génie Maritime, Genoa collection, image 1-0024)

also became a schooner.
  Dimensions & tons: 22.00m wl, 20.70m x 7.00m x 3.20m. 200 tons disp. Draught 2.54m mean.
  Guns: None.
Vigilant Brest Dyd. (Constructeur: Chedeville)
  K: 6.1841. L: 12.3.1842. Comm: 1.6.1843. C: 6.1843.
  Struck 11.1852. Became careening hulk (*ponton de carénage*) at Saint-Pierre et Miquelon. BU or sold there 1876.

PILOTE – 90 tons, schooner rig.
  Dimensions & tons: dimensions unknown. 150 disp.
  Guns: Probably none.
Pilote Brest Dyd
  K: 1839. L: 20.4.1840. C: 5.1840.
  Probably service or colonial craft until comm. 4.8.1846 and on fleet list 1846. Listed 1.1.1847 on local service in Senegal. Decomm. 24.9.1853 and struck 31.12.1854. This or another *Pilote* (listed as a service craft) was comm. at Saint-Louis de Senegal on 1.1.1861 and decomm. on 17.8.1862 and hulked there. Sold or BU 1865.

DORADE – 300 tons. Mercantile clipper ship purchased on the ways 1.1860 under a contract signed on 25.12.1859.
  Dimensions & tons: 35.90m, 32.90m x 8.20m, 8.40m ext x 4.67m. 300/480 tons. Draught 3.67m mean. Men: 30.
  Guns: 4 carronades.
Dorade Gustave Guibert, Bordeaux
  K: 1859. L: 28.2.1860. C: 4.1860. Comm: 21.5.1860
  Struck 10.2.1873, ponton-caserne at Saigon 1875-76, then BU there.

PURCHASED AND REQUISITIONED SMALLER TRANSPORTS. As for the previous periods, this miscellaneous collection of vessels was procured to meet the needs of the day. They are listed chronologically in order of entering service.
Anonyme (schooner comm. 17.6.1815 at Brest). Mentioned for the last time in the 11.1819 fleet list.

Diligent (mercantile brig from Saint-Malo comm. 17.7.1815 at Fort Royal, Martinique, 76 tons, 43 men). Decomm. 25.1.1816 at Brest, struck c1818 and became service craft.

Cormoran (Danish mercantile dogger *Wilhelmina* purchased 8.1822 and comm. 9.5.1823 at Brest).
  Dimensions & tons: 23.81m x 6.05m x 3.28m. 200 tons disp. Draught 2.90m aft.
  Guns: 4 x 12pdr carronades.
  Decomm. 26.2.1824 and transferred to the administration of French Guiana. Wrecked 1828 in the Mana River, off fleet list 1828.

Bisson (merchant vessel comm. at Brest 1.4.1828, probably for the Navarino campaign). Decomm. at Brest 1.5.1840. Not in fleet lists. Named after the commander of the prize *Panayoti*, who blew up his ship to prevent its capture.

Charmante (mercantile brig comm. at Brest 10.6.1828, probably for the Navarino campaign). Decomm. at Brest 9.5.1837 (crew transferred to *Adèle*). Not in fleet lists.

Trémentin (merchant vessel comm. at Brest 1.5.1828, probably for the Navarino campaign). Decomm. at Brest 13.5.1834, crew transferred to *Virginie* 14.5.1834. Not in fleet lists. Named for the second in command on *Panayoti* and that vessel's only French survivor.

Adèle (merchant vessel comm. at Brest 9.5.1837 with crew of *Charmante*). Decomm. 1.10.1844, recomm. 1.9.1845, from 1.1.1848 was annexe to *Aube*, hospital ship at Gabon. Decomm. 1.1.1849. Not in fleet lists.

Seudre (mercantile brig sometimes called a *brick-aviso* laid down at Bordeaux in 1842, purchased at Bordeaux in 1842 soon after launching and comm. 16.12.1843 at Rochefort). Recomm. 26.11.1844 with crew of *Laurier*. Decomm. 28.4.1853, struck 1854, probably BU 1856. Originally rated as a 262-ton gabarre, she was re-rated as a 130-ton transport c1844 and was then changed to 150 tons c1845, 200 tons in 1847, and 150 tons before 1853.

Mayottais (merchant cutter or schooner purchased at Île Bourbon (Réunion) 1843, on fleet list 1846 and comm. 1.1.1847, 150/212 tons but tonnage rating changed to 50 tons 1850). At Mayotte in 1847 and 1849. Hospital ship at Nossi-Bé in 1851. Redesignated *Mayottais No.2* in 1855. Condemned at Mayotte 18.7.1856, decomm. 5.10.1857.

Mayottais No.1 (Built in the USA, possibly *Sea Horse*, purchased at Reunion 1.1855, renamed *Mayottais* c3.1856, and comm. 7.6.1856, 300 tons, 16-39 men, carried 4 guns). Wrecked 11.11.1858 on the coast of Ste. Marie de Madagascar, struck and BU.

D'Zaoudzi (mercantile, built at London in 1852, purchased at Reunion 10.1855 and comm. 13.10.1855, 60/100 tons, 31-36 men, carried 2 guns). Station ship 1860-64, struck 29.10.1864, transferred to colonial account of Sainte-Marie de Madagascar 1.1.1865.

Bonite (mercantile *Mogador*, built 1851, lengthened and changed from two-masted brig to three-masted barque 1856, purchased 11.1859 from Charles Van Cauwenberghe of Dunkirk, comm. 18.11.1859 and named 23.11.1859, 292 tons, carried 2 guns). Struck 1.7.1872 at Noumea.

Ressource (merchant vessel built at Nantes, purchased 7.1860 and comm. 25.7.1860, 200 tons, 31 men). Wrecked 12.11.1861 on the Chilean coast, struck 6.5.1862.

Postscript: Broadside Ironclads

Ironclad frigates

On 20 February 1845 the 29-year old *ingénieur-constructeur* Stanislas-Charles-Laur (or Laurent) Dupuy de Lôme (known to his family as Henri), who had just returned from a trip to Britain to study iron shipbuilding there, submitted a 'project for a steam frigate combining the conditions of speed and strength. Screw machinery, armoured iron hull'. His ship's 68.30 metre iron hull was protected by 9cm of laminated armour consisting of six 15mm plates covering the entire waterline and a 40m battery amidships. It carried 12 x 30pdrs and 12 x 22cm shell guns in the battery and four more of these guns on the gaillards at the ends. Machinery of 600nhp was to produce a speed of 11 knots or more, while sails and crew were reduced to a bare minimum. On 14 April 1845 the Minister of Marine ordered trials of the proposed armour at the gunnery test range at Toulon, but on 9 June 1845 he suspended these tests until similar trials at the navy's gunnery test range at Gâvres were completed. These, as well as similar trials in Britain, showed that laminated armour could not withstand 30pdr shot or 22cm shells, and the British trials also showed that iron hulls when struck by projectiles shattered at the impact point and produced lethal shrapnel inside the ship. As a result both navies renounced iron hulls for combatant ships for the next decade.

Following the success of three *Dévastation* class floating batteries in the attack on the Russian fortification at Kinburn on 17 October 1855, French naval constructors submitted numerous proposals for seagoing ironclad warships and, impelled personally by Napoleon III, trials of armour intensified. On 1 January 1857 Stanislas-Charles-Henri Dupuy de Lôme was named Director of Matériel in charge of all French naval shipbuilding, and the success at Gâvres in October 1857 of an armour scheme developed by Camille Audinet cleared the way for him to design a successful seagoing armoured vessel.

GLOIRE Class. Wooden hulls. On 4 March 1858 the Minister of Marine ordered the construction of three armoured frigates of 900nhp, two at Toulon and one at Lorient. A fourth was added at Cherbourg on 3 September 1858 in anticipation of the 1859 building program. Plans by Dupuy de Lôme for *Gloire* were approved by the Minister of Marine on 20 March 1858 and were also used for *Invincible* and *Normandie*. The engines of *Gloire* were ordered from the Forges et Chantiers de la Méditerranée (FCM) by a contract approved on 4 June 1858. The engines of *Invincible* were ordered with those of the iron-hulled *Couronne* (below) from Mazeline by a contract approved on 4 June 1858, but they

Coloured engraving of the *Gloire*, the world's first seagoing ironclad, under both sail and steam. The ship is carrying the original light barquentine rig as completed; this was later replaced with a full ship rig in 1861 before being reduced to a barque in 1864. (Courtesy of Beverley R. Robinson Collection, US Naval Academy Museum)

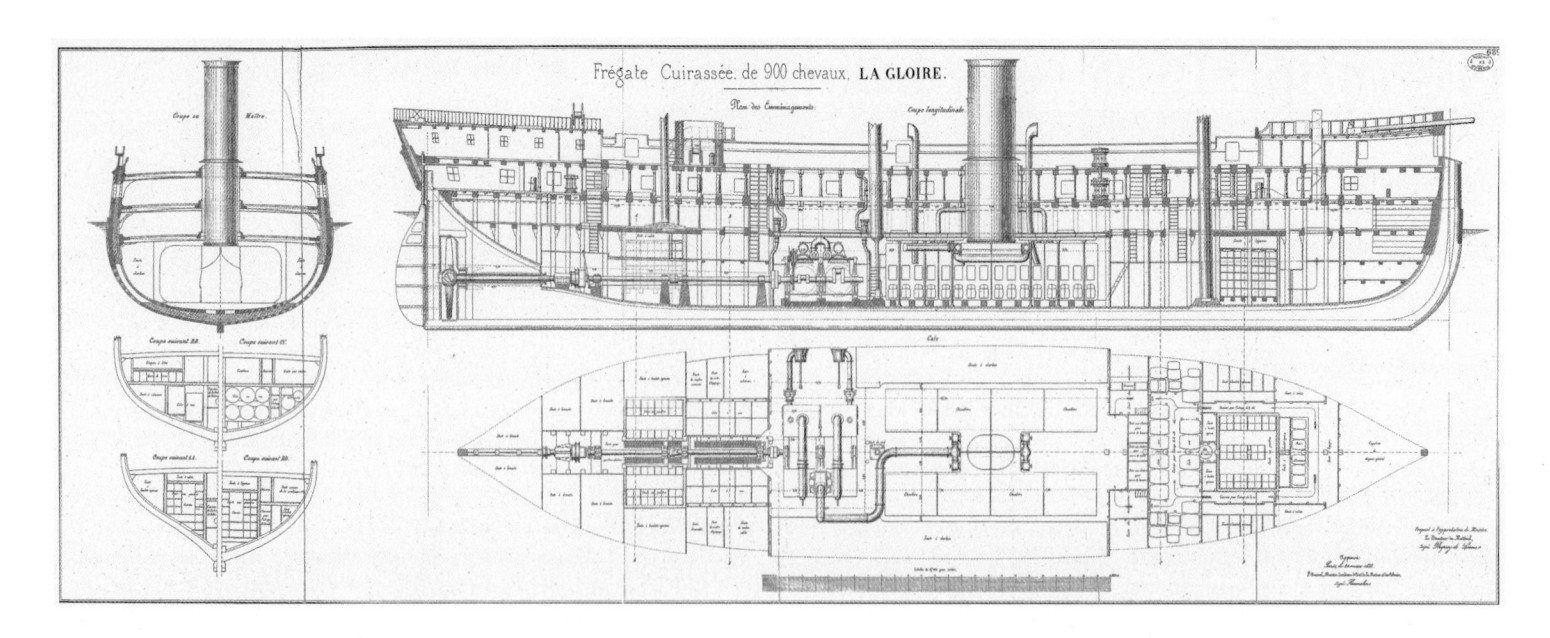

Official internal arrangement drawings of the *Gloire*, approved Paris 20 March 1858. (Atlas du Génie Maritime, French collection, plate 689)

were reassigned to *Napoléon* and new engines for *Invincible* were ordered from FCM by a contract approved on 18 May 1860. The engines of *Normandie* were ordered from Mazeline by a supplement approved on 22 September 1858 to Mazeline's contract for *Couronne*. The 900nhp engines in these ships were like those of *Algésiras* with some modifications. *Normandie*'s engines were reused in the 1870s in the coast defence ship *Tonnerre*.

Gloire was initially placed in commission (*ouverture de campagne*) on 26 December 1859 while still incomplete and ran preliminary trials in June 1860 and official trials on 20-21 August 1860. She escorted Napoleon III to Algiers in September 1860 and was the only escort able to remain with the royal yacht during a storm on the return trip. She then ran comparative trials with *Algésiras* (90). During her trials *Gloire* was criticised for rolling more than a ship of the line in calm seas, for shipping a lot of water in rough seas, and above all for the low height of her battery above the water of only 1.88 metres, but overall she was declared to be a masterpiece. She was originally given a light barquentine rig, but received a full ship rig of 27,000 sq.ft. during the winter of 1860-61 except for a pole bowsprit. All ironclads were re-rigged as barques in 1864. In 1869 the height of the battery of *Gloire* above the water was 2.03m.

Because of rapid changes in technology the armaments of these ships changed dramatically during their first few years, the calibres of the guns increasing and the numbers decreasing. The 16cm rifles initially fitted in these ships were muzzle-loaders. *Gloire* ran experimental gunnery trials in March 1862 with 17 breech-loading 16cm M1858 rifles on one side and 17 muzzle-loading 16cm M1858 rifles on the other side. The breech-loaders were clear winners, and in 1863 *Gloire* received a complete armament of 34 breech-loading 16cm rifles. In 1864 *Gloire* and *Invincible* had 32 x 16cm rifles and in 1865 *Normandie* had 12 x 50pdr (19cm) smoothbores and 12 to 16 x 16cm rifles. However none of these weapons could penetrate the armour carried by *Gloire*, and the new Model 1864 artillery was developed with calibres up to 27cm. In 1867 *Gloire* was rearmed with 6 x 24cm M1864 in the centre of the battery and 2 x 19cm M1864 on the gaillards, one forward and one aft, and the other two ships received similar armaments.

Dimensions & tons: (*Gloire*) 80.39m oa, 77.40m, 77.89m wl, 74.14m x 16.16m, 16.82m ext, 17.00m max x 8.16m. 5,617 tons. Draught 7.28/8.38m. Men: 570.

Machinery: 900nhp. Trials (*Gloire*, 1869) 2,699ihp = 12.31kts. 2 cylinders, 8 boilers. Coal 500-682 tons.

Armour: Side at waterline 120mm iron on 800mm wood backing from 2m below the wl to 0.5m above; battery 110mm iron armour on 660mm wood backing. Conning tower just forward of the mizzen mast.

Guns: UD 34 x 16cm M1858; SD 2 x 16cm M1858.

Gloire Toulon Dyd/FCM (Constructeur, Émile-Charles Dorian)
 Ord: 4.3.1858. Named: 8.3.1858. K: 5.1858. L: 24.11.1859. Comm: 26.12.1859. C: 8.1860.
 Comm. definitively 13.5.1862. Struck 27.12.1879 at Brest. BU 1883.

Invincible Toulon Dyd/FCM.
 Ord: 4.3.1858. Named: 8.3.1858. K: 5.1858. L: 4.4.1861. Comm: 6.4.1861 and 3.1862, C: 3.1863.
 Struck 12.8.1872 at Cherbourg. BU 1875-77.

Normandie Cherbourg Dyd/Mazeline.
 Ord: 3.9.1858. K: 14.9.1858. Named: 24.9.1858. L: 10.3.1860. Comm: 2.7.1860. C: 3.1862.
 Comm. definitively 13.5.1862. Struck 1.8.1871 at Toulon. BU 1871.

COURONNE. Iron hull. On 16 April 1858 Dupuy de Lôme wrote that his wooden-hulled *Gloire* should not be the exclusive model for all three of the ships ordered on 4 March 1858 but that other types of construction should also be considered. He proposed using the plans of *Gloire* for the second ship at Toulon, but for the ship at Lorient he recommended the iron-hulled design of Camille Audinet. The engines for this ship were ordered from Mazeline by a contract approved on 4 June 1858 and Audenet's plans were approved by the Minister of Marine on 1 September 1858.

As in the other early ironclads her armaments changed frequently during the 1860s. In 1865 she had 14 x 19cm M1864 in the battery and 4 x 16cm rifles on the gaillards, and by 1869 her armament had become 8 x 24cm M1864 in the battery and 4 x 19cm M1864 on the gaillards at the ends. The height of her battery above the water at this time was 1.88m.

Dimensions & tons: 81.85m, 80.00m wl, 75.00m x 16.50m, 16.70m ext x 8.60m. 6,004 tons. Draught 7.14m/8.69m. Men: 570.

Couronne, France's first iron-hulled armoured warship, carrying a full ship rig, so presumably photographed before the 1864 rationalisation that converted all ironclads to barque rig. (AAMM)

    Machinery: 900nhp. Trials (1862) 2,913ihp = 12.66kts. 2 cylinders, 8 boilers. Coal 650 tons.
    Armour: Side at waterline 100mm iron on 100mm wood backing on 40mm iron on 250mm wood on 10mm hull plating; battery 80mm iron on 100mm wood backing on 40mm iron on 280mm wood on 10mm hull plating.
    Guns: UD 10 x 50pdr (19cm) SB, 26 x 16cm M1858; SD 4 x 16cm M1858 (changed to 22cm rifled shell guns in 1864).
Couronne Lorient Dyd-Caudan/Mazeline (Constructeur, Audenet)
    Ord: 4.3.1858. Named: 24.9.1858. K: 14.2.1859. L: 28.3.1861. Comm: 11.10.1861 and 2.2.1862 (trials). C: 2.1862.
    Converted to a gunnery training ship 1881-85, a second gun deck being added and the armour and some boilers being removed. Replaced by *Gironde* 1.12.1908 and decommissioned 1.9.1909. Barracks ship for the main workshop of the fleet at Toulon 1908-1931. Struck 1914. Sold 25.10.1933, BU 1934 at La Seyne.

The building program for 1859 initially included four armoured frigates, of which one was ordered in advance at Cherbourg in September 1858 as a sister of *Gloire* to get work started right away. A Ministerial directive of October 1858 ordered constructors in the ports to submit plans for the other three armoured frigates (one each at Cherbourg, Brest, and Lorient), but on 26 April 1859 the Council of Works rejected all of these. On 10 June 1859 Dupuy de Lôme proposed that the Minister approve the Council's April rejection with the exception of a plan by Paul Picot de Moras which was 'very good'. It included 56 guns on two decks, engines of 1,200nhp for a speed of 13.5 knots, and a removable ram on the bow, and the Council's only criticisms were its excessive dimensions (91 x 17.88m) and the removable nature of the ram. Dupuy de Lôme proposed sending the plan back to Picot de Moras for revisions along the lines recommended by the Council and added that 'We can then build the ship at Cherbourg to either of his plans.' For the ships at Brest and Lorient Dupuy de Lôme took the two-deck battery and ram bow that had featured in several of the 1859 projects and produced the design for the 1,000nhp *Magenta* class. The Council on 30 Aug. 1859 again returned Picot de Moras' plan to him for revision but the Minister had already decided to limit 1859 ironclad construction to two ships. On 22 March 1860 the *Moniteur de la Flotte* reported in its unofficial section that the start of construction had been announced of a *vaisseau blindé* at Cherbourg that would have a length of 100 metres, an iron ram of 10 metres, an engine of 1,200nhp, and that would be named *Napoléon Ier*; this appears to have been a belated and mistaken reference to Picot's ship.

MAGENTA Class. Wooden hulls. These were the largest of France's broadside ironclads, with two gun decks and a bronze ram. They were identical in appearance except for a giant eagle figurehead on *Solférino*. *Solférino* was briefly called a *vaisseau cuirassé* when she was ordered and named on 15 June 1859, with the explanation that she had two covered batteries without gaillards and thus fell between frigates and ships of the line. However her original designation of *frégate cuirassée* was restored on 18 July 1859 because of her relatively small number of guns and because foreign equivalents were being called frigates. The plans by Stanislas-Charles-Henri Dupuy de Lôme were approved on 2 December 1859. The engines for both ships were ordered from Mazeline by a contract signed on 27 April 1860. *Magenta* received hull sheathing between September 1867 and May 1868. The height of the lower battery above the waterline was 1.60m.

Solférino at Brest in the early 1860s – before the 1864 order to rig all ironclads as barques – with eleven guns visible in the lower battery and twelve in the upper battery. By 1869 the lower battery in these ships was empty. Her large eagle figurehead is painted the same colour as the rest of the ship making it nearly invisible. (USN NH-43641)

Technology advances caused the batteries of these ships to decline from 52 to 14 guns by the end of the 1860s. In 1865 the upper battery armament of *Magenta* was altered to 4 x 24cm rifles and 4 x 19cm rifles with 4 x 19cm rifles and 2 x 22cm shell guns on the gaillards. By 1869 both ships had been rearmed with 10 x 24cm M1864/66 in the upper battery and 4 x 19cm M1864/66 on the gaillards, the lower battery being left vacant.

Dimensions & tons: (*Magenta*) 91.96m oa, 84.53m, 86.10m wl, 83.10m x 17.34m ext (18.30m after sheathing 1868) x 8.30m. 7,058 tons. Draught 7.03/8.63m. Men: 706.

Machinery: 1,000nhp. Trials (*Magenta*, 1869) 4,019ihp = 12.89kts. 2 cylinders, 8 boilers. Coal 625-800 tons.

Armour: Side 120mm iron on 830mm wood backing from 1.5m below to 1.6m above the waterline; battery 120mm iron on 670mm wood backing over a length of 45 metres. 100mm conning tower just aft of the funnel.

Guns: LD 16 x 50pdr (19cm) SB, 10 x 16cm rifles; UD 24 x 16cm rifles; SD 2 x 22cm shell.

Magenta Brest Dyd/Mazeline (Constructeur, Bernard-Charles Chariot)
  Ord: 15.6.1859. K: 22.6.1859. L: 22.6.1861. Comm: 22.5.1862. C: 5.1862.
  Began preparations for commissioning 18.9.1861, embarked her machinery 12.1861, comm. definitively 2.1.1863. Destroyed 31.10.1875 at Toulon when her after magazine blew up almost three hours after the ship caught fire. Struck 31.12.1875.

Solférino Lorient Dyd/Mazeline (Constructeur, Charles-Louis Duchalard)
  Ord: 15.6.1859 and named. K: 24.6.1859. L: 24.6.1861. Comm: 25.8.1862. C: 8.1862.
  Began preparations for commissioning 18.12.1861. Struck 21.7.1882 at Brest. Ordered BU 27.11.1882, BU completed 14.8.1884.

On 31 October 1859 the Council of Works discussed a 'project for the conversion of the ship of the line *Ville de Lyon* into an armoured ship [by M.] Guieysse' and decided not to pursue it. Other designs for armoured conversions that the Council of Works rejected at around this time were the conversion of the incomplete sailing frigate *Guerrière* to an armoured ram (28 April 1857), the conversion of the sailing two-decker *Jemmapes* to an armoured battery and ram for the defence of Cherbourg (first discussed 12 January 1858 and finally rejected 25 January 1859), and the conversion of the three-decker *Valmy* to an armoured frigate (5 July 1859). The *Valmy* project is described in the section on that ship.

PROVENCE Class. Wooden hulls. Napoleon III was very favorably impressed with the performance of *Gloire* when she escorted him to and from Algiers in September 1860 and decided upon his return to accelerate his naval building program based on this new type. On 22 September 1860 Stanislas-Charles-Henri Dupuy de Lôme proposed an immediate construction program of ten replicas of *Gloire*, nine with wooden hulls and one of iron. (This program also included 11 floating batteries as discussed below and the two *Vénus* class station frigates or corvettes listed in Chapter 6.). In his revised design, Dupuy de Lôme responded to the main criticism of *Gloire* by increasing the height of the battery above the water to 2.25 metres and modifying the bow for improved seakeeping, and he also increased the thickness of the armour in response to recent trials of 16cm rifles. The ten ships were ordered on 16 November 1860, their plans were approved on 19 November 1860, and they were named on 29 December 1860. Soon afterwards their nominal horsepower was increased from the 900 of *Gloire* to the 1,000 of *Magenta* to keep up with potential British competition by raising the designed speed from 13.6 to 14.0 knots. The specifications shown here for the class are from an 1865 sailing report (*devis*) for *Provence*, in which the height of her battery above the water was 2.22m.

The engines for seven ships (including the iron-hulled *Héroïne*, below) were ordered from FCM and Mazeline by contracts signed on 27 November 1861, while the other three ships were engined by Indret. Conventional two-cylinder engines based on those of *Algésiras* were begun for *Provence, Flandre, Guyenne, Surveillante,* and *Héroïne*, but the French then learned that the British *Warrior* had achieved 14.3 knots on trials and resolved to increase the designed speed of the other five to 14.5 knots by adding a third cylinder to their engines. All five received three horizontal cylinders of the same diameter, but in *Gauloise* and *Revanche* the steam was admitted simultaneously to all three cylinders while in *Savoie, Magnanime,* and *Valeureuse* it entered the middle cylinder and from there expanded into the other two. These three engines were an early form of double expansion or compound machinery, a type that soon replaced the original single expansion or simple engines. *Provence* ran her speed trials 14 February 1865, *Savoie* ran hers from 7 May to 9 June 1866, and *Magnanime* followed between 19 April 1866 and 15 May 1866.

The class was designed with 34 guns but, as Dupuy de Lôme later wrote, 'with the thought of reducing this figure when larger guns were available'. In fact, the armament of the class fell from 34 to 12 guns before the end of the 1860s. *Provence* and *Flandre* were completed with the mixed armament of 50pdr smoothbores and 16cm rifles shown below, two of the battery 16cm rifles being relocated in *Flandre* to the gaillards. *Gauloise, Guyenne, Héroïne, Revanche, Surveillante,* and *Valeureuse* were completed in 1867 with 4 x 24cm M1864 and 6 x 19cm M1864 in the battery and 1 x 19cm M1864 and 6 x 16cm M1858 on the gaillards. The battery armament of *Héroïne, Revanche,* and *Valeureuse* was probably soon modified to 8 x 24cm M1864. In 1869-70 *Provence, Flandre, Savoie, Magnanime,* and *Surveillante* carried 8 x 24cm M1864 in the battery and 4 x 19cm M1864 on the gaillards, firing forward from under the forecastle and aft from under the poop.

- Dimensions & tons: (*Provence*) 82.90m oa, 80.00m, 78.85m wl, 75.00m x 17.06m ext x 8.48m. 5,810 tons. Draught 7.00/8.40m. Men: 580-594.
- Machinery: 1,000nhp. Trials (*Flandre*, 1865) 3,537ihp = 14.34kts. 2 or 3 cylinders, 8 boilers (each with 4 furnaces). Coal 507-650 tons.
- Armour: Side at waterline 150mm iron on 750mm wood backing; battery 110mm iron on 610mm wood backing; conning tower 100mm just aft of the funnel.
- Guns: UD 10 x 50pdr (19cm) SB, 22 x 16cm M1864 rifles; SD 2 x 22cm shell.

Provence Toulon Dyd/FCM (Constructeur, Hyacinthe Joseph De Coppier)
- Ord: 16.11.1860. K: 3.1861. L: 29.10.1863. Comm: 25.2.1864. C: 3.1864.
- Comm. definitively 1.2.1865. Struck 3.5.1886 at Toulon, hulk used as gunnery target. Sold and BU 1893.

Flandre Cherbourg Dyd/Mazeline (Constructeur, Jean-Félix De Robert)
- Ord: 16.11.1860. Named: 29.12.1860. K: 28.1.1861. L: 21.6.1864. Comm: 20.2.1865. C: 5.1865.
- Struck 12.11.1886 at Cherbourg. BU 1887.

Savoie Toulon Dyd/FCM (Constructeurs, Louis Dutard and others)
- Ord: 16.11.1860. K: 3.1861. L: 29.9.1864. Comm: 25.3.1865 (trials). C: 4.1865.
- Struck 19.11.1888 at Cherbourg. BU 1889.

Magnanime Brest Dyd/Mazeline (Constructeurs, Émile-August-Leclert and Édouard Thomas Nouet)
- Ord: 16.11.1860. K: 27.2.1861. L: 19.8.1864. Comm: 1.11.1865 (trials). C: 11.1865.
- Comm. definitively 7.7.1866. Struck 19.6.1882. BU 1885.

Valeureuse Brest Dyd/Indret (Constructeurs, Émile Lisbonne and Édouard-Thomas Nouet)
- Ord: 16.11.1860. K: 13.5.1861. L: 18.8.1864. Comm: 27.2.1867 (trials). C: 2.1867.
- Comm. definitively 25.3.1867. Struck 26.2.1886 at Brest. BU 1888.

Gauloise Brest Dyd/Mazeline (Constructeur, Édouard Thomas Nouet)
- Ord: 16.11.1860. K: 21.1.1861. L: 26.4.1865. Comm: 12.4.1867. C: 4.1867.
- Comm. definitively 5.12.1867. Condemned 23.10.1883 at Cherbourg. BU 1884-86.

Guyenne Rochefort Dyd/Indret (Constructeurs, Henri Paul Denis de Senneville, Auguste Boden, and Henri De Lisleferme)
- Ord: 16.11.1860. K: 11.2.1861. L: 6.9.1865. Comm: 15.4.1867. C: 4.1867.
- Comm. definitively 6.11.1867. Struck 19.10.1882 at Toulon. On sale list 1883, BU 1887.

Revanche Toulon Dyd/FCM.
- Ord: 16.11.1860. K: 3.1861. L: 28.12.1865. Comm: 16.4.1867 and 1.5.1867. C: 5.1867.
- Annex to *Provençale* (station hulk at Toulon) 1889-91, headquarters for the mobile defence force (*Défense mobile*) at Algiers 1892. Struck 10.1.1893. BU 1893.

Surveillante Lorient Dyd/Indret (Constructeurs, Charles Louis Eugène Duchalard and Marie-Anne-Louis De Bussy)
- Ord: 16.11.1860. K: 28.1.1861. L: 18.8.1864. Comm: 13.5.1867. C: 5.1867.
- Comm. definitively 21.10.1867. Struck 13.5.1887 at Brest, headquarters ship for the reserves at Cherbourg. BU 1898.

HÉROÏNE. Iron hull. Although the Council of Works had recommended in 1859 using iron hulls in the new armoured fleet to the greatest extent possible, only one of the ten *Provence* class ships was built in this manner. *Héroïne* was laid down on the slip at Lorient vacated by the iron-hulled *Couronne*. Her engines were ordered from Mazeline by a contract signed on 27 November 1861. Her initial battery armament, shown below, was probably soon modified to 8 x 24cm M1864. The height of her battery above the water in 1867 was 2.12m.

- Dimensions & tons: 80.00m, 80.08m wl, 74.48m x 17.13m ext x 8.93m. 5,969 tons. Draught 7.77/8.27m. Men: 580-594.
- Machinery: 1000nhp. Trials (1867) 3230ihp = 13.05kts. 2 cylinders, 8 boilers. Coal 528-650 tons.
- Armour: Side at waterline 150mm iron on 380mm wood backing on

20mm hull plating; battery 110mm iron armour on 380mm wood backing on 20mm hull plating, conning tower 100mm.
Guns: (1867) UD 4 x 24cm M1864, 6 x 19cm M1864; SD 1 x 19cm M1864, 6 x 16cm M1858.

Héroïne Lorient Dyd-Caudan/Mazeline (Constructeur, Nicolas Le Moine)
Ord: 16.11.1860 and named. K: 10.6.1861. L: 10.12.1863. Comm: 1.4.1864 and 7.6.1865. C: 6.1865.
Struck 10.1.1893 and engines removed. Sent to Dakar under sail 1-2.1894 to be a station ship and floating workshop there. Floating fort 1.1898 to 1.1901. Scuttled off Dakar 29.12.1901 after an epidemic of yellow fever.

The only other seagoing broadside ironclad built for France, *Belliqueuse* (begun in 1863), falls just outside our period. A smaller vessel designed for overseas cruising, she was wooden-hulled with a complete 150cm wrought iron armour belt from the battery deck down to 1.5m below the waterline and 120cm side armour above it amidships over the guns. She was designed for twelve guns in the battery and two on the gaillards, all of the largest rifled type available, and was completed with 4 x 19cm M1864 and 4 x 16cm M1864 in the battery and 4 x 16cm M1864 on the gaillards. Like the *Magenta* class she carried a bronze ram at the bow.

Ironclad floating batteries

On 16 August 1820 the French naval lieutenant Jacques-Philippe Mérignon de Montgéry returned to France from a mission to the United States to collect information on the military aspects of steam propulsion for ships. Montgéry was particularly impressed by Robert Fulton's steam floating battery *Fulton I*, originally *Demologos*, and at the end of 1820 funds were included in the 1821 budget for construction of a similar vessel at Rochefort to defend the Île d'Aix, the British attack there in 1809 still being a recent painful memory. A tug to tow vessels on the

Surveillante probably near Cherbourg in the late 1860s. Five guns are visible in the starboard battery in alternating ports amidships, suggesting that she still has her original battery armament of ten guns (which increased to twelve guns in 1870). Note the conning tower just forward of the funnel. (USN NH-75901)

Charente between Rochefort and Île d'Aix was soon added to this program. A report dated 2 July 1821 of a Rochefort commission forwarded the preliminary design work of François Chanot on both the floating battery and the tug. The commission rejected high pressure machinery for the floating battery, recommending instead four low-pressure engines of 40nhp similar to the two in the tug design. The floating battery was soon abandoned on the recommendation of Montgéry, who had learned of serious problems with Fulton's floating battery, but the tug design was proceeded with leading to the *Coureur* class (see Chapter 11).

***PROTECTEUR* Class.** On 9 December 1846 the Ministry of Marine asked the dockyards to submit plans for two steam floating batteries to be laid down in 1847 under a seven-year naval program approved on 3 July 1846, *Protecteur* at Lorient and *Tonnant* at Brest. Their mission – similar to that of the contemporary British steam blockships – was to protect the entrances to important French rivers. They were to have a heavy armament of about 50 x 36pdr and 22cm No.1 shell guns, wood sides as thick as those of a 74-gun ship, a draught of not over five metres, and screw machinery capable of a speed of 6 knots. Of the two projects considered by the Council of Works on 23 June 1847 one submitted by Victor Gervaize was radically different, with a multi-layered iron hull, 30 guns, and a speed of 11 knots to permit use as a ram. The Council rejected both projects but was sufficiently interested in Gervaize's iron hull to add iron armour to its revised specifications for the ships and to order trials of metal targets at the artillery test range at Gâvres. These however were cancelled on 17 November 1847 because of doubts over the suitability of iron hulls and laminated armour for combatant ships.

In March 1848 the Council rejected another project for a floating battery submitted by Pierre Legrix and recommended using old ships of the line and frigates instead.

DÉVASTATION Class. Wooden hulls. At the outbreak of the Crimean War Napoleon III, wanting to attack Russian fortifications but realizing that wooden ships of the line could not withstand fire from Russian shell guns, ordered the resumption of the 1846 floating battery project. After trials showed that thick armour plates on a heavy wood backing could resist projectiles, the Minister of Marine on 28 and 29 July ordered the construction of 10 floating batteries (4 at Brest, 2 at Rochefort, 2 at Lorient, and 2 at Cherbourg). By contracts approved on 28 August 1854 armour was ordered from Schneider and from Petin Gaudet for five or ten batteries, and five 150nhp engines were ordered from Schneider with an option to add five more prior to 15 September 1854. However the navy found that French industry could not produce armour for ten batteries and suggested to the British on 15 August that they take on the construction of five of them. On 1 September 1854 the French reduced their program to five ships, which were designed by Pierre Armand Guieysse and named on 13 October 1854. During construction boiler power was increased to 225nhp but the official rating remained 150nhp and speed trials were disappointing. *Lave* began to go into commission for trials before she was launched. She, *Dévastation*, and *Tonnante* were towed to the Black Sea in about 45 days in August and September 1855 and proved the value of armour during the bombardment of the Russian forts at Kinburn on 17 October 1855. The other two were scheduled for use in the Baltic, but operations there were over before they were ready and they stayed at Cherbourg. The original sail area of *Tonnante* was 1,470 sq.yds on three masts with square sails on the fore and main, but the rig of the class was reduced to 419 sq. yd. after the Crimean War. The height of their battery above the water was 0.90m.

Dévastation or possibly *Lave* in reserve at Toulon, probably during the 1860s. Other ships laid up at Toulon at around this time included *Reine Hortense* (ex *Comte d'Eu*), *Roland*, *Colbert*, and *Tanger*, some of which may be visible in the background. (Marius Bar)

   Dimensions & tons: (*Tonnante*) 53.00m oa, 52.35m, 51.50m x 13.55m ext, 13.14m x 2.62m. 1,604 tons. Draught 2.50/2.80m. Men: 282.
   Machinery: 150nhp. Trials 317ihp = 3.70kts. 2 cylinders, 6 boilers, high pressure. 1 screw, 3 rudders, 3 removable masts. Coal 100 tons.
   Armour: Side at waterline 110mm, battery 100mm.
   Guns: (1855) UD 16 x 50pdr (19cm) SB. SD 2 x 18pdr or 12pdr carronades.

Dévastation Cherbourg Dyd/Schneider (Constructeur, Charles Eugène Antoine)
   Ord: 28.7.1854. K: 5.9.1854. L: 17.4.1855. Comm: 25.4.1855. C: 5.1855.
   Left Cherbourg 10.8.1855 for the Crimea under tow by the paddle frigate *Albatros*. In the Adriatic 6-7.1859. Annex to the gunnery training ship *Louis XIV* at Toulon 1866, as such carried 6-19cm. SD 2-24cm, 3-16cm M1860, and 1-22cm shell guns in her battery. Struck 9.5.1871 at Toulon. BU 1872.

Tonnante Brest Dyd/Schneider (Constructeur, Pierre Thomeuf)
   Ord: 28.7.1854. K: 5.9.1854. L: 17.3.1855. Comm: 23.4.1855. C: 4.1855.

Left Brest 30.7.1855 for the Crimea under tow by the paddle frigate *Darien*. In the Adriatic 6-7.1859. Struck 31.8.1871 at Toulon. BU 1873-74.

Lave Lorient Dyd/Schneider (Constructeur, probably Pierre Thomeuf)
Ord: 28.7.1854. K: 20.8.1854. L: 26.5.1855. Comm: 18.5.1855. C: 6.1855.

Left Lorient 6.8.1855 for the Crimea under tow by the paddle frigate *Magellan*. In the Adriatic 6-7.1859. Struck 9.5.1871 at Toulon. BU 1873.

Foudroyante Lorient Dyd/Schneider (Constructeur, Pierre Thomeuf)
Ord: 28.7.1854. K: 20.8.1854. L: 2.6.1855. Comm: 4.6.1855. C: 9.1855.

In 1859 carried 4 x 50pdrs and 12 x 16cm shell guns in the battery and a bronze 12cm shell gun on deck, and in 1870 had 10 x 16cm M1864 rifles in the battery and 2 x 14cm M1864 rifles on deck. Struck 29.11.1871 at Cherbourg. BU 1874.

Congrève Rochefort Dyd/Schneider (Constructeurs, Victorin Sabattier and Alfred François Lebelin de Dionne)
Ord: 28.7.1854. K: 4.9.1854. L: 1.6.1855. Comm: 2.6.1855. C: 8.1855.

Struck 13.5.1867 at Brest. BU 1868.

PALESTRO Class. Wooden hulls. These four vessels were built as replacements for the *Dévastation* class because of fears that the 1855 ships would deteriorate because they had been built hurriedly with poor timber. Their construction was decided upon at the end of 1858. A proposal to reuse the armour of the 1855 ships was rejected by the Council of Works on 29 March 1859, partly because the Council felt that 12cm armour (as in *Gloire*) was necessary. Stanislas-Charles-Henri Dupuy de Lôme then drafted plans that featured the smallest tonnage compatible with 12cm armour, reduced length to reduce the target offered by the ship, finer lines to increase speed, and twin screws with altered stern lines to improve manoeuverability. The Council of Works approved these plans in May 1859 and recommended that construction be assigned to the dockyards. These were overloaded with ironclad construction, however, and Dupuy de Lôme had two sets of plans prepared, one with a wooden hull to be built by Lucien Arman at Bordeaux and one with an iron hull to be built by the Forges et Chantiers de la Méditerranée (FCM) at La Seyne. One wooden-hulled battery, *Paixhans,* was ordered from Arman by a contract approved on 1 June 1859; the Minister of Marine approved ordering three more on 5 July 1859. These (*Saigon, Peiho,* and *Palestro,* in the original renderings of their names) were ordered from Arman by a supplemental contract approved on 18 July 1859 and named on 27 July 1859. The engines for all four ships were ordered from FCM by a contract signed on 9 September 1859. Construction was delayed by a series of design modifications, and *Paixhans* and *Palestro* were further delayed by late delivery of their armour (which had to be reordered in October 1860) and a fire in the shipyard's warehouses in January 1862. Trials were mediocre because of steering difficulties. The height of the battery of this class was 0.98m. The armament was later reduced to 10 x 16cm. When examined at Rochefort for recommissioning in 1867 they were found to be in bad condition, and they were disposed of at the same time as the *Dévastation* class.

Dimensions & tons: 47.50m, 46.40m wl?, 42.70m x 14.04m ext x 2.91m. 1,563 tons. Draught 3.06/3.22m. Men: 212.
Machinery: 150nhp. 580ihp = 7.50kts. 2 screws. Coal 40 tons.
Armour: Side at waterline 120mm, battery 110mm.
Guns: 12 x 16cm M1864.

Palestro Lucien Arman, Bordeaux/FCM (Constructeur at Bordeaux, Joseph Alexandre De Gasté)

Ord: 1.6.1859 (contract). K: 24.5.1859. L: 9.9.1862. Comm: 1.9.1862. C: 9.1862.

Fitted out at Rochefort 3-7.1863 by David Cazelles. To second category reserve 6.6.1863 and to third category reserve (out of commission) 7.4.1864. Struck 21.8.1871 at Rochefort. BU 8.1871-1.1872.

Paixhans Lucien Arman, Bordeaux/FCM (Constructeur at Bordeaux, Joseph Alexandre De Gasté)

Ord: 18.6.1859 (contract). K: 24.5.1859. L: 9.9.1862. Comm: 1.1.1863. C: 1.1863.

Fitted out at Rochefort 2-7.1863 by David Cazelles. To second category reserve 13.7.1863 and to third category reserve (out of commission) 16.4.1864. Struck 21.8.1871 at Rochefort. BU 8.1871-2.1872.

Peï-ho Lucien Arman, Bordeaux/FCM
Ord: 18.6.1859 (contract). K: 20.7.1859. L: 25.5.1861. Comm: 4.10.1862. C: 10.1862.

Began preparations for commissioning 15.7.1861, first comm. 5.10.1861. Fitted out at Rochefort from 3.1862 by Louis Marc Willotte. To second category reserve 24.3.1864 and to third category reserve (out of commission) 1.2.1865. Struck 15.11.1869 at Rochefort. BU 4.1870 to 10.1871.

Saïgon Lucien Arman, Bordeaux/FCM (Constructeur, Louis Marc Willotte at Rochefort in 1862)

Ord: 18.6.1859 (contract). K: 20.7.1859. L: 24.6.1861. Comm: 10.10.1862. C: 10.1862.

First comm. 10.10.1861. Fitted out at Rochefort 4-11.1862 by Louis Marc Willotte. To second category reserve 1.1.1863. Caught fire 15.11.1863 and sank in the Charente, refloated 30.11.1863, decomm. 1.1.1864, repairs completed 3.1864. Struck 21.8.1871 at Rochefort, partially BU and converted to embarkation hulk 1-4.1872, BU 1884.

REMPART Class (not built). Iron hulls. On 24 May 1860 a commission on coast defences recommended construction of eleven more floating batteries to give France a total of twenty for the defence of her main military and commercial ports (the nine already built or in hand were the five *Dévastation* class and the four *Palestro* class). The Council of Works insisted on iron hulls to make the units more durable, and on 16 November 1860 the navy decided to build five iron-hulled ships in the dockyards (*Rempart* and *Réveil* at Cherbourg, *Indomptable* and *Courageuse* at Lorient, and one unnamed at Brest) and six by contract.

The navy realised that the offensive use of floating batteries as in the Crimea was impracticable against England and that the main function of the ships would be defence of French coasts and ports. For this the ships need shorter batteries to reduce the target they offered plus the ability to fire forward and aft. The plans by Nicolas Le Moine that were ultimately used to build the *Implacable* class were given preliminary approval in July 1861 and eleven ships were ordered to them on 14 August 1861. In early November the orders were redistributed: *Rempart* to Cherbourg, *Indomptable* and *Courageuse* to Lorient, *Réveil* to Brest, and three *Implacable* class to Ernest Gouin at Nantes, and four *Embuscade* class to Lucien Arman at Bordeaux. The program was then curtailed for budgetary reasons by the cancellation of the four dockyard ships on 28 November 1861.

IMPLACABLE Class. Iron hulls. These ships were ordered from Ernest Gouin at Nantes by a contract signed on 13 September 1861. The final plans for this class by Nicolas Le Moine were dated 3 February 1862. Their engines were ordered from Schneider with those of the *Embuscade* class by a contract signed on 10 October 1862. The ends of the ship were cut down to permit fire ahead and astern; temporary bulkheads could be erected for transits at sea. Their designed height of the battery above the water was 1.45m; in service it was 1.32m. In 1870 *Opiniâtre* and *Implacable* were armed with 4 x 19cm M1864 in the battery and 2 x 16cm M1858 on the gaillards while *Arrogante* received 3 x 24cm M1864 in the battery and 4 x 12cm on deck.

Dimensions & tons: 44.08m, 44.00m wl, 43.00m x 14.60m, 14.76m ext x 3.17m. 1,440 tons. Draught 2.64/2.94m. Men: 200.
Machinery: 150nhp. Trials (*Opiniâtre*, 1865) 457ihp = 6.98kts. 2 cylinders, 4 boilers, 2 screws, 1 rudder. Coal 40 tons.
Armour: Side at waterline 120mm on 400mm wood on 12mm iron hull, battery 110mm on 400mm wood on 12mm iron hull
Guns: (1866) 4 x 16cm M1864, 6 x 16cm M1858-60

Implacable Ernest Gouin, Nantes/Schneider (Constructeurs, Charles Auxcousteaux and Charles Louis Duchalard)
Ord: 9.1861 (contract). K: 1.10.1861. L: 21.1.1864. Comm. 10.7.1864. C: 7.1864.
Replaced *Dévastation* in 1871 as annex to the gunnery training ship *Louis XIV* at Toulon, and as such carried in the battery 2 x 24cm M1870, 2 x 19cm M1870, 1 x 19cm M1864, 1 x 16cm M1860, 2 x 16cm M1864, and 6 x 14cm M1870 and on the gaillards 1 x 22cm rifled shell gun and 1 x 12cm. Continued this duty as annex to *Alexandre* 1874-77 and to *Souverain* 4.1879. Engineers' training ship 3.6.1880 to 1881. Struck 30.12.1884, became torpedo test platform at Toulon. BU 1908.

Opiniâtre Ernest Gouin, Nantes/Schneider (Constructeurs, Charles Auxcousteaux and Charles Louis Duchalard)
Ord: 9.1861 (contract). K: 10.3.1862. L: 23.3.1864. Comm. 10.1.1865. C: 1.1865.
To Brest from Lorient 1867-68 and to Cherbourg 1870. Designated 25.6.1881 to replace *Faon* as headquarters hulk of the mobile

Implacable seen from the starboard quarter in semi-derelict condition at Toulon, probably in the early 1880s. The low ends of this class gave it excellent end-on fire but limited its operations to harbours and other protected areas. A sister, *Arrogante*, was swamped and sunk in a sudden squall in 1879. (Marius Bar)

defence force (*Défense mobile*) at Cherbourg. Barracks for the *Défense Mobile* 1883, struck 19.3.1885 and continued service as barracks and support hulk. Support ship for a torpedo boat flotilla 1906-11. Sold at Cherbourg for BU 1912.

Arrogante Ernest Gouin, Nantes/Schneider (Constructeurs, Charles Auxcousteaux and Charles Louis Duchalard)
Ord: 9.1861 (contract). K: 20.3.1862. L: 26.6.1864. Comm. 25.1.1865. C: 9.1865.
To Brest from Lorient 1870 and to Toulon 1876. Gunnery training ship at Toulon 27.7.1877. Swamped and sank in a squall 19.3.1879 at La Badine, Hyères, raised 10.5.1879 and repaired. Struck 30.12.1884, headquarters hulk for the reserves at Toulon. Was tender to *Iéna*, guardship of the reserve, in 1896. Used as fleet gunnery target off Toulon 9.1898, Sold 1899.

EMBUSCADE Class. Iron hulls. These ships were ordered from Lucien Arman at Bordeaux by a contract signed on 13 September 1861. They were to have been built to the same plans as the *Implacable* class, but objections were raised that they needed to be able to operate in outer roadsteads as well as inner harbours and needed to match the increase in the armour thickness of the latest French ironclad frigates. The Minister of Marine had the plans for the Arman ships modified with a height of battery of 2 metres and armour of 14 centimetres. In addition the ends of the ships were raised to improve seaworthiness and the hull was shortened and widened, causing the number of guns to be reduced from

Refuge around the late 1880s as a hulk at Brest supporting the torpedo boats of the *Défense Mobile* there. This class, built at the same time as the *Implacable* class, was redesigned with raised ends to permit it to operate in open roadsteads. This photo has been attributed to Emile Mage who documented much naval activity at Brest between 1860 and 1900. (Marius Bar)

ten to eight. The resulting plans by Nicolas Le Moine for these ships were dated 30 January 1862. Their engines were ordered from Schneider with those of the *Implacable* class by a contract signed on 10 October 1862. The height of the battery above the water in the *Embuscade* class was recorded in service as 1.40m, barely more than that of the *Implacable* class. In 1870 *Imprenable* was armed with 2 x 24cm M1864 and 2 x 19cm M1864 in the battery and 2 x 12cm on the gaillards while the other three carried 4 x 19cm M1864 in the battery and no guns on deck.

Dimensions & tons: 39.65m, 39.50m wl, 38.50m x 15.60m, 15.80m ext x 3.92m. 1,449-1,600 tons. Draught 3.08/3.28m. Men: 180.
Machinery: 150nhp. Trials (*Protectrice* c1870) 409ihp = 7.40kts. 2 cylinders, 4 boilers, 2 screws. Coal 80 tons.
Armour: Side at waterline 140mm on 400mm wood on 10mm iron hull, battery 110mm on 400mm wood on 10mm iron hull
Guns: (1866) 4 x 16cm M1864, 4 x 16cm M1860.

Embuscade Lucien Arman, Bordeaux/Schneider (Constructeurs, Joseph Alexandre De Gasté, Adrien Charles Joyeux, and Louis Auguste Silvestre du Perron)
Ord: 9.1861 (contract). K: 25.2.1862. L: 18.11.1865. Comm. 22.1.1866 (trials). C: 1.1866.
Full commission 6.9.1866 and to Cherbourg. Back to Rochefort 1870. Struck 28.1.1885 at Rochefort. Headquarters hulk for the mobile defence force (*Défense mobile*) at Rochefort from 1884 until 1939. Sold for BU 1945.

Imprenable Lucien Arman, Bordeaux/Schneider (Constructeurs, Joseph Alexandre De Gasté, Adrien Charles Joyeux, and Louis Auguste Silvestre du Perron)
Ord: 9.1861 (contract). K: 25.2.1862. L: 17.12.1865. Comm. 1.2.1868. C: 2.1868.
From Lorient to Cherbourg c1870. Struck 7.3.1882, torpedo test and launch platform at Cherbourg. Sold for BU 1939.

Refuge Lucien Arman, Bordeaux/Schneider.
Ord: 9.1861 (contract). K: 25.2.1862. L: 1.5.1866. Comm. 1.10.1866 (trials). C: 10.1866.
To Brest 1868. Struck 5.7.1884 at Brest, barracks hulk for the mobile defence force (*Défense mobile*). Engineers' training hulk 1890. Listed as BU 1895, but hull was still in the Penfeld at Brest in 6-7.1940. BU 1945?

Protectrice Lucien Arman, Bordeaux/Schneider (Constructeurs, Joseph Alexandre De Gasté, Adrien Charles Joyeux, and Louis Auguste Silvestre du Perron)
Ord: 9.1861 (contract). K: 25.2.1862. L: 8.12.1866. Comm. 1.1.1867 (trials). C: 1.1867.
Full commission 24.8.1867 and to Cherbourg. Rammed a pier and sank in 1871, salvaged. Struck 9.8.1889 at Cherbourg, BU 1890.

Appendices

Appendix A   Standard Armaments of French Ships, 1786-1848

1. Ships of the line

Pre-1822 Designs		
118-gun	1786	LD 32 x 36pdrs; MD 34 x 24pdrs; UD 34 x 12pdrs; SD 18 x 8pdrs, 6 x 36pdr obusiers
	1807	LD 32 x 36pdrs; MD 34 x 24pdrs; UD 34 x 12pdrs; SD 14 x 8pdrs, 12 x 36pdr carr.
	1828	LD 32 x 36pdrs; MD 34 x 24pdrs; UD 34 x 36pdr carr.; SD 16 x 36pdr carr., 4 x 18pdrs long
	1838	As new 1st Class
110-gun	1786	LD 30 x 36pdrs; MD 32 x 24pdrs; UD 30 x 12pdrs; SD 18 x 8pdrs, 6 x 36pdr obusiers
	1807	LD 30 x 36pdrs; MD 32 x 24pdrs; UD 34 x 12pdrs; SD 12 x 8pdrs, 10 x 36pdr carr.
	1828	LD 30 x 36pdrs; MD 32 x 24pdrs; UD 32 x 36pdr carr.; SD 12 x 36pdr carr., 4 x 18pdrs long
80-gun	1786	LD 30 x 36pdrs; UD 32 x 24pdrs; SD 18 x 12pdrs, 6 x 36pdr obusiers
	1807	LD 30 x 36pdrs; UD 32 x 24pdrs; SD 14 x 12pdrs, 10 x 36pdr carr.
	1828	LD 30 x 36pdrs; UD 32 x 24pdrs; SD 20 x 36pdr carr., 4 x 18pdrs long
	1838	As new 3rd Class except 4 fewer carronades on the SD
74-gun	1786	LD 28 x 36pdrs; UD 30 x 18pdrs; SD 16 x 8pdrs, 6 x 24pdr obusiers
	1807	LD 28 x 36pdrs; UD 30 x 18pdrs; SD 14 x 8pdrs, 10 x 36pdr carr.
	1828	LD 28 x 36pdrs; UD 30 x 18pdrs; SD 20 x 36pdr carr., 4 x 18pdrs long
	1838	LD 24 x 36pdrs, 4 x 22cm shell; UD 26 x 18pdrs, 4 x 16cm shell; SD 20 x 36pdr carr., 4 x 18pdrs long
64-gun	1786	LD 26 x 24pdrs; UD 28 x 12pdrs; SD 10 x 8pdrs, 4 x 24pdr obusiers

Post-1822 Designs		
1st Rank	1828	LD 32 x 30pdrs No.1; MD 34 x 30pdrs No.2; UD 34 x 30pdr carr., SD 16 x 30pdr carr., 4 x 18pdrs long
	1838	LD 32 x 30pdrs No.1; MD 30 x 30pdrs No.2, 4 x 22cm No.1 shell; UD 34 x 16cm shell; SD 16 x 30pdr carr., 4 x 16cm shell
	1848	LD 24 x 30pdrs No.1, 8 x 22cm No 1 shell; MD 26 x 30pdrs No.2, 8 x 22cm No.2 shell; UD 34 x 16cm shell; SD 12 x 30pdr carr., 4 x 16cm shell
2nd Rank	1828	LD 32 x 30pdrs No.1; UD 34 x 30pdrs No.2; SD 30 x 30pdr carr., 4 x 18pdrs long
	1838	LD 28 x 30pdrs No.1, 4 x 22cm No 1 shell; UD 34 x 30pdrs No.2; SD 30 x 30pdr carr., 4 x 16cm shell
	1848	LD 24 x 30pdrs No.1, 8 x 22cm No.1 shell; UD 26 x 30pdrs No.2, 8 x 22cm No.2 shell; SD 26 x 30pdr carr., 4 x 16cm shell
3rd Rank	1828	LD 30 x 30pdrs No.1; UD 32 x 30pdrs No.2; SD 24 x 30pdr carr., 4 x 18pdrs long
	1838	LD 26 x 30pdrs No.1, 4 x 22cm No.1 shell; UD 32 x 30pdrs No.2; SD 24 x 30pdr carr., 4 x 16cm shell
	1848	LD 22 x 30pdrs No.1, 8 x 22cm No.1 shell; UD 24 x 30pdrs No.2, 8 x 22cm No.2 shell; SD 20 x 30pdr carr., 4 x 16cm shell
4th Rank	1828	LD 28 x 30pdrs No.1; UD 30 x 30pdrs No.2; SD 20 x 30pdr carr., 4 x 18pdrs long
	1838	LD 24 x 30pdrs No.1, 4 x 22cm No.1 shell; UD 30 x 30pdrs No.2; SD 18 x 30pdr carr., 4 x 16cm shell
	1848	LD 20 x 30pdrs No.1, 8 x 22cm No.1 shell; UD 22 x 30pdrs No.2, 8 x 22cm No.2 shell; SD 14 x 30pdr carr., 4 x 16cm shell

2. Frigates

Pre-1819 Designs		
18pdr	1786	UD 26 x 18pdrs; SD 10 x 8pdrs, 4 x 24pdr obusiers
	1807	UD 28 x 18pdrs; SD 8 x 8pdrs, 8 x 36pdr carr.,
	1817	UD 28 x 18pdrs; SD 14 x 24pdr carr., 2 x 8pdrs
	1828	UD 28 x 18pdrs; SD 16 x 24pdr carr., 2 x 18pdrs short
	1838	UD 24 x 18pdrs, 4 x 16cm shell; SD 16 x 24pdr carr., 2 x 18pdrs short
12pdr	1786	UD 26 x 12pdrs; SD 6 x 6pdrs, 4 x 18pdr obusiers

1819-1820 Designs		
36pdr (1820) rasée	1828	UD 28 x 36pdrs; SD 28 x 36pdr carr., 2 x 18pdrs long
	1838	UD 26 x 36pdrs, 2 x 22cm shell; SD 28 x 36pdr carron, 2 x 18pdrs long
24pdr (1819)	1828	UD 30 x 24pdrs; SD 26 x 24pdr carr., 2 x 18pdrs short
	1838	UD 30 x 24pdrs; SD 20 x 24pdr carr., 2 x 18pdrs long (*Calypso* and *Atalante*)

Post-1822 Designs		
1st Rank	1828	UD 30 x 30pdrs No.1; SD 28 x 30pdr carr., 2 x 18pdrs long
	1838	UD 28 x 30pdrs No.1, 2 x 22cm No.1 shell; SD 26 x 30pdr carr., 4 x 16cm shell
	1848	UD 26 x 30pdrs No.1, 4 x 22cm No.1 shell; SD 26 x 30pdr carr., 4 x 16cm shell
2nd Rank	1828	UD 28 x 24pdrs; SD 22 x 24pdr carr., 2 x 18pdrs short
	1838	UD 28 x 30pdrs No.2; SD 18 x 30pdr carr., 4 x 16cm shell
	1848	UD 24 x 30pdrs No.2, 4 x 22cm No.2 shell; SD 18 x 30pdr carr., 4 x 16cm shell
3rd Rank	1828	UD 28 x 18pdrs long; SD 16 x 30pdr carr., 2 x 18pdrs short
	1838	UD 22 x 30pdrs No.2, 4 x 16cm shell; SD 14 x 30pdr carr.
	1848	UD 24 x 30pdrs No.2, 2 x 22cm No.2 shell; SD 10 x 30pdr carr., 4 x 16cm shell

3. Corvettes

Pre-1822 Designs		
24-28 guns	1807	22 x 24pdr carr., 2 x 12pdrs
	1828	UD 20 x 24pdr carr.; SD 6 x 12pdr carr., 2 x 12pdrs
18-20 guns	1807	18 x 24pdr carr., 2 x 12pdrs
	1828	18 x 24pdr carr., 2 x 6pdrs (*Echo*)
	1838	18 x 24pdr carr., 2 x 16cm shell (*Echo* and *Camille* class)
Under 18 guns	1807	14 x 24pdr carr., 2 x 8pdrs

Post-1822 Designs		
Spardeck	1828	UD 20 x 30pdr carr., 4 x 18pdrs short; SD 8 x 30pdr carr.
	1838	UD 24 x 16cm shell; SD 6 x 18pdr carr.
	1848	UD 22 x 16cm shell, 2 x 22cm No.2 shell; SD 6 x 18pdr carr.
Open Battery	1828	20 x 30pdr carr., 4 x 18pdrs short
	1838	20 x 30pdr carr., 4 x 16cm shell
	1848	20 x 30pdr carr., 4 x 16cm shell
Corvette-Aviso	1828	16 x 18pdr carr., 2 x 8pdrs
	1838	14 x 18pdr carr., 2 x 12pdrs short
	1848	14 x 18pdr carr., 2 x 16cm shell

4. Brigs and avisos

Pre-1822 Designs		
Brig (16-gun)	1807	14 x 24pdr carr., 2 x 8pdrs
	1828	14 x 24pdr carr., 2 x 8pdrs
	1838	14 x 24pdr carr., 2 x 16cm shell

Post-1822 Designs		
Brig	1828	18 x 24pdr carr., 2 x 18pdrs short
	1838	18 x 24pdr carr., 2 x 16cm shell
	1848	18 x 24pdr carr., 2 x 16cm shell
Brig-Aviso	1828	16 x 18pdr carr.
	1838	8 x 18pdr carr., 2 x 12pdrs short
	1848	10 x 18pdr carr., 2 x 12pdrs short

Appendix B French Naval Artillery, 1786-1860

Designation	Cal.	Model	Lngth	Lngth	Weight		Notes
	mm.	Year	cm.	Cals.	Gun kg	Proj kg.	
Long Guns							
50pdr	194.0	1849	317.0	16.4	4624	25.15	
36pdr	174.8	1786	286.5	16.1	3520	18.28	Also M1856 (293.5cm)
30pdr No.1 (long)	164.7	1820	282.9	16.5	3035	15.34	Also M1849 (277.5cm)
30pdr No.2 (short)	"	1820	259.0	15.4	2487	"	Also M1849 (255.0cm)
30pdr No.3	"	1849	231.0	13.7	2140	"	
30pdr No.4	"	1849	223.0	13.3	1860	"	
24pdr long	152.5	1786	273.5	17.6	2504	12.08	
24pdr short	"	1824	253.9	16.3	2115	"	
18pdr long	138.7	1786	257.2	18.1	2062	9.12	
18pdr short	"	1824	240.1	17.0	1716	"	
12pdr long	120.7	1786	243.0	19.5	1466	6.09	
12pdr short	"	1824	221.5	18.8	1174	"	
12pdr No.3	"	1856	190.5	15.6	—	"	For small ships and boats
8pdr long	106.0	1786	259.8	24.0	1166	4.08	
8pdr short	"	1786	221.9	20.4	1005	"	
6pdr long	93.0	1786	227.3	23.8	840	—	
6pdr short	"	1786	200.3	20.8	630	—	
4pdr long	81.0	1786	179.2	21.4	540	—	
4pdr short	"	1786	153.8	18.2	390	—	
Pierrier (swivel)	53.0	1786	92.0	17.2	85	0.49	Also M1840
Obusier							
36pdr	174.8	1786	70.0	2.95	350	—	
Carronades							
36pdr	172.6	1825	143.3	7.9	1146	18.28	Also M1804, M1856
30pdr	163.0	1820	143.8	8.4	1011	15.34	
24pdr	150.8	1824	124.1	7.8	755	"	Also M1804
18pdr	137.6	1818	114.3	7.8	578	9.12	
12pdr	120.7	1818	98.6	7.6	381	6.09	Used in boats, etc.
Shell Guns							
27cm	274.4	1842	262.9	9.2	5200	—	Chamber as 36pdr
22cm No.1	223.3	1827	249.1	10.6	3636	25.86	Chamber as 24pdr
22cm No.1	"	1841	249.1	10.6	3636	"	Chamber as 30pdr
22cm No.1	"	1842	277.7	12.0	3614	"	Also M1849
22cm No.2	"	1842	246.4	10.6	2722	"	Also M1849
16cm	163.0	1827	217.6	13.0	1480	10.00	Also M1849
12cm No.1	120.5	(1849)	—	—	300	—	Field gun and small ships
12cm No.2	"	(1839)	86.0	6.8	100	3.9	Mountain gun in boats
32cm mortar	324.8	1840	124.4	3.0	4361	—	Also M1859
Muzzle-loading Rifles							
16cm	165.0	1855	249.1	14.3	3924	26.4	Conv. 22cm No.1 M1841
16cm	164.7	1858-60	293.5	16.7	3640	31.5	Also M1858
14cm No.1	140.0	(1864)	257.2	17.5	2300	18.7	Converted 18pdr long
14cm No.2	138.7	(1867)	240.1	16.5	1830	"	Converted 18pdr short
12cm	121.3	(1859)	191.0	15.4	610	10.8	Conv. Army field gun
Breech-loading Rifles							
16cm	164.7	1860	295.0	15.9	3640	31.5	
16cm	"	1864-66	338.5	19.2	5000	"	Also 45kg solid shot
14cm	138.7	1864-67	—	—	1900	18.7	

Notes: Lengths are nominal (face of muzzle to back of base ring) for muzzle-loaders, maximum for breech-loaders. Lengths of carronades, obusiers, and shell guns are close approximations. Weights of projectiles are for solid shot for long smoothbores and shells for the others. Shell guns were named after the solid shot that matched their bore: the 27cm, 22cm, and 16cm were also called 150pdr, 80pdr, and 30pdr shell guns respectively. Until 1862 the weight of the shell for 16cm M1858 and 1860 rifles was 30.4kg. The 36pdr obusier, the pierriers (swivels) and all three 12cm models were made of bronze. Smaller 24pdr and 18pdr obusiers were planned in 1786 but never produced.

Appendix C Resources Provided to the French Navy, 1786-1861

Year	Budget (as voted)	Spent (actual)	Men (actual)
1786	34.00	—	—
1787	45.00	—	—
1788	47.28	—	—
1789	—	—	—
1790	48.82	74.58	—
1791-1799	—	—	—
1800-1801	98.00	—	—
1801-1802	104.00	—	—
1802-1803	151.70	—	—
1803-1804	226.39	—	—
1804-1805	144.56	—	—
1805-1806	166.80	—	—
1807	105.84	—	—
1808	115.57	—	—
1809	110.48	—	—
1810	111.37	—	—
1811	157.00	—	—
1812	164.00	—	—
1813	147.37	—	—
1814	64.48	—	—
1815	39.62	—	—
1816	48.00	—	—
1817	44.00	—	—
1818	44.80	—	—
1819	44.55	—	—
1820 (with colonies)	50.00	49.42	—
1820 (Navy only)	43.93	44.31	10,782
1821	47.02	47.08	13,814
1822	54.13	55.16	12,596
1823	54.14	66.67	17,133
1824	53.83	58.72	17,159
1825	55.00	57.53	15,654
1826	56.00	58.90	18,912
1827	57.00	62.31	19,706
1828	57.00	81.18	30,210
1829	56.72	73.63	32,479
1830	58.11	83.33	32,339
1831	64.99	65.27	26,450
1832	58.31	57.24	20,572
1833	59.21	57.36	20,351
1834	55.67	55.02	19,943
1835	56.76	55.20	19,618
1836	54.88	61.06	25,588
1837	54.37	59.09	27,125
1838	57.38	64.47	28,892
1839	58.57	70.64	29,138
1840	62.10	87.97	36,901
1841	66.22	113.82	44,663
1842	118.03	114.01	41,152
1843	89.19	93.87	35,927
1844	91.23	99.13	34,775
1845	91.81	96.84	35,127
1846	94.32	111.51	35,325
1847	116.71	127.00	36,814
1848	115.68	124.03	33,748
1849	98.89	97.51	31,120
1850	91.31	84.49	29,432
1851	88.55	81.48	26,463
1852	95.79	86.01	29,662
1853	101.53	99.50	33,328
1854	179.19	173.76	56,768
1855	225.96	217.11	65,007
1856	226.60	209.02	52,548
1857	127.12	126.12	35,986
1858	115.18	134.94	35,871
1859	123.02	207.68	49,655
1860	123.50	203.99	48,771
1861	124.20	206.99	50,953

Notes: The amounts budgeted and actually spent are in millions of francs (livres tournois before 1790). Between 1791 and 1799, a period of economic chaos, provisional credits were provided to the navy but their attribution to fiscal years cannot be determined. The figures from 1786 to 1819 include colonial expenses, which were a little over 6 million francs in 1817-1819. Figures with and without colonial expenses are provided for 1820, thereafter the figures exclude the colonies. The figures from 1800 to 1815 may be actual rather than budgeted amounts.

Appendix D Strength of the French Navy 1789-1859

Year	Line of Battle Ships				Frigates				Steamers		Others	
	Active	*Inact.*	*Afloat*	*Bldg.*	*Active*	*Inact.*	*Afloat*	*Bldg.*	*Afloat*	*Bldg.*	*Afloat*	*Bldg.*
1.1789	—	—	70	12	—	—	65	10	0	0	97	0
1791	—	—	70	12	—	—	65	6	0	0	87	2
1792	—	—	76	7	—	—	71	6	0	0	81	0
4.1798	—	—	58	14	—	—	59	11	0	0	225	179
9.1801	34	12	46	5	31	5	36	7	0	0	187	5
9.1802	25	24	49	13	32	7	39	1	0	0	149	3
9.1803	36	12	48	12	27	6	33	12	0	0	137	17
9.1804	44	6	50	17	28	4	32	15	0	0	163	13
9.1805	49	2	51	23	33	0	33	11	0	0	209	15
1.1806	37	1	38	19	30	1	31	11	0	0	220	14
1.1807	32	5	37	23	29	1	30	13	0	0	259	11
1.1808	25	15	40	27	26	5	31	18	0	0	256	9
1.1809	39	3	42	19	29	5	34	14	0	0	313	14
1.1810	34	4	38	22	23	5	28	17	0	0	610	21
1.1811	37	9	46	26	25	5	30	23	0	0	328	24
1.1812	48	3	51	37	28	2	30	20	0	0	319	22
1.1813	53	4	57	39	34	3	37	20	0	0	400	18
1.1814	55	8	63	37	39	2	41	18	0	0	390	16
1815	—	—	56	16	—	—	31	10	0	0	293	6
1816	—	—	55	14	—	—	31	8	0	0	285	5
1817	—	—	54	14	—	—	32	6	0	0	264	7
1818	0	56	56	12	3	30	33	5	0	0	208	4
1819	1	47	48	10	5	24	29	5	0	0	177	4
1820	3	46	49	9	10	21	31	8	0	0	176	8
1821	4	42	46	9	15	19	34	6	0	0	168	6
1822	3	42	45	9	16	16	32	10	0	0	162	3
1823	4	39	43	9	25	10	35	5	0	0	181	4
1824	7	38	45	10	26	8	34	5	0	0	189	21
1825	7	35	42	13	23	11	34	7	6	0	209	18
1826	4	35	39	13	24	9	33	10	5	3	182	15
1827	7	29	36	20	25	10	35	16	5	3	185	20
1828	8	25	33	20	37	4	41	14	9	1	196	25
1829	8	25	33	20	34	6	40	22	10	3	182	25
1830	12	21	33	20	36	4	40	26	11	6	193	29
1831	7	26	33	20	23	17	40	26	12	5	192	26
1832	3	30	33	21	16	21	37	26	14	7	193	16
1833	5	24	29	23	15	20	35	26	17	4	192	19
1834	5	22	27	24	11	24	35	25	17	5	196	10
1835	8	19	27	26	11	24	35	27	16	7	196	4
1836	10	14	24	25	15	20	35	25	21	7	196	6
1837	11	11	22	26	15	21	36	23	24	7	188	3
1838	10	12	22	26	16	21	37	21	25	8	185	9
1839	13	8	21	25	16	20	36	20	29	4	203	4
1840	20	3	23	23	24	4	28	19	34	3	207	16
1841	20	3	23	23	21	8	29	16	40	5	206	9
1842	20	3	23	23	18	11	29	15	40	5	194	10
1843	11	12	23	23	17	12	29	17	43	6	190	5
1844	11	12	23	23	19	11	30	15	53	12	176	5
1845	10	13	23	23	18	13	31	18	55	19	170	3
1846	12	9	21	23	19	13	32	20	72	24	172	4
1847	9	15	24	22	19	20	39	19	82	19	163	16
1848	10	17	27	22	12	28	40	19	98	9	173	8

Year	Line of Battle Ships				Frigates				Steamers		Others	
	Active	Inact.	Afloat	Bldg.	Active	Inact.	Afloat	Bldg.	Afloat	Bldg.	Afloat	Bldg.
1849	8	18	26	23	13	26	39	18	102	7	172	8
1850	11	16	27	21	11	29	40	19	105	8	166	9
1851	11	16	27	22	14	25	39	18	106	5	153	8
1852	11	18	29	20	16	22	38	18	118	6	143	7
1853	14	—	—	—	14	—	—	—	—	—	—	—
1854	35	—	—	—	30	—	—	—	—	—	—	—
1855	37	—	—	—	32	—	—	—	—	—	—	—
1856	30	—	—	—	33	—	—	—	—	—	—	—
1857	25	—	—	—	19	—	—	—	—	—	—	—
1858	21	—	—	—	23	—	—	—	—	—	—	—
1859	26	16	42	5	27	18	45	17	203	50	86	5

Notes: Data after 1815 are as at the end of the year and are best compared with British figures for the beginning of the following year. Earlier data are as at the months indicated above when known. The 'others' category appears to be inflated in 1798 and 1810 by the inclusion of *bâtiments légers* and *canonnières* not included in other years. 'Ships of the Line' and 'Frigates' include screw ships; other steamers are in the steam column. The frigate figures for 1859 also include the first 'ironclad frigates'. Sources (all official) and counting rules varied during the period and the figures are best used to indicate trends rather than to show exact quantities.

Appendix E French Naval Programs, 1820-1857

1. Sailing Ship Programs

Program:	1820-24	1837	1846	1857
Ships of the Line				
1st Rank	10	10	10	1
2nd Rank	10	10	10	1
3rd Rank	15	15	15	4
4th Rank	5	5	5	4
TOTAL	40	40	40	10
Frigates				
1st Rank	17	17	15	5
2nd Rank	17	17	20	6
3rd Rank	16	16	15	9
TOTAL	50	50	50	20
Corvettes				
Spardeck	5	8	20	9
Open battery	5	12	20	5
Brigs and Avisos				
Large brigs	10	10	30	25
Corvette-avisos	30	30	—	—
Brig Avisos	15	20	20	9
Smaller types	—	50	30	44
Transports	—	50	16	25

Notes: The numbers refer to ships to be maintained essentially complete, either afloat or on the ways. The Programs of 1820 and 1837 also provided for 13 ships of the line and 16 frigates under construction, and the Program of 1846 included 4 and 16 respectively. The sailing ships listed in the 1857 program were those then in existence and were all expected to disappear without replacement during the next eight years.

2. Steam Vessel Programs

1 Feb 1837 (Program of 1837)

40 steamers of 150nhp and above

11 Feb 1842

5 steam frigates, 540nhp
15 steam frigates, 450nhp
20 steam corvettes, 320-220nhp
30 steamers of 160nhp and less

10 Nov 1845

10 combatant steamers, 1st Class (frigates), 600nhp
20 combatant steamers, 2nd Class (corvettes), 400nhp
20 light steamers, 1st Class, 300nhp
30 light steamers, 2nd Class, 200-180nhp
20 light steamers, 3rd Class, 100-90nhp

22 Nov 1846 (Program of 1846)

10 frigates, 600-450nhp, 30-20 guns
20 corvettes, 1st Class, 400-320nhp, 12-8 guns
20 corvettes, 2nd Class, 300-220nhp, 6-4 guns
30 avisos, 1st Class, 200-160nhp
20 avisos, 2nd Class, 120nhp and less
2 floating batteries, 500-400nhp, 50-40 guns

8 Jan 1857 (Program of 1857)
The Combat Fleet

25 ships of the line, large, 900nhp, 90 guns
15 ships of the line, small, 700nhp, 70 guns
20 frigates, 650nhp, 40 guns
30 corvettes, 400nhp, 14 guns
30 avisos, 1st Class, 250nhp, 4 guns
30 avisos, 2nd Class, 150nhp, 4 guns

The Transport Fleet (to carry 40,000 men)

27 sail frigates converted to screw transports,
250-200nhp, 4 guns
20 paddle frigates
47 other screw transports

The Transition Fleet (Existing, not to be replaced)

26 sail ships of the line converted to steam
3 'mixed propulsion corvettes' (*Biche, Sentinelle, Zélée*)
7 paddle corvettes
40 paddle avisos

Noites: The principal modifications to the Program of 1857 between January 1857 and its promulgation in November 1857 were the deletion of two ship of the line conversions (*Friedland* and *Jemmapes*) and the reduction in the number of sail frigates to be converted to transports from 27 to 5. Many of these were converted instead to steam frigates.

Appendix F   French Ministers of Marine, 1780-1870

Throughout most of the eighteenth century, the political head of the French Navy was the Secretary of State for the Navy (*Secrétaire d'État à la Marine*). From 1791 the post was designated that of Minister of Marine and the Colonies, a title which was maintained until 1893, when responsibility for France's colonies was separated off; an exception was between 20 April 1794 and 4 November 1795, when 'Minister' was altered to 'Commissioner'. The Minister also generally retained the title of Secretary of State. The holders of the post (irrespective of the actual title) from 1780 until 1870 were:

1780	(7 June)	Charles-Eugène-Gabriel de la Croix, marquis de Castries (marshal in 1783)
1787	(25 Aug)	Armand-Marc, comte de Montmorin Saint-Hérem (interim)
	(24 Dec)	César-Henri, comte de La Luzerne
1789	(12 July)	Arnaud de Laporte (absent)
	(16 July)	César-Henri, comte de La Luzerne (re-established)
1790	(26 Oct)	Charles-Pierre Claret de Fleurieu (resigned 15 Apr 1791)
1791	(16 May)	Antoine-Jean-Marie Thévenard (chef d'escadre)
	(18 Sept)	Claude Antoine de Valdec de Lessart (interim)
	(7 Oct)	Antoine-François de Bertrand de Molleville
1792	(16 Mar)	Jean de Lacoste
	(21 July)	Francois-Joseph de Gratet, vicomte du Bouchage
	(10 Aug)	Gaspard Monge
1793	(10 Apr)	Jean Dalbarade (capitaine de vaisseau, then rear admiral)
1795	(2 July)	Jean-Claude Redon de Beaupréau
	(4 Nov)	Laurent-Jean-François Truguet (vice admiral)
1797	(16 July)	Georges-René Pléville Le Pelley (rear admiral)
1798	(28 Apr)	Étienne Eustache Bruix (vice admiral)
1799	(4 Mar)	Charles-Joseph-Mathieu Lambrechts (interim)
	(27 Mar)	Charles-Maurice de Talleyrand-Périgord (interim)
	(2 July)	Marc-Antoine Bourdon de Vatry
	(22 Nov)	Pierre-Alexandre-Laurent Forfait
1801	(3 Oct)	Denis Decrès (rear admiral, then vice admiral)
1814	(3 Apr)	Pierre-Victor, baron Malouet
	(8 Sept)	Antoine-François-Claude, comte Ferrand (interim)
	(2 Dec)	Jacques-Claude, comte Beugnot
1815	(20 Mar)	Denis, duc Decrès (vice admiral)
	(9 July)	Arnail-François, comte de Jaucourt
	(27 Sept)	François-Joseph de Gratet, vicomte du Bouchage
1817	(23 June)	Laurent, comte de Gouvion-Saint-Cyr (marshal of France)
	(12 Sept)	Louis-Mathieu, comte Molé
1818	(29 Dec)	Pierre-Barthélémy, baron Portal d'Albarèdes
1821	(14 Dec)	Aimé-Marie-Gaspard, marquis de Clermont-Tonnerre
1824	(4 Aug)	Christophe, comte Chabrol de Crouzol
1828	(3 Mar)	Jean-Guillaume, baron Hyde de Neuville
1829	(8 Aug)	Henri Gauthier, comte de Rigny (vice admiral, did not accept)
	(8 Aug)	Jules-Auguste-Armand-Marie, prince de Polignac (interim)
	(23 Aug)	Charles Lemercier de Longpré, baron d'Haussez
1830	(31 July)	Henri Gauthier, comte de Rigny (absent)
	(11 Aug)	Horace François Bastien, comte Sébastiani della Porta
	(17 Nov)	Antoine-Maurice-Apollinaire, comte d'Argout
1831	(13 Mar)	Henri Gauthier, comte de Rigny
1834	(4 Apr)	Henri Gauthier, comte de Rigny (interim, after Vice Admiral Albin-Reine, baron Roussin, then negotiating a treaty, did not accept)
	(19 May)	Louis-Léon, comte Jacob (vice admiral)
	(10 Nov)	Pierre-Charles-François, baron Dupin
	(18 Nov)	Victor-Guy, baron Duperré (Admiral of France)
1836	(6 Sept)	Claude-Charles-Marie Ducampe de Rosamel (vice admiral)
1839	(31 Mar)	Jean-Marguerite, baron Tupinier
	(12 May)	Victor-Guy, baron Duperré (Admiral of France)
1840	(1 Mar)	Albin-Reine, baron Roussin (vice admiral)
	(29 Oct)	Victor-Guy, baron Duperré (Admiral of France)
1843	(7 Feb)	Albin-Reine, baron Roussin (Admiral of France)
	(24 July)	Ange-René-Armand, baron de Mackau (vice admiral)
1847	(9 May)	Napoléon Lannes, duc de Montebello
1848	(24 Feb)	François Arago
	(11 May)	Joseph-Grégoire Casy (vice admiral)
	(28 June)	Louis-François-Jean Le Blanc (vice admiral, did not accept)
	(29 June)	Jules Bastide
	(17 July)	Raymond-Jean-Baptiste de Verninac Saint-Maur (capitaine de vaisseau)
	(20 Dec)	Alexandre-César-Charles-Victor Destutt, marquis de Tracy
1849	(31 Oct)	Joseph-Romain Desfossés (rear admiral, also called Romain-Desfossés)
1851	(9 Jan)	Théodore Ducos
	(24 Jan)	Auguste-Nicolas Vaillant (rear admiral)
	(10 Apr)	Prosper, marquis de Chasseloup-Laubat
	(26 Oct)	Hippolyte Fortoul
	(2 Dec)	Théodore Ducos
1855	(27 Mar)	Jacques Pierre Abbatucci (interim)
	(19 Apr)	Ferdinand-Alphonse Hamelin (Admiral of France)
1860	(24 Nov)	Prosper, marquis de Chasseloup-Laubat
1867	(20 Jan)	Charles Rigault de Genouilly (Admiral of France)

Appendix G French Navy Shipbuilding Officials

1. Directors of Ports and Dockyards, 1777-1869

The position of *Directeur des Ports et Arsenaux*, immediately under the Secretary of State for the Navy, was created by Antoine de Sartine (the Navy Secretary) and Louis XVI in January 1777 specifically for Charles-Pierre Claret de Fleurieu, a naval officer and gifted scientist. The responsibilities of the office included managing the materiel of the navy, including the design and construction of ships, as well as other activities within the naval ports. Fleurieu held the position for fifteen years during which he assembled the fleets that fought during the War of American Independence and launched voyages of discovery, notably that of La Pérouse in 1785. Both the office and its incumbents remained remarkably stable over time except during the revolution. The first major change to the name of the position after 1815 came around 1850 when it became the *Direction des Travaux* (Directorate of Works), and by 1856 it had become the *Direction du Matériel* (Directorate of Materiel). The following individuals held this position between 1777 and 1869, the dates being approximate and some individuals with short incumbency possibly being missing:

1777	Charles-Pierre Claret de Fleurieu (chevalier de Fleurieu)
1790	Guillaume de Liberge de Granchain
1791	Joseph de Pouget de Saint André
1793	Taillevis, Tréhouart, Chappatte
1795	Jean-Marie-Théodore David
1797	Jacques-Antoine-Isidore Forestier
1800	Charles-Marie Jurien
1823	Jean-Marguerite, baron Tupinier
1843	Mathurin Boucher
1850	Gustave-Benôit Garnier
1856	Alexandre Auguste-Gustave Robiou de Lavrignais
1857	Stanislas-Charles-Henri-Laur Dupuy de Lôme (to 1869)

2. Inspectors of (Naval) Construction

In 1783 and 1784 Sartine's successor, the marquis de Castries, appointed the chevalier Jean-Charles de Borda as *Directeur de l'École des Ingénieurs de vaisseaux* and *Inspecteur des Constructions*, both posts being in Paris. The title of *Inspecteur des Constructions* originated in an ordinance of Louis XIV in 1689 and had previously been held between 1739 and 1781 by Henri-Louis Duhamel du Monceau, a botanist and expert in naval timber who had established the *École des Ingénieurs de vaisseaux* in 1765. Borda was a naval *capitaine de vaisseau* with extensive experience at sea and a noted scientist and savant. He had already participated in 1782 in the selection of Sané's design for the 74-gun ship as the standard for the French Navy, and in 1786 and 1787 he directed competitions that led to the selection of Sané's 118-gun and 80-gun designs as the standards for the other two types of French ships of the line. He retained his titles until just before his death in 1799. Sané became *inspecteur des constructions navales de l'Atlantique* in 1798 and then continued his oversight role as the navy's first *inspecteur général du génie maritime* (1800-1817). Borda's role as a naval educator was remembered in the assignment of his name to successive school ships of the French Naval Academy at Brest between 1839 and 1912.

3. Inspecteurs Généraux du Génie Maritime

The *Inspecteur général du Génie maritime* was the senior officer in his corps with a rank equivalent to Rear Admiral. The *inspecteurs généraux* after Sané concentrated on administration and usually did not take as prominent role in ship design as did some of their subordinate *directeurs des constructions*, *ingénieurs*, and *sous-ingénieurs*. The following were appointed to this position on the dates shown.

(27 April 1800)	Jacques-Noël Sané
12 November 1817	Pierre-Jacques-Nicolas Rolland
1 August 1837	Mathurin-François Boucher
2 December 1842	Jacques-Louis Bonard
29 October 1847	Mathurin-François Boucher
1 January 1851	Paul-Marie Leroux
12 April 1854	Gustave-Benoît Garnier
17 March 1858	Hippolyte-Louis-Édouard Prétot

In addition Baron Pierre-Charles-François Dupin was awarded the rank of *Inspecteur général du Génie maritime* on 10 July 1843 on an honorary basis and remained on the list until around 1848.

Appendix H Selected French Naval Constructors, 1786-1861

The following French naval constructors are mentioned in this book for work performed after 1785. A Royal Ordinance of 25 March 1765 created the title of *ingénieurs constructeurs de la Marine*, gave these former civilian naval constructors a military uniform, and defined the structure of the new corps. A law of 21 October 1795 decided that the engineers who built the navy's ships would henceforth be recruited from graduates of the new *École Polytechnique*, and regulation of 27 April 1800 introduced the name *Génie Maritime* for this corps. The dates that Polytechnique students selected the Génie are shown below – they were normally admitted to the corps as students (*élèves*) shortly thereafter. While every effort has been made to ensure accuracy in this table, no guarantee can be given that there are not errors or omissions

Last name	*Prénoms and service*
Abauzir	Jean-Jacques. Active at Toulon 1794-1798.
Alexandre	Charles-Robert. Polytechnique 1803, retired 1847.
Allix	Georges Baptiste François, 1808. Polytechnique 1830, retired 1870.
Antoine	Charles Eugène, 1823-1874. Polytechnique 1844.
Antoine	Louis Charles, 1825. Polytechnique 1844, retired 1886.
Arnaud	Antoine, 1775. Polytechnique 1796, retired 1825. Listed as Auguste-François from around 1813.
Aubert	Active at Cherbourg 1794-1801.
Audenet	Camille. Polytechnique 1843.
Auriol	Antoine, 1797. Polytechnique 1818, retired 1858.
Aurous	Jules, 1825. Polytechnique 1844, retired 1890.
Auxcousteaux	Charles Marie Hippolyte, 1820. Polytechnique 1842, retired 1869.
Baron	Jean, 1839. On leave 1882.
Barrallier	Louis Charles, 1780-1855.
Barthélemy	Jean-Louis-Henri (J.-B.-L.-H.-N.). Polytechnique 1800. Deceased 1810.
Baudry	Jean, 1758-1824.
Bayle	Jean Baptiste Gabriel Jules Aymeric, 1804. Polytechnique 1825, retired 1861.
Bayssellance	Jean Adrien, 1829. Polytechnique 1848, retired 1877.
Besuchet	Anne François Joseph, 1790-1858. Polytechnique 1812, retired 1842.
Binet	Philippe Thomas, 1788-1855. Polytechnique 1811, retired 1854.
Boden	Auguste Émile, 1834. Retired 1883.
Bonard	Jacques Louis, 1777-1848.
Bonjean	Antoine Nicolas François, 1778. Retired 1815.
Bonnet-Lescure	Antoine, 1777. Polytechnique 1800, retired 1831.
Boucher	Mathurin François, 1778-1851. Polytechnique 1797, retired 1851.
Boumard	Charles-Marc-Marie-Édouard. Polytechnique 1842.
Bretocq	Louis Jean Baptiste, 1774-1855.
Brun	Charles Marie, 1821-1897. Polytechnique 1840.
Brun Sainte-Catherine	Jacques Balthazar, 1759-?. Sous-ingénieur 1781.
Campaignac	Antoine Bernard, 1792-1866. Polytechnique 1813, retired 1841.
Carlet	Marie Pierre Honoré Félix, 1827. Polytechnique 1847, retired 1892.
Caro	François, 1730-1810.
Cazavan	Amédée, 1835. Polytechnique 1855.
Cazelles	David Jules Frédéric Émile, 1836-1880.
Chanot	François. Polytechnique 1809. Deceased in Egypt.
Chapelle	Joseph Véronique Charles, 1716, deceased after 1791.
Chariot	Bernard Charles Jacques, 1803. Retired 1863.
Chaumont	Jean François, 1774-1856. Polytechnique 1798, retired 1835.
Chedeville	Alexandre Louis, 1807. Polytechnique 1828, retired 1872.
Chevillard (aîné)	Henri, 1737 – c1810. Ingénieur ordinaire 1774.
Chevillard (cadet)	Jean Denis, 1738-1804. Ingénieur-constructeur en chef 1781.
Clarke	Jean-Georges-Luc. Polytechnique 1823, resigned 1839.
Cochon de Lapparent	Henri. Polytechnique 1828.
Compère-Desfontaines	Théophile Zéphirin, 1825. Polytechnique 1846-retired 1886.
Corrard	Louis Alexandre, 1817. Polytechnique 1837, retired 1871.
Coulomb	Joseph Marie Blaise, 1728, deceased after 1800.
Courbebaisse	Émile Marie Victor, 1825. Polytechnique 1840, retired 1890.
Courtin	Nicolas-Émile. Polytechnique 1838.
Cros	Joseph. Polytechnique 1827.
D'Ingler	Louis-Jules. Polytechnique 1824.

Last name	Prenoms and service
Daniel	Pierre Félix, 1783-1869. Polytechnique 1804, retired 1848.
Daviel	Joseph Anne Marie Simon Pierre, 1784-1847. Polytechnique 1806.
De Bussy	Marie-Anne-Louis. Polytechnique 1844.
De Coppier	Hyacinthe Joseph, 1818-1871. Polytechnique 1840.
De Gasté	Joseph Alexandre Adélaïde, 1811-1893. Polytechnique 1833.
De Gérando	Léon, 1832-1887.
De Lacalle	Eugène. At Rochefort in the 1860s.
De Lisleferme	Henri. Polytechnique 1838.
De Robert	Jean Félix, 1818-1881. Polytechnique 1840.
De Roussel	Anselme, 1821. Polytechnique 1842, retired 1880.
De Sandfort	Eugène-Jacques-Louis. Polytechnique 1843.
Degay	Pierre, 1758-1819.
Delacour	Marc-Henri-Victor. Polytechnique 1846.
Delamorinière	Jean François Henri, 1791-1878. Polytechnique 1811, retired 1844.
Delapoix de Freminville	Antoine-Joseph. Polytechnique 1842.
Delisleferme	Henri, 1816. Retired 1864.
Demouy	Marie Eugène, 1840-1874.
Denaix	Jean. Ingénieur (2nd Class) by 1801.
Denis de Senneville	Henri Paul Ernest, 1819. Polytechnique 1841-retired 1885.
Denÿs	Étienne Daniel, 1725-1800. Civilian shipbuilder at Dunkirk, made a sous-ingénieur without pay in 1771 and promoted to ingénieur ordinaire in 1786-88.
Desmarest	Charles Léger, 1780-1825. Polytechnique 1803.
Dorian	Émile Charles Frédéric, 1819. Polytechnique 1839, retired 1884.
Dreppe	Joseph Marie Gaspard, 1787. Polytechnique 1806, retired 1837.
Dubois	Louis Joseph Félix, 1787. Retired 1814.
Duchalard	Charles Louis Eugène. Polytechnique 1840.
Dufay	see Sanial-Dufay.
Duhamel	Sous-ingénieur 1782, at Rochefort 1786-1792, then at Saint-Malo.
Dumonteil	Jean, 1788-1853. Polytechnique 1809. Retired 1848.
Dupin	Pierre-Charles-François, 1784-1873.
Dupuy de Lôme	Stanislas Charles Henri Laur (or Laurent), 1816-1885. Polytechnique 1837.
Dutard	Louis. Polytechnique 1845.
Etesse	François Louis Anne, 1763-1814.
Etiennez	Émile, 1799-1845. Polytechnique 1821.
Fabien	Martin or Jacques. Premier maître charpentier nominated 1762 and active at Cherbourg and Le Havre 1788-1793.
Fabre d'Églantine	Louis Théodore Jules Vincent, 1779-1840. Polytechnique 1802, retired 1833.
Fauveau	Joseph Germain Chéri, 1795-1873. Polytechnique 1813.
Féraud	Jean Louis, 1750-1809.
Filhon	Paul, 1768. Retired 1830.
Forfait	Pierre Alexandre Laurent, 1752-1807. Sous-ingénieur 1777.
Forquenot	Armand, 1819. Polytechnique 1841, on leave 1865.
Garnier	Gustave Benoit, 1792-1859. Polytechnique 1813.
Garnier Saint-Maurice (cadet)	Honoré Maurice Philibert, 1760-1837. Sous-ingénieur in 1784.
Garrigues	Jean-Charles. Ingénieur (2nd Class) by 1801.
Gauthier (Gautier)	Jean François, 1733-1800. On the liste 1786-8 as Capitaine de Vaisseau, Director at Toulon.
Geoffroy	Antoine, 1772-1851.
Gervaize	Victor Charles Eudore, 1817. Polytechnique 1837, retired 1881.
Ginoux	Jean Joseph, 1723-1785. Ingénieur ordinaire 1765.
Graciot	Active at Rochefort 1789-1793.
Gréhan	François Toussaint, 1772-1821.
Greslé	Philippe, 1776. Polytechnique 1798, retired 1821.
Guède	Jules Philibert, 1824. Polytechnique 1845, retired 1884.
Guérin	Jean-Nicolas. Sous-ingénieur (1st Class) by 1803.
Guesnet	Achille Antoine, 1825. Polytechnique 1846, retired 1873.
Guieysse	Pierre Armand, 1810-1891. Polytechnique 1829.
Guignace	Léon Michel, 1731-1805. Ingénieur-constructeur en chef 1776.
Guillemard	Jean François, 1784. Polytechnique 1803, retired 1834.
Hamart	André. Polytechnique 1804. Killed in the Russian campaign 1812.
Haran	Raymond Antoine, 1748-?. Ingénieur ordinaire 1778.
Hérel	Jean-Baptiste (J.-B.-L.) Polytechnique 1796, resigned 1810.

Last name	Prenoms and service
Hubert	Jean Baptiste, 1781-1845. Polytechnique 1799.
Jaunez	Pierre Dieudonné. Polytechnique 1798, resigned 1812.
Jay	Charles Louis. Polytechnique 1846.
Jobart-Dumesnil	Claude-Marie. Polytechnique 1826, resigned 1837.
Jobert	Honoré Louis, 1789. Polytechnique 1808, retired 1817.
Joffre	Firmin Isidore, 1799. Polytechnique 1820, retired 1864.
Joyeux	Adrien Charles, 1825. Polytechnique 1846, retired 1880.
Kerris	Henri Jules, 1808. Polytechnique 1830, retired 1869.
Lafosse	Jean-François. Ingénieur ordinaire by 1798, active since 1794.
Laglaine	Active at Rochefort 1789-1793.
Laimant	Amédée. Polytechnique 1809. To the control service 1844, retired 1853.
Lair	Pierre Jacques Guillaume, 1769-1830.
Lamaëstre	Jean-Baptiste François. Polytechnique 1824.
Lambert	Louis-Philibert-Armand. Polytechnique 1830. Deceased 1839 in Mexico.
Lamothe fils (La Motte, La Mothe)	Jacques Augustin, 1762-1824. Sous-ingénieur 1782.
Lamothe (De La Motte, La Mothe)	Pierre-Augustin. Ingénieur ordinaire 1766.
Langlois	Noël François, 1775. Polytechnique 1796, retired 1830.
Larchevesque-Thibaut	Jean Baptiste, 1792-1852. Polytechnique 1812.
Lavrignais (de)	see Robiou de Lavrignais.
Layrle	Charles-Louis-Marie, 1831. Polytechnique 1853.
Le Déan	Aimé Jean Louis Nicolas René, 1776-1841. Polytechnique 1796.
Le Grix	Pierre Félix, 1790. Polytechnique 1811, retired 1848.
Le Jouteux	Jean Émile, 1802. Retired 1852.
Le Moine	Nicolas Marie Julien, 1827. Polytechnique 1848, on leave 1872.
Le Roy	Jean-Jacques. Ingénieur ordinaire 1778.
Lebas	Jean Baptiste Apollinaire, 1797. Polytechnique 1818, retired 1858.
Lebelin de Dionne	Alfred François, 1824. Polytechnique 1846, retired 1882.
Leboulleur de Courlon	Louis-Clément. Polytechnique 1843.
Lebreton	Clément-Marie. Sous-ingénieur (2nd Class) by 1813. Deceased 1819.
Leclert	Émile-August, 1834. Polytechnique 1854.
Lecointre	Louis-Édouard. Polytechnique 1841.
Lefébure de Cerisy	Louis Charles, 1789. Polytechnique 1809, retired 1837. Served in Egypt.
Lefebvre	Jean Baptiste, 1778-1851.
Legrand	Victor Pierre Justin Léon, 1825. Polytechnique 1846, retired 1890.
Leharivel-Durocher	Anne-Jean-Louis. Polytechnique 1800.
Lemarchand	Signed plans as a sous-ingénieur at Saint-Malo on 11 February 1793.
Lemoyne-Sérigny	Amédée-Ferdinand-Honoré-Marie. Polytechnique 1803, retired 1832. Was probably the Lemoine-Serigny first listed in 1808 as a sous-ingénieur (2nd Class) at Rochefort and the Jean-Baptiste active there from 1804 to 1810.
Leroux	Paul Marie, 1786-1853. Polytechnique 1808.
Lesage	Vital-François. Polytechnique 1819. Deceased 1832.
Lescure	see Bonnet-Lescure.
Levesque	Alphonse Ermecinde, 1799-1842. Polytechnique 1818.
Liénard	Alexandre, 1791. Polytechnique 1812, retired 1838.
Lisbonne	Émile Eliacinth, 1823. Polytechnique 1843, retired 1886.
Maillot	Étienne. Ingénieur ordinaire by 1798.
Mangin	Amédée Paul Théodore, 1818. Polytechnique 1839, retired 1877.
Marestier	Jean Baptiste, 1781-1832. Polytechnique 1803.
Marielle	Jules. Polytechnique 1838.
Masson	Guillaume-Cyr. Polytechnique 1836.
Masson	Paulin (Paul) Émile Jean François, 1836-1895.
Mimerel	Armand Florimond, 1790-1857. Polytechnique 1811, retired 1850.
Moissard	Louis Just, 1799-1849. Polytechnique 1820.
Moll	Charles Henri, 1815-1899. Polytechnique 1835.
Montety	Paulin-Jean-Charles. Polytechnique 1841.
Moras (de)	see Picot de Moras.
Moreau	Philippe Jacques, 1777. Polytechnique 1803, retired 1830.
Nettre	Charles Lamy, 1823. Polytechnique 1845, on leave 1869.
Niou	Joseph. Ingénieur ordinaire 1784.

Last name	Prenoms and service
Noël	Charles. Active at Cherbourg 1810-14, not on list of Génie officers.
Nosereau	Gabriel, 1789. Polytechnique 1811, retired 1849.
Notaire-Grandville	Alexandre Jean Louis, 1774-1813. Died in the Russian campaign.
Nouet	Édouard Thomas Marie, 1822-1902. Polytechnique 1843.
Ozanne	Pierre, 1737-1813. Sous-ingénieur 1778.
Pastoureau-Labesse	Jean Baptiste, 1818. Polytechnique 1840, on leave 1868.
Pénétreau (Pennetreau)	Pierre Joseph, 1758-1813. Sous-ingénieur 1782.
Penevert (Pennevert)	Hubert, 1754-1827. Sous-ingénieur 1786-88.
Perroy	Jean Baptiste Charles, 1781-1847. Polytechnique 1803, retired 1833.
Peschart d'Ambly	Charles Frédéric, 1825. Polytechnique 1847, retired 1893.
Pestel	François Timothée Benjamin, 1763-1828. Ingénieur (2nd Class) by 1801.
Picot de Moras	Paul Marie Étienne, 1816-1886. Polytechnique 1835.
Piedvache	Joseph Eugène, 1835. Polytechnique 1856.
Pironneau	Jean Baptiste Adolphe, 1801. Polytechnique 1821, retired 1886.
Poncet	François Frédéric, 1755-1830. Sous-ingénieur 1779.
Prétot	Hippolyte Louis Édouard, 1797. Polytechnique 1818, retired 1865.
Prouhet-Kérambour	Victor Joseph Marie, 1816-1841. Polytechnique 1835.
Reech	Frédéric. Polytechnique 1825.
Ricaud du Temple	Antoine Michel, 1757-1834. Sous-ingénieur 1784.
Rigault de Genouilly	Jean-Charles. Polytechnique 1797, retired 1840.
Robert	Charles Louis Napoléon, 1804. Polytechnique 1825, resigned 1837.
Robiou de Lavrignais	Alexandre Auguste Gustave, 1805-1886. Polytechnique 1827.
Roger	Antoine, 1812-1845. Polytechnique 1833.
Rolland (aîné)	Pierre-Élisabeth. Sous-ingénieur 1780.
Rolland (cadet)	Pierre Jacques Nicolas, 1769-1837.
Romagnesi	Napoléon Achille, 1836-1862.
Rossin	Pierre-Jean-Baptiste-Eugène. Polytechnique 1828.
Rougier	Camille-François-Pierre. Polytechnique 1820. Deceased 1837.
Royer	Active at Toulon 1803-1805, not on list of Génie officers.
Sabattier	Victorin Gabriel Justin Epiphanès, 1820. Polytechnique 1839, retired 1881.
Sané	Jacques Noël, 1740-1831. Ingénieur ordinaire 1774.
Sanial-Dufay	Louis Alcide, 1812. Polytechnique 1834, retired 1874.
Saussillon	Claude. Sous-ingénieur 1767, deceased 1785.
Schlumberger	Charles, 1825. Retired 1880.
Segondat	Jean Michel, 1779-1854.
Segondat-Duvernet	Charles-Jean-François, 1735-1816. Ingénieur-constructeur en chef 1783, retired 1811.
Senneville (de)	see Denis de Senneville.
Serpin-Dugué	Athanase-Marie. Polytechnique 1825. Deceased 1833.
Silvestre du Perron	Louis Auguste, 1820. Polytechnique 1841, retired 1866.
Simon	Charles Michel, 1776. Retired 1840.
Sochet	Prix Charles Jean Baptiste, 1803-1863. Polytechnique 1822.
Sollier	Louis Nicolas Frédéric, 1822. Polytechnique 1842, retired 1886.
Soulery	Paul-Marie-François. Polytechnique 1846.
Tellier	Charles Henri Pierre. Resigned around 1800.
Thomeuf	Pierre, 1801. Polytechnique 1830, retired 1859.
Train	Pierre. Sous-ingénieur 1776, deceased 1785.
Traon	Mathieu. Sous-ingénieur (2nd Class) by 1803.
Tupinier	Jean Marguerite, 1779-1850. Polytechnique 1796.
Vaneechout	Polydore Alexis. Polytechnique 1822.
Verny	François Léonce, 1837. Resigned 1880.
Vésignié	Louis-François-Octave. Polytechnique 1853.
Vial du Clairbois	Honoré-Sébastien. Ingénieur ordinaire 1783.
Vidal	Albin Abraham, 1826. Polytechnique 1847, retired 1891.
Villain	Jules Toussaint, 1822. Polytechnique 1843, retired 1880.
Villaret	Nathaniel Lucien Louis Jean Jacques, 1837-1919.
Vincent	Jean Antoine Aza, 1793-1853. Polytechnique 1813, retired 1849.
Vincent	Jean Pierre Séraphin, 1779-1818.
Willotte	Louis-Marc-Antoine-Émile. Polytechnique 1847.
Zani de Ferranty	Achille-Auguste. Polytechnique 1843.
Zédé	Gustave-Alexandre. Polytechnique 1845.

Appendix I French Naval Ship and Engine Builders, 1793-1861

1. Private Shipbuilders, 1793-1814

Name	Location	Dates	Types built
Aguillon fils	La Seyne	1804	small sail
Bastiat, Dufouc & fils	Bayonne	1793	corvettes
Blaise, Ménard	Marseille, La Ciotat	1806-7	small sail
Bourmaud (frères)	Nantes	1794-96	frigates
Capon (S., worked for Destouches)	Rochefort Dyd	1798-1802	line
Chaigneau (Arnaud)	Bordeaux-Lormont	1813	small sail
Chicallat & Jouvin	Marseille	1808-11	transports
Colin-Olivier (Michel)	Dieppe	1793-99	frigates, brigs, small sail, flotilla
Courau (François, Jean-Baptiste, & Laurent)	Bordeaux	1807-16	frigates, corvettes
Courtois	Honfleur	1794-95	corvettes
Crucy & Baudet (Louis & Antoine Crucy and Jean Baudet)	Basse-Indre, Paimboeuf	1793-95	frigates, corvettes
Crucy (Louis & Antoine)	Basse-Indre	1794-99	frigates, brigs
Crucy (Louis, Antoine, & Mathurin)	Basse-Indre, Nantes, Indret	1797-1805	frigates, brigs, small sail, transports
Crucy (Louis, Antoine, & Mathurin)	Lorient Dyd, Lorient Dyd-Caudan, Rochefort Dyd	1798-1809	line, frigates, brigs
Crucy (Mathurin & Antoine)	Basse-Indre, Indret	1805-11	frigates, brigs, small sail, transports
Crucy (Louis & Michel-Louis)	Paimboeuf	1806-14	frigates, brigs, transports
Crucy (Antoine)	Basse-Indre, Nantes	1808-12	brigs, small sail
Crucy (Michel-Louis)	Basse-Indre	1812-13	transports
Denise (Denis?)	Honfleur	1794-95	corvettes
Deros (Louis)	Le Havre, Honfleur	1787-95	frigates, corvettes, transports
Destouches (Entreprise)	Rochefort Dyd	1798-1802	line
Dubois (Benjamin)	Saint-Malo (Montmarin)	1777-91	frigates, corvettes, brigs, transports
Ethéart (Entreprise, may be Jacques Vulfran or Wulfren Ethéart)	Saint-Malo	1795-1808	frigates, brigs
Fortier (Pierre, Jacques & Nicolas)	Honfleur	1793-95	corvettes, brigs
Fouache (Jean)	Le Havre	1793-96	frigates, corvettes, small sail
Fouache & Reine (Jean Fouache & Louis-Michel Reine)	Le Havre, Honfleur	1793-97	corvettes, flotilla
Fouache and Thibaudier (Jean Fouache and Entreprise Thibaudier)	Le Havre	1799-1800	brigs
Gallon (Jean or Jean-Baptiste)	Honfleur	1793-95	brigs, flotilla
Gouel (Jean-François)	Le Havre	1787-88	transports
Grisard (may have used yards of Rondeaux or Piston)	Port-Napoléon (Port-Louis), Île de France	1805-10	brigs, small sail, transports
Guibert (André)	Bordeaux	1803-4	flotilla
Guibert (Auguste Snr)	Paimboeuf	1813-14	brigs
Guibert (Pierre)	Bordeaux	1794-95	frigates
Houssez (Jean-Marie, worked for Destouches)	Rochefort Dyd	1798-1801	line
Lerond Campion & Co.	Granville, Le Havre	1804-13	brigs
Loquet (Nicholas)	Honfleur	1794-1800	corvettes, flotilla
Mauger (Pierre)	Le Havre	1792-93	corvettes, small sail
Normand (André-François)	Honfleur	1793-94	corvettes
Normand (Louis-Jacques)	Cherbourg	1794-95	brigs
Normand (Joseph-Augustin)	Honfleur	1793-95	corvettes, brigs
Pelleteau (worked for Destouches)	Rochefort Dyd	1798-1802	line
Pestel (Jean-Louis, elder brother of François)	Honfleur	1793-1804	corvettes, transports
Reyboulet (Riboulet?)	La Ciotat	1802-6	corvettes
Ronsard (François-Michel, worked with Auguste Guibert Snr)	Paimboeuf	1813-14	brigs
Roustan	Toulon (at the dockyard?)	1813-14	flotilla
Vian, Velin, Riboulet, & Ménard	La Ciotat	1803-11	brigs, transports

The Crucy Brothers

Following the adoption of a law of January 1793 that allowed contractors to build warships for the navy, Louis and Antoine Crucy in association with Jean Baudet formed the Société Crucy-Baudet. They took over an inactive yard at Basse-Indre (on the Loire, close to Nantes) belonging to the Frères Bourmaud which had large supplies of timber and built hulls that were then taken to Navy dockyards for fitting out. The Committee of Public Safety seized the Basse-Indre yard in August 1794 and rented it back to the Crucys. The firm also established an annex to the Basse-Indre yard at Paimboeuf (downriver, between Nantes and St Nazaire).

In September 1796 the government returned to a system of contracting with private firms. Baudet left to start a caulking firm and Louis and Antoine Crucy re-occupied the Basse-Indre yard and took over the Paimboeuf yard. Now operating with a third brother, Mathurin, as the Société Louis Crucy et frères, they established another yard at Nantes (Chantenay, quai de la Piperie). Mathurin, a famous architect and urban planner at Nantes, resigned from his municipal activites in 1800 to assume an active role in the then-profitable shipbuilding firm. Between 1798 and 1803 the Crucys received contracts to build ships in the Lorient and Rochefort Dockyards. They also built some transports at the navy's facility at Indret across the river from Basse-Indre.

In 1806 the Crucy Brothers' firm was dissolved. Mathurin and Antoine took over the yards at Basse-Indre and Nantes and the contract at Indret as the Société Mathurin et Antoine Crucy while Louis on behalf of his young son Michel-Louis took over the Paimboeuf yard as the Société Michel Louis Crucy. Mathurin retired from the business in 1809 and in 1812 Antoine also retired and rented the Basse-Indre yard to Michel-Louis. By then Michel-Louis' firm was in financial difficulty and it was dissolved in 1813. It was to have been taken over by Auguste Guibert but in May 1814 the navy resumed the peacetime practice of building warships only in its own dockyards and stopped contract work. Guibert completed two brigs at Paimboeuf with François-Michel Ronsard, but two frigates on the ways there were dismantled and taken to the Lorient Dockyard for reassembly and completion.

The Normand Family

François Normand first appeared as a shipbuilder at Honfleur in 1688 and his son of the same name founded the family shipbuilding firm at Honfleur in 1728. The son of the second François, André-François Normand (1726-1812), was certified as a master shipbuilder in 1742 and inherited the family business in 1772. His son Joseph-Augustin (1753-1838) received his certification in 1771 and was in sole charge of the business by the end of the 1780s. He received orders for three corvettes and brigs during the 1790s, some in his father's name, and also built flotilla craft. His son, Augustin Normand (1792-1871) began his shipbuilding career as a carpenter in the dockyard at Le Havre in 1808 and joined his father when released from service in 1814. He moved the family business from Honfleur to Le Havre in 1820 and became famous for his work with screw steamers in the 1840s. Louis-Jacques Normand (1747-1817), a cousin to André François, moved in 1786 from Honfleur to Cherbourg where he helped the naval constructor Pierre Ozanne build the brig *Colombe*, in 1794-5.

2. Private Shipbuilders, 1822-1861

Name	Location	Dates	Types built
Bataille	La Mailleraye (Rouen)	1822-23	paddle
Malleux (Armand)	Rouen	1822-23	paddle
Thibault	Rouen	1824-26	paddle (*Serpent*)
Vandenbussche (Pierre-François)	Dunkirk	1827-28	small sail (*Vigilant*)
Cavé (François)	Asnières-sur-Seine (from Saint-Ouen 1843)	1842-52	paddle, screw corvette (*Chaptal*)
Benet (Louis)	La Ciotat	1843-44	paddle (*Narval*)
Chaigneau & Bichon (Chaigneau fils frères & Bichon or Arnaud Chaigneau & Jean Bichon or Arnaud & François Chaigneau et Jean Bichon)	Bordeaux-Lormont	1843-48	brig-avisos, small sail (*Iris*), sail transport (*Moselle*), paddle, small screw (including corvette *Sentinelle*),
Courau & Arman (Jean-Baptiste and Laurent Coureau and Lucien Arman)	Bordeaux-Lormont	1844-47	paddle
Malo (Gaspard)	Dunkirk	1844-49	paddle, small screw corvette (*Biche*)
Guibert (Louis-Auguste)	Nantes	1844-56	brig-avisos, small sail (*Églé*), sail transport (*Durance*), paddle, small screw, transports
Normand (Augustin)	Le Havre	1844-66	screw corvettes, small screw
Taylor (Philip)	La Seyne	1846-56	paddle (*Mouette*), transports
Baudet	Paimboeuf	1847-48	brig-aviso (*Rusé*)
Pivert	Saint-Malo	1847-48	brig-aviso (*Railleur*)
Gâche & Voruz (Vincent Gâche aîné & Jean-Simon Voruz aîné, Nantes)	Nantes	1848-49	paddle
Nillus (Charles-Michel)	Le Havre	1853-54	paddle (*Akba* class)
Arman (Lucien)	Bordeaux, Ajaccio, Paris	1854-66	small screw, transports, ironclads
Gouin (Ernest)	Nantes	1856-64	paddle, small screw, transports, ironclads
Forges et Chantiers de la Méditerranée (FCM)	La Seyne, Le Havre	1857-61	paddle, small screw
Chaigneau (Arnaud, François, & Charles)	Bordeaux-Lormont	1859	small sail
Cardon (Émile)	Honfleur	1859-60	small screw
Bichon (Gustave & Arnaud-Frédéric, plus Jean for *Tancrède*)	Bordeaux-Lormont	1859-62	small screw, transports

Name	Location	Dates	Types built
Moulinié & Labat (Arnaud Moulinié et frères & Thèodore Labat)	Bordeaux	1859-62	small screw, transports
Durenne	Asnières-sur-Seine	1860	small screw

3. Navy and Private Steam Engine Builders, 1819-1861

Name	Location	Dates	Max NHP
Périer (Scipion)	Paris (Chaillot)	1819	32
Manby (Aaron) & Wilson	Paris (Charenton)	1823-1827	160
Aitken & Steel	Paris (à la Gare)	1828	160
Gengembre (Philippe)	Paris	1828	160
Frimot	Landerneau	1830	160
Dumoulin (G.)	Paris	1831	60
Martin (Emile)	Fourchambault	1831	120
Pelletan & De la Barre	Paris	1832	40
INDRET	(Navy)	1832 etc.	1200
Hallette (Alexis)	Arras	1833-1848	450
Cavé (François)	Paris (St. Denis)	1833-1856	900
Villack (R. de)	Charenton	1839	160
Sudds, Adkins & Barker	Rouen	1839-1841	160
Schneider Bros.	Le Creusot	1841 etc.	650
Pauwels	Paris (St. Denis)	1842-1843	220
Stéhélin & Huber	Bitschwiller	1842-1843	220
Beslay	Paris	1843	80
Benet (Louis)	La Ciotat	1844-1851	450
CHERBOURG DOCKYARD	(Navy)	1844-1858	900
Mazeline Bros.	Le Havre	1844 etc.	650
Baboneau (J.-A.)	Nantes	1846-1847	180
Gâche (Vincent) & Voruz (Jean-Simon)	Nantes (2 firms)	1846-1854	200
LORIENT DOCKYARD	(Navy)	1846-1858	400
Taylor (Philip)	Marseille	1847	200
Nillus (Charles-Michel)	Le Havre	1848-1854	200
ROCHEFORT DOCKYARD	(Navy)	1848-1869	480
BREST DOCKYARD	(Navy)	1852-1856	500
TOULON DOCKYARD	(Navy)	1854-1858	900
Charbonnier, Bourguignon	Paris (Asnières)	1855	90
Gouin (Ernest)	Nantes	1855	90
Forges & Chantiers de la Mediterranee	La Seyne (FCM)	1855 etc.	600

Firms that built both engines and hulls carried out both functions at the same locations except for François Cavé, who built his hulls (and his engines after 1850) at Asnières near Paris, and Philip Taylor who built his hulls at La Seyne-sur-Mer near Toulon (the future Forges et Chantiers de la Méditerranée yard).

Foreign engine builders used by the navy were Fawcett & Preston of Liverpool (1829-41), Fenton, Murray & Jackson of Leeds (1836), Maudslay of London (1837), Miller & Ravenhill of London (1842), Rontgen of Fijenoord, Holland (1844-45) and Napier of Glasgow (1857).

Appendix J Composition of the Crew for a French Ship of the Line, 1795

The following is the composition of the équipage of ships of various rates as at 25 October 1795 (3 Brumaire An IV)

Designation	118-gun ship	110-gun ship	80-gun ship	74-gun ship
État-major (commissioned officers)				
Capitaine de vaisseau	1	1	1	1
Capitaine de frégate (executive officer)	1	1	1	1
Lieutenants de vaisseau	6	6	5	4
Enseignes de vaisseau	9	9	7	7
Officiers de la garnison (marine officers)	2	2	1	1
Commissaire de vaisseau (purser)	1	1	1	1
Chirurgien-major de vaisseau (surgeon)	1	1	1	1
Aspirants	9	9	9	7
Officiers-Mariniers (petty officers & artificers)				
Maître d'équipage (Master)	1	1	1	1
Premier Maître de manoeuvre	1	1	1	1
Second Maîtres de manoeuvre	3	3	2	2
Contre Maîtres de manoeuvre	4	4	3	3
Quartier Maîtres (quartermasters)	24	24	18	16
Maîtres de canonnage (master gunners)	4	4	3	3
Second Maîtres de canonnage	7	7	4	4
Maîtres Canonniers (gunners' mates)	66	62	48	42
Maîtres de timonerie (helmsmen)	2	2	2	2
Second Maîtres de timonerie	6	6	5	4
Ouvriers de timonerie (helmsmen's mates)	10	10	8	7
Pilotes-cotiers (harbour pilots)	2	2	1	1
Maître de charpentage (carpenter)	1	1	1	1
Second Maîtres de charpentage	2	2	2	1
Ouvriers de charpentage (carpenter's mates)	6	5	5	3
Maître de calfatage (caulker)	1	1	1	1
Second Maîtres de calfatage	2	2	2	1
Ouvriers de calfatage (caulker's mates)	6	5	5	3
Maître de voilerie (sailmaker)	1	1	1	1
Second Maître de voilerie	1	1	1	1
Ouvriers de voilerie (sailmaker's mates)	3	3	2	2
Matelots				
Premier class	121	114	95	76
Second class	121	114	95	76
Troisième class	121	114	95	76
Quatrième class	121	114	95	76
Novices	161	150	125	101
Mousses (boys)	80	75	60	50
Marine Artillery				
Cannoniers-matelots (marines/artillerymen)	180	170	130	100
Supernumeraires				
Capitaine d'armes (armourer)	1	1	1	1
Second captaine d'armes	1	1	1	1
Forgerons (blacksmiths)	2	2	-	-
Chaudronnier (coppersmith)	1	1	-	-
Ravitailleur (victualler)	1	1	-	-
Second chirurgiens (assistant surgeons)	2	2	2	2
Ouvriers de chirurgien (surgeon's mates)	2	2	-	-
Premier commissaires (stewards)	1	2	1	1
Second commissaires (second stewards)	3	2	2	1

Designation	118-gun ship	110-gun ship	80-gun ship	74-gun ship
Ouvriers de commissary (ration distributers)	2	2	2	2
Cuisiniers (cooks)	2	2	1	1
Boucher (butcher)	1	1	1	1
Boulanger (baker)	1	1	1	1
Tonneliers (coopers)	2	2	1	1
Plantons (officers' servants)	17	17	13	13
Total	1,130	1,070	866	706

Source: Terry Crowdy, *French Warship Crews, 1789-1805*, Osprey Publishing, 2005.

Index to Named Vessels

This index lists alphabetically all named vessels referenced in this book, but only for their primary entry (mention elsewhere in the book is not noted). Each is noted along with its year of launch (or of acquisition for ships not ordered for the French Navy) and the year on which it ceased to be known under that name, its original type, and the appropriate page number. Vessels which were renamed while remaining in French naval service (even if hulked) also appear under that new name. Vessels which were numbered only are not included; most of the thousands of small craft purchased for the Boulogne Flotilla (for the intended invasion of Britain) are also omitted for lack of space. Vessels that were built for or which served in 'dependent' forces such as the Napoleonic Italian Navy are included.

24 Février, 1850-1850, Screw two-decker, see *Napoléon* 1850-1886
À Propos, 1807-1808, Schooner, 259
Abeille, 1795-1796, Cutter, see *Bonnet Rouge* 1793-1795
Abeille, 1801-1858, 16-gun brig, 210
Abeille, 1802-1816, Schooner, 259
Abeille, 1814-1815, Felucca, 304
Abeille, 1844-1847, 18-gun brig, 233
Abeille, 1858-1871, Paddle aviso, 345
Abeille, 1871-1871, Screw aviso (hulked), see *Lutin* 1861-1871
Aberwrac'h, 1865-1874, 36pdr rasée frigate (hulked), see *Minerve* 1831-1865
Abondance, 1808-1814, Transport (schooner), 416
Abondance, 1833-1856, Flûte, see *Moselle* 1820-1833
Abondance, 1859-1866, Large transport, 398
Abondante, 1803-1806, Felucca, 304
Abordant, 1796-1797, Bateau-canonnier, 279
Aborigène, 1795-1795, Transport, see *Alerte* (prize) 1794-1796
Abraham-Jouanes, 1793-1797, Transport (galiote), 411
Absolu, 1795-1795, Transport, see *Alerte* (ship) 1794-1796
Accès, 1795-1795, Lugger, see *Angélique* 1793-1815
Achéron, 1813-1847, Mortar gunboat, 292
Achéron, 1828-1835, Bomb vessel, 312
Achéron, 1835-1872, Paddle vessel, 324
Achille, 1786-1794, Two-decker (74-gun), see *Annibal* 1778-1786
Achille, 1793-1801, Flûte, 376
Achille, 1804-1805, Two-decker (74-gun), 94
Achille, 1810-1810, Cutter, see *Principe Achille* 1810-1810
Achille, 1814-1816, Two-decker (74-gun), see *Dantzick* 1807-1814
Achille, 1827-1839, Two-decker (90-gun), see *Breslaw* 1839-1856
Achille, 1848-1850, Two-decker (90-gun), see *Saint Louis* 1854-1857
Actéon, 1804-1805, 16 x 6pdr brig, 214
Actéon, 1812-1822, 16-gun brig, 218
Actéon, 1827-1848, 20-gun brig, 230
Actif, 1779-1792, Schooner, 239
Actif, 1793-1794, 16-gun brig, 211
Actif, 1793-1795, Cutter, see *Malin* 1795-1806
Actif, 1793-1795, Cutter, 248
Actif, 1793-1800, Aviso, 244
Actif, 1794-1795, Aviso, 241
Actif, 1795-1796, Bateau-plat (galiote), 272
Actif, 1795-1796, Bateau-canonnier, 278
Actif, 1798-1802, Pink, 297
Actif, 1799-1830, Cutter, 246

Actif, 1808-1813, Gunboat, 292
Actif, 1821-1836, Cutter, 269
Actif, 1836-1861, Paddle tug (service craft), 321
Actif, 1839-1842, Cutter, 269
Actif, 1861-1919, Screw aviso, 362
Active, 1778-1795, 8pdr frigate (28-gun), 122
Active, 1808-1810, Transport, 416
Active, 1838-1839, Gabarre, 392
Active (Grande Gabarre Écurie No.5), 1812-1827, Gabarre, 390
Adelaide, 1792-1795, Transport (ship), 406
Adelaide, 1794-1794, Transport, 407
Adèle, 1797-1799, Bateau-canonnier, 278
Adèle, 1804-1813, Felucca gunboat, 304
Adèle, 1808-1834, Péniche, 293
Adèle, 1837-1849, Transport, 418
Admiral Tromp, 1810-1811, Two-decker (68-gun), 83
Adonis, 1786-?, Sloop (service craft), 406
Adonis, 1806-1823, 16-gun brig, 216
Adonis, 1827-1865, 20-gun brig, 230
Adonis, 1863-1907, Screw aviso, 361
Adour, 1802-1803, Gabarre, 385
Adour, 1819-1854, Flûte, 380
Adour, 1839-1846, Paddle tug (service craft), 321
Adour, 1856-1905, Screw transport, 400
Adria, 1806-1809, 12pdr frigate (34-gun), 133
Adrienne, 1809-1815, 18pdr frigate (44-gun), 150
Affranchi, 1795-1796, Cutter, see *Actif* 1793-1795
Affranchie, 1794-1794, Corvette, 178
Affronteur, 1795-1803, Lugger, 242
Africain, 1795-1795, Flûte, 378
Africain, 1819-1827, Paddle vessel, 315
Africain, 1832-1838, Paddle vessel, 321
Africain, 1858-1879, Paddle aviso, 350
Africain, 1879-1881, Paddle aviso (hulked), see *Arabe* 1858-1882
Africain, 1881-1883, Paddle aviso (hulked), see *Espadon* 1860-1881
Africaine, 1796-1796, 18-gun brig, 213
Africaine, 1798-1801, 18pdr frigate (44-gun), 140
Africaine, 1814-1814, 18pdr frigate (44-gun), see *Jahde* 1812-1815
Africaine, 1814-1822, 18pdr frigate (44-gun), see *Ems* 1812-1815
Africaine, 1827-1835, Balancelle or bateau, 308
Africaine, 1839-1871, 18pdr frigate (46-gun), 158
Agamemnon, 1812-1823, Two-decker (74-gun), 100
Agamemnon, 1828 cancelled, Two-decker (100-gun), 64
Agathe (Agate), 1833-1876, Corvette de charge, see *Saône* 1830-1833
Agathe (Agate), 1846-1852, Schooner, 266
Agathe-Marie, 1797-1799, Flûte, 378
Agile, 1797-1797, Schooner, 247
Agile, 1797-1798, Schooner, 242
Agile, 1799-1815, Schooner, 243
Agile, 1819-1837, Mortar gunboat, see *Terre* 1811-1819
Agile, 1843-1888, 10-gun brig-aviso, 233
Agilité, 1888-1891, 10-gun brig-aviso, see *Agile* 1843-1888
Aglaé, 1789-1789, Schooner, 249
Aglaé, 1795-1795, Lugger, see *Aimable Adélaide* 1793-1795
Aglaé, 1797-1798, Bomb vessel, 310
Aglaé, 1832-1843, Schooner, 268
Aglaë, 1788-1793, 12pdr frigate (32-gun), 129
Agricola, 1794-1803, 36pdr rasée frigate, 104
Aigle, 1793-1795, Schooner, 245

Aigle, 1800-1805, Two-decker (74-gun), 91
Aigle, 1813-1814, Xebec, 305
Aigle, 1814 cancelled, Two-decker (74-gun), 98
Aigle, 1853-1858, Screw aviso, 356
Aigle, 1858-1873, Paddle yacht, 352
Aigle d'Or, 1834-1846, Schooner, 268
Aigrette, 1756-1789, 8pdr frigate (32-gun), 121
Aigrette, 1811-1822, 20 x 24pdr corvette, 182
Aigrette, 1824-1832, 16-gun brig, 226
Aigrette, 1848 cancelled, Corvette-aviso, 193
Aigrette, 1855-1859, Screw gunboat, 365
Aigrette, 1862-1863, Screw gunboat, see *Le Brethon* 1864-1869
Aiguille, 1795-1803, Cutter, see *Montagne* 1793-1795
Aimable Adélaide, 1793-1795, Lugger, 248
Aimable Bristol, 1803-1815, Transport, see *Betsy* 1795-1803
Aimable Caroline, 1793-1801, 8-gun brig, see *Caroline* 1793-1801
Aimable Eulalie (Transport No. 330), 1803-1822, Transport (sloop), 412
Aimable Henriette, 1793-1794, Transport, 406
Aimable Lucile, 1794-1797, Transport, 408
Aimable Rose-Désirée, 1803-1814, Transport (sloop), 413
Aimée, 1793-1807, Aviso, 250
Air, 1810-1813, Gunboat, 291
Ajaccio, 1850-1871, Paddle aviso, 343
Ajax, 1774-1801, Two-decker (64-gun), 79
Ajax, 1794-1795, Transport, 407
Ajax, 1806-1818, Two-decker (74-gun), 94
Ajax, 1810-1813, Corvette, 184
Ajax, 1828 cancelled, Two-decker (90-gun), 65
Ajax, 1832-1839, Two-decker (100-gun), see *Austerlitz* 1839-1852
Ajax, 1865-1876, Two-decker (hulked), see *Suffren* 1829-1865
Akba, 1854-1859, Paddle aviso, 349
Akim, 1794-1795, Transport, 407
Alacrity, 1811-1822, 18-gun brig, 221
Alacrity, 1825-1851, 20-gun brig, 229
Alarme, 1855-1857, Screw gunboat, 365
Albanais, 1808-1814, Two-decker (74-gun), 96
Albanaise, 1790-1800, Tartane, 295
Albatros, 1844-1880, Paddle frigate, 332
Albo (*Albro*), 1796-1796, Transport (brig), 408
Alceste, 1780-1799, 12pdr frigate (32-gun), 125
Alceste, 1846-1891, 30pdr frigate (52-gun), 113
Alcibiade, 1826-1889, 20-gun brig, 230
Alcide, 1782-1795, Two-decker (74-gun), 86
Alcide, 1802-1802, Two-decker (74-gun), see *Courageux* 1806-1832
Alcide, 1802-1807, Two-decker (74-gun), see *D'Hautpoul* 1807-1809
Alcide, 1810 cancelled, 18pdr frigate (50-gun), 155
Alcide, 1814 cancelled, Two-decker (74-gun), 98
Alcinous, 1813-1813, Gunboat, 292
Alcion (*Alcyon*), 1795-1805, Cutter, 245
Alcmène, 1811-1814, 18pdr frigate (44-gun), 147
Alcmène, 1834-1851, 20 x 30pdr corvette, 189
Alcudia, 1793-1794, 20 x 6pdr corvette, 176
Alcyon, 1802-1803, 16-gun brig, 210
Alcyon, 1809-1814, 16-gun brig, 217
Alcyon (*Alcyone*), 1858-1892, Cutter, 268
Alcyone, 1825-1865, 16-gun brig, 227
Aldudes, 1794-1794, Cutter, 249
Alecton, 1814 cancelled, Gunboat, 291
Alecton, 1843-1854, Paddle aviso, 346
Alecton, 1861-1884, Paddle aviso, 345
Alerte, 1787-1799, 4pdr brig-aviso, 204
Alerte, 1794-1794, 16 x 6pdr corvette, 174
Alerte, 1794-1795, Felucca, 297

Alerte, 1794-1796, Transport (ship), 407
Alerte, 1794-1796, Transport (prize), 408
Alerte, 1795-1797, Transport (sloop), 408
Alerte, 1796-1796, Schooner, 249
Alerte, 1798-1803, 12 x 4pdr corvette, 176
Alerte, 1807-1815, Lugger or chasse-marée, see *Ami de Lorient* 1803-1806
Alerte, 1825-1865, 20-gun brig, 230
Alerte, 1855-1884, Screw gun launch, 368
Alexander, 1798-1803, Transport (galiote), 410
Alexandre, 1792-1793, Two-decker (74-gun), see *Jemmapes* 1794-1830
Alexandre, 1794-1795, Two-decker (74-gun), 92
Alexandre, 1794-1795, Flûte, 377
Alexandre, 1794-1795, Transport, 407
Alexandre, 1799-1799, 8/16-gun brig, 213
Alexandre, 1803-1806, Two-decker (80-gun), see *Indivisible* 1799-1803
Alexandre, 1809-1809, 12/16-gun brig, 224
Alexandre, 1814 cancelled, Two-decker (80-gun), 60
Alexandre, 1827-1839, Two-decker (90-gun), see *Donawerth* 1839-1857
Alexandre, 1848-1857, Two-decker (90-gun), 66
Alexandre, 1857-1900, Screw two-decker, 72
Alexandre 1er, 1855-1855, Large transport, see *Hérault* 1855-1862
Alexandrine, 1793-1805, Brigantine, 299
Alexandrine, 1802-1804, Transport (sloop), 412
Algéciras, 1804-1808, Two-decker (74-gun), 91
Alger, 1830-1882, Two-decker (74-gun), see *Provence* 1815-1830
Algérie, 1848-1867, 30pdr frigate (40-gun), 160
Algésiras, 1823-1847, Two-decker (80-gun), 58
Algésiras, 1855-1906, Screw two-decker, 71
Allantia, 1794-1796, 18 x 4pdr corvette, 176
Allègre, 1796-1797, Flûte, 378
Alliance, 1794-1795, Transport (galiote), 407
Alliance, 1799-1799, Transport (brig), 409
Alliance, 1799-1807, Two-decker (74-gun), see *Saint Sébastien* 1799-1799
Allier, 1828-1865, Corvette de charge, 382
Allier, 1861-1869, Screw transport, 403
Alligator, 1782-1783, 16 x 6pdr corvette, 166
Alligator, 1859-1868, Paddle corvette (hulked), see *Archimède* 1842-1859
Alon-Prah, 1860-1879, Screw aviso, 363
Alouette, 1786-1795, 20 x 6pdr corvette, 165
Alouette, 1807-1807, Lugger or chasse-marée, see *Ami National* 1803-1807
Alouette, 1812-1813, 20 x 24pdr corvette, 182
Alouette, 1839-1868, 4-gun gunbrig, 231
Alouette (Grande Gabarre Écurie No.6), 1812-1817, Gabarre, 390
Alsacienne, 1807-1809, Transport (half-xebec), 414
Alsacienne, 1823-1851, 8-gun gunbrig, 228
Al'tsinoye, 1809-1810, Corvette, 184
Amalthéa, 1803-1819, Transport (brig), 413
Amarante, 1793-1796, 6pdr brig, 205
Amarante (*Amaranthe*), 1817-1833, Schooner, 260
Amarante (*Amaranthe*), 1845-1869, Schooner, 266
Amazone, 1778-1797, 12pdr frigate (32-gun), 125
Amazone, 1793-1793, Tartane, 296
Amazone, 1794-1795, Transport, 407
Amazone, 1807-1808, 18pdr frigate (50-gun), 156
Amazone, 1807-1811, 18pdr frigate (44-gun), 146
Amazone, 1821-1842, 24pdr frigate (58-gun), 107
Amazone, 1845-1858, 30pdr frigate (50-gun), 114

Amazone, 1858-1873, Screw transport, 402
Ambitieuse, 1808-1810, Flûte, see *Mérinos* 1811-1812
Ambitieuse, 1813-1813, 18pdr frigate (44-gun), 152
Amélia, 1804-1807, Bomb vessel, 311
Amélie, 1808-1815, 18pdr frigate (44-gun), 150
America, 1782-1786, Two-decker (74-gun), 88
America, 1788-1794, Two-decker (74-gun), 89
Amérique, 1794-1795, Transport, 407
Améthyste, 1809-1809, 14-gun brig-aviso, 226
Ami de la Vertu, 1801-1814, Transport, 409
Ami de Lorient, 1803-1806, Lugger or chasse-marée, 258
Ami des Lois, 1793-1813, Chasse-marée, 242
Ami des Lois, 1794-1795, Transport, 407
Ami du Commerce, 1793-1800, Schooner, 240
Ami National, 1803-1807, Lugger or chasse-marée, 258
Amiral de Ruyter, 1810-1811, Two-decker (80-gun), 61
Amiral Evertsen, 1810-1811, Two-decker (80-gun), 61
Amiral Piet Hein, 1810-1811, Two-decker (74-gun), see *Piet Hein* 1811-1813
Amiral Piet Hein, 1811 cancelled, Two-decker (80-gun), 62
Amiral Zoutman, 1810-1811, Two-decker (80-gun), 61
Amis, 1795-1795, Transport (brig), see *Deux Amis* 1793-1795
Amis Fideles, 1786-?, Sloop (service craft), 406
Amis Réunis, 1786-?, Sloop (service craft), 406
Amitié, 1779-1791, Gabarre, 385
Amitié, 1793-1797, Tartane, 296
Amitié, 1794-1794, Brigantine, 297
Amitié, 1794-1816, 2-gun brig, 212
Amitié, 1803-1803, Cutter, 258
Amitié, 1804-1807, Schooner, 259
Amoureuse, 1798-1801, Half-galley, 300
Amphion, 1749-1787, Two-decker (50-gun), 76
Amphion, 1863-1866, Screw aviso, 361
Amphitrite, 1768-1791, 12pdr frigate (32-gun), 123
Amphitrite, 1782-1787, Gabarre, 385
Amphitrite, 1786-?, Sloop (service craft), 406
Amphitrite, 1803-1805, 18pdr frigate (44-gun), see *Milanaise* 1805-1815
Amphitrite, 1808-1809, 18pdr frigate (44-gun), 147
Amphitrite, 1811-1814, 18pdr frigate (44-gun), see *Anfitrite* 1811-1814
Amphitrite, 1814-1821, 18pdr frigate (44-gun), see *Saale* 1810-1815
Amphitrite, 1824-1836, 36pdr rasée frigate, 107
Amphitrite, 1848 cancelled, 30pdr frigate (60-gun), 115
Amstel, 1812-1813, 18pdr frigate (44-gun), 153
Amsterdam, 1795-1799, Transport (galiote), 411
Amsterdam, 1811-1814, Two-decker (80-gun), see *Commerce d'Amsterdam* 1810-1811
Ana, 1839-1842, Schooner, 269
Anacréon, 1845-1860, Paddle aviso, 339
Andorinha, 1807-1808, Corvette, 184
Andromaque, 1777-1796, 12pdr frigate (32-gun), 124
Andromaque, 1797-1797, Galley, 298
Andromaque, 1811-1812, 18pdr frigate (44-gun), 149
Andromaque, 1841-1905, 30pdr frigate (60-gun), 109
Andromède, 1806-1807, 18pdr frigate (44-gun), see *Saale* 1810-1815
Andromède, 1814 cancelled, 18pdr frigate (44-gun), 147
Andromède, 1833-1883, 24pdr frigate (52-gun), 111
Anémone, 1795-1798, Tartane, see *Cincinnatus* 1794-1795
Anémone, 1823-1824, Schooner, 262
Anfitrite, 1811-1814, 18pdr frigate (44-gun), 153
Ange, 1796-1799, Transport (galiote), 411
Angélique, 1793-1815, Lugger, 244
Angélique, 1794-1795, Transport, 408
Angélique, 1794-1797, Aviso, 299
Angenoria, 1795-1796, Lugger, see *Martinet* 1793-1795
Angerone, 1795-1795, Transport, see *Aimable Lucile* 1794-1797
Anguille, 1795-1795, Cutter, see *Marat* 1793-1795
Anna, 1843-1856, colonial brig, 236
Anna Suzanna, 1793-1795, Flûte, 375
Annapolis, 1786-?, Sloop (service craft), 406
Anne, 1799-1800, Lugger, 246
Anne-Émilie, 1794-1794, Transport, 407
Annetta Bella, 1797-1797, Galley, see *Chiaretta* 1797-1806
Annette, 1794-1795, Transport, 407
Annibal, 1778-1786, Two-decker (74-gun), 85
Annibal, 1782-1787, Two-decker (50-gun), 76
Annibal, 1795-1796, Bateau-canonnier, 278
Annibal, 1801-1824, Two-decker (74-gun), 93
Annibal, 1827-1854, Two-decker (100-gun), 64
Annonciation, 1792-1793, Brigantine, 296
Anonyme, 1793-1795, Lugger, 247
Anonyme, 1794-1794, Transport, 407
Anonyme, 1815-1819, Transport (schooner), 417
Antifédéraliste, 1794-1795, Two-decker (80-gun), see *Languedoc* 1763-1794
Antifédéraliste, 1794-1795, Flûte, 377
Antigone, 1816-1829, 18pdr frigate (44-gun), 147
Antigone, 1837 cancelled, 30pdr frigate (46-gun), 159
Antilope, 1810-1815, Schooner, 252
Antilope, 1823-1832, 16-gun brig, 226
Antilope, 1836-1843, Aviso, 265
Antilope, 1844-1851, Paddle aviso, 347
Antilope, 1855-1858, Paddle aviso, 344
Antoine, 1808-1809, Felucca, see *Saint Antoine* 1808-1809
Anversois, 1807-1815, Two-decker (74-gun), 95
Apollon, 1788-1797, Two-decker (74-gun), 89
Apollon, 1796-1801, Transport (brig), 410
Aquila, 1797-1814, 12pdr frigate (32-gun), 133
Aquilon, 1789-1798, Two-decker (74-gun), 89
Aquilon, 1803-1809, Two-decker (74-gun), see *Nestor* 1793-1797
Arabe, 1794-1803, 14-gun brig, 211
Arabe, 1797-1797, Schooner, 250
Arabe, 1858-1882, Paddle aviso, 350
Arach, 1838-1846, Balancelle, 308
Araïna (*Arraïna*), 1832-1845, Trincadour, 307
Arc (*No.12*), 1860-1873, Screw sectional gun launch, 369
Arc en Ciel, 1844-1887, 24pdr frigate (hulked), see *Artémise* 1828-1844
Archer, 1859-1871, Paddle aviso, 350
Archimède, 1791-1795, Gabarre, see *Espérance* 1787-1791
Archimède, 1842-1859, Paddle corvette, 330
Archimède, 1860-1883, Paddle aviso, 350
Arcole, 1810-1814, Two-decker (74-gun), 97
Arcole, 1855-1872, Screw two-decker, 71
Ardèche, 1861-1887, Screw transport, 403
Ardent, 1830-1881, Paddle vessel, 320
Ardente, 1793-1807, Gunboat, 275
Ardente, 1857-1871, Screw frigate, 116
Aréthuse, 1791-1793, 18pdr frigate (36-gun), 138
Aréthuse, 1798-1799, 18 x 8pdr brig, 208
Aréthuse, 1805-1807, 18pdr frigate (44-gun), see *Elbe* 1808-1815
Aréthuse, 1812-1833, 18pdr frigate (44-gun), 149
Aréthuse, 1834-1865, 22 x 30pdr rasée corvette, 191
Aréthuse (loaned), 1801-1802, 18pdr frigate (40-gun), 144
Aretusa, 1811-1814, Schooner, 254
Argo, 1793-1803, Gabarre, 386
Argo, 1795-1795, Felucca, see *Alerte* 1794-1795
Argonaute, 1781-1794, Two-decker (74-gun), 86
Argonaute, 1798-1806, Two-decker (74-gun), 89
Argonaute, 1838 cancelled, Two-decker (90-gun), 65
Argus, 1793-1795, Chasse-marée, 241
Argus, 1793-1796, Aviso, 240
Argus, 1795-1796, Bateau-canonnier, 278
Argus, 1800-1807, 16-gun brig, 209
Argus, 1814-1827, 10-gun gunbrig, see *Plumper* 1805-1815
Argus, 1832-1882, 16-gun brig, 228
Argus, 1860-1884, Screw aviso, 363
Ariane, 1811-1812, 18pdr frigate (44-gun), 149
Ariane, 1830-1866, 20 x 30pdr corvette, 189
Ariège, 1856-1896, Screw transport, 400
Ariège (*Arrìège*), 1812-1849, Flûte, 380
Ariel, 1779-1793, 8pdr frigate (20-gun), 122
Ariel, 1794-1796, Schooner, 245
Ariel, 1848-1875, Screw aviso, 354
Aristide, 1795-1796, Bateau-canonnier, 278
Ark (*Arc*), 1793-1801, Cutter, 244
Armande, 1793-1795, Schooner, 249
Armide, 1804-1806, 18pdr frigate (44-gun), 146
Armide, 1821-1866, 18pdr frigate (44-gun), 150
Armorique, 1857-1862, 30pdr frigate (40-gun), 159
Armorique, 1862-1911, Screw frigate, 162
Arquebuse, 1811-1829, Gunboat, 291
Arquebuse, 1855-1882, Screw gunboat, 366
Arrìège, 1812-1849, Flûte, see *Ariège* 1812-1849
Arrimeuse, 1795-1795, Gunboat (tartane), see *Dune Libre* 1794-1795
Arrogante, 1779-1792, Gunboat, see *Nantaise* 1779-1792
Arrogante, 1795-1798, Gunboat, see *Brave* 1793-1798
Arrogante, 1811-1813, Gunboat, 291
Arrogante, 1864-1899, Ironclad floating battery, 427
Arsa, 1812-1813, Péniche, 293
Artémise, 1794-1798, 12pdr frigate (32-gun), 129
Artémise, 1828-1844, 24pdr frigate (52-gun), 111
Artémise, 1846-1868, 30-gun corvette, 193
Artesien, 1765-1786, Two-decker (64-gun), 78
Artésienne, 1823-1836, Schooner, 261
Asie, 1809-1811, Two-decker (66-gun), 82
Asmodée, 1839-1841, Paddle frigate, see *Vauban* 1845-1866
Asmodée, 1841-1841, Paddle frigate, see *Gomer* 1841-1868
Asmodée, 1841-1866, Paddle frigate, 329
Aspic, 1795-1796, Cutter, see *Marat* 1793-1795
Assaillante, 1795-1797, Gunboat (tartane), see *Dorade* 1793-1794
Assemblée Nationale, 1793-1795, 14 x 8pdr corvette, 168
Assiduité, 1795-1795, training corvette, 178
Assistance, 1794-1797, Cutter, 245
Astrée, 1779-1795, 12pdr frigate (32-gun), 124
Astrée, 1786-?, Sloop (service craft), 406
Astrée, 1794-1795, Transport, 407
Astrée, 1809-1810, 18pdr frigate (44-gun), 151
Astrée, 1820-1845, 18pdr frigate (44-gun), 149
Astrée, 1845-1859, 30pdr frigate (50-gun), 114
Astrée, 1859-1913, Screw frigate, 120
Astrolabe, 1785-1788, Flûte, 374
Astrolabe, 1816-1827, Schooner, 259
Astrolabe, 1825-1852, Gabarre, see *Coquille* 1811-1825
Atalante, 1768-1794, 12pdr frigate (32-gun), 123
Atalante, 1794-1797, 16 x 6pdr brig, 207
Atalante, 1800-1803, Two-decker (74-gun), 93
Atalante, 1802-1806, 18pdr frigate (44-gun), 141
Atalante, 1812-1815, 18pdr frigate (44-gun), 151
Atalante, 1825-1850, 24pdr frigate (58-gun), 107
Athalante, 1796-1796, Transport, 410
Athénien, 1798-1800, Two-decker (64-gun), 82
Athénienne, 1796-1796, 14-gun brig, 213
Athlète, 1883-1887, 24pdr frigate (hulked), see *Andromède* 1833-1883
Atlas, 1803-1808, Two-decker (74-gun), see *Atalante* 1800-1803
Atlas, 1814 cancelled, Two-decker (80-gun), 60
Atlas, 1814-1819, Two-decker (74-gun), see *Ville de Berlin* 1807-1815
Attentive, 1794-1795, Coast defence vessel, 245
Aube, 1832-1852, Corvette de charge, 382
Aube, 1859-1875, Screw transport, 402
Audacieuse, 1804-1815, 8 x 24pdr corvette, 180
Audacieuse, 1856-1872, Screw frigate, 116
Audacieux, 1784-1803, Two-decker (74-gun), 87
Audacieux, 1799-1802, Aviso, 251
Audacieux, 1805-1807, Two-decker (74-gun), see *Pultusk* 1807-1814
Audacieux, 1812-1813, Two-decker (74-gun), 97
Auguste, 1778-1793, Two-decker (80-gun), 55
Auguste, 1783-1786, 22 x 6pdr corvette, 166
Auguste, 1792-1803, 16 x 8pdr corvette, 167
Auguste, 1793-1794, Brigantine, 296
Auguste, 1803-1814, 6-gun brig, 225
Auguste, 1811-1814, Two-decker (80-gun), 59
August-Félicité, 1794-1795, Transport, 407
Aurora, 1811-1814, Schooner, see *Principessa di Bologna* 1810-1811
Aurore, 1768-1793, 12pdr frigate (32-gun), 123
Aurore, 1786-?, Sloop (service craft), 406
Aurore, 1786-1793, Gabarre, 386
Aurore, 1794-1794, 12pdr frigate (32-gun), see *Artémise* 1794-1798
Aurore, 1799-1801, 16 x 8pdr corvette, 174
Aurore, 1803-1819, Cutter or sloop, 256
Aurore, 1806-1808, Schooner or cutter, 259
Aurore, 1810-1810, Corvette, 183
Aurore, 1810-1814, 18pdr frigate (40-gun), 154
Aurore, 1814-1849, 18pdr frigate (44-gun), see *Adrienne* 1809-1815
Aurore, 1860-1867, Schooner, 270
Austerlitz, 1806-1809, 12pdr frigate (34-gun), 133
Austerlitz, 1808-1837, Three-decker, 47
Austerlitz, 1839-1852, Two-decker (100-gun), 64
Austerlitz, 1852-1895, Screw two-decker, 67
Australie, 1844-1876, Paddle aviso, 339
Autruche, 1781-1785, Flûte, see *Astrolabe* 1785-1788
Autruche, 1795-1796, Gunboat, see *Montagne* 1794-1795
Autruche, 1807-1808, Transport, 414
Autruche, 1822-1832, Schooner, 261
Avalanche, 1855-1867, Screw gunboat, 365
Aventure, 1782-1786, Gabarre, 385
Aventure, 1795-1796, Bateau-canonnier, 278
Aventure, 1827-1830, 16-gun brig, 228
Aventure, 1852-1855, 30-gun corvette, 193
Aventure, 1862-1863, Screw gunboat, see *Tardif* 1864-1869
Aventurier, 1793-1798, 12 x 4pdr brig, 205
Aventurière, 1794-1795, Felucca, 297
Aventurière, 1798-1818, Half-galley, 300
Aventurière, 1801-1816, Schooner, 244
Averne, 1811-1829, Gunboat, 291
Averne, 1848-1880, Paddle aviso, 341
Aveyron, 1864-1884, Screw transport, 403
Avtroil, 1809-1810, 12pdr frigate (32-gun), 135
Aziz, 1794-1795, Transport, 407

Babet, 1793-1794, 20 x 6pdr corvette, 167
Babet, 1807-1814, Gabarre, 387
Baccante, 1813-1814, Gunboat (Italian), 288
Bacchante, 1795-1803, 20 x 18pdr corvette, 173
Bacchante, 1812-1824, Schooner, 254
Bache, 1865-1885, 24pdr frigate (hulked), see *Atalante* 1825-1850
Badine, 1780-1809, 20 x 8pdr corvette, 164
Badine, 1813 cancelled, 20 x 6pdr corvette, 182
Badine, 1827-1842, 16-gun brig, 228
Balance, 1795-1796, Flûte, see *Belle Angélique* 1793-1797
Balance, 1807-1816, Transport, 414
Balaou No.1, 1810-1811, Schooner, see *Postillon*

INDEX TO NAMED VESSELS 449

1810-1810
Balaou No.2, 1810-1813, Schooner, see *Faune* 1810-1810
Balaou No.3, 1810-1816, Schooner, see *Léger* 1810-1810
Balaou No.4, 1811-1811, Schooner, see *Moustique* 1810-1811
Balaou No.5, 1811-1814, Schooner, see *Sans-Façon* 1810-1811
Balaou No.6, 1811-1813, Schooner, see *Gabier* 1810-1811
Balaou No.7, 1811-1814, Schooner, see *Rapide* 1810-1811
Balaou No.8, 1811-1814, Schooner, see *Lama* 1810-1811
Baleine, 1779-1786, Flûte, 373
Baleine, 1793-1803, Transport (galiote), 411
Baleine, 1794-1795, Trincadour, 296
Baleine, 1807-1813, Flûte, 378
Baleine, 1830-1850, Gabarre, 391
Ballon, 1782-1795, Lugger, 239
Bamberg (*Bambery*), 1806-1814, Half-xebec, 305
Banel, 1797-1802, Two-decker (64-gun), 81
Banker, 1810-1813, Gunboat (Dutch), 288
Barbeau, 1782-1791, Flûte, 374
Barbude, 1782-1786, 6pdr 'frigate' (22-gun), 122
Barbue, 1777-1796, Gabarre, 384
Barbue, 1808-1808, Transport (yacht), 416
Barra, 1794-1795, Two-decker (74-gun), 90
Barra, 1794-1795, Gunboat, 275
Barra, 1794-1797, 20 x 6pdr corvette, see *Alcudia* 1793-1794
Barricade, 1848-1849, Two-decker (74-gun), see *Couronne* 1824-1848
Basilic, 1795-1796, Transport, see *Bec d'Ambez* 1794-1795
Basilic, 1843-1865, Paddle aviso, 346
Basilic, 1854-1873, Paddle aviso, 348
Basque, 1809-1809, 16-gun brig, 216
Basse-Ville, 1798-1799, Coast defence ship, 176
Batave, 1797-1807, Two-decker (74-gun), see *Jupiter* 1789-1797
Batave (*Transport No. 460*), 1804-1814, Transport, 412
Bateaux-canonniers Nos. 98-476, 1803-1814, Bateaux-canonniers, 285
Bateaux-Plats Nos. 1-12, 1798-1802, Bateaux-plats, 272
Batterie Flottante No.1, 1793-1794, Floating battery, see *Carpe* 1794-1795
Batterie Flottante No.2, 1793-1794, Floating battery, see *Brochet* 1794-1795
Baucis, 1825-1831, 16-gun brig, 227
Baucis, 1840-1880, Schooner, 265
Baudet, 1804-1814, Transport (sloop), 412
Bayadère, 1811-1833, 20 x 8pdr corvette, 179
Bayard, 1847-1858, Two-decker (90-gun), 65
Bayard, 1859-1876, Screw two-decker, 75
Bayonnais, 1817-1834, Gabarre, 391
Bayonnaise, 1779-1790, Gabarre, 384
Bayonnaise, 1793-1803, 24 x 8pdr corvette, 172
Bayonnaise, 1825-1835, 18-gun corvette-aviso, 186
Bayonnaise, 1846-1877, 30-gun corvette, 192
Béarnais, 1808-1809, 16-gun brig, 216
Béarnaise, 1820-1837, Schooner, 260
Béarnois (*Béarnais*), 1794-1795, Transport, 411
Beaulançon (*Beau-Lançon*), 1797-1802, Lugger, 242
Beaumanoir, 1853-1904, 18-gun brig, 233
Bec d'Ambez, 1794-1795, Gunboat, see *Gironde* 1793-1797
Bec d'Ambez, 1794-1795, Transport, 407
Belem, 1807-1808, Flûte, 381
Belette, 1781-1793, 20 x 8pdr corvette, 165
Belette, 1796-1801, Péniche, 278
Belette, 1797-1803, Bateau-canonnier, 278
Belette, 1836-1846, Schooner, 262
Bélier, 1800-1805, 16-gun brig, 209
Bella Chiaretta, 1797-1797, Galley, see *Chiaretta* 1797-1806
Bella Veneziana, 1806-1813, Gunboat (Italian), 287
Belle Angélique, 1793-1797, Flûte, 376
Belle Angélique, 1797-1798, Transport (brig), 408
Belle Gabrielle, 1828-1830, 30pdr frigate (60-gun), 108
Belle Hélène, 1837-1850, Trincadour, 308
Belle London, 1795-1797, 10 x 6pdr brig, 212
Belle Maltaise, 1798-1799, Transport (brig), 409
Belle Poule, 1802-1806, 18pdr frigate (44-gun), 140
Belle Poule, 1834-1865, 30pdr frigate (60-gun), 109
Belle Suzanne, 1794-1795, Transport, 407
Belle-Françoise, 1794-1795, Transport, 407
Belle-Poule, 1806-1813, Gunboat (Italian), 287
Belliqueuse, 1793-1797, 12pdr brig, 206
Belliqueux, 1814 cancelled, Two-decker (74-gun), 98
Bellislois, 1792-1802, Chasse-marée, 248
Bellislois (*Bellilois*), 1795-1823, Lugger, 242
Bellislois (*Bellilois*), 1806-1807, Lugger or chasse-marée, see *Ami de Lorient* 1803-1806
Bellona, 1808-1811, 32-gun corvette, 181
Bellone, 1778-1798, 12pdr frigate (32-gun), 125
Bellone, 1797-1807, 12pdr frigate (38-gun), 133
Bellone, 1808-1810, 18pdr frigate (44-gun), 145
Bellone, 1809-1814, Gunboat, 291
Bellone, 1814-1840, 18pdr frigate (44-gun), see *Pauline* 1807-1815
Bellone, 1853-1858, 30pdr frigate (50-gun), 114
Bellone, 1858-1895, Screw frigate, 117
Belmont, 1794-1797, Flûte, 376
Benjamin, 1807-1808, Corvette, 184
Berceau, 1794-1804, 22 x 8pdr corvette, 170
Berceau, 1834-1846, 20 x 30pdr corvette, 191
Bergère, 1794-1795, Transport, 407
Bergère, 1794-1806, 16 x 8pdr corvette, 170
Bergère, 1833-1865, 18 x 24pdr corvette-aviso, 188
Bernardus, 1811-1811, Transport (galiote), 413
Bérouse, 1798-1798, 12pdr frigate (32-gun), 133
Bérouse, 1798-1798, Transport, 409
Bertheaume, 1860-1888, 4-gun gunbrig (hulked), see *Vigie* 1839-1860
Berthollet, 1850-1866, Paddle corvette, 338
Berwick, 1795-1805, Two-decker (74-gun), 92
Beschutter, 1810-1813, Gunboat (Dutch), 288
Betsy, 1795-1803, Transport (galiote), 410
Betzy, 1793-1796, 18-gun brig, 211
Betzy (*Betsy*), 1796-1803, Brigantine, 300
Beyrand, 1797-1799, Two-decker (64-gun), 81
Bianca, 1811-1814, Péniche, 293
Biby (*Bibi*), 1797-1804, Bateau-canonnier, 278
Biche, 1796-1796, Corvette, 178
Biche, 1798-1801, Schooner, 242
Biche, 1801-1807, Schooner, 243
Biche, 1808-1830, Schooner, 254
Biche, 1836-1846, Aviso, 264
Biche, 1848-1868, Iron screw corvette, 197
Bien-Aimé, 1794-1795, Transport, 407
Bien-Aimé, 1794-1795, Transport, 407
Bienfaisant, 1794-1795, Transport (brig), 407
Bienvenue, 1788-1794, Flûte, 374
Bienvenue, 1803-1812, Gabarre, 386
Bigotte, 1791-1793, Schooner, 249
Bionda, 1811-1814, Péniche, 293
Biscayenne, 1793-1793, Brigantine, see *Annonciation* 1792-1793
Bisson, 1828-1840, Transport, 418
Bisson, 1830-1850, 20-gun brig, 231
Bisson, 1850-1872, Paddle aviso, 343
Blanche, 1794-1796, Gunboat (gabarre or dogger), 277
Blonde, 1781-1793, 20 x 8pdr corvette, 164
Blonde, 1796-1796, 16-gun brig, 213
Blonde, 1832-1849, 20 x 30pdr corvette, 187
Bloys (*Vice-admiraal*), 1810-1813, Gunboat (Dutch), 288
Bobérach, 1830-1858, Xebec, 308
Boccaise, 1810-1813, Péniche, 293
Bolognesa, 1813-1813, Gunboat (Italian), 288
Bombardier (*Bombe*), 1794-1803, Bomb vessel, 309
Bombe, 1811-1829, Mortar gunboat, 291
Bombe, 1855-1859, Bomb vessel, 312
Bon Destin, 1797-1810, Xebec, 298
Bon Espoir, 1793-1795, Cutter, 244
Bon Frère, 1794-1794, Transport (sloop), 407
Bon Patriote, 1811-1811, Half-xebec or balancelle, 307
Bon Père, 1794-1795, Transport, 407
Bona, 1830-1831, Schooner, 268
Bonaparte, 1797-1799, Lugger, 248
Bonaparte, 1801-1802, Yacht, 313
Bonheur, 1793-1793, 22 x 12pdr corvette, see *Jacobine* 1794-1794
Bonite, 1813-1843, Flûte, 380
Bonite, 1859-1872, Transport, 418
Bonne, 1808-1814, Transport (schooner), 416
Bonne Aventure, 1793-1798, Xebec, 296
Bonne Aventure, 1794-1795, Transport (brig), 407
Bonne Aventure, 1794-1796, Flûte, 376
Bonne Aventure, 1799-1799, Corvette, 178
Bonne Citoyenne, 1794-1796, 20 x 8pdr corvette, 170
Bonne Intention, 1796-1797, Gunboat (galiote), 277
Bonne Marie, 1833-1844, Schooner, 269
Bonne Société, 1786-?, Sloop (service craft), 406
Bonne-Espérance, 1793-1799, Transport (galiote), 411
Bonnet Rouge, 1793-1794, Two-decker (74-gun), see *Commerce de Bordeaux* 1785-1793
Bonnet Rouge, 1793-1795, Cutter, 241
Borda, 1832-1839, 16-gun brig, 228
Borda, 1839-1863, Three-decker (hulked), see *Commerce de Paris* 1806-1830
Borda, 1863-1890, Three-decker (hulked), see *Valmy* 1847-1863
Borda, 1889-1914, Two-decker (hulked), see *Intrépide* 1864-1889
Bordelaise, 1824-1841, 8-gun gunbrig, 229
Borée, 1785-1794, Two-decker (74-gun), 87
Borée, 1805-1828, Two-decker (74-gun), 95
Boston, 1793-1793, Schooner, 249
Boudeuse, 1766-1800, 12pdr frigate (32-gun), 123
Boudeuse, 1796-1796, Bateau-canonnier, 278
Bougainville, 1832-1865, 16-gun brig, 228
Bougainville, 1859-1890, Screw aviso, 358
Boulonnaise, 1777-1791, Gabarre, 384
Boulonnaise, 1839-1846, 4-gun gunbrig, 231
Bouncer, 1805-1815, 10-gun gunbrig, 222
Bourdais, 1864-1869, Screw gunboat, 367
Bourguignonne, 1807-1816, Transport (half-xebec), 414
Bourlos, 1798-1799, Gunboat, 281
Bourrasque, 1855-1867, Screw gun launch, 368
Boussole, 1785-1788, Flûte, 374
Boussole, 1804-1814, Hydrographic vessel, 313
Boussole, 1833-1848, 20 x 30pdr corvette, 189
Boutefeu (1), 1811-1812, Mortar gunboat, 292
Boutefeu (2), 1814-1837, Mortar gunboat, 292
Bouvines, 1831 cancelled, 30pdr frigate (46-gun), 158
Boyard, 1843-1880, Paddle tug (service craft), see *Pélican* 1828-1865
Brabançon, 1810-1815, Two-decker (80-gun), see *Neptune* 1818-1868
Brabant, 1810-1814, Two-decker (74-gun), 102
Brak, 1810-1813, Gunboat (Dutch), 288
Brakel (*Kapitein*), 1810-1813, Gunboat (Dutch), 288
Brandon, 1839-1841, Paddle vessel, 324
Brandon, 1846-1867, Paddle aviso, 338
Braque, 1809-?1815, 10 x 4pdr brig, see *Surveillant* 1793-1797
Brasier, 1833-1854, Paddle vessel, 324
Brave, 1746-1802, Galley, 294
Brave, 1781-1798, Two-decker (74-gun), 86
Brave, 1793-1795, Gunboat, 273
Brave, 1793-1798, 36pdr rasée frigate, 104
Brave, 1795-1796, Bateau-canonnier, 278
Brave, 1803-1806, Two-decker (74-gun), see *Cassard* 1795-1798
Brave, 1813-1814, Two-decker (74-gun), 100
Brave Sans Culotte, 1793-1795, Xebec or tartane, 296
Bravoure, 1795-1801, 12pdr frigate (40-gun), 131
Brême, 1795-1803, 24 x 8pdr corvette, see *Bayonnaise* 1793-1803
Brenta, 1811-1813, Péniche, 293
Bresciana, 1806-1813, Gunboat (Italian), 287
Brésil, 1808-1808, Two-decker (68-gun), see *Saint Sébastien* 1807-1808
Breslaw, 1808-1837, Two-decker (74-gun), 95
Breslaw, 1839-1856, Two-decker (90-gun), 65
Breslaw, 1856-1887, Screw two-decker, 73
Bressane, 1823-1833, 8-gun gunbrig, 229
Brestoise, 1815-1845, Schooner, 256
Bretagne, 1766-1793, Three-decker, 43
Bretagne, 1852 cancelled, Three-decker, 51
Bretagne, 1855-1880, Screw three-decker, 52
Bretagne, 1880-1894, Two-decker (hulked), see *Ville de Bordeaux* 1860-1880
Bretagne, 1894-1910, Two-decker (hulked), see *Fontenoy* 1858-1911
Breton, 1794-1795, Flûte, 377
Bretonne, 1780-1803, Gabarre, 384
Bretonne, 1807-1816, Xebec or half-xebec, 306
Bretonne, 1814-1815, Prame, see *Ville d'Anvers* 1804-1815
Bretonne, 1817-1830, Gabarre, 391
Briarée, 1824-1824, Two-decker (100-gun), see *Fleurus* 1830-1853
Brillant, 1774-1797, Two-decker (64-gun), 79
Brillant, 1812-1814, Two-decker (74-gun), 100
Brillante, 1797-1797, 12pdr frigate (38-gun), see *Montenotte* 1797-1801
Brillante, 1830-1875, 20 x 30pdr corvette, 187
Brilliant, 1794-1799, Lugger, 245
Brochet, 1794-1795, Floating battery, 312
Bruiteux, 1796-1796, Cutter, 249
Brûlante, 1794-1814, Gunboat, 275
Brûle Gueule, 1794-1800, 20 x 6pdr corvette, 169
Bruletout, 1796-1799, Bateau-canonnier, 279
Brumaire, 1794-1795, Gunboat (tartane), 278
Brune, 1781-1799, 20 x 8pdr corvette, 165
Brunswick, 1805-1805, Flûte, 380
Brutale, 1793-1793, Gunboat (chasse-marée), 276
Brutale, 1794-1809, Gunboat, 275
Brutus, 1792-1797, Two-decker (74-gun), see *Diadème* 1756-1792
Brutus, 1793-1795, 18 x 6pdr corvette, 177
Brutus, 1793-1797, 36pdr rasée frigate, 104
Brutus, 1794-1795, Transport, 407
Brutus, 1798-1803, Two-decker (74-gun), see *Impétueux* 1803-1806
Bucentaure, 1795-1795, Transport, see *Belle Suzanne* 1794-1795
Bucentaure, 1797-1814, Prame, 273
Bucentaure, 1803-1805, Two-decker (80-gun), 58
Bucentaure, 1833-1839, Two-decker (100-gun), see *Wagram* 1839-1854
Bucéphale, 1834-1873, Gabarre, 392
Bull-Dog, 1801-1801, 18 x 8pdr corvette, 175
Buse (*Buze*), 1793-1793, Tartane, 296
Bustler, 1808-1813, 14-gun gunbrig, 222
Buveur, 1795-1795, Transport, see *Bec d'Ambez* 1794-1795

Ça Ira, 1792-1796, Two-decker (80-gun), see *Couronne* 1781-1792
Ça Ira, 1794-1794, Two-decker (74-gun), see *Borée* 1785-1794
Ça Ira, 1794-1794, Gunboat, 277
Ça-Ira, 1795-1796, Bateau-canonnier, 278
Caboteur, 1794-1794, Transport, 407
Cabriole, 1814 cancelled, Schooner, 255
Cachelot, 1810-1813, Gunboat (Dutch), 288
Cacique, 1795-1795, Felucca, see *Constance* 1794-1795
Cacique, 1843-1868, Paddle frigate, 332
Cacique, 1893-1895, Two-decker (hulked), see *Saint Louis* 1857-1893
Cados, 1808-1812, Transport (half-xebec), 416

Caffarelli, 1847-1883, Paddle frigate, 335
Caïman, 1843-1854, Paddle corvette, 333
Calabrese, 1810-1815, 6-gun brig, 225
Calcul, 1795-1795, Felucca or tartane, see *Général Biron* 1793-1793
Calcutta, 1805-1809, Two-decker (56-gun), 77
Caledonia, 1795-1797, Flûte, 376
Calédonienne, 1858-1883, Schooner, 268
Calipso, 1808-1814, Gunboat (Italian), 287
Calliope, 1795-1797, 22 x 8pdr corvette, see *Cornélie* 1794-1795
Calvados, 1858-1887, Screw transport, 401
Calypso, 1785-1793, 12pdr frigate (32-gun), 128
Calypso, 1795-1797, 22 x 6pdr corvette, see *Duguay-Trouin* 1794-1795
Calypso, 1807-1814, 18pdr frigate (44-gun), 146
Calypso, 1812-1813, Speronare or galiote, 303
Calypso, 1814-1841, 18pdr frigate (44-gun), see *Elbe* 1808-1815
Calypso, 1830-1885, 24pdr frigate (58-gun), see *Marie Thérèse* 1823-1830
Camaret, 1865-1866, Gabarre (hulked), see *Robuste* 1828-1865
Caméléon, 1839-1865, Paddle corvette, 326
Camille, 1830-1851, 18 x 24pdr corvette-aviso, 188
Campechana, 1838-1840, Schooner, 268
Camphroust, 1793-1795, 8 x 4pdr corvette, 175
Canada, 1782-1797, Bomb vessel, 310
Canada, 1843-1878, Paddle frigate, 331
Cancer, 1795-1795, Lugger, see *Charlotte* 1793-1803
Canicule, 1795-1795, Felucca, see *Consolante* 1794-1795
Canonnière, 1803-1809, 18pdr frigate (42-gun), see *Minerve* 1794-1795
Canot de l'Empereur, 1848-, Yacht, see *Canot Impérial d'Anvers* 1810-1815
Canot Impérial d'Anvers, 1810-1815, Yacht, 314
Canot Royal de Brest, 1815-1848, Yacht, see *Canot Impérial d'Anvers* 1810-1815
Capélan, 1841-1892, Cutter, 265
Capri, 1810-1815, Two-decker (74-gun), 99
Capricciosa, 1806-1813, Gunboat (Italian), 287
Capricieuse, 1786-1800, 12pdr frigate (32-gun), 129
Capricieuse, 1795-1801, Tartane, see *Carmagnole* 1790-1795
Capricieuse, 1828-1836, 16-gun brig, 228
Capricieuse, 1849-1868, 30-gun corvette, 193
Carabine (*No.13*), 1860-1889, Screw sectional gun launch, 369
Caraïbe, 1842-1847, Paddle frigate, 332
Caravane, 1809-1817, Flûte, 378
Caravane, 1828-1864, Corvette de charge, 382
Caressante, 1795-1795, Felucca or tartane, see *Général Biron* 1793-1793
Carlotta, 1807-1808, 18pdr frigate (44-gun), 156
Carlotta, 1807-1810, 8-gun gunbrig, 219
Carmagnole, 1790-1795, Tartane, 295
Carmagnole, 1793-1794, Schooner, 249
Carmagnole, 1793-1800, 18pdr frigate (42-gun), 138
Carmagnole, 1794-1794, Schooner, 249
Carmagnole, 1795-1796, Bateau-canonnier, 278
Carnac, 1796-1796, Chasse-marée, 248
Carnation, 1808-1809, 18-gun brig, 221
Carolina, 1807-1814, 32-gun corvette, 181
Carolina, 1811-1815, 18pdr frigate (44-gun), 151
Caroline, 1792-1802, 16 x 8pdr corvette, 167
Caroline, 1793-1801, 8-gun brig, 211
Caroline, 1795-1800, Bateau-canonnier, 278
Caroline, 1798-1801, Biscayenne or trincadour, 297
Caroline, 1803-1815, Speronare or felucca, 304
Caroline, 1806-1809, 18pdr frigate (44-gun), 144
Caroline, 1824-1828, Paddle vessel, 316
Caroline, 1828-1830, 30pdr frigate (60-gun), see *Dryade* 1828-1838
Carpe, 1794-1795, Floating battery, 312
Carrère, 1797-1801, 18pdr frigate (44-gun), 143
Carthaginoise, 1798-1800, 12pdr frigate (32-gun), 133
Casabianca, 1859-1884, Paddle aviso, 345
Cassard, 1795-1796, Bateau-canonnier, 278
Cassard, 1795-1798, Two-decker (74-gun), 89
Cassard, 1803-1818, Two-decker (74-gun), 90
Cassard, 1832-1851, 20-gun brig, 231
Cassard, 1859-1867, Screw aviso, 357
Cassard, 1866-1866, Screw corvette, 200
Cassard, 1867-1893, Screw corvette, see *Comte d'Eu* 1846-1848
Cassauba, 1830-1835, 12-gun brig-aviso, 237
Casse-Tête (*No.16*), 1860-1867, Screw sectional gun launch, 370
Cassini, 1845-1869, Paddle corvette, 334
Cassius, 1795-1802, Half-xebec, see *Courrier d'Italie* 1794-1795
Castiglione, 1799-1801, Gunboat, 280
Castiglione, 1812-1814, Two-decker (74-gun), 96
Castiglione, 1835-1860, Two-decker (90-gun), 65
Castiglione, 1860-1900, Screw two-decker, 73
Castor, 1786-?, Sloop (service craft), 406
Castor, 1794-1794, 12pdr frigate (36-gun), 134
Castor, 1797-1797, 16 x 8pdr brig, 212
Castor, 1831-1855, Paddle vessel, 320
Castor, 1861-1894, Paddle aviso, 345
Castries, 1794-1794, Transport, 407
Casuarina, 1802-1803, Schooner, 259
Catharina Tholent, 1807-1807, Transport, see *Patiente* 1807-1814
Catherine, 1794-1795, Transport, 407
Catherine, 1796-1801, Flûte, see *Catherine-Marguerite* 1794-1796
Catherine, 1801-1807, Gabarre, 386
Catherine-Élisabeth, 1795-1796, Bateau-canonnier, 278
Catherine-Marguerite, 1794-1796, Flûte, 376
Catinat, 1851-1885, Paddle corvette, 335
Caton, 1794-1795, Transport (brig), 407
Caton, 1794-1801, Two-decker (80 gun), see *Duc de Bourgogne* 1751-1792
Caton, 1795-1796, Bateau-canonnier, 278
Caton, 1847-1875, Screw corvette, 195
Cauchoise, 1817-1838, Gabarre, 391
Causse, 1797-1801, Two-decker (66-gun), 80
Cécile-Charlotte, 1794-1795, Transport, 407
Cecilia-Anna, 1793-1797, Transport (galiote), 411
Célère, 1795-1795, 18 x 6pdr corvette, see *Brutus* 1793-1795
Célère, 1798-1800, Aviso, 243
Celeste, 1783-1792, Schooner, 239
Céleste, 1793-1795, 12 x 4pdr corvette, 171
Céleste Union, 1788-1788, Gabarre, 386
Censeur, 1782-1799, Two-decker (74-gun), 86
Centaure, 1782-1793, Two-decker (74-gun), 87
Centaure, 1818-1823, Two-decker (80-gun), 60
Cerbere, 1786-?, Sloop (service craft), 406
Cerbère, 1793-1796, Lugger, 248
Cerbère, 1795-1800, Gunboat, see *Chalier* 1794-1795
Cerbère, 1811-1829, Gunboat, 291
Cerbère, 1836-1865, Paddle vessel, 324
Céres, 1786-?, Sloop (service craft), 406
Cérès, 1779-1787, 12pdr frigate (32-gun), 125
Cérès, 1783-1791, 18 x 6pdr corvette, 166
Cérès, 1795-1798, 16 x 18pdr corvette, 172
Cérès, 1796-1798, Flûte, 376
Cérès, 1797-1797, 12pdr frigate (32-gun), see *Mantoue* 1797-1801
Cérès, 1812-1814, 18pdr frigate (44-gun), 153
Cérès, 1820-1823, 24pdr frigate (58-gun), see *Marie Thérèse* 1823-1830
Cérès, 1826-1840, 18-gun corvette-aviso, 186
Cérès, 1838-1838, Schooner?, 268
Cérès, 1847-1857, 30pdr frigate (40-gun), 160
Cérès, 1857-1896, Screw transport, 402
Cérès (loaned), 1801-1802, 18pdr frigate (40-gun), 143
Cerf, 1788-1795, 4pdr brig-aviso, 204
Cerf, 1797-1799, Bateau-canonnier, 279
Cerf, 1797-1800, Xebec, 297
Cerf, 1801-1803, 18-gun brig, 213
Cerf, 1807-1821, Schooner, 252
Cerf, 1833-1892, 16-gun brig, 228
Cerf-Volant, 1782-1786, Lugger, 239
Cerf-Volant, 1793-1796, 12-gun brig, 207
César, 1804-1806, 18-gun brig, 225
César, 1807-1814, Two-decker (74-gun), 95
Cesare, 1812-1814, 18-gun brig, 219
Ceylon, 1810-1819, 18pdr frigate (40-gun), 156
Ceylon (*Ceylan*), 1810-1810, Flûte, 381
Chacal, 1844-1862, Paddle aviso, 347
Chalier (*Chaslier*), 1794-1795, Gunboat, 275
Chaloupes-canonnières Nos. 22-445, 1803-1831, Gunboats, 284
Chameau, 1781-1796, Flûte, 374
Chameau, 1795-1796, Flûte, see *Antifédéraliste* 1794-1795
Chameau, 1795-1804, Bateau-plat, 272
Chameau, 1805 cancelled, Flûte, 378
Chameau, 1807-1813, Transport, 414
Chameau, 1818-1857, Gabarre, 391
Chamois, 1823-1849, Xebec or mistic, 308
Chamois, 1855-1878, Paddle aviso, 344
Champenoise, 1807-1809, Transport, see *Transport No. 2* 1806-1807
Champenoise, 1824-1834, 8-gun gunbrig, 229
Chandernagor, 1835-1895, Gabarre, 392
Chaptal, 1845-1862, Screw corvette, 194
Chardonneret, 1795-1795, Lugger, see *Oiseau* 1795-1796
Charente, 1803-1804, Gabarre, 385
Charente, 1809-1839, Gabarre, 388
Charente Inférieure, 1793-1794, 12pdr frigate (38-gun), 130
Chargeur, 1793-1803, Lugger, 248
Charlemagne, 1807-1814, Two-decker (74-gun), 95
Charlemagne, 1850-1851, Two-decker (90-gun), 65
Charlemagne, 1851-1884, Screw two-decker, 67
Charles, 1794-1795, Transport, 407
Charles, 1797-1798, Transport (sloop), 408
Charles, 1797-1799, Transport, 408
Charles-Honoré, 1798-1800, Transport (brig), see *Honoré* 1798-1800
Charlotte, 1793-1797, Lugger, see *Royal Charlotte* 1793-1797
Charlotte, 1793-1803, Lugger, 245
Charlotte, 1803-1814, Transport (packet), 413
Charlotte, 1805-1812, Transport, 414
Charlton, 1809-1810, Flûte, 380
Charmante, 1828-1837, Transport (brig), 418
Charmante-Rose, 1794-1795, Transport, 407
Charte, 1842-1848, 30pdr frigate (46-gun), 158
Chasseur, 1794-1797, Lugger, 248
Chasseur, 1803 cancelled, 16-gun brig, 215
Chasseur, 1805-1834, Lugger, see *Lougre No.3* 1803-1805
Chasseur, 1848-1887, 14-gun brig, 235
Chat, 1793-1799, Gunboat (chasse-marée), 276
Chatham, 1810-1814, Two-decker (80-gun), 61
Chercheur, 1795-1795, Cutter, see *Courrier* 1793-1795
Chéri, 1793-1796, Corvette, 177
'*Cherson* (*Herzon*, *Kerson*)', 1809-1811, Flûte, 381
Cheval Marin, 1797-1797, Galley, 298
Chevert, 1863-1873, 18-gun brig, 233
Chevre, 1782-1788, Gabarre, 384
Chevrette, 1795-1801, 20 x 8pdr corvette, see *Montagne* 1793-1795
Chevrette, 1843-1846, 4-gun gunbrig, 231
Chevrette, 1846-1866, Aviso (hulked), see *Biche* 1836-1846
Chevrette (*Grande Gabarre Écurie No.1*), 1811-1830, Gabarre, 389
Chevreuil, 1797-1799, Bateau-canonnier, 279
Chiaretta, 1797-1806, Galley, 299
Chicaneur, 1812 cancelled, Corvette, 182
Chien de Chasse, 1780-1787, Cutter, 239
Chien de Chasse, 1794-1798, Tartane, 295
Chiffonne, 1793-1804, Gunboat, 275
Chiffonne, 1799-1801, 12pdr frigate (38-gun), 131
Chimère, 1833-1871, Paddle vessel, 319
Chloé (*Cloé*), 1807-1814, Gabarre, 387
Choquante, 1795-1798, 16 x 8pdr brig, 206
Choria, 1834-1842, Trincadour, 307
Christiana, 1812-1812, Transport (sloop), 413
Christophe Colomb, 1843-1878, Paddle frigate, 332
Ciclope, 1808 uncertain, 10-gun brig, 220
Cicogne, 1794-1803, 14 x 18pdr corvette, 171
Cigale, 1836-1846, Schooner, 262
Cigogne, 1782-1791, Gabarre, 384
Cigogne, 1806-1807, Gabarre, 387
Cigogne, 1826-1865, 16-gun brig, 227
Cimeterre (*No.18*), 1860-1870, Screw sectional gun launch, 370
Cincinnatus, 1794-1795, Tartane, 296
Circe, 1810-1813, Gunboat (Dutch), 288
Circé, 1786-?, Sloop (service craft), 406
Circé, 1811-1831, 18pdr frigate (44-gun), 147
Circé, 1833-1844, 28 x 18pdr rasée corvette, 191
Circé, 1860-1875, Screw frigate, 120
Circulateur, 1795-1796, Cutter, see *Courrier de Lorient* 1793-1795
Cisalpin, 1797-1803, Two-decker (74-gun), see *Nestor* 1793-1797
Cisalpine, 1798-1799, Schooner, 250
Cisalpine, 1798-1799, Gunboat, see *Petite Cisalpine* 1798-1799
Cisalpine, 1798-1799, Felucca?, see *Romaine* 1798-1799
Citoyen, 1764-1793, Two-decker (74-gun), 84
Citoyen, 1793-1801, 22 x 8pdr corvette, 177
Citoyen, 1794-1794, Transport, 408
Citoyen, 1795-1795, Xebec or tartane, see *Brave Sans Culotte* 1793-1795
Citoyen, 1795-1796, Bateau-canonnier, 278
Citoyen, 1812 cancelled, Two-decker (74-gun), 97
Citoyenne, 1794-1802, 16 x 8pdr brig, 206
Citoyenne, 1800-1805, 12 x 4pdr brig, see *Citoyenne Française* 1795-1800
Citoyenne (*Citoyenne No.2*), 1793-1804, Gunboat, 273
Citoyenne Française, 1795-1800, 12 x 4pdr brig, 207
Clairvoyant, 1793-1800, Schooner, 240
Claudius Civilis, 1810-1811, 12-gun brig, 224
Clémentine, 1844-1844, Schooner, 270
Clémentine, 1848-1854, Schooner, 270
Cléomène, 1794-1796, Flûte, 377
Cléopâtre, 1781-1793, 12pdr frigate (32-gun), 127
Cléopâtre, 1805-1805, 12pdr frigate (38-gun), 135
Cléopâtre, 1817-1824, 18pdr frigate (44-gun), 147
Cléopâtre, 1838-1869, 30pdr frigate (50-gun), 112
Clorinde, 1800-1803, 18pdr frigate (40-gun), 143
Clorinde, 1808-1814, 18pdr frigate (44-gun), 149
Clorinde, 1821-1835, 24pdr frigate (58-gun), 107
Clorinde, 1838 cancelled, 30pdr frigate (52-gun), 113
Clorinde, 1845-1857, 30pdr frigate (40-gun), 159
Clorinde, 1857-1911, Screw frigate, 161
Cocarde, 1796-1803, 12pdr frigate (40-gun), see *Cocarde Nationale* 1794-1796
Cocarde Nationale, 1794-1796, 12pdr frigate (40-gun), 130
Coche, 1793-1802, Flûte, see *Miromesnil*
Cocyte, 1795-1795, Gunboat, see *Convention* 1794-1795
Cocyte, 1837-1875, Paddle vessel, 324
Coëtlogon, 1859-1879, Screw aviso, 360
Colbert, 1848-1867, Paddle corvette, 335

Colère, 1795-1796, Gunboat, see *Crocodile* 1793-1795
Colibri, 1802-1802, 16-gun brig, 210
Colibri, 1808-1809, 16-gun brig, 216
Colibri, 1817-1832, Schooner-aviso, see *Mouche No.16* 1808-1817
Colibri, 1822-1824, 20-gun brig, see *Alacrity* 1825-1851
Colibri, 1825-1833, Schooner, 269
Colibri, 1835-1845, colonial brig, 236
Coligny, 1850-1889, Paddle corvette, 336
Colomb, 1795-1796, Bateau-canonnier, 278
Colombe, 1794-1794, Transport, 407
Colombe, 1795-1803, 12 x 12pdr brig, 207
Colombe, 1796-1796, Aviso, 250
Colombe, 1809-1811, Felucca, 306
Colombe, 1814-1828, Schooner, see *Magpie* 1807-1815
Colombe, 1836-1847, Aviso, 265
Colombi, 1832-1842, Bateau or balancelle, 308
Colosse, 1813-1825, Two-decker (74-gun), 100
Colosse, 1865-1879, Three-decker (hulked), see *Friedland* 1840-1865
Comachiese, 1806-1812, Gunboat (Italian), 287
Comachiese (2), 1813-1813, Gunboat (Italian), 288
Comète, 1796-1810, 24pdr frigate (30-gun), 106
Comète, 1803-1804, Transport, 413
Comète, 1826-1859, 16-gun brig, 227
Comète, 1859-1880, Screw gunboat, 366
Cometta, 1824-1824, brig, 237
Commandant Bourdais, 1864-1869, Screw gunboat, see *Bourdais* 1864-1869
Commandant Fleuriau, 1819-1821, colonial brig, 236
Commerce, 1830-1839, Three-decker (110-gun), see *Commerce de Paris* 1806-1830
Commerce d'Amsterdam, 1810-1811, Two-decker (80-gun), 61
Commerce de Bordeaux, 1782-1783, Three-decker (projected), 44
Commerce de Bordeaux, 1785-1793, Two-decker (74-gun), 87
Commerce de Lyon, 1782-1783, Three-decker (projected), 44
Commerce de Lyon, 1807-1831, Two-decker (74-gun), 95
Commerce de Marseille, 1788-1793, Three-decker, 46
Commerce de Paris, 1806-1830, Three-decker (110-gun), 49
Commerce de Rotterdam, 1810-1811, Two-decker (68-gun), 83
Commerce du Havre, 1828-1829, Paddle vessel, 318
Commission, 1793-1795, Gabarre, see *Pluvier* 1776-1793
Commode, 1793-1793, Tartane, 296
Commode, 1803-1803, Gunboat, see *Méchante* 1793-1803
Commune, 1871-1871, Screw sectional armoured floating battery, see *Sectional Floating Battery No.5*
Comte d'Artois, 1814-1830, Three-decker, see *Ville de Paris* 1850-1858
Comte d'Eu, 1842-1844, Paddle aviso, 338
Comte d'Eu, 1846-1848, Screw corvette, 195
Conception, 1786-?, Sloop (service craft), 406
Concorde, 1791-1800, 18pdr frigate (44-gun), 137
Concorde, 1794-1795, Transport, 407
Concorde, 1798-1802, 14-gun brig, 212
Concorde, 1804-1811, Transport, 413
Confiance, 1794-1795, 16 x 6pdr corvette, 177
Confiante, 1797-1798, 20 x 18pdr corvette, 173
Conflict, 1804-1815, 10-gun gunbrig, 222
Congrève, 1855-1868, Ironclad floating battery, 426
Conquérant, 1765-1798, Two-decker (74-gun), 84
Conquérant, 1800-1816, Two-decker (74-gun), 93
Conquérant, 1812-1842, Two-decker (80-gun), 59

Conquête, 1794-1795, Transport, 408
Conquête de l'Amérique, 1794-1795, Transport, 407
Conscrit, 1804-1814, Transport (sloop), see *Zélé Conscrit* 1804-1814
Consolante, 1775-1804, 24pdr frigate (38-gun), 103
Consolante, 1794-1795, Felucca, 297
Consolante, 1800-1803, 18pdr frigate (44-gun), 141
Consolateur, 1808-1808, 3-gun brig, 226
Constance, 1794-1795, Felucca, 297
Constance, 1794-1797, 22 x 8pdr corvette, 169
Constance, 1798-1798, Gunboat, 280
Constance, 1812-1843, 18pdr frigate (44-gun), 153
Constance, 1815-1843, Sloop or cutter, 256
Constantine, 1851-1894, 30-gun corvette, 193
Constitutie, 1810-1811, Flûte, 382
Constitution, 1793-1795, Floating battery, 312
Constitution, 1794-1795, Felucca or tartane, see *Général Biron* 1793-1793
Constitution, 1795-1803, Two-decker (74-gun), 91
Constitution, 1848-1882, 30pdr frigate (46-gun), see *Charte* 1842-1848
Constitution de 1793, 1793-1794, Felucca or tartane, see *Général Biron* 1793-1793
Contente, 1797-1797, Gunboat, 280
Contrariant, 1795-1795, Lugger, see *Cerbère* 1793-1796
Convention, 1792-1800, Two-decker (74-gun), see *Sceptre* 1780-1792
Convention, 1794-1795, Gunboat, 276
Convention, 1796-1796, Transport (lugger), 408
Convention Nationale, 1793-1793, Schooner, 249
Cook, 1795-1802, Bateau-canonnier, 278
Copenhague, 1810-1814, 4-gun brig, 225
Coq, 1797-1799, Bateau-canonnier, 279
Coquette, 1798-1801, Half-galley, 300
Coquette, 1809-1822, 20 x 6pdr corvette, 182
Coquette, 1838-1853, 18 x 24pdr corvette-aviso, 188
Coquille, 1794-1798, 12pdr frigate (40-gun), 131
Coquille, 1813 cancelled, 20 x 6pdr corvette, 182
Coquille (Grande Gabarre Écurie No.2), 1811-1825, Gabarre, 389
Coraggiosa, 1806-1814, Gunboat (Italian), 287
Corbineau, 1808 not built, 18pdr frigate (44-gun), 154
Corcyre, 1809-1811, 18pdr frigate (38-gun), 157
Cordelière, 1828-1831, 20 x 30pdr corvette, see *Naïade* 1830-1851
Cordelière, 1858-1876, 30-gun corvette, 194
Cormoran, 1776-1789, Transport (chasse-marée), 405
Cormoran, 1798-1798, Lugger, 248
Cormoran, 1798-1800, Flûte, 378
Cormoran, 1822-1828, Transport (dogger), 418
Cormoran, 1841-1872, Gabarre, 393
Cormoran, 1880-1887, Paddle aviso (hulked), see *Goéland* 1848-1887
Cormorandière, 1850-1914, 20-gun brig (hulked), see *Bisson* 1830-1850
Cornaline, 1812-1823, Flûte, 380
Cornaline, 1834-1870, 20 x 30pdr corvette, 190
Cornelia, 1793-1794, Aviso, 247
Cornélie, 1794-1795, 22 x 8pdr corvette, 168
Cornélie, 1797-1808, 18pdr frigate (44-gun), 140
Cornélie, 1814 cancelled, 18pdr frigate (44-gun), 147
Cornélie, 1825-1846, 18-gun corvette-aviso, 186
Cornélie, 1858-1909, 30-gun corvette, 193
Cornish Hero, 1797-1798, 18-gun brig, 211
Corona, 1807-1811, 18pdr frigate (44-gun), 150
Corona, 1812-1814, 18pdr frigate (44-gun), 153
Corrèze, 1868-1896, Screw transport, 403
Corse, 1797-1798, Xebec, 297
Corse, 1850-1903, Screw aviso, 355
Corvettes de pêche Nos. 1-81, 1803-1814, Transport, 412

Cosmao, 1861-1882, Screw corvette, 200
Côte d'Or, 1793-1793, Three-decker, see *États de Bourgogne* 1790-1793
Coulebas, 1796-1799, Bateau-canonnier, 279
Couleuvrine, 1855-1868, Screw gun launch, 368
Courageuse, 1778-1799, 12pdr frigate (32-gun), 124
Courageuse, 1794-1795, 18pdr frigate (44-gun), see *Justice* 1795-1801
Courageuse, 1811-1813, Transport (galiote), 413
Courageuse, 1861 cancelled, Ironclad floating battery, 426
Courageux, 1793-1797, Lugger, 241
Courageux, 1795-1796, Bateau-canonnier, 278
Courageux, 1798-1800, Brigantine, 297
Courageux, 1802-1802, Two-decker (74-gun), see *D'Hautpoul* 1807-1809
Courageux, 1806-1832, Two-decker (74-gun), 91
Coureur, 1786-1792, Schooner, 249
Coureur, 1792-1798, Corvette, see *Duc de Chartres* 1782-1792
Coureur, 1794-1795, Schooner, 249
Coureur, 1804-1814, Transport (sloop), see *Alexandrine* 1802-1804
Coureur, 1808-1814, 16-gun brig, 217
Coureur, 1823-1849, Paddle vessel, 316
Coureuse, 1794-1795, Schooner, 249
Coureuse, 1801-1804, Schooner, 244
Couronne, 1781-1792, Two-decker (80-gun), 55
Couronne, 1807-1812, Two-decker (74-gun), see *Duc de Berry* 1818-1830
Couronne, 1813-1813, Two-decker (74-gun), 97
Couronne, 1824-1848, Two-decker (74-gun), 99
Couronne, 1861-1934, Ironclad frigate, 421
Courrier, 1782-1794, Lugger, 239
Courrier, 1793-1795, Cutter, 241
Courrier, 1794-1796, Cutter, 245
Courrier, 1799-1807, Schooner, 243
Courrier, 1811-1813, Cutter, 258
Courrier d'Italie, 1794-1795, Half-xebec, 296
Courrier de l'Europe, 1783-1789, Packet, see *Serin* 1771-1783
Courrier de Lorient, 1783-1789, Packet, see *Fortune* 1780-1783
Courrier de Lorient, 1793-1795, Cutter, 249
Courrier de Nantes, 1793-1793, Cutter, see *Courrier* 1793-1795
Courrier de New York, 1783-1789, Packet, see *Alligator* 1782-1783
Courrier National, 1795-1795, Cutter, see *Courrier* 1793-1795
Coursier, 1836-1843, Paddle vessel, 325
Courtois, 1795-1797, 12 x 6pdr brig, 212
Cousine, 1786-1807, Schooner, 240
Coutelas (No.19), 1860-1889, Screw sectional gun launch, 370
Coventry, 1783-1786, 8pdr frigate (28-gun), 122
Cowley, 1798-1798, Transport, see *Lowlay* 1798-1798
Crac (Craak), 1808-1813, Transport, 414
Crachefeu, 1794-1795, Gunboat, 275
Crachefeu, 1797-1799, Bateau-canonnier, 279
Créole, 1797-1803, 18pdr frigate (44-gun), 141
Créole, 1805-1809, 12-gun brig, 222
Créole, 1808-1823, 8-gun brig-schooner, 226
Créole, 1824-1838, colonial brig, 236
Créole, 1829-1845, 20 x 30pdr corvette, 186
Crescent, 1781-1786, 8pdr frigate (28-gun), 122
Creuse, 1863-1891, Screw transport, 403
Creutzen, 1794-1795, Lugger, 248
Crocodil, 1810-1813, Gunboat (Dutch), 288
Crocodile, 1793-1795, Gunboat, 275
Crocodile, 1794-1795, Gunboat, 277
Crocodile, 1832-1856, Paddle vessel, 319
Crocodile, 1858-1869, Paddle aviso, 350
Croiseur, 1855-1866, Screw aviso, 362
Cruelle, 1793-1800, Gunboat, 274
Crul (Schout-bij-nacht), 1810-1813, Gunboat (Dutch), 288
Cuirassier, 1822-1843, 18-gun brig, 226
Cultivateur, 1794-1795, Transport, 407
Cumberland, 1804-1809, Schooner, 256

Cupidon, 1829-1843, Schooner, 268
Curieuse, 1795-1796, Gunboat, see *Chiffonne* 1793-1804
Curieuse, 1794-1799, Biscayenne, 297
Curieuse, 1799-1800, Schooner or biscayenne, 250
Curieux, 1799-1801, 16 x 8pdr brig, 209
Curieux, 1788-1793, 4pdr brig-aviso, 204
Curieux, 1795-1796, Bateau-canonnier, 278
Curieux, 1800-1804, 16 x 6pdr brig, 209
Curieux, 1814-1833, 16-gun brig, see *Mercure* 1806-1810
Curieux, 1860-1879, Screw aviso, 360
Curiosa, 1807-1808, Schooner, 257
Curiosa, 1812-1813, Felucca, 302
Cuvier, 1842-1848, Paddle corvette, 330
Cuvier, 1860-1893, Screw aviso, 361
Cyane, 1805-1805, 18 x 6pdr corvette, 183
Cybèle, 1789-1809, 18pdr frigate (44-gun), 137
Cybèle, 1797-1799, Schooner, 246
Cybèle, 1816-1833, 18pdr frigate (44-gun), 149
Cybèle, 1836-1850, 24 x 18pdr rasée corvette, 191
Cyclope, 1805-1810, 16-gun brig, 215
Cyclope, 1828-1879, Bomb vessel, 312
Cyclope, 1886-1897, Two-decker (hulked), see *Donawerth* 1857-1868
Cygne, 1795-1796, Cutter, 244
Cygne, 1795-1796, Transport (brig), see *Caton* 1794-1795
Cygne, 1806-1808, 16-gun brig, 215
Cygne, 1825-1865, 20-gun brig, 229

D'Zaoudzi, 1855-1865, Transport, 418
Dague (No.20), 1860-1879, Screw sectional gun launch, 370
Dahlmann, 1808 not built, 18pdr frigate (44-gun), 154
Daim, 1849-1885, Paddle aviso, 342
Dalmate, 1808-1815, Two-decker (74-gun), 96
Dame Anna, 1793-1797, Transport (galiote), 411
Dame Arentina, 1793-1797, Transport (galiote), 411
Dame de Grace, 1798-1799, Transport (brig), 409
Dame Madeleine, 1796-1802, Gunboat (dogger or lugger), see *Madeleine* 1794-1802
Dame Marie, 1793-1802, Transport (galiote), 411
Dame Petronilla, 1793-1797, Transport (galiote), 411
Dame-Alida, 1795-1807, Transport (galiote), 411
Dame-Angelina, 1795-1807, Transport (galiote), 411
Dame-Catherine, 1793-1795, Transport, 411
Dame-Elsina, 1793-1797, Transport (galiote), 411
Dame-Francina, 1793-1797, Transport (galiote), 411
Dame-Gertrude, 1793-1797, Transport (galiote), 411
Dame-Girardina, 1793-1797, Transport (galiote), 411
Danae, 1786-?, Sloop (service craft), 406
Danaé, 1798-1801, 20 x 8pdr corvette, see *Vaillante* 1796-1798
Danaé, 1838-1858, 30pdr frigate (50-gun), 112
Danaé, 1856-1879, Screw frigate, 117
Danaë, 1782-1796, 18pdr frigate (36-gun), 135
Danaë, 1807-1812, 18pdr frigate (44-gun), 145
Danaë, 1814-1818, 18pdr frigate (44-gun), see *Vistule* 1808-1815
Danaïde, 1832-1865, 20 x 30pdr corvette, 187
Dangereuse, 1795-1799, Tartane, see *Duguay-Trouin* 1794-1795
Danois, 1861-1868, Schooner (hulked), see *Décidée* 1840-1861
Dantzick, 1807-1815, Two-decker (74-gun), 95
Danube, 1808-1826, Two-decker (74-gun), 94
Daphné, 1794-1797, 20 x 8pdr corvette, 175
Daphné (1), 1824-1833, Schooner, 261
Daphné (2), 1836-1866, Schooner, 261

Darien, 1842-1869, Paddle frigate, 331
Dart, 1798-1803, 6-gun brig, 211
Das, 1810-1813, Gunboat (Dutch), 288
D'Assas, 1830-1852, 20-gun brig, 231
D'Assas, 1854-1893, Screw corvette, 198
Dauphin, 1807-1807, Schooner, 259
Dauphin, 1809-1819, Lugger or chasse-marée, see *Deux Amis* 1802-1809
Dauphin, 1846-1868, Paddle aviso, 339
Dauphin Royal, 1782-1787, Gabarre, 385
Dauphin Royal, 1791-1792, Three-decker, 46
Dauphin Royal, 1824-1830, Two-decker (100-gun), see *Fleurus* 1830-1853
Dauphine, 1829-1830, 18pdr frigate (44-gun), see *Adrienne* 1809-1815
Dauphinoise, 1823-1851, Schooner, 261
David, 1779-1786, 6pdr corvette, 166
David, 1794-1795, Transport (sloop), 407
David, 1812-1812, brig, 226
De Gelder (Admiraal), 1810-1813, Gunboat (Dutch), 288
De Haan (Admiraal), 1810-1813, Gunboat (Dutch), 289
De Haas (Schout-bij-nacht), 1810-1813, Gunboat (Dutch), 289
De Liefde (Admiraal), 1810-1813, Gunboat (Dutch), 289
De Ruyter, 1811-1814, Two-decker (80-gun), see *Amiral de Ruyter* 1810-1811
Dea, 1806-1813, Gunboat (Italian), 287
Décade, 1794-1794, Transport, 407
Décade, 1794-1795, 20 x 6pdr corvette, 175
Décade, 1795-1798, 12pdr frigate (38-gun), see *Décade Française* 1794-1795
Décade Française, 1794-1795, 12pdr frigate (38-gun), 130
Décidée, 1798-1818, Half-galley, 300
Décidée, 1804-1814, 6 x 24pdr corvette, 181
Décidée, 1840-1861, Schooner, 265
Décidée, 1862-1885, Screw gunboat, 366
Décius, 1795-1796, 16 x 8pdr corvette, 170
Découverte, 1793-1795, Transport (sloop), 406
Découverte, 1795-1797, 4pdr brig-aviso, see *Papillon* 1786-1795
Découverte, 1798-1800, Schooner, 243
Découverte, 1800-1803, Schooner, 243
Decrès, 1866-1910, Screw corvette, 200
Dédaigneuse, 1793-1826, Gunboat, 274
Dédegneuse, 1797-1801, 12pdr frigate (40-gun), 131
Défiante, 1794-1795, 16 x 4pdr corvette, 176
Dego, 1797-1798, Mortar boat, 310
Dego, 1798-1800, Two-decker (64-gun), 82
Delphine, 1811-1817, Half-xebec or felucca, 305
Démocrate, 1795-1795, Two-decker (74-gun), see *Jupiter* 1789-1797
D'Entrecasteaux, 1858-1876, Screw aviso, 358
Département de la Manche, 1806-1810, 18pdr frigate (44-gun), 144
Département des Landes, 1804-1830, 20 x 8pdr corvette, 178
Département du Nord, 1803-1807, Schooner, 259
Département du Var, 1794-1795, Gunboat (tartane), see *Dorade* 1793-1794
Deplaisante, 1795-1797, Gunboat, see *Dédaigneuse* 1793-1826
Dépôt, 1865-1875, Bomb vessel (hulked), see *Vulcain* 1828-1865
Déroulède, 1860-1868, Paddle aviso, 351
Derzkiy, 1809-1810, Corvette, 184
Desaix, 1800-1802, Two-decker (74-gun), see *Tyrannicide* 1793-1800
Desaix, 1802-1804, Two-decker (74-gun), 94
Desaix, 1852 cancelled, Three-decker, 51
Desaix, 1858 cancelled, Two-decker (70-gun), 102
Desaix, 1870-1894, Screw corvette, 200
Descartes, 1844-1867, Paddle frigate, 328
Désintéressé, 1795-1795, Transport, see *Notre Dame des Carmes* 1794-1795
Désirée, 1783-1788, Flûte, 374
Désirée, 1795-1801, Bateau-canonnier, 278
Désirée, 1796-1800, 24pdr frigate (30-gun), 106
Désirée, 1803-1838, Gabarre, 386
D'Estaing, 1859-1876, Screw aviso, 359
Destin, 1777-1793, Two-decker (74-gun), 85
Destin, 1794-1795, Flûte, 377
Destruction, 1797-1797, Bomb vessel, 310
Deux Amis, 1793-1795, Transport (brig), 406
Deux Amis, 1793-1796, Floating battery, 312
Deux Amis, 1802-1809, Lugger or chasse-marée, 258
Deux Amis, 1803-1803, Schooner, 259
Deux Amis, 1808-1814, Bateau, 304
Deux Amis, 1824-1835, Cutter or sloop, 269
Deux Associés, 1794-1795, Flûte, 377
Deux Colombes, 1793-1797, Aviso, 245
Deux Frères, 1784-1792, Two-decker (80-gun), 56
Deux Frères, 1794-1795, Transport (galiote), 407
Deux Frères, 1794-1795, Transport, see *Frères* 1794-1795
Deux Frères, 1798-1799, Tartane, 297
Deux Hélènes, 1781-1786, Gabarre, 385
Deux Soeurs, 1793-1797, Transport (galiote), 411
Deux Soeurs, 1800-1818, Transport (sloop), 409
Deux Soeurs, 1803-1822, Transport (dogger), 413
Deux Soeurs Créoles, 1794-1795, Transport, 407
Dévastation, 1855-1872, Ironclad floating battery, 425
Devin, 1795-1795, Flûte, see *Duras* 1794-1795
D'Hautpoul, 1807-1809, Two-decker (74-gun), 91
Diadème, 1756-1792, Two-decker (74-gun), 84
Diadème, 1811-1868, Two-decker (80-gun), 58
Dialmath, 1855-1865, Paddle aviso, 350
Diamant, 1861-1879, Screw aviso, 360
Diamante, 1797-1814, Two-decker (64-gun), 81
Diana, 1806-1806, Gunboat (Italian), 287
Diane, 1786-?, Sloop (service craft), 406
Diane, 1796-1800, 18pdr frigate (44-gun), 141
Diane, 1808-1831, 20 x 8pdr corvette, 179
Diane (Transport No.51), 1798-1798, Transport, 408
Dictateur, 1782-1793, Two-decker (74-gun), 86
Didon, 1785-1792, 18pdr frigate (36-gun), 136
Didon, 1799-1805, 18pdr frigate (44-gun), 141
Didon, 1810-1815, 18pdr frigate (44-gun), see *Duchesse de Berry* 1816-1830
Didon, 1828-1867, 30pdr frigate (60-gun), 110
Difficile, 1793-1796, 20 x 6pdr corvette, 177
Digue, 1805-1807, Transport (sloop), 412
Diligence, 1799-1804, Transport (brig), 409
Diligent, 1795-1797, Bateau-plat, 272
Diligent, 1800-1806, 16-gun brig, 209
Diligent, 1803-1817, Transport (brig), 413
Diligent, 1815-1818, Transport (brig), 418
Diligente, 1793-1794, Transport, 407
Diligente, 1794-1800, 12 x 18pdr corvette, 168
Diligente, 1801-1854, 14 x 6pdr corvette, 174
Diligente, 1808-1809, Corvette, 185
Diligente, 1808-1814, Péniche, 293
Diligente, 1810-1810, Flûte, 382
Diligente, 1810-1813, Gunboat, 291
Diligente, 1864-1893, Screw gunboat, 366
Diomède, 1803-1806, Two-decker (74-gun), see *Union* 1799-1803
Diomède, 1809-1813, Flûte, 381
Diomède, 1828 cancelled, Two-decker (90-gun), 65
Diomède, 1831-1839, Two-decker (90-gun), see *Tilsitt* 1839-1856
Discovery, 1809-1809, Corvette, 183
Divette, 1875-1887, Transport (hulked), see *Pourvoyeur* 1840-1875
Dix-Août, 1798-1803, Two-decker (74-gun), see *Cassard* 1795-1798
Dix-huit Fructidor, 1797-1800, Two-decker (80-gun), see *Foudroyant* 1800-1834
Dix-Huit Fructidor, 1799-1799, Transport (lugger), 409
Dnepr, 1809-1811, Transport, 413
Doggersbank, 1810-1814, Two-decker (68-gun), 83
Dolphin, 1795-1796, 10 x 4pdr brig, 212
Donawerth, 1808-1824, Two-decker (80-gun), 58
Donawerth, 1839-1857, Two-decker (90-gun), 65
Donawerth, 1857-1868, Screw two-decker, 73
Donawerth, 1868-1869, Screw two-decker, see *Jean Bart* 1852-1868
Dorade, 1764-1789, Gabarre, 383
Dorade, 1793-1794, Gunboat (tartane), 276
Dorade, 1795-1798, Schooner, 249
Dorade, 1799-1799, 4-gun brig, 213
Dorade, 1807-1812, Gabarre, 387
Dorade, 1822-1844, Schooner, 262
Dorade, 1860-1876, Transport (clipper ship), 417
Dordogne, 1781-1788, Gabarre, 384
Dordogne, 1794-1795, Transport, 407
Dordogne, 1803-1806, Gabarre, 386
Dordogne, 1811-1811, Flûte, see *Tarn* 1818-1842
Dordogne, 1828-1845, Corvette de charge, 382
Dordogne, 1855-1893, Screw transport, 399
Dore, 1828-1851, Bomb vessel, 312
Doris, 1836-1846, Schooner, 261
Double Marin, 1794-1794, Aviso, 250
Doucereuse, 1795-1795, 16 x 8pdr corvette, see *Décius* 1795-1796
Douze Avril, 1829-1830, 30pdr frigate (46-gun), see *Charte* 1842-1848
Dragomire, 1798-1799, Coast defence ship, 176
Dragon, 1793-1800, Cutter, 241
Dragon, 1803 cancelled, 16-gun brig, 215
Dragon, 1822-1865, 18-gun brig, 226
Dragon, 1865-1865, Screw transport, see *Allier* 1861-1869
Dragon, 1865-1869, Corvette de charge (hulked), see *Allier* 1828-1865
Dragon, 1869-1879, Corvette (hulked), see *Triomphante* 1834-1869
Dragonne, 1855-1867, Screw gunboat, 365
Dragut, 1797-1797, Aviso, 250
Droits de l'Homme, 1798-1798, Aviso, 250
Droits de L'Homme, 1794-1797, Two-decker (74-gun), 89
Droits du Peuple, 1795-1795, 12pdr frigate (36-gun), 134
Dromadaire, 1781-1805, Flûte, 374
Dromadaire, 1805 cancelled, Flûte, 378
Dromadaire, 1810-1811, Flûte, 379
Dromadaire, 1821-1843, Large transport, 396
Dromadaire, 1845-1870, Gabarre, see *Mahé* 1835-1845
Dromadaire, 1873-1877, Screw transport (hulked), see *Loire* 1855-1873
Drôme, 1862-1875, Screw transport, 403
Drouot, 1852 cancelled, 18-gun brig, 233
Druide, 1877-1888, 30pdr frigate (hulked), see *Iphigénie* 1827-1877
Dryade, 1783-1801, 18pdr frigate (36-gun), 136
Dryade, 1812-1815, 18pdr frigate (44-gun), 151
Dryade, 1828-1838, 30pdr frigate (60-gun), 110
Dryade, 1847-1856, 30pdr frigate (50-gun), 114
Dryade, 1856-1886, Screw transport, 402
Du Chayla, 1855-1890, Screw corvette, 199
Dubois, 1797-1801, Two-decker (64-gun), 81
Duc d'Angoulême, 1814-1830, Three-decker (110-gun), 49
Duc de Berry, 1818-1830, Two-decker (74-gun), 98
Duc de Bordeaux, 1820-1830, Three-decker, see *Friedland* 1840-1865
Duc de Bourgogne, 1751-1792, Two-decker (80-gun), 55
Duc de Chartres, 1782-1792, Corvette, 166
Duchesse, 1742-1792, Galley, 294
Duchesse d'Angoulême, 1814-1825, 18pdr frigate (44-gun), see *Atalante* 1812-1815
Duchesse de Berry, 1815-1830, 18pdr frigate (44-gun), 151
Duchesse d'Orléans, 1829-1848, 30pdr frigate (60-gun), see *Victoire* 1848-1861
Ducouëdic, 1829-1867, 20-gun brig, 230
Dugommier, 1797-1805, Two-decker (74-gun), see *Pluton* 1778-1797
Duguay Trouin, 1854-1857, Two-decker (100-gun), 64
Duguay Trouin, 1857-1872, Screw two-decker, 74
Duguay-Trouin, 1788-1793, Two-decker (74-gun), 89
Duguay-Trouin, 1793-1794, 12pdr frigate (34-gun), 134
Duguay-Trouin, 1794-1795, 22 x 6pdr corvette, 177
Duguay-Trouin, 1794-1795, Tartane, 296
Duguay-Trouin, 1800-1805, Two-decker (74-gun), 91
Duguay-Trouin, 1813-1826, Two-decker (74-gun), 100
Duguesclin, 1807-1820, Two-decker (74-gun), 95
Duguesclin, 1848-1858, Two-decker (90-gun), 65
Duguesclin, 1858-1860, Screw two-decker, 74
Dune Libre, 1794-1795, Gunboat (tartane), 278
Dunkerque, 1794-1795, Transport, 408
Dunois, 1830-1842, 16-gun brig, 228
Duperré, 1849-1870, Two-decker (74-gun), see *Couronne* 1824-1848
Dupetit Thouars, 1830-1867, 16-gun brig, 228
Dupetit-Thouars, 1799-1804, Bomb vessel, 310
Dupleix, 1861-1890, Screw corvette, 199
Duquesne, 1788-1803, Two-decker (74-gun), 90
Duquesne, 1794-1795, Flûte, 377
Duquesne, 1795-1796, Bateau-canonnier, 278
Duquesne, 1810-1811, Two-decker (74-gun), see *Duguay-Trouin* 1813-1826
Duquesne, 1810-1814, Two-decker (74-gun), 97
Duquesne, 1811-1833, Two-decker (74-gun), see *Moscou* 1809-1811
Duquesne, 1814-1858, Two-decker (80-gun), see *Zélandais* 1813-1815
Duquesne, 1847-1853, Two-decker (90-gun), 65
Duquesne, 1853-1872, Screw two-decker, 69
Durance, 1781-1791, Gabarre, 384
Durance, 1805-1838, Gabarre, 386
Durance, 1847 cancelled, Gabarre, 393
Durance, 1848-1854, Large transport, 397
Durance, 1855-1875, Screw transport, 398
Duras, 1794-1795, Flûte, 377
Duroc, 1852-1856, Screw aviso, 355
Dyle, 1803 cancelled, Flûte, 378

Eau, 1810-1820, Gunboat, 291
Ebe, 1811-1814, 18pdr frigate (44-gun), 153
Ébrié, 1853-1856, Paddle aviso, 348
Écho, 1810-1844, 20 x 6pdr corvette, 182
Écho, 1848 cancelled, Corvette-aviso, 193
Écho, 1860-1865, Paddle aviso, see *Saïgon* 1860-1860
Éclair, 1771-1793, 18 x 6pdr corvette, 163
Éclair, 1793-1795, Gunboat (chasse-marée), 276
Éclair, 1793-1796, Cutter or lugger, 248
Éclair, 1798-1799, Gunboat (tartane), 280
Éclair, 1799-1801, Schooner, 243
Éclair, 1808-1814, Schooner, 259
Éclair, 1818-1825, Schooner-aviso, see *Mouche No.15* 1808-1818
Éclair, 1835-1858, Bomb vessel, see *Achéron* 1828-1835
Éclair, 1838-1848, Schooner, 269
Éclair, 1855-1872, Screw gunboat, 364
Éclaireur, 1811-1821, 16-gun brig, 217
Éclaireur, 1834-1835, Paddle vessel, 325
Éclaireur, 1847-1868, Paddle aviso, 341
Éclat, 1794-1795, Gunboat (tartane), see *Hecla* 1794-1795
Éclatant, 1794-1796, Flûte, 377
Éclatante, 1793-1803, Gunboat, 273
Éclipse, 1826-1865, 16-gun brig, 227
Écluse, 1764-1788, Gabarre, 383
Économe, 1855-1874, Paddle aviso, 349
Écrevisse, 1795-1796, Flûte, see *Deux Associés* 1794-1795

Écureuil, 1794-1796, Lugger, 242
Écureuil, 1799-1802, Lugger, 243
Écureuil, 1806-1810, 16-gun brig, 215
Écureuil, 1814-1827, 10-gun gunbrig, see *Bouncer* 1805-1815
Écureuil (*Écureuil No. 1*), 1829-1872, Cutter, 263
Écureuil No. 2, 1846-1859, Schooner, 266
Écurie, 1866-1894, 30pdr frigate (hulked), see *Belle Gabrielle* 1828-1830
Effronté, 1793-1793, Tartane, 296
Effroyable, 1795-1796, Gunboat, see *Etna* 1793-1797
Égalité, 1793-1795, Floating battery, 312
Égalité, 1793-1796, Chasse-marée, 248
Égalité, 1797-1798, 20-gun corvette, 178
Égérie, 1803-1804, 20 x 8pdr corvette, see *Département des Landes* 1803-1830
Égérie, 1811-1830, 20 x 8pdr corvette, 179
Égérie, 1834-1873, Corvette de charge, see *Lozère* 1832-1834
Egida, 1813-1814, Gunboat (Italian), 288
Églantine, 1839-1885, 4-gun gunbrig, 231
Églantine (*Grande Gabarre Écurie No.3*), 1812-1828, Gabarre, 390
Églé, 1826-1843, 18-gun corvette-aviso, 186
Églé, 1846-1860, Schooner, 266
Égyptien, 1799-1799, Gabarre, 386
Égyptien, 1800-1804, Half-xebec, 297
Égyptienne, 1799-1801, 24pdr frigate (50-gun), 105
Égyptienne, 1812-1815, Flûte, 380
Élan, 1795-1822, Transport (dogger), 406
Élan, 1843-1851, Paddle corvette, 333
Elbe, 1808-1815, 18pdr frigate (44-gun), 149
Elbine, 1813-1814, 20 x 24pdr corvette, 182
Eldorado, 1843-1875, Paddle frigate, 332
Elena, 1811-1814, Péniche, 293
Éléphant, 1795-1803, Bateau-plat, 272
Éléphant, 1811-1833, Flûte, 379
Éléphant, 1873-1886, Two-decker (hulked), see *Turenne* 1858-1875
Éléphantine, 1799-1801, Felucca or djerme, 301
Elisa, 1799-1801, Transport (brig), 410
Élisa, 1808-1810, 18pdr frigate (44-gun), 149
Elisa (*Eliza*), 1804-1805, Schooner, 257
Élisabeth, 1792-1793, Schooner, see *Coureur* 1786-1792
Élisabeth, 1794-1796, Flûte, see *Tigre* 1793-1794
Élisabeth-Judith, 1794-1794, Transport, 407
Elise, 1793-1794, 22 x 6pdr corvette, 175
Élizabeth, 1810-1813, Schooner, 257
Elus, 1786-?, Sloop (service craft), 406
Elvetia, 1813-1813, Gunboat (Italian), 288
Embucade, 1798-1803, 12pdr frigate (38-gun), 134
Embuscade, 1789-1798, 12pdr frigate (34-gun), 130
Embuscade, 1837-1862, 20 x 30pdr corvette, 189
Embuscade, 1865-1945, Ironclad floating battery, 428
Émeraude, 1779-1797, 12pdr frigate (32-gun), 124
Émeraude, 1793-1793, Tartane, 296
Émeraude, 1814 cancelled, 18pdr frigate (44-gun), 147
Émeraude, 1823-1843, Schooner, 262
Emilia-Louisa, 1793-1796, Transport (galiote), 411
Émilie, 1794-1795, Transport, 407
Émilie (*Émile*), 1795-1801, Bateau-canonnier, 278
Ems, 1812-1815, 18pdr frigate (44-gun), 153
Émulation, 1794-1795, Transport, see *Jeune Louis* 1794-1794
Émulation, 1862-1883, Corvette (hulked), see *Embuscade* 1837-1862
Émulation (*Grande Gabarre Écurie No.12*), 1811-1845, Gabarre, 391
Encantador, 1824-1824, brig-schooner, 236
Encelade, 1811-1854, Mortar gunboat, 292
Encourageante, 1795-1800, Felucca, 295
Endymion, 1805-1814, 16-gun brig, 215
Endymion, 1824-1840, 18-gun brig, 226
Énea, 1797-1808, Half-xebec, 298
Énéas, 1809-1816, 18-gun brig, 223
Enfant, 1792-1795, Lugger, 240
Enfant de la Patrie, 1797-1798, 16 x 18pdr corvette, see *Cérès* 1795-1798
Enfant Prodigue, 1796-1803, Schooner, 250
Enfante de la Patrie, 1795-1797, 12 x 6pdr corvette, 178
Enflammée, 1793-1803, Gunboat, 275
Engageante, 1766-1794, 12pdr frigate (32-gun), 123
Énigme, 1795-1803, Gunboat, see *Etna* 1794-1795
Enjouée, 1795-1796, Schooner, see *Coureur* 1794-1795
Enjouée, 1797-1797, Gunboat, 280
Entrepôt, 1866-1888, 18pdr frigate (hulked), see *Armide* 1821-1866
Entreprenant, 1787-1803, Two-decker (74-gun), 88
Entreprenant, 1800-1801, Bateau, 297
Entreprenant, 1807-1808, Felucca or patmar, 303
Entreprenant, 1808-1810, 12-gun brig, 220
Entreprenant, 1849-1909, 14-gun brig, 235
Entreprenante, 1829-1858, 30pdr frigate (60-gun), 113
Entreprenante, 1858-1896, Screw transport, 402
Entreprise, 1792-1795, Aviso, 250
Entreprise, 1796-1796, Transport (brig), 408
Entreprise, 1809-1813, Galeotta or half-galley, 306
Envie, 1808-1815, Half-xebec, 305
Éole, 1789-1811, Two-decker (74-gun), 89
Éole, 1794-1794, Transport, 407
Éole, 1797-1797, Two-decker (66-gun), see *Robert* 1797-1818
Éole, 1799-1799, 16 x 8pdr corvette, 178
Éole, 1799-1803, Xebec, 301
Éole, 1814-1819, Two-decker (74-gun), see *Anversois* 1807-1815
Éole, 1833-1839, Two-decker (100-gun), see *Eylau* 1839-1856
Epée (*No.22*), 1860-1867, Screw sectional gun launch, 370
Éperlan, 1837-1851, Cutter, 264
Épervier, 1788-1797, 4pdr brig-aviso, 204
Épervier, 1795-1797, Cutter, 245
Épervier, 1795-1798, Aviso, 250
Épervier, 1802-1803, 16-gun brig, 210
Épervier, 1805 cancelled, 16-gun brig, 215
Épervier, 1810-1822, 16-gun brig, 217
Épervier, 1836-1841, Aviso, 265
Épervier, 1847-1857, Paddle aviso, 339
Épervier, 1858-1858, Screw aviso, see *Aigle* 1853-1858
Epi, 1795-1795, Corvette, see *Félicité* 1794-1795
Érèbe, 1837-1850, Paddle vessel, 325
Érèbe, 1861-1869, Paddle tug (service craft), 321
Éridan, 1843-1847, Paddle aviso, 346
Eridano, 1810-1814, 16-gun brig, see *Écureuil* 1806-1810
Érigone, 1803 cancelled, 20 x 8pdr corvette, 178
Érigone, 1812-1825, 18pdr frigate (44-gun), 152
Érigone, 1836-1879, 18pdr frigate (46-gun), 158
Ernéa, 1834-1842, Trincadour, 308
Escaut, 1795-1795, 14 x 6pdr brig, 213
Escaut, 1803-1815, Flûte, 375
Espadon, 1842-1854, Paddle corvette, 333
Espadon, 1860-1881, Paddle aviso, 350
Espagnol, 1794-1795, Cutter, 247
Espérance, 1787-1791, Gabarre, 385
Espérance, 1791-1794, Gabarre, see *Durance* 1781-1791
Espérance, 1793-1793, Flûte, see *Miromesnil* 1793-1793
Espérance, 1793-1795, Aviso, 250
Espérance, 1793-1795, Bomb vessel, 310
Espérance, 1794-1795, 22 x 6pdr corvette, see *Elise* 1793-1794
Espérance, 1794-1795, Transport, 407
Espérance, 1795-1795, Transport (galiote), 411
Espérance, 1795-1802, Schooner, 249
Espérance, 1798-1801, Gunboat, 280
Espérance, 1802-1802, Xebec, see *Saint Hilaire* 1798-1802
Espérance, 1804-1808, Hydrographic vessel, 313
Espérance, 1817-1827, 20 x 8pdr corvette, 179
Espérance, 1825-1843, Schooner, 269
Esperanza, 1839-1842, Schooner, 269
Espiègle, 1788-1793, 4pdr brig-aviso, 204
Espiègle, 1793-1794, 4pdr brig, 206
Espiègle, 1795-1797, Cutter, 242
Espiègle, 1804-1808, 16-gun brig, 215
Espiègle, 1834-1888, Cutter, 264
Espingole (*No.23*), 1860-1879, Screw sectional gun launch, 370
Espion, 1794-1795, 18 x 6pdr corvette, 175
Espion, 1795-1797, Aviso, see *Épervier* 1795-1798
Espoir, 1788-1797, 4pdr brig-aviso, 204
Estafette, 1810-1836, Schooner, 254
Estafette, 1842-1868, Schooner, 261
Esteck, 1794-1802, Lugger, see *Steck* 1794-1802
Estelle, 1802-1815, Schooner, 259
Esther, 1794-1795, Flûte, 376
États de Bourgogne, 1790-1793, Three-decker, 46
Étienne Marchand, 1829-1831, 16-gun brig, see *Argus* 1832-1882
Étincelle, 1814 cancelled, Schooner, 256
Étincelle, 1823-1836, Balancelle or bateau, 308
Étincelle, 1855-1864, Screw gunboat, 364
Etna, 1754-1786, Bomb vessel, 309
Etna, 1793-1797, Gunboat, 273
Etna, 1794-1795, Gunboat, 275
Etna, 1794-1795, Gunboat (tartane), 278
Etna, 1795-1796, 16 x 18pdr corvette, 172
Etna, 1800-1833, 6 x 18pdr corvette, 174
Etna, 1801-1815, Gunboat, 280
Etna, 1836-1847, Paddle vessel, 324
Étoile, 1783-1796, Flûte, 374
Étoile, 1798-1798, Transport, 409
Étoile, 1798-1799, Gunboat (tartane), 280
Étoile, 1807-1809, Flûte, 382
Étoile, 1813-1814, 18pdr frigate (44-gun), 149
Étoile, 1814-1849, Schooner, 259
Étoile, 1858-1879, Paddle aviso, 345
Étoile du Matin, 1793-1795, Aviso, 244
Étoile-Brillante, 1794-1795, Transport, 407
Étonnante, 1795-1795, Gunboat (tartane), see *Etna* 1794-1795
Étonnante, 1795-1806, 16 x 18pdr corvette, 173
Étourdi, 1799-1801, Aviso, 251
Étourdi, 1808-1811, 16-gun brig, 217
Étourdie, 1794-1798, 12pdr brig, 206
Étourdie, 1799-1802, Schooner, 250
Eugénie, 1794-1796, 16 x 6pdr brig, 213
Eugénie, 1837-1851, Trincadour, 308
Eugenio, 1810-1814, Xebec, 303
Euménide, 1813-1825, Gunboat, 291
Euménide, 1848-1907, Paddle corvette, 336
Euphrate, 1839-1862, Paddle vessel, 324
Euphrate, 1893-1933, Corvette (hulked), see *D'Assas* 1854-1893
Eure, 1862-1877, Screw transport, 403
Europe, 1794-1795, Transport, 407
Europe (*Europa*), 1809-1809, Flûte, 380
Européen, 1859-1911, Screw transport, 404
Euryale, 1806 cancelled, 16-gun brig, 215
Euryale, 1813-1846, 16-gun brig, 218
Euryale, 1863-1870, 18-gun brig, 233
Eurydice, 1795-1796, Schooner, see *Armande* 1793-1795
Eurydice, 1809-1811, 18pdr frigate (44-gun), see *Atalante* 1812-1815
Eurydice, 1810-1814, 18pdr frigate (40-gun), 154
Eurydice, 1814-1825, 18pdr frigate (44-gun), see *Prégel* 1810-1815
Eurydice, 1849-1877, 30-gun corvette, 193
Eveillé, 1772-1786, Two-decker (64-gun), 78
Eveillé, 1788-1795, 4pdr brig-aviso, 205
Éveillé, 1797-1798, Lugger, 248
Éveillé, 1809-1814, 8-gun brig, see *Surveillant* 1804-1809
Evertsen, 1811-1814, Two-decker (80-gun), see *Amiral Evertsen* 1810-1811
Evertsen (*Admiraal*), 1810-1813, Gunboat (Dutch), 289
Exange (*Exauge*), 1794-1795, Flûte, 376
Expéditif, 1798-1801, Half-xebec, 295
Expédition, 1788-1795, 4pdr brig-aviso, 204
Expédition, 1794-1795, 16 x 6pdr corvette, 176
Expédition, 1794-1795, 14-gun brig, 211
Expédition, 1794-1795, Cutter or sloop, 249
Expédition, 1798-1799, Gunboat (tartane), 280
Expéditive, 1809-1824, Gabarre, 388
Expéditive, 1834-1884, Gabarre, 392
Experiment, 1779-1800, Two-decker (50-gun), 76
Exterminateur, 1794-1795, Felucca, 296
Extraordinaire, 1795-1796, Cutter or sloop, see *Expédition* 1794-1795
Eylau, 1808-1829, Two-decker (80-gun), 58
Eylau, 1839-1856, Two-decker (100-gun), 64
Eylau, 1856-1905, Screw two-decker, 72

Fabert, 1833-1838, 16-gun brig, 228
Fabert, 1848-1872, 6-gun brig-aviso, 236
Fabius, 1793-1796, 20 x 6pdr corvette, 177
Fabius, 1795-1796, Bateau-canonnier, 278
Fabuleux, 1795-1796, Transport (chasse-marée), see *Félicité* 1781-1795
Faisceau, 1796-1797, Aviso, 250
Fama, 1806-1815, Corvette, 183
Fama, 1808-1816, Schooner, 257
Fame of Pool, 1798-1806, Transport, 410
Fanfaron, 1781-1802, Cutter, 238
Fanfaron, 1795-1799, Bateau-canonnier, 278
Fanfaron, 1804-1809, 16-gun brig, 215
Fanfaron, 1842-1843, 18-gun brig, see *Olivier* 1884-1887
Fanny, 1793-1794, Aviso, 244
Fanny, 1795-1796, Bateau-canonnier, 278
Fantôme, 1795-1795, Gunboat, see *Foudre* 1793-1798
Fantôme, 1795-1795, Gunboat (tartane), see *Foudre* 1794-1795
Faon, 1847-1881, Screw aviso, 356
Farceur, 1795-1797, Gunboat (chasse-marée), see *Furet* 1793-1795
Fardeau, 1794-1815, Gabarre, 385
Fatalité, 1795? cancelled, 24pdr frigate (30-gun), 105
Faucon, 1825-1848, 20-gun brig, 230
Fauçon, 1811-1819, Transport, 414
Fauconneau (*No.24*), 1860-1870, Screw sectional gun launch, 370
Faulx (*No.27*), 1860-1879, Screw sectional gun launch, 370
Faune, 1804-1805, 16-gun brig, 215
Faune, 1810-1810, Schooner, 258
Faune, 1811-1832, 16-gun brig, 217
Faune, 1843-1844, 18-gun brig, see *Abeille* 1844-1847
Faune, 1847-1869, 14-gun brig, 235
Faune, 1893-1920, Screw corvette (hulked), see *Comte d'Eu* 1846-1848
Fauvette, 1783-1815, 20 x 6pdr corvette, 165
Fauvette, 1824-1836, Schooner, 261
Fauvette, 1842-1876, Schooner, 265
Faveur, 1795-1796, Flûte, see *Fille Unique* 1785-1804
Favori, 1799-1806, Cutter, 246
Favori, 1806-1809, 16-gun brig, 214
Favori, 1814-1831, 10-gun gunbrig, see *Mallard* 1804-1815
Favori, 1842-1860, Cutter, 265
Favori, 1861-1887, Screw aviso, 363
Favorita, 1808-1811, 18pdr frigate (44-gun), 150
Favorite, 1785-1795, 20 x 6pdr corvette, 165
Favorite, 1806-1807, 18 x 6pdr corvette, 183
Favorite, 1809-1810, 20 x 6pdr corvette, see *Écho* 1810-1844
Favorite, 1829-1853, 20 x 30pdr corvette, 187
Favorite, 1870-1887, Corvette-transport, 194

Fée, 1780-1790, 12pdr frigate (32-gun), 125
Fée, 1795-1795, Felucca, see *Fidèle* 1794-1795
Félicité, 1781-1795, Transport (chasse-marée), 405
Félicité, 1785-1809, 12pdr frigate (32-gun), 128
Félicité, 1794-1795, Corvette, 177
Félicité, 1798-1801, Aviso, 250
Félix Méritis, 1794-1795, Flûte, 377
Fenice, 1809-1809, 18-gun brig, 224
Fenice, 1812-1814, Schooner, 254
Ferme, 1740-1814, Galley, 294
Ferme, 1785-1792, Two-decker (74-gun), 87
Ferme, 1794-1795, Flûte, 377
Ferrarese, 1810-1813, Gunboat (Italian), 287
Ferreter, 1807-1813, 16-gun gunbrig, 222
Fertile, 1795-1796, Felucca, see *Furet* 1794-1795
Festin, 1795-1813, 12 x 18pdr corvette, see *Fraternité* 1793-1795
Feu, 1811-1819, Gunboat, 291
Feu Roulant, 1797-1799, Bateau-canonnier, 279
Fiamma, 1811-1814, Péniche, 293
Fidèle, 1789-1813, 12pdr frigate (32-gun), 128
Fidèle, 1794-1795, Felucca, 297
Fidèle, 1809-1809, 18pdr frigate (44-gun), 149
Fidèle, 1813-1813, 18pdr frigate (44-gun), 153
Figuières, 1794-1795, Two-decker (80-gun), see *Formidable* 1795-1805
Fille Unique, 1785-1804, Flûte, 374
Fils Unique, 1838-1840, Schooner, 268
Fine, 1779-1794, 12pdr frigate (32-gun), 124
Fine, 1801-1809, Schooner, 243
Fine, 1836-1850, Schooner, 261
Fine, 1860-1871, Schooner, 270
Finistère, 1828-1865, Bomb vessel, 312
Finistère, 1859-1921, Screw transport, 402
Finistèrre, 1803-1816, Two-decker (74-gun), see *Thésée* 1790-1793
Firmesa, 1839-1842, Schooner, 269
Flamande, 1814-1827, Prame, see *Ville de Genève* 1804-1815
Flambart, 1849-1865, Paddle aviso, 342
Flambeau, 1837-1880, Paddle vessel, 325
Flamberge (*No.28*), 1860-1885, Screw sectional gun launch, 370
Flamme, 1809-1826, Gunboat, see *Surveillante* 1807-1809
Flamme, 1855-1878, Screw gunboat, 364
Flandre, 1864-1887, Ironclad frigate, 423
Fléche, 1768-1794, 18 x 6pdr corvette, 163
Flèche, 1799-1801, 16 x 8pdr brig, 209
Flèche, 1799-1802, 6 x 4pdr schooner/Aviso, see *Hirondelle* 1793-1799
Flèche, 1808-1813, Schooner, 252
Flèche, 1825-1852, 16-gun brig, 227
Flèche, 1855-1883, Screw gunboat, 365
Fleur de Lis, 1814-1830, 18pdr frigate (44-gun), see *Dryade* 1812-1815
Fleur de Lys, 1785-1792, 12pdr frigate (32-gun), 126
Fleuret (*No.29*), 1860-1886, Screw sectional gun launch, 371
Fleurian, 1819-1821, colonial brig, see *Commandant Fleuriau* 1819-1821
Fleurus, 1830-1853, Two-decker (100-gun), 64
Fleurus, 1853-1877, Screw two-decker, 69
Flibustier, 1793-1795, 36pdr rasée frigate, 104
Flibustier, 1797-1799, Bateau-canonnier, 279
Flibustier, 1810-1813, 16-gun brig, 217
Flore, 1768-1787, 8pdr frigate (32-gun), 122
Flore, 1787-1795, 12pdr frigate (32-gun), see *Flore Americaine* 1784-1787
Flore, 1798 not built, 8pdr brig, 208
Flore, 1806-1811, 18pdr frigate (44-gun), 147
Flore, 1814-1840, 18pdr frigate (44-gun), see *Hortense* 1803-1815
Flore, 1847-1869, 30pdr frigate (50-gun), 115
Flore, 1869-1901, Screw frigate, 120
Flore Americaine, 1784-1787, 12pdr frigate (32-gun), 127
Floréal, 1794-1796, Gunboat (tartane), 278
Floris, 1810-1813, Gunboat (Dutch), 289
Flottante, 1795-1796, Tartane, see *François de Paule* 1794-1795
Flûte Impériale, 1810-1810, Flûte, see *Diligente* 1810-1810
Folgore, 1806-1813, Gunboat (Italian), 287
Folle, 1795-1795, Gunboat, see *Barra* 1794-1795
Fontenoy, 1827-1858, Two-decker (90-gun), 65
Fontenoy, 1858-1894, Screw two-decker, 73
Forbin, 1795-1796, Bateau-canonnier, 278
Forbin, 1859-1885, Screw aviso, 357
Forcalquier (*Fort-Calquier*), 1793-1793, Cutter or chasse-marée, 249
Force (*Forte*), 1794-1802, Gunboat (tartane), 278
Forfait, 1859-1875, Screw aviso, 357
Formidable, 1795-1795, Two-decker (74-gun), see *Marat* 1794-1795
Formidable, 1795-1805, Two-decker (80-gun), 57
Formidable, 1828-1836, Three-decker, see *Valmy* 1847-1863
Fort, 1795-1796, Bateau-canonnier, 278
Fort, 1796-1797, Flûte, 378
Fort, 1866-1920, Bomb vessel (hulked), see *Bombe* 1855-1859
Fortanatus, 1797-1799, Xebec, 300
Forte, 1781-1787, Gabarre, 384
Forte, 1794-1799, 24pdr frigate (50-gun), 105
Forte, 1811-1814, Péniche, 293
Forte, 1838-1841, Schooner, 269
Forte, 1841-1894, 30pdr frigate (60-gun), 109
Fortitude, 1794-1808, 8-gun brig, 212
Fort-Samson, 1794-1795, Transport, 407
Fortune, 1780-1783, 16 x 6pdr corvette, 166
Fortune, 1798-1813, Half-xebec, 301
Fortune, 1799-1803, Transport (brig), 409
Fortune, 1833-1874, Corvette de charge, see *Var* 1832-1833
Fortune, 1839-1842, Schooner, 269
Fortuné, 1795-1797, Aviso, see *Sans Culotte* 1793-1795
Fortuné (*Fortunée*), 1800-1810, Half-xebec or tartane, 302
Fortunée, 1791-1794, 12pdr frigate (32-gun), 128
Fortunée, 1793-1793, Tartane, see *Trompette* 1793-1793
Foudre, 1793-1798, Gunboat, 274
Foudre, 1794-1795, Gunboat (tartane), 278
Foudre, 1796-1800, Aviso, 242
Foudre, 1804-1813, 8 x 24pdr corvette, 180
Foudre, 1820-1837, Gunboat, see *Eau* 1810-1820
Foudre, 1856-1891, Screw frigate, 115
Foudroyant, 1799-1803, Prame, 272
Foudroyant, 1800-1834, Two-decker (80-gun), 57
Foudroyante, 1794-1806, Prame, 272
Foudroyante, 1855-1874, Ironclad floating battery, 426
Fougueux, 1785-1805, Two-decker (74-gun), 87
Fougueux, 1814 cancelled, Two-decker (80-gun), 60
Fouine, 1796-1798, Lugger, 248
Fourmi, 1797-1799, Bateau-canonnier, 278
Fournaise, 1814 cancelled, Gunboat, 291
Fournaise, 1855-1858, Bomb vessel, 312
Fournaise, 1885-1896, Screw aviso (hulked), see *Forbin* 1859-1885
Framée (*No.30*), 1860-1892, Screw sectional gun launch, 371
Franchise, 1797-1803, 12pdr frigate (40-gun), 131
François de Paule, 1794-1795, Tartane, 297
Françoise, 1795-1799, Bateau-canonnier, 278
François-Marie, 1793-1794, Transport (cutter), 407
Franklin, 1797-1798, Two-decker (80-gun), 57
Fraternité, 1793-1795, 12 x 18pdr corvette, 168
Fraternité, 1793-1802, 12pdr frigate (32-gun), see *Aglaë* 1788-1793
Fraternité, 1797-1797, Transport, 408
Frédéric, 1795-1801, Bomb vessel, see *Galiote Hollandaise* 1793-1793
Frédéric, 1812-1813, Cutter, 258
Frédéric Guillaume, 1793-1793, Bomb vessel, see *Galiote Hollandaise* 1793-1793
Frères, 1794-1795, Transport, 407
Friedland, 1807-1808, 18-gun brig, 219
Friedland, 1810-1814, Two-decker (80-gun), 59
Friedland, 1840-1865, Three-decker, 48
Frimaire, 1794-1799, Gunboat (tartane), 278
Friponne, 1780-1796, 12pdr frigate (32-gun), 127
Friponne, 1810 -1820, 20 x 6pdr corvette, 182
Frise, 1810-1814, 12pdr frigate (40-gun), 154
Frontin, 1797-1825, Two-decker (66-gun), 80
Fructidor, 1794-1796, Gunboat (tartane), 278
Fructueux, 1799-1799, Transport (brig), 409
Fulminante, 1793-1796, Gunboat, 273
Fulminante, 1798-1798, Cutter, 249
Fulminante, 1814 cancelled, Gunboat, 291
Fulminante, 1855-1879, Screw gunboat, 365
Fulton, 1833-1867, Paddle vessel, 322
Furet, 1786-1795, 4pdr brig-aviso, 203
Furet, 1793-1795, Gunboat (chasse-marée), 276
Furet, 1794-1795, Felucca, 296
Furet, 1796-1812, Péniche, 278
Furet, 1799-1801, Cutter, 249
Furet, 1801-1806, 16-gun brig, 210
Furet, 1822-1850, Cutter, 262
Furie, 1814 cancelled, Gunboat, 291
Furieuse, 1797-1809, 18pdr frigate (44-gun), 139
Furieuse, 1810-1812, Gunboat, 291
Fusée, 1855-1869, Screw gunboat, 365
Fusta, 1797-1806, Galley, 299

Gaad (or *Haac*?), 1810-1813, Gunboat (Dutch), 289
Gabier, 1810-1811, Schooner, 258
Gabier, 1838-1868, school brig, see *Gazelle* 1822-1837
Gaité, 1796-1797, 20 x 8pdr corvette, 170
Gaivota do Mar, 1807-1808, 24-gun brig, 223
Galatée, 1779-1795, 12pdr frigate (32-gun), 126
Galatée, 1796-1797, Aviso, 250
Galatée, 1800-1800, 20 x 18pdr corvette, 173
Galatée, 1812-1838, 18pdr frigate (44-gun), 151
Galatée, 1845-1893, 30-gun corvette, 193
Galathée, 1786-?, Sloop (service craft), 406
Galathée, 1794-1795, Transport, 407
Galibi, 1786-1794, Schooner, 240
Galibi, 1823-1824, Paddle vessel, see *Caroline* 1824-1828
Galibi, 1841-1865, Paddle aviso, 345
Galilée, 1851-1890, Paddle aviso, 343
Galiote Hollandaise, 1793-1793, Bomb vessel, 310
Gange, 1794-1795, Transport, 407
Gardien, 1865-1867, Paddle vessel (hulked), see *Cerbère* 1836-1865
Garonne, 1798-1799, Bateau-canonnier, 280
Garonne, 1803-1806, Gabarre, 386
Garonne, 1821-1837, Gabarre, 391
Garonne, 1845 cancelled, Gabarre, 392
Garonne, 1858-1891, Screw transport, 401
Gasconne, 1807-1816, Transport (pink), 414
Gasparin, 1794-1795, Two-decker (74-gun), see *Apollon* 1788-1797
Gasparin, 1794-1795, Gunboat (tartane), 277
Gassendi, 1840-1866, Paddle corvette, 326
Gaulois, 1797-1805, Two-decker (74-gun), see *Trajan* 1792-1797
Gaulois, 1812-1831, Two-decker (74-gun), 98
Gauloise, 1804-1808, Tartane gunboat, 302
Gauloise, 1865-1886, Ironclad frigate, 423
Gave, 1781-1792, Gabarre, 384
Gavotte, 1808-1811, Transport (yacht), 414
Gazelle, 1806-1814, Felucca, 304
Gazelle, 1822-1837, 16-gun brig, 226
Gazelle, 1842-1859, Schooner, 261
Gazelle, 1860-1883, Schooner, 268
Général Biron, 1793-1793, Felucca or tartane, 296
Général Brun, 1800-1801, 14-gun corvette, 178
Général Magallon, 1821-1830, Lugger, 269
Général Stuart, 1799-1802, Balancelle, 296
Généralities, 1782-1783, Three-decker (projected), 44
Généreux, 1785-1800, Two-decker (74-gun), 87
Généreux, 1831-1865, Two-decker (74-gun), 100
Généreux (*Généreuse*), 1810-1814, Flûte, 381
Génie, 1794-1796, Gunboat (tartane), 278
Génie, 1808-1833, 16-gun brig, 216
Génie, 1842-1889, 18-gun brig, 232
Génois, 1805-1821, Two-decker (74-gun), 95
Gentil, 1794-1795, Flûte, 377
Gentille, 1778-1795, 12pdr frigate (32-gun), 125
Gentille, 1794-1795, Transport, 407
Gentille, 1804-1811, Tartane gunboat, 302
Gentille, 1840-1876, Schooner, 265
Géographe, 1800-1819, 24 x 12pdr corvette, 173
Georges, 1803-1816, Cutter, 256
Gerardina-Maria, 1793-1802, Transport (galiote), see *Girardina-Maria* 1793-1802
Gerfaut, 1782-1796, Lugger, 239
Germinal, 1794-1796, Gunboat (tartane), 278
Gertrude, 1807-1814, Gabarre, 387
Gijzel or *Gyssel* (*Vice-admiraal Arnoud*), 1810-1813, Gunboat (Dutch), 289
Girafe (*Giraffe*), 1809-1811, Flûte, 379
Girafe (*Giraffe*), 1834-1868, Gabarre, 391
Girardina-Maria, 1793-1802, Transport (galiote), 411
Gironde, 1793-1797, Gunboat, 274
Gironde, 1808-1837, Gabarre, 388
Gironde, 1849 cancelled, Large transport, 397
Gironde, 1855-1867, Screw transport, 399
Girouette, 1809-1839, Gabarre, 388
Glaive (*No.31*), 1860-1886, Screw sectional gun launch, 371
Gliata, 1810-1814, Péniche, 293
Globe, 1797-1827, Lugger, 242
Gloire, 1778-1798, 12pdr frigate (32-gun), 125
Gloire, 1797-1797, Two-decker (64-gun), see *Banel* 1797-1802
Gloire, 1797-1797, Galley, 298
Gloire, 1803-1806, 18pdr frigate (44-gun), 145
Gloire, 1811-1829, 18pdr frigate (44-gun), 149
Gloire, 1837-1847, 30pdr frigate (46-gun), 112
Gloire, 1859-1883, Ironclad frigate, 420
Gloria, 1807-1814, Schooner, 252
Glorieux, 1794-1795, Transport, 407
Glorieux, 1798-1798, Two-decker (74-gun), see *Cassard* 1803-1818
Glorieux, 1805-1807, Two-decker (74-gun), see *Polonais* 1808-1815
Glorieux, 1812-1814, Two-decker (74-gun), see *Duc de Berry* 1818-1830
Gloriole, 1821-1822, Corvette, 194
Gloriole, 1822-1823, Schooner, 261
Goacchino, 1812-1815, Two-decker (74-gun), 99
Gobe-Mouche, 1806-1808, Schooner, 251
Godefroi, 1844 cancelled, Paddle frigate, 334
Goëland, 1787-1793, 4pdr brig-aviso, 204
Goëland, 1801-1803, 16-gun brig, 210
Goëland, 1811-1819, Schooner, 259
Goëland, 1848-1887, Paddle aviso, 341
Goëland, 1827-1845, Cutter, 263
Golo, 1811-1829, Flûte, 379
Golymin, 1809-1814, Two-decker (74-gun), 94
Gomer, 1839-1841, Paddle frigate, see *Descartes* 1844-1867
Gomer, 1841-1841, Paddle frigate, see *Mogador* 1848-1880
Gomer, 1841-1868, Paddle frigate, 329
Good Intent, 1793-1801, Xebec, 299
Good Union, 1799-1801, Xebec, 301
Gorgone, 1848-1869, Paddle corvette, 336
Gotiche, 1793-1795, Gunboat (dogger), 277
Goulu, 1793-1795, 10 x 4pdr corvette, 177
Goze, 1801-1803, Schooner, 244
Gracieuse, 1787-1793, 12pdr frigate (32-gun), 129
Grand Bassam, 1852-1868, Paddle aviso, 348
Grande Gabarres Écurie Nos. 1-12, 1811-1814, Gabarres, 388
Granval, 1794-1795, Transport, 407
Granville, 1793-1820, Cutter, 241
Granville, 1794-1795, Cutter, see *London* 1794-

1797
Grappler, 1806-1809, 10-gun brig, 223
Grasshopper, 1811-1813, 18-gun brig, 221
Grégeois, 1839-1865, Paddle vessel, 324
Grenade, 1811-1837, Mortar gunboat, 292
Grenade, 1855-1871, Screw gunboat, 365
Grenadier, 1796-1797, Bateau-canonnier, 279
Grenadier, 1825-1865, 20-gun brig, 230
Griffon, 1806-1808, 16-gun brig, 215
Griffon, 1829-1865, 20-gun brig, 230
Griffon, 1858-1869, Paddle aviso, 350
Grigoriy Velikiya Armenii, 1809-1810, 18pdr frigate (50-gun), 156
Groenland, 1843-1844, Paddle frigate, 332
Grondeur, 1795-1795, Transport, see *Glorieux* 1794-1795
Grondeur, 1839-1875, Paddle vessel, 324
Grondin, 1778-1789, Transport (chasse-marée), 405
Grondin, 1808-1809, Transport (brig), 413
Grondin, 1815-1826, Transport, see *Betsy* 1795-1803
Growler, 1798-1809, Gunboat, 280
Guadeloupe, 1783-1786, 8pdr frigate (20-gun), 122
Guadeloupe, 1794-1806, Schooner, see *Guadeloupienne* 1793-1794
Guadeloupe, 1829-1831, 20 x 30pdr corvette, see *Triomphante* 1834-1869
Guadeloupienne, 1793-1794, Schooner, 249
Guardien (*Gardien*), 1854-1862, Large transport (hulked), see *Durance* 1848-1854
Guêpe, 1795-1795, Gunboat (tartane), see *Gasparin* 1794-1795
Guêpe, 1808-1814, Transport (snow or brig), 415
Guêpe (No.11), 1859-1898, Screw gun launch, 369
Guerrier, 1755-1798, Two-decker (74-gun), 84
Guerrier, 1796-1797, Bateau-canonnier, 279
Guerrier, 1800-1800, Half-xebec, 296
Guerriera, 1811-1814, 18pdr frigate (44-gun), 153
Guerrière, 1799-1806, 18pdr frigate (44-gun), 142
Guerrière, 1811-1814, 18pdr frigate (44-gun), see *Guerriera* 1811-1814
Guerrière, 1821-1840, 36pdr rasée frigate, 107
Guerrière, 1848-1860, 30pdr frigate (60-gun), 115
Guerrière, 1860-1912, Screw frigate, 118
Guet N'Dar, 1848-1854, Paddle aviso, 348
Guet N'Dar, 1854-1857, Paddle aviso, 349
Guillaume Tell, 1795-1800, Two-decker (80-gun), 57
Guillaume-Tell, 1794-1795, Transport, 407
Gustave, 1812-1813, Cutter, 258
Guyane, 1777-1788, Gabarre, 384
Guyenne, 1865-1887, Ironclad frigate, 423

Haai, 1810-1813, 7-gun gunbrig, 224
Haleur, 1860-1882, Paddle aviso (hulked), see *Var* 1844-1860
Hamach, 1794-1797, Flûte, see *Hannach* 1794-1797
Hambourgeoise, 1813-1814, 20 x 24pdr corvette, 182
Hannach (*Hamach*), 1794-1797, Flûte, 376
Harcourt, 1794-1795, Flûte, 376
Hardi, 1750-1794, Two-decker (64-gun), 78
Hardi, 1797-1799, Bateau-canonnier, 279
Hardi (*Hardy*), 1794-1803, Cutter, 242
Hargneuse, 1793-1803, Gunboat, 274
Harmonie, 1794-1795, Flûte, 377
Harmonie, 1795-1797, 18pdr frigate (44-gun), 140
Harpie, 1795-1796, Flûte, see *Harcourt* 1794-1795
Hasard, 1788-1796, 4pdr brig-aviso, 204
Havik, 1810-1813, 7-gun gunbrig, 224
Hazard, 1803-1804, Corvette, 183
Hébé, 1782-1782, 18pdr frigate (38-gun), 136
Hébé, 1786-?, Sloop (service craft), 406
Hébé, 1803 cancelled, 20 x 8pdr corvette, 178

Hébé, 1808-1809, 20 x 8pdr corvette, 179
Hébé, 1811-1814, 18pdr frigate (44-gun), see *Ebe* 1811-1814
Hébé, 1822-1835, 28-gun corvette, 185
Hecla, 1794-1795, Gunboat (tartane), 278
Hécla, 1826-1851, Bomb vessel, 312
Hector, 1814-1820, Two-decker (74-gun), see *Dalmate* 1808-1815
Hector, 1828 cancelled, Two-decker (100-gun), 64
Hector, 1834-1850, Two-decker (90-gun), see *Charlemagne* 1850-1851
Heemskerk (*Admiraal*), 1810-1813, Gunboat (Dutch), 289
Helena, 1795-1799, Flûte, see *Henri* 1793-1795
Hélène, 1791-1793, 12pdr frigate (32-gun), 129
Hélène, 1798-1801, Gunboat (djerme), see *Sainte-Hélène* 1798-1801
Héliopolis, 1798-1801, 12 x 6pdr corvette, 176
Héliopolis, 1847-1887, 30pdr frigate (46-gun), 158
Hendrick, 1794-1795, Flûte, 376
Henri, 1793-1795, Lugger, 244
Henri (*Henry*), 1793-1795, Flûte, 375
Henri IV, 1848-1854, Two-decker (100-gun), 64
Henriette, 1795-1801, Bateau-canonnier, 278
Hérault, 1855-1862, Large transport, 398
Hérault, 1880-1903, Screw aviso (hulked), see *Marceau* 1852-1880
Hercule, 1778-1795, Two-decker (74-gun), 85
Hercule, 1793-1794, Transport, 407
Hercule, 1797-1798, Two-decker (74-gun), 89
Hercule, 1798-1798, Bomb vessel, 310
Hercule, 1799-1804, Transport (brig), 410
Hercule, 1803-1814, Bomb vessel, 311
Hercule, 1815-1815, Two-decker (74-gun), see *Provence* 1815-1830
Hercule, 1836-1875, Two-decker (100-gun), 64
Herminie, 1828-1838, 30pdr frigate (60-gun), 108
Hermione, 1779-1793, 12pdr frigate (32-gun), 124
Hermione, 1794-1797, 6-gun brig, 211
Hermione, 1803-1803, 18pdr frigate (46-gun), 147
Hermione, 1804-1808, 18pdr frigate (44-gun), 144
Hermione, 1814-1841, 18pdr frigate (44-gun), see *Illyrienne* 1811-1815
Hermione, 1847-1860, 30pdr frigate (50-gun), 115
Hermione, 1860-1892, Screw frigate, 119
Hernoux, 1794-1795, Flûte, 377
Héroïne, 1830-1861, 20 x 30pdr corvette, 189
Héroïne, 1863-1901, Ironclad frigate, 424
Héron, 1808-1811, Gabarre, 388
Héron, 1847-1874, Paddle aviso, 340
Héros, 1778-1794, Two-decker (74-gun), 86
Héros, 1794-1795, Transport, 407
Héros, 1801-1808, Two-decker (74-gun), 91
Héros, 1813-1828, Three-decker, 48
Herzon, 1809-1811, Flûte, see *Cherson* 1809-1811
Heureuse, 1793-1794, 22 x 6pdr corvette, see *Sans Culotide* 1794-1795
Heureuse, 1798-1799, 12pdr frigate (38-gun), 131
Heureuse, 1804-1813, 6 x 24pdr corvette, 181
Heureuse Rencontre, 1794-1794, Schooner, 249
Heureux, 1782-1798, Two-decker (74-gun), 87
Heureux, 1803-1832, Yacht, 314
Hippopotame, 1817 cancelled, Flûte, 380
Hirondelle, 1762-1794, 16 x 6pdr corvette, 163
Hirondelle, 1786-1788, Cutter, 248
Hirondelle, 1792-1792, Schooner, 249
Hirondelle, 1793-1794, Lugger, 248
Hirondelle, 1793-1795, Cutter, 245
Hirondelle, 1793-1799, 6 x 4pdr brig, 213
Hirondelle, 1793-1799, Aviso, 250
Hirondelle, 1794-1794, 12-gun brig, 213
Hirondelle, 1795-1795, Transport, 408
Hirondelle, 1796-1818, Felucca, 295
Hirondelle, 1798-1799, Gunboat (tartane), 280

Hirondelle, 1820-1837, Schooner, 260
Hirondelle, 1843-1865, Schooner, 261
Hirton, 1794-1795, Flûte, 376
Historique, 1795-1795, Flûte, see *Harmonie* 1794-1795
Hoche, 1797-1798, Two-decker (74-gun), see *Barra* 1794-1795
Hoche, 1798-1799, Lugger, 248
Hoche, 1870-1872, Screw two-decker, see *Prince Jérôme* 1853-1870
Hollandais, 1811-1814, Two-decker (80-gun), see *Royal Hollandais* 1810-1811
Hong Kong, 1860-1869, Paddle aviso, 351
Honoré, 1798-1800, Transport (brig), 409
Hook, 1793-1794, Lugger, 245
Hoop, 1793-1815, Cutter, 245
Hoope, 1798-1807, Transport, 410
Hope, 1793-1815, Cutter, see *Hoop* 1793-1815
Horsel, 1810-1813, Gunboat (Dutch), 288
Hortense, 1803-1815, 18pdr frigate (44-gun), 144
Hortense, 1852-1852, Screw corvette, see *Roland* 1850-1870
Hortentia, 1807-1808, Schooner, see *Ortensia* 1807-1808
Hulst (*Vice-admiraal*), 1810-1813, Gunboat (Dutch), 289
Hunter, 1796-1797, Transport, 410
Huron, 1814-1822, 16-gun brig, 218
Hussard, 1796-1797, Bateau-canonnier, 279
Hussard, 1809-1822, 16-gun brig, 217
Hussard, 1827-1876, 20-gun brig, 230
Hydre, 1794-1797, 36pdr rasée frigate, 104
Hydre, 1797-1814, Prame, 273
Hydrographe, 1851-1859, Schooner, 270
Hyène, 1793-1796, 22 x 8pdr corvette, 174
Hyène, 1810-1813, 15-gun brig, 224
Hymen, 1814 cancelled, Three-decker (110-gun), 49
Hymenée, 1809-1810, 18pdr frigate (44-gun), see *Étoile* 1813-1814
Hypocrite, 1781-1789, 6pdr corvette, 166

Ibis, 1845-1857, Schooner, 270
Ida, 1807-1819, Transport, 414
Idas, 1810-1814, Cutter, 257
Idra (Venetian), 1797-1806, Prame, see *Hydre* 1797-1814
Iéna, 1806-1814, 18-gun brig, 219
Iéna, 1808-1810, Corvette, 185
Iéna, 1830-1886, Three-decker (110-gun), see *Duc d'Angoulême* 1814-1830
Iéna, 1886-1897, Screw transport (hulked), see *Dryade* 1856-1886
Iguala, 1838-1843, 16-gun corvette-aviso, 191
Île d'Aix, 1853-1866, Schooner, 267
Île d'Énet, 1853-1862, Schooner, 267
Île d'Oléron, 1846-1858, Schooner, 267
Île d'Yeu (*Île Dieu*), 1793-1821, Gunboat, 274
Île de Bourbon, 1829-1831, 20 x 30pdr corvette, see *Danaïde* 1832-1865
Île de France, 1793-1793, Corvette, 176
Île de la Réunion, 1799-1799, Transport, 409
Île de Ré, 1793-1797, Gunboat, 274
Île Madame, 1851-1861, Schooner, 267
Île Républicaine, 1794-1795, Gunboat, see *Île de Ré* 1793-1797
Illustre, 1781-1791, Two-decker (74-gun), 86
Illustre, 1811-1814, Two-decker (80-gun), 59
Illustre, 1814-1827, Two-decker (80-gun), see *Auguste* 1811-1814
Illyrienne, 1811-1815, 18pdr frigate (44-gun), 151
Immortalité, 1795-1798, 24pdr frigate (30-gun), 105
Immortel, 1801-1804, Transport, see *Necker Immortel* 1801-1804
Immortel, 1813-1813, 18pdr frigate (44-gun), 152
Impatient, 1788-1803, 4pdr brig-aviso, 204
Impatiente, 1795-1796, 24pdr frigate (30-gun), 105
Imperatrice Eugénie, 1856-1870, Screw frigate, 115

Impérial, 1805-1806, Three-decker, see *Vengeur* 1803-1805
Impérial, 1811-1815, Three-decker, 47
Impérial, 1856-1870, Screw two-decker, 71
Impérial (*Impériale*), 1805-1806, Schooner-aviso, 259
Imperial (*Ymperial*), 1794-1795, Flûte, 376
Impérieuse, 1787-1793, 18pdr frigate (36-gun), 137
Impérieuse, 1848 cancelled, 30pdr frigate (60-gun), 115
Impérieuse, 1856-1874, Screw frigate, 116
Impétueux, 1787-1794, Two-decker (74-gun), 89
Impétueux, 1803-1806, Two-decker (74-gun), 91
Impétueux, 1814 cancelled, Two-decker (74-gun), 98
Implacable, 1864-1908, Ironclad floating battery, 427
Importune, 1796-1798, Corvette, 178
Imposant, 1795-1796, Bateau-canonnier, 278
Imprenable, 1865-1939, Ironclad floating battery, 428
Inabordable, 1793-1803, Gunboat, 275
Incendiaire, 1796-1797, Bateau-canonnier, 279
Incendiaire, 1813-1821, Mortar gunboat, 292
Incommode, 1793-1803, Gunboat, 275
Inconnue, 1793-1794, 12pdr brig, 206
Inconstant, 1811-1843, 16-gun brig, 218
Inconstant, 1848-1868, 6-gun brig-aviso, 236
Inconstante, 1790-1793, 12pdr frigate (32-gun), 129
Inconstante, 1812-1814, 18pdr frigate (44-gun), 152
Incorruptible, 1795-1830, 24pdr frigate (30-gun), 105
Incorruttibile, 1806-1807, Gunboat (Italian), 287
Indépendant, 1795-1800, Pink or half-xebec, see *Intrépide* 1794-1795
Indépendante, 1830-1866, 30pdr frigate (60-gun), see *Belle Gabrielle* 1828-1830
Indiano, 1808-1814, 12-gun brig, 220
Indien, 1794-1798, Flûte, 377
Indien, 1808-1813, Flûte, 382
Indien, 1808-1814, 12-gun brig, see *Indiano* 1808-1814
Indienne, 1794-1794, Gunboat, see *Île d'Yeu* 1793-1821
Indienne, 1796-1809, 18pdr frigate (44-gun), 139
Indienne, 1835-1863, Gabarre, 392
Indivisible, 1799-1803, Two-decker (80-gun), 57
Indomptable, 1790-1805, Two-decker (80-gun), 57
Indomptable, 1811-1813, Gunboat, 291
Indomptable, 1824-1824, Two-decker (100-gun), see *Jemmapes* 1840-1890
Indomptable, 1861 cancelled, Ironclad floating battery, 426
Industrie, 1794-1795, Transport, 408
Industrie, 1807-1814, Transport, 414
Inévitable, 1795-1796, Gunboat (brig or dogger), see *Saint-Jacques* 1794-1799
Infante, 1793-1798, 18 x 6pdr brig, 212
Infatigable, 1799-1806, 18pdr frigate (44-gun), 142
Infatigable, 1843-1862, Gabarre, 392
Infatigable (*Grande Gabarre Écurie No.11*), 1811-1837, Gabarre, 391
Infernal, 1843-1861, Paddle frigate, 327
Infernale, 1804-1814, Bomb vessel, 310
Inflexible, 1805-1807, Two-decker (74-gun), see *Golymin* 1809-1814
Inflexible, 1812-1820, Three-decker, see *Friedland* 1840-1865
Inflexible, 1839-1875, Two-decker (90-gun), 65
Inondée, 1795-1796, Felucca, see *Jeune Barra* 1794-1795
Inquiète, 1793-1803, Gunboat, 273
Insolente, 1796-1800, 14-18 x 6pdr corvette, 174
Insolente (*Insolent*), 1793-1803, Gunboat, 274
Instituteur, 1794-1795, 20 x 4pdr corvette, see *Lord Gordon* 1793-1798
Insurgente, 1793-1799, 12pdr frigate (32-gun),

130
Intercepté, 1795-1795, Transport, see *Jeune Auguste* 1794-1795
Intrépide, 1794-1795, Pink or half-xebec, 296
Intrépide, 1794-1796, 22 x 8pdr corvette, 177
Intrépide, 1794-1797, 12 x 12pdr brig, 213
Intrépide, 1795-1796, Bateau-canonnier, 278
Intrépide, 1800-1805, Two-decker (74-gun), 93
Intrépide, 1864-1889, Screw two-decker, 71
Intrépide, 1890-1891, Three-decker (hulked), see *Valmy* 1847-1863
Invidia, 1808-1815, Half-xebec, see *Envie* 1808-1815
Invincible, 1780-1808, Three-decker, 44
Invincible, 1795-1795, Transport (sloop), 408
Invincible, 1795-1796, Bateau-canonnier, 278
Invincible, 1861-1877, Ironclad frigate, 420
Iphigénie, 1777-1795, 12pdr frigate (32-gun), 124
Iphigénie, 1786-1791, Schooner, 249
Iphigénie, 1805-1807, 18pdr frigate (44-gun), see *Oder* 1813-1815
Iphigénie, 1810-1810, 18pdr frigate (42-gun), 156
Iphigénie, 1810-1814, 18pdr frigate (44-gun), 151
Iphigénie, 1827-1877, 30pdr frigate (60-gun), 109
Irene, 1810-1813, 6-gun gunbrig, 224
Iris, 1781-1793, 12pdr frigate (32-gun), 125
Iris, 1798 not built, 8pdr brig, 208
Iris, 1806-1809, 20 x 8pdr corvette, 179
Iris, 1810-1813, Corvette, 184
Iris, 1818-1844, Schooner, 260
Iris, 1846-1855, Schooner, 266
Isère, 1832-1865, Corvette de charge, 382
Isère, 1855-1860, Screw transport, 399
Isis, 1799-1799, Aviso, 251
Isis, 1822-1833, 18-gun corvette-aviso, 185
Isis, 1851-1900, 30pdr frigate (40-gun), 159
Isle de France, 1770-1790, Flûte, 374
Isly, 1849-1875, Screw frigate, 161
Isolé, 1795-1796, Brigantine, see *Jeune Émilie* 1794-1796
Isonzo, 1799-1801, Gunboat, 280
Istrienne, 1813 cancelled, 18pdr frigate (44-gun), 154
Italienne, 1806-1816, 18pdr frigate (44-gun), 145

Jacinthe, 1823-1841, Schooner, 262
Jacoba Catharina, 1795-1796, Floating battery, see *Carpe* 1794-1795
Jacobin, 1793-1794, Two-decker (80-gun), see *Auguste* 1778-1793
Jacobin, 1794-1795, Tartane, see *Petit Jacobin* 1794-1795
Jacobin, 1795-1795, Xebec, see *Bonne Aventure* 1793-1798
Jacobine, 1794-1794, 22 x 12pdr corvette, 169
Jacques, 1794-1795, Gunboat (brig or dogger), see *Saint-Jacques* 1794-1799
Jahde, 1812-1815, 18pdr frigate (44-gun), 152
Jalouse, 1794-1797, 12pdr brig, 206
Jalouse, 1804-1816, Tartane gunboat, 302
James, 1793-1796, Transport (brig), 409
Janus, 1805-1814, 8-gun brig, 223
Janus, 1848-1914, 18-gun brig, 232
Japon, 1859-1903, Screw transport, 404
Jardin de la Paix, 1797-1799, Flûte, 378
Jaseur, 1806-1807, 14-gun brig, 226
Jason, 1797-1797, 20 x 8pdr brig, 212
Jason, 1805-1819, Transport, 414
Javan, 1810-1811, Corvette, 185
Jean, 1794-1794, Transport, 407
Jean Bart, 1790-1809, Two-decker (74-gun), 89
Jean Bart, 1792-1793, Gunboat (tartane), 276
Jean Bart, 1793-1795, 18 x 6pdr corvette, 167
Jean Bart, 1793-1800, Lugger, 245
Jean Bart, 1820-1833, Two-decker (74-gun), 100
Jean Bart, 1848-1852, Two-decker (90-gun), 66
Jean Bart, 1852-1868, Screw two-decker, 68
Jean Bart, 1868-1886, Screw two-decker, see *Donawerth* 1857-1868
Jean Bart No.2, 1794-1795, Corvette, 177
Jean de Vienne, 1829-1831, 20-gun brig, see *Oreste* 1833-1875
Jean de Witt, 1810-1814, Two-decker (68-gun), 83
Jean Hachette, 1828-1831, 20 x 30pdr corvette, see *Blonde* 1832-1849
Jean Leep, 1805-1814, Transport, 413
Jean-Baptiste, 1797-1799, Transport (brig), 408
Jean-Bart, 1795-1796, Bateau-canonnier, 278
Jean-Jacob, 1799-1802, Flûte, 378
Jean-Jacques Rousseau, 1795-1802, Two-decker (74-gun), 91
Jean-Johannes (*Jean-Jouannez*), 1793-1800, Transport (galiote), 411
Jeanne, 1793-1794, Transport (brig), 407
Jeanne, 1806-1823, Gabarre, 387
Jeanne d'Albret, 1831 cancelled, 30pdr frigate (60-gun), 113
Jeanne d'Arc, 1820-1850, 24pdr frigate (58-gun), 107
Jeanne d'Arc, 1847-1865, 30pdr frigate (46-gun), 158
Jeanne Hachette, 1853 cancelled, 30-gun corvette, 194
Jeannette, 1792-1793, Schooner, 249
Jemmapes, 1794-1830, Two-decker (74-gun), 89
Jemmapes, 1840-1890, Two-decker (100-gun), 64
Jérôme Napoléon, 1860-1866, Screw aviso, see *Cassard* 1859-1867
Jérôme Napoléon, 1866-1870, Screw corvette-yacht, see *Cassard* 1866-1866
Jeune Alexandrine, 1794-1795, Transport, 407
Jeune André, 1794-1794, Transport, 407
Jeune Ange, 1799-1814, Transport (galiote), see *Ange* 1796-1799
Jeune Auguste, 1794-1795, Transport, 407
Jeune Barra, 1794-1795, Felucca, 297
Jeune Charles, 1794-1795, Flûte, 377
Jeune Édouard, 1803-1807, Transport (sloop), 413
Jeune Édouard (*Transport No.34*), 1798-1798, Transport, 408
Jeune Élisabeth, 1794-1794, Transport, see *Élisabeth-Judith* 1794-1794
Jeune Émile, 1797-1800, Transport, 408
Jeune Émilie, 1794-1796, Brigantine, 297
Jeune Émilie, 1795-1795, Transport, 408
Jeune Eugénie, 1794-1795, Transport, 407
Jeune Louis, 1794-1794, Transport, 407
Jeune Louis, 1794-1794, Transport, 407
Jeune Sophie, 1803-1806, Cutter, 258
Jeune Thérèse (*Transport No. 301*), 1803-1814, Transport, 412
Jeune Victoire, 1794-1795, Transport, 407
Jeune-Adélaide, 1794-1795, Transport, 407
Jeune-Camille, 1794-1795, Transport, 407
Jeune-Jouwerc, 1793-1797, Transport (galiote), 411
Jeune-Robert, 1794-1795, Transport, 407
Jeune-Sophie, 1794-1795, Transport, 407
Johanna-Anna, 1812-1814, Flûte, 382
Joie, 1795-1804, 12 x 12pdr corvette, 171
Joie, 1804-1807, Half-xebec (hulked), see *Égyptien* 1800-1804
Jonk Cleander, 1793-1803, Transport (galiote), see *Leander* 1793-1797
Jonker Slewig (*Joncker Slewigh*), 1795-1802, Floating battery, see *Brochet* 1794-1795
Jonk-Jouwert, 1793-1797, Transport (galiote), see *Jeune-Jouwerc* 1793-1797
Jonquille, 1823-1830, Schooner, 262
Jonquille, 1845-1857, Schooner, 266
Joseph, 1794-1797, 14 x 6pdr corvette, 176
Joseph, 1809-1809, Felucca, 305
Joséphine, 1794-1794, Transport, 407
Joubert, 1799-1809, Xebec, 301
Joubert, 1803-1842, Chasse-marée, 251
Joubert, 1806-1814, Bomb vessel, 311
Jouvence, 1866-1886, Bomb vessel (hulked), see *Fournaise* 1855-1858
Jouvencelle, 1841-1867, Schooner, 265
Joyeuse, 1793-1795, Tartane, 296
Joyeux, 1795-1796, Lugger, see *Jean Bart* 1793-1800
Julie, 1803-1807, Transport (brig), 413
Julie, 1806-1808, Felucca, 302
Juliette, 1783-1787, Corvette, 166
Jumeaux, 1797-1799, Flûte, 378
Junon, 1782-1799, 18pdr frigate (36-gun), 136
Junon, 1786-?, Sloop (service craft), 406
Junon, 1797-1797, Galley, 298
Junon, 1806-1809, 18pdr frigate (44-gun), 146
Junon, 1814-1842, 18pdr frigate (44-gun), see *Amélie* 1808-1815
Junon, 1847-1861, 30pdr frigate (50-gun), 115
Junon, 1861-1876, Screw frigate, 119
Jupiter, 1789-1797, Two-decker (74-gun), 89
Jupiter, 1803-1806, Two-decker (74-gun), see *Constitution* 1795-1803
Jupiter, 1831-1870, Two-decker (80-gun), 60
Jupiter, 1870-1897, Two-decker (hulked), see *Impérial* 1856-1870
Jura, 1858-1888, Screw transport, 401
Juriam-William, 1793-1797, Transport (galiote), 411
Juste, 1792-1794, Two-decker (80-gun), see *Deux Frères* 1784-1792
Juste, 1794-1795, Gabarre, 386
Juste, 1794-1795, Transport, 407
Justice, 1795-1801, 18pdr frigate (44-gun), 140
Justine, 1796-1796, Flûte, 378

Kamchatka, 1851-1851, Schooner, see *Kaméhaméha* 1851-1859
Kaméhaméha, 1851-1859, Schooner, 269
Karsus, 1795-1796, Bateau-canonnier, 278
Kemphaan, 1810-1813, Gunboat (Dutch), 289
Kenau Hasselaar, 1810-1814, 12pdr frigate (40-gun), 154
Kenney, 1863-1869, Screw gunboat, 367
Kep, 1885-1887, Screw gunboat (hulked), see *Surprise* 1863-1885
Kermorvant, 1852-1866, 20-gun brig (hulked), see *D'Assas* 1830-1852
Kerson, 1809-1811, Flûte, see *Cherson* 1809-1811
Ketty, 810-1813, 6-gun gunbrig, 224
Kien-Chan, 1860-1876, Paddle aviso, 351
Kléber, 1870-1891, Screw aviso, see *Cassard* 1859-1867
Knorhaan, 1810-1813, Gunboat (Dutch), 288
Krekel, 1810-1813, Gunboat (Dutch), 288
Kremlin, 1812-1815, Two-decker (74-gun), see *Provence* 1815-1830

La Bourdonnais, 1856-1873, Screw aviso, see *Labourdonnaye* 1856-1873
La Ciotat, 1811-1816, Gabarre, 388
La Tour d'Auvergne, 1832 cancelled, Two-decker (74-gun), 102
Laborieuse, 1796-1827, Transport (gabarre), 406
Laborieuse, 1855-1871, Schooner, 267
Laborieux, 1848-1879, Paddle corvette, 336
Labourdonnaye, 1856-1873, Screw aviso, 362
Labrador, 1839-1842, Schooner, 269
Labrador, 1842-1878, Paddle frigate, 332
'Lacrosser, Senhora da Solidao', 1810-1811, Transport (galiote), see *Nossa Senhora da Solidao* 1808-1810
Laharpe (*La Harpe*), 1797-1809, Two-decker (74-gun), 93
Lahire, 1829-1831, 16-gun brig, see *Lutin* 1833-1865
Lama, 1810-1811, Schooner, 258
Lambert, 1794-1795, Flûte, 377
Lamotte-Picquet, 1859-1892, Screw aviso, 360
Lamproie, 1782-1793, Flûte, 374
Lamproie (*Grande Gabarre Écurie No.8*), 1812-1850, Gabarre, 390
Lamproie (*Lamproye*), 1804-1809, Gabarre, 386
Lance, 1855-1863, Screw gunboat, 365
Lancier, 1811-1821, 16-gun brig, 217
Lancier, 1822-1855, 18-gun brig, 226
Languedoc, 1763-1794, Two-decker (80-gun), 55
Languedocienne, 1807-1811, Xebec, 306
Lanninon, 1865-1866, 18pdr frigate (hulked), see *Thétis* 1819-1865
Lapérouse, 1832-1875, 20-gun brig, 231
Lapeyrouse, 1795-1796, Bateau-canonnier, 278
Lapin, 1801-1812, Transport, 409
Laplace, 1852-1880, Screw corvette, 198
Lark (*Larck*), 1793-1801, Cutter, see *Ark* 1793-1801
Larmour, 1876-1899, 20-gun brig (hulked), see *Hussard* 1827-1876
Las Casas, 1794-1796, 18 x 6pdr corvette, 176
Latitude, 1795-1796, Gunboat, see *Légère* 1794-1799
Latouche-Tréville, 1860-1887, Screw aviso, 359
Laurel, 1803-1806, 12-gun brig, 222
Laurel, 1808-1809, 22 x 9pdr corvette, 183
Laurette, 1793-1795, Gunboat, 276
Laurier, 1811-1832, 16-gun brig, 217
Laurier, 1832-1865, 16-gun brig, 228
Lave, 1855-1873, Ironclad floating battery, 426
Lavoisier, 1838-1886, Paddle corvette, 326
Laybach, 1811-1814, Péniche, 293
Lazouski, 1793-1795, 4pdr brig-aviso, see *Espoir* 1788-1797
Le Brethon, 1864-1869, Screw gunboat, 367
Leander, 1793-1797, Transport (galiote), 411
Leander, 1798-1799, Two-decker (50-gun), 77
Léger, 1794-1797, 16-gun brig, 213
Léger, 1803-1818, Half-xebec, 304
Léger, 1810-1810, Schooner, 258
Léger, 1844-1875, 10-gun brig-aviso, 234
Légère, 1784-1786, Schooner, 239
Légère, 1785-1786, Schooner, 240
Légère, 1788-1793, Schooner, 240
Légère, 1793-1793, 6pdr 'frigate' (22-gun), see *Barbude* 1782-1786
Légère, 1794-1798, Felucca, 297
Légère, 1794-1799, Gunboat, 277
Légère, 1799-1811, Felucca, 301
Légère, 1801-1803, Schooner, 243
Légère, 1806-1816, Balancelle or felucca, 304
Légère, 1825-1850, Schooner, 263
Lejoille, 1799-1805, Xebec, 302
Lente, 1795-1795, Felucca, see *Légère* 1794-1798
Leoben, 1810-1811, Schooner, 254
Léoben, 1797-1801, 12pdr frigate (38-gun), 133
Léonidas, 1794-1799, Felucca or half-galley, 299
Léopard, 1787-1793, Two-decker (74-gun), 87
Lepanto, 1809-1814, 8-gun brig, 220
Lepeletier, 1793-1795, Cutter, see *Pelletier* 1793-1795
Les Jumeaux, 1797-1799, Flûte, see *Jumeaux* 1797-1799
Letizia, 1812-1815, 24 x 24pdr corvette, 182
Letun, 1809-1809, 12-gun brig, 224
Levrette, 1779-1806, Cutter, 238
Levrette, 1784-1792, Schooner, 239
Levrette, 1794-1795, 18 x 6pdr corvette, 175
Levrette, 1808-1823, Schooner, 254
Levrette, 1836-1846, Schooner, 261
Levrier, 1794-1799, Xebec, 297
Lévrier, 1786-?, Sloop (service craft), 406
Lévrier, 1816-1822, Schooner, see *Léger* 1810-1810
Lévrier, 1823-1833, Xebec, 308
Lévrier, 1837-1887, Cutter, 265
Lézard, 1793-1795, Lugger, 248
Lézard, 1875-1877, 20-gun brig, see *Lapérouse* 1832-1875
Lézard (*Petit Gabarre Écurie No.1*), 1809-1867, Gabarre, 388
Liamone, 1821-1847, Mortar gunboat, see *Incendiaire* 1813-1821
Liamone, 1844-1867, Paddle aviso, 348
Libérateur d'Italie, 1797-1797, Lugger or tartane, 248
Liberté, 1792-1793, Felucca, 296
Liberté, 1793-1794, Corvette, 177
Liberté, 1793-1796, Chasse-marée, 248
Liberté, 1793-1797, Floating battery, 312
Liberté, 1794-1794, Transport, 407
Liberté, 1794-1795, 18 x 6pdr brig, see *Infante* 1793-1798

INDEX TO NAMED VESSELS

Liberté, 1794-1796, Schooner, 249
Liberté, 1795-1795, 16 x 4pdr corvette, 178
Liberté des Mers, 1793-1799, Three-decker (projected), 45
Libre, 1796-1805, 24pdr frigate (30-gun), 105
Libre, 1798-1799, Péniche, 278
Licorne, 1795-1804, Flûte, see *Lambert* 1794-1795
Licorne, 1811-1826, Flûte, 379
Licorne, 1834-1894, Gabarre, 392
Ligurie, 1805-1814, 10-gun brig, 223
Ligurienne, 1798-1800, 14 x 6pdr brig, 207
Lilloise, 1823-1833, 8-gun gunbrig, 229
Lily, 1858-1876, Paddle aviso, 351
Linnet, 1813-1813, 14-gun brig, 221
Linotte, 1804-1816, Felucca, 302
Lion, 1751-1785, Two-decker (64-gun), 78
Lion, 1794-1798, Two-decker (74-gun), see *Cassard* 1803-1818
Lion, 1804-1809, Two-decker (74-gun), 94
Lion, 1808-1809, Cutter, 257
Lionne, 1784-1808, Gabarre, 384
Lionne (*Grande Gabarre Écurie No.10*), 1811-1852, Gabarre, 390
Lise, 1795-1804, Bateau-canonnier, 278
Lochrist, 1860-1888, 4-gun gunbrig (hulked), see *Tactique* 1839-1860
Lodi, 1797-1803, 18 x 6pdr brig, see *Jason* 1797-1797
Lodi (*Lody*), 1803-1815, Lugger or chasse-marée, 258
Loi, 1793-1801, Lugger, 248
Loire, 1780-1793, Gabarre, 384
Loire, 1796-1798, 18pdr frigate (44-gun), 140
Loire, 1803-1809, Flûte, 378
Loire, 1814-1838, Flûte, see *Généreux* 1810-1814
Loire, 1840-1852, Gabarre, 393
Loire, 1855-1873, Screw transport, 398
Loire, 1872-1897, Transport (sail), see *Prince Jérôme* 1853-1870
Loire-Inférieure, 1798-1798, Gunboat, 280
Loiret, 1803 not built, 30-gun corvette, 178
Loiret, 1820-1844, Gabarre, see *Portefaix* 1809-1820
Loiret, 1856-1883, Screw transport, 400
Lombardo, 1810-1814, Two-decker (74-gun), 97
Lonato, 1797-1797, Half-xebec, 298
Lonato, 1797-1799, 8pdr frigate (38-gun), 133
London, 1794-1795, Felucca, 299
London, 1794-1797, Cutter, 245
Longitudinale, 1795-1815, Bomb vessel, see *Louise* 1792-1795
Lord Gordon, 1793-1798, 20 x 4pdr corvette, 175
Loterie, 1798-1801, Lugger, 246
Lougre No.1, 1803-1804, Lugger, 258
Lougre No.2, 1803-1805, Lugger, 258
Lougre No.3, 1803-1805, Lugger, 258
Lougre No.6, 1803-1808, Lugger, see *Marie-Joseph* 1803-1808
Lougre No.9, 1802-1809, Lugger or chasse-marée, see *Deux Amis* 1802-1809
Louis XIV, 1854-1857, Three-decker, 48
Louis XIV, 1857-1882, Screw three-decker, 53
Louise, 1784-1786, Schooner, 239
Louise, 1792-1795, Bomb vessel, 309
Louise, 1794-1795, Transport, 407
Louise, 1806-1816, Gabarre, 387
Louise, 1828-1834, Paddle vessel, see *Caroline* 1824-1828
Loup, 1795-1795, Tartane, see *Petit Jacobin* 1794-1795
Loup de Mer, 1796-1799, Bateau-canonnier, 279
Louqsor, 1830-1837, Large transport, see *Luxor* 1830-1837
Lourde, 1781-1797, Flûte, 374
Loutre, 1808-1812, Transport (snow), 415
Lowlay, 1798-1798, Transport, 408
Loyauté, 1795-1798, Cutter, 249
Lozère, 1847 cancelled, Gabarre, 393
Lozère, 1832-1834, Corvette de charge, 382
Lucifer, 1853-1887, Screw aviso, 356
Lupin, 1866-1887, Bomb vessel (hulked), see *Torche* 1855-1858
Lutin, 1788-1793, 4pdr brig-aviso, 204
Lutin, 1804-1806, 16-gun brig, 215
Lutin, 1810-1810, Schooner, 255
Lutin, 1814-1820, Cutter, see *Hoop* 1793-1815
Lutin, 1833-1865, 16-gun brig, 228
Lutin, 1861-1871, Screw aviso, 360
Lutin, 1871-1871, Paddle aviso (hulked), see *Abeille* 1858-1871
Lutine, 1779-1793, 12pdr frigate (32-gun), 125
Lutine, 1796-1796, Bateau-canonnier, 278
Luxor (*Louqsor*), 1830-1837, Large transport, 397
Lybio, 1810-1842, Flûte, 379
Lybio, 1849 cancelled, Large transport, 397
Lydia, 1795-1797, Flûte, 376
Lynx, 1779-1797, Gunboat, 271
Lynx, 1804-1807, 16 x 6pdr brig, 214
Lynx, 1811-1813, Corvette, 184
Lynx, 1814-1834, 10-gun gunbrig, see *Conflict* 1804-1815
Lynx, 1848-1858, 6-gun brig-aviso, 236
Lynx, 1861-1866, Screw aviso, 361
Lyonnaise, 1821-1838, Schooner, 260
Lys, 1785-1792, Two-decker (74-gun), 87
Lys, 1794-1794, Transport, 407
Lys, 1814-1826, Two-decker (74-gun), see *Polonais* 1808-1815
Lys, 1815-1827, Schooner-aviso, see *Mouche No.29* 1810-1815
Lys, 1825-1830, Two-decker (100-gun), see *Ulm* 1830-1854

Madagascar, 1828-1866, Gabarre, 391
Madeleine, 1794-1795, Transport, 407
Madeleine, 1794-1802, Gunboat (dogger or lugger), 277
Madone de Grace de Saint Antoine de Padoue, 1798-1800, Transport (barque), 409
Magdelaine, 1794-1795, Transport, 407
Magellan, 1843-1884, Paddle frigate, 332
Magenta, 1861-1875, Ironclad frigate, 422
Magicien, 1861-1890, Paddle aviso, 345
Magicienne, 1798-1799, Schooner, 247
Magicienne, 1824-1840, 18pdr frigate (44-gun), 147
Magicienne, 1845-1861, 30pdr frigate (50-gun), 114
Magicienne, 1861-1900, Screw frigate, 119
Magnanime, 1779-1793, Two-decker (74-gun), 86
Magnanime, 1794-1798, Two-decker (74-gun), see *Vétéran* 1803-1842
Magnanime, 1803-1816, Two-decker (74-gun), 94
Magnanime, 1864-1885, Ironclad frigate, 423
Magnifique, 1814-1837, Two-decker (80-gun), 58
Magpie, 1807-1815, Schooner, 256
Mahé, 1835-1845, Gabarre, 392
Mahé, 1873-1876, Screw aviso (hulked), see *Labourdonnaye* 1856-1873
Majestueux, 1780-1797, Three-decker, 44
Majestueux, 1803-1839, Three-decker, see *République Française* 1802-1803
Makalos, 1786-?, Sloop (service craft), 406
Malabar, 1794-1809, Flûte, 377
Malicieuse, 1795-1806, 16 x 12pdr corvette, 173
Malin, 1781-1786, Cutter, 238
Malin, 1795-1806, Cutter, 245
Mallard, 1804-1815, 10-gun gunbrig, 222
Malo, 1799-1799, Transport (brig), 409
Malouine, 1823-1868, 8-gun gunbrig, 229
Mamelouck, 1810-1815, 16-gun brig, 217
Mamelucco, 1808-1814, 10-gun brig, 220
Mameluck, 1808-1814, 10-gun brig, see *Mamelucco* 1808-1814
Manche, 1806-1810, 18pdr frigate (44-gun), see *Département de la Manche* 1806-1810
Mantoue, 1797-1797, Half-xebec, 298
Mantoue, 1797-1801, 12pdr frigate (32-gun), 133
Mantovana, 1806-1814, Gunboat (Italian), 287
Marabout, 1852-1869, Paddle aviso, 348
Marat, 1793-1795, Cutter, 240
Marat, 1794-1795, Two-decker (74-gun), 89
Maraudier, 1797-1799, Bateau-canonnier, 279
Marc, 1803-1814, Hydrographic vessel, 313
Marceau, 1797-1798, Two-decker (74-gun), see *Apollon* 1788-1797
Marceau, 1852-1880, Screw aviso, 355
Maréchal de Castries, 1785-1793, 18 x 6pdr corvette, 166
Marengo, 1800-1811, Two-decker (74-gun), see *Sceptre* 1780-1792
Marengo, 1802-1806, Two-decker (74-gun), see *Jean-Jacques Rousseau* 1795-1802
Marengo, 1810-1865, Two-decker (74-gun), 94
Marengo, 1814-1815, Three-decker, see *Ville de Paris* 1850-1870
Marguerite, 1794-1807, Gunboat (galiote), 276
Marguerite, 1798-1798, Gunboat (tartane), 280
Marguerite, 1808-1808, 10-gun brig, 223
Marguerite (*Grande Gabarre Écurie No.4*), 1812-1817, Gabarre, 390
Marguérite Adélaïde, 1794-1795, Bomb vessel, 310
Marguerite-Unie, 1794-1795, Transport, 407
Maria, 1808-1809, 12/14-gun brig, 221
Maria, 1810-1814, 18pdr frigate (40-gun), 154
Maria, 1824-1824, Schooner, 268
Maria Primeira, 1807-1808, Two-decker (74-gun), 101
Marianne, 1834-1842, Trincadour, 308
Marianne (*Marie-Anne*), 1798-1799, Transport (brig), 409
Marie, 1794-1795, Transport (brig), 407
Marie, 1798-1798, Transport, 409
Marie, 1801-1804, Transport (brig), 409
Marie, 1806-1807, Transport (brig), 413
Marie, 1808-1816, Gabarre, 387
Marie, 1808-1811, Transport (brig), see *Mathilde* 1808-1811
Marie (*Marie-Rose*), 1798-1799, Tartane, 297
Marie Fibrick, 1793-1797, Transport (galiote), 411
Marie Graty (*Mary Graty*), 1795-1814, Transport (brig), 410
Marie Guiton, 1793-1795, 20 x 6pdr corvette, see *Alouette* 1786-1795
Marie Thérèse, 1823-1830, 24pdr frigate (58-gun), 107
Marie Vaudelours (*Vandelaar*), 1793-1797, Transport (galiote), 411
Marie-André, 1796-1796, Aviso, 250
Marie-Angélique, 1794-1794, Transport, 407
Marie-Anne Guillemette, 1800-1827, Transport (brig), 409
Marie-Dorothée, 1795-1796, Transport (galiote), see *Baleine* 1793-1803
Marie-Flore (*Transport No.4*), 1798-1800, Transport, 408
Marie-Françoise, 1778-1789, Transport (chasse-marée), 405
Marie-Françoise, 1794-1794, Transport, 407
Marie-Françoise-Providence, 1794-1795, Transport, 407
Marie-Jeanne, 1794-1794, Transport, 407
Marie-Jeanne, 1799-1803, Transport, 409
Marie-Joseph, 1794-1795, Transport, 407
Marie-Joseph (*Marie-Josephe*), 1803-1808, Lugger, 258
Marie-Louise, 1794-1795, Transport, 407
Marie-Thérèse, 1794-1795, Transport, 407
Marie-Thérèse, 1799-1801, Transport, 409
Marin, 1796-1797, Bateau-canonnier, 279
Maringouin, 1793-1808, Gunboat (chasse-marée), 276
Maritime, 1795-1795, Gunboat (chasse-marée), see *Mouche Sans Raison* 1793-1795
Marmotte, 1808-1809, Transport (yacht), 415
Marne, 1826-1841, Corvette de charge, 382
Marne, 1855-1894, Screw transport, 399
Marquis de Castries, 1781-1791, Gabarre, 385
Mars, 1803-1807, Cutter, 258
Mars, 1804-1832, Cutter, 257
Mars, 1814 cancelled, Two-decker (80-gun), 60
Marseillais, 1766-1794, Two-decker (74-gun), 84
Marsouin, 1787-1795, Gabarre, 385
Marsouin, 1842-1865, Gabarre, 393
Marsouin (*Petit Gabarre Écurie No.2*), 1809-1834, Gabarre, 388
Marthe, 1794-1795, Transport, 407
Marthe, 1796-1800, Péniche, 278
Martin Garcia, 1839-1842, Schooner, 269
Martinet, 1793-1795, Lugger, 245
Martinet, 1793-1795, Lugger, 247
Martinique, 1779-1792, Gunboat, 271
Martinique, 1829-1831, 20 x 30pdr corvette, see *Alcmène* 1834-1851
Massafran, 1838-1844, Balancelle, 308
Masséna, 1860-1906, Screw two-decker, 73
Masséna, 1850-1860, Two-decker (90-gun), 65
Mathilde, 1808-1811, Transport (brig), 415
Maure, 1794-1794, Transport, 407
Mayenne, 1821-1845, Gabarre, 391
Mayenne, 1857-1876, Screw transport, 400
Mayottais (*Mayottais No.2*), 1843-1857, Transport (cutter or schooner), 418
Mayottais No.1, 1855-1858, Transport, 418
Méchante, 1793-1805, Gunboat, 275
Mécontent, 1808-1809, Transport (schooner), 415
Médée?, 1778-1800, 12pdr frigate (32-gun), 125
Médée, 1786-?, Sloop (service craft), 406
Médée, 1797-1797, Two-decker (66-gun), see *Frontin* 1797-1825
Médée, 1811-1850, 18pdr frigate (44-gun), 151
Medusa, 1797-1797, Galley, 299
Medusa, 1810-1814, Gunboat (Italian), 287
Méduse, 1782-1796, 18pdr frigate (36-gun), 136
Méduse, 1797-1797, 12pdr frigate (38-gun), see *Léoben* 1797-1801
Méduse, 1810-1816, 18pdr frigate (44-gun), 149
Mégère, 1779-1795, Gunboat, 271
Mégère, 1794-1796, Gunboat (tartane), 278
Mégère, 1853-1901, Screw aviso, 356
Meilleur, 1794-1796, Bomb vessel, see *Marguérite Adélaïde* 1794-1795
Mélanie, 1803-1823, Transport (cutter), 412
Méléagre, 1830-1883, 20-gun brig, 231
Mélodieux, 1795-1796, Gunboat (dogger or lugger), see *Madeleine* 1794-1802
Mélomane, 1794-1794, Transport, 407
Melpomène, 1789-1794, 18pdr frigate (36-gun), 137
Melpomène, 1812-1815, 18pdr frigate (44-gun), 150
Melpomène, 1828-1865, 30pdr frigate (60-gun), 108
Melpomène, 1848 cancelled, 30pdr frigate (60-gun), 115
Menaçante, 1795-1800, Bomb vessel, 309
Ménagère, 1819-1856, Gabarre, 391
Ménagère, 1859-1889, Large transport, 398
Mentor, 1794-1795, Transport, 407
Menzaleh, 1798-1799, Aviso, 250
Mercure, 1783-1798, Two-decker (74-gun), 87
Mercure, 1794-1795, Transport, 407
Mercure, 1806-1810, 16-gun brig, 216
Mercure, 1811-1814, 12-gun brig, 226
Mercure, 1842-1888, 18-gun brig, 233
Mercure de Londres, 1796-1798, 16 x 4pdr corvette, see *Mercury of London* 1793-1794
Mercurio, 1808 uncertain, 10-gun brig, 220
Mercurio, 1810-1812, 16-gun brig, see *Cyclope* 1805-1810
Mercurius, 1794-1795, Transport, 410
Mercury of London, 1793-1794, 16 x 4pdr corvette, 175
Mère Duchêsne, 1799-1799, Schooner, 248
Méridienne, 1795-1797, Gunboat, see *Mégère* 1779-1795
Mérinos, 1811-1812, Flûte, 379
Mérinos, 1838-1838, Gabarre, see *Active* 1838-1839
Merle, 1795-1818, Half-xebec, see *Montagne* 1794-1795
Merle, 1801-1818, Balancelle or pink, 297
Merope, 1797-1797, Galley, 298
Mérope, 1797-1799, Schooner, 247
Mers el Kebir, 1830-1831, Schooner, 268

Mésange, 1823-1851, Schooner, 261
Mesnil, 1794-1794, Transport, 407
Messager, 1795-1803, Cutter or chasse-marée, see *Forcalquier* 1793-1793
Messager, 1811-1822, Schooner, 255
Messager, 1841-1865, 16-gun brig, 228
Messidor, 1794-1796, Gunboat (tartane), 278
Météore, 1833-1874, Paddle vessel, 323
Meurthe, 1842-1854, Corvette de charge, 383
Meurthe, 1855-1872, Screw transport, 399
Meurtrière, 1855-1868, Screw gun launch, 368
Meuse, 1803 cancelled, Flûte, 378
Meuse, 1811-1814, 18pdr frigate (44-gun), 152
Meuse, 1825-1836, Corvette de charge, 382
Meuse, 1847 cancelled, Gabarre, 392
Meuse, 1855-1904, Screw transport, 399
Microcosme, 1795-1795, Lugger, see *Martinet* 1793-1795
Mignonne, 1767-1794, 8pdr frigate (32-gun), 121
Mignonne, 1795-1803, 16 x 18pdr corvette, 173
Mignonne, 1840-1849, Schooner, 265
Mikhail, 1809-1810, 18pdr frigate (48-gun), 156
Milan, 1807-1809, 16-gun brig, 215
Milan, 1849-1866, Paddle aviso, 342
Milanaise, 1805-1815, 18pdr frigate (44-gun), 148
Milanese, 1806-1813, Gunboat (Italian), 287
Millesimo, 1799-1801, Gunboat, 280
Mincio, 1797-1797, Xebec, 297
Minerva, 1797-1799, Two-decker (58 gun), 77
Minerve, 1782-1794, 18pdr frigate (36-gun), 135
Minerve, 1786-?, Sloop (service craft), 406
Minerve, 1794-1795, 18pdr frigate (42-gun), 138
Minerve, 1794-1795, Transport, 407
Minerve, 1794-1802, Corvette, see *Spartiate* 1794-1794
Minerve, 1805-1806, 18pdr frigate (44-gun), 146
Minerve, 1807-1808, 18pdr frigate (50-gun), 156
Minerve, 1810-1814, 18pdr frigate (40-gun), 154
Minerve, 1831-1834, Two-decker (74-gun), see *Duc de Berry* 1818-1830
Minerve, 1831-1865, 36pdr rasée frigate, 107
Minerve, 1865-1897, Screw corvette, 202
Minerve (loaned), 1801-1801, 18pdr frigate (40-gun), 144
Miquelonnaise, 1815-1819, Schooner, 256
Mirage, 1860-1868, Schooner, 270
Mirmidon, 1841-1882, Cutter, 264
Miromesnil, 1793-1793, Flûte, 376
Mitraille, 1855-1869, Screw gunboat, 365
Modenese, 1806-1813, Gunboat (Italian), 287
Modeste, 1786-1793, 12pdr frigate (32-gun), 129
Mogador, 1848-1880, Paddle frigate, 330
Mohawk, 1801-1814, 16 x 12pdr corvette, 176
Moineau, 1794-1797, Corvette, see *Spartiate* 1794-1794
Molène, 1858-1866, 16-gun brig (hulked), see *Abeille* 1801-1858
Mollusque, 1868-1872, Schooner (hulked), see *Estafette* 1842-1868
Momus, 1799-1799, Transport (brig), 409
Momus, 1810-1838, Schooner, 254
Monarque, 1814 cancelled, Three-decker (110-gun), 49
Mondovi, 1797-1798, 16 x 8pdr brig, see *Pollux* 1797-1797
Monge, 1841-1841, Paddle frigate, see *Asmodée* 1841-1866
Monge, 1841-1844, Paddle frigate, see *Mogador* 1848-1880
Monge, 1848 cancelled, Paddle corvette, 337
Monge, 1859-1868, Screw aviso, 357
Monro, 1794-1795, Chasse-marée, 245
Mont Blanc, 1793-1805, Two-decker (74-gun), see *Pyrrhus* 1791-1793
Mont Blanc, 1806-1807, Two-decker (74-gun), see *Mont Saint Bernard* 1811-1814
Mont Saint Bernard, 1811-1814, Two-decker (74-gun), 96
Montagnard, 1794-1795, Two-decker (74-gun), see *Jupiter* 1789-1797
Montagne, 1793-1795, Three-decker, see *États de Bourgogne* 1790-1793
Montagne, 1793-1795, 20 x 8pdr corvette, 172
Montagne, 1793-1795, Cutter, 240
Montagne, 1793-1795, Cutter or lugger, 248
Montagne, 1793-1795, Xebec, see *Good Intent* 1793-1801
Montagne, 1794-1794, 18pdr frigate (44-gun), 139
Montagne, 1794-1795, Gunboat, 275
Montagne, 1794-1795, Half-xebec, 299
Montagne, 1794-1796, Cutter, see *Pensée* 1793-1796
Montebello, 1810-1810, Two-decker (74-gun), see *Duquesne* 1810-1814
Montebello, 1812-1814, Three-decker, 48
Montebello, 1852-1889, Screw three-decker, 52
Montecuccoli, 1809-1814, 18-gun brig, 219
Montenotte, 1797-1798, Mortar boat, 310
Montenotte, 1797-1801, 12pdr frigate (38-gun), 132
Montenotte, 1810-1814, Two-decker (74-gun), 97
Montesquieu, 1795-1795, Felucca, see *Petit Barra* 1795-1795
Montézuma, 1843-1863, Paddle frigate, 332
Montréal, 1779-1793, 12pdr frigate (32-gun), 127
Mora, 1811-1813, Felucca, 306
Morbihan, 1793-1795, Cutter or chasse-marée, see *Forcalquier* 1793-1793
Morbihan, 1794-1794, Flûte, 377
Morlaque, 1810-1814, Péniche, 293
Mortier, 1895-1803, Bomb vessel, 309
Moscava, 1813-1814, 18pdr frigate (44-gun), 153
Moscou, 1809-1811, Two-decker (74-gun), 101
Moselle, 1788-1794, Gabarre, 385
Moselle, 1805-1808, Gabarre, 386
Moselle, 1820-1833, Flûte, 380
Moselle, 1847 cancelled, Gabarre, 393
Moselle, 1848-1856, Large transport, 397
Moselle, 1859-1887, Screw transport, 402
Moskowa, 1813-1814, 18pdr frigate (44-gun), see *Moscava* 1813-1814
Mouche, 1787-1797, 4pdr brig-aviso, 204
Mouche, 1803-1822, Gunboat (chasse-marée), see *Mouche Sans Raison* 1793-1795
Mouche, 1804 cancelled, 16-gun brig, 210
Mouche, 1814-1815, Felucca, 304
Mouche, 1840-1873, Schooner, 265
Mouche No.1, 1808-1808, Schooner-aviso, see *Villaret* 1806-1807
Mouche No.10, 1808-1817, Schooner-aviso, 252
Mouche No.11, 1808-1810, Schooner-aviso, 252
Mouche No.12, 1808-1817, Schooner-aviso, 252
Mouche No.13, 1808-1809, Schooner-aviso, 252
Mouche No.14, 1808-1815, Schooner-aviso, 252
Mouche No.15, 1808-1818, Schooner-aviso, 252
Mouche No.16, 1808-1817, Schooner-aviso, 252
Mouche No.17 (*Goélette No.17*), 1808-1814, Schooner-aviso, 252
Mouche No.18 (*Goélette No.18*), 1808-1814, Schooner-aviso, 252
Mouche No.19 (*Goélette No.19*), 1808-1817, Schooner-aviso, 252
Mouche No.2, 1808-1808, Schooner-aviso, 252
Mouche No.20, 1809-1818, Schooner-aviso, 252
Mouche No.21, 1809-1818, Schooner-aviso, 252
Mouche No.22, 1809-1814, Schooner-aviso, 253
Mouche No.23, 1809-1810, Schooner-aviso, 253
Mouche No.24, 1809-1817, Schooner-aviso, 253
Mouche No.25, 1810-1810, Schooner-aviso, 253
Mouche No.26, 1809-1810, Schooner-aviso, 253
Mouche No.27, 1809-1811, Schooner-aviso, 253
Mouche No.28, 1809-1810, Schooner-aviso, 253
Mouche No.29, 1810-1815, Schooner-aviso, 253
Mouche No.3, 1808-1808, Schooner-aviso, 252
Mouche No.4, 1808-1809, Schooner-aviso, 252
Mouche No.5, 1808-1809, Schooner-aviso, 252
Mouche No.6, 1808-1809, Schooner-aviso, 252
Mouche No.7, 1808-1809, Schooner-aviso, 252
Mouche No.8, 1808-1817, Schooner-aviso, 252
Mouche No.9, 1808-1817, Schooner-aviso, 252
Mouche Sans Raison, 1793-1795, Gunboat (chasse-marée), 276
Moucheron, 1818-1830, Schooner-aviso, see *Mouche No.21* 1809-1818
Mouette, 1796-1796, Corvette, 178
Mouette, 1847-1867, Paddle aviso, 340
Mousquito, 1803-1807, Schooner, 259
Mousse, 1867-1878, 16-gun brig, see *Dupetit Thouars* 1830-1867
Moustique, 1793-1826, Gunboat (chasse-marée), 276
Moustique, 1810-1811, Schooner, 258
Moustique, 1834-1893, Cutter, 264
Mucius, 1793-1804, Two-decker (74-gun), see *Orion* 1787-1793
Mucius Scévola, 1791-1794, Two-decker (74-gun), see *Illustre* 1781-1791
Mucius Scévola, 1793-1793, Two-decker (74-gun), see *Orion* 1787-1793
Muiron, 1797-1850, 18pdr frigate (44-gun), 143
Muiron, 1850-1882, 18pdr frigate (hulked), see *Médée* 1811-1850
Mulet, 1782-1795, Flûte, 374
Mulet, 1795-1802, Bateau-plat, 272
Mulet, 1807-1811, Transport, 414
Munro, 1794-1795, Chasse-marée, see *Monro* 1794-1795
Musette, 1793-1795, 20 x 6pdr corvette, 177
Musette, 1803-1809, Schooner-aviso, 259
Musquito, 1803-1807, Schooner, see *Mousquito* 1803-1807
Mutin, 1845-1851, Cutter, see *Passe-Partout* 1837-1845
Mutine, 1794-1797, 12pdr brig, 206
Mutine, 1797-1799, Bateau-canonnier, 278
Mutine, 1799-1803, 16 x 8pdr corvette, 174
Mutine, 1808-1814, Péniche, 293
Mutine, 1824-1841, Schooner, 263
Mutine, 1855-1883, Screw gun launch, 368

Nageur, 1827-1838, Paddle vessel, 317
Naïade, 1793-1805, 12 x 12pdr corvette, 168
Naïade, 1812-1813, 20 x 24pdr corvette, 182
Naïade, 1830-1851, 20 x 30pdr corvette, 187
Nancy, 1797-1803, Transport, see *Nancy de Lins* 1794-1797
Nancy de Greenock, 1794-1794, Transport, 410
Nancy de Lins, 1794-1797, Transport (brig), 410
Nanine, 1795-1804, Bateau-canonnier, 278
Nantaise, 1779-1792, Gunboat, 271
Nantaise, 1813-1828, Gabarre, 391
Napoléon, 1806-1806, Schooner, 256
Napoléon, 1850-1886, Screw two-decker, 67
Napoléon Ier, 1860 not built, Ironclad frigate, 421
Narcisse, 1793-1794, Cutter, 240
Narenta, 1811-1814, Péniche, 293
Narval, 1844-1877, Paddle aviso, 339
Nathalie, 1794-1802, 10 x 4pdr brig, 213
Nathalie, 1808-1815, Gabarre, 388
Nativité, 1798-1798, Tartane, 297
Naturaliste, 1800-1811, Bomb vessel, see *Menaçante* 1795-1800
Nausicaa, 1813-1814, Speronare or galiote, 303
Navalo, 1808-1811, Transport (snow), 415
Navarin, 1832-1854, Two-decker (100-gun), 64
Navarin, 1854-1908, Screw two-decker, 70
Navigateur, 1794-1796, Corvette, 178
Néarque, 1804-1806, 16-gun brig, 215
Nécessaire, 1783-1792, Flûte, 374
Nécessité, 1795-1810, Flûte, see *Normande* 1789-1795
Necker Immortel, 1801-1804, Transport, 409
Négative (*No.14*), 1795-1797, Gunboat, 278
Négligente (*No.12*), 1795-1795, Gunboat, 278
Négresse, 1798-1799, Gunboat (tartane), 280

Némésis, 1795-1796, 24 x 8pdr corvette, 175
Némésis, 1847-1888, 30pdr frigate (52-gun), 112
Neptune, 1778-1795, Two-decker (74-gun), 85
Neptune, 1793-1794, Transport, 406
Neptune, 1793-1797, Corvette, 177
Neptune, 1794-1794, Transport, 408
Neptune, 1794-1798, Lugger, 247
Neptune, 1803-1808, Two-decker (80-gun), 58
Neptune, 1805-1816, Xebec or half-xebec, 304
Neptune, 1807-1816, Transport, 414
Neptune, 1814 cancelled, Three-decker (110-gun), 49
Neptune, 1818-1868, Two-decker (80-gun), 58
Neptune Fortuné, 1796-1798, Lugger, 248
Neptune Hardi, 1794-1796, Cutter, 249
Néréide, 1779-1810, 12pdr frigate (32-gun), 124
Néréide, 1803 cancelled, 18pdr frigate (44-gun), 144
Néréide, 1809-1811, 18pdr frigate (44-gun), 145
Néréide, 1814-1830, 18pdr frigate (44-gun), see *Rancune* 1813-1815
Néréide, 1836-1896, 30pdr frigate (50-gun), 111
Nestor, 1793-1797, Two-decker (74-gun), 90
Nestor, 1810-1865, Two-decker (74-gun), 99
Nestor, 1873-1778, Two-decker (hulked), see *Tourville* 1853-1873
Netley, 1806-1807, 18-gun brig, 221
Nettuno, 1807-1808, 18-gun brig, 219
Neuf Thermidor, 1794-1795, Two-decker (80-gun), see *Auguste* 1778-1793
Newton, 1848-1857, Paddle corvette, 335
Nicodème, 1795-1801, Flûte, see *Société* 1793-1794
Niémen, 1808-1809, 18pdr frigate (44-gun), 147
Nièvre, 1828-1838, Corvette de charge, 382
Nièvre, 1855-1874, Screw transport, 399
Nil, 1798-1799, Felucca, 297
Ninfa, 1806-1809, Gunboat (Italian), 287
Nini, 1809-1814, Transport (chaloupe), 413
Niobé, 1825 cancelled, 18-gun corvette-aviso, 186
Niobé, 1827-1839, 30pdr frigate (50-gun), see *Virginie* 1842-1888
Nisus, 1805-1809, 16-gun brig, 215
Nisus, 1826-1844, 20-gun brig, 230
Nisus, 1850-1915, 18-gun brig, 232
Nivôse, 1794-1797, Gunboat (tartane), see *Sainte-Marie* 1794-1794
No.11, 1859-1898, Screw gun launch, 369
No.1-10, 1859-1919, Screw gun launches, 368
No.12-31, 1860-1892, Screw sectional gun launches, 369
No.1-5, 1859-1923, Screw sectional armoured floating batteries, 371
Noirmoutier, 1793-1793, Gunboat, 274
Nord-Est, 1795-1799, 4pdr brig, see *Zéphir* 1793-1799
Normande, 1789-1795, Flûte, 375
Normande, 1807-1809, Transport (pink), 414
Normande, 1810-1810, Flûte, see *Salamandre* 1811-1826
Normande, 1814-1833, Flûte, see *Égyptienne* 1812-1815
Normandie, 1794-1795, Flûte, see *Société* 1793-1794
Normandie, 1860-1871, Ironclad frigate, 420
Northumberland, 1780-1794, Two-decker (74-gun), 85
Norzagaray, 1859-1866, Screw aviso, 363
Nossa Senhora da Solidao, 1808-1810, Transport (galiote), 416
Notre Dame de Grace, 1793-1793, Tartane, 299
Notre Dame des Carmes, 1794-1795, Transport, 408
Notre Dame des Carmes, 1798-1799, Transport, 409
Notre Dame des Douleurs, 1794-1795, Transport, 408
Notre Dame des Martyrs, 1807-1808, Two-decker

INDEX TO NAMED VESSELS

(74-gun), 101
Nourrice, 1792-1811, Flûte, 375
Nouvelle, 1795? cancelled, 24pdr frigate (30-gun), 105
Nouvelle, 1797-1799, 16 x 8pdr corvette, see *Mutine* 1799-1803
Nouvelle Entreprise, 1797-1798, Flûte, 378
Nouvelle Entreprise de Dantzig, 1782-1789, Flûte, 374
Nouvelle Étoile, 1794-1794, Transport, 407
Nouvelle Résolution, 1793-1800, Transport (galiote), see *Nouvelle Révolution* 1793-1800
Nouvelle Révolution, 1793-1800, Transport (galiote), 411
Novateur, 1795-1795, Transport, see *Notre Dame des Douleurs* 1794-1795
Noviciat, 1794-1796, 16 x 4pdr corvette, see *Mercury of London* 1793-1794
Nue (No.9), 1795-1795, Gunboat, 278
Nu-Hiva, 1851-1865, Schooner, 270
Nuit (No.6), 1795-1795, Gunboat, 278
Nymphe, 1782-1793, 18pdr frigate (34-gun), 136
Nymphe, 1785-1788, Schooner, 240
Nymphe, 1803-1807, 18pdr frigate (44-gun), see *Vistule* 1808-1815
Nymphe, 1810-1873, 18pdr frigate (44-gun), 149
Nymphe, 1836 cancelled, 30pdr frigate (46-gun), 158

O Hydra, 1794-1795, Xebec, 300
Obligado, 1845-1846, Schooner, 269
Obligado, 1850-1910, 14-gun brig, 235
Observateur, 1800-1806, 16-gun brig, 209
Observateur, 1808-1826, Gunboat, 291
Observateur, 1839-1854, 16-gun brig, see *Laurier* 1832-1839
Obusiera, 1806-1809, Felucca, 305
Océan, 1795-1855, Three-decker, see *États de Bourgogne* 1790-1793
Océan, 1803-1804, Schooner, 259
Oder, 1813-1815, 18pdr frigate (44-gun), 148
Oenone, 1808-1811, Transport (schooner), 415
Oise, 1803 cancelled, Flûte, 378
Oise, 1825-1863, Corvette de charge, 382
Oiseau, 1793-1793, Chasse-marée, 248
Oiseau, 1793-1795, 16 x 6pdr corvette, 176
Oiseau, 1794-1795, Lugger, 248
Oiseau, 1794-1801, 18 x 6pdr brig, 213
Oiseau, 1795-1796, Lugger, 248
Oiseau, 1801-1803, Schooner, 243
Oiseleur, 1810-1834, Lugger, 255
Olive, 1806-1807, Flûte, 380
Olivier, 1814-1823, 16-gun brig, see *Mamelouck* 1810-1815
Olivier, 1829-1831, 6-gun brig-aviso, 231
Olivier, 1844-1887, 18-gun brig, 233
Olympe, 1795-1795, Lugger, see *Oiseau* 1794-1795
Ondine, 1851-1851, Cutter (hulked), see *Passe-Partout* 1837-1845
Ondine, 1860-1871, Paddle aviso, 351
Opiniâtre, 1864-1912, Ironclad floating battery, 427
Opinion, 1794-1796, Gunboat (tartane), 278
Orage, 1795-1796, 18 x 6pdr brig, see *Oiseau* 1794-1801
Orage, 1799-1799, Lugger, 248
Oran, 1830-1831, Schooner, 268
Oranger, 1798-1799, Bomb vessel, 310
Orénoque, 1843-1880, Paddle frigate, 332
Oreste, 1796-1816, Transport (dogger), 406
Oreste, 1797-1797, Cutter, 247
Oreste, 1805-1810, 16-gun brig, 214
Oreste, 1833-1875, 20-gun brig, 231
Orevizana, 1813-1813, Gunboat (Italian), 288
Orient, 1795-1798, Three-decker, see *Dauphin Royal* 1791-1792
Oriflamme, 1829-1831, 18pdr frigate (46-gun), see *Érigone* 1836-1879
Orion, 1787-1793, Two-decker (74-gun), 87
Orion, 1813-1841, Two-decker (74-gun), 99
Orione, 1806-1810, Bomb vessel, see *Destruction* 1797-1797

Orione, 1855-1883, Large transport, 398
Orne, 1862-1891, Screw transport, 403
Orphée, 1786-?, Sloop (service craft), 406
Ortensia, 1807-1808, Schooner, 252
Orythie, 1827-1844, 18-gun corvette-aviso, 186
Osiris, 1799-1800, Half-xebec, 295
Osiris, 1800-1813, Half-xebec, 297
Osterley, 1799-1800, Flûte, 376
Otello, 1812-1814, 20-gun brig, 220
Otway, 1806-1806, Corvette, 183
Ouessant, 1859-1880, school brig, see *Comète* 1826-1859
Ouessant, 1878-1893, school brig, see *Dupetit Thouars* 1830-1867
Outarde, 1794-1796, Flûte, 373
Ovidor, 1809-1810, Flûte, see *Généreux* 1810-1814
Oyapock, 1852-1865, Paddle aviso, 348

Pacificateur, 1804 cancelled, Two-decker (74-gun), 92
Pacificateur, 1811-1824, Two-decker (80-gun), 59
Padovana, 1806-1814, Gunboat (Italian), 287
Paix, 1794-1796, Transport (brig), 407
Paix, 1796-1797, Aviso, 250
Paix, 1797-1797, Galley, 298
Paixhans, 1862-1872, Ironclad floating battery, 426
Palestro, 1862-1872, Ironclad floating battery, 426
Palinure, 1804-1808, 16-gun brig, 215
Palinure, 1825-1887, 20-gun brig, 229
Pallade, 1797-1797, 12pdr frigate (38-gun), 132
Pallas, 1794-1794, Transport, 407
Pallas, 1798-1800, 18pdr frigate (40-gun), 142
Pallas, 1808-1824, 18pdr frigate (44-gun), 149
Pallas, 1825-1827, Two-decker (74-gun), see *Colosse* 1813-1825
Pallas, 1825-1854, 36pdr rasée frigate, 107
Pallas, 1848-1860, 30pdr frigate (60-gun), 115
Pallas, 1860-1910, Screw frigate, 118
Palmer, 1845-1847, Schooner, 269
Palme, 1797-1797, 8pdr frigate (38-gun), see *Lonato* 1797-1799
Panama, 1843-1897, Paddle frigate, 332
Panayoti, 1827-1827, brig, 237
Pandore, 1846-1858, 30pdr frigate (52-gun), 112
Pandore, 1858-1893, Screw frigate, 117
Pandour, 1780-1795, Cutter, 238
Pandour, 1804-1806, 16-gun brig, 215
Pandour, 1843-1850, 10-gun brig-aviso, 234
Panthère, 1806-1833, Gabarre, 386
Panthère, 1844-1888, 4-gun gunbrig, 231
Paon, 1808-1808, Flûte, see *Lybio* 1810-1842
Papeïti, 1848-1859, Schooner, 270
Papillon, 1781-1789, Cutter, 238
Papillon, 1786-1795, 4pdr brig-aviso, 203
Papillon, 1793-1803, 12-gun brig, 207
Papillon, 1807-1809, 16-gun brig, 216
Papillon, 1817-1817, Schooner-aviso, see *Mouche No.24* 1809-1817
Papillon, 1841-1841, Cutter, see *Capélan* 1841-1892
Papillon, 1841-1851, 16-gun brig, 228
Papin, 1836-1845, Paddle vessel, 324
Paraskeva, 1809-1811, Two-decker (74-gun), 101
Parisien, 1848-1853, Yacht, see *Reine Amélie* 1835-1848
Parisienne, 1798-1814, Gunboat, 280
Parleur, 1795-1795, 4pdr brig-aviso, see *Papillon* 1786-1795
Pas-de-Charge, 1797-1799, Bateau-canonnier, 279
Passage du Po, 1797-1798, Mortar boat, 310
Passe Partout, 1795-1815, Schooner, 242
Passe Partout, 1845-1845, Paddle aviso, see *Anacréon* 1845-1860
Passe Partout, 1846-1870, Screw aviso, 353
Passe-Partout, 1803-1804, Chasse-marée, 258

Passe-Partout, 1837-1845, Cutter, 264
Patience, 1792-1814, Galley, 294
Patiente, 1807-1814, Transport, 414
Patriote, 1785-1821, Two-decker (74-gun), 87
Patriote, 1794-1796, Chasse-marée, 248
Patriote, 1798-1798, Flûte, 378
Patriote, 1799-1800, Bomb vessel, 310
Patriote, 1848-1853, Screw corvette, see *Comte d'Eu* 1846-1848
Pauline, 1793-1798, Gunboat (galiote), 277
Pauline, 1807-1815, 18pdr frigate (44-gun), 144
Pavel, 1809-1810, Corvette, 184
Pavillon National, 1793-1793, Gunboat, 276
Pêcheur, 1795-1795, 4-gun brig, 213
Pégase, 1795-1797, Two-decker (74-gun), see *Barra* 1794-1795
Peggy, 1799-1805, Cutter, 246
Peggy de Greenock (Grenoch), 1794-1795, Flûte, 376
Peï-Ho, 1858-1861, Screw aviso, 363
Peï-ho, 1861-1871, Ironclad floating battery, 426
Pélagie, 1795-1807, 8 x 4pdr brig, 213
Pélican, 1828-1865, Paddle vessel, 317
Pélican, 1847-1885, Screw aviso, 354
Pelletier, 1793-1795, Two-decker (74-gun), see *Séduisant* 1783-1796
Pelletier, 1793-1795, Cutter, 240
Pelletier, 1794-1795, Tartane, 295
Pelopidas, 1794-1796, Flûte, 376
Peltier, 1794-1795, Tartane, see *Pelletier* 1794-1795
Pénélope, 1787-1788, 18pdr frigate (36-gun), 137
Pénélope, 1806-1829, 18pdr frigate (44-gun), 146
Pénélope, 1840-1889, 30pdr frigate (46-gun), 158
Péniches Nos. 1-542, 1803-1813, Péniches, 286
Pensée, 1793-1796, Cutter, 245
Pensée, 1795-1804, 18pdr frigate (44-gun), see *Spartiate* 1794-1795
Pensée, 1796-1796, Cutter, 249
Perçante, 1795-1796, 20 x 8pdr corvette, 170
Perche, 1808-1808, Transport (brig), 415
Perche, 1808-1814, Transport (snow), 415
Perdrix, 1784-1795, 20 x 6pdr corvette, 165
Perdrix, 1813-1813, 20 x 24pdr corvette, 182
Perdrix, 1840-1901, Gabarre, 392
Père Duchêne, 1793-1794, Cutter, 241
Perle, 1790-1793, 18pdr frigate (36-gun), 138
Perle, 1795-1795, Schooner, 259
Perle, 1807-1808, 18pdr frigate (44-gun), see *Pérola* 1807-1808
Perle, 1813-1823, 18pdr frigate (44-gun), 148
Perle, 1859-1869, 18-gun corvette-aviso, 186
Perle, 1860-1863, Schooner, 268
Permuteur, 1795-1795, Brigantine, see *Petite Colette* 1795-1795
Perola, 1794-1795, Transport, 411
Pérola, 1807-1808, 18pdr frigate (44-gun), 156
Pérou, 1781-1792, Flûte, 374
Pérou, 1786-?, Sloop (service craft), 406
Pérou, 1799-1799, Coast defence vessel, 251
Perrier (Le Perier), 1794-1794, Transport, 407
Persane, 1809-1811, Flûte, 379
Persévérante, 1847-1868, 30pdr frigate (60-gun), 113
Pescado, 1830-1830, 16-gun brig-schooner, 237
Pétillante, 1814 cancelled, Gunboat, 291
Petit Barra, 1795-1795, Felucca, 297
Petit Boston, 1793-1793, Schooner, see *Boston* 1793-1793
Petit Cousin, 1782-1786, Gabarre, 385
Petit Diable, 1793-1797, Cutter, 241
Petit Gabarre Écurie No. 4, 1810-1814, Gabarre, 388
Petit Gabarres Écurie Nos. 1-3, 1809-1814, Gabarres, 388
Petit Jacobin, 1793-1794, brig, 213
Petit Jacobin, 1794-1795, Tartane, 297
Petit Page, 1806-1818, Felucca or balancelle, 306

Petit Sans Culotte, 1793-1795, Xebec or tartane, see *Brave Sans Culotte* 1793-1795
Petite Aurore, 1786-1793, Gabarre, see *Aurore* 1786-1793
Petite Cisalpine, 1798-1799, Gunboat, 280
Petite Colette, 1795-1795, Brigantine, 297
Petite Victoire, 1793-1795, Aviso, 250
Pétrel, 1846-1855, Paddle aviso, 339
Péronille, 1794-1795, Transport, 407
Peuple, 1792-1794, Two-decker (80 gun), see *Duc de Bourgogne* 1751-1792
Peuple, 1794-1794, Three-decker, see *Vengeur* 1803-1805
Peuple, 1795-1795, Three-decker, see *États de Bourgogne* 1790-1793
Peuple Souverain, 1792-1798, Two-decker (74-gun), see *Souverain* 1757-1792
Phaeton, 1804-1806, 16-gun brig, 215
Phaéton, 1837-1859, Paddle vessel, 324
Phaéton, 1860-1879, Paddle aviso, 351
Phare, 1835-1865, Paddle vessel, 323
Phénix, 1793-1826, 20 x 6pdr corvette, 175
Phénix, 1797-1797, Galley, 298
Phénix, 1807-1808, 18pdr frigate (44-gun), 156
Phénix, 1848-1874, Paddle aviso, 341
Philippine, 1788-1791, Schooner, 240
Philomèle, 1822-1836, Schooner, 261
Phlégéton, 1853-1868, Screw corvette, 198
Phocéen, 1794-1795, Transport, 407
Phocion, 1792-1793, Two-decker (74-gun), see *Ferme* 1785-1792
Phoenix (Phénix), 1793-1794, Transport, 407
Phoque, 1842-1859, Paddle corvette, 333
Phoque, 1860-1886, Paddle aviso, 350
Physicienne, 1820-1821, Corvette, 194
Piave, 1812-1814, 18pdr frigate (44-gun), 153
Picarde (Picardie), 1814-1827, Prame, see *Ville de Liège* 1806-1815
Piémontaise, 1804-1808, 18pdr frigate (44-gun), 145
Pierre, 1795-1798, Xebec, 295
Piet Hein, 1811-1813, Two-decker (74-gun), 97
Pieter Floriszoon or *Pieter Florisz (Schout-bij-nacht)*, 1810-1813, Gunboat (Dutch), 289
Pilade (Pylade), 1797-1803, Transport (dogger), 406
Pilote, 1840-1865, Transport (schooner), 417
Pilote des Indes, 1778-1790, 10 x 6pdr corvette, 166
Pingouin, 1844-1856, Screw aviso, 362
Pingouin, 1859-1878, Paddle corvette (hulked), see *Phoque* 1842-1859
Pingre de Tesdal, 1805-1795, Transport, 408
Pintade, 1779-1787, Gabarre, 384
Pintade, 1807-1816, Bomb vessel, 311
Pintade, 1818-1887, Gabarre, 391
Pionnier, 1859-1873, Paddle vessel, 350
Pique, 1792-1795, 12pdr frigate (32-gun), see *Fleur de Lys* 1785-1792
Pique, 1794-1794, Transport, 407
Pique, 1862-1895, Screw gunboat, 366
Pivert, 1782-1787, Lugger, 239
Pivert, 1795-1796, Cutter or lugger, see *Montagne* 1793-1795
Platon, 1795-1795, Polacre, 300
Platon, 1845-1846, Paddle corvette, see *Caffarelli* 1847-1883
Pleiade, 1755-1786, 8pdr frigate (32-gun), 121
Plougastel, 1861-1867, Corvette (hulked), see *Héroïne* 1830-1861
Plowers, 1806-1806, Corvette, 183
Plume, 1795-1795, Transport, see *Angélique* 1794-1795
Plumper, 1805-1815, 10-gun gunbrig, 222
Pluton, 1778-1797, Two-decker (74-gun), 85
Pluton, 1786-?, Sloop (service craft), 406
Pluton, 1805-1808, Two-decker (74-gun), 95
Pluton, 1841-1854, Paddle corvette, 326
Pluton, 1865-1873, Two-decker (74-gun), see *Marengo* 1810-1865
Pluvier, 1776-1793, Gabarre, 383
Pluvier, 1795-1801, Tartane, see *Pelletier* 1794-1795
Pluvier, 1808-1811, 16-gun brig, 217

Pluvier, 1837-1869, Cutter, 265
Pluviôse, 1794-1795, Gunboat (tartane), 278
Plymouth, 1799-1801, Lugger, 246
Podor, 1855-1875, Paddle aviso, 349
Poisson Volant, 1782-1786, Cutter, 239
Poisson Volant, 1794-1802, Cutter, 241
Poisson Volant, 1806-1814, Balancelle, 306
Poisson-Volant (*Corvette de pêche No. 10*), 1803-1814, Transport, 413
Polacre No.3, 1811-1814, Transport (polacre), 414
Polasky, 1803-1813, 10-gun brig, 225
Polluce, 1806-1812, 16 x 8pdr brig, see *Castor* 1797-1797
Pollux, 1786-?, Sloop (service craft), 406
Pollux, 1797-1797, 16 x 8pdr brig, 212
Pollux, 1859-1859, Paddle aviso, see *Magicien* 1861-1890
Polonais, 1808-1815, Two-decker (74-gun), 94
Polyphème, 1812-1813, Two-decker (74-gun), 97
Polyphème, 1824-1828, Two-decker (100-gun), see *Tage* 1847-1857
Poméranienne, 1812-1813, Schooner, 259
Pomone, 1785-1794, 24pdr frigate (32-gun), 103
Pomone, 1805-1811, 18pdr frigate (44-gun), 144
Pomone, 1821-1831, 28-gun corvette, 185
Pomone, 1836 cancelled, 30pdr frigate (46-gun), 158
Pomone, 1845-1887, Screw frigate, 160
Pompée, 1791-1793, Two-decker (74-gun), 90
Pompée, 1795-1796, Bateau-canonnier, 278
Pondichéry, 1794-1809, Flûte, see *Morbihan* 1794-1794
Pont d'Arcole, 1803-1816, Lugger or chasse-marée, 258
Ponton, 1865-1875, Bomb vessel (hulked), see *Finistère* 1828-1865
Portefaix, 1782-1785, Flûte, see *Boussole* 1785-1788
Portefaix, 1796-1814, Transport (gabarre), 406
Portefaix (*Petit Gabarre Écurie No.3*), 1809-1820, Gabarre, 388
Porteuse, 1785-1797, Gabarre, 384
Porteuse, 1796-1814, Transport (gabarre), 406
Porteuse, 1810-1810, Gabarre, 388
Portland, 1793-1799, Sloop, 245
Portugaise, 1798-1799, Bomb vessel, 310
Portugaise, 1808-1808, Two-decker (68-gun), see *Princesse de Beira* 1807-1808
Postillon, 1818-1828, colonial brig, 236
Postillon, 1795-1796, Polacre, 300
Postillon, 1799-1813, Felucca, 302
Postillon, 1810-1810, Schooner, 257
Poudre, 1855-1884, Screw gunboat, 365
Poudrière, 1865-1888, 30pdr frigate (hulked), see *Belle Poule* 1834-1865
Poulette, 1781-1793, 20 x 8pdr corvette, 165
Poulette, 1808-1811, Transport (yacht), 416
Poursuivante, 1796-1807, 24pdr frigate (30-gun), 106
Poursuivante, 1844-1891, 30pdr frigate (52-gun), 112
Pourvoyeur, 1793-1826, 4pdr brig, 205
Pourvoyeur, 1840-1875, Transport (brig), 417
Pourvoyeuse, 1772-1786, 24pdr frigate (38-gun), 103
Pourvoyeuse, 1794-1798, Felucca, 297
Pourvoyeuse, 1803-1815, Gabarre, 386
Pourvoyeuse, 1834-1835, Gabarre, see *Recherche* 1835-1868
Pourvoyeuse, 1855-1880, Schooner, 267
Prairial, 1794-1797, Gunboat (tartane), 278
Précieuse, 1778-1816, 12pdr frigate (32-gun), 125
Précieuse, 1812-1814, 18pdr frigate (44-gun), 152
Prégel, 1810-1815, 18pdr frigate (44-gun), 151
Prégent, 1857-1887, Screw aviso, 359
Preneuse, 1795-1799, 18pdr frigate (44-gun), 140
Président, 1804-1806, 18pdr frigate (44-gun), 145
Prévoyant, 1795-1796, Bateau-canonnier, 278
Prévoyante, 1793-1795, Flûte, 375

Prévoyante, 1803-1817, Gabarre, 386
Prévoyante, 1834-1886, Gabarre, 392
Prima, 1799-1800, Galley, see *Raggio* 1799-1800
Primauguet, 1829-1831, 16-gun brig, see *Sylphe* 1831-1857
Primauguet, 1852-1884, Screw corvette, 198
Prince, 1811-1814, Two-decker (80-gun), see *Prince Royal* 1810-1811
Prince Eugène, 1857 not built, Screw two-decker, 75
Prince Impérial, 1857 not built, Screw two-decker, 75
Prince Jérôme, 1853-1870, Screw two-decker, 69
Prince Royal, 1810-1811, Two-decker (80-gun), 61
Princesa Real, 1807-1808, Flûte, 381
Princesse Auguste, 1806-1814, 18-gun brig, see *Principessa Augusta* 1806-1814
Princesse de Beira, 1807-1808, Two-decker (68-gun), 82
Princesse de Bologne, 1811-1814, 18pdr frigate (44-gun), see *Principessa di Bologna* 1811-1814
Princesse Royale, 1795-1801, Corvette, 176
Principe Achille, 1810-1810, Cutter, 258
Principessa Augusta, 1806-1814, 18-gun brig, 218
Principessa di Bologna, 1810-1811, Schooner, 254
Principessa di Bologna, 1811-1814, 18pdr frigate (44-gun), 153
Printemps, 1795-1815, Cutter, see *Pelletier* 1793-1795
Procida, 1845-1846, 3-gun brig-schooner, 237
Prodigiosa, 1806-1813, Gunboat (Italian), 287
Prométhée, 1848-1868, Paddle aviso, 341
Prompt, 1793-1795, 16-gun corvette, 175
Prompte, 1792-1793, 20 x 6pdr corvette, 167
Prony, 1847-1861, Paddle corvette, 335
Prosélyte, 1786-1793, 12pdr frigate (32-gun), 128
Proserpina, 1807-1814, Felucca, 302
Proserpine, 1783-1796, 18pdr frigate (36-gun), 136
Proserpine, 1797-1797, Galley, 298
Proserpine, 1809-1866, 18pdr frigate (40-gun), 156
Protecteur, 1760-1789, Two-decker (74-gun), 84
Protecteur, 1799-1799, Coast defence vessel, 251
Protecteur, 1847 cancelled, Ironclad floating battery, 424
Protectrice, 1793-1803, Gunboat, 274
Protectrice, 1866-1890, Ironclad floating battery, 428
Protée, 1786-?, Sloop (service craft), 406
Protée, 1860-1868, Paddle aviso, 351
Provençal, 1804-1816, Tartane gunboat, 302
Provençale, 1821-1828, Schooner, 261
Provençale, 1841-1892, Gabarre, 392
Provence, 1815-1830, Two-decker (74-gun), 100
Provence, 1863-1893, Ironclad frigate, 423
Providence, 1793-1794, Brigantine, 296
Providence, 1796-1796, Lugger, 248
Providence, 1798-1803, Schooner, 250
Providence, 1845 cancelled, Gabarre, 392
Prudence, 1865-1898, 30pdr frigate (hulked), see *Jeanne d'Arc* 1847-1865
Prudent, 1794-1794, Transport, 407
Prudent (*Prudence*), 1795-1797, Bateau-plat, 272
Prudente, 1790-1799, 12pdr frigate (32-gun), 129
Prudente, 1810-1844, Gabarre, 388
Prudente, 1842-1855, Gabarre, 392
Psiche, 1807-1808, Schooner, 252
Psyche, 1837 cancelled, 30pdr frigate (46-gun), 159
Psyché, 1798-1805, 12pdr frigate (36-gun), 134
Psyché, 1807-1808, Schooner, see *Psiche* 1807-1808
Psyché, 1814-1821, 18pdr frigate (44-gun), see *Jahde* 1812-1815
Psyché, 1831 cancelled, 30pdr frigate (46-gun), 158
Psyché, 1844-1879, 30pdr frigate (40-gun), 159

Puce, 1808-1815, Transport (galiote), 416
Puissant, 1782-1793, Two-decker (74-gun), 86
Pultusk, 1807-1814, Two-decker (74-gun), 95
Pulvérisateur (*Pulvériseur*), 1801-1801, Bomb vessel, 310
Pygmée, 1860-1873, Paddle aviso, 351
Pylade, 1797-1797, Cutter, 247
Pylade, 1805-1808, 16-gun brig, 214
Pylade, 1833-1865, 20-gun brig, 231
Pyrrhus, 1791-1793, Two-decker (74-gun), 89

Quartidi, 1794-1803, Cutter, 245
Quartier Morin, 1794-1794, Flûte, 377
Quatorze Juillet, 1795-1808, Two-decker (74-gun), see *Tonnerre* 1808-1809
Quatorze Juillet, 1798-1798, Two-decker (74-gun), 91
Quatorze Juillet, 1798-1802, Two-decker (74-gun), see *Vétéran* 1803-1842
Quatre Frères, 1794-1794, Transport (galiote), 407
Quatre-Soeurs, 1794-1795, Transport, 407
Qui-Vive, 1796-1799, Bateau-canonnier, 279

Rafale, 1855-1865, Screw gun launch, 367
Raffermie, 1795-1799, Flûte, see *Républicaine* 1795-1795
Rafleur, 1793-1794, Lugger, 248
Raggio, 1799-1800, Galley, 302
Ragusaise, 1810-1814, Péniche, 293
Ragusas, 1810-1813, Transport, 416
Railleur, 1795-1798, 14-gun brig, see *Républicain* 1793-1795
Railleur, 1810-1822, 16-gun brig, 217
Railleur, 1848-1862, 6-gun brig-aviso, 236
Railleuse, 1779-1798, 12pdr frigate (32-gun), 126
Railleuse, 1825-1839, 16-gun brig, 227
Raison, 1794-1795, Flûte, 377
Rameur, 1831-1878, Paddle vessel, 321
Ramier, 1818-1828, Schooner-aviso, see *Mouche No.20* 1809-1818
Ramier, 1834-1847, Paddle vessel, 325
Rance, 1845 cancelled, Gabarre, 392
Rancune, 1813-1815, 18pdr frigate (44-gun), 151
Ranger, 1794-1797, Cutter, 245
Rapace, 1804-1827, Lugger, see *Lougre No.1* 1803-1804
Rapide, 1807-1808, Schooner-aviso, see *Villaret* 1806-1807
Rapide, 1810-1811, Schooner, 258
Rapide, 1823-1840, Paddle vessel, 316
Rapide, 1841-1860, Paddle aviso, 346
Rapide, 1873-1891, Paddle yacht, 352
'*Raschgoun* (*Rasgouhn, Rachgoun*)', 1832-1844, Balancelle, 308
Rassurante, 1795-1798, 18pdr frigate (42-gun), see *Carmagnole* 1793-1800
Ravisseur, 1795-1796, Cutter, see *Renommée* 1794-1801
Rayon, 1795-1798, Lugger, see *Républicain* 1793-1795
Reale Italiano, 1812-1814, Two-decker (74-gun), 96
Rebecca, 1799-1799, Chasse-marée, 248
Rebecca, 1800-1815, Transport (sloop), 409
Receleur, 1795-1795, Lugger, see *Républicaine* 1794-1795
Recherche, 1791-1794, Gabarre, see *Truite* 1787-1791
Recherche, 1804-1805, Hydrographic vessel, see *Marc* 1803-1814
Recherche, 1816-1827, Schooner, 259
Recherche, 1835-1868, Gabarre, 392
Réciproque, 1794-1795, Flûte, 377
Récompense, 1794-1798, Gunboat (tartane), 277
Reconnaissant, 1799-1801, Aviso, 250
Redbridge (*Red-Bridge*), 1803-1814, Schooner-gunboat, 256
Redoutable, 1795-1805, Two-decker (74-gun), see *Suffren* 1791-1795
Redoutable, 1803-1805, Half-xebec, 304
Redoutable, 1855-1874, Screw two-decker, 71

Redoute, 1855-1879, Screw gunboat, 365
Réfléchi, 1776-1793, Two-decker (64-gun), 79
Reflex, 1795-1795, Lugger, see *Résolue* 1794-1795
Réformateur, 1795-1795, Xebec, see *Saint Ramond* 1794-1794
Refuge, 1866-1940, Ironclad floating battery, 428
Régénérateur, 1811-1814, Two-decker (74-gun), see *Rigeneratore* 1811-1814
Régénéré, 1794-1795, Xebec, see *Saint Ramond* 1794-1794
Régénérée, 1794-1801, 12pdr frigate (40-gun), 131
Régénérée, 1797-1797, Transport, 408
Régulus, 1805-1814, Two-decker (74-gun), 91
Reine, 1795-1798, Flûte, 376
Reine, 1810-1811, 18pdr frigate (50-gun), 155
Reine Amélie, 1835-1848, Yacht, 314
Reine Blanche, 1837-1865, 30pdr frigate (52-gun), 113
Reine Hortense, 1852-1853, Screw corvette, see *Roland* 1850-1870
Reine Hortense, 1853-1867, Screw corvette, see *Comte d'Eu* 1846-1848
Reine Hortense, 1867-1870, Screw aviso, see *Cassard* 1859-1867
Réjouie, 1795-1809, 6 x 24pdr corvette, 171
Réjouissant, 1795-1795, Half-xebec, see *Revanche* 1794-1800
Remise, 1850-1894, Corvette (hulked), see *Cybèle* 1836-1850
Remorqueur, 1832-1841, Paddle vessel, 321
Rempart, 1861 cancelled, Ironclad floating battery, 426
Renard, 1793-1803, Lugger, 241
Renard, 1810-1814, 16-gun brig, 217
Renard, 1829-1847, Cutter, 264
Renau (*Renaud*), 1798-1815, Cutter, 246
Renaudin, 1857-1879, Screw aviso, 359
René-Marie, 1794-1795, Transport, 408
Renommée, 1794-1801, Cutter, 249
Renommée, 1795-1796, 12pdr frigate (38-gun), see *Républicaine Française* 1794-1795
Renommée, 1797-1797, Two-decker (64-gun), see *Dubois* 1797-1801
Renommée, 1804-1816, Transport (paquebot), 412
Renommée, 1808-1811, 18pdr frigate (44-gun), 149
Renommée, 1847-1858, 30pdr frigate (60-gun), 110
Renommée, 1856-1898, Screw frigate, 117
Réolaise, 1793-1800, 18 x 4pdr corvette, 175
Reprise, 1795-1797, 20 x 6pdr corvette, see *Révolutionnaire* 1793-1795
Reprise, 1800-1805, Felucca or bateau, 302
Reptile, 1795-1795, Felucca, see *Républicaine* 1793-1795
Républicain, 1792-1794, Three-decker, see *Royal Louis* 1780-1792
Républicain, 1793-1793, Aviso, 250
Républicain, 1793-1794, 18 x 8pdr corvette, 171
Républicain, 1793-1795, 14-gun brig, 213
Républicain, 1793-1795, Lugger, 248
Républicain, 1793-1799, Three-decker (projected), 45
Républicain, 1794-1794, Transport, 407
Républicain, 1794-1795, Flûte, 377
Républicain, 1794-1795, Transport, 408
Républicain, 1795-1796, Two-decker (74-gun), see *Pyrrhus* 1791-1793
Républicain, 1797-1808, Three-decker, see *Majestueux* 1780-1797
Républicain, 1798-1798, Transport (brig), 409
Républicaine, 1793-1795, Felucca, 296
Républicaine, 1794-1795, Lugger, 248
Républicaine, 1794-1799, 22 x 8pdr corvette, 168
Républicaine, 1795-1795, 18 x 4pdr corvette, 178
Républicaine, 1795-1795, 12 x 4pdr brig, see *Citoyenne Française* 1795-1800
Républicaine, 1795-1795, Flûte, 377

Républicaine, 1799-1799, Transport, 409
Républicaine Française, 1794-1795, 12pdr frigate (38-gun), 130
Républicaine No.2, 1794-1795, Corvette, 177
République, 1793-1800, Floating battery, 312
République, 1795-1795, Tartane, see *République Française* 1793-1795
République Française, 1793-1795, Tartane, 296
République Française, 1802-1803, Three-decker, 46
République Italienne, 1803-1803, 18pdr frigate (44-gun), see *Hermione* 1804-1808
Requin, 1793-1795, Cutter, 241
Requin, 1798-1799, Felucca, 297
Requin, 1801 cancelled, 16-gun brig, 211
Requin, 1806-1808, 16-gun brig, 217
Requin, 1808-1822, Lugger, see *Marie-Joseph* 1803-1808
Requin, 1828-1837, Paddle vessel, 318
Requin, 1847-1874, Paddle aviso, 340
Réserve, 1805-1806, Two-decker (74-gun), see *Zélé* 1763-1805
Réservoir (hulk), 1860-1869, Cutter (hulked), see *Favori* 1842-1860
Résistance, 1795-1797, 24pdr frigate (48-gun), 105
Résistance, 1845-1847, 16-gun brig, 237
Résolue, 1778-1798, 12pdr frigate (32-gun), 124
Résolue, 1794-1795, Lugger, 248
Résolue, 1795-1795, Xebec, see *O Hydra* 1794-1795
Résolue, 1830-1833, 18pdr frigate (44-gun), see *Dryade* 1812-1815
Résolue, 1863-1869, 30pdr frigate (40-gun), 160
Résolue, 1869-1913, Screw frigate, 162
Résolution, 1784-1789, Two-decker (50-gun), see *Romulus* 1781-1784
Résolution, 1793-1794, 16-gun brig, 211
Résolution, 1795-1796, Bateau-canonnier, 278
Resplendissante, 1795-1795, Felucca, see *Surveillante* 1793-1795
Ressource, 1805-1809, Transport, 413
Ressource, 1860-1861, Transport, 418
Ressouvenir, 1795-1795, Transport, see *René-Marie* 1794-1795
Réunion, 1786-1793, 12pdr frigate (32-gun), 129
Revanche, 1794-1800, Half-xebec, 299
Revanche, 1795-1824, 24pdr frigate (30-gun), 105
Revanche, 1798-1813, Felucca gunboat, 296
Revanche, 1865-1893, Ironclad frigate, 423
Réveil, 1861 cancelled, Ironclad floating battery, 426
Révolution, 1793-1795, Bomb vessel, see *Galiote Hollandaise* 1793-1793
Révolution, 1793-1803, Two-decker (74-gun), see *Thésée* 1790-1793
Révolution, 1794-1794, 20 x 6pdr corvette, 178
Révolutionnaire, 1793-1794, Tartane, 296
Révolutionnaire, 1793-1794, Xebec, 296
Révolutionnaire, 1793-1795, 20 x 6pdr corvette, 167
Révolutionnaire, 1793-1796, Three-decker, see *Bretagne* 1766-1793
Révolutionnaire, 1794-1794, 18pdr frigate (44-gun), 139
Révolutionnaire, 1794-1794, Transport, 407
Révolutionnaire, 1795-1796, Bateau-canonnier, 278
Reynst (Admiraal), 1810-1813, Gunboat (Dutch), 289
Rhin, 1802-1806, 18pdr frigate (44-gun), 140
Rhin, 1841-1854, Corvette de charge, 383
Rhin, 1855-1910, Screw transport, 399
Rhinocéros, 1794-1816, Gabarre, 385
Rhinocéros, 1812-1815, Flûte, 380
Rhinocéros, 1821-1843, Large transport, 396
Rhône, 1781-1790, Gabarre, 384
Rhône, 1805-1836, Flûte, 375
Rhône, 1847 cancelled, Gabarre, 393
Rhône, 1859-1899, Screw transport, 401
Richemont, 1781-1793, 12pdr frigate (32-gun), 127

Ridder van Unie, 1810 cancelled, 18pdr frigate (50-gun), 155
Rigeneratore, 1811-1814, Two-decker (74-gun), 96
Rivale, 1795-1795, Gunboat (chasse-marée), see *Tonnerre* 1793-1795
Rivoli, 1797-1799, 16 x 8pdr brig, see *Castor* 1797-1797
Rivoli, 1806-1807, 16-gun brig, see *Serpent* 1807-1808
Rivoli, 1810-1812, Two-decker (74-gun), 96
Rob, 1810-1813, Gunboat (Dutch), 288
Robert, 1797-1818, Two-decker (66-gun), 80
Robuste, 1793-1796, 10-gun brig, 213
Robuste, 1806-1809, Two-decker (80-gun), 58
Robuste, 1828-1865, Gabarre, 391
Robuste, 1836-1836, Gabarre, see *Charente* 1809-1839
Rochefort, 1787-?, Yacht, 313
Rochefort, 1797-1798, Gabarre, 385
Rôdeur, 1822-1850, Cutter, 262
Rôdeur, 1855-1866, Screw aviso, 362
Roemer Vlack, 1810-1813, Gunboat (Dutch), 289
Roland, 1850-1870, Screw corvette, 196
Rolla, 1805-1806, 10-gun brig, 222
Romaine, 1794-1816, 24pdr frigate (30-gun), 105
Romaine, 1798-1799, Felucca gunboat, 296
Romaine, 1798-1801, Half-galley, 300
Romulus, 1781-1784, Two-decker (50 gun), 76
Romulus, 1812-1821, Two-decker (74-gun), 99
Ronco, 1808-1808, 18-gun brig, 219
Rondinella, 1799-1809, 18 x 12pdr corvette, 176
Rose, 1797-1797, Galley, see *Andromaque* 1797-1797
Rose, 1810-1815, Schooner, 254
Rose, 1823-1844, Schooner, 262
Rose-Éléonore, 1794-1795, Transport, 407
Rosette, 1795-1803, Bateau-canonnier, 278
Rosine, 1794-1813, 10-gun brig, 212
Rossignol, 1769-1796, 16 x 6pdr corvette, 163
Rossignol, 1817-1817, Schooner-aviso, see *Mouche No.12* 1808-1817
Rossignol, 1843-1865, 10-gun brig-aviso, 234
Rossolis, 1808-1809, Corvette, 185
Rotterdam, 1811-1814, Two-decker (68-gun), see *Commerce de Rotterdam* 1810-1811
Rouget, 1814-1815, Transport, see *Marie Graty* 1795-1814
Rousse, 1793-1803, Bomb vessel, 309
Rovignoise, 1810-1814, Péniche, 293
Royal, 1806-1808, Two-decker (74-gun), see *Royal Hollandais* 1808-1809
Royal Charles, 1824-1830, Two-decker (100-gun), see *Jemmapes* 1840-1890
Royal Charlotte, 1793-1797, Lugger, 245
Royal Dauphin, 1782-1787, Gabarre, see *Dauphin Royal* 1782-1787
Royal Hollandais, 1808-1809, Two-decker (74-gun), 96
Royal Hollandais, 1810-1811, Two-decker (80-gun), 61
Royal Hollandais, 1810-1814, 12-gun brig, 225
Royal Italien, 1812-1814, Two-decker (74-gun), see *Reale Italiano* 1812-1814
Royal Louis, 1780-1792, Three-decker, 44
Royal Louis, 1814-1825, Three-decker, see *Impérial* 1811-1815
Royaliste, 1792-1793, Flûte, see *Bienvenue* 1788-1794
Rubis, 1812-1813, 18pdr frigate (44-gun), 149
Rubis, 1841-1865, Paddle aviso, 347
Ruby, 1810-1810, 12-gun brig, 225
Ruche, 1808-1814, Transport (schooner), 416
Rude, 1793-1795, Gunboat, 275
Ruisseleuse, 1794-1795, Tartane, see *Républicaine Française* 1793-1795
Ruither, 1795-1796, Bateau-canonnier, 278
Ruppel, 1812-1814, 18pdr frigate (44-gun), 152
Rusé, 1794-1795, Lugger, 248
Rusé, 1814-1835, 16-gun brig, 218
Rusé, 1848-1862, 6-gun brig-aviso, 236

Rusée, 1778-1793, Gunboat, 271
Rustique, 1795-1795, Bomb vessel, see *Galiote Hollandaise* 1793-1793
Rutlan, 1794-1794, Aviso, 250
Rutland, 1794-1796, Lugger, 245

Saale, 1810-1815, 18pdr frigate (44-gun), 147
Sabine, 1834-1854, 20 x 30pdr corvette, 189
Sagesse, 1794-1803, 20 x 8pdr corvette, 170
Sagittaire, 1761-1788, Two-decker (50-gun), 76
Saïgon, 1860-1860, Paddle aviso, 345
Saïgon, 1861-1884, Ironclad floating battery, 426
Saint Antoine, 1800-1801, Two-decker (74-gun), 93
Saint Antoine, 1808-1809, Felucca, 306
Saint Esprit, 1765-1794, Two-decker (80-gun), 55
Saint François, 1778-1789, Transport (chasse-marée), 405
Saint François, 1792-1793, Tartane, 296
Saint Genard, 1800-1803, Two-decker (74-gun), 93
Saint Georges, 1797-1797, Two-decker (66-gun), see *Sandos* 1797-1807
Saint Georges, 1797-1797, Half-xebec, 298
Saint Guillaume, 1784-1789, Transport (chasse-marée), 405
Saint Hilaire, 1798-1802, Xebec, 300
Saint Jean, 1789-1789, Transport (chasse-marée), 405
Saint Jean-Baptiste, 1796-1802, Transport (chasse-marée), 408
Saint Jean-Baptiste, 1798-1799, Transport (bombarde), 409
Saint Jean-Baptiste, 1801-1801, Gunboat, see *Espérance* 1798-1801
Saint Louis, 1828-1832, Two-decker (100-gun), see *Tage* 1847-1857
Saint Louis, 1854-1857, Two-decker (90-gun), 66
Saint Louis, 1857-1893, Screw two-decker, 73
Saint Martin, 1839-1841, 5-gun brig-schooner, 237
Saint Martin, 1845-1846, 22-gun brig, 237
Saint Michel, 1741-1787, Two-decker (64-gun), 78
Saint Nicolas, 1796-1796, Transport, 408
Saint Philippe, 1798-1799, 2 x 12pdr brig, 212
Saint Pierre, 1795-1795, Cutter, see *Trois Couleurs* 1793-1796
Saint Pierre, 1802-1813, 16-gun brig, see *Colibri* 1802-1802
Saint Pierre, 1809-1819, Two-decker (74-gun), 101
Saint Ramond, 1794-1794, Xebec, 297
Saint Sébastien, 1799-1799, Two-decker (74-gun), 93
Saint Sébastien, 1807-1808, Two-decker (68-gun), 82
Sainte Anne, 1798-1799, Transport, 409
Sainte Anne (No.14), 1860-1872, Screw sectional gun launch, 370
Sainte Catherine, 1787-1787, 18 x 6pdr corvette, see *Subtile* 1777-1791
Sainte Croix, 1793-1793, Schooner, 249
Sainte Lucie, 1779-1801, Gunboat, 271
Sainte Marie (No.21), 1860-1872, Screw sectional gun launch, 370
Sainte-Barbe, 1855-1865, Screw gunboat, 365
Sainte-Hélène, 1798-1801, Gunboat (djerme), 280
Sainte-Marie, 1794-1794, Gunboat (tartane), 277
Saint-Esprit, 1798-1798, Transport (brig), 409
Saint-Jacques, 1794-1799, Gunboat (brig or dogger), 277
Saint-Ouen, 1829-1831, 20-gun brig, see *Pylade* 1833-1865
Saint-Pierre, 1794-1795, Transport (lugger), 407
Saint-Vincent, 1794-1795, Transport, 408
Saisissante, 1795-1795, Flûte, see *Suffren* 1794-1797

Saisson, 1795-1796, 16 x 8pdr corvette, see *Spartiate* 1793-1795
Sakalave, 1855-1869, Schooner, 270
Salamandre, 1754-1791, Bomb vessel, 309
Salamandre, 1793-1806, Bomb vessel, 309
Salamandre, 1811-1826, Flûte, 379
Salamandre, 1833-1835, Paddle vessel, 319
Salamandre, 1847-1871, Screw aviso, 353
Salamine, 1798-1799, 18 x 6pdr brig, see *Infante* 1793-1798
Salamine, 1812-1813, Gunboat (felucca or trincadour), 292
Sally, 1795-1801, 8 x 6pdr brig, 212
Sally, 1797-1797, Cutter, 246
Salona, 1810-1814, Péniche, 293
Salpêtre, 1811-1837, Gunboat, 291
Salve, 1855-1875, Screw gunboat, 366
San Nicola, 1798-1799, Galley, see *Santa Ferma* 1798-1799
Sandos, 1797-1807, Two-decker (66-gun), 80
Sandwich, 1799-1803, Cutter, 246
Sané, 1847-1859, Paddle frigate, 329
Sans Abus, 1795-1795, Transport, see *Sans Culotte* 1794-1795
Sans Crainte, 1795-1797, Tartane, see *Sans Peur* 1794-1795
Sans Culotide, 1794-1795, 22 x 6pdr corvette, 171
Sans Culotte, 1792-1795, Three-decker, see *Dauphin Royal* 1791-1792
Sans Culotte, 1793-1794, brig, 213
Sans Culotte, 1793-1795, Aviso, 247
Sans Culotte, 1794-1795, Transport, 407
Sans Culotte, 1795-1795, 18-gun corvette, 178
Sans Pareil, 1793-1794, Two-decker (80-gun), 57
Sans Pareil, 1813 cancelled, Three-decker, 48
Sans Pareille, 1798-1801, 18 x 8pdr corvette, 174
Sans Peur, 1794-1795, Tartane, 295
Sans Peur, 1794-1797, 12 x 6pdr brig, 213
Sans Quartier, 1794-1799, Lugger, 241
Sans-Culotte, 1793-1795, Brigantine, 296
Sans-Culotte de Calais, 1794-1795, Transport, 407
Sans-Façon, 1810-1811, Schooner, 258
Sans-Peur, 1797-1798, Bateau-canonnier, 279
Sans-Peur, 1807-1807, 20 x 24pdr corvette, 183
Sans-Pitié, 1798-1815, Prame, 272
Sans-Quartier, 1801-1801, Tartane?, see *Joyeuse* 1793-1795
Sans-Souci, 1788-1793, 4pdr brig-aviso, 204
Sans-Souci, 1794-1803, Cutter, 242
Sans-Souci, 1811-1814, 16-gun brig, 218
Santa Ferma, 1798-1799, Galley, 301
Santa Lucia, 1798-1800, Galley, 301
Santa Marina, 1798-1798, Transport (brig), 409
Santander, 1808-1812, Lugger, 257
Santi Petri, 1823-1862, Two-decker (80-gun), see *Centaure* 1818-1823
Santo Christo, 1823-1823, Schooner, 268
Saône, 1798-1799, Bateau-canonnier, 280
Saône, 1830-1833, Corvette de charge, 382
Saône, 1855-1875, Screw transport, 399
Sapeur, 1812-1814, 16-gun brig, 218
Sapho, 1809-1825, 20 x 8pdr corvette, 179
Sapho, 1831-1843, 20 x 30pdr corvette, 189
Sarcelle, 1808-1829, Gabarre, 388
Sarcelle, 1838-1860, Gabarre, 392
Sardine, 1771-1796, 16 x 6pdr corvette, 164
Sardine, 1794-1795, Trincadour, 297
Sardine, 1801 cancelled, 16-gun brig, 211
Sardine, 1806-1807, Transport, 413
Sardine, 1814-1815, Transport, see *Jean Leep* 1805-1814
Sarthe, 1862-1901, Screw transport, 403
Saturne, 1805-1807, Two-decker (80-gun), see *Eylau* 1804-1829
Saturne, 1814 cancelled, Two-decker (80 gun), 60
Satyre, 1795-1795, Lugger, see *Surveillant* 1793-1795
Saumon, 1776-1787, Gabarre, 384
Saumon, 1795-1803, Lugger, 242

Saumon, 1805-1813, Transport (brig), 414
Saumon, 1822-1847, Transport (brig), 417
Sauterelle, 1817-1819, Schooner, 260
Sauterne, 1813-1819, Schooner, see *Soterne* 1813-1819
Savant, 1795-1796, Aviso, see *Société Populaire* 1793-1795
Savoie, 1864-1889, Ironclad frigate, 423
Sceptre, 1780-1792, Two-decker (74-gun), 86
Sceptre, 1810-1830, Two-decker (80-gun), 58
Sceptre, 1835-1850, Two-decker (90-gun), see *Masséna* 1850-1860
Scévola, 1793-1796, 36pdr rasée frigate, 104
Schram (*Vice-admiraal*), 1810-1813, Gunboat (Dutch), 289
Schrijver (*Admiraal*), 1810-1813, Gunboat (Dutch), 289
Scipion, 1778-1782, Two-decker (74-gun), 85
Scipion, 1790-1793, Two-decker (74-gun), 90
Scipion, 1794-1795, Two-decker (80-gun), see *Saint Esprit* 1765-1794
Scipion, 1801-1805, Two-decker (74-gun), 91
Scipion, 1813-1846, Two-decker (74-gun), 100
Scorpion, 1794-1803, 14-16 x 6pdr corvette, 175
Scout, 1794-1795, 16-gun brig, 211
Sébastopol, 1858 cancelled, Two-decker (70-gun), 102
Sed el Bahr, 1809-1811, Two-decker (80-gun), 61
Séduisant, 1783-1796, Two-decker (74-gun), 87
Seine, 1783-1788, Flûte, 374
Seine, 1793-1798, 18pdr frigate (42-gun), 139
Seine, 1806-1809, Flûte, 378
Seine, 1814-1835, Flûte, see *Escaut* 1803-1815
Seine, 1845-1846, Corvette de charge, 383
Seine, 1856-1885, Screw transport, 400
Sémillante, 1780-1787, 20 x 8pdr corvette, 164
Sémillante, 1791-1808, 12pdr frigate (32-gun), 130
Sémillante, 1841-1855, 30pdr frigate (60-gun), 109
Sémiramis, 1797-1797, Galley, 298
Sémiramis, 1829-1861, 30pdr frigate (60-gun), 110
Sémiramis, 1861-1895, Screw frigate, 118
Sémiramis, 1895-1899, Screw frigate (hulked), see *Magicienne* 1861-1899
Semmering, 1810-1814, Two-decker (74-gun), see *Sigmaring* 1810-1814
Sénateur, 1795-1801, Flûte, see *Sultana* 1794-1801
Sénégal, 1800-1801, 18-gun brig, 213
Sensible, 1787-1798, 12pdr frigate (32-gun), 129
Sentinelle, 1793-1827, Cutter, 240
Sentinelle, 1798-1803, Felucca, 297
Sentinelle, 1807-1810, Schooner, 259
Sentinelle, 1831-1845, Trincadour, see *Trincadour No.6* 1823-1831
Sentinelle, 1848-1877, Iron screw corvette, 197
Septentrion, 1793-1794, Transport, 407
Sérieuse, 1779-1798, 12pdr frigate (32-gun), 125
Sérieuse, 1793-1794, 12pdr brig, 206
Sérieuse, 1848-1889, 30-gun corvette, 193
Serin, 1771-1783, 14 x 6pdr corvette, 163
Serin, 1788-1794, 4pdr brig-aviso, 204
Serin, 1804 cancelled, 16-gun brig, 210
Serin, 1817-1817, Schooner-aviso, see *Mouche No.8* 1808-1817
Serpent, 1807-1808, 16-gun brig, 216
Serpent, 1826-1839, Paddle vessel, 317
Serpent, 1843-1865, Paddle aviso, 346
Serpent, 1852-1865, Paddle aviso, 348
Serpente, 1795-1815, 20 x 18pdr corvette, 173
Serpentin, 1793-1803, Cutter, 241
Sesostris, 1851-1896, Paddle aviso, 343
Seudre, 1842-1856, Transport (brig), 418
Severo, 1806-1807, Two-decker (74-gun), see *Rigeneratore* 1811-1814
Sèvre, 1857-1871, Screw transport, 400
Seybouse, 1837-1839, Balancelle, 308
Shamrock, 1859-1876, Paddle aviso, 351
Sibylle, 1791-1794, 18pdr frigate (42-gun), 138
Sibylle, 1847-1883, 30pdr frigate (52-gun), 112
Sibylle (loaned), 1801-1803, 18pdr frigate (40-gun), see *Minerve* 1801-1801
Sidi-Ferruch, 1830-1835, 14-gun brig-schooner, 237
Siècle, 1797-1809, 10 x 4pdr brig, see *Surveillant* 1793-1797
Sigmaring, 1810-1814, Two-decker (74-gun), 97
Silène, 1814-1830, 16-gun brig, 218
Simplon, 1810-1815, 16-gun brig, see *Mercure* 1806-1810
Sincère, 1784-1793, 16 x 6pdr corvette, 166
Sincère, 1794-1795, Flûte, 377
Sinon, 1793-1816, Gunboat (chasse-marée), 276
Sirène, 1782-1787, Gabarre, 385
Sirène, 1795-1825, 12pdr frigate (40-gun), 131
Sirène, 1814-1837, 18pdr frigate (44-gun), see *Milanaise* 1805-1815
Sirène, 1823-1871, 24pdr frigate (58-gun), 107
Sirène (*Syrène*), 1808-1814, Xebec or half-xebec, 305
Sirène (*Syrène*), 1809-1809, Half-xebec, 306
Six Frères, 1794-1794, Transport (galiote), 411
Six Soeurs, 1794-1795, Schooner, 245
Société, 1793-1794, Flûte, 376
Société, 1795-1811, 16 x 8pdr corvette, see *Société Populaire* 1794-1795
Société d'Ayeau, 1793-1793, Brigantine, 296
Société Populaire, 1793-1795, Aviso, 250
Société Populaire, 1794-1795, 16 x 8pdr corvette, 170
Socrate, 1844-1846, Paddle corvette, see *Prony* 1847-1861
Soeurs, 1794-1795, Flûte, 377
Soigneux (*Sougneuse*), 1795-1795, Brigantine, see *Sans-Culotte* 1793-1795
Soldat, 1796-1798, Bateau-canonnier, 279
Solférino, 1861-1884, Ironclad frigate, 422
Solide, 1811-1814, Transport (galiote), see *Nossa Senhora da Solidao* 1808-1810
Solon, 1846-1879, Paddle aviso, 338
Somerset, 1794-1795, Lugger, 245
Somme, 1840-1851, Corvette de charge, 382
Somme, 1856-1887, Screw transport, 400
Sophie, 1794-1794, Transport, 407
Sophie, 1794-1795, 20 x 8pdr corvette, 177
Sophie, 1795-1797, Aviso, 250
Sophie, 1811-1813, brig or polacre, 226
Sorcier, 1808-1813, Transport (brig), 416
Sorro, 1794-1795, Transport, 411
Soterne, 1813-1819, Schooner, 256
Soucieuse, 1795-1816, 22 x 6pdr corvette, see *Sans Culotide* 1794-1795
Souffleur, 1794-1814, Cutter, 241
Souffleur, 1828-1865, Paddle vessel, 317
Souffleur, 1849-1900, Paddle corvette, 337
Souris, 1793-1798, Gunboat (chasse-marée), 276
Souris, 1808-1813, Transport (yacht), 416
Souris, 1846-1855, Schooner, 266
Soute, 1869-1871, Paddle aviso (hulked), see *Marabout* 1852-1869
Souverain, 1757-1792, Two-decker (74-gun), 84
Souverain, 1819-1854, Three-decker, 48
Souverain, 1854-1905, Screw three-decker, 53
Souveraine, 1856-1892, Screw frigate, 116
Sovrana, 1806-1814, Gunboat (Italian), 287
Spartiate, 1793-1795, 16 x 8pdr corvette, 177
Spartiate, 1794-1794, Corvette, 177
Spartiate, 1794-1794, Corvette, 177
Spartiate, 1794-1795, 18pdr frigate (44-gun), 139
Spartiate, 1798-1798, Two-decker (74-gun), 91
Sparviero, 1806-1810, 12-gun brig, 223
Speedy, 1794-1802, 14-gun brig, 211
Speranza, 1807-1807, 32-gun corvette, see *Carolina* 1807-1814
Sphinx, 1776-1802, Two-decker (64-gun), 79
Sphinx, 1813-1814, 16-gun brig, 218
Sphinx, 1829-1845, Paddle vessel, 319
Sphinx, 1860-1873, Paddle aviso, 351
Spongeux, 1795-1795, Trincadour, see *Sardine* 1794-1795
Staghouwer (*Schout-bij-nacht*), 1810-1813, Gunboat (Dutch), 289
Stanislas, 1794-1794, Transport, 407
Stationnaire, 1799-1799, Coast defence vessel, 251
Steck (*Steeck*), 1794-1802, Lugger, 245
Stengel, 1797-1799, Two-decker (64-gun), 81
Stoicien, 1795-1795, Transport (lugger), see *Saint-Pierre* 1794-1795
Streatham, 1809-1809, Flûte, 380
Strela, 1809-1814, Cutter, 258
Stridente, 1855-1859, Screw gun launch, 368
Styx, 1834-1867, Paddle vessel, 323
Suappop, 1812-1813, 12-gun brig, 226
Subtil, 1793-1797, 4pdr brig, 206
Subtile, 1777-1791, 18 x 6pdr corvette, 164
Subtile, 1793-1826, Gunboat, 274
Subtile, 1799-1799, Aviso, 251
Succes, 1793-1797, Cutter, 244
Succes, 1801-1807, Cutter, 246
Succès, 1801-1801, 12pdr frigate (38-gun), 134
Suffisant, 1782-1793, Two-decker (74-gun), 86
Suffisant, 1793-1795, 6pdr brig, 205
Suffren, 1791-1795, Two-decker (74-gun), 89
Suffren, 1793-1808, Flûte, 376
Suffren, 1794-1797, Flûte, 377
Suffren, 1799-1799, Schooner, 250
Suffren, 1803-1823, Two-decker (74-gun), 91
Suffren, 1829-1865, Two-decker (90-gun), 65
Sultan, 1794-1795, Flûte, see *Sultana* 1794-1801
Sultana, 1794-1801, Flûte, 376
Sultane, 1765-1793, 12pdr frigate (32-gun), 123
Sultane, 1803-1805, 18pdr frigate (44-gun), see *Italienne* 1806-1816
Sultane, 1813-1814, 18pdr frigate (44-gun), 149
Sultane, 1847-1855, Schooner, 270
Superbe, 1784-1795, Two-decker (74-gun), 87
Superbe, 1794-1795, Flûte, 377
Superbe, 1805-1807, Two-decker (74-gun), see *Breslaw* 1808-1837
Superbe, 1814-1833, Two-decker (74-gun), 98
Surcouf, 1858-1885, Screw aviso, 358
Surprenant, 1795-1795, Transport, see *Saint-Vincent* 1794-1795
Surprise, 1783-1789, Cutter, 239
Surprise, 1793-1803, Gunboat, 275
Surprise, 1794-1794, Cutter, 245
Surprise, 1825-1865, 16-gun brig, 227
Surprise, 1863-1885, Screw gunboat, 366
Surveillant, 1786-1786, Schooner, 240
Surveillant, 1793-1795, Lugger, 245
Surveillant, 1793-1797, 4 x 4pdr cutter, 213
Surveillant, 1795-1796, Bateau-canonnier, 278
Surveillant, 1797-1801, Bateau-canonnier, 279
Surveillant, 1800-1811, 16-gun brig, 209
Surveillant, 1804-1809, 8-gun brig, 225
Surveillant, 1855-1868, Paddle aviso, 349
Surveillante, 1778-1797, 12pdr frigate (32-gun), 124
Surveillante, 1793-1795, Felucca, 299
Surveillante, 1794-1795, 6-gun brig, 212
Surveillante, 1794-1795, Schooner, 245
Surveillante, 1796-1796, Aviso, 250
Surveillante, 1802-1803, 18pdr frigate (44-gun), 140
Surveillante, 1807-1809, Gunboat, 291
Surveillante, 1819-1837, Gunboat, see *Feu* 1811-1819
Surveillante, 1825-1845, 30pdr frigate (60-gun), 108
Surveillante, 1864-1898, Ironclad frigate, 423
Suzanne, 1794-1796, Transport, 407
Swan, 1795-1796, Cutter, see *Cygne* 1795-1796
Swift No.1, 1794-1795, Transport, 410
Swift No.2, 1794-1795, Transport, 410
Swiftsure, 1801-1805, Two-decker (74-gun), 92
Sylphe, 1782-1788, 4pdr brig, 203
Sylphe, 1804-1808, 16-gun brig, 216
Sylphe, 1831-1857, 16-gun brig, 228
Sylphe, 1861-1887, Screw aviso, 363
Sylphide, 1823-1829, 18-gun corvette-aviso, 186
Syrène, 1823-1871, 24pdr frigate (58-gun), see *Sirène* 1823-1871
Syzygie, 1795-?, Tartane, see *Joyeuse* 1793-1795

Tactique, 1795-1815, 18 x 6pdr corvette, see *Tigre* 1795-1795
Tactique, 1839-1860, 4-gun gunbrig, 231
Tactique, 1863-1886, Screw gunboat, 366
Tafna, 1837-1852, Balancelle, 308
Tage, 1847-1857, Two-decker (100-gun), 64
Tage, 1857-1885, Screw two-decker, 74
Tagliamento, 1799-1799, Gunboat, 280
Talbot, 1794-1803, Lugger, 245
Talisman, 1862-1909, Screw aviso, 362
Tamerlan, 1844 cancelled, Paddle frigate, 334
Tamise, 1793-1796, 12pdr frigate (36-gun), 134
Tanche, 1808-1808, Transport (brig), 416
Tancrède, 1794-1795, Transport, 408
Tancrède, 1861-1867, Screw aviso, 361
Tane Manou, 1852-1859, Schooner, 270
Tanger, 1849-1889, Paddle corvette, 337
Tantale, 1849-1850, Paddle aviso, see *Bisson* 1850-1872
Tapageuse, 1795-1806, 12 x 12pdr corvette, 171
Tardif, 1864-1869, Screw gunboat, 367
Tarleton, 1782-1793, 14 x 6pdr brig, 203
Tarn, 1818-1842, Flûte, 380
Tarn, 1863-1905, Screw transport, 403
Tartare, 1836-1867, Paddle vessel, 324
Tartaria, 1811-1814, Péniche, 293
Teazer, 1805-1811, 10-gun gunbrig, 222
Télégraphe, 1799-1815, Schooner, 243
Téméraire, 1782-1803, Two-decker (74-gun), 87
Téméraire, 1794-1795, Xebec, see *Révolutionnaire* 1793-1794
Téméraire, 1803-1817, Schooner, 259
Tempesta, 1806-1813, Gunboat (Italian), 287
Tempête, 1726-1786, Bomb vessel, 309
Tempête, 1793-1803, Gunboat, 273
Tempête, 1799-1807, Half-galley, 295
Tempête, 1855-1866, Screw gunboat, 365
Temps, 1795-1800, Flûte, see *Destin* 1794-1795
Ténare, 1840-1861, Paddle vessel, 325
Terpsichore, 1812-1814, 18pdr frigate (44-gun), 151
Terpsichore, 1827-1839, 30pdr frigate (60-gun), 110
Terre, 1811-1819, Mortar gunboat, 292
Terreur, 1794-1795, Gunboat (tartane), 278
Terreur, 1794-1804, Cutter, see *Père Duchèsne* 1793-1794
Terreur, 1799-1801, Felucca, 297
Terrible, 1780-1804, Three-decker, 44
Terrible, 1793-1804, Gunboat, 273
Terrible, 1799-1804, Gunboat, 281
Terrible, 1814 cancelled, Three-decker (110-gun), 49
Teulié, 1808-1808, 18-gun brig, 219
Thalie, 1795-1795, 10 x 4pdr corvette, see *Thétis* 1793-1795
Thames, 1794-1795, Transport, see *Thomas* 1794-1795
Thébaïde, 1801-1801, Gunboat (djerme), see *Espérance* 1798-1801
Thémis, 1786-?, Sloop (service craft), 406
Thémis, 1799-1814, 12pdr frigate (40-gun), 131
Thémis, 1814-1832, 18pdr frigate (44-gun), see *Oder* 1813-1815
Thémis, 1836 cancelled, 30pdr frigate (46-gun), 159
Thémis, 1847-1862, 30pdr frigate (50-gun), 114
Thémis, 1862-1931, Screw frigate, 119
Thémistocle, 1791-1793, Two-decker (74-gun), 89
Thémistocle, 1794-1795, Transport, 407
Thémistocle, 1795-1796, Bateau-canonnier, 278
Thérèse, 1799-1800, Coast defence ship, 176
Thermidor, 1794-1795, Gunboat (tartane), 278
Thésée, 1790-1793, Two-decker (74-gun), 89
Thésée, 1806-1807, Two-decker (74-gun), see *Ville de Berlin* 1807-1815
Thétis, 1788-1808, 18pdr frigate (34-gun), 137
Thétis, 1793-1795, 10 x 4pdr corvette, 175
Thétis, 1819-1865, 18pdr frigate (44-gun), 151
Thévenard, 1798-1799, Xebec, 301

INDEX TO NAMED VESSELS 463

Thévenard, 1799-1803, Bomb vessel, 310
Thisbé, 1830-1865, 20 x 30pdr corvette, 190
Thisbé, 1849-1871, 30-gun corvette, 193
Thisbé (Thysbé), 1807-1818, Felucca, 302
Thomas, 1794-1795, Transport, 408
Thomas of Bristol, 1893-1814, Flûte, 375
Tibre, 1814 cancelled, Two-decker (80-gun), 60
Tibre, 1911-1922, Screw frigate (hulked), see *Clorinde* 1857-1911
Tiercelet, 1782-1797, Lugger, 239
Tigre, 1793-1794, Flûte, 376
Tigre, 1793-1795, Two-decker (74-gun), 90
Tigre, 1794-1795, 18 x 6pdr corvette, 167
Tilsit, 1810-1814, Two-decker (80-gun), 59
Tilsitt, 1839-1856, Two-decker (90-gun), 65
Tilsitt, 1856-1887, Screw two-decker, 73
Timoléon, 1794-1798, Two-decker (74-gun), see *Commerce de Bordeaux* 1785-1793
Tirailleuse, 1855-1876, Screw gun launch, 367
Tirone (Tyronne), 1793-1801, Flûte, 375
Tisifone (Tisiphone), 1807-1812, Felucca, 302
Tisiphone, 1851-1875, Paddle corvette, 337
Titan, 1844-1896, Paddle corvette, 334
Titus, 1795-1816, Chasse-marée, see *Argus* 1793-1795
Tjalque Vlyt, 1811-1813, Transport (tjalk), 412
Tjerk Hiddes de Vries (Vice-admiraal), 1810-1813, Gunboat (Dutch), 289
Tocsin, 1811-1837, Gunboat, 291
Tocsin, 1855-1875, Bomb vessel, 312
Tonnant, 1789-1798, Two-decker (80-gun), 57
Tonnant, 1804-1807, Two-decker (80-gun), see *Ville de Varsovie* 1808-1809
Tonnant, 1847 cancelled, Ironclad floating battery, 424
Tonnante, 1799-1813, Half-galley, 295
Tonnante, 1810-1813, Gunboat (half-galley), 292
Tonnante, 1855-1874, Ironclad floating battery, 425
Tonnerre, 1793-1795, Gunboat (chasse-marée), 276
Tonnerre, 1808-1809, Two-decker (74-gun), 91
Tonnerre, 1838-1873, Paddle vessel, 324
Topaze, 1790-1793, 12pdr frigate (32-gun), 129
Topaze, 1805-1809, 18pdr frigate (44-gun), 146
Topaze, 1823-1838, Schooner, 262
Topaze, 1844-1857, Schooner, 261
Torche, 1795-1805, 16 x 18pdr corvette, 172
Torche, 1812-1837, Schooner, 255
Torche, 1855-1858, Bomb vessel, 312
Torpille, 1795-1796, Gunboat (tartane), see *Volcan* 1794-1795
Torre Chica, 1830-1835, 10-gun brig-aviso, 237
Torride, 1795-1797, Gunboat (tartane), see *Union* 1794-1797
Torride, 1797-1799, Cutter, see *Sally* 1797-1797
Tortue, 1795-1798, Gunboat (tartane), see *Vipère* 1794-1795
Tortue, 1807-1814, Bomb vessel, 311*
Toulinguet, 1859-1875, Schooner (hulked), see *Gazelle* 1842-1859
Toulonnaise, 1823-1843, Schooner, 261
Touraine, 1870-1887, Screw frigate, see *Imperatrice Eugénie* 1856-1870
Tourmente, 1795-1795, Gunboat (tartane), see *Terreur* 1794-1795
Tourmente, 1855-1869, Screw gunboat, 365
Tourtereau, 1782-1787, 18 x 6pdr corvette, 165
Tourterelle, 1794-1795, 22 x 8pdr corvette, 168
Tourville, 1788-1841, Two-decker (74-gun), 89
Tourville, 1795-1796, Bateau-canonnier, 278
Tourville, 1811-1822, Two-decker (74-gun), see *Saint Genard* 1800-1803
Tourville, 1847-1853, Two-decker (90-gun), 65
Tourville, 1853-1873, Screw two-decker, 69
Tout-Coeur, 1796-1797, Bateau-canonnier, 279
Traineau, 1795-1795, Transport, see *Thomas* 1794-1795
Trajan, 1792-1797, Two-decker (74-gun), 89
Trajan, 1793-1795, Flûte, 376
Trajan, 1811-1829, Two-decker (74-gun), 98
Transport No. 1, 1806-1809, Transport, 413
Transport No. 2, 1806-1807, Transport (pink), 413
Transport No. 274, 1803-1821, Transport, 412
Transport No. 281, 1804-1821, Transport, 412
Transport No. 3, 1806-1811, Transport (brig), 413
Transport No. 4, 1806-1814, Transport, 413
Transport No. 5, 1806-1807, Transport, 413
Transport No. 6, 1806-1807, Transport, 413
Transport No. 639, 1803-1814, Transport, 412
Transport No. 665, 1803-1814, Transport, 412
Transport No. 698, 1803-1814, Transport, 412
Transport No. 7, 1806-1807, Transport, 413
Transport No. 703, 1803-1814, Transport, 412
Transport No. 964, 1804-1816, Transport, 412
Transports Nos. 1-1165, 1803-1814, Transport, 412
Travail, 1794-1795, Gunboat (tartane), 277
Travailleuse, 1865-1878, 30pdr frigate (hulked), see *Melpomène* 1828-1865
Trave, 1812-1813, 18pdr frigate (44-gun), 152
Treizième (Canonnière No.13), 1803-1804, Bomb vessel, see *Rousse* 1793-1803
Trémentin, 1828-1834, Transport, 418
Trente et un Mai, 1794-1795, Two-decker (74-gun), see *Pyrrhus* 1791-1793
Trevigiana, 1806-1813, Gunboat (Italian), 287
Tribune, 1794-1796, 12pdr frigate (38-gun), see *Charente Inférieure* 1793-1794
Tricolore, 1792-1793, Two-decker (74-gun), see *Lys* 1785-1792
Tricolore, 1794-1794, Aviso, 250
Tricolore, 1799-1803, Schooner, 243
Trident, 1812-1875, Two-decker (74-gun), 99
Triestin, 1810-1813, Transport, 416
Triestine, 1811-1814, Péniche, 293
Trimeuse, 1805-1807, Schooner, 259
Trincadour No.1, 1813-1832, Trincadour, 303
Trincadour No.2, 1813-1832, Trincadour, 303
Trincadour No.3, 1819-1832, Trincadour, 307
Trincadour No.4, 1819-1832, Trincadour, 307
Trincadour No.5, 1819-1832, Trincadour, 307
Trincadour No.6, 1823-1831, Trincadour, 307
Trincadour No.7, 1823-1823, Trincadour, 307
Triomphant, 1779-1806, Two-decker (80-gun), 55
Triomphant, 1809-1825, Two-decker (74-gun), 94
Triomphante, 1804-1817, 6 x 24pdr corvette, 180
Triomphante, 1834-1869, 20 x 30pdr corvette, 187
Triple Alliance, 1786-?, Sloop (service craft), 406
Triton, 1747-1794, Two-decker (64-gun), 78
Triton, 1786-?, Sloop (service craft), 406
Triton, 1794-1797, Transport, 410
Triton, 1796-1796, Flûte, 376
Triton, 1803-1807, Floating battery, 312
Triton, 1807-1808, 12pdr frigate (42-gun), 135
Triton, 1810-1813, Gunboat (Dutch), 289
Triton, 1823-1870, Two-decker (74-gun), 98
Triton, 1876-1879, Two-decker (hulked), see *Bayard* 1859-1876
Trocadéro, 1824-1836, Three-decker, 48
Trois Amis, 1797-1799, Transport, 408
Trois Amis, 1803-1821, Transport (lugger), 413
Trois Couleurs, 1793-1796, Cutter, 241
Trombe, 1795-1795, Gunboat, see *Terrible* 1793-1804
Trombe, 1855-1870, Bomb vessel, 312
Tromp, 1811-1814, Two-decker (68-gun), see *Admiral Tromp* 1810-1811
Tromp (Admiraal Cornelis), 1810-1813, Gunboat (Dutch), 289
Trompette, 1793-1793, Tartane, 296
Trompeur, 1794-1796, Lugger, see *Neptune* 1794-1798
Trompeuse, 1793-1794, 16 x 6pdr brig, 205
Trompeuse, 1809-1813, Half-xebec, see *Sirène* 1809-1809
Troubadour, 1811-1816, Half-xebec or balancelle, see *Bon Patriote* 1811-1811
Truite, 1787-1791, Gabarre, 385
Truite, 1791-1795, Gabarre, 385
Truite, 1795-1796, Flûte, see *Trajan* 1793-1795
Truite, 1859-1898, Large transport, 398
Truite (Grande Gabarre Écurie No.9), 1811-1832, Gabarre, 390
Turbot, 1776-1789, Transport (chasse-marée), 405
Turbot, 1804-1821, Transport (sloop), 412
Turbot, 1805-1811, Transport, 414
Turbot, 1822-1835, Sloop, 262
Turbulent, 1794-1801, Tartanç, 295
Turenne, 1854-1858, Two-decker (100-gun), 64
Turenne, 1858-1875, Screw two-decker, 75
Turgot, 1794-1795, Transport, 407
Turlurette, 1804-1809, Felucca, 302
Turot, 1793-?, Two-decker (64-gun), see *Réfléchi* 1776-1793
Turquoise, 1824-1829, Schooner, 261
Turquoise, 1830-1864, Schooner, 265
Tympan, 1795-1795, Xebec, see *Révolutionnaire* 1793-1794
Tyrannicide, 1793-1800, Two-decker (74-gun), 89
Tyrannicide, 1794-1795, Flûte, 377
Tyrol, 1797-1797, Half-xebec, 298
Tyronne, 1793-1801, Flûte, see *Tirone* 1793-1801

Ulloa, 1842-1888, Paddle frigate, 331
Ulloa, 1891-1895, Screw frigate (hulked), see *Foudre* 1856-1891
Ulm, 1809-1830, Two-decker (74-gun), 94
Ulm, 1830-1854, Two-decker (100-gun), 64
Ulm, 1854-1890, Screw two-decker, 69
Ulysse, 1803-1811, Two-decker (74-gun), see *Saint Genard* 1800-1803
Ulysse, 1810-1812, Transport (galiote), 413
Union, 1793-1793, Tartane, 296
Union, 1793-1793, Transport (sloop), 406
Union, 1794-1795, Transport (brigantine), 407
Union, 1794-1797, Gunboat (tartane), 277
Union, 1794-1801, Cutter, 245
Union, 1798-1802, Transport, 409
Union, 1799-1803, Two-decker (74-gun), 91
Unité, 1793-1796, 12pdr frigate (32-gun), see *Gracieuse* 1787-1793
Unité, 1794-1796, 22 x 8pdr corvette, 168
Unité, 1797-1797, Transport, 408
Unité, 1800-1815, Transport (sloop), 409
United Kingdom, 1809-1810, Flûte, 380
Uranie, 1788-1796, 18pdr frigate (44-gun), 138
Uranie, 1800-1814, 18pdr frigate (44-gun), 142
Uranie, 1805-1816, Lugger, see *Lougre No.2* 1803-1805
Uranie, 1816-1820, Gabarre, see *La Ciotat* 1811-1816
Uranie, 1832-1883, 30pdr frigate (60-gun), 110
Urbins, 1786-?, Sloop (service craft), 406
Uriil, 1809-1811, Two-decker (80-gun), 60
Urne, 1795-1795, Gunboat (tartane), see *Vertu* 1794-1795
Utile, 1784-1796, Gabarre, 384
Utile, 1794-1804, Aviso, 250
Utile, 1798-1798, Gunboat, 281
Utile, 1801-1806, Gabarre, see *Princesse Royale* 1795-1801
Utile, 1819-1830, Aviso or cutter, 269
Utile, 1831-1835, Aviso or sloop, 269
Utile, 1846-1852, 24pdr frigate (hulked), see *Vénus* 1823-1846
Utilité, 1794-1794, Transport (brig), 408
Utrecht, 1810-1813, Two-decker (68-gun), 83

Va et Vient, 1777-1787, Schooner, 239
Vaillante, 1793-1796, Gunboat, 273
Vaillante, 1796-1798, 20 x 8pdr corvette, 170
Vaillante, 1804-1814, 6 x 24pdr corvette, 181
Vaillante Hirondelle, 1797-1801, Transport, 408
Vainqueur, 1795-1795, Cutter, see *Vigilant* 1793-1795
Valentine, 1831 cancelled, 30pdr frigate (60-gun), 113
Valeureuse, 1798-1806, 18pdr frigate (44-gun), 142
Valeureuse, 1864-1888, Ironclad frigate, 423
Valmy, 1847-1863, Three-decker, 50
Van der Does (Vice-admiraal), 1810-1813, Gunboat (Dutch), 289
Van der Werff, 1812-1814, 18pdr frigate (50-gun), 155
Van Galen (Commandeur), 1810-1813, Gunboat (Dutch), 290
Van Gendt (Schout-bij-nacht), 1810-1813, Gunboat (Dutch), 290
Van Nes (Vice-admiraal), 1810-1813, Gunboat (Dutch), 290
Van Wassenaar (Luitenant-admiraal), 1810-1813, Gunboat (Dutch), 290
Vanneau, 1782-1793, Lugger, 239
Var, 1806-1809, Flûte, 378
Var, 1832-1833, Corvette de charge, 382
Var, 1844-1860, Paddle aviso, 348
Var, 1863-1896, Screw transport, 403
Vasco da Gama, 1807-1808, Two-decker (74-gun), 101
Vauban, 1845-1866, Paddle frigate, 328
Vaubois, 1798-1798, Galley, 301
Vautour, 1795-1803, Lugger, 242
Vautour, 1806-1809, 16-gun brig, 217
Vautour, 1834-1866, Paddle vessel, 321
Vedetta No.1, 1808-1814, Schooner-aviso, 254
Vedetta No.2, 1808-1814, Schooner-aviso, 254
Vedetta No.3, 1809-1814, Schooner-aviso, 254
Vedetta No.4, 1809-1814, Schooner-aviso, 254
Vedette, 1793-1794, Aviso, 250
Vedette, 1795-1795, Gunboat, see *Vésuve* 1793-1795
Vedette, 1796-1800, Cutter, see *Pensée* 1793-1796
Vedette, 1796-1801, Cutter, see *Pensée* 1796-1796
Vedette, 1799-1804, Chasse-marée, 248
Vedette, 1808-1817, Schooner or cutter, see *Aurore* 1806-1808
Vedette, 1839-1842, 4-gun gunbrig, 231
Vedette, 1844-1856, Paddle aviso, see *Comte d'Eu* 1842-1844
Veilleur, 1872-1888, Two-decker (hulked), see *Duquesne* 1853-1872
Véloce, 1809-1813, Transport (galiote), 413
Véloce, 1838-1860, Paddle corvette, 326
Vem, 1901-1911, Screw transport (hulked), see *Sarthe* 1862-1901
Vencador, 1806-1808, Two-decker (74-gun), 100
Vendémiaire, 1794-1795, Gunboat (tartane), 278
Venere, 1813-1814, 18pdr frigate (44-gun), 153
Vengeance, 1794-1795, 22 x 8pdr corvette, 172
Vengeance, 1794-1800, 24pdr frigate (48-gun), 105
Vengeance, 1810-1818, Half-xebec, 307
Vengeance, 1848-1898, 30pdr frigate (60-gun), 113
Vengeur, 1789-1793, Two-decker (74-gun), 89
Vengeur, 1794-1794, 16-gun corvette, 175
Vengeur, 1795-1796, Bateau-canonnier, 278
Vengeur, 1798-1799, Schooner, 244
Vengeur, 1803-1805, Three-decker, 46
Vengeur du Peuple, 1794-1794, Two-decker (74-gun), see *Marseillais* 1766-1794
Vénitien, 1806-1815, Two-decker (74-gun), see *Triton* 1823-1870
Venteux, 1795-1803, Gunboat, see *Volage* 1793-1795
Ventôse, 1794-1796, Gunboat (tartane), 278
Venturie, 1793-1793, Tartane, 296
Venturier, 1797-1797, Cutter, see *Ranger* 1794-1797
Vénus, 1782-1788, 18pdr frigate (34-gun), 136
Vénus, 1786-?, Sloop (service craft), 406
Vénus, 1795-1800, 22 x 8pdr corvette, see *Vengeance* 1794-1795
Vénus, 1797-1797, Galley, 298
Vénus, 1803 cancelled, 18pdr frigate (44-gun), 144
Vénus, 1806-1810, 18pdr frigate (44-gun), 146
Vénus, 1807-1808, 12pdr frigate (36-gun), 135
Vénus, 1808-1809, 14 x 12pdr corvette, 185

Vénus, 1811-1814, Corvette, 184
Vénus, 1813-1814, 18pdr frigate (44-gun), see *Venere* 1813-1814
Vénus, 1823-1846, 24pdr frigate (58-gun), 107
Vénus, 1845-1845, Schooner, see *Palmar* 1845-1847
Vénus, 1848 cancelled, 30pdr frigate (60-gun), 115
Vénus, 1864-1909, Screw corvette, 202
Vérificateur, 1795-1795, Bomb vessel, see *Victoire Sophie* 1794-1795
Vérité, 1795-1795, Gunboat, see *Volage* 1794-1795
Veronese, 1806-1813, Gunboat (Italian), 287
Verschoor, 1810-1813, Gunboat (Dutch), 290
Verseau, 1795-1796, Aviso, see *Utile* 1794-1804
Verona, 1809-1810, Corvette, 184
Vertu, 1794-1795, Gunboat (tartane), 278
Vertu, 1794-1803, 18pdr frigate (44-gun), 139
Vertu, 1803-1803, Schooner, 259
Vestale, 1780-1799, 12pdr frigate (32-gun), 125
Vestale, 1813-1813, 18pdr frigate (44-gun), 153
Vestale, 1822-1834, 24pdr frigate (58-gun), 107
Vésuve, 1793-1795, Gunboat, 273
Vésuve, 1794-1795, Gunboat (tartane), 278
Vésuve, 1795-1830, 16 x 18pdr corvette, 172
Vésuve, 1825-1840, Bomb vessel, 311
Vesuvio, 1813 cancelled, Two-decker (80-gun), 60
Vétéran, 1803-1842, Two-decker (74-gun), 90
Vétéran, 1872-1877, Two-decker (hulked), see *Duguay Trouin* 1857-1872
Vétéran, 1885-1896, Two-decker (hulked), see *Tage* 1857-1885
Viala, 1794-1795, Two-decker (74-gun), see *Constitution* 1795-1803
Vicentina, 1806-1813, Gunboat (Italian), 287
Victoire, 1770-1792, Two-decker (74-gun), 85
Victoire, 1795-1799, Two-decker (80-gun), see *Languedoc* 1763-1794
Victoire, 1798-1800, Galley, 300
Victoire, 1798-1801, Gunboat, 281
Victoire, 1799-1807, Schooner, 250
Victoire, 1800-1814, Schooner, 250
Victoire, 1802-1814, Schooner, 259
Victoire, 1830-1841, 18pdr frigate (44-gun), see *Duchesse de Berry* 1816-1830
Victoire, 1848-1861, 30pdr frigate (60-gun), 114
Victoire, 1861-1882, Screw frigate, 118
Victoire Sophie, 1794-1795, Bomb vessel, 310
Victor, 1849-1881, 18-gun brig, 232
Victorieuse, 1794-1795, 12pdr brig, 206
Victorieuse, 1806-1847, 20 x 8pdr corvette, 179
Victorieux (*Transport No. 960*), 1803-1817, Transport, 412
Victorine, 1804-1805, 18-gun brig, 221
Victorine, 1808-1814, Transport (schooner), 416
Vierge de Grace, 1798-1799, Transport (brig), see *Dame de Grace* 1798-1799
Vierge de la Garde, 1798-1799, Tartane, 297
Vierge du Rosaire, 1798-1799, Transport, 409
Vieux Catharina, 1795-1796, Bateau-canonnier, see *Catherine-Élisabeth* 1795-1796
Vif, 1798-1800, Aviso, 250
Vigie, 1799-1810, Schooner, 243
Vigie, 1839-1860, 4-gun gunbrig, 231
Vigie, 1861-1885, Screw aviso, 363
Vigilance, 1794-1798, 22 x 8pdr corvette, 176
Vigilant, 1793-1795, Cutter, 240
Vigilant, 1797-1799, Bateau-canonnier, 279
Vigilant, 1797-1801, Cutter, 249
Vigilant, 1800-1803, 16-gun brig, 209
Vigilant, 1810-1826, Lugger, 255
Vigilant, 1828-1842, Sloop, 263
Vigilant, 1842-1876, Transport (brig), 417
Vigilante, 1783-1796, 16 x 6pdr corvette, 165
Vigilante, 1792-1795, Felucca, 296
Vigilante, 1810-1813, Gunboat, 291
Vigilante, 1838-1840, Schooner, 268
Vigilante, 1855-1869, Schooner, 267
Vigilanza (*Vigilante*), 1806-1813, Felucca, 306
Vigogne, 1828-1836, Gabarre, 391
Vigogne, 1847 cancelled, Gabarre, 393

Vigoreux, 1865-1885, 30pdr frigate (hulked), see *Reine Blanche* 1837-1865
Villaret, 1806-1807, Schooner-aviso, 256
Ville Commune de Lorient, 1794-1794, Flûte, see *Ville de Lorient* 1793-1797
Ville d'Aix, 1804-1814, Prame, 282
Ville d'Aix La Chapelle, 1804 cancelled, Prame, 282
Ville d'Amiens, 1805-1815, Prame, 283
Ville d'Angers, 1803 cancelled, Prame, 282
Ville d'Anvers, 1804-1815, Prame, 282
Ville d'Arcangel, 1794-1795, Transport, 407
Ville d'Avignon, 1804 cancelled, Prame, 282
Ville d'Orléans, 1805-1827, Prame, 283
Ville d'Ostende, 1804 cancelled, Prame, 282
Ville de Berlin, 1807-1815, Two-decker (74-gun), 95
Ville de Besançon, 1804-1819, Prame, 283
Ville de Bordeaux, 1860-1880, Screw two-decker, 71
Ville de Bordeaux, 1880-1881, Three-decker (hulked), see *Bretagne* 1855-1880
Ville de Brest, 1803-1814, Prame, see *Éléphant* 1795-1803
Ville de Bruxelles, 1804-1814, Prame, 282
Ville de Caen, 1804-1816, Prame, 283
Ville de Cambrai, 1804-1814, Prame, 283
Ville de Chambéry, 1804-1815, Prame, 284
Ville de Clermont-Ferrand, 1804 cancelled, Prame, 282
Ville de Cognac or *Ville de Coignac*, 1804-1804, Prame, 282
Ville de Dijon, 1804 cancelled, Prame, 282
Ville de Gand, 1803-1814, Prame, 282
Ville de Genève, 1804-1815, Prame, 282
Ville de Grenoble, 1804 cancelled, Prame, 282
Ville de Liège, 1806-1815, Prame, 283
Ville de Lille, 1803-1814, Prame, see *Foudroyant* 1799-1803
Ville de Limoges, 1804 cancelled, Prame, 282
Ville de Lisbonne, 1808-1809, Two-decker (74-gun), see *Maria Primeira* 1807-1808
Ville de Lorient, 1793-1795, Flûte, 376
Ville de Lorient, 1793-1797, Flûte, 376
Ville de Lyon, 1803-1804, Two-decker (74-gun), see *Commerce de Lyon* 1807-1831
Ville de Lyon, 1804-1811, Prame, 283
Ville de Lyon, 1861-1885, Screw two-decker, 72
Ville de Marseille, 1798-1800, Flûte, 378
Ville de Marseille, 1812-1877, Two-decker (74-gun), 100
Ville de Mayence, 1804-1814, Prame, 282
Ville de Metz, 1804 cancelled, Prame, 282
Ville de Milan, 1803-1805, 18pdr frigate (46-gun), see *Hermione* 1803-1803
Ville de Milan, 1804 cancelled, 18pdr frigate (44-gun), 146
Ville de Montpellier, 1804-1814, Prame, 282
Ville de Nantes, 1858-1887, Screw two-decker, 71
Ville de Nice, 1860 not built, Screw frigate, 120
Ville de Paris, 1782-1783, Three-decker (projected), 44
Ville de Paris, 1850-1858, Three-decker, 47
Ville de Paris, 1858-1898, Screw three-decker, 54
Ville de Pau, 1804-1814, Prame, 282
Ville de Perpignan, 1804 cancelled, Prame, 283
Ville de Poitiers, 1804 cancelled, Prame, 282
Ville de Reims, 1803 cancelled, Prame, 282
Ville de Rennes, 1804 cancelled, Prame, 282
Ville de Rouen, 1794-1795, Transport (brig), 407
Ville de Rouen, 1804-1818, Prame, 283
Ville de Strasbourg, 1804-1816, Prame, 283
Ville de Toulouse, 1804 cancelled, Prame, 282
Ville de Tours, 1804-1814, Prame, 282
Ville de Turin, 1803 cancelled, Prame, 282
Ville de Varsovie, 1808-1809, Two-decker (80-gun), 58
Ville de Vienne, 1815-1815, Three-decker, see *Ville de Paris* 1850-1858
Ville du Havre, 1804-1814, Prame, 283
Ville du Havre, 1829-1843, Paddle vessel, see *Commerce du Havre* 1828-1829

Violente, 1778-1793, Gunboat, 271
Violente, 1795-1796, Gunboat, see *Vaillante* 1793-1796
Vipère, 1793-1794, 4pdr brig, 205
Vipère, 1794-1795, Gunboat (tartane), 278
Virginie, 1794-1796, 18pdr frigate (44-gun), 140
Virginie, 1803-1808, Transport (cutter), 413
Virginie, 1823-1830, Schooner, 269
Virginie, 1842-1888, 30pdr frigate (50-gun), 112
Visible, 1795-1797, Cutter, see *Union* 1794-1801
Vistule, 1808-1815, 18pdr frigate (44-gun), 148
Vittoria, 1797-1797, Two-decker (66-gun), 80
Vittoria, 1798-1799, Galley, see *Santa Ferma* 1798-1799
Vittoria, 1806-1808, Felucca, 306
Vittoria, 1806-1813, Gunboat (Italian), 287
Vive, 1795-1795, Gunboat (tartane), see *Vésuve* 1794-1795
Vlack, 1810-1813, Gunboat (Dutch), 290
Vlug or *Vlugh* (*Vice-admiraal*), 1810-1813, Gunboat (Dutch), 290
Vogue, 1795-1795, Felucca, see *Vigilante* 1792-1795
Volage, 1793-1795, Gunboat, 274
Volage, 1794-1795, Gunboat, 277
Volage, 1795-1797, 22 x 8pdr corvette, 172
Volage, 1801-1816, Schooner, 244
Volage, 1825-1865, 16-gun brig, 227
Volante, 1796-1800, Schooner, 250
Volcan, 1793-1796, Gunboat, 275
Volcan, 1794-1795, Gunboat (tartane), 278
Volcan, 1800-1802, Gunboat, 280
Volcan, 1811-1830, Gunboat, 291
Volcan, 1826-1856, Bomb vessel, 312
Volontaire, 1794-1794, 18pdr frigate (44-gun), see *Montagne* 1794-1794
Volontaire, 1796-1806, 18pdr frigate (44-gun), 140
Volontaire (*Transport No. 749*), 1803-1815, Transport (brig), 412
Volpe, 1812-1814, Felucca, 302
Volpe, 1813-1813, Gunboat (Italian), 288
Volta, 1851-1855, Screw corvette, see *Du Chayla* 1855-1890
Voltaire, 1795-1795, Two-decker (74-gun), see *Constitution* 1795-1803
Volteggiatore, 1807-1814, Yacht, 314
Voltigeant, 1794-1794, Transport, 408
Voltigeur, 1793-1797, 4pdr brig, 213
Voltigeur, 1804-1806, 16-gun brig, 215
Voltigeur, 1827-1865, 20-gun brig, 230
Voyageur, 1795-1795, Flûte, see *Ville de Lorient* 1793-1797
Voyageur, 1819-1831, Paddle vessel, 315
Voyageur, 1841-1872, Paddle aviso, 346
Vraye Humanité, 1786-?, Sloop (service craft), 406
Vulcain, 1795-1810, Prame, 272
Vulcain, 1797-1797, Two-decker (66-gun), see *Causse* 1797-1801
Vulcain, 1828-1865, Bomb vessel, 312
Vulcain, 1863-1885, Three-decker (hulked), see *Commerce de Paris* 1806-1830

Wagram, 1810-1837, Three-decker, 47
Wagram, 1839-1854, Two-decker (100-gun), 64
Wagram, 1854-1887, Screw two-decker, 69
Warmond or *Warmont* (*Vice-admiraal*), 1810-1813, Gunboat (Dutch), 290
Warren Hastings, 1806-1810, Flûte, 380
Washington, 1794-1796, Flûte, 377
Waterhoud, 1810-1813, Gunboat (Dutch), 290
Watigny, 1794-1809, Two-decker (74-gun), see *Wattignies* 1794-1809
Wattignies, 1794-1809, Two-decker (74-gun), 89
Wendor, 1796-1798, Cutter, 246
Weser, 1812-1813, 18pdr frigate (44-gun), 152
Weser, 1859-1861, Screw transport, 404
Wilding, 1798-1798, Transport, 410
William, 1796-1799, Transport (brig), 410

William-Anna, 1796-1797, Transport (sloop), 408
Windham, 1809-1810, Flûte, 381
Witte Cornelisz de With (*Vice-admiraal*), 1810-1813, Gunboat (Dutch), 290
Wrou-Madalena, 1795-1797, Transport (galiote), 411

Yacht de la Reine, 1785-1793, Yacht, 313
Ymperial, 1794-1795, Flûte, see *Imperial* 1794-1795
Yonne, 1855-1918, Screw transport, 399
Yssel, 1811-1814, 18pdr frigate (44-gun), 152

Zaire, 1797-1806, Galley, 298
Zèbre, 1810-1849, 16-gun brig, 217
Zèbre, 1854-1896, 18-gun brig, 233
Zeemeeuw, 1810-1813, 7-gun gunbrig, 224
Zélandais, 1813-1815, Two-decker (80-gun), 59
Zélé, 1763-1805, Two-decker (74-gun), 84
Zélé Conscrit, 1804-1814, Transport (sloop), 412
Zélée, 1854-1887, Screw transport, 398
Zélée (*Grande Gabarre Écurie No. 7*), 1812-1854, Gabarre, 390
Zénobie, 1847-1858, 30pdr frigate (52-gun), 112
Zénobie, 1858-1868, Screw frigate, 117
Zéphir, 1793-1799, 4pdr brig, 206
Zéphir, 1794-1795, Transport, 407
Zéphir No.2, 1799-1804, 4pdr brig, see *Zéphir* 1793-1799
Zéphyr, 1804 cancelled, 18pdr frigate (44-gun), 140
Zéphyr, 1806-1809, Corvette, 183
Zéphyr, 1813-1823, 16-gun brig, 218
Zéphyr, 1848-1858, 6-gun brig-aviso, 236
Zibeline, 1795-1795, Gabarre, see *Utile* 1784-1808
Zoé, 1795-1801, Bateau-canonnier, 278
Zone, 1795-1798, Flûte, see *Ville de Lorient* 1793-1795
Zoutman, 1811-1814, Two-decker (80 gun), see *Amiral Zoutman* 1810-1811